Hershman & McFarlane
Children Act Handbook

2022/23

Hershman & McFarlane
Children Act Handbook

2022/23

Bloomsbury Professional

LONDON · DUBLIN · EDINBURGH · NEW YORK · NEW DELHI · SYDNEY

BLOOMSBURY PROFESSIONAL
Bloomsbury Publishing Plc
50 Bedford Square, London, WC1B 3DP, UK
1385 Broadway, New York, NY 10018, USA
29 Earlsfort Terrace, Dublin 2, Ireland

BLOOMSBURY and the Diana logo are trademarks of Bloomsbury Publishing Plc

First published in Great Britain 2022

© Bloomsbury Professional 2022

British Library Cataloguing-in-Publication Data

A catalogue record for this book is available from the British Library.

ISBN:	PB:	978 1 52652 473 7
	ePDF:	978 1 52652 475 1
	ePub:	978 1 52652 474 4

Typeset by Evolution Design and Digital Ltd (Kent)
Printed and bound by CPI Group (UK) Ltd, Croydon, CR0 4YY

To find out more about our authors and books visit www.bloomsburyprofessional.com. Here you will find extracts, author information, details of forthcoming events and the option to sign up for our newsletters

PREFACE TO THE FIRST EDITION

In the ten years since the publication of Children Law and Practice, one drawback of the layout of the text has been that, in order to have both the commentary and the statutory material at court, it has been necessary for users to carry both volumes of the work with them. This modestly sized handbook is being published in order to ease the physical burden on users by providing core statutory material in a portable supplement.

We hope that this handbook will be a useful addition to the family law library and that the selection that we have made is sufficient to meet both the need for portability and the need to provide essential core material. Any suggestions for additional material are welcome.

The Children Act Handbook will be updated each year and issued as part of the subscription package to all Children Law and Practice subscribers. In addition, the Handbook will be available for sale separately to non-subscribers.

David Hershman and
Andrew McFarlane

August 2001

CONTENTS

Part IV – Miscellaneous

Part I
STATUTES

ADOPTION AND CHILDREN ACT 2002

ss 1, 18–29, 52

ARRANGEMENT OF SECTIONS

PART 1
ADOPTION

Chapter 1
Introductory

1 Considerations applying to the exercise of powers

(1) [Subsections (2) to (4) apply]² whenever a court or adoption agency is coming to a decision relating to the adoption of a child.

(2) The paramount consideration of the court or adoption agency must be the child's welfare, throughout his life.

(3) The court or adoption agency must at all times bear in mind that, in general, any delay in coming to the decision is likely to prejudice the child's welfare.

(4) The court or adoption agency must have regard to the following matters (among others) –

(a)   the child's ascertainable wishes and feelings regarding the decision (considered in the light of the child's age and understanding),

(b)   the child's particular needs,

(c)   the likely effect on the child (throughout his life) of having ceased to be a member of the original family and become an adopted person,

(d)   the child's age, sex, background and any of the child's characteristics which the court or agency considers relevant,

(e)   any harm (within the meaning of the Children Act 1989) which the child has suffered or is at risk of suffering,

(f)   the relationship which the child has with relatives, [with any person who is a prospective adopter with whom the child is placed,]³ and with any other person in relation to whom the court or agency considers the relationship to be relevant, including –

    (i)   the likelihood of any such relationship continuing and the value to the child of its doing so,

    (ii)   the ability and willingness of any of the child's relatives, or of any such person, to provide the child with a secure environment in which the child can develop, and otherwise to meet the child's needs,

    (iii)   the wishes and feelings of any of the child's relatives, or of any such person, regarding the child.

(5) [In placing a child for adoption, an adoption agency in Wales]² must give due consideration to the child's religious persuasion, racial origin and cultural and linguistic background.

(6) [In coming to a decision relating to the adoption of a child, a court or adoption agency]² must always consider the whole range of powers available to it in the child's case (whether under this Act or the Children Act 1989); and the court must not make any order under this Act unless it considers that making the order would be better for the child than not doing so.

(7) In this section, 'coming to a decision relating to the adoption of a child', in relation to a court, includes –

(a)   coming to a decision in any proceedings where the orders that might be made by the court include an adoption order (or the revocation of such an order), a placement order (or the revocation of such an order) or an order under section 26 [or 51A]¹ (or the revocation or variation of such an order),

(b)   coming to a decision about granting leave in respect of any action (other than the initiation of proceedings in any court) which may be taken by an adoption agency or individual under this Act,

but does not include coming to a decision about granting leave in any other circumstances.

(8) For the purposes of this section –

(a)   references to relationships are not confined to legal relationships,

(b)   references to a relative, in relation to a child, include the child's mother and father.

[(9) In this section 'adoption agency in Wales' means an adoption agency that is –

(a) a local authority in Wales, or

(b) a registered adoption society whose principal office is in Wales.][2]

NOTES

Amendment.[1] Words inserted: Children and Families Act 2014, s 9(2).[2] Words substituted and subsection inserted: Children and Families Act 2014, s 3.[3] Words inserted: Children and Social Work Act 2017, s 9.

****

Chapter 3
Placement for Adoption and Adoption Orders
Placement of children by adoption agency for adoption

18 Placement for adoption by agencies

(1) An adoption agency may –

(a) place a child for adoption with prospective adopters, or

(b) where it has placed a child with any persons (whether under this Part or not), leave the child with them as prospective adopters,

but, except in the case of a child who is less than six weeks old, may only do so under section 19 or a placement order.

(2) An adoption agency may only place a child for adoption with prospective adopters if the agency is satisfied that the child ought to be placed for adoption.

(3) A child who is placed or authorised to be placed for adoption with prospective adopters by a local authority is looked after by the authority.

(4) If an application for an adoption order has been made by any persons in respect of a child and has not been disposed of –

(a) an adoption agency which placed the child with those persons may leave the child with them until the application is disposed of, but

(b) apart from that, the child may not be placed for adoption with any prospective adopters.

'Adoption order' includes a Scottish or Northern Irish adoption order.

(5) References in this Act (apart from this section) to an adoption agency placing a child for adoption –

(a) are to its placing a child for adoption with prospective adopters, and

(b) include, where it has placed a child with any persons (whether under this Act or not), leaving the child with them as prospective adopters;

and references in this Act (apart from this section) to a child who is placed for adoption by an adoption agency are to be interpreted accordingly.

(6) References in this Chapter to an adoption agency being, or not being, authorised to place a child for adoption are to the agency being or (as the case may be) not being authorised to do so under section 19 or a placement order.

(7) This section is subject to sections 30 to 35 (removal of children placed by adoption agencies).

19 Placing children with parental consent

(1) Where an adoption agency is satisfied that each parent or guardian of a child has consented to the child –

    (a)   being placed for adoption with prospective adopters identified in the consent, or

    (b)   being placed for adoption with any prospective adopters who may be chosen by the agency,

and has not withdrawn the consent, the agency is authorised to place the child for adoption accordingly.

(2) Consent to a child being placed for adoption with prospective adopters identified in the consent may be combined with consent to the child subsequently being placed for adoption with any prospective adopters who may be chosen by the agency in circumstances where the child is removed from or returned by the identified prospective adopters.

(3) Subsection (1) does not apply where –

    (a)   an application has been made on which a care order might be made and the application has not been disposed of, or

    (b)   a care order or placement order has been made after the consent was given.

(4) References in this Act to a child placed for adoption under this section include a child who was placed under this section with prospective adopters and continues to be placed with them, whether or not consent to the placement has been withdrawn.

(5) This section is subject to section 52 (parental etc consent).

20 Advance consent to adoption

(1) A parent or guardian of a child who consents to the child being placed for adoption by an adoption agency under section 19 may, at the same or any subsequent time, consent to the making of a future adoption order.

(2) Consent under this section –

    (a)   where the parent or guardian has consented to the child being placed for adoption with prospective adopters identified in the consent, may be consent to adoption by them, or

    (b)   may be consent to adoption by any prospective adopters who may be chosen by the agency.

(3) A person may withdraw any consent given under this section.

(4) A person who gives consent under this section may, at the same or any subsequent time, by notice given to the adoption agency –

    (a)   state that he does not wish to be informed of any application for an adoption order, or

    (b)   withdraw such a statement.

(5) A notice under subsection (4) has effect from the time when it is received by the adoption agency but has no effect if the person concerned has withdrawn his consent.

(6) This section is subject to section 52 (parental etc consent).

21 Placement orders

(1) A placement order is an order made by the court authorising a local authority to place a child for adoption with any prospective adopters who may be chosen by the authority.

(2) The court may not make a placement order in respect of a child unless –

    (a)   the child is subject to a care order,

    (b)   the court is satisfied that the conditions in section 31(2) of the 1989 Act (conditions for making a care order) are met, or

    (c)   the child has no parent or guardian.

(3) The court may only make a placement order if, in the case of each parent or guardian of the child, the court is satisfied –

    (a)   that the parent or guardian has consented to the child being placed for adoption with any prospective adopters who may be chosen by the local authority and has not withdrawn the consent, or

    (b)   that the parent's or guardian's consent should be dispensed with.

This subsection is subject to section 52 (parental etc consent).

(4) A placement order continues in force until –

    (a)   it is revoked under section 24,

    (b)   an adoption order is made in respect of the child, or

    (c)   the child marries[, forms a civil partnership][1] or attains the age of 18 years.

'Adoption order' includes a Scottish or Northern Irish adoption order.

NOTES

Amendments.[1] Words inserted: Civil Partnership Act 2004, s 79(1), (2).

22 Applications for placement orders

(1) A local authority must apply to the court for a placement order in respect of a child if –

(a)   the child is placed for adoption by them or is being provided with accommodation by them,

(b)   no adoption agency is authorised to place the child for adoption,

(c)   the child has no parent or guardian or the authority consider that the conditions in section 31(2) of the 1989 Act are met, and

(d)   the authority are satisfied that the child ought to be placed for adoption.

(2) If –

(a)   an application has been made (and has not been disposed of) on which a care order might be made in respect of a child, or

(b)   a child is subject to a care order and the appropriate local authority are not authorised to place the child for adoption,

the appropriate local authority must apply to the court for a placement order if they are satisfied that the child ought to be placed for adoption.

(3) If –

(a)   a child is subject to a care order, and

(b)   the appropriate local authority are authorised to place the child for adoption under section 19,

the authority may apply to the court for a placement order.

(4) If a local authority –

(a)   are under a duty to apply to the court for a placement order in respect of a child, or

(b)   have applied for a placement order in respect of a child and the application has not been disposed of,

the child is looked after by the authority.

(5) Subsections (1) to (3) do not apply in respect of a child –

(a)   if any persons have given notice of intention to adopt, unless the period of four months beginning with the giving of the notice has expired without them applying for an adoption order or their application for such an order has been withdrawn or refused, or

(b)   if an application for an adoption order has been made and has not been disposed of.

'Adoption order' includes a Scottish or Northern Irish adoption order.

(6) Where –

(a)   an application for a placement order in respect of a child has been made and has not been disposed of, and

(b)   no interim care order is in force,

the court may give any directions it considers appropriate for the medical or psychiatric examination or other assessment of the child; but a child who is of sufficient understanding to make an informed decision may refuse to submit to the examination or other assessment.

(7) The appropriate local authority –

    (a)   in relation to a care order, is the local authority in whose care the child is placed by the order, and

    (b)   in relation to an application on which a care order might be made, is the local authority which makes the application.

23 Varying placement orders

(1) The court may vary a placement order so as to substitute another local authority for the local authority authorised by the order to place the child for adoption.

(2) The variation may only be made on the joint application of both authorities.

24 Revoking placement orders

(1) The court may revoke a placement order on the application of any person.

(2) But an application may not be made by a person other than the child or the local authority authorised by the order to place the child for adoption unless –

    (a)   the court has given leave to apply, and

    (b)   the child is not placed for adoption by the authority.

(3) The court cannot give leave under subsection (2)(a) unless satisfied that there has been a change in circumstances since the order was made.

(4) If the court determines, on an application for an adoption order, not to make the order, it may revoke any placement order in respect of the child.

(5) Where –

    (a)   an application for the revocation of a placement order has been made and has not been disposed of, and

    (b)   the child is not placed for adoption by the authority,

the child may not without the court's leave be placed for adoption under the order.

25 Parental responsibility

(1) This section applies while –

    (a)   a child is placed for adoption under section 19 or an adoption agency is authorised to place a child for adoption under that section, or

    (b)   a placement order is in force in respect of a child.

(2) Parental responsibility for the child is given to the agency concerned.

(3) While the child is placed with prospective adopters, parental responsibility is given to them.

(4) The agency may determine that the parental responsibility of any parent or guardian, or of prospective adopters, is to be restricted to the extent specified in the determination.

PART I – Statutes

26 Contact

(1) On an adoption agency being authorised to place a child for adoption, or placing a child for adoption who is less than six weeks old[–

  (a)   any contact provision in a child arrangements order under section 8 of the 1989 Act ceases to have effect,

  (b)   any order under section 34 of that Act (parental etc contact with children in care) ceases to have effect, and

  (c)   any activity direction made in proceedings for the making, variation or discharge of a child arrangements order with respect to the child, or made in other proceedings that relate to such an order, is discharged.][2]

(2) While an adoption agency is so authorised or a child is placed for adoption –

  (a)   no application may be made for[–

    (i)   a child arrangements order under section 8 of the 1989 Act containing contact provision, or

    (ii)   an order under section 34 of that Act, but][2]

  (b)   the court may make an order under this section requiring the person with whom the child lives, or is to live, to allow the child to visit or stay with the person named in the order, or for the person named in the order and the child otherwise to have contact with each other.

(3) An application for an order under this section may be made by –

  (a)   the child or the agency,

  (b)   any parent, guardian or relative,

  (c)   any person in whose favour there was provision …[2] which ceased to have effect by virtue of subsection [(1)(a) or an order which ceased to have effect by virtue of subsection (1)(b)][2],

  (d)   if a [child arrangements][3] order was in force immediately before the adoption agency was authorised to place the child for adoption or (as the case may be) placed the child for adoption at a time when he was less than six weeks old, [any person named in the order as a person with whom the child was to live][2],

  (e)   if a person had care of the child immediately before that time by virtue of an order made in the exercise of the High Court's inherent jurisdiction with respect to children, that person,

  (f)   any person who has obtained the court's leave to make the application.

(4) When making a placement order, the court may on its own initiative make an order under this section.

(5) …[1]

[(5A) In this section 'contact provision' means provision which regulates arrangements relating to –

  (a)   with whom a child is to spend time or otherwise have contact, or

  (b)   when a child is to spend time or otherwise have contact with any person;

but in paragraphs (a) and (b) a reference to spending time or otherwise having contact with a person is to doing that otherwise than as a result of living with the person.

(6) In this section 'activity direction' has the meaning given by section 11A of the 1989 Act.][2]

NOTES

Amendments.[1] Subsection omitted: Children and Families Act 2014, s 9(3).[2] Paragraphs and subparagraphs inserted, words omitted and subsections (5A) and (6) substituted for subsection (6): Children and Families Act 2014, s 12, Sch 2, paras 59, 60.

27 Contact: supplementary

(1) An order under section 26 –

   (a)   has effect while the adoption agency is authorised to place the child for adoption or the child is placed for adoption, but

   (b)   may be varied or revoked by the court on an application by the child, the agency or a person named in the order.

(2) The agency may refuse to allow the contact that would otherwise be required by virtue of an order under that section if –

   (a)   it is satisfied that it is necessary to do so in order to safeguard or promote the child's welfare, and

   (b)   the refusal is decided upon as a matter of urgency and does not last for more than seven days.

(3) Regulations may make provision as to –

   (a)   the steps to be taken by an agency which has exercised its power under subsection (2),

   (b)   the circumstances in which, and conditions subject to which, the terms of any order under section 26 may be departed from by agreement between the agency and any person for whose contact with the child the order provides,

   (c)   notification by an agency of any variation or suspension of arrangements made (otherwise than under an order under that section) with a view to allowing any person contact with the child.

(4) Before making a placement order the court must –

   (a)   consider the arrangements which the adoption agency has made, or proposes to make, for allowing any person contact with the child, and

   (b)   invite the parties to the proceedings to comment on those arrangements.

(5) An order under section 26 may provide for contact on any conditions the court considers appropriate.

28 Further consequences of placement

(1) Where a child is placed for adoption under section 19 or an adoption agency is authorised to place a child for adoption under that section –

(a)   a parent or guardian of the child may not apply for a [child arrangements order regulating the child's living arrangements][1] unless an application for an adoption order has been made and the parent or guardian has obtained the court's leave under subsection (3) or (5) of section 47,

(b)   if an application has been made for an adoption order, a guardian of the child may not apply for a special guardianship order unless he has obtained the court's leave under subsection (3) or (5) of that section.

(2) Where –

(a)   a child is placed for adoption under section 19 or an adoption agency is authorised to place a child for adoption under that section, or

(b)   a placement order is in force in respect of a child,

then (whether or not the child is in England and Wales) a person may not do either of the following things, unless the court gives leave or each parent or guardian of the child gives written consent.

(3) Those things are –

(a)   causing the child to be known by a new surname, or
(b)   removing the child from the United Kingdom.

(4) Subsection (3) does not prevent the removal of a child from the United Kingdom for a period of less than one month by a person who provides the child's home.

[(5) For the purposes of subsection (1)(a), a child arrangements order regulates a child's living arrangements if the arrangements regulated by the order consist of, or include, arrangements which relate to either or both of the following –

(a)   with whom the child is to live, and
(b)   when the child is to live with any person.][1]

NOTES

Amendments.[1] Words substituted and subsection inserted: Children and Families Act 2014, s 12, Sch 2, paras 59, 61.

29 Further consequences of placement orders

(1) Where a placement order is made in respect of a child and either –

(a)   the child is subject to a care order, or
(b)   the court at the same time makes a care order in respect of the child,

the care order does not have effect at any time when the placement order is in force.

(2) On the making of a placement order in respect of a child, any order mentioned in section 8(1) of the 1989 Act, and any supervision order in respect of the child, ceases to have effect.

(3) Where a placement order is in force –

(a)   no prohibited steps order …[1] or specific issue order, and
(b)   no supervision order or child assessment order,

may be made in respect of the child.

(4) [Where a placement order is in force, a child arrangements order may be made with respect to the child's living arrangements only if –][1]

   (a)   an application for an adoption order has been made in respect of the child, and

   (b)   the [child arrangements][1] order is applied for by a parent or guardian who has obtained the court's leave under subsection (3) or (5) of section 47 or by any other person who has obtained the court's leave under this subsection.

[(4A) For the purposes of subsection (4), a child arrangements order is one made with respect to a child's living arrangements if the arrangements regulated by the order consist of, or include, arrangements which relate to either or both of the following –

   (a)   with whom the child is to live, and

   (b)   when the child is to live with any person.][1]

(5) Where a placement order is in force, no special guardianship order may be made in respect of the child unless –

   (a)   an application has been made for an adoption order, and

   (b)   the person applying for the special guardianship order has obtained the court's leave under this subsection or, if he is a guardian of the child, has obtained the court's leave under section 47(5).

(6) Section 14A(7) of the 1989 Act applies in respect of an application for a special guardianship order for which leave has been given as mentioned in subsection (5)(*b*) with the omission of the words 'the beginning of the period of three months ending with'.

(7) Where a placement order is in force –

   (a)   section 14C(1)(b) of the 1989 Act (special guardianship: parental responsibility) has effect subject to any determination under section 25(4) of this Act,

   (b)   section 14C(3) and (4) of the 1989 Act (special guardianship: removal of child from UK etc) does not apply.

NOTES

Amendments.[1] Words omitted and substituted and subsection inserted: Children and Families Act 2014, s 12, Sch 2, paras 59, 62.

****

[Post-adoption contact

51A Post-adoption contact

(1) This section applies where –

   (a)   an adoption agency has placed or was authorised to place a child for adoption, and

   (b)   the court is making or has made an adoption order in respect of the child.

(2) When making the adoption order or at any time afterwards, the court may make an order under this section –

    (a)   requiring the person in whose favour the adoption order is or has been made to allow the child to visit or stay with the person named in the order under this section, or for the person named in that order and the child otherwise to have contact with each other, or

    (b)   prohibiting the person named in the order under this section from having contact with the child.

(3) The following people may be named in an order under this section –

    (a)   any person who (but for the child's adoption) would be related to the child by blood (including half-blood), marriage or civil partnership;

    (b)   any former guardian of the child;

    (c)   any person who had parental responsibility for the child immediately before the making of the adoption order;

    (d)   any person who was entitled to make an application for an order under section 26 in respect of the child (contact with children placed or to be placed for adoption) by virtue of subsection (3)(c), (d) or (e) of that section;

    (e)   any person with whom the child has lived for a period of at least one year.

(4) An application for an order under this section may be made by –

    (a)   a person who has applied for the adoption order or in whose favour the adoption order is or has been made,

    (b)   the child, or

    (c)   any person who has obtained the court's leave to make the application.

(5) In deciding whether to grant leave under subsection (4)(c), the court must consider –

    (a)   any risk there might be of the proposed application disrupting the child's life to such an extent that he or she would be harmed by it (within the meaning of the 1989 Act),

    (b)   the applicant's connection with the child, and

    (c)   any representations made to the court by –

        (i)   the child, or

        (ii)   a person who has applied for the adoption order or in whose favour the adoption order is or has been made.

(6) When making an adoption order, the court may on its own initiative make an order of the type mentioned in subsection (2)(b).

(7) The period of one year mentioned in subsection (3)(e) need not be continuous but must not have begun more than five years before the making of the application.

(8) Where this section applies, an order under section 8 of the 1989 Act may not make provision about contact between the child and any person who may be named in an order under this section.][1]

PART I – Statutes

NOTES
Amendment.[1] Section and heading preceding it inserted: Children and Families Act 2014, s 9(1).

[51B Orders under section 51A: supplementary

(1) An order under section 51A –

    (a)   may contain directions about how it is to be carried into effect,

    (b)   may be made subject to any conditions the court thinks appropriate,

    (c)   may be varied or revoked by the court on an application by the child, a person in whose favour the adoption order was made or a person named in the order, and

    (d)   has effect until the child's 18th birthday, unless revoked.

(2) Subsection (3) applies to proceedings –

    (a)   on an application for an adoption order in which –

        (i)   an application is made for an order under section 51A, or

        (ii)   the court indicates that it is considering making such an order on its own initiative;

    (b)   on an application for an order under section 51A;

    (c)   on an application for such an order to be varied or revoked.

(3) The court must (in the light of any rules made by virtue of subsection (4)) –

    (a)   draw up a timetable with a view to determining without delay whether to make, (or as the case may be) vary or revoke an order under section 51A, and

    (b)   give directions for the purpose of ensuring, so far as is reasonably practicable, that that timetable is adhered to.

(4) Rules of court may –

    (a)   specify periods within which specified steps must be taken in relation to proceedings to which subsection (3) applies, and

    (b)   make other provision with respect to such proceedings for the purpose of ensuring, so far as is reasonably practicable, that the court makes determinations about orders under section 51A without delay.][1]

NOTES
Amendment.[1] Section inserted: Children and Families Act 2014, s 9(1).

Placement and adoption: general

52 Parental etc consent

(1) The court cannot dispense with the consent of any parent or guardian of a child to the child being placed for adoption or to the making of an adoption order in respect of the child unless the court is satisfied that –

    (a)   the parent or guardian cannot be found or [lacks capacity (within the meaning of the Mental Capacity Act 2005) to give consent][1], or

    (b)   the welfare of the child requires the consent to be dispensed with.

(2) ...²

(3) Any consent given by the mother to the making of an adoption order is ineffective if it is given less than six weeks after the child's birth.

(4) The withdrawal of any consent to the placement of a child for adoption, or of any consent given under section 20, is ineffective if it is given after an application for an adoption order is made.

(5) 'Consent' means consent given unconditionally and with full understanding of what is involved; but a person may consent to adoption without knowing the identity of the persons in whose favour the order will be made.

(6) 'Parent' (except in subsections (9) and (10) below) means a parent having parental responsibility.

(7) Consent under section 19 or 20 must be given in the form prescribed by rules, and the rules may prescribe forms in which a person giving consent under any other provision of this Part may do so (if he wishes).

(8) Consent given under section 19 or 20 must be withdrawn –

    (a)   in the form prescribed by rules, or
    (b)   by notice given to the agency.

(9) Subsection (10) applies if –

    (a)   an agency has placed a child for adoption under section 19 in pursuance of consent given by a parent of the child, and
    (b)   at a later time, the other parent of the child acquires parental responsibility for the child.

(10) The other parent is to be treated as having at that time given consent in accordance with this section in the same terms as those in which the first parent gave consent.

NOTES

Amendments.[1] Words substituted: Mental Capacity Act 2005, s 67(1), Sch 6, para 45.[2] Subsection omitted: Crime and Courts Act 2013, s 17, Sch 11, paras 151, 153.

****

CHILDREN ACT 1989

ARRANGEMENT OF SECTIONS

PART IV
CARE AND SUPERVISION

PART I – Statutes

PART X

CHILD MINDING AND DAY CARE FOR YOUNG CHILDREN

[PART XA1
CHILD MINDING AND DAY CARE FOR CHILDREN IN …² WALES

PART XII
MISCELLANEOUS AND GENERAL

An Act to reform the law relating to children; to provide for local authority services for children in need and others; to amend the law with respect to children's homes, community homes, voluntary homes and voluntary organisations; to make provision with respect to fostering, child minding and day care for young children and adoption; and for connected purposes. [16 November 1989]

PART I
INTRODUCTORY

1 Welfare of the child

(1) When a court determines any question with respect to –

  (a)   the upbringing of a child; or
  (b)   the administration of a child's property or the application of any income arising from it,

the child's welfare shall be the court's paramount consideration.

(2) In any proceedings in which any question with respect to the upbringing of a child arises, the court shall have regard to the general principle that any delay in determining the question is likely to prejudice the welfare of the child.

[(2A) A court, in the circumstances mentioned in subsection (4)(a) or (7), is as respects each parent within subsection (6)(a) to presume, unless the contrary is shown, that involvement of that parent in the life of the child concerned will further the child's welfare.

(2B) In subsection (2A) 'involvement' means involvement of some kind, either direct or indirect, but not any particular division of a child's time.][2]

(3) In the circumstances mentioned in subsection (4), a court shall have regard in particular to –

    (a)   the ascertainable wishes and feelings of the child concerned (considered in the light of his age and understanding);

    (b)   his physical, emotional and educational needs;

    (c)   the likely effect on him of any change in his circumstances;

    (d)   his age, sex, background and any characteristics of his which the court considers relevant;

    (e)   any harm which he has suffered or is at risk of suffering;

    (f)   how capable each of his parents, and any other person in relation to whom the court considers the question to be relevant, is of meeting his needs;

    (g)   the range of powers available to the court under this Act in the proceedings in question.

(4) The circumstances are that –

    (a)   the court is considering whether to make, vary or discharge a section 8 order, and the making, variation or discharge of the order is opposed by any party to the proceedings; or

    (b)   the court is considering whether to make, vary or discharge [a special guardianship order or][1] an order under Part IV.

(5) Where a court is considering whether or not to make one or more orders under this Act with respect to a child, it shall not make the order or any of the orders unless it considers that doing so would be better for the child than making no order at all.

[(6) In subsection (2A) 'parent' means parent of the child concerned; and, for the purposes of that subsection, a parent of the child concerned –

    (a)   is within this paragraph if that parent can be involved in the child's life in a way that does not put the child at risk of suffering harm; and

    (b)   is to be treated as being within paragraph (a) unless there is some evidence before the court in the particular proceedings to suggest that involvement of that parent in the child's life would put the child at risk of suffering harm whatever the form of the involvement.

(7) The circumstances referred to are that the court is considering whether to make an order under section 4(1)(c) or (2A) or 4ZA(1)(c) or (5) (parental responsibility of parent other than mother).][2]

NOTES

Amendments.[1] Words inserted: Adoption and Children Act 2002, s 115(2), (3).[2] Subsections (2A), (2B), (6) and (7) inserted: Children and Families Act 2014, s 11.

Definitions. 'A section 8 order': s 8(2); 'child': s 105(1); 'harm': ss 31(9), 105(1); 'the court': s 92(7); 'upbringing': s 105(1).

2 Parental responsibility for children

(1) Where a child's father and mother were married to[, or civil partners of,][3] each other at the time of his birth, they shall each have parental responsibility for the child.

[(1A) Where a child –

    (a)   has a parent by virtue of section 42 of the Human Fertilisation and Embryology Act 2008; or

    (b)   has a parent by virtue of section 43 of that Act and is a person to whom section 1(3) of the Family Law Reform Act 1987 applies,

the child's mother and the other parent shall each have parental responsibility for the child.][2]

(2) Where a child's father and mother were not married to[, or civil partners of,][3] each other at the time of his birth –

    (a)   the mother shall have parental responsibility for the child;

    (b)   the father [shall have parental responsibility for the child if he has acquired it (and has not ceased to have it)][1] in accordance with the provisions of this Act.

[(2A) Where a child has a parent by virtue of section 43 of the Human Fertilisation and Embryology Act 2008 and is not a person to whom section 1(3) of the Family Law Reform Act 1987 applies –

    (a)   the mother shall have parental responsibility for the child;

    (b)   the other parent shall have parental responsibility for the child if she has acquired it (and has not ceased to have it) in accordance with the provisions of this Act.][2]

(3) References in this Act to a child whose father and mother were, or (as the case may be) were not, married to[, or civil partners of,][3] each other at the time of his birth must be read with section 1 of the Family Law Reform Act 1987 (which extends their meaning).

(4) The rule of law that a father is the natural guardian of his legitimate child is abolished.

(5) More than one person may have parental responsibility for the same child at the same time.

(6) A person who has parental responsibility for a child at any time shall not cease to have that responsibility solely because some other person subsequently acquires parental responsibility for the child.

(7) Where more than one person has parental responsibility for a child, each of them may act alone and without the other (or others) in meeting that responsibility; but nothing in this Part shall be taken to affect the operation of any enactment which requires the consent of more than one person in a matter affecting the child.

PART I – Statutes

(8) The fact that a person has parental responsibility for a child shall not entitle him to act in any way which would be incompatible with any order made with respect to the child under this Act.

(9) A person who has parental responsibility for a child may not surrender or transfer any part of that responsibility to another but may arrange for some or all of it to be met by one or more persons acting on his behalf.

(10) The person with whom any such arrangement is made may himself be a person who already has parental responsibility for the child concerned.

(11) The making of any such arrangement shall not affect any liability of the person making it which may arise from any failure to meet any part of his parental responsibility for the child concerned.

NOTES

Amendments.[1] Words substituted: Adoption and Children Act 2002, s 111(5).[2] Subsections inserted: Human Fertilisation and Embryology Act 2008, s 56, Sch 6, Pt 1, para 26.[3] Words inserted: SI 2019/1458, reg 15(1), (2).
Definitions. 'Child': s 105(1); 'married … at the time of his birth': s 2(3); 'parental responsibility': s 3.

3 Meaning of 'parental responsibility'

(1) In this Act 'parental responsibility' means all the rights, duties, powers, responsibilities and authority which by law a parent of a child has in relation to the child and his property.

(2) It also includes the rights, powers and duties which a guardian of the child's estate (appointed, before the commencement of section 5, to act generally) would have had in relation to the child and his property.

(3) The rights referred to in subsection (2) include, in particular, the right of the guardian to receive or recover in his own name, for the benefit of the child, property of whatever description and wherever situated which the child is entitled to receive or recover.

(4) The fact that a person has, or does not have, parental responsibility for a child shall not affect –

  (a)   any obligation which he may have in relation to the child (such as a statutory duty to maintain the child); or
  (b)   any rights which, in the event of the child's death, he (or any other person) may have in relation to the child's property.

(5) A person who –

  (a)   does not have parental responsibility for a particular child; but
  (b)   has care of the child,

may (subject to the provisions of this Act) do what is reasonable in all the circumstances of the case for the purpose of safeguarding or promoting the child's welfare.

NOTES

Definitions. 'Child': s 105(1); 'parental responsibility': s 3.

4 Acquisition of parental responsibility by father

(1) Where a child's father and mother were not married to[, or civil partners of,]⁵ each other at the time of his birth [, the father shall acquire parental responsibility for the child if –

  (a) he becomes registered as the child's father under any of the enactments specified in subsection (1A);
  (b) he and the child's mother make an agreement (a 'parental responsibility agreement') providing for him to have parental responsibility for the child; or
  (c) the court, on his application, orders that he shall have parental responsibility for the child.]¹

[(1A) The enactments referred to in subsection (1)(a) are –

  (a) paragraphs (a), (b) and (c) of section 10(1) and of section 10A(1) of the Births and Deaths Registration Act 1953;
  (b) paragraphs (a), (b)(i) and (c) of section 18(1), and sections 18(2)(b) and 20(1)(a) of the Registration of Births, Deaths and Marriages (Scotland) Act 1965; and
  (c) sub-paragraphs (a), (b) and (c) of Article 14(3) of the Births and Deaths Registration (Northern Ireland) Order 1976.

(1B) The [Secretary of State]⁴ may by order amend subsection (1A) so as to add further enactments to the list in that subsection.]²

(2) No parental responsibility agreement shall have effect for the purposes of this Act unless –

  (a) it is made in the form prescribed by regulations made by the Lord Chancellor; and
  (b) where regulations are made by the Lord Chancellor prescribing the manner in which such agreements must be recorded, it is recorded in the prescribed manner.

[(2A) A person who has acquired parental responsibility under subsection (1) shall cease to have that responsibility only if the court so orders.

(3) The court may make an order under subsection (2A) on the application –

  (a) of any person who has parental responsibility for the child, or
  (b) with leave of the court, of the child himself,

subject, in the case of parental responsibility acquired under subsection (1)(c), to section 12(4).]³

(4) The court may only grant leave under subsection (3)(b) if it is satisfied that the child has sufficient understanding to make the proposed application.

NOTES

Amendments.¹ Words substituted: Adoption and Children Act 2002, s 111(1), (2).² Subsections (1A), (1B) inserted: Adoption and Children Act 2002, s 111(1), (3).³ Subsections (2A), (3) inserted: Adoption and Children Act 2002, s 111(1), (4).⁴ Words substituted: SI 2003/3191, arts 3(a), 6, Sch, para 1.⁵ Words inserted: SI 2019/1458, reg 15(1), (3).

Definitions. 'Child': s 105(1); 'parental responsibility': s 3; 'parental responsibility agreement': s 4(1)(b); 'prescribed': s 105(1); 'the court': s 92(7).

[4ZA Acquisition of parental responsibility by second female parent

(1) Where a child has a parent by virtue of section 43 of the Human Fertilisation and Embryology Act 2008 and is not a person to whom section 1(3) of the Family Law Reform Act 1987 applies, that parent shall acquire parental responsibility for the child if –

(a)   she becomes registered as a parent of the child under any of the enactments specified in subsection (2);

(b)   she and the child's mother make an agreement providing for her to have parental responsibility for the child; or

(c)   the court, on her application, orders that she shall have parental responsibility for the child.

(2) The enactments referred to in subsection (1)(a) are –

(a)   paragraphs (a), (b) and (c) of section 10(1B) and of section 10A(1B) of the Births and Deaths Registration Act 1953;

(b)   paragraphs (a), (b) and (d) of section 18B(1) and sections 18B(3)(a) and 20(1)(a) of the Registration of Births, Deaths and Marriages (Scotland) Act 1965; and

(c)   sub-paragraphs (a), (b) and (c) of Article 14ZA(3) of the Births and Deaths Registration (Northern Ireland) Order 1976.

(3) The Secretary of State may by order amend subsection (2) so as to add further enactments to the list in that subsection.

(4) An agreement under subsection (1)(b) is also a 'parental responsibility agreement', and section 4(2) applies in relation to such an agreement as it applies in relation to parental responsibility agreements under section 4.

(5) A person who has acquired parental responsibility under subsection (1) shall cease to have that responsibility only if the court so orders.

(6) The court may make an order under subsection (5) on the application –

(a)   of any person who has parental responsibility for the child; or

(b)   with the leave of the court, of the child himself,

subject, in the case of parental responsibility acquired under subsection (1)(c), to section 12(4).

(7) The court may only grant leave under subsection (6)(b) if it is satisfied that the child has sufficient understanding to make the proposed application.][1]

NOTES

Amendments.[1] Section inserted: Human Fertilisation and Embryology Act 2008, s 56, Sch 6, Pt 1, para 27.

[4A Acquisition of parental responsibility by step-parent

(1) Where a child's parent ('parent A') who has parental responsibility for the child is married to[, or a civil partner of,]² a person who is not the child's parent ('the step-parent') –

PART I – Statutes

   (a)   parent A or, if the other parent of the child also has parental responsibility for the child, both parents may by agreement with the step-parent provide for the step-parent to have parental responsibility for the child; or
   (b)   the court may, on the application of the step-parent, order that the step-parent shall have parental responsibility for the child.

(2) An agreement under subsection (1)(a) is also a 'parental responsibility agreement', and section 4(2) applies in relation to such agreements as it applies in relation to parental responsibility agreements under section 4.

(3) A parental responsibility agreement under subsection (1)(a), or an order under subsection (1)(b), may only be brought to an end by an order of the court made on the application –

   (a)   of any person who has parental responsibility for the child; or
   (b)   with the leave of the court, of the child himself.

(4) The court may only grant leave under subsection (3)(b) if it is satisfied that the child has sufficient understanding to make the proposed application.]¹

NOTES

Amendments.¹ Section inserted: Adoption and Children Act 2002, s 112.² Words inserted: Civil Partnership Act 2004, s 75(1), (2).

5 Appointment of guardians

(1) Where an application with respect to a child is made to the court by any individual, the court may by order appoint that individual to be the child's guardian if –

   (a)   the child has no parent with parental responsibility for him; or
   (b)   a [parent, guardian or special guardian of the child's was named in a child arrangements order as a person with whom the child was to live and]³ has died while the order was in force[; or
   (c)   paragraph (b) does not apply, and the child's only or last surviving special guardian dies.]²

(2) The power conferred by subsection (1) may also be exercised in any family proceedings if the court considers that the order should be made even though no application has been made for it.

(3) A parent who has parental responsibility for his child may appoint another individual to be the child's guardian in the event of his death.

(4) A guardian of a child may appoint another individual to take his place as the child's guardian in the event of his death[; and a special guardian of a child may appoint another individual to be the child's guardian in the event of his death]².

(5) An appointment under subsection (3) or (4) shall not have effect unless it is made in writing, is dated and is signed by the person making the appointment or –

    (a)   in the case of an appointment made by a will which is not signed by the testator, is signed at the direction of the testator in accordance with the requirements of section 9 of the Wills Act 1837; or

    (b)   in any other case, is signed at the direction of the person making the appointment, in his presence and in the presence of two witnesses who each attest the signature.

(6) A person appointed as a child's guardian under this section shall have parental responsibility for the child concerned.

(7) Where –

    (a)   on the death of any person making an appointment under subsection (3) or (4), the child concerned has no parent with parental responsibility for him; or

    (b)   immediately before the death of any person making such an appointment, a [child arrangements order was in force in which the person was named as a person with whom the child was to live or the person][3] [was the child's only (or last surviving) special guardian][2]

the appointment shall take effect on the death of that person.

(8) Where, on the death of any person making an appointment under subsection (3) or (4) –

    (a)   the child concerned has a parent with parental responsibility for him; and

    (b)   subsection (7)(b) does not apply,

the appointment shall take effect when the child no longer has a parent who has parental responsibility for him.

(9) Subsections (1) and (7) do not apply if the [child arrangements][3] order referred to in paragraph (b) of those subsections [also named][3] a surviving parent of the child [as a person with whom the child was to live][3].

(10) Nothing in this section shall be taken to prevent an appointment under subsection (3) or (4) being made by two or more persons acting jointly.

(11) Subject to any provision made by rules of court, no court shall exercise the High Court's inherent jurisdiction to appoint a guardian of the estate of any child.

(12) Where the rules of court are made under subsection (11) they may prescribe the circumstances in which, and conditions subject to which, an appointment of such a guardian may be made.

(13) A guardian of a child may only be appointed in accordance with the provisions of this section.

PART I – Statutes

NOTES

Amendments.[1] Words substituted: Adoption and Children Act 2002, s 115(2), (4)(a)(i).[2] Words inserted: Adoption and Children Act 2002, s 115(2), (4)(a)(ii), (b), (c).[3] Words substituted: Children and Families Act 2014, s 12, Sch 2, paras 1, 2.

Definitions. 'Child': s 105(1); 'family proceedings': s 8(3); 'guardian of a child': s 105(1); 'parental responsibility': s 3; 'residence order': s 8(1); 'signed': s 105(1); 'the court': s 92(7).

6 Guardians: revocation and disclaimer

(1) An appointment under section 5(3) or (4) revokes an earlier such appointment (including one made in an unrevoked will or codicil) made by the same person in respect of the same child, unless it is clear (whether as the result of an express provision in the later appointment or by any necessary implication) that the purpose of the later appointment is to appoint an additional guardian.

(2) An appointment under section 5(3) or (4) (including one made in an unrevoked will or codicil) is revoked if the person who made the appointment revokes it by a written and dated instrument which is signed –

   (a)   by him; or
   (b)   at his direction, in his presence and in the presence of two witnesses who each attest the signature.

(3) An appointment under section 5(3) or (4) (other than one made in a will or codicil) is revoked if, with the intention of revoking the appointment, the person who made it –

   (a)   destroys the instrument by which it was made; or
   (b)   has some other person destroy that instrument in his presence.

[(3A) An appointment under section 5(3) or (4) (including one made in an unrevoked will or codicil) is revoked if the person appointed is the spouse of the person who made the appointment and either –

   (a)   ...[3] a court of civil jurisdiction in England and Wales dissolves or annuls the marriage, or
   (b)   the marriage is dissolved or annulled and the divorce or annulment is entitled to recognition in England and Wales by virtue of Part II of the Family Law Act 1986,

unless a contrary intention appears by the appointment.][1]

[(3B) An appointment under section 5(3) or (4) (including one made in an unrevoked will or codicil) is revoked if the person appointed is the civil partner of the person who made the appointment and either –

   (a)   an order of a court of civil jurisdiction in England and Wales dissolves or annuls the civil partnership, or
   (b)   the civil partnership is dissolved or annulled and the dissolution or annulment is entitled to recognition in England and Wales by virtue of Chapter 3 of Part 5 of the Civil Partnership Act 2004,

unless a contrary intention appears by the appointment.][2]

(4) For the avoidance of doubt, an appointment under section 5(3) or (4) made in a will or codicil is revoked if the will or codicil is revoked.

(5) A person who is appointed as a guardian under section 5(3) or (4) may disclaim his appointment by an instrument in writing signed by him and made within a reasonable time of his first knowing that the appointment has taken effect.

(6) Where regulations are made by the Lord Chancellor prescribing the manner in which such disclaimers must be recorded, no such disclaimer shall have effect unless it is recorded in the prescribed manner.

(7) Any appointment of a guardian under section 5 may be brought to an end at any time by order of the court –

>   (a) on the application of any person who has parental responsibility for the child;
>   (b) on the application of the child concerned, with leave of the court; or
>   (c) in any family proceedings, if the court considers that it should be brought to an end even though no application has been made.

NOTES

Amendments.[1] Subsection inserted: Law Reform (Succession) Act 1995, s 4(1).[2] Subsection inserted: Civil Partnership Act 2004, s 76.[3] Words revoked: Divorce, Dissolution and Separation Act 2020, s 6(1), Schedule, para 52.
Definitions. 'Child': s 105(1); 'family proceedings': s 8(3); 'parental responsibility': s 3; 'signed': s 105(1); 'the court': s 92(7).

7 Welfare reports

(1) A court considering any question with respect to a child under this Act may –

>   (a) ask [an officer of the Service][1] [or a Welsh family proceedings officer][2]; or
>   (b) ask a local authority to arrange for –
>   (i)   an officer of the authority; or
>   (ii)   such other person (other than [an officer of the service][1] [or a Welsh family proceedings officer][2]) as the authority considers appropriate,

to report to the court on such matters relating to the welfare of that child as are required to be dealt with in the report.

(2) The Lord Chancellor may[, after consulting the Lord Chief Justice,][3] make regulations specifying matters which, unless the court orders otherwise, must be dealt with in any report under this section.

(3) The report may be made in writing, or orally, as the court requires.

(4) Regardless of any enactment or rule of law which would otherwise prevent it from doing so, the court may take account of –

>   (a) any statement contained in the report; and
>   (b) any evidence given in respect of the matters referred to in the report,

in so far as the statement or evidence is, in the opinion of the court, relevant to the question which it is considering.

(5) It shall be the duty of the authority or [an officer of the Service][1] [or a Welsh family proceedings officer][2] to comply with any request for a report under this section.

[(6) The Lord Chief Justice may nominate a judicial office holder (as defined in section 109(4) of the Constitutional Reform Act 2005) to exercise his functions under subsection (2).][4]

NOTES

Amendments.[1] Words substituted: Criminal Justice and Court Services Act 2000, s 74, Sch 7, paras 87, 88.[2] Words inserted: Children Act 2004, s 40, Sch 3, paras 5, 6.[3] Words inserted: Constitutional Reform Act 2005, s 15(1), Sch 4, Pt 1, paras 203, 204(1), (2).[4] Subsection inserted: Constitutional Reform Act 2005, s 15(1), Sch 4, Pt 1, paras 203, 204(1), (3).
Definitions. 'Child': s 105(1); 'local authority': s 105(1); 'the court': s 92(7).

PART II
ORDERS WITH RESPECT TO CHILDREN IN FAMILY AND OTHER PROCEEDINGS

General

8 [Child arrangements orders][6] and other orders with respect to children

(1) In this Act –

['child arrangements order' means an order regulating arrangements relating to any of the following –
    (a) with whom a child is to live, spend time or otherwise have contact, and
    (b) when a child is to live, spend time or otherwise have contact with any person;][5]

...[5]

'a prohibited steps order' means an order that no step which could be taken by a parent in meeting his parental responsibility for a child, and which is of a kind specified in the order, shall be taken by any person without the consent of the court;

...[5]

'a specific issue order' means an order giving directions for the purpose of determining a specific question which has arisen, or which may arise, in connection with any aspect of parental responsibility for a child.

(2) In this Act 'a section 8 order' means any of the orders mentioned in subsection (1) and any order varying or discharging such an order.

(3) For the purposes of this Act 'family proceedings' means any proceedings –

    (a) under the inherent jurisdiction of the High Court in relation to children; and
    (b) under the enactments mentioned in subsection (4),

but does not include proceedings on an application for leave under section 100(3).

(4) The enactments are –

    (a)   Parts I, II and IV of this Act;
    (b)   the Matrimonial Causes Act 1973;
    [(ba) Schedule 5 to the Civil Partnership Act 2004;][4]
    (c)   ...[1]
    [(d) the Adoption and Children Act 2002;][3]
    (e)   the Domestic Proceedings and Magistrates' Courts Act 1978;
    [(ea) Schedule 6 to the Civil Partnership Act 2004;][4]
    (f)   ...[1]
    (g)   Part III of the Matrimonial and Family Proceedings Act 1984;
    [(h) the Family Law Act 1996][1];
    [(i)   sections 11 and 12 of the Crime and Disorder Act 1998;][2]
    [(j)   Part 1 of Schedule 2 to the Female Genital Mutilation Act 2003 (other than paragraph 3 of that Schedule).][7]

NOTES

Amendments.[1] Paragraphs inserted or repealed: Family Law Act 1996, s 66(1), Sch 8, Pt III, para 60.[2] Paragraph inserted: Crime and Disorder Act 1998, s 119, Sch 8, para 68.[3] Paragraph substituted: Adoption and Children Act 2002, s 139(1), Sch 3, paras 54, 55.[4] Paragraphs inserted: Civil Partnership Act 2004, s 261(1), Sch 27, para 129(1)–(3).[5] Definition inserted and definitions omitted: Children and Families Act 2014, s 12(1), (2).[6] Words inserted: Children and Families Act 2014, s 12, Sch 2, paras 1, 3.[7] Paragraph inserted: Children Act 1989 (Amendment) (Female Genital Mutilation) Act 2019, s 1.
Definitions. 'A section 8 order': s 8(2); 'child': s 105(1); 'contact order': s 8(1); 'family proceedings': s 8(3); 'parental responsibility': s 3; 'prohibited steps order': s 8(1); 'residence order': s 8(1); 'specific issue order': s 8(1).

9 Restrictions on making section 8 orders

(1) No court shall make any section 8 order, other than a [child arrangements order to which subsection (6B) applies][6], with respect to a child who is in the care of a local authority.

(2) No application may be made by a local authority for a [child arrangements][6] order and no court shall make such an order in favour of a local authority.

(3) A person who is, or was at any time within the last six months, a local authority foster parent of a child may not apply for leave to apply for a section 8 order with respect to the child unless –

    (a)   he has the consent of the authority;
    (b)   he is relative of the child; or
    (c)   the child has lived with him for at least [one year][1] preceding the application.

(4) ...[2]

(5) No court shall exercise its powers to make a specific issue order or prohibited steps order –

    (a)   with a view to achieving a result which could be achieved by making a [child arrangements][6] order [or an order under section 51A of the Adoption and Children Act 2002 (post-adoption contact)][5]; or

(b) in any way which is denied to the High Court (by section 100(2)) in the exercise of its inherent jurisdiction with respect to children.

(6) [No court shall make a [section 8][6] order][4] is to have effect for a period which will end after the child has reached the age of sixteen unless it is satisfied that the circumstances of the case are exceptional.

[(6A) Subsection (6) does not apply to a child arrangements order to which subsection (6B) applies.

(6B) This subsection applies to a child arrangements order if the arrangements regulated by the order relate only to either or both of the following –

(a) with whom the child concerned is to live, and
(b) when the child is to live with any person.][6]

(7) No court shall make any section 8 order, other than one varying or discharging such an order, with respect to a child who has reached the age of sixteen unless it is satisfied that the circumstances of the case are exceptional.

NOTES

Amendments.[1] Words substituted: Adoption and Children Act 2002, s 113(a).[2] Subsection repealed: Adoption and Children Act 2002, s 113(b), 139(3), Sch 5.[3] Words inserted: Adoption and Children Act 2002, s 114(2).[4] Words substituted: Children and Young Persons Act 2008, s 37(1).[5] Words inserted: Children and Families Act 2014, s 9(7).[6] Words substituted and subsections inserted: Children and Families Act 2014, s 12, Sch 2, paras 1, 4.
Definitions. 'A section 8 order': s 8(2); 'child': s 105(1); 'contact order': s 8(1); 'local authority': s 105(1); 'local authority foster parent': s 23(3); 'prohibited steps order': s 8(1); 'relative': s 105(1); 'residence order': s 8(1); 'specific issue order': s 8(1); 'the court': s 92(7).

10 Power of court to make section 8 orders

(1) In any family proceedings in which a question arises with respect to the welfare of any child, the court may make a section 8 order with respect to the child if –

(a) an application for the order has been made by a person who –
   (i) is entitled to apply for a section 8 order with respect to the child; or
   (ii) has obtained the leave of the court to make the application; or
(b) the court considers that the order should be made even though no such application has been made.

(2) The court may also make a section 8 order with respect to any child on the application of a person who –

(a) is entitled to apply for a section 8 order with respect to the child; or
(b) has obtained the leave of the court to make the application.

(3) This section is subject to the restrictions imposed by section 9.

(4) The following persons are entitled to apply to the court for any section 8 order with respect to a child –

(a) any parent[, guardian or special guardian][1] of the child;
[(aa) any person who by virtue of section 4A has parental responsibility for the child;][2]

[(b)   any person who is named, in a child arrangements order that is in force with respect to the child, as a person with whom the child is to live.]⁶

(5)   The following persons are entitled to apply for a [child arrangements]⁶ order with respect to a child –

(a)   any party to a marriage (whether or not subsisting) in relation to whom the child is a child of the family;

[(aa)   any civil partner in a civil partnership (whether or not subsisting) in relation to whom the child is a child of the family;]⁴

(b)   any person with whom the child has lived for a period of at least three years;

(c)   any person who –

  [(i)   in any case where a child arrangements order in force with respect to the child regulates arrangements relating to with whom the child is to live or when the child is to live with any person, has the consent of each of the persons named in the order as a person with whom the child is to live;]⁶

  (ii)   in any case where the child is in the care of a local authority, has the consent of that authority; or

  (iii)   in any other case, has the consent of each of those (if any) who have parental responsibility for the child.

[(d)   any person who has parental responsibility for the child by virtue of provision made under section 12(2A).]⁶

[(5A)   A local authority foster parent is entitled to apply for a [child arrangements order to which subsection (5C) applies]⁶ with respect to a child if the child has lived with him for a period of at least one year immediately preceding the application.]³

[(5B)   A relative of a child is entitled to apply for a [child arrangements order to which subsection (5C) applies]⁶ with respect to the child if the child has lived with the relative for a period of at least one year immediately preceding the application.]⁵

[(5C)   This subsection applies to a child arrangements order if the arrangements regulated by the order relate only to either or both of the following –

(a)   with whom the child concerned is to live, and

(b)   when the child is to live with any person.]⁶

(6)   A person who would not otherwise be entitled (under the previous provisions of this section) to apply for the variation or discharge of a section 8 order shall be entitled to do so if –

(a)   the order was made on his application; or

(b)   in the case of a [child arrangements]⁶ order, he is named in [provisions of the order regulating arrangements relating to –

  (i)   with whom the child concerned is to spend time or otherwise have contact, or

  (ii)   when the child is to spend time or otherwise have contact with any person.]⁶

(7) Any person who falls within a category of person prescribed by rules of court is entitled to apply for any such section 8 order as may be prescribed in relation to that category of person.

[(7A) If a special guardianship order is in force with respect to a child, an application for a [child arrangements order to which subsection (7B) applies][6] may only be made with respect to him, if apart from this subsection the leave of the court is not required, with such leave.][3]

[(7B) This subsection applies to a child arrangements order if the arrangements regulated by the order consist of, or include, arrangements which relate to either or both of the following –

    (a)   with whom the child concerned is to live, and
    (b)   when the child is to live with any person.][6]

(8) Where the person applying for leave to make an application for a section 8 order is the child concerned, the court may only grant leave if it is satisfied that he has sufficient understanding to make the proposed application for the section 8 order.

(9) Where the person applying for leave to make an application for a section 8 order is not the child concerned, the court shall, in deciding whether or not to grant leave, have particular regard to –

    (a)   the nature of the proposed application for the section 8 order;
    (b)   the applicant's connection with the child;
    (c)   any risk there might be of that proposed application disrupting the child's life to such an extent that he would be harmed by it; and
    (d)   where the child is being looked after by a local authority –
        (i)   the authority's plans for the child's future; and
        (ii)   the wishes and feelings of the child's parents.

(10) The period of three years mentioned in subsection (5)(b) need not be continuous but must not have begun more than five years before, or ended more than three months before, the making of the application.

NOTES

Amendments.[1] Words substituted: Adoption and Children Act 2002, s 139(1), Sch 3, paras 54, 56(a).[2] Paragraph inserted: Adoption and Children Act 2002, s 139(1), Sch 3, paras 54, 56(b).[3] Subsection inserted: Adoption and Children Act 2002, s 139(1), Sch 3, paras 54, 56(c), (d).[4] Paragraph inserted: Civil Partnership Act 2004, s 77.[5] Subsection inserted: Children and Young Persons Act 2008, s 36.[6] Paragraphs substituted and inserted; subparagraph substituted; words substituted; subsections inserted: Children and Families Act 2014, s 12, Sch 2, paras 1, 5.

Definitions. 'A section 8 order': s 8(2); 'child': s 105(1); 'child who is looked after by a local authority': s 22(1); 'child of the family': s 105(1); 'contact order': s 8(1); 'family proceedings': s 8(3); 'guardian of a child': s 105(1); 'harm': ss 31(a), 105(1); 'local authority': s 105(1); 'parental responsibility': s 3; 'residence order': s 8(1); 'the court': s 92(7).

11 General principles and supplementary provisions

(1) In proceedings in which any question of making a section 8 order, or any other question with respect to such an order, arises, the court shall (in the light of any [provision in rules of court that is of the kind mentioned in subsection (2) (a) or (b))][2] –

(a)   draw up a timetable with a view to determining the question without delay; and

(b)   give such directions as it considers appropriate for the purpose of ensuring, so far as is reasonably practicable, that that timetable is adhered to.

(2) Rules of court may –

(a)   specify periods within which specified steps must be taken in relation to proceedings in which such questions arise; and

(b)   make other provision with respect to such proceedings for the purpose of ensuring, so far as is reasonably practicable, that such questions are determined without delay.

(3) Where a court has power to make a section 8 order, it may do so at any time during the course of the proceedings in question even though it is not in a position to dispose finally of those proceedings.

(4) ...[1]

(5) Where –

(a)   a [child arrangements][1] order has been made with respect to a child; and

(b)   [the child has][1] two parents who each have parental responsibility for him,

the [order, so far as it has the result that there are times when the child lives or is to live with one of the parents,][1] shall cease to have effect if the parents live together for a continuous period of more than six months.

(6) [A child arrangements order made with respect to a child, so far as it provides for the child to spend time or otherwise have contact with one of the child's parents at times when the child is living with the child's other parent,][1] shall cease to have effect if the parents live together for a continuous period of more than six months.

(7) A section 8 order may –

(a)   contain directions about how it is to be carried into effect;

(b)   impose conditions which must be complied with by any person –

[(i)   who is named in the order as a person with whom the child concerned is to live, spend time or otherwise have contact;][1]

(ii)   who is a parent of the child ...[1];

(iii) who is not a parent of his but who has parental responsibility for him; or

(iv) with whom the child is living,

and to whom the conditions are expressed to apply;

(c)   be made to have effect for a specified period, or contain provisions which are to have effect for a specified period;

(d)   make such incidental, supplemental or consequential provision as the court thinks fit.

PART I – Statutes

NOTES

Amendments.[1] Subsection omitted, words substituted and omitted, and subparagraph substituted: Children and Families Act 2014, s 12, Sch 2, paras 1, 6.[2] Words substituted: Children and Families Act 2014, s 14(1), (5).

Definitions. 'A section 8 order': s 8(2); 'child': s 105(1); 'contact order': s 8(1); 'parental responsibility': s 3; 'residence order': s 8(1); 'the court': s 92(7).

[11A ...[2] Activity directions

[(1) Subsection (2) applies in proceedings in which the court is considering whether to make provision about one or more of the matters mentioned in subsection (1A) by making –

    (a)   a child arrangements order with respect to the child concerned, or

    (b)   an order varying or discharging a child arrangements order with respect to the child concerned.

(1A) The matters mentioned in this subsection are –

    (a)   with whom a child is to live,

    (b)   when a child is to live with any person,

    (c)   with whom a child is to spend time or otherwise have contact, and

    (d)   when a child is to spend time or otherwise have contact with any person.

(2) The court may make an activity direction in connection with the provision that the court is considering whether to make.

(2A) Subsection (2B) applies in proceedings in which subsection (2) does not apply and in which the court is considering –

    (a)   whether a person has failed to comply with a provision of a child arrangements order, or

    (b)   what steps to take in consequence of a person's failure to comply with a provision of a child arrangements order.

(2B) The court may make an activity direction in connection with that provision of the child arrangements order.

(3) An activity direction is a direction requiring an individual who is a party to the proceedings concerned to take part in an activity that would, in the court's opinion, help to establish, maintain or improve the involvement in the life of the child concerned of –

    (a)   that individual, or

    (b)   another individual who is a party to the proceedings.][2]

(4) The direction is to specify the activity and the person providing the activity.

(5) The activities that may be so required include, in particular –

    (a)   programmes, classes and counselling or guidance sessions of a kind that –

(i)   may assist a person as regards establishing, maintaining or improving [involvement in a child's life][2];

(ii) may, by addressing a person's violent behaviour, enable or facilitate [involvement in a child's life][2];

(b)   sessions in which information or advice is given as regards making or operating arrangements for [involvement in a child's life][2], including making arrangements by means of mediation.

(6) No individual may be required by [an][2] activity direction –

(a)   to undergo medical or psychiatric examination, assessment or treatment;
(b)   to take part in mediation.

(7) A court may not on the same occasion –

(a)   make [an activity direction under subsection (2)][2], and
(b)   dispose finally of the proceedings as they relate to [the matters mentioned in subsection (1A) in connection with which the activity direction is made][2].

[(7A) A court may not on the same occasion –

(a)   make an activity direction under subsection (2B), and
(b)   dispose finally of the proceedings as they relate to failure to comply with the provision in connection with which the activity direction is made.][2]

(8) [Each of subsections (2) and (2B)][2] has effect subject to the restrictions in sections 11B and 11E.

(9) In considering whether to make [an][2] activity direction, the welfare of the child concerned is to be the court's paramount consideration.][1]

NOTES

Amendments.[1] Section inserted: Children and Adoption Act 2006, s 1.[2] Subsections substituted, subsection inserted, words substituted and word omitted: Children and Families Act 2014, s 12, Sch 2, paras 1, 7.

[11B ...[3] Activity directions: further provision

(1) A court may not make [an activity direction under section 11A(2) in connection with any matter mentioned in section 11A(1A)][3] unless there is a dispute as regards the provision [about that matter][3] that the court is considering whether to make in the proceedings.

(2) A court may not make [an][3] activity direction requiring an individual who is a child to take part in an activity unless the individual is a parent of the child in relation to whom the court is considering provision [about a matter mentioned in section 11A(1A)][3].

(3) A court may not make [an activity][3] direction in connection with the making, variation or discharge of a [child arrangements order][3], if the [child arrangements order][3] is, or would if made be, an excepted order.

(4) A [child arrangements order][3] with respect to a child is an excepted order if –

(a) it is made in proceedings that include proceedings on an application for a relevant adoption order in respect of the child; or

(b) it makes provision as regards contact between the child and a person who would be a parent or relative of the child but for the child's adoption by an order falling within subsection (5).

(5) An order falls within this subsection if it is –

(a) a relevant adoption order;

(b) an adoption order, within the meaning of section 72(1) of the Adoption Act 1976, other than an order made by virtue of section 14 of that Act on the application of a married couple one of whom is the mother or the father of the child;

(c) a Scottish adoption order, within the meaning of the Adoption and Children Act 2002, other than an order made –

   (i) by virtue of section 14 of the Adoption (Scotland) Act 1978 on the application of a married couple one of whom is the mother or the father of the child, or

   (ii) by virtue of section 15(1)(aa) of that Act; or

   [(iii) by virtue of an application under section 30 of the Adoption and Children (Scotland) Act 2007 where subsection (3) of that section applies; or]²

(d) a Northern Irish adoption order, within the meaning of the Adoption and Children Act 2002, other than an order made by virtue of Article 14 of the Adoption (Northern Ireland) Order 1987 on the application of a married couple one of whom is the mother or the father of the child.

(6) A relevant adoption order is an adoption order, within the meaning of section 46(1) of the Adoption and Children Act 2002, other than an order made –

(a) on an application under section 50 of that Act by a couple (within the meaning of that Act) one of whom is the mother or the father of the person to be adopted, or

(b) on an application under section 51(2) of that Act.

(7) A court may not make [an]³ activity direction in relation to an individual unless the individual is habitually resident in England and Wales; and a direction ceases to have effect if the individual subject to the direction ceases to be habitually resident in England and Wales.]¹

NOTES

Amendments.¹ Section inserted: Children and Adoption Act 2006, s 1.² Paragraph inserted: Adoption and Children (Scotland) Act 2007 (Consequential Modifications) Order 2011, SI 2011/1740, art 2, Sch 1, Pt 1, para 3(1), (2).³ Words substituted and word omitted: Children and Families Act 2014, s 12, Sch 2, paras 1, 8.

[11C ...² Activity conditions

(1) This section applies if in any family proceedings the court makes –

   [(a) a child arrangements order containing –
      (i) provision for a child to live with different persons at different times,

    (ii)   provision regulating arrangements relating to with whom a child is to spend time or otherwise have contact, or

    (iii) provision regulating arrangements relating to when a child is to spend time or otherwise have contact with any person; or

  (b)   an order varying a child arrangements order so as to add, vary or omit provision of a kind mentioned in paragraph (a)(i), (ii) or (iii).][2]

(2) The [child arrangements order][2] may impose, or the [child arrangements order][2] may be varied so as to impose, a condition ['an activity condition')][2] requiring an individual falling within subsection (3) to take part in an activity that [would, in the court's opinion, help to establish, maintain or improve the involvement in the life of the child concerned of –

  (a)   that individual, or

  (b)   another individual who is a party to the proceedings.][2].

(3) An individual falls within this subsection if he is –

  (a)   for the purposes of the [child arrangements order][2] so made or varied, [a person][2] with whom the child concerned lives or is to live;

  (b)   [a person][2] whose contact with the child concerned is provided for in that order; or

  (c)   a person upon whom that order imposes a condition under section 11(7)(b).

(4) The condition is to specify the activity and the person providing the activity.

(5) Subsections (5) and (6) of section 11A have effect as regards the activities that may be required by [an][2] activity condition as they have effect as regards the activities that may be required by [an][2] activity direction.

(6) Subsection (2) has effect subject to the restrictions in sections 11D and 11E.][1]

NOTES

Amendments.[1] Section inserted: Children and Adoption Act 2006, s 1.[2] Paragraphs and words substituted and word omitted: Children and Families Act 2014, s 12, Sch 2, paras 1, 9.

[11D …[2] Activity conditions: further provision

(1) A [child arrangements order][2] may not impose [an activity][2] condition on an individual who is a child unless the individual is a parent of the child concerned.

(2) If a [child arrangements order][2] is an excepted order (within the meaning given by section 11B(4)), it may not impose (and it may not be varied so as to impose) [an activity][2] condition.

(3) A [child arrangements order][2] may not impose [an activity][2] condition on an individual unless the individual is habitually resident in England and Wales; and a condition ceases to have effect if the individual subject to the condition ceases to be habitually resident in England and Wales.][1]

NOTES

Amendments.[1] Section inserted: Children and Adoption Act 2006, s 1.[2] Words substituted and word omitted: Children and Families Act 2014, s 12, Sch 2, paras 1, 10.

[11E ...² Activity directions and conditions: making

(1) Before making [an activity]² direction (or imposing [an activity]² condition by means of a [child arrangements order]²), the court must satisfy itself as to the matters falling within subsections (2) to (4).

(2) The first matter is that the activity proposed to be specified is appropriate in the circumstances of the case.

(3) The second matter is that the person proposed to be specified as the provider of the activity is suitable to provide the activity.

(4) The third matter is that the activity proposed to be specified is provided in a place to which the individual who would be subject to the direction (or the condition) can reasonably be expected to travel.

(5) Before making such a direction (or such an order), the court must obtain and consider information about the individual who would be subject to the direction (or the condition) and the likely effect of the direction (or the condition) on him.

(6) Information about the likely effect of the direction (or the condition) may, in particular, include information as to –

    (a)   any conflict with the individual's religious beliefs;
    (b)   any interference with the times (if any) at which he normally works or attends an educational establishment.

(7) The court may ask an officer of the Service or a Welsh family proceedings officer to provide the court with information as to the matters in subsections (2) to (5); and it shall be the duty of the officer of the Service or Welsh family proceedings officer to comply with any such request.

(8) In this section 'specified' means specified in [an]² activity direction (or in [an]² activity condition).]¹

NOTES

Amendments.¹ Section inserted: Children and Adoption Act 2006, s 1.² Words substituted and word omitted: Children and Families Act 2014, s 12, Sch 2, paras 1, 11.

[11F ...² Activity directions and conditions: financial assistance

(1) The Secretary of State may by regulations make provision authorising him to make payments to assist individuals falling within subsection (2) in paying relevant charges or fees.

(2) An individual falls within this subsection if he is required by [an activity]² direction or condition to take part in an activity that [is expected to help to establish, maintain or improve the involvement of that or another individual in the life of]² a child, not being a child ordinarily resident in Wales.

(3) The National Assembly for Wales may by regulations make provision authorising it to make payments to assist individuals falling within subsection (4) in paying relevant charges or fees.

(4) An individual falls within this subsection if he is required by [an activity]² direction or condition to take part in an activity that [is expected to help to establish, maintain or improve the involvement of that or another individual in the life of]² a child who is ordinarily resident in Wales.

(5) A relevant charge or fee, in relation to an activity required by [an activity]² direction or condition, is a charge or fee in respect of the activity payable to the person providing the activity.

(6) Regulations under this section may provide that no assistance is available to an individual unless –

  (a)   the individual satisfies such conditions as regards his financial resources as may be set out in the regulations;

  (b)   the activity in which the individual is required by [an activity]² direction or condition to take part is provided to him in England or Wales;

  (c)   where the activity in which the individual is required to take part is provided to him in England, it is provided by a person who is for the time being approved by the Secretary of State as a provider of activities required by [an activity]² direction or condition;

  (d)   where the activity in which the individual is required to take part is provided to him in Wales, it is provided by a person who is for the time being approved by the National Assembly for Wales as a provider of activities required by [an activity]² direction or condition.

(7) Regulations under this section may make provision –

  (a)   as to the maximum amount of assistance that may be paid to or in respect of an individual as regards an activity in which he is required by [an activity]² direction or condition to take part;

  (b)   where the amount may vary according to an individual's financial resources, as to the method by which the amount is to be determined;

  (c)   authorising payments by way of assistance to be made directly to persons providing activities required by [an activity]² direction or condition.]¹

NOTES

Amendments.¹ Section inserted: Children and Adoption Act 2006, s 1.² Words substituted and word omitted: Children and Families Act 2014, s 12, Sch 2, paras 1, 12.

[11G ...² Activity directions and conditions: monitoring

(1) This section applies if in any family proceedings the court –

  (a)   makes [an activity]² direction in relation to an individual, or

  (b)   makes a [child arrangements order]² that imposes, or varies a [child arrangements order]² so as to impose, [an activity]² condition on an individual.

(2) The court may on making the direction (or imposing the condition by means of a [child arrangements order]²) ask an officer of the Service or a Welsh family proceedings officer –

(a)   to monitor, or arrange for the monitoring of, the individual's compliance with the direction (or the condition);

(b)   to report to the court on any failure by the individual to comply with the direction (or the condition).

(3) It shall be the duty of the officer of the Service or Welsh family proceedings officer to comply with any request under subsection (2).][1]

NOTES

Amendments.[1] Section inserted: Children and Adoption Act 2006, s 1.[2] Words substituted and word omitted: Children and Families Act 2014, s 12, Sch 2, paras 1, 13.

[11H Monitoring contact [and shared residence][2]

(1) This section applies if in any family proceedings the court makes –

[(a) a child arrangements order containing provision of a kind mentioned in section 11C(1)(a)(i), (ii) or (iii), or

(b)   an order varying a child arrangements order so as to add, vary or omit provision of any of those kinds.][2]

(2) The court may ask an officer of the Service or a Welsh family proceedings officer –

(a)   to monitor whether an individual falling within subsection (3) complies with [each provision of any of those kinds that is contained in the child arrangements order (or in the child arrangements order as varied);][2]

(b)   to report to the court on such matters relating to the individual's compliance as the court may specify in the request.

(3) An individual falls within this subsection if the [child arrangements order][2] so made (or the [child arrangements order][2] as so varied) –

[(za) provides for the child concerned to live with different persons at different times and names the individual as one of those persons;

(a)   imposes requirements on the individual with regard to the child concerned spending time or otherwise having contact with some other person;

(b)   names the individual as a person with whom the child concerned is to spend time or otherwise have contact; or][2]

(c)   imposes a condition under section 11(7)(b) on the individual.

(4) If the [child arrangements order][2] (or the [child arrangements order][2] as varied) includes [an activity][2] condition, a request under subsection (2) is to be treated as relating to the provisions of the order other than [the contact activity][2] condition.

(5) The court may make a request under subsection (2) –

(a)   on making the [child arrangements order][2] (or the order varying the [child arrangements order][2]), or

(b)   at any time during the subsequent course of the proceedings as they relate to contact with the child concerned [or to the child's living arrangements][2].

(6) In making a request under subsection (2), the court is to specify the period for which the officer of the Service or Welsh family proceedings officer is to monitor compliance with the order; and the period specified may not exceed twelve months.

(7) It shall be the duty of the officer of the Service or Welsh family proceedings officer to comply with any request under subsection (2).

(8) The court may order any individual falling within subsection (3) to take such steps as may be specified in the order with a view to enabling the officer of the Service or Welsh family proceedings officer to comply with the court's request under subsection (2).

(9) But the court may not make an order under subsection (8) with respect to an individual who is a child unless he is a parent of the child with respect to whom the order falling within subsection (1) was made.

(10) A court may not make a request under subsection (2) in relation to a [child arrangements][2] order that is an excepted order (within the meaning given by section 11B(4)).][1]

NOTES

Amendments.[1] Section inserted: Children and Adoption Act 2006, s 2.[2] Words substituted and inserted: Children and Families Act 2014, s 12, Sch 2, paras 1, 14.

[11I [Child arrangements][2] orders: warning notices

Where the court makes (or varies) a [child arrangements][2] order, it is to attach to the [child arrangements][2] order (or the order varying the [child arrangements][2] order) a notice warning of the consequences of failing to comply with the [child arrangements][2] order.][1]

NOTES

Amendments.[1] Section inserted: Children and Adoption Act 2006, s 3.[2] Words substituted: Children and Families Act 2014, s 12, Sch 2, paras 1, 15.

[11J Enforcement orders

(1) This section applies if a [child arrangements][2] order with respect to a child has been made.

(2) If the court is satisfied beyond reasonable doubt that a person has failed to comply with [a provision of the child arrangements][2] order, it may make an order (an 'enforcement order') imposing on the person an unpaid work requirement.

(3) But the court may not make an enforcement order if it is satisfied that the person had a reasonable excuse for failing to comply with the [provision][2].

(4) The burden of proof as to the matter mentioned in subsection (3) lies on the person claiming to have had a reasonable excuse, and the standard of proof is the balance of probabilities.

PART I – Statutes

(5) The court may make an enforcement order in relation to the [child arrangements order]² only on the application of –

    (a)   [a person]² who is, for the purposes of the [child arrangements order]², [a person]² with whom the child concerned lives or is to live;

    (b)   [a person]² whose contact with the child concerned is provided for in the [child arrangements order]²;

    (c)   any individual subject to a condition under section 11(7)(b) or [an activity]² condition imposed by the [child arrangements order]²; or

    (d)   the child concerned.

(6) Where the person proposing to apply for an enforcement order in relation to a [child arrangements]² order is the child concerned, the child must obtain the leave of the court before making such an application.

(7) The court may grant leave to the child concerned only if it is satisfied that he has sufficient understanding to make the proposed application.

(8) Subsection (2) has effect subject to the restrictions in sections 11K and 11L.

(9) The court may suspend an enforcement order for such period as it thinks fit.

(10) Nothing in this section prevents a court from making more than one enforcement order in relation to the same person on the same occasion.

(11) Proceedings in which any question of making an enforcement order, or any other question with respect to such an order, arises are to be regarded for the purposes of section 11(1) and (2) as proceedings in which a question arises with respect to a section 8 order.

(12) In Schedule A1 –

    (a)   Part 1 makes provision as regards an unpaid work requirement;

    (b)   Part 2 makes provision in relation to the revocation and amendment of enforcement orders and failure to comply with such orders.

(13) …³]¹

NOTES

Amendments.¹ Section inserted: Children and Adoption Act 2006, s 4(1).² Words substituted: Children and Families Act 2014, s 12, Sch 2, paras 1, 16.³ Subsection omitted: Crime and Courts Act 2013, s 17, Sch 11, paras 102, 103.

[11K Enforcement orders: further provision

(1) A court may not make an enforcement order against a person in respect of a failure to comply with a [provision of a child arrangements order]² unless it is satisfied that before the failure occurred the person had been given (in accordance with rules of court) a copy of, or otherwise informed of the terms of –

    (a)   in the case of a failure to comply with [a provision of a child arrangements order where the order]² was varied before the failure occurred, a notice under section 11I relating to the order varying [the child arrangements]² order or, where more than one such order has been made, the last order preceding the failure in question;

(b)   in any other case, a notice under section 11I relating to the [child arrangements]² order.

(2) A court may not make an enforcement order against a person in respect of any failure to comply with a [provision of a child arrangements]² order occurring before the person attained the age of 18.

(3) A court may not make an enforcement order against a person in respect of a failure to comply with a [provision of a child arrangements order where the child arrangements order]² is an excepted order (within the meaning given by section 11B(4)).

(4) A court may not make an enforcement order against a person unless the person is habitually resident in England and Wales; and an enforcement order ceases to have effect if the person subject to the order ceases to be habitually resident in England and Wales.]¹

NOTES

Amendments.¹ Section inserted: Children and Adoption Act 2006, s 4(1).² Words substituted: Children and Families Act 2014, s 12, Sch 2, paras 1, 17.

[11L   Enforcement orders: making

(1) Before making an enforcement order as regards a person in breach of [a provision of a child arrangements]² order, the court must be satisfied that –

(a)   making the enforcement order proposed is necessary to secure the person's compliance with the [child arrangements]² order or any [child arrangements]² order that has effect in its place;

(b)   the likely effect on the person of the enforcement order proposed to be made is proportionate to the seriousness of the breach …².

(2) Before making an enforcement order, the court must satisfy itself that provision for the person to work under an unpaid work requirement imposed by an enforcement order can be made in the local justice area in which the person in breach resides or will reside.

(3) Before making an enforcement order as regards a person in breach of a [provision of a child arrangements]² order, the court must obtain and consider information about the person and the likely effect of the enforcement order on him.

(4) Information about the likely effect of the enforcement order may, in particular, include information as to –

(a)   any conflict with the person's religious beliefs;

(b)   any interference with the times (if any) at which he normally works or attends an educational establishment.

(5) A court that proposes to make an enforcement order may ask an officer of the Service or a Welsh family proceedings officer to provide the court with information as to the matters in subsections (2) and (3).

(6) It shall be the duty of the officer of the Service or Welsh family proceedings officer to comply with any request under this section.

(7) In making an enforcement order in relation to a [child arrangements]² order, a court must take into account the welfare of the child who is the subject of the [child arrangements]² order.]¹

NOTES

Amendments.¹ Section inserted: Children and Adoption Act 2006, s 4(1). ² Words substituted and omitted: Children and Families Act 2014, s 12, Sch 2, paras 1, 18.

[11M Enforcement orders: monitoring

(1) On making an enforcement order in relation to a person, the court is to ask an officer of the Service or a Welsh family proceedings officer –

 (a) to monitor, or arrange for the monitoring of, the person's compliance with the unpaid work requirement imposed by the order;
 (b) to report to the court if a report under paragraph 8 of Schedule A1 is made in relation to the person;
 (c) to report to the court on such other matters relating to the person's compliance as may be specified in the request;
 (d) to report to the court if the person is, or becomes, unsuitable to perform work under the requirement.

(2) It shall be the duty of the officer of the Service or Welsh family proceedings officer to comply with any request under this section.]¹

NOTES

Amendments.¹ Section inserted: Children and Adoption Act 2006, s 4(1).

[11N Enforcement orders: warning notices

Where the court makes an enforcement order, it is to attach to the order a notice warning of the consequences of failing to comply with the order.]¹

NOTES

Amendments.¹ Section inserted: Children and Adoption Act 2006, s 4(1).

[11O Compensation for financial loss

(1) This section applies if a [child arrangements]² order with respect to a child has been made.

(2) If the court is satisfied that –

 (a) an individual has failed to comply with the [a provision of the child arrangements]² order, and
 (b) a person falling within subsection (6) has suffered financial loss by reason of the breach,

it may make an order requiring the individual in breach to pay the person compensation in respect of his financial loss.

(3) But the court may not make an order under subsection (2) if it is satisfied that the individual in breach had a reasonable excuse for failing to comply with the [particular provision of the child arrangements][2] order.

(4) The burden of proof as to the matter mentioned in subsection (3) lies on the individual claiming to have had a reasonable excuse.

(5) An order under subsection (2) may be made only on an application by the person who claims to have suffered financial loss.

(6) A person falls within this subsection if he is –

    (a)   [a person][2] who is, for the purposes of the [child arrangements order][2], [a person][2] with whom the child concerned lives or is to live;

    (b)   [a person][2] whose contact with the child concerned is provided for in the [child arrangements order][2];

    (c)   an individual subject to a condition under section 11(7)(b) or [an activity][2] condition imposed by the [child arrangements order][2]; or

    (d)   the child concerned.

(7) Where the person proposing to apply for an order under subsection (2) is the child concerned, the child must obtain the leave of the court before making such an application.

(8) The court may grant leave to the child concerned only if it is satisfied that he has sufficient understanding to make the proposed application.

(9) The amount of compensation is to be determined by the court, but may not exceed the amount of the applicant's financial loss.

(10) In determining the amount of compensation payable by the individual in breach, the court must take into account the individual's financial circumstances.

(11) An amount ordered to be paid as compensation may be recovered by the applicant as a civil debt due to him.

(12) Subsection (2) has effect subject to the restrictions in section 11P.

(13) Proceedings in which any question of making an order under subsection (2) arises are to be regarded for the purposes of section 11(1) and (2) as proceedings in which a question arises with respect to a section 8 order.

(14) In exercising its powers under this section, a court is to take into account the welfare of the child concerned.][1]

NOTES

Amendments.[1] Section inserted: Children and Adoption Act 2006, s 5.[2] Words substituted: Children and Families Act 2014, s 12, Sch 2, paras 1, 19.

PART I – Statutes

[11P Orders under section 11O(2): further provision

(1) A court may not make an order under section 11O(2) requiring an individual to pay compensation in respect of a failure by him to comply with a [provision of a child arrangements][2] unless it is satisfied that before the failure occurred the individual had been given (in accordance with rules of court) a copy of, or otherwise informed of the terms of –

(a) in the case of a failure to comply with [a provision of a child arrangements order where the order][2] was varied before the failure occurred, a notice under section 11I relating to the order varying the [child arrangements][2] order or, where more than one such order has been made, the last order preceding the failure in question;

(b) in any other case, a notice under section 11I relating to the [child arrangements][2] order.

(2) A court may not make an order under section 11O(2) requiring an individual to pay compensation in respect of a failure by him to comply with a [provision of a child arrangements][2] order where the failure occurred before the individual attained the age of 18.

(3) A court may not make an order under section 11O(2) requiring an individual to pay compensation in respect of a failure by him to comply with a contact order that is an excepted order (within the meaning given by section 11B(4)).][1]

NOTES

Amendments.[1] Section inserted: Children and Adoption Act 2006, s 5.[2] Words substituted: Children and Families Act 2014, s 12, Sch 2, paras 1, 20.

12 [Child arrangements][4] orders and parental responsibility

[(1) Where –

(a) the court makes a child arrangements order with respect to a child,

(b) the father of the child, or a woman who is a parent of the child by virtue of section 43 of the Human Fertilisation and Embryology Act 2008, is named in the order as a person with whom the child is to live, and

(c) the father, or the woman, would not otherwise have parental responsibility for the child,

the court must also make an order under section 4 giving the father, or under section 4ZA giving the woman, that responsibility.

(1A) Where –

(a) the court makes a child arrangements order with respect to a child,

(b) the father of the child, or a woman who is a parent of the child by virtue of section 43 of the Human Fertilisation and Embryology Act 2008, is named in the order as a person with whom the child is to spend time or otherwise have contact but is not named in the order as a person with whom the child is to live, and

(c)   the father, or the woman, would not otherwise have parental responsibility for the child,

the court must decide whether it would be appropriate, in view of the provision made in the order with respect to the father or the woman, for him or her to have parental responsibility for the child and, if it decides that it would be appropriate for the father or the woman to have that responsibility, must also make an order under section 4 giving him, or under section 4ZA giving her, that responsibility.]⁶

(2) Where the court makes a [child arrangements order and a person who is not a]⁶ parent or guardian of the child concerned [is named in the order as a person with whom the child is to live,]⁶ that person shall have parental responsibility for the child while the [order remains in force so far as providing for the child to live with that person]⁶.

[(2A) Where the court makes a child arrangements order and –

(a)   a person who is not the parent or guardian of the child concerned is named in the order as a person with whom the child is to spend time or otherwise have contact, but

(b)   the person is not named in the order as a person with whom the child is to live,

the court may provide in the order for the person to have parental responsibility for the child while paragraphs (a) and (b) continue to be met in the person's case.]⁶

(3) Where a person has parental responsibility for a child as a result of subsection (2) [or (2A)]⁶, he shall not have the right –

(a)   …¹

(b)   to agree, or refuse to agree, to the making of an adoption order, or an order under [section 84 of the Adoption and Children Act 2002]², with respect to the child; or

(c)   to appoint a guardian for the child.

(4) Where subsection (1) [...⁶]⁴ requires the court to make an order under section 4 [or 4ZA]⁴ [in respect of a]⁶ [parent]⁴ of a child, the court shall not bring that order to an end at any time while the [child arrangements order concerned remains in force so far as providing for the child to live with that parent]⁶.

[(5) …⁵

(6) …⁵]³

NOTES

Amendments.¹ Paragraph repealed: Adoption and Children Act 2002, s 139(1), (3), Sch 3, paras 54, 57(a), Sch 5.² Words substituted: Adoption and Children Act 2002, s 139(1), (3), Sch 3, paras 54, 57(b).³ Subsections inserted: Adoption and Children Act 2002, s 114(1).⁴ Subsection inserted, words inserted and word substituted: Human Fertilisation and Embryology Act 2008, s 56, Sch 6, Pt 1, para 28.⁵ Subsections repealed: Children and Young Persons Act 2008, ss 36, 42, Sch 4.⁶ Subsections substituted and inserted, words substituted, inserted and omitted: Children and Families Act 2014, s 12, Sch 2, paras 1, 21.

Definitions. 'Child': s 105(1); 'guardian of a child': s 105(1); 'parental responsibility': s 3; 'residence order': s 8(1); 'the court': s 92(7).

PART I – Statutes

13 Change of child's name or removal from jurisdiction

(1) Where a [child arrangements order to which subsection (4) applies][1] is in force with respect to a child, no person may –

(a)   cause the child to be known by a new surname; or
(b)   remove him from the United Kingdom;

without either the written consent of every person who has parental responsibility for the child or the leave of the court.

(2) Subsection (1)(b) does not prevent the removal of a child, for a period of less than one month, by [a person named in the child arrangements order as a person with whom the child is to live][1].

(3) In making a [child arrangements order to which subsection (4) applies,][1] the court may grant the leave required by subsection (1)(b), either generally or for specified purposes.

[(4) This subsection applies to a child arrangements order if the arrangements regulated by the order consist of, or include, arrangements which relate to either or both of the following –

(a)   with whom the child concerned is to live, and
(b)   when the child is to live with any person.][1]

NOTES

Amendments.[1] Words substituted and subsection inserted: Children and Families Act 2014, s 12, Sch 2, paras 1, 22.
Definitions. 'Child': s 105(1); 'parental responsibility': s 3; 'residence order': s 8(1); 'the court': s 92(7).

14 Enforcement of residence orders

...[1]

NOTES

Amendment.[1] Section omitted: Children and Families Act 2014, s 12, Sch 2, paras 1, 23.

[Special guardianship

14A Special guardianship orders

(1) A 'special guardianship order' is an order appointing one or more individuals to be a child's 'special guardian' (or special guardians).

(2) A special guardian –

(a)   must be aged eighteen or over; and
(b)   must not be a parent of the child in question,

and subsections (3) to (6) are to be read in that light.

(3) The court may make a special guardianship order with respect to any child on the application of an individual who –

(a) is entitled to make such an application with respect to the child; or
(b) has obtained the leave of the court to make the application,

or on the joint application of more than one such individual.

(4) Section 9(3) applies in relation to an application for leave to apply for a special guardianship order as it applies in relation to an application for leave to apply for a section 8 order.

(5) The individuals who are entitled to apply for a special guardianship order with respect to a child are –

(a) any guardian of the child;
(b) any individual [who is named in a child arrangements order as a person with whom the child is to live;]³
(c) any individual listed in subsection (5)(b) or (c) of section 10 (as read with subsection (10) of that section);
(d) a local authority foster parent with whom the child has lived for a period of at least one year immediately preceding the application[;
(e) a relative with whom the child has lived for a period of at least one year immediately preceding the application]².

(6) The court may also make a special guardianship order with respect to a child in any family proceedings in which a question arises with respect to the welfare of the child if –

(a) an application for the order has been made by an individual who falls within subsection (3)(a) or (b) (or more than one such individual jointly); or
(b) the court considers that a special guardianship order should be made even though no such application has been made.

(7) No individual may make an application under subsection (3) or (6)(a) unless, before the beginning of the period of three months ending with the date of the application, he has given written notice of his intention to make the application –

(a) if the child in question is being looked after by a local authority, to that local authority, or
(b) otherwise, to the local authority in whose area the individual is ordinarily resident.

(8) On receipt of such a notice, the local authority must investigate the matter and prepare a report for the court dealing with –

(a) the suitability of the applicant to be a special guardian;
(b) such matters (if any) as may be prescribed by the Secretary of State; and
(c) any other matter which the local authority consider to be relevant.

(9) The court may itself ask a local authority to conduct such an investigation and prepare such a report, and the local authority must do so.

(10) The local authority may make such arrangements as they see fit for any person to act on their behalf in connection with conducting an investigation or preparing a report referred to in subsection (8) or (9).

(11) The court may not make a special guardianship order unless it has received a report dealing with the matters referred to in subsection (8).

(12) Subsections (8) and (9) of section 10 apply in relation to special guardianship orders as they apply in relation to section 8 orders.

(13) This section is subject to section 29(5) and (6) of the Adoption and Children Act 2002.][1]

NOTES

Amendments.[1] Section inserted: Adoption and Children Act 2002, s 115(1).[2] Paragraph inserted: Children and Young Persons Act 2008, s 38.[3] Words substituted: Children and Families Act 2014, s 12, Sch 2, paras 1, 24.

[14B Special guardianship orders: making

(1) Before making a special guardianship order, the court must consider whether, if the order were made –

(a) a [child arrangements order containing contact provision][3] should also be made with respect to the child, ...[2]

(b) any section 8 order in force with respect to the child should be varied or discharged.

[(c) where [provision contained in a child arrangements order][3] made with respect to the child is not discharged, any enforcement order relating to [that provision][3] should be revoked, and

(d) where an activity direction has been made –

(i) in proceedings for the making, variation or discharge of a child arrangements order with respect to the child, or

(ii) in other proceedings that relate to such an order,

that direction should be discharged.][3][2]

[(1A) In subsection (1) 'contact provision' means provision which regulates arrangements relating to –

(a) with whom a child is to spend time or otherwise have contact, or

(b) when a child is to spend time or otherwise have contact with any person;

but in paragraphs (a) and (b) a reference to spending time or otherwise having contact with a person is to doing that otherwise than as a result of living with the person.][3]

(2) On making a special guardianship order, the court may also –

(a) give leave for the child to be known by a new surname;

(b) grant the leave required by section 14C(3)(b), either generally or for specified purposes.][1]

NOTES

Amendments.[1] Section inserted: Adoption and Children Act 2002, s 115(1).[2] Word repealed and paragraphs inserted: Children and Adoption Act 2006, s 15, Sch 2, paras 7, 8, Sch 3.[3] Words and paragraph substituted, and subsection inserted: Children and Families Act 2014, s 12, Sch 2, paras 1, 25.

[14C   Special guardianship orders: effect

(1) The effect of a special guardianship order is that while the order remains in force –

    (a)   a special guardian appointed by the order has parental responsibility for the child in respect of whom it is made; and

    (b)   subject to any other order in force with respect to the child under this Act, a special guardian is entitled to exercise parental responsibility to the exclusion of any other person with parental responsibility for the child (apart from another special guardian).

(2) Subsection (1) does not affect –

    (a)   the operation of any enactment or rule of law which requires the consent of more than one person with parental responsibility in a matter affecting the child; or

    (b)   any rights which a parent of the child has in relation to the child's adoption or placement for adoption.

(3) While a special guardianship order is in force with respect to a child, no person may –

    (a)   cause the child to be known by a new surname; or

    (b)   remove him from the United Kingdom,

without either the written consent of every person who has parental responsibility for the child or the leave of the court.

(4) Subsection (3)(b) does not prevent the removal of a child, for a period of less than three months, by a special guardian of his.

(5) If the child with respect to whom a special guardianship order is in force dies, his special guardian must take reasonable steps to give notice of that fact to –

    (a)   each parent of the child with parental responsibility; and

    (b)   each guardian of the child,

but if the child has more than one special guardian, and one of them has taken such steps in relation to a particular parent or guardian, any other special guardian need not do so as respects that parent or guardian.

(6) This section is subject to section 29(7) of the Adoption and Children Act 2002.][1]

NOTES

Amendments.[1] Section inserted: Adoption and Children Act 2002, s 115(1).

[14D Special guardianship orders: variation and discharge

(1) The court may vary or discharge a special guardianship order on the application of –

(a) the special guardian (or any of them, if there are more than one);

(b) any parent or guardian of the child concerned;

(c) any individual [who is named in a child arrangements order as a person with whom the child is to live;]²

(d) any individual not falling within any of paragraphs (a) to (c) who has, or immediately before the making of the special guardianship order had, parental responsibility for the child;

(e) the child himself; or

(f) a local authority designated in a care order with respect to the child.

(2) In any family proceedings in which a question arises with respect to the welfare of a child with respect to whom a special guardianship order is in force, the court may also vary or discharge the special guardianship order if it considers that the order should be varied or discharged, even though no application has been made under subsection (1).

(3) The following must obtain the leave of the court before making an application under subsection (1) –

(a) the child;

(b) any parent or guardian of his;

(c) any step-parent of his who has acquired, and has not lost, parental responsibility for him by virtue of section 4A;

(d) any individual falling within subsection (1)(d) who immediately before the making of the special guardianship order had, but no longer has, parental responsibility for him.

(4) Where the person applying for leave to make an application under subsection (1) is the child, the court may only grant leave if it is satisfied that he has sufficient understanding to make the proposed application under subsection (1).

(5) The court may not grant leave to a person falling within subsection (3)(b)(c) or (d) unless it is satisfied that there has been a significant change in circumstances since the making of the special guardianship order.]¹

NOTES

Amendments.¹ Section inserted: Adoption and Children Act 2002, s 115(1).² Words substituted: Children and Families Act 2014, s 12, Sch 2, paras 1, 26.

[14E Special guardianship orders: supplementary

(1) In proceedings in which any question of making, varying or discharging a special guardianship order arises, the court shall (in the light of any [provision in rules of court that is of the kind mentioned in section 11(2)(a) or (b))]² –

(a) draw up a timetable with a view to determining the question without delay; and

(b)   give such directions as it considers appropriate for the purpose of ensuring, so far as is reasonably practicable, that the timetable is adhered to.

(2) Subsection (1) applies also in relation to proceedings in which any other question with respect to a special guardianship order arises.

(3) The power to make rules in subsection (2) of section 11 applies for the purposes of this section as it applies for the purposes of that.

(4) A special guardianship order, or an order varying one, may contain provisions which are to have effect for a specified period.

(5) Section 11(7) (apart from paragraph (c)) applies in relation to special guardianship orders and orders varying them as it applies in relation to section 8 orders.][1]

NOTES

Amendments.[1] Section inserted: Adoption and Children Act 2002, s 115(1).[2] Words substituted: Children and Families Act 2014, s 14(1), (6).

[14F   Special guardianship support services

(1) Each local authority must make arrangements for the provision within their area of special guardianship support services, which means –

(a)   counselling, advice and information; and
(b)   such other services as are prescribed,

in relation to special guardianship.

(2) The power to make regulations under subsection (1)(b) is to be exercised so as to secure that local authorities provide financial support.

(3) At the request of any of the following persons –

(a)   a child with respect to whom a special guardianship order is in force;
(b)   a special guardian;
(c)   a parent;
(d)   any other person who falls within a prescribed description,

a local authority may carry out an assessment of that person's needs for special guardianship support services (but, if the Secretary of State so provides in regulations, they must do so if he is a person of a prescribed description, or if his case falls within a prescribed description, or if both he and his case fall within prescribed descriptions).

(4) A local authority may, at the request of any other person, carry out an assessment of that person's needs for special guardianship support services.

(5) Where, as a result of an assessment, a local authority decide that a person has needs for special guardianship support services, they must then decide whether to provide any such services to that person.

(6) If –

(a) a local authority decide to provide any special guardianship support services to a person, and

(b) the circumstances fall within a prescribed description,

the local authority must prepare a plan in accordance with which special guardianship support services are to be provided to him, and keep the plan under review.

(7) The Secretary of State may by regulations make provision about assessments, preparing and reviewing plans, the provision of special guardianship support services in accordance with plans and reviewing the provision of special guardianship support services.

(8) The regulations may in particular make provision –

(a) about the type of assessment which is to be carried out, or the way in which an assessment is to be carried out;

(b) about the way in which a plan is to be prepared;

(c) about the way in which, and the time at which, a plan or the provision of special guardianship support services is to be reviewed;

(d) about the considerations to which a local authority are to have regard in carrying out an assessment or review or preparing a plan;

(e) as to the circumstances in which a local authority may provide special guardianship support services subject to conditions (including conditions as to payment for the support or the repayment of financial support);

(f) as to the consequences of conditions imposed by virtue of paragraph (e) not being met (including the recovery of any financial support provided);

(g) as to the circumstances in which this section may apply to a local authority in respect of persons who are outside that local authority's area;

(h) as to the circumstances in which a local authority may recover from another local authority the expenses of providing special guardianship support services to any person.

(9) A local authority may provide special guardianship support services (or any part of them) by securing their provision by –

(a) another local authority; or

(b) a person within a description prescribed in regulations of persons who may provide special guardianship support services,

and may also arrange with any such authority or person for that other authority or that person to carry out the local authority's functions in relation to assessments under this section.

(10) A local authority may carry out an assessment of the needs of any person for the purposes of this section at the same time as an assessment of his needs is made under any other provision of this Act or under any other enactment.

(11) Section 27 (co-operation between authorities) applies in relation to the exercise of functions of a local authority [in England][2] under this section as it applies in relation to the exercise of functions of a local authority under Part 3

[and see sections 164 and 164A of the Social Services and Well-being (Wales) Act 2014 for provision about co-operation between local authorities in Wales and other bodies]².]¹

NOTES

Amendments.¹ Section inserted: Adoption and Children Act 2002, s 115(1).² Words inserted: SI 2016/413, regs 55, 56.

[14G

…²]¹

NOTES

Amendments.¹ Section inserted: Adoption and Children Act 2002, s 115(1).² Section repealed: Health and Social Care (Community Health and Standards) Act 2003, ss 117(2), 196, Sch 14, Pt 2.

Financial relief

15   Orders for financial relief with respect to children

(1) Schedule 1 (which consists primarily of the re-enactment, with consequential amendments and minor modifications, of provisions of [section 6 of the Family Law Reform Act 1969]¹, the Guardianship of Minors Acts 1971 and 1973, the Children Act 1975 and of sections 15 and 16 of the Family Law Reform Act 1987) makes provision in relation to financial relief for children.

(2) …²

NOTES

Amendments.¹ Words inserted: Courts and Legal Services Act 1990, s 116, Sch 16, para 10(1).² Subsection omitted: Crime and Courts Act 2013, s 17, Sch 11, paras 102, 105.

Family assistance orders

16   Family assistance orders

(1) Where, in any family proceedings, the court has power to make an order under this Part with respect to any child, it may (whether or not it makes such an order) make an order requiring –

(a) [an officer of the Service]¹ [or a Welsh family proceedings officer]² to be made available; or
(b) a local authority to make an officer of the authority available,

to advise, assist and (where appropriate) befriend any person named in the order.

(2) The persons who may be named in an order under this section ('a family assistance order') are –

(a) any parent [, guardian or special guardian]³ of the child;
(b) any person with whom the child is living or [who is named in a child arrangements order as a person with whom the child is to live, spend time or otherwise have contact]⁵;
(c) the child himself.

PART I – Statutes

(3) No court may make a family assistance order unless –

(a) ...[4]

(b) it has obtained the consent of every person to be named in the order other than the child.

(4) A family assistance order may direct –

(a) the person named in the order; or

(b) such of the persons named in the order as may be specified in the order,

to take such steps as may be so specified with a view to enabling the officer concerned to be kept informed of the address of any person named in the order and to be allowed to visit any such person.

[(4A) If the court makes a family assistance order with respect to a child and the order is to be in force at the same time as [contact provision contained in a child arrangements order][5] made with respect to the child, the family assistance order may direct the officer concerned to give advice and assistance as regards establishing, improving and maintaining contact to such of the persons named in the order as may be specified in the order.][4]

[(4B) In subsection (4A) 'contact provision' means provision which regulates arrangements relating to –

(a) with whom a child is to spend time or otherwise have contact, or

(b) when a child is to spend time or otherwise have contact with any person.][5]

(5) Unless it specifies a shorter period, a family assistance order shall have effect for a period of [twelve months][4] beginning with the day on which it is made.

[(6) If the court makes a family assistance order with respect to a child and the order is to be in force at the same time as a section 8 order made with respect to the child, the family assistance order may direct the officer concerned to report to the court on such matters relating to the section 8 order as the court may require (including the question whether the section 8 order ought to be varied or discharged).][4]

(7) A family assistance order shall not be made so as to require a local authority to make an officer of theirs available unless –

(a) the authority agree; or

(b) the child concerned lives or will live within their area.

(8), (9) ...[1]

NOTES

Amendments.[1] Words substituted or subsections omitted: Criminal Justice and Court Services Act 2000, s 74, Sch 7, paras 87, 89, Sch 8.[2] Words inserted: Children Act 2004, s 40, Sch 3, paras 5, 7.[3] Words substituted: Adoption and Children Act 2002, s 139(1), Sch 3, paras 54, 58.[4] Paragraph repealed, subsections inserted and substituted, and words substituted: Children and Adoption Act 2006, ss 6(1)–(5), 15(2), Sch 3.[5] Words substituted and subsection inserted: Children and Families Act 2014, s 12, Sch 2, paras 1, 27.

Definitions. 'A section 8 order': s 8(2); 'child': s 105(1); 'contact order': s 8(1); 'family assistance order': s 16(2); 'family proceedings': s 8(3); 'guardian of a child': s 105(1); 'local authority': s 105(1); 'the court': s 92(7).

[16A Risk assessments

(1) This section applies to the following functions of officers of the Service or Welsh family proceedings officers –

(a)   any function in connection with family proceedings in which the court has power to make an order under this Part with respect to a child or in which a question with respect to such an order arises;

(b)   any function in connection with an order made by the court in such proceedings.

(2) If, in carrying out any function to which this section applies, an officer of the Service or a Welsh family proceedings officer is given cause to suspect that the child concerned is at risk of harm, he must –

(a)   make a risk assessment in relation to the child, and

(b)   provide the risk assessment to the court.

(3) A risk assessment, in relation to a child who is at risk of suffering harm of a particular sort, is an assessment of the risk of that harm being suffered by the child.][1]

NOTES

Amendments.[1] Section inserted: Children and Adoption Act 2006, s 7.

[PART III
SUPPORT FOR CHILDREN AND FAMILIES PROVIDED BY LOCAL AUTHORITIES IN ENGLAND][1]

[Application to local authorities in England

16B Application to local authorities in England

(1) This Part applies in relation to local authorities in England.

(2) Accordingly, unless the contrary intention appears, a reference in this Part to a local authority means a local authority in England.]

NOTES

Amendments.[1] Part heading substituted, section and cross head inserted: SI 2016/413, regs 55, 57.

Provision of services for children and their families

17 Provision of services for children in need, their families and others

(1) It shall be the general duty of every local authority (in addition to the other duties imposed on them by this Part) –

(a)   to safeguard and promote the welfare of children within their area who are in need; and

(b)   so far as is consistent with that duty, to promote the upbringing of such children by their families,

by providing a range and level of services appropriate to those children's needs.

(2) For the purpose principally of facilitating the discharge of their general duty under this section, every local authority shall have the specific duties and powers set out in Part 1 of Schedule 2.

(3) Any service provided by an authority in the exercise of functions conferred on them by this section may be provided for the family of a particular child in need or for any member of his family, if it is provided with a view to safeguarding or promoting the child's welfare.

(4) The [Secretary of State]⁷ may by order amend any provision of Part I of Schedule 2 or add any further duty or power to those for the time being mentioned there.

[(4A) Before determining what (if any) services to provide for a particular child in need in the exercise of functions conferred on them by this section, a local authority shall, so far as is reasonably practicable and consistent with the child's welfare –

(a) ascertain the child's wishes and feelings regarding the provision of those services; and

(b) give due consideration (having regard to his age and understanding) to such wishes and feelings of the child as they have been able to ascertain.]⁶

(5) Every local authority –

(a) shall facilitate the provision by others (including in particular voluntary organisations) of services which [it is a function of the authority]⁹ to provide by virtue of this section, or section 18, 20, [[22A to 22C]⁹, 23B to 23D, 24A or 24B]³; and

(b) may make such arrangements as they see fit for any person to act on their behalf in the provision of any such service.

(6) The services provided by a local authority in the exercise of functions conferred on them by this section may include [providing accommodation and]⁴ giving assistance in kind or …¹⁰ in cash.

(7) Assistance may be unconditional or subject to conditions as to the repayment of the assistance or of its value (in whole or in part).

(8) Before giving any assistance or imposing any conditions, a local authority shall have regard to the means of the child concerned and of each of his parents.

(9) No person shall be liable to make any repayment of assistance or of its value at any time when he is in receipt [of universal credit (except in such circumstances as may be prescribed),]¹¹ of income support [under]⁵ [Part VII of the Social Security Contributions and Benefits Act 1992]¹[, of any element of child tax credit other than the family element, of working tax credit]⁵ [or of an income-based jobseeker's allowance]².

(10) For the purposes of this Part a child shall be taken to be in need if –

(a) he is unlikely to achieve or maintain, or to have the opportunity of achieving or maintaining, a reasonable standard of health or development without the provision for him of services by a local authority under this Part;

(b) his health or development is likely to be significantly impaired, or further impaired, without the provision for him of such services; or

(c) he is disabled,

and 'family', in relation to such a child, includes any person who has parental responsibility for the child and any other person with whom he has been living.

(11) For the purposes of this Part, a child is disabled if he is blind, deaf or dumb or suffers from mental disorder of any kind or is substantially and permanently handicapped by illness, injury or congenital deformity or such other disability as may be prescribed; and in this Part –

'development' means physical, intellectual, emotional, social or behavioural development; and

'health' means physical or mental health.

[(12) The Treasury may by regulations prescribe circumstances in which a person is to be treated for the purposes of this Part (or for such of those purposes as are prescribed) as in receipt of any element of child tax credit other than the family element or of working tax credit][, of an income-based jobseeker's allowance or of an income-related employment and support allowance][8].

[(13) The duties imposed on a local authority by virtue of this section do not apply in relation to a child in the authority's area who is being looked after by a local authority in Wales in accordance with Part 6 of the Social Services and Well-being (Wales) Act 2014.][12]

NOTES

Amendments.[1] Words substituted: Disability Living Allowance and Disability Working Allowance Act 1991, s 7(2), Sch 3, Pt II, para 13.[2] Words substituted: Social Security (Consequential Provisions) Act 1992, s 4, Sch 2, para 108.[3] Words substituted: Children (Leaving Care) Act 2000, s 7(1), (2).[4] Words inserted: Adoption and Children Act 2002, s 116(1).[5] Words substituted and subsection inserted: Tax Credits Act 2002, s 47, Sch 3, paras 15 and 16.[6] Subsection inserted: Children Act 2004, s 53(1).[7] Words substituted: SI 2016/413, regs 55, 58.[8] Words inserted: Welfare Reform Act 2007, s 28(1), Sch 3, para 6(1), (2).[9] Words substituted: Children and Young Persons Act 2008, s 8(2), Sch 1, para 1.[10] Words repealed: Children and Young Persons Act 2008, ss 24, 42, Sch 4.[11] Words inserted: Welfare Reform Act 2012, s 31, Sch 2, para 1.[12] Subsection inserted: SI 2016/413, regs 55, 58.

Definitions. 'Child': s 105(1); 'child in need': s 17(10); 'development': s 17(11); 'disabled': s 17(11); 'family': s 17(10); 'functions': s 105(1); 'health': s 17(11); 'local authority': s 105(1); 'parental responsibility': s 3; 'prescribed': s 105(1); 'service': s 105(1); 'upbringing': s 105(1); 'voluntary organisation': s 105(1).

[17ZA Young carers' needs assessments…][3]

(1) A local authority …[3] must assess whether a young carer within their area has needs for support and, if so, what those needs are, if –

(a) it appears to the authority that the young carer may have needs for support, or

(b) the authority receive a request from the young carer or a parent of the young carer to assess the young carer's needs for support.

(2) An assessment under subsection (1) is referred to in this Part as a 'young carer's needs assessment'.

(3) In this Part 'young carer' means a person under 18 who provides or intends to provide care for another person (but this is qualified by section 17ZB(3)).

(4) Subsection (1) does not apply in relation to a young carer if the local authority have previously carried out a care-related assessment of the young carer in relation to the same person cared for.

(5) But subsection (1) does apply (and so a young carer's needs assessment must be carried out) if it appears to the authority that the needs or circumstances of the young carer or the person cared for have changed since the last care-related assessment.

(6) 'Care-related assessment' means –

    (a)   a young carer's needs assessment;

    (b)   an assessment under any of the following –

        (i)   section 1 of the Carers (Recognition and Services) Act 1995;

        (ii)   section 1 of the Carers and Disabled Children Act 2000;

        (iii) section 4(3) of the Community Care (Delayed Discharges) Act 2003;

        [(iv) Part 1 of the Care Act 2014.][2]

(7) A young carer's needs assessment must include an assessment of whether it is appropriate for the young carer to provide, or continue to provide, care for the person in question, in the light of the young carer's needs for support, other needs and wishes.

(8) A local authority, in carrying out a young carer's needs assessment, must have regard to –

    (a)   the extent to which the young carer is participating in or wishes to participate in education, training or recreation, and

    (b)   the extent to which the young carer works or wishes to work.

(9) A local authority, in carrying out a young carer's needs assessment, must involve –

    (a)   the young carer,

    (b)   the young carer's parents, and

    (c)   any person who the young carer or a parent of the young carer requests the authority to involve.

(10) A local authority that have carried out a young carer's needs assessment must give a written record of the assessment to –

    (a)   the young carer,

    (b)   the young carer's parents, and

    (c)   any person to whom the young carer or a parent of the young carer requests the authority to give a copy.

PART I – Statutes

(11) Where the person cared for is under 18, the written record must state whether the local authority consider him or her to be a child in need.

(12) A local authority …[3] must take reasonable steps to identify the extent to which there are young carers within their area who have needs for support.][1]

NOTES

Amendments.[1] Section inserted: Children and Families Act 2014, s 96(1).[2] Sub-paragraph inserted: Care Act 2014 and Children and Families Act 2014 (Consequential Amendments) Order 2015, SI 2015/914, art 2, Sch, paras 43, 44.[3] Words omitted: SI 2016/413, regs 55, 59.

[17ZB   Young carers' needs assessments: supplementary

(1) This section applies for the purposes of section 17ZA.

(2) 'Parent', in relation to a young carer, includes –

    (a)   a parent of the young carer who does not have parental responsibility for the young carer, and

    (b)   a person who is not a parent of the young carer but who has parental responsibility for the young carer.

(3) A person is not a young carer if the person provides or intends to provide care –

    (a)   under or by virtue of a contract, or

    (b)   as voluntary work.

(4) But in a case where the local authority consider that the relationship between the person cared for and the person under 18 providing or intending to provide care is such that it would be appropriate for the person under 18 to be regarded as a young carer, that person is to be regarded as such (and subsection (3) is therefore to be ignored in that case).

(5) The references in section 17ZA and this section to providing care include a reference to providing practical or emotional support.

(6) Where a local authority –

    (a)   are required to carry out a young carer's needs assessment, and

    (b)   are required or have decided to carry out some other assessment of the young carer or of the person cared for;

the local authority may, subject to subsection (7), combine the assessments.

(7) A young carer's needs assessment may be combined with an assessment of the person cared for only if the young carer and the person cared for agree.

(8) The Secretary of State may by regulations make further provision about carrying out a young carer's needs assessment; the regulations may, in particular –

    (a)   specify matters to which a local authority is to have regard in carrying out a young carer's needs assessment;

(b)   specify matters which a local authority is to determine in carrying out a young carer's needs assessment;

(c)   make provision about the manner in which a young carer's needs assessment is to be carried out;

(d)   make provision about the form a young carer's needs assessment is to take.

(9) The Secretary of State may by regulations amend the list in section 17ZA(6)(b) so as to –

(a)   add an entry,

(b)   remove an entry, or

(c)   vary an entry.]¹

NOTES

Amendment.¹ Section inserted: Children and Families Act 2014, s 96(1).

[17ZC Consideration of young carers' needs assessments

A local authority that carry out a young carer's needs assessment must consider the assessment and decide –

(a)   whether the young carer has needs for support in relation to the care which he or she provides or intends to provide;

(b)   if so, whether those needs could be satisfied (wholly or partly) by services which the authority may provide under section 17; and

(c)   if they could be so satisfied, whether or not to provide any such services in relation to the young carer.]¹

NOTES

Amendment.¹ Section inserted: Children and Families Act 2014, s 96(1).

[17ZD Parent carers' needs assessments...³

(1) A local authority ...³ must, if the conditions in subsections (3) and (4) are met, assess whether a parent carer within their area has needs for support and, if so, what those needs are.

(2) In this Part 'parent carer' means a person aged 18 or over who provides or intends to provide care for a disabled child for whom the person has parental responsibility.

(3) The first condition is that –

(a)   it appears to the authority that the parent carer may have needs for support, or

(b)   the authority receive a request from the parent carer to assess the parent carer's needs for support.

(4) The second condition is that the local authority are satisfied that the disabled child cared for and the disabled child's family are persons for whom they may provide or arrange for the provision of services under section 17.

(5) An assessment under subsection (1) is referred to in this Part as a 'parent carer's needs assessment'.

(6) Subsection (1) does not apply in relation to a parent carer if the local authority have previously carried out a care-related assessment of the parent carer in relation to the same disabled child cared for.

(7) But subsection (1) does apply (and so a parent carer's needs assessment must be carried out) if it appears to the authority that the needs or circumstances of the parent carer or the disabled child cared for have changed since the last care-related assessment.

(8) 'Care-related assessment' means –

    (a)   a parent carer's needs assessment;
    (b)   an assessment under any of the following –
        (i)   section 1 of the Carers (Recognition and Services) Act 1995;
        (ii)   section 6 of the Carers and Disabled Children Act 2000;
        (iii)   section 4(3) of the Community Care (Delayed Discharges) Act 2003;
        [(iv) Part 1 of the Care Act 2014.][2]

(9) A parent carer's needs assessment must include an assessment of whether it is appropriate for the parent carer to provide, or continue to provide, care for the disabled child, in the light of the parent carer's needs for support, other needs and wishes.

(10) A local authority in carrying out a parent carer's needs assessment must have regard to –

    (a)   the well-being of the parent carer, and
    (b)   the need to safeguard and promote the welfare of the disabled child cared for and any other child for whom the parent carer has parental responsibility.

(11) In subsection (10) 'well-being' has the same meaning as in Part 1 of the Care Act 2014.

(12) A local authority, in carrying out a parent carer's needs assessment, must involve –

    (a)   the parent carer,
    (b)   any child for whom the parent carer has parental responsibility, and
    (c)   any person who the parent carer requests the authority to involve.

(13) A local authority that have carried out a parent carer's needs assessment must give a written record of the assessment to –

    (a)   the parent carer, and
    (b)   any person to whom the parent carer requests the authority to give a copy.

(14) A local authority ...[3] must take reasonable steps to identify the extent to which there are parent carers within their area who have needs for support.][1]

PART I – Statutes

NOTES

Amendments.[1] Section inserted: Children and Families Act 2014, s 97(1).[2] Sub-paragraph inserted: Care Act 2014 and Children and Families Act 2014 (Consequential Amendments) Order 2015, SI 2015/914, art 2, Sch, paras 43, 45.[3] Words omitted: SI 2016/413, regs 55, 60.

[17ZE Parent carers' needs assessments: supplementary

(1) This section applies for the purposes of section 17ZD.

(2) The references in section 17ZD to providing care include a reference to providing practical or emotional support.

(3) Where a local authority –

    (a)   are required to carry out a parent carer's needs assessment, and

    (b)   are required or have decided to carry out some other assessment of the parent carer or of the disabled child cared for,

the local authority may combine the assessments.

(4) The Secretary of State may by regulations make further provision about carrying out a parent carer's needs assessment; the regulations may, in particular –

    (a)   specify matters to which a local authority is to have regard in carrying out a parent carer's needs assessment;

    (b)   specify matters which a local authority is to determine in carrying out a parent carer's needs assessment;

    (c)   make provision about the manner in which a parent carer's needs assessment is to be carried out;

    (d)   make provision about the form a parent carer's needs assessment is to take.

(5) The Secretary of State may by regulations amend the list in section 17ZD(8) (b) so as to –

    (a)   add an entry,

    (b)   remove an entry, or

    (c)   vary an entry.][1]

NOTES

Amendment.[1] Section inserted: Children and Families Act 2014, s 97(1).

[17ZF Consideration of parent carers' needs assessments

A local authority that carry out a parent carer's needs assessment must consider the assessment and decide –

    (a)   whether the parent carer has needs for support in relation to the care which he or she provides or intends to provide;

    (b)   whether the disabled child cared for has needs for support;

    (c)   if paragraph (a) or (b) applies, whether those needs could be satisfied (wholly or partly) by services which the authority may provide under section 17; and

(d)   if they could be so satisfied, whether or not to provide any such services in relation to the parent carer or the disabled child cared for.][1]

NOTES

Amendment.[1] Section inserted: Children and Families Act 2014, s 97(1).

[17ZG   Section 17 services: continued provision where EHC plan maintained

(1) This section applies where, immediately before a child in need reaches the age of 18 –

(a)   a local authority …[3] is providing services for the child in the exercise of functions conferred by section 17, and

(b)   an EHC plan is maintained for the child.

(2) The local authority may continue to provide services for the child in the exercise of those functions after the child reaches the age of 18, but may not continue to do so after the EHC plan has ceased to be maintained[, except in so far as the authority is required to do so under section 17ZH or 17ZI][2].

(3) In this section 'EHC plan' means a plan within section 37(2) of the Children and Families Act 2014.][1]

NOTES

Commencement. 1 September 2014, SI 2014/889, art 7.
Amendment.[1] Section inserted: Children and Families Act 2014, s 50.[2] Words inserted: Care Act 2014, s 66(2).[3] Words omitted: SI 2016/413, regs 55, 61.

[17ZH   Section 17 services: transition for children to adult care and support

(1) Subsections (2) to (4) apply where a local authority …[2] providing services for a child in need in the exercise of functions conferred by section 17 –

(a)   are required by section 58(1) or 63(1) of the Care Act 2014 to carry out a child's needs assessment or young carer's assessment in relation to the child, or

(b)   are required by section 60(1) of that Act to carry out a child's carer's assessment in relation to a carer of the child.

(2) If the local authority carry out the assessment before the child reaches the age of 18 and decide to treat it as a needs or carer's assessment in accordance with section 59(6), 61(6) or 64(7) of the Care Act 2014 (with Part 1 of that Act applying to the assessment as a result), the authority must continue to comply with section 17 after the child reaches the age of 18 until they reach a conclusion in his case.

(3) If the local authority carry out the assessment before the child reaches the age of 18 but decide not to treat it as a needs or carer's assessment in accordance with section 59(6), 61(6) or 64(7) of the Care Act 2014 –

(a)   they must carry out a needs or carer's assessment (as the case may be) after the child reaches the age of 18, and

(b) they must continue to comply with section 17 after he reaches that age until they reach a conclusion in his case.

(4) If the local authority do not carry out the assessment before the child reaches the age of 18, they must continue to comply with section 17 after he reaches that age until –

(a) they decide that the duty under section 9 or 10 of the Care Act 2014 (needs or carer's assessment) does not apply, or

(b) having decided that the duty applies and having discharged it, they reach a conclusion in his case.

(5) Subsection (6) applies where a local authority …[2] providing services for a child in need in the exercise of functions conferred by section 17 –

(a) receive a request for a child's needs assessment or young carer's assessment to be carried out in relation to the child or for a child's carer's assessment to be carried out in relation to a carer of the child, but

(b) have yet to be required by section 58(1), 60(1) or 63(1) of the Care Act 2014 to carry out the assessment.

(6) If the local authority do not decide, before the child reaches the age of 18, whether or not to comply with the request, they must continue to comply with section 17 after he reaches that age until –

(a) they decide that the duty under section 9 or 10 of the Care Act 2014 does not apply, or

(b) having decided that the duty applies and having discharged it, they reach a conclusion in his case.

(7) A local authority reach a conclusion in a person's case when –

(a) they conclude that he does not have needs for care and support or for support (as the case may be), or

(b) having concluded that he has such needs and that they are going to meet some or all of them, they begin to do so, or

(c) having concluded that he has such needs, they conclude that they are not going to meet any of those needs (whether because those needs do not meet the eligibility criteria or for some other reason).

(8) In this section, 'child's needs assessment', 'child's carer's assessment', 'young carer's assessment', 'needs assessment', 'carer's assessment' and 'eligibility criteria' each have the same meaning as in Part 1 of the Care Act 2014.][1]

NOTES

Commencement. 1 April 2015, SI 2015/993, art 2.
Amendment.[1] Section inserted: Care Act 2014, s 66(1).[2] Words omitted: SI 2016/413, regs 55, 62.

[17ZI Section 17 services: provision after EHC plan no longer maintained

(1) This section applies where a local authority … providing services for a person in the exercise, by virtue of section 17ZG, of functions conferred by section 17 are required to carry out a needs assessment in that person's case.

(2) If the EHC plan for the person ceases to be maintained before the local authority reach a conclusion in the person's case, they must continue to comply with section 17 until they do reach a conclusion in his case.

(3) The references to the local authority reaching a conclusion in a person's case are to be read with section 17ZH(7).

(4) In this section, 'needs assessment' has the same meaning as in Part 1 of the Care Act 2014.]¹

NOTES

Commencement. 1 April 2015, SI 2015/993, art 2.
Amendment.¹ Section inserted: Care Act 2014, s 66(1).² Words omitted: SI 2016/413, regs 55, 63.

[17A Direct payments

(1) The [Secretary of State]⁴ may by regulations make provision for and in connection with requiring or authorising the responsible authority in the case of a person of a prescribed description who falls within subsection (2) to make, with that person's consent, such payments to him as they may determine in accordance with the regulations in respect of his securing the provision of the service mentioned in that subsection.

(2) A person falls within this subsection if he is –

   (a)   a person with parental responsibility for a disabled child,
   (b)   a disabled person with parental responsibility for a child, or
   (c)   a disabled child aged 16 or 17,

and a local authority ('the responsible authority') have decided for the purposes of section 17 that the child's needs (or, if he is such a disabled child, his needs) call for the provision by them of a service in exercise of functions conferred on them under that section.

[(3) Regulations under this section may, in particular, make provision –

   (a)   specifying circumstances in which the responsible authority are not required or authorised to make any payments under the regulations to a person, whether those circumstances relate to the person in question or to the particular service mentioned in subsection (2);
   (b)   for any payments required or authorised by the regulations to be made to a person by the responsible authority ('direct payments') to be made to that person ('the payee') as gross payments or alternatively as net payments;
   (c)   for the responsible authority to make for the purposes of subsection (3A) or (3B) such determination as to –
          (i)   the payee's means, and
          (ii)   the amount (if any) which it would be reasonably practicable for the payee to pay to the authority by way of reimbursement or contribution,
          as may be prescribed;
   (d)   as to the conditions falling to be complied with by the payee which must or may be imposed by the responsible authority in relation to the direct payments (and any conditions which may not be so imposed);

(e) specifying circumstances in which the responsible authority –
    (i) may or must terminate the making of direct payments,
    (ii) may require repayment (whether by the payee or otherwise) of the whole or part of the direct payments;

(f) for any sum falling to be paid or repaid to the responsible authority by virtue of any condition or other requirement imposed in pursuance of the regulations to be recoverable as a debt due to the authority;

(g) displacing functions or obligations of the responsible authority with respect to the provision of the service mentioned in subsection (2) only to such extent, and subject to such conditions, as may be prescribed;

(h) authorising direct payments to be made to any prescribed person on behalf of the payee;

(j) as to matters to which the responsible authority must, or may, have regard when making a decision for the purposes of a provision of the regulations;

(k) as to steps which the responsible authority must, or may, take before, or after, the authority makes a decision for the purposes of a provision of the regulations;

(l) specifying circumstances in which a person who has fallen within subsection (3D) but no longer does so (whether because of fluctuating capacity, or regaining or gaining of capacity) is to be treated, or may be treated, as falling within subsection (3D) for purposes of this section or for purposes of regulations under this section.

(3A) For the purposes of subsection (3)(b) 'gross payments' means payments –

(a) which are made at such a rate as the authority estimate to be equivalent to the reasonable cost of securing the provision of the service concerned; but

(b) which may be made subject to the condition that the payee pays to the responsible authority, by way of reimbursement, an amount or amounts determined under the regulations.

(3B) For the purposes of subsection (3)(b) 'net payments' means payments –

(a) which are made on the basis that the payee will pay an amount or amounts determined under the regulations by way of contribution towards the cost of securing the provision of the service concerned; and

(b) which are accordingly made at such a rate below that mentioned in subsection (3A)(a) as reflects any such contribution by the payee.

(3C) Regulations made for the purposes of subsection (3)(a) may provide that direct payments shall not be made in respect of the provision of residential accommodation for any person for a period in excess of a prescribed period.

(3D) A person falls within this subsection if the person lacks capacity, within the meaning of the Mental Capacity Act 2005, to consent to the making of direct payments.][6]

(4) Regulations under this section shall provide that, where payments are made under the regulations to a person falling within subsection (5) –

PART I – Statutes

(a)   the payments shall be made at the rate mentioned in subsection [(3A)(a)][6]; and

(b)   subsection [(3A)(b)][6] shall not apply.

(5) A person falls within this subsection if he is –

(a)   a person falling within subsection (2)(a) or (b) and the child in question is aged 16 or 17, or

(b)   a person who is in receipt [of universal credit (except in such circumstances as may be prescribed),][5] of income support, ...[2] under Part 7 of the Social Security Contributions and Benefits Act 1992[, of any element of child tax credit other than the family element, of working tax credit][2] [, of an income-based jobseeker's allowance or of an income-related employment and support allowance][3].

(6) In this section –

...[6]

'disabled' in relation to an adult has the same meaning as that given by section 17(11) in relation to a child;

'prescribed' means specified in or determined in accordance with regulations under this section ...[6].][1]

NOTES

Amendments.[1] Section inserted: Carers and Disabled Children Act 2000, s 7(1); and subsequently substituted: Health and Social Care Act 2001, s 58 (applies to England only).[2] Words repealed or inserted: Tax Credits Act 2002, s 47, Sch 3, s 60, paras 15, 17, Sch 6.[3] Words substituted: Welfare Reform Act 2007, s 28(1), Sch 3, para 6(1), (3).[4] Words substituted: SI 2016/413, regs 55, 64.[5] Words inserted: Welfare Reform Act 2012, s 31, Sch 2, para 1.[6] Subsections and words substituted and words omitted: Care Act 2014 and Children and Families Act 2014 (Consequential Amendments) Order 2015, SI 2015/914, art 2, Sch, paras 43, 46.

Definitions. 'Accommodation': s 22(2); 'child': s 105(1); 'local authority': s 105(1).

[17B ...[2]][1]

NOTES

Amendments.[1] Section inserted in relation to England: Carers and Disabled Children Act 2000, s 7(1).[2] Section omitted: SI 2016/413, regs 55, 65.

Definitions. 'child': s 105(1); 'disabled': s 17(11); 'local authority': s 105(1); 'parental responsibility': s 3.

18 Day care for pre-school and other children

(1) Every local authority shall provide such day care for children in need within their area who are –

(a)   aged five or under; and

(b)   not yet attending schools,

as is appropriate.

(2) ...[1]

(3) A local authority may provide facilities (including training, advice, guidance and counselling) for those –

(a)   caring for children in day care; or

(b)   who at any time accompany such children while they are in day care.

(4) In this section 'day care' means any form of care or supervised activity provided for children during the day (whether or not it is provided on a regular basis).

(5) Every local authority shall provide for children in need within their area who are attending any school such care or supervised activities as is appropriate –

(a)   outside school hours; or

(b)   during school holidays.

(6) …[1]

(7) In this section 'supervised activity' means an activity supervised by a responsible person.

NOTES

Amendments.[1] Subsections omitted: SI 2016/413, regs 55, 66.
Definitions. 'Child': s 105(1); 'child in need': s 17(10); 'day care': s 18(4); 'local authority': s 105(1); 'school': s 105(1); 'supervised activity': s 18(7).

19

…[1]

NOTES

Amendments.[1] Section repealed: Education Act 2002, s 149(2).

Provision of accommodation for children

20 Provision of accommodation for children: general

(1) Every local authority shall provide accommodation for any child in need within their area who appears to them to require accommodation as a result of –

(a)   there being no person who has parental responsibility for him;

(b)   his being lost or having been abandoned; or

(c)   the person who has been caring for him being prevented (whether or not permanently, and for whatever reason) from providing him with suitable accommodation or care.

(2) Where a local authority provide accommodation under subsection (1) for a child who is ordinarily resident in the area of another local authority, that other local authority may take over the provision of accommodation for the child within –

(a)   three months of being notified in writing that the child is being provided with accommodation; or

(b)   such other longer period as may be prescribed [in regulations made by the Secretary of State][4].

[(2A) Where a local authority in Wales provide accommodation under section 76(1) of the Social Services and Well-being (Wales) Act 2014 (accommodation for children without parents or who are lost or abandoned etc.) for a child who is ordinarily resident in the area of a local authority in England, that local authority in England may take over the provision of accommodation for the child within –

(a)   three months of being notified in writing that the child is being provided with accommodation; or

(b)   such other longer period as may be prescribed in regulations made by the Secretary of State.][4]

(3) Every local authority shall provide accommodation for any child in need within their area who has reached the age of sixteen and whose welfare the authority consider is likely to be seriously prejudiced if they do not provide him with accommodation.

(4) A local authority may provide accommodation for any child within their area (even though a person who has parental responsibility for him is able to provide him with accommodation) if they consider that to do so would safeguard or promote the child's welfare.

(5) A local authority may provide accommodation for any person who has reached the age of sixteen but is under twenty-one in any community home which takes children who have reached the age of sixteen if they consider that to do so would safeguard or promote his welfare.

(6) Before providing accommodation under this section, a local authority shall, so far as is reasonably practicable and consistent with the child's welfare –

(a)   ascertain the child's wishes [and feelings][1] regarding the provision of accommodation; and

(b)   give due consideration (having regard to his age and understanding) to such wishes [and feelings][1] of the child as they have been able to ascertain.

(7) A local authority may not provide accommodation under this section for any child if any person who –

(a)   has parental responsibility for him; and
(b)   is willing and able to –
    (i)   provide accommodation for him; or
    (ii) arrange for accommodation to be provided for him,

objects.

(8) Any person who has parental responsibility for a child may at any time remove the child from accommodation provided by or on behalf of the local authority under this section.

(9) Subsections (7) and (8) do not apply while any person –

[(a)   who is named in a child arrangements order as a person with whom the child is to live;][3]

[(aa) who is a special guardian of the child; or][2]

(b)   who has care of the child by virtue of an order made in the exercise of the High Court's inherent jurisdiction with respect to children,

agrees to the child being looked after in accommodation provided by or on behalf of the local authority.

(10) Where there is more than one such person as is mentioned in subsection (9), all of them must agree.

(11) Subsections (7) and (8) do not apply where a child who has reached the age of sixteen agrees to being provided with accommodation under this section.

NOTES

Amendments.[1] Words inserted: Children Act 2004, s 53(2).[2] Paragraph inserted: Adoption and Children Act 2002, s 139(1), Sch 3, paras 54, 59.[3] Paragraph substituted: Children and Families Act 2014, s 12, Sch 2, paras 1, 28.[4] Words and subsection inserted: SI 2016/413, regs 55, 67.

Definitions. 'Child': s 105(1); 'child in need': s 17(10); 'community home': s 53(1); 'local authority': s 105(1); 'ordinary residence': s 105(6); 'parental responsibility': s 3; 'prescribed': s 105(1); 'residence order': s 8(1).

21 Provision of accommodation for children in police protection or detention or on remand, etc

(1) Every local authority shall make provision for the reception and accommodation of children who are removed or kept away from home under Part V.

(2) Every local authority shall receive, and provide accommodation for, children –

(a)   in police protection whom they are requested to receive under section 46(3)(f);

(b)   whom they are requested to receive under section 38(6) of the Police and Criminal Evidence Act 1984;

(c)   who are –

(i)   ...[9]

[(ia) remanded to accommodation provided by or on behalf of a local authority by virtue of [paragraph 5 of Schedule 4 or paragraph 7 of Schedule 5 to the Sentencing Code][12] (breach etc of referral orders and reparation orders);][7]

[(ii) remanded to accommodation provided by or on behalf of a local authority by virtue of [paragraph 25 of Schedule 7 to the Code][12] (breach etc of youth rehabilitation orders); ...[8]

[(iia) remanded to accommodation provided by or on behalf of a local authority by virtue of paragraph 10 of the Schedule to the Street Offences Act 1959 (breach of orders under section 1(2A) of that Act)][8]

(iii) the subject of a youth rehabilitation order imposing a local authority residence requirement or a youth rehabilitation order with fostering,][7]

and with respect to whom they are the designated authority.

[[(2A) In subsection (2)(c)(iii) –

'local authority residence requirement' has the meaning given by paragraph 24 of Schedule 6 to the Sentencing Code;

'youth rehabilitation order' has the meaning given by section 173 of that Code;

'youth rehabilitation order with fostering' has the meaning given by section 176 of that Code.]¹²]⁷

(3) Where a child has been –

    (a)   removed under Part V; or

    (b)   detained under section 38 of the Police and Criminal Evidence Act 1984,

and he is not being provided with accommodation by a local authority [or by a local authority in Wales]¹¹ or in a hospital vested in the [Secretary of State or]¹⁰ [the Welsh Ministers]⁶ [...¹⁰]³ [or otherwise made available pursuant to arrangements made by [the Secretary of State, the National Health Service Commissioning Board or a clinical commissioning group under the National Health Service Act 2006 or]¹⁰ a [[Local Health Board]⁵]²]¹ [...¹⁰]³, any reasonable expenses of accommodating him shall be recoverable from the local authority[, or local authority in Wales,]¹¹ in whose area he is ordinarily resident.

NOTES

Amendments.¹ Words inserted: National Health Service and Community Care Act 1990, s 66(1), Sch 36, para 1.² Words substituted: Health Authorities Act 1995, s 2(1), Sch 1, Pt III, para 118(1), (3).³ Words inserted: Health Act 1999 (Supplementary, Consequential etc Provisions) Order 2000, SI 2000/90.⁴ Words substituted: Powers of Criminal Courts (Sentencing) Act 2000, s 165(1), Sch 9, para 126.⁵ Words substituted: SI 2007/961.⁶ Children and Young Persons Act 2008, s 39, Sch 3, paras 1, 5.⁷ Paragraphs inserted and substituted, and subsection inserted: Criminal Justice and Immigration Act 2008, ss 6(2), (3), 149, Sch 4, Pt 1, paras 33, 34(1)–(3), Pt 2, para 105, Sch 28, Pt 1.⁸ Word omitted and paragraph inserted: Policing and Crime Act 2009, s 112, Sch 7, Pt 3, para 21, Sch 8, Pt 2.⁹ Paragraph omitted: Legal aid, Sentencing and Punishment of Offenders Act 2012, s 105, Sch 12, paras 23, 24.¹⁰ Words substituted, omitted and inserted: Health and Social Care Act 2012, s 55(2), Sch 5, Pt 1, paras 47, 48.¹¹ Words inserted: SI 2016/413, regs 55, 68. ¹² Words and subsection substituted: Sentencing Act 2020, s 410, Sch 24, para 108.

Definitions. 'Accommodation': s 22(2); 'child': s 105(1); 'clinical commissioning group': s 105(1); 'hospital': s 105(1); 'local authority': s 105(1); 'police protection': s 46(2); 'supervision order': s 31(11).

Duties of local authorities in relation to children looked after by them

22 General duty of local authority in relation to children looked after by them

(1) [In this section]⁵, any reference to a child who is looked after by a local authority is a reference to a child who is –

    (a)   in their care; or

    (b)   provided with accommodation by the authority in the exercise of any functions (in particular those under this Act) which [are social services functions within the meaning of]¹ the Local Authority Social Services Act 1970 [, apart from functions under sections [17]³ 23B and 24B]².

(2) In subsection (1) 'accommodation' means accommodation which is provided for a continuous period of more than 24 hours.

(3) It shall be the duty of a local authority looking after any child –

    (a)   to safeguard and promote his welfare; and

PART I – Statutes

(b)   to make such use of services available for children cared for by their own parents as appears to the authority reasonable in his case.

[(3A) The duty of a local authority under subsection (3)(a) to safeguard and promote the welfare of a child looked after by them includes in particular a duty to promote the child's educational achievement.][4]

[(3B) A local authority ...[5] must appoint at least one person for the purpose of discharging the duty imposed by virtue of subsection (3A).

(3C) A person appointed by a local authority under subsection (3B) must be an officer employed by that authority or another local authority ...[5].][6]

(4) Before making any decision with respect to a child whom they are looking after, or proposing to look after, a local authority shall, so far as is reasonably practicable, ascertain the wishes and feelings of –

(a)   the child;
(b)   his parents;
(c)   any person who is not a parent of his but who has parental responsibility for him; and
(d)   any other person whose wishes and feelings the authority consider to be relevant,

regarding the matter to be decided.

(5) In making any such decision a local authority shall give due consideration –

(a)   having regard to his age and understanding, to such wishes and feelings of the child as they have been able to ascertain;
(b)   to such wishes and feelings of any person mentioned in subsection (4) (b) to (d) as they have been able to ascertain; and
(c)   to the child's religious persuasion, racial origin and cultural and linguistic background.

(6) If it appears to a local authority that it is necessary, for the purposes of protecting members of the public from serious injury, to exercise their powers with respect to a child whom they are looking after in a manner which may not be consistent with their duties under this section, they may do so.

(7) If the [Secretary of State][5] considers it necessary, for the purpose of protecting members of the public from serious injury, to give directions to a local authority with respect to the exercise of their powers with respect to a child whom they are looking after, [Secretary of State][5] may give such directions to [the authority][5].

(8) Where any such directions are given to an authority they shall comply with them even though doing so is inconsistent with their duties under this section.

NOTES

Amendments.[1] Words substituted: Local Government Act 2000, s 107, Sch 5, para 19.[2] Words inserted: Children (Leaving Care) Act 2000, s 2(2).[3] Reference inserted: Adoption and Children Act 2002, s 116(2).[4] Subsection inserted: Children Act 2004, s 52.[5] Words substituted and omitted: SI 2016/413, regs 55, 69.[6] Subsections inserted: Children and Families Act 2014, s 99.

Definitions. 'Accommodation': s 22(2); 'child': s 105(1); 'child who is looked after by a local authority': s 22(1); 'functions': s 105(1); 'local authority': s 105(1); 'parental responsibility': s 3; 'service': s 105(1).

[22A Provision of accommodation for children in care

When a child is in the care of a local authority, it is their duty to provide the child with accommodation.][1]

NOTES

Amendments.[1] Section substituted together with ss 22B–22F for s 23: Children and Young Persons Act 2008, s 8(1).

Definitions. 'Accommodation': s 22(2); 'child': s 105(1); 'local authority': s 105(1).

[22B Maintenance of looked after children

It is the duty of a local authority to maintain a child they are looking after in other respects apart from the provision of accommodation.][1]

NOTES

Amendments.[1] Section substituted together with ss 22A, 22C–22F for s 23: Children and Young Persons Act 2008, s 8(1).

Definitions. 'Accommodation': s 22(2); 'child': s 105(1); 'local authority': s 105(1).

[22C Ways in which looked after children are to be accommodated and maintained

(1) This section applies where a local authority are looking after a child ('C').

(2) The local authority must make arrangements for C to live with a person who falls within subsection (3) (but subject to subsection (4)).

(3) A person ('P') falls within this subsection if –

   (a)   P is a parent of C;
   (b)   P is not a parent of C but has parental responsibility for C; or
   (c)   in a case where C is in the care of the local authority and there was [a child arrangements order][2] in force with respect to C immediately before the care order was made, P was a person [named in the child arrangements order as a person with whom C was to live][2].

(4) Subsection (2) does not require the local authority to make arrangements of the kind mentioned in that subsection if doing so –

   (a)   would not be consistent with C's welfare; or
   (b)   would not be reasonably practicable.

(5) If the local authority are unable to make arrangements under subsection (2), they must place C in the placement which is, in their opinion, the most appropriate placement available.

(6) In subsection (5) 'placement' means –

   (a)   placement with an individual who is a relative, friend or other person connected with C and who is also a local authority foster parent;
   (b)   placement with a local authority foster parent who does not fall within paragraph (a);

(c)   placement in a children's home in respect of which a person is registered under Part 2 of the Care Standards Act 2000 [or Part 1 of the Regulation and Inspection of Social Care (Wales) Act 2016 (anaw 2)][5]; or

(d)   subject to section 22D, placement in accordance with other arrangements which comply with any regulations made for the purposes of this section.

(7) In determining the most appropriate placement for C, the local authority must, subject to [subsection (9B) and][3] the other provisions of this Part (in particular, to their duties under section 22) –

(a)   give preference to a placement falling within paragraph (a) of subsection (6) over placements falling within the other paragraphs of that subsection;

(b)   comply, so far as is reasonably practicable in all the circumstances of C's case, with the requirements of subsection (8); and

(c)   comply with subsection (9) unless that is not reasonably practicable.

(8) The local authority must ensure that the placement is such that –

(a)   it allows C to live near C's home;

(b)   it does not disrupt C's education or training;

(c)   if C has a sibling for whom the local authority are also providing accommodation, it enables C and the sibling to live together;

(d)   if C is disabled, the accommodation provided is suitable to C's particular needs.

(9) The placement must be such that C is provided with accommodation within the local authority's area.

[(9A) Subsection (9B) applies (subject to subsection (9C)) where the local authority are …[4] –

(a)   are considering adoption for C, or

(b)   are satisfied that C ought to be placed for adoption but are not authorised under section 19 of the Adoption and Children Act 2002 (placement with parental consent) or by virtue of section 21 of that Act (placement orders) to place C for adoption.

(9B) Where this subsection applies –

(a)   subsections (7) to (9) do not apply to the local authority,

(b)   the local authority must consider placing C with an individual within subsection (6)(a), and

(c)   where the local authority decide that a placement with such an individual is not the most appropriate placement for C, the local authority must consider placing C with a local authority foster parent who has been approved as a prospective adopter.

(9C) Subsection (9B) does not apply where the local authority have applied for a placement order under section 21 of the Adoption and Children Act 2002 in respect of C and the application has been refused.][3]

(10) The local authority may determine –

PART I – Statutes

(a)   the terms of any arrangements they make under subsection (2) in relation to C (including terms as to payment); and

(b)   the terms on which they place C with a local authority foster parent (including terms as to payment but subject to any order made under section 49 of the Children Act 2004).

(11) The [Secretary of State][4] may make regulations for, and in connection with, the purposes of this section.

[(12) For the meaning of 'local authority foster parent' see section 105(1).][4]][1]

NOTES

Amendments.[1] Section substituted together with ss 22A, 22B, 22D–22F for s 23: Children and Young Persons Act 2008, s 8(1).[2] Words substituted: Children and Families Act 2014, s 12, Sch 2, paras 1, 29.[3] Words and subsections inserted: Children and Families Act 2014, s 2, with effect from 25 July 2014, SI 2014/889, art 6.[4] Words omitted and substituted and subsection substituted: SI 2016/413, regs 55, 70.[5] Words inserted: Regulation and Inspection of Social Care (Wales) Act 2016 (Consequential Amendments) Regulations 2018, SI 2018/195, regs 8, 9.

Definitions. 'Accommodation': s 22(2); 'child': s 105(1); 'local authority': s 105(1); 'looked after by a local authority': s 22(1); 'parental responsibility': s 3.

[22D Review of child's case before making alternative arrangements for accommodation

(1) Where a local authority are providing accommodation for a child ('C') other than by arrangements under section 22C(6)(d), they must not make such arrangements for C unless they have decided to do so in consequence of a review of C's case carried out in accordance with regulations made under section 26.

(2) But subsection (1) does not prevent a local authority making arrangements for C under section 22C(6)(d) if they are satisfied that in order to safeguard C's welfare it is necessary –

(a)   to make such arrangements; and
(b)   to do so as a matter of urgency.]][1]

NOTES

Amendments.[1] Section substituted together with ss 22A–22C, 22E, 22F for s 23: Children and Young Persons Act 2008, s 8(1).

Definitions. 'Accommodation': s 22(2); 'child': s 105(1); 'local authority': s 105(1).

[22E Children's homes provided by Secretary of State or Welsh Ministers.

Where a local authority place a child they are looking after in a children's home provided, equipped and maintained by the Secretary of State or the Welsh Ministers under section 82(5), they must do so on such terms as the Secretary of State or the Welsh Ministers (as the case may be) may from time to time determine.]][1]

NOTES

Amendments.[1] Section substituted: SI 2016/413, regs 55, 71.

Definitions. 'Child': s 105(1); 'children's home': s 23; 'local authority': s 105(1).

[22F Regulations as to children looked after by local authorities

Part 2 of Schedule 2 has effect for the purposes of making further provision as to children looked after by local authorities and in particular as to the regulations which may be made under section 22C(11).][1]

NOTES

Amendments.[1] Section substituted together with ss 22A–22E for s 23: Children and Young Persons Act 2008, s 8(1).

[22G General duty of local authority to secure sufficient accommodation for looked after children

(1) It is the general duty of a local authority to take steps that secure, so far as reasonably practicable, the outcome in subsection (2).

(2) The outcome is that the local authority are able to provide the children mentioned in subsection (3) with accommodation that –

    (a)   is within the authority's area; and
    (b)   meets the needs of those children.

(3) The children referred to in subsection (2) are those –

    (a)   that the local authority are looking after,
    (b)   in respect of whom the authority are unable to make arrangements under section 22C(2), and
    (c)   whose circumstances are such that it would be consistent with their welfare for them to be provided with accommodation that is in the authority's area.

(4) In taking steps to secure the outcome in subsection (2), the local authority must have regard to the benefit of having –

    (a)   a number of accommodation providers in their area that is, in their opinion, sufficient to secure that outcome; and
    (b)   a range of accommodation in their area capable of meeting different needs that is, in their opinion, sufficient to secure that outcome.

(5) In this section 'accommodation providers' means –

local authority foster parents; and

children's homes in respect of which a person is registered under Part 2 of the Care Standards Act 2000.][1]

NOTES

Amendments.[1] Section inserted in relation to England: Children and Young Persons Act 2008, s 9.
Definitions. 'Accommodation': s 22(2); 'children's home': s 23; 'local authority': s 105(1); 'local authority foster parents': s 22C(12).

[23

…[2]][1]

NOTES

Amendments.[1] Section substituted by ss 22A–22F in relation to England: Children and Young Persons Act 2008, s 8(1).

[Educational achievement of previously looked after children

23ZZA Information and advice for promoting educational achievement

(1) A local authority in England must make advice and information available in accordance with this section for the purpose of promoting the educational achievement of each relevant child educated in their area.

(2) The advice and information must be made available to –

    (a)   any person who has parental responsibility for the child,

    (b)   the member of staff at the child's school designated under section 20A of the Children and Young Persons Act 2008 or by virtue of section 2E of the Academies Act 2010, and

    (c)   any other person that the local authority consider appropriate.

(3) A local authority in England may do anything else that they consider appropriate with a view to promoting the educational achievement of relevant children educated in their area.

(4) A local authority in England must appoint at least one person for the purpose of discharging the duty imposed by subsection (1).

(5) The person appointed for that purpose must be an officer employed by the authority or another local authority in England.

(6) In this section –

    'relevant child' means –

        (a)   a child who was looked after by the local authority or another local authority in England or Wales but ceased to be so looked after as a result of –

            (i)   a child arrangements order which includes arrangements relating to with whom the child is to live, or when the child is to live with any person,

            (ii)   a special guardianship order, or

            (iii)   an adoption order within the meaning given by section 72(1) of the Adoption Act 1976 or section 46(1) of the Adoption and Children Act 2002, or

        (b)   a child who appears to the local authority –

            (i)   to have been in state care in a place outside England and Wales because he or she would not otherwise have been cared for adequately, and

            (ii)   to have ceased to be in that state care as a result of being adopted.

(7) For the purposes of this section a child is educated in a local authority's area if—

    (a)   the child is receiving early years provision secured by the local authority under section 7(1) of the Childcare Act 2006, or

    (b)   the child is of compulsory school age and—

        (i)   the child attends a school in the local authority's area, or

        (ii)   if the child does not attend school, the child receives all or most of his or her education in the local authority's area.

(8) For the purposes of this section a child is in 'state care' if he or she is in the care of, or accommodated by—

    (a)   a public authority,

    (b)   a religious organisation, or

    (c)   any other organisation the sole or main purpose of which is to benefit society.][1]

NOTES

Amendments.[1] Section and preceding cross-heading inserted: Children and Social Work Act 2017, s 4.

[Visiting

23ZA Duty of local authority to ensure visits to, and contact with, looked after children and others

(1) This section applies to –

    (a)   a child looked after by a local authority;

    (b)   a child who was looked after by a local authority but who has ceased to be looked after by them as a result of prescribed circumstances.

(2) It is the duty of the local authority –

    (a)   to ensure that a person to whom this section applies is visited by a representative of the authority ('a representative');

    (b)   to arrange for appropriate advice, support and assistance to be available to a person to whom this section applies who seeks it from them.

(3) The duties imposed by subsection (2) –

    (a)   are to be discharged in accordance with any regulations made for the purposes of this section by the [Secretary of State][2];

    (b)   are subject to any requirement imposed by or under an enactment applicable to the place in which the person to whom this section applies is accommodated.

(4) Regulations under this section for the purposes of subsection (3)(a) may make provision about –

    (a)   the frequency of visits;

    (b)   circumstances in which a person to whom this section applies must be visited by a representative; and

    (c)   the functions of a representative.

(5) In choosing a representative a local authority must satisfy themselves that the person chosen has the necessary skills and experience to perform the functions of a representative.][1]

NOTES

Amendments.[1] Section and preceding cross-heading inserted: Children and Young Persons Act 2008, s 15.[2] Words substituted: SI 2016/413, regs 55, 72.

[23ZB Independent visitors for children looked after by a local authority

(1) A local authority looking after a child must appoint an independent person to be the child's visitor if –

  (a)   the child falls within a description prescribed in regulations made by the [Secretary of State][2]; or
  (b)   in any other case, it appears to them that it would be in the child's interests to do so.

(2) A person appointed under this section must visit, befriend and advise the child.

(3) A person appointed under this section is entitled to recover from the appointing authority any reasonable expenses incurred by that person for the purposes of that person's functions under this section.

(4) A person's appointment as a visitor in pursuance of this section comes to an end if –

  (a)   the child ceases to be looked after by the local authority;
  (b)   the person resigns the appointment by giving notice in writing to the appointing authority; or
  (c)   the authority give him notice in writing that they have terminated it.

(5) The ending of such an appointment does not affect any duty under this section to make a further appointment.

(6) Where a local authority propose to appoint a visitor for a child under this section, the appointment shall not be made if –

  (a)   the child objects to it; and
  (b)   the authority are satisfied that the child has sufficient understanding to make an informed decision.

(7) Where a visitor has been appointed for a child under this section, the local authority shall terminate the appointment if –

  (a)   the child objects to its continuing; and
  (b)   the authority are satisfied that the child has sufficient understanding to make an informed decision.

(8) If the local authority give effect to a child's objection under subsection (6) or (7) and the objection is to having anyone as the child's visitor, the authority does not have to propose to appoint another person under subsection (1) until the objection is withdrawn.

(9) The [Secretary of State][2] may make regulations as to the circumstances in which a person is to be regarded for the purposes of this section as independent of the appointing authority.][1]

NOTES

Amendments.[1] Section inserted: Children and Young Persons Act 2008, s 16(1).[2] Words substituted: SI 2016/413, regs 55, 73.

Advice and assistance for certain children [and young persons][1]

[23A The responsible authority and relevant children

(1) The responsible local authority shall have the functions set out in section 23B in respect of a relevant child.

(2) In subsection (1) 'relevant child' means (subject to subsection (3)) a child who –

    (a)   is not being looked after [by any local authority in England or by any local authority in Wales][3];

    (b)   was, before last ceasing to be looked after, an eligible child for the purposes of paragraph 19B of Schedule 2; and

    (c)   is aged sixteen or seventeen.

(3) The [Secretary of State][3] may prescribe –

    (a)   additional categories of relevant children; and

    (b)   categories of children who are not to be relevant children despite falling within subsection (2).

(4) In subsection (1) the 'responsible local authority' is the one which last looked after the child.

(5) If under subsection (3)(a) the [Secretary of State][3] prescribes a category of relevant children which includes children who do not fall within subsection (2) (b) (for example, because they were being looked after by a local authority in Scotland), [the [Secretary of State][3]][2] may in the regulations also provide for which local authority is to be the responsible local authority for those children.][1]

NOTES

Amendments.[1] Section inserted: Children (Leaving Care) Act 2000, s 2(4).[2] Words substituted: Children and Young Persons Act 2008, s 39, Sch 3, paras 1, 8.[3] Words substituted: SI 2016/413, regs 55, 74.

[23B Additional functions of the responsible authority in respect of relevant children

(1) It is the duty of each local authority to take reasonable steps to keep in touch with a relevant child for whom they are the responsible authority, whether he is within their area or not.

(2) It is the duty of each local authority to appoint a personal adviser for each relevant child (if they have not already done so under paragraph 19C of Schedule 2).

(3) It is the duty of each local authority, in relation to any relevant child who does not already have a pathway plan prepared for the purposes of paragraph 19B of Schedule 2 –

(a) to carry out an assessment of his needs with a view to determining what advice, assistance and support it would be appropriate for them to provide him under this Part; and

(b) to prepare a pathway plan for him.

[(4)–(7) ...]³

(8) The responsible local authority shall safeguard and promote the child's welfare and, unless they are satisfied that his welfare does not require it, support him by –

(a) maintaining him;

(b) providing him with or maintaining him in suitable accommodation; and

(c) providing support of such other descriptions as may be prescribed.

(9) Support under subsection (8) may be in cash.

(10) The [Secretary of State]² may by regulations make provision about the meaning of 'suitable accommodation' and in particular about the suitability of landlords or other providers of accommodation.

(11) If the local authority have lost touch with a relevant child, despite taking reasonable steps to keep in touch, they must without delay –

(a) consider how to re-establish contact; and

(b) take reasonable steps to do so,

and while the child is still a relevant child must continue to take such steps until they succeed.

(12) Subsections (7) to (9) of section 17 apply in relation to support given under this section as they apply in relation to assistance given under that section.

(13) Subsections (4) and (5) of section 22 apply in relation to any decision by a local authority for the purposes of this section as they apply in relation to the decisions referred to in that section.]¹

NOTES

Amendments.¹ Section inserted: Children (Leaving Care) Act 2000, s 2(4).² Words substituted: SI 2016/413, regs 55, 75.³ Subsections (4)–(7) repealed: Children and Young Persons Act 2008, ss 22(1), 42, Sch 4.

[23C Continuing functions in respect of former relevant children

(1) Each local authority shall have the duties provided for in this section towards –

(a) a person who has been a relevant child for the purposes of section 23A (and would be one if he were under eighteen), and in relation to whom they were the last responsible authority; and

(b) a person who was being looked after by them when he attained the age of eighteen, and immediately before ceasing to be looked after was an eligible child,

and in this section such a person is referred to as a 'former relevant child'.

(2) It is the duty of the local authority to take reasonable steps –

    (a)   to keep in touch with a former relevant child whether he is within their area or not; and

    (b)   if they lose touch with him, to re-establish contact.

(3) It is the duty of the local authority –

    (a)   to continue the appointment of a personal adviser for a former relevant child; and

    (b)   to continue to keep his pathway plan under regular review.

(4) It is the duty of the local authority to give a former relevant child –

    (a)   assistance of the kind referred to in section 24B(1), to the extent that his welfare requires it;

    (b)   assistance of the kind referred to in section 24B(2), to the extent that his welfare and his educational or training needs require it;

    (c)   other assistance, to the extent that his welfare requires it.

(5) The assistance given under subsection (4)(c) may be in kind or, in exceptional circumstances, in cash.

[(5A) It is the duty of the local authority to pay the relevant amount to a former relevant child who pursues higher education in accordance with a pathway plan prepared for that person.

(5B) The [Secretary of State][4] may by regulations –

    (a)   prescribe the relevant amount for the purposes of subsection (5A);

    (b)   prescribe the meaning of 'higher education' for those purposes;

    (c)   make provision as to the payment of the relevant amount;

    (d)   make provision as to the circumstances in which the relevant amount (or any part of it) may be recovered by the local authority from a former relevant child to whom a payment has been made.

(5C) The duty set out in subsection (5A) is without prejudice to that set out in subsection (4)(b).][2]

(6) Subject to subsection (7), the duties set out in subsections (2), (3) and (4) subsist until the former relevant child reaches the age of twenty-one.

(7) If the former relevant child's pathway plan sets out a programme of education or training which extends beyond his twenty-first birthday –

    (a)   the duty set out in subsection (4)(b) continues to subsist for so long as the former relevant child continues to pursue that programme; and

    (b)   the duties set out in subsections (2) and (3) continue to subsist concurrently with that duty.

(8) For the purposes of subsection (7)(a) there shall be disregarded any interruption in a former relevant child's pursuance of a programme of education or training if the local authority are satisfied that he will resume it as soon as is reasonably practicable.

(9) Section 24B(5) applies in relation to a person being given assistance under subsection (4)(b) [or who is in receipt of a payment under subsection (5A)][3] as it applies in relation to a person to whom section 24B(3) applies.

(10) Subsections (7) to (9) of section 17 apply in relation to assistance given under this section as they apply in relation to assistance given under that section.][1]

NOTES

Amendments.[1] Section inserted: Children (Leaving Care) Act 2000, s 2(4).[2] Subsections inserted: Children and Young Persons Act 2008, s 21(1), (2).[3] Words inserted: Children and Young Persons Act 2008, s 21(1), (3).[4] Words substituted: SI 2016/413, regs 55, 76.

[23CZA Arrangements for certain former relevant children to continue to live with former foster parents

(1) Each local authority ...[2] have the duties provided for in subsection (3) in relation to a staying put arrangement.

(2) A 'staying put arrangement' is an arrangement under which –

> (a)   a person who is a former relevant child by virtue of section 23C(1)(b), and
>
> (b)   a person (a 'former foster parent') who was the former relevant child's local authority foster parent immediately before the former relevant child ceased to be looked after by the local authority,

continue to live together after the former relevant child has ceased to be looked after.

(3) It is the duty of the local authority (in discharging the duties in section 23C(3) and by other means) –

> (a)   to monitor the staying put arrangement, and
>
> (b)   to provide advice, assistance and support to the former relevant child and the former foster parent with a view to maintaining the staying put arrangement.

(4) Support provided to the former foster parent under subsection (3)(b) must include financial support.

(5) Subsection (3)(b) does not apply if the local authority consider that the staying put arrangement is not consistent with the welfare of the former relevant child.

(6) The duties set out in subsection (3) subsist until the former relevant child reaches the age of 21.][1]

NOTES

Amendment.[1] Section inserted: Children and Families Act 2014, s 98(1), (2).[2] Words omitted: SI 2016/413, regs 55, 77.

[23CZB England: further advice and support

(1) This section applies to a former relevant child if –

> (a)   he or she has reached the age of 21 but not the age of 25, and

PART I – Statutes

(b) a local authority in England had duties towards him or her under section 23C (whether or not some of those duties continue to subsist by virtue of subsection (7) of that section).

(2) If the former relevant child informs the local authority that he or she wishes to receive advice and support under this section, the local authority has the duties provided for in subsections (3) to (6).

(3) The local authority must provide the former relevant child with a personal adviser until the former relevant child –

(a) reaches the age of 25, or
(b) if earlier, informs the local authority that he or she no longer wants a personal adviser.

(4) The local authority must –

(a) carry out an assessment in relation to the former relevant child under subsection (5), and
(b) prepare a pathway plan for the former relevant child.

(5) An assessment under this subsection is an assessment of the needs of the former relevant child with a view to determining –

(a) whether any services offered by the local authority (under this Act or otherwise) may assist in meeting his or her needs, and
(b) if so, what advice and support it would be appropriate for the local authority to provide for the purpose of helping the former relevant child to obtain those services.

(6) The local authority must provide the former relevant child with advice and support that it would be appropriate to provide as mentioned in subsection (5)(b).

(7) Where a former relevant child to whom this section applies is not receiving advice and support under this section, the local authority must offer such advice and support –

(a) as soon as possible after he or she reaches the age of 21, and
(b) at least once in every 12 months.

(8) In this section 'former relevant child' has the meaning given by section 23C(1).][1]

NOTES

Amendment. [1] Section inserted: Children and Social Work Act 2017, s 3(1), (2).

[23CA Further assistance to pursue education or training

(1) This section applies to a person if –

(a) he is under the age of twenty-five or of such lesser age as may be prescribed by the [Secretary of State][2];
(b) he is a former relevant child (within the meaning of section 23C) towards whom the duties imposed by subsections (2), (3) and (4) of that section no longer subsist; and

(c)   he has informed the responsible local authority that he is pursuing, or wishes to pursue, a programme of education or training.

[(2) It is the duty of the responsible local authority to provide a personal adviser for a person to whom this section applies.]³

(3) It is the duty of the responsible local authority –

(a)   to carry out an assessment of the needs of a person to whom this section applies with a view to determining what assistance (if any) it would be appropriate for them to provide to him under this section; and
(b)   to prepare a pathway plan for him.

(4) It is the duty of the responsible local authority to give assistance of a kind referred to subsection (5) to a person to whom this section applies to the extent that his educational or training needs require it.

(5) The kinds of assistance are –

(a)   contributing to expenses incurred by him in living near the place where he is, or will be, receiving education or training; or
(b)   making a grant to enable him to meet expenses connected with his education and training.

(6) If a person to whom this section applies pursues a programme of education or training in accordance with the pathway plan prepared for him, the duties of the local authority under this section (and under any provision applicable to the pathway plan prepared under this section for that person) subsist for as long as he continues to pursue that programme.

(7) For the purposes of subsection (6), the local authority may disregard any interruption in the person's pursuance of a programme of education or training if they are satisfied that he will resume it as soon as is reasonably practicable.

(8) Subsections (7) to (9) of section 17 apply to assistance given to a person under this section as they apply to assistance given to or in respect of a child under that section, but with the omission in subsection (8) of the words 'and of each of his parents'.

(9) Subsection (5) of section 24B applies to a person to whom this section applies as it applies to a person to whom subsection (3) of that section applies.

(10) Nothing in this section affects the duty imposed by subsection (5A) of section 23C to the extent that it subsists in relation to a person to whom this section applies; but the duty to make a payment under that subsection may be taken into account in the assessment of the person's needs under subsection (3)(a).

(11) In this section 'the responsible local authority' means, in relation to a person to whom this section applies, the local authority which had the duties provided for in section 23C towards him.]¹

NOTES

Amendments.¹ Section inserted: Children and Young Persons Act 2008, s 22(2).² Words substituted: SI 2016/413, regs 55, 78.³ Subsection substituted: Children and Social Work Act 2017, s 3(1), (3). **Definitions.** 'responsible local authority': s 23CA(11).

[Personal advisers and pathway plans

23D Personal advisers

(1) The [Secretary of State][2] may by regulations require local authorities to appoint a personal adviser for children or young persons of a prescribed description who have reached the age of sixteen but not the age of [twenty-five][3] who are not –

(a)   children who are relevant children for the purposes of section 23A;
(b)   the young persons referred to in section 23C; or
(c)   the children referred to in paragraph 19C of Schedule 2[; or
(d)   persons to whom section 23CA applies][3].

(2) Personal advisers appointed under or by virtue of this Part shall (in addition to any other functions) have such functions as the [Secretary of State][2] prescribes.

[(3) Where a local authority in England ceases to be under a duty to provide a personal adviser for a person under any provision of this Part, that does not affect any other duty under this Part to provide a personal adviser for the person.

(4) Where a local authority in England has more than one duty under this Part to provide a personal adviser for a person, each duty is discharged by the provision of the same personal adviser (the local authority are not required to provide more than one personal adviser for the person).][4]][1]

NOTES

Amendments.[1] Cross-heading and section inserted: Children (Leaving Care) Act 2000, s 3.[2] Words substituted: SI 2016/413, regs 55, 79.[3] Words substituted, and paragraph and preceding word inserted: Children and Young Persons Act 2008, s 23(1).[4] Subsections inserted: Children and Social Work Act 2017, s 3(1), (4).

[23E Pathway plans

(1) In this Part, a reference to a 'pathway plan' is to a plan setting out –

(a)   in the case of a plan prepared under paragraph 19B of Schedule 2 –
 (i)   the advice, assistance and support which the local authority intend to provide a child under this Part, both while they are looking after him and later; and
 (ii)   when they might cease to look after him;

[(aa) in the case of a plan prepared under section 23CZB, the advice and support that the local authority intend to provide;][6] and
(b)   in the case of a plan prepared under section 23B [or 23CA][4], the advice, assistance and support which the local authority intend to provide under this Part,

and dealing with such other matters (if any) as may be prescribed [in regulations made by the Secretary of State][2].

[(1ZA) A local authority may carry out an assessment under section 23CZB(5) of a person's needs at the same time as any assessment of the person's needs is made under section 23CA(3).][6]

[(1A) A local authority may carry out an assessment under section 23B(3)[, 23CZB(5)]⁶ or 23CA(3) of a person's needs at the same time as any assessment of his needs is made under –

(a)   the Chronically Sick and Disabled Persons Act 1970;
(b)   Part 4 of the Education Act 1996 [or Part 3 of the Children and Families Act 2014]⁵ (in the case of an assessment under section 23B(3));
[(ba) Part 2 of the Additional Learning Needs and Education Tribunal (Wales) Act 2018;]⁷
(c)   the Disabled Persons (Services, Consultation and Representation) Act 1986; or
(d)   any other enactment.

(1B) The [Secretary of State]² may by regulations make provision as to assessments for the purposes of section 23B(3)[, 23CZB(5)]⁶ or 23CA.

(1C) Regulations under subsection (1B) may in particular make provision about –

(a)   who is to be consulted in relation to an assessment;
(b)   the way in which an assessment is to be carried out, by whom and when;
(c)   the recording of the results of an assessment;
(d)   the considerations to which a local authority are to have regard in carrying out an assessment.

(1D) A local authority shall keep each pathway plan prepared by them under section 23B[, 23CZB]⁶ or 23CA under review.]³

(2) The [Secretary of State]² may by regulations make provision about pathway plans and their review.]¹

NOTES

Amendments.¹ Section inserted: Children (Leaving Care) Act 2000, s 3.² Words inserted and substituted: SI 2016/413, regs 55, 80.³ Subsections inserted: Children and Young Persons Act 2008, s 22(3), (5).⁴ Words inserted: Children and Young Persons Act 2008, s 22(3), (4).⁵ Words inserted: Children and Families Act 2014, s 82, Sch 3, para 65(1), (2).⁶ Paragraph, subsection and words inserted: Children and Social Work Act 2017, s 3(1), (5)-(10).⁷ Paragraph inserted: Additional Learning Needs and Education Tribunal (Wales) Act 2018, s 96, Sch 1, para 2(1), (2)(b).

[24 Persons qualifying for advice and assistance

[(1) In this Part 'a person qualifying for advice and assistance' means a person to whom subsection (1A) or (1B) applies.

(1A) This subsection applies to a person –

(a)   who has reached the age of sixteen but not the age of twenty-one;
(b)   with respect to whom a special guardianship order is in force (or, if he has reached the age of eighteen, was in force when he reached that age); and
(c)   who was, immediately before the making of that order, looked after by a local authority.

(1B) This subsection applies to a person to whom subsection (1A) does not apply, and who –

(a)   is under twenty-one; and

(b)   at any time after reaching the age of sixteen but while still a child was, but is no longer, looked after, accommodated or fostered.]³

(2) In [subsection (1B)(b)]⁴, 'looked after, accommodated or fostered' means –

    (a)   looked after by a local authority [(without subsequently being looked after by a local authority in Wales)]⁷;

    (b)   accommodated by or on behalf of a voluntary organisation;

    (c)   accommodated in a private children's home;

    (d)   accommodated for a consecutive period of at least three months –

        (i)   by any [Local Health Board]⁶, Special Health Authority [...⁹ or by a local authority in the exercise of education functions]⁸, or

        (ii)   in any care home or independent hospital or in any accommodation provided [pursuant to arrangements made by the Secretary of State, the National Health Service Commissioning Board or a clinical commissioning group under the National Health Service Act 2006 or]⁹ by a National Health Service trust [or an NHS foundation trust]²[, or by a local authority in Wales in the exercise of education functions]⁷; or

    (e)   privately fostered.

(3) Subsection (2)(d) applies even if the period of three months mentioned there began before the child reached the age of sixteen.

(4) In the case of a person qualifying for advice and assistance by virtue of subsection (2)(a), it is the duty of the local authority which last looked after him to take such steps as they think appropriate to contact him at such times as they think appropriate with a view to discharging their functions under sections 24A and 24B.

(5) In each of sections 24A and 24B, the local authority under the duty or having the power mentioned there ('the relevant authority') is –

    [(za) in the case of a person to whom subsection (1A) applies, a local authority determined in accordance with regulations made by the [Secretary of State]⁷;]⁵

    (a)   in the case of a person qualifying for advice and assistance by virtue of subsection (2)(a), the local authority which last looked after him; or

    (b)   in the case of any other person qualifying for advice and assistance, the local authority within whose area the person is (if he has asked for help of a kind which can be given under section 24A or 24B).]¹

NOTES

Amendments.¹ Section and words in cross-heading inserted: Children (Leaving Care) Act 2000, ss 2(3), 4(1).² Words inserted: Health and Social Care (Community Health and Standards) Act 2003, s 34, Sch 4, paras 75, 76.³ Subsection substituted: Adoption and Children Act 2002, s 139(1), Sch 3, paras 54, 60(a).⁴ Words substituted: Adoption and Children Act 2002, s 139(1), Sch 3, paras 54, 60(b).⁵ Paragraph inserted: Adoption and Children Act 2002, s 139(1), Sch 3, paras 54, 60(c).⁶ Words substituted: SI 2007/961.⁷ Words inserted and substituted: SI 2016/413, regs 55, 81.⁸ Words substituted: SI 2010/1158.⁹ Words omitted and inserted: Health and Social Care Act 2012, s 55(2), Sch 5, Pt 1, paras 47, 49.

[24A Advice and assistance

(1) The relevant authority shall consider whether the conditions in subsection (2) are satisfied in relation to a person qualifying for advice and assistance.

(2) The conditions are that –

    (a)   he needs help of a kind which they can give under this section or section 24B; and

    (b)   in the case of a person [to whom section 24(1A) applies, or to whom section 24(1B) applies and][3] who was not being looked after by any local authority, [or local authority in Wales][5] they are satisfied that the person by whom he was being looked after does not have the necessary facilities for advising or befriending him.

(3) If the conditions are satisfied –

    (a)   they shall advise and befriend him if [he is a person to whom section 24(1A) applies, or he is a person to whom section 24(1B) applies and][4] he was being looked after by a local authority [(without subsequently being looked after by a local authority in Wales),][5] or was accommodated by or on behalf of a voluntary organisation; and

    (b)   in any other case they may do so.

(4) Where as a result of this section a local authority are under a duty, or are empowered, to advise and befriend a person, they may also give him assistance.

(5) The assistance may be in kind [and, in exceptional circumstances, assistance may be given –

    (a)   by providing accommodation, if in the circumstances assistance may not be given in respect of the accommodation under section 24B, or

    (b)   in cash][2].

(6) Subsections (7) to (9) of section 17 apply in relation to assistance given under this section or section 24B as they apply in relation to assistance given under that section.][1]

NOTES

Amendments.[1] Section inserted: Children (Leaving Care) Act 2000, s 4(1).[2] Words substituted: Adoption and Children Act 2002, s 116(3).[3] Words inserted: Adoption and Children Act 2002, s 139(1), Sch 3, paras 54, 61(a).[4] Words inserted: Adoption and Children Act 2002, s 139(1), Sch 3, paras 54, 61(b).[5] Words inserted: SI 2016/413, regs 55, 82.

[24B Employment, education and training

(1) The relevant local authority may give assistance to any person who qualifies for advice and assistance by virtue of [section 24(1A) or][2] section 24(2)(a) by contributing to expenses incurred by him in living near the place where he is, or will be, employed or seeking employment.

(2) The relevant local authority may give assistance to a person to whom subsection (3) applies by –

    (a)   contributing to expenses incurred by the person in question in living near the place where he is, or will be, receiving education or training; or

    (b)   making a grant to enable him to meet expenses connected with his education or training.

PART I – Statutes

(3) This subsection applies to any person who –

    (a)   is under [twenty-five][4]; and

    (b)   qualifies for advice and assistance by virtue of [section 24(1A) or][2] section 24(2)(a), or would have done so if he were under twenty-one.

(4) Where a local authority are assisting a person under subsection (2) they may disregard any interruption in his attendance on the course if he resumes it as soon as is reasonably practicable.

(5) Where the local authority are satisfied that a person to whom subsection (3) applies who is in full-time further or higher education needs accommodation during a vacation because his term-time accommodation is not available to him then, they shall give him assistance by –

    (a)   providing him with suitable accommodation during the vacation; or

    (b)   paying him enough to enable him to secure such accommodation himself.

(6) The [Secretary of State][3] may prescribe the meaning of 'full-time', 'further education', 'higher education' and 'vacation' for the purposes of subsection (5).][1]

NOTES

Amendments.[1] Section inserted: Children (Leaving Care) Act 2000, s 4(1).[2] Words inserted: Adoption and Children Act 2002, s 139(1), Sch 3, paras 54, 62.[3] Words substituted: SI 2016/413, regs 55, 83.[4] Words substituted: Children and Young Persons Act 2008, s 23(2).

[24C Information

(1) Where it appears to a local authority that a person –

    (a)   with whom they are under a duty to keep in touch under section 23B, 23C or 24; or

    (b)   whom they have been advising and befriending under section 24A; or

    (c)   to whom they have been giving assistance under section 24B,

proposes to live, or is living, in the area of another local authority[, or in the area of a local authority in Wales][3], they must inform that other authority.

[(2) Where a child who is accommodated in England –

    (a)   by a voluntary organisation or in a private children's home;

    (b)   by or on behalf of any Local Health Board or Special Health Authority;

    (c)   by or on behalf of a clinical commissioning group or the National Health Service Commissioning Board;

    (d)   by or on behalf of a local authority in the exercise of education functions;

    (e)   by or on behalf of a local authority in Wales in the exercise of education functions;

    (f)   in any care home or independent hospital; or

    (g)   in any accommodation provided by or on behalf of a National Health Service trust or by or on behalf of an NHS Foundation Trust,

ceases to be so accommodated after reaching the age of 16, the person by whom or on whose behalf the child was accommodated or who carries on or manages the home or hospital (as the case may be) must inform the local authority or local authority in Wales within whose area the child proposes to live.][3]

(3) Subsection (2) only applies, by virtue of [any of paragraphs (b) to (g)][3], if the accommodation has been provided for a consecutive period of at least three months.][1]

[(4) In a case where a child was accommodated by or on behalf of a local authority, or a local authority in Wales, in the exercise of education functions, subsection (2) applies only if the authority who accommodated the child is different from the authority within whose area the child proposes to live.][2, 3]

NOTES

Amendments.[1] Section inserted: Children (Leaving Care) Act 2000, s 4(1).[2] Subsection inserted: SI 2010/1158.[3] Words substituted and inserted and subsections substituted: SI 2016/413, regs 55, 84.

[24D Representations: sections 23A to 24B

(1) Every local authority shall establish a procedure for considering representations (including complaints) made to them by –

  (a)   a relevant child for the purposes of section 23A or a young person falling within section 23C;

  (b)   a person qualifying for advice and assistance; or

  (c)   a person falling within section 24B(2),

about the discharge of their functions under this Part in relation to him.

[(1A) Regulations may be made by the [Secretary of State][3] imposing time limits on the making of representations under subsection (1).][2]

(2) In considering representations under subsection (1), a local authority shall comply with regulations (if any) made by the [Secretary of State][3] for the purposes of this subsection.][1]

NOTES

Amendments.[1] Section inserted: Children (Leaving Care) Act 2000, s 5.[2] Subsection inserted: Adoption and Children Act 2002, s 117(1).[3] Words substituted: SI 2016/413, regs 55, 85.

Secure accommodation

25 Use of accommodation for restricting liberty

(1) Subject to the following provisions of this section, a child who is being looked after by a local authority [in England or Wales][3] may not be placed, and, if placed, may not be kept, in accommodation [in England][2] [or Scotland][3] provided for the purpose of restricting liberty ('secure accommodation') unless it appears –

  (a)   that –
    (i)   he has a history of absconding and is likely to abscond from any other description of accommodation; and
    (ii)   if he absconds, he is likely to suffer significant harm; or

  (b)   that if he is kept in any other description of accommodation he is likely to injure himself or other persons.

(2) The [Secretary of State]² may by regulations –

    (a)   specify a maximum period –

        (i)   beyond which a child may not be kept in secure accommodation [in England]² [or Scotland]³ without the authority of the court; and

        (ii)   for which the court may authorise a child to be kept in secure accommodation [in England]² [or Scotland]³;

    (b)   empower the court from time to time to authorise a child to be kept in secure accommodation [in England]² [or Scotland]³ for such further period as the regulations may specify; and

    (c)   provide that applications to the court under this section shall be made only by local authorities [in England or Wales]³.

(3) It shall be the duty of a court hearing an application under this section to determine whether any relevant criteria for keeping a child in secure accommodation are satisfied in his case.

(4) If a court determines that any such criteria are satisfied, it shall make an order authorising the child to be kept in secure accommodation and specifying the maximum period for which he may be so kept.

(5) On any adjournment of the hearing of an application under this section, a court may make an interim order permitting the child to be kept during the period of the adjournment in secure accommodation.

[(5A) Where a local authority in England or Wales are authorised under this section to keep a child in secure accommodation in Scotland, the person in charge of the accommodation may restrict the child's liberty to the extent that the person considers appropriate, having regard to the terms of any order made by a court under this section.]³

(6) No court shall exercise the powers conferred by this section in respect of a child who is not legally represented in that court unless, having been informed of his right to apply for [the provision of representation under Part 1 of the Legal Aid, Sentencing and Punishment of Offenders Act 2012]¹ and having had the opportunity to do so, he refused or failed to apply.

(7) The [Secretary of State]² may by regulations provide that –

    (a)   this section shall or shall not apply to any description of children specified in the regulations;

    (b)   this section shall have effect in relation to children of a description specified in the regulations subject to such modifications as may be so specified;

    (c)   such other provisions as may be so specified shall have effect for the purpose of determining whether a child of a description specified in the regulations may be placed or kept in secure accommodation [in England]² [or Scotland]³;

    [(d)   a child may only be placed in secure accommodation that is of a description specified in the regulations (and the description may in particular be framed by reference to whether the accommodation, or the person providing it, has been approved by the Secretary of State or the Scottish Ministers).]³

(8) The giving of an authorisation under this section shall not prejudice any power of any court in England and Wales or Scotland to give directions relating to the child to whom the authorisation relates.

[(8A) Sections 168 and 169(1) to (4) of the Children's Hearings (Scotland) Act 2011 (asp 1) (enforcement and absconding) apply in relation to an order under subsection (4) above as they apply in relation to the orders mentioned in section 168(3) or 169(1)(a) of that Act.][3]

(9) This section is subject to section 20(8).

NOTES

Amendments.[1] Words substituted: Legal Aid, Sentencing and Punishment of Offenders Act 2012, s 39, Sch 5, Pt 1, para 38.[2] Words substituted: SI 2016/413,regs 55, 86.[3] Words substituted and inserted, subsections and paragraphs inserted: Children and Social Work Act 2017, s 10, Sch 1, paras 1, 2.
Definitions. 'Child': s 105(1); 'child who is looked after by a local authority': s 22(1); 'harm': ss 31(9), 105(1); 'local authority': s 105(1); 'secure accommodation': s 25(1); 'significant harm': ss 31(9), (10), 105(1); 'the court': s 92(7).

[Independent reviewing officers

25A Appointment of independent reviewing officer

(1) If a local authority are looking after a child, they must appoint an individual as the independent reviewing officer for that child's case.

(2) The initial appointment under subsection (1) must be made before the child's case is first reviewed in accordance with regulations made under section 26.

(3) If a vacancy arises in respect of a child's case, the local authority must make another appointment under subsection (1) as soon as is practicable.

(4) An appointee must be of a description prescribed in regulations made by the [Secretary of State][2].][1]

NOTES

Amendments.[1] Section and preceding cross-heading inserted: Children and Young Persons Act 2008, s 10(1).[2] Words substituted: SI 2016/413, regs 55, 87.

[25B Functions of the independent reviewing officer

(1) The independent reviewing officer must –

    (a)   monitor the performance by the local authority of their functions in relation to the child's case;

    (b)   participate, in accordance with regulations made by the [Secretary of State][2], in any review of the child's case;

    (c)   ensure that any ascertained wishes and feelings of the child concerning the case are given due consideration by the local authority;

    (d)   perform any other function which is prescribed in regulations made by the [Secretary of State][2].

(2) An independent reviewing officer's functions must be performed –

    (a)   in such manner (if any) as may be prescribed in regulations made by the [Secretary of State][2]; and

(b)   having regard to such guidance as that authority may issue in relation to the discharge of those functions.

(3) If the independent reviewing officer considers it appropriate to do so, the child's case may be referred by that officer to –

(a)   an officer of the Children and Family Court Advisory and Support Service; ...²

(b)   ...²

(4) If the independent reviewing officer is not an officer of the local authority, it is the duty of the authority –

(a)   to co-operate with that individual; and

(b)   to take all such reasonable steps as that individual may require of them to enable that individual's functions under this section to be performed satisfactorily.]¹

NOTES

Amendments.¹ Section and preceding cross-heading inserted: Children and Young Persons Act 2008, s 10(1).² Words substituted and omitted and paragraph omitted: SI 2016/413, regs 55, 88.

[25C   Referred cases

(1) In relation to children whose cases are referred to officers under section 25B(3), the Lord Chancellor may by regulations –

(a)   extend any functions of the officers in respect of family proceedings (within the meaning of section 12 of the Criminal Justice and Court Services Act 2000) to other proceedings;

(b)   require any functions of the officers to be performed in the manner prescribed by the regulations.

(2) ...²]¹

NOTES

Amendments.¹ Section inserted in relation to England: Children and Young Persons Act 2008, s 10(2).² Subsection omitted: SI 2016/413, regs 55, 89.

Supplemental

26   Review of cases and inquiries into representations

(1) The [Secretary of State]⁶ may make regulations requiring the case of each child who is being looked after by a local authority to be reviewed in accordance with the provisions of the regulations.

(2) The regulations may, in particular, make provision –

(a)   as to the manner in which each case is to be reviewed;

(b)   as to the considerations to which the local authority are to have regard in reviewing each case;

(c)   as to the time when each case is first to be reviewed and the frequency of subsequent reviews;

PART I – Statutes

(d) requiring the authority, before conducting any review, to seek the views of –
   (i) the child;
   (ii) his parents;
   (iii) any person who is not a parent of his but who has parental responsibility for him; and
   (iv) any other person whose views the authority consider to be relevant, including, in particular, the views of those persons in relation to any particular matter which is to be considered in the course of the review;

(e) requiring the authority ...[1], in the case of a child who is in their care [–
   (i) to keep the section 31A plan for the child under review and, if they are of the opinion that some change is required, to revise the plan, or make a new plan, accordingly;
   (ii) to consider][1] whether an application should be made to discharge the care order;

(f) requiring the authority ...[1], in the case of a child in accommodation provided by the authority [–
   (i) if there is no plan for the future care of the child, to prepare one,
   (ii) if there is such a plan for the child, to keep it under review and, if they are of the opinion that some change is required, to revise the plan or make a new plan, accordingly,
   (iii) to consider][1] whether the accommodation accords with the requirements of this Part;

(g) requiring the authority to inform the child, so far as is reasonably practicable, of any steps he may take under this Act;

(h) requiring the authority to make arrangements, including arrangements with such other bodies providing services as it considers appropriate, to implement any decision which they propose to make in the course, or as a result, of the review;

(i) requiring the authority to notify details of the result of the review and of any decision taken by them in consequence of the review to –
   (i) the child;
   (ii) his parents;
   (iii) any person who is not a parent of his but who has had parental responsibility for him; and
   (iv) any other person whom they consider ought to be notified;

(j) requiring the authority to monitor the arrangements which they have made with a view to ensuring that they comply with the regulations;

[(k) ...[7]][1]

[(2A) ...[7]

(2B) ...[7]

(2C) ...[7]][1]

[(2D) ...[7]][2]

(3) Every local authority shall establish a procedure for considering any representations (including any complaint) made to them by –

(a)   any child who is being looked after by them or who is not being looked after by them but is in need;

(b)   a parent of his;

(c)   any person who is not a parent of his but who has parental responsibility for him;

(d)   any local authority foster parent;

(e)   such other person as the authority consider has a sufficient interest in the child's welfare to warrant his representations being considered by them,

about the discharge by the authority of any of their [qualifying functions][3] in relation to the child.

[(3A) The following are qualifying functions for the purposes of subsection (3) –

(a)   functions under this Part,

(b)   such functions under Part 4 or 5 as are specified by the [Secretary of State][6] in regulations.

(3B) The duty under subsection (3) extends to representations (including complaints) made to the authority by –

(a)   any person mentioned in section 3(1) of the Adoption and Children Act 2002 (persons for whose needs provision is made by the Adoption Service) and any other person to whom arrangements for the provision of adoption support services (within the meaning of that Act) extend,

(b)   such other person as the authority consider has sufficient interest in a child who is or may be adopted to warrant his representations being considered by them,

about the discharge by the authority of such functions under the Adoption and Children Act 2002 as are specified by the [Secretary of State][6] in regulations.][4]

[(3C) The duty under subsection (3) extends to any representations (including complaints) which are made to the authority by –

(a)   a child with respect to whom a special guardianship order is in force,

(b)   a special guardian or a parent of such a child,

(c)   any other person the authority consider has a sufficient interest in the welfare of such a child to warrant his representations being considered by them, or

(d)   any person who has applied for an assessment under section 14F(3) or (4),

about the discharge by the authority of such functions under section 14F as may be specified by the [Secretary of State][6] in regulations.][5]

(4) The procedure shall ensure that at least one person who is not a member or officer of the authority takes part in –

(a)   the consideration; and

(b)   any discussions which are held by the authority about the action (if any) to be taken in relation to the child in the light of the consideration.

[but this subsection is subject to subsection (5A).]⁴

[(4A) Regulations may be made by the [Secretary of State]⁶ imposing time limits on the making of representations under this section.]⁴

(5) In carrying out any consideration of representations under this section a local authority shall comply with any regulations made by the [Secretary of State]⁶ for the purpose of regulating the procedure to be followed.

[(5A) Regulations under subsection (5) may provide that subsection (4) does not apply in relation to any consideration or discussion which takes place as part of a procedure for which provision is made by the regulations for the purpose of resolving informally the matters raised in the representations.]⁴

(6) The [Secretary of State]⁶ may make regulations requiring local authorities to monitor the arrangements that they have made with a view to ensuring that they comply with any regulations made for the purposes of subsection (5).

(7) Where any representation has been considered under the procedure established by a local authority under this section, the authority shall –

    (a)   have due regard to the findings of those considering the representation; and

    (b)   take such steps as are reasonably practicable to notify (in writing) –
        (i)   the person making the representation;
        (ii)   the child (if the authority consider that he has sufficient understanding); and
        (iii)   such other persons (if any) as appear to the authority to be likely to be affected,

of the authority's decision in the matter and their reasons for taking that decision and of any action which they have taken, or propose to take.

(8) Every local authority shall give such publicity to their procedure for considering representations under this section as they consider appropriate.

NOTES

Amendments.¹ Subsections and paragraph inserted, and words inserted or repealed: Adoption and Children Act 2002, s 118.² Subsection inserted: Children Act 2004, s 40, Sch 3, paras 5, 8.³ Words substituted: Adoption and Children Act 2002, s 117(2), (3).⁴ Subsections and words inserted: Adoption and Children Act 2002, s 117(2), (4), (5).⁵ Subsection inserted: Health and Social Care (Community Health and Standards) Act 2003, s 117(1).⁶ Words substituted: SI 2016/413, regs 55, 90.⁷ Paragraph (2) (k) and subsections (2A)–(2D) repealed: Children and Young Persons Act 2008, ss 10(3), 42, Sch 4 with savings (SI 2010/2981, art 5 and SI 2016/452, art 3).
Definitions. 'Accommodation': s 22(2); 'care order': s 31(11); 'child': s 105(1); 'child in need': s 17(10); 'child who is looked after by the local authority': s 22(1); 'functions': s 105(1); 'local authority': s 105(1); 'local authority foster parent': s 23(3); 'parental responsibility': s 3.

[26ZA

...²]¹

NOTES

Amendments.¹ Section prospectively inserted: Health and Social Care (Community Health and Standards) Act 2003, s 116(1), from a date to be appointed.² Section repealed: Education and Inspections Act 2006, ss 157, 184, Sch 14, paras 9, 10, Sch 18, Pt 5.

[26ZB

...²]¹

NOTES

Amendments.¹ Section inserted: Health and Social Care (Community Health and Standards) Act 2003, s 116(2).² Section omitted: SI 2016/413, regs 55,91.

[26A Advocacy services

(1) Every local authority shall make arrangements for the provision of assistance to –

    (a)   persons who make or intend to make representations under section 24D; and

    (b)   children who make or intend to make representations under section 26.

(2) The assistance provided under the arrangements shall include assistance by way of representation.

[(2A) ...³]²

(3) The arrangements –

    (a)   shall secure that a person may not provide assistance if he is a person who is prevented from doing so by regulations made by the [Secretary of State]³; and

    (b)   shall comply with any other provision made by the regulations in relation to the arrangements.

(4) The [Secretary of State]³ may make regulations requiring local authorities to monitor the steps that they have taken with a view to ensuring that they comply with regulations made for the purposes of subsection (3).

(5) Every local authority shall give such publicity to their arrangements for the provision of assistance under this section as they consider appropriate.]¹

NOTES

Amendments.¹ Section inserted: Adoption and Children Act 2002, s 119.² Subsection inserted in relation to Wales: Health and Social Care (Community Health and Standards) Act 2003, s 116(3).³ Subsection omitted and words substituted: SI 2016/413, regs 55, 92.

27 Co-operation between authorities

(1) Where it appears to a local authority that any authority ...¹ mentioned in subsection (3) could, by taking any specified action, help in the exercise of any of their functions under this Part, they may request the help of that other authority ...¹, specifying the action in question.

(2) An authority whose help is so requested shall comply with the request if it is compatible with their own statutory or other duties and obligations and does not unduly prejudice the discharge of any of their functions.

(3) The [authorities]² are –

    (a)   any local authority;

(b)   ...[9]

(c)   any local housing authority;

[(ca) the National Health Service Commissioning Board;][10]

(d)   any [clinical commissioning group,][10] [[Local Health Board][7], Special Health Authority][4] ...[10]][5] [, National Health Service trust or NHS foundation trust][6]; and

[(da) any local authority in Wales;][11]

(e)   any person authorised by the [Secretary of State][8] for the purposes of this section.

[(3A) The Secretary of State must not authorise the Welsh Ministers under subsection (3)(e) without their consent.][11]

(4) ...[3]

NOTES

Amendments.[1] Words repealed: Courts and Legal Services Act 1990, ss 116, 125(7), Sch 16, para 14(a), Sch 20.[2] Words substituted or inserted: Courts and Legal Services Act 1990, s 116, Sch 16, para 14(b).[3] Subsection repealed: Education Act 1993, s 307, Sch 19, para 147.[4] Words substituted: Health Authorities Act 1995, s 2(1), Sch 1, Pt III, para 118(1), (5).[5] Words inserted: Health Act 1999 (Supplementary, Consequential etc Provisions) Order 2000, SI 2000/90.[6] Words inserted: Health and Social Care (Community Health and Standards) Act 2003, s 34, Sch 4, paras 75, 78.[7] Words substituted: SI 2007/961.[8] Words substituted: SI 2016/413, regs 55, 93.[9] Paragraph repealed: SI 2010/1158.[10] Paragraph inserted, words inserted and omitted: Health and Social Care Act 2012, s 55(2), Sch 5, Pt 1, paras 47, 51.[11] Paragraph and subsection inserted: SI 2016/413, regs 55, 93.
Definitions. 'Child'; 'clinical commissioning group'; 'functions'; 'health authority'; 'local authority'; 'local education authority'; 'local housing authority'; 'special educational needs': s 105(1).

28

...[1]

NOTES

Amendments.[1] Section repealed: SI 2010/1158.

29 Recoupment of cost of providing services etc

(1) Where a local authority provide any service under section 17 or 18, other than advice, guidance or counselling, they may recover from a person specified in subsection (4) such charge for the service as they consider reasonable.

(2) Where the authority are satisfied that that person's means are insufficient for it to be reasonably practicable for him to pay the charge, they shall not require him to pay more than he can reasonably be expected to pay.

(3) No person shall be liable to pay any charge under subsection (1) [for a service provided under section 17 or section 18(1) or (5)][8] at any time when he is in receipt [of universal credit (except in such circumstances as may be prescribed),][17] of income support [under][10] [Part VII of the Social Security Contributions and Benefits Act 1992][3][, of any element of child tax credit other than the family element, of working tax credit][10][, of an income-based jobseeker's allowance or of an income-related employment and support allowance][14].

[(3A) No person shall be liable to pay any charge under subsection (1) for a service provided under section 18(2) or (6) at any time when he is in receipt of income support under Part VII of the Social Security and Benefits Act 1992[, of an income-based jobseeker's allowance or of an income-related employment and support allowance][14].]7

[(3B) No person shall be liable to pay any charge under subsection (1) for a service provided under section 18(2) or (6) at any time when –

    (a)   he is in receipt of guarantee state pension credit under section 1(3)(a) of the State Pension Credit Act 2002, or

    (b)   he is a member of a [couple][12] (within the meaning of that Act) the other member of which is in receipt of guarantee state pension credit.][11]

(4) The persons are –

    (a)   where the service is provided for a child under sixteen, each of his parents;

    (b)   where it is provided for a child who has reached the age of sixteen, the child himself; and

    (c)   where it is provided for a member of the child's family, that member.

(5) Any charge under subsection (1) may, without prejudice to any other method of recovery, be recovered summarily as a civil debt.

(6) Part III of Schedule 2 makes provision in connection with contributions towards the maintenance of children who are being looked after by local authorities and consists of the re-enactment with modifications of provisions in Part V of the Child Care Act 1980.

(7) Where a local authority provide any accommodation under section 20(1) for a child who was (immediately before they began to look after him) ordinarily resident within the area of another local authority [or the area of a local authority in Wales][18], they may recover from that other authority any reasonable expenses incurred by them in providing the accommodation and maintaining him.

(8) Where a local authority provide accommodation under section 21(1) or (2) (a) or (b) for a child who is ordinarily resident within the area of another local authority [or the area of a local authority in Wales][18] and they are not maintaining him in –

    (a)   a community home provided by them;

    (b)   a controlled community home; or

    (c)   a hospital vested in the [Secretary of State or][16] [the Welsh Ministers][15] [...[16]][6], [or any other hospital made available pursuant to arrangements made by [the Secretary of State, the National Health Service Commissioning Board or a clinical commissioning group under the National Health Service Act 2006 or by][16] [...[16]][9] a [[Local Health Board][13]][4]][1] [...[16]][6],

they may recover from that other authority any reasonable expenses incurred by them in providing the accommodation and maintaining him.

(9) [Except where subsection (10) [or subsection (11)][18] applies,][8] where a local authority comply with any request under section 27(2) [or section 164A(2) of the

Social Services and Well-being (Wales) Act 2014 (duty of other persons to co-operate and provide information)][18] in relation to a child or other person who is not ordinarily resident within their area, they may recover from the local authority [or a local authority in Wales][18] in whose area the child or person is ordinarily resident any [reasonable expenses][2] incurred by them in respect of that person.

[(10) Where a local authority ('authority A') comply with any request under section 27(2) from another local authority ('authority B') in relation to a child or other person –

  (a)   whose responsible authority is authority B for the purposes of section 23B or 23C; or

  (b)   whom authority B are advising or befriending or to whom they are giving assistance by virtue of section 24(5)(a),

authority A may recover from authority B any reasonable expenses incurred by them in respect of that person.][8]

[(11) Where a local authority ('authority A') comply with any request under section 164A(2) of the Social Services and Well-being (Wales) Act 2014 (duty of other persons to co-operate and provide information) from a local authority in Wales ('authority B') in relation to a person, and authority B are the responsible local authority for that person (within the meaning of section 104(5)(b) (except for category 4 young persons) or (d) of that Act), then authority A may recover from authority B any reasonable expenses incurred by them in respect of that person.][18]

NOTES

Amendments.[1] Words inserted: National Health Service and Community Care Act 1990, s 66(1), Sch 9, para 36(3).[2] Words substituted: Courts and Legal Services Act 1990, s 116, Sch 16, para 15.[3] Words substituted: Social Security (Consequential Provisions) Act 1992, s 4, Sch 2, para 108.[4] Words substituted: Health Authorities Act 1995, s 2(1), Sch 1, Pt III, para 118(1), (6).[5] Words inserted: Jobseekers Act 1995, s 41(4), Sch 2, para 19.[6] Words inserted: Health Act 1999 (Supplementary, Consequential etc Provisions) Order 2000, SI 2000/90.[7] Words and subsection inserted: Local Government Act 2000, s 103.[8] Words and subsection inserted: Children (Leaving Care) Act 2000, s 7(3).[9] Words inserted: National Health Service Reform and Health Care Professions Act 2002 (Supplementary, Consequential etc Provisions) Regulations 2002, SI 2002/2469, reg 4, Sch 1, para 16(1), (2).[10] Word substituted: Tax Credits Act 2002, s 47, Sch 3, paras 15, 18.[11] Subsection inserted: State Pension Credit Act 2002, s 14, Sch 2, Pt 3, para 30.[12] Word substituted: Civil Partnership Act 2004 (Overseas Relationships and Consequential, etc Amendments) Order 2005, SI 2005/3129, art 4(4), Sch 4, para 9.[13] Words substituted: SI 2007/961.[14] Words substituted: Welfare Reform Act 2007, s 28(1), Sch 3, para 6(1), (4).[15] Words inserted: Children and Young Persons Act 2008, s 39, Sch 3, paras 1, 20.[16] Words substituted, omitted and inserted: Health and Social Care Act 2012, s 55(2), Sch 5, Pt 1, paras 47, 52.[17] Words inserted: Welfare Reform Act 2012, s 31, Sch 2, para 1.[18] Words and subsection inserted: SI 2016/413, regs 55, 94.

Definitions. 'Child': s 105(1); 'child who is looked after by a local authority': s 22(1); 'clinical commissioning group': s 105(1); 'community home': s 53(1); 'controlled community home': s 53(4); 'hospital': s 105(1); 'local authority': s 105(1); 'ordinary residence': s 105(6); 'service': s 105(1).

30 Miscellaneous

(1) Nothing in this Part shall affect any duty imposed on a local authority by or under any other enactment.

(2) Any question arising under section 20(2), 21(3) or 29(7) to (9) as to the ordinary residence of a child shall be determined by agreement between the local authorities concerned or, in default of agreement, by the [Secretary of State][3] [but see subsection (2C)][3].

[(2A) ...

(2B) ...³]¹

[(2C) Any question arising as to whether a child is ordinarily resident –

    (a)   in the area of a local authority under section 20(2), 21(3) or 29(7) to (9), or

    (b)   in the area of a local authority in Wales under section 76(2), 77(4) or (5), or 193(3) to (6) of the Social Services and Well-being (Wales) Act 2014,

shall be determined by the local authority and local authority in Wales concerned, or in default of agreement, by the Secretary of State.

(2D) The Secretary of State must consult the Welsh Ministers before making a determination under subsection (2C).]

(3) ...²

(4) The [Secretary of State]³ may make regulations for determining, as respects any [education]² functions specified in the regulations, whether a child who is being looked after by a local authority is to be treated, for purposes so specified, as a child of parents of sufficient resources or as a child of parents without resources.

NOTES

Amendments.¹ Subsections inserted: Children and Young Persons Act 2008, s 39, Sch 3, paras 1, 21.² Subsection repealed and word substituted: SI 2010/1158.³ Subsections omitted and inserted, words substituted and inserted: SI 2016/413, regs 55, 95.

Definitions. 'Child who is looked after by a local authority': s 22(1); 'functions': s 105(1); 'local authority': s 105(1); 'ordinary residence': s 105(6).

[30A

...²]¹

NOTES

Amendments.¹ Section inserted: Children and Young Persons Act 2008, s 39, Sch 3, paras 1, 22.² Section omitted: SI 2016/413, regs 55, 96.

PART IV
CARE AND SUPERVISION

General

31 Care and supervision orders

(1) On the application of any local authority or authorised person, the court may make an order –

    (a)   placing the child with respect to whom the application is made in the care of a designated local authority; or

    (b)   putting him under the supervision of a designated local authority ...².

(2) A court may only make a care order or supervision order if it is satisfied –

(a)   that the child concerned is suffering, or is likely to suffer, significant harm; and

(b)   that the harm, or likelihood of harm, is attributable to –

   (i)   the care given to the child, or likely to be given to him if the order were not made, not being what it would be reasonable to expect a parent to give to him; or

   (ii)   the child's being beyond parental control.

(3) No care order or supervision order may be made with respect to a child who has reached the age of seventeen (or sixteen, in the case of a child who is married).

[(3A) A court deciding whether to make a care order –

(a)   is required to consider the permanence provisions of the section 31A plan for the child concerned, but

(b)   is not required to consider the remainder of the section 31A plan, subject to section 34(11).

[(3B) For the purposes of subsection (3A), the permanence provisions of a section 31A plan are –

(a)   such of the plan's provisions setting out the long-term plan for the upbringing of the child concerned as provide for any of the following –

   (i)   the child to live with any parent of the child's or with any other member of, or any friend of, the child's family;

   (ii)   adoption;

   (iii)   long-term care not within sub-paragraph (i) or (ii);

(b)   such of the plan's provisions as set out any of the following –

   (i)   the impact on the child concerned of any harm that he or she suffered or was likely to suffer;

   (ii)   the current and future needs of the child (including needs arising out of that impact);

   (iii)   the way in which the long-term plan for the upbringing of the child would meet those current and future needs.][7]

(3C) The Secretary of State may by regulations amend this section for the purpose of altering what for the purposes of subsection (3A) are the permanence provisions of a section 31A plan.][6]][4]

(4) An application under this section may be made on its own or in any other family proceedings.

(5) The court may –

(a)   on an application for a care order, make a supervision order;

(b)   on an application for a supervision order, make a care order.

(6) Where an authorised person proposes to make an application under this section he shall –

(a)   if it is reasonably practicable to do so; and

(b)   before making the application,

consult the local authority appearing to him to be the authority in whose area the child concerned is ordinarily resident.

(7) An application made by an authorised person shall not be entertained by the court if, at the time when it is made, the child concerned is –

    (a)   the subject of an earlier application for a care order, or supervision order, which has not been disposed of; or

    (b)   subject to –

        (i)   a care order or supervision order;

        [(ii) a youth rehabilitation order within [the meaning given by section 173 of the Sentencing Code][8]; or][5]

        (iii) a supervision requirement within the meaning of [Part II of the Children (Scotland) Act 1995][1].

(8) The local authority designated in a care order must be –

    (a)   the authority within whose area the child is ordinarily resident; or

    (b)   where the child does not reside in the area of a local authority, the authority within whose area any circumstances arose in consequence of which the order is being made.

(9) In this section –

'authorised person' means –

    (a)   the National Society for the Prevention of Cruelty to Children and any of its officers; and

    (b)   any person authorised by order of the Secretary of State to bring proceedings under this section and any officer of a body which is so authorised;

'harm' means ill-treatment or the impairment of health or development [including, for example, impairment suffered from seeing or hearing the ill-treatment of another][3];

'development' means physical, intellectual, emotional, social or behavioural development;

'health' means physical or mental health; and

'ill-treatment' includes sexual abuse and forms of ill-treatment which are not physical.

(10) Where the question of whether harm suffered by a child is significant turns on the child's health or development, his health or development shall be compared with that which could reasonably be expected of a similar child.

(11) In this Act –

'a care order' means (subject to section 105(1)) an order under subsection (1)(a) and (except where express provision to the contrary is made) includes an interim care order made under section 38; and

'a supervision order' means an order under subsection (1)(b) and (except where express provision to the contrary is made) includes an interim supervision order made under section 38.

NOTES

Amendments.[1] Words substituted: Children (Scotland) Act 1995, s 105(4), Sch 4, para 48(1), (2).[2] Words omitted: Criminal Justice and Court Services Act 2000, ss 74, 75, Sch 7, paras 87, 90, Sch 8.[3] Words inserted: Adoption and Children Act 2002, s 120.[4] Subsection inserted: Adoption and Children Act 2002, s 121(1).[5] Paragraph substituted: Criminal Justice and Immigration Act 2008, s 6(2), Sch 4, Pt 1, paras 33, 35.[6] Subsections (3A)–(3C) substituted for subsection (3A): Children and Families Act 2014, s 15(1).[7] Subsection substituted: Children and Social Work Act 2017, s 8.[8] Words substituted: Sentencing Act 2020, s 410, Sch 24, para 109.

Definitions. 'Authorised person': s 31(9); 'care order': ss 31(11), 105(1); 'child': s 105(1); 'designated local authority': s 31(8); 'development': s 31(9); 'family proceedings': s 8(3); 'harm': s 31(9); 'health': s 31(9); 'ill-treatment': s 31(9); 'local authority': s 105(1); 'ordinary residence': s 105(6); 'significant harm': s 31(10); 'supervision order': s 31(11); 'the court': s 92(7).

[31A Care orders: care plans

(1) Where an application is made on which a care order might be made with respect to a child, the appropriate local authority must, within such time as the court may direct, prepare a plan ('a care plan') for the future care of the child.

(2) While the application is pending, the authority must keep any care plan prepared by them under review and, if they are of the opinion some change is required, revise the plan, or make a new plan, accordingly.

(3) A care plan must give any prescribed information and do so in the prescribed manner.

(4) For the purposes of this section, the appropriate local authority, in relation to a child in respect of whom a care order might be made, is the local authority proposed to be designated in the order.

(5) In section 31(3A) and this section, references to a care order do not include an interim care order.

(6) A plan prepared, or treated as prepared, under this section is referred to in this Act as a 'section 31A plan'.][1]

Amendments.[1] Section inserted: Adoption and Children Act 2002, s 121(2).

32 Period within which application for order under this Part must be disposed of

(1) A court [in which an application for an order under this Part is proceeding][1] shall (in the light of any [provision in rules of court that is of the kind mentioned in subsection (2)(a) or (b))][1] –

    (a)   draw up a timetable with a view to [disposing of the application –
        (i)   without delay, and
        (ii)   in any event within twenty-six weeks beginning with the day on which the application was issued; and][1]
    (b)   give such directions as it considers appropriate for the purpose of ensuring, so far as is reasonably practicable, that that timetable is adhered to.

(2) Rules of court may –

    (a)   specify periods within which specified steps must be taken in relation to such proceedings; and

(b) make other provision with respect to such proceedings for the purpose of ensuring, so far as is reasonably practicable, that they are disposed of without delay.

[(3) A court, when drawing up a timetable under subsection (1)(a), must in particular have regard to –

(a) the impact which the timetable would have on the welfare of the child to whom the application relates; and

(b) the impact which the timetable would have on the conduct of the proceedings.

(4) A court, when revising a timetable drawn up under subsection (1)(a) or when making any decision which may give rise to a need to revise such a timetable (which does not include a decision under subsection (5)), must in particular have regard to –

(a) the impact which any revision would have on the welfare of the child to whom the application relates; and

(b) the impact which any revision would have on the duration and conduct of the proceedings.

(5) A court in which an application under this Part is proceeding may extend the period that is for the time being allowed under subsection (1)(a)(ii) in the case of the application, but may do so only if the court considers that the extension is necessary to enable the court to resolve the proceedings justly.

(6) When deciding whether to grant an extension under subsection (5), a court must in particular have regard to –

(a) the impact which any ensuing timetable revision would have on the welfare of the child to whom the application relates, and

(b) the impact which any ensuing timetable revision would have on the duration and conduct of the proceedings;

and here 'ensuing timetable revision' means any revision, of the timetable under subsection (1)(a) for the proceedings, which the court considers may ensue from the extension.

(7) When deciding whether to grant an extension under subsection (5), a court is to take account of the following guidance: extensions are not to be granted routinely and are to be seen as requiring specific justification.

(8) Each separate extension under subsection (5) is to end no more than eight weeks after the later of –

(a) the end of the period being extended; and

(b) the end of the day on which the extension is granted.

(9) The Lord Chancellor may by regulations amend subsection (1)(a)(ii), or the opening words of subsection (8), for the purpose of varying the period for the time being specified in that provision.

(10) Rules of court may provide that a court –

(a)   when deciding whether to exercise the power under subsection (5), or

(b)   when deciding how to exercise that power,

must, or may or may not, have regard to matters specified in the rules, or must take account of any guidance set out in the rules.][1]

NOTES

Amendments.[1] Words substituted and subsections inserted: Children and Families Act 2014, s 14(1)–(3), (7).

Definition. 'The court': s 92(7).

Care orders

33 Effect of care order

(1) Where a care order is made with respect to a child it shall be the duty of the local authority designated by the order to receive the child into their care and to keep him in their care while the order remains in force.

(2) Where –

(a)   a care order has been made with respect to a child on the application of an authorised person; but

(b)   the local authority designated by the order was not informed that that person proposed to make the application,

the child may be kept in the care of that person until received into the care of the authority.

(3) While a care order is in force with respect to a child, the local authority designated by the order shall –

(a)   have parental responsibility for the child; and

(b)   have the power (subject to the following provisions of this section) to determine the extent to which [a parent or guardian of the child]

[(i)   a parent, guardian or special guardian of the child; or

(ii)   a person who by virtue of section 4A has parental responsibility for the child,][1]

may meet his parental responsibility for him.

(4) The authority may not exercise the power in subsection (3)(b) unless they are satisfied that it is necessary to do so in order to safeguard or promote the child's welfare.

(5) Nothing in subsection (3)(b) shall prevent [a person mentioned in that provision who has care of the child][1] from doing what is reasonable in all the circumstances of the case for the purpose of safeguarding or promoting his welfare.

(6) While a care order is in force with respect to a child, the local authority designated by the order shall not –

(a)   cause the child to be brought up in any religious persuasion other than that in which he would have been brought up if the order had not been made; or

(b) have the right –
   [(i) to consent or refuse to consent to the making of an application with respect to the child under section 18 of the Adoption Act 1976;][2]
   (ii) to agree or refuse to agree to the making of an adoption order, or an order under [section 84 of the Adoption and Children Act 2002][3], with respect to the child; or
   (iii) to appoint a guardian for the child.

(7) While a care order is in force with respect to a child, no person may –

(a) cause the child to be known by a new surname; or
(b) remove him from the United Kingdom,

without either the written consent of every person who has parental responsibility for the child or the leave of the court.

(8) Subsection (7)(b) does not –

(a) prevent the removal of such a child, for a period of less than one month, by the authority in whose care he is; or
(b) apply to arrangements for such a child to live outside England and Wales (which are governed by paragraph 19 of Schedule 2 [in England, and section 124 of the Social Services and Well-being (Wales) Act 2014 in Wales][4]).

(9) The power in subsection (3)(b) is subject (in addition to being subject to the provisions of this section) to any right, duty, power, responsibility or authority which [a person mentioned in that provision][3] has in relation to the child and his property by virtue of any other enactment.

NOTES

Amendments.[1] Words substituted: Adoption and Children Act 2002, s 139(1), Sch 3, paras 54, 63(a), (b).[2] Subparagraph repealed: Adoption and Children Act 2002, s 139(1), Sch 3, paras 54, 63(c)(i).[3] Words substituted: Adoption and Children Act 2002, s 139(1), Sch 3, paras 54, 63(c)(ii), (d).[4] Words inserted: SI 2016/413, regs 55, 97.

Definitions. 'Authorised person': s 31(9); 'care order': ss 31(11), 105(1); 'designated local authority': s 31(8); 'guardian of the child': s 105(1); 'local authority': s 105(1); 'parental responsibility': s 3; 'the court': s 92(7).

34 Parental contact etc with children in care

(1) Where a child is in the care of a local authority, the authority shall (subject to the provisions of this section [and their duty under section 22(3)(a)][3] [or, where the local authority is in Wales, under section 78(1)(a) of the Social Services and Well-being (Wales) Act 2014][4]) allow the child reasonable contact with –

(a) his parents;
(b) any guardian [or special guardian][1] of his;
[(ba) any person who by virtue of section 4A has parental responsibility for him;][1]
(c) where there was a [child arrangements][2] order in force with respect to the child immediately before the care order was made, [any person named in the child arrangements order as a person with whom the child was to live][2]; and

PART I – Statutes

(d)   where, immediately before the care order was made, a person had care of the child by virtue of an order made in the exercise of the High Court's inherent jurisdiction with respect to children, that person.

(2)   On an application made by the authority or the child, the court may make such order as it considers appropriate with respect to the contact which is to be allowed between the child and any named person.

(3)   On an application made by –

(a)   any person mentioned in paragraphs (a) to (d) of subsection (1); or
(b)   any person who has obtained the leave of the court to make the application,

the court may make such order as it considers appropriate with respect to the contact which is to be allowed between the child and that person.

(4)   On an application made by the authority or the child, the court may make an order authorising the authority to refuse to allow contact between the child and any person who is mentioned in paragraphs (a) to (d) of subsection (1) and named in the order.

(5)   When making a care order with respect to a child, or in any family proceedings in connection with a child who is in the care of a local authority, the court may make an order under this section, even though no application for such an order has been made with respect to the child, if it considers that the order should be made.

(6)   An authority may refuse to allow the contact that would otherwise be required by virtue of subsection (1) or an order under this section if –

(a)   they are satisfied that it is necessary to do so in order to safeguard or promote the child's welfare; and
(b)   the refusal –
(i)   is decided upon as a matter of urgency; and
(ii)   does not last for more than seven days.

[(6A) Where (by virtue of an order under this section, or because subsection (6) applies) a local authority in England are authorised to refuse to allow contact between the child and a person mentioned in any of paragraphs (a) to (c) of paragraph 15(1) of Schedule 2, paragraph 15(1) of that Schedule does not require the authority to endeavour to promote contact between the child and that person.][3]

[(6B) Where (by virtue of an order under this section, or because subsection (6) applies) a local authority in Wales is authorised to refuse contact between the child and a person mentioned in any of paragraphs (a) to (c) of section 95(1) of the Social Services and Well-being (Wales) Act 2014, section 95(1) of that Act does not require the authority to promote contact between the child and that person.][4]

(7)   An order under this section may impose such conditions as the court considers appropriate.

(8)   The Secretary of State may by regulations make provision as to –

[(za) what a local authority in England must have regard to in considering whether contact between a child and a person mentioned in any of paragraphs (a) to (d) of subsection (1) is consistent with safeguarding and promoting the child's welfare;][3]

(a) the steps to be taken by a local authority who have exercised their powers under subsection (6);

(b) the circumstances in which, and conditions subject to which, the terms of any order under this section may be departed from by agreement between the local authority and the person in relation to whom the order is made;

(c) notification by a local authority of any variation or suspension of arrangements made (otherwise than under an order under this section) with a view to affording any person contact with a child to whom this section applies.

(9) The court may vary or discharge any order made under this section on the application of the authority, the child concerned or the person named in the order.

(10) An order under this section may be made either at the same time as the care order itself or later.

(11) Before [making, varying or discharging an order under this section or][3] making a care order with respect to any child the court shall –

(a) consider the arrangements which the authority have made, or propose to make, for affording any person contact with a child to whom this section applies; and

(b) invite the parties to the proceedings to comment on those arrangements.

NOTES

Amendments.[1] Words and paragraph inserted: Adoption and Children Act 2002, s 139(1), Sch 3, paras 54, 64(a), (b).[2] Words substituted: Children and Families Act 2014, s 12, Sch 2, paras 1, 31.[3] Words, subsection and paragraph inserted: Children and Families Act 2014, s 8, with effect from 25 July 2014, SI 2014/889, art 14.[4] Words and subsection inserted: SI 2016/413, regs 55, 98.

Definitions. 'Care order': ss 31(11), 105(1); 'child': s 105(1); 'family proceedings': s 8(3); 'guardian of a child': s 105(1); 'local authority': s 105(1); 'residence order': s 8(1); 'the court': s 92(7).

Supervision orders

35 Supervision orders

(1) While a supervision order is in force it shall be the duty of the supervisor –

(a) to advise, assist and befriend the supervised child;

(b) to take such steps as are reasonably necessary to give effect to the order; and

(c) where –

(i) the order is not wholly complied with; or

(ii) the supervisor considers that the order may no longer be necessary,

to consider whether or not to apply to the court for its variation or discharge.

(2) Parts I and II of Schedule 3 make further provision with respect to supervision orders.

NOTES

Definitions. 'Supervised child', 'supervisor': s 105(1); 'supervision order': s 31(11); 'the court': s 92(7).

36 Education supervision orders

(1) On the application of any [local authority]⁴, the court may make an order putting the child with respect to whom the application is made under the supervision of a designated [local authority]⁴.

(2) In this Act 'an education supervision order' means an order under subsection (1).

(3) A court may only make an education supervision order if it is satisfied that the child concerned is of compulsory school age and is not being properly educated.

(4) For the purposes of this section, a child is being properly educated only if he is receiving efficient full-time education suitable to his age, ability and aptitude and any special educational needs he may have.

(5) Where a child is –

    (a)   the subject of a school attendance order which is in force under [section 437 of the Education Act 1996]² and which has not been complied with; or

  [(b) is not attending regularly within the meaning of section 444 of that Act –
      (i)   a school at which he is a registered pupil,
      (ii) any place at which education is provided for him in the circumstances mentioned in subsection (1) [or (1A)] of section 444ZA of that Act, or
      (iii) any place which he is required to attend in the circumstances mentioned in subsection [(1B) or] (2) of that section]³,

then, unless it is proved that he is being properly educated, it shall be assumed that he is not.

(6) An education supervision order may not be made with respect to a child who is in the care of a local authority.

(7) The [local authority]⁴ designated in an education supervision order must be –

    (a)   the authority within whose area the child concerned is living or will live; or

    (b)   where –
      (i)   the child is a registered pupil at a school; and
      (ii) the authority mentioned in paragraph (a) and the authority within whose area the school is situated agree,
  the latter authority.

(8) Where a [local authority]⁴ propose to make an application for an education supervision order they shall, before making the application, consult the …¹ appropriate local authority [if different]⁴.

(9) The appropriate local authority is –

(a) in the case of a child who is being provided with accommodation by, or on behalf of, a local authority, that authority; and

(b) in any other case, the local authority within whose area the child concerned lives, or will live.

(10) Part III of Schedule 3 makes further provision with respect to education supervision orders.

[(11) Where, for the purposes of the Additional Learning Needs and Education Tribunal (Wales) Act 2018, a local authority in Wales is responsible for a child or a child is looked after by a local authority in Wales, the reference to special educational needs in subsection (4) is to be interpreted as a reference to additional learning needs (which has the same meaning as in that Act).][6]

NOTES

Amendments.[1] Words repealed: Education Act 1993, s 307, Sch 19, para 149, Sch 21, Part II.[2] Words substituted: Education Act 1996, s 582(1), Sch 37, para 85.[3] Paragraph substituted: Education Act 2005, s 117, Sch 18, para 1.[4] Words substituted and inserted: SI 2010/1158.[5] Words inserted: Education and Skills Act 2008, s 169, Sch 1, para 43.[6] Subsection inserted: Additional Learning Needs and Education Tribunal (Wales) Act 2018, s 96, Sch 1, para 2(1), (3).
Definitions. 'Appropriate local authority': s 36(9); 'child': s 105(1); 'education supervision order': s 36(2); 'local authority': s 105(1); 'local education authority': s 105(1); 'properly educated': s 36(4); 'registered pupil': s 105(1); 'school': s 105(1); 'special educational needs': s 105(1); 'the court': s 92(7).

Powers of court

37 Powers of court in certain family proceedings

(1) Where, in any family proceedings in which a question arises with respect to the welfare of any child, it appears to the court that it may be appropriate for a care or supervision order to be made with respect to him, the court may direct the appropriate authority to undertake an investigation of the child's circumstances.

(2) Where the court gives a direction under this section the local authority concerned shall, when undertaking the investigation, consider whether they should –

(a) apply for a care order or for a supervision order with respect to the child;

(b) provide services or assistance for the child or his family; or

(c) take any other action with respect to the child.

(3) Where a local authority undertake an investigation under this section, and decide not to apply for a care order or supervision order with respect to the child concerned, they shall inform the court of –

(a) their reasons for so deciding;

(b) any service or assistance which they have provided, or intend to provide, for the child and his family; and

(c) any other action which they have taken, or propose to take, with respect to the child.

(4) The information shall be given to the court before the end of the period of eight weeks beginning with the date of the direction, unless the court otherwise directs.

PART I – Statutes

(5) The local authority named in a direction under subsection (1) must be –

> (a)   the authority in whose area the child is ordinarily resident; or
> (b)   where the child [is not ordinarily resident]¹ in the area of a local authority, the authority within whose area any circumstances arose in consequence of which the direction is being given.

(6) If, on the conclusion of any investigation or review under this section, the authority decide not to apply for a care order or supervision order with respect to the child –

> (a)   they shall consider whether it would be appropriate to review the case at a later date; and
> (b)   if they decide that it would be, they shall determine the date on which that review is to begin.

NOTES

Amendments.¹ Words substituted: Courts and Legal Services Act 1990, s 116, Sch 16, para 16.
Definitions. 'Appropriate authority': s 37(5); 'care order': ss 31(11), 105(1); 'child': s 105(1); 'family proceedings': s 8(3); 'local authority': s 105(1); 'ordinary residence': s 105(6); 'supervision order': s 31(11); 'the court': s 92(7).

38   Interim orders

(1) Where –

> (a)   in any proceedings on an application for a care order or supervision order, the proceedings are adjourned; or
> (b)   the court gives a direction under section 37(1),

the court may make an interim care order or an interim supervision order with respect to the child concerned.

(2) A court shall not make an interim care order or interim supervision order under this section unless it is satisfied that there are reasonable grounds for believing that the circumstances with respect to the child are as mentioned in section 31(2).

(3) Where, in any proceedings on an application for a care order or supervision order, a court makes a [child arrangements order with respect to the living arrangements of]² the child concerned, it shall also make an interim supervision order with respect to him unless satisfied that his welfare will be satisfactorily safeguarded without an interim order being made.

[(3A) For the purposes of subsection (3), a child arrangements order is one made with respect to the living arrangements of the child concerned if the arrangements regulated by the order consist of, or include, arrangements which relate to either or both of the following –

> (a)   with whom the child is to live, and
> (b)   when the child is to live with any person.]²

(4) An interim order made under or by virtue of this section shall have effect for such period as may be specified in the order, but shall in any event cease to have effect on whichever of the following events first occurs –

(a) ...[3]

(b) ...[3]

(c) in a case which falls within subsection (1)(a), the disposal of the application;

(d) in a case which falls within subsection (1)(b), the disposal of an application for a care order or supervision order made by the authority with respect to the child;

[(da) in a case which falls within subsection (1)(b) and in which –
  (i) no direction has been given under section 37(4), and
  (ii) no application for a care order or supervision order has been made with respect to the child,
  the expiry of the period of eight weeks beginning with the date on which the order is made;][3]

(e) in a case which falls within subsection (1)(b) and in which –
  (i) the court has given a direction under section 37(4), but
  (ii) no application for a care order or supervision order has been made with respect to the child,
  the expiry of the period fixed by that direction.

(5) ...[3]

(6) Where the court makes an interim care order, or interim supervision order, it may give such directions (if any) as it considers appropriate with regard to the medical or psychiatric examination or other assessment of the child; but if the child is of sufficient understanding to make an informed decision he may refuse to submit to the examination or other assessment.

(7) A direction under subsection (6) may be to the effect that there is to be –

(a) no such examination or assessment; or

(b) no such examination or assessment unless the court directs otherwise.

[(7A) A direction under subsection (6) to the effect that there is to be a medical or psychiatric examination or other assessment of the child may be given only if the court is of the opinion that the examination or other assessment is necessary to assist the court to resolve the proceedings justly.

(7B) When deciding whether to give a direction under subsection (6) to that effect the court is to have regard in particular to –

(a) any impact which any examination or other assessment would be likely to have on the welfare of the child, and any other impact which giving the direction would be likely to have on the welfare of the child,

(b) the issues with which the examination or other assessment would assist the court,

(c) the questions which the examination or other assessment would enable the court to answer,

(d) the evidence otherwise available,

(e) the impact which the direction would be likely to have on the timetable, duration and conduct of the proceedings,

(f) the cost of the examination or other assessment, and

(g)   any matters prescribed by Family Procedure Rules.][1]

(8) A direction under subsection (6) may be –

(a)   given when the interim order is made or at any time while it is in force; and

(b)   varied at any time on the application of any person falling within any class of person prescribed by rules of court for the purposes of this subsection.

(9) Paragraphs 4 and 5 of Schedule 3 shall not apply in relation to an interim supervision order.

(10) Where a court makes an order under or by virtue of this section it shall, in determining the period for which the order is to be in force, consider whether any party who was, or might have been, opposed to the making of the order was in a position to argue his case against the order in full.

NOTES

Amendments.[1] Subsections inserted: Children and Families Act 2014, s 13.[2] Words substituted and subsection inserted: Children and Families Act 2014, s 12, Sch 2, paras 1, 32.[3] Paragraphs omitted, subsection inserted and omitted: Children and Families Act 2014, s 14(1), (4).
Definitions. 'Care order': s 31(11); 'child': s 105(1); 'relevant period': s 38(5); 'residence order': s 8(1); 'supervision order': s 31(11); 'the court': s 92(7).

[38A Power to include exclusion requirement in interim care order

(1) Where –

(a)   on being satisfied that there are reasonable grounds for believing that the circumstances with respect to a child are as mentioned in section 31(2) (a) and (b)(i), the court makes an interim care order with respect to a child, and

(b)   the conditions mentioned in subsection (2) are satisfied,

the court may include an exclusion requirement in the interim care order.

(2) The conditions are –

(a)   that there is reasonable cause to believe that, if a person ('the relevant person') is excluded from a dwelling-house in which the child lives, the child will cease to suffer, or cease to be likely to suffer, significant harm, and

(b)   that another person living in the dwelling-house (whether a parent of the child or some other person) –
(i)   is able and willing to give to the child the care which it would be reasonable to expect a parent to give him, and
(ii)   consents to the inclusion of the exclusion requirement.

(3) For the purposes of this section an exclusion requirement is any one or more of the following –

(a)   a provision requiring the relevant person to leave a dwelling-house in which he is living with the child,

(b) a provision prohibiting the relevant person from entering a dwelling-house in which the child lives, and

(c) a provision excluding the relevant person from a defined area in which a dwelling-house in which the child lives is situated.

(4) The court may provide that the exclusion requirement is to have effect for a shorter period than the other provisions of the interim care order.

(5) Where the court makes an interim care order containing an exclusion requirement, the court may attach a power of arrest to the exclusion requirement.

(6) Where the court attaches a power of arrest to an exclusion requirement of an interim care order, it may provide that the power of arrest is to have effect for a shorter period than the exclusion requirement.

(7) Any period specified for the purposes of subsection (4) or (6) may be extended by the court (on one or more occasions) on an application to vary or discharge the interim care order.

(8) Where a power of arrest is attached to an exclusion requirement of an interim care order by virtue of subsection (5), a constable may arrest without warrant any person whom he has reasonable cause to believe to be in breach of the requirement.

(9) Sections 47(7), (11) and (12) and 48 of, and Schedule 5 to, the Family Law Act 1996 shall have effect in relation to a person arrested under subsection (8) of this section as they have effect in relation to a person arrested under section 47(6) of that Act.

(10) If, while an interim care order containing an exclusion requirement is in force, the local authority have removed the child from the dwelling-house from which the relevant person is excluded to other accommodation for a continuous period of more than 24 hours, the interim care order shall cease to have effect in so far as it imposes the exclusion requirement.][1]

NOTES

Amendments.[1] Section inserted: Family Law Act 1996, s 52, Sch 6, para 1.

[38B Undertakings relating to interim care orders

(1) In any case where the court has power to include an exclusion requirement in an interim care order, the court may accept an undertaking from the relevant person.

(2) No power of arrest may be attached to any undertaking given under subsection (1).

(3) An undertaking given to a court under subsection (1) –

(a) shall be enforceable as if it were an order of the court, and

(b) shall cease to have effect if, while it is in force, the local authority have removed the child from the dwelling-house from which the relevant person is excluded to other accommodation for a continuous period of more than 24 hours.

(4) This section has effect without prejudice to the powers of the High Court and [family court]² apart from this section.

(5) In this section 'exclusion requirement' and 'relevant person' have the same meaning as in section 38A.]¹

NOTES

Amendments.¹ Section inserted: Family Law Act 1996, s 52, Sch 6, para 1.² Words substituted: Crime and Courts Act 2013, s 17, Sch 11, paras 102, 106.

39 Discharge and variation etc of care orders and supervision orders

(1) A care order may be discharged by the court on the application of –

   (a)   any person who has parental responsibility for the child;
   (b)   the child himself; or
   (c)   the local authority designated by the order.

(2) A supervision order may be varied or discharged by the court on the application of –

   (a)   any person who has parental responsibility for the child;
   (b)   the child himself; or
   (c)   the supervisor.

(3) On the application of a person who is not entitled to apply for the order to be discharged, but who is a person with whom the child is living, a supervision order may be varied by the court in so far as it imposes a requirement which affects that person.

[(3A) On the application of a person who is not entitled to apply for the order to be discharged, but who is a person to whom an exclusion requirement contained in the order applies, an interim care order may be varied or discharged by the court in so far as it imposes the exclusion requirement.

(3B) Where a power of arrest has been attached to an exclusion requirement of an interim care order, the court may, on the application of any person entitled to apply for the discharge of the order so far as it imposes the exclusion requirement, vary or discharge the order in so far as it confers a power of arrest (whether or not any application has been made to vary or discharge any other provision of the order).]¹

(4) Where a care order is in force with respect to a child the court may, on the application of any person entitled to apply for the order to be discharged, substitute a supervision order for the care order.

(5) When a court is considering whether to substitute one order for another under subsection (4) any provision of this Act which would otherwise require section 31(2) to be satisfied at the time when the proposed order is substituted or made shall be disregarded.

NOTES

Amendments.¹ Subsections inserted: Family Law Act 1996, s 52, Sch 6, para 2.
Definitions. 'Care order': ss 31(11), 105(1); 'child': s 105(1); 'local authority': s 105(1); 'supervision order': s 31(11); 'supervisor': s 105(1); 'the court': s 92(7).

40 Orders pending appeals in cases about care or supervision orders

(1) Where –

(a)   a court dismisses an application for a care order; and
(b)   at the time when the court dismisses the application, the child concerned is the subject of an interim care order,

the court may make a care order with respect to the child to have effect subject to such directions (if any) as the court may see fit to include in the order.

(2) Where –

(a)   a court dismisses an application for a care order, or an application for a supervision order; and
(b)   at the time when the court dismisses the application, the child concerned is the subject of an interim supervision order,

the court may make a supervision order with respect to the child to have effect subject to such directions (if any) as the court may see fit to include in the order.

(3) Where a court grants an application to discharge a care order or supervision order, it may order that –

(a)   its decision is not to have effect; or
(b)   the care order, or supervision order, is to continue to have effect but subject to such directions as the court sees fit to include in the order.

(4) An order made under this section shall only have effect for such period, not exceeding the appeal period, as may be specified in the order.

(5) Where –

(a)   an appeal is made against any decision of a court under this section; or
(b)   any application is made to the appellate court in connection with a proposed appeal against that decision,

the appellate court may extend the period for which the order in question is to have effect, but not so as to extend it beyond the end of the appeal period.

(6) In this section 'the appeal period' means –

(a)   where an appeal is made against the decision in question, the period between the making of that decision and the determination of the appeal; and
(b)   otherwise, the period during which an appeal may be made against the decision.

NOTES

Definitions. 'Appeal period': s 40(6); 'care order': ss 31(11), 105(1); 'child': s 105(1); 'the court': s 92(7).

[Representation of child]²

41 Representation of child and of his interests in certain proceedings

(1) For the purpose of any specified proceedings, the court shall appoint [an officer of the Service]² [or a Welsh family proceedings officer]³ for the child

concerned unless satisfied that it is not necessary to do so in order to safeguard his interests.

(2) The [officer of the Service][2] [or Welsh family proceedings officer][3] shall –

    (a)   be appointed in accordance with rules of court; and

    (b)   be under a duty to safeguard the interests of the child in the manner prescribed by such rules.

(3) Where –

    (a)   the child concerned is not represented by a solicitor; and

    (b)   any of the conditions mentioned in subsection (4) is satisfied,

the court may appoint a solicitor to represent him.

(4) The conditions are that –

    (a)   no [officer of the Service][2] [or Welsh family proceedings officer][3] has been appointed for the child;

    (b)   the child has sufficient understanding to instruct a solicitor and wishes to do so;

    (c)   it appears to the court that it would be in the child's best interests for him to be represented by a solicitor.

(5) Any solicitor appointed under or by virtue of this section shall be appointed, and shall represent the child, in accordance with rules of court.

(6) In this section 'specified proceedings' means any proceedings –

    (a)   on an application for a care order or supervision order;

    (b)   in which the court has given a direction under section 37(1) and has made, or is considering whether to make, an interim care order;

    (c)   on an application for the discharge of a care order or the variation or discharge of a supervision order;

    (d)   on an application under section 39(4);

    (e)   in which the court is considering whether to make a [child arrangements order with respect to the living arrangements of][5] a child who is the subject of a care order;

    (f)   with respect to contact between a child who is the subject of a care order and any other person;

    (g)   under Part V;

    (h)   on an appeal against –

        (i)   the making of, or refusal to make, a care order, supervision order or any order under section 34;

        (ii)   the making of, or refusal to make, a [child arrangements order with respect to the living arrangements of][6] a child who is the subject of a care order; or

        (iii)   the variation or discharge, or refusal of an application to vary or discharge, an order of a kind mentioned in sub-paragraph (i) or (ii);

        (iv)   the refusal of an application under section 39(4);

        (v)   the making of, or refusal to make, an order under Part V; or [(hh) on an application for the making or revocation of a placement order (within the meaning of section 21 of the Adoption and Children Act 2002);][5]

(i) which are specified for the time being, for the purposes of this section, by rules of court.

[(6A) The proceedings which may be specified under subsection (6)(i) include (for example) proceedings for the making, varying or discharging of a section 8 order.][4]

[(6B) For the purposes of subsection (6), a child arrangements order is one made with respect to the living arrangements of a child if the arrangements regulated by the order consist of, or include, arrangements which relate to either or both of the following –

(a) with whom the child is to live, and

(b) when the child is to live with any person.][5]

(7)–(9) ...[2]

(10) Rules of court may make provision as to –

(a) the assistance which any [officer of the Service][2] [or Welsh family proceedings officer][3] may be required by the court to give to it;

(b) the consideration to be given by any [officer of the Service][2] [or Welsh family proceedings officer][3], where an order of a specified kind has been made in the proceedings in question, as to whether to apply for the variation or discharge of the order;

(c) the participation of [officers of the Service][2] [or Welsh family proceedings officers][3] in reviews, of a kind specified in the rules, which are conducted by the court.

(11) Regardless of any enactment or rule of law which would otherwise prevent it from doing so, the court may take account of –

(a) any statement contained in a report made by [an officer of the Service][2] [or a Welsh family proceedings officer][3] who is appointed under this section for the purpose of the proceedings in question; and

(b) any evidence given in respect of the matters referred to in the report,

in so far as the statement or evidence is, in the opinion of the court, relevant to the question which the court is considering.

[(12) ...[2]][1]

NOTES

Amendments.[1] Subsection inserted: Courts and Legal Services Act 1990, s 116, Sch 16, para 17.[2] Words substituted or omitted: Criminal Justice and Court Services Act 2000, ss 74, 75, Sch 7, paras 87, 91, Sch 8.[3] Words inserted: Children Act 2004, s 40, Sch 3, paras 5, 9.[4] Subsection inserted: Adoption and Children Act 2002, s 122(1)(b).[5] Paragraph inserted: Adoption and Children Act 2002, s 122(1)(a).[6] Words substituted and subsection inserted: Children and Families Act 2014, s 12, Sch 2, paras 1, 33.

Definitions. 'Care order': ss 31(11), 105(1); 'child': s 105(1); 'local authority': s 105(1); 'residence order': s 8(1); 'specified proceedings': s 41(6); 'supervision order': s 31(11); 'the court': s 92(7).

42 [Right of officer of the Service to have access to local authority records][5]

(1) Where [an officer of the Service][5] [or Welsh family proceedings officer][7] has been appointed [under section 41][5] he shall have the right at all reasonable times to examine and take copies of –

(a)   any records of, or held by, a local authority [or an authorised person][1] which were compiled in connection with the making, or proposed making, by any person of any application under this Act with respect to the child concerned; …[2]

(b)   any …[2] records of, or held by, a local authority which were compiled in connection with any functions which [are social services functions within the meaning of][6] the Local Authority Social Services Act 1970 [or for the purposes of the Social Services and Well-being (Wales) Act 2014][8], so far as those records relate to that child [; or

(c)   any records of, or held by, an authorised person which were compiled in connection with the activities of that person, so far as those records relate to that child.][3]

(2) Where [an officer of the Service][5] [or Welsh family proceedings officer][7] takes a copy of any record which he is entitled to examine under this section, that copy or any part of it shall be admissible as evidence of any matter referred to in any –

(a)   report which he makes to the court in the proceedings in question; or
(b)   evidence which he gives in those proceedings.

(3) Subsection (2) has effect regardless of any enactment or rule of law which would otherwise prevent the record in question being admissible in evidence.

[(4) In this section 'authorised person' has the same meaning as in section 31.][4]

NOTES

Amendments.[1] Words inserted: Courts and Legal Services Act 1990, s 116, Sch 16, para 18(2).[2] Words repealed: Courts and Legal Services Act 1990, s 125(7), Sch 20.[3] Words inserted: Courts and Legal Services Act 1990, s 116, Sch 16, para 18(3).[4] Words inserted: Courts and Legal Services Act 1990, s 116, Sch 16, para 18(4).[5] Words substituted: Criminal Justice and Court Services Act 2000, s 74, Sch 7, paras 87, 92.[6] Words substituted: Local Government Act 2000, s 107, Sch 5, para 20.[7] Words inserted: Children Act 2004, s 40, Sch 3, paras 5, 10.[8] Words inserted: SI 2016/413, regs 55, 99.
Definitions. 'Child': s 105(1); 'functions': s 105(1); 'local authority': s 105(1).

PART V
PROTECTION OF CHILDREN

43 Child assessment orders

(1) On the application of a local authority or authorised person for an order to be made under this section with respect to a child, the court may make the order if, but only if, it is satisfied that –

(a)   the applicant has reasonable cause to suspect that the child is suffering, or is likely to suffer, significant harm;

PART I – Statutes

(b) an assessment of the state of the child's health or development, or of the way in which he has been treated, is required to enable the applicant to determine whether or not the child is suffering, or is likely to suffer, significant harm; and

(c) it is unlikely that such an assessment will be made, or be satisfactory, in the absence of an order under this section.

(2) In this Act 'a child assessment order' means an order under this section.

(3) A court may treat an application under this section as an application for an emergency protection order.

(4) No court shall make a child assessment order if it is satisfied –

(a) that there are grounds for making an emergency protection order with respect to the child; and

(b) that it ought to make such an order rather than a child assessment order.

(5) A child assessment order shall –

(a) specify the date by which the assessment is to begin; and

(b) have effect for such period, not exceeding 7 days beginning with that date, as may be specified in the order.

(6) Where a child assessment order is in force with respect to a child it shall be the duty of any person who is in a position to produce the child –

(a) to produce him to such person as may be named in the order; and

(b) to comply with such directions relating to the assessment of the child as the court thinks fit to specify in the order.

(7) A child assessment order authorises any person carrying out the assessment, or any part of the assessment, to do so in accordance with the terms of the order.

(8) Regardless of subsection (7), if the child is of sufficient understanding to make an informed decision he may refuse to submit to a medical or psychiatric examination or other assessment.

(9) The child may only be kept away from home –

(a) in accordance with directions specified in the order;

(b) if it is necessary for the purposes of the assessment; and

(c) for such period or periods as may be specified in the order.

(10) Where the child is to be kept away from home, the order shall contain such directions as the court thinks fit with regard to the contact that he must be allowed to have with other persons while away from home.

(11) Any person making an application for a child assessment order shall take such steps as are reasonably practicable to ensure that notice of the application is given to –

(a) the child's parents;

(b) any person who is not a parent of his but who has parental responsibility for him;

(c)   any other person caring for the child;

[(d)   any person named in a child arrangements order as a person with whom the child is to spend time or otherwise have contact;][1]

(e)   any person who is allowed to have contact with the child by virtue of an order under section 34; and

(f)   the child,

before the hearing of the application.

(12) Rules of court may make provision as to the circumstances in which –

(a)   any of the persons mentioned in subsection (11); or

(b)   such other person as may be specified in the rules,

may apply to the court for a child assessment order to be varied or discharged.

(13) In this section 'authorised person' means a person who is an authorised person for the purposes of section 31.

NOTES

Amendment.[1] Paragraph substituted: Children and Families Act 2014, s 12, Sch 2, paras 1, 34.
Definitions. 'Authorised person': s 43(13); 'child': s 105(1); 'child assessment order': s 43(2); 'contact order': s 8(1); 'emergency protection order': s 44(4); 'harm': s 31(9); 'local authority': s 105(1); 'parental responsibility': s 3; 'significant harm': s 31(10); 'the court': s 92(7).

44 Orders for emergency protection of children

(1) Where any person ('the applicant') applies to the court for an order to be made under this section with respect to a child, the court may make the order if, but only if, it is satisfied that –

(a)   there is reasonable cause to believe that the child is likely to suffer significant harm if –

(i)   he is not removed to accommodation provided by or on behalf of the applicant; or

(ii)   he does not remain in the place in which he is then being accommodated;

(b)   in the case of an application made by a local authority –

(i)   enquiries are being made with respect to the child under section 47(1)(b); and

(ii)   those enquiries are being frustrated by access to the child being unreasonably refused to a person authorised to seek access and that the applicant has reasonable cause to believe that access to the child is required as a matter of urgency; or

(c)   in the case of an application made by an authorised person –

(i)   the applicant has reasonable cause to suspect that a child is suffering, or is likely to suffer, significant harm;

(ii)   the applicant is making enquiries with respect to the child's welfare; and

(iii)   those enquiries are being frustrated by access to the child being unreasonably refused to a person authorised to seek access and the applicant has reasonable cause to believe that access to the child is required as a matter of urgency.

(2) In this section –

(a) 'authorised person' means a person who is an authorised person for the purposes of section 31; and

(b) 'a person authorised to seek access' means –

   (i) in the case of an application by a local authority, an officer of the local authority or a person authorised by the authority to act on their behalf in connection with the enquiries; or

   (ii) in the case of an application by an authorised person, that person.

(3) Any person –

(a) seeking access to a child in connection with enquiries of a kind mentioned in subsection (1); and

(b) purporting to be a person authorised to do so,

shall, on being asked to do so, produce some duly authenticated document as evidence that he is such a person.

(4) While an order under this section ('an emergency protection order') is in force it –

(a) operates as a direction to any person who is in a position to do so to comply with any request to produce the child to the applicant;

(b) authorises –

   (i) the removal of the child at any time to accommodation provided by or on behalf of the applicant and his being kept there; or

   (ii) the prevention of the child's removal from any hospital, or other place, in which he was being accommodated immediately before the making of the order; and

(c) gives the applicant parental responsibility for the child.

(5) Where an emergency protection order is in force with respect to a child, the applicant –

(a) shall only exercise the power given by virtue of subsection (4)(b) in order to safeguard the welfare of the child;

(b) shall take, and shall only take, such action in meeting his parental responsibility for the child as is reasonably required to safeguard or promote the welfare of the child (having regard in particular to the duration of the order); and

(c) shall comply with the requirements of any regulations made by the Secretary of State for the purposes of this subsection.

(6) Where the court makes an emergency protection order, it may give such directions (if any) as it considers appropriate with respect to –

(a) the contact which is, or is not, to be allowed between the child and any named person;

(b) the medical or psychiatric examination or other assessment of the child.

(7) Where any direction is given under subsection (6)(b), the child may, if he is of sufficient understanding to make an informed decision, refuse to submit to the examination or other assessment.

(8) A direction under subsection (6)(a) may impose conditions and one under subsection (6)(b) may be to the effect that there is to be –

(a)   no such examination or assessment; or
(b)   no such examination or assessment unless the court directs otherwise.

(9) A direction under subsection (6) may be –

(a)   given when the emergency protection order is made or at any time while it is in force; and
(b)   varied at any time on the application of any person falling within any class of person prescribed by rules of court for the purposes of this subsection.

(10) Where an emergency protection order is in force with respect to a child and –

(a)   the applicant has exercised the power given by subsection (4)(b)(i) but it appears to him that it is safe for the child to be returned; or
(b)   the applicant has exercised the power given by subsection (4)(b)(ii) but it appears to him that it is safe for the child to be allowed to be removed from the place in question,

he shall return the child or (as the case may be) allow him to be removed.

(11) Where he is required by subsection (10) to return the child the applicant shall –

(a)   return him to the care of the person from whose care he was removed; or
(b)   if that is not reasonably practicable, return him to the care of –
    (i)   a parent of his;
    (ii)   any person who is not a parent of his but who has parental responsibility for him; or
    (iii)   such other person as the applicant (with the agreement of the court) considers appropriate.

(12) Where the applicant has been required by subsection (10) to return the child, or to allow him to be removed, he may again exercise his powers with respect to the child (at any time while the emergency protection order remains in force) if it appears to him that a change in the circumstances of the case makes it necessary for him to do so.

(13) Where an emergency protection order has been made with respect to a child, the applicant shall, subject to any direction given under subsection (6), allow the child reasonable contact with –

(a)   his parents;
(b)   any person who is not a parent of his but who has parental responsibility for him;
(c)   any person with whom he was living immediately before the making of the order;
[(d)   any person named in a child arrangements order as a person with whom the child is to spend time or otherwise have contact;][1]

(e)   any person who is allowed to have contact with the child by virtue of an order under section 34; and

(f)   any person acting on behalf of any of those persons.

(14) Wherever it is reasonably practicable to do so, an emergency protection order shall name the child; and where it does not name him it shall describe him as clearly as possible.

(15) A person shall be guilty of an offence if he intentionally obstructs any person exercising the power under subsection (4)(b) to remove, or prevent the removal of, a child.

(16) A person guilty of an offence under subsection (15) shall be liable on summary conviction to a fine not exceeding level 3 on the standard scale.

NOTES

Amendment.[1] Paragraph substituted: Children and Families Act 2014, s 12, Sch 2, paras 1, 35.
Definitions. 'Authorised person': s 44(2); 'child': s 105(1); 'contact order': s 8(1); 'emergency protection order': s 44(4); 'harm': s 31(9); 'hospital': s 105(1); 'local authority': s 105(1); 'parental responsibility': s 3; 'person authorised to seek access': s 44(2); 'significant harm': s 31(10); 'the applicant': s 44(1); 'the court': s 92(7).

[44A Power to include exclusion requirement in emergency protection order

(1) Where –

(a)   on being satisfied as mentioned in section 44(1)(a), (b) or (c), the court makes an emergency protection order with respect to a child, and

(b)   the conditions mentioned in subsection (2) are satisfied,

the court may include an exclusion requirement in the emergency protection order.

(2) The conditions are –

(a)   that there is reasonable cause to believe that, if a person ('the relevant person') is excluded from a dwelling-house in which the child lives, then –

(i)   in the case of an order made on the ground mentioned in section 44(1)(a), the child will not be likely to suffer significant harm, even though the child is not removed as mentioned in section 44(1)(a)(i) or does not remain as mentioned in section 44(1)(a)(ii), or

(ii)   in the case of an order made on the ground mentioned in paragraph (b) or (c) of section 44(1), the enquiries referred to in that paragraph will cease to be frustrated, and

(b)   that another person living in the dwelling-house (whether a parent of the child or some other person) –

(i)   is able and willing to give to the child the care which it would be reasonable to expect a parent to give him, and

(ii)   consents to the inclusion of the exclusion requirement.

(3) For the purposes of this section an exclusion requirement is any one or more of the following –

(a)   a provision requiring the relevant person to leave a dwelling-house in which he is living with the child,

(b)   a provision prohibiting the relevant person from entering a dwelling-house in which the child lives, and

(c)   a provision excluding the relevant person from a defined area in which a dwelling-house in which the child lives is situated.

(4) The court may provide that the exclusion requirement is to have effect for a shorter period than the other provisions of the order.

(5) Where the court makes an emergency protection order containing an exclusion requirement, the court may attach a power of arrest to the exclusion requirement.

(6) Where the court attaches a power of arrest to an exclusion requirement of an emergency protection order, it may provide that the power of arrest is to have effect for a shorter period than the exclusion requirement.

(7) Any period specified for the purposes of subsection (4) or (6) may be extended by the court (on one or more occasions) on an application to vary or discharge the emergency protection order.

(8) Where a power of arrest is attached to an exclusion requirement of an emergency protection order by virtue of subsection (5), a constable may arrest without warrant any person whom he has reasonable cause to believe to be in breach of the requirement.

(9) Sections 47(7), (11) and (12) and 48 of, and Schedule 5 to, the Family Law Act 1996 shall have effect in relation to a person arrested under subsection (8) of this section as they have effect in relation to a person arrested under section 47(6) of that Act.

(10) If, while an emergency protection order containing an exclusion requirement is in force, the applicant has removed the child from the dwelling-house from which the relevant person is excluded to other accommodation for a continuous period of more than 24 hours, the order shall cease to have effect in so far as it imposes the exclusion requirement.][1]

NOTES

Amendments.[1] Section inserted: Family Law Act 1996, s 52, Sch 6, para 3.

[44B   Undertakings relating to emergency protection orders

(1) In any case where the court has power to include an exclusion requirement in an emergency protection order, the court may accept an undertaking from the relevant person.

(2) No power of arrest may be attached to any undertaking given under subsection (1).

(3) An undertaking given to a court under subsection (1) –

(a)   shall be enforceable as if it were an order of the court, and (b)　shall cease to have effect if, while it is in force, the applicant has removed the child from the dwelling-house from which the relevant person is excluded to other accommodation for a continuous period of more than 24 hours.

(4) This section has effect without prejudice to the powers of the High Court and [family court][2] apart from this section.

(5) In this section 'exclusion requirement' and 'relevant person' have the same meaning as in section 44A.][1]

NOTES

Amendments.[1] Section inserted: Family Law Act 1996, s 52, Sch 6, para 3.[2] Words substituted: Crime and Courts Act 2013, s 17, Sch 11, paras 102, 107.

45 Duration of emergency protection orders and other supplemental provisions

(1) An emergency protection order shall have effect for such period, not exceeding eight days, as may be specified in the order.

(2) Where –

(a)　the court making an emergency protection order would, but for this subsection, specify a period of eight days as the period for which the order is to have effect; but

(b)　the last of those eight days is a public holiday (that is to say, Christmas Day, Good Friday, a bank holiday or a Sunday),

the court may specify a period which ends at noon on the first later day which is not such a holiday.

(3) Where an emergency protection order is made on an application under section 46(7), the period of eight days mentioned in subsection (1) shall begin with the first day on which the child was taken into police protection under section 46.

(4) Any person who –

(a)　has parental responsibility for a child as the result of an emergency protection order; and

(b)　is entitled to apply for a care order with respect to the child,

may apply to the court for the period during which the emergency protection order is to have effect to be extended.

(5) On an application under subsection (4) the court may extend the period during which the order is to have effect by such period, not exceeding seven days, as it thinks fit, but may do so only if it has reasonable cause to believe that the child concerned is likely to suffer significant harm if the order is not extended.

(6) An emergency protection order may only be extended once.

(7) Regardless of any enactment or rule of law which would otherwise prevent it from doing so, a court hearing an application for, or with respect to, an emergency protection order may take account of –

    (a)   any statement contained in any report made to the court in the course of, or in connection with, the hearing; or

    (b)   any evidence given during the hearing,

which is, in the opinion of the court, relevant to the application.

(8) Any of the following may apply to the court for an emergency protection order to be discharged –

    (a)   the child;

    (b)   a parent of his;

    (c)   any person who is not a parent of his but who has parental responsibility for him; or

    (d)   any person with whom he was living immediately before the making of the order.

[(8A) On the application of a person who is not entitled to apply for the order to be discharged, but who is a person to whom an exclusion requirement contained in the order applies, an emergency protection order may be varied or discharged by the court in so far as it imposes the exclusion requirement.

(8B) Where a power of arrest has been attached to an exclusion requirement of an emergency protection order, the court may, on the application of any person entitled to apply for the discharge of the order so far as it imposes the exclusion requirement, vary or discharge the order in so far as it confers a power of arrest (whether or not any application has been made to vary or discharge any other provision of the order).][2]

(9) ...[5]

[(10) No appeal may be made against –

    (a)   the making of, or refusal to make, an emergency protection order;

    (b)   the extension of, or refusal to extend, the period during which such an order is to have effect;

    (c)   the discharge of, or refusal to discharge, such an order; or

    (d)   the giving of, or refusal to give, any direction in connection with such an order.][1]

(11) Subsection (8) does not apply –

    (a)   where the person who would otherwise be entitled to apply for the emergency protection order to be discharged –

        (i)   was given notice (in accordance with rules of court) of the hearing at which the order was made; and

        (ii)   was present at that hearing; or

    (b)   to any emergency protection order the effective period of which has been extended under subsection (5).

(12) A court making an emergency protection order may direct that the applicant may, in exercising any powers which he has by virtue of the order, be accompanied by a registered medical practitioner, registered nurse or [registered midwife][4], if he so chooses.

[(13) The reference in subsection (12) to a registered midwife is to such a midwife who is also registered in the Specialist Community Public Health Nurses' Part of the register maintained under article 5 of the Nursing and Midwifery Order 2001.][3]

NOTES

Amendments.[1] Words substituted: Courts and Legal Services Act 1990, s 116, Sch 16, para 19.[2] Subsections inserted: Family Law Act 1996, s 52, Sch 6, para 4.[3] Subsection inserted: SI 2004/1771.[4] Words substituted: Nursing and Midwifery Order 2001 [*sic*], SI 2002/253, art 54(3), Sch 5, para 10(a).[5] Subsection repealed: Children and Young Persons Act 2008, ss 30, 42, Sch 4.

Definitions. 'Bank holiday': s 105(1); 'care order': ss 31(11), 105(1); 'child': s 105(1); 'emergency protection order': s 44(4); 'harm': s 31(9); 'parental responsibility': s 3; 'significant harm': s 31(10); 'the court': s 92(7).

46 Removal and accommodation of children by police in cases of emergency

(1) Where a constable has reasonable cause to believe that a child would otherwise be likely to suffer significant harm, he may –

   (a)   remove the child to suitable accommodation and keep him there; or
   (b)   take such steps as are reasonable to ensure that the child's removal from any hospital, or other place, in which he is then being accommodated is prevented.

(2) For the purposes of this Act, a child with respect to whom a constable has exercised his powers under this section is referred to as having been taken into police protection.

(3) As soon as is reasonably practicable after taking a child into police protection, the constable concerned shall –

   (a)   inform the local authority within whose area the child was found of the steps that have been, and are proposed to be, taken with respect to the child under this section and the reasons for taking them;
   (b)   give details to the authority within whose area the child is ordinarily resident ('the appropriate authority') of the place at which the child is being accommodated;
   (c)   inform the child (if he appears capable of understanding) –
       (i)   of the steps that have been taken with respect to him under this section and of the reasons for taking them; and
       (ii)   of the further steps that may be taken with respect to him under this section;
   (d)   take such steps as are reasonably practicable to discover the wishes and feelings of the child;
   (e)   secure that the case is inquired into by an officer designated for the purposes of this section by the chief officer of the police area concerned; and

(f)   where the child was taken into police protection by being removed to accommodation which is not provided –

  (i)   by or on behalf of a local authority; or

  (ii)   as a refuge, in compliance with the requirements of section 51,

secure that he is moved to accommodation which is so provided.

(4) As soon as is reasonably practicable after taking a child into police protection, the constable concerned shall take such steps as are reasonably practicable to inform –

(a)   the child's parents;

(b)   every person who is not a parent of his but who has parental responsibility for him; and

(c)   any other person with whom the child was living immediately before being taken into police protection,

of the steps that he has taken under this section with respect to the child, the reasons for taking them and the further steps that may be taken with respect to him under this section.

(5)   On completing any inquiry under subsection (3)(e), the officer conducting it shall release the child from police protection unless he considers that there is still reasonable cause for believing that the child would be likely to suffer significant harm if released.

(6)   No child may be kept in police protection for more than 72 hours.

(7)   While a child is being kept in police protection, the designated officer may apply on behalf of the appropriate authority for an emergency protection order to be made under section 44 with respect to the child.

(8)   An application may be made under subsection (7) whether or not the authority know of it or agree to its being made.

(9)   While a child is being kept in police protection –

(a)   neither the constable concerned nor the designated officer shall have parental responsibility for him; but

(b)   the designated officer shall do what is reasonable in all the circumstances of the case for the purpose of safeguarding or promoting the child's welfare (having regard in particular to the length of the period during which the child will be so protected).

(10) Where a child has been taken into police protection, the designated officer shall allow –

(a)   the child's parents;

(b)   any person who is not a parent of the child but who has parental responsibility for him;

(c)   any person with whom the child was living immediately before he was taken into police protection;

[(d)   any person named in a child arrangements order as a person with whom the child is to spend time or otherwise have contact;][1]

(e) any person who is allowed to have contact with the child by virtue of an order under section 34; and

(f) any person acting on behalf of any of those persons,

to have such contact (if any) with the child as, in the opinion of the designated officer, is both reasonable and in the child's best interests.

(11) Where a child who has been taken into police protection is in accommodation provided by, or on behalf of, the appropriate authority, subsection (10) shall have effect as if it referred to the authority rather than to the designated officer.

NOTES

Amendment.[1] Paragraph substituted: Children and Families Act 2014, s 12, Sch 2, paras 1, 36.
Definitions. 'Appropriate authority': s 46(3)(b); 'child': s 105(1); 'contact order': s 8(1); 'designated officer': s 46(3)(e); 'emergency protection order': s 44(4); 'harm': s 31(9); 'hospital': s 105(1); 'local authority': s 105(1); 'ordinary residence': s 105(6); 'police protection': s 46(2); 'significant harm': s 31(10).

47 Local authority's duty to investigate

(1) Where a local authority –

(a) are informed that a child who lives, or is found, in their area –
   (i) is the subject of an emergency protection order; or
   (ii) is in police protection; ...[8]
   [(iii) ...[8]][2]

(b) have reasonable cause to suspect that a child who lives, or is found, in their area is suffering, or is likely to suffer, significant harm,

the authority shall make, or cause to be made, such enquiries as they consider necessary to enable them to decide whether they should take any action to safeguard or promote the child's welfare.

[...[8]][2]

(2) Where a local authority have obtained an emergency protection order with respect to a child, they shall make, or cause to be made, such enquiries as they consider necessary to enable them to decide what action they should take to safeguard or promote the child's welfare.

(3) The enquiries shall, in particular, be directed towards establishing –

[(a) whether the authority should –
   (i) make any application to court under this Act;
   (ii) exercise any of their other powers under this Act;
   (iii) exercise any of their powers under section 11 of the Crime and Disorder Act 1998 (child safety orders); or
   (iv) (where the authority is a local authority in Wales) exercise any of their powers under the Social Services and Well-being (Wales) Act 2014;
with respect to the child;][10]

(b) whether, in the case of a child –
   (i) with respect to whom an emergency protection order has been made; and

(ii)   who is not in accommodation provided by or on behalf of the authority,

it would be in the child's best interests (while an emergency protection order remains in force) for him to be in such accommodation; and

(c)   whether, in the case of a child who has been taken into police protection, it would be in the child's best interests for the authority to ask for an application to be made under section 46(7).

(4) Where enquiries are being made under subsection (1) with respect to a child, the local authority concerned shall (with a view to enabling them to determine what action, if any, to take with respect to him) take such steps as are reasonably practicable –

(a)   to obtain access to him; or

(b)   to ensure that access to him is obtained, on their behalf, by a person authorised by them for the purpose,

unless they are satisfied that they already have sufficient information with respect to him.

(5) Where, as a result of any such enquiries, it appears to the authority that there are matters connected with the child's education which should be investigated, they shall consult [the local authority (as defined in section 579(1) of the Education 1996), if different, specified in subsection (5ZA).

(5ZA) The local authority referred to in subsection (5) is –

(a)   the local authority who –
      (i)   maintain any school at which the child is a pupil, or
      (i)   make arrangements for the provision of education for the child otherwise than at school pursuant to section 19 of the Education Act 1996, or

(b)   in a case where the child is a pupil at a school which is not maintained by a local authority, the local authority in whose area the school is situated.][7]

[(5A) For the purposes of making a determination under this section as to the action to be taken with respect to a child, a local authority shall, so far as is reasonably practicable and consistent with the child's welfare –

(a)   ascertain the child's wishes and feelings regarding the action to be taken with respect to him; and

(b)   give due consideration (having regard to his age and understanding) to such wishes and feelings of the child as they have been able to ascertain.][5]

(6) Where, in the course of enquiries made under this section –

(a)   any officer of the local authority concerned; or

(b)   any person authorised by the authority to act on their behalf in connection with those enquiries –
      (i)   is refused access to the child concerned; or
      (ii)   is denied information as to his whereabouts,

the authority shall apply for an emergency protection order, a child assessment order, a care order or a supervision order with respect to the child unless they are satisfied that his welfare can be satisfactorily safeguarded without their doing so.

(7) If, on the conclusion of any enquiries or review made under this section, the authority decide not to apply for an emergency protection order, a care order, a child assessment order or a supervision order they shall –

    (a)   consider whether it would be appropriate to review the case at a later date; and

    (b)   if they decide that it would be, determine the date on which that review is to begin.

(8) Where, as a result of complying with this section, a local authority conclude that they should take action to safeguard or promote the child's welfare they shall take that action (so far as it is both within their power and reasonably practicable for them to do so).

(9) Where a local authority are conducting enquiries under this section, it shall be the duty of any person mentioned in subsection (11) to assist them with those enquiries (in particular by providing relevant information and advice) if called upon by the authority to do so.

(10) Subsection (9) does not oblige any person to assist a local authority where doing so would be unreasonable in all the circumstances of the case.

(11) The persons are –

    (a)   any local authority;

    (b)   ...[7]

    (c)   any local housing authority;

    [(ca) the National Health Service Commissioning Board;][9]

    (d)   any [clinical commissioning group,][9] [[Local Health Board][6], Special Health Authority][1][...[9]][3][, National Health Service trust or NHS foundation trust][4]; and

    (e)   any person authorised by the Secretary of State for the purposes of this section.

(12) Where a local authority are making enquiries under this section with respect to a child who appears to them to be ordinarily resident within the area of another authority, they shall consult that other authority, who may undertake the necessary enquiries in their place.

NOTES

Amendments.[1] Words substituted: Health Authorities Act 1995, s 2(1), Sch 1, Pt III, para 118(1), (7).[2] Words inserted: Crime and Disorder Act 1998, ss 15(4), 119, Sch 8, para 69.[3] Words inserted: Health Act 1999 (Supplementary, Consequential etc Provisions) Order 2000, SI 2000/90.[4] Words substituted: Health and Social Care (Community Health and Standards) Act 2003, s 34, Sch 4, paras 75, 79.[5] Subsection inserted: Children Act 2004, s 53(3).[6] Words substituted: SI 2007/961.[7] Words and subsection substituted and paragraph repealed: SI 2010/1158.[8] Paragraph and word repealed: Policing and Crime Act 2009, s 112(2), Sch 8, Pt 13.[9] Paragraph inserted, words inserted and omitted: Health and Social Care Act 2012, s 55(2), Sch 5, Pt 1, paras 47, 53.[10] Subsection substituted: SI 2016/413, regs 55, 100.

Definitions. 'Care order': s 31(11); 'child': s 105(1); 'child assessment order': s 43(2); 'clinical commissioning group': s 105(1); 'emergency protection order': s 44(4); 'harm': s 31(9); 'health authority': s 105(1); 'local authority': s 105(1); 'local education authority': s 105(1); 'local housing

PART I – Statutes

authority': s 105(1); 'ordinary residence': s 105(6); 'police protection': s 46(2); 'significant harm': s 31(10); 'supervision order': s 31(11); 'the court': s 92(7).

48 Powers to assist in discovery of children who may be in need of emergency protection

(1) Where it appears to a court making an emergency protection order that adequate information as to the child's whereabouts –

    (a)   is not available to the applicant for the order; but

    (b)   is available to another person,

it may include in the order a provision requiring that other person to disclose, if asked to do so by the applicant, any information that he may have as to the child's whereabouts.

(2) No person shall be excused from complying with such a requirement on the ground that complying might incriminate him or his spouse [or civil partner][3] of an offence; but a statement or admission made in complying shall not be admissible in evidence against either of them in proceedings for any offence other than perjury.

(3) An emergency protection order may authorise the applicant to enter premises specified by the order and search for the child with respect to whom the order is made.

(4) Where the court is satisfied that there is reasonable cause to believe that there may be another child on those premises with respect to whom an emergency protection order ought to be made, it may make an order authorising the applicant to search for that other child on those premises.

(5) Where –

    (a)   an order has been made under subsection (4);

    (b)   the child concerned has been found on the premises; and

    (c)   the applicant is satisfied that the grounds for making an emergency protection order exist with respect to him,

the order shall have effect as if it were an emergency protection order.

(6) Where an order has been made under subsection (4), the applicant shall notify the court of its effect.

(7) A person shall be guilty of an offence if he intentionally obstructs any person exercising the power of entry and search under subsection (3) or (4).

(8) A person guilty of an offence under subsection (7) shall be liable on summary conviction to a fine not exceeding level 3 on the standard scale.

(9) Where, on an application made by any person for a warrant under this section, it appears to the court –

    (a)   that a person attempting to exercise powers under an emergency protection order has been prevented from doing so by being refused entry to the premises concerned or access to the child concerned; or

(b)   that any such person is likely to be so prevented from exercising any such powers,

it may issue a warrant authorising any constable to assist the person mentioned in paragraph (a) or (b) in the exercise of those powers, using reasonable force if necessary.

(10) Every warrant issued under this section shall be addressed to, and executed by, a constable who shall be accompanied by the person applying for the warrant if –

(a)   that person so desires; and
(b)   the court by whom the warrant is issued does not direct otherwise.

(11) A court granting an application for a warrant under this section may direct that the constable concerned may, in executing the warrant, be accompanied by a registered medical practitioner, registered nurse or [registered midwife][2] if he so chooses.

[(11A) The reference in subsection (11) to a registered midwife is to such a midwife who is also registered in the Specialist Community Public Health Nurses' Part of the register maintained under article 5 of the Nursing and Midwifery Order 2001.][1]

(12) An application for a warrant under this section shall be made in the manner and form prescribed by rules of court.

(13) Wherever it is reasonably practicable to do so, an order under subsection (4), an application for a warrant under this section and any such warrant shall name the child; and where it does not name him it shall describe him as clearly as possible.

NOTES

Amendments.[1] Words substituted and subsection inserted: SI 2004/1771.[2] Words substituted: Nursing and Midwifery Order 2001 [*sic*], SI 2002/253, art 54(3), Sch 5, para 10(b).[3] Words inserted: Civil Partnership Act 2004, s 261(1), Sch 27, para 130.
Definitions. 'Child': s 105(1); 'emergency protection order': s 44(4); 'the applicant': s 44(1); 'the court': s 92(7).

49 Abduction of children in care etc

(1) A person shall be guilty of an offence if, knowingly and without lawful authority or reasonable excuse, he –

(a)   takes a child to whom this section applies away from the responsible person;
(b)   keeps such a child away from the responsible person; or
(c)   induces, assists or incites such a child to run away or stay away from the responsible person.

(2) This section applies in relation to a child who is –

(a)   in care;
(b)   the subject of an emergency protection order; or

    (c)   in police protection,

and in this section 'the responsible person' means any person who for the time being has care of him by virtue of the care order, the emergency protection order, or section 46, as the case may be.

(3) A person guilty of an offence under this section shall be liable on summary conviction to imprisonment for a term not exceeding six months, or to a fine not exceeding level 5 on the standard scale, or to both.

NOTES

Definitions. 'Care order': ss 31(11), 105(1); 'child': s 105(1); 'emergency protection order': s 44(4); 'police protection': s 46(2); 'responsible person': s 49(2).

50 Recovery of abducted children etc

(1) Where it appears to the court that there is reason to believe that a child to whom this section applies –

    (a)   has been unlawfully taken away or is being unlawfully kept away from the responsible person;
    (b)   has run away or is staying away from the responsible person; or
    (c)   is missing,

the court may make an order under this section ('a recovery order').

(2) This section applies to the same children to whom section 49 applies and in this section 'the responsible person' has the same meaning as in section 49.

(3) A recovery order –

    (a)   operates as a direction to any person who is in a position to do so to produce the child on request to any authorised person;
    (b)   authorises the removal of the child by any authorised person;
    (c)   requires any person who has information as to the child's whereabouts to disclose that information, if asked to do so, to a constable or an officer of the court;
    (d)   authorises a constable to enter any premises specified in the order and search for the child, using reasonable force if necessary.

(4) The court may make a recovery order only on the application of –

    (a)   any person who has parental responsibility for the child by virtue of a care order or emergency protection order; or
    (b)   where the child is in police protection, the designated officer.

(5) A recovery order shall name the child and –

    (a)   any person who has parental responsibility for the child by virtue of a care order or emergency protection order; or
    (b)   where the child is in police protection, the designated officer.

(6) Premises may only be specified under subsection (3)(d) if it appears to the court that there are reasonable grounds for believing the child to be on them.

(7) In this section –

'an authorised person' means –
  (a)   any person specified by the court;
  (b)   any constable;
  (c)   any person who is authorised –
     (i)   after the recovery order is made; and
     (ii)   by a person who has parental responsibility for the child by virtue of a care order or an emergency protection order,
  to exercise any power under a recovery order; and

'the designated officer' means the officer designated for the purposes of section 46.

(8) Where a person is authorised as mentioned in subsection (7)(c) –

  (a)   the authorisation shall identify the recovery order; and
  (b)   any person claiming to be so authorised shall, if asked to do so, produce some duly authenticated document showing that he is so authorised.

(9) A person shall be guilty of an offence if he intentionally obstructs an authorised person exercising the power under subsection (3)(b) to remove a child.

(10) A person guilty of an offence under this section shall be liable on summary conviction to a fine not exceeding level 3 on the standard scale.

(11) No person shall be excused from complying with any request made under subsection (3)(c) on the ground that complying with it might incriminate him or his spouse [or civil partner][1] of an offence; but a statement or admission made in complying shall not be admissible in evidence against either of them in proceedings for an offence other than perjury.

(12) Where a child is made the subject of a recovery order whilst being looked after by a local authority, any reasonable expenses incurred by an authorised person in giving effect to the order shall be recoverable from the authority.

(13) A recovery order shall have effect in Scotland as if it had been made by the Court of Session and as if that court had had jurisdiction to make it.

(14) In this section 'the court', in relation to Northern Ireland, means a magistrates' court within the meaning of the Magistrates' Courts (Northern Ireland) Order 1981.

NOTES

Amendments.[1] Words inserted: Civil Partnership Act 2004, s 261(1), Sch 27, para 131.
Definitions. 'Authorised person': s 50(7); 'care order': s 31(11); 'child': s 105(1); 'child who is looked after by a local authority': s 22(1); 'emergency protection order': s 44(4); 'local authority': s 105(1); 'parental responsibility': s 3; 'police protection': s 46(2); 'recovery order': s 50(1); 'responsible person': s 49(2); 'the court': s 92(7); 'the designated officer': s 50(7).

51 Refuges for children at risk

(1) Where it is proposed to use a voluntary home or [private][2] children's home to provide a refuge for children who appear to be at risk of harm, the Secretary of State may issue a certificate under this section with respect to that home.

(2) Where a local authority or voluntary organisation arrange for a foster parent to provide such a refuge, the Secretary of State may issue a certificate under this section with respect to that foster parent.

(3) In subsection (2) 'foster parent' means a person who is, or who from time to time is, a local authority foster parent or a foster parent with whom children are placed by a voluntary organisation.

(4) The Secretary of State may by regulations –

    (a)   make provision as to the manner in which certificates may be issued;
    (b)   impose requirements which must be complied with while any certificate is in force; and
    (c)   provide for the withdrawal of certificates in prescribed circumstances.

(5) Where a certificate is in force with respect to a home, none of the provisions mentioned in subsection (7) shall apply in relation to any person providing a refuge for any child in that home.

(6) Where a certificate is in force with respect to a foster parent, none of those provisions shall apply in relation to the provision by him of a refuge for any child in accordance with arrangements made by the local authority or voluntary organisation.

(7) The provisions are –

    (a)   section 49;
    [(b)   sections 82 (recovery of certain fugitive children) and 83 (harbouring) of the Children (Scotland) Act 1995, so far as they apply in relation to anything done in England and Wales;][1]
    (c)   section 32(3) of the Children and Young Persons Act 1969 (compelling, persuading, inciting or assisting any person to be absent from detention, etc), so far as it applies in relation to anything done in England and Wales;
    (d)   section 2 of the Child Abduction Act 1984.

NOTES

Amendments.[1] Subsection substituted: Children (Scotland) Act 1995, s 105(4), Sch 4, para 48(1), (3).[2] Word substituted: Care Standards Act 2000, s 116, Sch 4, para 14.
Definitions. 'Child': s 105(1); 'foster parent': s 51(3); 'harm': s 31(9); 'local authority': s 105(1); 'local authority foster parent': s 23(3); 'prescribed': s 105(1); 'voluntary home': s 60(3); 'voluntary organisation': s 105(1).

52 Rules and regulations

(1) Without prejudice to section 93 or any other power to make such rules, rules of court may be made with respect to the procedure to be followed in connection with proceedings under this Part.

(2) The rules may in particular make provision –

    (a)   as to the form in which any application is to be made or direction is to be given;
    (b)   prescribing the persons who are to be notified of –

PART I – Statutes

    (i)   the making, or extension, of an emergency protection order; or

    (ii)   the making of an application under section 45(4) or (8) or 46(7); and

  (c)   as to the content of any such notification and the manner in which, and person by whom, it is to be given.

(3) The Secretary of State may by regulations provide that, where –

  (a)   an emergency protection order has been made with respect to a child;

  (b)   the applicant for the order was not the local authority within whose area the child is ordinarily resident; and

  (c)   that local authority are of the opinion that it would be in the child's best interests for the applicant's responsibilities under the order to be transferred to them,

that authority shall (subject to their having complied with any requirements imposed by the regulations) be treated, for the purposes of this Act, as though they and not the original applicant had applied for, and been granted, the order.

(4) Regulations made under subsection (3) may, in particular, make provision as to –

  (a)   the considerations to which the local authority shall have regard in forming an opinion as mentioned in subsection (3)(c); and

  (b)   the time at which responsibility under any emergency protection order is to be treated as having been transferred to a local authority.

NOTES

Definitions. 'Child': s 105(1); 'emergency protection order': s 44(4); 'local authority': s 105(1); 'ordinary residence': s 105(6).

PART VI
COMMUNITY HOMES

53 Provision of community homes by local authorities

(1) Every local authority shall make such arrangements as they consider appropriate for securing that homes ('community homes') are available –

  (a)   for the care and accommodation of children looked after by them; and

  (b)   for purposes connected with the welfare of children (whether or not looked after by them),

and may do so jointly with one or more other local authorities.

(2) In making such arrangements, a local authority shall have regard to the need for ensuring the availability of accommodation –

  (a)   of different descriptions; and

  (b)   which is suitable for different purposes and the requirements of different descriptions of children.

(3) A community home may be a home –

(a)   provided, [equipped, maintained and (subject to subsection (3A)) managed][1] by a local authority; or

(b)   provided by a voluntary organisation but in respect of which a local authority and the organisation –

    (i)   propose that, in accordance with an instrument of management, the [equipment, maintenance and (subject to subsection (3B)) management][1] of the home shall be the responsibility of the local authority; or

    (ii)   so propose that the management, equipment and maintenance of the home shall be the responsibility of the voluntary organisation.

[(3A) A local authority may make arrangements for the management by another person of accommodation provided by the local authority for the purpose of restricting the liberty of children.

(3B) Where a local authority are to be responsible for the management of a community home provided by a voluntary organisation, the local authority may, with the consent of the body of managers constituted by the instrument of management for the home, make arrangements for the management by another person of accommodation provided for the purpose of restricting the liberty of children.][1]

(4) Where a local authority are to be responsible for the management of a community home provided by a voluntary organisation, the authority shall designate the home as a controlled community home.

(5) Where a voluntary organisation are to be responsible for the management of a community home provided by the organisation, the local authority shall designate the home as an assisted community home.

(6) Schedule 4 shall have effect for the purpose of supplementing the provisions of this Part.

NOTES

Amendments.[1] Words or subsections inserted: Criminal Justice and Public Order Act 1994, s 22.
Definitions. 'Assisted community home': s 53(5); 'child': s 105(1); 'child who is looked after by the local authority': s 22(1); 'community home': s 53(1); 'controlled community home': s 53(4); 'local authority': s 105(1); 'voluntary organisation': s 105(1).

54

… [1]

NOTES

Amendments.[1] Section repealed: Care Standards Act 2000, s 117, Sch 6.

55 Determination of disputes relating to controlled and assisted community homes

(1) Where any dispute relating to a controlled community home arises between the local authority specified in the home's instrument of management and –

(a)   the voluntary organisation by which the home is provided; or

(b) any other local authority who have placed, or desire or are required to place, in the home a child who is looked after by them,

the dispute may be referred by either party to the Secretary of State for his determination.

(2) Where any dispute relating to an assisted community home arises between the voluntary organisation by which the home is provided and any local authority who have placed, or desire to place, in the home a child who is looked after by them, the dispute may be referred by either party to the Secretary of State for his determination.

(3) Where a dispute is referred to the Secretary of State under this section he may, in order to give effect to his determination of the dispute, give such directions as he thinks fit to the local authority or voluntary organisation concerned.

(4) This section applies even though the matter in dispute may be one which, under or by virtue of Part II of Schedule 4, is reserved for the decision, or is the responsibility, of –

(a) the local authority specified in the home's instrument of management; or
(b) (as the case may be) the voluntary organisation by which the home is provided.

(5) Where any trust deed relating to a controlled or assisted community home contains provision whereby a bishop or any other ecclesiastical or denominational authority has power to decide questions relating to religious instruction given in the home, no dispute which is capable of being dealt with in accordance with that provision shall be referred to the Secretary of State under this section.

(6) In this Part 'trust deed', in relation to a voluntary home, means any instrument (other than an instrument of management) regulating –

(a) the maintenance, management or conduct of the home; or
(b) the constitution of a body of managers or trustees of the home.

NOTES

Definitions. 'Assisted community home': s 53(5); 'child': s 105(1); 'child who is looked after by a local authority': s 22(1); 'community home': s 53(1); 'controlled community home': s 53(4); 'local authority': s 105(1); 'trust deed': s 55(6); 'voluntary home': s 60(3); 'voluntary organisation': s 105(1).

56 Discontinuance by voluntary organisation of controlled or assisted community home

(1) The voluntary organisation by which a controlled or assisted community home is provided shall not cease to provide the home except after giving to the Secretary of State and the local authority specified in the home's instrument of management not less than two years' notice in writing of their intention to do so.

(2) A notice under subsection (1) shall specify the date from which the voluntary organisation intend to cease to provide the home as a community home.

(3) Where such a notice is given and is not withdrawn before the date specified in it, the home's instrument of management shall cease to have effect on that

date and the home shall then cease to be a controlled or assisted community home.

(4) Where a notice is given under subsection (1) and the home's managers give notice in writing to the Secretary of State that they are unable or unwilling to continue as its managers until the date specified in the subsection (1) notice, the Secretary of State may by order –

    (a)   revoke the home's instrument of management; and

    (b)   require the local authority who were specified in that instrument to conduct the home until –

        (i)   the date specified in the subsection (1) notice; or

        (ii) such earlier date (if any) as may be specified for the purposes of this paragraph in the order,

as if it were a community home provided by the local authority.

(5) Where the Secretary of State imposes a requirement under subsection (4)(b) –

    (a)   nothing in the trust deed for the home shall affect the conduct of the home by the local authority;

    (b)   the Secretary of State may by order direct that for the purposes of any provision specified in the direction and made by or under any enactment relating to community homes (other than this section) the home shall, until the date or earlier date specified as mentioned in subsection (4)(b), be treated as a controlled or assisted community home;

    (c)   except in so far as the Secretary of State so directs, the home shall until that date be treated for the purposes of any such enactment as a community home provided by the local authority; and

    (d)   on the date or earlier date specified as mentioned in subsection (4)(b) the home shall cease to be a community home.

NOTES

Definitions. 'Assisted community home': s 53(5); 'community home': s 53(1); 'controlled community home': s 53(4); 'local authority': s 105(1); 'trust deed': s 55(6); 'voluntary organisation': s 105(1).

57 Closure by local authority of controlled or assisted community home

(1) The local authority specified in the instrument of management for a controlled or assisted community home may give –

    (a)   the Secretary of State; and

    (b)   the voluntary organisation by which the home is provided,

not less than two years' notice in writing of their intention to withdraw their designation of the home as a controlled or assisted community home.

(2) A notice under subsection (1) shall specify the date ('the specified date') on which the designation is to be withdrawn.

(3) Where –

(a) a notice is given under subsection (1) in respect of a controlled or assisted community home;
(b) the home's managers give notice in writing to the Secretary of State that they are unable or unwilling to continue as managers until the specified date; and
(c) the managers' notice is not withdrawn,

the Secretary of State may by order revoke the home's instrument of management from such date earlier than the specified date as may be specified in the order.

(4) Before making an order under subsection (3), the Secretary of State shall consult the local authority and the voluntary organisation.

(5) Where a notice has been given under subsection (1) and is not withdrawn, the home's instrument of management shall cease to have effect on –

(a) the specified date; or
(b) where an earlier date has been specified under subsection (3), that earlier date,

and the home shall then cease to be a community home.

NOTES

Definitions. 'Assisted community home': s 53(5); 'controlled community home': s 53(4); 'community home': s 53(1); 'local authority': s 105(1); 'the specified date': s 57(2); 'voluntary organisation': s 105(1).

58 Financial provisions applicable on cessation of controlled or assisted community home or disposal etc of premises

(1) Where –

(a) the instrument of management for a controlled or assisted community home is revoked or otherwise ceases to have effect under section ...[3] 56(3) or (4)(a) or 57(3) or (5); or
(b) any premises used for the purposes of such a home are (at any time after 13th January 1987) disposed of, or put to use otherwise than for those purposes,

the proprietor shall become liable to pay compensation ('the appropriate compensation') in accordance with this section.

(2) Where the instrument of management in force at the relevant time relates –

(a) to a controlled community home; or
(b) to an assisted community home which, at any time before the instrument came into force, was a controlled community home,

the appropriate compensation is a sum equal to that part of the value of any premises which is attributable to expenditure incurred in relation to the premises, while the home was a controlled community home, by the authority who were then the responsible authority.

(3) Where the instrument of management in force at the relevant time relates –

(a) to an assisted community home; or

(b)   to a controlled community home which, at any time before the instrument came into force, was an assisted community home,

the appropriate compensation is a sum equal to that part of the value of the premises which is attributable to the expenditure of money provided by way of grant under section 82, section 65 of the Children and Young Persons Act 1969 or section 82 of the Child Care Act 1980.

(4) Where the home is, at the relevant time, conducted in premises which formerly were used as an approved school or were an approved probation hostel or home, the appropriate compensation is a sum equal to that part of the value of the premises which is attributable to the expenditure –

(a)   of sums paid towards the expenses of the managers of an approved school under section 104 of the Children and Young Persons Act 1933; ...[2]

(b)   of sums paid under section 51(3)(c) of the Powers of Criminal Courts Act 1973 [or section 20(1)(c) of the Probation Service Act 1993][1] in relation to expenditure on approved probation hostels or homes [; or

(c)   of sums paid under section 3, 5 or 9 of the Criminal Justice and Court Services Act 2000 in relation to expenditure on approved premises (within the meaning of Part I of that Act).][2]

(5) The appropriate compensation shall be paid –

(a)   in the case of compensation payable under subsection (2), to the authority who were the responsible authority at the relevant time; and

(b)   in any other case, to the Secretary of State.

(6) In this section –

'disposal' includes the grant of a tenancy and any other conveyance, assignment, transfer, grant, variation or extinguishment of an interest in or right over land, whether made by instrument or otherwise;

'premises' means any premises or part of premises (including land) used for the purposes of the home and belonging to the proprietor;

'the proprietor' means –
(a)   the voluntary organisation by which the home is, at the relevant time, provided; or
(b)   if the premises are not, at the relevant time, vested in that organisation, the persons in whom they are vested;

'the relevant time' means the time immediately before the liability to pay arises under subsection (1); and

'the responsible authority' means the local authority specified in the instrument of management in question.

(7) For the purposes of this section an event of a kind mentioned in subsection (1)(b) shall be taken to have occurred –

(a) in the case of a disposal, on the date on which the disposal was completed or, in the case of a disposal which is effected by a series of transactions, the date on which the last of those transactions was completed;

(b) in the case of premises which are put to different use, on the date on which they first begin to be put to their new use.

(8) The amount of any sum payable under this section shall be determined in accordance with such arrangements –

(a) as may be agreed between the voluntary organisation by which the home is, at the relevant time, provided and the responsible authority or (as the case may be) the Secretary of State; or

(b) in default of agreement, as may be determined by the Secretary of State.

(9) With the agreement of the responsible authority or (as the case may be) the Secretary of State, the liability to pay any sum under this section may be discharged, in whole or in part, by the transfer of any premises.

(10) This section has effect regardless of –

(a) anything in any trust deed for a controlled or assisted community home;

(b) the provisions of any enactment or instrument governing the disposition of the property of a voluntary organisation.

NOTES

Amendments.[1] Words inserted: Probation Service Act 1993, s 32, Sch 3, para 9(2).[2] Word omitted or words inserted: Criminal Justice and Court Services Act 2000, ss 74, 75, Sch 7, paras 87, 93, Sch 8.[3] Word repealed: Care Standards Act 2000, s 117, Sch 6.

Definitions. 'Appropriate compensation': s 58(1)–(4); 'assisted community home': s 53(5); 'community home': s 53(1); 'controlled community home': s 53(4); 'disposal': s 58(6); 'local authority': s 105(1); 'premises': s 58(6); 'the proprietor': s 58(6); 'the relevant time': s 58(6); 'the responsible authority': s 58(6); 'trust deed': s 55(6); 'voluntary organisation': s 105(1).

PART VII
VOLUNTARY HOMES AND VOLUNTARY ORGANISATIONS

59 Provision of accommodation by voluntary organisations

(1) Where a voluntary organisation provide accommodation for a child, they shall do so by –

(a) placing him (subject to subsection (2)) with –
   (i) a family;
   (ii) a relative of his; or
   (iii) any other suitable person,
   on such terms as to payment by the organisation and otherwise as the organisation may determine [(subject to section 49 of the Children Act 2004)][2];

[(aa) maintaining him in [a children's home in respect of which a person is registered under Part 2 of the Care Standards Act 2000][5] [or Part 1 of the Regulation and Inspection of Social Care (Wales) Act 2016][7];

(b)–(e)   ...]¹
(f)   making such other arrangements (subject to subsection (3)) as seem appropriate to them.

[(1A) Where under subsection (1)(aa) a [voluntary organisation]⁵ maintains a child in a home provided, equipped and maintained by [an appropriate national authority]³ under section 82(5), it shall do so on such terms as [that national authority]³ may from time to time determine.]¹

(2) The [appropriate national authority]³ may make regulations as to the placing of children with foster parents by voluntary organisations ....⁴

(3) The [appropriate national authority]³ may make regulations as to the arrangements which may be made under subsection (1)(f) ....⁴

[(3A) Regulations [made in relation to England]⁶ under subsection (2) or (3) may in particular make provision which (with any necessary modifications) is similar to that which may be made under section 22C by virtue of any of paragraphs 12B, 12E and 12F of Schedule 2.]⁴

[(3B) Regulations made in relation to Wales under subsection (2) or (3) may in particular make provision which (with any necessary modifications) is similar to that which may be made under sections 81 or 87 of the Social Services and Well-being (Wales) Act 2014, including provision which may be made under section 87 in accordance with the examples given in sections 89, 92 and 93 of that Act.]⁶

(4) The [appropriate national authority]³ may make regulations requiring any voluntary organisation who are providing accommodation for a child –

(a)   to review his case; and
(b)   to consider any representations (including any complaint) made to them by any person falling within a prescribed class of person,

in accordance with the provisions of the regulations.

[(5A) Regulations [made in relation to England]⁶ under subsection (4) may, in particular –

(a)   apply with modifications any provision of section 25A or 25B;
(b)   make provision which (with any necessary modifications) is similar to any provision which may be made under section 25A, 25B or 26.]⁴

[(5B) Regulations made in relation to Wales under subsection (4) may in particular make provision which (with any necessary modifications) is similar to that which may be made under sections 99, 100 or 102 of the Social Services and Well-being (Wales) Act 2014.]⁶

(6) Regulations under subsections (2) to (4) may provide that any person who, without reasonable excuse, contravenes or fails to comply with a regulation shall be guilty of an offence and liable on summary conviction to a fine not exceeding level 4 on the standard scale.

[(7) In this Part 'appropriate national authority' means –

   (a)   in relation to England, the Secretary of State; and

   (b)   in relation to Wales, the Welsh Ministers.][3]

NOTES

Amendments.[1] Paragraph (aa) substituted for paras (b)–(e) and subsection inserted: Care Standards Act 2000, s 116, Sch 4, para 14(8).[2] Words inserted: Children Act 2004, s 49(4).[3] Words substituted and subsection inserted: Children and Young Persons Act 2008, s 39, Sch 3, paras 1, 23.[4] Words omitted, subsection (3A) inserted and subsection (5A) substituted for (5): Children and Young Persons Act 2008, s 8(2), Sch 1, paras 2(1), (4)–(7).[5] Words substituted: Children and Young Persons Act 2008, s 8(2), Sch 1, para 2(1)–(3).[6] Words and subsections inserted: SI 2016/413, regs 55, 101.[7] Words inserted: Regulation and Inspection of Social Care (Wales) Act 2016 (Consequential Amendments) Regulations 2018, SI 2018/195, regs 8, 10.

Definitions. 'Child': s 105(1); 'community home': s 53(1); 'relative': s 105(1); 'voluntary home': s 60(2); 'voluntary organisation': s 105(1).

60 [Voluntary homes][1]

(1), (2) ...[2]

[(3) In this Act 'voluntary home' means a children's home which is carried on by a voluntary organisation but does not include a community home.][1]

(4) Schedule 5 shall have effect for the purpose of supplementing the provisions of this Part.

NOTES

Amendments.[1] Section heading and subsection substituted: Care Standards Act 2000, s 116, Sch 4, para 14(1), (9).[2] Subsections repealed: Care Standards Act 2000, s 117, Sch 6.

Definitions. 'voluntary home': s 60(3); 'voluntary organisation': s 105(1).

61 Duties of voluntary organisations

(1) Where a child is accommodated by or on behalf of a voluntary organisation, it shall be the duty of the organisation –

   (a)   to safeguard and promote his welfare;

   (b)   to make such use of the services and facilities available for children cared for by their own parents as appears to the organisation reasonable in his case; and

   (c)   to advise, assist and befriend him with a view to promoting his welfare when he ceases to be so accommodated.

(2) Before making any decision with respect to any such child the organisation shall, so far as is reasonably practicable, ascertain the wishes and feelings of –

   (a)   the child;

   (b)   his parents;

   (c)   any person who is not a parent of his but who has parental responsibility for him; and

   (d)   any other person whose wishes and feelings the organisation consider to be relevant,

regarding the matter to be decided.

(3) In making any such decision the organisation shall give due consideration –

    (a)   having regard to the child's age and understanding, to such wishes and feelings of his as they have been able to ascertain;

    (b)   to such other wishes and feelings mentioned in subsection (2) as they have been able to ascertain; and

    (c)   to the child's religious persuasion, racial origin and cultural and linguistic background.

NOTES

Definitions. 'Child': s 105(1); 'parental responsibility': s 3; 'voluntary organisation': s 105(1).

62 Duties of local authorities

(1) Every local authority shall satisfy themselves that any voluntary organisation providing accommodation –

    (a)   within the authority's area for any child; or

    (b)   outside that area for any child on behalf of the authority,

are satisfactorily safeguarding and promoting the welfare of the children so provided with accommodation.

(2) Every local authority shall arrange for children who are accommodated within their area by or on behalf of voluntary organisations to be visited, from time to time, in the interests of their welfare.

(3) The [appropriate national authority][3] may make regulations –

    (a)   requiring every child who is accommodated within a local authority's area, by or on behalf of a voluntary organisation, to be visited by an officer of the authority –

        (i)   in prescribed circumstances; and

        (ii)   on specified occasions or within specified periods; and

    (b)   imposing requirements which must be met by any local authority, or officer of a local authority, carrying out functions under this section.

(4) Subsection (2) does not apply in relation to community homes.

(5) Where a local authority are not satisfied that the welfare of any child who is accommodated by or on behalf of a voluntary organisation is being satisfactorily safeguarded or promoted they shall –

    (a)   unless they consider that it would not be in the best interests of the child, take such steps as are reasonably practicable to secure that the care and accommodation of the child is undertaken by –

        (i)   a parent of his;

        (ii)   any person who is not a parent of his but who has parental responsibility for him; or

        (iii)   a relative of his; and

    (b)   consider the extent to which (if at all) they should exercise any of their functions with respect to the child.

(6) Any person authorised by a local authority may, for the purpose of enabling the authority to discharge their duties under this section –

    (a)   enter, at any reasonable time, and inspect any premises in which children are being accommodated as mentioned in subsection (1) or (2);

    (b)   inspect any children there;

    (c)   require any person to furnish him with such records of a kind required to be kept by regulations made under [section 22 of the Care Standards Act 2000][1] [or section 20 of the Health and Social Care Act 2008][4][, or section 27 of the Regulation and Inspection of Social Care (Wales) Act 2016 (anaw 2)][6] (in whatever form they are held), or allow him to inspect such records, as he may at any time direct.

(7) Any person exercising the power conferred by subsection (6) shall, if asked to do so, produce some duly authenticated document showing his authority to do so.

(8) Any person authorised to exercise the power to inspect records conferred by subsection (6) –

    (a)   shall be entitled at any reasonable time to have access to, and inspect and check the operation of, any computer and any associated apparatus or material which is or has been in use in connection with the records in question; and

    (b)   may require –

        (i)   the person by whom or on whose behalf the computer is or has been so used; or

        (ii)   any person having charge of, or otherwise concerned with the operation of, the computer, apparatus or material,

to afford him such assistance as he may reasonably require.

(9) Any person who intentionally obstructs another in the exercise of any power conferred by subsection (6) or (8) shall be guilty of an offence and liable on summary conviction to a fine not exceeding level 3 on the standard scale.

[(10) This section does not apply in relation to any voluntary organisation which is an institution within the further education sector, as defined in section 91 of the Further and Higher Education Act 1992, [a 16 to 19 Academy][5] or a school.][2]

NOTES

Amendments.[1] Words substituted: Care Standards Act 2000, s 116, Sch 4, para 14(10).[2] Subsection inserted: Care Standards Act 2000, s 105(5).[3] Words substituted: Children and Young Persons Act 2008, s 39, Sch 3, paras 1, 24.[4] Words inserted: SI 2010/813.[5] Words inserted: Education Act 2011, s 54(1), Sch 13, para 6(1), (2).[6] Words inserted: SI 2019/772, regs 2, 3.

Definitions. 'Child': s 105(1); 'community home': s 53(1); 'functions', 'local authority': s 105(1); 'parental responsibility': s 3; 'prescribed', 'relative', 'voluntary organisation': s 105(1).

PART VIII
REGISTERED CHILDREN'S HOMES

63 [Private children's homes etc]2

(1)–(10) ...[1]

(11) Schedule 6 shall have effect with respect to [private][2] children's homes.

(12) Schedule 7 shall have effect for the purpose of setting out the circumstances in which a person may foster more than three children without being treated –][3]

> [(a)][3] for the purposes of this Act and the Care Standards Act 2000,][2] as carrying on a children's home[; and
>
> [(b) for the purposes of the Regulation and Inspection of Social Care (Wales) Act 2016, as providing a care home service within the meaning of Part 1 of that Act][3].

NOTES

Amendments.[1] Subsections repealed: Care Standards Act 2000, s 117, Sch 6.[2] Section heading substituted and words inserted: Care Standards Act 2000, s 116, Sch 4, para 14(1), (11).[3] Words substituted and inserted: Regulation and Inspection of Social Care (Wales) Act 2016 (Consequential Amendments) Regulations 2018, SI 2018/195, regs 8, 11.

Definitions. 'children's home': s 23.

64 Welfare of children in children's homes

(1) Where a child is accommodated in a [private][1] children's home, it shall be the duty of the person carrying on the home to –

    (a)   safeguard and promote the child's welfare;

    (b)   make such use of the services and facilities available for children cared for by their own parents as appears to that person reasonable in the case of the child; and

    (c)   advise, assist and befriend him with a view to promoting his welfare when he ceases to be so accommodated.

(2) Before making any decision with respect to any such child the person carrying on the home shall, so far as is reasonably practicable, ascertain the wishes and feelings of –

    (a)   the child;

    (b)   his parents;

    (c)   any other person who is not a parent of his but who has parental responsibility for him; and

    (d)   any person whose wishes and feelings the person carrying on the home considers to be relevant,

regarding the matter to be decided.

(3) In making any such decision the person concerned shall give due consideration –

    (a)   having regard to the child's age and understanding, to such wishes and feelings of his as he has been able to ascertain;

(b) to such other wishes and feelings mentioned in subsection (2) as he has been able to ascertain; and

(c) to the child's religious persuasion, racial origin and cultural and linguistic background.

(4) Section 62, except subsection (4), shall apply in relation to any person who is carrying on a [private]¹ children's home as it applies in relation to any voluntary organisation.

NOTES

Amendments.¹ Word inserted: Care Standards Act 2000, s 116, Sch 4, para 14(12).
Definitions. 'Child': s 105(1); 'children's home': s 23; 'parental responsibility': s 3; 'voluntary organisation': s 105(1).

65 Persons disqualified from carrying on, or being employed in, children's homes

[(A1) A person ('P') who is disqualified (under section 68) from fostering a child privately must not carry on, or be otherwise concerned in the management of, or have any financial interest in, a children's home in England unless –

(a) P has, within the period of 28 days beginning with the day on which P became aware of P's disqualification, disclosed to the appropriate authority the fact that P is so disqualified, and

(b) P has obtained the appropriate authority's written consent.

(A2) A person ('E') must not employ a person ('P') who is so disqualified in a children's home in England unless –

(a) E has, within the period of 28 days beginning with the day on which E became aware of P's disqualification, disclosed to the appropriate authority the fact that P is so disqualified, and

(b) E has obtained the appropriate authority's written consent.]⁵

(1) A person who is disqualified (under section 68) from fostering a child privately shall not carry on, or be otherwise concerned in the management of, or have any financial interest in, a children's home [in Wales]⁵ unless he has –

(a) disclosed to [the appropriate authority]¹ the fact that he is so disqualified; and

(b) obtained [its]¹ written consent.

(2) No person shall employ a person who is so disqualified in a children's home [in Wales]⁵ unless he has –

(a) disclosed to [the appropriate authority]¹ the fact that that person is so disqualified; and

(b) obtained [its]¹ written consent.

(3) Where [the appropriate authority refuses to give its consent under this section, it]¹ shall inform the applicant by a written notice which states –

(a) the reason for the refusal;

[(b) the applicant's right to appeal under section 65A against the refusal to the [First-tier Tribunal]⁴]¹; and

(c) the time within which he may do so.

(4) Any person who contravenes subsection [(A1), (A2),]⁵ (1) or (2) shall be guilty of an offence and liable on summary conviction to imprisonment for a term not exceeding six months or to a fine not exceeding level 5 on the standard scale or to both.

(5) Where a person contravenes subsection [(A2) or]⁵ (2) he shall not be guilty of an offence if he proves that he did not know, and had no reasonable grounds for believing, that the person whom he was employing was disqualified under section 68.

[(6) In this section and section 65A 'appropriate authority' means–

(a) in relation to England, [[Her Majesty's Chief Inspector of Education, Children's Services and Skills]³]²; and

(b) in relation to Wales, the National Assembly for Wales.]¹

NOTES

Amendments.¹ Words substituted and subsection inserted: Care Standards Act 2000, s 116, Sch 4, para 14(13).² Words substituted: Health and Social Care (Community Health and Standards) Act 2003, s 147, Sch 9, para 10(1), (2).³ Words substituted: Education and Inspections Act 2006, s 157, Sch 14, paras 9, 12.⁴ Words substituted: SI 2008/2833.⁵ Subsections and words inserted: Children and Families Act 2014, s 105.

Definitions. 'Child': s 105(1); 'children's home': s 23; 'responsible authority': Sch 6, para 3(1); 'to foster a child privately': s 66(1)(b).

[65A Appeal against refusal of authority to give consent under section 65

(1) An appeal against a decision of an appropriate authority under section 65 shall lie to the [First-tier Tribunal]².

(2) On an appeal the Tribunal may confirm the authority's decision or direct it to give the consent in question.]¹

NOTES

Amendments.¹ Section inserted: Care Standards Act 2000, s 116, Sch 4, para 14(14).² Words substituted: SI 2008/2833.

PART IX
PRIVATE ARRANGEMENTS FOR FOSTERING CHILDREN

66 Privately fostered children

(1) In this Part –

(a) 'a privately fostered child' means a child who is under the age of sixteen and who is cared for, and provided with accommodation [in their own home]¹ by, someone other than –

(i) a parent of his;

(ii) a person who is not a parent of his but who has parental responsibility for him; or

(iii)   a relative of his; and

(b)   'to foster a child privately' means to look after the child in circumstances in which he is a privately fostered child as defined by this section.

(2) A child is not a privately fostered child if the person caring for and accommodating him –

(a)   has done so for a period of less than 28 days; and
(b)   does not intend to do so for any longer period.

(3) Subsection (1) is subject to –

(a)   the provisions of section 63; and
(b)   the exceptions made by paragraphs 1 to 5 of Schedule 8.

(4) In the case of a child who is disabled, subsection (1)(a) shall have effect as if for 'sixteen' there were substituted 'eighteen'.

[(4A) The Secretary of State may by regulations make provision as to the circumstances in which a person who provides accommodation to a child is, or is not, to be treated as providing him with accommodation in the person's own home.][1]

(5) Schedule 8 shall have effect for the purposes of supplementing the provision made by this Part.

NOTES

Amendments.[1] Words and subsection inserted: Care Standards Act 2000, s 116, Sch 4, para 14(1), (15).
Definitions. 'Child': s 105(1); 'disabled': s 17(11); 'parental responsibility': s 3; 'privately fostered child': s 66(1); 'relative': s 105(1); 'to foster a child privately': s 66(1).

67 Welfare of privately fostered children

(1) It shall be the duty of every local authority to satisfy themselves that the welfare of children who are [or are proposed to be][1] privately fostered within their area is being [or will be][1] satisfactorily safeguarded and promoted and to secure that such advice is given to those [concerned with][1] them as appears to the authority to be needed.

(2) The Secretary of State may make regulations –

(a)   requiring every child who is privately fostered within a local authority's area to be visited by an officer of the authority –
(i)   in prescribed circumstances; and
(ii)   on specified occasions or within specified periods; and
(b)   imposing requirements which are to be met by any local authority, or officer of a local authority, in carrying out functions under this section.

[(2A) Regulations under subsection (2)(b) may impose requirements as to the action to be taken by a local authority for the purposes of discharging their duty under subsection (1) where they have received notification of a proposal that a child be privately fostered.][1]

(3) Where any person who is authorised by a local authority [for the purpose][1] has reasonable cause to believe that –

    (a)   any privately fostered child is being accommodated in premises within the authority's area; or

    (b)   it is proposed to accommodate any such child in any such premises,

he may at any reasonable time inspect those premises and any children there.

(4) Any person exercising the power under subsection (3) shall, if so required, produce some duly authenticated document showing his authority to do so.

(5) Where a local authority are not satisfied that the welfare of any child who is [or is proposed to be][1] privately fostered within their area is being [or will be][1] satisfactorily safeguarded or promoted they shall –

    (a)   unless they consider that it would not be in the best interests of the child, take such steps as are reasonably practicable to secure that the care and accommodation of the child is undertaken by –
        (i)   a parent of his;
        (ii)   any person who is not a parent of his but who has parental responsibility for him; or
        (iii)   a relative of his; and

    (b)   consider the extent to which (if at all) they should exercise any of their functions under this Act with respect to the child.

[(6) The Secretary of State may make regulations requiring a local authority to monitor the way in which the authority discharge their functions under this Part (and the regulations may in particular require the authority to appoint an officer for that purpose).][1]

NOTES

Amendments.[1] Words inserted or substituted and subsections inserted: Children Act 2004, s 44.
Definitions. 'Child': s 105(1); 'functions': s 105(1); 'local authority': s 105(1); 'parental responsibility': s 3; 'prescribed': s 105(1); 'privately fostered child': s 66(1); 'relative': s 105(1).

68   Persons disqualified from being private foster parents

(1) Unless he has disclosed the fact to the appropriate local authority and obtained their written consent, a person shall not foster a child privately if he is disqualified from doing so by regulations made by the Secretary of State for the purposes of this section.

(2) The regulations may, in particular, provide for a person to be so disqualified where –

    (a)   an order of a kind specified in the regulations has been made at any time with respect to him;

    (b)   an order of a kind so specified has been made at any time with respect to any child who has been in his care;

    (c)   a requirement of a kind so specified has been imposed at any time with respect to any such child, under or by virtue of any enactment;

    (d)   he has been convicted of any offence of a kind so specified, or ...[1] discharged absolutely or conditionally for any such offence;

(e) a prohibition has been imposed on him at any time under section 69 or under any other specified enactment;

(f) his rights and powers with respect to a child have at any time been vested in a specified authority under a specified enactment.

[(2A) A conviction in respect of which a probation order was made before 1st October 1992 (which would not otherwise be treated as a conviction) is to be treated as a conviction for the purposes of subsection (2)(d).][1]

(3) Unless he has disclosed the fact to the appropriate local authority and obtained their written consent, a person shall not foster a child privately if –

(a) he lives in the same household as a person who is himself prevented from fostering a child by subsection (1); or

(b) he lives in a household at which any such person is employed.

[(3A) A person shall not foster a child privately if –

(a) he is barred from regulated activity relating to children (within the meaning of section 3(2) of the Safeguarding Vulnerable Groups Act 2006); or

(b) he lives in the same household as a person who is barred from such activity.][2]

(4) Where an authority refuse to give their consent under this section, they shall inform the applicant by a written notice which states –

(a) the reason for the refusal;

(b) the applicant's right under paragraph 8 of Schedule 8 to appeal against the refusal; and

(c) the time within which he may do so.

(5) In this section –

'the appropriate authority' means the local authority within whose area it is proposed to foster the child in question; and

'enactment' means any enactment having effect, at any time, in any part of the United Kingdom.

NOTES

Amendments.[1] Words repealed and subsection inserted: Criminal Justice Act 2003, ss 304, 332, Sch 32, Pt 1, paras 59, 60, Sch 37, Pt 7.[2] Subsection inserted: Safeguarding Vulnerable Groups Act 2006, s 63(1), Sch 9, Pt 2, para 12.

Definitions. 'Appropriate authority': s 68(5); 'child': s 105(1); 'enactment': s 68(5); 'local authority': s 105(1); 'to foster a child privately': s 66(1).

69 Power to prohibit private fostering

(1) This section applies where a person –

(a) proposes to foster a child privately; or

(b) is fostering a child privately.

(2) Where the local authority for the area within which the child is proposed to be, or is being, fostered are of the opinion that –

(a)   he is not a suitable person to foster a child;

(b)   the premises in which the child will be, or is being, accommodated are not suitable; or

(c)   it would be prejudicial to the welfare of the child for him to be, or continue to be, accommodated by that person in those premises,

the authority may impose a prohibition on him under subsection (3).

(3) A prohibition imposed on any person under this subsection may prohibit him from fostering privately –

(a)   any child in any premises within the area of the local authority; or

(b)   any child in premises specified in the prohibition;

(c)   a child identified in the prohibition, in premises specified in the prohibition.

(4) A local authority who have imposed a prohibition on any person under subsection (3) may, if they think fit, cancel the prohibition –

(a)   of their own motion; or

(b)   on an application made by that person,

if they are satisfied that the prohibition is no longer justified.

(5) Where a local authority impose a requirement on any person under paragraph 6 of Schedule 8, they may also impose a prohibition on him under subsection (3).

(6) Any prohibition imposed by virtue of subsection (5) shall not have effect unless –

(a)   the time specified for compliance with the requirement has expired; and

(b)   the requirement has not been complied with.

(7) A prohibition imposed under this section shall be imposed by notice in writing addressed to the person on whom it is imposed and informing him of –

(a)   the reason for imposing the prohibition;

(b)   his right under paragraph 8 of Schedule 8 to appeal against the prohibition; and

(c)   the time within which he may do so.

NOTES

Definitions. 'Child': s 105(1); 'local authority': s 105(1); 'to foster a child privately': s 66(1).

70 Offences

(1) A person shall be guilty of an offence if –

(a)   being required, under any provision made by or under this Part, to give any notice or information –

(i)   he fails without reasonable excuse to give the notice within the time specified in that provision; or

(ii)   he fails without reasonable excuse to give the information within a reasonable time; or

    (iii)   he makes, or causes or procures another person to make, any statement in the notice or information which he knows to be false or misleading in a material particular;

(b)   he refuses to allow a privately fostered child to be visited by a duly authorised officer of a local authority;

(c)   he intentionally obstructs another in the exercise of the power conferred by section 67(3);

(d)   he contravenes section 68;

(e)   he fails without reasonable excuse to comply with any requirement imposed by a local authority under this Part;

(f)   he accommodates a privately fostered child in any premises in contravention of a prohibition imposed by a local authority under this Part;

(g)   he knowingly causes to be published, or publishes, an advertisement which he knows contravenes paragraph 10 of Schedule 8.

(2) Where a person contravenes section 68(3), he shall not be guilty of an offence under this section if he proves that he did not know, and had no reasonable ground for believing, that any person to whom section 68(1) applied was living or employed in the premises in question.

(3) A person guilty of an offence under subsection (1)(a) shall be liable on summary conviction to a fine not exceeding level 5 on the standard scale.

(4) A person guilty of an offence under subsection (1)(b), (c) or (g) shall be liable on summary conviction to a fine not exceeding level 3 on the standard scale.

(5) A person guilty of an offence under subsection (1)(d) or (f) shall be liable on summary conviction to imprisonment for a term not exceeding six months, or to a fine not exceeding level 5 on the standard scale, or to both.

(6) A person guilty of an offence under subsection (1)(e) shall be liable on summary conviction to a fine not exceeding level 4 on the standard scale.

(7) If any person who is required, under any provision of this Part, to give a notice fails to give the notice within the time specified in that provision, proceedings for the offence may be brought at any time within six months from the date when evidence of the offence came to the knowledge of the local authority.

(8) Subsection (7) is not affected by anything in section 127(1) of the Magistrates' Courts Act 1980 (time limit for proceedings).

NOTES

Definitions. 'Child': s 105(1); 'local authority': s 105(1); 'privately fostered child': s 66(1).

PART X
CHILD MINDING AND DAY CARE FOR YOUNG CHILDREN

...[1]

NOTES

Amendments.[1] Part X repealed in relation to England and Wales: Care Standards Act 2000, s 79(5).

[PART XA1
CHILD MINDING AND DAY CARE FOR CHILDREN IN ...²
WALES

NOTES

Amendments.¹ Part XA repealed in relation to Wales: Children and Families (Wales) Measure 2010, s 73, Sch 2 (with transitional provisions and savings, SI 2010/2582, Schs 2, 3).² Words omitted: Childcare Act 2006, s 103, Sch 2, para 5, Sch 3, Pt 2.

Introductory

[79A Child minders and day care providers

(1) This section and section 79B apply for the purposes of this Part.

(2) 'Act as a child minder' means (subject to the following subsections) look after one or more children under the age of eight on domestic premises for reward; and 'child minding' shall be interpreted accordingly.

(3) A person who –

   (a)   is the parent, or a relative, of a child;
   (b)   has parental responsibility for a child;
   (c)   is a local authority foster parent in relation to a child;
   (d)   is a foster parent with whom a child has been placed by a voluntary organisation; or
   (e)   fosters a child privately,

does not act as a child minder when looking after that child.

(4) Where a person –

   (a)   looks after a child for the parents ('P1'), or
   (b)   in addition to that work, looks after another child for different parents ('P2'),

and the work consists (in a case within paragraph (a)) of looking after the child wholly or mainly in P1's home or (in a case within paragraph (b)) of looking after the children wholly or mainly in P1's home or P2's home or both, the work is not to be treated as child minding.

(5) In subsection (4), 'parent', in relation to a child, includes –

   (a)   a person who is not a parent of the child but who has parental responsibility for the child;
   (b)   a person who is a relative of the child.

(6) 'Day care' means care provided at any time for children under the age of eight on premises other than domestic premises.

(7) This Part does not apply in relation to a person who acts as a child minder, or provides day care on any premises, unless the period, or the total of the periods, in any day which he spends looking after children or (as the case may be) during which the children are looked after on the premises exceeds two hours.

PART I – Statutes

(8) In determining whether a person is required to register under this Part for child minding, any day on which he does not act as a child minder at any time between 2 am and 6 pm is to be disregarded.]¹

NOTES

Amendments.¹ Part XA repealed in relation to Wales: Children and Families (Wales) Measure 2010, s 73, Sch 2 (with transitional provisions and savings, SI 2010/2582, Schs 2, 3).

[79B Other definitions, etc

(1) ...⁵

[(2) In this Act 'the Assembly' means the National Assembly for Wales.]⁵

(3) A person is qualified for registration for child minding if –

   (a)   he, and every other person looking after children on any premises on which he is or is likely to be child minding, is suitable to look after children under the age of eight;

   (b)   every person living or employed on the premises in question is suitable to be in regular contact with children under the age of eight;

   (c)   the premises in question are suitable to be used for looking after children under the age of eight, having regard to their condition and the condition and appropriateness of any equipment on the premises and to any other factor connected with the situation, construction or size of the premises; and

   (d)   he is complying with regulations under section 79C and with any conditions imposed [under this Part]².

(4) A person is qualified for registration for providing day care on particular premises if –

   [(a)   he has made adequate arrangements to ensure that –

      (i)   every person (other than himself and the responsible individual) looking after children on the premises is suitable to look after children under the age of eight; and

      (ii)   every person (other than himself and the responsible individual) living or working on the premises is suitable to be in regular contact with children under the age of eight;

   (b)   the responsible individual –

      (i)   is suitable to look after children under the age of eight, or

      (ii)   if he is not looking after such children, is suitable to be in regular contact with them;]³

   (c)   the premises are suitable to be used for looking after children under the age of eight, having regard to their condition and the condition and appropriateness of any equipment on the premises and to any other factor connected with the situation, construction or size of the premises; and

   (d)   he is complying with regulations under section 79C and with any conditions imposed [under this Part]².

(5) For the purposes of subsection [(4)(a)]³ a person is not treated as working on the premises in question if –

(a)   none of his work is done in the part of the premises in which children are looked after; or

(b)   he does not work on the premises at times when children are looked after there.

[(5ZA) For the purposes of subsection (4), 'the responsible individual' means –

(a)   in a case of one individual working on the premises in the provision of day care, that person;

(b)   in a case of two or more individuals so working, the individual so working who is in charge.]³

[(5A) Where, for the purposes of determining a person's qualification for registration under this Part –

(a)   [the Assembly]⁵ requests any person ('A') to consent to the disclosure to the authority by another person ('B') of any information relating to A which is held by B and is of a prescribed description, and

(b)   A does not give his consent (or withdraws it after having given it),

[the Assembly]⁵ may, if regulations so provide and it thinks it appropriate to do so, regard A as not suitable to look after children under the age of eight, or not suitable to be in regular contact with such children.]¹

(6) 'Domestic premises' means any premises which are wholly or mainly used as a private dwelling and 'premises' includes any area and any vehicle.

[(7) 'Regulations' means regulations made by the Assembly.]⁵

(8) ...⁶

(9) Schedule 9A (which supplements the provisions of this Part) shall have effect.]⁷

NOTES

Amendments.¹ Subsection inserted: Education Act 2002, s 152, Sch 13, para 1.² Words substituted: Children Act 2004, s 48, Sch 4, paras 1, 2.³ Subsection inserted and paragraphs and words substituted: Children Act 2004, s 48, Sch 4, paras 1, 6.⁴ Words substituted: Education and Inspections Act 2006, s 157, Sch 14, paras 9, 13.⁵ Subsections repealed and substituted and words substituted: Childcare Act 2006, s 103, Sch 2, paras 6, 7, Sch 3, Pt 2.⁶ Subsection repealed: SI 2008/2833.⁷ Part XA repealed in relation to Wales: Children and Families (Wales) Measure 2010, s 73, Sch 2 (with transitional provisions and savings, SI 2010/2582, Schs 2, 3).

Regulations

[79C   Regulations etc governing child minders and day care providers

(1) ...¹

(2) The Assembly may make regulations governing the activities of registered persons who act as child minders, or provide day care, on premises in Wales.

(3) The regulations under this section may deal with the following matters (among others) –

(a)   the welfare and development of the children concerned;
(b)   suitability to look after, or be in regular contact with, children under the age of eight;
(c)   qualifications and training;
(d)   the maximum number of children who may be looked after and the number of persons required to assist in looking after them;
(e)   the maintenance, safety and suitability of premises and equipment;
(f)   the keeping of records;
(g)   the provision of information.

(4), (5) ...[1]

(6) If the regulations require any person (other than [the Assembly][1]) to have regard to or meet factors, standards and other matters prescribed by or referred to in the regulations, they may also provide for any allegation that the person has failed to do so to be taken into account –

(a)   by [the Assembly][1] in the exercise of its functions under this Part, or
(b)   in any proceedings under this Part.

(7) Regulations may provide –

(a)   that a registered person who without reasonable excuse contravenes, or otherwise fails to comply with, any requirement of the regulations shall be guilty of an offence; and
(b)   that a person guilty of the offence shall be liable on summary conviction to a fine not exceeding level 5 on the standard scale.][2]

NOTES

Amendments.[1] Subsections repealed and words substituted: Childcare Act 2006, s 103, Sch 2, paras 6, 8, Sch 3, Pt 2.[2] Part XA repealed in relation to Wales: Children and Families (Wales) Measure 2010, s 73, Sch 2 (with transitional provisions and savings, SI 2010/2582, Schs 2, 3).

Registration

[79D Requirement to register

[(1) No person shall act as a child minder in Wales unless he is registered under this Part for child minding by the Assembly.][1]

(2) Where it appears to [the Assembly][1] that a person has contravened subsection (1), the authority may serve a notice ('an enforcement notice') on him.

(3) An enforcement notice shall have effect for a period of one year beginning with the date on which it is served.

(4) If a person in respect of whom an enforcement notice has effect contravenes subsection (1) without reasonable excuse ...[1], he shall be guilty of an offence.

(5) No person shall provide day care on any premises [in Wales][1] unless he is registered under this Part for providing day care on those premises by [the Assembly][1].

PART I – Statutes

(6) If any person contravenes subsection (5) without reasonable excuse, he shall be guilty of an offence.

(7) A person guilty of an offence under this section shall be liable on summary conviction to a fine not exceeding level 5 on the standard scale.][2]

NOTES

Amendments.[1] Subsection substituted, and words substituted and inserted: Childcare Act 2006, s 103(1), Sch 2, paras 6, 9, Sch 3, Pt 2.[2] Part XA repealed in relation to Wales: Children and Families (Wales) Measure 2010, s 73, Sch 2 (with transitional provisions and savings, SI 2010/2582, Schs 2, 3).

[79E   Applications for registration

(1) A person who wishes to be registered under this Part shall make an application to [the Assembly][2].

(2) The application shall –

   (a)   give prescribed information about prescribed matters;
   (b)   give any other information which [the Assembly][2] reasonably requires the applicant to give
   [(c)   be accompanied by the prescribed fee][1].

(3) Where a person provides, or proposes to provide, day care on different premises, he shall make a separate application in respect of each of them.

(4) Where [the Assembly][2] has sent the applicant notice under section 79L(1) of its intention to refuse an application under this section, the application may not be withdrawn without the consent of the authority.

(5) A person who, in an application under this section, knowingly makes a statement which is false or misleading in a material particular shall be guilty of an offence and liable, on summary conviction, to a fine not exceeding level 5 on the standard scale.][3]

NOTES

Amendments.[1] Paragraph inserted: Children Act 2004, s 48, Sch 4, paras 1, 3(1).[2] Words substituted: Childcare Act 2006, s 103(1), Sch 2, para 6.[3] Part XA repealed in relation to Wales: Children and Families (Wales) Measure 2010, s 73, Sch 2 (with transitional provisions and savings, SI 2010/2582, Schs 2, 3).

[79F   Grant or refusal of registration

(1) If, on an application [under section 79E][1] by a person for registration for child minding –

   (a)   [the Assembly][3] is of the opinion that the applicant is, and will continue to be, qualified for registration for child minding (so far as the conditions of section 79B(3) are applicable); ...[2]
   (b)   ...[2]

[the Assembly][3] shall grant the application; otherwise, it shall refuse it.

(2) If, on an application [under section 79E][1] by any person for registration for providing day care on any premises –

(a) [the Assembly]³ is of the opinion that the applicant is, and will continue to be, qualified for registration for providing day care on those premises (so far as the conditions of section 79B(4) are applicable); …²

(b) …²

[the Assembly]³ shall grant the application; otherwise, it shall refuse it.

(3) An application may, as well as being granted subject to any conditions [the Assembly]³ thinks necessary or expedient for the purpose of giving effect to regulations under section 79C, be granted subject to any other conditions [the Assembly]³ thinks fit to impose.

(4) [The Assembly]³ may as it thinks fit vary or remove any condition to which the registration is subject or impose a new condition.

(5) Any register kept by [the Assembly]³ of persons who act as child minders or provide day care shall be open to inspection by any person at all reasonable times.

(6) A registered person who without reasonable excuse contravenes, or otherwise fails to comply with, any condition imposed on his registration shall be guilty of an offence.

(7) A person guilty of an offence under subsection (6) shall be liable on summary conviction to a fine not exceeding level 5 on the standard scale.]⁴

NOTES

Amendments.¹ Words inserted: Children Act 2004, s 48, Sch 4, paras 1, 3(2)(a).² Words or paragraphs repealed: Children Act 2004, ss 48, 64, Sch 4, paras 1, 3(2)(b), Sch 5, Pt 2.³ Words substituted: Childcare Act 2006, s 103(1), Sch 2, para 6.⁴ Part XA repealed in relation to Wales: Children and Families (Wales) Measure 2010, s 73, Sch 2 (with transitional provisions and savings, SI 2010/2582, Schs 2, 3).

[79G Cancellation of registration

(1) [The Assembly]³ may cancel the registration of any person if –

(a) in the case of a person registered for child minding, [the Assembly]³ is of the opinion that the person has ceased or will cease to be qualified for registration for child minding;

(b) in the case of a person registered for providing day care on any premises, [the Assembly]³ is of the opinion that the person has ceased or will cease to be qualified for registration for providing day care on those premises,

or if [a fee]² which is due from the person has not been paid.

(2) Where a requirement to make any changes or additions to any services, equipment or premises has been imposed on a registered person …¹, his registration shall not be cancelled on the ground of any defect or insufficiency in the services, equipment or premises if –

(a) the time set for complying with the requirements has not expired; and

(b) it is shown that the defect or insufficiency is due to the changes or additions not having been made.

(3) Any cancellation under this section must be in writing.][4]

NOTES

Amendments.[1] Words repealed: Children Act 2004, ss 48, 64, Sch 4, paras 1, 2(2), Sch 5, Pt 2.[2] Words substituted: Children Act 2004, s 48, Sch 4, paras 1, 4(1).[3] Words substituted: Childcare Act 2006, s 103(1), Sch 2, para 6.[4] Part XA repealed in relation to Wales: Children and Families (Wales) Measure 2010, s 73, Sch 2 (with transitional provisions and savings, SI 2010/2582, Schs 2, 3).

[79H Suspension of registration

(1) Regulations may provide for the registration of any person for acting as a child minder or providing day care to be suspended for a prescribed period by [the Assembly][2] in prescribed circumstances.

(2) Any regulations made under this section shall include provision conferring on the person concerned a right of appeal to the [First-tier][3] Tribunal against suspension.

[(3) ...[2]

(4) A person registered under this Part for child minding by the Assembly shall not act as a child minder in Wales at a time when that registration is so suspended.

(5) A person registered under this Part for providing day care on any premises shall not provide day care on those premises at any time when that registration is so suspended.

(6) If any person contravenes subsection (3), (4) or (5) without reasonable excuse, he shall be guilty of an offence and liable on summary conviction to a fine not exceeding level 5 on the standard scale.][1]][4]

NOTES

Amendments.[1] Subsections inserted: Education Act 2002, s 152, Sch 13, para 2.[2] Words substituted and subsection repealed: Childcare Act 2006, s 103, Sch 2, paras 6, 10, Sch 3, Pt 2.[3] Words inserted: SI 2008/2833.[4] Part XA repealed in relation to Wales: Children and Families (Wales) Measure 2010, s 73, Sch 2 (with transitional provisions and savings, SI 2010/2582, Schs 2, 3).

[79J Resignation of registration

(1) A person who is registered for acting as a child minder or providing day care may by notice in writing to [the Assembly][1] resign his registration.

(2) But a person may not give a notice under subsection (1) –

  (a) if [the Assembly][1] has sent him a notice under section 79L(1) of its intention to cancel the registration, unless the authority has decided not to take that step; or

  (b) if [the Assembly][1] has sent him a notice under section 79L(5) of its decision to cancel the registration and the time within which an appeal may be brought has not expired or, if an appeal has been brought, it has not been determined.][2]

NOTES

Amendments.[1] Words substituted: Childcare Act 2006, s 103(1), Sch 2, para 6.[2] Part XA repealed in relation to Wales: Children and Families (Wales) Measure 2010, s 73, Sch 2 (with transitional provisions and savings, SI 2010/2582, Schs 2, 3).

[79K Protection of children in an emergency

(1) If, in the case of any person registered [under this Part]¹ for acting as a child minder or providing day care –

    (a)   [the Assembly]¹ applies to a justice of the peace for an order –

        (i)   cancelling the registration;

        (ii) varying or removing any condition to which the registration is subject; or

        (iii) imposing a new condition; and

    (b)   it appears to the justice that a child who is being, or may be, looked after by that person, or (as the case may be) in accordance with the provision for day care made by that person, is suffering, or is likely to suffer, significant harm,

the justice may make the order.

(2) The cancellation, variation, removal or imposition shall have effect from the time when the order is made.

(3) An application under subsection (1) may be made without notice.

(4) An order under subsection (1) shall be made in writing.

(5) Where an order is made under this section, [the Assembly]¹ shall serve on the registered person, as soon as is reasonably practicable after the making of the order –

    (a)   a copy of the order;

    (b)   a copy of any written statement of [the Assembly's]¹ reasons for making the application for the order which supported that application; and

    (c)   notice of any right of appeal conferred by section 79M.

(6) Where an order has been so made, [the Assembly]¹ shall, as soon as is reasonably practicable after the making of the order, notify the local authority in whose area the person concerned acts or acted as a child minder, or provides or provided day care, of the making of the order.]²

NOTES

Amendments.¹ Words inserted and substituted: Childcare Act 2006, s 103(1), Sch 2, paras 6, 11.² Part XA repealed in relation to Wales: Children and Families (Wales) Measure 2010, s 73, Sch 2 (with transitional provisions and savings, SI 2010/2582, Schs 2, 3).

[79L Notice of intention to take steps

(1) Not less than 14 days before –

    (a)   refusing an application for registration;

    (b)   cancelling a registration;

    (c)   removing or varying any condition to which a registration is subject or imposing a new condition; or

    (d)   refusing to grant an application for the removal or variation of any condition to which a registration is subject, [the Assembly]¹ shall send to the applicant, or (as the case may be) registered person, notice in writing of its intention to take the step in question.

(2) Every such notice shall –

    (a)   give [the Assembly's]¹ reasons for proposing to take the step; and

    (b)   inform the person concerned of his rights under this section.

(3) Where the recipient of such a notice informs [the Assembly]¹ in writing of his desire to object to the step being taken, [the Assembly]¹ shall afford him an opportunity to do so.

(4) Any objection made under subsection (3) may be made orally or in writing, by the recipient of the notice or a representative.

(5) If [the Assembly]¹, after giving the person concerned an opportunity to object to the step being taken, decides nevertheless to take it, it shall send him written notice of its decision.

(6) A step of a kind mentioned in subsection (1)(b) or (c) shall not take effect until the expiry of the time within which an appeal may be brought under section 79M or, where such an appeal is brought, before its determination.

(7) Subsection (6) does not prevent a step from taking effect before the expiry of the time within which an appeal may be brought under section 79M if the person concerned notifies [the Assembly]¹ in writing that he does not intend to appeal.]²

NOTES

Amendments.¹ Words substituted: Childcare Act 2006, s 103(1), Sch 2, para 6.² Part XA repealed in relation to Wales: Children and Families (Wales) Measure 2010, s 73, Sch 2 (with transitional provisions and savings, SI 2010/2582, Schs 2, 3).

[79M Appeals

(1) An appeal against –

    (a)   the taking of any step mentioned in section 79L(1); ...¹

    (b)   an order under section 79K, [or

    (c)   a determination made by [the Assembly]² under this Part (other than one falling within paragraph (a) or (b)) which is of a prescribed description,]¹

shall lie to the [First-tier]³ Tribunal.

(2) On an appeal, the [First-tier]³ Tribunal may –

    (a)   confirm the taking of the step or the making of the order [or determination]¹ or direct that it shall not have, or shall cease to have, effect; and

    (b)   impose, vary or cancel any condition.]⁴

NOTES

Amendments.¹ Words repealed and inserted: Education Act 2002, ss 149(2), 152, 215(2), Sch 13, para 3, Sch 22, Pt 3.² Words substituted: Childcare Act 2006, s 103(1), Sch 2, para 6.³ Words inserted: SI 2008/2833.⁴ Part XA repealed in relation to Wales: Children and Families (Wales) Measure 2010, s 73, Sch 2 (with transitional provisions and savings, SI 2010/2582, Schs 2, 3).

Inspection: England

79N

...¹

NOTES

Amendments.¹ Section repealed: Childcare Act 2006, s 103, Sch 2, para 12, Sch 3, Pt 2.

79P

...¹

NOTES

Amendments.¹ Section repealed: Education Act 2005, ss 53, 123, Sch 7, Pt 1, para 2, Sch 19, Pt 1.

79Q

...¹

NOTES

Amendments.¹ Section repealed: Childcare Act 2006, s 103, Sch 2, para 12, Sch 3, Pt 2.

79R

...¹

NOTES

Amendments.¹ Section repealed: Childcare Act 2006, s 103, Sch 2, para 12, Sch 3, Pt 2.

Inspection: Wales

[79S General functions of the Assembly

(1) The Assembly may secure the provision of training for persons who provide or assist in providing child minding or day care, or intend to do so.

(2) In relation to child minding and day care provided in Wales, the Assembly shall have any additional function specified in regulations made by the Assembly; ...¹]²

NOTES

Amendments.¹ Words repealed: Childcare Act 2006, s 103, Sch 2, para 13, Sch 3, Pt 2.² Part XA repealed in relation to Wales: Children and Families (Wales) Measure 2010, s 73, Sch 2 (with transitional provisions and savings, SI 2010/2582, Schs 2, 3).

[79T Inspection: Wales

(1) The Assembly may at any time require any registered person to provide it with any information connected with the person's activities as a child minder or provision of day care which the Assembly considers it necessary to have for the purposes of its functions under this Part.

(2) The Assembly may by regulations make provision –

(a) for the inspection of ...¹ child minding provided in Wales by registered persons and of day care provided by registered persons on premises in Wales;

(b)   for the publication of reports of the inspections in such manner as the Assembly considers appropriate.

(3) The regulations may provide for the inspections to be organised by –

(a)   the Assembly; or
(b)   Her Majesty's Chief Inspector of Education and Training in Wales, or any other person, under arrangements made with the Assembly.

(4) The regulations may provide for subsections (2) to (4) of [section 29 of the Education Act 2005][1] to apply with modifications in relation to the publication of reports under the regulations.][2]

NOTES

Amendments.[1] Words omitted and substituted: Education Act 2005, ss 53, 123, Sch 7, para 5, Sch 19, Pt 1.[2] Part XA repealed in relation to Wales: Children and Families (Wales) Measure 2010, s 73, Sch 2 (with transitional provisions and savings, SI 2010/2582, Schs 2, 3).

Supplementary

[79U   Rights of entry etc

(1) [Any person authorised for the purposes of this subsection by [the Assembly][3]][1] may at any reasonable time enter any premises in …[3] Wales on which child minding or day care is at any time provided.

(2) Where [a person authorised for the purposes of this subsection by [the Assembly][3]][1] has reasonable cause to believe that a child is being looked after on any premises in contravention of this Part, he may enter those premises at any reasonable time.

[(2A) Authorisation under subsection (1) or (2) –

(a)   may be given for a particular occasion or period;
(b)   may be given subject to conditions.][1]

(3) [A person entering premises under this section may (subject to any conditions imposed under subsection (2A)(b)][1] –

(a)   inspect the premises;
(b)   inspect, and take copies of –
      (i)   any records kept by the person providing the child minding or day care; and
      (ii) any other documents containing information relating to its provision;
(c)   seize and remove any document or other material or thing found there which he has reasonable grounds to believe may be evidence of a failure to comply with any condition or requirement imposed by or under this Part;
(d)   require any person to afford him such facilities and assistance with respect to matters within the person's control as are necessary to enable him to exercise his powers under this section;
(e)   take measurements and photographs or make recordings;

PART I – Statutes

(f)   inspect any children being looked after there, and the arrangements made for their welfare;

(g)   interview in private the person providing the child minding or day care; and

(h)   interview in private any person looking after children, or living or working, there who consents to be interviewed.

(4) [Section 58 of the Education Act 2005][2] (inspection of computer records for purposes of Part I of that Act) shall apply for the purposes of subsection (3) as it applies for the purposes of Part I of that Act.

(5) ...[1]

(6) A person exercising any power conferred by this section shall, if so required, produce some duly authenticated document showing his authority to do so.

(7) It shall be an offence wilfully to obstruct a person exercising any such power.

(8) Any person guilty of an offence under subsection (7) shall be liable on summary conviction to a fine not exceeding level 4 on the standard scale.

(9) In this section –

...[1]

'documents' and 'records' each include information recorded in any form.][4]

NOTES

Amendments.[1] Words and subsection inserted, and subsection and definition repealed: Education Act 2002, s 152, Sch 13, para 5.[2] Words substituted: Education Act 2005, s 53, Sch 7, Pt 1, para 6.[3] Words repealed and substituted: Childcare Act 2006, s 103, Sch 2, paras 6, 14, Sch 3, Pt 2.[4] Part XA repealed in relation to Wales: Children and Families (Wales) Measure 2010, s 73, Sch 2 (with transitional provisions and savings, SI 2010/2582, Schs 2, 3).

[79V Function of local authorities

Each local authority [in Wales][1] shall, in accordance with regulations, secure the provision –

(a)   of information and advice about child minding and day care; and

(b)   of training for persons who provide or assist in providing child minding or day care.][2]

NOTES

Amendments.[1] Words inserted: Childcare Act 2006, s 103(1), Sch 2, para 15.[2] Part XA repealed in relation to Wales: Children and Families (Wales) Measure 2010, s 73, Sch 2 (with transitional provisions and savings, SI 2010/2582, Schs 2, 3).

Checks on suitability of persons working with children over the age of seven

[79W Requirement for certificate of suitability

(1) This section applies to any person not required to register under this Part who looks after, or provides care for, children [in Wales][1] and meets the following conditions.

References in this section to children are to those under the age of 15 or (in the case of disabled children) 17.

(2) The first condition is that the period, or the total of the periods, in any week which he spends looking after children or (as the case may be) during which the children are looked after exceeds five hours.

(3) The second condition is that he would be required to register under this Part (or, as the case may be, this Part if it were subject to prescribed modifications) if the children were under the age of eight.

(4) Regulations may require a person to whom this section applies to hold a certificate issued by [the Assembly][2] as to his suitability, and the suitability of each prescribed person, to look after children.

(5) The regulations may make provision about –

    (a)   applications for certificates;
    (b)   the matters to be taken into account by [the Assembly][2] in determining whether to issue certificates;
    (c)   the information to be contained in certificates;
    (d)   the period of their validity.

(6) The regulations may provide that a person to whom this section applies shall be guilty of an offence –

    (a)   if he does not hold a certificate as required by the regulations; or
    (b)   if, being a person who holds such a certificate, he fails to produce it when reasonably required to do so by a prescribed person.

(7) The regulations may provide that a person who, for the purpose of obtaining such a certificate, knowingly makes a statement which is false or misleading in a material particular shall be guilty of an offence.

(8) The regulations may provide that a person guilty of an offence under the regulations shall be liable on summary conviction to a fine not exceeding level 5 on the standard scale.][3]

NOTES

Amendments.[1] Words inserted: Childcare Act 2006, s 103(1), Sch 2, para 16.[2] Words substituted: Childcare Act 2006, s 103(1), Sch 2, para 6.[3] Part XA repealed in relation to Wales: Children and Families (Wales) Measure 2010, s 73, Sch 2 (with transitional provisions and savings, SI 2010/2582, Schs 2, 3).

Time limit for proceedings

[79X Time limit for proceedings

Proceedings for an offence under this Part or regulations made under it may be brought within a period of six months from the date on which evidence sufficient in the opinion of the prosecutor to warrant the proceedings came to his knowledge; but no such proceedings shall be brought by virtue of this section more than three years after the commission of the offence.][1][2]

NOTES

Amendments.[1] Part inserted: Care Standards Act 2000, s 79(1).[2] Part XA repealed in relation to Wales: Children and Families (Wales) Measure 2010, s 73, Sch 2 (with transitional provisions and savings, SI 2010/2582, Schs 2, 3).

PART XI
SECRETARY OF STATE'S SUPERVISORY FUNCTIONS AND RESPONSIBILITIES

80 Inspection of children's homes etc by persons authorised by [the Appropriate National Authority][14]

(1) The [Appropriate National Authority][14] may cause to be inspected from time to time any –

    (a) [private][4] children's home [in England][14];

    (b) premises in which a child who is being looked after by a local authority is living;

    (c) premises in which a child who is being accommodated by or on behalf of a [local authority in the exercise of education functions or a][9] voluntary organisation is living;

    (d) premises in which a child who is being accommodated by or on behalf of a [[Local Health Board][8], Special Health Authority][2][...[13]][3][, National Health Service trust or NHS foundation trust][6] [or pursuant to arrangements made by the Secretary of State, the National Health Service Commissioning Board or a clinical commissioning group under the National Health Service Act 2006][13] is living;

    (e) ...[7]

    (f) ...[7]

    (g) premises in which a privately fostered child, or child who is treated as a foster child by virtue of paragraph 9 of Schedule 8, is living or in which it is proposed that he will live;

    (h) premises on which any person is acting as a child minder;

    [(i) *premises with respect to which a person is registered under section 71(1)(b) [or with respect to which a person is registered for providing day care under Part XA]*[4]*;*][11]

    (j) [care home [in England][14] or independent hospital used to accommodate children;][4]

    (k) premises which are provided by a local authority and in which any service is provided by that authority under Part III;

    (l) [school or college][5] providing accommodation for any child.

(2) An inspection under this section shall be conducted by a person authorised to do so by the [Appropriate National Authority][14].

(3) An officer of a local authority shall not be authorised except with the consent of that authority.

(4) The [Appropriate National Authority][14] may require any person of a kind mentioned in subsection (5) to furnish [it][14] with such information, or allow [it][14] to inspect such records (in whatever form they are held), relating to –

(a)   any premises to which subsection (1) or, in relation to Scotland, subsection (1)(h) or (i) applies;

(b)   any child who is living in any such premises;

(c)   the discharge by the [Appropriate National Authority][14] of any of [its][14] functions under this Act;

(d)   the discharge by any local authority of any of their functions under this Act,

as the [Appropriate National Authority][14] may at any time direct.

(5) The persons are any –

(a)   local authority;

(b)   voluntary organisation;

(c)   person carrying on a [private][4] children's home [in England][14];

(d)   proprietor of an independent school [or governing body of any other school][5];

[(da) governing body of an institution designated under section 28 of the Further and Higher Education Act 1992;

(db) further education corporation;][5]

[(dc) sixth form college corporation;][10]

[(dd) proprietor of a 16 to 19 Academy;][12]

(e)   person fostering any privately fostered child or providing accommodation for a child on behalf of a local authority, …[9] [[Local Health Board][8], Special Health Authority][2][[13]][3][, National Health Service trust][1] [, NHS foundation trust][6] or voluntary organisation;

[(ea) person providing accommodation for a child pursuant to arrangements made by the Secretary of State, the National Health Service Commissioning Board or a clinical commissioning group under the National Health Service Act 2006;][13]

(f)   …[9]

(g)   person employed in a teaching or administrative capacity at any educational establishment (whether or not maintained by [a local authority][9]) at which a child is accommodated on behalf of a local authority …[9];

[(h) person who is the occupier of any premises in which any person acts as a child minder (within the meaning of Part X) or provides day care for young children (within the meaning of that Part);][11]

[(hh) person who is the occupier of any premises –

(i)   in which any person required to be registered for child minding under Part XA acts as a child minder (within the meaning of that Part); or

(ii)   with respect to which a person is required to be registered under that Part for providing day care;][4, 11]

(i)   person carrying on any home of a kind mentioned in subsection (1)(j);

[(j)   person carrying on a fostering agency.][5]

(6) Any person inspecting any home or other premises under this section may –

(a)   inspect the children there; and

(b)   make such examination into the state and management of the home or premises and the treatment of the children there as he thinks fit.

(7) Any person authorised by the [Appropriate National Authority][14] to exercise the power to inspect records conferred by subsection (4) –

(a)   shall be entitled at any reasonable time to have access to, and inspect and check the operation of, any computer and any associated apparatus or material which is or has been in use in connection with the records in question; and
(b)   may require –
(i)   the person by whom or on whose behalf the computer is or has been so used; or
(ii)   any person having charge of, or otherwise concerned with the operation of, the computer, apparatus or material,

to afford him such reasonable assistance as he may require.

(8) A person authorised to inspect any premises under this section shall have a right to enter the premises for that purpose, and for any purpose specified in subsection (4), at any reasonable time.

(9) Any person exercising that power shall, if so required, produce some duly authenticated document showing his authority to do so.

(10) Any person who intentionally obstructs another in the exercise of that power shall be guilty of an offence and liable on summary conviction to a fine not exceeding level 3 on the standard scale.

(11) The [Appropriate National Authority][14] may by order provide for subsections (1), (4) and (6) not to apply in relation to such homes, or other premises, as may be specified in the order.

[(11A) But subsections (1), (4) and (6) do not apply if –

(a)   the Appropriate National Authority is the Welsh Ministers; and
(b)   the inspection relates to a private children's home or a care home (see, instead the Regulation and Inspection of Social Care (Wales) Act 2016 (anaw 2)).][14]

(12) Without prejudice to section 104, any such order may make different provision with respect to each of those subsections.

[(13) In this section –

'college' means an institution within the further education sector as defined in section 91 of the Further and Higher Education Act 1992 [or a 16 to 19 Academy][12];
'fostering agency' has the same meaning as in the Care Standards Act 2000;
'further education corporation' has the same meaning as in the Further and Higher Education Act 1992.
['sixth form college corporation' has the same meaning as in that Act.][10]][5]
['proprietor' has the same meaning as in the Education Act 1996.][12]

[(14) In this section 'Appropriate National Authority' means –

(a)   in relation to England, the Secretary of State; and

(b)   in relation to Wales, the Welsh Ministers.][14]

NOTES

Amendments.[1] Words inserted: National Health Service and Community Care Act 1990, s 66(1), Sch 9, para 36(4)(b).[2] Words substituted: Health Authorities Act 1995, s 2(1), Sch 1, Pt III, para 118(1), (9).[3] Words inserted: Health Act 1999 (Supplementary, Consequential etc Provisions) Order 2000, SI 2000/90.[4] Paragraph and words inserted or substituted: Care Standards Act 2000, ss 116, 117(2), Sch 4, paras 14(1), (16).[5] Subsection, paragraphs and words inserted or substituted: Care Standards Act 2000, s 109 (applies to England only).[6] Words substituted or inserted: Health and Social Care (Community Health and Standards) Act 2003, s 34, Sch 4, paras 75, 80.[7] Paragraphs repealed: Adoption and Children Act 2002, s 139(1), (3), Sch 3, paras 54, 65, Sch 5.[8] Words substituted: SI 2007/961.[9] Words substituted and repealed, and words and paragraph repealed: SI 2010/1158.[10] Paragraph and definition inserted: SI 2010/1080.[11] Paragraphs omitted in relation to Wales: Children and Families (Wales) Measure 2010, ss 72, 73, Sch 1, paras 5, 6, Sch 2.[12] Paragraph and words inserted: Education Act 2011, s 54(1), Sch 13, para 6(1), (3).[13] Paragraph inserted, words inserted and omitted: Health and Social Care Act 2012, s 55(2), Sch 5, Pt 1, paras 47, 54.[14] Words substituted, subsections and words inserted: SI 2019/772, regs 2, 4.

Definitions. 'Adoption agency': s 105(1); 'child': s 105(1); 'child minder': s 71(2)(a); 'child who is looked after by a local authority': s 22(1); 'children's home': s 23; 'clinical commissioning group': s 105(1); 'day care': ss 18, 71(2)(b); 'functions': s 105(1); 'health authority': s 105(1); 'independent school': s 105(1); 'local authority': s 105(1); 'local education authority': s 105(1); 'mental nursing home': s 105(1); 'nursing home': s 105(1); 'privately fostered child': s 105(1); 'residential care home': s 105(1); 'voluntary home': s 60(3); 'voluntary organisation': s 105(1).

81

…[1]

NOTES

Amendments.[1] Section repealed: Inquiries Act 2005, ss 48(1), 49(2), Sch 2, Pt 1, para 12, Sch 3.

82 Financial support by Secretary of State

(1) The Secretary of State may (with the consent of the Treasury) defray or contribute towards –

(a)   any fees or expenses incurred by any person undergoing approved child care training;

(b)   any fees charged, or expenses incurred, by any person providing approved child care training or preparing material for use in connection with such training; or

(c)   the cost of maintaining any person undergoing such training.

(2) The Secretary of State may make grants to local authorities in respect of expenditure incurred by them in providing secure accommodation in community homes other than assisted community homes.

(3) Where –

(a)   a grant has been made under subsection (2) with respect to any secure accommodation; but

(b)   the grant is not used for the purpose for which it was made or the accommodation is not used as, or ceases to be used as, secure accommodation, the Secretary of State may (with the consent of the Treasury) require the authority concerned to repay the grant, in whole or in part.

(4) The Secretary of State may make grants to voluntary organisations towards –

(a) expenditure incurred by them in connection with the establishment, maintenance or improvement of voluntary homes which, at the time when the expenditure was incurred –
  (i) were assisted community homes; or
  (ii) were designated as such; or
(b) expenses incurred in respect of the borrowing of money to defray any such expenditure.

(5) The Secretary of State may arrange for the provision, equipment and maintenance of homes for the accommodation of children who are in need of particular facilities and services which –

(a) are or will be provided in those homes; and
(b) in the opinion of the Secretary of State, are unlikely to be readily available in community homes.

(6) In this Part –

'child care training' means training undergone by any person with a view to, or in the course of –
  (a) his employment for the purposes of any of the functions mentioned in section 83(9) or in connection with the adoption of children or with the accommodation of children in a [care home or independent hospital][1]; or
  (b) his employment by a voluntary organisation for similar purposes;

'approved child care training' means child care training which is approved by the Secretary of State; and

'secure accommodation' means accommodation provided for the purpose of restricting the liberty of children.

(7) Any grant made under this section shall be of such amount, and shall be subject to such conditions, as the Secretary of State may (with the consent of the Treasury) determine.

NOTES

Amendments.[1] Words substituted: Care Standards Act 2000, s 116, Sch 4, para 14(18).
Definitions. 'Approved child care training': s 82(6); 'assisted community home': s 53(5); 'child': s 105(1); 'child care training': s 82(6); 'community home': s 53(1); 'functions': s 105(1); 'mental nursing home': s 105(1); 'nursing home': s 105(1); 'residential care home': s 105(1); 'secure accommodation': s 82(6); 'voluntary home': s 60(3); 'voluntary organisation': s 105(1).

83 Research and returns of information

(1) The Secretary of State may conduct, or assist other persons in conducting, research into any matter connected with –

(a) his functions, or the functions of local authorities, under the enactments mentioned in subsection (9);

[(aa) the functions [of –
    (i)   the Child Safeguarding Practice Review Panel;
    (ii)   safeguarding partners (within the meaning given by section 16E(3) of the Children Act 2004) in relation to local authority areas in England;
    (iii) child death review partners (within the meaning given by section 16Q(2) of the Children Act 2004) in relation to local authority areas in England;][6]4
  (b)   the adoption of children; or
  (c)   the accommodation of children in a [care home or independent hospital]1.

(2) Any local authority may conduct, or assist other persons in conducting, research into any matter connected with –

  (a)   their functions under the enactments mentioned in subsection (9);
[(aa) ...6;]4
  (b)   the adoption of children; or
  (c)   the accommodation of children in a [care home or independent hospital]1.

(3) Every local authority shall, at such times and in such form as the Secretary of State may direct, transmit to him such particulars as he may require with respect to –

  (a)   the performance by the local authority of all or any of their functions –
    (i)   under the enactments mentioned in subsection (9); or
    (ii)   in connection with the accommodation of children in a [care home or independent hospital]1; and
  (b)   the children in relation to whom the authority have exercised those functions[; ...6
  (c)   ...6]4.

(4) Every voluntary organisation shall, at such times and in such form as the Secretary of State may direct, transmit to him such particulars as he may require with respect to children accommodated by them or on their behalf.

[(4A) Particulars required to be transmitted under subsection (3) or (4) may include particulars relating to and identifying individual children.]2

(5) The Secretary of State may direct [an officer of the family court]5 to transmit –

  (a)   to such person as may be specified in the direction; and
  (b)   at such times and in such form as he may direct,

such particulars as he may require with respect to proceedings of the court which relate to children.

(6) The Secretary of State shall in each year lay before Parliament a consolidated and classified abstract of the information transmitted to him under subsections (3) to (5).

(7) The Secretary of State may institute research designed to provide information on which requests for information under this section may be based.

(8) The Secretary of State shall keep under review the adequacy of the provision of child care training and for that purpose shall receive and consider any information from or representations made by –

(a) the Central Council for Education and Training in Social Work;

(b) such representatives of local authorities as appear to him to be appropriate; or

(c) such other persons or organisations as appear to him to be appropriate,

concerning the provision of such training.

(9) The enactments are –

(a) this Act;

(b) the Children and Young Persons Acts 1933 to 1969;

(c) section 116 of the Mental Health Act 1983 (so far as it relates to children looked after by local authorities);

[(ca) Part 1 of the Adoption and Children Act 2002;

(cb) the Children Act 2004;

(cc) the Children and Young Persons Act 2008;][4]

(d) ...[3]

NOTES

Amendments.[1] Words substituted: Care Standards Act 2000, s 116, Sch 4, para 14(19).[2] Subsection inserted: Children Act 2004, s 54.[3] Paragraph repealed: SI 2005/2078, art 16(1), Sch 3.[4] Paragraphs inserted: Children and Young Persons Act 2008, s 33(1)–(5).[5] Words substituted: Crime and Courts Act 2013, s 17, Sch 11, paras 102, 108.[6] Paragraphs and words substituted and paragraphs and words repealed: Children and Social Work Act 2017, s 11, 31, Sch 2, para 8.

Definitions. 'Child': s 105(1); 'child care training': s 82(6); 'functions': s 105(1); 'local authority': s 105(1); 'mental nursing home': s 105(1); 'nursing home': s 105(1); 'residential care home': s 105(1); 'voluntary organisation': s 105(1).

84 Local authority failure to comply with statutory duty: default power of Secretary of State

(1) If the Secretary of State is satisfied that any local authority has failed, without reasonable excuse, to comply with any of the duties imposed on them by or under this Act he may make an order declaring that authority to be in default with respect to that duty.

(2) An order under subsection (1) shall give the Secretary of State's reasons for making it.

(3) An order under subsection (1) may contain such directions for the purpose of ensuring that the duty is complied with, within such period as may be specified in the order, as appear to the Secretary of State to be necessary.

(4) Any such direction shall, on the application of the Secretary of State, be enforceable by mandamus.

PART XII
MISCELLANEOUS AND GENERAL

Notification of children accommodated in certain establishments

85 Children accommodated by health authorities and local education authorities

(1) Where a child is provided with accommodation [in England][8] by any [...[8],Special Health Authority][2], [...[7]][3] [National Health Service trust][1] [or NHS foundation trust or by a local authority [in England][8] in the exercise of education functions][5] ('the accommodating authority') –

   (a)   for a consecutive period of at least three months; or
   (b)   with the intention, on the part of that authority, of accommodating him for such a period,

the accommodating authority shall notify [the appropriate officer of][6] the responsible authority.

(2) Where subsection (1) applies with respect to a child, the accommodating authority shall also notify [the appropriate officer of][6] the responsible authority when they cease to accommodate the child.

[(2ZA) Where a child is provided with accommodation –

   (a)   by a body which is not mentioned in subsection (1), and
   (b)   pursuant to arrangements made by the Secretary of State, the National Health Service Commissioning Board or a clinical commissioning group under the National Health Service Act 2006,

subsections (1) and (2) apply in relation to the Secretary of State, the Board or (as the case may be) the clinical commissioning group as if it were the accommodating authority.][7]

[(2A) In a case where the child is [provided with accommodation in England by a local authority in England][8] in the exercise of education functions, subsections (1) and (2) apply only if the local authority providing the accommodation is different from the responsible authority.][5]

(3) In this section 'the responsible authority' means –

   (a)   the local authority appearing to the accommodating authority to be the authority within whose area the child was ordinarily resident immediately before being accommodated; or
   (b)   where it appears to the accommodating authority that a child was not ordinarily resident within the area of any local authority, the local authority within whose area the accommodation is situated.

[(3A) In this section and sections 86 and 86A 'the appropriate officer' means –

   (a)   in relation to a local authority in England, their director of children's services; and

(b)   in relation to a local authority in Wales, their [director of social services][8].][6]

(4) Where [the appropriate officer of a][6] [local authority in England has been notified under this section, or under section 120 of the Social Services and Well-being (Wales) Act 2014 (assessment of children accommodated by health authorities and education authorities)][8], [the local authority][6] shall –

(a)   take such steps as are reasonably practicable to enable them to determine whether the child's welfare is adequately safeguarded and promoted while he is accommodated by the accommodating authority; and

(b)   consider the extent to which (if at all) they should exercise any of their functions under this Act with respect to the child.

[(5) For the purposes of subsection (4)(b), if the child is not in the area of the local authority, they must treat him as if he were in that area.][6]

NOTES

Amendments.[1] Words inserted: National Health Service and Community Care Act 1990, s 66(1), Sch 9, para 36(5).[2] Words inserted: Health Authorities Act 1995, s 2(1), Sch 1, Pt III, para 118(1), (9).[3] Words inserted: Health Act 1999 (Supplementary, Consequential etc Provisions) Order 2000, SI 2000/90.[4] Words substituted: SI 2007/961.[5] Words substituted and subsection inserted: SI 2010/1158.[6] Words inserted and substituted and subsections inserted: Children and Young Persons Act 2008, s 17(1)–(5).[7] Subsection inserted and words omitted: Health and Social Care Act 2012, s 55(2), Sch 5, Pt 1, paras 47, 55.[8] Words inserted, omitted and substituted: SI 2016/413, regs 55, 102.

Definitions. 'Child': s 105(1); 'clinical commissioning group': s 105(1); 'functions': s 105(1); 'health authority': s 105(1); 'local authority': s 105(1); 'local education authority': s 105(1); 'the accommodating authority': s 85(1); 'the responsible authority': s 85(3).

86 [Children accommodated in care homes or independent hospitals][1]

(1) Where a child is provided with accommodation [in England][3] in any [care home or independent hospital][1] –

(a)   for a consecutive period of at least three months; or

(b)   with the intention, on the part of the person taking the decision to accommodate him, of accommodating him for such period,

the person carrying on [the establishment in question][2] shall notify [the appropriate officer of][2] the local authority within whose area [the establishment][2] is carried on.

(2) Where subsection (1) applies with respect to a child, the person carrying on [the establishment][2] shall also notify [the appropriate officer of][2] that authority when he ceases to accommodate the child in [the establishment][2].

(3) Where [the appropriate officer of a local authority has][2] been notified under this section, [the local authority][2] shall –

(a)   take such steps as are reasonably practicable to enable them to determine whether the child's welfare is adequately safeguarded and promoted while he is accommodated in [the establishment in question][2]; and

(b)   consider the extent to which (if at all) they should exercise any of their functions under this Act with respect to the child.

(4) If the person carrying on any [care home or independent hospital]² fails, without reasonable excuse, to comply with this section he shall be guilty of an offence.

(5) A person authorised by a local authority [in England]³ may enter any [care home or independent hospital]¹ within the authority's area for the purpose of establishing whether the requirements of this section have been complied with.

(6) Any person who intentionally obstructs another in the exercise of the power of entry shall be guilty of an offence.

(7) Any person exercising the power of entry shall, if so required, produce some duly authenticated document showing his authority to do so.

(8) Any person committing an offence under this section shall be liable on summary conviction to a fine not exceeding level 3 on the standard scale.

NOTES

Amendments.[1] Words substituted: Care Standards Act 2000, s 116, Sch 4, para 14(20).[2] Words substituted and inserted: Children and Young Persons Act 2008, s 17(6)–(10).[3] Words inserted: SI 2016/413, regs 55, 103.

Definitions. 'Child': s 105(1); 'functions': s 105(1); 'local authority': s 105(1); 'mental nursing home': s 105(1); 'nursing home': s 105(1); 'residential care home': s 105(1).

[86A Visitors for children notified to local authority ...²

(1) This section applies if the appropriate officer of a local authority [in England]² –

  (a)   has been notified with respect to a child under section 85(1) or 86(1)[, or under section 120(2)(a) of the Social Services and Well-being (Wales) Act 2014]²; and

  (b)   has not been notified with respect to that child under section 85(2) [or under section 120(2)(b) of the Social Services and Well-being (Wales) Act 2014, as the case may be]².

(2) The local authority must, in accordance with regulations made under this section, make arrangements for the child to be visited by a representative of the authority ('a representative').

(3) It is the function of a representative to provide advice and assistance to the local authority on the performance of their duties under section 85(4) or, as the case may be, 86(3).

(4) Regulations under this section may make provision about –

  (a)   the frequency of visits under visiting arrangements;
  (b)   circumstances in which visiting arrangements must require a child to be visited; and
  (c)   additional functions of a representative.

(5) Regulations under this section are to be made by the Secretary of State ...².

(6) In choosing a representative a local authority must satisfy themselves that the person chosen has the necessary skills and experience to perform the functions of a representative.

(7) In this section 'visiting arrangements' means arrangements made under subsection (2).][1]

NOTES

Amendments.[1] Section inserted: Children and Young Persons Act 2008, s 18.[2] Words inserted, substituted and omitted: SI 2016/413, regs 55, 104.

87 [Welfare of children in boarding schools and colleges][1]

[(1) Where a school or college provides accommodation for any child, it shall be the duty of the relevant person to safeguard and promote the child's welfare.

[(1A) For the purposes of this section and sections 87A to 87D, a school or college provides accommodation for a child if –

(a) it provides accommodation for the child on its own premises, or

(b) it arranges for accommodation for the child to be provided elsewhere (other than in connection with a residential trip away from the school).][7]

(2) Subsection (1) does not apply in relation to a school or college which is a children's home or care home.

(3) Where accommodation is provided for a child by any school or college the appropriate authority shall take such steps as are reasonably practicable to enable them to determine whether the child's welfare is adequately safeguarded and promoted while [accommodation for the child is provided][7] by the school or college.

[(3A) Where accommodation is provided for a child by a school or college in England, the Secretary of State may at any time (including a time when the duty under subsection (3) is suspended by virtue of section 87A) direct the Chief Inspector for England to take the steps referred to in subsection (3).

(3B) Where accommodation is provided for a child by a school or college in Wales, the Welsh Ministers may, at any time when the duty under subsection (3) is suspended by virtue of section 87A, take the steps referred to in subsection (3).][7]

(4) Where the [the Chief Inspector for England is][4] of the opinion that there has been a failure to comply with subsection (1) in relation to a child provided with accommodation by a school or [college in England, he shall][4] –

(a) in the case of a school other than an independent school[, an alternative provision Academy that is not an independent school][8] or a special school, notify the [local authority][5] for the area in which the school is situated;

(b) in the case of a special school which is maintained by a [local authority][5], notify that authority;

(c) in any other case, notify the Secretary of State.

(4A) Where the National Assembly for Wales are of the opinion that there has been a failure to comply with subsection (1) in relation to a child provided with accommodation by a school or college [in Wales][4], they shall –

    (a)   in the case of a school other than an independent school or a special school, notify the [local authority]⁵ for the area in which the school is situated;

    (b)   in the case of a special school which is maintained by a [local authority]⁵, notify that authority;

(5) Where accommodation is, or is to be, provided for a child by any school or college, a person authorised by the appropriate authority may, for the purpose of enabling that authority to discharge [any of its functions]⁷ under this section, enter at any time premises which are, or are to be, premises of the school or college.]¹

(6) Any person [exercising]¹ the power conferred by subsection (5) may carry out such inspection of premises, children and records as is prescribed by regulations made by the Secretary of State for the purposes of this section.

(7) Any person exercising that power shall, if asked to do so, produce some duly authenticated document showing his authority to do so.

(8) Any person authorised by the regulations to inspect records –

    (a)   shall be entitled at any reasonable time to have access to, and inspect and check the operation of, any computer and any associated apparatus or material which is or has been in use in connection with the records in question; and

    (b)   may require –

        (i)   the person by whom or on whose behalf the computer is or has been so used; or

        (ii)   any person having charge of, or otherwise concerned with the operation of, the computer, apparatus or material,

to afford him such assistance as he may reasonably require.

(9) Any person who intentionally obstructs another in the exercise of any power conferred by this section or the regulations shall be guilty of an offence and liable on summary conviction to a fine not exceeding level 3 on the standard scale.

[(9A) Where [the Chief Inspector for England]⁴ or the National Assembly for Wales exercises the power conferred by subsection (5) in relation to a child, [that authority must]⁴ publish a report on whether the child's welfare is adequately safeguarded and promoted while [accommodation for the child is provided]⁷ by the school or college.

(9B) Where [the Chief Inspector for England]⁴ or the National Assembly for Wales publishes a report under this section, [that authority must]⁴ –

    (a)   send a copy of the report to the school or college concerned; and

    (b)   make copies of the report available for inspection at its offices by any person at any reasonable time.

(9C) Any person who requests a copy of a report published under this section is entitled to have one on payment of such reasonable fee (if any) as [the Chief Inspector for England]⁴ or the National Assembly for Wales (as the case may be) considers appropriate.]²

[(10) In this section and sections 87A to 87D –

'the 1992 Act' means the Further and Higher Education Act 1992;
'appropriate authority' means –

    (a)   in relation to England, [[the Chief Inspector for England][4]][3];

    (b)   in relation to Wales, the National Assembly for Wales;

['the Chief Inspector for England' means Her Majesty's Chief Inspector of Education, Children's Services and Skills;][4]
'college' means an institution within the further education sector as defined in section 91 of the 1992 Act [or a 16 to 19 Academy][9];
…[4];
'further education corporation' has the same meaning as in the 1992 Act;
'[local authority][5]' and 'proprietor' have the same meanings as in the Education Act 1996.
['sixth form college corporation' has the same meaning as in the 1992 Act.][6]

(11) In this section and sections 87A and 87D 'relevant person' means –

    (a)   in relation to an independent school [or an alternative provision Academy that is not an independent school][8], the proprietor of the school;

    (b)   in relation to any other school, or an institution designated under section 28 of the 1992 Act, the governing body of the school or institution;

    (c)   in relation to an institution conducted by a further education corporation [or sixth form college corporation][6], the corporation.

    [(d)   in relation to a 16 to 19 Academy, the proprietor of the Academy.][9]

(12) Where a person other than the proprietor of an independent school [or an alternative provision Academy that is not an independent school][8] is responsible for conducting the school, references in this section to the relevant person include references to the person so responsible.][1]

NOTES

Amendments.[1] Subsections and words substituted: Care Standards Act 2000, ss 105, 116, Sch 4, para 14(1), (21).[2] Subsections inserted: Health and Social Care (Community Health and Standards) Act 2003, s 111.[3] Words substituted: Health and Social Care (Community Health and Standards) Act 2003, s 147, Sch 9, para 10(1), (3).[4] Words inserted, substituted and repealed: Education and Inspections Act 2006, s 157, Sch 14, paras 9, 16(1)–(5), Sch 18, Pt 5.[5] Words substituted: SI 2010/1158.[6] Definition and words inserted: SI 2010/1080.[7] Subsections inserted and words substituted: Education Act 2011, s 43(1), (2).[8] Words inserted: SI 2012/976.[9] Words and paragraph inserted: Education Act 2011, s 54(1), Sch 13, para 6(1), (4). **Definitions.** 'Child': s 105(1); 'children's home': s 23; 'independent school': s 105(1); 'local authority': s 105(1); 'proprietor': s 87(10); 'residential care home': s 105(1).

[87A Suspension of duty under section 87(3)

(1) The Secretary of State may appoint a person to be an inspector for the purposes of this section if –

    (a)   that person already acts as an inspector for other purposes in relation to schools or colleges to which section 87(1) applies, and

    (b)   the Secretary of State is satisfied that the person is an appropriate person to determine whether the welfare of children provided with

PART I – Statutes

accommodation by such schools or colleges is adequately safeguarded and promoted while [accommodation for the children is provided]² by them.

(2) Where –

    (a)   the relevant person enters into an agreement in writing with a person appointed under subsection (1),

    (b)   the agreement provides for the person so appointed to have in relation to the school or college the function of determining whether section 87(1) is being complied with, and

    (c)   the appropriate authority receive from the person mentioned in paragraph (b) ('the inspector') notice in writing that the agreement has come into effect,

the authority's duty under section 87(3) in relation to the school or college shall be suspended.

(3) Where the appropriate authority's duty under section 87(3) in relation to any school or college is suspended under this section, it shall cease to be so suspended if the appropriate authority receive –

    (a)   a notice under subsection (4) relating to the inspector, or

    (b)   a notice under subsection (5) relating to the relevant agreement.

(4) The Secretary of State shall terminate a person's appointment under subsection (1) if –

    (a)   that person so requests, or

    (b)   the Secretary of State ceases, in relation to that person, to be satisfied that he is such a person as is mentioned in paragraph (b) of that subsection,

and shall give notice of the termination of that person's appointment to the appropriate authority.

[(4A) The Secretary of State may by regulations specify matters that must be taken into account in deciding whether to appoint a person to be an inspector for the purposes of this section in relation to schools or colleges in England, or to terminate the appointment of such a person under subsection (4)(b).]

(5) Where –

    (a)   the appropriate authority's duty under section 87(3) in relation to any school or college is suspended under this section, and

    (b)   the relevant agreement ceases to have effect,

the inspector shall give to the appropriate authority notice in writing of the fact that it has ceased to have effect.

(6) In this section references to the relevant agreement, in relation to the suspension of the appropriate authority's duty under section 87(3) as regards any school or college, are to the agreement by virtue of which the appropriate authority's duty under that provision as regards that school or college is suspended.]¹

NOTES

Amendments.[1] Section substituted: Care Standards Act 2000, s 106(1).[2] Words substituted and subsection inserted: Education Act s 43(1), (3).

[87B Duties of inspectors under section 87A

(1) The Secretary of State may impose on a person appointed under section 87A(1) ('an authorised inspector') such requirements relating to, or in connection with, the carrying out under substitution agreements of the function mentioned in section 87A(2)(b) as the Secretary of State thinks fit.

(2) Where, in the course of carrying out under a substitution agreement the function mentioned in section 87A(2)(b), it appears to an authorised inspector that there has been a failure to comply with section 87(1) in the case of a child provided with accommodation by the school [or college][2] to which the agreement relates, the inspector shall give notice of that fact –

[(a) in the case of a school other than an independent school[, an alternative provision Academy that is not an independent school][4] or a special school, to the [local authority][3] for the area in which the school is situated;
(b) in the case of a special school which is maintained by a [local authority][3], to that authority;
(c) in any other case, to the Secretary of State.][2]

(3) Where, in the course of carrying out under a substitution agreement the function mentioned in section 87A(2)(b), it appears to an authorised inspector that a child provided with accommodation by the school [or college][2] to which the agreement relates is suffering, or is likely to suffer, significant harm, the inspector shall –

(a) give notice of that fact to the local authority in whose area the school is situated, and
(b) where the inspector is required to make inspection reports to the Secretary of State, supply that local authority with a copy of the latest inspection report to have been made by the inspector to the Secretary of State in relation to the school.

[(4) In this section 'substitution agreement' means an agreement by virtue of which the duty of the appropriate authority under section 87(3) in relation to a school or college is suspended.][2]][1]

NOTES

Amendments.[1] Section inserted: Deregulation and Contracting Out Act 1994, s 38.[2] Subsection substituted and words inserted: Care Standards Act 2000, s 106.[3] Words substituted: SI 2010/1158.[4] Words inserted: SI 2012/976.

[87BA Quality assurance of inspectors under section 87A

(1) The Chief Inspector for England must, at intervals of no more than a year, prepare and send to the Secretary of State a report about inspectors who are appointed under section 87A in relation to schools or colleges in England.

(2) In preparing a report under this section the Chief Inspector for England must have regard to such matters as the Secretary of State may direct.

(3) The Secretary of State may in particular give directions about –

(a)   matters to be taken into account in preparing a report, and

(b)   the form and contents of a report.][1]

NOTES

Amendments.[1] Section inserted: Education Act 2011, s 43(1), (4).

[87C Boarding schools: national minimum standards

(1) The Secretary of State may prepare and publish statements of national minimum standards for safeguarding and promoting the welfare of children for whom accommodation is provided [by][2] a school or college.

(2) The Secretary of State shall keep the standards set out in the statements under review and may publish amended statements whenever he considers it appropriate to do so.

(3) Before issuing a statement, or an amended statement which in the opinion of the Secretary of State effects a substantial change in the standards, the Secretary of State shall consult any persons he considers appropriate.

(4) The standards shall be taken into account –

(a)   in the making by the appropriate authority of any determination under section 87(4) or (4A);

(b)   in the making by a person appointed under section 87A(1) of any determination under section 87B(2); and

(c)   in any proceedings under any other enactment in which it is alleged that the person has failed to comply with section 87(1).][1]

NOTES

Amendments.[1] Section inserted: Care Standards Act 2000, s 107.[2] Word substituted: Education Act 2011, s 43(1), (5).

[87D Annual fee for boarding school inspections

(1) Regulations under subsection (2) may be made in relation to any school or college in respect of which the appropriate authority is required to take steps under section 87(3).

(2) The Secretary of State may by regulations require the relevant person to pay the appropriate authority an annual fee of such amount, and within such time, as the regulations may specify.

(3) A fee payable by virtue of this section may, without prejudice to any other method of recovery, be recovered summarily as a civil debt.][1]

NOTES

Amendments.[1] Section inserted: Care Standards Act 2000, s 108.

Adoption

88

(1) ...[1]

(2) ...²

NOTES

Amendments.¹ Subsection repealed: Adoption and Children Act 2002, s 139(1), (3), Sch 3, paras 54, 67, Sch 5.² Subsection repealed: Adoption and Children (Scotland) Act 2007, s 120(2), Sch 3 (repeal extended to England, Wales and Northern Ireland by Adoption and Children (Scotland) Act 2007 (Consequential Modifications) Order 2011, SI 2011/1740, art 3, Sch 2, Pt 3).

89

...¹

NOTES

Amendments.¹ Section repealed: Child Support, Pensions and Social Security Act 2000, s 85, Sch 9, Part IX.

Criminal care and supervision orders

90 Care and supervision orders in criminal proceedings

(1) The power of a court to make an order under subsection (2) of section 1 of the Children and Young Persons Act 1969 (care proceedings in [youth courts]¹) where it is of the opinion that the condition mentioned in paragraph (f) of that subsection ('the offence condition') is satisfied is hereby abolished.

(2) The powers of the court to make care orders –

    (a)   under section 7(7)(a) of the Children and Young Persons Act 1969 (alteration in treatment of young offenders etc.); and

    (b)   under section 15(1) of that Act, on discharging a supervision order made under section 7(7)(b) of that Act,

are hereby abolished.

(3) The powers given by that Act to include requirements in supervision orders shall have effect subject to amendments made by Schedule 12.

NOTES

Amendments.¹ Words substituted: Criminal Justice Act 1991, s 100, Sch 11, para 40(1), (2)(r).

Effect and duration of orders etc

91 Effect and duration of orders etc

(1) The making of a [child arrangements order with respect to the living arrangements of]⁸ a child who is the subject of a care order discharges the care order.

[(1A) For the purposes of subsection (1), a child arrangements order is one made with respect to the living arrangements of a child if the arrangements regulated by the order consist of, or include, arrangements which relate to either or both of the following –

    (a)   with whom the child is to live, and

    (b)   when the child is to live with any person.]⁸

PART I – Statutes

(2) The making of a care order with respect to a child who is the subject of any section 8 order discharges that order.

[(2A) Where [an][8] activity direction has been made [with respect to][8] a child, the making of a care order with respect to the child discharges the direction.][5]

(3) The making of a care order with respect to a child who is the subject of a supervision order discharges that other order.

(4) The making of a care order with respect to a child who is a ward of court brings that wardship to an end.

(5) The making of a care order with respect to a child who is the subject of a school attendance order made under [section 437 of the Education Act 1996][1] discharges the school attendance order.

[(5A) The making of a special guardianship order with respect to a child who is the subject of –

  (a)   a care order; or
  (b)   an order under section 34,

discharges that order.][2]

(6) Where an emergency protection order is made with respect to a child who is in care, the care order shall have effect subject to the emergency protection order.

(7) Any order made under section 4(1) [4ZA(1),][6] [4A(1)][3] or 5(1) shall continue in force until the child reaches the age of eighteen, unless it is brought to an end earlier.

(8) Any –

  (a)   agreement under section 4[, 4ZA][6] [or 4A][3]; or
  (b)   appointment under section 5(3) or (4),

shall continue in force until the child reaches the age of eighteen, unless it is brought to an end earlier.

(9) An order under Schedule 1 has effect as specified in that Schedule.

(10) A section 8 order [...[8]][7] shall, if it would otherwise still be in force, cease to have effect when the child reaches the age of sixteen, unless it is to have effect beyond that age by virtue of section 9(6) [...[7]][4].

[(10A) Subsection (10) does not apply to provision in a child arrangements order which regulates arrangements relating to –

  (a)   with whom a child is to live, or
  (b)   when a child is to live with any person.][8]

(11) Where a section 8 order has effect with respect to a child who has reached the age of sixteen, it shall, if it would otherwise still be in force, cease to have effect when he reaches the age of eighteen.

(12) Any care order, other than an interim care order, shall continue in force until the child reaches the age of eighteen, unless it is brought to an end earlier.

(13) Any order made under any other provision of this Act in relation to a child shall, if it would otherwise still be in force, cease to have effect when he reaches the age of eighteen.

(14) On disposing of any application for an order under this Act, the court may (whether or not it makes any other order in response to the application) order that no application for an order under this Act of any specified kind may be made with respect to the child concerned by any person named in the order without leave of the court.

(15) Where an application ('the previous application') has been made for –

   (a)   the discharge of a care order;
   (b)   the discharge of a supervision order;
   (c)   the discharge of an education supervision order;
   (d)   the substitution of a supervision order for a care order; or
   (e)   a child assessment order,

no further application of a kind mentioned in paragraphs (a) to (e) may be made with respect to the child concerned, without leave of the court, unless the period between the disposal of the previous application and the making of the further application exceeds six months.

(16) Subsection (15) does not apply to applications made in relation to interim orders.

(17) Where –

   (a)   a person has made an application for an order under section 34;
   (b)   the application has been refused; and
   (c)   a period of less than six months has elapsed since the refusal,

that person may not make a further application for such an order with respect to the same child, unless he has obtained the leave of the court.

NOTES

Amendments.[1] Words substituted: Education Act 1996, s 582(1), Sch 37, Pt I, para 90.[2] Subsection inserted: Adoption and Children Act 2002, s 139(a), (3), Sch 3, paras 54, 68(a).[3] Words inserted: Adoption and Children Act 2002, s 139(a), (3), Sch 3, paras 54, 68(b), (c).[4] Words inserted: Adoption and Children Act 2002, s 114(3).[5] Subsection inserted: Children and Adoption Act 2006, s 15(1), Sch 2, paras 7, 9.[6] References inserted: Human Fertilisation and Embryology Act 2008, s 56, Sch 6, Pt 1, para 29.[7] Words inserted or repealed: Children and Young Persons Act 2008, ss 37(3)(a), 42, Sch 4.[8] Words substituted and omitted and subsections inserted: Children and Families Act 2014, s 12, Sch 2, paras 1, 37.
Definitions. 'A section 8 order': s 8(2); 'care order': ss 31(11), 105(1); 'child': s 105(1); 'child assessment order': s 43(2); 'education supervision order': s 36(2); 'emergency protection order': s 44(4); 'residence order': s 8(1); 'supervision order': s 31(11); 'the court': s 92(7).

Jurisdiction and procedure etc

92 Jurisdiction of courts

(1)–(6) ...[2]

(7) For the purposes of this Act 'the court' means [the High Court or the family court][2].

(8) Subsection (7) is subject to …[2] any express provision as to the jurisdiction of any court made by any other provision of this Act.

(9) …[2]

(10) …[2]

[(10A) …[2]][1]

(11) Part II of Schedule 11 makes amendments consequential on this section.

NOTES

Amendments.[1] Words and subsection inserted: Constitutional Reform Act 2005, s 15(1), Sch 4, Pt 1, paras 203, 205(1)–(4).[2] Words substituted and omitted, and subsections omitted: Crime and Courts Act 2013, s 17, Sch 11, paras 102, 109.
Definitions. 'Family panel': s 92(1); 'family proceedings': s 92(2); 'family proceedings court': s 92(1); 'the court': s 92(7).

93 Rules of Court

(1) An authority having power to make rules of court may make such provision for giving effect to –

(a)   this Act;
(b)   the provisions of any statutory instrument made under this Act; or
(c)   any amendment made by this Act in any other enactment,

as appears to that authority to be necessary or expedient.

(2) The rules may, in particular, make provision –

(a)   with respect to the procedure to be followed in any relevant proceedings (including the manner in which any application is to be made or other proceedings commenced);
(b)   as to the persons entitled to participate in any relevant proceedings, whether as parties to the proceedings or by being given the opportunity to make representations to the court;
[(bb) for children to be separately represented in relevant proceedings,][2]
(c)   with respect to the documents and information to be furnished, and notices to be given, in connection with any relevant proceedings;
(d)   …[3]
(e)   with respect to preliminary hearings;
(f)   …[3]
(g)   …[3]
(h)   enabling the court, in such circumstances as may be prescribed, to proceed on any application even though the respondent has not been given notice of the proceedings;
(i)   …[3]
(j)   …[3]

(3) In subsection (2) –

'notice of proceedings' means a summons or such other notice of proceedings as is required; and 'given', in relation to a summons, means 'served';

'prescribed' means prescribed by the rules; and

'relevant proceedings' means any application made, or proceedings brought, under any of the provisions mentioned in paragraphs (a) to (c) of subsection (1) and any part of such proceedings.

(4) This section and any other power in this Act to make rules of court are not to be taken as in any way limiting any other power of the authority in question to make rules of court.

(5) When making any rules under this section an authority shall be subject to the same requirements as to consultation (if any) as apply when the authority makes rules under its general rule making power.

NOTES

Amendments.[1] Words substituted and inserted: Courts and Legal Services Act 1990, s 116, Sch 16, para 22.[2] Paragraph inserted: Adoption and Children Act 2002, s 122(2).[3] Paragraphs omitted: Crime and Courts Act 2013, s 17, Sch 11, paras 102, 110.

Definitions. 'Notice of proceedings': s 93(3); 'prescribed': s 93(3); 'relevant proceedings': s 93(3); 'the court': s 92(7).

94

...[1]

NOTES

Amendments.[1] Section repealed: Crime and Courts Act 2013, s 17, Sch 11, paras 102, 111.

95 Attendance of child at hearing under Part IV or V

(1) In any proceedings in which a court is hearing an application for an order under Part IV or V, or is considering whether to make any such order, the court may order the child concerned to attend such stage or stages of the proceedings as may be specified in the order.

(2) The power conferred by subsection (1) shall be exercised in accordance with rules of court.

(3) Subsections (4) to (6) apply where –

    (a)   an order under subsection (1) has not been complied with; or

    (b)   the court has reasonable cause to believe that it will not be complied with.

(4) The court may make an order authorising a constable, or such person as may be specified in the order –

    (a)   to take charge of the child and to bring him to the court; and

    (b)   to enter and search any premises specified in the order if he has reasonable cause to believe that the child may be found on the premises.

(5) The court may order any person who is in a position to do so to bring the child to the court.

(6) Where the court has reason to believe that a person has information about the whereabouts of the child it may order him to disclose it to the court.

NOTES
Definitions. 'Child': s 105(1); 'the court': s 92(7).

96 Evidence given by, or with respect to, children

(1) Subsection (2) applies in any civil proceedings where a child who is called as a witness in any civil proceedings does not, in the opinion of the court, understand the nature of an oath.

(2) The child's evidence may be heard by the court if, in its opinion –

  (a)   he understands that it is his duty to speak the truth; and
  (b)   he has sufficient understanding to justify his evidence being heard.

(3) The Lord Chancellor may[, with the concurrence of the Lord Chief Justice,]² by order make provision for the admissibility of evidence which would otherwise be inadmissible under any rule of law relating to hearsay.

(4) An order under subsection (3) may only be made with respect to –

  (a)   civil proceedings in general or such civil proceedings, or class of civil proceedings, as may be prescribed; and
  (b)   evidence in connection with the upbringing, maintenance or welfare of a child.

(5) An order under subsection (3) –

  (a)   may, in particular, provide for the admissibility of statements which are made orally or in a prescribed form or which are recorded by any prescribed method of recording;
  (b)   may make different provision for different purposes and in relation to different descriptions of court; and
  (c)   may make such amendments and repeals in any enactment relating to evidence (other than in this Act) as the Lord Chancellor considers necessary or expedient in consequence of the provision made by the order.

(6) Subsection (5)(b) is without prejudice to section 104(4).

(7) In this section –

  ['civil proceedings' means civil proceedings, before any tribunal, in relation to which the strict rules of evidence apply, whether as a matter of law or by agreement of the parties, and references to 'the court' shall be construed accordingly;]¹ and

  'prescribed' means prescribed by an order under subsection (3).

NOTES
Amendments.¹ Definition substituted: Civil Evidence Act 1995, s 15(1), Sch 1, para 16.² Words inserted: Constitutional Reform Act 2005, s 15(1), Sch 4, Pt 1, paras 203, 207.
Definitions. 'Child': s 105(1); 'civil proceedings': s 96(7); 'court': s 92(7); 'prescribed': s 96(7); 'upbringing': s 105(1).

PART I – Statutes

97 Privacy for children involved in certain proceedings

(1) ...[10]

(2) No person shall publish [to the public at large or any section of the public][5] any material which is intended, or likely, to identify –

(a) any child as being involved in any proceedings before [the High Court][4] or the family court][10] in which any power under this Act [or the Adoption and Children Act 2002][6] may be exercised by the court with respect to that or any other child; or

(b) an address or school as being that of a child involved in any such proceedings.

(3) In any proceedings for an offence under this section it shall be a defence for the accused to prove that he did not know, and had no reason to suspect, that the published material was intended, or likely, to identify the child.

(4) The court or the [Lord Chancellor][3] may, if satisfied that the welfare of the child requires it [and, in the case of the Lord Chancellor, if the Lord Chief Justice agrees][7], by order dispense with the requirements of subsection (2) to such extent as may be specified in the order.

(5) For the purposes of this section –

'publish' includes –
(a) include in a programme service (within the meaning of the Broadcasting Act 1990);][1] or
(b) cause to be published; and

'material' includes any picture or representation.

(6) Any person who contravenes this section shall be guilty of an offence and liable, on summary conviction, to a fine not exceeding level 4 on the standard scale.

[(6A) It is not a contravention of this section to –

(a) enter material in the Adoption and Children Act Register (established under section 125 of the Adoption and Children Act 2002), or

(b) permit persons to search and inspect that register pursuant to regulations made under section 128A of that Act.][9]

(7) ...[10]

(8) ...[10]

[(9) The Lord Chief Justice may nominate a judicial office holder (as defined in section 109(4) of the Constitutional Reform Act 2005) to exercise his functions under subsection (4).][7]

NOTES

Amendments.[1] Words substituted: Broadcasting Act 1990, s 203(1), Sch 20, para 53.[2] Words substituted: Courts and Legal Services Act 1990, s 116, Sch 16, para 24.[3] Words substituted: Transfer of Functions (Magistrates' Courts and Family Law) Order 1992, SI 1992/709.[4] Words inserted: Access to Justice

Act 1999, s 72.[5] Words inserted: Children Act 2004, s 62(1).[6] Words inserted: Adoption and Children Act 2002, s 101(3).[7] Words and subsection inserted: Constitutional Reform Act 2005, s 15(1), Sch 4, Pt 1, paras 203, 208(1)–(3).[8] Words substituted and paragraph omitted: Courts Act 2003, s 109(1), (3), Sch 8, para 337, Sch 10.[9] Subsection inserted: Children and Families Act 2014, s 7(7).[10] Subsections omitted and words substituted: Crime and Courts Act 2013, s 17, Sch 10, para 75.
Definitions. 'Child': s 105(1); 'material': s 97(5); 'publish': s 97(5); 'school': s 105(1); 'the court': s 92(7).

98 Self-incrimination

(1) In any proceedings in which a court is hearing an application for an order under Part IV or V, no person shall be excused from –

(a)   giving evidence on any matter; or

(b)   answering any question put to him in the course of his giving evidence,

on the ground that doing so might incriminate him or his spouse [or civil partner][1] of an offence.

(2) A statement or admission made in such proceedings shall not be admissible in evidence against the person making it or his spouse [or civil partner][1] in proceedings for an offence other than perjury.

NOTES

Amendments.[1] Words inserted: Civil Partnership Act 2004, s 261(1), Sch 27, para 132.

99

... [1]

NOTES

Amendments.[1] Section repealed: Access to Justice Act 1999, s 106, Sch 15, Pt I.

100 Restrictions on use of wardship jurisdiction

(1) Section 7 of the Family Law Reform Act 1969 (which gives the High Court power to place a ward of court in the care, or under the supervision, of a local authority) shall cease to have effect.

(2) No court shall exercise the High Court's inherent jurisdiction with respect to children –

(a)   so as to require a child to be placed in the care, or put under the supervision, of a local authority;

(b)   so as to require a child to be accommodated by or on behalf of a local authority;

(c)   so as to make a child who is the subject of a care order a ward of court; or

(d)   for the purpose of conferring on any local authority power to determine any question which has arisen, or which may arise, in connection with any aspect of parental responsibility for a child.

(3) No application for any exercise of the court's inherent jurisdiction with respect to children may be made by a local authority unless the authority have obtained the leave of the court.

PART I – Statutes

(4) The court may only grant leave if it is satisfied that –

  (a)   the result which the authority wish to achieve could not be achieved through the making of any order of a kind to which subsection (5) applies; and

  (b)   there is reasonable cause to believe that if the court's inherent jurisdiction is not exercised with respect to the child he is likely to suffer significant harm.

(5) This subsection applies to any order –

  (a)   made otherwise than in the exercise of the court's inherent jurisdiction; and

  (b)   which the local authority is entitled to apply for (assuming, in the case of any application which may only be made with leave, that leave is granted).

NOTES

Definitions. 'Care order': ss 31(11), 105(1); 'child': s 105(1); 'harm': s 31(9); 'local authority': s 105(1); 'parental responsibility': s 3; 'significant harm': s 31(10); 'the court': s 92(7).

101 Effect of orders as between England and Wales and Northern Ireland, the Channel Islands or the Isle of Man

(1) The Secretary of State may make regulations providing –

  (a)   for prescribed orders which –

    (i)   are made by a court in Northern Ireland; and

    (ii)   appear to the Secretary of State to correspond in their effect to orders which may be made under any provision of this Act,

to have effect in prescribed circumstances, for prescribed purposes of this Act, as if they were orders of a prescribed kind made under this Act;

  (b)   for prescribed orders which –

    (i)   are made by a court in England and Wales; and

    (ii)   appear to the Secretary of State to correspond in their effect to orders which may be made under any provision in force in Northern Ireland,

to have effect in prescribed circumstances, for prescribed purposes of the law of Northern Ireland, as if they were orders of a prescribed kind made in Northern Ireland.

(2) Regulations under subsection (1) may provide for the order concerned to cease to have effect for the purposes of the law of Northern Ireland, or (as the case may be) the law of England and Wales, if prescribed conditions are satisfied.

(3) The Secretary of State may make regulations providing for prescribed orders which –

  (a)   are made by a court in the Isle of Man or in any of the Channel Islands; and

  (b)   appear to the Secretary of State to correspond in their effect to orders which may be made under this Act, to have effect in prescribed circumstances for prescribed purposes of this Act, as if they were orders of a prescribed kind made under this Act.

(4) Where a child who is in the care of a local authority is lawfully taken to live in Northern Ireland, the Isle of Man or in any of the Channel Islands, the care order in question shall cease to have effect if the conditions prescribed in regulations by the Secretary of State are satisfied.

(5) Any regulations made under this section may –

   (a)   make such consequential amendments (including repeals) in –
       (i)   section 25 of the Children and Young Persons Act 1969 (transfers between England and Wales and Northern Ireland); or
       (ii) section 26 (transfers between England and Wales and Channel Islands or Isle of Man) of that Act,
       as the Secretary of State considers necessary or expedient; and
   (b)   modify any provision of this Act, in its application (by virtue of the regulations) in relation to an order made otherwise than in England and Wales.

NOTES

Definitions. 'Care order': ss 31(11), 105(1); 'child': s 105(1); 'local authority': s 105(1); 'prescribed': s 105(1); 'the court': s 92(7).

Search warrants

102 Power of constable to assist in exercise of certain powers to search for children or inspect premises

(1) Where, on an application made by any person for a warrant under this section, it appears to the court –

   (a)   that a person attempting to exercise powers under any enactment mentioned in subsection (6) has been prevented from doing so by being refused entry to the premises concerned or refused access to the child concerned; or
   (b)   that any such person is likely to be so prevented from exercising any such powers,

it may issue a warrant authorising any constable to assist that person in the exercise of those powers, using reasonable force if necessary.

(2) Every warrant issued under this section shall be addressed to, and executed by, a constable who shall be accompanied by the person applying for the warrant if –

   (a)   that person so desires; and
   (b)   the court by whom the warrant is issued does not direct otherwise.

(3) A court granting an application for a warrant under this section may direct that the constable concerned may, in executing the warrant, be accompanied by a registered medical practitioner, registered nurse or [registered midwife][1] if he so chooses.

[(3A) The reference in subsection (3) to a registered midwife is to such a midwife who is also registered in the Specialist Community Public Health Nurses' Part of the register maintained under article 5 of the Nursing and Midwifery Order 2001.][2]

(4) An application for a warrant under this section shall be made in the manner and form prescribed by rules of court.

(5) Where –

  (a) an application for a warrant under this section relates to a particular child; and

  (b) it is reasonably practicable to do so,

the application and any warrant granted on the application shall name the child; and where it does not name him it shall describe him as clearly as possible.

(6) The enactments are –

  (a) sections 62, 64, 67, 76, 80, 86 and 87;

  (b) paragraph 8(1)(b) and (2)(b) of Schedule 3;

  (c) ...[3]

NOTES

Amendments.[1] Words substituted: SI 2002/253.[2] Subsection inserted: SI 2004/1771.[3] Paragraph repealed: Adoption and Children Act 2002, s 139(1), (3), Sch 3, paras 54, 69, Sch 5.
Definitions. 'Child': s 105(1); 'the court': s 92(7).

General

103 Offences by bodies corporate

(1) This section applies where any offence under this Act is committed by a body corporate.

(2) If the offence is proved to have been committed with the consent or connivance of or to be attributable to any neglect on the part of any director, manager, secretary or other similar officer of the body corporate, or any person who was purporting to act in any such capacity, he (as well as the body corporate) shall be guilty of the offence and shall be liable to be proceeded against and punished accordingly.

104 Regulations and orders

(1) Any power of the Lord Chancellor[, the Treasury][2][, the Secretary of State or the National Assembly for Wales][4] under this Act to make an order, regulations, or rules, except an order under section ...[1] 56(4)(a), 57(3), 84 or 97(4) or paragraph 1(1) of Schedule 4, shall be exercisable by statutory instrument.

(2) Any such statutory instrument, except one made under section [4(1)(b),][3] [4ZA(3),][6] 17(4), 107 or 108(2) [or one containing regulations which fall within subsection [(3AA),][13] [(3AB),][14] (3B)[, (3BA)][12] or (3C)][7], shall be subject to annulment in pursuance of a resolution of either House of Parliament.

[(2A) ...[8]][5]

[(3A) An order under section 4(1B)[, 4ZA(3)][11] or 17(4) or regulations which fall within subsection [(3AA),][13] [(3AB),][14] (3B)[, (3BA)][12][, (3BB)][15] or (3C) shall not be made by the Secretary of State unless a draft of the statutory instrument containing the order or regulations has been laid before, and approved by a resolution of, each House of Parliament.

[(3AA) Regulations fall within this subsection if they are regulations made in the exercise of the power conferred by section 17ZB(9).][13]

[(3AB) Regulations fall within this subsection if they are regulations made in the exercise of the power conferred by section 17ZE(5).][14]

(3B) Regulations fall within this subsection if they are the first regulations to be made by the Secretary of State in the exercise of the power conferred by section 23C(5B)(b).

[(3BA) Regulations fall within this subsection if they are regulations made in the exercise of the power conferred by section 31(3C) or 32(9).][12]

[(3BB) Regulations fall within this subsection if they are regulations made in the exercise of the power conferred by paragraph 3B(4) of Schedule A1.][15]

(3C) Regulations fall within this subsection if they are the first regulations to be made by the Secretary of State in the exercise of the power conferred by paragraph 6(2) of Schedule 2.][9]

(4) Any statutory instrument made under this Act may –

    (a)   make different provision for different cases;
    (b)   provide for exemptions from any of its provisions; and
    (c)   contain …[10] incidental, supplemental and transitional provisions …[10].

NOTES

Amendments.[1] Word repealed: Care Standards Act 2000, s 117, Sch 6.[2] Words inserted: Tax Credits Act 2002, s 47, Sch 3.[3] Words inserted: Adoption and Children Act 2002, s 111(6).[4] Words substituted: Children and Adoption Act 2006, s 15(1), Sch 2, paras 7, 10(a).[5] Subsection inserted: Children and Adoption Act 2006, s 15(1), Sch 2, paras 7, 10(b).[6] Reference inserted: Human Fertilisation and Embryology Act 2008, s 56, Sch 6, Pt 1, para 30(a).[7] Words inserted: Children and Young Persons Act 2008, s 39, Sch 3, paras 1, 25(1), (2).[8] Subsection repealed: Children and Young Persons Act 2008, ss 39, 42, Sch 3, paras 1, 25(1), (3), Sch 4.[9] Subsections substituted: Children and Young Persons Act 2008, s 39, Sch 3, paras 1, 25(1), (4).[10] Words repealed: Children and Young Persons Act 2008, ss 39, 42, Sch 3, paras 1, 25(1), (5), Sch 4.[11] Reference inserted: SI 2009/1892.[12] Words and subsection inserted: Children and Families Act 2014, s 16(1).[13] Subsection numbers and subsection inserted: Children and Families Act 2014, s 96(2).[14] Subsection numbers and subsection inserted: Children and Families Act 2014, s 97(2).[15] Words and subsection inserted: Sentencing Act 2020, s 410, Sch 24, para 110.

[104A   Regulations made by the Welsh Ministers under section 31A or Part 7

(1) Any power of the Welsh Ministers under section 31A or Part 7 to make regulations shall be exercisable by statutory instrument.

(2) Any such statutory instrument shall be subject to annulment in pursuance of a resolution of the National Assembly for Wales.][1, 2]

NOTES

Amendments.[1] Section inserted: Children and Young Persons Act 2008, s 39, Sch 3, paras 1, 26.[2] Section substituted: SI 2016/413, regs 55, 105.

105 Interpretation

(1) In this Act –

['activity condition' has the meaning given by section 11C;
'activity direction' has the meaning given by section 11A;][32]
'adoption agency' means a body which may be referred to as an adoption agency by virtue of [section 2 of the Adoption and Children Act 2002][16];
[...][12, 29]
'bank holiday' means a day which is a bank holiday under the Banking and Financial Dealings Act 1971;
[['care home' –

    (a)   has the same meaning as in the Care Standards Act 2000 in respect of a care home in England; and

    (b)   means a place in Wales at which a care home service within the meaning of Part 1 of the Regulation and Inspection of Social Care (Wales) Act 2016 is provided wholly or mainly to persons aged 18 or over;][34]][12]

'care order' has the meaning given by section 31(11) and also includes any order which by or under any enactment has the effect of, or is deemed to be, a care order for the purposes of this Act; and any reference to a child who is in the care of an authority is a reference to a child who is in their care by virtue of a care order;
'child' means, subject to paragraph 16 of Schedule 1, a person under the age of eighteen;
['child arrangements order' has the meaning given by section 8(1);][32]
'child assessment order' has the meaning given by section 43(2);
'child minder' has the meaning given by section 71;
['child of the family', in relation to parties to a marriage, or to two people who are civil partners of each other, means –

    (a)   a child of both of them, and

    (b)   any other child, other than a child placed with them as foster parents by a local authority or voluntary organisation, who has been treated by both of them as a child of their family;][19]

[['children's home'–

    (a)   has the same meaning as it has for the purposes of the Care Standards Act 2000 in respect of a children's home in England (see section 1 of that Act); and

    [(b)   means a place in Wales at which –

        (i)   a care home service is provided wholly or mainly to children, or

        (ii)   a secure accommodation service is provided,

and in this paragraph 'care home service' and 'secure accommodation service' have the meaning given in Part 1 of the Regulation and Inspection of Social Care (Wales) Act 2016 (anaw 2);][35]][34]][29]

['clinical commissioning group' means a body established under section 14D of the National Health Service Act 2006;][31]
'community home' has the meaning given by section 53;
[...][32]

...[32]][22]

...[32]

'day care' [(*except in Part XA*)][11, 30] has the same meaning as in section 18;
'disabled', in relation to a child, has the same meaning as in section 17(11);
...[3]
'domestic premises' has the meaning given by section 71(12);
['dwelling-house' includes –
  (a)   any building or part of a building which is occupied as a dwelling;
  (b)   any caravan, house-boat or structure which is occupied as a dwelling; and any yard, garage or outhouse belonging to it and occupied with it;][6]

['education functions' has the meaning given by section 579(1) of the Education Act 1996;][27]
'education supervision order' has the meaning given in section 36;
'emergency protection order' means an order under section 44;
['enforcement order' has the meaning given by section 11J;][22]
'family assistance order' has the meaning given in section 16(2);
'family proceedings' has the meaning given by section 8(3);
'functions' includes powers and duties;
'guardian of a child' means a guardian (other than a guardian of the estate of a child) appointed in accordance with the provisions of section 5;
'harm' has the same meaning as in section 31(9) and the question of whether harm is significant shall be determined in accordance with section 31(10);
[...[20]][3]
'health service hospital' [means a health service hospital within the meaning given by the National Health Service Act 2006 or the National Health Service (Wales) Act 2006][20];
'hospital' [(*except in Schedule 9A*)][12, 30] has the same meaning as in the Mental Health Act 1983, except that it does not include a [hospital at which high security psychiatric services within the meaning of that Act are provided][7];
'ill-treatment' has the same meaning as in section 31(9);
['income-based jobseeker's allowance' has the same meaning as in the Jobseekers Act 1995;][4]
['income-related employment and support allowance' means an income-related allowance under Part 1 of the Welfare Reform Act 2007 (employment and support allowance);][23]
['independent hospital' –
  (a)   in relation to England, means a hospital as defined by section 275 of the National Health Service Act 2006 that is not a health service hospital as defined by that section; and
  (b)   in relation to Wales, has the same meaning as in the Care Standards Act 2000;][28]

'independent school' has the same meaning as in [the Education Act 1996][5];
'local authority' means, in relation to England ...[2], the council of a county, a metropolitan district, a London Borough or the Common Council of the City of London [, in relation to Wales, the council of a county or a county borough][2] and, in relation to Scotland, a local authority within the meaning of section 1(2) of the Social Work (Scotland) Act 1968;

['local authority foster parent' means a person authorised as such in accordance with regulations made by virtue of –
  (a)   paragraph 12F of Schedule 2; or
  (b)   sections 87 and 93 of the Social Services and Well-being (Wales) Act 2014 (regulations providing for approval of local authority foster parents);][33]

['Local Health Board' means a Local Health Board established under section 11 of the National Health Service (Wales) Act 2006;][21]
... [27]

'local housing authority' has the same meaning as in the Housing Act 1985;
... [12]

['officer of the Service' has the same meaning as in the Criminal Justice and Court Services Act 2000;][9]

'parental responsibility' has the meaning given in section 3;

'parental responsibility agreement' has the meaning given in [sections 4(1)[, 4ZA(4)][24] and 4A(2)][16];

'prescribed' means prescribed by regulations made under this Act;

['private children's home' means a children's home in respect of which a person is registered under Part II of the Care Standards Act 2000 [or Part 1 of the Regulation and Inspection of Social Care (Wales) Act 2016][34] which is not a community home or a voluntary home;][12]

['...[31]][20];][7]

'privately fostered child' and 'to foster a child privately' have the same meaning as in section 66;

'prohibited steps order' has the meaning given by section 8(1);
... [18]
... [12]

'registered pupil' has the same meaning as in [the Education Act 1996][5];

'relative', in relation to a child, means a grandparent, brother, sister, uncle or aunt (whether of the full blood or half blood or [by marriage or civil partnership)][19] or step-parent;
... [32]
... [12]

'responsible person', in relation to a child who is the subject of a supervision order, has the meaning given in paragraph 1 of Schedule 3;

'school' has the same meaning as in [the Education Act 1996][5] or, in relation to Scotland, in the Education (Scotland) Act 1980;

['section 31A plan' has the meaning given by section 31A(6);][17]

'service', in relation to any provision made under Part III, includes any facility;

'signed', in relation to any person, includes the making by that person of his mark;

'special educational needs' has the same meaning as in [the Education Act 1993][5];

['special guardian' and 'special guardianship order' have the meaning given by section 14A;][17]

['Special Health Authority' means a Special Health Authority established under [section 28 of the National Health Service Act 2006 or section 22 of the National Health Service (Wales) Act 2006,][20];][3]

'specific issue order' has the meaning given by section 8(1);

PART I – Statutes

...[31][20],][13]
'supervision order' has the meaning given by section 31(11);
'supervised child' and 'supervisor', in relation to a supervision order or an education supervision order, mean respectively the child who is (or is to be) under supervision and the person under whose supervision he is (or is to be) by virtue of the order;
'upbringing', in relation to any child, includes the care of the child but not his maintenance;
'voluntary home' has the meaning given by section 60;
'voluntary organisation' means a body (other than a public or local authority) whose activities are not carried on for profit.
['Welsh family proceedings officer' has the meaning given by section 35 of the Children Act 2004][15].

(2) References in this Act to a child whose father and mother were, or (as the case may be) were not, married to[, or civil partners of,][36] each other at the time of his birth must be read with section 1 of the Family Law Reform Act 1987 (which extends the meaning of such references).

(3) ...[32]

[(4) References in this Act to a child who is looked after –

(a) in relation to a child who is looked after by a local authority in England, has the meaning given in section 22; and

(b) in relation to a child who is looked after by a local authority in Wales, has the meaning given in section 74 of the Social Services and Well-being (Wales) Act 2014 (child or young person looked after by a local authority).][33]

(5) References in this Act to accommodation provided by or on behalf of a local authority are references to accommodation so provided in the exercise of functions [of that or any other local authority which are social services functions...[33]][10] ...[33].

[(5A) References in this Act to a child minder shall be construed –

(a) ...[14]

(b) in relation to ...[25] Wales, in accordance with section 79A.][11, 30]

[(5B) In subsection (5) 'social services functions' means –

(a) in England, social services functions within the meaning of the Local Authority Social Services Act 1970, and

(b) in Wales, social services functions within the meaning of the Social Services and Well-being (Wales) Act 2014.][33]

(6) In determining the 'ordinary residence' of a child for any purpose of this Act, there shall be disregarded any period in which he lives in any place –

(a) which is a school or other institution;

(b) in accordance with the requirements of a supervision order under this Act ...[26]

[(ba) in accordance with the requirements of a youth rehabilitation order under [Chapter 1 of Part 9 of the Sentencing Code][37]; or][26]

(c) while he is being provided with accommodation by or on behalf of a local authority.

(7) References in this Act to children who are in need shall be construed in accordance with section 17.

[(7A) References in this Act to a hospital or accommodation made available or provided pursuant to arrangements made by the Secretary of State under the National Health Service Act 2006 are references to a hospital or accommodation made available or provided pursuant to arrangements so made in the exercise of the public health functions of the Secretary of State (within the meaning of that Act).

(7B) References in this Act to arrangements made by the National Health Service Commissioning Board or a clinical commissioning group under the National Health Service Act 2006 include references to arrangements so made by virtue of section 7A of that Act.][31](8) Any notice or other document required under this Act to be served on any person may be served on him by being delivered personally to him, or being sent by post to him in a registered letter or by the recorded delivery service at his proper address.

(9) Any such notice or other document required to be served on a body corporate or a firm shall be duly served if it is served on the secretary or clerk of that body or a partner of that firm.

(10) For the purposes of this section, and of section 7 of the Interpretation Act 1978 in its application to this section, the proper address of a person –

(a) in the case of a secretary or clerk of a body corporate, shall be that of the registered or principal office of that body;

(b) in the case of a partner of a firm, shall be that of the principal office of the firm; and

(c) in any other case, shall be the last known address of the person to be served.

NOTES

Amendments.[1] Words inserted: Registered Homes (Amendment) Act 1991, s 2(6).[2] Words repealed or inserted: Local Government (Wales) Act 1994, Sch 10, para 13, Sch 18.[3] Definitions repealed or substituted: Health Authorities Act 1995, ss 2(1), 5(1), Sch 1, Pt III, para 118(1), (10).[4] Definition inserted: Jobseekers Act 1995, s 41(4), Sch 2, para 19.[5] Words substituted: Education Act 1996, s 582(1), Sch 37, Pt I, para 91.[6] Definition inserted: Family Law Act 1996, s 52, Sch 6, para 5.[7] Definitions inserted or amended: Health Act 1999 (Supplementary, Consequential etc Provisions) Order 2000, SI 2000/90.[8] Words substituted: Powers of Criminal Courts (Sentencing) Act 2000, s 165(1), Sch 9, para 128.[9] Definition inserted: Criminal Justice and Court Services Act 2000, s 74, Sch 7, paras 87, 95.[10] Words substituted: Local Government Act 2000, s 107, Sch 5, para 22.[11] Definition amended and subsection inserted: Care Standards Act 2000, s 116, Sch 4, para 14(1), 23.[12] Definitions and words repealed, definition inserted: Care Standards Act 2000, s 116, Sch 4, para 14(23).[13] Definition inserted: National Health Service Reform and Health Care Professions Act 2002 (Supplementary, Consequential etc Provisions) Regulations 2002, SI 2002/2469.[14] Paragraph repealed and subsection inserted: Regulation of Care (Scotland) Act 2001, s 79, Sch 3, para 15.[15] Definition inserted: Children Act 2004, s 40, Sch 3, paras 5, 11.[16] Words substituted: Adoption and Children Act 2002, s 139(1), Sch 3, paras 54, 70(a),(c).[17] Definition inserted: Adoption and Children Act 2002, s 139(1), Sch 3, paras 54, 70(b), (e).[18] Definition repealed: Adoption and Children Act 2002, s 139(1), Sch 3, paras 54, 70(d).[19] Definition and words substituted: Civil Partnership Act 2004, s 75(1), (3), (4).[20] Words repealed and substituted: National Health Service (Consequential Provisions)

Act 2006, s 2, Sch 1, paras 124, 125.[21] Definition inserted: SI 2007/961.[22] Definitions inserted: Children and Adoption Act 2006, s 15(1), Sch 2, paras 7, 11.[23] Definition inserted: Welfare Reform Act 2007, s 28(1), Sch 3, para 6(1), (5).[24] Reference inserted: Human Fertilisation and Embryology Act 2008, s 56, Sch 6, Pt 1, para 31.[25] Words repealed: Childcare Act 2006, s 103, Sch 2, para 17, Sch 3, Pt 2.[26] Words repealed and paragraph inserted: Criminal Justice and Immigration Act 2008, ss 6(2), 149, Sch 4, Pt 1, paras 33, 36, Sch 28, Pt 1.[27] Definitions inserted and repealed: SI 2010/1158.[28] Definition 'independent hospital' substituted: SI 2010/813.[29] Definition 'appropriate children's home' repealed and definition 'children's home' substituted: Children and Young Persons Act 2008, ss 8(2), 42, Sch 1, para 3, Sch 4.[30] Words in italics omitted and subsection (5A) omitted in relation to Wales: Children and Families (Wales) Measure 2010, ss 72, 73, Sch 1, paras 5, 7, Sch 2.[31] Subsections inserted and definitions inserted and omitted: Health and Social Care Act 2012, s 55(2), Sch 5, Pt 1, paras 47, 56.[32] Definitions inserted and omitted and subsection omitted: Children and Families Act 2014, s 12, Sch 2, paras 1, 38.[33] Definition substituted, subsections substituted and inserted, words omitted: SI 2016/413, regs 55, 106.[34] Definitions substituted and words inserted: Regulation and Inspection of Social Care (Wales) Act 2016 (Consequential Amendments) Regulations 2018, SI 2018/195, regs 8, 12.[35] Paragraph substituted: SI 2019/772, regs 2, 5.[36] Words inserted: SI 2019/1458, reg 15(1), (4).[37] Words substituted: Sentencing Act 2020, s 410, Sch 24, para 111.

106 Financial provisions

(1) Any –

- (a)   grants made by the Secretary of State under this Act; and
- (b)   any other expenses incurred by the Secretary of State under this Act,

shall be payable out of money provided by Parliament.

(2) Any sums received by the Secretary of State under section 58, or by way of the repayment of any grant made under section 82(2) or (4) shall be paid into the Consolidated Fund.

107 Application to the Channel Islands

Her Majesty may by Order in Council direct that any of the provisions of this Act shall extend to any of the Channel Islands with such exceptions and modifications as may be specified in the Order.

108 Short title, commencement, extent, etc

(1) This Act may be cited as the Children Act 1989.

(2) Sections 89 and 96(3) to (7), and paragraph 35 of Schedule 12, shall come into force on the passing of this Act and paragraph 36 of Schedule 12 shall come into force at the end of the period of two months beginning with the day on which this Act is passed but otherwise this Act shall come into force on such date as may be appointed by order made by the Lord Chancellor or the Secretary of State, or by both acting jointly.

(3) Different dates may be appointed for different provisions of this Act in relation to different cases.

(4) The minor amendments set out in Schedule 12 shall have effect.

(5) The consequential amendments set out in Schedule 13 shall have effect.

(6) The transitional provisions and savings set out in Schedule 14 shall have effect.

(7) The repeals set out in Schedule 15 shall have effect.

(8) An order under subsection (2) may make such transitional provisions or savings as appear to the person making the order to be necessary or expedient in connection with the provisions brought into force by the order, including –

(a) provisions adding to or modifying the provisions of Schedule 14; and
(b) such adaptations –
   (i) of the provisions brought into force by the order; and
   (ii) of any provisions of this Act then in force,
   as appear to him necessary or expedient in consequence of the partial operation of this Act.

(9) The Lord Chancellor may by order make such amendments or repeals, in such enactments as may be specified in the order, as appear to him to be necessary or expedient in consequence of any provision of this Act.

(10) This Act shall, in its application to the Isles of Scilly, have effect subject to such exceptions, adaptations and modifications as the Secretary of State may by order prescribe.

(11) The following provisions of this Act extend to Scotland –

. . .²
section 25(8);
section 50(13)
. . .²
section 88;
section 104 (so far as necessary);
section 105 (so far as necessary);
subsections (1) to (3), (8) and (9) and this subsection;
in Schedule 2, paragraph 24;
in Schedule 12, paragraphs 1, 7 to 10, 18, 27, 30(a) and 41 to 44;
in Schedule 13, paragraphs 18 to 23, 32, 46, 47, 50, 57, 62, 63, 68(a) and (b) and 71;
in Schedule 14, paragraphs 1, 33 and 34;
in Schedule 15, the entries relating to –
   (a) the Custody of Children Act 1891;
   (b) the Nurseries and Child Minders Regulation Act 1948;
   (c) section 53(3) of the Children and Young Persons Act 1963;
   (d) section 60 of the Health Services and Public Health Act 1968;
   (e) the Social Work (Scotland) Act 1968;
   (f) the Adoption (Scotland) Act 1978;
   (g) the Child Care Act 1980;
   (h) the Foster Children (Scotland) Act 1984;
   (i) the Child Abduction and Custody Act 1985; and
   (j) the Family Law Act 1986.

(12) The following provisions of this Act extend to Northern Ireland –

section 101(1)(b), (2) and (5)(a)(i);
subsections (1) to (3), (8) and (9) and this subsection;

in Schedule 2, paragraph 24;

in Schedule 12, paragraphs 7 to 10, 18 and 27;

in Schedule 13, paragraphs 21, 22, 46, 47, 57, 62, 63, 68(c) to (e) and 69 to 71;

in Schedule 14, paragraphs ...[1] 28 to 30 and 38(a); and

in Schedule 15, the entries relating to the Guardianship of Minors Act 1971, the Children Act 1975, the Child Care Act 1980, and the Family Law Act 1986.

NOTES

Amendments.[1] Word repealed: Courts and Legal Services Act 1990, ss 116, 125(7), Sch 16, para 25, Sch 20.[2] Words repealed: Regulation of Care (Scotland) Act 2001, s 80(1), Sch 4.

[SCHEDULE A1
ENFORCEMENT ORDERS

[PART 1:
UNPAID WORK REQUIREMENT

1 The responsible officer etc

(1) For the purposes of this Part of this Schedule –

'the responsible officer', in relation to a relevant person, means the person who is for the time being responsible for discharging the functions conferred by this Part of this Schedule on the responsible officer in accordance with arrangements made by the Secretary of State;

'relevant person', in relation to an enforcement order, means a person subject to the order.

(2) The responsible officer must be an officer of a provider of probation services.

2 Obligations of responsible officer

(1) This paragraph applies where an enforcement order is in force.

(2) The responsible officer must –

(a)   make any arrangements that are necessary in connection with the requirements imposed by the order, and

(b)   promote the relevant person's compliance with those requirements.

(3) Sub-paragraph (4) applies where –

(a)   an enforcement order is in force, and

(b)   an officer of the Children and Family Court Advisory and Support Service or a Welsh family proceedings officer (as defined in section 35 of the Children Act 2004) is required under section 11M to report on matters relating to the order.

(4) The officer of the Service or the Welsh family proceedings officer ('the family officer') may request the responsible officer to report to the family officer on such matters relating to the order as the family officer may require for the purpose of

making a report under section 11M(1)(c) or (d); and it shall be the duty of the responsible officer to comply with such a request.

3 Enforcement order to specify relevant person's home local justice area

(1) An enforcement order must specify which local justice area is the relevant person's home local justice area.

(2) The area specified must be the local justice area in which the relevant person resides or will reside.

3A Requirement and obligation of relevant person

(1) In this Part of this Schedule 'unpaid work requirement', in relation to an enforcement order, means a requirement that the relevant person must perform unpaid work in accordance with the instructions of the responsible officer as to –

(a) the work to be performed, and
(b) the times, during a period of 12 months, at which the person is to perform it.

(2) Sub-paragraph (1)(b) is subject to paragraphs 7 and 9.

(3) But the period of 12 months is not to run while the enforcement order is suspended under section 11J(9).

3B Number of hours of unpaid work to be specified in order

(1) The number of hours which a person may be required to work under an unpaid work requirement –

(a) must be specified in the relevant order, and
(b) must, in aggregate, be –
    (i)   not less than 40, and
    (ii) not more than 200.

(2) Sub-paragraph (3) applies where on the same occasion and in relation to the same person the court makes more than one enforcement order imposing an unpaid work requirement.

(3) The court may direct that the hours of work specified in any of those requirements is to be –

(a) concurrent with, or
(b) additional to,

those specified in any other of those orders.

But the total number of hours which are not concurrent must not exceed the maximum number (see sub-paragraph (1)(b)(ii)).

(4) The Secretary of State may by regulations substitute the maximum number of hours for the time being specified in sub-paragraph (1)(b).

3C Duty to keep in touch with responsible officer

(1) This paragraph applies where an enforcement order is in force.

(2) The relevant person –

    (a)   must keep in touch with the responsible officer in accordance with any instructions the responsible officer may give the relevant person from time to time, and

    (b)   must notify the responsible officer of any change of address.

(3) An obligation imposed by sub-paragraph (2) is enforceable as if it were a requirement of the enforcement order.

3D Rules relating to enforcement orders

The power of the Secretary of State to make rules under section 394 of the Sentencing Code in relation to persons subject to community orders or suspended sentence orders may also be exercised in relation to persons subject to enforcement orders.]²]¹

NOTES

Amendments.¹ Schedule inserted: Children and Adoption Act 2006, s 4(2), Sch 1 (SI 2008/2870, art 2(2)(b)).² Part substituted: Sentencing Act 2020, s 410, Sch 24, para 112(1), (2).

PART 2
REVOCATION, AMENDMENT OR BREACH OF ENFORCEMENT ORDER

Power to revoke

4. (1) This paragraph applies where a court has made an enforcement order in respect of a person's failure to comply with a [provision of a child arrangements]² order and the enforcement order is in force.

(2) The court may revoke the enforcement order if it appears to the court that –

    (a)   in all the circumstances no enforcement order should have been made,

    (b)   having regard to circumstances which have arisen since the enforcement order was made, it would be appropriate for the enforcement order to be revoked, or

    (c)   having regard to the person's satisfactory compliance with the [child arrangements]² order or any [child arrangements]² order that has effect in its place, it would be appropriate for the enforcement order to be revoked.

(3) The enforcement order may be revoked by the court under sub-paragraph (2) of its own motion or on an application by the person subject to the enforcement order.

(4) In deciding whether to revoke the enforcement order under sub-paragraph (2)(b), the court is to take into account –

(a)   the extent to which the person subject to the enforcement order has complied with it, and

(b)   the likelihood that the person will comply with the [child arrangements]² order or any [child arrangements]² order that has effect in its place in the absence of an enforcement order.

(5) In deciding whether to revoke the enforcement order under sub-paragraph (2)(c), the court is to take into account the likelihood that the person will comply with the [child arrangements]² order or any [child arrangements]² order that has effect in its place in the absence of an enforcement order.

NOTES

Amendments.¹ Schedule inserted: Children and Adoption Act 2006, s 4(2), Sch 1.² Words substituted: Children and Families Act 2014, s 12, Sch 2, paras 1, 39.

Amendment by reason of change of residence

5. (1) This paragraph applies where a court has made an enforcement order in respect of a person's failure to comply with a [provision of a child arrangements]² order and the enforcement order is in force.

(2) If the court is satisfied that the person has changed, or proposes to change, his residence from the local justice area specified in the order to another local justice area, the court may amend the order by substituting the other area for the area specified.

(3) The enforcement order may be amended by the court under sub-paragraph (2) of its own motion or on an application by the person subject to the enforcement order.

NOTES

Amendments.¹ Schedule inserted: Children and Adoption Act 2006, s 4(2), Sch 1.² Words substituted: Children and Families Act 2014, s 12, Sch 2, paras 1, 39.

Amendment of hours specified under unpaid work requirement

6. (1) This paragraph applies where a court has made an enforcement order in respect of a person's failure to comply with a [provision of a child arrangements]² order and the enforcement order is in force.

(2) If it appears to the court that, having regard to circumstances that have arisen since the enforcement order was made, it would be appropriate to do so, the court may reduce the number of hours specified in the order (but not below the minimum specified in [paragraph 3B(1)(b)(i)]³).

(3) In amending the enforcement order under sub-paragraph (2), the court must be satisfied that the effect on the person of the enforcement order as proposed to be amended is no more than is required to secure his compliance with the [child arrangements]² order or any [child arrangements]² order that has effect in its place.

(4) The enforcement order may be amended by the court under sub-paragraph (2) of its own motion or on an application by the person subject to the enforcement order.

NOTES
Amendments.[1] Schedule inserted: Children and Adoption Act 2006, s 4(2), Sch 1.[2] Words substituted: Children and Families Act 2014, s 12, Sch 2, paras 1, 39.[3] Words substituted: Sentencing Act 2020, s 410, Sch 24, para 112(1), (3).

Amendment to extend unpaid work requirement

7. (1) This paragraph applies where a court has made an enforcement order in respect of a person's failure to comply with a [provision of a child arrangements][2] order and the enforcement order is in force.

(2) If it appears to the court that, having regard to circumstances that have arisen since the enforcement order was made, it would be appropriate to do so, the court may, in relation to the order, extend the period of twelve months specified in [paragraph 3A(1)(b)][3].

(3) The period may be extended by the court under sub-paragraph (2) of its own motion or on an application by the person subject to the enforcement order.

NOTES
Amendments.[1] Schedule inserted: Children and Adoption Act 2006, s 4(2), Sch 1.[2] Words substituted: Children and Families Act 2014, s 12, Sch 2, paras 1, 39.[3] Words substituted: Sentencing Act 2020, s 410, Sch 24, para 112(1), (4).

Warning and report following breach

8. (1) This paragraph applies where a court has made an enforcement order in respect of a person's failure to comply with a [provision of a child arrangements][2] order.

(2) If the responsible officer is of the opinion that the person has failed without reasonable excuse to comply with the unpaid work requirement imposed by the enforcement order, the officer must give the person a warning under this paragraph unless –

    (a)   the person has within the previous twelve months been given a warning under this paragraph in relation to a failure to comply with the unpaid work requirement, or

    (b)   the responsible officer reports the failure to the appropriate person.

(3) A warning under this paragraph must –

    (a)   describe the circumstances of the failure,

    (b)   state that the failure is unacceptable, and

    (c)   inform the person that, if within the next twelve months he again fails to comply with the unpaid work requirement, the warning and the subsequent failure will be reported to the appropriate person.

(4) The responsible officer must, as soon as practicable after the warning has been given, record that fact.

(5) If –

    (a)   the responsible officer has given a warning under this paragraph to a person subject to an enforcement order, and

(b)   at any time within the twelve months beginning with the date on which the warning was given, the responsible officer is of the opinion that the person has since that date failed without reasonable excuse to comply with the unpaid work requirement imposed by the enforcement order,

the officer must report the failure to the appropriate person.

(6) A report under sub-paragraph (5) must include a report of the warning given to the person subject to the enforcement order.

(7) The appropriate person, in relation to an enforcement order, is the officer of the Service or the Welsh family proceedings officer who is required under section 11M to report on matters relating to the enforcement order.

(8) 'Responsible officer', in relation to a person subject to an enforcement order, has [the meaning given by paragraph 1][3].

NOTES

Amendments.[1] Schedule inserted: Children and Adoption Act 2006, s 4(2), Sch 1.[2] Words substituted: Children and Families Act 2014, s 12, Sch 2, paras 1, 39.[3] Words substituted: Sentencing Act 2020, s 410, Sch 24, para 112(1), (5).

Breach of an enforcement order

9. (1) This paragraph applies where a court has made an enforcement order ('the first order') in respect of a person's failure to comply with a [provision of a child arrangements][2] order.

(2) If the court is satisfied beyond reasonable doubt that the person has failed to comply with the unpaid work requirement imposed by the first order, the court may –

(a)   amend the first order so as to make the requirement more onerous, or

(b)   make an enforcement order ('the second order') in relation to the person and (if the first order is still in force) provide for the second order to have effect either in addition to or in substitution for the first order.

(3) But the court may not exercise its powers under sub-paragraph (2) if it is satisfied that the person had a reasonable excuse for failing to comply with the unpaid work requirement imposed by the first order.

(4) The burden of proof as to the matter mentioned in sub-paragraph (3) lies on the person claiming to have had a reasonable excuse, and the standard of proof is the balance of probabilities.

(5) The court may exercise its powers under sub-paragraph (2) in relation to the first order only on the application of a person who would be able to apply under section 11J for an enforcement order if the failure to comply with the first order were a failure to comply with [a provision of the child arrangements][2] order to which the first order relates.

(6) Where the person proposing to apply to the court is the child with respect to whom the [child arrangements][2] order was made, subsections (6) and (7) of section 11J have effect in relation to the application as they have effect in relation to an application for an enforcement order.

(7) An application to the court to exercise its powers under sub-paragraph (2) may only be made while the first order is in force.

(8) The court may not exercise its powers under sub-paragraph (2) in respect of a failure by the person to comply with the unpaid work requirement imposed by the first order unless it is satisfied that before the failure occurred the person had been given (in accordance with rules of court) a copy of, or otherwise informed of the terms of, a notice under section 11N relating to the first order.

(9) In dealing with the person under sub-paragraph (2)(a), the court may –

    (a)   increase the number of hours specified in the first order (but not above the maximum specified in [paragraph 3B(1)(b)(ii)]³;

    (b)   in relation to the order, extend the period of twelve months specified in [paragraph 3A(1)(b)]³.

(10) In exercising its powers under sub-paragraph (2), the court must be satisfied that, taking into account the extent to which the person has complied with the unpaid work requirement imposed by the first order, the effect on the person of the proposed exercise of those powers –

    (a)   is no more than is required to secure his compliance with the [child arrangements]² order or any [child arrangements]² order that has effect in its place, and

    (b)   is no more than is proportionate to the seriousness of his failures to comply with the [provisions of the child arrangements order and with]² the first order.

(11) Where the court exercises its powers under sub-paragraph (2) by making an enforcement order in relation to a person who has failed to comply with another enforcement order –

    (a)   sections 11K(4), 11L(2) to (7), 11M and 11N have effect as regards the making of the order in relation to the person as they have effect as regards the making of an enforcement order in relation to a person who has failed to comply with a [provision of a child arrangements]² order;

    (b)   this Part of this Schedule has effect in relation to the order so made as if it were an enforcement order made in respect of the failure for which the other order was made.

(12) Sub-paragraph (2) is without prejudice to section 63(3) of the Magistrates' Courts Act 1980 as it applies in relation to enforcement orders.

NOTES

Amendments.¹ Schedule inserted: Children and Adoption Act 2006, s 4(2), Sch 1.² Words substituted: Children and Families Act 2014, s 12, Sch 2, paras 1, 39.³ Words substituted: Sentencing Act 2020, s 410, Sch 24, para 112(1), (6).

Provision relating to amendment of enforcement orders

10. Sections 11L(2) to (7) and 11M have effect in relation to the making of an order under paragraph 6(2), 7(2) or 9(2)(a) amending an enforcement order as they have effect in relation to the making of an enforcement order; and references in sections 11L(2) to (7) and 11M to an enforcement order are to be read accordingly.][1]

NOTES

Amendments.[1] Schedule inserted: Children and Adoption Act 2006, s 4(2), Sch 1.

SCHEDULE 1
FINANCIAL PROVISION FOR CHILDREN

Section 15(1)

Orders for financial relief against parents

1. (1) On an application made by a parent[, guardian or special guardian][2] of a child, or by any person [who is named in a child arrangements order as a person with whom a child is to live][4], the court [may make one or more of the orders mentioned in sub-paragraph (2).][5]

   (a) ...[5]
   (b) ...[5]

(2) The orders referred to in sub-paragraph (1) are –

   (a) an order requiring either or both parents of a child –
      (i) to make to the applicant for the benefit of the child; or
      (ii) to make to the child himself,
     such periodical payments, for such term, as may be specified in the order;
   (b) an order requiring either or both parents of a child –
      (i) to secure to the applicant for the benefit of the child; or
      (ii) to secure to the child himself,
     such periodical payments, for such term, as may be so specified;
   (c) an order requiring either or both parents of a child –
      (i) to pay to the applicant for the benefit of the child; or
      (ii) to pay to the child himself,
     such lump sum as may be so specified;
   (d) an order requiring a settlement to be made for the benefit of the child, and to the satisfaction of the court, of property –
      (i) to which either parent is entitled (either in possession or in reversion); and
      (ii) which is specified in the order;
   (e) an order requiring either or both parents of a child –
      (i) to transfer to the applicant, for the benefit of the child; or
      (ii) to transfer to the child himself,
     such property to which the parent is, or the parents are, entitled (either in possession or in reversion) as may be specified in the order.

(3) The powers conferred by this paragraph may be exercised at any time.

(4) An order under sub-paragraph (2)(a) or (b) may be varied or discharged by a subsequent order made on the application of any person by or to whom payments were required to be made under the previous order.

(5) Where a court makes an order under this paragraph –

   (a)   it may at any time make a further such order under sub-paragraph (2)(a), (b) or (c) with respect to the child concerned if he has not reached the age of eighteen;

   (b)   it may not make more than one order under sub-paragraph (2)(d) or (e) against the same person in respect of the same child.

(6) On making, varying or discharging ...[4] [...[4] a special guardianship order][3][, or on making, varying or discharging provision in a child arrangements order with respect to the living arrangements of a child,][4] the court may exercise any of its powers under this Schedule even though no application has been made to it under this Schedule.

[(6A) For the purposes of sub-paragraph (6) provision in a child arrangements order is with respect to the living arrangements of a child if it regulates arrangements relating to –

   (a)   with whom the child is to live, or

   (b)   when the child is to live with any person.][4]

[(7) Where a child is a ward of court, the court may exercise any of its powers under this Schedule even though no application has been made to it.][1]

NOTES

Amendments.[1] Sub-paragraph added: Courts and Legal Services Act 1990, s 116, Sch 16, para 10(2).[2] Words substituted: Adoption and Children Act 2002, s 139(1), Sch 3, paras 54, 71(a)(i).[3] Words inserted: Adoption and Children Act 2002, s 139(1), Sch 3, paras 54, 71(a)(ii).[4] Words substituted, omitted and inserted, and subparagraph inserted: Children and Families Act 2014, s 12, Sch 2, paras 1, 40.[5] Words substituted and paragraphs repealed: Crime and Courts Act 2013, s 17, Sch 11, paras 102, 112, 113. **Definitions.** 'Child': s 105(1); 'parent': Sch 1, para 16(2); 'residence order': s 8(1); 'the court': s 92(7).

Orders for financial relief for persons over eighteen

2. (1) If, on an application by a person who has reached the age of eighteen, it appears to the court –

   (a)   that the applicant is, will be or (if an order were made under this paragraph) would be receiving instruction at an educational establishment or undergoing training for a trade, profession or vocation, whether or not while in gainful employment; or

   (b)   that there are special circumstances which justify the making of an order under this paragraph,

the court may make one or both of the orders mentioned in sub-paragraph (2).

(2) The orders are –

   (a)   an order requiring either or both of the applicant's parents to pay to the applicant such periodical payments, for such term, as may be specified in the order;

   (b)   an order requiring either or both of the applicant's parents to pay to the applicant such lump sum as may be so specified.

(3) An applicant may not be made under this paragraph by any person if, immediately before he reached the age of sixteen, a periodical payments order was in force with respect to him.

(4) No order shall be made under this paragraph at a time when the parents of the applicant are living with each other in the same household.

(5) An order under sub-paragraph (2)(a) may be varied or discharged by a subsequent order made on the application of any person by or to whom payments were required to be made under the previous order.

(6) In sub-paragraph (3) 'periodical payments order' means an order made under –

    (a)   this Schedule;
    (b)   …[1]
    (c)   section 23 or 27 of the Matrimonial Causes Act 1973;
    (d)   Part I of the Domestic Proceedings and Magistrates' Courts Act 1978,
    [(e)   Part 1 or 9 of Schedule 5 to the Civil Partnership Act 2004 (financial relief in the High Court or a county court etc);
    (f)   Schedule 6 to the 2004 Act (financial relief in the magistrates' courts etc),][2]
for the making or securing of periodical payments.

(7) The powers conferred by this paragraph shall be exercisable at any time.

(8) Where the court makes an order under this paragraph it may from time to time while that order remains in force make a further such order.

NOTES

Amendments.[1] Words repealed: Child Support Act 1991, s 58(14).[2] Subparagraphs inserted: Civil Partnership Act 2004, s 78(1), (2).
Definitions. 'Periodical payments order': Sch 1, para 2(6); 'the court': s 92(7).

Duration of orders for financial relief

3. (1) The term to be specified in an order for periodical payments made under paragraph 1(2)(a) or (b) in favour of a child may begin with the date of the making of an application for the order in question or any later date [or a date ascertained in accordance with sub-paragraph (5) or (6)][1] but –

    (a)   shall not in the first instance extend beyond the child's seventeenth birthday unless the court thinks it right in the circumstances of the case to specify a later date; and
    (b)   shall not in any event extend beyond the child's eighteenth birthday.

(2) Paragraph (b) of sub-paragraph (1) shall not apply in the case of a child if it appears to the court that –

    (a)   the child is, or will be (if an order were made without complying with that paragraph) would be receiving instruction at an educational establishment or undergoing training for a trade, profession or vocation, whether or not while in gainful employment; or
    (b)   there are special circumstances which justify the making of an order without complying with that paragraph.

(3) An order for periodical payments made under paragraph 1(2)(a) or 2(2)(a) shall, notwithstanding anything in the order, cease to have effect on the death of the person liable to make payments under the order.

(4) Where an order is made under paragraph 1(2)(a) or (b) requiring periodical payments to be made or secured to the parent of a child, the order shall cease to have effect if –

(a)   any parent making or securing the payments; and
(b)   any parent to whom the payments are made or secured,

live together for a period of more than six months.

[(5) Where –

(a)   a [maintenance calculation]² ('the [current calculation]²') is in force with respect to a child; and
(b)   an application is made for an order under paragraph 1(2)(a) or (b) of this Schedule for periodical payments in favour of that child –
       (i)   in accordance with section 8 of the Child Support Act 1991; and
       (ii)   before the end of the period of 6 months beginning with the making of the [current calculation]²,

the term to be specified in any such order made on that application may be expressed to begin on, or at any time after, the earliest permitted date.

(6) For the purposes of subsection (5) above, 'the earliest permitted date' is whichever is the later of –

(a)   the date 6 months before the application is made; or
(b)   the date on which the [current calculation]² took effect or, where successive [maintenance calculations]² have been continuously in force with respect to a child, on which the first of [those calculations]² took effect.

(7) Where –

(a)   a [maintenance calculation]² ceases to have effect …² by or under any provision of the Child Support Act 1991, and
(b)   an application is made, before the end of the period of 6 months beginning with the relevant date, for an order for periodical payments under paragraph 1(2)(a) or (b) in favour of a child with respect to whom that [maintenance calculation]² was in force immediately before it ceased to have effect …²,

the term to be specified in any such order, or in any interim order under paragraph 9, made on that application may begin with the date on which that [maintenance calculation]² ceased to have effect …², or any later date.

(8) In sub-paragraph (7)(b) –

(a)   where the [maintenance calculation]² ceased to have effect, the relevant date is the date on which it so ceased; and
(b)   …².

NOTES
Amendments.[1] Words and subparagraphs inserted: Maintenance Orders (Backdating) Order 1993, SI 1993/623.[2] Words substituted and words and paragraphs repealed: Child Support, Pensions and Social Security Act 2000, ss 26, 85, Sch 3, para 10(1), (2), Sch 9, Pt I.

Matters to which court is to have regard in making orders for financial relief

4. (1) In deciding whether to exercise its powers under paragraph 1 or 2, and if so in what manner, the court shall have regard to all the circumstances including –

   (a)   the income, earning capacity, property and other financial resources which each person mentioned in sub-paragraph (4) has or is likely to have in the foreseeable future;

   (b)   the financial needs, obligations and responsibilities which each person mentioned in sub-paragraph (4) has or is likely to have in the foreseeable future;

   (c)   the financial needs of the child;

   (d)   the income, earning capacity (if any), property and other financial resources of the child;

   (e)   any physical or mental disability of the child;

   (f)   the manner in which the child was being, or was expected to be, educated or trained.

(2) In deciding whether to exercise its powers under paragraph 1 against a person who is not the mother or father of the child, and if so in what manner, the court shall in addition have regard to –

   (a)   whether that person had assumed responsibility for the maintenance of the child, and, if so, the extent to which and basis on which he assumed that responsibility and the length of the period during which he met that responsibility;

   (b)   whether he did so knowing that the child was not his child;

   (c)   the liability of any other person to maintain the child.

(3) Where the court makes an order under paragraph 1 against a person who is not the father of the child, it shall record in the order that the order is made on the basis that the person against whom the order is made is not the child's father.

(4) The persons mentioned in sub-paragraph (1) are –

   (a)   in relation to a decision whether to exercise its powers under paragraph 1, any parent of the child;

   (b)   in relation to a decision whether to exercise its powers under paragraph 2, the mother and father of the child;

   (c)   the applicant for the order;

   (d)   any other person in whose favour the court proposes to make the order.

[(5) In the case of a child who has a parent by virtue of section 42 or 43 of the Human Fertilisation and Embryology Act 2008, any reference in sub-paragraph (2), (3) or (4) to the child's father is a reference to the woman who is a parent of the child by virtue of that section.][1]

NOTES

Amendments.[1] Subparagraph inserted: Human Fertilisation and Embryology Act 2008, s 56, Sch 6, Pt 1, para 32(1), (2).

Provisions relating to lump sums

5. (1) Without prejudice to the generality of paragraph 1, an order under that paragraph for the payment of a lump sum may be made for the purpose of enabling any liabilities or expenses –

    (a)   incurred in connection with the birth of the child or in maintaining the child; and

    (b)   reasonably incurred before the making of the order,

to be met.

(2) ...[2]

(3) The power of the court under paragraph 1 or 2 to vary or discharge an order for the making or securing of periodical payments by a parent shall include power to make an order under that provision for the payment of a lump sum by that parent.

(4) ...[2]

(5) An order made under paragraph 1 or 2 for the payment of a lump sum may provide for the payment of that sum by instalments.

(6) Where the court provides for the payment of a lump sum by instalments the court, on an application made either by the person liable to pay or the person entitled to receive that sum, shall have power to vary that order by varying –

    (a)   the number of instalments payable;

    (b)   the amount of any instalment payable;

    (c)   the date on which any instalment becomes payable.

[(7) The Lord Chief Justice may nominate a judicial office holder (as defined in section 109(4) of the Constitutional Reform Act 2005) to exercise his functions under this paragraph.][1]

NOTES

Amendments.[1] Subparagraph inserted: Constitutional Reform Act 2005, s 15(1), Sch 4, Pt 1, paras 203, 209(1), (3).[2] Subparagraphs omitted: Crime and Courts Act 2013, s 17, Sch 11, paras 102, 112, 114. **Definitions.** 'Child': s 105(1), Sch 1, para 16(1); 'parent': Sch 1, para 16(2); 'the court': s 92(7).

Variation etc of orders for periodical payments

6. (1) In exercising its powers under paragraph 1 or 2 to vary or discharge an order for the making or securing of periodical payments the court shall have regard to all the circumstances of the case, including any change in any of the matters to which the court was required to have regard when making the order.

(2) The power of the court under paragraph 1 or 2 to vary an order for the making or securing of periodical payments shall include power to suspend any provision of the order temporarily and to revive any provision so suspended.

(3) Where on an application under paragraph 1 or 2 for the variation or discharge of an order for the making or securing of periodical payments the court varies the payments required to be made under that order, the court may provide that the payments as so varied shall be made from such date as the court may specify [except that, subject to sub-paragraph (9), the date shall not be][1] earlier than the date of the making of the application.

(4) An application for the variation of an order made under paragraph 1 for the making or securing of periodical payments to or for the benefit of a child may, if the child has reached the age of sixteen, be made by the child himself.

(5) Where an order for the making or securing of periodical payments made under paragraph 1 ceases to have effect on the date on which the child reaches the age of sixteen, or at any time after that date but before or on the date on which he reaches the age of eighteen, the child may apply to the court which made the order for an order for its revival.

(6) If on such an application it appears to the court that –

  (a)   the child is, will be or (if an order were made under this sub-paragraph) would be receiving instruction at an educational establishment or undergoing training for a trade, profession or vocation, whether or not while in gainful employment; or

  (b)   there are special circumstances which justify the making of an order under this paragraph,

the court shall have power by order to revive the order from such date as the court may specify, not being earlier than the date of the making of the application.

(7) Any order which is revived by an order under sub-paragraph (5) may be varied or discharged under that provision, on the application of any person by whom or to whom payments are required to be made under the revived order.

(8) An order for the making or securing of periodical payments made under paragraph 1 may be varied or discharged, after the death of either parent, on the application of a guardian [or special guardian][3] of the child concerned.

[(9) Where –

  (a)   an order under paragraph 1(2)(a) or (b) for the making or securing of periodical payments in favour of more than one child ('the order') is in force;

  (b)   the order requires payments specified in it to be made to or for the benefit of more than one child without apportioning those payments between them;

  (c)   a [maintenance calculation][2] ('[the calculation][2]') is made with respect to one or more, but not all, of the children with respect to whom those payments are to be made; and

  (d)   an application is made, before the end of the period of 6 months beginning with the date on which [the calculation][2] was made, for the variation or discharge of the order,

the court may, in exercise of its powers under paragraph 1 to vary or discharge the order, direct that the variation or discharge shall take effect from the date on which [the calculation][2] took effect or any later date.][1]

NOTES

Amendments.[1] Words substituted or subparagraph inserted: Maintenance Orders (Backdating) Order 1993, SI 1993/623.[2] Words substituted: Child Support, Pensions and Social Security Act 2000, s 26, Sch 3, para 10(1), (3).[3] Words inserted: Adoption and Children Act 2002, s 139(1), Sch 3, paras 54, 71(b).

[Variation of orders for periodical payments etc made by magistrates' courts

6A. (1) Subject to [sub-paragraph (7)][2], the power of [the family][2] court –

(a)   under paragraph 1 or 2 to vary an order for the making of periodical payments, or

(b)   under paragraph 5(6) to vary an order for the payment of a lump sum by instalments,

shall include power, if the court is satisfied that payment has not been made in accordance with the order, to exercise one of its powers under [section 1(4) and (4A) of the Maintenance Enforcement Act 1991][2].

(2) ...[2]

(3) ...[2]

(4) ...[2]

(5) ...[2]

(6) [Subsection (6) of section 1 of the Maintenance Enforcement Act 1991][2] (power of court to order that account be opened) shall apply for the purposes of [sub-paragraph (1)][2] as it applies for the purposes of that section.

(7) Before varying the order by exercising one of its powers under [section 1(4) and (4A) of the Maintenance Enforcement Act 1991][2], the court shall have regard to any representations made by the parties to the application.

(8) ...[2]

(9) None of the powers of the court ...[2] conferred by this paragraph shall be exercisable in relation to an order under this Schedule for the making of periodical payments, or for the payment of a lump sum by instalments, [unless at the time when the order was made the person required to make the payments was ordinarily resident in England and Wales.][2]

(10) ...[2]][1]

NOTES

Amendments.[1] Paragraph inserted: Maintenance Enforcement Act 1991, s 6.[2] Words substituted and omitted, and subparagraphs omitted: Crime and Courts Act 2013, s 17, Sch 11, paras 102, 112, 115.

Variation of orders for secured periodical payments after death of parent

7. (1) Where the parent liable to make payments under a secured periodical payments order has died, the persons who may apply for the variation or discharge of the order shall include the personal representatives of the deceased parent.

(2) No application for the variation of the order shall, except with the permission of the court, be made after the end of the period of six months from the date on which representation in regard to the estate of that parent is first taken out.

(3) The personal representatives of a deceased person against whom a secured periodical payments order was made shall not be liable for having distributed any part of the estate of the deceased after the end of the period of six months referred to in sub-paragraph (2) on the ground that they ought to have taken into account the possibility that the court might permit an application for variation to be made after that period by the person entitled to payments under the order.

(4) Sub-paragraph (3) shall not prejudice any power to recover any part of the estate so distributed arising by virtue of the variation of an order in accordance with this paragraph.

(5) Where an application to vary a secured periodical payments order is made after the death of the parent liable to make payments under the order, the circumstances to which the court is required to have regard under paragraph 6(1) shall include the changed circumstances resulting from the death of the parent.

[(6) The following are to be left out of account when considering for the purposes of sub-paragraph (2) when representation was first taken out –

  (a)   a grant limited to settled land or to trust property,
  (b)   any other grant that does not permit any of the estate to be distributed,
  (c)   a grant limited to real estate or to personal estate, unless a grant limited to the remainder of the estate has previously been made or is made at the same time,
  (d)   a grant, or its equivalent, made outside the United Kingdom (but see sub-paragraph (6A)).

(6A) A grant sealed under section 2 of the Colonial Probates Act 1892 counts as a grant made in the United Kingdom for the purposes of sub-paragraph (6), but is to be taken as dated on the date of sealing.]¹

(7) In this paragraph 'secured periodical payments order' means an order for secured periodical payments under paragraph 1(2)(b).

NOTES
Amendments.¹ Sub-paragraphs (6) and (6A) substituted for sub-paragraph (6): Inheritance and Trustees' Powers Act 2014, s 7, Sch 3, para 4(1), (2).
Definitions. 'Child': s 105(1), Sch 1, para 16(1); 'parent': Sch 1, para 16(2); 'secured periodical payments order': Sch 1, para 7(7); 'the court': s 92(7).

Financial relief under other enactments

8. (1) This paragraph applies where a [child arrangements order to which sub-paragraph (1A) applies]² [or a special guardianship order]¹ is made with respect to a child at a time when there is in force an order ('the financial relief order') made under any enactment other than this Act and requiring a person to contribute to the child's maintenance.

[(1A) This sub-paragraph applies to a child arrangements order if the arrangements regulated by the order consist of, or include, arrangements which relate to either or both of the following –

> (a)   with whom the child concerned is to live, and
>
> (b)   when the child is to live with any person.][2]

(2)   Where this paragraph applies, the court may, on the application of –

> (a)   any person required by the financial relief order to contribute to the child's maintenance; or
>
> (b)   any person [who is named in a child arrangements order as a person with whom the child is to live or][2] in whose favour ...[2] [...[2] a special guardianship order][1] with respect to the child is in force,

make an order revoking the financial relief order, or varying it by altering the amount of any sum payable under that order or by substituting the applicant for the person to whom any such sum is otherwise payable under that order.

NOTES

Amendments.[1] Words inserted: Adoption and Children Act 2002, s 139(1), Sch 3, paras 54, 71(c).[2] Words substituted, omitted and inserted and subparagraph inserted: Children and Families Act 2014, s 12, Sch 2, paras 1, 40.

Interim orders

9. (1)   Where an application is made under paragraph 1 or 2 the court may, at any time before it disposes of the application, make an interim order –

> (a)   requiring either or both parents to make such periodical payments, at such times and for such term as the court thinks fit; and
>
> (b)   giving any direction which the court thinks fit.

(2)   An interim order made under this paragraph may provide for payments to be made from such date as the court may specify [except that, subject to paragraph 3(5) and (6), the date shall not be][1] earlier than the date of the making of the application under paragraph 1 or 2.

(3)   An interim order made under this paragraph shall cease to have effect when the application is disposed of or, if earlier, on the date specified for the purposes of this paragraph in the interim order.

(4)   An interim order in which a date has been specified for the purposes of subparagraph (3) may be varied by substituting a later date.

NOTES

Amendments.[1] Words substituted: Maintenance Orders (Backdating) Order 1993, SI 1993/623.
Definitions. 'Child': s 105(1); 'parent': Sch 1, para 16(2); 'residence order': s 8(1); 'the court': s 92(7); 'the financial relief order': Sch 1, para 8(1).

Alteration of maintenance agreements

10. (1)   In this paragraph and in paragraph 11 'maintenance agreement' means any agreement in writing made with respect to a child, whether before or after the commencement of this paragraph, which –

> (a)   is or was made between the father and mother of the child; and
>
> (b)   contains provision with respect to the making or securing of payments, or the disposition or use of any property, for the maintenance or education of the child,

and any such provisions are in this paragraph, and paragraph 11, referred to as 'financial arrangements'.

(2) [Subject to sub-paragraph (2A), where]² a maintenance agreement is for the time being subsisting and each of the parties to the agreement is for the time being either domiciled or resident in England and Wales, then, either party may apply for an order under this paragraph.

[(2A) If an application or part of an application relates to a matter [in relation to which Article 18 of the 2007 Hague Convention applies, the court may not entertain the application or that part of it except where permitted by Article 18]⁴.

(2B) In sub-paragraph (2A), ['the 2007 Hague Convention' means the Convention on the International Recovery of Child Support and Other Forms of Family Maintenance concluded on 23 November 2007 at The Hague]⁴.]²

(3) If the court to which the application is made is satisfied either –

    (a)   that, by reason of a change in the circumstances in the light of which any financial arrangements contained in the agreement were made (including a change foreseen by the parties when making the agreement), the agreement should be altered so as to make different financial arrangements; or

    (b)   that the agreement does not contain proper financial arrangements with respect to the child,

then that court may by order make such alterations in the agreement by varying or revoking any financial arrangements contained in it as may appear to it to be just having regard to all the circumstances.

(4) If the maintenance agreement is altered by an order under this paragraph, the agreement shall have effect thereafter as if the alteration had been made by agreement between the parties and for valuable consideration.

(5) Where a court decides to make an order under this paragraph altering the maintenance agreement –

    (a)   by inserting provision for the making or securing by one of the parties to the agreement of periodical payments for the maintenance of the child; or

    (b)   by increasing the rate of periodical payments required to be made or secured by one of the parties for the maintenance of the child,

then, in deciding the term for which under the agreement as altered by the order the payments or (as the case may be) the additional payments attributable to the increase are to be made or secured for the benefit of the child, the court shall apply the provisions of sub-paragraphs (1) and (2) of paragraph 3 as if the order were an order under paragraph 1(2)(a) or (b).

(6) …³

(7) For the avoidance of doubt it is hereby declared that nothing in this paragraph affects any power of a court before which any proceedings between the parties

PART I – Statutes

to a maintenance agreement are brought under any other enactment to make an order containing financial arrangements or any right of either party to apply for such an order in such proceedings.

[(8) In the case of a child who has a parent by virtue of section 42 or 43 of the Human Fertilisation and Embryology Act 2008, the reference in sub-paragraph (1)(a) to the child's father is a reference to the woman who is a parent of the child by virtue of that section.]¹

NOTES

Amendments.¹ Subparagraph inserted: Human Fertilisation and Embryology Act 2008, s 56, Sch 6, Pt 1, para 32(1), (3).² Words substituted and sub-paragraphs inserted: Civil Jurisdiction and Judgments (Maintenance) Regulations 2011, SI 2011/1484, reg 9, Sch 7, para 12.³ Subparagraph omitted: Crime and Courts Act 2013, s 17, Sch 11, paras 102, 112, 116.⁴ Words substituted: Jurisdiction and Judgments (Family) (Amendment etc.) (EU Exit) Regulations 2019, SI 2019/519, reg 7, Schedule, para 17(1), (2) (as amended by the Jurisdiction, Judgments and Applicable Law (Amendment) (EU Exit) Regulations 2020, SI 2020/1574, reg 5(1), (3)(g)).

11. (1) Where a maintenance agreement provides for the continuation, after the death of one of the parties, of payments for the maintenance of a child and that party dies domiciled in England and Wales, the surviving party or the personal representatives of the deceased party may apply to the High Court or [the family court]¹ for an order under paragraph 10.

(2) If a maintenance agreement is altered by a court on an application under this paragraph, the agreement shall have effect thereafter as if the alteration had been made, immediately before the death, by agreement between the parties and for valuable consideration.

(3) An application under this paragraph shall not, except with leave of the High Court or [the family court]¹, be made after the end of the period of six months beginning with the day on which representation in regard to the estate of the deceased is first taken out.

[(4) The following are to be left out of account when considering for the purposes of sub-paragraph (3) when representation was first taken out –

(a)   a grant limited to settled land or to trust property,
(b)   any other grant that does not permit any of the estate to be distributed,
(c)   a grant limited to real estate or to personal estate, unless a grant limited to the remainder of the estate has previously been made or is made at the same time,
(d)   a grant, or its equivalent, made outside the United Kingdom (but see sub-paragraph (4A)).

(4A) A grant sealed under section 2 of the Colonial Probates Act 1892 counts as a grant made in the United Kingdom for the purposes of sub-paragraph (4), but is to be taken as dated on the date of sealing.]²

(5) …¹

(6) The provisions of this paragraph shall not render the personal representatives of the deceased liable for having distributed any part of the estate of the deceased after the expiry of the period of six months referred to in sub-paragraph (3) on

PART I – Statutes

the ground that they ought to have taken into account the possibility that a court might grant leave for an application by virtue of this paragraph to be made by the surviving party after that period.

(7) Sub-paragraph (6) shall not prejudice any power to recover any part of the estate so distributed arising by virtue of the making of an order in pursuance of this paragraph.

NOTES

Amendments.[1] Words substituted and subparagraph omitted: Crime and Courts Act 2013, s 17, Sch 11, paras 102, 112, 117.[2] Sub-paragraphs (4) and (4A) substituted for sub-paragraph (4): Inheritance and Trustees' Powers Act 2014, s 7, Sch 3, para 4(1), (3).
Definitions. 'Child': s 105(1); 'financial arrangements': Sch 1, para 10(1); 'maintenance agreement': Sch 1, para 10(1); 'the court': s 92(7).

Enforcement of orders for maintenance

12. (1) Any person for the time being under an obligation to make payments in pursuance of any order for the payment of money made by [the family court][1] under this Act shall give notice of any change of address to such person (if any) as may be specified in the order.

(2) Any person failing without reasonable excuse to give such a notice shall be guilty of an offence and liable on summary conviction to a fine not exceeding level 2 on the standard scale.

(3) ...[1]

NOTES

Amendments.[1] Words substituted and subparagraph omitted: Crime and Courts Act 2013, s 17, Sch 11, paras 102, 112, 118.

Direction for settlement of instrument by conveyancing counsel

13. Where the High Court or [the family court][1] decides to make an order under this Act for the securing of periodical payments or for the transfer or settlement of property, it may direct that the matter be referred to one of the conveyancing counsel of the court to settle a proper instrument to be executed by all necessary parties.

NOTES

Amendments.[1] Words substituted: Crime and Courts Act 2013, s 17, Sch 11, paras 102, 112, 119.

[Jurisdiction ...3][2]

[14. (1) The court has jurisdiction in relation to an application under paragraph 1 in respect of a child if any of the following persons are habitually resident or domiciled in England and Wales on the date of the application –

   (a)   a parent of the child;
   (b)   a guardian or special guardian of the child;
   (c)   a person who is named in a child arrangements order as a person with whom the child is to live;
   (d)   the child.

(2) The court has jurisdiction in relation to an application under paragraph 2 if the applicant or a parent against whom the order is sought or made is habitually resident or domiciled in England and Wales on the date of the application.][1]

NOTES

Amendments.[1] Paragraph substituted: Civil Jurisdiction and Judgments (Maintenance) Regulations 2011, SI 2011/1484, reg 9, Sch 7, para 12.[2] Heading substituted: International Recovery of Maintenance (Hague Convention 2007 etc.) Regulations 2012, SI 2012/2814, reg 9, Sch 5, para 3.[3] Words omitted repealed and paragraph substituted: Jurisdiction and Judgments (Family) (Amendment etc.) (EU Exit) Regulations 2019, SI 2019/519, reg 7, Schedule, para 17(1), (2A), (3) (as amended by the Jurisdiction and Judgments (Family) (Amendment etc.) (EU Exit) (No. 2) Regulations 2019, SI 2019/836, reg 2(1), (2)).

Local authority contribution to child's maintenance

15. (1) Where a child lives, or is to live, with a person as the result of a [child arrangements order][2], a local authority may make contributions to that person towards the cost of the accommodation and maintenance of the child.

(2) Sub-paragraph (1) does not apply where the person with whom the child lives, or is to live, is a parent of the child or the husband or wife [or civil partner][1] of a parent of the child.

NOTES

Amendments.[1] Words inserted: Civil Partnership Act 2004, s 78(1), (3).[2] Words substituted: Children and Families Act 2014, s 12, Sch 2, paras 1, 40.

Interpretation

16. (1) In this Schedule 'child' includes, in any case where an application is made under paragraph 2 or 6 in relation to a person who has reached the age of eighteen, that person.

[(2) In this Schedule, except paragraphs 2 and 15, 'parent' includes –

    (a)   any party to a marriage (whether or not subsisting) in relation to whom the child concerned is a child of the family, and

    (b)   any civil partner in a civil partnership (whether or not subsisting) in relation to whom the child concerned is a child of the family;

and for this purpose any reference to either parent or both parents shall be read as a reference to any parent of his and to all of his parents.][3]

[(3) In this Schedule, '[maintenance calculation][2]' has the same meaning as it has in the Child Support Act 1991 by virtue of section 54 of that Act as read with any regulations in force under that section.][1]

NOTES

Amendments.[1] Words added: Maintenance Orders (Backdating) Order 1993, SI 1993/623.[2] Words substituted: Child Support, Pensions and Social Security Act 2000, s 26, Sch 3, para 10(1), (4).[3] Subparagraph substituted: Civil Partnership Act 2004, s 78(1), (4).

Definitions. 'Child': s 105(1), Sch 1, para 16(1); 'child of the family': s 105(1); 'local authority': s 105(1); 'parent': Sch 1, para 16(2); 'residence order': s 8(1).

[SCHEDULE 2
SUPPORT FOR CHILDREN AND FAMILIES PROVIDED BY LOCAL AUTHORITIES IN ENGLAND][13]

Sections 17, 23 and 29

[Application to local authorities in England][8]

A1. (1) This Schedule applies only in relation to local authorities in England.

(2) Accordingly, unless the contrary intention appears, a reference in this Schedule to a local authority means a local authority in England.][8]

PART I
PROVISION OF SERVICES FOR FAMILIES

Identification of children in need and provision of information

1. (1) Every local authority shall take reasonable steps to identify the extent to which there are children in need within their area.

(2) Every local authority shall –

    (a)   publish information
        (i)   about services provided by them under sections 17, 18, [20 [and 23D][14]][1]; and
        (ii) where they consider it appropriate, about the provision by others (including, in particular, voluntary organisations) of services which the authority have power to provide under those sections; and
    (b)   take such steps as are reasonably practicable to ensure that those who might benefit from the services receive the information relevant to them.

1A. ...[2]

Maintenance of a register of disabled children

2. (1) Every local authority shall open and maintain a register of disabled children within their area.

(2) The register may be kept by means of a computer.

Assessment of children's needs

3. Where it appears to a local authority that a child within their area is in need, the authority may assess his needs for the purposes of this Act at the same time as any assessment of his needs is made under –

    (a)   the Chronically Sick and Disabled Persons Act 1970;
    (b)   [Part IV of the Education Act 1996][3];
    [(ba) Part 3 of the Children and Families Act 2014;][7]
    (c)   the Disabled Persons (Services, Consultation and Representation) Act 1986; or
    (d)   any other enactment.

Prevention of neglect and abuse

4. (1) Every local authority shall take reasonable steps, through the provision of services under Part III of this Act, to prevent children within their area suffering ill-treatment or neglect.

(2) Where a local authority believe that a child who is at any time within their area –

  (a)   is likely to suffer harm; but
  (b)   lives or proposes to live in the area of another local authority [or in the area of a local authority in Wales]⁹ they shall inform that other local authority [or the local authority in Wales, as the case may be]⁹.

(3) When informing that other local authority [or the local authority in Wales]⁹ they shall specify –

  (a)   the harm that they believe he is likely to suffer; and
  (b)   (if they can) where the child lives or proposes to live.

Provision of accommodation in order to protect child

5. (1) Where –

  (a)   it appears to a local authority that a child who is living on particular premises is suffering, or is likely to suffer, ill treatment at the hands of another person who is living on those premises; and
  (b)   that other person proposes to move from the premises,

the authority may assist that other person to obtain alternative accommodation.

(2) Assistance given under this paragraph may be in cash.

(3) Subsections (7) to (9) of section 17 shall apply in relation to assistance given under this paragraph as they apply in relation to assistance given under that section.

Provision for disabled children

6. [(1)]⁵ Every local authority shall provide services designed –

  (a)   to minimise the effect on disabled children within their area of their disabilities; ...⁵
  (b)   to give such children the opportunity to lead lives which are as normal as possible[; and
  (c)   to assist individuals who provide care for such children to continue to do so, or to do so more effectively, by giving them breaks from caring]⁵.

[(2) The duty imposed by sub-paragraph (1)(c) shall be performed in accordance with regulations made by the [Secretary of State]¹⁰.]⁴

Provision to reduce need for care proceedings etc.

7. Every local authority shall take reasonable steps designed –

(a)   to reduce the need to bring –
   (i)   proceedings for care or supervision orders with respect to children within their area;
   (ii)   criminal proceedings against such children;
   (iii) any family or other proceedings with respect to such children which might lead to them being placed in the authority's care; or
   (iv)   proceedings under the inherent jurisdiction of the High Court with respect to children;
(b)   to encourage children within their area not to commit criminal offences; and
(c)   to avoid the need for children within their area to be placed in secure accommodation [within the meaning given in section 25 and in section 119 of the Social Services and Well-being (Wales) Act 2014][11].

Provision for children living with their families

8. Every local authority shall make such provision as they consider appropriate for the following services to be available with respect to children in need within their area while they are living with their families –

(a)   advice, guidance and counselling;
(b)   occupational, social, cultural or recreational activities;
(c)   home help (which may include laundry facilities);
(d)   facilities for, or assistance with, travelling to and from home for the purpose of taking advantage of any other service provided under this Act or of any similar service;
(e)   assistance to enable the child concerned and his family to have a holiday.

[Provision for accommodated children

8A (1) Every local authority shall make provision for such services as they consider appropriate to be available with respect to accommodated children.

(2) 'Accommodated children' are those children in respect of whose accommodation the local authority have been notified under section 85 or 86 [or under section 120 of the Social Services and Well-being (Wales) Act 2014 (assessment of children accommodated by health authorities and education authorities)][12].

(3) The services shall be provided with a view to promoting contact between each accommodated child and that child's family.

(4) The services may, in particular, include –

(a)   advice, guidance and counselling;
(b)   services necessary to enable the child to visit, or to be visited by, members of the family;
(c)   assistance to enable the child and members of the family to have a holiday together.

(5) Nothing in this paragraph affects the duty imposed by paragraph 10.][6]

PART I – Statutes

Family centres

9. (1) Every local authority shall provide such family centres as they consider appropriate in relation to children within their area.

(2) 'Family centre' means a centre at which any of the persons mentioned in sub-paragraph (3) may –

(a)   attend for occupational, social, cultural or recreational activities;

(b)   attend for advice, guidance or counselling; or

(c)   be provided with accommodation while he is receiving advice, guidance or counselling.

(3) The persons are –

(a)   a child;

(b)   his parents;

(c)   any person who is not a parent of his but who has parental responsibility for him;

(d)   any other person who is looking after him.

Maintenance of the family home

10. Every local authority shall take such steps as are reasonably practicable, where any child within their area who is in need and whom they are not looking after is living apart from his family –

(a)   to enable him to live with his family; or

(b)   to promote contact between him and his family,

if, in their opinion, it is necessary to do so in order to safeguard or promote his welfare.

Duty to consider racial groups to which children in need belong

11. Every local authority shall, in making any arrangements –

(a)   for the provision of day care within their area; or

(b)   designed to encourage persons to act as local authority foster parents,

have regard to the different racial groups to which children within their area who are in need belong.

NOTES

Amendments.[1] Words substituted: Children (Leaving Care) Act 2000, s 7(1), (4).[2] Paragraph repealed: Children Act 2004, s 64, Sch 5, Pt 1.[3] Words substituted: Education Act 1996, s 582(1), Sch 37, Pt I, para 92.[4] Subparagraph inserted: Children and Young Persons Act 2008, s 25(1), (4).[5] Subsection designated (1), word omitted and paragraph inserted: Children and Young Persons Act, ss 25(1)–(3), 42, Sch 4.[6] Paragraph inserted: Children and Young Persons Act 2008, s 19.[7] Paragraph inserted: Children and Families Act 2014, s 82, Sch 3, para 65(1), (3), with effect from 1 September 2014.[8] Headings and paragraph inserted: SI 2016/413, regs 55, 107.[9] Words inserted: SI 2016/413, regs 55, 108.[10] Words inserted: SI 2016/413, regs 55, 109.[11] Words inserted: SI 2016/413, regs 55, 110.[12] Words inserted: SI 2016/413, regs 55, 111.[13] Heading substituted: SI 2016/413, regs 55, 121.[14] Words substituted: Children and Social Work Act 2017, ss 11, 31, Sch 2, paras 1, 2.

Definitions. 'Care order': ss 31(11), 105(1); 'child': s 105(1); 'child in need': s 17(10); 'day care': ss 18(4), 105(1); 'disabled': ss 17(11), 105(1); 'family': s 17(10); 'family centre': Sch 2, para 9(2); 'family

PART I – Statutes

proceedings': s 8(3); 'harm': ss 31(9), 105(1); 'ill-treatment': ss 31(9), 105(1); 'local authority': s 105(1); 'local authority foster parent': s 23(3); 'parental responsibility': s 3; 'secure accommodation': s 25(1); 'significant harm': ss 31(10), 105(1); 'supervision order': s 31(11); voluntary organisation': s 105(1).

PART II
CHILDREN LOOKED AFTER BY LOCAL AUTHORITIES [IN ENGLAND]¹²

[Regulations as to conditions under which child in care is allowed to live with parent, etc

12A. Regulations under section 22C may, in particular, impose requirements on a local authority as to –

(a) the making of any decision by a local authority to allow a child in their care to live with any person falling within section 22C(3) (including requirements as to those who must be consulted before the decision is made and those who must be notified when it has been made);
(b) the supervision or medical examination of the child concerned;
(c) the removal of the child, in such circumstances as may be prescribed, from the care of the person with whom the child has been allowed to live;
(d) the records to be kept by local authorities.

Regulations as to placements of a kind specified in section 22C(6)(d)

12B. Regulations under section 22C as to placements of the kind specified in section 22C(6)(d) may, in particular, make provision as to –

(a) the persons to be notified of any proposed arrangements;
(b) the opportunities such persons are to have to make representations in relation to the arrangements proposed;
(c) the persons to be notified of any proposed changes in arrangements;
(d) the records to be kept by local authorities;
(e) the supervision by local authorities of any arrangements made.

Placements out of area

12C. Regulations under section 22C may, in particular, impose requirements which a local authority must comply with –

(a) before a child looked after by them is provided with accommodation at a place outside the area of the authority; or
(b) if the child's welfare requires the immediate provision of such accommodation, within such period of the accommodation being provided as may be prescribed.

Avoidance of disruption in education

12D. (1) Regulations under section 22C may, in particular, impose requirements which a local authority must comply with before making any decision concerning a child's placement if he is in the fourth key stage.

(2) A child is 'in the fourth key stage' if he is a pupil in the fourth key stage for the purposes of Part 6 or 7 of the Education 2002 (see section 82 and 103 of that Act).

Regulations as to placing of children with local authority foster parents

12E. Regulations under section 22C may, in particular, make provision –

(a)   with regard to the welfare of children placed with local authority foster parents;

(b)   as to the arrangements to be made by local authorities in connection with the health and education of such children;

(c)   as to the records to be kept by local authorities;

(d)   for securing that where possible the local authority foster parent with whom a child is to be placed is –

(i)   of the same religious persuasion as the child; or

(ii)   gives an undertaking that the child will be brought up in that religious persuasion;

(e)   for securing the children placed with local authority foster parents, and the premises in which they are accommodated, will be supervised and inspected by a local authority and that the children will be removed from those premises if their welfare appears to require it.

12F. (1) Regulations under section 22C may, in particular, also make provision –

(a)   for securing that a child is not placed with a local authority foster parent unless that person is for the time being approved as a local authority foster parent by such local authority as may be prescribed [in regulations made by the Secretary of State][13];

(b)   establishing a procedure under which any person in respect of whom a qualifying determination has been made may apply to the [Secretary of State][13] for a review of that determination by a panel constituted by [the Secretary of State][13].

(2) A determination is a qualifying determination if –

(a)   it relates to the issue of whether a person should be approved, or should continue to be approved, as a local authority foster parent; and

(b)   it is of a prescribed description.

(3) Regulations made by virtue of sub-paragraph (1)(b) may include provision as to –

(a)   the duties and powers of a panel;

(b)   the administration and procedures of a panel;

(c)   the appointment of members of a panel (including the number, or any limit on the number, of members who may be appointed and any conditions for appointment);

(d)   the payment of fees to members of a panel;

(e)   the duties of any person in connection with a review conducted under the regulations;

(f)   the monitoring of any such reviews.

(4) Regulations made by virtue of sub-paragraph (3)(e) may impose a duty to pay to the [Secretary of State][13] such sum as that national authority may determine; but such a duty may not be imposed upon a person who has applied for a review of a qualifying determination.

(5) The [Secretary of State][13] must secure that, taking one financial year with another, the aggregate of the sums which become payable to it under regulations made by virtue of sub-paragraph (4) does not exceed the cost to it of performing its independent review functions.

(6) The [Secretary of State][13] may make an arrangement with an organisation under which independent review functions are performed by the organisation on the national authority's behalf.

(7) If the [Secretary of State][13] makes such an arrangement with an organisation, the organisation is to perform its functions under the arrangement in accordance with any general or special directions given by that national authority.

(8) The arrangement may include provision for payments to be made to the organisation by the [Secretary of State][13].

(9) Payments made by the [Secretary of State][13] in accordance with such provision shall be taken into account in determining (for the purpose of sub-paragraph (5)) the cost to that national authority of performing its independent review functions.

(10) …[13]

(11) In this paragraph –

'financial year' means a period of twelve months ending with 31st March;

'independent review function' means a function conferred or imposed on a national authority by regulations made by virtue of sub-paragraph (1)(b);

'organisation' includes [the Welsh Ministers,][13] a public body and a private or voluntary organisation.

12G. Regulations under section 22C may, in particular, also make provision as to the circumstances in which local authorities may make arrangements for duties imposed on them by the regulations to be discharged on their behalf.][9]

Promotion and maintenance of contact between child and family

15. (1) Where a child is being looked after by a local authority, the authority shall, unless it is not reasonably practicable or consistent with his welfare, endeavour to promote contact between the child and –

(a) his parents;
(b) any person who is not a parent of his but who has parental responsibility for him; and
(c) any relative, friend or other person connected with him.

(2) Where a child is being looked after by a local authority –

(a)   the authority shall take such steps as are reasonably practicable to secure that
    (i)   his parents; and
    (ii) any person who is not a parent of his but who has parental responsibility for him,
    are kept informed of where he is being accommodated; and
(b)   every such person shall secure that the authority are kept informed of his or her address.

(3) Where a local authority ('the receiving authority') take over the provision of accommodation for a child from another local authority [or a local authority in Wales][14] ('the transferring authority') under section 20(2) –

(a)   the receiving authority shall (where reasonably practicable) inform
    (i)   the child's parents; and
    (ii) any person who is not a parent of his but who has parental responsibility for him;
(b)   sub-paragraph (2)(a) shall apply to the transferring authority, as well as the receiving authority, until at least one such person has been informed of the change; and
(c)   sub-paragraph (2)(b) shall not require any person to inform the receiving authority of his address until he has been so informed.

(4) Nothing in this paragraph requires a local authority to inform any person of the whereabouts of a child if –

(a)   the child is in the care of the authority; and
(b)   the authority has reasonable cause to believe that informing the person would prejudice the child's welfare.

(5) Any person who fails (without reasonable excuse) to comply with sub-paragraph (2)(b) shall be guilty of an offence and liable on summary conviction to a fine not exceeding level 2 on the standard scale.

(6) It shall be a defence in any proceedings under sub-paragraph (5) to prove that the defendant was residing at the same address as another person who was the child's parent or had parental responsibility for the child and had reasonable cause to believe that the other person had informed the appropriate authority that both of them were residing at that address.

Visits to or by children: expenses

16. (1) This paragraph applies where –

(a)   a child is being looked after by a local authority; and
(b)   the conditions mentioned in sub-paragraph (3) are satisfied.

(2) The authority may –

(a)   make payments to –
    (i)   a parent of the child;
    (ii) any person who is not a parent of his but who has parental responsibility for him; or

     (iii)   any relative, friend or other person connected with him,

     in respect of travelling, subsistence or other expenses incurred by that person in visiting the child; or

  (b)   make payments to the child, or to any person on his behalf, in respect of travelling, subsistence or other expenses incurred by or on behalf of the child in his visiting –

     (i)   a parent of his;

     (ii)   any person who has parental responsibility for him; or

     (iii)   any relative, friend or other person connected with him.

(3) The conditions are that –

  (a)   it appears to the authority that the visit in question could not otherwise be made without undue financial hardship; and

  (b)   the circumstances warrant the making of the payments.

17. ...[10]

Power to guarantee apprenticeship deeds etc

18. (1) While a child is being looked after by a local authority, or is a person qualifying for advice and assistance, the authority may undertake any obligation by way of guarantee under any deed of apprenticeship or articles of clerkship which he enters into.

(2) Where a local authority have undertaken any such obligation under any deed or articles they may at any time (whether or not they are still looking after the person concerned) undertake the like obligation under any supplemental deed or articles.

Arrangements to assist children to live abroad

19. (1) A local authority may only arrange for, or assist in arranging for, any child in their care to live outside England and Wales with the approval of the court.

(2) A local authority may, with the approval of every person who has parental responsibility for the child arrange for, or assist in arranging for, any other child looked after by them to live outside England and Wales.

(3) The court shall not give its approval under sub-paragraph (1) unless it is satisfied that –

  (a)   living outside England and Wales would be in the child's best interests;

  (b)   suitable arrangements have been, or will be, made for his reception and welfare in the country in which he will live;

  (c)   the child has consented to living in that country; and

  (d)   every person who has parental responsibility for the child has consented to his living in that country.

(4) Where the court is satisfied that the child does not have sufficient understanding to give or withhold his consent, it may disregard sub-paragraph (3)(c) and give its approval if the child is to live in the country concerned with a parent, guardian, [special guardian,]⁴ or other suitable person.

(5) Where a person whose consent is required by sub-paragraph (3)(d) fails to give his consent, the court may disregard that provision and give its approval if it is satisfied that that person –

(a)   cannot be found;
(b)   is incapable of consenting; or
(c)   is withholding his consent unreasonably.

(6) [Section 85 of the Adoption and Children Act 2002 (which imposes restrictions on taking children out of the United Kingdom)]⁵ shall not apply in the case of any child who is to live outside England and Wales with the approval of the court given under this paragraph.

(7) Where a court decides to give its approval under this paragraph it may order that its decision is not to have effect during the appeal period.

(8) In sub-paragraph (7) 'the appeal period' means –

(a)   where an appeal is made against the decision, the period between the making of the decision and the determination of the appeal; and
(b)   otherwise, the period during which an appeal may be made against the decision.

[(9) This paragraph does not apply[–

(a)   to a local authority placing a child in secure accommodation in Scotland under section 25, or
(b)]¹⁷ to a local authority placing a child for adoption with prospective adopters.]⁶

[Preparation for ceasing to be looked after

19A. It is the duty of the local authority looking after a child to advise, assist and befriend him with a view to promoting his welfare when they have ceased to look after him.

19B. (1) A local authority shall have the following additional functions in relation to an eligible child whom they are looking after.

(2) In sub-paragraph (1) 'eligible child' means, subject to sub-paragraph (3), a child who –

(a)   is aged sixteen or seventeen; and
(b)   has been looked after by a local authority [or by a local authority in Wales]⁸ for a prescribed period, or periods amounting in all to a prescribed period, which began after he reached a prescribed age and ended after he reached the age of sixteen.

(3) The [Secretary of State][8] may prescribe –

    (a)   additional categories of eligible children; and

    (b)   categories of children who are not to be eligible children despite falling within sub-paragraph (2).

(4) For each eligible child, the local authority shall carry out an assessment of his needs with a view to determining what advice, assistance and support it would be appropriate for them to provide him under this Act –

    (a)   while they are still looking after him; and

    (b)   after they cease to look after him,

and shall then prepare a pathway plan for him.

(5) The local authority shall keep the pathway plan under regular review.

(6) Any such review may be carried out at the same time as a review of the child's case carried out by virtue of section 26.

(7) The [Secretary of State][8] may by regulations make provision as to assessments for the purposes of sub-paragraph (4).

(8) The regulations may in particular provide for the matters set out in section 23B(6).

[Preparation for ceasing to be looked after: staying put arrangements

19BA. (1) This paragraph applies in relation to an eligible child (within the meaning of paragraph 19B) who has been placed by a local authority …[15] with a local authority foster parent.

(2) When carrying out the assessment of the child's needs in accordance with paragraph 19B(4), the local authority must determine whether it would be appropriate to provide advice, assistance and support under this Act in order to facilitate a staying put arrangement, and with a view to maintaining such an arrangement, after the local authority cease to look after him or her.

(3) The local authority must provide advice, assistance and support under this Act in order to facilitate a staying put arrangement if –

    (a)   the local authority determine under sub-paragraph (2) that it would be appropriate to do so, and

    (b)   the eligible child and the local authority foster parent wish to make a staying put arrangement.

(4) In this paragraph, 'staying put arrangement' has the meaning given by section 23CZA.][11]

Personal advisers

19C. A local authority shall arrange for each child whom they are looking after who is an eligible child for the purposes of paragraph 19B to have a personal adviser.][2]

Death of children being looked after by local authorities

20. (1) If a child who is being looked after by a local authority dies, the authority –

(a) [shall notify the Secretary of State and Her Majesty's Chief Inspector of Education, Children's Services and Skills;][13]

(b) shall, so far as is reasonably practicable, notify the child's parents and every person who is not a parent of his but who has parental responsibility for him;

(c) may, with the consent (so far as it is reasonably practicable to obtain it) of every person who has parental responsibility for the child, arrange for the child's body to be buried or cremated; and

(d) may, if the conditions mentioned in sub-paragraph (2) are satisfied, make payments to any person who has parental responsibility for the child, or any relative, friend or other person connected with the child, in respect of travelling, subsistence or other expenses incurred by that person in attending the child's funeral.

(2) The conditions are that –

(a) it appears to the authority that the person concerned could not otherwise attend the child's funeral without undue financial hardship; and

(b) that the circumstances warrant the making of the payments.

(3) Sub-paragraph (1) does not authorise cremation where it does not accord with the practice of the child's religious persuasion.

(4) Where a local authority have exercised their power under sub-paragraph (1) (c) with respect to a child who was under sixteen when he died, they may recover from any parent of the child any expenses incurred by them.

(5) Any sums so recoverable shall, without prejudice to any other method of recovery, be recoverable summarily as a civil debt.

(6) Nothing in this paragraph affects any enactment regulating or authorising the burial, cremation or anatomical examination of the body of a deceased person.

NOTES

Amendments.[1] Sub-paragraph added: Courts and Legal Services Act 1990, s 116, Sch 16, para 27.[2] Paragraphs inserted: Children (Leaving Care) Act 2000, s 1.[4] Words inserted: Adoption and Children Act 2002, s 139(1), Sch 3, paras 54, 72(a).[5] Words substituted: Adoption and Children Act 2002, s 139(1), Sch 3, paras 54, 72(b).[6] Subparagraph inserted: Adoption and Children Act 2002, s 139(1), Sch 3, paras 54, 72(c).[8] Words substituted and inserted: SI 2016/413, regs 55, 115.[9] Paras 12A–12G substituted for paras 12–14 as originally enacted: Children and Young Persons Act 2008, s 8(2), Sch 1, para 4.[10] Paragraph repealed: Children and Young Persons Act 2008, ss 16(2), 42, Sch 4.[11] Paragraph 19BA inserted: Children and Families Act 2014, s 98(1), (3).[12] Words inserted: SI 2016/413, regs 55, 112.[13] Words inserted and substituted, and paragraph omitted: SI 2016/413, regs 55, 113.[14] Words inserted: SI 2016/413, regs 55, 114.[15] Words omitted: SI 2016/413, regs 55, 116.[16] Paragraph substituted: SI 2016/413, regs 55, 117.[17] Words inserted: Children and Social Work Act 2017, s 10, Sch 1, paras 1, 3.

Definitions. 'Child': s 105(1); 'child who is looked after by a local authority': s 22(1); 'functions': s 105(1); 'local authority': s 105(1); 'local authority foster parent': s 23(3); 'parental responsibility': s 3; 'person qualifying for advice and assistance': s 24(2); 'prescribed': s 105(1); 'relative': s 105(1); 'receiving authority': Sch 2, para 15(3); 'the appeal period': Sch 2, para 19(8); 'the court': s 92(7); 'the transferring authority': Sch 2, para 15(3).

PART III
CONTRIBUTIONS TOWARDS MAINTENANCE OF CHILDREN [IN ENGLAND][10]

Liability to contribute

21. (1) Where a local authority are looking after a child (other than in the cases mentioned in sub-paragraph (7)) they shall consider whether they should recover contributions towards the child's maintenance from any person liable to contribute ('a contributor').

(2) An authority may only recover contributions from a contributor if they consider it reasonable to do so.

(3) The persons liable to contribute are –

    (a)   where the child is under sixteen, each of his parents;

    (b)   where he has reached the age of sixteen, the child himself.

(4) A parent is not liable to contribute during any period when he is in receipt of [of universal credit (except in such circumstances as may be prescribed),][8] income support [under][2] [Part VII of the Social Security Contributions and Benefits Act 1992][1][, of any element of child tax credit other than the family element, of working tax credit][2][, of an income-based jobseeker's allowance or of an income-related employment and support allowance][4].

(5) A person is not liable to contribute towards the maintenance of a child in the care of a local authority in respect of any period during which the child is [living with, under arrangements made by the authority in accordance with section 22C,][5] a parent of his.

(6) A contributor is not obliged to make any contribution towards a child's maintenance except as agreed or determined in accordance with this Part of this Schedule.

(7) The cases are where the child is looked after by a local authority under –

    (a)   section 21;

    (b)   an interim care order;

    (c)   [section 92 of the Powers of Criminal Courts (Sentencing) Act 2000][3] [or section 260 of the Sentencing Code][12].

Agreed contributions

22. (1) Contributions towards a child's maintenance may only be recovered if the local authority have served a notice ('a contribution notice') on the contributor specifying –

    (a)   the weekly sum which they consider that he should contribute; and

    (b)   arrangements for payment.

(2) The contribution notice must be in writing and dated.

(3) Arrangements for payment shall, in particular, include –

(a)   the date on which liability to contribute begins (which must not be earlier than the date of the notice);
(b)   the date on which liability under the notice will end (if the child has not before that date ceased to be looked after by the authority); and
(c)   the date on which the first payment is to be made.

(4) The authority may specify in a contribution notice a weekly sum which is a standard contribution determined by them for all children looked after by them.

(5) The authority may not specify in a contribution notice a weekly sum greater than that which they consider –

(a)   they would normally be prepared to pay if they had placed a similar child with local authority foster parents; and
(b)   it is reasonably practicable for the contributor to pay (having regard to his means).

(6) An authority may at any time withdraw a contribution notice (without prejudice to their power to serve another).

(7) Where the authority and the contributor agree –

(a)   the sum which the contributor is to contribute; and
(b)   arrangements for payment,

(whether as specified in the contribution notice or otherwise) and the contributor notifies the authority in writing that he so agrees, the authority may recover summarily as a civil debt any contribution which is overdue and unpaid.

(8) A contributor may, by serving a notice in writing on the authority, withdraw his agreement in relation to any period of liability falling after the date of service of the notice.

(9) Sub-paragraph (7) is without prejudice to any other method of recovery.

Contribution orders

23. (1) Where a contributor has been served with a contribution notice and has –

(a)   failed to reach any agreement with the local authority as mentioned in paragraph 22(7) within the period of one month beginning with the day on which the contribution notice was served; or
(b)   served a notice under paragraph 22(8) withdrawing his agreement,

the authority may apply to the court for an order under this paragraph.

(2) On such an application the court may make an order ('a contribution order') requiring the contributor to contribute a weekly sum towards the child's maintenance in accordance with arrangements for payment specified by the court.

PART I – Statutes

(3) A contribution order –

(a) shall not specify a weekly sum greater than that specified in the contribution notice; and

(b) shall be made with due regard to the contributor's means.

(4) A contribution order shall not –

(a) take effect before the date specified in the contribution notice; or

(b) have effect while the contributor is not liable to contribute (by virtue of paragraph 21); or

(c) remain in force after the child has ceased to be looked after by the authority who obtained the order.

(5) An authority may not apply to the court under sub-paragraph (1) in relation to a contribution notice which they have withdrawn.

(6) Where –

(a) a contribution order is in force;

(b) the authority serve another contribution notice; and

(c) the contributor and the authority reach an agreement under paragraph 22(7) in respect of that other contribution notice,

the effect of the agreement shall be to discharge the order from the date on which it is agreed that the agreement shall take effect.

(7) Where an agreement is reached under sub-paragraph (6) the authority shall notify the court –

(a) of the agreement; and

(b) of the date on which it took effect.

(8) A contribution order may be varied or revoked on the application of the contributor or the authority.

(9) In proceedings for the variation of a contribution order, the authority shall specify –

(a) the weekly sum which, having regard to paragraph 22, they propose that the contributor should contribute under the order as varied; and

(b) the proposed arrangements for payment.

(10) Where a contribution order is varied, the order –

(a) shall not specify a weekly sum greater than that specified by the authority in the proceedings for variation; and

(b) shall be made with due regard to the contributor's means.

(11) An appeal shall lie in accordance with rules of court from any order made under this paragraph.

Enforcement of contribution orders etc

24. (1) ...[9]

(2) Where a contributor has agreed, or has been ordered, to make contributions to a local authority, any other local authority within whose area the contributor is for the time being living may –

    (a)   at the request of the local authority who served the contribution notice; and
    (b)   subject to agreement as to any sum to be deducted in respect of services rendered,

collect from the contributor any contributions due on behalf of the authority who served the notice.

(3) In sub-paragraph (2) the reference to any other local authority includes a reference to –

    [(aa) a local authority in Wales;][11]
    (a)   a local authority within the meaning of section 1(2) of the Social Work (Scotland) Act 1968; and
    (b)   a Health and Social Services Board established under Article 16 of the Health and Personal Social Services (Northern Ireland) Order 1972.

(4) The power to collect sums under sub-paragraph (2) includes the power to –

    (a)   receive and give a discharge for any contributions due; and
    (b)   (if necessary) enforce payment of any contributions,

even though those contributions may have fallen due at a time when the contributor was living elsewhere.

(5) Any contributions collected under sub-paragraph (2) shall be paid (subject to any agreed deduction) to the local authority who served the contribution notice.

(6) In any proceedings under this paragraph, a document which purports to be –

    (a)   a copy of an order made by a court under or by virtue of paragraph 23; and
    (b)   certified as a true copy by the [designated officer for][6] the court,

shall be evidence of the order.

(7) In any proceedings under this paragraph, a certificate which –

    (a)   purports to be signed by the clerk or some other duly authorised officer of the local authority who obtained the contribution order; and
    (b)   states that any sum due to the authority under the order is overdue and unpaid,

shall be evidence that the sum is overdue and unpaid.

Regulations

25. The [Secretary of State][7] may make regulations –

    (a)   as to the considerations which a local authority must take into account in deciding –
        (i)   whether it is reasonable to recover contributions; and
        (ii) what the arrangements for payment should be;

(b) as to the procedures [they][7] must follow in reaching agreements with –

    (i) contributors (under paragraph 22 and 23); and

    [(ii) any other local authority under paragraph 24(2).][7]

NOTES

Amendments.[1] Words substituted: Social Security (Consequential Provisions) Act 1992, s 4, Sch 2, para 108.[2] Words substituted or inserted: Tax Credits Act 2002, s 47, Sch 3, paras 15, 20.[3] Words substituted: Powers of Criminal Courts (Sentencing) Act 2000, s 165(1), Sch 9, para 131.[4] Words substituted: Welfare Reform Act 2007, s 28(1), Sch 3, para 6(1), (6).[5] Words substituted: Children and Young Persons Act 2008, s 8(2), Sch 1, para 5.[6] Words substituted: Courts Act 2003, s 109(1), Sch 8, para 340.[7] Words and subparagraph substituted: SI 2016/413, regs 55, 120.[8] Words inserted: Welfare Reform Act 2012, s 31, Sch 2, para 1.[9] Subparagraph omitted: Crime and Courts Act 2013, s 17, Sch 11, paras 102, 120.[10] Words inserted: SI 2016/413, regs 55, 118.[11] Paragraph inserted: SI 2016/413, regs 55, 119.[12] Words inserted: Sentencing Act 2020, s 410, Sch 24, para 113.

Definitions. 'Child': s 105(1); 'child who is looked after by a local authority': s 22(1); 'contribution notice': Sch 2, para 22(1); 'contribution order': Sch 2, para 23(2); 'contributor': Sch 2, para 21(1); 'local authority': s 105(1); 'local authority foster parent': s 23(3); 'signed': s 105(1); 'the court': s 92(7).

SCHEDULE 3
SUPERVISION ORDERS

Sections 35 and 36

PART I
GENERAL

Meaning of 'responsible person'

1. In this Schedule, 'the responsible person', in relation to a supervised child, means –

(a) any person who has parental responsibility for the child; and

(b) any other person with whom the child is living.

Power of supervisor to give directions to supervised child

2. (1) A supervision order may require the supervised child to comply with any directions given from time to time by the supervisor which require him to do all or any of the following things –

(a) to live at a place or places specified in the directions for a period or periods so specified;

(b) to present himself to a person or persons specified in the directions at a place or places and on a day or days so specified;

(c) to participate in activities specified in the directions on a day or days so specified.

(2) It shall be for the supervisor to decide whether, and to what extent, he exercises his power to give directions and to decide the form of any directions which he gives.

(3) Sub-paragraph (1) does not confer on a supervisor power to give directions in respect of any medical or psychiatric examination or treatment (which are matters dealt with in paragraphs 4 and 5).

Imposition of obligations on responsible person

3. (1) With the consent of any responsible person, a supervision order may include a requirement –

  (a)   that he take all reasonable steps to ensure that the supervised child complies with any direction given by the supervisor under paragraph 2;
  (b)   that he take all reasonable steps to ensure that the supervised child complies with any requirement included in the order under paragraph 4 or 5;
  (c)   that he comply with any directions given by the supervisor requiring him to attend at a place specified in the directions for the purpose of taking part in activities so specified.

(2) A direction given under sub-paragraph (1)(c) may specify the time at which the responsible person is to attend and whether or not the supervised child is required to attend with him.

(3) A supervision order may require any person who is a responsible person in relation to the supervised child to keep the supervisor informed of his address, if it differs from the child's.

Psychiatric and medical examinations

4. (1) A supervision order may require the supervised child –

  (a)   to submit to a medical or psychiatric examination; or
  (b)   to submit to any such examination from time to time as directed by the supervisor.

(2) Any such examination shall be required to be conducted –

  (a)   by, or under the direction of, such registered medical practitioner as may be specified in the order;
  (b)   at a place specified in the order and at which the supervised child is to attend as a non-resident patient; or
  (c)   at –
        (i)   a health service hospital; or
        (ii) in the case of a psychiatric examination, a hospital [, independent hospital or care home][1],
        at which the supervised child is, or is to attend as, a resident patient.

(3) A requirement of a kind mentioned in sub-paragraph (2)(c) shall not be included unless the court is satisfied, on the evidence of a registered medical practitioner, that –

  (a)   the child may be suffering from a physical or mental condition that requires, and may be susceptible to, treatment; and
  (b)   a period as a resident patient is necessary if the examination is to be carried out properly.

(4) No court shall include a requirement under this paragraph in a supervision order unless it is satisfied that –

(a)　where the child has sufficient understanding to make an informed decision, he consents to its inclusion; and

(b)　satisfactory arrangements have been, or can be, made for the examination.

Psychiatric and medical treatment

5. (1) Where a court which proposes to make or vary a supervision order is satisfied, on the evidence of a registered medical practitioner approved for the purposes of section 12 of the Mental Health Act 1983, that the mental condition of the supervised child –

(a)　is such as requires, and may be susceptible to, treatment; but

(b)　is not such as to warrant his detention in pursuance of a hospital order under Part III of that Act,

the court may include in the order a requirement that the supervised child shall, for a period specified in the order, submit to such treatment as is so specified.

(2) The treatment specified in accordance with sub-paragraph (1) must be –

(a)　by, or under the direction of, such registered medical practitioner as may be specified in the order;

(b)　as a non-resident patient at such a place as may be so specified; or

(c)　as a resident patient in a hospital [, independent hospital or care home][1].

(3) Where a court which proposes to make or vary a supervision order is satisfied, on the evidence of a registered medical practitioner, that the physical condition of the supervised child is such as requires, and may be susceptible to, treatment, the court may include in the order a requirement that the supervised child shall, for a period specified in the order, submit to such treatment as is so specified.

(4) The treatment specified in accordance with sub-paragraph (3) must be –

(a)　by, or under the direction of, such registered medical practitioner as may be specified in the order;

(b)　as a non-resident patient at such place as may be so specified; or

(c)　as a resident patient in a health service hospital.

(5) No court shall include a requirement under this paragraph in a supervision order unless it is satisfied –

(a)　where the child has sufficient understanding to make an informed decision, that he consents to its inclusion; and

(b)　that satisfactory arrangements have been, or can be, made for the treatment.

(6) If a medical practitioner by whom or under whose direction a supervised person is being treated in pursuance of a requirement included in a supervision order by virtue of this paragraph is unwilling to continue to treat or direct the treatment of the supervised child or is of the opinion that –

(a)　the treatment should be continued beyond the period specified in the order;

(b)　the supervised child needs different treatment;

PART I – Statutes

    (c)   he is not susceptible to treatment; or

    (d)   he does not require further treatment,

the practitioner shall make a report in writing to that effect to the supervisor.

(7) On receiving a report under this paragraph the supervisor shall refer it to the court, and on such a reference the court may make an order cancelling or varying the requirement.

NOTES

Amendments.[1] Words substituted: Care Standards Act 2000, s 116, Sch 4, para 14(24).
Definitions. 'Child': s 105(1); 'health service hospital': s 105(1); 'hospital': s 105(1); 'mental nursing home': s 105(1); 'parental responsibility': s 3; 'supervised child': s 105(1); 'supervision order': s 31(11); 'supervisor': s 105(1); 'the court': s 92(7); 'the responsible person': Sch 3, para 1.

PART II
MISCELLANEOUS

Life of supervision order

6. (1) Subject to sub-paragraph (2) and section 91, a supervision order shall cease to have effect at the end of the period of one year beginning with the date on which it was made.

(2) A supervision order shall also cease to have effect if an event mentioned in section 25(1)(a) or (b) of the Child Abduction and Custody Act 1985 (termination of existing orders) occurs with respect to the child.

(3) Where the supervisor applies to the court to extend, or further extend, a supervision order the court may extend the order for such period as it may specify.

(4) A supervision order may not be extended so as to run beyond the end of the period of three years beginning with the date on which it was made.

7. ...[1]

Information to be given to supervisor etc.

8. (1) A supervision order may require the supervised child –

    (a)   to keep the supervisor informed of any change in his address; and
    (b)   to allow the supervisor to visit him at the place where he is living.

(2) The responsible person in relation to any child with respect to whom a supervision order is made shall –

    (a)   if asked by the supervisor, inform him of the child's address (if it is known to him); and
    (b)   if he is living with the child, allow the supervisor reasonable contact with the child.

Selection of supervisor

9. (1) A supervision order shall not designate a local authority as the supervisor unless –

(a) the authority agree; or

(b) the supervised child lives or will live within their area.

(2)–(5) ...²

Effect of supervision order on earlier orders

10. The making of a supervision order with respect to any child brings to an end any earlier care or supervision order which –

(a) was made with respect to that child; and

(b) would otherwise continue in force.

Local authority functions and expenditure

11. (1) The Secretary of State may make regulations with respect to the exercise by a local authority of their functions where a child has been placed under their supervision by a supervision order.

(2) Where a supervision order requires compliance with directions given by virtue of this section, any expenditure incurred by the supervisor for the purposes of the directions shall be defrayed by the local authority designated in the order.

NOTES

Amendments.¹ Paragraph repealed: Courts and Legal Services Act 1990, ss 116, 125(7), Sch 16, para 27, Sch 20.² Subparagraphs omitted: Criminal Justice and Court Services Act 2000, ss 74, 75, Sch 7, paras 87, 96, Sch 8.

Definitions. 'Care order': ss 31(11), 105(1); 'child': s 105(1); 'local authority': s 105(1); 'supervised child': s 105(1); 'supervision order': s 31(11); 'supervisor': s 105(1); 'the appropriate authority': Sch 3, para 9(3); 'the responsible person': Sch 3, para 1.

PART III
EDUCATION SUPERVISION ORDERS

Effect of orders

12. (1) Where an education supervision order is in force with respect to a child, it shall be the duty of the supervisor –

(a) to advise, assist and befriend, and give directions to –

(i) the supervised child; and

(ii) his parents;

in such a way as will, in the opinion of the supervisor, secure that he is properly educated;

(b) where any such directions given to

(i) the supervised child; or

(ii) a parent of his,

have not been complied with, to consider what further steps to take in the exercise of the supervisor's powers under this Act.

(2) Before giving any directions under sub-paragraph (1) the supervisor shall, so far as is reasonably practicable, ascertain the wishes and feelings of –

(a)   the child; and
(b)   his parents;

including, in particular, their wishes as to the place at which the child should be educated.

(3) When settling the terms of any such directions, the supervisor shall give due consideration –

(a)   having regard to the child's age and understanding, to such wishes and feelings of his as the supervisor has been able to ascertain; and
(b)   to such wishes and feelings of the child's parents as he has been able to ascertain.

(4) Directions may be given under this paragraph at any time while the education supervision order is in force.

13. (1) Where an education supervision order is in force with respect to a child, the duties of the child's parents under [sections 7 and 444 of the Education Act 1996 (duties to secure education of children and][1] to secure regular attendance of registered pupils) shall be superseded by their duty to comply with any directions in force under the education supervision order.

(2) Where an education supervision order is made with respect to a child –

(a)   any school attendance order –
(i)   made under [section 437 of the Education Act 1996][1] with respect to the child; and
(ii)   in force immediately before the making of the education supervision order,
shall cease to have effect; and
(b)   while the education supervision order remains in force, the following provisions shall not apply with respect to the child –
(i)   [section 437][1] of that Act (school attendance orders);
(ii)   [section 9 of that Act][1] (pupils to be educated in accordance with wishes of their parents);
(iii)   [sections 411 and 423 of that Act][1] (parental preference and appeals against admission decisions);
[(c)   a youth rehabilitation order made under [Chapter 1 of Part 9 of the Sentencing Code][4] with respect to the child, while the education supervision order is in force, may not include an education requirement (within the meaning of that Part);][3]
(d)   any education requirement of a kind mentioned in paragraph (c), which was in force with respect to the child immediately before the making of the education supervision order, shall cease to have effect.

Effect where child also subject to supervision order

14. (1) This paragraph applies where an education supervision order and a supervision order, or [youth rehabilitation order (within [the meaning given by section 173 of the Sentencing Code][4])][3], are in force at the same time with respect to the same child.

(2) Any failure to comply with a direction given by the supervisor under the education supervision order shall be disregarded if it would not have been reasonably practicable to comply with it without failing to comply with a direction [or instruction]³ given under the other order.

Duration of orders

15. (1) An education supervision order shall have effect for a period of one year, beginning with the date on which it is made.

(2) An education supervision order shall not expire if, before it would otherwise have expired, the court has (on the application of the authority in whose favour the order was made) extended the period during which it is in force.

(3) Such an application may not be made earlier than three months before the date on which the order would otherwise expire.

(4) The period during which an education supervision order is in force may be extended under sub-paragraph (2) on more than one occasion.

(5) No one extension may be for a period of more than three years.

(6) An education supervision order shall cease to have effect on –

    (a)   the child's ceasing to be of compulsory school age; or
    (b)   the making of a care order with respect to the child;

and sub-paragraphs (1) to (4) are subject to this sub-paragraph.

Information to be given to supervisor etc.

16. (1) An education supervision order may require the child –

    (a)   to keep the supervisor informed of any change in his address; and
    (b)   to allow the supervisor to visit him at the place where he is living.

(2) A person who is the parent of a child with respect to whom an education supervision order has been made shall –

    (a)   if asked by the supervisor, inform him of the child's address (if it is known to him); and
    (b)   if he is living with the child, allow the supervisor reasonable contact with the child.

Discharge of orders

17. (1) The court may discharge any education supervision order on the application of –

    (a)   the child concerned;
    (b)   a parent of his; or
    (c)   [the local authority designated in the order]⁴.

PART I – Statutes

(2) On discharging an education supervision order, the court may direct the local authority within whose area the child lives, or will live, to investigate the circumstances of the child.

Offences

18. (1) If a parent of a child with respect to whom an education supervision order is in force persistently fails to comply with a direction given under the order he shall be guilty of an offence.

(2) It shall be a defence for any person charged with such an offence to prove that –

    (a)   he took all reasonable steps to ensure that the direction was complied with;

    (b)   the direction was unreasonable; or

    (c)   he had complied with –

        (i)   a requirement included in a supervision order made with respect to the child; or

        (ii) directions given under such a requirement,

        and that it was not reasonably practicable to comply both with the direction and with the requirement or directions mentioned in this paragraph.

(3) A person guilty of an offence under this paragraph shall be liable on summary conviction to a fine not exceeding level 3 on the standard scale.

Persistent failure of child to comply with directions

19. (1) Where a child with respect to whom an education supervision order is in force persistently fails to comply with any direction given under the order, [the local authority designated in the order shall notify the appropriate local authority, if different][4].

(2) Where a local authority have been notified under sub-paragraph (1) they shall investigate the circumstances of the child.

(3) In this paragraph 'the appropriate local authority' has the same meaning as in section 36.

Miscellaneous

20. The Secretary of State may by regulations make provision modifying, or displacing, the provisions of any enactment about education in relation to any child with respect to whom an education supervision order is in force to such extent as appears to the Secretary of State to be necessary or expedient in consequence of the provision made by this Act with respect to such orders.

Interpretation

21. In this part of this Schedule 'parent' has the same meaning as in [the Education Act 1996][1].

NOTES

Amendments.[1] Words substituted: Education Act 1996, s 582(1), Sch 37, Pt I, para 93.[2] Words substituted: Powers of Criminal Courts (Sentencing) Act 2000, s 165(1), Sch 9, para 131.[3] Subparagraph and words substituted, and words inserted: Criminal Justice and Immigration Act 2008, s 6(2), Sch 4, Pt 1, paras 33, 37(1)–(3).[4] Words substituted: SI 2010/1158.[5] Words substituted: Sentencing Act 2020, s 410, Sch 24, para 114.

Definitions. 'Care order': ss 31(11), 105(1); 'child': s 105(1); 'education supervision order': s 36(2); 'local education authority': s 105(1); 'parent': Sch 3, para 21; 'supervised child': s 105(1); 'supervision order': s 31(11); 'supervisor': s 105(1); 'the appropriate local authority': Sch 3, para 19(3); 'the court': s 92(7).

PART I – Statutes

SCHEDULE 4
MANAGEMENT AND CONDUCT OF COMMUNITY HOMES

Section 53(6)

PART I
INSTRUMENTS OF MANAGEMENT

Instruments of management for controlled and assisted community homes

1. (1) The Secretary of State may by order make an instrument of management providing for the constitution of a body of managers for any …[1] home which is designated as a controlled or assisted community home.

(2) Sub-paragraph (3) applies where two or more …[1] homes are designated as controlled community homes or as assisted community homes.

(3) If –

    (a)   those homes are, or are to be, provided by the same voluntary organisation; and

    (b)   the same local authority is to be represented on the body of managers for those homes,

a single instrument of management may be made by the Secretary of State under this paragraph constituting one body of managers for those homes or for any two or more of them.

(4) The number of persons who, in accordance with an instrument of management, constitute the body of managers for a …[1] home shall be such number (which must be a multiple of three) as may be specified in the instrument.

(5) The instrument shall provide that the local authority specified in the instrument shall appoint –

    (a)   in the case of a …[1] home which is designated as a controlled community home, two-thirds of the managers; and

    (b)   in the case of a …[1] home which is designated as an assisted community home, one-third of them.

(6) An instrument of management shall provide that the foundation managers shall be appointed, in such manner and by such persons as may be specified in the instrument –

    (a)   so as to represent the interests of the voluntary organisation by which the home is, or is to be, provided; and

    (b)   for the purpose of securing that

         (i)   so far as is practicable, the character of the home ...[1] will be preserved; and

         (ii) subject to paragraph 2(3), the terms of any trust deed relating to the home are observed.

(7) An instrument of management shall come into force on such date as it may specify.

(8) If an instrument of management is in force in relation to a ...[1] home the home shall be (and be known as) a controlled community home or an assisted community home, according to its designation.

(9) In this paragraph –

'foundation managers', in relation to a ...[1] home, means those of the managers of the home who are not appointed by a local authority in accordance with sub-paragraph (5); and
'designated' means designated in accordance with section 53.

2. (1) An instrument of management shall contain such provisions as the Secretary of State considers appropriate.

(2) Nothing in the instrument of management shall affect the purposes for which the premises comprising the home are held.

(3) Without prejudice to the generality of sub-paragraph (1), an instrument of management may contain provisions –

    (a)   specifying the nature and purpose of the home (or each of the homes) to which it relates;

    (b)   requiring a specified number or proportion of the places in that home (or those homes) to be made available to local authorities and to any other body specified in the instrument; and

    (c)   relating to the management of that home (or those homes) and the charging of fees with respect to –

         (i)   children placed there; or

         (ii) places made available to any local authority or other body.

(4) Subject to sub-paragraphs (1) and (2), in the event of any inconsistency between the provisions of any trust deed and an instrument of management, the instrument of management shall prevail over the provisions of the trust deed in so far as they relate to the home concerned.

(5) After consultation with the voluntary organisation concerned and with the local authority specified in its instrument of management, the Secretary of State may by order vary or revoke any provisions of the instrument.

NOTES

Amendments.[1] Words repealed: Courts and Legal Services Act 1990, ss 116, 125(7), Sch 16, para 28, Sch 20.

Definitions. 'Assisted community home': s 53(5); 'child': s 105(1); 'community home': s 53(1); 'controlled community home': s 53(4); 'designated': Sch 4, para 1(9); 'foundation managers': Sch 4, para 1(9); 'local authority': s 105(1); 'trust deed': s 55(6); 'voluntary home': s 60(3); 'voluntary organisation': s 105(1).

PART II
MANAGEMENT OF CONTROLLED AND ASSISTED COMMUNITY HOMES

3. (1) The management, equipment and maintenance of a controlled community home shall be the responsibility of the local authority specified in its instrument of management.

(2) The management, equipment and maintenance of an assisted community home shall be the responsibility of the voluntary organisation by which the home is provided.

(3) In this paragraph –

'home' means a controlled community home or (as the case may be) assisted community home; and

'the managers', in relation to a home, means the managers constituted by its instrument of management; and

'the responsible body', in relation to a home, means the local authority or (as the case may be) voluntary organisation responsible for its management, equipment and maintenance.

(4) The functions of a home's responsible body shall be exercised through the managers [, except in so far as, under section 53(3B), any of the accommodation is to be managed by another person][1].

(5) Anything done, liability incurred or property acquired by a home's managers shall be done, incurred or acquired by them as agents of the responsible body [; and similarly, to the extent that a contract so provides, as respects anything done, liability incurred or property acquired by a person by whom, under section 53(3B), any of the accommodation is to be managed][1].

(6) In so far as any matter is reserved for the decision of a home's responsible body by –

(a)   sub-paragraph (8);

(b)   the instrument of management;

(c)   the service by the body on the managers, or any of them, of a notice reserving any matter,

that matter shall be dealt with by the body and not by the managers.

(7) In dealing with any matter so reserved, the responsible body shall have regard to any representations made to the body by the managers.

(8) The employment of persons at a home shall be a matter reserved for the decision of the responsible body.

(9) Where the instrument of management of a controlled community home so provides, the responsible body may enter into arrangements with the voluntary

organisation by which that home is provided whereby, in accordance with such terms as may be agreed between them and the voluntary organisation, persons who are not in the employment of the responsible body shall undertake duties at that home.

(10) Subject to sub-paragraph (11) –

(a)   where the responsible body for an assisted community home proposes to engage any person to work at that home or to terminate without notice the employment of any person at that home, it shall consult the local authority specified in the instrument of management and, if that authority so direct, the responsible body shall not carry out its proposal without their consent; and

(b)   that local authority may, after consultation with the responsible body, require that body to terminate the employment of any person at that home.

(11) Paragraphs (a) and (b) of sub-paragraph (10) shall not apply –

(a)   in such cases or circumstances as may be specified by notice in writing given by the local authority to the responsible body; and

(b)   in relation to the employment of any persons or class of persons specified in the home's instrument of management.

(12) The accounting year of the managers of a home shall be such as may be specified by the responsible body.

(13) Before such date in each accounting year as may be so specified, the managers of a home shall submit to the responsible body estimates, in such form as the body may require, of expenditure and receipts in respect of the next accounting year.

(14) Any expenses incurred by the managers of a home with the approval of the responsible body shall be defrayed by that body.

(15) The managers of a home shall keep –

(a)   proper accounts with respect to the home; and
(b)   proper records in relation to the accounts.

(16) Where an instrument of management relates to more than one home, one set of accounts and records may be kept in respect of all the homes to which it relates.

NOTES

Amendments.[1] Words inserted: Criminal Justice and Public Order Act 1994, s 22.
Definitions. 'Assisted community home': s 53(5); 'community home': s 53(1); 'controlled community home': s 53(4); 'functions': s 105(1); 'home': Sch 4, para 3(3); 'local authority': s 105(1); 'the managers': Sch 4, para 3(3); 'the responsible body': Sch 4, para 3(3).

PART III
REGULATIONS

4. (1) The Secretary of State may make regulations –

(a)   as to the placing of children in community homes;

(b)–(c) ...[1]

(2), (3) ...[1]

NOTES

Amendments.[1] Paragraphs repealed: Care Standards Act 2000, s 117, Sch 6.

SCHEDULE 5
VOLUNTARY HOMES AND VOLUNTARY ORGANISATIONS

Section 60(4)

PART I
REGISTRATION OF VOLUNTARY HOMES

1.–6. ...[1]

NOTES

Amendments.[1] Part repealed: Care Standards Act 2000, s 117, Sch 6

PART II
REGULATIONS AS TO VOLUNTARY HOMES

Regulations as to conduct of voluntary homes

7. (1) The [appropriate national authority][2] may make regulations –

    (a)   as to the placing of children in voluntary homes;
    (b)–(c) ...[1]

(2)–(4) ...[1]

8. ...[1]

NOTES

Amendments.[1] Paragraph and sub-paragraphs repealed: Care Standards Act 2000, s 117, Sch 6.[2] Words substituted: Children and Young Persons Act 2008, s 39, Sch 3, paras 1, 28.

SCHEDULE 6
[PRIVATE CHILDREN'S HOMES][1]

Section 63(11)

PART I
REGISTRATION

1.–9. ...[2]

NOTES

Amendments.[1] Heading substituted: Care Standards Act 2000, s 116, Sch 4, para 14(1), (25) (a).[2] Part repealed: Care Standards Act 2000, s 117, Sch 6.

PART II
REGULATIONS

10. (1) The Secretary of State may make regulations –

PART I – Statutes

(a)   as to the placing of children in [private][1] children's homes;

(b)–(c) …[2]

(2) The regulations may in particular –

(a)–(k) …[2]

(l)   make provision similar to that made by regulations under section 26.

(3), (4) …[2]

NOTES

Amendments.[1] Word substituted: Care Standards Act 2000, s 116, Sch 4, para 14(25).[2] Paragraphs and sub-paragraphs repealed: Care Standards Act 2000, s 117, Sch 6.

SCHEDULE 7
FOSTER PARENTS: LIMITS ON NUMBER OF FOSTER CHILDREN

Section 63(12)

Interpretation

1. For the purposes of this Schedule, a person fosters a child if –

(a)   he is a local authority foster parent in relation to the child;

(b)   he is a foster parent with whom the child has been placed by a voluntary organisation; or

(c)   he fosters the child privately.

The usual fostering limit

2. Subject to what follows, a person may not foster more than three children ('the usual fostering limit').

Siblings

3. A person may exceed the usual fostering limit if the children concerned are all siblings with respect to each other.

Exemption by local authority

4. (1) A person may exceed the usual fostering limit if he is exempted from it by the local authority within whose area he lives.

(2) In considering whether to exempt a person, a local authority shall have regard, in particular, to –

(a)   the number of children whom the person proposes to foster;

(b)   the arrangements which the person proposes for the care and accommodation of the fostered children;

(c)   the intended and likely relationship between the person and the fostered children;

(d)   the period of time for which he proposes to foster the children; and
(e)   whether the welfare of the fostered children (and of any other children who are or will be living in the accommodation) will be safeguarded and promoted.

(3) Where a local authority exempt a person, they shall inform him by notice in writing –

(a)   that he is so exempted;
(b)   of the children, described by name, whom he may foster; and
(c)   of any condition to which the exemption is subject.

(4) A local authority may at any time by notice in writing –

(a)   vary or cancel an exemption; or
(b)   impose, vary or cancel a condition to which the exemption is subject,

and, in considering whether to do so, they shall have regard in particular to the considerations mentioned in sub-paragraph (2).

(5) The Secretary of State may make regulations amplifying or modifying the provisions of this paragraph in order to provide for cases where children need to be placed with foster parents as a matter of urgency.

Effect of exceeding fostering limit

5. [(A1) This paragraph applies to a person fostering in England.][2]

(1) A person shall cease to be treated [, for the purposes of this Act and the Care Standards Act 2000][1] as fostering and shall be treated as carrying on a children's home if –

(a)   he exceeds the usual fostering limit; or
(b)   where he is exempted under paragraph 4 –
    (i)   he fosters any child not named in the exemption; and
    (ii)   in so doing, he exceeds the usual fostering limit.

(2) Sub-paragraph (1) does not apply if the children concerned are all siblings in respect of each other.

[**5A.** (1) This paragraph applies to a person (P) fostering in Wales.

(2) Sub-paragraph (3) applies where—

(a)   P exceeds the usual fostering limit and is not exempted under paragraph 4;
(b)   P is exempted under paragraph 4 and exceeds the usual fostering limit by fostering a child not named in the exemption.

(3) Where this paragraph applies, P is not to be treated as fostering and is to be treated for the purposes of the Regulation and Inspection of Social Care (Wales) Act 2016 as providing a care home service.

(4) But sub-paragraph (3) does not apply if the children fostered are all siblings in respect of each other.][2]

NOTES

Amendments.[1] Words inserted: Care Standards Act 2000, s 116, Sch 4, para 14(26).[2] Sub-paragraph and paragraph inserted: Regulation and Inspection of Social Care (Wales) Act 2016 (Consequential Amendments) Regulations 2018, SI 2018/195, regs 8, 13.

Complaints etc

6. (1) Every local authority shall establish a procedure for considering any representations (including any complaint) made to them about the discharge of their functions under paragraph 4 by a person exempted or seeking to be exempted under that paragraph.

(2) In carrying out any consideration of representations under subparagraph (1), a local authority shall comply with any regulations made by the Secretary of State for the purposes of this paragraph.

NOTES

Definitions. 'Child': s 105(1); 'children's home': s 23; 'foster': Sch 7, para 1; 'local authority': s 105(1); 'local authority foster parent': s 23(3); 'the usual fostering limit': Sch 7, para 2; 'voluntary organisation': s 105(1).

SCHEDULE 8
PRIVATELY FOSTERED CHILDREN

Section 66(5)

Exemptions

1. A child is not a privately fostered child while he is being looked after by a local authority.

2. (1) A child is not a privately fostered child while he is in the care of any person –

    (a)   in premises in which any –
        (i)   parent of his;
        (ii) person who is not a parent of his but who has parental responsibility for him; or
        (iii) person who is a relative of his and who has assumed responsibility for his care,
        is for the time being living;
    (b)   ...[1]
    (c)   in accommodation provided by or on behalf of any voluntary organisation;
    (d)   in any school in which he is receiving full-time education;
    (e)   in any health service hospital;
    (f)   [in any care home or independent hospital;][2]
    (g)   in any home or institution not specified in this paragraph but provided, equipped and maintained by the Secretary of State.

(2) Sub-paragraph [(1)(c)][1] to (g) does not apply where the person caring for the child is doing so in his personal capacity and not in the course of carrying out his duties in relation to the establishment mentioned in the paragraph in question.

PART I – Statutes

NOTES

Amendments.[1] Sub-paragraph repealed and word substituted: Care Standards Act 2000, s 116, Sch 4, para 14(27).[2] Sub-paragraph substituted: Care Standards Act 2000, s 116, Sch 4, para 14(28).

3. A child is not a privately fostered child while he is in the care of any person in compliance with –

[(a) a youth rehabilitation order made under [Chapter 1 of Part 9 of the Sentencing Code][3];][2]; or

(b) a supervision requirement within the meaning of [Part II of the Children (Scotland) Act 1995][1].

NOTES

Amendments.[1] Words substituted: Children (Scotland) Act 1995, s 105(4), Sch 4, para 48(1), (5).[2] Subparagraph substituted: Criminal Justice and Immigration Act 2008, s 6(2), Sch 4, Pt 1, paras 33, 38.[3] Words substituted: Sentencing Act 2020, s 410, Sch 24, para 115.

4. A child is not a privately fostered child while he is liable to be detained, or subject to guardianship, under the Mental Health Act 1983.

5. A child is not a privately fostered child while [he is placed in the care of a person who proposes to adopt him under arrangements made by an adoption agency within the meaning of –

(a) section 2 of the Adoption and Children Act 2002;

[(b) section 119 of the Adoption and Children (Scotland) Act 2007; or][3]

(c) Article 3 of the Adoption (Northern Ireland) Order 1987][1]

[or while he is a child in respect of whom a local authority have functions by virtue of regulations under section 83(6)(b) of the Adoption and Children Act 2002 (which relates to children brought into the United Kingdom for adoption), or corresponding functions by virtue of regulations under section 1 of the Adoption (Intercountry Aspects) Act 1999 (regulations to give effect to Hague Convention on Protection of Children and Co-operation in respect of Intercountry Adoption)][2]

NOTES

Amendments.[1] Words substituted: Adoption and Children Act 2002, s 139(1), Sch 3, paras 54, 73.[2] Words inserted: Children and Adoption Act 2006, s 14(3).[3] Sub-paragraph substituted: Adoption and Children (Scotland) Act 2007 (Consequential Modifications) Order 2011, SI 2011/1740, art 2, Sch 1, Pt 1, para 3(1), (3).

Power of local authority to impose requirements

6. (1) Where a person is fostering any child privately, or proposes to foster any child privately, the appropriate local authority may impose on him requirements as to –

(a) the number, age and sex of the children who may be privately fostered by him;

(b) the standard of the accommodation and equipment to be provided for them;

(c) the arrangements to be made with respect to their health and safety; and

(d) particular arrangements which must be made with respect to the provision of care for them, and it shall be his duty to comply with any such requirement before the end of such period as the authority may specify unless, in the case of a proposal, the proposal is not carried out.

(2) A requirement may be limited to a particular child, or class of child.

(3) A requirement (other than one imposed under sub-paragraph (1)(a)) may be limited by the authority so as to apply only when the number of children fostered by the person exceeds a specified number.

(4) A requirement shall be imposed by notice in writing addressed to the person on whom it is imposed and informing him of –

    (a)   the reason for imposing the requirement;
    (b)   his right under paragraph 8 to appeal against it; and
    (c)   the time within which he may do so.

(5) A local authority may at any time vary any requirement, impose any additional requirement or remove any requirement.

(6) In this Schedule –

    (a)   'the appropriate local authority' means –
        (i)   the local authority within whose area the child is being fostered; or
        (ii) in the case of a proposal to foster a child, the local authority within whose area it is proposed that he will be fostered; and
    (b)   'requirement', in relation to any person, means a requirement imposed on him under this paragraph.

Regulations requiring notification of fostering etc

7. (1) The Secretary of State may by regulations make provision as to –

    (a)   the circumstances in which notification is required to be given in connection with children who are, have been or are proposed to be fostered privately; and
    (b)   the manner and form in which such notification is to be given.

(2) The regulations may, in particular –

    (a)   require any person who is, or proposes to be, involved (whether or not directly) in arranging for a child to be fostered privately to notify the appropriate authority;
    (b)   require any person who is –
        (i)   a parent of a child; or
        (ii) a person who is not a parent of his but who has parental responsibility for a child,
        and who knows that it is proposed that the child should be fostered privately, to notify the appropriate authority;
    (c)   require any parent of a privately fostered child, or person who is not a parent of such a child but who has parental responsibility for him, to notify the appropriate authority of any change in his address;
    (d)   require any person who proposes to foster a child privately, to notify the appropriate authority of his proposal;

(e) require any person who is fostering a child privately, or proposes to do so, to notify the appropriate authority of –

    (i) any offence of which he has been convicted;

    (ii) any disqualification imposed on him under section 68; or

    (iii) any prohibition imposed on him under section 69;

(f) require any person who is fostering a child privately, to notify the appropriate authority of any change in his address;

(g) require any person who is fostering a child privately to notify the appropriate authority in writing of any person who begins, or ceases, to be part of his household;

(h) require any person who has been fostering a child privately, but has ceased to do so, to notify the appropriate authority (indicating, where the child has died, that that is the reason).

[7A. Every local authority must promote public awareness in their area of requirements as to notification for which provision is made under paragraph 7.][1]

NOTES

Amendments.[1] Paragraph inserted in relation to England: Children Act 2004, s 44(7).

Appeals

8. (1) A person aggrieved by –

(a) a requirement imposed under paragraph 6;

(b) a refusal of consent under section 68;

(c) a prohibition imposed under section 69;

(d) a refusal to cancel such a prohibition;

(e) a refusal to make an exemption under paragraph 4 of Schedule 7;

(f) a condition imposed in such an exemption; or

(g) a variation or cancellation of such an exemption,

may appeal to the court.

(2) The appeal must be made within fourteen days from the date on which the person appealing is notified of the requirement, refusal, prohibition, condition, variation or cancellation.

(3) Where the appeal is against –

(a) a requirement imposed under paragraph 6;

(b) a condition of an exemption imposed under paragraph 4 of Schedule 7; or

(c) a variation or cancellation of such an exemption,

the requirement, condition, variation or cancellation shall not have effect while the appeal is pending.

(4) Where it allows an appeal against a requirement or prohibition, the court may, instead of cancelling the requirement or prohibition –

(a) vary the requirement, or allow more time for compliance with it; or

(b)   if an absolute prohibition has been imposed, substitute for it a prohibition on using the premises after such time as the court may specify unless such specified requirements as the local authority had power to impose under paragraph 6 are complied with.

(5) Any requirement or prohibition specified or substituted by a court under this paragraph shall be deemed for the purposes of Part IX (other than this paragraph) to have been imposed by the local authority under paragraph 6 or (as the case may be) section 69.

(6) Where it allows an appeal against a refusal to make an exemption, a condition imposed in such an exemption or a variation or cancellation of such an exemption, the court may –

(a)   make an exemption;
(b)   impose a condition; or
(c)   vary the exemption.

(7) Any exemption made or varied under sub-paragraph (6), or any condition imposed under that sub-paragraph, shall be deemed for the purposes of Schedule 7 (but not for the purposes of this paragraph) to have been made, varied or imposed under that Schedule.

(8) Nothing in sub-paragraph (1)(e) to (g) confers any right of appeal on –

(a)   a person who is, or would be if exempted under Schedule 7, a local authority foster parent; or
(b)   a person who is, or would be if so exempted, a person with whom a child is placed by a voluntary organisation.

Extension of Part IX to certain school children during holidays

9. (1) Where a child under sixteen who is a pupil at a school . . .[1] lives at the school during school holidays for a period of more than two weeks, Part IX shall apply in relation to the child as if –

(a)   while living at the school, he were a privately fostered child; and
(b)   paragraphs [2(1)(c) and (d)][2] and 6 were omitted.

[But this sub-paragraph does not apply to a school which is [a children's home in respect of which a person is registered under Part 2 of the Care Standards Act 2000][3] [or Part 1 of the Regulation and Inspection of Social Care (Wales) Act 2016][4].][2]

(2) Sub-paragraph (3) applies to any person who proposes to care for and accommodate one or more children at a school in circumstances in which some or all of them will be treated as private foster children by virtue of this paragraph.

(3) That person shall, not less than two weeks before the first of those children is treated as a private foster child by virtue of this paragraph during the holiday in question, give written notice of his proposal to the local authority within whose area the child is ordinarily resident ('the appropriate authority'), stating the estimated number of the children.

(4) A local authority may exempt any person from the duty of giving notice under sub-paragraph (3).

(5) Any such exemption may be granted for a special period or indefinitely and may be revoked at any time by notice in writing given to the person exempted.

(6) Where a child who is treated as a private foster child by virtue of this paragraph dies, the person caring for him at the school shall, not later than 48 hours after the death, give written notice of it –

   (a)   to the appropriate local authority; and

   (b)   where reasonably practicable, to each parent of the child and to every person who is not a parent of his but who has parental responsibility for him.

(7) Where a child who is treated as a foster child by virtue of this paragraph ceases for any other reason to be such a child, the person caring for him at the school shall give written notice of the fact to the appropriate local authority.

NOTES

Amendments.[1] Words repealed: Care Standards Act 2000, s 110.[2] Words inserted and substituted: Care Standards Act 2000, s 116, Sch 4, para 14(27).[3] Words substituted: Children and Young Persons Act 2008, s 8(2), Sch 1, para 6.[4] Words inserted: Regulation and Inspection of Social Care (Wales) Act 2016 (Consequential Amendments) Regulations 2018, SI 2018/195, regs 8, 14.

Prohibition of advertisements relating to fostering

10. No advertisement indicating that a person will undertake, or will arrange for, a child to be privately fostered shall be published, unless it states that person's name and address.

Avoidance of insurances on lives of privately fostered children

11. A person who fosters a child privately and for reward shall be deemed for the purposes of the Life Assurance Act 1774 to have no interest in the life of the child.

NOTES

Definitions. 'Child': s 105(1); 'child who is looked after by a local authority': s 22(1); 'children's home': s 23; 'health service hospital': s 105(1); 'local authority': s 105(1); 'local authority foster parent': s 23(3); 'local education authority': s 105(1); 'mental nursing home': s 105(1); 'nursing home': s 105(1); 'parental responsibility': s 3; 'privately fostered child': s 66; 'relative': s 105(1); 'requirement': Sch 8, para 6(6); 'residential care home': s 105(1); 'school': s 105(1); 'the appropriate local authority': Sch 8, para 6(6); 'the court': s 92(7); 'to foster a child privately': s 66; 'voluntary organisation': s 105(1).

[Schedule 9 ceases to extend to England and Wales.]

[SCHEDULE 9A[1]
CHILD MINDING AND DAY CARE FOR YOUNG CHILDREN [IN WALES][2]

NOTES

Amendments.[1] Schedule 9A repealed in relation to Wales: Children and Families (Wales) Measure 2010, s 73, Sch 2 (with transitional and savings provisions, SI 2010/2582, Schs 2, 3).[2] Words inserted: Childcare Act 2006, s 103(1), Sch 2, para 18(1), (2).

[Exemption of certain schools

1. (1) Except in prescribed circumstances, Part XA does not apply to provision of day care within sub-paragraph (2) for any child looked after in –

    (a)   a maintained school;

    (b)   a school assisted by a [local authority][2];

    (c)   a school in respect of which payments are made by …[1] the Assembly under section 485 of the Education Act 1996;

    (d)   an independent school.

(2) The provision mentioned in sub-paragraph (1) is provision of day care made by –

    (a)   the person carrying on the establishment in question as part of the establishment's activities; or

    (b)   a person employed to work at that establishment and authorised to make that provision as part of the establishment's activities.

(3) In sub-paragraph (1) –

'assisted' has the same meaning as in the Education Act 1996;

'maintained school' has the meaning given by section 20(7) of the School Standards and Framework Act 1998.][3]

NOTES

Amendments.[1] Words repealed: Childcare Act 2006, s 103, Sch 2, para 18(1), (3), Sch 3, Pt 2.[2] Words substituted: SI 2010/1158.[3] Schedule 9A repealed in relation to Wales: Children and Families (Wales) Measure 2010, s 73, Sch 2 (with transitional and savings provisions, SI 2010/2582, Schs 2, 3).

[Exemption for other establishments

2. (1) Part XA does not apply to provision of day care within sub-paragraph (2) for any child looked after –

    (a)   in *an appropriate children's home* [a children's home in respect of which a person is registered under Part 2 of the Care Standards Act 2000][3];

    (b)   in a care home;

    (c)   as a patient in a hospital (within the meaning of the Care Standards Act 2000);

    (d)   in a residential family centre.

(2) The provision mentioned in sub-paragraph (1) is provision of day care made by –

    (a)   the department, authority or other person carrying on the establishment in question as part of the establishment's activities; or

    (b)   a person employed to work at that establishment and authorised to make that provision as part of the establishment's activities.

[2A. (1) Part XA does not apply to provision of day care in a hotel, guest house or other similar establishment for children staying in that establishment where –

(a)   the provision takes place only between 6pm and 2 am; and

(b)   the person providing the care is doing so for no more than two different clients at the same time.

(2) For the purposes of sub-paragraph (1)(b), a 'client' is a person at whose request (or persons at whose joint request) day care is provided for a child.]¹]²

NOTES

Amendments.¹ Paragraph inserted: Children Act 2004, s 48, Sch 4, paras 1, 7.² Schedule 9A repealed in relation to Wales: Children and Families (Wales) Measure 2010, s 73, Sch 2 (with transitional and savings provisions, SI 2010/2582, Schs 2, 3).³ Words in italics substituted by words in square brackets: Children and Young Persons Act 2008, s 8(2), Sch 1, para 7.

[Exemption for occasional facilities

3. (1) Where day care is provided on particular premises on less than six days in any year, that provision shall be disregarded for the purposes of Part XA if the person making it has notified [the Assembly]¹ in writing before the first occasion on which the premises concerned are so used in that year.

(2) In sub-paragraph (1) 'year' means the year beginning with the day (after the commencement of paragraph 5 of Schedule 9) on which the day care in question was or is first provided on the premises concerned and any subsequent year.]²

NOTES

Amendments.¹ Words substituted: Childcare Act 2006, s 103(1), Sch 2, para 6.² Schedule 9A repealed in relation to Wales: Children and Families (Wales) Measure 2010, s 73, Sch 2 (with transitional and savings provisions, SI 2010/2582, Schs 2, 3).

[Disqualification for registration

4. (1) Regulations may provide for a person to be disqualified for registration for child minding or providing day care [in Wales]⁶.

(2) The regulations may, in particular, provide for a person to be disqualified where –

(a)   he is included in the list kept under section 1 of the Protection of Children Act 1999;

[(b)   he is subject to a direction under section 142 of the Education Act 2002, given on the grounds that he is unsuitable to work with children [or on grounds relating to his health]⁵]²;

[(ba) he is barred from regulated activity relating to children (within the meaning of section 3(2) of the Safeguarding Vulnerable Groups Act 2006);]⁷

(c)   an order of a prescribed kind has been made at any time with respect to him;

(d)   an order of a prescribed kind has been made at any time with respect to any child who has been in his care;

(e)   a requirement of a prescribed kind has been imposed at any time with respect to such a child, under or by virtue of any enactment;

(f)   he has at any time been refused registration under Part X or Part XA[, or Part 3 of the Childcare Act 2006,]⁶ or any prescribed enactment or had any such registration cancelled;

(g)   he has been convicted of any offence of a prescribed kind, or has been …[4] discharged absolutely or conditionally for any such offence;

[(ga) he has been given a caution in respect of any offence of a prescribed kind;][5]

(h)   he has at any time been disqualified from fostering a child privately;

(j)   a prohibition has been imposed on him at any time under section 69, section 10 of the Foster Children (Scotland) Act 1984 or any prescribed enactment;

(k)   his rights and powers with respect to a child have at any time been vested in a prescribed authority under a prescribed enactment.

(3) Regulations may provide for a person who lives –

(a)   in the same household as a person who is himself disqualified for registration for child minding or providing day care [in Wales]; or

(b)   in a household at which any such person is employed,

to be disqualified for registration for child minding or providing day care [in Wales].

[(3A) Regulations under this paragraph may provide for a person not to be disqualified for registration [(and may in particular provide for a person not to be disqualified for registration for the purposes of sub-paragraphs (4) and (5))][3] by reason of any fact which would otherwise cause him to be disqualified if –

(a)   he has disclosed the fact to [the Assembly][6], and

(b)   [the Assembly][6] has consented in writing …[3] and has not withdrawn that consent.][1]

(4) A person who is disqualified for registration for providing day care [in Wales][6] shall not provide day care, or be [directly][3] concerned in the management of …[3] any provision of day care [in Wales][6].

(5) No person shall employ, in connection with the provision of day care [in Wales][6], a person who is disqualified for registration for providing day care [in Wales][6].

[(6) In this paragraph –

'caution' includes a reprimand or warning within the meaning of section 65 of the Crime and Disorder Act 1998;

'enactment' means any enactment having effect, at any time, in any part of the United Kingdom.][5]

[(7) A conviction in respect of which a probation order was made before 1st October 1992 (which would not otherwise be treated as a conviction) is to be treated as a conviction for the purposes of this paragraph.][4][8]

NOTES

Amendments.[1] Sub-paragraph inserted: Education Act 2002, s 152, Sch 13, para 6.[2] Subparagraph substituted: Education Act 2002, s 215(1), Sch 21, para 9.[3] Words inserted or repealed in relation to England: Children Act 2004, ss 48, 64, Sch 4, paras 1, 5, 8, Sch 5, Pt 2.[4] Words repealed and subparagraph inserted: Criminal Justice Act 2003, ss 304, 332, Sch 32, Pt 1, paras 59, 61(1)–(3), Sch 37, Pt 7.[5] Words

PART I – Statutes

and subparagraph inserted, and subparagraph substituted: Childcare Act 2006, s 102(1), (2)(a).[6] Words inserted and substituted: Childcare Act 2006, s 103(1), Sch 2, paras 6, 18(1), (4).[7] Subparagraph inserted: Safeguarding Vulnerable Groups Act 2006, s 63(1), Sch 9, Pt 1, para 1.[8] Schedule 9A repealed in relation to Wales: Children and Families (Wales) Measure 2010, s 73, Sch 2 (with transitional and savings provisions, SI 2010/2582, Schs 2, 3).

[5. (1) If any person –

    (a)   acts as a child minder [in Wales][1] at any time when he is disqualified for registration for child minding [in Wales][1]; or

    (b)   contravenes [sub-paragraph (4) or (5)][2] of paragraph 4,

he shall be guilty of an offence.

[(2) A person who contravenes sub-paragraph (4) of paragraph 4 shall not be guilty of an offence under this paragraph if –

    (a)   he is disqualified for registration by virtue only of regulations made under sub-paragraph (3) of paragraph 4, and

    (b)   he proves that he did not know, and had no reasonable grounds for believing, that he was living in the same household as a person who was disqualified for registration or in a household in which such a person was employed.][2]

(3) Where a person contravenes sub-paragraph (5) of paragraph 4, he shall not be guilty of an offence under this paragraph if he proves that he did not know, and had no reasonable grounds for believing, that the person whom he was employing was disqualified.

(4) A person guilty of an offence under this paragraph shall be liable on summary conviction to imprisonment for a term not exceeding six months, or to a fine not exceeding level 5 on the standard scale, or to both.][3]

NOTES

Amendments.[1] Words inserted: Childcare Act 2006, s 103(1), Sch 2, para 18(1), (5).[2] Words and subparagraph substituted in relation to England: Childcare Act 2006, s 103(1), Sch 2, para 18(1), (5).[3] Schedule 9A repealed in relation to Wales: Children and Families (Wales) Measure 2010, s 73, Sch 2 (with transitional and savings provisions, SI 2010/2582, Schs 2, 3).

[Provision of day care: unincorporated associations

5A. (1) References in Part XA to a person, so far as relating to the provision of day care, include an unincorporated association.

(2) Proceedings for an offence under Part XA which is alleged to have been committed by an unincorporated association must be brought in the name of the association (and not in that of any of its members).

(3) For the purpose of any such proceedings, rules of court relating to the service of documents are to have effect as if the association were a body corporate.

(4) In proceedings for an offence under Part XA brought against an unincorporated association, section 33 of the Criminal Justice Act 1925 and Schedule 3 to the Magistrates' Courts Act 1980 (procedure) apply as they do in relation to a body corporate.

(5) A fine imposed on an unincorporated association on its conviction of an offence under Part XA is to be paid out of the funds of the association.

(6) If an offence under Part XA committed by an unincorporated association is shown –

    (a)   to have been committed with the consent or connivance of an officer of the association or a member of its governing body, or

    (b)   to be attributable to any neglect on the part of such an officer or member,

the officer or member as well as the association is guilty of the offence and liable to proceeded against and punished accordingly.][1, 2]

NOTES

Amendments.[1] Paragraph inserted: Children Act 2004, s 48, Sch 4, paras 1, 9.[2] Schedule 9A repealed in relation to Wales: Children and Families (Wales) Measure 2010, s 73, Sch 2 (with transitional and savings provisions, SI 2010/2582, Schs 2, 3).

[Certificates of registration

6. (1) If an application for registration is granted, [the Assembly][1] shall give the applicant a certificate of registration.

(2) A certificate of registration shall give prescribed information about prescribed matters.

(3) Where, due to a change of circumstances, any part of the certificate requires to be amended, [the Assembly][1] shall issue an amended certificate.

(4) Where [the Assembly][1] is satisfied that the certificate has been lost or destroyed, the authority shall issue a copy, on payment by the registered person of any prescribed fee.

(5) For the purposes of Part XA, a person is –

    (a)   registered for providing child minding [in Wales][1]; or

    (b)   registered for providing day care on any premises [in Wales][1],

if a certificate of registration to that effect is in force in respect of him.][2]

NOTES

Amendments.[1] Words substituted and inserted: Childcare Act 2006, s 103(1), Sch 2, paras 6, 18(1), (6).[2] Schedule 9A repealed in relation to Wales: Children and Families (Wales) Measure 2010, s 73, Sch 2 (with transitional and savings provisions, SI 2010/2582, Schs 2, 3).

[...[1] Fees

7. Regulations may require registered persons to pay to [the Assembly][2][, at or by the prescribed times, fees of the prescribed amounts in respect of the discharge by [the Assembly][2] of its functions under Part XA][1].][3]

NOTES

Amendments.[1] Word repealed and words substituted: Children Act 2004, ss 48, 64, Sch 4, paras 1, 4(2), Sch 5, Pt 2.[2] Words substituted: Childcare Act 2006, s 103(1), Sch 2, para 6.[3] Schedule 9A repealed in relation to Wales: Children and Families (Wales) Measure 2010, s 73, Sch 2 (with transitional and savings provisions, SI 2010/2582, Schs 2, 3).

[Co-operation between authorities

8. (1) …[1]

(2) Where it appears to the Assembly that any local authority in Wales could, by taking any specified action, help in the exercise of any of its functions under Part XA, the Assembly may request the help of that authority specifying the action in question.

(3) An authority whose help is so requested shall comply with the request if it is compatible with their own statutory or other duties and obligations and does not unduly prejudice the discharge of any of their functions.][2]][3]

NOTES

Amendments.[1] Subparagraph repealed: Childcare Act 2006, s 103, Sch 2, para 18(1), (7), Sch 3, Pt 2.[2] Schedule inserted: Care Standards Act 2000, s 79(2), Sch 3.[3] Schedule 9A repealed in relation to Wales: Children and Families (Wales) Measure 2010, s 73, Sch 2 (with transitional and savings provisions, SI 2010/2582, Schs 2, 3).

SCHEDULE 10
AMENDMENTS OF ADOPTION LEGISLATION

[not reproduced]

SCHEDULE 11
JURISDICTION

Section 92

PART I

…[1]

NOTES

Amendments.[1] Schedule 11, Part 1 repealed: Crime and Courts Act 2013, s 17, Sch 11, paras 102, 121.

PART II
CONSEQUENTIAL AMENDMENTS

[not reproduced]

SCHEDULE 12
MINOR AMENDMENTS

[not reproduced]

SCHEDULE 13
CONSEQUENTIAL AMENDMENTS

[not reproduced]

SCHEDULE 14
TRANSITIONALS AND SAVINGS

Section 108(6)

Pending Proceedings, etc

1. (1) [Subject to sub-paragraphs (1A) and (4)]¹, nothing in any provision of this Act (other than the repeals mentioned in sub-paragraph (2)) shall affect any proceedings which are pending immediately before the commencement of that provision.

[(1A) Proceedings pursuant to section 7(2) of the Family Law Reform Act 1969 (committal or wards of court to care of local authority) or in the exercise of the High Court's inherent jurisdiction with respect to children which are pending in relation to a child who has been placed or allowed to remain in the care of a local authority shall not be treated as pending proceedings after 13th October 1992 for the purposes of this Schedule if no final order has been made by that date pursuant to section 7(2) of the 1969 Act or in the exercise of the High Court's inherent jurisdiction in respect of the child's care.]¹

(2) The repeals are those of –

(a)   section 42(3) of the Matrimonial Causes Act 1973 (declaration by court that party to marriage unfit to have custody of children of family); and

(b)   section 38 of the Sexual Offences Act 1956 (power of court to divest person of authority over girl or boy in cases of incest).

(3) For the purposes of the following provisions of this Schedule, any reference to an order in force immediately before the commencement of a provision of this Act shall be construed as including a reference to an order made after that commencement in proceedings pending before that commencement.

(4) Sub-paragraph (3) is not to be read as making the order in question have effect from a date earlier than that on which it was made.

(5) An order under section 96(3) may make such provision with respect to the application of the order in relation to proceedings which are pending when the order comes into force as the Lord Chancellor considers appropriate.

2. Where, immediately before the day on which Part IV comes into force, there was in force an order under section 3(1) of the Children and Young Persons Act 1963 (order directing a local authority to bring a child or young person before a [youth court]⁶ under section 1 of the Children and Young Persons Act 1969), the order shall cease to have effect on that day.

Custody orders, etc

Cessation of declarations of unfitness, etc.

3. Where, immediately before the day on which Parts I and II come into force, there was in force –

(a) a declaration under section 42(3) of the Matrimonial Causes Act 1973 (declaration by court that party to marriage unfit to have custody of children of family); or

(b) an order under section 38(1) of the Sexual Offences Act 1956 divesting a person of authority over a girl or boy in a case of incest;

the declaration or, as the case may be, the order shall cease to have effect on that day.

The Family Law Reform Act 1987 (c. 42)

Conversion of orders under section 4

4. Where, immediately before the day on which Parts I and II come into force, there was in force an order under section 4(1) of the Family Law Reform Act 1987 (order giving father parental rights and duties in relation to a child), then, on and after that day, the order shall be deemed to be an order under section 4 of this Act giving the father parental responsibility for the child.

Orders to which paragraphs 6 to 11 apply

5. (1) In paragraphs 6 to 11 'an existing order' means any order which –

(a) is in force immediately before the commencement of Parts I and II;
(b) was made under any enactment mentioned in sub-paragraph (2);
(c) determines all or any of the following –
  (i) who is to have custody of a child;
  (ii) who is to have care and control of a child;
  (iii) who is to have access to a child;
  (iv) any matter with respect to a child's education or upbringing; and
(d) is not an order of a kind mentioned in paragraph 15(1).

(2) The enactments are –

(a) the Domestic Proceedings and Magistrates' Courts Act 1978;
(b) the Children Act 1975;
(c) the Matrimonial Causes Act 1973;
(d) the Guardianship of Minors Acts 1971 and 1973;
(e) the Matrimonial Causes Act 1965;
(f) the Matrimonial Proceedings (Magistrates' Courts) Act 1960.

(3) For the purposes of this paragraph and paragraphs 6 to 11 'custody' includes legal custody and joint as well as sole custody but does not include access.

Parental responsibility of parents

6. (1) Where –

(a) a child's father and mother were married to each other at the time of his birth; and
(b) there is an existing order with respect to the child,

each parent shall have parental responsibility for the child in accordance with section 2 as modified by sub-paragraph (3).

(2) Where –

(a)   a child's father and mother were not married to each other at the time of his birth; and

(b)   there is an existing order with respect to the child,

section 2 shall apply as modified by sub-paragraphs (3) and (4).

(3) The modification is that for section 2(8) there shall be substituted –

'(8) The fact that a person has parental responsibility for a child does not entitle him to act in a way which would be incompatible with any existing order or any order made under this Act with respect to the child'.

(4) The modifications are that –

(a)   for the purposes of section 2(2), where the father has custody or care and control of the child by virtue of any existing order, the court shall be deemed to have made (at the commencement of that section) an order under section 4(1) giving him parental responsibility for the child; and

(b)   where by virtue of paragraph (a) a court is deemed to have made an order under section 4(1) in favour of a father who has care and control of a child by virtue of an existing order, the court shall not bring the order under section 4(1) to an end at any time while he has care and control of the child by virtue of the order.

Persons who are not parents but who have custody or care and control

7. (1) Where a person who is not the parent or guardian of a child has custody or care and control of him by virtue of an existing order, that person shall have parental responsibility for him so long as he continues to have that custody or care and control by virtue of the order.

(2) Where sub-paragraph (1) applies, [Parts I and II and paragraph 15 of Schedule 1][1] shall have effect as modified by this paragraph.

(3) The modifications are that –

(a)   for section 2(8) there shall be substituted –

'(8) The fact that a person has parental responsibility for a child does not entitle him to act in a way which would be incompatible with any existing order or with any order made under this Act with respect to the child';

(b)   at the end of section 9(4) there shall be inserted –

'(c)   any person who has custody or care and control of a child by virtue of any existing order'; and

(c)   at the end of section 34(1)(c) there shall be inserted –

'(cc) where immediately before the care order was made there was an existing order by virtue of which a person had custody or care and control of the child, that person.'

[(d)   for paragraph 15 of Schedule I there shall be substituted –

'**15.** Where a child lives with a person as the result of a custodianship order within the meaning of section 33 of the Children Act 1975, a local authority may make contributions to that person towards the cost of the accommodation and maintenance of the child so long as that person continues to have legal custody of that child by virtue of the order.']¹

Persons who have care and control

8. (1) Sub-paragraphs (2) to (6) apply where a person has care and control of a child by virtue of an existing order, but they shall cease to apply when that order ceases to have effect.

(2) Section 5 shall have effect as if –

(a)   for any reference to a residence order in favour of a parent or guardian there were substituted a reference to any existing order by virtue of which the parent or guardian has care and control of the child; and

(b)   for subsection (9) there were substituted –

'(9) Subsections (1) and (7) do not apply if the existing order referred to in paragraph (b) of those subsections was one by virtue of which a surviving parent of the child also had care and control of him.'

(3) Section 10 shall have effect as if for subsection (5)(c)(i) there were substituted –

'(i)   in any case where by virtue of an existing order any person or persons has or have care and control of the child, has the consent of that person or each of those persons'.

(4) Section 20 shall have effect as if for subsection (9)(a) there were substituted 'who has care and control of the child by virtue of an existing order.'

(5) Section 23 shall have effect as if for subsection (4)(c) there were substituted –

'(c)   where the child is in care and immediately before the care order was made there was an existing order by virtue of which a person had care and control of the child, that person.'

(6) In Schedule 1, paragraphs 1(1) and 14(1) shall have effect as if for the words 'in whose favour a residence order is in force with respect to the child' there were substituted 'who has been given care and control of the child by virtue of an existing order'.

Persons who have access

9. (1) Sub-paragraphs (2) to (4) apply where a person has access by virtue of an existing order.

(2) Section 10 shall have effect as if after subsection (5) there were inserted –

'(5A) Any person who has access to a child by virtue of an existing order is entitled to apply for a contact order.'

(3) Section 16(2) shall have effect as if after paragraph (b) there were inserted –

'(bb) any person who has access to the child by virtue of an existing order.'

(4) Sections 43(11), 44(13) and 46(10), shall have effect as if in each case after paragraph (d) there were inserted –

'(dd) any person who has been given access to him by virtue of an existing order.'

Enforcement of certain existing orders

10. ...[8]

Discharge of existing orders

11. (1) The making of a residence order or a care order with respect to a child who is the subject of an existing order discharges the existing order.

(2) Where the court makes any section 8 order (other than a residence order) with respect to a child with respect to whom any existing order is in force, the existing order shall have effect subject to the section 8 order.

(3) The court may discharge an existing order which is in force with respect to a child –

(a)   in any family proceedings relating to the child or in which any question arises with respect to the child's welfare; or
(b)   on the application of –
(i)   any parent or guardian of the child;
(ii)   the child himself; or
(iii)   any person named in the order.

(4) A child may not apply for the discharge of an existing order except with the leave of the court.

(5) The power in sub-paragraph (3) to discharge an existing order includes the power to discharge any part of the order.

(6) In considering whether to discharge an order under the power conferred by sub-paragraph (3) the court shall, if the discharge of the order is opposed by any party to the proceedings, have regard in particular to the matters mentioned in section 1(3).

GUARDIANS

Existing guardians to be guardians under this Act

12. (1) Any appointment of a person as guardian of a child which –

(a)   was made –
(i)   under sections 3 to 5 of the Guardianship of Minors Act 1971;

(ii)   under section 38(3) of the Sexual Offences Act 1956; or

(iii)   under the High Court's inherent jurisdiction with respect to children; and

(b)   has taken effect before the commencement of section 5(4),

shall (subject to sub-paragraph (2)) be deemed, on and after the commencement of section 5(4), to be an appointment made and having effect under that section.

(2) Where an appointment of a person as guardian of a child has effect under section 5 by virtue of sub-paragraph (1)(a)(ii), the appointment shall not have effect for a period which is longer than any period specified in the order.

Appointment of guardian not yet in effect

13. Any appointment of a person to be a guardian of a child –

(a)   which was made as mentioned in paragraph 12(1)(a)(i); but

(b)   which, immediately before the commencement of section 5(4), had not taken effect,

shall take effect in accordance with section 5 (as modified, where it applies, by paragraph 8(2)).

Persons deemed to be appointed as guardians under existing wills

14. For the purposes of the Wills Act 1837 and of this Act any disposition by will and testament or devise of the custody and tuition of any child, made before the commencement of section 5(4) and paragraph 1 of Schedule 13, shall be deemed to be an appointment by will of a guardian of the child.

CHILDREN IN CARE

Children in compulsory care

15. (1) Sub-paragraph (2) applies where, immediately before the day on which Part IV comes into force, a person was –

(a)   in care by virtue of –

(i)   a care order under section 1 of the Children and Young Persons Act 1969;

(ii)   a care order under section 15 of that Act, on discharging a supervision order made under section 1 of that Act; or

(iii)   an order or authorisation under section 25 or 26 of that Act;

(b)   ...[5]

to be the subject of a care order under the Children and Young Persons Act 1969;

(c)   in care –

(i)   under section 2 of the Child Care Act 1980; or

(ii)   by virtue of paragraph 1 of Schedule 4 to that Act (which extends the meaning of a child in care under section 2 to include children in care under section 1 of the Children Act 1948), and a child in respect of whom a resolution under section 3 of the Act of 1980 or section 2 of the Act of 1948 was in force;

(d)   a child in respect of whom a resolution had been passed under section 65 of the Child Care Act 1980;

(e)   in care by virtue of an order under –

(i)   section 2(1)(e) of the Matrimonial Proceedings (Magistrates' Courts) Act 1960;

(ii)   section 7(2) of the Family Law Reform Act 1969;

(iii)   section 43(1) of the Matrimonial Causes Act 1973; or

(iv)   section 2(2)(b) of the Guardianship Act 1973;

(v)   section 10 of the Domestic Proceedings and Magistrates' Courts Act 1978,

(orders having effect for certain purposes as if the child had been received into care under section 2 of the Child Care Act 1980);

(f)   in care by virtue of an order made, on the revocation of a custodianship order, under section 36 of the Children Act 1975; ...[2]

(g)   in care by virtue of an order made, on the refusal of an adoption order, under section 26 of the Adoption Act 1976 or any order having effect (by virtue of paragraph 1 of Schedule 2 to that Act) as if made under that section [; or

(h)   in care by virtue of an order of the court made in the exercise of the High Court's inherent jurisdiction with respect to children.][2]

(2) Where this sub-paragraph applies, then, on and after the day on which Part IV commences –

(a)   the order or resolution in question shall be deemed to be a care order;

(b)   the authority in whose care the person was immediately before that commencement shall be deemed to be the authority designated in that deemed care order; and

(c)   any reference to a child in the care of a local authority shall include a reference to a person who is the subject of such a deemed care order,

and the provisions of this Act shall apply accordingly, subject to paragraph 16.

Modifications

16. (1) Sub-paragraph (2) only applies where a person who is the subject of a care order by virtue of paragraph 15(2) is a person falling within sub-paragraph (1)(a) ...[5] of that paragraph.

(2) Where the person would otherwise have remained in care until reaching the age of nineteen, by virtue of –

(a)   section 20(3)(a) or 21(1) of the Children and Young Persons Act 1969;
...[5]

(b)   ...[5]

this Act applies as if in section 91(12) for the word 'eighteen' there were substituted 'nineteen'.

(3) ...[5]

[(3A) Where in respect of a child who has been placed or allowed to remain in the care of a local authority pursuant to section 7(2) of the Family Law Reform Act 1969 or in the exercise of the High Court's inherent jurisdiction and the child is still in the care of a local authority, proceedings have ceased by virtue of paragraph 1(1A) to be treated as pending, paragraph 15(2) shall apply on 14th October 1992 as if the child was in care pursuant to an order as specified in paragraph 15(1)(e)(ii) or (h) as the case may be.][1]

(4) [Sub-paragraphs (5) and (6) only apply][3] where a child who is the subject of a care order by virtue of paragraph 15(2) is a person falling within sub-paragraph (1)(e) to [(h)][2] of that paragraph.

(5) [Subject to sub-paragraph (6),][3] where a court, on making the order, or at any time thereafter, gave directions under –

[(a) section 4(4)(a) of the Guardianship Act 1973;
(b) section 43(5)(a) of the Matrimonial Causes Act 1973; or
(c) in the exercise of the High Court's inherent jurisdiction with respect to children,][2]

as to the exercise by the authority of any powers, those directions shall[, subject to the provisions of section 25 of this Act and of any regulations made under that section,][3] continue to have effect (regardless of any conflicting provision in this Act [other than section 25][3]) until varied or discharged by a court under this sub-paragraph.

[(6) Where directions referred to in sub-paragraph (5) are to the effect that a child be placed in accommodation provided for the purpose of restricting liberty then the directions shall cease to have effect upon the expiry of the maximum period specified by regulations under section 25(2)(a) in relation to children of his description, calculated from 14th October 1991.][3]

Cessation of wardship where ward in care

[16A. (1) Where a child who is a ward of court is in care by virtue of –

(a) an order under section 7(2) of the Family Law Reform Act 1969; or
(b) an order made in the exercise of the High Court's inherent jurisdiction with respect to children,

he shall, on the day on which Part IV commences, cease to be a ward of court.][2]

[(2) Where immediately before the day on which Part IV commences a child was in the care of a local authority and as the result of an order –

(a) pursuant to section 7(2) of the Family Law Reform Act 1969; or
(b) made in the exercise of the High Court's inherent jurisdiction with respect to children,

continued to be in the care of a local authority and was made a ward of court, he shall on the day on which Part IV commences, cease to be a ward of court.

(3) Sub-paragraphs (1) and (2) do not apply in proceedings which are pending.][1]

Children placed with parent etc. while in compulsory care

17. (1) This paragraph applies where a child is deemed by paragraph 15 to be in the care of a local authority under an order or resolution which is deemed by that paragraph to be a care order.

(2) If, immediately before the day on which Part III comes into force, the child was allowed to be under the charge and control of –

(a)   a parent or guardian under section 21(2) of the Child Care Act 1980; or
(b)   a person who, before the child was in the authority's care, had care and control of the child by virtue of an order falling within paragraph 5,

on and after that day the provision made by and under section 23(5) shall apply as if the child had been placed with the person in question in accordance with that provision.

Orders for access to children in compulsory care

18. (1) This paragraph applies to any access order –

(a)   made under section 12C of the Child Care Act 1980 (access orders with respect to children in care of local authorities); and
(b)   in force immediately before the commencement of Part IV

(2) On and after the commencement of Part IV, the access order shall have effect as an order made under section 34 in favour of the person named in the order.

[**18A.** (1) This paragraph applies to any decision of a local authority to terminate arrangements for access or to refuse to make such arrangements –

(a)   of which notice has been given under, and in accordance with, section 12B of the Child Care Act 1980 (termination of access); and
(b)   which is in force immediately before the commencement of Part IV.

(2) On and after the commencement of Part IV, a decision to which this paragraph applies shall have effect as a court order made under section 34(4) authorising the local authority to refuse to allow contact between the child and the person to whom notice was given under section 12B of the Child Care Act 1980.][3]

19. (1) This paragraph applies where, immediately before the commencement of Part IV, an access order made under section 12C of the Act of 1980 was suspended by virtue of an order made under section 12E of that Act (suspension of access orders in emergencies).

(2) The suspending order shall continue to have effect as if this Act had not been passed.

(3) If –

(a)   before the commencement of Part IV; and
(b)   during the period for which the operation of the access order is suspended,

the local authority concerned made an application for its variation or discharge to an appropriate juvenile court, its operation shall be suspended until the date on which the application to vary or discharge it is determined or abandoned.

Children in voluntary care

20. (1) This paragraph applies where, immediately before the day on which Part III comes into force –

    (a)   a child was in the care of a local authority –
        (i)   under section 2(1) of the Child Care Act 1980; or
        (ii) by virtue of paragraph 1 of Schedule 4 to that Act (which extends the meaning of references to children in care under section 2 to include references to children in care under section 1 of the Children Act 1948); and
    (b)   he was not a person in respect of whom a resolution under section 3 of the Act of 1980 or section 2 of the Act of 1948 was in force.

(2) Where this paragraph applies, the child shall, on and after the day mentioned in sub-paragraph (1), be treated for the purposes of this Act as a child who is provided with accommodation by the local authority under Part III, but he shall cease to be so treated once he ceases to be so accommodated in accordance with the provisions of Part III.

(3) Where –

    (a)   this paragraph applies; and
    (b)   the child, immediately before the day mentioned in sub-paragraph (1), was (by virtue of section 21(2) of the Act of 1980) under the charge and control of a person falling within paragraph 17(2)(a) or (b),

the child shall not be treated for the purposes of this Act as if he were being looked after by the authority concerned.

Boarded out children

21. (1) Where, immediately before the day on which Part III comes into force, a child in the care of a local authority –

    (a)   was –
        (i)   boarded out with a person under section 21(1)(a) of the Child Care Act 1980; or
        (ii) placed under the charge and control of a person, under section 21(2) of that Act; and
    (b)   the person with whom he was boarded out, or (as the case may be) placed, was not a person falling within paragraph 17(2)(a) or (b),

on and after that day, he shall be treated (subject to sub-paragraph (2)) as having been placed with a local authority foster parent and shall cease to be so treated when he ceases to be placed with that person in accordance with the provisions of this Act.

(2) Regulations made under section 23(2)(a) shall not apply in relation to a person who is a local authority foster parent by virtue of sub-paragraph (1) before the end of the period of twelve months beginning with the day on which Part III comes into force and accordingly that person shall for that period be subject –

(a)   in a case falling within sub-paragraph (1)(a)(i), to terms and regulations mentioned in section 21(1)(a) of the Act of 1980; and

(b)   in a case falling within sub-paragraph (1)(a)(ii), to terms fixed under section 21(2) of that Act and regulations made under section 22A of that Act,

as if that Act had not been repealed by this Act.

Children in care to qualify for advice and assistance

22. Any reference in Part III to a person qualifying for advice and assistance shall be construed as including a reference to a person within the area of the local authority in question who is under twenty-one and who was, at any time after reaching the age of sixteen but while still a child –

(a)   a person falling within –
(i)   any of paragraphs (a) to [(h)]² of paragraph 15(1); or
(ii)   paragraph 20(1); or

(b)   the subject of a criminal care order (within the meaning of paragraph 34).

Emigration of children in care

23. Where –

(a)   the Secretary of State has received a request in writing from a local authority that he give his consent under section 24 of the Child Care Act 1980 to the emigration of a child in their care; but

(b)   immediately before the repeal of the Act of 1980 by this Act, he has not determined whether or not to give his consent,

section 24 of the Act of 1980 shall continue to apply (regardless of that repeal) until the Secretary of State has determined whether or not to give his consent to the request.

Contributions for maintenance of children in care

24. (1) Where, immediately before the day on which Part III of Schedule 2 comes into force, there was in force an order made (or having effect as if made) under any of the enactments mentioned in sub-paragraph (2), then, on and after that day –

(a)   the order shall have effect as if made under paragraph 23(2) of Schedule 2 against a person liable to contribute; and

(b)   Part III of Schedule 2 shall apply to the order, subject to the modifications in sub-paragraph (3).

(2) The enactments are –

(a)   section 11(4) of the Domestic Proceedings and Magistrates' Courts Act 1978;

(b)   section 26(2) of the Adoption Act 1976;

(c)   section 36(5) of the Children Act 1975;

(d)   section 2(3) of the Guardianship Act 1973;

(e)   section 2(1)(h) of the Matrimonial Proceedings (Magistrates' Courts) Act 1960,

(provisions empowering the court to make an order requiring a person to make periodical payments to a local authority in respect of a child in care).

(3) The modifications are that, in paragraph 23 of Schedule 2 –

(a)   in sub-paragraph (4), paragraph (a) shall be omitted;

(b)   for sub-paragraph (6) there shall be substituted –

'(6) Where –

(a)   a contribution order is in force;

(b)   the authority serve a contribution notice under paragraph 22; and

(c)   the contributor and the authority reach an agreement under paragraph 22(7) in respect of the contribution notice,

the effect of the agreement shall be to discharge the order from the date on which it is agreed that the agreement shall take effect'; and

(c)   at the end of sub-paragraph (10) there shall be inserted –

'and

(c)   where the order is against a person who is not a parent of the child, shall be made with due regard to –

(i)   whether that person had assumed responsibility for the maintenance of the child, and, if so, the extent to which and basis on which he assumed that responsibility and the length of the period during which he met that responsibility;

(ii)   whether he did so knowing that the child was not his child;

(iii)   the liability of any other person to maintain the child.'

SUPERVISION ORDERS

Orders under section 1(3)(b) or 21(2) of the 1969 Act

25. (1) This paragraph applies to any supervision order –

(a)   made –

(i)   under section 1(3)(b) of the Children and Young Persons Act 1969; or

(ii)   under section 21(2) of that Act on the discharge of a care order made under section 1(3)(c) of that Act; and

(b)   in force immediately before the commencement of Part IV.

(2) On and after the commencement of Part IV, the order shall be deemed to be a supervision order made under section 31 and –

(a) any requirement of the order that the child reside with a named individual shall continue to have effect while the order remains in force, unless the court otherwise directs

(b) any other requirement imposed by the court, or directions given by the supervisor, shall be deemed to have been imposed or given under the appropriate provisions of Schedule 3.

(3) Where, immediately before the commencement of Part IV, the order had been in force for a period of [six months or more][3], it shall cease to have effect at the end of the period of six months beginning with the day on which Part IV comes into force unless –

(a) the court directs that it shall cease to have effect at the end of a different period (which shall not exceed three years);

(b) it ceased to have effect earlier in accordance with section 91; or

(c) it would have ceased to have had effect earlier had this Act not been passed.

(4) Where sub-paragraph (3) applies, paragraph 6 of Schedule 3 shall not apply.

(5) Where, immediately before the commencement of Part IV, the order had been in force for less than six months it shall cease to have effect in accordance with section 91 and paragraph 6 of Schedule 3 unless –

(a) the court directs that it shall cease to have effect at the end of a different period (which shall not exceed three years); or

(b) it would have ceased to have had effect earlier had this Act not been passed.

Other supervision orders

26. (1) This paragraph applies to any order for the supervision of a child which was in force immediately before the commencement of Part IV and was made under –

(a) section 2(1)(f) of the Matrimonial Proceedings (Magistrates' Courts) Act 1960;

(b) section 7(4) of the Family Law Reform Act 1969;

(c) section 44 of the Matrimonial Causes Act 1973;

(d) section 2(2)(a) of the Guardianship Act 1973;

(e) section 34(5) or 36(3)(b) of the Children Act 1975;

(f) section 26(1)(a) of the Adoption Act 1976; or

(g) section 9 of the Domestic Proceedings and Magistrates' Courts Act 1978.

(2) The order shall not be deemed to be a supervision order made under any provision of this Act but shall nevertheless continue in force for a period of one year beginning with the day on which Part IV comes into force unless –

(a) the court directs that it shall cease to have effect at the end of a lesser period; or

(b) it would have ceased to have had effect earlier had this Act not been passed.

PLACE OF SAFETY ORDERS

27. (1) This paragraph applies to –

(a) any order or warrant authorising the removal of a child to a place of safety which –
   (i) was made, or issued, under any of the enactments mentioned in sub-paragraph (2); and
   (ii) was in force immediately before the commencement of Part IV; and

(b) any interim order made under section 23(5) of the Children and Young Persons Act 1963 or section 28(6) of the Children and Young Persons Act 1969.

(2) The enactments are –

(a) section 40 of the Children and Young Persons Act 1933 (warrant to search for or remove child);

(b) section 28(1) of the Children and Young Persons Act 1969 (detention of child in place of safety);

(c) section 34(1) of the Adoption Act 1976 (removal of protected children from unsuitable surroundings);

(d) section 12(1) of the Foster Children Act 1980 (removal of foster children kept in unsuitable surroundings).

(3) The order or warrant shall continue to have effect as if this Act had not been passed.

(4) Any enactment repealed by this Act shall continue to have effect in relation to the order or warrant so far as is necessary for the purposes of securing that the effect of the order is what it would have been had this Act not been passed.

(5) Sub-paragraph (4) does not apply to the power to make an interim order or further interim order given by section 23(5) of the Children and Young Persons Act 1963 or section 28(6) of the Children and Young Persons Act 1969.

(6) Where, immediately before section 28 of the Children and Young Persons Act 1969 is repealed by this Act, a child is being detained under the powers granted by that section, he may continue to be detained in accordance with that section but subsection (6) shall not apply.

RECOVERY OF CHILDREN

28. The repeal by this Act of subsection (1) of section 16 of the Child Care Act 1980 (arrest of child absent from compulsory care) shall not affect the operation of that section in relation to any child arrested before the coming into force of the repeal.

29. (1) This paragraph applies where –

(a) a summons has been issued under section 15 or 16 of the Child Care Act 1980 (recovery of children in voluntary or compulsory care); and

(b) the child concerned is not produced in accordance with the summons before the repeal of that section by this Act comes into force.

(2) The summons, any warrant issued in connection with it and section 15 or (as the case may be) section 16, shall continue to have effect as if this Act had not been passed.

30. The amendment by paragraph 27 of Schedule 12 of section 32 of the Children and Young Persons Act 1969 (detention of absentees) shall not affect the operation of that section in relation to –

(a) any child arrested; or

(b) any summons or warrant issued,

under that section before the coming into force of that paragraph.

VOLUNTARY ORGANISATIONS: PARENTAL RIGHTS RESOLUTIONS

31. (1) This paragraph applies to a resolution –

(a) made under section 64 of the Child Care Act 1980 (transfer of parental rights and duties to voluntary organisations); and

(b) in force immediately before the commencement of Part IV.

(2) The resolution shall continue to have effect until the end of the period of six months beginning with the day on which Part IV comes into force unless it is brought to an end earlier in accordance with the provisions of the Act of 1980 preserved by this paragraph.

(3) While the resolution remains in force, any relevant provisions of, or made under, the Act of 1980 shall continue to have effect with respect to it.

(4) Sub-paragraph (3) does not apply to –

(a) section 62 of the Act of 1980 and any regulations made under that section (arrangements by voluntary organisations for emigration of children); or

(b) section 65 of the Act of 1980 (duty of local authority to assume parental rights and duties).

(5) Section 5(2) of the Act of 1980 (which is applied to resolutions under Part VI of that Act by section 64(7) of that Act) shall have effect with respect to the resolution as if the reference in paragraph (c) to an appointment of a guardian under section 5 of the Guardianship of Minors Act 1971 were a reference to an appointment of a guardian under section 5 of this Act.

FOSTER CHILDREN

32. (1) This paragraph applies where –

(a) immediately before the commencement of Part VIII, a child was a foster child within the meaning of the Foster Children Act 1980; and

(b) the circumstances of the case are such that, had Parts VIII and IX then been in force, he would have been treated for the purposes of this Act as a child who was being provided with accommodation in a children's home and not as a child who was being privately fostered.

(2) If the child continues to be cared for and provided with accommodation as before, section 63(1) and (10) shall not apply in relation to him if –

(a) an application for registration of the home in question is made under section 63 before the end of the period of three months beginning with the day on which Part VIII comes into force; and

(b) the application has not been refused or, if it has been refused –
    (i)   the period for an appeal against the decision has not expired; or
    (ii) an appeal against the refusal has been made but has not been determined or abandoned.

(3) While section 63(1) and (10) does not apply, the child shall be treated as a privately fostered child for the purposes of Part IX.

NURSERIES AND CHILD MINDING

33. (1) Sub-paragraph (2) applies where, immediately before the commencement of Part X, any premises are registered under section 1(1)(a) of the Nurseries and Child-Minders Regulation Act 1948 (registration of premises, other than premises wholly or mainly used as private dwellings, where children are received to be looked after).

(2) During the transitional period, the provisions of the Act of 1948 shall continue to have effect with respect to those premises to the exclusion of Part X.

(3) Nothing in sub-paragraph (2) shall prevent the local authority concerned from registering any person under section 71(1)(b) with respect to the premises.

(4) In this paragraph 'the transitional period' means the period ending with –

(a) the first anniversary of the commencement of Part X; or
(b) if earlier, the date on which the local authority concerned registers any person under section 71(1)(b) with respect to the premises.

34. (1) Sub-paragraph (2) applies where, immediately before the commencement of Part X –

(a) a person is registered under section 1(1)(b) of the Act of 1948 (registration of persons who for reward receive into their homes children under the age of five to be looked after); and

(b) all the children looked after by him as mentioned in section 1(1)(b) of that Act are under the age of five.

(2) During the transitional period, the provisions of the Act of 1948 shall continue to have effect with respect to that person to the exclusion of Part X.

(3) Nothing in sub-paragraph (2) shall prevent the local authority concerned from registering that person under section 71(1)(a).

(4) In this paragraph 'the transitional period' means the period ending with –

    (a)   the first anniversary of the commencement of Part X; or
    (b)   if earlier, the date on which the local authority concerned registers that person under section 71(1)(a).

CHILDREN ACCOMMODATED IN CERTAIN ESTABLISHMENTS

35. In calculating, for the purposes of section 85(1)(a) or 86(1)(a), the period of time for which a child has been accommodated any part of that period which fell before the day on which that section came into force shall be disregarded.

CRIMINAL CARE ORDERS

36. (1) This paragraph applies where, immediately before the commencement of section 90(2) there was in force an order ('a criminal care order') made –

    (a)   under section 7(7)(a) of the Children and Young Persons Act 1969 (alteration in treatment of young offenders etc.); or
    (b)   under section 15(1) of that Act, on discharging a supervision order made under section 7(7)(b) of that Act.

(2) The criminal care order shall continue to have effect until the end of the period of six months beginning with the day on which section 90(2) comes into force unless it is brought to an end earlier in accordance with –

    (a)   the provisions of the Act of 1969 preserved by sub-paragraph (3)(a); or
    (b)   this paragraph.

(3) While the criminal care order remains in force, any relevant provisions –

    (a)   of the Act of 1969; and
    (b)   of the Child Care Act 1980,

shall continue to have effect with respect to it.

(4) While the criminal care order remains in force, a court may, on the application of the appropriate person, make –

    (a)   a residence order;
    (b)   a care order or a supervision order under section 31;
    (c)   an education supervision order under section 36 (regardless of subsection (6) of that section); or
    (d)   an order falling within sub-paragraph (5),

and shall, on making any of those orders, discharge the criminal care order.

(5) The order mentioned in sub-paragraph (4)(d) is an order having effect as if it were a supervision order of a kind mentioned in section 12AA of the Act of 1969 (as inserted by paragraph 23 of Schedule 12), that is to say, a supervision order –

(a)   imposing a requirement that the child shall live for a specified period in local authority accommodation; but

(b)   in relation to which the conditions mentioned in [subsection (6)]² of section 12AA are not required to be satisfied.

(6) The maximum period which may be specified in an order made under sub-paragraph (4)(d) is six months and such an order may stipulate that the child shall not live with a named person.

(7) ...⁹

(8) In sub-paragraph (4) 'appropriate person' means –

(a)   in the case of an application for a residence order, any person (other than a local authority) who has the leave of the court;

(b)   in the case of an application for an education supervision order, a local education authority; and

(c)   in any other case, the local authority to whose care the child was committed by the order.

MISCELLANEOUS

Consents under the Marriage Act 1949 (c. 76)

37. (1) In the circumstances mentioned in sub-paragraph (2), section 3 of and Schedule 2 to the Marriage Act 1949 (consents to marry) shall continue to have effect regardless of the amendment of that Act by paragraph 5 of Schedule 12.

(2) The circumstances are that –

(a)   immediately before the day on which paragraph 5 of Schedule 12 comes into force, there is in force –
   (i)   an existing order, as defined in paragraph 5(1); or
   (ii)   an order of a kind mentioned in paragraph 16(1); and

(b)   section 3 of and Schedule 2 to the Act of 1949 would, but for this Act, have applied to the marriage of the child who is the subject of the order.

The Children Act 1975 (c. 72)

38. The amendments of other enactments made by the following provisions of the Children Act 1975 shall continue to have effect regardless of the repeal of the Act of 1975 by this Act –

(a)   section 68(4), (5) and (7) (amendments of section 32 of the Children and Young Persons Act 1969); and

(b)   in Schedule 3 –
   (i)   paragraph 13 (amendments of Births and Deaths Registration Act 1953);
   (ii)   paragraph 43 (amendment of Perpetuities and Accumulations Act 1964);
   (iii) paragraphs 46 and 47 (amendments of Health Services and Public Health Act 1968); and

PART I – Statutes

> (iv) paragraph 77 (amendment of Parliamentary and Other Pensions Act 1972).

The Child Care Act 1980 (c. 5)

39. The amendment made to section 106(2)(a) of the Children and Young Persons Act 1933) by paragraph 26 of Schedule 5 to the Child Care Act 1980 shall continue to have effect regardless of the repeal of the Act of 1980 by this Act.

Legal aid

40. ...[7]

NOTES

Amendments.[1] Words inserted or substituted: SI 1991/1990, amending SI 1991/828.[2] Words repealed, inserted or substituted: Courts and Legal Services Act 1990, ss 116, 125(7), Sch 16, para 33, Sch 20.[3] Words inserted or substituted: Children Act 1989 (Commencement and Transitional Provisions) Order 1991, SI 1991/828, art 4, Sch.[4] References in paras 12, 13 and 14 to 'the commencement of section 5' shall be construed as references to the commencement of ss (1)–(10) and (13) of that section (14 Oct 1991) except in relation to the appointment of a guardian of the estate of any child in which case they shall be construed as a reference to the commencement of ss (11) and (12) of that section (1 Feb 1992): SI 1991/1990, amending SI 1991/828.[5] Words repealed: Armed Forces Act 1991, s 26(2), Sch 3.[6] Words substituted: Criminal Justice Act 1991, s 100, Sch 11, para 40(2)(r).[7] Paragraph repealed: Access to Justice Act 1999, s 106, Sch 15, Pt I.[8] Paragraph omitted: Children and Families Act 2014, s 12, Sch 2, paras 1, 41.[9] Sub-paragraph repealed: Legal Aid, Sentencing and Punishment of Offenders Act 2012, s 141(10), Sch 25, Pt 2.

Definitions. 'A section 8 order': s 8(2); 'actual custody': Sch 14, para 10(3); 'appropriate person': Sch 14, para 36(8); 'care order': ss 31(11), 105(1); 'child': s 105(1); 'children's home': s 23; 'contact order': s 8(1); 'contribution notice': Sch 2, para 22(1); 'contribution order': Sch 2, para 23(2); 'contributor': Sch 2, para 21(1); 'criminal care order': Sch 14, para 36(1); 'custody': Sch 14, para 5(3); 'education supervision order': s 36(2); 'existing order': Sch 14, para 5(1), (2); 'family proceedings': s 8(3); 'local authority': s 105(1); 'local authority foster parent': s 23(3); 'local education authority': s 105(1); 'order in force immediately before the commencement of ... this Act': Sch 14, para (1), (3), (4); 'parental responsibility': s 3; 'privately fostered child': s 66(1); 'residence order': s 8(1); 'supervision order': s 31(11); 'supervisor': s 105(1); 'the transitional period': Sch 14, para 33(4); 'upbringing': s 105(1).

CHILDREN AND FAMILIES ACT 2014

****

13 Control of expert evidence, and of assessments, in children proceedings

(1) A person may not without the permission of the court instruct a person to provide expert evidence for use in children proceedings.

(2) Where in contravention of subsection (1) a person is instructed to provide expert evidence, evidence resulting from the instructions is inadmissible in children proceedings unless the court rules that it is admissible.

(3) A person may not without the permission of the court cause a child to be medically or psychiatrically examined or otherwise assessed for the purposes of the provision of expert evidence in children proceedings.

(4) Where in contravention of subsection (3) a child is medically or psychiatrically examined or otherwise assessed, evidence resulting from the examination or other assessment is inadmissible in children proceedings unless the court rules that it is admissible.

(5) In children proceedings, a person may not without the permission of the court put expert evidence (in any form) before the court.

(6) The court may give permission as mentioned in subsection (1), (3) or (5) only if the court is of the opinion that the expert evidence is necessary to assist the court to resolve the proceedings justly.

(7) When deciding whether to give permission as mentioned in subsection (1), (3) or (5) the court is to have regard in particular to –

  (a) any impact which giving permission would be likely to have on the welfare of the children concerned, including in the case of permission as mentioned in subsection (3) any impact which any examination or other assessment would be likely to have on the welfare of the child who would be examined or otherwise assessed,
  (b) the issues to which the expert evidence would relate,
  (c) the questions which the court would require the expert to answer,
  (d) what other expert evidence is available (whether obtained before or after the start of proceedings),
  (e) whether evidence could be given by another person on the matters on which the expert would give evidence,
  (f) the impact which giving permission would be likely to have on the timetable for, and duration and conduct of, the proceedings,
  (g) the cost of the expert evidence, and
  (h) any matters prescribed by Family Procedure Rules.

(8) References in this section to providing expert evidence, or to putting expert evidence before a court, do not include references to –

    (a)   the provision or giving of evidence –
- (i)   by a person who is a member of the staff of a local authority or of an authorised applicant,
- (ii) in proceedings to which the authority or authorised applicant is a party, and
- (iii) in the course of the person's work for the authority or authorised applicant,

    (b)   the provision or giving of evidence –
- (i)   by a person within a description prescribed for the purposes of subsection (1) of section 94 of the Adoption and Children Act 2002 (suitability for adoption etc.), and
- (ii) about the matters mentioned in that subsection,

    (c)   the provision or giving of evidence by an officer of the Children and Family Court Advisory and Support Service when acting in that capacity, or

    (d)   the provision or giving of evidence by a Welsh family proceedings officer (as defined by section 35(4) of the Children Act 2004) when acting in that capacity.

(9) In this section –

'authorised applicant' means –
- (a)   the National Society for the Prevention of Cruelty to Children, or
- (b)   a person authorised by an order under section 31 of the Children Act 1989 to bring proceedings under that section;

'child' means a person under the age of 18;

'children proceedings' has such meaning as may be prescribed by Family Procedure Rules;

'the court', in relation to any children proceedings, means the court in which the proceedings are taking place;

'local authority' –
- (a)   in relation to England means –
  - (i)   a county council,
  - (ii) a district council for an area for which there is no county council,
  - (iii) a London borough council,
  - (iv) the Common Council of the City of London, or
  - (v) the Council of the Isles of Scilly, and
- (b)   in relation to Wales means a county council or a county borough council.

(10) The preceding provisions of this section are without prejudice to sections 75 and 76 of the Courts Act 2003 (power to make Family Procedure Rules).

Part II

STATUTORY INSTRUMENTS

FAMILY COURT (COMPOSITION AND DISTRIBUTION OF BUSINESS) RULES 2014

SI 2014/840

ARRANGEMENT OF RULES

PART 1
INTRODUCTORY PROVISIONS

1 Citation, commencement and interpretation

These Rules may be cited as the Family Court (Composition and Distribution of Business) Rules 2014 and come into force on 22 April 2014.

2

(1) In these Rules –

'the 1991 Act' means the Child Support Act 1991;

'appeal' includes an application seeking permission to appeal and an application in the course of the appeal proceedings;
...[1]

'authorised', except in the context of references to an authorised court officer, means authorised by the President of the Family Division or nominated by or on behalf of the Lord Chief Justice to conduct particular business in the family court, in accordance with Part 3;

'authorised court officer' has the meaning assigned to it by rule 44.1 of the Civil Procedure Rules 1998 as applied to family proceedings by rule 28.2(1) of the Family Procedure Rules 2010;

'costs judge' means –

    (a)   the Chief Taxing Master;

    (b)   a taxing master of the Senior Courts; or

    (c)   a person appointed to act as deputy for the person holding office referred to in paragraph (b) or to act as a temporary additional officer for any such office;

'financial remedy' has the meaning assigned to it by rule 2.3 of the Family Procedure Rules 2010;

'judge of circuit judge level' means –

    (a)   a circuit judge who, where applicable, is authorised;

    (b)   a Recorder who, where applicable, is authorised;

    (c)   any other judge of the family court authorised to sit as a judge of circuit judge level in the family court;

'judge of district judge level' means –

    (a)   the Senior District Judge of the Family Division;

    (b)   a district judge of the Principal Registry of the Family Division;

    (c)   a person appointed to act as deputy for the person holding office referred to in paragraph (b) or to act as a temporary additional officer for any such office;

    (d)   a district judge who, where applicable, is authorised;

    (e)   a deputy district judge appointed under section 102 of the Senior Courts Act 1981 or section 8 of the County Courts Act 1984 who, where applicable, is authorised;

    (f)   an authorised District Judge (Magistrates' Courts);

    (g)   any other judge of the family court authorised to sit as a judge of district judge level in the family court.

'judge of High Court judge level' means –

    (a)   a deputy judge of the High Court;

    (b)   a puisne judge of the High Court;

    (c)   a person who has been a judge of the Court of Appeal or a puisne judge of the High Court who may act as a judge of the family court by virtue of section 9 of the Senior Courts Act 1981;

    (d)   the Senior President of Tribunals;

    (e)   the Chancellor of the High Court;

    (f)   an ordinary judge of the Court of Appeal (including the vice-president, if any, of either division of that court);

    (g)   the President of the Queen's Bench Division;

    (h)   the President of the Family Division;

    (i)   the Master of the Rolls;

    (j)   the Lord Chief Justice;

'judge of the family court' means a judge referred to in section 31C(1) of the Matrimonial and Family Proceedings Act 1984;

…[1] and

'lay justice' means an authorised justice of the peace who is not a District Judge (Magistrates' Courts).

(2) In these Rules, references to provisions of the Adoption and Children Act 2002 include, as applicable, references to those provisions as modified by the Human Fertilisation and Embryology (Parental Orders) Regulations 2010.

NOTES

Amendment.[1] Definition repealed: SI 2020/100.

PART 2
COMPOSITION OF THE FAMILY COURT

3 Composition: general

(1) Subject to rules in this Part, the family court shall be composed of –

    (a)   one of the following –

        (i)   a judge of district judge level;

        (ii)   a judge of circuit judge level; or

        (iii)   a judge of High Court judge level; or

    (b)   two or three lay justices.

(2) Where paragraph (1)(b) applies, the court shall include, so far as is practicable, both a man and a woman.

4 Composition: allocation decision

When making a decision on allocation to which rule 20 applies, the family court shall be composed of one or more of the following –

    (a)   a judge of district judge level;

    (b)   a judge of circuit judge level.

PART II – Statutory instruments

5 Composition: appeals heard by a judge of district judge level

(1) Subject to rule 7, the family court shall be composed of a judge of district judge level when hearing an appeal from the decision of the Secretary of State where an appeal is brought under –

- (a)   regulation 25AB(1) of the Child Support (Collection and Enforcement) Regulations 1992 (Appeals);
- (b)   section 20(1) (a) or (b) of the 1991 Act to a court by virtue of article 3 of the Child Support Appeals (Jurisdiction of Courts) Order 2002 (Parentage appeals to be made to courts).

(2) The family court may be composed of a judge of district judge level when hearing applications in the course of appeal proceedings against decisions of persons referred to in rule 6(2)(b) to (d) or decisions of the court referred to in rule 6(3).

(3) The family court shall be composed of a costs judge or a district judge of the High Court when hearing an appeal against the decision of an authorised court officer.

6 Composition: appeals heard by a judge of circuit judge level or a judge of High Court level

(1) Subject to rule 7, when hearing an appeal from the decisions of persons referred to in paragraph (2) or the court referred to in paragraph (3), the family court shall be composed of –

- (a)   a judge of circuit judge level; or
- (b)   a judge of High Court level where there is a need for such a level of judge to hear the appeal to make most effective and efficient use of local judicial resource and the resource of the High Court bench.

(2) The persons referred to in paragraph (1) are –

- (a)   a judge of district judge level;
- (b)   two or three lay justices;
- (c)   a lay justice; or
- (d)   [a person nominated by the Lord Chancellor who is authorised to exercise functions under section 31O(1) of the Matrimonial and Family Proceedings Act 1984][1].

(3) The court referred to in paragraph (1) is a magistrates' court where an appeal is brought under section 111A of the Magistrates' Courts Act 1980 (appeals on ground of error of law in child support proceedings).

NOTES

Amendment.[1] Words substituted: SI 2020/100.

7 Composition: appeals heard by a judge of High Court level

(1) The family court shall be composed of a judge of High Court level when hearing an appeal from the decision of –

(a)   the Senior District Judge of the Family Division in financial remedy proceedings;

(b)   ...[1]

(c)   a costs judge; or

(d)   the Gender Recognition Panel where an appeal is brought under section 8(1) of the Gender Recognition Act 2004 (Appeals etc.).

(2) The family court shall be composed of a judge of High Court level (instead of a judge of district judge level or a judge of circuit judge level) where there is –

(a)   an appeal against a decision referred to in rules 5 and 6; and

(b)   the Designated Family Judge or a judge of High Court level considers that the appeal would raise an important point of principle or practice.

NOTES

Amendment.[1] Words omitted repealed: SI 2021/505.

8 Composition: matters part heard

(1) Paragraph (2) applies where a hearing –

(a)   was before two or three lay justices; and

(b)   was part heard.

(2) The court which resumes the hearing shall, wherever possible, be composed of the same lay justices as dealt with the previous part of the hearing.

PART 3
AUTHORISATIONS

9 Powers to grant authorisations

(1) Paragraph (2) applies to business in such categories as may be specified from time to time by the President of the Family Division.

(2) A judge of district judge level or a judge of circuit judge level may conduct business to which this paragraph applies in the family court only if authorised by the President of the Family Division to do so.

(3) The President of the Family Division may specify the matters referred to in paragraph (1) in directions, after consulting the Lord Chancellor.

(4) A lay justice may conduct business in the family court only if authorised by the Lord Chief Justice to do so.

PART 4
LAY JUSTICES: CHAIRMANSHIP OF THE FAMILY COURT

[10 Interpretation of this Part

In this Part, '2016 Rules' means the Justices of the Peace Rules 2016.][1]

NOTES

Amendment.[1] Rule substituted: SI 2016/709.

PART II – Statutory instruments

11 Chairman

(1) When the family court is composed of two or three lay justices, it shall sit under the chairmanship of a lay justice who [has been approved to preside in accordance with the 2016 Rules][1].

(2) A lay justice may preside before being [approved to preside in accordance with the 2016 Rules][1] only if that lay justice is –

    (a)   under the supervision of another authorised lay justice who is [approved to preside in accordance with the 2016 Rules][1]; and

    (b)   has completed the training course required by [rule 19 of the 2016 Rules][1].

(3) …[1]

(4) This rule and rule 12 are subject to sections 18(1) and (2) of the Courts Act 2003.

NOTES

Amendment.[1] Words substituted and paragraph repealed: SI 2016/709.

12 Absence of authorised lay justice entitled to preside

(1) The lay justices present may appoint one of their number to preside in the family court to deal with any case in the absence of a lay justice entitled to preside under rule 11 if –

    (a)   before making such appointment the lay justices present are satisfied as to the suitability for this purpose of the lay justice proposed; and

    (b)   expect as mentioned in paragraph (2), the lay justice proposed has completed or is undergoing a chairman training course in accordance with [rule 19(f) of the 2016 Rules][1].

(2) The condition in paragraph (1)(b) does not apply if by reason of illness, circumstances unforeseen when the lay justices to sit were chosen, or other emergency, no lay justice who complies with that condition is present.

NOTES

Amendment.[1] Words substituted: SI 2016/709.

PART 5
DISTRIBUTION OF BUSINESS OF THE FAMILY COURT

[12A Interpretation of this Part

In this Part –

    'incoming protection measure' means a protection measure that has been ordered in a Member State of the European Union other than the United Kingdom or Denmark;
    'protection measure' has the meaning given to it in the Protection Measures Regulation;

'Protection Measures Regulation' means Regulation (EU) No 606/2013 of the European Parliament and of the Council of 12th June 2013 on mutual recognition of protection measures in civil matters.][1]

NOTES

Amendment.[1] Rule inserted: SI 2014/3297.

13 General

(1) This Part makes provision for the distribution of business of the family court among the judges of the family court.

(2) Rules 15 and 20 are subject to rule 17.

(3) Rules 15, 16, 17, 18, 19 and 20 make provision regarding the level of judge of the family court to which a matter is to be allocated initially.

(Rule 29.19 of the Family Procedure Rules 2010 makes provision for a judge of the family court to determine that a matter should be heard by a different level of judge of the family court.)

14 Persons who may exercise jurisdiction of the family court

Subject to the provisions of this Part or of any other enactment, any jurisdiction and powers conferred by any enactment on the family court, or on a judge of the family court, may be exercised by any judge of the family court.

15 Allocation of proceedings in Schedule 1

(1) An application in a type of proceedings listed in the first column of the table in Schedule 1 shall be allocated to be heard by a judge of the level listed in the second column of that table.

(2) Paragraph (1) and the provisions of Schedule 1 are subject to the need to take into account the need to make the most effective and efficient use of local judicial resource and the resource of the High Court bench that is appropriate given the nature and type of the application.

16 Allocation of emergency applications

(1) In this rule –

'the 1986 Act' means the Family Law Act 1986;

'the 1989 Act' means the Children Act 1989; and

'the 1996 Act' means the Family Law Act 1996.

(2) An application of a type referred to in paragraph (3) shall be allocated to the first available judge of the family court who –

(a)   where applicable, is authorised to conduct the type of business to which the application relates; and

(b)   would not be precluded by Schedule 2 from dealing with the application.

(3) The types of applications are those –

(a) under –

    (i) section 33 of the 1986 Act (disclosure of information as to the whereabouts of a child);

    (ii) section 34 of the 1986 Act (order authorising the taking charge and delivery of a child);

    (iii) section 44(1) of the 1989 Act (emergency protection order);

    (iv) section 44(9)(b) of the 1989 Act (varying a direction in an emergency protection order given under section 44(6) of the 1989 Act);

    (v) section 45(4) of the 1989 Act (extending the period during which an emergency protection order is to have effect);

    (vi) section 45(8) of the 1989 Act (to discharge an emergency protection order);

    (vii) section 45(8A) of the 1989 Act (to vary or discharge an emergency protection order in so far as it imposes an exclusion requirement on a person who is not entitled to apply for the order to be discharged);

    (viii) section 45(8B) of the 1989 Act (to vary or discharge an emergency protection order in so far as it confers powers of arrest attached to an exclusion requirement);

    (ix) section 48(9) of the 1989 Act (warrant to assist in discovery of children who may be in need of emergency protection);

    (x) section 50 of the 1989 Act (recovery of abducted children);

    (xi) section 102(1) of the 1989 Act (warrant for a constable to assist in the exercise of certain powers to search for children or inspect premises);

    (xii) Part 4 of the 1996 Act which are made without notice, except where the applicant is under 18 or where an application for an occupation order under section 33 of that Act requires a determination of a question of property ownership;

    (xiii) section 41 of the Adoption and Children Act 2002 (recovery order); ...[1]

    (xiv) section 79 of the Childcare Act 2006 (warrant for a constable to assist in the exercise of powers of entry); ...[1]

    [(xv) the Protection Measures Regulation made within or in connection with an application under sub-paragraph (xii); or

    (xvi) Article 11 of the Protection Measures Regulation for adjustment of an incoming protection measure except where the applicant is aged under 18; or][1]

(b) which are not referred to in paragraph (a) but which require the immediate attention of the court.

(4) An application of a type listed in paragraph (5) shall be allocated to the first available judge of the family court, other than lay justices, who, where applicable, is authorised to conduct the type of business to which the application relates.

(5) The types of application are those under –

(a) Part 4 of the 1996 Act which are made without notice and where the applicant is aged under 18 or where an application for an occupation order under section 33 of that Act requires a determination of a question of property ownership;

(b) Part 4A of the 1996 Act which are made without notice[;][1]

[(c) the Protection Measures Regulation made within or in connection with an application under sub-paragraph (a) or (b);

(d) Article 11 of the Protection Measures Regulation for adjustment of an incoming protection measure where the applicant is aged under 18.][1]

[(e) Part 1 of Schedule 2 to the Female Genital Mutilation Act 2003 which are made without notice.][2]

NOTES

Amendments. [1] Words omitted, punctuation substituted and sub-paragraphs inserted: SI 2014/3297.[2] Paragraph inserted: SI 2015/1421.

17 Allocation: applications in existing proceedings or in connection with proceedings that have concluded

(1) Subject to paragraphs (3) to (5), an application made within existing proceedings in the family court shall be allocated to the level of judge who is dealing with the existing proceedings to which the application relates.

(2) Subject to paragraphs (3) to (5), an application made in connection with proceedings in the family court that have concluded shall be allocated to the level of judge who last dealt with those proceedings.

(3) In Schedule 2 –

(a) the remedies listed in tables 1, 2 and 3 may not be granted by lay justices;

(b) the remedies listed in tables 2 and 3 may not be granted by a judge of district judge level;

(c) the remedies listed in table 3 may not be granted by a judge of circuit judge level, subject to any exception stated in that table.

(4) Where the effect of Schedule 2 is that an application for a particular remedy may not be granted by the level of judge referred to in paragraph (1) or (2), then that application shall be allocated to a level of judge who is able to grant that remedy.

(5) Any power of the family court to make an order for committal in respect of a breach of a judgment, order or undertaking to do or abstain from doing an act may only be made by a judge of the same level as, or of a higher level than, the judge who make the judgment or order, or who accepted the undertaking, as the case may be.

18 Allocation: costs

Subject to any direction of the court, an application for detailed assessment of a bill of costs shall be allocated to an authorised court officer, a district judge or a costs judge.

PART II – Statutory instruments

19 Allocation: appeals

An appeal shall be allocated to a judge in accordance with rules 5 to 7.

20 Allocation: all other proceedings

(1) An application of a type not referred to in other rules in this Part or in Schedule 1 or Schedule 2 shall be allocated by one or more of the persons referred to in rule 4.

(2) When deciding which level of judge to allocate such an application to, the decision must be based on consideration of the relative significance of the following factors –

    (a)   the need to make the most effective and efficient use of the local judicial resource and the resource of the High Court bench that is appropriate, given the nature and type of application;

    (b)   the need to avoid delay;

    (c)   the need for judicial continuity;

    (d)   the location of the parties or of any child relevant to the proceedings; and

    (e)   complexity.

PART 6
GUIDANCE

21 Guidance on distribution of business of the family court

(1) The President of the Family Division may, after consulting the Lord Chancellor, issue guidance on the application or interpretation of Part 5.

(2) Where the Lord Chancellor determines that the guidance has significant implications for resources, it may only be issued with the agreement of the Lord Chancellor.

(3) If the Lord Chancellor does not agree the guidance, the Lord Chancellor must provide the President of the Family Division with written reasons why the Lord Chancellor does not agree the guidance.

SCHEDULE 1
ALLOCATION

Type of proceedings	Level of judge
1. Proceedings under –	**Lay justices**
(a) the Maintenance Orders (Facilities for Enforcement) Act 1920;	
(b) the Marriage Act 1949;	
(c) the Maintenance Orders Act 1950;	
(d) the Maintenance Orders Act 1958;	

Type of proceedings	Level of judge
(e) the Maintenance Orders (Reciprocal Enforcement) Act 1972; (f) the Domestic Proceedings and Magistrates' Courts Act 1978; (g) the Civil Jurisdiction and Judgments Act 1982; (h) the Family Law Act 1986, section 55A (declarations of parentage); (i) the Child Support Act 1991, except section 32L or appeals; (j) the Crime and Disorder Act 1998, section 11 (child safety order); (k) Council Regulation (EC) No 44/2001 (known as the Judgments Regulation); (l) section 34 of the Children and Families (Wales) Measure 2010; (m) Schedule 6 to the Civil Partnership Act 2004; (n) the Childcare Act 2006, except section 79; (o) the Human Fertilisation and Embryology Act 2008, section 54 [or section 54A]2, where the child's place of birth was in England and Wales and where all respondents agree to the making of the order; (p) Council Regulation (EC) No 4/2009 (known as the Maintenance Regulation)[;]¹ [(q) the Protection Measures Regulation for enforcement of an incoming protection measure.]¹	
2. Proceedings under –	**Judge of district judge level**

(a) the Married Women's Property Act 1882;
 	
(b) the Matrimonial Causes Act 1973;
 	
(c) the Matrimonial and Family Proceedings Act 1984 sections 13 and 12 (permission and substantive application) …³;
 	
(d) the Children Act 1989, Schedule 1;
 	
(e) the Gender Recognition Act 2004, except appeals under section 8(1) and referrals to the court under section 8(5);
 	
(f) the Civil Partnership Act 2004, except under –
 	
  (i) Schedule 6 (financial provision corresponding to provision made by the Domestic Proceedings and Magistrates' Courts Act 1978)[.]³
 	
  (ii) …³	

PART II – Statutory instruments

Type of proceedings	Level of judge
3. Proceedings under –	**Judge of circuit judge level**
(a) the Family Law Act 1986 section 55 (declarations as to marital status), 56 (declarations as to legitimacy or legitimation) or 57 (declarations as to adoptions effected overseas); (b) the Child Support Act 1991 under section 32L (orders preventing avoidance); (c) the Human Fertilisation and Embryology Act 2008, section 54 [or section 54A][2], where the child's place of birth was in England and Wales but where not all respondents agree to the making of the order.	
4. Proceedings under –	**Judge of High Court judge level**
(a) …3 (b) the Adoption and Children Act 2002, section 60(3) (order to disclose or to prevent disclosure of information to an adopted person); (c) the Adoption and Children Act 2002, section 79(4) (order for Registrar General to give information); (d) the Civil Partnership Act 2004, paragraphs 4 and 9 of Schedule 7 (permission and substantive application) where – 　(i) the parties do not consent to permission being granted; or 　(ii) the parties consent to permission being granted but do not consent to the substantive order sought; (e) referrals to the court under section 8(5) of the Gender Recognition Act 2004; (f) the Human Fertilisation and Embryology Act 2008, section 54 [or section 54A][2], where the child's place of birth was outside of England and Wales[;][1] [(g) Article 13 of the Protection Measures Regulation.][1]	
5. Proceedings under the Adoption and Children Act 2002 under –	**Level of judge who is dealing with, or has dealt with, proceedings relating to the same child or, if there are or were no such proceedings, to lay justices.**

Type of proceedings	Level of judge

(a) section 21 (placement order);
 	
(b) section 23 (order varying a placement order);
 	
(c) section 24 (order revoking a placement order);
 	
(d) ...[3]
 	
(e) section 27 (order varying or revoking a contact order);
 	
(f) section 28(2) or (3) (order permitting the child's name to be changed or the removal of the child from the United Kingdom);
 	
(g) section 46(c) (adoption order) except where –
 	
  (i) a local authority is a party to the application;
 	
  (ii) the application is for an overseas adoption within the meaning given in section 87 of the Adoption and Children Act 2002; or
 	
  (iii) the application is for a Convention adoption within the meaning given in section 66(1)(c) of the Adoption and Children Act 2002;
 	
(h) section 51A(2)(a) or (b)(d) (postadoption contact);
 	
(i) section 55(e) (revocation of adoption on legitimation);
 	
(j) paragraph 4 of Schedule 1 (amendment of orders).	

6. Proceedings under the Adoption and Children Act 2002 under section 46 (adoption order) where –	**Level of judge who is dealing with, or dealt with, proceedings relating to the same child or, if there are or were no such proceedings, to a judge of district judge level**
(a) a local authority is a party to the application; (b) the application is for an overseas adoption within the meaning given in section 87 of the Adoption and Children Act 2002; or (c) the application is for a Convention adoption within the meaning given in section 66(1)(c) of the Adoption and Children Act 2002.	

NOTES

Amendments.[1] Punctuation substituted and sub-paragraphs inserted: SI 2014/3297. [2] Words inserted: SI 2018/1413.[3] Words and paragraphs omitted repealed, and word substituted: SI 2021/505.

SCHEDULE 2
REMEDIES

Table 1

Remedies which may not be granted by lay justices in the family court

1. Charging order.

2. Order (known as a 'freezing injunction') restraining a party from:

    (a) removing from the jurisdiction assets located there;

    (b) dealing with any assets whether located in the jurisdiction or not.

3. Interim injunction.

4. Interim declaration.

5. Order under section 34 Senior Courts Act 1981 or section 53 County Courts Act 1984, as applied to the family court under section 31E Matrimonial and Family Proceedings Act 1984, for disclosure of documents or inspection of property against a non-party.

6. Order for a specified fund to be paid into court where there is a dispute over a party's right to the fund.

7. Order permitting a party seeking to recover personal property to pay money into court pending the outcome of the proceedings and directing that, if money is paid into court, the property must be given to that party.

8. Order directing a party to provide information about the location of relevant property or assets or to provide information about relevant property or assets, which are or may be the subject of an application for a freezing injunction.

9. Order directing a party to prepare and file accounts relating to the dispute.

10. Order directing an account to be taken or enquiry to be made by the court.

11. Third party debt order.

12. Order for –

    (a) detention, custody or preservation of relevant property;

    (b) inspection of relevant property;

    (c) taking of a sample of relevant property;

    (d) carrying out an experiment on or with relevant property;

    (e) sale of relevant property which is of a perishable nature or which for any other good reason it is desirable to sell quickly;

    (f) the payment of income from relevant property until an application is decided.

13. Order authorising a person to enter any land or building in the possession of a party for the purposes of carrying out an order referred to in paragraph 12.

14. Warrant of delivery.

Remedies which may not be granted by lay justices in the family court

15. Warrant of control.

16. Warrant for the possession of land.

17. Order to deliver up goods under section 4 of the Torts (Interference with Goods) Act 1977.

Table 2

Remedies which may not be granted by lay justices or judges of district judge level in the family court

1. Civil restraint order (limited).

Table 3

Remedies which may not be granted by lay justices, judges of district judge level or judges of circuit judge level in the family court

1. Civil restraint order (extended or general), except that such orders may be granted by a Designated Family Judge or a deputy Designated Family Judge.

2. Search order requiring a party to admit another party to premises for the purposes of preserving evidence etc (section 7 Civil Procedure Act 1997).

3. Claims in respect of a judicial act under the Human Rights Act 1998.

4. Action in respect of the interference with the due administration of justice.

5. Warrants of sequestration to enforce a judgment, order or undertaking in the family court.

[6. Order under Article 13 of the Protection Measures Regulation refusing to recognise or enforce an incoming protection measure.][1]

NOTES

Amendment.[1] Paragraph inserted: SI 2014/3297.

FAMILY PROCEDURE RULES 2010

SI 2010/2955

RELEVANT CORE RULES AND PRACTICE DIRECTIONS

ARRANGEMENT OF RULES

PART II – Statutory instruments

PART 6
SERVICE

Chapter 1
Scope of this Part and Interpretation

Practice Direction 6C –

PART 8
PROCEDURE FOR MISCELLANEOUS APPLICATIONS

Chapter 1
Procedure

Chapter 5
Declarations

Chapter 9
Application for Consent to Marriage of a Child or to Registration of Civil Partnership of a Child

PART 9
APPLICATIONS FOR A FINANCIAL REMEDY

Chapter 3
Applications for Financial Remedies for Children

PART 12
[CHILDREN PROCEEDINGS][1] EXCEPT PARENTAL ORDER PROCEEDINGS AND PROCEEDINGS FOR APPLICATIONS IN ADOPTION, PLACEMENT AND RELATED PROCEEDINGS

Chapter 1
Interpretation and Application of this Part

Chapter 2
General Rules

PART II – Statutory instruments

PART II – Statutory instruments

PART 14
PROCEDURE FOR APPLICATIONS IN ADOPTION,
PLACEMENT AND RELATED PROCEEDINGS

PART 16
REPRESENTATION OF CHILDREN AND REPORTS
IN PROCEEDINGS INVOLVING CHILDREN

Chapter 1
Application of this Part

Chapter 2
Child as Party in Family Proceedings

Chapter 3
When a Children's Guardian or Litigation Friend will be Appointed

Chapter 4
Where a Children's Guardian or Litigation Friend is not Required

PART II – Statutory instruments

PART 27
HEARINGS AND DIRECTIONS APPOINTMENTS

PART II – Statutory instruments

[PART 38
RECOGNITION AND ENFORCEMENT OF PROTECTION MEASURES

Chapter 1
Scope and interpretation of this Part

PART 1
OVERRIDING OBJECTIVE

1.1 The overriding objective

(1) These rules are a new procedural code with the overriding objective of enabling the court to deal with cases justly, having regard to any welfare issues involved.

(2) Dealing with a case justly includes, so far as is practicable –

  (a)   ensuring that it is dealt with expeditiously and fairly;
  (b)   dealing with the case in ways which are proportionate to the nature, importance and complexity of the issues;
  (c)   ensuring that the parties are on an equal footing;
  (d)   saving expense; and
  (e)   allotting to it an appropriate share of the court's resources, while taking into account the need to allot resources to other cases.

1.2 Application by the court of the overriding objective

The court must seek to give effect to the overriding objective when it –

  (a)   exercises any power given to it by these rules; or
  (b)   interprets any rule.

1.3 Duty of the parties

The parties are required to help the court to further the overriding objective.

1.4 Court's duty to manage cases

(1) The court must further the overriding objective by actively managing cases.

[(2) Active case management includes –

  (a)   setting timetables or otherwise controlling the progress of the case;
  (b)   identifying at an early stage –
    (i)   the issues; and
    (ii)   who should be a party to the proceedings;
  (c)   deciding promptly –
    (i)   which issues need full investigation and hearing and which do not; and
    (ii)   the procedure to be followed in the case;
  (d)   deciding the order in which issues are to be resolved;
  (e)   controlling the use of expert evidence;
  (f)   encouraging the parties to use [a non-court dispute resolution][2] procedure if the court considers that appropriate and facilitating the use of such procedure;
  (g)   helping the parties to settle the whole or part of the case;
  (h)   encouraging the parties to co-operate with each other in the conduct of proceedings;

PART II – Statutory instruments

(i)   considering whether the likely benefits of taking a particular step justify the cost of taking it;

(j)   dealing with as many aspects of the case as it can on the same occasion;

(k)   dealing with the case without the parties needing to attend at court;

(l)   making use of technology; and

(m)   giving directions to ensure that the case proceeds quickly and efficiently.][1]

NOTES

Amendments.[1] Paragraph substituted: SI 2012/3061. [2] Words substituted: SI 2014/843.

[1.5 The Welsh language

(1) Nothing in the overriding objective undermines the principles provided by section 1 of the Welsh Language (Wales) Measure 2011 that the Welsh language has official status in Wales or by section 22 of the Welsh Language Act 1993 that in any legal proceedings in Wales the Welsh language may be used by any person who desires to use it.

(2) The parties are required to assist the court to put into effect the principles set out in paragraph (1).][1]

NOTES

Amendments.[1] Paragraph inserted: SI 2018/1172.

PART 2
APPLICATION AND INTERPRETATION OF THE RULES

[2.1 Application of these Rules

Unless the context otherwise requires, these rules apply to family proceedings in –

(a)   the High Court; and

(b)   the family court.][1]

NOTES

Amendment.[1] Rule substituted: SI 2013/3204.

2.2 The glossary

(1) The glossary at the end of these rules is a guide to the meaning of certain legal expressions used in the rules, but is not to be taken as giving those expressions any meaning in the rules which they do not have in the law generally.

(2) Subject to paragraph (3), words in these rules which are included in the glossary are followed by 'GL'.

(3) The word 'service', which appears frequently in the rules, is included in the glossary but is not followed by 'GL'.

2.3 Interpretation

(1) In these rules –

['the 1958 Act' means the Maintenance Orders Act 1958;][1]

'the 1973 Act' means the Matrimonial Causes Act 1973;

'the 1978 Act' means the Domestic Proceedings and Magistrates' Courts 1978;

'the 1980 Hague Convention' means the Convention on the Civil Aspects of International Child Abduction which was signed at The Hague on 25 October 1980;

'the 1984 Act' means the Matrimonial and Family Proceedings Act 1984;

'the 1986 Act' means the Family Law Act 1986;

'the 1989 Act' means the Children Act 1989;

'the 1990 Act' means the Human Fertilisation and Embryology Act 1990;

'the 1991 Act' means the Child Support Act 1991;

'the 1996 Act' means the Family Law Act 1996;

'the 1996 Hague Convention' means the Convention on Jurisdiction, Applicable Law, Recognition, Enforcement and Co-Operation in Respect of Parental Responsibility and Measures for the Protection of Children;

'the 2002 Act' means the Adoption and Children Act 2002;

'the 2004 Act' means the Civil Partnership Act 2004;

'the 2005 Act' means the Mental Capacity Act 2005;

['the 2007 Hague Convention' means the Convention on the International Recovery of Child Support and other forms of Family Maintenance done at The Hague on 23 November 2007;][5]

'the 2008 Act' means the Human Fertilisation and Embryology Act 2008;

['the 2014 Act' means the Children and Families Act 2014;][10]

'adoption proceedings' means proceedings for an adoption order under the 2002 Act;

...[8]

...[10]

'application form' means a document in which the applicant states his intention to seek a court order other than in accordance with the Part 18 procedure;

'application notice' means a document in which the applicant states his intention to seek a court order in accordance with the Part 18 procedure;

['Article 11 form' means a form published by the Permanent Bureau of the Hague Conference under Article 11(4) of the 2007 Hague Convention for use in relation to an application under Article 10 of that Convention, and includes a Financial Circumstances Form as defined in rule 9.3(1) which accompanies such an application;][5]

'Assembly' means the National Assembly for Wales;

'bank holiday' means a bank holiday under the Banking and Financial Dealings Act 1971 –

    (a)   for the purpose of service of a document within the United Kingdom, in the part of the United Kingdom where service is to take place; and

    (b)   for all other purposes, in England and Wales.

'business day' means any day other than –

    (a)   a Saturday, Sunday, Christmas Day or Good Friday; or

    (b)   a bank holiday;

'care order' has the meaning assigned to it by section 31(11) of the 1989 Act;

'CCR' means the County Court Rules 1981, as they appear in Schedule 2 to the CPR [...[9]][4];

'child' means a person under the age of 18 years who is the subject of the proceedings; except that –

(a)   in adoption proceedings, it also includes a person who has attained the age of 18 years before the proceedings are concluded; and

(b)   in proceedings brought under ...[14] the 1980 Hague Convention or the European Convention, it means a person under the age of 16 years who is the subject of the proceedings;

['child arrangements order' has the meaning given to it by section 8(1) of the 1989 Act;][10]

'child of the family' has the meaning given to it by section 105(1) of the 1989 Act;

'children and family reporter' means an officer of the Service or a Welsh family proceedings officer who has been asked to prepare a welfare report under section 7(1)(a) of the 1989 Act or section 102(3)(b) of the 2002 Act;

'children's guardian' means –

(a)   in relation to a child who is the subject of and a party to specified proceedings or proceedings to which Part 14 applies, the person appointed in accordance with rule 16.3(1); and

(b)   in any other case, the person appointed in accordance with rule 16.4;

'civil partnership order' means one of the orders mentioned in section 37 of the 2004 Act;

'civil partnership proceedings' means proceedings for a civil partnership order;

...[8]

'civil restraint order' means an order restraining a party –

(a)   from making any further applications in current proceedings (a limited civil restraint order);

(b)   from making certain applications in specified courts (an extended civil restraint order); or

(c)   from making any application in specified courts (a general civil restraint order);

...[3]

'consent order' means an order in the terms applied for to which the respondent agrees;

...[10]

...[14]

'court' means, subject to any rule or other enactment which provides otherwise, the High Court [or the family court][8];

(rule 2.5 relates to the power to perform functions of the court.)

...[8]

'court officer' means [a member of court staff][8];

'CPR' means the Civil Procedure Rules 1998;

'deputy' has the meaning given in section 16(2)(b) of the 2005 Act;

...[8]

'detailed assessment proceedings' means the procedure by which the amount of costs is decided in accordance with Part 47 of the CPR;

'directions appointment' means a hearing for directions;

... [8]

... [8]

... [8]

'the European Convention' means the European Convention on Recognition and Enforcement of Decisions concerning Custody of Children and on the Restoration of Custody of Children which was signed in Luxembourg on 20 May 1980;

'filing', in relation to a document, means delivering it, by post or otherwise, to the court office;

'financial order' means –

    (a)   an avoidance of disposition order;

    (b)   an order for maintenance pending suit;

    (c)   an order for maintenance pending outcome of proceedings;

    (d)   an order for periodical payments or lump sum provision as mentioned in section 21(1) of the 1973 Act, except an order under section 27(6) of that Act;

    (e)   an order for periodical payments or lump sum provision as mentioned in paragraph 2(1) of Schedule 5 to the 2004 Act, made under Part 1 of Schedule 5 to that Act;

    (f)   a property adjustment order;

    (g)   a variation order;

    (h)   a pension sharing order; ... [7]

    (i)   a pension compensation sharing order[; or

    (j)   an order for payment in respect of legal services;][7]

('variation order', 'pension compensation sharing order' and 'pension sharing order' are defined in rule 9.3)

'financial remedy' means –

    (a)   a financial order;

    (b)   an order under Schedule 1 to the 1989 Act;

    (c)   an order under Part 3 of the 1984 Act [except an application under section 13 of the 1984 Act for permission to apply for a financial remedy][2];

    (d)   an order under Schedule 7 to the 2004 Act [except an application under paragraph 4 of Schedule 7 to the 2004 Act for permission to apply for an order under paragraph 9 or 13 of that Schedule][2];

    (e)   an order under section 27 of the 1973 Act;

    (f)   an order under Part 9 of Schedule 5 to the 2004 Act;

    (g)   an order under section 35 of the 1973 Act;

    (h)   an order under paragraph 69 of Schedule 5 to the 2004 Act;

    (i)   an order under Part 1 of the 1978 Act;

    (j)   an order under Schedule 6 to the 2004 Act;

    (k)   an order under section 10(2) of the 1973 Act; or

    (l)   an order under section 48(2) of the 2004 Act;

'hearing' includes a directions appointment;

PART II – Statutory instruments

'hearsay' means a statement made, otherwise than by a person while giving oral evidence in proceedings, which is tendered as evidence of the matters stated, and references to hearsay include hearsay of whatever degree;

['incoming protection measure' means a protection measure that has been ordered in a Member State of the European Union other than …[14] Denmark;][11]

'inherent jurisdiction' means the High Court's power to make any order or determine any issue in respect of a child, including in wardship proceedings, where it would be just and equitable to do so unless restricted by legislation or case law;

(Practice Direction 12D (Inherent Jurisdiction (including Wardship Proceedings)) provides examples of inherent jurisdiction proceedings.)

['judge' means –

    (a)   in the High Court, a judge or a district judge of that court (including a district judge of the principal registry) or a person authorised to act as such; and

    (b)   in the family court, a person who is –

        (i)   the Lord Chief Justice;

        (ii)   the Master of the Rolls;

        (iii)   the President of the Queen's Bench Division;

        (iv)   the President of the Family Division;

        (v)   the Chancellor of the High Court;

        (vi)   an ordinary judge of the Court of Appeal (including the vice-president, if any, of either division of that court);

        (vii)   the Senior President of Tribunals;

        (viii) a puisne judge of the High Court;

        (ix)   a deputy judge of the High Court;

        (x)   a person who has been a judge of the Court of Appeal or a puisne judge of the High Court who may act as a judge of the family court by virtue of section 9 of the Senior Courts Act 1981;

        (xi)   the Chief Taxing Master;

        (xii)   a taxing master of the Senior Courts;

        (xiii)   a person appointed to act as a deputy for the person holding office referred to in sub-paragraph (xii) or to act as a temporary additional officer for any such office;

        (xiv)   a circuit judge;

        (xv)   a Recorder;

        (xvi)   the Senior District Judge of the Family Division;

        (xvii) a district judge of the principal registry;

        (xviii) a person appointed to act as a deputy for the person holding office referred to in sub-paragraph (xvii) or to act as a temporary additional office holder for any such office;

        (xix)   a district judge;

        (xx)   a deputy district judge appointed under section 102 of the Senior Courts Act 1981 or section 8 of the County Courts Act 1984;

        (xxi)   a District Judge (Magistrates' Courts);

        (xxii) a lay justice;

  (xxiii) any other judge referred to in section 31C(1) of the 1984 Act who is authorised by the President of the Family Division to conduct particular business in the family court;][9]

'jurisdiction' means, unless the context requires otherwise, England and Wales and any part of the territorial waters of the United Kingdom adjoining England and Wales;

['justices' legal adviser' means a person authorised to exercise functions under section 67B of the Courts Act 2003 who has such qualifications as are prescribed by the Authorised Court Staff (Legal Advice Functions) Qualifications Regulations 2020;][13]

['lay justice' means a justice of the peace who is not a District Judge (Magistrates' Courts);][9]

'legal representative' means a –

 (a) barrister;

 (b) solicitor;

 (c) solicitor's employee;

 (d) manager of a body recognised under section 9 of the Administration of Justice Act 1985; or

 (e) person who, for the purposes of the Legal Services Act 2007, is an authorised person in relation to an activity which constitutes the conduct of litigation (within the meaning of the Act),

who has been instructed to act for a party in relation to proceedings;

'litigation friend' has the meaning given –

 (a) in relation to a protected party, by Part 15; and

 (b) in relation to a child, by Part 16;

[...[14]][1]

'matrimonial cause' means proceedings for a matrimonial order;

'matrimonial order' means –

 (a) a [divorce order][15] made under section 1 of the 1973 Act;

 (b) a [nullity of marriage order][15] made on one of the grounds set out in [section 11, 12 or 12A][12] of the 1973 Act;

 (c) a [judicial separation order][15] made under section 17 of the 1973 Act;

['non-court dispute resolution' means methods of resolving a dispute, including mediation, other than through the normal court process;][10]

'note' includes a record made by mechanical means;

'officer of the Service' has the meaning given by section 11(3) of the Criminal Justice and Court Services Act 2000;

'order' includes directions of the court;

'order for maintenance pending outcome of proceedings' means an order under paragraph 38 of Schedule 5 to the 2004 Act;

'order for maintenance pending suit' means an order under section 22 of the 1973 Act;

['order for payment for legal services' means an order under section 22ZA of the 1973 Act or an order under paragraph 38A of Part 8 of Schedule 5 to the 2004 Act;][7]

'parental order proceedings' has the meaning assigned to it by rule 13.1;

'parental responsibility' has the meaning assigned to it by section 3 of the 1989 Act;

'placement proceedings' means proceedings for the making, varying or revoking of a placement order under the 2002 Act;

'principal registry' means the principal registry of the Family Division of the High Court;

'proceedings' means, unless the context requires otherwise, family proceedings as defined in section 75(3) of the Courts Act 2003;

'professional acting in furtherance of the protection of children' includes –

    (a)   an officer of a local authority exercising child protection functions;

    (b)   a police officer who is –

        (i)   exercising powers under section 46 of the Act of 1989; or

        (ii)   serving in a child protection unit or a paedophile unit of a police force,

    (c)   any professional person attending a child protection conference or review in relation to a child who is the subject of the proceedings to which the information regarding the proceedings held in private relates[;][2]

    (d)   an officer of the National Society for the Prevention of Cruelty to Children; [or][2]

    [(e)   a member or employee of the [Disclosure and Barring Service]6, being the body established under [section 87(1) of the Protection of Freedoms Act 2012][6];][2]

'professional legal adviser' means a –

    (a)   barrister;

    (b)   solicitor;

    (c)   solicitor's employee;

    (d)   manager of a body recognised under section 9 of the Administration of Justice Act 1985; or

    (e)   person who, for the purposes of the Legal Services Act 2007, is an authorised person in relation to an activity which constitutes the conduct of litigation (within the meaning of that Act),

who is providing advice to a party but is not instructed to represent that party in the proceedings;

'property adjustment order' means –

    (a)   in proceedings under the 1973 Act, any of the orders mentioned in section 21(2) of that Act;

    (b)   in proceedings under the 1984 Act, an order under section 17(1)(a)(ii) of that Act;

    (c)   in proceedings under Schedule 5 to the 2004 Act, any of the orders mentioned in paragraph 7(1); or

    (d)   in proceedings under Schedule 7 to the 2004 Act, an order for property adjustment under paragraph 9(2) or (3);

'protected party' means a party, or an intended party, who lacks capacity (within the meaning of the 2005 Act) to conduct proceedings;

['protection measure' has the meaning given to it in the Protection Measures Regulation;

'Protection Measures Regulation' means the Regulation (EU) No 606/2013 of the European Parliament and of the Council of 12th June 2013 on mutual recognition of protection measures in civil matters;][11]

'reporting officer' means an officer of the Service or a Welsh family proceedings officer appointed to witness the documents which signify a parent's or guardian's consent to the placing of the child for adoption or to the making of an adoption order or a section 84 order;

'risk assessment' has the meaning assigned to it by section 16A(3) of the 1989 Act;

...[8]

'RSC' means the Rules of the Supreme Court 1965 as they appear in Schedule 1 to the CPR [...[9]][4];

'section 8 order' has the meaning assigned to it by section 8(2) of the 1989 Act;

'section 84 order' means an order made by the High Court under section 84 of the 2002 Act giving parental responsibility prior to adoption abroad;

'section 89 order' means an order made by the High Court under section 89 of the 2002 Act –

   (a)   annulling a Convention adoption or Convention adoption order;

   (b)   providing for an overseas adoption or determination under section 91 of the 2002 Act to cease to be valid; or

   (c)   deciding the extent, if any, to which a determination under section 91 of the 2002 Act has been affected by a subsequent determination under that section;

'Service' has the meaning given by section 11 of the Criminal Justice and Court Services Act 2000;

...[14]

'specified proceedings' has the meaning assigned to it by section 41(6) of the 1989 Act and rule 12.27;

'welfare officer' means a person who has been asked to prepare a report under section 7(1)(b) of the 1989 Act;

'Welsh family proceedings officer' has the meaning given by section 35(4) of the Children Act 2004.

(2) In these rules a reference to –

   (a)   an application for a matrimonial order or a civil partnership order is to be read as a reference to [an application][15] for –

      (i)   a matrimonial order; [or][11]

      (ii) ...[11]

      (iii) a civil partnership order,

   and includes [an application][15] by a respondent asking for such an order;

   (b)   'financial order' in matrimonial proceedings is to be read as a reference to 'ancillary relief';

   (c)   'matrimonial proceedings' is to be read as a reference to a matrimonial cause ...[11].

(3) [Where[9]][4] these rules apply the CPR, they apply the CPR as amended from time to time.

(4) ...[9]

NOTES

Amendments.[1] Definitions inserted: SI 2011/1328. [2] Words and subparagraph inserted and punctuation substituted: SI 2012/679. [3] Definition omitted: SI 2012/2007. [4] Words inserted: SI 2012/2046. [5] Definitions inserted: SI 2012/2806. [6] Words substituted: SI 2012/3006. [7] Word omitted, subparagraph inserted and definition inserted: SI 2013/1472. [8] Definitions omitted and words substituted: SI 2013/3204. [9] Words deleted and substituted, definitions inserted and substituted, paragraph omitted: SI 2014/667. [10] Definitions inserted and omitted: SI 2014/843. [11] Definitions inserted, word inserted, words omitted and paragraph omitted: SI 2014/3296. [12] Words substituted: SI 2015/913. [13] Definition substituted: SI 2020/135. [14] Words omitted repealed: SI 2019/517. [15] Words substituted: SI 2022/44.

2.4 Modification of rules in application to serial numbers etc.

If a serial number has been assigned under rule 14.2 or the name or other contact details of a party is not being revealed in accordance with rule 29.1 –

   (a) any rule requiring any party to serve any document will not apply; and
   (b) the court will give directions about serving any document on the other parties.

2.5 Power to perform functions conferred on the court by these rules and practice directions

(1) Where these rules or a practice direction provide for the court to perform any function then, except where any rule or practice direction [or any other enactment]1 provides otherwise, that function may be performed –

   (a) in relation to proceedings in the High Court or in a district registry, by any judge or district judge of that Court including a district judge of the principal registry;
   [(b) in relation to proceedings in the family court –
      (i) by the court composed in accordance with rules made under section 31D of the 1984 Act; or
      (ii) where Practice Direction 2A applies, by a single lay justice who is authorised as specified in rules made under section 31D of the 1984 Act.][2]

   (c) ...[1]

   [...[3]][1]

[(1A) The functions of the family court or a judge of the family court listed in Practice Direction 2C may be exercised by a justices' legal adviser.][3]

(2) A deputy High Court judge and a district judge, including a district judge of the principal registry, may not try a claim for a declaration of incompatibility in accordance with section 4 of the Human Rights Act 1998.

NOTES

Amendments.[1] Words substituted and paragraph omitted: SI 2013/3204. [2] Paragraph substituted: SI 2014/667. [3] Words repealed and paragraph inserted: SI 2020/135.

2.6 Powers of the single justice to perform functions under the 1989 Act, the 1996 Act, the 2002 Act and the Childcare Act 2006

(1) [A single lay justice who is authorised as specified in rules made under section 31D of the 1984 Act may perform the functions of the family court –][1]

(a)   where an application without notice is made under sections 10, 44(1), 48(9), 50(4) and 102(1) of the 1989 Act;

(b)   subject to paragraph (2), under sections 11(3) or 38(1) of the 1989 Act;

(c)   under sections 4(3)(b), 4A(3)(b), 4ZA(6)(b), 7, 34(3)(b), 41, 44(9)(b) and (11)(b)(iii), 48(4), 91(15) or (17) or paragraph 11(4) of Schedule 14 of the 1989 Act;

(d)   …[1]

(e)   where an application without notice is made under section 41(2) of the 2002 Act (recovery orders);

(f)   where an application without notice is made for an occupation order or a non molestation order under Part 4 of the 1996 Act; or

(g)   where an application is made for a warrant under section 79 of the Childcare Act 2006;

(2) A single [lay justice][1] may make an order under section 11(3) or 38(1) of the 1989 Act where –

(a)   a previous such order has been made in the same proceedings;

(b)   the terms of the order sought are the same as those of the last such order made; and

(c)   a written request for such an order has been made and –

(i)   the other parties and any children's guardian consent to the request and they or their legal representatives have signed the request; or

(ii)   at least one of the other parties and any children's guardian consent to the request and they or their legal representatives have signed the request, and the remaining parties have not indicated that they either consent to or oppose the making of the order.

(3) The proceedings referred to in paragraph [(1)(a) and (c)][1] are proceedings which are prescribed for the purposes of section 93(2)(i) of the 1989 Act.

NOTES

Amendment.[1] Words substituted and sub-paragraph omitted: SI 2014/667.
Modification. Rule 2.6 modified in certain applications under the Children Act 1989, in respect of enforcement of contact orders, by the Magistrates' Courts (Enforcement or Variation of Orders Made in Family Proceedings and Miscellaneous Provisions) Rules 2011, SI 2011/1329, rr 76, 83.

[2.7 Single lay justice: power to refer to the family court

Where a single lay justice –

(a)   is performing a function of the family court in accordance with rule 2.5(1)(b)(ii) or rule 2.6(1) or (2); and

(b)   considers, for whatever reason, that it is inappropriate to perform the function,

the single lay justice must refer the matter to the family court.][1]

PART II – Statutory instruments

NOTES

Amendment.[1] Rule substituted: SI 2014/667.

2.8 Court's discretion as to where it deals with cases

The court may deal with a case at any place that it considers appropriate.

2.9 Computation of time

(1) This rule shows how to calculate any period of time for doing any act which is specified –

    (a)   by these rules;

    (b)   by a practice direction; or

    (c)   by a direction or order of the court.

(2) A period of time expressed as a number of days must be computed as clear days.

(3) In this rule 'clear days' means that in computing the numbers of days –

    (a)   the day on which the period begins; and

    (b)   if the end of the period is defined by reference to an event, the day on which that event occurs,

are not included.

(4) Where the specified period is 7 days or less and includes a day which is not a business day, that day does not count.

(5) When the period specified –

    (a)   by these rules or a practice direction; or

    (b)   by any direction or order of the court,

for doing any act at the court office ends on a day on which the office is closed, that act will be in time if done on the next day on which the court office is open.

2.10 Dates for compliance to be calendar dates and to include time of day

(1) Where the court makes an order or gives a direction which imposes a time limit for doing any act, the last date for compliance must, wherever practicable –

    (a)   be expressed as a calendar date; and

    (b)   include the time of day by which the act must be done.

(2) Where the date by which an act must be done is inserted in any document, the date must, wherever practicable, be expressed as a calendar date.

(3) Where 'month' occurs in any order, direction or other document, it means a calendar month.

Practice Direction –
Practice Directions relating to Family Proceedings in force before 6th April 2011 which support the Family Procedure Rules 2010

Introduction and the Existing Practice Directions

1.1 The Family Procedure Rules 2010 ('the FPR 2010') come into force on 6th April 2011.The purpose of this practice direction is to inform court users of the practice directions relating (only) to family proceedings which date from before 6th April 2011 ('existing Practice Directions') but will continue to apply after that date.

1.2 The table in the Annex to this practice direction lists those existing Practice Directions which will continue to apply. The listed existing Practice Directions will apply to family proceedings on and after 6th April 2011 –

(a) with the modifications outlined in the Annex (in particular that the numbering of the existing Practice Directions will be as set out in column one of the table in the Annex) and any other modifications necessary in consequence of the FPR 2010 coming into force; and

(b) subject to the FPR 2010 and any other practice directions supporting those rules.

Application of Practice Direction 23B of the Civil Procedure Rules 1998

2.1 Paragraphs 1.1, 1.2, 1.4 and 1.5 of CPR Practice Direction 23B apply to applications under Part III of the Family Law Reform Act 1969 for the use of scientific tests to determine parentage. These applications will be made using the procedure in Part 18 of the FPR 2010 (Procedure for Other Applications in Proceedings).

Annex

Number	Title	Date	Court	Updated rule references
PD6C	Practice Direction (Disclosure of Addresses by Government Departments) (amending Practice Direction of 13th February 1989) (NB this practice direction does not apply to requests for disclosure from HMRC and related agencies which are covered by 'Disclosure Orders against the Inland Revenue-Guidance from the President's Office (November 2003)'	20 July 1995	High Court, county court and magistrates' court	

PART II – Statutory instruments

Number	Title	Date	Court	Updated rule references
PD7D	Gender Recognition Act 2004	5 April 2005	High Court and county court	
PD12A	Public Law Proceedings Guide to Case Management: April 2010	April 2010	High Court, county court and magistrates' court	
PD12B	The Revised Private Law Programme	April 2010	High Court, county court and magistrates' court	
PD12I	Applications for Reporting Restriction Orders (nb this practice direction applies to information about children and protected parties)	18 March 2005	High Court	
PD12J	Residence and Contact Orders: Domestic Violence and Harm	14 January 2009	High Court, county court and magistrates' court	In paragraph 10, for 'the Family Proceedings Rules 1991, rule 4.17AA and by the Family Proceedings Courts (Children Act 1989) Rules 1991, rule 17AA', substitute, 'rule 12.34 of the Family Procedure Rules 2010'
PD12K	President's Direction (Children Act 1989: Exclusion Requirement)	17 December 1997	High Court, county court and magistrates' court	
PD12L	Children Act 1989:Risk Assessments under Section 16A	3 September 2007	High Court, county court and magistrates' court	
PD12M	Family Assistance Orders: Consultation	3 September 2007	High Court, county court and magistrates' court	
PD12N	Enforcement of Children Act 1989 Contact Orders: Disclosure of Information to Officers of the National Probation Service (High Court and county court)	6 November 2008	High Court and county court (The Lord Chief Justice issued a Practice Direction on this subject for the magistrates' courts mirroring the one for the High Court and county courts)	
PD12O	Practice Direction (Arrival of Child in England by Air)	18 January 1980	High Court and county court	
PD12P	Registrar's Direction (Removal from jurisdiction: issue of Passports)	15 May 1987	High Court and county court	

Number	Title	Date	Court	Updated rule references
PD14A	Who Receives a Copy of the Application Form for Orders in Proceedings		High Court, county court and magistrates' court	In the heading, for 'Part 5,rule 24(1)(b)(ii) of the Family Procedure (Adoption) Rules 2005', substitute 'Part 14, rule 14.6(1)(b)(ii) of the Family Procedure Rules 2010'
PD14B	The First Directions Hearing-Adoptions with a Foreign Element		High Court, county court and magistrates' court	In the heading, for 'Part 5,rule 26(3) of the Family Procedure (Adoption) Rules 2005', substitute 'Part 14, rule 14.8(3) of the Family Procedure Rules 2010'; and in paragraph 2, for 'rule 26(1)', substitute 'rule 14.8(1)'
PD14C	Reports by the Adoption Agency or Local Authority		High Court, county court and magistrates' court	In the heading for 'Part 5,rule 29(3) of the Family Procedure (Adoption) Rules 2005', substitute 'Part 14, rule 14.11(3) of the Family Procedure Rules 2010'
PD14D	Reports by a Registered Medical Practitioner ('Health Reports')		High Court, county court and magistrates' court	In the heading for 'Part 5,rule 30(2) of the Family Procedure(Adoption) Rules 2005',substitute 'Part 14, rule 14.12(2) of the Family Procedure Rules 2010'; and in paragraph 1.1, for 'rule 30(1)', substitute 'rule 14.12(1)'
PD14E	Communication of Information Relating to the Proceedings		High Court, county court and magistrates' court	In the heading for 'Part 8,rule 78(1)(b) of the Family Procedure (Adoption) Rules 2005', substitute 'Part 14, rule 14.14(b) of the Family Procedure Rules 2010'; and in paragraph 1.1, for 'rule 78', substitute 'rule 14.14'
PD14F	Disclosing Information to an Adopted Adult		High Court, county court and magistrates' court	In the heading for 'Part 8,rule 84(1)(d) of the Family Procedure (Adoption) Rules 2005', substitute 'Part 14, rule 14.18(1)(d) of the Family Procedure Rules 2010'; in paragraphs 1,1 and 1.2, for 'rule 84', substitute 'rule 14.18'; and in paragraph 1.2, for 'rule 17', substitute 'rule 5'

PART II – Statutory instruments

Number	Title	Date	Court	Updated rule references
PD27A	Family Proceedings: Court Bundles (Universal Practice to be applied in All Courts other than the Family Proceedings Court)	27 July 2006	High Court and county court	
PD27B	Attendance of Media Representatives at Hearings in Family Proceedings (High Court and county courts) (This practice direction should be read as if amended by *Re X (a child) (residence and contact: rights of media attendance)* (2009) EWHC 1728 (Fam) [87])	20 April 2009	High Court and county courts	For references to 'rule 10.28 of the Family Proceedings Rules 1991', substitute 'rule 27.11 of the Family Procedure Rules 2010'; in paragraph 2.2 for 'paragraphs (4) to (6)', substitute 'paragraphs (3) to (5)'; in paragraph 2.3, for 'Part 11 of the Family Proceedings Rules 1991', substitute 'Part 12,Chapter 7 of the Family Procedure Rules 2010 and Practice Direction 12G'; in paragraph 4.2, for 'paragraph (8)',substitute 'paragraph (7)'; in paragraph 4.3, for 'paragraph (3)(f)', substitute 'paragraph 2(f)' and for 'paragraph 3(g)', substitute 'paragraph (2) (g)'; in paragraph 5.1,for paragraph(4), substitute paragraph (3); in paragraph 5.2, for 'paragraph (4)',substitute 'paragraph (3)' and for 'paragraph (4)(a)', substitute 'paragraph 3(a)'; in paragraph 5.3, for 'paragraph 4(a)(iii)', substitute 'paragraph 3(a) (iii)'; in paragraph 5.4, for 'paragraph 4(b)', substitute 'paragraph 3(b)'; and in paragraph 6.1, for 'paragraph (6)' substitute 'paragraph (5)'

Number	Title	Date	Court	Updated rule references
PD27C	Attendance of Media Representatives at Hearings in Family Proceedings (Family Proceedings Court) (This practice direction should be read as if amended by *Re X (a child) (residence and contact: rights of media attendance)* (2009) EWHC 1728 (Fam) at [87]	20 April 2009	Magistrates' courts	In paragraph 1.1, for 'rule 16A of the Family Proceedings Courts (Children Act 1989) Rules 1991 ('the Rules')', substitute 'rule 27.11 of the Family Procedure Rules 2010 ('the Rules')'; in paragraph 2.1, for references to 'rule 16A(2)' where it occurs, substitute 'rule 27.11(1)' and for 'paragraphs (3) to (5) of rule 16A', substitute; 'paragraphs (3) to(5) of rule 27.11'; in paragraph 2.2, for 'rule 16A(2)', substitute 'rule 27.11(1)'; in paragraph 2.3 for 'Part 11C (rules relating to disclosure to third parties)', substitute 'Part 12, Chapter 7 of the Family Procedure Rules 2010 and Practice Direction 12G'; in paragraph 2.4, for 'rule 16A', substitute 'rule 27.11';and in paragraph 4.3, for 'paragraph (1)(f)', substitute 'paragraph 2(f)' and for 'paragraph (1)(g)' substitute ' paragraph 2(g)'
PD29B	Human Rights Act 1998	24 July 2000	High Court, county court and magistrates' court	
PD34B	Practice Note Tracing Payers Overseas	10 February 1976	High Court and county court	

NOTES

The list of Practice Directions above is no longer up to date and is yet to be formally amended.

Practice Direction 2A –
Functions of the Court in the Family Procedure Rules 2010 and Practice Directions which may be Performed by a Single Lay Justice

This Practice Direction supplements FPR Part 2, rule 2.5(1)(b)(ii) (Power to perform functions conferred on the court by these rules and practice directions)

1.1 Where the FPR or a practice direction provide for the court to perform any function, that function may be performed by a single lay justice who is authorised as specified in rules made under section 31D of the 1984 Act except that such a justice cannot perform the functions listed in:

(a)   column 2 of Table 1 in accordance with the rules listed in column 1; and

(b)   column 2 of Table 2 in accordance with the paragraph of the practice direction listed in column 1.

1.2 For the avoidance of doubt, unless a rule, practice direction or other enactment provides otherwise, a single lay justice cannot make the decision of the family court at the final hearing of an application for a substantive order. For example, a single lay justice cannot make a child arrangements order on notice, placement order, adoption or care order. However, a single lay justice can discharge the functions of the family court under the statutory provisions listed in rule 2.6 of the FPR.

Table 1

Rule	Nature of function
3.10	Determining whether a MIAM exemption has been validly claimed.
4.1(3)(g)	Stay the whole or part of any proceedings or judgment either generally or until a specified date or event.
4.1(3)(l)	Exclude an issue from consideration.
4.1(3)(m)	Dismiss or give a decision on an application after a decision on a preliminary issue.
4.1(4)(a)	When the court makes an order, making that order subject to conditions.
4.1(6)	Varying and revoking an order (other than directions which the court has made).
4.3(1)	Ability of the court to make orders (other than directions) of its own initiative.
4.3(7)	Recording a decision to strike out a statement of case or dismiss an application (including an application for permission to appeal) and considering whether it is appropriate to make a civil restraint order where the court considers that the application is totally without merit.
4.4, 4.5 and 4.6	All the powers of the family court under these rules (power to strike out statement of case, sanctions have effect unless defaulting party obtains relief from sanctions).
Part 7	The duties and powers of the family court in this Part.
Part 8	The duties and powers of the family court in this Part otherwise than specified in rule 8.20(4) and except in relation to applications for a declaration of parentage under section 55A of the 1986 Act.
8.20(4)	A direction that a child should be made a respondent to the application for a declaration of parentage under section 55A of the Family Law Act 1986, except where the parties consent to the child being made a respondent.

Rule	Nature of function
9.11(2)	Direction that a child be separately represented on an application.
9.12(1)	The duties of the family court upon the issue of an application for financial remedies for children.
9.15	The duties and powers of the family court in respect of the first appointment relating to applications for financial remedies for children.
9.16(1)	Giving permission for the production of further documents between the first appointment and FDR appointment in applications for financial remedies for children.
9.16(2)	Giving further directions or directing that parties attend an FDR appointment.
9.17(8)	Making an appropriate consent order at the conclusion of an FDR appointment.
9.17(9)	Giving directions for the future course of proceedings for financial remedies for children where it does not make an appropriate consent order.
9.17(10)	Giving directions that the parties need not personally attend an FDR appointment.
9.18A(5)(a)	Determining whether the standard procedure or the fast-track procedure should apply to an application for a financial remedy.
9.22	All the powers of the family court under this rule (relating to proceedings by or against a person outside England and Wales for variation or revocation of orders under section 20 of the 1978 Act or paragraphs 30 to 34 of Schedule 6 to the 2004 Act).
9.26B	The powers of the family court in respect of adding parties to, or removing parties from, proceedings for a financial remedy.
9.33(6)	Giving notice of the date of the first appointment or other hearing in an application for a financial remedy where the applicant or respondent is the party with pension rights.
9.34(3)(b)	Giving directions that a person objecting to a consent order for pension attachment attends court of furnish written details of the objection.
9.36	The duties of the family court in respect of making a pension sharing order or a pension attachment order.
10.11(2)	Determining, following an arrest, whether the facts and circumstances leading to an arrest amount to breach of an occupation order or non-molestation order and deciding whether to adjourn proceedings.

PART II – Statutory instruments

Rule	Nature of function
10.14	Adjourning hearings for consideration of the penalty to be imposed for contempt of court.
10.17(1)	The taking of recognizance.
Part 11	The duties and powers of the family court in this Part.
12.3(2)	Where the person with parental responsibility is a child, a direction for that child be made a party, except where the parties consent to that child being made a party.
12.3(3)	Direction that a child be made a party to proceedings or that a child who is a party be removed, except where the parties consent to the child being made a party or to the removal of that party.
12.3(4)	Consequential directions following the addition or removal of a party except where a single justice is able to make such a direction under rule 12.3(2) and (3).
12.8(2)	Directing that an applicant effect service in section 8 private law proceedings.
12.22	Drawing up a timetable for public law proceedings.
12.25	The duties and powers of the family court in respect of case management hearings.
12.26	The duties and powers of the family court in respect of discussions between advocates.
12.26C(1)	Giving reasons for, and an explanation of the impact on the welfare of the child of, decisions to extend time limits.
12.61(1) and (2)	Considering the transfer of proceedings to the court of another [Contracting State][1], directions in relation to the manner in which parties may make representations and power to deal with question of transfer without a hearing with the consent of parties.
12.64(1)	Exercising court's powers under …[1] Article 8 of the 1996 Hague Convention.
12.68(1)	Staying the proceedings.
12.68(3)	Giving reasons for the court's decision, making a finding of fact and stating a finding of fact where such a finding has been made.
12.70(1)	Contemplating the placement of a child in another [Contracting State][1].
12.70(3)	Sending request directly to the central authority or other authority having jurisdiction in the other …[1] State.
12.70(4)	Sending request to Central Authority for England and Wales for onward transmission.
12.70(5)	Considering the documents which should accompany the request.

Rule	Nature of function
13.3(3)	Where the person with parental responsibility is a child, a direction for that child be made a party, except where the parties consent to that child being made a party.
13.3(4)	Direction that a child be made a party to proceedings or that a child who is a party be removed, except where the parties consent to the child being made a party or to the removal of that party.
13.3(5)	Consequential directions following the addition or removal of a party except where a single justice is able to make such a direction under rule 13.3(3) and (4).
13.9(7)	Variation or revocation of direction following transfer, except where a single justice would be able to make the direction in question under rule 13.9(1).
13.15(3)	Determination of the probable date of the child's birth.
13.20(1)	Specifying a later date by which a parental order takes effect.
14.2(4)	Giving directions regarding the removal of serial numbers.
14.3(2)	Direction that a child be made a respondent, except where the parties consent to the child being made a respondent.
14.3(3)(b)	Direction that a child who is a party be removed, except where the parties consent to the child being made a respondent.
14.3(4)	Consequential directions following the addition or removal of a party except where a single justice is able to make such a direction under rule 14.3(2) and (3)
14.8(3)	Any of the directions listed in PD14B in proceedings for – (a) a Convention adoption order (b) a section 84 order (c) a section 88 direction (d) a section 89 order; or (e) an adoption order where section 83(1) of the 2002 Act applies (restriction on bringing children in)
14.16(8)	Making an adoption order under section 50 of the 2002 Act after personal attendance of one only of the applicants if there are special circumstances.
14.16(9)	Not making a placement order unless the legal representative of the applicant attends the final hearing.
14.17(4)	Determination of the probable date of the child's birth.
14.25(1)	Specifying a later date by which an order takes effect.
15.3(1)	Permission to a person to take steps before the protected party has a litigation friend.

PART II – Statutory instruments

Rule	Nature of function
15.3(2)	Permission to a party to take steps (where during proceedings a person lacks capacity to continue to conduct proceedings) before the protected party has a litigation friend.
15.3(3)	Making an order that a step taken before a protected party has a litigation friend has effect.
15.6(1)	Making an order appointing a person as a litigation friend.
15.6(6)	Court may not appoint a litigation friend unless it is satisfied that the person complies with the conditions in rule 15.4(3).
15.7	Direction that a person may not act as a litigation friend, termination of an appointment, appointment of a litigation friend in substitution for an existing one.
16.2	Power of court to make a child a party to proceedings if it considers it is in the best interests of the child to do so.
16.6(3)(a)	Permission to a child to conduct proceedings without a children's guardian or litigation friend.
16.6(6)	Power of the court to grant an application under paragraph (3)(a) or (5) if the court considers that the child has sufficient understanding to conduct the proceedings.
16.6(7)	Power of the court to require the litigation friend or children's guardian to take such part in proceedings (referred to in paragraph (6)) as the court directs.
16.6(8)	Power of the court to revoke permission granted under paragraph (3) in specified circumstances.
16.6(10)	Power of the court, in specified circumstances, to appoint a person to be the child's litigation friend or children's guardian.
16.8(2)	Permission to a person to take steps before the child has a litigation friend.
16.8(3)	Making an order that a step taken before the child has a litigation friend has effect.
16.11(1)	Making an order appointing a person as a litigation friend.
16.12	Direction that a person may not act as a litigation friend, termination of an appointment, appointment of a litigation friend in substitution for an existing one.
16.23(2)	Permission to a person to take steps before the child has a children's guardian.
18.3(1)(c)	Direction that a child be a respondent to an application under Part 18.

Rule	Nature of function
18.9(1)(a)	Power of court to deal with a Part 18 application without a hearing.
18.12	Power of the court to proceed in absence of a party, except where a single justice has the power to make the relevant order applied for.
19.8(2)	The court's power to require or permit a party to give oral evidence at the hearing.
Part 20	The duties and powers of the family court in this Part.
21.3	Power of court relating to withholding inspection or disclosure of a document.
22.1(2) to (4)	Power to exclude evidence that would otherwise be admissible, power to permit a party to adduce evidence, or to seek to rely on a document, in respect of which that party has failed to comply with requirements of Part 22 and power to limit cross examination.
22.6	Court's powers relating to use at final hearing of witness statements which have been served.
22.12	Power of court to require evidence by affidavit instead of or in addition to a witness statement.
22.15(4)	Permission for a party to amend or withdraw any admission made by that party on such terms as the court thinks just.
22.20(3)(a)	Permission for a witness statement in proceedings in the family court under Part 9 to be used for a purpose other than the proceedings in which it is served.
…1	…1
…1	…1
25.4	Giving permission to put expert evidence before the family court.
25.5(1)	Having regard to any failure to comply with rule 25.6 or any direction of the family court about expert evidence when deciding whether to give permission mentioned in section 13(1), (3) or (5) of the 2014 Act or to give a direction under section 38(6) of the 1989 Act.
25.6(1)	Giving directions in respect of permission mentioned in section 13(1), (3) or (5) of the 2014 Act or rule 25.4(2).
27.5	Granting applications to set aside judgments or orders following failure to attend.
27.10(1)(b)	Direction that proceedings to which the Rules apply will not be held in private, expect that a single justice may give such a direction in relation to a hearing which that single justice is conducting.

PART II – Statutory instruments

Rule	Nature of function
27.11(2)(g)	Power of the court to permit any other person to be present during any hearing, except that a single justice may give such permission in relation to a hearing which that single justice is conducting.
27.11(3)	Direction that persons within rule 27.11(2)(f) shall not attend the proceedings or any part of them.
28.3(6)	Making an order requiring one party to pay the costs of another party.
29.8(1)	Court's opinion that it would be prevented by section 8 or 9 of the Child Support Act 1991 from making an order.
29.8(2)	Court's consideration of the matter without a hearing.
29.8(10)	Power of the court to determine that it would be prevented by sections 8 or 9 of the 1991 Act from making an order, and to dismiss the application.
29.8(11)	The court must give written reasons for its decision.
29.9(2)	Direction that the document will be treated as if it contained the application and directions as the court considers appropriate as to the subsequent conduct of the proceedings.
29.12(1)	Permission for inspection of a document, except where no party to the proceedings to which that document relates objects
29.13(1)	Direction for a court officer not to serve a copy of an order (other than directions that the single justice has made) to every party affected by it.
29.15	Specifying alternative date for an order to take effect, except an order which the single justice has made.
29.16	Correcting an accidental slip or omission in an order, except where that order was made by a single justice.
29.17	Functions in relation to the transfer of proceedings to another court.
29.19(3)	Giving directions in respect of requests for reconsideration of decisions on the allocation of proceedings.
29.91(5)	Reconsidering decisions in respect of allocation of proceedings.
Part 30	Any power of the magistrates' court (where it is the lower court) to grant or refuse permission to appeal, except where a single justice has the power to make the order which is subject to the appeal.
31.9	Power for court to stay the proceedings.

Rule	Nature of function
32.22B	Powers in relation to methods of payment for means of payment orders.
32.22C(2)	Notifying interested parties of the outcome of an application for a variation of a method of payment.
32.22C(3)	Recording variations of methods of payment on the order to which the variation relates.
Part 33	The duties and powers of the family court in this Part.
Part 34	The duties and powers of the family court in this Part in so far as they relate to enforcement.
Part 37	The duties and powers of the family court in this Part.
Part 38	Recognition and Enforcement of Protection Measures
Part 39	The duties and powers of the family court in this Part.
Part 40	The duties and powers of the family court in this Part.

NOTES

Amendment.[1] Words substituted, and words and entries omitted repealed: FPR Update, March 2019.

Table 2

PD3A – Family Mediation Information and Assessment Meetings (MIAMS) – Paragraphs 7, 36 and 37	Under paragraph 7 if an applicant claims a MIAM exemption, the family court will issue proceedings but will inquire into the exemption claimed. At the first hearing the family court may review any supporting evidence in order to ensure that the MIAM exemption was validly claimed. If a MIAM exemption has not been validly claimed, the family court may direct the applicant or the parties to attend a MIAM, and may adjourn proceedings for that purpose.
	Under paragraph 36 the family court may adjourn proceedings where evidence is not available or may give directions about how and when evidence is to be filed.
	Under paragraph 37, if the family court determines that the MIAM exemption was not validly claimed, the court may direct the applicant, or the parties, to attend a MIAM and may adjourn proceedings pending MIAM attendance.
PD4B – Civil Restraint Orders	Generally, the family court's functions in respect of applications for civil restraint orders.

PART II – Statutory instruments

PD7A – Procedure for Applications in Matrimonial and Civil Partnership Proceedings – Paragraphs 3.4, 5.3 and 7.1	Under paragraph 3.4 the family court may give permission to file an application without the required documentation.
	Under paragraph 5.3 the family court may direct a period within which a party must file with the court an amended application for a matrimonial or civil partnership order or an amended answer.
	Under paragraph 7.1 the family court may made an order for the disclosure of documents under rule [7.17(2)(c)][2] where an application for a matrimonial or civil partnership order is not being dealt with as an [standard][2] case.
PD7B – Medical Examinations on Applications for Annulment of a Marriage – Paragraph 1.1	Under paragraph 1.1 where a defended application is made for the annulment of a marriage based on the incapacity of one of the parties to consummate, the family court should not appoint a medical examiner unless it appears necessary to do so for the proper disposal of the case.
PD7C – Polygamous Marriages – paragraph 2.4	Under paragraph 2.4 the family court may give an additional spouse notice of any of the proceedings to which this practice direction applies and make an additional spouse a party to such proceedings.
PD8A – Where to Start Certain Proceedings – Paragraph 1.2	Under paragraph 1.2 the family court may make a direction in respect of whether a matter will be heard in the same location of the family court as existing (or proposed) proceedings.
PD12J – Child Arrangements and Contact Order: Domestic Violence and Harm.	Generally, the family court's functions in respect of applications in respect of child arrangements orders, about where a child should live or about contact between a child and a parent or other family member except the functions in the first three bullets points in paragraph 6 and paragraphs 8, 15 and 21.
PD12M – Family Assistance Orders: Consultation – paragraphs 1.2, 1.3 and 1.5	Under paragraph 1.2 the family court must have obtained the opinion of the appropriate officer about whether it would be in the best interests of the child in question for a family assistance order to be made and, if so, how the family assistance order could operate and for what period

	Under paragraph 1.3 the family court decides on the category of officer required to be made available under the family assistance order
	Under paragraph 1.5 the family court must give to the person it proposes to name in the order an opportunity to comment
PD14B – The First Directions Hearing – adoptions with a Foreign Element – Paragraph 2	Under paragraph 2 the court's consideration of:
	(a) whether the requirements of the Adoption and Children Act 2002 and the Adoptions with a Foreign Element Regulations 2005 (S.I. 2005/392) appear to have been complied with and, if not, consider whether or not it is appropriate to transfer the case to the High Court;
	(b) whether all relevant documents are translated into English and, if not, fix a timetable for translating any outstanding documents;
	(c) whether the applicant needs to file an affidavit setting out the full details of the circumstances in which the child was brought to the United Kingdom, of the attitude of the parents to the application and confirming compliance with the requirements of The Adoptions with a Foreign Element Regulations 2005; and
	(d) give directions about:
	(i) the production of the child's passport and visa;
	(ii) the need for the Official Solicitor and a representative of the Home office to attend future hearings; and
	(iii) personal service on the parents (via the Central Authority in the case of an application for a Convention Adoption Order) including information about the role of the Official Solicitor and availability of legal aid to be represented within the proceedings; and
	(e) consider fixing a further directions no later than 6 weeks after the date of the first directions appointment and timetable a date by which the Official Solicitor should file an interim report in advance of that further appointment.

PART II – Statutory instruments

PD15A – Protected Parties – Paragraph 4.2(b)	Under paragraph 4.2(b) court directions on service on protected party.
PD16A – Representation of Children – [Paragraph 6.8][1]	Under paragraph 6.8 the children's guardian must –
	(a) unless the court otherwise directs, file a written report advising on the interests of the child in accordance with the timetable set by the court; and
	(b) in proceedings to which Part 14 applies, where practicable, notify any person the joining of whom as a party to those proceedings would be likely, in the opinion of the children's guardian, to safeguard the interests of the child, of the court's power to join that person as a party under rule 14.3 and must inform the court
	(i) of any notification;
	(ii) of anyone whom the child's guardian attempted to notify under this paragraph but was unable to contact; and
	(iii) of anyone whom the children's guardian believes may wish to be joined to the proceedings
	Under paragraph 7.5 the court may, at the same time as deciding whether to join the child as a party, consider whether the proceedings should be transferred to another court taking into account the provisions of Part 3 of the Allocation and Transfer of Proceedings Order 2008.
PD18A – Other Applications in Proceedings Paragraphs 4.1 to 4.4(a)	Under paragraph 4.1 on receipt of an application notice containing a request for a hearing, unless the court considers that the application is suitable for consideration without a hearing, the court officer will, if serving a copy of the application notice, notify the applicant of the time and date fixed for the hearing of the application.
	Under paragraph 4.2 on receipt of an application notice containing a request that the application be dealt with without a hearing, the court will decide whether the application is suitable for consideration without a hearing.

	Under paragraph 4.3 where the court considers that the application is suitable for consideration without a hearing but is not satisfied that it has sufficient material to decide the application immediately it may give directions for the filing of evidence and will inform the applicant and the respondent(s) of its decision.
	Under paragraph 4.4(a) where the court does not consider that the application is suitable for consideration without a hearing it may give directions as to the filing of evidence.
PD20A – Interim Remedies	Generally, the family court's functions in respect of applications for interim remedies.
PD22A – Written Evidence – Paragraphs 1.6, 14.1 and 14.2	Under paragraph 1.6 the court may give a direction under rule 22.12 that evidence shall be given by affidavit instead of or in addition to a witness statement on its own initiative; or after any party has applied to the court for such a direction.
	Under paragraph 14.1 where an affidavit, a witness statement or an exhibit to either an affidavit or a witness statement does not comply with Part 22 or PD22A in relation to its form, the court may refuse to admit it as evidence and may refuse to allow the costs arising from its preparation.
	Under paragraph 14.2 permission to file a defective affidavit or witness statement or to use a defective exhibit may be obtained from the court where the case is proceeding.
...[1]	...[1]
PD27A – Family Proceedings: Court Bundles (Universal Practice to be Applied in all Courts other than the Family Proceedings Court)	Generally, the family court's functions in respect of court bundles.
PD27B – Attendance of Media Representatives at Hearings in Family Proceedings	Generally the family court's discretion to exclude media representatives from attending hearings or part of hearings (other than where a Single Lay Justice is conducting the hearing).
PD37A – Applications and Proceedings in relation to contempt of court	Generally, the family court's functions in respect of applications and proceedings in relation to contempt of court.
...[1]	

| PD 40A – Charging Orders, Stop Orders and Stop Notices | Generally, the family court's functions in respect of applications and proceedings for charging orders, stop orders and stop notices. |

NOTES

Amendments.[1] Entries omitted repealed: FPR Update, March 2019. [2] Words substituted: FPR Update No 2 of 2022, 23 February 2022.

[Practice Direction 2B –
References in the Rules to Actions Done by the Court or by a Court Officer

In the past, where the Rules have provided for an action to be done by the court or by a court officer, they have often provided that the court or court officer 'will' do that action.

From and including 11th January 2015, and including amendments coming into force on that date, where an amendment is made to these Rules to insert a new provision or alter an existing one, and that amendment provides for an action to be done by the court, or by a court officer, the Rules will generally provide that the court or court officer 'must' do the action, rather than 'will'. This is to make it clearer where an obligation lies with the court or court officer to do something. Occasionally in the future, it may still be appropriate to use the word 'will', for example in a statement of future intent, and on those occasions, 'will' will be used.

This does not affect the meaning of 'will' and 'must' in the Rules before 11th January 2015.][1]

NOTES

Amendment.[1] Practice direction inserted: President's Direction, January 2015.

[Practice Direction 2C –
Justices' legal adviser

This Practice Direction supplements FPR Part 2, rule 2.5(1A).

Functions which may be carried out by a justices' legal adviser

1) The functions of the family court or a judge of the family court that may be carried out by a justices' legal adviser are the functions of the family court or of a judge of the court specified in the provisions listed in column 1 of the table subject to the exceptions or restrictions specified in column 2 in relation to particular functions.

Duty to refer if inappropriate to carry out function

2) When considering a function specified in the table—

    a)   a justices' legal adviser must consider whether in the particular circumstances it would be inappropriate to carry out the function; and

b)   if a justices' legal adviser determines that it would be inappropriate to
carry out the function, the justices' legal adviser must refer the matter to
the court.

Table

Column 1	Column 2
FPR rule 3.3	
FPR rule 3.4	
FPR rule 3.10	
FPR rule 4.1(3)(a)	Except any extensions in public law proceedings that would have the effect that disposal of the application would occur later than the end of twenty-six weeks beginning with the day on which the application was issued.
FPR rule 4.1(3)(b), (c), (d), (f), (h), (j), (k), (n), (o)	
FPR rule 4.3(2)	
FPR rule 4.3(5)	
FPR rule 4.7(a) and (b)	
FPR rule 6.14(4) and (6)	
FPR rule 6.16(1)	
FPR rule 6.19	
FPR rule 6.20	
FPR rule 6.24(2)	
FPR rule 6.26(5)	
FPR rule 6.32	
FPR rule 6.36	
...[2]	...[2]
the 1973 Act, section [1(3),][2] 1(4) and (5)	Only in [standard][2] cases, and only the making '[final][2]' of [conditional orders][2] of divorce
the 1973 Act, section 6(2)	Only where the parties consent to the adjournment
the 1973 Act, section 10A(2) and (3)	Only in an application under section 10A(2) to which the other party consents
the 1973 Act, section [17(1B)][2]	Only in [standard][2] cases
the 1973 Act, section 37(1)(a) and (d)	Only in [standard][2] cases, and only the making 'final' of such orders
the 1973 Act, section 42(3)	Only where the parties consent to the adjournment

Column 1	Column 2
the 1973 Act, section 44...[2](4)	Only in [standard][2] cases
...[2]	...[2]
FPR rule [7.8(3)(b)][2]	...[2]
FPR rule [7.8(4)][2]	...[2]
...[2]	...[2]
...[2]	...[2]
FPR rule [7.10(2)][2]	
FPR rule [7.10(3)][2]	
FPR rule [7.10(4)][2]	
...[2]	...[2]
...[2]	...[2]
FPR rule [7.23]2(1)(d)(ii) and (3)	Only where the application under section 10A(2) was made on consent
FPR rule [7.19(4)][2]	
FPR rule 8.20(4)	Only where the parties consent to the person being made a respondent and where the person is not a child
FPR rule 9.18	
FPR rule 9.20	
FPR rule 9.26	
FPR rule 9.46(2)	
FPR rule 10.3(1)	
FPR rule 10.6(2)	
FPR rule 10.7	
FPR rule 12.3(2)	Only where the parties consent to the person being made a respondent and where the person is not a child
FPR rule 12.3(3)	Only where the parties consent to the person being made a respondent and where the person is not a child
FPR rule 12.3(4)	Only where otherwise authorised to add or remove the person as a party
FPR rule 12.4(5)	Only where the parties consent to the person being made a respondent and where the person is not a child
FPR rule 12.5(1)	
the 1989 act, section 32(1)	

Column 1	Column 2
the 1989 act, section 32(4)	Except that the carrying out of such function must not have the direct or indirect effect of extending the timetable for the proceedings with the effect that the disposal of the application would occur later than the end of twenty-six weeks beginning with the day on which the application was issued
FPR rule 12.5(2)	Except at an Issues Resolution Hearing for which Practice Direction 12A makes provision, and except the carrying out of any function that has the direct or indirect effect of extending the timetable for the proceedings with the effect that the disposal of the application would occur later than the end of twenty-six weeks beginning with the day on which the application was issued
FPR rule 12.6(a)	
the 1989 act, section 7(1) and FPR rule 12.6(d)	
FPR rule 12.12	Except at an Issues Resolution Hearing for which Practice Direction 12A makes provision, and except any direction in public law proceedings that has the direct or indirect effect of extending the timetable for the proceedings with the effect that the disposal of the application would occur later than the end of twenty-six weeks beginning with the day on which the application was issued
FPR rule 12.13	Except that in any public law proceedings, the carrying out of such function must not have the direct or indirect effect of extending the timetable for the proceedings with the effect that the disposal of the application would occur later than the end of twenty-six weeks beginning with the day on which the application was issued
FPR rule 12.14(3) and (4)	
FPR rule 12.15	Except any direction in a public law proceeding that has the direct or indirect effect of extending the timetable for the proceedings with the effect that the disposal of the application would occur later than the end of twenty-six weeks beginning with the day on which the application was issued

PART II – Statutory instruments

Column 1	Column 2
FPR rule 12.16(6)	
FPR rule 12.16(7)	
FPR rule 12.19(2) and (3)	
FPR rule 12.21(1)	
FPR rule 12.22	
FPR rule 12.73(1)(b)	
Practice Direction 12G, paragraph 1.2	
Practice Direction 12J, paragraph 6, first three bullet points only	
Practice Direction 12J, paragraph 8	
Practice Direction 12J, paragraph 15	
Practice Direction 12J, paragraph 21	
FPR rule 12.24	
FPR rule 12.25(1), (2) and (5)	
FPR rule 12.26	
FPR rule 12.29	
FPR rule 12.30	
the 1989 Act, section 41	

Column 1	Column 2
the 1989 Act, sections 10(1) and (2)	Only where – (a) a previous such order has been made in the same proceedings; (b) the terms of the order sought are the same as those of the last such order made; (c) the order is an order in the course of proceedings and does not Dispose finally of the proceedings; and (d) a written request for such an order has been made and – (i) the other parties and any children's guardian consent to the request and they or their legal representatives have signed the request; or (ii) at least one of the other parties and any children's guardian consent to the request and they or their legal representatives have signed the request, and the remaining parties have not indicated that they either consent to or oppose the making of the order.
the 1989 Act, section 38(1)	Only where – (a) a previous such order has been made in the same proceedings; (b) the terms of the order sought are the same as those of the last such order made; and (c) a written request for such an order has been made and – (i) the other parties and any children's guardian consent to the request and they or their legal representatives have signed the request; or (ii) at least one of the other parties and any children's guardian consent to the request and they or their legal representatives have signed the request, and the remaining parties have not indicated that they either consent to or oppose the making of the order.
FPR rule 12.31	
FPR rule 13.3(3)	
FPR rule 13.3(4)	

PART II – Statutory instruments

Column 1	Column 2
FPR rule 13.3(5)	
FPR rule 13.5	
FPR rule 13.8	
FPR rule 13.9(1)	Except 13.9(1)(e) and (f)
FPR rule 13.9(3)	
FPR rule 13.9(6)	
FPR rule 13.9(8)	
FPR rule 13.9(9)	
FPR rule 13.11(1)	
FPR rule 13.14	
FPR rule 13.16	
FPR rule 13.17	
FPR rule 13.21(1)	
FPR rule 13.21(4)	
FPR rule 13.22(4)	
FPR rule 14.2(3)	Only where the applicant consents to the removal
FPR rule 14.3(2)	Only where the parties consent to the child being made a respondent
FPR rule 14.3(3)	Only where the parties consent to the person or body being made a respondent or to a party being removed, as the case may be, and only where the person being made a respondent or being removed as a party is not a child
FPR rule 14.3(4)	Only where such directions are consequential on directions made under FPR rule 14.3(2) or (3)
FPR rule 14.5(2)(b) and (3)	
FPR rule 14.6(1)	
FPR rule 14.6(2)(a)	
FPR rule 14.6(2)(b)	
FPR rule 14.6(3)(b)	
FPR rule 14.6(4)	
FPR rule 14.7	
the 2002 Act, section 51B(3)	
FPR rule 14.8(1)	Except 14.8(1)(d)
FPR rule 14.8(4)	

Column 1	Column 2
FPR rule 14.8(6)	
FPR rule 14.8(7)	
FPR rule 14.9(4)(b)	
FPR rule 14.10(2)	
FPR rule 14.14	
FPR rule 14.16(4) and (7)	
FPR rule 14.18	
FPR rule 14.20	
FPR rule 14.26(1)	
FPR rule 14.27(2)	
Practice Direction 14E, paragraph 1.2	
FPR rule 15.6(3)	
FPR rule 15.6(5)	
FPR rule 15.8(1)(b)	
FPR rule 15.9	
Practice Direction 15B	
FPR rule 16.3(1)	
FPR rule 16.3(2), (3) and (4)	Only in relation to specified proceedings as defined in the 1989 Act, section 41(6)
FPR rule 16.4	
FPR rule 16.11(3)	
FPR rule 16.11(5) and (6)	
FPR rule 16.21	
FPR rule 16.24	
FPR rule 16.30	
FPR rule 16.33	
FPR rule 16.34	
FPR rule 17.3(2)	
FPR rule 17.4	
FPR rule 17.5	
FPR rule 18.3(1)(c)	Only where the parties consent to the person being made a respondent and where the person being made a respondent is not a child
FPR rule 18.4(2)(b)	
FPR rule 18.5(2)(c)	

PART II – Statutory instruments

Column 1	Column 2
FPR rule 18.8(4)	
FPR rule 18.9(1)	Only where authorised by this Practice Direction to deal with the application with a hearing
Practice Direction 18A, paragraph 8.1	
Practice Direction 18A, paragraph 10.1	
Practice Direction 18A, paragraph 11.2	
FPR rule 19.1(3)	
FPR rule 19.4(4)	
FPR rule 19.6(2)	
FPR rule 19.8(1)(b)	
FPR rule 19.8(3)	
FPR rule 19.9(2)	
Practice Direction 19A, paragraphs 4.1 and 4.4	
FPR rule 21.2(3)	Only where the parties consent to the application for disclosure
Practice Direction 21A, paragraph 2.4	
FPR rule 22.1(1)	
FPR rule 22.3	
FPR rule 22.5	
FPR rule 22.7(1)	
FPR rule 22.9	
FPR rule 22.10	
Practice Direction 22A, paragraph 5.3	
FPR rule 23.4(1)	
FPR rule 23.6(8)	
the 1984 Act, section 31G(2)	
FPR rule 23.9	
FPR rule 24.3	
FPR rule 24.4(2)	
FPR rule 24.7	
FPR rule 24.8	

Column 1	Column 2
FPR rule 24.9	
FPR rule 24.10	
FPR rule 24.11(3)	
FPR rule 24.13	
the 2014 Act, section 13	
FPR rule 25.4	
FPR rule 25.8	
FPR rule 25.9	
FPR rule 25.10(2)	
FPR rule 25.10(3)	
FPR rule 25.10(4)	
FPR rule 25.11	
FPR rule 25.12	
FPR rule 25.13	
FPR rule 25.16	
FPR rule 25.17	
FPR rule 25.18	
FPR rule 25.19	
Practice Direction 25A, paragraph 2.1	
Practice Direction 25B, paragraphs 10.1 and 10.2	
Practice Direction 25E, paragraph 4.1	
FPR rule 26.3	
FPR rule 26.4	
FPR rule 27.3	
FPR rule 27.4	
FPR rule 27.7	
FPR rule 29.1	
FPR rule 29.4	
FPR rule 29.11	
FPR rule 29.14	
FPR rule 29.15	Only where the order in question is one which the justices' legal adviser made
FPR rule 29.16	Only where the order in question is one which a justices' legal adviser made

PART II – Statutory instruments

Column 1	Column 2
FPR rule 29.19(5)	
FPR rule 37.9(3)	
The Family Court (Composition and Distribution of Business) Rules 2014, rule 20][1]	

NOTES

Amendment.[1] Practice Direction inserted: Practice Direction, April 2020. [2] Words substituted, entries and words omitted repealed, and words inserted: FPR Update No 2 of 2022, 23 February 2022.

[PART 3
NON-COURT DISPUTE RESOLUTION

Chapter 1
Interpretation

3.1

In this Part –

'allocation' means allocation of proceedings other than appeal proceedings to a level of judge;

['authorised family mediator' means a person identified by the Family Mediation Council as qualified to conduct a MIAM;][2]

'domestic violence' means any incident, or pattern of incidents, of controlling, coercive or threatening behaviour, violence or abuse (whether psychological, physical, sexual, financial or emotional) between the prospective applicant and another prospective party;

'family mediation information and assessment meeting' has the meaning given to it in section 10(3) of the 2014 Act.

'harm' has the meaning given to it in section 31 of the Children Act 1989;

'mediator's exemption' has the meaning given to it in Rule 3.8(2);

'MIAM' means a family mediation information and assessment meeting;

'MIAM exemption' has the meaning given to it in Rule 3.8(1);

'MIAM requirement' is the requirement in section 10(1) of the 2014 Act for a person to attend a MIAM before making a relevant family application;

'private law proceedings' has the meaning given to it in Rule 12.2;

'prospective applicant' is the person who is considering making a relevant family application;

'prospective party' is a person who would be likely to be a party to the proceedings in the relevant family application;

'prospective respondent' is a person who would be a likely respondent to the proceedings in the relevant family application; and

'relevant family application' has the meaning given to it in section 10(3) of the 2014 Act.][1]

NOTES

Amendments.[1] Part 3 substituted: SI 2014/843 (as amended). [2] Definition substituted: SI 2015/1868.

[Chapter 2
The Court's Duty and Powers Generally

3.2 Scope of this Chapter

This Chapter contains the court's duty and powers to encourage and facilitate the use of non-court dispute resolution.

3.3 The court's duty to consider non-court dispute resolution

(1) The court must consider, at every stage in proceedings, whether non-court dispute resolution is appropriate.

(2) In considering whether non-court dispute resolution is appropriate in proceedings which were commenced by a relevant family application, the court must take into account –

  (a)   whether a MIAM took place;
  (b)   whether a valid MIAM exemption was claimed or mediator's exemption was confirmed; and
  (c)   whether the parties attempted mediation or another form of non-court dispute resolution and the outcome of that process.

3.4 When the court will adjourn proceedings or a hearing in proceedings

(1) If the court considers that non-court dispute resolution is appropriate, it may direct that the proceedings, or a hearing in the proceedings, be adjourned for such specified period as it considers appropriate –

  (a)   to enable the parties to obtain information and advice about[, and consider using]² non-court dispute resolution; and
  (b)   where the parties agree, to enable non-court dispute resolution to take place.

(2) The court may give directions under this rule on an application or of its own initiative.

(3) Where the court directs an adjournment under this rule, it will give directions about the timing and method by which the parties must tell the court if any of the issues in the proceedings have been resolved.

(4) If the parties do not tell the court if any of the issues have been resolved as directed under paragraph (3), the court will give such directions as to the management of the case as it considers appropriate.

(5) The court or court officer will –

  (a)   record the making of an order under this rule; and
  (b)   arrange for a copy of the order to be served as soon as practicable on the parties.

(6) Where the court proposes to exercise its powers of its own initiative, the procedure set out in rule 4.3(2) to (6) applies.]¹

PART II – Statutory instruments

NOTES

Amendments.[1] Part 3 substituted: SI 2014/843 (as amended). [2] Words inserted: SI 2014/3296.

[Chapter 3
Family Mediation Information and Assessment Meetings (MIAMs)

3.5 Scope of this Chapter

This Chapter contains Rules about the requirement in section 10(1) of the 2014 Act to attend a MIAM.

3.6 Applications to which the MIAM requirement applies

(1) The MIAM requirement applies to any application to initiate the proceedings specified in paragraph (2), unless a MIAM exemption or a mediator's exemption applies.

(2) The specified proceedings are –

   (a)   the private law proceedings relating to children specified in Practice Direction 3A; and

   (b)   the proceedings for a financial remedy specified in Practice Direction 3A.

3.7 Making an application

An application to initiate any of the proceedings specified in Rule 3.6 must contain, or be accompanied by, a form containing, either –

   (a)   a confirmation from an authorised family mediator that the prospective applicant has attended a MIAM;

   (b)   a claim by the prospective applicant that one of the MIAM exemptions applies; or

(A list of MIAM exemptions is set out in Rule 3.8(1) below.)

   (c)   a confirmation from an authorised family mediator that a mediator's exemption applies.

(A list of mediator's exemptions is set out in Rule 3.8(2) below.)

3.8 Circumstances in which the MIAM requirement does not apply (MIAM exemptions and mediator's exemptions)

The MIAM requirement does not apply if –

(1) a prospective applicant claims in the relevant form that any of the following circumstances (a 'MIAM exemption') applies –

Domestic violence

   (a)   there is evidence of domestic violence, as specified in Practice Direction 3A; or

Child protection concerns

   (b)

      (i)   – a child would be the subject of the application; and

      (ii)   that child or another child of the family who is living with that child is currently –

          (aa) the subject of enquiries by a local authority under section 47 of the 1989 Act; or

          (ab) the subject of a child protection plan put in place by a local authority; or

Urgency

   (c)   the application must be made urgently because –

      (i)   there is risk to the life, liberty or physical safety of the prospective applicant or his or her family or his or her home; or

      (ii)   any delay caused by attending a MIAM would cause –

          (aa) a risk of harm to a child;

          (ab) a risk of unlawful removal of a child from the United Kingdom, or a risk of unlawful retention of a child who is currently outside England and Wales;

          (ac) a significant risk of a miscarriage of justice;

          (ad) unreasonable hardship to the prospective applicant; or

          (ae) irretrievable problems in dealing with the dispute (including the irretrievable loss of significant evidence); or

      (iii) there is a significant risk that in the period necessary to schedule and attend a MIAM, proceedings relating to the dispute will be brought in another state in which a valid claim to jurisdiction may exist, such that a court in that other State would be seised of the dispute before a court in England and Wales; or

Previous MIAM attendance or MIAM exemption

   (d) –

      (i)   in the 4 months prior to making the application, the person attended a MIAM or participated in another form of non-court dispute resolution relating to the same or substantially the same dispute; or

      (ii)   at the time of making the application, the person is participating in another form of non-court dispute resolution relating to the same or substantially the same dispute; or

   (e) –

      (i)   in the 4 months prior to making the application, the person filed a relevant family application confirming that a MIAM exemption applied; and

      (ii)   that application related to the same or substantially the same dispute; or

   (f) –

      (i)   the application would be made in existing proceedings which are continuing; and

PART II – Statutory instruments

(ii)   the prospective applicant attended a MIAM before initiating those proceedings; or

(g) –

(i)   the application would be made in existing proceedings which are continuing; and

(ii)   a MIAM exemption applied to the application for those proceedings; or

Other

(h) –

(i)   there is evidence that the prospective applicant is bankrupt, as specified in Practice Direction 3A; and

(ii)   the proceedings would be for a financial remedy; or

(i)   the prospective applicant does not have sufficient contact details for any of the prospective respondents to enable a family mediator to contact any of the prospective respondents for the purpose of scheduling the MIAM; or

(j)   the application would be made without notice; or

(Paragraph 5.1 of Practice Direction 18A sets out the circumstances in which applications may be made without notice.)

(k) –

(i)   the prospective applicant is or all of the prospective respondents are subject to a disability or other inability that would prevent attendance at a MIAM unless appropriate facilities can be offered by an authorised mediator;

(i)   the prospective applicant has contacted as many authorised family mediators as have an office within fifteen miles of his or home (or three of them if there are three or more), and all have stated that they are unable to provide such facilities; and

(iii)   the names, postal addresses and telephone numbers or e-mail addresses for such authorised family mediators, and the dates of contact, can be provided to the court if requested; or

(l)   the prospective applicant or all of the prospective respondents cannot attend a MIAM because he or she is, or they are, as the case may be –

(i)   in prison or any other institution in which he or she is or they are required to be detained;

(ii)   subject to conditions of bail that prevent contact with the other person; or

(iii)   subject to a licence with a prohibited contact requirement in relation to the other person; or

(m)   the prospective applicant or all of the prospective respondents are not habitually resident in England and Wales; or

(n)   a child is one of the prospective parties by virtue of Rule 12.3(1); or

(o) –

(i)   the prospective applicant has contacted as many authorised family mediators as have an office within fifteen miles of his or her home (or three of them if there are three or more), and all of them have stated that they are not available to conduct a MIAM within fifteen business days of the date of contact; and

        (ii)   the names, postal addresses and telephone numbers or e-mail addresses for such authorised family mediators, and the dates of contact, can be provided to the court if requested; or

   (p)   there is no authorised family mediator with an office within fifteen miles of the prospective applicant's home; or

(2) an authorised family mediator confirms in the relevant form (a 'mediator's exemption') that he or she is satisfied that –

   (a)   mediation is not suitable as a means of resolving the dispute because none of the respondents is willing to attend a MIAM; or

   (b)   mediation is not suitable as a means of resolving the dispute because all of the respondents failed without good reason to attend a MIAM appointment; or

   (c)   mediation is otherwise not suitable as a means of resolving the dispute.

3.9 Conduct of MIAMs

(1) Only an authorised family mediator may conduct a MIAM.

(2) At the MIAM, the authorised family mediator must –

   (a)   provide information about the principles, process and different models of mediation, and information about other methods of non-court dispute resolution;

   (b)   assess the suitability of mediation as a means of resolving the dispute;

   (c)   assess whether there has been, or is a risk of, domestic violence; and

   (d)   assess whether there has been, or is a risk of, harm by a prospective party to a child that would be a subject of the application.

3.10 MIAM exemption not validly claimed

(1) If a MIAM exemption has been claimed, the court will, if appropriate when making a decision on allocation, and in any event at the first hearing, inquire into whether the exemption was validly claimed.

(2) If a court finds that the MIAM exemption was not validly claimed, the court will –

   (a)   direct the applicant, or direct the parties to attend a MIAM; and

   (b)   if necessary, adjourn the proceedings to enable a MIAM to take place;

unless the court considers that in all the circumstances of the case, the MIAM requirement should not apply to the application in question.

(3) In making a decision under Rule 3.10(2), the court will have particular regard to –

   (a)   any applicable time limits;

   (b)   the reason or reasons why the MIAM exemption was not validly claimed;

   (c)   the applicability of any other MIAM exemptions; and

   (d)   the number and nature of issues that remain to be resolved in the proceedings.][1]

NOTES

Amendment.[1] Part 3 substituted: SI 2014/843 (as amended).

Practice Direction 3A –
Family Mediation Information and Assessment
Meetings (MIAMS)

This Practice Direction supplements FPR Part 3

Summary

1 The purpose of this Practice Direction is to supplement the MIAM Rules in the Family Procedure Rules and to set out good practice to be followed by prospective respondents who are expected to also attend a MIAM.

2 Under section 10(1) of the Children and Families Act 2014, it is now a requirement for a person to attend a MIAM before making certain kinds of applications to obtain a court order. (A list of these applications is set out in Rule 3.6 and in paragraphs 12 and 13 below.) The person who would be the respondent to the application is expected to attend the MIAM. The court has a general power to adjourn proceedings in order for non-court dispute resolution to be attempted, including attendance at a MIAM to consider family mediation and other options.

3 A MIAM is a short meeting that provides information about mediation as a way of resolving disputes. A MIAM is conducted by a trained mediator who will assess whether mediation is appropriate in the circumstances. A MIAM should be held within 15 business days of contacting the mediator.

4 There are exemptions to the MIAM requirement. These are set out in the MIAM Rules (see Chapter 3 to Part 3 of the Family Procedure Rules), and are explained in more detail in this Practice Direction.

5 The effect of the MIAM requirement and accompanying Rules is that a person who wishes to make certain kinds of applications to the court must first attend a MIAM unless a 'MIAM exemption' or a 'mediator's exemption' applies. These exemptions are set out in Rule 3.8.

6 When making certain kinds of applications (see paragraphs 12 and 13 below), an applicant must therefore provide on the application form, or on a separate form, one of the following: (i) confirmation from a mediator that she or he has attended a MIAM; (ii) confirmation from a mediator that a 'mediator's exemption' applies; or (iii) a claim that a MIAM exemption applies. An applicant who claims an exemption from the MIAM requirement is not required to attach any supporting evidence with their application, but should bring any supporting evidence to the first hearing.

7 If an applicant claims a MIAM exemption, the court will issue proceedings but will inquire into the exemption claimed, either at the stage at which the case is allocated or at the first hearing. At the first hearing, the court may review any

supporting evidence in order to ensure that the MIAM exemption was validly claimed. As set out in more detail below, if a MIAM exemption has not been validly claimed, the court may direct the applicant or the parties to attend a MIAM, and may adjourn proceedings for that purpose.

Background: Consideration of mediation and other non-court dispute resolution

8 The adversarial court process is not always best suited to the resolution of family disputes. Such disputes are often best resolved through discussion and agreement, where that can be managed safely and appropriately.

9 Family mediation is one way of settling disagreements. A trained mediator can help the parties to reach an agreement. A mediator who conducts a MIAM is a qualified independent facilitator who can also discuss other forms of dispute resolution if mediation is not appropriate.

10 Attendance at a MIAM provides an opportunity for the parties to a dispute to receive information about the process of mediation and to understand the benefits it can offer as a way to resolve disputes. At that meeting, a trained mediator will discuss with the parties the nature of their dispute and will explore with them whether mediation would be a suitable way to resolve the issues on which there is disagreement.

The applications to which the MIAM requirement applies

11 In accordance with section 10 of the 2014 Act, and Rule 3.6, the proceedings to which the MIAM requirement applies are the private law proceedings relating to children listed in paragraph 12 and the proceedings for a financial remedy listed in paragraph 13 below.

Private law proceedings relating to children

12

(1) The private law proceedings relating to children referred to in paragraph 11 are proceedings for the following orders, unless one of the circumstances specified in sub-paragraph (2) applies –

(a) a child arrangements order and other orders with respect to a child or children under section 8 of the Children Act 1989;

(b) a parental responsibility order (under sections 4(1)(c), 4ZA(1)(c) or 4A(1)(b) of the Children Act 1989) or an order terminating parental responsibility (under sections 4(2A), 4ZA(5) or 4A(3) of that Act);

(c) an order appointing a child's guardian (under section 5(1) of the Children Act 1989) or an order terminating the appointment (under section 6(7) of that Act);

(d) an order giving permission to change a child's surname or remove a child from the United Kingdom (under sections 13(1) or 14C of the Children Act 1989);

(e)   a special guardianship order; and

(f)   an order varying or discharging such an order (under section 14D of the Children Act 1989).

(2) The circumstances referred to in sub-paragraph (1) are that the proceedings –

(a)   are for a consent order;

(b)   are for an order relating to a child or children in respect of whom there are ongoing emergency proceedings, care proceedings or supervision proceedings; or

(c)   are for an order relating to a child or children who are the subject of an emergency protection order, a care order or a supervision order.

Proceedings for a financial remedy

13

(1) The proceedings for a financial remedy referred to in paragraph 11 are proceedings for the following orders, unless one of the circumstances specified in sub-paragraph (2) applies –

(a)   the following financial orders:

(i)   an order for maintenance pending suit;

(ii)   an order for maintenance pending outcome of proceedings;

(iii) an order for periodical payments or lump sum provision as mentioned in section 21(1) of the Matrimonial Causes Act 1973, except an order under section 27(6) of that Act;

(iv)   an order for periodical payments or lump sum provision as mentioned in paragraph 2(1) of Schedule 5 to the Civil Partnership Act 2004, made under Part 1 of Schedule 5 to that Act;

(v)   a property adjustment order;

(vi)   a variation order;

(vii) a pension sharing order; or

(viii) a pension compensation sharing order;

(b)   an order for financial provision for children (under Schedule 1 to the Children Act 1989);

(c)   an order for financial provision in a case of neglect to maintain (under section 27 of the Matrimonial Causes Act 1973 or under Part 9 of Schedule 5 to the Civil Partnership Act 2004);

(d)   an order for alteration of a maintenance agreement (under section 35 of the Matrimonial Causes Act 1973 or under paragraph 69 of Schedule 5 to the 2004 Act);

(e)   an order for financial provision for failure to maintain for parties to a marriage and children of the family (under Part 1 of the Domestic Proceedings and Magistrates' Courts Act 1978 or an order under Schedule 6 to the Civil Partnership Act 2004); and

(f)   an order for special protection for respondent in certain separation cases (under section 10(2) of the Matrimonial Causes Act 1973 or under section 48(2) of the Civil Partnership Act 2004).

(2) The circumstances referred to in sub-paragraph (1) are that the proceedings –

(a)   are for a consent order; or

(b)   are for enforcement of any order made in proceedings for a financial remedy or of any agreement made in or in contemplation of proceedings for a financial remedy.

Making an application

14 An application to the court in any of the proceedings specified above must be on the relevant court form which must contain either: (a) a confirmation from a mediator that the applicant has attended a MIAM; (b) a claim by the applicant that a MIAM exemption applies (the list of MIAM exemptions is set out in Rule 3.8(1)); or (c) a confirmation from a mediator that a mediator's exemption applies (the list of circumstances that qualify for a mediator's exemption is in Rule 3.8(2)).

15 Relevant application forms are available from the HMCTS form finder service at www.justice.gov.uk/forms/hmcts. For matters concerning children you can find out which form to use by reading the leaflet CB1 – Making an application – Children and the Family Courts'. Leaflet CB7 – Guide for separated parents: children and the family courts also provides guidance on the court process.

16 The relevant form can be completed either by the applicant or his or her legal representative. Any reference in this Practice Direction or in the Rules to completion of the form by an applicant includes a reference to completion by a legal representative.

MIAM exemptions

17 FPR Rule 3.8(1) sets out the circumstances in which the MIAM requirement does not apply. These are called MIAM exemptions.

18 In order to claim that a MIAM exemption applies, an applicant will need to tick the appropriate MIAM exemption boxes on the relevant form.

19 Applicants should note that some of the MIAM exemptions require that certain evidence is available. The next section of the Practice Direction specifies those forms of evidence. This evidence does not need to be provided with the application but applicants should bring such evidence to the first hearing because the court will inquire into such evidence in order to determine whether the MIAM exemption has been validly claimed.

MIAM exemption – Domestic violence

20

(1) The forms of evidence referred to in Rule 3.8(1)(a) are –

[(a)   evidence that a prospective party has been arrested for a relevant domestic violence offence;

(b)   evidence of a relevant police caution for a domestic violence offence

(c)   evidence of relevant criminal proceedings for a domestic violence offence which have not concluded;

(d)   evidence of a relevant conviction for a domestic violence offence;

(e)   a court order binding a prospective party over in connection with a domestic violence offence;

(f)   a domestic violence protection notice issued under section 24 of the Crime and Security Act 2010 against a prospective party;

(g)   a relevant protective injunction;

(h)   an undertaking given in England and Wales under section 46 or 63E of the Family Law Act 1996 (or given in Scotland or Northern Ireland in place of a protective injunction) by a prospective party, provided that a cross-undertaking relating to domestic violence was not given by another prospective party;

(i)   a copy of a finding of fact, made in proceedings in the United Kingdom, that there has been domestic violence by a prospective party;

(j)   an expert report produced as evidence in proceedings in the United Kingdom for the benefit of a court or tribunal confirming that a person with whom a prospective party is or was in a family relationship, was assessed as being, or at risk of being, a victim of domestic violence by that prospective party;

(k)   a letter or report from an appropriate health professional confirming that –

    (i)   that professional, or another appropriate health professional, has examined a prospective party in person; and

    (ii)   in the reasonable professional judgment of the author or the examining appropriate health professional, that prospective party has, or has had, injuries or a condition consistent with being a victim of domestic violence;

(l)   a letter or report from–

    (i)   the appropriate health professional who made the referral described below;

    (ii)   an appropriate health professional who has access to the medical records of the prospective party referred to below; or

    (iii) the person to whom the referral described below was made; confirming that there was a referral by an appropriate health professional of a prospective party to a person who provides specialist support or assistance for victims of, or those at risk of, domestic violence;

(m)   a letter from any person who is a member of a multi-agency risk assessment conference (or other suitable local safeguarding forum) confirming that a prospective party, or a person with whom that prospective party is in a family relationship, is or has been at risk of harm from domestic violence by another prospective party;

(n)   a letter from an independent domestic violence advisor confirming that they are providing support to a prospective party;

(o)   a letter from an independent sexual violence advisor confirming that they are providing support to a prospective party relating to sexual violence by another prospective party;

(p)   a letter from an officer employed by a local authority or housing association (or their equivalent in Scotland or Northern Ireland) for the purpose of supporting tenants containing

      (i)   a statement to the effect that, in their reasonable professional judgment, a person with whom a prospective party is or has been in a family relationship is, or is at risk of being, a victim of domestic violence by that prospective party;

      (ii) a description of the specific matters relied upon to support that judgment; and

      (iii) a description of the support they provided to the victim of domestic violence or the person at risk of domestic violence by that prospective party;

(q) a letter which –

      (i)   is from an organisation providing domestic violence support services, or a registered charity, which letter confirms that it –

          (aa) is situated in England and Wales,

          (bb) has been operating for an uninterrupted period of six months or more; and

          (cc) provided a prospective party with support in relation to that person's needs as a victim, or a person at risk, of domestic violence; and

      (ii) contains –

          (aa) a statement to the effect that, in the reasonable professional judgment of the author of the letter, the prospective party is, or is at risk of being, a victim of domestic violence;

          (bb) a description of the specific matters relied upon to support that judgment;

          (cc) a description of the support provided to the prospective party; and

          (dd) a statement of the reasons why the prospective party needed that support;

(r) a letter or report from an organisation providing domestic violence support services in the United Kingdom confirming –

      (i)   that a person with whom a prospective party is or was in a family relationship was refused admission to a refuge;

      (ii) the date on which they were refused admission to the refuge; and

      (iii) they sought admission to the refuge because of allegations of domestic violence by the prospective party referred to in paragraph (i);

(s) a letter from a public authority confirming that a person with whom a prospective party is or was in a family relationship, was assessed as being, or at risk of being, a victim of domestic violence by that prospective party (or a copy of that assessment);

(t) a letter from the Secretary of State for the Home Department confirming that a prospective party has been granted leave to remain in the United Kingdom under paragraph 289B of the Rules made by the Home Secretary under section 3(2) of the Immigration Act 1971, which can be found at https://www.gov.uk/guidance/immigration-rules/immigration-rules-index;

(u) evidence which demonstrates that a prospective party has been, or is at risk of being, the victim of domestic violence by another prospective party in the form of abuse which relates to financial matters.][5]

PART II – Statutory instruments

MIAM exemption – Bankruptcy

21 The forms of evidence referred to in Rule 3.8(1)(h) are –

(a)   [application][4] by the prospective applicant for a bankruptcy order;

(b)   petition by a creditor of the prospective applicant for a bankruptcy order; or

(c)   a bankruptcy order in respect of the prospective applicant.

Finding an authorised family mediator

22 As set out in Rule 3.9, a MIAM must be conducted by an authorised family mediator. [Under that rule, an authorised family mediator is a person identified by the Family Mediation Council as qualified to conduct a MIAM.][3]

23 A list of authorised family mediators, including their location, can be found using the 'Find your local mediator' search engine at: www.familymediationcouncil.org.uk

24 The expectation is that a prospective applicant should be able to find an authorised family mediator within 15 miles of his or her home. As stated in Rule 3.8(1)(o) a MIAM exemption is available if:

(i)   the prospective applicant has contacted as many authorised family mediators as have an office within fifteen miles of his or her home (or three of them if there are three or more), and all of them have stated that they are not available to conduct a MIAM within fifteen business days of the date of contact; and

(ii)   the names, postal addresses and telephone numbers or e-mail addresses for such authorised family mediators, and the dates of contact, can be provided to the court if requested.

25 Rule 3.8(1)(p) also provides an exemption if there is no authorised family mediator with an office within fifteen miles of the prospective applicant's home.

26 To determine whether a mediator is within the distance of 15 miles from their home, applicants can use the 'Find your local mediator' search engine to type in their own post code and then use the distance option to display only family mediators within a 15 mile distance.

27 The applicant will need to be prepared to produce at the first hearing the names, contact information and details of the dates of contact with the authorised family mediators.

28 Information about the Family Mediation Council, including its code of conduct can also be found at www.familymediationcouncil.org.uk

Funding attendance at a MIAM

29 The cost of attending a MIAM will depend on whether the prospective parties attend separately or together and whether at least one of the prospective parties is eligible for Legal Aid. If at least one party is eligible for Legal Aid then the

total cost of MIAM attendance can be met by the Legal Aid Agency, whether the parties attend the same MIAM or separate MIAMs.

30 If neither party is eligible for Legal Aid then the mediator will agree with the prospective parties how the cost of MIAM attendance is to be met.

31 Parties can find out whether they are eligible for Legal Aid by using the calculator tool available at www.gov.uk/legal-aid.

Attending a MIAM

32 Prospective respondents are expected to attend a MIAM, either with the prospective applicant or separately. A respondent may choose to attend a MIAM separately but this should usually be with the same authorised family mediator.

33 The prospective applicant should provide contact details for the prospective respondent to an authorised family mediator for the purpose of the mediator contacting them to discuss their willingness to attend a MIAM and, if appropriate, to schedule their attendance at a MIAM.

34 If the mediator contacts the prospective respondent and determines that he or she is unwilling to attend a MIAM, a prospective applicant should ask the mediator to confirm this as a ground for MIAM exemption in the relevant section of the application form, which should then be returned signed to the applicant.

MIAM exemption: Inquiries by the court

35 Where a MIAM exemption requires that certain evidence is available, the evidence does not need to be provided with the application form. Applicants should instead bring [any][4] such evidence to the first hearing because the court will inquire into such evidence in order to determine whether the MIAM exemption was validly claimed.

36 The court may if appropriate adjourn proceedings where such evidence is not available or may give directions about how and when such evidence is to be filed with the court.

37 If the court determines that the MIAM exemption was not validly claimed, the court may direct the applicant, or the parties, to attend a MIAM and may adjourn proceedings pending MIAM attendance.

Definitions

38 For the purpose of this Practice Direction –

['accommodated' [in paragraph 20(1)(k)(i)] does not require a stay of a minimum time period;][2]
'care order' has the meaning given to it in Rule 2.3 of the FPR;
'care proceedings' has the meaning given to it in Rule 12.2 of the FPR;
'consent order' has the meaning given to it in Rule 2.3 of the FPR;
'emergency proceedings' has the meaning given to it in Rule 12.2 of the FPR;
'emergency protection order' has the meaning given to it in Rule 12.2 of the FPR;

PART II – Statutory instruments

'FPR' means the Family Procedure Rules 2010;

'financial order' has the meaning given to it in Rule 2.3 of the FPR;

'financial remedy' has the meaning given to it in Rule 2.3 of the FPR;

'health professional' means a registered –

(a)   medical practitioner who holds a licence to practise;

(b)   nurse;

(c)   midwife; or

(d)   practitioner psychologist who holds a licence to practise;

'mediator's exemption' has the meaning given to it in Rule 3.1 of the FPR;

'MIAM' means a family mediation information and assessment meeting;

'MIAM exemption' has the meaning given to it in Rule 3.1 of the FPR;

'MIAM requirement' has the meaning given to it in Rule 3.1 of the FPR;

'non-court dispute resolution' has the meaning given to it in Rule 2.3 of the FPR;

'pension compensation sharing order' has the meaning given in Rule 9.3 of the FPR;

'pension sharing order' has the meaning given in Rule 9.3 of the FPR;

'private law proceedings' has the meaning given to it in Rule 12.2 of the FPR;

'prospective applicant' has the meaning given to it in Rule 3.1 of the FPR;

'prospective party' has the meaning given to it in Rule 3.1 of the FPR;

'prospective respondent' has the meaning given to it in Rule 3.1 of the FPR;

'protective injunction' means –

(a)   a non-molestation order under section 42 of the 1996 Act or article 20 of the Family Homes and Domestic Violence (Northern Ireland) Order 1998;

(b)   an occupation order under section 33, 35, 36, 37 or 38 of the 1996 Act or article 11, 13, 14, 15 or 16 of the Family Homes and Domestic Violence (Northern Ireland) Order 1998;

(c)   an exclusion order under section 4 of the Matrimonial Homes (Family Protection) (Scotland) Act 1981 or section 104 of the 2004 Act;

(d)   a forced marriage protection order or interim forced marriage protection order under any of the following provisions –

(i)   Part 4A of the 1996 Act;

(ii)   section 2 of, and paragraph 1 of Schedule 1 to, the Forced Marriage (Civil Protection) Act 2007;

(iii) section 1 of the Forced Marriage etc. (Protection & Jurisdiction) (Scotland) Act 2011; and

(iv)   section 5 of the Forced Marriage etc. (Protection & Jurisdiction) (Scotland) Act 2011;

[(da) an injunction under section 3A of the Protection From Harassment Act 1997;][2]

(e)   a restraining order under section 5 or 5A of the Protection from Harassment Act 1997;

(f)   a restraining injunction under article 5 or a restraining order under article 7 or 7A of the Protection from Harassment (Northern Ireland) Order 1997;

(g)   a non-harassment order under section 234A of the Criminal Procedure (Scotland) Act 1995 or section 8 or 8A of the Protection from Harassment Act 1997;

(h)   a common law injunction;
(i)   any of the following interdicts –
  (i)   a matrimonial interdict within the meaning of section 14 of the Matrimonial Homes (Family Protection) (Scotland) Act 1981;
  (ii) a domestic interdict within the meaning of section 18A of the Matrimonial Homes (Family Protection) (Scotland) Act 1981;
  (iii) an interdict for civil partners within the meaning of section 113 of the Civil Partnership Act 2004;
  (iv) an interdict that has been determined to be a domestic abuse interdict within the meaning of section 3 of the Domestic Abuse (Scotland) Act 2001; and
  (v)   a common law interdict;

['refuge' means a refuge established for the purpose of providing accommodation for victims of, or those at risk of, domestic violence;][2]
'relevant' in paragraph 20 of this Practice Direction means that the evidence –
  (a) identifies a prospective party as being, or at risk of being, the victim of domestic violence unless the evidence –
    (i) is in a form described in paragraph 20 (1)(a) to (c), (f), (n) or (o); and
    (ii) relates to a domestic violence offence which does not identify the victim; and
  (b) identifies another party as being –
    (i)   for evidence described in paragraph 20(1)(a) to (c) and (f), convicted of, cautioned with, on police bail for, or charged with the domestic violence offence; and
    (ii) for evidence described in paragraph 20(1)(d), the respondent to the protective injunction;
    (iii) for evidence described in paragraph 20(1)(n), the person against whom the notice or order has been issued or made; and
    (iv) for evidence described in paragraph 20(1)(o), the person against whom the order binding over has been made.

'supervision order' has the meaning given to it in Rule 12.2 of the FPR;
'supervision proceedings' has the meaning given to it in Rule 12.2 of the FPR; and
'variation order' has the meaning given to it in Rule 9.3 of the FPR.][1]

NOTES

Amendment.[1] PD3A substituted: FPR Update, April 2014. [2] Paragraph, subparagraph and definitions inserted, subparagraph substituted, words substituted and omitted: FPR Update, July 2015. [3] Words substituted: FPR Update, November 2015. [4] Words substituted and inserted and paragraphs inserted: FPR Update October 2016. [5] Paragraph inserted, sub-paragraphs substituted, definitions omitted and inserted: FPR Update January 2018.

[PART 3A
VULNERABLE PERSONS: PARTICIPATION IN PROCEEDINGS AND GIVING EVIDENCE

3A.1 Interpretation

In this Part –

'child' means a person under the age of 18 years whether or not the child is the subject of the proceedings, except that –

    (a)   in adoption proceedings, it also includes a person who is the subject of proceedings and has attained the age of 18 years before the proceedings are concluded; and

    (b)   in proceedings brought under …[2] the 1980 Hague Convention or the European Convention, it means a person under the age of 16 years who is the subject of proceedings;

['domestic abuse' has the meaning given in section 1 of the Domestic Abuse Act 2021;][3]

'intermediary' means a person whose function is to –

    (a)   communicate questions put to a witness or party;

    (b)   communicate to any person asking such questions the answers given by the witness or party in reply to them; and

    (c)   explain such questions or answers so far as is necessary to enable them to be understood by the witness or party or by the person asking such questions;

'live link' means a live television link or other arrangement whereby a witness or party, while absent from the courtroom or other place where the proceedings are being held, is able to see and hear a person there and to be seen and heard by the judge, legal representatives acting in the proceedings and other persons appointed to assist a witness or party;

'mental disorder' has the meaning given in section 1 of the Mental Health Act 1983;

'participation direction' means –

    (a)   a general case management direction made for the purpose of assisting a witness or party to give evidence or participate in proceedings; or

    (b)   a direction that a witness or party should have the assistance of one or more of the measures in rule 3A.8; and

['relative' has the meaning given by section 63(1) of the 1996 Act;

'victim' includes a child to whom section 3(2) of the Domestic Abuse Act 2021 applies; and][3]

references to 'quality of evidence' are to its quality in terms of completeness, coherence and accuracy; and for this purpose 'coherence' refers to a witness's or a party's ability in giving evidence to give answers which address the questions put to the witness or the party and which can be understood both individually and collectively.][1]

NOTES

Amendments.[1] Part 3A inserted: SI 2017/1033. [2] Words omitted repealed: SI 2019/517. [3] Definitions inserted: SI 2021/875.

[3A.2 Application of provisions in this Part

(1) Rule 3A.4 does not apply to a party who is a child.

(2) Rules 3A.3 to 3A.5 do not apply to a party who is a protected party.

[(3) Rules 3A.3 to 3A.5 do not apply to a party or witness who—

    (a)   falls within the assumption set out at rule 3A.2A(1); and
    (b)   has not made a request of a kind referred to in rule 3A.2A(2).][2]][1]

NOTES

Amendments.[1] Part 3A inserted: SI 2017/1033.[2] Paragraph inserted: SI 2021/875.

[3A.2A Court's duty to consider making participation directions: victims of domestic abuse

(1) Subject to paragraph (2), where it is stated that a party or witness is, or is at risk of being, a victim of domestic abuse carried out by a party, a relative of another party, or a witness in the proceedings, the court must assume that the following matters are diminished—

    (a)   the quality of the party's or witness's evidence;
    (b)   in relation to a party, their participation in the proceedings.

(2) The party or witness concerned can request that the assumption set out in paragraph (1) does not apply to them if they do not wish it to.

(3) Where the assumption set out in paragraph (1) applies, the court must consider whether it is necessary to make one or more participation directions.][1]

NOTES

Amendments.[1] Rule inserted: SI 2021/875.

[3A.3 Court's duty to consider vulnerability of [other parties or witnesses][2]

(1) When considering the vulnerability of a party or witness as mentioned in rule 3A.4 or 3A.5, the court must have regard in particular to the matters set out in paragraphs (a) to (j) and (m) of rule 3A.7.

(2) Practice Direction 3AA gives guidance about vulnerability.][1]

NOTES

Amendments.[1] Part 3A inserted: SI 2017/1033.[2] Words substituted: SI 2021/875.

[3A.4 Court's duty to consider how a party can participate in the proceedings

(1) The court must consider whether a party's participation in the proceedings (other than by way of giving evidence) is likely to be diminished by reason of vulnerability and, if so, whether it is necessary to make one or more participation directions.

(2) Before making such participation directions, the court must consider any views expressed by the party about participating in the proceedings.][1]

NOTES

Amendments.[1] Part 3A inserted: SI 2017/1033.

[3A.5 Court's duty to consider how a party or a witness can give evidence

(1) The court must consider whether the quality of evidence given by a party or witness is likely to be diminished by reason of vulnerability and, if so, whether it is necessary to make one or more participation directions.

(2) Before making such participation directions, the court must consider any views expressed by the party or witness about giving evidence.][1]

NOTES

Amendments.[1] Part 3A inserted: SI 2017/1033.

[3A.6 Protected parties

(1) The court must consider whether it is necessary to make one or more participation directions to assist –

(a)   the protected party participating in proceedings; or
(b)   the protected party giving evidence.

(2) Before making such participation directions, the court must consider any views expressed by the protected party's litigation friend about the protected party's participation in the proceedings or that party giving evidence.

(Part 15 contains rules about representation of a protected party. Practice Direction 15B contains provisions about the ability of a protected party to give evidence.)][1]

NOTES

Amendments.[1] Part 3A inserted: SI 2017/1033.

[3A.7 What the court must have regard to

When deciding whether to make one or more participation directions the court must have regard in particular to–

(a)   the impact of any actual or perceived intimidation, including any behaviour towards the party or witness on the part of –
(i)   any other party or other witness to the proceedings or members of the family or associates of that other party or other witness; or
(ii)   any members of the family of the party or witness;
(b)   whether the party or witness –
(i)   suffers from mental disorder or otherwise has a significant impairment of intelligence or social functioning;
(ii)   has a physical disability or suffers from a physical disorder; or
(iii)   is undergoing medical treatment;
(c)   the nature and extent of the information before the court;

(d) the issues arising in the proceedings including (but not limited to) any concerns arising in relation to abuse;

(e) whether a matter is contentious;

(f) the age, maturity and understanding of the party or witness;

(g) the social and cultural background and ethnic origins of the party or witness;

(h) the domestic circumstances and religious beliefs of the party or witness;

(i) any questions which the court is putting or causing to be put to a witness in accordance with section 31G(6) of the 1984 Act;

(j) any characteristic of the party or witness which is relevant to the participation direction which may be made;

(k) whether any measure is available to the court;

(l) the costs of any available measure; and

(m) any other matter set out in Practice Direction 3AA.][1]

NOTES

Amendments.[1] Part 3A inserted: SI 2017/1033.

[3A.8 Measures

(1) The measures referred to in this Part are those which –

(a) prevent a party or witness from seeing another party or witness;

(b) allow a party or witness to participate in hearings and give evidence by live link;

(c) provide for a party or witness to use a device to help communicate;

(d) provide for a party or witness to participate in proceedings with the assistance of an intermediary;

(e) provide for a party or witness to be questioned in court with the assistance of an intermediary; or

(f) do anything else which is set out in Practice Direction 3AA.

(2) If the family court makes a direction for a measure which is not available where the court is sitting, it may direct that the court will sit at the nearest or most convenient location where the family court sits and the measure is available.

(3) If the High Court makes a direction for a measure which is not available where the court is sitting, it may direct that the court will sit at the nearest or most convenient location where the High Court sits and the measure is available.

(4) Nothing in these rules gives the court power to direct that public funding must be available to provide a measure.

(5) If a direction for a measure is considered by the court to be necessary but the measure is not available to the court, the court must set out in its order the reasons why the measure is not available.][1]

NOTES

Amendments.[1] Part 3A inserted: SI 2017/1033.

PART II – Statutory instruments

[3A.9 When the duties of the court apply and recording reasons for decisions made under this Part

(1) The court's duties under rules 3A.3 to 3A.6 apply as soon as possible after the start of proceedings and continue until the resolution of the proceedings.

(2) The court must set out its reasons on the court order for –

    (a)   making, varying or revoking directions referred to in this Part; or

    (b)   deciding not to make, vary or revoke directions referred to in this Part, in proceedings that involve a vulnerable person or protected party.][1]

NOTES

Amendments.[1] Part 3A inserted: SI 2017/1033.

[3A.10 Application for directions under this Part

(1) An application for directions under this Part may be made on the application form initiating the proceedings or during the proceedings by any person filing an application notice.

(2) The application form or application notice must contain the matters set out in Practice Direction 3AA.

(3) Subject to paragraph (2), the Part 18 procedure applies to an application for directions made during the proceedings.

(4) This rule is subject to any direction of the court.][1]

NOTES

Amendments.[1] Part 3A inserted: SI 2017/1033.

[3A.11 Procedure where the court makes directions of its own initiative

Where the court proposes to make a participation direction of its own initiative the procedure set out in rule 4.3(2) to (6) applies.][1]

NOTES

Amendments.[1] Part 3A inserted: SI 2017/1033.

[3A.12 Functions of officers of the Service and Welsh family proceedings officers

Nothing in this Part gives the court power to direct that an officer of the Service or a Welsh family proceedings officer should perform any function beyond the functions conferred upon such officers by any other enactment.][1]

NOTES

Amendments.[1] Part 3A inserted: SI 2017/1033.

[3A.13 Prohibition of cross-examination in person under Part 4B of the 1984 Act

A practice direction may make provision in relation to the prohibition of cross-examination in person under Part 4B of the 1984 Act.][1]

NOTES
Amendments.[1] Rule inserted: SI 2022/44.

Practice Direction 3AA –
Vulnerable Persons: Participation in Proceedings and Giving Evidence

This Practice Direction supplements FPR Part 3A.

Preamble and interpretation

1.1 Part 3A FPR makes provision in relation to vulnerable persons (parties and witnesses), including protected parties, in family proceedings.

[– Rule 3A.2A FPR sets out the assumption that where it is stated that a party or witness is, or is at risk of being, a victim of domestic abuse carried out by a party, relative of another party, or a witness in the proceedings, they are vulnerable. Where the assumption applies, the court must consider whether it is necessary to make a participation direction.][1]

– Rule 3A.4 FPR places a duty on the court to consider whether a party's participation in the proceedings is likely to be diminished by reason of vulnerability and, if so whether it is necessary to make one or more participation directions (as defined in rule 3A.1 FPR). Rule 3A.4 FPR does not apply to a child or to a party who is a protected party[, or to those who fall within the assumption at rule 3A.2A FPR][1].

– Rule 3A.5 FPR places a duty on the court to consider whether the quality of evidence given by a party or witness is likely to be diminished by reason of vulnerability and, if so whether it is necessary to make one or more participation directions. Rule 3A.5 FPR does not apply to a party who is a protected party[, or to those who fall within the assumption at rule 3A.2A FPR][1].

– Rule 3A.6 FPR places a duty on the court to consider whether it is necessary to make one or more participation directions to assist a protected party in proceedings, or a protected party giving evidence.

[1.1A For the avoidance of doubt, it should be noted that the assumption that a person is vulnerable, as referred to in rule 3A.2A FPR and in paragraph 1.1 above, only applies for the purposes of the court considering whether it is necessary to make a participation direction and not for any other purpose.][1]

1.2 This Practice Direction sets out the procedure and practice to be followed to achieve a fair hearing by providing for appropriate measures to be put in place to ensure that the participation of parties and the quality of the evidence of the parties and other witnesses is not diminished by reason of their vulnerability.

1.3 It is the duty of the court (under rules 1.1(2); 1.2 & 1.4 and Part 3A FPR) and of all parties to the proceedings (rule 1.3 FPR) to identify any party or witness who is a vulnerable person at the earliest possible stage of any family proceedings.

1.4 All parties and their representatives are required to work with the court and each other to ensure that each party or witness can participate in proceedings without the quality of their evidence being diminished and without being put in fear or distress by reason of their vulnerability as defined with reference to the circumstances of each person and to the nature of the proceedings.

1.5 In applying the provisions of Part 3A FPR and the provisions of this Practice Direction, the court and the parties must also have regard to all other relevant rules and Practice Directions and in particular those referred to in the Annex to this Practice Direction.

NOTES

Amendments.[1] Sub-paragraph, words and paragraph inserted: FPR Update, 15 July 2021.

Factors to which the court has to have regard when considering the vulnerability of a party or witness mentioned: rule 3A.3(1) FPR

2.1 Rule 3A.3 FPR makes clear that when considering the vulnerability of a party or witness for the purposes of rule 3A.4 FPR (the court's duty to consider how a vulnerable party other than a child can participate in the proceedings) or rule 3A.5 FPR (the court's duty to consider how a vulnerable party or witness can give evidence), the court must have regard in particular to the matters set out in paragraphs (a) to (j) and (m) of rule 3A.7 FPR. Where rule 3A.7(d) refers to questions of abuse, this includes any concerns arising in relation to any of the following –

    (a)   domestic abuse …[1];
    (b)   sexual abuse;
    (c)   physical and emotional abuse;
    (d)   racial and/or cultural abuse or discrimination;
    (e)   forced marriage or so called 'honour based violence';
    (f)   female genital or other physical mutilation;
    (g)   abuse or discrimination based on gender or sexual orientation; and
    (h)   human trafficking.

[2.2 As provided by rule 3A.2A FPR, where it is stated that a party or witness is, or as at risk of being, a victim of domestic abuse carried out by certain third parties, it is to be automatically assumed for the purposes of Part 3A FPR that they are vulnerable. For such parties and witnesses, the court should proceed directly to a consideration of whether a participation direction is necessary.][1]

NOTES

Amendments.[1] Words omitted repealed and paragraph inserted: FPR Update, 15 July 2021.

Guidance about vulnerability: rule 3A.3(2) FPR

3.1 Rule 3A.3 FPR requires the court to have regard in particular to the matters set out in paragraphs (a) to (j) and (m) of rule 3A.7 FPR when considering the vulnerability of a party or witness other than a protected party [or victim of domestic abuse][1]. The court should require the assistance of relevant parties in the case when considering whether these factors or any of them may mean that the participation of any party or witness in the case is likely to be diminished by reason of vulnerability. When addressing this question, the court should consider the ability of the party or witness to –

(a) understand the proceedings, and their role in them, when in court;

(b) put their views to the court;

(c) instruct their representative/s before, during and after the hearing; and

(d) attend the hearing without significant distress.

NOTES

Amendments.[1] Words inserted: FPR Update, 15 July 2021.

Participation directions: participation other than by way of giving evidence

4.1 This section of the Practice Direction applies where [the assumption at rule 3A.2A FPR applies to a party, or where][1] a court has concluded that a party's participation in proceedings (other than by way of giving evidence) is likely to be diminished by reason of vulnerability, including cases where a party might be participating in proceedings by way of asking questions of a witness.

4.2 The court will consider whether it is necessary to make one or more participation directions, as required by rule 3A.4 [and rule 3A.2A][1]. The court may make such directions for the measures specified in rule 3A.8. In addition, the court may use its general case management powers as it considers appropriate to facilitate the party's participation. For example, the court may decide to make directions in relation to matters such as the structure and the timing of the hearing, the formality of language to be used in the court and whether (if facilities allow for it) the parties should be enabled to enter the court building through different routes and use different waiting areas.

NOTES

Amendments.[1] Words inserted: FPR Update, 15 July 2021.

Participation directions: the giving of evidence by a vulnerable party, vulnerable witness or protected party

5.1 This section of the Practice Direction applies where a court has concluded that a vulnerable party, vulnerable witness or protected party [(including those deemed vulnerable by virtue of the assumption at rule 3A.2A FPR)][1] should give evidence. In reaching its conclusion as to whether a child should give evidence to the court, the court must apply the guidance from relevant caselaw and the guidance of the Family Justice Council in relation to children giving evidence in family proceedings.

NOTES

Amendments.[1] Words inserted: FPR Update, 15 July 2021.

Ground rules hearings

5.2 When the court has decided that a vulnerable party, vulnerable witness or protected party should give evidence there shall be a 'ground rules hearing' prior to any hearing at which evidence is to be heard, at which any necessary participation directions will be given –

(a)   as to the conduct of the advocates and the parties in respect of the evidence of that person, including the need to address the matters referred to in paragraphs 5.3 to 5.7, and

(b)   to put any necessary support in place for that person.

The ground rules hearing does not need to be a separate hearing to any other hearing in the proceedings.

5.3 If the court decides that a vulnerable party, vulnerable witness or protected party should give evidence to the court, consideration should be given to the form of such evidence, for example whether it should be oral or other physical evidence, such as through sign language or another form of direct physical communication.

5.4 The court must consider the best way in which the person should give evidence, including considering whether the person's oral evidence should be given at a point before the hearing, recorded and, if the court so directs, transcribed, or given at the hearing with, if appropriate, participation directions being made.

5.5 In all cases in which it is proposed that a vulnerable party, vulnerable witness or protected party is to be cross-examined (whether before or during a hearing) the court must consider whether to make participation directions, including prescribing the manner in which the person is to be cross-examined. The court must consider whether to direct that- –

(a)   any questions that can be asked by one advocate should not be repeated by another without the permission of the court;

(b)   questions or topics to be put in cross-examination should be agreed prior to the hearing;

(c)   questions to be put in cross-examination should be put by one legal representative or advocate alone, or, if appropriate, by the judge; and

(d)   the taking of evidence should be managed in any other way.

5.6 The court must also consider whether a vulnerable party, vulnerable witness or protected party has previously –

(a)   given evidence, and been cross-examined, in criminal proceedings and whether that evidence and cross-examination has been pre-recorded (see sections 27 and 28 of the Youth Justice and Criminal Evidence Act 1999); or

(b)   given an interview which was recorded but not used in previous criminal or family proceedings.

If so, and if any such recordings are available, the court should consider their being used in the family proceedings.

5.7 All advocates (including those who are litigants in person) are expected to be familiar with and to use the techniques employed by the toolkits and approach of the Advocacy Training Council. The toolkits are available at www.theadvocatesgateway.org/toolkits. Further guidance for advocates is available from the Ministry of Justice at http://www.justice.gov.uk/guidance.htm.

Matters to be included in an application form for directions: rule 3A.10(2) FPR

6.1 An application for directions under Part 3A FPR should contain the following information, as applicable:

(a) why the party or witness would benefit from assistance;

[(aa) whether the party or witness falls within the assumption at rule 3A.2A FPR;][1]

(b) the measure or measures that would be likely to maximise as far as practicable the quality of that evidence;

(c) why the measure or measures sought would be likely to improve the person's ability to participate in the proceedings; and

(d) why the measure or measures sought would be likely to improve the quality of the person's evidence.

NOTES

Amendments.[1] Sub-paragraph inserted: FPR Update, 15 July 2021.

Annex

As noted at paragraph 1.5, in applying the provisions of Part 3A FPR and the provisions of this Practice Direction, the court and the parties must also have regard to all other relevant rules and Practice Directions and in particular –

- Part 1 FPR (Overriding Objective);
- Part 4 FPR (General Case Management Powers);
- Part 12 FPR and Practice Direction 12J
- Part 15 FPR (Representation of Protected Parties) and Practice Direction 15B (Adults Who May Be Protected Parties and Children Who May Become Protected Parties in Family Proceedings);
- Part 18 FPR (Procedure for Other Applications in Proceedings);
- Part 22 FPR (Evidence);

NOTES

Amendment.[1] Practice Direction 3AA inserted: FPR Update, 27 November 2017.

PART 4
GENERAL CASE MANAGEMENT POWERS

4.1 The court's general powers of management

(1) In this Part, 'statement of case' means the whole or part of, an application form or answer.

(2) The list of powers in this rule is in addition to any powers given to the court by any other rule or practice direction or by any other enactment or any powers it may otherwise have.

(3) Except where these rules provide otherwise, the court may –

(a) extend or shorten the time for compliance with any rule, practice direction or court order (even if an application for extension is made after the time for compliance has expired);

PART II – Statutory instruments

(b)   make such order for disclosure and inspection, including specific disclosure of documents, as it thinks fit;

[(bb) direct that any proceedings in the High Court be heard by a Divisional Court of the High Court;]2

(c)   adjourn or bring forward a hearing;

(d)   require a party or a party's legal representative to attend the court;

(e)   hold a hearing and receive evidence by telephone or by using any other method of direct oral communication;

(f)   direct that part of any proceedings be dealt with as separate proceedings;

(g)   stay(GL) the whole or part of any proceedings or judgment either generally or until a specified date or event;

(h)   consolidate proceedings;

(i)   hear two or more applications on the same occasion;

(j)   direct a separate hearing of any issue;

(k)   decide the order in which issues are to be heard;

(l)   exclude an issue from consideration;

(m)   dismiss or give a decision on an application after a decision on a preliminary issue;

(n)   direct any party to file and serve an estimate of costs; and

(o)   take any other step or make any other order for the purpose of managing the case and furthering the overriding objective.

(Rule 21.1 explains what is meant by disclosure and inspection.)

[(Rule 37.15(6)(b) makes specific provision in relation to Divisional Courts.)]2

(4) When the court makes an order, it may –

(a)   make it subject to conditions, including a condition to pay a sum of money into court; and

(b)   specify the consequence of failure to comply with the order or a condition.

[(4A) Where the court has made a direction in accordance with paragraph (3)(bb) the proceedings shall be heard by a Divisional Court of the High Court and not be a single judge.]2

(5) Where the court gives directions it will take into account whether or not a party has complied with any relevant pre-action protocol(GL).

(6) A power of the court under these rules to make an order includes a power to vary or revoke the order.

(7) Any provision in these rules –

(a)   requiring or permitting directions to be given by the court is to be taken as including provision for such directions to be varied or revoked; and

(b)   requiring or permitting a date to be set is to be taken as including provision for that date to be changed or cancelled.

(8) The court may not extend the period within which [an application for]1 a section 89 order must be made.

NOTES

Amendments.1 Words inserted: SI 2012/679. [2] Paragraph, sub-paragraph and words inserted: SI 2018/440.

4.2 Court officer's power to refer to the court

Where a step is to be taken by a court officer –

(a)   the court officer may consult the court before taking that step;
(b)   the step may be taken by the court instead of the court officer.

4.3 Court's power to make order of its own initiative

(1) Except where an enactment provides otherwise, the court may exercise its powers on an application or of its own initiative.

(Part 18 sets out the procedure for making an application.)

(2) [Subject to rule 29.17, where][1] the court proposes to make an order of its own initiative –

(a)   it may give any person likely to be affected by the order an opportunity to make representations; and
(b)   where it does so it must specify the time by and the manner in which the representations must be made.

(3) Where the court proposes –

(a)   to make an order of its own initiative; and
(b)   to hold a hearing to decide whether to make the order,

it must give each party likely to be affected by the order at least 5 days' notice of the hearing.

(4) The court may make an order of its own initiative without hearing the parties or giving them an opportunity to make representations.

(5) Where the court has made an order under paragraph 4 –

(a)   a party affected by the order may apply to have it set aside[(GL)], varied or stayed[(GL)]; and
(b)   the order must contain a statement of the right to make such an application.

(6) An application under paragraph (5)(a) must be made –

(a)   within such period as may be specified by the court; or
(b)   if the court does not specify a period, within 7 days beginning with the date on which the order was served on the party making the application.

(7) If [the court][1] of its own initiative strikes out a statement of case or dismisses an application (including an application for permission to appeal) and it considers that the application is totally without merit –

(a)   the court's order must record that fact; and

PART II – Statutory instruments

(b)   the court must at the same time consider whether it is appropriate to make a civil restraint order.

NOTES

Amendments.[1] Words substituted: SI 2013/3204.

4.4 Power to strike out a statement of case

(1) Except in proceedings to which Parts 12 to 14 apply, the court may strike out[(GL)] a statement of case if it appears to the court –

(a)   that the statement of case discloses no reasonable grounds for bringing or defending the application;

(b)   that the statement of case is an abuse of the court's process or is otherwise likely to obstruct the just disposal of the proceedings;

(c)   that there has been a failure to comply with a rule, practice direction or court order; or

(d)   in relation to applications for matrimonial and civil partnership orders and answers to such applications, that the parties to the proceedings consent.

[(1A) When the court is considering whether to exercise the power to strike out a statement of case, it must take into account any written evidence filed in relation to the application or answer.][2]

(2) When the court strikes out a statement of case it may make any consequential order it considers appropriate.

(3) Where –

(a)   the court has struck out an applicant's statement of case;

(b)   the applicant has been ordered to pay costs to the respondent; and

(c)   before paying those costs, the applicant starts another application against the same respondent, arising out of facts which are the same or substantially the same as those relating to the application in which the statement of case was struck out,

the court may, on the application of the respondent, stay[(GL)] that other application until the costs of the first application have been paid.

(4) Paragraph (1) does not limit any other power of the court to strike out[(GL)] a statement of case.

(5) If [the court][1] strikes out an applicant's statement of case and it considers that the application is totally without merit –

(a)   the court's order must record that fact; and

(b)   the court must at the same time consider whether it is appropriate to make a civil restraint order.

NOTES

Amendment.[1] Words substituted: SI 2013/3204.[2] Paragraph inserted: SI 2016/355.

4.5 Sanctions have effect unless defaulting party obtains relief

(1) Where a party has failed to comply with a rule, practice direction or court order, any sanction for failure to comply imposed by the rule, practice direction or court order has effect unless the party in default applies for and obtains relief from the sanction.

(Rule 4.6 sets out the circumstances which the court may consider on an application to grant relief from a sanction.)

(2) Where the sanction is the payment of costs, the party in default may only obtain relief by appealing against the order for costs.

(3) Where a rule, practice direction or court order –

(a) requires a party to do something within a specified time; and
(b) specifies the consequence of failure to comply,

the time for doing the act in question may not be extended by agreement between the parties.

4.6 Relief from sanctions

(1) On an application for relief from any sanction imposed for a failure to comply with any rule, practice direction or court order the court will consider all the circumstances including –

(a) the interests of the administration of justice;
(b) whether the application for relief has been made promptly;
(c) whether the failure to comply was intentional;
(d) whether there is a good explanation for the failure;
(e) the extent to which the party in default has complied with other rules, practice directions, court orders and any relevant pre –action protocol(GL);
(f) whether the failure to comply was caused by the party or the party's legal representative;
(g) whether the hearing date or the likely hearing date can still be met if relief is granted;
(h) the effect which the failure to comply had on each party; and
(i) the effect which the granting of relief would have on each party or a child whose interest the court considers relevant.

(2) An application for relief must be supported by evidence.

4.7 General power of the court to rectify matters where there has been an error of procedure

Where there has been an error of procedure such as a failure to comply with a rule or practice direction –

(a) the error does not invalidate any step taken in the proceedings unless the court so orders; and
(b) the court may make an order to remedy the error.

4.8 Power of the court to make civil restraint orders

Practice Direction 4B sets out –

    (a)   the circumstances in which [the court][1] has the power to make a civil restraint order against a party to proceedings;

    (b)   the procedure where a party applies for a civil restraint order against another party; and

    (c)   the consequences of the court making a civil restraint order.

NOTES

Amendment.[1] Words substituted: SI 2013/3204.

Practice Direction 4A – Striking Out a Statement of Case

This Practice Direction supplements FPR Part 4, rule 4.4 (Power to strike out a statement of case)

Introduction

1.1 Rule 4.4 enables the court to strike out the whole or part of a statement of case which discloses no reasonable grounds for bringing or defending the application (rule 4.4(1)(a)), or which is an abuse of the process of the court or otherwise likely to obstruct the just disposal of the proceedings (rule 4.4(1)(b)). These powers may be exercised on an application by a party or on the court's own initiative.

[1.1A Before exercising these powers the court must take into account any written evidence filed in relation to the application or answer (rule 4.4(1A)). For example, the court must take into account the financial statement (Form E) filed in relation to an application for a property adjustment order, pension sharing order and other financial orders.][1]

1.2 This practice direction sets out the procedure a party should follow to make an application for an order under rule 4.4.

NOTES

Amendment.[1] Paragraph inserted: FPR Update, April 2016.

Examples of cases within the rule

2.1 The following are examples of cases where the court may conclude that an application falls within rule 4.4(1)(a) –

    (a)   those which set out no facts indicating what the application is about;

    (b)   those which are incoherent and make no sense;

    (c)   those which contain a coherent set of facts but those facts, even if true, do not disclose any legally recognisable application against the respondent.

2.2 An application may fall within rule 4.4(1)(b) where it cannot be justified, for example because it is frivolous, scurrilous or obviously ill-founded.

2.3 An answer may fall within rule 4.4(1)(a) where it consists of a bare denial or otherwise sets out no coherent statement of facts.

2.4 …[1]

2.5 The examples set out above are intended only as illustrations.

2.6 Where a rule, practice direction or order states 'shall be struck out or dismissed' or 'will be struck out or dismissed' this means that the order striking out or dismissing the proceedings will itself bring the proceedings to an end and that no further order of the court is required.

NOTES

Amendment.[1] Paragraph omitted: FPR Update, July 2015.

Applications which appear to fall within rule 4.4(1)(a) or (b)

3.1 A court officer who is asked to issue an application form but believes the application may fall within rule 4.4(1)(a) or (b) should issue the application form, but may then consult the court (under rule 4.2) before returning the form to the applicant or taking any other step to serve the respondent. The court may of its own initiative make an immediate order designed to ensure that the application is disposed of or (as the case may be) proceeds in a way that accords with the rules.

3.2 The court may allow the applicant a hearing before deciding whether to make such an order.

3.3 Orders the court may make include –

    (a)   an order that the application be stayed until further order;

    (b)   an order that the application form be retained by the court and not served until the stay is lifted;

    (c)   an order that no application by the applicant to lift the stay be heard unless the applicant files such further documents (for example a witness statement or an amended application form) as may be specified in the order.

3.4 Where the court makes any such order or, subsequently, an order lifting the stay, it may give directions about the service on the respondent of the order and any other documents on the court file.

3.5 The fact that the court allows an application referred to it by a court officer to proceed does not prejudice the right of any party to apply for any order against the applicant.

Answers which appear to fall within rule 4.4(1)(a) or (b)

4.1 A court officer may similarly consult the court about any document filed which purports to be an answer and which the officer believes may fall within rule 4.4(1)(a) or (b).

4.2 If the court decides that the document falls within rule 4.4(1)(a) or (b) it may on its own initiative make an order striking it out. Where the court does so it may extend the time for the respondent to file a proper answer.

PART II – Statutory instruments

4.3 The court may allow the respondent a hearing before deciding whether to make such an order.

4.4 Alternatively the court may make an order requiring the respondent within a stated time to clarify the answer or to give additional information about it. The order may provide that the answer will be struck out if the respondent does not comply.

4.5 The fact that the court does not strike out an answer on its own initiative does not prejudice the right of the applicant to apply for any order against the respondent.

General provisions

5.1 The court may exercise its powers under rule 4.4(1)(a) or (b) on application by a party to the proceedings or on its own initiative at any time.

5.2 Where the court at a hearing strikes out all or part of a party's statement of case it may enter such judgment for the other party as that party appears entitled to.

Applications for orders under rule 4.4(1)

6.1 Attention is drawn to Part 18 (Procedure for Other Applications in Proceedings) and to the practice direction that supplements it. The practice direction requires all applications to be made as soon as possible.

6.2 While many applications under rule 4.4(1) can be made without evidence in support, the applicant should consider whether facts need to be proved and, if so, whether evidence in support should be filed and served.

Practice Direction 4B –
Civil Restraint Orders

This Practice Direction supplements FPR rule 4.8

Introduction

1.1 This practice direction applies where the court is considering whether to make –

    (a)   a limited civil restraint order;
    (b)   an extended civil restraint order; or
    (c)   a general civil restraint order,

against a party who has made applications which are totally without merit.

Rules 4.3(7), 4.4(5) and 18.13 provide that where a statement of case or application is struck out or dismissed and is totally without merit, the court order must specify that fact and the court must consider whether to make a civil restraint order. Rule 30.11(5) makes similar provision where the appeal court refuses an application for permission to appeal, strikes out an appellant's notice or dismisses an appeal.

The powers of the court to make civil restraint orders are separate from and do not replace the powers given to the court by section 91(14) of the Children Act 1989.

Limited civil restraint orders

2.1 A limited civil restraint order may be made ...[1] where a party has made 2 or more applications which are totally without merit.

2.2 Where the court makes a limited civil restraint order, the party against whom the order is made –

    (a)   will be restrained from making any further applications in the proceedings in which the order is made without first obtaining the permission of a judge identified in the order;

    (b)   may apply for amendment or discharge of the order, but only with the permission of a judge identified in the order; and

    (c)   may apply for permission to appeal the order and if permission is granted, may appeal the order.

2.3 Where a party who is subject to a limited civil restraint order –

    (a)   makes a further application in the proceedings in which the order is made without first obtaining the permission of a judge identified in the order, such application will automatically be dismissed –

        (i)   without the judge having to make any further order; and

        (ii)   without the need for the other party to respond to it; and

    (b)   repeatedly makes applications for permission pursuant to that order which are totally without merit, the court may direct that if the party makes any further application for permission which is totally without merit, the decision to dismiss the application will be final and there will be no right of appeal, unless the judge who refused permission grants permission to appeal.

2.4 A party who is subject to a limited civil restraint order may not make an application for permission under paragraphs 2.2(a) or (b) without first serving notice of the application on the other party in accordance with paragraph 2.5.

2.5 A notice under paragraph 2.4 must –

    (a)   set out the nature and grounds of the application; and

    (b)   provide the other party with at least 7 days within which to respond.

2.6 An application for permission under paragraphs 2.2(a) or (b) –

    (a)   must be made in writing;

    (b)   must include the other party's written response, if any, to the notice served under paragraph 2.4; and

    (c)   will be determined without a hearing.

2.7 ...[1]

2.8 Where a party makes an application for permission under paragraphs 2.2(a) or (b) and permission is refused, any application for permission to appeal –

    (a)   must be made in writing; and

    (b)   will be determined without a hearing.

2.9 A limited civil restraint order –

    (a)   is limited to the particular proceedings in which it is made;

    (b)   will remain in effect for the duration of the proceedings in which it is made, unless the court orders otherwise; and

    (c)   must identify the judge or judges to whom an application for permission under paragraphs 2.2(a), 2.2(b) or 2.8 should be made.

NOTES

Amendments.[1] Text omitted: FPR Update, April 2014.

Extended civil restraint orders

3.1 An extended civil restraint order may be made ...[1] where a party has persistently made applications which are totally without merit.

3.2 Unless the court orders otherwise, where the court makes an extended civil restraint order, the party against whom the order is made –

    (a)   will be restrained from making applications in any court concerning any matter involving or relating to or touching upon or leading to the proceedings in which the order is made without first obtaining the permission of a judge identified in the order;

    (b)   may apply for amendment or discharge of the order, but only with the permission of a judge identified in the order; and

    (c)   may apply for permission to appeal the order and if permission is granted, may appeal the order.

3.3 Where a party who is subject to an extended civil restraint order –

    (a)   makes an application in a court identified in the order concerning any matter involving or relating to or touching upon or leading to the proceedings in which the order is made without first obtaining the permission of a judge identified in the order, the application will automatically be struck out or dismissed –

        (i)   without the judge having to make any further order; and

        (ii)   without the need for the other party to respond to it; and

    (b)   repeatedly makes applications for permission pursuant to that order which are totally without merit, the court may direct that if the party makes any further application for permission which is totally without merit, the decision to dismiss the application will be final and there will be no right of appeal, unless the judge who refused permission grants permission to appeal.

3.4 A party who is subject to an extended civil restraint order may not make an application for permission under paragraphs 3.2(a) or (b) without first serving notice of the application on the other party in accordance with paragraph 3.5.

3.5 A notice under paragraph 3.4 must –

(a) set out the nature and grounds of the application; and

(b) provide the other party with at least 7 days within which to respond.

3.6 An application for permission under paragraphs 3.2(a) or (b) –

(a) must be made in writing;

(b) must include the other party's written response, if any, to the notice served under paragraph 3.4; and

(c) will be determined without a hearing.

3.7 ...[1]

3.8 Where a party makes an application for permission under paragraphs 3.2(a) or (b) and permission is refused, any application for permission to appeal –

(a) must be made in writing; and

(b) will be determined without a hearing.

3.9 An extended civil restraint order –

(a) will be made for a specified period not exceeding 2 years;

(b) must identify the courts in which the party against whom the order is made is restrained from making applications; and

(c) must identify the judge or judges to whom an application for permission under paragraphs 3.2(a), 3.2(b) or 3.8 should be made.

3.10 The court may extend the duration of an extended civil restraint order, if it considers it appropriate to do so, but the duration of the order must not be extended for a period greater than 2 years on any given occasion.

NOTES

Amendments.[1] Text omitted: FPR Update, April 2014.

General civil restraint orders

4.1 A general civil restraint order may be made ...[1] where, the party against whom the order is made persists in making applications which are totally without merit, in circumstances where an extended civil restraint order would not be sufficient or appropriate.

4.2 Unless the court otherwise orders, where the court makes a general civil restraint order, the party against whom the order is made –

(a) will be restrained from making any application in any court without first obtaining the permission of a judge identified in the order;

(b) may apply for amendment or discharge of the order, but only with the permission of a judge identified in the order; and

(c) may apply for permission to appeal the order and if permission is granted, may appeal the order.

4.3 Where a party who is subject to a general civil restraint order –

(a)   makes an application in any court without first obtaining the permission of a judge identified in the order, the application will automatically be struck out or dismissed –

   (i)   without the judge having to make any further order; and

   (ii)   without the need for the other party to respond to it; and

(b)   repeatedly makes applications for permission pursuant to that order which are totally without merit, the court may direct that if the party makes any further application for permission which is totally without merit, the decision to dismiss that application will be final and there will be no right of appeal, unless the judge who refused permission grants permission to appeal.

4.4 A party who is subject to a general civil restraint order may not make an application for permission under paragraphs 4.2(a) or (b) without first serving notice of the application on the other party in accordance with paragraph 4.5.

4.5 A notice under paragraph 4.4 must –

(a)   set out the nature and grounds of the application; and

(b)   provide the other party with at least 7 days within which to respond.

4.6 An application for permission under paragraphs 4.2(a) or (b) –

(a)   must be made in writing;

(b)   must include the other party's written response, if any, to the notice served under paragraph 4.4; and

(c)   will be determined without a hearing.

4.7 …[1]

4.8 Where a party makes an application for permission under paragraphs 4.2(a) or (b) and permission is refused, any application for permission to appeal –

(a)   must be made in writing; and

(b)   will be determined without a hearing.

4.9 A general civil restraint order –

(a)   will be made for a specified period not exceeding 2 years;

(b)   must identify the courts in which the party against whom the order is made is restrained from making applications; and

(c)   must identify the judge or judges to whom an application for permission under paragraphs 4.2(a), 4.2(b) or 4.8 should be made.

4.10 The court may extend the duration of a general civil restraint order, if it considers it appropriate to do so, but he duration of the order must not be extended for a period greater than 2 years on any given occasion.

NOTES

Amendments.[1] Text omitted: FPR Update, April 2014.

General

5.1 The other party or parties to the proceedings may apply for any civil restraint order.

5.2 An application under paragraph 5.1 must be made using the procedure in Part 18 unless the court otherwise directs and the application must specify which type of civil restraint order is sought.

****

PART 6
SERVICE

Chapter 1
Scope of this Part and Interpretation

6.1 Part 6 rules about service apply generally

This Part applies to the service of documents, except where –

    (a)   another Part, any other enactment or a practice direction makes a different provision; or

    (b)   the court directs otherwise.

6.2 Interpretation

In this Part 'solicitor' includes any person who, for the purposes of the Legal Services Act 2007, is an authorised person in relation to an activity which constitutes the conduct of litigation (within the meaning of that Act).

****

Chapter 3
Service of Documents other than an Application for a Matrimonial Order or Civil Partnership Order in the United Kingdom

6.23 Method of service

A document may be served by any of the following methods –

    (a)   personal service, in accordance with rule 6.25;

    (b)   first class post, document exchange or other service which provides for delivery on the next business day, in accordance with Practice Direction 6A;

    (c)   leaving it at a place specified in rule 6.26; or

    (d)   fax or [e-mail][1] in accordance with Practice Direction 6A.

    (Rule 6.35 provides for the court to permit service by an alternative method or at an alternative place.)

NOTES

Amendment.[1] Words substituted: SI 2015/1868.

6.24 Who is to serve

(1) A party to proceedings will serve a document which that party has prepared, or which the court has prepared or issued on behalf of that party, except where –

(a)   a rule or practice direction provides that the court will serve the document; or

(b)   the court directs otherwise.

(2) Where a court officer is to serve a document, it is for the court to decide which method of service is to be used.

(3) Where the court officer is to serve a document prepared by a party, that party must provide a copy for the court and for each party to be served.

6.25 Personal service

(1) Where required by another Part, any other enactment, a practice direction or a court order, a document must be served personally.

(2) In other cases, a document may be served personally except where the party to be served has given an address for service under rule 6.26(2)(a).

(3) A document is served personally on an individual by leaving it with that individual.

6.26 Address for service

(1) A party to proceedings must give an address at which that party may be served with documents relating to those proceedings.

(2) Subject to paragraph (4), a party's address for service must be –

(a)   the business address either within the United Kingdom …[2] of a solicitor acting for the party to be served; or

(b)   where there is no solicitor acting for the party to be served, an address within the United Kingdom at which the party resides or carries on business.

…[2]

(3) Where there is no solicitor acting for the party to be served and the party does not have an address within the United Kingdom at which that party resides or carries on business, the party must, subject to paragraph (4), give an address for service within the United Kingdom.

(4) A party who –

(a)   has been served with an application for a matrimonial or civil partnership order outside the United Kingdom; and

(b)   apart from acknowledging service of the application, does not take part in the proceedings,

need not give an address for service within the United Kingdom.

(5) Any document to be served in proceedings must be sent, or transmitted to, or left at, the party's address for service unless it is to be served personally or the court orders otherwise.

(6) Where, in accordance with Practice Direction 6A, a party indicates or is deemed to have indicated that they will accept service by fax, the fax number given by that party must be at the address for service.

(7) Where a party indicates in accordance with Practice Direction 6A, that they will accept service by [e-mail][1], the e-mail address …[1] given by that party will be deemed to be …[1] the address for service.

(8) This rule does not apply where an order made by the court under rule 6.35 (service by an alternative method or at an alternative place) specifies where a document may be served.

NOTES

Amendment.[1] Words substituted and omitted: SI 2015/1868.2 Words omitted repealed: SI 2019/517.

6.27 Change of address for service

Where the address for service of a party changes, that party must give notice in writing of the change, as soon as it has taken place, to the court and every other party.

6.28 Service of an application form commencing proceedings on children and protected parties

(1) This rule applies to the service of an application form commencing proceedings other than an application for a matrimonial or civil partnership order.

(2) An application form commencing proceedings which would otherwise be served on a child or protected party must be served –

    (a)   where the respondent is a child, in accordance with rule 6.14(1); and

    (b)   where the respondent is a protected party, in accordance with rule 6.14(2).

6.29 Service of other documents on or by children and protected parties where a litigation friend has been or will be appointed

(1) This rule applies to –

    (a)   a protected party; or

    (b)   a child to whom the provisions of rule 16.5 and Chapter 5 of Part 16 apply (litigation friends).

(2) An application for an order appointing a litigation friend where a protected party or child has no litigation friend must be served in accordance with rule 15.8 or rule 16.13 as the case may be.

(3) Any other document which would otherwise be served on or by a child or protected party must be served on or by the litigation friend conducting the proceedings on behalf of the child or protected party.

6.30 Service on or by children where a children's guardian has been or will be appointed under rule 16.4

(1) This rule applies to a child to whom the provisions of rule 16.4 and Chapter 7 apply.

(2) An application for an order appointing a children's guardian where a child has no children's guardian must be served in accordance with rule 16.26.

(3) Any other document which would otherwise be served on or by a child must be served on or by the children's guardian conducting the proceedings on behalf of the child.

6.31 Service on or by children where a children's guardian has been appointed under rule 16.3

(1) This rule applies where a children's guardian has been appointed for a child in accordance with rule 16.3.

(2) Any document which would otherwise be served on the child must be served on –

    (a)   the solicitor appointed by the court in accordance with section 41(3) of the 1989 Act; and

    (b)   the children's guardian.

(3) Any document which would otherwise be served by the child must be served by –

    (a)   the solicitor appointed by the court in accordance with section 41(3) of the 1989 Act or by the children's guardian; or

    (b)   if no solicitor has been appointed as mentioned in paragraph (a), the children's guardian.

6.32 Supplementary provisions relating to service on children and protected parties

(1) The court may direct that a document be served on a protected party or child or on some person other than a person upon whom it would be served under rules 6.28 to 6.31 above.

(2) The court may direct that, although a document has been sent or given to someone other than a person upon whom it should be served under rules 6.28 to 6.31 above, the document is to be treated as if had been properly served.

(3) This rule and rules 6.28 to 6.31 do not apply where the court has made an order under rule 16.6 allowing a child to conduct proceedings without a children's guardian or litigation friend.

6.33 Supplementary provision relating to service on children

(1) This rule applies to proceedings to which Part 12 applies.

(2) Where a rule requires –

    (a)   a document to be served on a party;

    (b)   a party to be notified of any matter; or

    (c)   a party to be supplied with a copy of a document,

in addition to the persons to be served in accordance with rules 6.28 to 6.32, the persons or bodies mentioned in paragraph (3) must be served, notified or supplied with a copy of a document, as applicable, unless the court directs otherwise.

(3) The persons or bodies referred to in paragraph (2) are –

    (a)   such of the following who are appointed in the proceedings –

        (i)   the children's guardian (if the children's guardian is not otherwise to be served);

        (ii)   the welfare officer;

        (iii)   the children and family reporter;

        (iv)   the officer of the Service, Welsh family proceedings officer or local authority officer acting under a duty referred to in rule 16.38; and

    (b)   a local authority preparing a report under section 14A(8) or (9) of the 1989 Act.

6.34 Deemed service

A document, other than an application for a matrimonial or civil partnership order, served in accordance with these rules or a practice direction is deemed to be served on the day shown in the following table –

Method of service	Deemed day of service
First class post (or other service which provides for delivery on the next business day)	The second day after it was posted, left with, delivered to or collected by the relevant service provider, provided that day is a business day; or, if not, the next business day after that day
Document exchange	The second day after it was left with, delivered to or collected by the relevant service provider, provided that day is a business day; or, if not, the next business day after that day.
Delivering the document to or leaving it at a permitted address	If it is delivered to or left at the permitted address on a business day before 4.30p.m., on that day; or in any other case, on the next business day after that day.
Fax	If the transmission of the fax is completed on a business day before 4.30p.m., on that day; or, in any other case, the next business day after the day on which it was transmitted.

Method of service	Deemed day of service
Other electronic method	If the e-mail or other electronic transmission is sent on a business day before 4.30p.m., on that day; or in any other case, on the next business day after the day on which it was sent.
Personal service	If the document is served personally before 4.30p.m. on a business day, on that day; or, in any other case, on the next business day after that day.

(Practice Direction 6A contains examples of how the date of deemed service is calculated.)

6.35 Service by an alternative method or at an alternative place

Rule 6.19 applies to any document in proceedings as it applies to an application for a matrimonial or civil partnership order and reference to the respondent in that rule is modified accordingly.

6.36 Power to dispense with service

The court may dispense with the service of any document which is to be served in proceedings.

6.37 Certificate of service

(1) Where a rule, practice direction or court order requires a certificate of service, the certificate must state the details set out in the following table –

Method of service	Details to be certified
Personal service	Date and time of personal service and method of identifying the person served.
First class post, document exchange or other service which provides for delivery on the next business day.	Date of posting, leaving with, delivering to or collection by the relevant service provider.
Delivery of document to or leaving it at a permitted place.	Date and time when the document was delivered to or left at the permitted place.
Fax.	Date and time of completion of transmission.
Other electronic method	Date and time of sending the email or other electronic transmission.
Alternative method or place permitted by court	As required by the court.

(2) An applicant who is required to file a certificate of service of an application form must do so at or before the earlier of –

(a)   the first directions appointment in; or

(b)   the hearing of,

the proceedings unless a rule or practice direction provides otherwise.

(Rule 17.2 requires a certificate of service to contain a statement of truth.)

6.38 Notification of outcome of service by the court

Where –

(a)   a document to be served by a court officer is served by post or other service which provides for delivery on the next working day; and

(b)   the document is returned to the court,

the court officer will send notification to the party who requested service that the document has been returned.

6.39 Notification of non-service by bailiff

Where –

(a)   the bailiff is to serve a document; and

(b)   the bailiff is unable to serve it,

the court officer must send notification to the party who requested service.

Chapter 4
Service Out of the Jurisdiction

6.40 Scope and interpretation

(1) This Chapter contains rules about –

(a)   service of application forms and other documents out of the jurisdiction; and

(b)   the procedure for service.

('Jurisdiction' is defined in rule 2.3.)

(2) In this Chapter –

.   'application form' includes an application notice;

'Commonwealth State' means a State listed in Schedule 3 to the British Nationality Act 1981; and

'the Hague Convention' means the Convention on the service abroad of judicial and extra-judicial documents in civil or commercial matters signed at the Hague on November 15, 1965.

6.41 Permission to serve not required

Any document to be served for the purposes of these rules may be served out of the jurisdiction without the permission of the court.

PART II – Statutory instruments

[6.41A Time for serving an application for a matrimonial or civil partnership order out of the jurisdiction

(1) The applicant must complete the step required by the table in paragraph (2) or (3), as applicable, in relation to the method of service chosen before 12.00 midnight on the day 28 days after the date of issue of the application.

(2) Where service of an application for a matrimonial or civil partnership order is to be effected on a party in Scotland or Northern Ireland—

Method of service	Step required
First class post, document exchange or other service which provides for delivery on the next business day	Posting, leaving with, delivering to or collection by the relevant service provider
Personal service under rule 6.7, by someone other than the applicant personally	Leaving it with the person to be served
Email service under rule 6.7A	Sending the application by e-mail and sending the notice required by rule 6.7A(2) by posting, leaving with, delivering to or collection by the relevant service provider

(3) Where service of an application for a matrimonial or civil partnership order is to be effected on a respondent out of the United Kingdom—

Method of service	Step required
Where service is to be effected by a method provided for by rule 6.45	The steps required by rule 6.46(2)
Where service is to be effected by another method permitted by the law of the country in which it is to be served	Sending or delivering the application to, or leaving it with, the person to be served or taking such other such steps to effect service as are permitted by the law of the country in which it is to be served][1]

NOTES

Amendments.[1] Rule inserted: SI 2022/44.

[6.41B Extension of time for serving the application for a matrimonial or civil partnership order

(1) The applicant may apply for an order extending the time for compliance with rule 6.41A.

(2) The general rule is that an application under paragraph (1) must be made—

(a)   within the period for service specified by rule 6.41A; or
(b)   where an order has been made under this rule, within the period specified by that order.

(3) Where an applicant asserts that they have a good reason for not making an application under paragraph (1) within the periods specified in paragraph (2) an application under paragraph (1) may be made—

    (a)   after the period for service specified by rule 6.41A; or

    (b)   where an order has been made under this rule, after the period specified by that order.

(4) On an application under paragraph (1), the court must consider all the circumstances including whether—

    (a)   the applicant has taken reasonable steps to comply with rule 6.41A; and

    (b)   the applicant has acted promptly.

(5) An application for an order extending the time for compliance with rule 6.41A—

    (a)   must be supported by evidence; and

    (b)   may be made without notice.][1]

NOTES

Amendments.[1] Rule inserted: SI 2022/44.

6.42 Period for acknowledging service or responding to application where application is served out of the jurisdiction

(1) This rule applies where, under these rules, a party is required to file –

    (a)   an acknowledgment of service; or

    (b)   an answer to an application,

and sets out the time period for doing so where the application is served out of the jurisdiction.

(2) Where the applicant serves an application on a respondent in –

    (a)   Scotland or Northern Ireland; or

    (b)   a …1 Hague Convention country within Europe,

the period for filing an acknowledgment of service or an answer to an application is 21 days after service of the application.

(3) Where the applicant serves an application on a respondent in a Hague Convention country outside Europe, the period for filing an acknowledgment of service or an answer to an application is 31 days after service of the application.

(4) Where the applicant serves an application on a respondent in a country not referred to in paragraphs (2) and (3), the period for filing an acknowledgment of service or an answer to an application is set out in Practice Direction 6B.

NOTES

Amendments.[1] Words omitted repealed: SI 2019/517.

PART II – Statutory instruments

6.43 Method of service – general provisions

(1) This rule contains general provisions about the method of service of an application for a matrimonial or civil partnership order, or other document, on a party out of the jurisdiction.

Where service is to be effected on a party in Scotland or Northern Ireland

(2) Where a party serves an application form or other document on a party in Scotland or Northern Ireland, it must be served by a method permitted by Chapter 2 (and references to 'jurisdiction' in that Chapter are modified accordingly) or Chapter 3 of this Part and rule 6.26(5) applies.

Where service is to be effected on a respondent out of the United Kingdom

(3) Where the applicant wishes to serve an application form, or other document, on a respondent out of the United Kingdom, it may be served by any method –

    [(a)   provided for by rule 6.45 (service through foreign governments, judicial authorities and British Consular authorities); or][1]

    (b)   permitted by the law of the country in which it is to be served.

(4) Nothing in paragraph (3) or in any court order authorises or requires any person to do anything which is contrary to the law of the country where the application form, or other document, is to be served.

NOTES

Amendments.[1] Paragraph substituted: SI 2021/155.

6.44 ...[1]

...[1]

NOTES

Amendments.[1] Rule repealed: SI 2019/517.

6.45 Service through foreign governments, judicial authorities and British Consular authorities

(1) Where the applicant wishes to serve an application form, or other document, on a respondent in any country which is a party to the Hague Convention, it may be served –

    (a)   through the authority designated under the Hague Convention in respect of that country; or

    (b)   if the law of that country permits –

        (i)   through the judicial authorities of that country; or

        (ii)   through a British Consular authority in that country.

(2) Where the applicant wishes to serve an application form, or other document, on a respondent in any country which is not a party to the Hague Convention, it may be served, if the law of that country so permits –

(a)   through the government of that country, where that government is willing to serve it; or

(b)   through a British Consular authority in that country.

(3) Where the applicant wishes to serve an application form, or other document, in –

(a)   any Commonwealth State which is not a party to the Hague Convention;

(b)   the Isle of Man or the Channel Islands; or

(c)   any British Overseas Territory,

the methods of service permitted by paragraphs (1)(b) and (2) are not available and the applicant or the applicant's agent must effect service on a respondent in accordance with rule 6.43 unless Practice Direction 6B provides otherwise.

(4) ...1

NOTES

Amendments.[1] Paragraph repealed: SI 2019/517.

6.46 Procedure where service is to be through foreign governments, judicial authorities and British Consular authorities

(1) This rule applies where the applicant wishes to serve an application form, or other document, under rule 6.45(1) or (2).

(2) Where this rule applies, the applicant must file –

(a)   a request for service of the application form, or other document, by specifying one or more of the methods in rule 6.45(1) or (2);

(b)   a copy of the application form or other document;

(c)   any other documents or copies of documents required by Practice Direction 6B; and

(d)   any translation required under rule 6.47.

(3) When the applicant files the documents specified in paragraph (2), the court officer will –

(a)   seal[(GL)], or otherwise authenticate with the stamp of the court, the copy of the application form or other document; and

(b)   forward the documents to the Senior Master of the Queen's Bench Division.

(4) The Senior Master will send documents forwarded under this rule –

(a)   where the application form, or other document, is being served through the authority designated under the Hague Convention, to that authority; or

(b)   in any other case, to [the Foreign, Commonwealth and Development Office][1] with a request that it arranges for the application form or other document to be served.

(5) An official certificate which –

PART II – Statutory instruments

   (a)   states that the method requested under paragraph (2)(a) has been performed and the date of such performance;

   (b)   states, where more than one method is requested under paragraph (2)(a), which method was used; and

   (c)   is made by –

      (i)   a British Consular authority in the country where the method requested under paragraph (2)(a) was performed;

      (ii)   the government or judicial authorities in that country; or

      (iii)   the authority designated in respect of that country under the Hague Convention,

is evidence of the facts stated in the certificate.

(6) A document purporting to be an official certificate under paragraph (5) is to be treated as such a certificate, unless it is proved not to be.

NOTES

Amendments.[1] Words substituted: SI 2020/942.

6.47 Translation of application form or other document

(1) Except where paragraphs (4) and (5) apply, every copy of the application form, or other document, filed under rule 6.45 (service through foreign governments, judicial authorities and British Consular authorities) must be accompanied by a translation of the application form or other document.

(2) The translation must be –

   (a)   in the official language of the country in which it is to be served; or

   (b)   if there is more than one official language of that country, in any official language which is appropriate to the place in the country where the application form or other document is to be served.

(3) Every translation filed under this rule must be accompanied by a statement by the person making it that it is a correct translation, and the statement must include that person's name, address and qualifications for making the translation.

(4) The applicant is not required to file a translation of the application form, or other document, filed under rule 6.45 where it is to be served in a country of which English is an official language.

(5) The applicant is not required to file a translation of the application form or other document filed under rule 6.45 where –

   (a)   the person on whom the document is to be served is able to read and understand English; and

   (b)   service of the document is to be effected directly on that person.

...[1]

NOTES

Amendments.[1] Words omitted repealed: SI 2019/517.

6.48 Undertaking to be responsible for expenses of [the Foreign, Commonwealth and Development Office][1]

Every request for service filed under rule 6.46 (procedure where service is to be through foreign governments, judicial authorities etc.) must contain an undertaking by the person making the request –

(a) to be responsible for all expenses incurred by [the Foreign, Commonwealth and Development Office][1] or foreign judicial authority; and

(b) to pay those expenses to [the Foreign, Commonwealth and Development Office]1 or foreign judicial authority on being informed of the amount.

NOTES

Amendments.[1] Words substituted: SI 2020/942.

Practice Direction 6A –
Service within the Jurisdiction

This Practice Direction supplements FPR Part 6, Chapters 2 and 3

General Provisions

Scope of this Practice Direction

1.1 This Practice Direction supplements the following provisions of Part 6 –

(a) Chapter 2 (service of the application for a matrimonial order or civil partnership order in the jurisdiction);

(b) Chapter 3 (service of documents other than an application for a matrimonial order or civil partnership order in the United Kingdom); and

(c) rule 6.43(2) in relation to the method of service on a party in Scotland or Northern Ireland.

(Practice Direction B supplementing Part 6 contains provisions relevant to service on a party in Scotland or Northern Ireland, including provisions about the period for responding to an application notice.)

When service may be by document exchange

2.1 Subject to the provisions of rule 6.4 (which provides when an application for a matrimonial or civil partnership order may be served by document exchange) service by document exchange (DX) may take place only where –

(a) the address at which the party is to be served includes a numbered box at a DX; or

(b) the writing paper of the party who is to be served or of the solicitor acting for that party sets out a DX box number; and

(c) the party or the solicitor acting for that party has not indicated in writing that they are unwilling to accept service by DX.

PART II – Statutory instruments

How service is effected by post, an alternative service provider or DX

3.1 Service by post, DX or other service which provides for delivery on the next business day is effected by –

(a)   placing the document in a post box;

(b)   leaving the document with or delivering the document to the relevant service provider; or

(c)   having the document collected by the relevant service provider.

Service by fax or [e-mail][1]

4.1 [Paragraphs 4.2 to 4.6 apply][1] to the service [by the court or by a party][1] of a document other than an application for a matrimonial or civil partnership order and documents in adoption proceedings and parental order proceedings.

[4.2 Subject to the provisions of rule 6.26(6) and (7), where a document is to be served by fax or e-mail –

(a)   the party who is to be served or the solicitor acting for that party must previously have indicated in writing to the court or party serving, whichever is applicable –

(i)   that the party to be served or the solicitor is willing to accept service by fax or e-mail; and

(ii)   the fax number or e-mail address to which it must be sent; and

(b)   the following are to be taken as sufficient written indications for the purposes of paragraph 4.2(a) –

(i)   a fax number set out on the letterhead or website of the solicitor acting for the party to be served;

(ii)   an e-mail address set out on the letterhead or website of the solicitor acting for the party to be served but only where it is stated that the e-mail address may be used for service;

(iii)   a fax number or e-mail address set out on a statement of case or an answer to a claim filed with the court by the party to be served; or

(iv)   an e-mail or other correspondence from the party to be served, to the court or party serving, confirming that they are willing to accept service by e-mail.][1]

[4.3 Where a party intends to –

(a)   serve a document by e-mail; or

(b)   request that the court serve a document by e-mail

that party must first ask the party who is to be served whether there are any limitations to the recipient's agreement to accept service by such means (for example, the format in which documents are to be sent and the maximum size of attachments that may be received).][1]

4.4 Where a document is served by [e-mail][1], the party serving the document need not in addition send or deliver a hard copy.

[4.5 Where a party requests the court to serve a document by e-mail and has received notification of limitations to the recipient's agreement to accept service pursuant to paragraph 4.3, that party must communicate those limitations to the court when requesting the court to serve.

4.6 Where limitations have been communicated by a party pursuant to paragraph 4.3, service on that party must comply with those limitations.]¹

NOTES

Amendment.¹ Words substituted and inserted and paragraphs substituted: FPR Update, November 2015.

[Service by email of an application for a matrimonial order or civil partnership order in the jurisdiction under rule 6.7A

4A.1 Where the respondent does not provide an email address rule 6.7A provides for email service by sending it to the respondent's usual email address. This is generally considered to be the email address actively used by the respondent for personal emails. Email service to a respondent's business email address should be avoided where possible.]¹

NOTES

Amendment.¹ Paragraph inserted: FPR Update No 2 of 2022, 23 February 2022.

Service on members of the Regular Forces and United States Air Force

5.1 The provisions that apply to service on members of the regular forces (within the meaning of the Armed Forces Act 2006) and members of the United States Air Force are annexed to this practice direction.

Application for an order for service by an alternative method or at an alternative place

6.1 An application ...¹ for an order under rule 6.19 may be made without notice.

6.2 Where an application for an order under rule 6.19 is made before the document is served, the application must be supported by evidence stating –

    (a)   the reason why an order is sought;

    (b)   what alternative method or place is proposed; and

    (c)   why the applicant believes that the document is likely to reach the person to be served by the method or at the place proposed.

6.3 Where the application for an order is made after the applicant has taken steps to bring the document to the attention of the person to be served by an alternative method or at an alternative place, the application must be supported by evidence stating –

    (a)   the reason why the order is sought;

    (b)   what alternative method or alternative place was used;

    (c)   when the alternative method or place was used; and

    (d)   why the applicant believes that the document is likely to have reached the person to be served by the alternative method or at the alternative place.

6.4 Examples –

(a)   an application to serve by posting or delivering to an address of a person who knows the other party must be supported by evidence that if posted or delivered to that address, the document is likely to be brought to the attention of the other party;

(b)   an application to serve by sending a SMS text message or leaving a voicemail message at a particular telephone number saying where the document is must be accompanied by evidence that the person serving the document has taken, or will take, appropriate steps to ensure that the party being served is using that telephone number and is likely to receive the message.

NOTES

Amendment.[1] Text omitted: FPR Update, April 2014.

Applications for an order to dispense with service

7.1 An application ...[1] for an order under rule 6.36 (power to dispense with service) may be made without notice.

NOTES

Amendment.[1] Text omitted: FPR Update, April 2014.

Deemed service of a document other than an application for a matrimonial or civil partnership order

8.1 Rule 6.34 contains provisions about deemed service of a document other than an application for a matrimonial or civil partnership order. Examples of how deemed service is calculated are set out below.

Example 1

8.2 Where the document is posted (by first class post) on a Monday (a business day), the day of deemed service is the following Wednesday (a business day).

Example 2

8.3 Where the document is left in a numbered box at the DX on a Friday (a business day), the day of deemed service is the following Monday (a business day).

Example 3

8.4 Where the document is sent by fax on a Saturday and the transmission of that fax is completed by 4.30p.m. on that day, the day of deemed service is the following Monday (a business day).

Example 4

8.5 Where the document is served personally before 4.30p.m. on a Sunday, the day of deemed service is the next day (Monday, a business day).

Example 5

8.6 Where the document is delivered to a permitted address after 4.30p.m. on the Thursday (a business day) before Good Friday, the day of deemed service is the following Tuesday (a business day) as the Monday is a bank holiday.

Example 6

8.7 Where the document is posted (by first class post) on a bank holiday Monday, the day of deemed service is the following Wednesday (a business day).

Service of application on children and protected parties

9.1 Rule 16.14(1) and (2) are applied to service of an application form (other than an application for a matrimonial or civil partnership order) commencing proceedings on children and protected parties by rule 6.28. Rule 6.14(7) makes provision as to how an application form must be served where the respondent is a child or protected party. A document served in accordance with rule 6.14(7) must be endorsed with the following notice which is set out in Form D5 –

Important Notice
The contents or purport of this document are to be communicated to the Respondent
[or as the case may be], [full name of Respondent]
if s/he is over 16 [add if the person to be served lacks capacity within the meaning of the Mental Capacity Act 2005 to conduct the proceedings] unless you are satisfied [after consultation with the responsible medical officer within the meaning of the Mental Health Act 1983 or, if s/he is not liable to be detained or subject to guardianship under that Act, his/her medical attendant]* that communication will be detrimental to his/her mental condition].

Provisions relating to Applications for Matrimonial and Civil Partnership Orders

Acknowledgment of service to be sent to applicant

10.1 Where the court office receives an acknowledgment of service the court officer must send a photographic [or scanned][1] copy of it to the applicant.

NOTES

Amendment.[1] Words inserted: FPR Update, November 2015.

Personal service of application by bailiff

11.1 The court will only consider a request for personal service of the application by a bailiff if the address for service is in England and Wales.

11.2 In normal circumstances, a request should only be made if [email service (if applicable) and][1] postal service has been attempted. In this case, if –

   (a)   a signed acknowledgment of service is not returned to the court within 14 days after posting; and

---

(b)   the applicant reasonably believes the respondent is still living at the stated address,

the applicant may make a request to the court for personal service by a bailiff.

11.3 A request for personal service by a bailiff should be made in writing to the court officer on the prescribed form and accompanied by the relevant fee. The request should also be accompanied by-

(a)   evidence that [email service (if applicable) and][1] postal service has been attempted and failed; or
(b)   if postal service has not been attempted, an explanation as to why postal service is not considered appropriate in the circumstances of the case.

11.4 A request will rarely be granted where the applicant is legally represented and it will be necessary for the representative to show why service by bailiff is required rather than by a process server.

NOTES

Amendments.[1] Words inserted: FPR Update No 2 of 2022, 23 February 2022.

Proof of personal service by bailiff

12.1 Once service of the application has been effected or attempted by the bailiff he must file a certificate of service in the issuing court.

12.2 If the respondent fails to sign and return an acknowledgment of service to the court office and –

(a)   the certificate contains a signature of receipt of the application by the respondent; or
(b)   the identity of the respondent is to be proved by a photograph supplied by the applicant,

the applicant must prove the signature or photograph in the [statement][1] filed by the applicant under rule 7.19(4).

NOTES

Amendments.[1] Word substituted: FPR 2010 2nd Update, 6 April 2012.

****

Service of application on children and protected parties

14.1 A document served in accordance with rule 6.14(7) must be endorsed with the notice contained in paragraph 9.1.

ANNEX

Service on Members of the Regular Forces

1 The following information is for litigants and legal representatives who wish to serve legal documents in civil proceedings in the courts of England and Wales on parties to the proceedings who are (or who, at the material time, were) members of the regular forces (as defined in the Armed Forces Act 2006).

2 The proceedings may take place in the [family][1] court or the High Court, and the documents to be served may be claim forms, interim application notices and pre-action application notices. Proceedings for divorce or maintenance and proceedings in the Family Courts generally are subject to special rules as to service which are explained in a practice direction issued by the Senior District Judge of the Principal Registry on 26 June 1979.

(now see Practice Direction 1 Maintenance Orders: Service Personnel; 2 Disclosure of Addresses [1995] 2 FLR 813.)

3 In this Annex, the person wishing to effect service is referred to as the 'claimant' and the member of the regular forces to be served is referred to as 'the member'; the expression 'overseas' means outside the United Kingdom.

Enquiries as to address

4 As a first step, the claimant's legal representative will need to find out where the member is serving, if this is not already known. For this purpose the claimant's legal representative should write to the appropriate officer of the Ministry of Defence as specified in paragraph 10 below.

5 The letter of enquiry should in every case show that the writer is a legal representative and that the enquiry is made solely with a view to the service of legal documents in civil proceedings.

6 In all cases the letter must give the full name, service number, rank or rate, and Ship, Arm or Trade, Regiment or Corps and Unit or as much of this information as is available. Failure to quote the service number and the rank or rate may result either in failure to identify the member or in considerable delay.

7 The letter must contain an undertaking by the legal representative that, if the address is given, it will be used solely for the purpose of issuing and serving documents in the proceedings and that so far as is possible the legal representative will disclose the address only to the court and not to the claimant or to any other person or body. A legal representative in the service of a public authority or private company must undertake that the address will be used solely for the purpose of issuing and serving documents in the proceedings and that the address will not be disclosed so far as is possible to any other part of the legal representative's employing organisation or to any other person but only to the court. Normally on receipt of the required information and undertaking the appropriate office will give the service address.

8 If the legal representative does not give the undertaking, the only information that will be given is whether the member is at that time serving in England or Wales, Scotland, Northern Ireland or overseas.

9 It should be noted that a member's address which ends with a British Forces Post Office address and reference (BFPO) will nearly always indicate that the member is serving overseas.

10 The letter of enquiry should be addressed as follows –

Royal Navy and Royal Marine Officers, Ratings and Other Ranks
Director Naval Personnel
Fleet Headquarters
MP 3.1
Leach Building
Whale Island
Portsmouth
Hampshire
PO2 8BY

Army Officers and other Ranks –
Army Personnel Centre
Disclosures 1
MP 520
Kentigern House
65 Brown Street
Glasgow
G2 8EX

Royal Air Force Officers and Other Ranks –
Manning 22E
RAF Disclosures
Room 221B
Trenchard Hall
RAF Cranwell
Sleaford
Lincolnshire
NG34 8HB

Assistance in serving documents on members

11 Once the claimant's legal representative has ascertained the member's address, the legal representative may use that address as the address for service by post, in cases where this method of service is allowed by the Civil Procedure Rules. There are, however, some situations in which service of the proceedings, whether in the High Court or in the [family][1] court, must be effected personally; in these cases an appointment will have to be sought, through the Commanding Officer of the Unit, Establishment or Ship concerned, for the purpose of effecting service. The procedure for obtaining an appointment is described below, and it applies whether personal service is to be effected by the claimant's legal representative or the legal representative's agent or by a court bailiff, or, in the case of proceedings served overseas (with the leave of the court) through the British Consul or the foreign judicial authority.

12 The procedure for obtaining an appointment to effect personal service is by application to the Commanding Officer of the Unit, Establishment or Ship in which the member is serving. The Commanding Officer may grant permission for the document server to enter the Unit, Establishment or Ship but if this is not appropriate the Commanding Officer may offer arrangements for the member to attend at a place in the vicinity of the Unit, Establishment or Ship in order that the member may be served. If suitable arrangements cannot be made the legal

representative will have evidence that personal service is impracticable, which may be useful in an application for service by an alternative method or at an alternative place.

General

13 Subject to the procedure outlined in paragraphs 11 and 12, there are no special arrangements to assist in the service of legal documents when a member is outside the United Kingdom. The appropriate office will, however, give an approximate date when the member is likely to return to the United Kingdom.

14 It sometimes happens that a member has left the regular forces by the time an enquiry as to address is made. If the claimant's legal representative confirms that the proceedings result from an occurrence when the member was in the regular forces and the legal representative gives the undertaking referred to in paragraph 7, the last known private address after discharge will normally be provided. In no other case, however, will the Ministry of Defence disclose the private address of a member of the regular forces.

Service on Members of United States Air Force

15 In addition to the information contained in the memorandum of 26 July 1979, and after some doubts having been expressed as to the correct procedure to be followed by persons having civil claims against members of the United States Air Force in England and Wales, the Lord Chancellor's Office (as it was then) issued the following notes for guidance with the approval of the appropriate United States authorities.

16 Instructions have been issued by the United States authorities to the commanding officers of all their units in England and Wales that every facility is to be given for the service of documents in civil proceedings on members of the United States Air Force. The proper course to be followed by a creditor or other person having a claim against a member of the United States Air Force is for that person to communicate with the commanding officer or, where the unit concerned has a legal officer, with the legal officer of the defendant's unit requesting the provision of facilities for the service of documents on the defendant. It is not possible for the United States authorities to act as arbitrators when a civil claim is made against a member of their forces. It is, therefore, essential that the claim should either be admitted by the defendant or judgment should be obtained on it, whether in the High Court or [the family]1 court. If a claim has been admitted or judgment has been obtained and the claimant has failed to obtain satisfaction within a reasonable period, the claimant's proper course is then to write to: Office of the Staff Judge Advocate, Headquarters, Third Air Force, R.A.F. Mildenhall, Suffolk, enclosing a copy of the defendant's written admission of the claim or, as the case may be, a copy of the judgment. Steps will then be taken by the Staff Judge Advocate to ensure that the matter is brought to the defendant's attention with a view to prompt satisfaction of the claim.

NOTES

Amendments.[1] Text substituted: FPR Update, April 2014.

PART II – Statutory instruments

Practice Direction 6B –
Service out of the Jurisdiction

This Practice Direction supplements FPR Part 6, Chapters 4

Contents of this Practice Direction

Scope of this Practice Direction	Paragraph 1
...[1]	...[1]
Documents to be filed under rule 6.46(2)(c)	Paragraph 3
Service in a Commonwealth State or British Overseas Territory	Paragraph 4
Period for responding to an application form	Paragraph 5
Service of application notices and orders	Paragraph 6
Period for responding to an application notice	Paragraph 7
Further information	Paragraph 8

NOTES

Amendment.[1] Entries omitted repealed: FPR Update, March 2019.

Scope of this Practice Direction

1.1 This Practice Direction supplements Chapter 4 (service out of the jurisdiction) of Part 6.

> (Practice Direction 6A contains relevant provisions supplementing rule 6.43(2) in relation to the method of service on a party in Scotland or Northern Ireland.)

...[1]

2.1 ...[1]

2.2 ...[1]

2.3 ...[1]

NOTES

Amendment.[1] Paragraphs omitted repealed: FPR Update, March 2019.

Documents to be filed under rule 6.46(2)

3.1 A duplicate of –

   (a)   the application form or other document to be served under rule 6.45(1) or (2);
   (b)   any documents accompanying the application or other document referred to in paragraph (a); and
   (c)   any translation required by rule 6.47;

must be provided for each party to be served out of the jurisdiction, together with forms for responding to the application.

3.2 Some countries require legalisation of the document to be served and some require a formal letter of request which must be signed by the Senior Master. Any queries on this should be addressed to the Foreign Process Section (Room E02) at the Royal Courts of Justice.

Service in a Commonwealth State or British Overseas Territory

4.1 The judicial authorities of certain Commonwealth States which are not a party to the Hague Convention require service to be in accordance with rule 6.45(1) (b)(i) and not 6.45(3). A list of such countries can be obtained from the Foreign Process Section (Room E02) at the Royal Courts of Justice.

4.2 The list of British overseas territories is contained in Schedule 6 to the British Nationality Act 1981. For ease of reference these are –

   (a)   Anguilla;
   (b)   Bermuda;
   (c)   British Antarctic Territory;
   (d)   British Indian Ocean Territory;
   (e)   Cayman Islands;
   (f)   Falkland Islands;
   (g)   Gibraltar;
   (h)   Montserrat;
   (i)   Pitcairn, Henderson, Ducie and Oeno Islands;
   (j)   St. Helena, Ascension and Tristan da Cunha;
   (k)   South Georgia and the South Sandwich Islands;
   (l)   Sovereign Base Areas of Akrotiri and Dhekelia;
   (m)   Turks and Caicos Islands;
   (n)   Virgin Islands.

Period for responding to an application form

5.1 Where rule 6.42 applies, the period within which the respondent must file an acknowledgment of service or an answer to the application is the number of days listed in the Table after service of the application.

5.2 Where an application is served out of the jurisdiction any statement as to the period for responding to the claim contained in any of the forms required by the Family Procedure Rules to accompany the application must specify the period prescribed under rule 6.42.

Service of application notices and orders

6.1 The provisions of Chapter 4 of Part 6 (special provisions about service out of the jurisdiction) also apply to service out of the jurisdiction of an application notice or order.

6.2 Where an application notice is to be served out of the jurisdiction in accordance with Chapter 4 of Part 6 the court must have regard to the country in which the application notice is to be served in setting the date for the hearing of the application and giving any direction about service of the respondent's evidence.

PART II – Statutory instruments

Period for responding to an application notice

7.1 Where an application notice or order is served out of the jurisdiction, the period for responding is 7 days less than the number of days listed in the Table.

Further information

8.1 Further information concerning service out of the jurisdiction can be obtained from the Foreign Process Section, Room E02, Royal Courts of Justice, Strand, London WC2A 2LL (telephone 020 7947 6691).

TABLE

Place or country	Number of days
Afghanistan	23
Albania	25
Algeria	22
Andorra	21
Angola	22
Anguilla	31
Antigua and Barbuda	23
Antilles (Netherlands)	31
Argentina	22
Armenia	21
Ascension Island	31
Australia	25
Austria	21
Azerbaijan	22
Azores	23
Bahamas	22
Bahrain	22
Balearic Islands	21
Bangladesh	23
Barbados	23
Belarus	21
Belgium	21
Belize	23
Benin	25
Bermuda	31
Bhutan	28
Bolivia	23

Place or country	Number of days
Bosnia and Herzegovina	21
Botswana	23
Brazil	22
British Virgin Islands	31
Brunei	25
Bulgaria	23
Burkina Faso	23
Burma	23
Burundi	22
Cambodia	28
Cameroon	22
Canada	22
Canary Islands	22
Cape Verde	25
Caroline Islands	31
Cayman Islands	31
Central African Republic	25
Chad	25
Chile	22
China	24
China (Hong Kong)	31
China (Macau)	31
China (Taiwan)	23
China (Tibet)	34
Christmas Island	27
Cocos (Keeling) Islands	41
Colombia	22
Comoros	23
Congo (formerly Congo Brazzaville or French Congo)	25
Congo (Democratic Republic)	25
Corsica	21
Costa Rica	23
Croatia	21
Cuba	24
Cyprus	31
Czech Republic	21

PART II – Statutory instruments

Place or country	Number of days
Denmark	21
Djibouti	22
Dominica	23
Dominican Republic	23
East Timor	25
Ecuador	22
Egypt	22
El Salvador	25
Equatorial Guinea	23
Eritrea	22
Estonia	21
Ethiopia	22
Falkland Islands and Dependencies	31
Faroe Islands	31
Fiji	23
Finland	24
France	21
French Guyana	31
French Polynesia	31
French West Indies	31
Gabon	25
Gambia	22
Georgia	21
Germany	21
Ghana	22
Gibraltar	31
Greece	21
Greenland	31
Grenada	24
Guatemala	24
Guernsey	21
Guinea	22
Guinea-Bissau	22
Guyana	22
Haiti	23
Holland (Netherlands)	21

Place or country	Number of days
Honduras	24
Hungary	22
Iceland	22
India	23
Indonesia	22
Iran	22
Iraq	22
Ireland (Republic of)	21
Ireland (Northern)	21
Isle of Man	21
Israel	22
Italy	21
Ivory Coast	22
Jamaica	22
Japan	23
Jersey	21
Jordan	23
Kazakhstan	21
Kenya	22
Kiribati	23
Korea (North)	28
Korea (South)	24
Kosovo	21
Kuwait	22
Kyrgyzstan	21
Laos	30
Latvia	21
Lebanon	22
Lesotho	23
Liberia	22
Libya	21
Liechtenstein	21
Lithuania	21
Luxembourg	21
Macedonia	21
Madagascar	23

PART II – Statutory instruments

Place or country	Number of days
Madeira	31
Malawi	23
Malaysia	24
Maldives	26
Mali	25
Malta	21
Mariana Islands	26
Marshall Islands	32
Mauritania	23
Mauritius	22
Mexico	23
Micronesia	23
Moldova	21
Monaco	21
Mongolia	24
Montenegro	21
Montserrat	31
Morocco	22
Mozambique	23
Namibia	23
Nauru	36
Nepal	23
Netherlands	21
Nevis	24
New Caledonia	31
New Zealand	26
New Zealand Island Territories	50
Nicaragua	24
Niger (Republic of)	25
Nigeria	22
Norfolk Island	31
Norway	21
Oman (Sultanate of)	22
Pakistan	23
Palau	23
Panama	26

Place or country	Number of days
Papua New Guinea	26
Paraguay	22
Peru	22
Philippines	23
Pitcairn, Henderson, Ducie and Oeno Islands	31
Poland	21
Portugal	21
Portuguese Timor	31
Puerto Rico	23
Qatar	23
Reunion	31
Romania	22
Russia	21
Rwanda	23
Sabah	23
St. Helena	31
St. Kitts and Nevis	24
St. Lucia	24
St. Pierre and Miquelon	31
St. Vincent and the Grenadines	24
Samoa (U.S.A. Territory) (See also Western Samoa)	30
San Marino	21
Sao Tome and Principe	25
Sarawak	28
Saudi Arabia	24
Scotland	21
Senegal	22
Serbia	21
Seychelles	22
Sierra Leone	22
Singapore	22
Slovakia	21
Slovenia	21
Society Islands (French Polynesia)	31
Solomon Islands	29
Somalia	22

PART II – Statutory instruments

Place or country	Number of days
South Africa	22
South Georgia (Falkland Island Dependencies)	31
South Orkneys	21
South Shetlands	21
Spain	21
Spanish Territories of North Africa	31
Sri Lanka	23
Sudan	22
Surinam	22
Swaziland	22
Sweden	21
Switzerland	21
Syria	23
Tajikistan	21
Tanzania	22
Thailand	23
Togo	22
Tonga	30
Trinidad and Tobago	23
Tristan Da Cunha	31
Tunisia	22
Turkey	21
Turkmenistan	21
Turks & Caicos Islands	31
Tuvalu	23
Uganda	22
Ukraine	21
United Arab Emirates	22
United States of America	22
Uruguay	22
Uzbekistan	21
Vanuatu	29
Vatican City State	21
Venezuela	22
Vietnam	28
Virgin Islands – U.S.A	24

Place or country	Number of days
Wake Island	25
Western Samoa	34
Yemen (Republic of)	30
Zaire	25
Zambia	23
Zimbabwe	22

ANNEX – ...[1]

...[1]

NOTES
Amendment.[1] Annex omitted repealed: FPR Update, March 2019.

Practice Direction 6C –
Disclosure of Addresses by Government Departments 13 February 1989 [as amended by Practice Direction 20 July 1995]

This Practice Direction supplements FPR Part 6

The arrangements set out in the Registrar's Direction of 26 April 1988 whereby the court may request the disclosure of addresses by government departments have been further extended. These arrangements will now cover:

(a) tracing the address of a person in proceedings against whom another person is seeking to obtain or enforce an order for financial provision either for himself or herself or for the children of the former marriage; and,

(b) tracing the whereabouts of a child, or the person with whom the child is said to be, in proceedings under the Child Abduction and Custody Act 1985 or in which a [Part I order] is being sought or enforced.

Requests for such information will be made officially by the [district judge]. The request, in addition to giving the information mentioned below, should certify:

1 In financial provision applications either

(a) that a financial provision order is in existence, but cannot be enforced because the person against whom the order has been made cannot be traced; or

(b) that the applicant has filed or issued a notice, [application][1] or originating summons containing an application for financial provision which cannot be served because the respondent cannot be traced.

[A 'financial provision order' means any of the orders mentioned in s 21 of the Matrimonial Causes Act 1973, except an order under s 27(6) of that Act].

2 *In wardship proceedings* that the child is the subject of wardship proceedings and cannot be traced, and is believed to be with the person whose address is sought.

3 (*deleted*)

The following notes set out the information required by those departments which are likely to be of the greatest assistance to an applicant.

NOTES

Amendment.[1] Word substituted: FPR Update No 2 of 2022, 23 February 2022.

(1) Department of Social Security

The department most likely to be able to assist is the Department of Social Security, whose records are the most comprehensive and complete. The possibility of identifying one person amongst so many will depend on the particulars given. An address will not be supplied by the department unless it is satisfied from the particulars given that the record of the person has been reliably identified.

The applicant or his solicitor should therefore be asked to supply as much as possible of the following information about the person sought:

(i)   National Insurance number;
(ii)   surname;
(iii)   forenames in full;
(iv)   date of birth (or, if not known, approximate age);
(v)   last known address, with date when living there;
(vi)   any other known address(es) with dates;
(vii)   if the person sought is a war pensioner, his war pension and service particulars (if known);

and in applications for financial provision:

(viii) the exact date of the marriage and the wife's forenames.

Enquiries should be sent by the [district judge] to:

Contribution Agency
Special Section A, Room 101B
Longbenton
Newcastle upon Tyne
NE98 1YX

The department will be prepared to search if given full particulars of the person's name and date of birth, but the chances of accurate identification are increased by the provision of more identifying information.

Second requests for records to be searched, provided that a reasonable interval has elapsed, will be met by the Department of Social Security.

Income Support [/Supplementary Benefit]

Where, in the case of applications for financial provision, the wife is or has been in receipt of [income support/supplementary benefit], it would be advisable in the first instance to make enquiries of the manager of the local Social Security office for the area in which she resides in order to avoid possible duplication of enquiries.

(2) [Office for National Statistics]

National Health Service Central Register

[The Office for National Statistics] administers the National Health Service Central Register for the Department of Health. The records held in the Central Register include individuals' names, with dates of birth and National Health Service number, against a record of the Family Practitioner Committee area where the patient is currently registered with a National Health Service doctor. The Central Register does not hold individual patients' addresses, but can advise courts of the last Family Practitioner Committee area registration. Courts can then apply for information about addresses to the appropriate Family Practitioner Committee for independent action.

When application is made for the disclosure of Family Practitioner Committee area registrations from these records the applicant or his solicitor should supply as much as possible of the following information about the person sought:

(i)   National Health Service number;
(ii) surname;
(iii) forenames in full;
(iv) date of birth (or, if not known, approximate age);
(v)   last known address;
(vi) mother's maiden name.

Enquiries should be sent by the [district judge] to:

[The Office for National Statistics]
National Health Service Central Register
Smedley Hydro, Trafalgar Road
Southport
Merseyside PR8 2HH

(3) Passport Office

If all reasonable enquiries, including the aforesaid methods, have failed to reveal an address, or if there are strong grounds for believing that the person sought may have made a recent application for a passport, enquiries may be made to the Passport Office. The applicant or his solicitor should provide as much of the following information about the person as possible:

(i)   surname;
(ii) forenames in full;
(iii) date of birth (or, if not known, approximate age);
(iv) place of birth;
(v)   occupation;
(vi) whether known to have travelled abroad, and, if so, the destination and dates;

PART II – Statutory instruments

(vii) last known address, with date living there;
(viii) any other known address(es), with dates.

The applicant or his solicitor must also undertake in writing that information given in response to the enquiry will be used solely for the purpose for which it was requested, ie to assist in tracing the husband in connection with the making or enforcement of a financial provision order or in tracing a child in connection with a [Part 1 order] or wardship proceedings, as the case may be.

Enquiries should be sent to:

The Chief Passport Officer
[UK Passport Agency]
Home Office
Clive House, Petty France
London SW1H 9HD

(4) Ministry of Defence

In cases where the person sought is known to be serving or to have recently served in any branch of HM Forces, the solicitor representing the applicant may obtain the address for service of financial provision or [Part I] and wardship proceedings direct from the appropriate service department. In the case of army servicemen, the solicitor can obtain a list of regiments and of the various manning and record offices from the Officer in Charge, Central Manning Support Office, Higher Barracks, Exeter EC4 4ND.

The solicitor's request should be accompanied by a written undertaking that the address will be used for the purpose of service of process in those proceedings and that so far as is possible the solicitor will disclose the address only to the court and not to the applicant or any other person, except in the normal course of the proceedings.

Alternatively, if the solicitor wishes to serve process on the person's commanding officer under the provisions contained in s 101 of the Naval Act 1957, s 153 of the Army Act 1955 and s 153 of the Air Force Act 1955 (all of which as amended by s 62 of the Armed Forces Act 1971) he may obtain that officer's address in the same way.

Where the applicant is acting in person the appropriate service department is prepared to disclose the address of the person sought, or that of his commanding officer, to a [district judge] on receipt of an assurance that the applicant has given an undertaking that the information will be used solely for the purpose of serving process in the proceedings.

In all cases, the request should include details of the person's full name, service number, rank or rating, and his ship, arm or trade, corps, regiment or unit or as much of this information as is available. The request should also include details of his date of birth, or, if not known, his age, his date of entry into the service and, if no longer serving, the date of discharge, and any other information, such as his last known address. Failure to quote the service number and the rank or rating may result in failure to identify the serviceman or at least in considerable delay.

Enquiries should be addressed as follows:

[(*a*) Officers of Royal Navy and Women's Royal Naval Service

The Naval Secretary
Room 161
Victory Building
HM Naval Base
Portsmouth
Hants PO1 3LS

Ratings in the Royal Navy
WRNS Ratings
QARNNS Ratings

Captain
Naval Drafting
Centurion Building
Grange Road
Gosport
Hants PO13 9XA

RN Medical and Dental Officers

The Medical Director General (Naval)
Room 114
Victory Building
HM Naval Base
Portsmouth
Hants PO1 3LS

Naval Chaplains

Director General
Naval Chaplaincy Service
Room 201
Victory Building
HM Naval Base
Portsmouth
Hants PO1 3LS

(*b*) Royal Marine Officers

The Naval Secretary
Room 161
Victory Building
HM Naval Base
Portsmouth
Hants PO1 3LS

Royal Marine Ranks

HQRM (DRORM)
West Battery
Whale Island
Portsmouth
Hants PO2 8DX

(*c*) Army Officers (including WRAC and QARANC)

Army Officer Documentation Office
Index Department
Room F7
Government Buildings
Stanmore
Middlesex

Other Ranks, Army	The Manning and Record Office which is appropriate to the Regiment or Corps
(d) Royal Air Force Officers and Other Ranks Women's Royal Air Force Officers and Other Ranks (including PMRA FNS)	Ministry of Defence RAF Personnel Management 2b1(a) (RAF) Building 248 RAF Innsworth Gloucester GL3 1EZ]

General notes

Records held by other departments are less likely to be of use, either because of their limited scope or because individual records cannot readily be identified. If, however, the circumstances suggest that the address may be known to another department, application may be made to it by the [district judge], all relevant particulars available being given.

When the department is able to supply the address of the person sought to the [district judge], it will be passed on by him to the applicant's solicitor (or, in proper cases, direct to the applicant if acting in person) on an understanding to use it only for the purpose of the proceedings.

Nothing in this practice direction affects the service in matrimonial causes of petitions which do not contain any application for financial provision, etc. The existing arrangements whereby the Department of Social Security will at the request of the solicitor forward a letter by ordinary post to a party's last known address remain in force in such cases.

The Registrar's Direction of 26 April 1988 is hereby revoked.

Issued [in its original form] with the concurrence of the Lord Chancellor.

NOTES

Amendments. FPR PD6C.

****

PART 8
PROCEDURE FOR MISCELLANEOUS APPLICATIONS

Chapter 1
Procedure

8.1 Procedure

Subject to rules 8.13 and 8.24, applications to which this Part applies must be made in accordance with the Part 19 procedure.

****

Chapter 5
Declarations

8.18 Scope of this Chapter

The rules in this Chapter apply to applications made in accordance with –

(a) section 55 of the 1986 Act (declarations as to marital status) and section 58 of the 2004 Act (declarations as to civil partnership status);

(b) section 55A of the 1986 Act (declarations of parentage);

(c) section 56(1)(b) and (2) of the 1986 Act (declarations of legitimacy or legitimation); and

(d) section 57 of the 1986 Act (declaration as to adoptions effected overseas).

8.19

…[1]

NOTES

Amendment.[1] Rule omitted: SI 2013/3204.

8.20 Who the parties are

(1) In relation to the proceedings set out in column 1 of the following table, column 2 sets out who the respondents to those proceedings will be.

Proceedings	*Respondent*
Applications for declarations as to marital or civil partnership status.	The other party to the marriage or civil partnership in question or, where the applicant is a third party, both parties to the marriage or civil partnership.
Applications for declarations of parentage.	[(i) The person whose parentage is in issue [except where that person is a child][2]; and (ii) any person who is or is alleged to be the parent of the person whose parentage is in issue, except where that person is the applicant [or is a child][2].][1]
Applications for declarations of legitimacy or legitimation.	The applicant's father and mother or the survivor of them.
Applications for declarations as to adoption effected overseas.	The person(s) whom the applicant is claiming are or are not the applicant's adoptive parents.

[(Under rule 16.2 the court may make a child a party to certain proceedings (including applications for declarations of parentage) where it considers that to be in the best interests of the child.)][2]

(2) The applicant must include in his application particulars of every person whose interest may be affected by the proceedings and his relationship to the applicant.

(3) The acknowledgment of service filed under rule 19.5 must give details of any other persons the respondent considers should be made a party to the application or be given notice of the application.

(4) Upon receipt of the acknowledgment of service, the court must give directions as to any other persons who should be made a respondent to the application or be given notice of the proceedings.

(5) A person given notice of proceedings under paragraph (4) may, within 21 days beginning with the date on which the notice was served, apply to be joined as a party.

(6) No directions may be given as to the future management of the case under rule 19.9 until the expiry of the notice period in paragraph (5).

NOTES

Amendments.[1] Words substituted: SI 2012/679. 2 Words inserted: SI 2016/901.

8.21 The role of the Attorney General

(1) The applicant must, except in the case of an application for a declaration of parentage, send a copy of the application and all accompanying documents to the Attorney General at least one month before making the application.

(2) The Attorney General may, when deciding whether to intervene in the proceedings, inspect any document filed at court relating to any family proceedings mentioned in the declaration proceedings.

(3) If the court is notified that the Attorney General wishes to intervene in the proceedings, a court officer must send the Attorney General a copy of any subsequent documents filed at court.

(4) The court must, when giving directions under rule 8.20(4), consider whether to ask the Attorney General to argue any question relating to the proceedings.

(5) If the court makes a request to the Attorney General under paragraph (4) and the Attorney General agrees to that request, the Attorney General must serve a summary of the argument on all parties to the proceedings.

8.22 Declarations of parentage

(1) If the applicant or the person whose parentage or parenthood is in issue, is known by a name other than that which appears in that person's birth certificate, that other name must also be stated in any order and declaration of parentage.

(2) A court officer must send a copy of a declaration of parentage and the application to the Registrar General within 21 days beginning with the date on which the declaration was made.

****

Chapter 9
Application for Consent to Marriage of a Child or to Registration of Civil
Partnership of a Child

8.41 Scope of this Chapter

The rules in this Chapter apply to an application under –

(a)   section 3 of the Marriage Act 1949; or
(b)   paragraph 3, 4 or 10 of Schedule 2 to the 2004 Act.

8.42 Child acting without a children's guardian

The child may bring an application without a children's guardian, unless the court directs otherwise.

8.43 Who the respondents are

Where an application follows a refusal to give consent to –

(a)   the marriage of a child; or
(b)   a child registering as the civil partner of another person,

every person who has refused consent will be a respondent to the application.

PART 9
APPLICATIONS FOR A FINANCIAL REMEDY

****

Chapter 3
Applications for Financial Remedies for Children

9.10 Application by parent, guardian etc for financial remedy in respect of children

(1) The following people may apply for a financial remedy in respect of a child –

(a)   a parent, guardian or special guardian of any child of the family;
(b)   any person [who is named in a child arrangements order as a person with whom a child of the family is to live]², and any applicant for such an order;
(c)   any other person who is entitled to apply for [a child arrangements order which names that person as a person with whom a child is to live]²;
(d)   a local authority, where an order has been made under section 31(1)(a) of the 1989 Act placing a child in its care;
(e)   the Official Solicitor, if appointed the children's guardian of a child of the family under rule 16.24; and
(f)   [subject to paragraph (1A),]¹ a child of the family who has been given permission to apply for a financial remedy.

PART II – Statutory instruments

[(1A) Where the application is –

(a)   for the variation of an order under section 2(1)(c), 6 or 7 of the 1978 Act or paragraph 2(1)(c) of, or Part 2 or 3 of, Schedule 6 to the 2004 Act for periodical payments in respect of a child;

(b)   the application is made by the child in question; and

(c)   the child in question is aged 16 or over,

the child does not require permission to make the application.][1]

(2) …[2]

NOTES

Amendments.[1] Words and paragraph inserted: SI 2013/3204. [2] Words substituted and paragraph omitted: SI 2014/843.

Modification. Rule 9.10 modified in the application for variation of a maintenance order under s 20 of the Domestic Proceedings and Magistrates' Courts Act 1978 or Sch 6 to the Civil Partnership Act 2004 by the Magistrates' Courts (Enforcement or Variation of Orders Made in Family Proceedings and Miscellaneous Provisions) Rules 2011, SI 2011/1329, rr 69, 83.

9.11 Children to be separately represented on certain applications

(1) Where an application for a financial remedy includes an application for an order for a variation of settlement, the court must, unless it is satisfied that the proposed variation does not adversely affect the rights or interests of any child concerned, direct that the child be separately represented on the application.

(2) On any other application for a financial remedy the court may direct that the child be separately represented on the application.

(3) Where a direction is made under paragraph (1) or (2), the court may if the person to be appointed so consents, appoint –

(a)   a person other than the Official Solicitor; or

(b)   the Official Solicitor,

to be a children's guardian and rule 16.24(5) and (6) and rules 16.25 to 16.28 apply as appropriate to such an appointment.

****

PART 12
[CHILDREN PROCEEDINGS][1] EXCEPT PARENTAL ORDER PROCEEDINGS AND PROCEEDINGS FOR APPLICATIONS IN ADOPTION, PLACEMENT AND RELATED PROCEEDINGS

Amendments.[1] Words substituted: SI 2012/3061.

Chapter 1
Interpretation and Application of this Part

12.1 Application of this Part

(1) The rules in this Part apply to –

(a) emergency proceedings;
(b) private law proceedings;
(c) public law proceedings;
(d) proceedings relating to the exercise of the court's inherent jurisdiction (other than applications for the court's permission to start such proceedings);
(e) proceedings relating to child abduction and the recognition and enforcement of decisions relating to custody under the European Convention;
(f) proceedings relating to ...[2] the 1996 Hague Convention in respect of children; and
(g) any other proceedings which may be referred to in a practice direction.

(Part 18 sets out the procedure for making an application for permission to bring proceedings.)
(Part 31 sets out the procedure for making applications for recognition and enforcement of judgments under ...[2] the 1996 Hague Convention.)

(2) The rules in Chapter 7 of this Part also apply to family proceedings which are not within paragraph (1) but which otherwise relate wholly or mainly to the maintenance or upbringing of a minor.

[(3) This Part is subject to any provision made by or pursuant to Part 41 (proceeding by electronic means).][1]

NOTES

Amendments.[1] Paragraph inserted: SI 2020/135. [2] Words omitted repealed: SI 2019/517.

12.2 Interpretation

In this Part –

'the 2006 Act' means the Childcare Act 2006;
['activity condition' has the meaning given to it by section 11C(2) of the 1989 Act;
'activity direction' has the meaning given to it by section 11A(3) of the 1989 Act;][1]
'advocate' means a person exercising a right of audience as a representative of, or on behalf of, a party;
'care proceedings' means proceedings for a care order under section 31(1)(a) of the 1989 Act;
['Case Management Order' means an order in the form referred to in Practice Direction 12A;][1]
'child assessment order' has the meaning assigned to it by section 43(2) of the 1989 Act;
...[1]
...[1]
'contribution order' has the meaning assigned to it by paragraph 23(2) of Schedule 2 to the 1989 Act;
'education supervision order' has the meaning assigned to it by section 36(2) of the 1989 Act;
'emergency proceedings' means proceedings for –

PART II – Statutory instruments

(a) the disclosure of information as to the whereabouts of a child under section 33 of the 1986 Act;

(b) an order authorising the taking charge of and delivery of a child under section 34 of the 1986 Act;

(c) an emergency protection order;

(d) an order under section 44(9)(b) of the 1989 Act varying a direction in an emergency protection order given under section 44(6) of that Act;

(e) an order under section 45(5) of the 1989 Act extending the period during which an emergency protection order is to have effect;

(f) an order under section 45(8) of the 1989 Act discharging an emergency protection order;

(g) an order under section 45(8A) of the 1989 Act varying or discharging an emergency protection order in so far as it imposes an exclusion requirement on a person who is not entitled to apply for the order to be discharged;

(h) an order under section 45(8B) of the 1989 Act varying or discharging an emergency protection order in so far as it confers a power of arrest attached to an exclusion requirement;

(i) warrants under sections 48(9) and 102(1) of the 1989 Act and under section 79 of the 2006 Act; or

(j) a recovery order under section 50 of the 1989 Act;

'emergency protection order' means an order under section 44 of the 1989 Act;

'enforcement order' has the meaning assigned to it by section 11J(2) of the 1989 Act;

'financial compensation order' means an order made under section 11O(2) of the 1989 Act;

'interim order' means an interim care order or an interim supervision order referred to in section 38(1) of the 1989 Act;

['Part 4 proceedings' means proceedings for –

(a) a care order, or the discharge of such an order, under section 39(1) of the 1989 Act;

(b) an order giving permission to change a child's surname or remove a child from the United Kingdom under section 33(7) of the 1989 Act;

(c) a supervision order, the discharge or variation of such an order under section 39(2) of the 1989 Act, or the extension of such an order under paragraph 6(3) of Schedule 3 to that Act;

(d) an order making provision regarding contact under section 34(2) to (4) of the 1989 Act or an order varying or discharging such an order under section 34(9) of that Act;

(e) an education supervision order, the extension of an education supervision order under paragraph 15(2) of Schedule 3 to the 1989 Act, or the discharge of such an order under paragraph 17(1) of Schedule 3 to that Act;

(f) an order varying directions made with an interim care order or interim supervision order under section 38(8)(b) of the 1989 Act;

(g)   an order under section 39(3) of the 1989 Act varying a supervision order in so far as it affects a person with whom the child is living but who is not entitled to apply for the order to be discharged;

(h)   an order under section 39(3A) of the 1989 Act varying or discharging an interim care order in so far as it imposes an exclusion requirement on a person who is not entitled to apply for the order to be discharged;

(i)   an order under section 39(3B) of the 1989 Act varying or discharging an interim care order in so far as it confers a power of arrest attached to an exclusion requirement; or

(j)   the substitution of a supervision order for a care order under section 39(4) of the 1989 Act;][1]

'private law proceedings' means proceedings for –

[(a)   a section 8 order except a child arrangements order to which section 9(6B) of the 1989 Act applies with respect to a child who is in the care of a local authority;][1]

(b)   a parental responsibility order under sections 4(1)(c), 4ZA(1)(c) or 4A(1)(b) of the 1989 Act or an order terminating parental responsibility under sections 4(2A), 4ZA(5) or 4A(3) of that Act;

(c)   an order appointing a child's guardian under section 5(1) of the 1989 Act or an order terminating the appointment under section 6(7) of that Act;

(d)   an order giving permission to change a child's surname or remove a child from the United Kingdom under sections 13(1) or 14C(3) of the 1989 Act;

(e)   a special guardianship order except where that order relates to a child who is subject of a care order;

(f)   an order varying or discharging such an order under section 14D of the 1989 Act;

(g)   an enforcement order;

(h)   a financial compensation order;

(i)   an order under paragraph 9 of Schedule A1 to the 1989 Act following a breach of an enforcement order;

(j)   an order under Part 2 of Schedule A1 to the 1989 Act revoking or amending an enforcement order; or

(k)   an order that a warning notice be attached to a [child arrangements order][1];

'public law proceedings' means [Part 4 proceedings and][1] proceedings for –

[(a)   a child arrangements order to which section 9(6B) of the 1989 Act applies with respect to a child who is in the care of a local authority;][1]

(b)   a special guardianship order relating to a child who is the subject of a care order;

(c)   a secure accommodation order under section 25 of the 1989 Act;

(d)–(m) ...[1]

(n)   a child assessment order, or the variation or discharge of such an order under section 43(12) of the 1989 Act;

PART II – Statutory instruments

(o)   an order permitting the local authority to arrange for any child in its care to live outside England and Wales under paragraph 19(1) of Schedule 2 to the 1989 Act;

(p)   a contribution order, or revocation of such an order under paragraph 23(8) of Schedule 2 to the 1989 Act;

(q)   an appeal under paragraph 8(1) of Schedule 8 to the 1989 Act;

'special guardianship order' has the meaning assigned to it by section 14A(1) of the 1989 Act;

'supervision order' has the meaning assigned to it by section 31(11) of the 1989 Act;

'supervision proceedings' means proceedings for a supervision order under section 31(1)(b) of the 1989 Act;

'warning notice' means a notice attached to an order pursuant to section 8(2) of the Children and Adoption Act 2006.

(The 1980 Hague Convention, the 1996 Hague Convention, the Council Regulation, and the European Convention are defined in rule 2.3.)

NOTES

Amendments.[1] Definitions inserted, substituted and omitted, sub-paragraphs substituted and omitted, words inserted and substituted: SI 2014/843.

Modification. Rule 12.2 modified in an application under para 23(8) of Sch 2 to the Children Act 1989 to vary a contribution order by the Magistrates' Courts (Enforcement or Variation of Orders Made in Family Proceedings and Miscellaneous Provisions) Rules 2011, SI 2011/1329, rr 78, 83.

Chapter 2
General Rules

12.3 Who the parties are

(1) In relation to the proceedings set out in column 1 of the following table, column 2 sets out who may make the application and column 3 sets out who the respondents to those proceedings will be.

Proceedings for	*Applicants*	*Respondents*
A parental responsibility order (section 4(1)(c), 4ZA(1)(c), or section 4A(1)(b) of the 1989 Act).	The child's father; the step parent; or the child's parent (being a woman who is a parent by virtue of section 43 of the Human Fertilisation and Embryology Act 2008 and who is not a person to whom section 1(3) of the Family Law Reform Act 1987 applies) (sections 4(1)(c), 4ZA(1)(c) and 4A(1)(b) of the 1989 Act).	Every person whom the applicant believes to have parental responsibility for the child; where the child is the subject of a care order, every person whom the applicant believes to have had parental responsibility immediately prior to the making of the care order;

Proceedings for	Applicants	Respondents
		in the case of an application to extend, vary or discharge an order, the parties to the proceedings leading to the order which it is sought to have extended, varied or discharged;
		in the case of specified proceedings, the child.
An order terminating a parental responsibility order or agreement (section 4(2A), 4ZA(5) or section 4A(3) of the 1989 Act).	Any person who has parental responsibility for the child; or with the court's permission, the child (section 4(3), 4ZA(6) and section 4A(3) of the 1989 Act).	As above.
An order appointing a guardian (section 5(1) of the 1989 Act).	An individual who wishes to be appointed as guardian (section 5(1) of the 1989 Act).	As above.
An order terminating the appointment of a guardian (section 6(7) of the 1989 Act).	Any person who has parental responsibility for the child; or with the court's permission, the child (section 6(7) of the 1989 Act).	As above.
A section 8 order.	Any person who is entitled to apply for a section 8 order with respect to the child (section 10(4) to (7) of the 1989 Act); or with the court's permission, any person (section 10(2)(b) of the 1989 Act).	As above.
An enforcement order (section 11J of the 1989 Act).	A person who is, for the purposes of the [child arrangements order]², a person with whom the child concerned lives or is to live;	The person the applicant alleges has failed to comply with the [child arrangements order]².
	any person whose contact with the child concerned is provided for in the [child arrangements order]²;	
	any individual subject to a condition under section 11(7)(b) of the 1989 Act or [an activity]2 condition imposed by a [child arrangements order]²; or	

PART II – Statutory instruments

Proceedings for	Applicants	Respondents
	with the court's permission, the child (section 11J(5) of the 1989 Act).	
A financial compensation order (section 11O of the 1989 Act).	Any person who is, for the purposes of the [child arrangements order]², a person with whom the child concerned lives or is to live;	The person the applicant alleges has failed to comply with the [child arrangements order]².
	any person whose contact with the child concerned is provided for in the [child arrangements order]²;	
	any individual subject to a condition under section 11(7)(b) of the 1989 Act or [an activity]2 condition imposed by a [child arrangements order]²; or	
	with the court's permission, the child (section 11O(6) of the 1989 Act).	
An order permitting the child's name to be changed or the removal of the child from the United Kingdom (section 13(1), 14C(3) or 33(7) of the 1989 Act).	Any person (section 13(1), 14C(3), 33(7) of the 1989 Act).	As for a parental responsibility order.
A special guardianship order (section 14A of the 1989 Act).	Any guardian of the child; any individual [who is named in a child arrangements order as a person with whom the child is to live]²;	As above, and if a care order is in force with respect to the child, the child.
	any individual listed in subsection (5)(b) or (c) of section 10 (as read with subsection (10) of that section) of the 1989 Act;	
	a local authority foster parent with whom the child has lived for a period of at least one year immediately preceding the application; or	
	any person with the court's permission (section 14A(3) of the 1989 Act) (more than one such individual can apply jointly (section 14A(3) and (5) of that Act)).	

Proceedings for	Applicants	Respondents
Variation or discharge of a special guardianship order (section 14D of the 1989 Act).	The special guardian (or any of them, if there is more than one);	As above.
	any individual [who is named in a child arrangements order as a person with whom the child is to live;][2]	
	any individual within section 14D(1)(d) of the 1989 Act who has parental responsibility for the child;	
	the child, any parent or guardian of the child and any step-parent of the child who has acquired, and has not lost, parental responsibility by virtue of section 4A of that Act with the court's permission; or	
	any individual within section 14D(1)(d) of that Act who immediately before the making of the special guardianship order had, but no longer has, parental responsibility for the child with the court's permission.	
A secure accommodation order (section 25 of the 1989 Act).	The local authority which is looking after the child; or the Health Authority, [Secretary of State, National Health Service Commissioning Board, clinical commissioning group,][1] National Health Service Trust established under section 25 of the National Health Service Act 2006 or section 18(1) of the National Health Service (Wales) Act 2006, National Health Service Foundation Trust or any local authority providing [or arranging][1] accommodation for the child (unless the child is looked after by a local authority).	As above.

PART II – Statutory instruments

Proceedings for	Applicants	Respondents
A care or supervision order (section 31 of the 1989 Act).	Any local authority; the National Society for the Prevention of Cruelty to Children and any of its officers (section 31(1) of the 1989 Act); or any authorised person.	As above.
An order varying directions made with an interim care or interim supervision order (section 38(8)(b) of the 1989 Act).	The parties to proceedings in which directions are given under section 38(6) of the 1989 Act; or any person named in such a direction.	As above.
An order discharging a care order (section 39(1) of the 1989 Act).	Any person who has parental responsibility for the child; the child; or the local authority designated by the order (section 39(1) of the 1989 Act).	As above.
An order varying or discharging an interim care order in so far as it imposes an exclusion requirement (section 39(3A) of the 1989 Act).	A person to whom the exclusion requirement in the interim care order applies who is not entitled to apply for the order to be discharged (section 39(3A) of the 1989 Act).	As above.
An order varying or discharging an interim care order in so far as it confers a power of arrest attached to an exclusion requirement (section 39(3B) of the 1989 Act).	Any person entitled to apply for the discharge of the interim care order in so far as it imposes the exclusion requirement (section 39(3B) of the 1989 Act).	As above.
An order substituting a supervision order for a care order (section 39(4) of the 1989 Act).	Any person entitled to apply for a care order to be discharged under section 39(1) (section 39(4) of the 1989 Act).	As above.
A child assessment order (section 43(1) of the 1989 Act).	Any local authority; the National Society for the Prevention of Cruelty to Children and any of its officers; or	As above.
	any person authorised by order of the Secretary of State to bring the proceedings and any officer of a body who is so authorised (section 43(1) and (13) of the 1989 Act).	

Proceedings for	Applicants	Respondents
An order varying or discharging a child assessment order (section 43(12) of the 1989 Act).	The applicant for an order that has been made under section 43(1) of the 1989 Act; or	As above.
	the persons referred to in section 43(11) of the 1989 Act (section 43(12) of that Act).	
An emergency protection order (section 44(1) of the 1989 Act).	Any person (section 44(1) of the 1989 Act).	As for a parental responsibility order.
An order extending the period during which an emergency protection order is to have effect (section 45(4) of the 1989 Act).	Any person who – has parental responsibility for a child as the result of an emergency protection order; and	As above.
	is entitled to apply for a care order with respect to the child (section 45(4) of the 1989 Act).	
An order discharging an emergency protection order (section 45(8) of the 1989 Act).	The child; a parent of the child; any person who is not a parent of the child but who has parental responsibility for the child; or	As above.
	any person with whom the child was living before the making of the emergency protection order (section 45(8) of the 1989 Act).	
An order varying or discharging an emergency protection order in so far as it imposes the exclusion requirement (section 45(8A) of the 1989 Act).	A person to whom the exclusion requirement in the emergency protection order applies who is not entitled to apply for the emergency protection order to be discharged (section 45(8A) of the 1989 Act).	As above.
An order varying or discharging an emergency protection order in so far as it confers a power of arrest attached to an exclusion requirement (section 45(8B) of the 1989 Act).	Any person entitled to apply for the discharge of the emergency protection order in so far as it imposes the exclusion requirement (section 45(8B) of the 1989 Act).	As above.

Proceedings for	Applicants	Respondents
An emergency protection order by the police (section 46(7) of the 1989 Act).	The officer designated officer for the purposes of section 46(3)(e) of the 1989 Act (section 46(7) of the 1989 Act).	As above.
A warrant authorising a constable to assist in exercise of certain powers to search for children and inspect premises (section 48 of the 1989 Act).	Any person attempting to exercise powers under an emergency protection order who has been or is likely to be prevented from doing so by being refused entry to the premises concerned or refused access to the child concerned (section 48(9) of the 1989 Act).	As above.
A warrant authorising a constable to assist in exercise of certain powers to search for children and inspect premises (section 102 of the 1989 Act).	Any person attempting to exercise powers under the enactments mentioned in section 102(6) of the 1989 Act who has been or is likely to be prevented from doing so by being refused entry to the premises concerned or refused access to the child concerned (section 102(1) of that Act).	As above.
An order revoking an enforcement order (paragraph 4 of Schedule A1 to the 1989 Act).	The person subject to the enforcement order.	The person who was the applicant for the enforcement order; and where the child was a party to the proceedings in which the enforcement order was made, the child.
An order amending an enforcement order (paragraphs 5 to 7 of Schedule A1 to the 1989 Act).	The person subject to the enforcement order.	The person who was the applicant for the enforcement order. (Rule 12.33 makes provision about applications under paragraph 5 of Schedule A1 to the 1989 Act.)
An order following breach of an enforcement order (paragraph 9 of Schedule A1 to the 1989 Act).	Any person who is, for [the purposes of the child arrangements order]², the person with whom the child lives or is to live; any person whose contact with the child concerned is [provided for in the child arrangements order]²;	The person the applicant alleges has failed to comply with the unpaid work requirement imposed by an enforcement order; and where the child was a party to the proceedings in which the enforcement order was made, the child.

Proceedings for	Applicants	Respondents
	any individual subject to a condition under section 11(7)(b) of the 1989 Act or [an activity condition imposed by a child arrangements order;]² or	
	with the court's permission, the child (paragraph 9 of Schedule A1 to the 1989 Act).	
An order permitting the local authority to arrange for any child in its care to live outside England and Wales (Schedule 2, paragraph 19(1), to the 1989 Act).	The local authority (Schedule 2, paragraph 19(1), to the 1989 Act).	As for a parental responsibility order.
A contribution order (Schedule 2, paragraph 23(1), to the 1989 Act).	The local authority (Schedule 2, paragraph 23(1), to the 1989 Act).	As above and the contributor.
An order revoking a contribution order (Schedule 2, paragraph 23(8), to the 1989 Act).	The contributor; or the local authority.	As above.
An order relating to contact with the child in care and any named person (section 34(2) of the 1989 Act) or permitting the local authority to refuse contact (section 34(4) of that Act).	The local authority; or the child (section 34(2) or 34(4) of the 1989 Act).	As above; and the person whose contact with the child is the subject of the application.
An order relating to contact with the child in care (section 34(3) of the 1989 Act).	The child's parents; any guardian or special guardian of the child;	As above; and the person whose contact with the child is the subject of the application.
	any person who by virtue of section 4A of the 1989 Act has parental responsibility for the child;	
	[where there was a child arrangements order in force with respect to the child immediately before the care order was made, any person named in that order as a person with whom the child was to live;]2	

Proceedings for	Applicants	Respondents
	a person who by virtue of an order made in the exercise of the High Court's inherent jurisdiction with respect to children had care of the child immediately before the care order was made (section 34(3)(a) of the 1989 Act); or	
	with the court's permission, any person (section 34(3)(b) of that Act).	
An order varying or discharging an order for contact with a child in care under section 34 (section 34((9) of the 1989 Act).	The local authority; the child; or any person named in the order (section 34(9) of the 1989 Act).	As above; and the person whose contact with the child is the subject of the application.
An education supervision order (section 36 of the 1989 Act).	Any local authority (section 36(1) of the 1989 Act).	As above; and the child.
An order varying or discharging a supervision order (section 39(2) of the 1989 Act).	Any person who has parental responsibility for the child; the child; or the supervisor (section 39(2) of the 1989 Act).	As above; and the supervisor.
An order varying a supervision order in so far as it affects the person with whom the child is living (section 39(3) of the 1989 Act).	The person with whom the child is living who is not entitled to apply for the order to be discharged (section 39(3) of the 1989 Act).	As above; and the supervisor.
An order varying a direction under section 44(6) of the 1989 Act in an emergency protection order (section 44(9)(b) of that Act).	The parties to the application for the emergency protection order in respect of which it is sought to vary the directions; the children's guardian; the local authority in whose area the child is ordinarily resident; or any person who is named in the directions.	As above, and the parties to the application for the order in respect of which it is sought to vary the directions; any person who was caring for the child prior to the making of the order; and any person [named in a child arrangements order as a person with whom the child is to spend time or otherwise have contact and who][2] is affected by the direction which it is sought to have varied.

Proceedings for	Applicants	Respondents
A recovery order (section 50 of the 1989 Act).	Any person who has parental responsibility for the child by virtue of a care order or an emergency protection order; or	As above; and the person whom the applicant alleges to have effected or to have been or to be responsible for the taking or keeping of the child.
	where the child is in police protection the officer designated for the purposes of section 46(3)(e) of the 1989 Act (section 50(4) of the 1989 Act).	
An order discharging an education supervision order (Schedule 3, paragraph 17(1), to the 1989 Act).	The child concerned; a parent of the child; or the local authority concerned (Schedule 3, paragraph 17(1), to the 1989 Act).	As above; and the local authority concerned; and the child.
An order extending an education supervision order (Schedule 3, paragraph 15(2), to the 1989 Act).	The local authority in whose favour the education supervision order was made (Schedule 3, paragraph 15(2), to the 1989 Act).	As above; and the child.
An appeal under paragraph (8) of Schedule 8 to the 1989 Act.	A person aggrieved by the matters listed in paragraph 8(1) of Schedule 8 to the 1989 Act.	The appropriate local authority.
An order for the disclosure of information as to the whereabouts of a child under section 33 of the 1986 Act.	Any person with a legitimate interest in proceedings for an order under Part 1 of the 1986 Act; or	Any person alleged to have information as to the whereabouts of the child.
	a person who has registered an order made elsewhere in the United Kingdom or a specified dependent territory.	
An order authorising the taking charge of and delivery of a child under section 34 of the 1986 Act.	The person to whom the child is to be given up under section 34(1) of the 1986 Act.	As above; and the person who is required to give up the child in accordance with section 34(1) of the 1986 Act.
An order relating to the exercise of the court's inherent jurisdiction (including wardship proceedings).	A local authority (with the court's permission); any person with a genuine interest in or relation to the child; or the child (wardship proceedings only).	The parent or guardian of the child; any other person who has an interest in or relationship to the child; and the child (wardship proceedings only and with the court's permission as described at rule 12.37).

Proceedings for	Applicants	Respondents
A warrant under section 79 of the 2006 Act authorising any constable to assist Her Majesty's Chief Inspector for Education, Children's Services and Skills in the exercise of powers conferred on him by section 77 of the 2006 Act.	Her Majesty's Chief Inspector for Education, Children's Services and Skills.	Any person preventing or likely to prevent Her Majesty's Chief Inspector for Education, Children's Services and Skills from exercising powers conferred on him by section 77 of the 2006 Act.
An order in respect of a child under the 1980 Hague Convention.	Any person, institution or body who claims that a child has been removed or retained in breach of rights of custody or claims that there has been a breach of rights of access in relation to the child.	The person alleged to have brought the child into the United Kingdom; the person with whom the child is alleged to be; any parent or guardian of the child who is within the United Kingdom and is not otherwise a party;
		any person in whose favour a decision relating to custody has been made if that person is not otherwise a party; and any other person who appears to the court to have sufficient interest in the welfare of the child.
An order concerning the recognition and enforcement of decisions relating to custody under the European Convention.	Any person who has a court order giving that person rights of custody in relation to the child.	As above.
An application for the High Court to request transfer of jurisdiction under ...[3] Article 9 of the 1996 Hague Convention (rule 12.65).	Any person with sufficient interest in the welfare of the child and who would be entitled to make a proposed application in relation to that child, or who intends to seek the permission of the court to make such application if the transfer is agreed.	As directed by the court in accordance with rule 12.65.

Proceedings for	Applicants	Respondents
An application under rule 12.71 for a declaration as to the existence, or extent, of parental responsibility under Article 16 of the 1996 Convention.	Any interested person including a person who holds, or claims to hold, parental responsibility for the child under the law of another State which subsists in accordance with Article 16 of the 1996 Hague Convention following the child becoming habitually resident in a territorial unit of the United Kingdom.	Every person whom the applicant believes to have parental responsibility for the child; any person whom the applicant believes to hold parental responsibility for the child under the law of another State which subsists in accordance with Article 16 of the 1996 Hague Convention following the child becoming habitually resident in a territorial unit of the United Kingdom; and
		where the child is the subject of a care order, every person whom the applicant believes to have had parental responsibility immediately prior to the making of the care order.
A warning notice.	The person who is, for the purposes of the [child arrangements order]², the person with whom the child concerned lives or is to live; the person whose contact with the child concerned is provided for in the [child arrangements order]²;	Any person who was a party to the proceedings in which the [child arrangements]² order was made. (Rule 12.33 makes provision about applications for warning notices).
	any individual subject to a condition under section 11(7)(b) of the 1989 Act or [an activity]² condition imposed by the [child arrangements order]²; or with the court's permission, the child.	

PART II – Statutory instruments

(2) The court will direct that a person with parental responsibility be made a party to proceedings where that person requests to be one.

(3) Subject to rule 16.2, the court may at any time direct that –

    (a)   any person or body be made a party to proceedings; or

    (b)   a party be removed.

(4) If the court makes a direction for the addition or removal of a party under this rule, it may give consequential directions about –

    (a)   the service of a copy of the application form or other relevant documents on the new party;

(b)   the management of the proceedings.

(5) In this rule –

'a local authority foster parent' has the meaning assigned to it by section 23(3) of the 1989 Act; and

'care home', 'independent hospital', 'local authority' and ['clinical commissioning group'] have the meanings assigned to them by section 105 of the 1989 Act.

(Part 16 contains the rules relating to the representation of children.)

NOTES

Amendments.[1] Words substituted and inserted: SI 2013/235. [2] Words substituted: SI 2014/843.[3] Words omitted repealed: SI 2019/517.

Modifications. Rule 12.3(1) modified in an application under para 23(8) of Sch 2 to the Children Act 1989 to vary a contribution order by the Magistrates' Courts (Enforcement or Variation of Orders Made in Family Proceedings and Miscellaneous Provisions) Rules 2011, SI 2011/1329, rr 78, 83.

12.4 Notice of proceedings to person with foreign parental responsibility

(1) This rule applies where a child is subject to proceedings to which this Part applies and –

(a)   a person holds or is believed to hold parental responsibility for the child under the law of another State which subsists in accordance with Article 16 of the 1996 Hague Convention following the child becoming habitually resident in a territorial unit of the United Kingdom; and

(b)   that person is not otherwise required to be joined as a respondent under rule 12.3.

(2) [Subject to paragraph (2A),][1] the applicant shall give notice of the proceedings to any person to whom the applicant believes paragraph (1) applies in any case in which a person whom the applicant believed to have parental responsibility under the 1989 Act would be a respondent to those proceedings in accordance with rule 12.3.

[(2A) Notice shall not be given to a person to whom the applicant believes paragraph (1) applies if the court directs that such notice is not necessary.][1]

(3) [Unless a direction has been made under paragraph (2A),][1] the applicant and every respondent to the proceedings shall provide such details as they possess as to the identity and whereabouts of any person they believe to hold parental responsibility for the child in accordance with paragraph (1) to the court officer, upon making, or responding to the application as appropriate.

(4) Where the existence of a person who is believed to have parental responsibility for the child in accordance with paragraph (1) only becomes apparent to a party at a later date during the proceedings, that party must notify the court officer of those details at the earliest opportunity.

(5) Where a person to whom paragraph (1) applies receives notice of proceedings, that person may apply to the court to be joined as a party using the Part 18 procedure.

NOTES
Amendments.[1] Words and paragraph inserted: SI 2020/135.

12.5 What the court will do when the application has been issued

[(1)]1 When …[1] proceedings [other than public law proceedings][1] have been issued the court will consider –

(a) setting a date for –
  (i) a directions appointment;
  (ii) in private law proceedings, a First Hearing Dispute Resolution Appointment; [or][1]
  (iii) …[1]
  (iv) the hearing of the application …[1],
  and if the court sets a date it will do so in accordance with rule 12.13 and [Practice Direction 12B][1];

(b) giving any of the directions listed in rule 12.12 or, where Chapter 6, section 1 applies, rule 12.48; and

(c) doing anything else which is set out in [Practice Direction 12B][1] or any other practice direction.

[(2) When Part 4 proceedings and in so far as practicable other public law proceedings have been issued the court will –

(a) set a date for the Case Management Hearing in accordance with Practice Direction 12A;

(b) set a date for the hearing of an application for an interim order if necessary;

(c) give any directions listed in rule 12.12; and

(d) do anything else which is set out in Practice Direction 12A.][1]

[(Practice Direction 12A sets out details relating to the Case Management Hearing. Practice Direction 12B supplementing this Part sets out details relating to the First Hearing Dispute Resolution Appointment.)][1]

NOTES
Amendments.[1] Words inserted, omitted and substituted, paragraph inserted and sub-paragraph omitted: SI 2014/843.

12.6 Children's guardian, solicitor and reports under section 7 of the 1989 Act

[Within a day of the issue of Part 4 proceedings or the transfer of Part 4 Proceedings to the court and as][1] soon as practicable after the issue of [other][1] proceedings or the transfer of the [other][1] proceedings to the court, the court will –

(a) in specified proceedings, appoint a children's guardian under rule 16.3(1) unless –
  (i) such an appointment has already been made by the court which made the transfer and is subsisting; or
  (ii) the court considers that such an appointment is not necessary to safeguard the interests of the child;

PART II – Statutory instruments

(b)   where section 41(3) of the 1989 Act applies, consider whether a solicitor should be appointed to represent the child, and if so, appoint a solicitor accordingly;

(c)   consider whether to ask an officer of the service or a Welsh family proceedings officer for advice relating to the welfare of the child;

(d)   consider whether a report relating to the welfare of the child is required, and if so, request such a report in accordance with section 7 of the 1989 Act.

(Part 16 sets out the rules relating to representation of children.)

NOTES

Amendments.[1] Words inserted and substituted: SI 2014/843.

12.7 What a court officer will do

(1) As soon as practicable after the issue of proceedings the court officer will return to the applicant the copies of the application together with the forms referred to in Practice Direction 5A.

(2) As soon as practicable after the issue of proceedings or the transfer of proceedings to the court or at any other stage in the proceedings the court officer will –

(a)   give notice of any hearing set by the court to the applicant; and

(b)   do anything else set out in Practice Directions 12A or 12B or any other practice direction.

[12.8 Service

(1) After the issue of proceedings under this Part, the documents specified in paragraph (5) must be served on the respondent or respondents.

(2) In section 8 private law proceedings, service under paragraph (1) will be effected by the court officer, unless –

(a)   the applicant requests to do so; or

(b)   the court directs the applicant to do so.

(3) In this Rule, 'section 8 private law proceedings' are proceedings for a section 8 order except proceedings for a child arrangements order to which section 9(6B) of the 1989 Act applies with respect to a child who is in the care of a local authority.

(4) In any other proceedings to which this Part applies, service under paragraph (1) must be effected by the applicant.

(5) The documents are –

(a)   the application together with the documents referred to in Practice Direction 12C; and

(b)   notice of any hearing set by the court.

(6) Service under this rule must be carried out in accordance with Practice Direction 12C.

(7) The general rules about service in Part 6 apply but are subject to this rule.

(Practice Direction 12C (Service of Application in Children Proceedings) provides that in Part 4 proceedings (except proceedings for an interim order) the minimum number of days prior to the Case Management Hearing for service of the application and accompanying documents is 7 days. The Court has discretion to extend or shorten this time (see rule 4.1(3)(a)).][1]

NOTES

Amendment.[1] Rule substituted: SI 2014/843.

12.9

...[1]

NOTES

Amendment.[1] Rule omitted: SI 2013/3204.

12.10

...[1]

NOTES

Amendment.[1] Rule omitted: SI 2013/3204.

12.11

...[1]

NOTES

Amendment.[1] Rule omitted: SI 2013/3204.

12.12 Directions

(1) This rule does not apply to proceedings under Chapter 6 of this Part.

(2) At any stage in the proceedings, the court may give directions about the conduct of the proceedings including –

(a) the management of the case;
(b) the timetable for steps to be taken between the giving of directions and the final hearing;
(c) the joining of a child or other person as a party to the proceedings in accordance with rules 12.3(2) and (3);
(d) the attendance of the child;
(e) the appointment of a children's guardian or of a solicitor under section 41(3) of the 1989 Act;
(f) the appointment of a litigation friend;
(g) the service of documents;
(h) the filing of evidence including experts' reports; and
(i) the exercise by an officer of the Service, Welsh family proceedings officer or local authority officer of any duty referred to in rule 16.38(1).

(3) Paragraph (4) applies where –

(a)   an officer of the Service or a Welsh family proceedings officer has filed a report or a risk assessment as a result of exercising a duty referred to in rule 16.38(1)(a); or

(b)   a local authority officer has filed a report as a result of exercising a duty referred to in rule 16.38(1)(b).

(4) The court may –

(a)   give directions setting a date for a hearing at which that report or risk assessment will be considered; and

(b)   direct that the officer who prepared the report or risk assessment attend any such hearing.

(5) The court may exercise the powers in paragraphs (2) and (4) on an application or of its own initiative.

(6) Where the court proposes to exercise its powers of its own initiative the procedure set out in rule 4.3(2) to (6) applies.

(7) Directions of a court which are still in force immediately prior to the transfer of proceedings to another court will continue to apply following the transfer subject to –

(a)   any changes of terminology which are required to apply those directions to the court to which the proceedings are transferred; and

(b)   any variation or revocation of the direction.

(8) The court or court officer will –

(a)   take a note of the giving, variation or revocation of a direction under this rule; and

(b)   as soon as practicable serve a copy of the note on every party.

(Rule 12.48 provides for directions in proceedings under the 1980 Hague Convention and the European Convention.)

12.13 Setting dates for hearings and setting or confirming the timetable and date for the final hearing

(1) At the –

(a)   transfer to a court of proceedings;

(b)   postponement or adjournment of any hearing; or

(c)   conclusion of any hearing at which the proceedings are not finally determined,

the court will set a date for the proceedings to come before the court again for the purposes of giving directions or for such other purposes as the court directs.

(2) At any hearing the court may –

(a) confirm a date for the final hearing or the week within which the final hearing is to begin (where a date or period for the final hearing has already been set);

(b) set a timetable for the final hearing unless a timetable has already been fixed, or the court considers that it would be inappropriate to do so; or

(c) set a date for the final hearing or a period within which the final hearing of the application is to take place.

(3) The court officer will notify the parties of –

(a) the date of a hearing fixed in accordance with paragraph (1);

(b) the timetable for the final hearing; and

(c) the date of the final hearing or the period in which it will take place.

(4) Where the date referred to in paragraph (1) is set at the transfer of proceedings, the date will be as soon as possible after the transfer.

(5) The requirement in paragraph (1) to set a date for the proceedings to come before the court again is satisfied by the court setting or confirming a date for the final hearing.

12.14 Attendance at hearings

(1) This rule does not apply to proceedings under Chapter 6 of this Part except for proceedings for a declaration under rule 12.71.

(2) Unless the court directs otherwise and subject to paragraph (3), the persons who must attend a hearing are –

(a) any party to the proceedings;

(b) any litigation friend for any party or legal representative instructed to act on that party's behalf; and

(c) any other person directed by the court or required by Practice Directions 12A or 12B or any other practice direction to attend.

(3) Proceedings or any part of them will take place in the absence of a child who is a party to the proceedings if –

(a) the court considers it in the interests of the child, having regard to the matters to be discussed or the evidence likely to be given; and

(b) the child is represented by a children's guardian or solicitor.

(4) When considering the interests of the child under paragraph (3) the court will give –

(a) the children's guardian;

(b) the solicitor for the child; and

(c) the child, if of sufficient understanding,

an opportunity to make representations.

(5) Subject to paragraph (6), where at the time and place appointed for a hearing, the applicant appears but one or more of the respondents do not, the court may proceed with the hearing.

PART II – Statutory instruments

(6) The court will not begin to hear an application in the absence of a respondent unless the court is satisfied that –

(a)   the respondent received reasonable notice of the date of the hearing; or
(b)   the circumstances of the case justify proceeding with the hearing.

(7) Where, at the time and place appointed for a hearing one or more of the respondents appear but the applicant does not, the court may –

(a)   refuse the application; or
(b)   if sufficient evidence has previously been received, proceed in the absence of the applicant.

(8) Where at the time and place appointed for a hearing neither the applicant nor any respondent appears, the court may refuse the application.

(9) Paragraphs (5) to (8) do not apply to a hearing where the court –

(a)   is considering –
   (i)   whether to make [an activity]1 direction or to attach [an activity]1 condition to a [child arrangements order]1; or
   (ii)   an application for a financial compensation order, an enforcement order or an order under paragraph 9 of Schedule A1 to the 1989 Act following a breach of an enforcement order; and

(b)   has yet to obtain sufficient evidence from, or in relation to, the person who may be the subject of the direction, condition or order to enable it to determine the matter.

(10) ...2

NOTES

Amendments.1 Words substituted: SI 2014/843.2 Words omitted repealed: SI 2019/517.

12.15 Steps taken by the parties

If –

(a)   the parties or any children's guardian agree proposals for the management of the proceedings (including a proposed date for the final hearing or a period within which the final hearing is to take place); and
(b)   the court considers that the proposals are suitable,

it may approve them without a hearing and give directions in the terms proposed.

[(Practice Direction 12A gives guidance as to the application of this rule to Part 4 proceedings in the light of the period that is for the time being allowed under section 32(1)(a)(ii) of the 1989 Act)]1

NOTES

Amendment.1 Words in parentheses inserted: SI 2014/843.

12.16 Applications without notice

(1) This rule applies to –

(a)   proceedings for a section 8 order;

(b)   emergency proceedings; and

(c)   proceedings relating to the exercise of the court's inherent jurisdiction (other than an application for the court's permission to start such proceedings and proceedings for collection, location and passport orders where Chapter 6 applies).

(2) An application in proceedings referred to in paragraph (1) may ...[1] be made without notice in which case the applicant must file the application –

(a)   where the application is made by telephone, the next business day after the making of the application; or

(b)   in any other case, at the time when the application is made.

(3) ...[1]

(4) Where –

(a)   a section 8 order;

(b)   an emergency protection order;

(c)   an order for the disclosure of information as to the whereabouts of a child under section 33 of the 1986 Act; or

(d)   an order authorising the taking charge of and delivery of a child under section 34 of the 1986 Act,

is made without notice, the applicant must serve a copy of the application on each respondent within 48 hours after the order is made.

(5) Within 48 hours after the making of an order without notice, the applicant must serve a copy of the order on –

(a)   the parties, unless the court directs otherwise;

(b)   any person who has actual care of the child or who had such care immediately prior to the making of the order; and

(c)   in the case of an emergency protection order and a recovery order, the local authority in whose area the child lives or is found.

(6) Where the court refuses to make an order on an application without notice it may direct that the application is made on notice in which case the application will proceed in accordance with rules 12.3 to 12.15.

(7) Where the hearing takes place outside the hours during which the court office is normally open, the court or court officer will take a note of the proceedings.

(Practice Direction 12E (Urgent Business) provides further details of the procedure for out of hours applications. See also Practice Direction 12D (Inherent Jurisdiction (including Wardship Proceedings).)

(Rule 12.47 provides for without-notice applications in proceedings under Chapter 6, section 1 of this Part, (proceedings under the 1980 Hague Convention and the European Convention).)

NOTES

Amendments.[1] Words and paragraph omitted: SI 2013/3204.

PART II – Statutory instruments

12.17 Investigation under section 37 of the 1989 Act

(1) This rule applies where a direction is given to an appropriate authority by the court under section 37(1) of the 1989 Act.

(2) On giving the direction the court may adjourn the proceedings.

(3) As soon as practicable after the direction is given the court will record the direction.

(4) As soon as practicable after the direction is given the court officer will –

    (a)   serve the direction on –
       (i)   the parties to the proceedings in which the direction is given; and
       (ii) the appropriate authority where it is not a party;

    (b)   serve any documentary evidence directed by the court on the appropriate authority.

(5) Where a local authority informs the court of any of the matters set out in section 37(3)(a) to (c) of the 1989 Act it will do so in writing.

(6) Unless the court directs otherwise, the court officer will serve a copy of any report to the court under section 37 of the 1989 Act on the parties.

    (Section 37 of the 1989 Act refers to the appropriate authority and section 37(5) of that Act sets out which authority should be named in a particular case.)

12.18 Disclosure of a report under section 14A(8) or (9) of the 1989 Act

(1) In proceedings for a special guardianship order, the local authority must file the report under section 14A(8) or (9) of the 1989 Act within the timetable fixed by the court.

(2) The court will consider whether to give a direction that the report under section 14A(8) or (9) of the 1989 Act be disclosed to each party to the proceedings.

(3) Before giving a direction for the report to be disclosed, the court must consider whether any information should be deleted from the report.

(4) The court may direct that the report must not be disclosed to a party.

(5) The court officer must serve a copy of the report in accordance with any direction under paragraph (2).

(6) In paragraph (3), information includes information which a party has declined to reveal under rule 29.1(1).

12.19 Additional evidence

(1) This rule applies to proceedings for a section 8 order or a special guardianship order.

(2) Unless the court directs otherwise, a party must not –

(a) file or serve any document other than in accordance with these rules or any practice direction;

(b) in completing a form prescribed by these rules or any practice direction, give information or make a statement which is not required or authorised by that form; or

(c) file or serve at a hearing –

   (i) any witness statement of the substance of the oral evidence which the party intends to adduce; or

   (ii) any copy of any document (including any experts' report) which the party intends to rely on.

(3) Where a party fails to comply with the requirements of this rule in relation to any witness statement or other document, the party cannot seek to rely on that statement or other document unless the court directs otherwise.

12.20

...[1]

Amendments.[1] Rule omitted: SI 2012/3061.

12.21 Hearings

(1) The court may give directions about the order of speeches and the evidence at a hearing.

(2) Subject to any directions given under paragraph (1), the parties and the children's guardian must adduce their evidence at a hearing in the following order –

(a) the applicant;

(b) any party with parental responsibility for the child;

(c) other respondents;

(d) the children's guardian;

(e) the child, if the child is a party to proceedings and there is no children's guardian.

Chapter 3
Special Provisions about Public Law Proceedings

[12.22 Timetable for the proceedings

In public law proceedings other than Part 4 proceedings, in so far as practicable the court will draw up the timetable for the proceedings or revise that timetable with a view to disposing of the application without delay and in any event within 26 weeks beginning with the date on which the application is issued.

(In relation to Part 4 proceedings, section 32(1)(a) of the 1989 Act requires the court to draw up a timetable with a view to disposing of the application without delay and in any event within 26 weeks beginning with the day on which the application is issued.)][1]

NOTES

Amendment.[1] Rule substituted: SI 2014/843.

[12.23 Application of rules 12.24 to 12.26C

Rules 12.24 to 12.26C apply to Part 4 proceedings and in so far as practicable other public law proceedings.][1]

NOTES

Amendment.[1] Rule substituted: SI 2014/843.

12.24 Directions

The court will direct the parties to –

    (a)   monitor compliance with the court's directions; and
    (b)   tell the court or court officer about –
        (i)   any failure to comply with a direction of the court; and
        (ii) any other delay in the proceedings.

[12.25 The Case Management Hearing and the Issues Resolution Hearing

(1) The court will conduct the Case Management Hearing with the objective of –

    (a)   confirming the level of judge to which the proceedings have been allocated;
    (b)   drawing up a timetable for the proceedings including the time within which the proceedings are to be resolved;
    (c)   identifying the issues; and
    (d)   giving directions in accordance with rule 12.12 and Practice Direction 12A to manage the proceedings.

(2) The court may hold a further Case Management Hearing only where this hearing is necessary to fulfil the objectives of the Case Management Hearing set out in paragraph (1).

(3) The court will conduct the Issues Resolution Hearing with the objective of –

    (a)   identifying the remaining issues in the proceedings;
    (b)   as far as possible resolving or narrowing those issues; and
    (c)   giving directions to manage the proceedings to the final hearing in accordance with rule 12.12 and Practice Direction 12A.

(4) Where it is possible for all the issues in the proceedings to be resolved at the Issues Resolution Hearing, the court may treat the Issues Resolution Hearing as a final hearing and make orders disposing of the proceedings.

(5) The court may set a date for the Case Management Hearing, a further Case Management Hearing and the Issues Resolution Hearing at the times referred to in Practice Direction 12A.

(6) The matters which the court will consider at the hearings referred to in this rule are set out in Practice Direction 12A.

(Rule 25.6 (experts: when to apply for the court's permission) provides that unless the court directs otherwise, parties must apply for the court's permission as mentioned in section 13(1), (3) and (5) of the 2014 Act as soon as possible and in Part 4 proceedings and in so far as practicable other public law proceedings no later than the Case Management Hearing.)][1]

NOTES

Amendment.[1] Rule substituted: SI 2014/843.

[12.26 Discussion between advocates

(1) When setting a date for the Case Management Hearing or the Issues Resolution Hearing the court will direct a discussion between the parties' advocates to –

   (a)   discuss the provisions of a draft of the Case Management Order; and

   (b)   consider any other matter set out in Practice Direction 12A.

(2) Where there is a litigant in person the court will give directions about how that person may take part in the discussions between the parties' advocates.

(3) Unless the court directs otherwise –

   (a)   any discussion between advocates must take place no later than 2 days before the Case Management Hearing; and

   (b)   a draft of the Case Management Order must be filed with the court no later than 11a.m. on the day before the Case Management Hearing.

(4) Unless the court directs otherwise –

   (a)   any discussion between advocates must take place no later than 7 days before the Issues Resolution Hearing; and

   (b)   a draft of the Case Management Order must be filed with the court no later than 11a.m. on the day before the Issues Resolution Hearing.

(5) For the purposes of this rule 'advocate' includes a litigant in person.][1]

NOTES

Amendment.[1] Rule substituted: SI 2014/843.

[12.26A Application for extension of the time limit for disposing of the application

(1) An application requesting the court to grant an extension must state –

   (a)   the reasons for the request;

   (b)   the period of extension being requested; and

   (c)   a short explanation of –

      (i)   why it is necessary for the request to be granted to enable the court to resolve the proceedings justly;

      (ii)   the impact which any ensuing timetable revision would have on the welfare of the child to whom the application relates;

      (iii)   the impact which any ensuing timetable revision would have on the duration and conduct of the proceedings; and

PART II – Statutory instruments

(iv)   the reasons for the grant or refusal of any previous request for extension.

(2) Part 18 applies to an application requesting the grant of an extension.

(3) In this rule

'ensuing timetable revision' has the meaning given to it by section 32(6) of the 1989 Act;

'extension' means an extension of the period for the time being allowed under section 32(1)(a)(ii) of the 1989 Act which is to end no more than 8 weeks after the later of the times referred to in section 32(8) of that Act.][1]

NOTES

Amendment.[1] Rule inserted: SI 2014/843 (as amended).

[12.26B Disapplication of rule 4.1(3)(a) court's power to extend or shorten the time for compliance with a rule

Rule 4.1(3)(a) does not apply to any period that is for the time being allowed under section 32(1)(a)(ii) of the 1989 Act.][1]

NOTES

Amendment.[1] Rule inserted: SI 2014/843.

[12.26C Extension of time limit: reasons for court's decision

(1) When refusing or granting an extension of the period that is for the time being allowed under section 32(1)(a)(ii) in the case of the application, the court will announce its decision and –

(a)   the reasons for that decision; and

(b)   where an extension is granted or refused, a short explanation of the impact which the decision would have on the welfare of the child.

(2) The court office will supply a copy of the order granting or refusing the extension including the reasons for the court's decision and the period of any extension and short explanation given under paragraph (1)(b) to –

(a)   the parties; and

(b)   any person who has actual care of the child who is the subject of the proceedings.][1]

NOTES

Amendment.[1] Rule inserted: SI 2014/843.

12.27 Matters prescribed for the purposes of the Act

(1) Proceedings for an order under any of the following provisions of the 1989 Act –

(a)   a secure accommodation order under section 25;

(b)   an order giving permission to change a child's surname or remove a child from the United Kingdom under section 33(7);

(c)   an order permitting the local authority to arrange for any child in its care to live outside England and Wales under paragraph 19(1) of Schedule 2;

(d)   the extension or further extension of a supervision order under paragraph 6(3) of Schedule 3;

(e)   appeals against the determination of proceedings of a kind set out in sub-paragraphs (a) to (d);

are specified for the purposes of section 41 of that Act in accordance with section 41(6)(i) of that Act.

(2) The persons listed as applicants in the table set out in rule 12.3 to proceedings for the variation of directions made with interim care or interim supervision orders under section 38(8) of the 1989 Act are the prescribed class of persons for the purposes of that section.

(3) The persons listed as applicants in the table set out in rule 12.3 to proceedings for the variation of a direction made under section 44(6) of the 1989 Act in an emergency protection order are the prescribed class of persons for the purposes of section 44(9) of that Act.

12.28 Exclusion requirements: interim care orders and emergency protection orders

(1) This rule applies where the court includes an exclusion requirement in an interim care order or an emergency protection order.

(2) The applicant for an interim care order or emergency protection order must –

(a)   prepare a separate statement of the evidence in support of the application for an exclusion requirement;

(b)   serve the statement personally on the relevant person with a copy of the order containing the exclusion requirement (and of any power of arrest which is attached to it);

(c)   inform the relevant person of that person's right to apply to vary or discharge the exclusion requirement.

(3) Where a power of arrest is attached to an exclusion requirement in an interim care order or an emergency protection order, the applicant will deliver –

(a)   a copy of the order; and

(b)   a statement showing that the relevant person has been served with the order or informed of its terms (whether by being present when the order was made or by telephone or otherwise),

to the officer for the time being in charge of the police station for the area in which the dwelling-house in which the child lives is situated (or such other police station as the court may specify).

(4) Rules 10.6(2) and 10.10 to 10.17 will apply, with the necessary modifications, for the service, variation, discharge and enforcement of any exclusion requirement to which a power of arrest is attached as they apply to an order made on an application under Part 4 of the 1996 Act.

PART II – Statutory instruments

(5) The relevant person must serve the parties to the proceedings with any application which that person makes for the variation or discharge of the exclusion requirement.

(6) Where an exclusion requirement ceases to have effect whether –

(a) as a result of the removal of a child under section 38A(10) or 44A(10) of the 1989 Act;

(b) because of the discharge of the interim care order or emergency protection order; or

(c) otherwise,

the applicant must inform –

(i) the relevant person;

(ii) the parties to the proceedings;

(iii) any officer to whom a copy of the order was delivered under paragraph (3); and

(iv) (where necessary) the court.

(7) Where the court includes an exclusion requirement in an interim care order or an emergency protection order of its own motion, paragraph (2) will apply with the omission of any reference to the statement of the evidence.

(8) In this rule, 'the relevant person' has the meaning assigned to it by sections 38A(2) and 44A(2) of the 1989 Act.

12.29 Notification of consent

(1) Consent for the purposes of the following provisions of the 1989 Act –

(a) section 16(3);

(b) section 38A(2)(b)(ii) or 44A(2)(b)(ii); or

(c) paragraph 19(3)(c) or (d) of Schedule 2,

must be given either –

(i) orally to the court; or

(ii) in writing to the court signed by the person giving consent.

(2) Any written consent for the purposes of section 38A(2) or 44A(2) of the 1989 Act must include a statement that the person giving consent –

(a) is able and willing to give to the child the care which it would be reasonable to expect a parent to give; and

(b) understands that the giving of consent could lead to the exclusion of the relevant person from the dwelling-house in which the child lives.

12.30 Proceedings for secure accommodation orders: copies of reports

In proceedings under section 25 of the 1989 Act, the court will, if practicable, arrange for copies of all written reports filed in the case to be made available before the hearing to –

(a)   the applicant;

(b)   the parent or guardian of the child to whom the application relates;

(c)   any legal representative of the child;

(d)   the children's guardian; and

(e)   the child, unless the court directs otherwise,

and copies of the reports may, if the court considers it desirable, be shown to any person who is entitled to notice of any hearing in accordance with Practice Direction 12C.

Chapter 4
Special Provisions about Private Law Proceedings

12.31 The First Hearing Dispute Resolution Appointment

(1) The court may set a date for the First Hearing Dispute Resolution Appointment after the proceedings have been issued.

(2) The court officer will give notice of any of the dates so fixed to the parties.

(Provisions relating to the timing of and issues to be considered at the First Hearing Dispute Resolution Appointment are contained in Practice Direction 12B.)

12.32 Answer

A respondent must file and serve on the parties an answer to the application for an order in private law proceedings within 14 days beginning with the date on which the application is served.

12.33 Applications for warning notices or applications to amend enforcement orders by reason of change of residence

(1) This rule applies in relation to an application …[1] for –

(a)   a warning notice to be attached to a [child arrangements][1] order; or

(b)   an order under paragraph 5 of Schedule A1 to the 1989 Act to amend an enforcement order by reason of change of residence.

(2) The application must be made without notice.

(3) The court may deal with the application without a hearing.

(4) If the court decides to deal with the application at a hearing, rules 12.5, 12.7 and 12.8 will apply.

NOTES

Amendment.[1] Words omitted: SI 2013/3204. [2] Words substituted: SI 2014/843.

Modification. Rule 12.33 modified in certain applications under the Children Act 1989 in respect of enforcement of contact orders, by the Magistrates' Courts (Enforcement or Variation of Orders Made in Family Proceedings and Miscellaneous Provisions) Rules 2011, SI 2011/1329, rr 76, 83.

12.34 Service of a risk assessment

(1) Where an officer of the Service or a Welsh family proceedings officer has filed a risk assessment with the court, subject to paragraph (2), the court officer will as soon as practicable serve copies of the risk assessment on each party.

(2) Before serving the risk assessment, the court must consider whether, in order to prevent a risk of harm to the child, it is necessary for –

   (a)   information to be deleted from a copy of the risk assessment before that copy is served on a party; or
   (b)   service of a copy of the risk assessment (whether with information deleted from it or not) on a party to be delayed for a specified period,

and may make directions accordingly.

12.35 Service of enforcement orders or orders amending or revoking enforcement orders

(1) Paragraphs (2) and (3) apply where [the court][1] makes –

   (a)   an enforcement order; or
   (b)   an order under paragraph 9(2) of Schedule A1 to the 1989 Act (enforcement order made following a breach of an enforcement order).

(2) As soon as practicable after an order has been made, a copy of it must be served by the court officer on –

   (a)   the parties, except the person against whom the order is made;
   (b)   the officer of the Service or the Welsh family proceedings officer who is to comply with a request under section 11M of the 1989 Act to monitor compliance with the order; and
   (c)   the responsible officer.

(3) Unless the court directs otherwise, the applicant must serve a copy of the order personally on the person against whom the order is made.

(4) The court officer must send a copy of an order made under paragraph 4, 5, 6 or 7 of Schedule A1 to the 1989 Act (revocation or amendment of an enforcement order) to –

   (a)   the parties;
   (b)   the officer of the Service or the Welsh family proceedings officer who is to comply with a request under section 11M of the 1989 Act to monitor compliance with the order;
   (c)   the responsible officer; and
   (d)   in the case of an order under paragraph 5 of Schedule A1 to the 1989 Act (amendment of enforcement order by reason of change of residence), the responsible officer in the former local justice area.

(5) In this rule, 'responsible officer' has the meaning given in paragraph 8(8) of Schedule A1 to the 1989 Act.

NOTES

Amendment.[1] Words omitted: SI 2013/3204.

Modification. Rule 12.35 modified in certain applications under the Children Act 1989 in respect of enforcement of contact orders by the Magistrates' Courts (Enforcement or Variation of Orders Made in Family Proceedings and Miscellaneous Provisions) Rules 2011, SI 2011/1329, rr 76, 83.

Chapter 5
Special Provisions about Inherent Jurisdiction Proceedings

12.36 Where to start proceedings

(1) An application for proceedings under the Inherent Jurisdiction of the court must be started in the High Court.

(2) Wardship proceedings, except applications for an order that a child be made or cease to be a ward of court, may be transferred to the [family court][1] unless the issues of fact or law make them more suitable for hearing in the High Court.

(The question of suitability for hearing in the High Court is explained in Practice Direction 12D (Inherent Jurisdiction (including Wardship Proceedings)).)

NOTES

Amendments.[1] Words substituted: SI 2013/3204.

12.37 Child as respondent to wardship proceedings

(1) A child who is the subject of wardship proceedings must not be made a respondent to those proceedings unless the court gives permission following an application under paragraph (2).

2) Where nobody other than the child would be a suitable respondent to wardship proceedings, the applicant may apply without notice for permission to make the wardship application –

(a) without notice; or
(b) with the child as the respondent.

12.38 Registration requirements

The court officer will send a copy of every application for a child to be made a ward of court to the principal registry for recording in the register of wards.

12.39 Notice of child's whereabouts

(1) Every respondent, other than a child, must file with the acknowledgment of service a notice stating –

(a) the respondent's address; and
(b) either –
    (i) the whereabouts of the child; or
    (ii) that the respondent is unaware of the child's whereabouts if that is the case.

PART II – Statutory instruments

(2) Unless the court directs otherwise, the respondent must serve a copy of that notice on the applicant.

(3) Every respondent other than a child must immediately notify the court in writing of –

  (a)   any subsequent changes of address; or
  (b)   any change in the child's whereabouts,

and, unless the court directs otherwise, serve a copy of that notice on the applicant.

(4) In this rule a reference to the whereabouts of a child is a reference to –

  (a)   the address at which the child is living;
  (b)   the person with whom the child is living; and
  (c)   any other information relevant to where the child may be found.

12.40 Enforcement of orders in wardship proceedings

The High Court may secure compliance with any direction relating to a ward of court by an order addressed to the tipstaff.

  (The role of the tipstaff is explained in Practice Direction 12D (Inherent Jurisdiction (including Wardship Proceedings)).)

12.41 Child ceasing to be ward of court

(1) A child who, by virtue of section 41(2) of the Senior Courts Act 1981, automatically becomes a ward of court on the making of a wardship application will cease to be a ward on the determination of the application unless the court orders that the child be made a ward of court.

(2) Nothing in paragraph (1) affects the power of the court under section 41(3) of the Senior Courts Act 1981 to order that any child cease to be a ward of court.

12.42 Adoption of a child who is a ward of court

An application for permission –

  (a)   to start proceedings to adopt a child who is a ward of court;
  (b)   to place such a child for adoption with parental consent; or
  (c)   to start proceedings for a placement order in relation to such a child,

may be made without notice in accordance with Part 18.

[12.42A Application for a writ of habeas corpus for release in relation to a minor

(1) Part 87 of the CPR applies in respect of an application for a writ of habeas corpus for release in relation to a minor –

  (a)   as if –
      (i)   for rule 87.2(1)(a) of the CPR there were substituted –
            '(a)   an application notice; and'; and

(ii) for rule 87.2(4) of the CPR there were substituted –
     '(4) The application notice must be filed in the Family Division of the High Court.'; and

(b) subject to any additional necessary modifications.

(2) Rules 12.5 to 12.8, 12.12 to 12.16, 12.21 and 12.39 do not apply to an application to which this rule applies.

(The term 'application notice' is defined in rule 2.3(1).)][1]

NOTES

Amendment.[1] Rule inserted: SI 2014/3296.

[12.42B Application to set aside an inherent jurisdiction order

(1) In this rule –

'inherent jurisdiction order' means an order, declaration or judgment made under the inherent jurisdiction, and includes –
   (a) a part of such an order, declaration or judgment; or
   (b) a consent order; and

'set aside' means to set aside pursuant to section 17(2) of the Senior Courts Act 1981 and this rule.

(2) A party may apply under this rule to set aside an inherent jurisdiction order where no error of the court is alleged.

(3) An application under this rule must be made within the proceedings in which the inherent jurisdiction order was made.

(4) An application under this rule must be made in accordance with the Part 18 procedure, subject to the modifications contained in this rule.

(5) Where the court decides to set aside an inherent jurisdiction order, it shall give directions for a rehearing or make such other orders as may be appropriate to dispose of the application.

(6) This rule is without prejudice to any power the High Court has to vary, revoke, discharge or set aside other orders, declarations or judgments where no error of the court is alleged.][1]

NOTES

Amendment.[1] Rule inserted: SI 2020/135.

Chapter 6
Proceedings under the 1980 Hague Convention, the European Convention, ...[2] and the 1996 Hague Convention

12.43 Scope

This Chapter applies to –

(a) [children proceedings][1] under the 1980 Hague Convention or the European Convention; and

(b) applications relating to ...[2] the 1996 Hague Convention in respect of children.

NOTES

Amendments.[1] Words substituted: SI 2012/3061.[2] Words omitted repealed: SI 2019/517.

Section 1
Proceedings under the 1980 Hague Convention or the European Convention

12.44 Interpretation

In this section –

'the 1985 Act' means the Child Abduction and Custody Act 1985;
'Central Authority' means, in relation to England and Wales, the Lord Chancellor;
'Contracting State' has the meaning given in –
> (a) section 2 of the 1985 Act in relation to the 1980 Hague Convention; and
> (b) section 13 of the 1985 Act in relation to the European Convention; and

'decision relating to custody' has the same meaning as in the European Convention.
('the 1980 Hague Convention' and the 'the European Convention' are defined in rule 2.3.)

12.45 Where to start proceedings

Every application under the 1980 Hague Convention or the European Convention must be –

(a) made in the High Court and issued in the principal registry; and
(b) heard by a Judge of the High Court unless the application is –
> (i) to join a respondent; or
> (ii) to dispense with service or extend the time for acknowledging service.

12.46 Evidence in support of application

Where the party making an application under this section does not produce the documents referred to in Practice Direction 12F, the court may –

(a) fix a time within which the documents are to be produced;
(b) accept equivalent documents; or
(c) dispense with production of the documents if the court considers it has sufficient information.

12.47 Without-notice applications

(1) This rule applies to applications –

(a) commencing or in proceedings under this section;
(b) for interim directions under section 5 or 19 of the 1985 Act;
(c) for the disclosure of information about the child and for safeguarding the child's welfare, under rule 12.57;
(d) for the disclosure of relevant information as to where the child is, under section 24A of the 1985 Act; or
(e) for a collection order, location order or passport order.

(2) Applications under this rule may be made without notice, in which case the applicant must file the application –

(a) where the application is made by telephone, the next business day after the making of the application; or
(b) in any other case, at the time when the application is made.

(3) Where an order is made without notice, the applicant must serve a copy of the order on the other parties as soon as practicable after the making of the order, unless the court otherwise directs.

(4) Where the court refuses to make an order on an application without notice, it may direct that the application is made on notice.

(5) Where any hearing takes place outside the hours during which the court office is usually open –

(a) if the hearing takes place by telephone, the applicant's solicitors will, if practicable, arrange for the hearing to be recorded; and
(b) in all other cases, the court or court officer will take a note of the proceedings.

(Practice Direction 12E (Urgent Business) provides further details of the procedure for out of hours applications. See also Practice Direction 12D (Inherent Jurisdiction (including Wardship Proceedings)).)

12.48 Directions

(1) As soon as practicable after an application to which this section applies has been made, the court may give directions as to the following matters, among others –

(a) whether service of the application may be dispensed with;
(b) whether the proceedings should be transferred to another court under rule 12.54;
(c) expedition of the proceedings or any part of the proceedings (and any direction for expedition may specify a date by which the court must issue its final judgment in the proceedings or a specified part of the proceedings);
(d) the steps to be taken in the proceedings and the time by which each step is to be taken;
(e) whether the child or any other person should be made a party to the proceedings;

PART II – Statutory instruments

   (f)   if the child is not made a party to the proceedings, the manner in which the child's wishes and feelings are to be ascertained, having regard to the child's age and maturity and in particular whether an officer of the Service or a Welsh family proceedings officer should report to the court for that purpose;

   (g)   where the child is made a party to the proceedings, the appointment of a children's guardian for that child unless a children's guardian has already been appointed;

   (h)   the attendance of the child or any other person before the court;

   (i)   the appointment of a litigation friend for a child or for any protected party, unless a litigation friend has already been appointed;

   (j)   the service of documents;

   (k)   the filing of evidence including expert evidence; and

   (l)   whether the parties and their representatives should meet at any stage of the proceedings and the purpose of such a meeting.

(Rule 16.2 provides for when the court may make the child a party to the proceedings and rule 16.4 for the appointment of a children's guardian for the child who is made a party. Rule 16.5 (without prejudice to rule 16.6) requires a child who is a party to the proceedings but not the subject of those proceedings to have a litigation friend.)

(2) Directions of a court which are in force immediately prior to the transfer of proceedings to another court under rule 12.54 will continue to apply following the transfer subject to –

   (a)   any changes of terminology which are required to apply those directions to the court to which the proceedings are transferred; and

   (b)   any variation or revocation of the directions.

(3) The court or court officer will –

   (a)   take a note of the giving, variation or revocation of directions under this rule; and

   (b)   as soon as practicable serve a copy of the directions order on every party.

12.49 Answer

(1) Subject to paragraph (2) and to any directions given under rule 12.48, a respondent must file and serve on the parties an answer to the application within 7 days beginning with the date on which the application is served.

(2) The court may direct a longer period for service where the respondent has been made a party solely on one of the following grounds –

   (a)   a decision relating to custody has been made in the respondent's favour; or

   (b)   the respondent appears to the court to have sufficient interest in the welfare of the child.

12.50 Filing and serving written evidence

(1) The respondent to an application to which this section applies may file and serve with the answer a statement verified by a statement of truth, together with any further evidence on which the respondent intends to rely.

(2) The applicant may, within 7 days beginning with the date on which the respondent's evidence was served under paragraph (1), file and serve a statement in reply verified by a statement of truth, together with any further evidence on which the applicant intends to rely.

12.51 Adjournment

The court will not adjourn the hearing of an application to which this section applies for more than 21 days at any one time.

12.52 Stay of proceedings upon notification of wrongful removal etc.

(1) In this rule and in rule 12.53 –

    (a) 'relevant authority' means –
        (i)   the High Court;
        (ii) [the family court][1];
        (iii) ...[1]
        (iv) the Court of Session;
        (v)   a sheriff court;
        [(vi) a children's hearing within the meaning of the Children's Hearings (Scotland) Act 2011;][2]
        (vii) the High Court in Northern Ireland;
        (viii) a county court in Northern Ireland;
        (ix) a court of summary jurisdiction in Northern Ireland;
        (x)   the Royal Court of Jersey;
        (xi) a court of summary jurisdiction in Jersey;
        (xii) the High Court of Justice of the Isle of Man;
        (xiii) a court of summary jurisdiction in the Isle of Man; or
        (xiv) the Secretary of State; and

    (b) 'rights of custody' has the same meaning as in the 1980 Hague Convention.

(2) Where a party to proceedings under the 1980 Hague Convention knows that an application relating to the merits of rights of custody is pending in or before a relevant authority, that party must file within the proceedings under the 1980 Hague Convention a concise statement of the nature of that application, including the relevant authority in or before which it is pending.

(3) On receipt of a statement filed in accordance with paragraph (2) above, a court officer will notify the relevant authority in or before which the application is pending and will subsequently notify the relevant authority of the result of the proceedings.

PART II – Statutory instruments

(4) On receipt by the relevant authority of a notification under paragraph (3) from the High Court or equivalent notification from the Court of Session, the High Court in Northern Ireland or the High Court of Justice of the Isle of Man –

(a)   all further proceedings in the action will be stayed[GL] unless and until the proceedings under the 1980 Hague Convention in the High Court, Court of Session, the High Court in Northern Ireland or the High Court of Justice of the Isle of Man are dismissed; and

(b)   the parties to the action will be notified by the court officer of the stay[GL] and dismissal.

NOTES

Amendments.[1] Words substituted and omitted: SI 2013/3204.2 Paragraph substituted: SI 2013/1465.

[12.52A   Application to set aside a return order under the 1980 Hague Convention

(1) In this rule—

'return order' means an order for the return or non-return of a child made under the 1980 Hague Convention and includes a consent order;

'set aside' means to set aside a return order pursuant to section 17(2) of the Senior Courts Act 1981 and this rule.

(2) A party may apply under this rule to set aside a return order where no error of the court is alleged.

(3) An application under this rule must be made within the proceedings in which the return order was made.

(4) An application under this rule must be made in accordance with the Part 18 procedure, subject to the modifications contained in this rule.

(5) Where the court decides to set aside a return order, it shall give directions for a rehearing or make such other orders as may be appropriate to dispose of the application.

(6) This rule is without prejudice to any power the High Court has to vary, revoke, discharge or set aside other orders, declarations or judgments which are not specified in this rule and where no error of the court is alleged.][1]

NOTES

Amendment.[1] Rule inserted: SI 2020/135.

12.53   Stay of proceedings where application made under s 16 of the 1985 Act (registration of decisions under the European Convention)

(1) A person who –

(a)   is a party to –

(i)   proceedings under section 16 of the 1985 Act; or

(ii)   proceedings as a result of which a decision relating to custody has been registered under section 16 of the 1985 Act; and

(b)   knows that an application is pending under –

    (i)   section 20(2) of the 1985 Act;

    (ii)   Article 21(2) of the Child Abduction and Custody (Jersey) Law 2005; or

    (iii)   section 42(2) of the Child Custody Act 1987 (an Act of Tynwald),

must file within the proceedings under section 16 of the 1985 Act a concise statement of the nature of the pending application.

(2) On receipt of a statement filed in accordance with paragraph (1) above, a court officer will notify the relevant authority in or before which the application is pending and will subsequently notify the relevant authority of the result of the proceedings.

(3) On receipt by the relevant authority of a notification under paragraph (2) from the High Court or equivalent notification from the Court of Session, the High Court in Northern Ireland or the High Court of Justice of the Isle of Man, the court officer will notify the parties to the action.

12.54   Transfer of proceedings

(1) At any stage in proceedings under the 1985 Act the court may –

    (a)   of its own initiative; or

    (b)   on the application of a party with a minimum of two days' notice;

order that the proceedings be transferred to a court listed in paragraph (4).

(2) Where the court makes an order for transfer under paragraph (1) –

    (a)   the court will state its reasons on the face of the order;

    (b)   a court officer will send a copy of the order, the application and the accompanying documents (if any) and any evidence to the court to which the proceedings are transferred; and

    (c)   the costs of the proceedings both before and after the transfer will be at the discretion of the court to which the proceedings are transferred.

(3) Where proceedings are transferred to the High Court from a court listed in paragraph (4), a court officer will notify the parties of the transfer and the proceedings will continue as if they had been commenced in the High Court.

(4) The listed courts are the Court of Session, the High Court in Northern Ireland, the Royal Court of Jersey or the High Court of Justice of the Isle of Man.

12.55   Revocation and variation of registered decisions

(1) This rule applies to decisions which –

    (a)   have been registered under section 16 of the 1985 Act; and

    (b)   are subsequently varied or revoked by an authority in the Contracting State in which they were made.

PART II – Statutory instruments

(2) The court will, on cancelling the registration of a decision which has been revoked, notify –

(a)   the person appearing to the court to have care of the child;
(b)   the person on whose behalf the application for registration of the decision was made; and
(c)   any other party to the application.

(3) The court will, on being informed of the variation of a decision, notify –

(a)   the party appearing to the court to have care of the child; and
(b)   any party to the application for registration of the decision;

and any such person may apply to make representations to the court before the registration is varied.

(4) Any person appearing to the court to have an interest in the proceedings may apply for the registration of a decision for the cancellation or variation of the decision referred to in paragraph (1).

12.56 The central index of decisions registered under the 1985 Act

A central index of decisions registered under section 16 of the 1985 Act, together with any variation of those decisions made under section 17 of that Act, will be kept by the principal registry.

12.57 Disclosure of information in proceedings under the European Convention

At any stage in proceedings under the European Convention the court may, if it has reason to believe that any person may have relevant information about the child who is the subject of those proceedings, order that person to disclose such information and may for that purpose order that the person attend before it or file affidavit[(GL)] evidence

Section 2
Applications relating to ...[2] the 1996 Hague Convention

12.58 Interpretation

(1) In this section –

...[1]

'Contracting State' means a State party to the 1996 Hague Convention;
['domestic Central Authority' means –
(a)   ...[2]
(b)   where the matter relates to the 1996 Hague Convention in England, the Lord Chancellor;
(c)   where the matter relates to the 1996 Hague Convention in Wales, the Welsh Ministers;][1]

...[2]

...²

'parental responsibility' has the meaning given in –

    (a)   ...²

    (b)   Article 1(2) of the 1996 Hague Convention in relation to proceedings under that Convention; and

...²

(2) In rules 12.59 to 12.70, references to the court of another ...² Contracting State include ...² authorities of Contracting States which have jurisdiction to take measures directed to the protection of the person or property of the child within the meaning of the 1996 Hague Convention.

NOTES

Amendments.¹ Definitions omitted and inserted: SI 2012/2046.² Words omitted repealed: SI 2019/517.

12.59 ...¹

...¹

NOTES

Amendments.¹ Rule repealed: SI 2019/517.

12.60 ...¹

...¹

NOTES

Amendments.¹ Words omitted repealed: SI 2019/517.

12.61 Transfer of proceedings under ...¹ Article 8 of the 1996 Hague Convention

(1) Where the court is considering the transfer of proceedings to the court of another ...¹ Contracting State under rules 12.62 to 12.64 it will –

    (a)   fix a date for a hearing for the court to consider the question of transfer; and

    (b)   give directions as to the manner in which the parties may make representations.

(2) The court may, with the consent of all parties, deal with the question of transfer without a hearing.

(3) Directions which are in force immediately prior to the transfer of proceedings to a court in another ...¹ Contracting State under rules 12.62 to 12.64 will continue to apply until the court in that other State accepts jurisdiction in accordance with the provisions of ...¹ the 1996 Hague Convention ...¹, subject to any variation or revocation of the directions.

(4) The court or court officer will –

    (a)   take a note of the giving, variation or revocation of directions under this rule; and

(b)   as soon as practicable serve a copy of the directions order on every party.

(5) A register of all applications and requests for transfer of jurisdiction to or from another ...[1] Contracting State will be kept by the principal registry.

NOTES

Amendments.[1] Words omitted repealed: SI 2019/517.

12.62 Application by a party for transfer of the proceedings

(1) A party may apply to the court ...[1] under Article 8(1) of the 1996 Hague Convention –

(a)   to stay[(GL)] the proceedings or a specified part of the proceedings and to invite the parties to introduce a request before a court of another ...[1] Contracting State; or

(b)   to make a request to a court of ...[1] another Contracting State to assume jurisdiction for the proceedings, or a specified part of the proceedings.

(2) An application under paragraph (1) must be made –

(a)   to the court in which the relevant parental responsibility proceedings are pending; and

(b)   using the Part 18 procedure.

(3) The applicant must file the application notice and serve it on the respondents [not less than 42 days before the hearing of the application][1].

NOTES

Amendments.[1] Words omitted repealed and words substituted: SI 2019/517.

12.63 Application by a court of ...[2] another Contracting State for transfer of the proceedings

(1) This rule applies where a court of ...[2] another Contracting State makes an application under ...[2] Article 9 of the 1996 Hague Convention that the court having jurisdiction in relation to the proceedings transfer the proceedings or a specific part of the proceedings to the applicant court.

(2) When the court receives the application, the court officer will –

(a)   as soon as practicable, notify the [domestic Central Authority][1] of the application; and

(b)   serve the application, and notice of the hearing on all other parties in England and Wales not less than 5 days before the hearing of the application.

NOTES

Amendments.[1] Words substituted: SI 2012/2046.[2] Words omitted repealed: SI 2019/517.

12.64 Exercise by the court of its own initiative of powers to seek to transfer the proceedings

(1) The court having jurisdiction in relation to the proceedings may exercise its powers of its own initiative under ...[1] Article 8 of the 1996 Hague Convention in relation to the proceedings or a specified part of the proceedings.

(2) Where the court proposes to exercise its powers, the court officer will give the parties not less than 5 days' notice of the hearing.

NOTES

Amendments.[1] Words omitted repealed: SI 2019/517.

12.65 Application to High Court to make request under ...[1] Article 9 of the 1996 Hague Convention to request transfer of jurisdiction

(1) An application for the court to request transfer of jurisdiction in a matter concerning a child from ...[1] another Contracting State under ...[1] Article 9 of the 1996 Hague Convention ...[1] must be made to the principal registry and heard in the High Court.

(2) An application must be made without notice to any other person and the court may give directions about joining any other party to the application.

(3) Where there is agreement between the court and the court or competent authority to which the request under paragraph (1) is made to transfer the matter to the courts of England and Wales, the court will consider with that other court or competent authority the specific timing and conditions for the transfer.

(4) Upon receipt of agreement to transfer jurisdiction from the court or other competent authority in the ...[1] Contracting State to which the request has been made, the court officer will serve on the applicant a notice that jurisdiction has been accepted by the courts of England and Wales.

(5) The applicant must attach the notice referred to in subparagraph (3) to any subsequent application in relation to the child.

(6) Nothing in this rule requires an application with respect to a child commenced following a transfer of jurisdiction to be made to or heard in the High Court.

(7) Upon allocation, the court to which the proceedings are allocated must immediately fix a directions hearing to consider the future conduct of the case.

NOTES

Amendments.[1] Words omitted repealed: SI 2019/517.

12.66 Procedure where the court receives a request from the authorities of another ...[1] Contracting State to assume jurisdiction in a matter concerning a child

(1) Where any court other than the High Court receives a request to assume jurisdiction in a matter concerning a child from a court or other authority which has jurisdiction in another ...[1] Contracting State, that court must immediately

PART II – Statutory instruments

refer the request to a Judge of the High Court for a decision regarding acceptance of jurisdiction to be made.

(2) Upon the High Court agreeing to the request under paragraph (1), the court officer will notify the parties to the proceedings before the other ...[1] Contracting State of that decision, and the case must be allocated as if the application had been made in England and Wales.

(3) Upon allocation, the court to which the proceedings are allocated must immediately fix a directions hearing to consider the future conduct of the case.

(4) The court officer will serve notice of the directions hearing on all parties to the proceedings in the other ...[1] Contracting State no later than 5 days before the date of that hearing.

NOTES

Amendments.[1] Words omitted repealed: SI 2019/517.

12.67 Service of the court's order or request relating to transfer of jurisdiction under ...[2] the 1996 Hague Convention

The court officer will serve an order or request relating to transfer of jurisdiction on all parties, the Central Authority of the other ...[2] Contracting State, and the [domestic Central Authority][1].

NOTES

Amendments.[1] Words substituted: SI 2012/2046.[2] Words omitted repealed: SI 2019/517.

12.68 Questions as to the court's jurisdiction or whether the proceedings should be stayed

(1) If at any time after issue of the application it appears to the court that under ...[1] Article 13 of the 1996 Hague Convention it is or may be required to stay[(GL)] the proceedings or to decline jurisdiction, the court must –

  (a)   stay[(GL)] the proceedings; and
  (b)   fix a date for a hearing to determine jurisdiction or whether there should be a stay[(GL)] or other order.

(2) The court officer will serve notice of the hearing referred to at paragraph (1)(b) on the parties to the proceedings.

(3) The court must, in writing –

  (a)   give reasons for its decision under paragraph (1); and
  (b)   where it makes a finding of fact, state such finding.

(4) The court may with the consent of all the parties deal with any question as to the jurisdiction of the court, or as to whether the proceedings should be stayed[(GL)], without a hearing.

NOTES

Amendments.[1] Words omitted repealed: SI 2019/517.

12.69 Request for consultation as to contemplated placement of child in England and Wales

(1) This rule applies to a request made –

    (a) ...[2]

    (b) under Article 33 of the 1996 Hague Convention by a court in another Contracting State

for consultation on or consent to the contemplated placement of a child in England and Wales.

(2) Where the court receives a request directly from a court in another ...[2] Contracting State, the court shall, as soon as practicable after receipt of the request, notify the [domestic Central Authority][1] of the request and take the appropriate action under paragraph (4).

(3) Where it appears to the court officer that no proceedings relating to the child are pending before a court in England and Wales, the court officer must inform the [domestic Central Authority][1] of that fact and forward to the Central Authority all documents relating to the request sent by the court in the other ...[2] Contracting State.

(4) Where the court receives a request forwarded by the [domestic Central Authority][1], the court must, as soon as practicable after receipt of the request, either –

    (a) where proceedings relating to the child are pending before the court, fix a directions hearing; or

    (b) where proceedings relating to the child are pending before another court in England and Wales, send a copy of the request to that court.

NOTES

Amendments.[1] Words substituted: SI 2012/2046.[2] Words omitted repealed: SI 2019/517.

12.70 Request made by court in England and Wales for consultation as to contemplated placement of child in another ...[2] Contracting State

(1) This rule applies where the court is contemplating the placement of a child in another ...[2] Contracting State under Article 33 of the 1996 Hague Convention, and proposes to send a request for consultation with or for the consent of the central authority or other authority having jurisdiction in the other State in relation to the contemplated placement.

(2) In this rule, a reference to 'the request' includes a reference to a report prepared for purposes of Article 33 of the 1996 Hague Convention where the request is made under that Convention.

(3) Where the court sends the request directly to the central authority or other authority having jurisdiction in the other State, it shall at the same time send a copy of the request to the [domestic Central Authority][1].

(4) The court may send the request to the [domestic Central Authority]1 for onward transmission to the central authority or other authority having jurisdiction in the other ...² State.

(5) The court should give consideration to the documents which should accompany the request.

>(See Chapters 1 to 3 of this Part generally, for the procedure governing applications for an order under paragraph 19(1) of Schedule 2 to the 1989 Act permitting a local authority to arrange for any child in its care to live outside England and Wales.)
>
>(Part 14 sets out the procedure governing applications for an order under section 84 (giving parental responsibility prior to adoption abroad) of the Adoption and Children Act 2002.)

NOTES

Amendments.¹ Words substituted: SI 2012/2046.² Words omitted repealed: SI 2019/517.

12.71 Application for a declaration as to the extent, or existence, of parental responsibility in relation to a child under Article 16 of the 1996 Hague Convention

(1) Any interested person may apply for a declaration –

>(a)   that a person has, or does not have, parental responsibility for a child; or
>
>(b)   as to the extent of a person's parental responsibility for a child,

where the question arises by virtue of the application of Article 16 of the 1996 Hague Convention.

(2) An application for a declaration as to the extent, or existence of a person's parental responsibility for a child by virtue of Article 16 of the 1996 Hague Convention must be made in the principal registry and heard in the High Court.

(3) An application for a declaration referred to in paragraph (1) may not be made where the question raised is otherwise capable of resolution in any other family proceedings in respect of the child.

Chapter 7
Communication of Information: [Children Proceedings]¹

NOTES

Amendments.¹ Words substituted: SI 2012/3061.

12.72 Interpretation

In this Chapter 'independent reviewing officer' means a person appointed in respect of a child in accordance with regulation 2A of the Review of Children's Cases Regulations 1991, or regulation 3 of the Review of Children's Cases (Wales) Regulations 2007.

12.73 Communication of information: general

(1) For the purposes of the law relating to contempt of court, information relating to proceedings held in private (whether or not contained in a document filed with the court) may be communicated –

    (a)   where the communication is to –

        (i)   a party;

        (ii)   the legal representative of a party;

        (iii)   a professional legal adviser;

        (iv)   an officer of the service or a Welsh family proceedings officer;

        (v)   the welfare officer;

        (vi)   [the Director of Legal Aid Casework (within the meaning of section 4 of the Legal Aid, Sentencing and Punishment of Offenders Act 2012)][1];

        (vii)   an expert whose instruction by a party has been authorised by the court for the purposes of the proceedings;

        (viii) a professional acting in furtherance of the protection of children;

        (ix)   an independent reviewing officer appointed in respect of a child who is, or has been, subject to proceedings to which this rule applies;

    (b)   where the court gives permission; or

    (c)   subject to any direction of the court, in accordance with rule 12.75 and Practice Direction 12G.

(2) Nothing in this Chapter permits the communication to the public at large, or any section of the public, of any information relating to the proceedings.

(3) Nothing in rule 12.75 and Practice Direction 12G permits the disclosure of an unapproved draft judgment handed down by any court.

NOTES

Amendments.[1] Words substituted: SI 2013/534.

12.74

…[1]

NOTES

Amendments.[1] Rule omitted: SI 2012/3061.

12.75 Communication of information for purposes connected with the proceedings

(1) A party or the legal representative of a party, on behalf of and upon the instructions of that party, may communicate information relating to the proceedings to any person where necessary to enable that party –

    (a)   by confidential discussion, to obtain support, advice or assistance in the conduct of the proceedings;

    [(b)   to attend a mediation information and assessment meeting, or to engage in mediation or other forms of non-court dispute resolution;][1]

(c)   to make and pursue a complaint against a person or body concerned in the proceedings; or

(d)   to make and pursue a complaint regarding the law, policy or procedure relating to a category of proceedings to which this Part applies.

(2) Where information is communicated to any person in accordance with paragraph (1)(a) of this rule, no further communication by that person is permitted.

(3) When information relating to the proceedings is communicated to any person in accordance with paragraphs (1)(b), (c) or (d) of this rule –

(a)   the recipient may communicate that information to a further recipient, provided that –
(i)   the party who initially communicated the information consents to that further communication; and
(ii)   the further communication is made only for the purpose or purposes for which the party made the initial communication; and

(b)   the information may be successively communicated to and by further recipients on as many occasions as may be necessary to fulfil the purpose for which the information was initially communicated, provided that on each such occasion the conditions in sub-paragraph (a) are met.

NOTES

Amendment.[1] Sub-paragraph substituted: SI 2014/843.

Practice Direction 12A –
Care, Supervision and Other Part 4 Proceedings: Guide to Case Management

This Practice Direction supplements FPR Part 12

1 The key stages of the court process

1.1 The Public Law Outline set out in the Table below contains an outline of –

(1)   the order of the different stages of the process;
(2)   the matters to be considered at the main case management hearings;
(3)   the latest timescales within which the main stages of the process should take place in order to resolve the proceedings within 26 weeks.

1.2 In the Public Law Outline –

(1)   'CMH' means the Case Management Hearing;
(2)   'FCMH' means Further Case Management Hearing;
(3)   'ICO' means interim care order;
(4)   'IRH' means the Issues Resolution Hearing;
(5)   'LA' means the Local Authority which is applying for a care or supervision order or a final order in other Part 4 proceedings;
(6)   'OS' means the Official Solicitor.

1.3 In applying the provisions of FPR Part 12 and the Public Law Outline the court and the parties must also have regard to –

- (1) all other relevant rules and Practice Directions and in particular –
  - FPR Part 1 (Overriding Objective);
  - [• FPR Part 2 and Practice Direction 2C (relating to justices' legal adviser functions);][1]
  - FPR Part 4 (General Case Management Powers);
  - FPR Part 15 (Representation of Protected Parties) and Practice Direction 15B (Adults Who May Be Protected Parties and Children Who May Become Protected Parties in Family Proceedings);
  - FPR Part 18 (Procedure for Other Applications in Proceedings);
  - FPR Part 22 (Evidence);
  - FPR Part 24 [(Witnesses and depositions generally)][1];
  - FPR Part 25 (Experts) and the Experts Practice Directions;
  - FPR 27.6 and Practice Direction 27A (Court Bundles);
  - FPR 30 (Appeals) and Practice Direction 30A (Appeals);

- (2) the Allocation Rules;
- (3) …[1]
- (4) President's Guidance issued from time to time on
  - Distribution of business of the family court;
  - Judicial continuity and deployment;
  - Prescribed templates and orders;

- (5) International instruments
  - …[1]
  - The 1996 Hague Convention;

- (6) Guidance relating to protected parties and others with a disability –
  - Protected Parties in Family Proceedings: Checklist For the Appointment of a Litigation Friend (including the Official Solicitor) (published in Family Law (January 2014);
  - The Mental Capacity Act 2005 (Transfer of Proceedings) Order 2007 SI 2007/1899, relating to young people over 16 where they are likely to lack decision-making capacity at age 18.

NOTES

Amendment.[1] Words substituted and words omitted repealed: FPR Update, March 2019.

Public Law Outline

PRE-PROCEEDINGS	
PRE-PROCEEDINGS CHECKLIST	
Annex Documents are the documents specified in the Annex to the Application Form which are to be attached to that form and filed with the court:	Checklist documents (already existing on the LA's files) are – (a) Evidential documents including –

PART II – Statutory instruments

PRE-PROCEEDINGS	
PRE-PROCEEDINGS CHECKLIST	
• Social Work Chronology • Social Work Statement and Genogram • The current assessments relating to the child and/or the family and friends of the child to which the Social Work Statement refers and on which the LA relies • Care Plan • Index of Checklist Documents	• Previous court orders including foreign orders and judgments/reasons • Any assessment materials relevant to the key issues including capacity to litigate, section 7 and 37 reports • Single, joint or inter-agency materials (e.g., health and education/Home Office and Immigration Tribunal documents); (b) Decision-making records including – • Records of key discussions with the family • Key LA minutes and records for the child • Pre-existing care plans (e.g., child in need plan, looked after child plan and child protection plan) • Letters Before Proceedings Only Checklist documents in *(a) are to be served* with the application form Checklist Documents in *(b) are to be disclosed on request* by any party Checklist documents are *not* to be – • filed with the court unless the court directs otherwise; and • older than 2 years before the date of issue of the proceedings unless reliance is placed on the same in the LA's evidence [Evidence in support of directions sought – • Evidence in support of any directions sought by Day 2 (see Stage 1 table below). Evidence in support of any directions sought by Day 2 should be filed with the court and served with the application form.][1]

STAGE 1 – ISSUE AND ALLOCATION
DAY 1 AND DAY 2 (see interpretation section)
On Day 1 (Day of issue):
• The LA files the Application Form and Annex Documents and sends copies to Cafcass/CAFCASS Cymru
• The LA notifies the court of the need for an urgent preliminary case management hearing or an urgent contested ICO hearing where this is known or expected
• Court officer issues application
Within a day of issue (Day 2):
• Court considers jurisdiction in a case with an international element
• Court considers initial allocation to specified level of judge, in accordance with the Allocation Rules and any President's Guidance on the distribution of business
[• Court considers any application for directions on exceptions from notification or automatic party status rules and issues any directions for or related to further hearing.]1
• LA serves the Application Form, Annex Documents and evidential Checklist Documents on the parties together with the notice of date and time of CMH and any urgent hearing
• Court gives standard directions on Issue and Allocation including:
– Checking compliance with Pre-Proceedings Checklist including service of any missing Annex Documents
– Appointing Children's Guardian (to be allocated by Cafcass/CAFCASS Cymru)
– Appointing solicitor for the child only if necessary
– Appointing (if the person to be appointed consents) a litigation friend for any protected party or any non subject child who is a party, including the OS where appropriate
– Identifying whether a request has been made or should be made to a Central Authority or other competent authority in a foreign state or a consular authority in England and Wales in a case with an international element
– Filing and service of a LA Case Summary
– Filing and service of a Case Analysis by the Children's Guardian
– Filing and Serving the Parents' Response
– Sending a request for disclosure to, e.g., the police or health service body
– Filing and serving an application for permission relating to experts under Part 25 on a date prior to the advocates meeting for the CMH
– Directing the solicitor for the child to arrange an advocates' meeting no later than 2 business days before the CMH

PART II – Statutory instruments

STAGE 1 – ISSUE AND ALLOCATION
DAY 1 AND DAY 2 (see interpretation section)
– Listing the CMH
• Court considers any request for an urgent preliminary case management hearing or an urgent contested ICO hearing and where necessary lists the hearing and gives additional directions.
• Court officer sends copy Notice of Hearing of the CMH and any urgent hearing by email to Cafcass/ CAFCASS Cymru.

STAGE 2 – CASE MANAGEMENT HEARING	
ADVOCATES' MEETING	CASE MANAGEMENT HEARING
(including any litigants in person)	
No later than 2 business days before CMH (or FCMH if it is necessary)	CMH: Not before day 12 and not later than day 18
	A FCMH is to be held only if necessary, it is to be listed as soon as possible and in any event no later than day 25

• Consider information on the Application Form and Annex documents, the LA Case Summary, and the Case Analysis
 	
• Identify the parties' positions to be recited in the draft Case Management Order
 	
• Identify the parties' positions about jurisdiction, in particular arising out of any international element
 	
• If necessary, identify proposed experts and draft questions in accordance with Part 25 and the Experts Practice Directions
 	
• Identify any disclosure that in the advocates' views is necessary
 	
• Immediately notify the court of the need for a contested ICO hearing and any issue about allocation
	• Court gives detailed case management directions, including:
	
	  – Considering jurisdiction in a case with an international element;
	
	  – Confirming allocation
	
	  – Drawing up the timetable for the child and the timetable for the proceedings and considering if an extension is necessary
	
	  – Identifying additional parties, intervenors and representation (including confirming that Cafcass/CAFCASS Cymru have allocated a Children's Guardian and that a litigation friend is appointed for any protected party or non-subject child)
	
	  – Giving directions for the determination of any disputed issue about litigation capacity

STAGE 2 – CASE MANAGEMENT HEARING	
ADVOCATES' MEETING	**CASE MANAGEMENT HEARING**
• LA advocate to file a draft Case Management Order in prescribed form with court by 11a.m. on the business day before the CMH and/or FCMH	– Identifying the key issues
	– Identifying the evidence necessary to enable the court to resolve the key issues
	– Deciding whether there is a real issue about threshold to be resolved
	– Determining any application made under Part 25 and otherwise ensuring compliance with Part 25 where it is necessary for expert(s) to be instructed
	– Identifying any necessary disclosure and if appropriate giving directions
	– Giving directions for any concurrent or proposed placement order proceedings
	– Ensuring compliance with the court's directions
	– If a FCMH is necessary, directing an advocates' meeting and Case Analysis if required
	– Directing filing of any threshold agreement, final evidence and Care Plan and responses to those documents for the IRH
	– Directing a Case Analysis for the IRH
	– Directing an advocates' meeting for the IRH
	– Listing (any FCMH) IRH, Final Hearing (including early Final Hearing) as appropriate
	– Giving directions for special measures and/or interpreters and intermediaries
	– Issuing the Case Management Order

PART II – Statutory instruments

STAGE 3 – ISSUES RESOLUTION HEARING	
ADVOCATES' MEETING (including any litigants in person)	**IRH**
No later than 7 business days before the IRH • Review evidence and the positions of the parties • Identify the advocates' views of – – the remaining key issues and how the issues may be resolved or narrowed at the IRH including by the making of final orders – the further evidence which is required to be heard to enable the key issues to be resolved or narrowed at the IRH – the evidence that is relevant and the witnesses that are required at the final hearing – the need for a contested hearing and/or time for oral evidence to be given at the IRH • LA advocate to – – notify the court immediately of the outcome of the discussion at the meeting – file a draft Case Management Order with the court by 11a.m. on the business day before the IRH	As directed by the court, in accordance with the timetable for the proceedings • Court identifies the key issue(s) (if any) to be determined and the extent to which those issues can be resolved or narrowed at the IRH • Court considers whether the IRH can be used as a final hearing • Court resolves or narrows the issues by hearing evidence • Court identifies the evidence to be heard on the issues which remain to be resolved at the final hearing • Court gives final case management directions including: – Any extension of the timetable for the proceedings which is necessary – Filing of the threshold agreement or a statement of facts/issues remaining to be determined – Filing of: ○ Final evidence and Care Plan ○ Case Analysis for Final Hearing (if required) ○ Witness templates ○ Skeleton arguments – Judicial reading list/reading time, including time estimate and an estimate for judgment writing time – Ensuring Compliance with PD27A (the Bundles Practice Direction) – Listing the Final Hearing • Court issues Case Management Order

NOTES

Amendment.[1] Words inserted and subparagraph repealed: Practice Direction, April 2020.

2 Flexible powers of the court

2.1 Attention is drawn to the flexible powers of the court either following the issue of the application or at any other stage in the proceedings.

2.2 The court may give directions without a hearing including setting a date for the Final Hearing or a period within which the Final Hearing will take place. The steps, which the court will ordinarily take at the various stages of the proceedings provided for in the Public Law Outline, may be taken by the court at another stage in the proceedings if the circumstances of the case merit this approach.

2.3 The flexible powers of the court include the ability for the court to cancel or repeat a particular hearing. For example, if the issue on which the case turns can with reasonable practicability be crystallised and resolved by taking evidence at an IRH then such a flexible approach must be taken in accordance with the overriding objective and to secure compliance with section 1(2) of the 1989 Act and resolving the proceedings within 26 weeks or the period for the time being specified by the court.

2.4 Where a party has requested an urgent hearing a) to enable the court to give immediate directions or orders to facilitate any case management issue which is to be considered at the CMH, or b) to decide whether an ICO is necessary, the court may list such a hearing at any appropriate time before the CMH and give directions for that hearing. It is anticipated that an urgent preliminary case management hearing will only be necessary to consider issues such as jurisdiction, parentage, party status, capacity to litigate, disclosure and whether there is, or should be, a request to a Central Authority or other competent authority in a foreign state or consular authority in England and Wales in an international case. It is not intended that any urgent hearing will delay the CMH.

2.5 Where it is anticipated that oral evidence may be required at the CMH, FCMH or IRH, the court must be notified in accordance with Stages 2 and 3 of the Public Law Outline well in advance and directions sought for the conduct of the hearing.

2.6 It is expected that full case management will take place at the CMH. It follows that the parties must be prepared to deal with all relevant case management issues, as identified in Stage 2 of the Public Law Outline. A FCMH should only be directed where necessary and must not be regarded as a routine step in proceedings.

3 Compliance with pre-proceedings checklist

3.1 It is recognised that in a small minority of cases the circumstances are such that the safety and welfare of the child may be jeopardised if the start of proceedings is delayed until all of the documents appropriate to the case and referred to in the Pre-proceedings Checklist are available. The safety and welfare of the child should never be put in jeopardy by delaying issuing proceedings whether because of lack of documentation or otherwise. (Nothing in this Practice Direction affects an application for an emergency protection order under section 44 of the 1989 Act). Also, where an application for an interim order is urgent, then the hearing of that application is NOT expected to be postponed until the Case Management Hearing. The Case Management Hearing is still to be held not before day 12 and not later than day 18 in accordance with the Public Law Outline and guidance in this Practice Direction. If an urgent preliminary Case Management Hearing or an urgent contested ICO hearing is held before the CMH, the court should not dispense with the CMH unless all of the parties have been sufficiently prepared and the court has been able to deal with all case management issues which would have come before it at the CMH.

3.2 The court recognises that preparation may need to be varied to suit the circumstances of the case. In cases where any of the Annex Documents required to be attached to the Application Form are not available at the time of issue of the application, the court will consider making directions on issue about when any missing documentation is to be filed. The expectation is that there must be a good reason why one or more of the documents are not available. Further directions relating to any missing documentation will also be made at the Case Management Hearing.

[3.3 Directions may be sought in the initial application for an exception to notification requirements under paragraph 3.1 of Practice Direction 12C or rule 12.4, or for party status under rule 12.3, and evidence in support should as far as possible be included with the application (which would be made separately under Part 18). Before deciding whether to seek such an exception or not, the Local Authority should discuss the issue with the other parties to the proceedings, before proceedings are issued.][1]

NOTES

Amendment.[1] Paragraph inserted: Practice Direction, April 2020.

4 Allocation

4.1 The court considers the allocation of proceedings in accordance with the Allocation Rules and any Guidance issued by the President on distribution of business of the family court. The [justices' legal adviser]1 (with responsibility for gatekeeping and allocation of proceedings) will discuss initial allocation with a district judge (with responsibility for allocation and gatekeeping of proceedings) as provided for in any Guidance issued by the President on distribution of business of the family court. The expectation is that, wherever possible, any question relating to allocation of the proceedings will be considered at the CMH.

NOTES

Amendment.[1] Words substituted: Practice Direction, April 2020.

5 The timetable for the child and the timetable for proceedings

5.1 The timetable for the proceedings:

(1) The court will draw up a timetable for the proceedings with a view to disposing of the application –
   (a) without delay; and

   (b)   in any event within 26 weeks beginning with the day on which the application was issued in accordance with section 32(1)(a)(ii) of the Children Act 1989.

(2)   The court, when drawing up or revising a timetable under paragraph (1), will in particular have regard to –
   (a)   the impact which the timetable or any revised timetable would have on the welfare of the child to whom the application relates; and
   (b)   the impact which the timetable or any revised timetable would have on the duration and conduct of the proceedings.

5.2 The impact which the timetable for the proceedings, any revision or extension of that timetable would have on the welfare of the child to whom the application relates are matters to which the court is to have particular regard. The court will use the Timetable for the Child to assess the impact of these matters on the welfare of the child and to draw up and revise the timetable for the proceedings.

5.3 The 'Timetable for the Child' is the timetable set by the court which takes into account dates which are important to the child's welfare and development.

5.4 The timetable for the proceedings is set having particular regard to the Timetable for the Child and the Timetable for the Child needs to be reviewed regularly. Where adjustments are made to the Timetable for the Child, the timetable for the proceedings will have to be reviewed consistently with resolving the proceedings within 26 weeks or the period for the time being specified by the court.

5.5 Examples of the dates the court will record and take into account when setting the Timetable for the Child are the dates of –

   (1)   any formal review by the Local Authority of the case of a looked after child (within the meaning of section 22(1) of the 1989 Act);
   (2)   any significant educational steps, including the child taking up a place at a new school and, where applicable, any review by the Local Authority of a statement of the child's special educational needs;
   (3)   any health care steps, including assessment by a paediatrician or other specialist;
   (4)   any review of Local Authority plans for the child, including any plans for permanence through adoption, Special Guardianship or placement with parents or relatives;
   (5)   any change or proposed change of the child's placement;
   (6)   any significant change in the child's social or family circumstances; or
   (7)   any timetable for the determination of an issue in a case with an international element.

5.6 To identify the Timetable for the Child, the applicant is required to provide the information needed about the significant steps in the child's life in the Application Form and the Social Work Statement and to update this information regularly taking into account information received from others involved in the child's life such as the parties, members of the child's family, the person who is caring for the child, the children's guardian, the Independent Reviewing Officer,

PART II – Statutory instruments

the child's key social worker and any Central Authority or competent authority in a foreign state or a consular authority in England and Wales in a case with an international element.

5.7 Where more than one child is the subject of the proceedings, the court should consider and will set a Timetable for the Child for each child. The children may not all have the same timetable, and the court will consider the appropriate progress of the proceedings in relation to each child.

5.8 Where there are parallel care proceedings and criminal proceedings against a person connected with the child for a serious offence against the child, linked directions hearings should where practicable take place as the case progresses. The timing of the proceedings in a linked care and criminal case should appear in the Timetable for the Child. The time limit of resolving the proceedings within 26 weeks applies unless a longer timetable has been set by the court in order to resolve the proceedings justly in accordance with section 32(1)(a)(ii) and (5) of the 1989 Act. Early disclosure and listing of hearings is necessary in proceedings in a linked care and criminal case.

6 Extensions to the timetable for proceedings

6.1 The court is required to draw up a timetable for proceedings with a view to disposing of the application without delay and in any event within 26 weeks. If proceedings can be resolved earlier, then they should be. A standard timetable and process is expected to be followed in respect of the giving of standard directions on issue and allocation and other matters which should be carried out by the court on issue, including setting and giving directions for the Case Management Hearing.

6.2 Having regard to the circumstances of the particular case, the court may consider that it is necessary to extend the time by which the proceedings are to be resolved beyond 26 weeks to enable the court to resolve the proceedings justly (see section 32(5) of the 1989 Act). When making this decision, the court is to take account of the guidance that extensions are not to be granted routinely and are to be seen as requiring specific justification (see section 32(7) of the 1989 Act). The decision and reason(s) for extending a case should be recorded in writing (in the Case Management Order) and orally stated in court, so that all parties are aware of the reasons for delay in the case (see FPR 12.26C). The Case Management Order must contain a record of this information, as well as the impact of the court's decision on the welfare of the child.

6.3 The court may extend the period within which proceedings are intended to be resolved on its own initiative or on application. Applications for an extension should, wherever possible, only be made so that they are considered at any hearing for which a date has been fixed or for which a date is about to be fixed. Where a date for a hearing has been fixed, a party who wishes to make an application at that hearing but does not have sufficient time to file an application notice should as soon as possible inform the court (if possible in writing) and, if possible, the other parties of the nature of the application and the reason for it. The party should then make the application orally at the hearing.

6.4 If the court agrees an extension is necessary, an initial extension to the time limit may be granted for up to eight weeks (or less if directed) in order to resolve the case justly (see section 32(8) of the 1989 Act). If more time is necessary, in order to resolve the proceedings justly, a further extension of up to eight weeks may be agreed by the court. There is no limit on the number of extensions that may be granted in a particular case.

6.5 If the court considers that the timetable for the proceedings will require an extension beyond the next eight week period in order to resolve the proceedings justly, the Case Management Order should –

(1)   state the reason(s) why it is necessary to have a further extension;
(2)   fix the date of the next effective hearing (which might be in a period shorter than a further eight weeks); and
(3)   indicate whether it is appropriate for the next application for an extension of the timetable to be considered on paper.

6.6 The expectation is that, subject to paragraph 6.5, extensions should be considered at a hearing and that a court will not approve proposals for the management of a case under FPR 12.15 where the consequence of those proposals is that the case is unlikely to be resolved within 26 weeks or other period for the time being allowed for resolution of the proceedings. In accordance with FPR 4.1(3)(e), the court may hold a hearing and receive evidence by telephone or by using any other method of direct oral communication. When deciding whether to extend the timetable, the court must have regard to the impact of any ensuing timetable revision on the welfare of the child (see section 32(6) of the 1989 Act).

7 Interpretation

7.1 In this Practice Direction –

'Allocation Rules' mean any rules relating to composition of the court and distribution of business made under section 31D of the Matrimonial and Family Proceedings Act 1984;

'Care Plan' is a separate document from the evidence that is filed by the local authority. It is a 'section 31A plan' referred to in section 31A of the 1989 Act which complies with guidance as to content issued by the Secretary of State;

'Case Analysis' means a written or, if there is insufficient time for a written, an oral outline of the case from the perspective of the child's best interests prepared by the children's guardian or Welsh family proceedings officer for the CMH or FCMH (where one is necessary) and IRH or as otherwise directed by the court, incorporating an analysis of the key issues that need to be resolved in the case including –

(a)   a threshold analysis;
(b)   a case management analysis, including an analysis of the timetable for the proceedings, an analysis of the Timetable for the Child and the evidence which any party proposes is necessary to resolve the issues;
(c)   a parenting capability analysis;

(d)   a child impact analysis, including an analysis of the ascertainable wishes and feelings of the child and the impact on the welfare of the child of any application to adjourn a hearing or extend the timetable for the proceedings;

(e)   an early permanence analysis including an analysis of the proposed placements and contact framework; by reference to a welfare and proportionality analysis;

(f)   whether and if so what communication it is proposed there should be during the proceedings with the child by the court;

'Case Management Order' is the prescribed form of order referred to in any Guidance issued by the President from time to time on prescribed templates and orders;

'Day' means 'business day'. 'Day 1' is the day of issue and 'Day 2' is the next business day following the day of issue of proceedings. 'Day 12', 'Day 18' and 'Day 25' are respectively the 11th, 17th and the 24th business days after the day of issue of proceedings (Day 1). '26 weeks' means 26 calendar weeks beginning on the day of issue of proceedings (Day 1);

'Experts Practice Directions' mean –

(a)   Practice Direction 25A (Experts – Emergencies and Pre Proceedings Instructions);

(b)   Practice Direction 25B (The Duties of An Expert, The Expert's Report and Arrangements For An Expert To Attend Court);

(c)   Practice Direction 25C (Children's Proceedings – The Use Of Single Joint Experts and The Process Leading to An Expert Being Instructed or Expert Evidence Being Put Before the Court);

(d)   Practice Direction 25E (Discussions Between Experts in Family Proceedings);

'Genogram' means a family tree, setting out in diagrammatic form the child's family and extended family members and their relationship with the child;

'Index of Checklist Documents' means a list of Checklist Documents referred to in the Public Law Outline Pre-Proceedings Checklist which is divided into two parts with Part A being the documents referred to in column 2, paragraph (a) of the Pre-Proceedings Checklist and Part B being those referred to in column 2, paragraph (b) of the Pre-Proceedings Checklist;

'International instruments'

...[3]

'The 1996 Hague Convention' means the Convention on Jurisdiction, Applicable Law, Recognition, Enforcement and Co-operation in Respect of Parental Responsibility and Measures for the Protection of Children;

...[2]

'Letter Before Proceedings' means any letter from the Local Authority containing written notification to the parents and others with parental responsibility for the child of the Local Authority's likely intention to apply to court for a care or supervision order and any related subsequent correspondence confirming the Local Authority's position;

'Local Authority Case Summary' means a document prepared by the Local Authority legal representative for each case management hearing in the form referred to in any Guidance issued by the President from time to time on prescribed templates and orders;

'Parents' Response' means a document from either or both of the parents containing

> (a) in no more than two pages, the parents' response to the Threshold Statement, and
>
> (b) the parents' placement proposals including the identity and whereabouts of all relatives and friends they propose be considered by the court;
>
> (c) Information which may be relevant to a person's capacity to litigate including information about any referrals to mental health services and adult services;

'Section 7 report' means any report under section 7 of the 1989 Act;

'Section 37 report' means any report by the Local Authority to the court as a result of a direction under section 37 of the 1989 Act;

'Social Work Chronology' means a schedule containing –

> (a) a succinct summary of the length of involvement of the local authority with the family and in particular with the child;
>
> (b) a succinct summary of the significant dates and events in the child's life in chronological order – i.e. a running record up to the issue of the proceedings; providing such information under the following headings –
>
>> (i) serial number;
>> (ii) date;
>> (iii) event-detail;
>> (iv) witness or document reference (where applicable);

'Social Work Statement' means a statement prepared by the Local Authority limited to the following evidence –

Summary
> (a) The order sought;
> (b) Succinct summary of reasons with reference as appropriate to the Welfare Checklist;

Family
> (c) Family members and relationships especially the primary carers and significant adults/other children;
> (d) Genogram;

Threshold
> (e) Precipitating events;
> (f) Background circumstances;
> (i) summary of children's services involvement cross-referenced to the chronology;
> (ii) previous court orders and emergency steps;
> (iii) previous assessments;
> (g) Summary of significant harm and or likelihood of significant harm which the LA will seek to establish by evidence or concession;

Parenting capability

(h)   Assessment of child's needs;

(i)   Assessment of parental capability to meet needs;

(j)   Analysis of why there is a gap between parental capability and the child's needs;

(k)   Assessment of other significant adults who may be carers;

Child impact

(l)   Wishes and feelings of the child(ren);

(m)   Timetable for the Child;

(n)   Delay and timetable for the proceedings;
      Permanence and contact

(o)   Parallel planning;

(p)   Realistic placement options by reference to a welfare and proportionality analysis;

(q)   Contact framework;

Case Management

(r)   Evidence and assessments necessary and outstanding;

(s)   Any information about any person's litigation capacity, mental health issues, disabilities or vulnerabilities that is relevant to their capability to participate in the proceedings; and

(t)   Case management proposals.

'Standard Directions on Issue and Allocation' means directions given by the court on issue and upon allocation in the prescribed form referred to in any Guidance issued by the President from time to time on prescribed templates and orders;

'Threshold Statement' means a written outline by the legal representative of the LA in the application form of the facts which the LA will seek to establish by evidence or concession to satisfy the threshold criteria under s 31(2) of the 1989 Act limited to no more than 2 pages;

'Welfare Checklist' means the list of matters which is set out in section 1(3) of the 1989 Act and to which the court is to have particular regard in accordance with section (1)(3) and (4).]¹

NOTES

Amendment. ¹ PD12A, FPR Update, April 2014.² Words substituted: Practice Direction, April 2020.³ Definition omitted repealed: FPR Update, March 2019.

See over for Public Law Outline 2014 (26 Weeks).

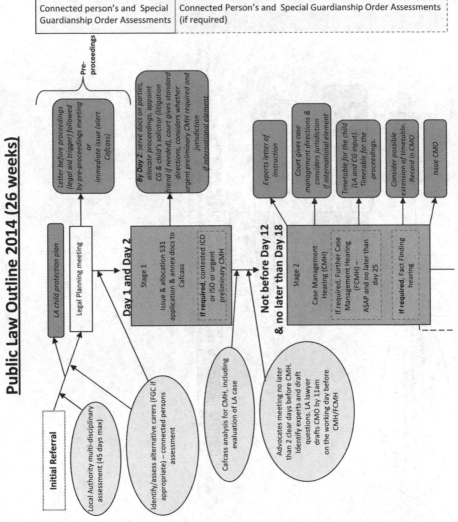

Public Law Outline 2014 (26 weeks)

Initial Referral

Local Authority multi-disciplinary assessment (45 days max)

Identify/assess alternative carers (FGC if appropriate) – connected persons assessment

LA child protection plan

Legal Planning meeting

Letter before proceedings (legal aid trigger) followed by pre-proceedings meeting *or* immediate issue (alert Cafcass)

Pre-proceedings

Connected person's and Special Guardianship Order Assessments

Connected Person's and Special Guardianship Order Assessments (if required)

Day 1 and Day 2

Stage 1

Issue & allocation S31 application & annex docs to Cafcass

If required, contested ICO or ISO or urgent preliminary CMH

By Day 2: serve docs on parties, allocate proceedings, appoint CG & child's solicitor litigation friend (if needed), court gives standard directions, considers whether urgent preliminary CMH required and jurisdiction if international element

Cafcass analysis for CMH, including evaluation of LA case

Advocates meeting no later than 2 clear days before CMH. Identify experts and draft questions. LA lawyer drafts CMO by 11am on the working day before CMH/FCMH

Not before Day 12 & no later than Day 18

Stage 2

Case Management Hearing (CMH)

If required, Further Case Management Hearing (FCMH) – ASAP and no later than day 25

If required, Fact Finding hearing

Experts letter of instruction

Court gives case management directions & considers jurisdiction if international element

Timetable for the child (LA and CG input). Timetable for the proceedings.

Consider possible extension of timetable. Record in CMO

Issue CMO

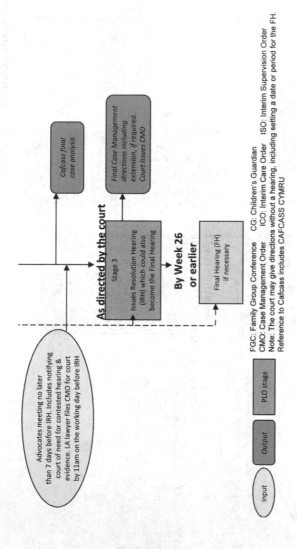

Advocates meeting no later than 7 days before IRH. Includes notifying court of need for contested hearing & evidence. LA lawyer files CMO for court by 11am on the working day before IRH

As directed by the court

Stage 3

Issues Resolution Hearing (IRH) which could also become the Final Hearing

By Week 26 or earlier

Final Hearing (FH) if necessary

Cafcass final case analysis

Final Case Management directions including extension, if required. Court issues CMO

FGC: Family Group Conference   CG: Children's Guardian   ICO: Interim Care Order   ISO: Interim Supervision Order
CMO: Case Management Order
Note: The court may give directions without a hearing, including setting a date or period for the FH.
Reference to Cafcass includes CAFCASS CYMRU

Output

PLO stage

Input

[Practice Direction 12B –
Child Arrangements Programme

This Practice Direction supplements FPR Part 12

Amendments—Substituted by FPR Update 12.

1 When does the Child Arrangements Programme Apply?

1.1 The Child Arrangements Programme (the 'CAP') applies where a dispute arises between separated parents and/or families about arrangements concerning children.

1.2 The CAP is designed to assist families to reach safe and child-focused agreements for their child, where possible out of the court setting. If parents / families are unable to reach agreement, and a court application is made, the CAP encourages swift resolution of the dispute through the court.

1.3 It is well-recognised that negotiated agreements between adults generally enhance long-term co-operation, and are better for the child concerned. Therefore, separated parents and families are strongly encouraged to attempt to resolve their disputes concerning the child outside of the court system. This may also be quicker and cheaper.

2 Signposting Services, Parenting Plans, & Public Funding

2.1 **Services:** Where a dispute arises in relation to a child, or children, parents and families are encouraged to obtain advice and support as soon as possible.

2.2 There are many services available for such families, who seek advice about resolving disputes concerning their child.

2.3 The following services are recommended:

(1) For more information about family mediation and to find the nearest mediation service (including those providing a MIAM): www.familymediationcouncil.org.uk;

(2) For a Guide about children and the family courts for separating parents (including representing yourself in court): the form 'CB7': http://www.cafcass.gov.uk/media/168195/cb7-eng.pdf

(3) For Cafcass (England): www.cafcass.gov.uk;

(4) For CAFCASS Cymru (Wales): www.wales.gov.uk/cafcasscymru;

(5) To find a legal adviser or family mediator: http://find-legal-advice.justice.gov.uk;

(6) To check whether you can get financial help (legal aid) to pay for non-court dispute resolution, &/or advice and representation at court, and to find a legal aid solicitor or mediator: https://www.gov.uk/check-legal-aid

(7) For general advice about sorting out arrangements for children, the use of post-separation mediation, &/or going to court: http://www.advicenow.org.uk; http://www.advicenow.org.uk/advicenow-guides/family/sorting-out-arrangements-for-your-children/

PART II – Statutory instruments

(8)   For general advice on separation services and options for resolving disputes: www.sortingoutseparation.org.uk;

(9)   For general advice about sorting out arrangements for children: http://theparentconnection.org.uk/

(10) For advice about Contact Centres, which are neutral places where children of separated families can enjoy contact with their non-resident parents and sometimes other family members, in a comfortable and safe environment; and information about where they are: www.naccc.org.uk;

(11) For the form to apply for a child arrangements order: https://www.gov.uk/looking-after-children-divorce/apply-for-court-order;

(12) For help with taking a case to court without a lawyer, the Personal Support Unit: http://thepsu.org/;

(13) For guidance on representing yourself at court, including a list of commonly used terms that you may come across: http://www.barcouncil.org.uk/instructing-a-barrister/representing-yourself-in-court/;

(14) For advice about finding and using a family law solicitor see: Law Society http://www.lawsociety.org.uk, and Resolution (family law solicitors): http://www.resolution.org.uk;

(15) For advice about finding using a family law barrister: see http://www.barcouncil.org.uk/about-the-bar/find-a-barrister/, and for arrangements for using a barrister directly see http://www.barcouncil.org.uk/instructing-a-barrister/public-access/.

2.4 **Parenting Plan:** A Parenting Plan is widely recognised as being a useful tool for separated parents to identify, agree and set out in writing arrangements for their children; such a plan could appropriately be used as the basis for discussion about a dispute which has arisen. It is likely to be useful in any event for assisting arrangements between separated parents.

2.5 The Parenting Plan should cover all practical aspects of care for the child, and should reflect a shared commitment to the child and his/her future, with particular emphasis on parental communication (learning how to deal with differences), living arrangements, money, religion, education, health care and emotional well-being.

2.6 A Parenting Plan is designed to help separated parents (and their families) to work out the best possible arrangements for the child; the plan should be understood by everyone, including (where the child is of an appropriate age and understanding) the child concerned.

2.7 For help on preparing a Parenting Plan, see:

(1)   Cafcass 'Putting Your Children First: A Guide for Separated Parents' (see also paragraph 4 below);

(2)   A draft of a Parenting Plan for parents or families to complete: http://www.cafcass.gov.uk/download/4365

[(3) A draft of a Parenting Plan prepared by CAFCASS Cymru for parents or families to complete: http://gov.wales/docs/cafcass/publications/071015ParentingPlanEn.pdf(thislinkstothedraftplaninEnglish) or http://gov.wales/docs/cafcass/publications/071015ParentingPlanCy.pdf (this links to the draft plan in Welsh).][1]

NOTES

Amendment.[1] Subparagraph inserted: FPR Update, April 2016.

2.8 **Publicly funded mediation and/or legal advice:** If parents need access to mediation, and legal advice in support of that mediation, they may be eligible for public funding. The Legal Aid Agency (LAA) will provide funding for Mediation Information and Assessment Meetings (MIAMs) and family mediation for all those who are eligible:

(1)   Where at least one party is eligible, the LAA will cover the costs of both parties to attend a MIAM to encourage any non-eligible client to find out about the benefits and suitability of mediation without incurring any costs.

(2)   The LAA will provide public funding for eligible parties to participate in family mediation and they may also receive some independent legal advice connected to the mediation process and where a settlement is reached can receive legal assistance to draft and issue proceedings to obtain a consent order.

(3)   Parties may find out if they are likely to be eligible for legal aid at the following link: https://www.gov.uk/check-legal-aid

(4)   To find the nearest publicly funded mediation service a client can use the search at http://find-legal-advice.justice.gov.uk. Publicly funded legal advisors can be found at: https://www.gov.uk/check-legal-aid

2.9 Public funding for legal advice and/or representation at court is available in limited circumstances. Further information can be found here: http://www.justice.gov.uk/legal-aid-for-private-family-matters

3 Explanation of terms

3.1 Some of the terms used in this document, and in the websites referred to above, may not be familiar to those who seek help and support.

3.2 A guide to some of the relevant terms is attached in the Annex at the end of this document.

4 The child in the dispute

4.1 In making any arrangements with respect to a child, the child's welfare must be the highest priority.

4.2 Children and young people should be at the centre of all decision-making. This accords with the Family Justice Young People's Board Charter (https://www.cafcass.gov.uk/media/179714/fjypb_national_charter_1013.pdf).

4.3 The child or young person should feel that their needs, wishes and feelings have been considered in the arrangements which are made for them.

4.4 Children should be involved, to the extent which is appropriate given their age and level of understanding, in making the arrangements which affect them. This is just as relevant where:

(1)   the parties are making arrangements between themselves (which may be recorded in a Parenting Plan),

as when:

(2)   arrangements are made in the context of dispute resolution outside away from the court,

and/or

(3)   the court is required to make a decision about the arrangements for the child.

4.5 If an application for a court order has been issued, the judge may want to know the child's view. This may be communicated to the judge in one of a number of ways:

(1)   By a Cafcass officer (in Wales, a Welsh Family Proceedings Officer (WFPO)) providing a report to the court which sets out the child's wishes and feelings;

(2)   By the child being encouraged (by the Cafcass officer or WFPO, or a parent or relative) to write a letter to the court;

(3)   In the limited circumstances described in paragraph 18 below, by the child being a party to the proceedings;

and/or:

(4)   By the judge meeting with the child, in accordance with approved Guidance (currently the FJC Guidelines for Judges Meeting Children subject to Family Proceedings (April 2010)). http://www.judiciary. gov.uk/JCO%2fDocuments%2fFJC%2fvoc%2fGuidelines_+Judges_ seeing_+Children.pdf

5 Non-court resolution of disputed arrangements for children

5.1 Dispute resolution services, including mediation, are available to provide opportunities for parents and families to work in a positive and constructive way, and should be actively considered and attempted where it is safe and appropriate to do so. Information about mediation and other non-court dispute resolution is available widely (see 'Signposting Services for Families' – paragraph 2 above).

5.2 It is not expected that those who are the victims of domestic violence should attempt to mediate or otherwise participate in forms of non-court dispute resolution. It is also recognised that drug and/or alcohol misuse and/or mental illness are likely to prevent couples from making safe use of mediation or similar services; these risk factors (which can be discussed at a MIAM – see below, paragraph 5.3) are likely to have an impact on arrangements for the child. Court Orders, including those made by consent, must be scrutinised to ensure that they are safe and take account of any risk factors, in accordance with Practice Direction 12J FPR.

5.3 Attendance at Mediation Information and Assessment Meeting ('MIAM'): Subject to paragraph 5.6 (below), before making a family application to the court (a 'relevant family application' as defined in paragraph 23 below), the person who is considering making such application must attend a family MIAM. A prospective respondent is expected to attend a MIAM – whether this is a separate MIAM or the same MIAM attended by the prospective applicant. At the MIAM, information will be provided about mediation of disputes of the kind to which the application relates, ways in which the dispute may be resolved otherwise than by the court, and the suitability of mediation (or any other way of resolving the dispute) for trying to resolve the dispute. The mediator will also assess whether there has been, or is a risk of,

(1) domestic violence, and/or
(2) harm by a prospective party to a child that would be the subject of the application.

5.4 It is the responsibility of the prospective applicant (or that person's legal representative) to contact a family mediator to arrange attendance at a MIAM.

5.5 Only an authorised family mediator can carry out a MIAM. [An authorised family mediator is a person identified by the Family Mediation Council as qualified to conduct a MIAM.][1]

5.6 A prospective applicant is not required to attend a MIAM where one of the circumstances set out in rule 3.8(1) or 3.8(2) FPR applies.

5.7 Information on [how to find an authorised family mediator]1 may be obtained from www.familymediationcouncil.org.uk website which hosts the 'find a local family mediator' database (see also 'Signposting Services for Families' – paragraph 2 above).

5.8 The prospective applicant (or the prospective applicant's legal representative) should provide the mediator with contact details for the other party or parties to the dispute ('the prospective respondent(s)'), so that the mediator can contact the prospective respondent(s) to discuss their willingness and availability to attend a MIAM.

5.9 The prospective applicant and, where they agree to do so, the prospective respondent(s), should then attend a MIAM arranged by the mediator. If the parties are willing to attend together and where it is assessed by the mediator to be safe, the meeting may be conducted jointly; otherwise, separate meetings will be held.

5.10 The Family Mediation Council sets the requirements for mediators who conduct MIAMs. In summary, a mediator who arranges a MIAM with one or more parties to a dispute should consider any risk factors present and how these should be managed, and should also consider with the party or parties concerned whether public funding may be available to meet the cost of the meeting and any subsequent mediation. Where neither of the parties is eligible for, or wishes to seek, public funding, any charge made by the mediator for the MIAM will be the responsibility of the party or parties attending, in accordance with any agreement made with the mediator.

5.11 Mediation is a confidential process; none of the parties to the mediation may provide information to the court as to the content of any discussions held in mediation and/or the reasons why agreement was not reached. Similarly, the mediator may not provide such information, unless the mediator considers that a safeguarding issue arises.

5.12 However, it is important that the parties, or either of them, introduce at the MIAM (or any subsequent court application) any other evidence of attempts to resolve a dispute and to focus on the needs of the child.

NOTES

Amendments.[1] Words substituted: FPR Update, November 2015.

6 Resolution of disputed arrangements for children through the Court

6.1 The judge is obliged to consider, at every stage of court proceedings, whether non-court dispute resolution is appropriate.

6.2 The parties should also actively consider non-court dispute resolution even if proceedings are issued and are ongoing.

6.3 If the court considers that another form of dispute resolution is appropriate, the court may direct that the proceedings, or a hearing in the proceedings, be adjourned for such specified period as it considers appropriate:

(1)   to enable the parties to obtain information and advice about non-court dispute resolution; and

(2)   where the parties agree, to enable non-court dispute resolution to take place.

6.4 Where the court adjourns proceedings, it shall give directions about the timing and method by which the parties must tell the court if any of the issues in the proceedings have been resolved.

6.5 It is to be noted that some courts operate an at-court mediation scheme, and at-court MIAMs, with providers contracted to the Legal Aid Agency. Some mediators may prefer to conduct mediation outside of the court premises. A mediation assessment may be possible at court; alternatively, the court may help in making an appointment with a local mediator for a MIAM or for mediation. Information about mediation arrangements should be advertised in the local court.

7 Local Good Practice

7.1 The CAP is designed to provide a framework for a consistent approach to the resolution of the issues in private family law in England & Wales.

7.2 Local practices and initiatives can be operated in addition to, and within, the framework

8 Application to court

8.1 Unless one of the MIAM exemptions applies (see rule 3.8 FPR), an application to court for determination of most issues concerning a child (see the definition of 'relevant family application' in rule 3.6 FPR and paragraphs 11 and 12 of PD3A) can be made only after a MIAM has taken place (at which meeting mediation and other forms of non-court dispute resolution will have been considered). One of the exemptions may be that the case is urgent, in which case see 'Urgent and Without Notice Applications' in paragraph 12 below. The grounds for urgency are defined in rule 3.8(c) FPR.

8.2 The application for a child arrangements order or other Children Act 1989 private law order shall be made on the relevant prescribed form.

8.3 For section 8 Children Act 1989 applications, the applicant will be required, on the form C100, to confirm attendance at a MIAM or specify that an exemption applies unless the application is for a consent order, or if the application concerns a child who is the subject of ongoing emergency proceedings, care proceedings or supervision proceedings, or if the child concerned is already the subject of an emergency protection order, care order or supervision order (see paragraphs 11 and 12 of PD3A).

8.4 The relevant part of the form C100 must be completed showing that either:

(1) the applicant has attended a MIAM; or

(2) the applicant has not attended a MIAM and claims one of the exemptions (rule 3.8(1) FPR) – exemptions include (but are not limited to) evidence of domestic violence, child protection concerns, urgency, previous MIAM attendance or exemption; or

(3) an authorised family mediator confirms in the form that he or she is satisfied that

(a) mediation is not suitable because the respondents is (if more than one respondent, any one of them is) unwilling to attend a MIAM;

(b) mediation is not suitable as a means of resolving the dispute because the respondent (if more than one, any of them) failed without good reason to attend a MIAM; or

(c) mediation is otherwise not suitable as a means of resolving the dispute.

8.5 The C100 form may be obtained from the Family Court or from www.gov.uk.

8.6 If the parties have previously prepared a Parenting Plan, this shall be attached to the Form C100.

8.7 If possible at the time of issue, and in any event by no later than one working day after issue, or in courts where applications are first considered on paper by no later than two working days after issue, the court shall send or hand to the Applicant the following:

(i) A copy of the application form C100 (together with the Supplemental Information Form C1A),

(ii) The Notice of Hearing;

(iii) The Acknowledgment Form C7;

(iv) A blank Form C1A, (if required);

(v) Information leaflets for the parties (which must include the CB7 leaflet)

8.8 Unless the applicant requests to do so, or the court directs the applicant to do so, the Court will serve the respondent(s) with:

(i) A copy of the application form C100 (together with Supplemental Information Form C1A, if provided);

(ii) The Notice of Hearing;

(iii) The Acknowledgement Form C7;

PART II – Statutory instruments

    (iv)   A blank form C1A;
    (v)   Information leaflet for the parties (which must include the CB7 leaflet).

8.9 The court shall send to Cafcass/CAFCASS Cymru a copy of the Form C100 (and the form C1A, if supplied), and the C6 Notice of Hearing no later than 2 working days after the date of issue. This will be in electronic format where possible.

8.10 The court shall not send to Cafcass/CAFCASS Cymru any other application under the Children Act 1989, or any other private law application, unless the Court has made a specific direction requesting the assistance of Cafcass/CAFCASS Cymru. Therefore, any application which is not in Form C100 or which does not contain a direction to Cafcass/CAFCASS Cymru will be returned to the court at which the application has been issued.

8.11 The respondent(s) must send the Acknowledgement Form C7 and, where applicable, the Supplemental Information Form C1A, to the court within 14 days after receiving the application, unless the court has specified a shorter time.

8.12 On receipt of the Acknowledgement Form C7 and any Form C1A filed by the respondent(s), the court shall send a copy of each form to Cafcass / CAFCASS Cymru, in electronic format where possible, and shall send copies to the applicant.

9 Allocation and Gatekeeping

9.1 It is important that the form C100 is fully completed (including the provision of telephone numbers of the relevant parties), otherwise there may be a delay in processing the application; where the form is not fully completed, the court staff may request further information before the application form is accepted for issue. It is also important that the form C100, the Acknowledgement Form C7 and, where applicable, any Supplemental Information Form C1A are fully and accurately completed to enable the court to make appropriate decisions about allocation and case management.

9.2 The application shall be considered by a nominated Legal Adviser &/or nominated District Judge ('the Gatekeeper(s)') within one working day of the date of receipt in accordance with the appropriate Rules of Procedure.

9.3 An application for a relevant family order shall be allocated to a level of judge in the Family Court in accordance with the Guidance issued by the President on Allocation and Gatekeeping for Proceedings under Part II of the Children Act 1989 (Private Law Proceedings) and the Family Court (Composition and Distribution of Business) Rules 2014, together with the Allocation Schedule.

9.4 Gatekeepers shall be able to issue Directions on Issue in the following circumstances:

    (1)   where, on the basis of information provided on the application form and any additional information provided on a C1A Supplemental Information Form, the Gatekeeper finds that the exemption from attending a MIAM has not validly been claimed, the Gatekeeper will

direct the applicant, or direct the parties to attend a MIAM before the FHDRA, unless the Gatekeeper considers that in all the circumstances of the case the MIAM requirement should not apply to the application in question; the Gatekeeper will have particular regard to the matters set out in rule 3.10(3) FPR when making this decision;

(2) where it appears that an urgent issue requires determination, the Gatekeeper may give directions for an accelerated hearing;

(3) exceptionally, where it appears that directions need to be given for the service and filing of evidence, he/she may give directions for the filing of evidence.

10 Judicial continuity

10.1 All private law cases will be allocated to a level of judge within the Family Court upon issue.

10.2 Continuity of Judicial involvement in the conduct of proceedings from the FHDRA to the making of a final order should be the objective in all cases.

10.3 Where the case has been allocated to be heard before lay justices, the expectation of judicial continuity should apply where:

(1) There has been a hearing to determine findings of fact,

(2) A decision yet to be made in the interests of a child by a court depends upon rulings or judicial assessments already made in the proceedings,

in which case, wherever possible, the hearing shall be listed before the same lay justices; alternatively, it shall be listed before the same legal adviser and at least one lay justice (preferably the chairman) to provide that continuity. Where a case is adjourned part-heard the court which resumes the hearing shall, wherever possible, be composed of the same lay justices as dealt with the previous part of the hearing (see rule 8 of the Family Court (Composition and Distribution of Business) Rules 2014).

11 Key welfare principles

11.1 Section 1 of the Children Act 1989 applies to all applications for orders concerning the upbringing of children. This means that:

(1) the child's welfare is the court's paramount consideration;

(2) delay is likely to be prejudicial to the welfare of the child, and

(3) a court order shall not be made unless the court considers that making an order would be better for the child than making no order at all.

11.2 Parties, and the court, must also have regard to the FPR in particular the following:

(1) FPR Rule 1. The 'overriding objective' will apply, so that the court will deal with a case justly, having regard to the welfare issues involved and specifically will:

(a) Ensure that the case is dealt with expeditiously and fairly;

(b) Deal with the case in ways which are proportionate to the nature, importance and complexity of the issues;

    (c)   Ensure that the parties are on an equal footing;

    (d)   Save expense;

    (e)   Allot to each case an appropriate share of the court's resources, while taking account of the need to allot resources to other cases.

(2)   Rule 3, and Practice Direction 3A;

(3)   FPR Part 4 'General Case Management Powers';

(4)   FPR Part 15 (Representation of Protected Parties) and Practice Direction 15B (Adults Who May Be Protected Parties and Children Who May Become Protected Parties in Family Proceedings);

(5)   FPR Part 16 (Representation of Children) (and see also paragraph 18 below);

(6)   FPR Part 18 (procedure for Other Applications in proceedings);

(7)   FPR Part 22 (Evidence);

(8)   …[1]

(9)   FPR Part 25 (Experts) and the Experts Practice Directions;

(10) FPR 27.6 and Practice Direction 27A (Court Bundles).

11.3 Where a fact-finding hearing is required, this shall take place in accordance with revised Practice Direction 12J FPR.

11.4 The court shall exercise its powers flexibly. The flexible powers of the court include the ability for the court to cancel or repeat a particular hearing.

NOTES

Amendment.[1] Paragraph omitted repealed: FPR Update, March 2019.

12 Urgent and Without Notice Applications

12.1 **Urgent:** Where an order is sought as a matter of urgency, an application may be made to the Court for an emergency order without the requirement for the Applicant to have attended at a MIAM. The categories of urgent application justifying such an exemption are set out in rule 3.8(c) FPR and include cases in which:

(1)   There is a risk to the life, liberty, or the physical safety of the prospective applicant or his or her family, or his or her home;

(2)   Any delay caused by attending a MIAM would cause:

    (A)   A risk of harm to the child;

    (B)   A risk of unlawful removal of a child from the United Kingdom or a risk of unlawful retention of a child who is currently outside England and Wales;

    (C)   A significant risk of a miscarriage of justice;

(4)   Unreasonable hardship to the prospective applicant;

(5)   Irretrievable problems in dealing with the dispute (including the irretrievable loss of significant evidence).

(3)   There is a significant risk that in the period necessary to schedule and attend a MIAM, proceedings relating to the dispute will be brought in another state in which a valid claim to jurisdiction may exist, such that a court in that other State would be seised of the dispute before a court in England and Wales.

12.2 **'Without Notice':** Applications to court made 'Without Notice' to the respondent(s) shall be allocated in accordance with the Family Court

(Composition and Distribution of Business) Rules 2014, and determined by reference to the provisions of Practice Direction 18A, paragraph 5.1, with further regard to the principles set out in Practice Direction 20A, paragraph 4.3–4.5 FPR (noting particularly paragraph 4.3(c)).

12.3 Without Notice Orders should be made only exceptionally, and where:

(1) If the applicant were to give notice to the respondent(s) this would enable the respondent(s) to take steps to defeat the purpose of the injunction; cases where the application is brought without notice in order to conceal the step from the respondent(s) are very rare indeed; or

(2) The case is one of exceptional urgency; that is to say, that there has been literally no time to give notice (either by telephone, text or e-mail or otherwise) before the injunction is required to prevent the threatened wrongful act; or

(3) If the applicant gives notice to the respondent(s), this would be likely to expose the applicant or relevant child to unnecessary risk of physical or emotional harm.

12.4 Any Order which follows an emergency 'without notice' hearing should specify:

(1) the reason(s) why the order has been made without notice to the respondent(s),

(2) the outline facts alleged which have been relied upon by the court in making the order, unless the facts are clearly contained in the statement in support; and

(3) the right of the respondent(s) to apply to vary or discharge the order.

12.5 Gatekeeping decisions: Following any urgent or 'without notice' hearing, unless all issues have been determined or the application has been dismissed without any further directions given, the judge may make gatekeeping decisions, including allocation and venue of future hearing, (and if so, shall notify the Gatekeeping team responsible for the area in which the child resides), or shall refer the application to the relevant Gatekeeping team for a decision on allocation and venue of future hearing; in either event, a copy of the C100 shall be sent to Cafcass for safeguarding checks, and (depending on the Gatekeeping decision) the file shall be sent to the court where future hearings will take place (if at a different court centre from the court where the urgent hearing occurred).

13 Safeguarding

13.1 Where an application is made for a child arrangements order (but not necessarily for specific issue or prohibited steps orders), before the FHDRA (see paragraph 14 below) Cafcass/CAFCASS Cymru shall identify any safety issues by the steps outlined below.

13.2 Such steps shall be confined to matters of safety. The Cafcass Officer or (in Wales) the Welsh Family Proceedings Officer (WFPO) shall not discuss with either party before the FHDRA any matter other than one which relates to safety. The parties will not be invited to talk about other issues, for example relating to the substance of applications or replies or about issues concerning matters of welfare or the prospects of resolution. If such issues are raised by either party, they will be advised that such matters will be deferred to the FHDRA when there is equality between the parties and full discussion can take place which will be a time when any safety issues that have been identified can also be taken into account.

13.3 In order to inform the court of possible risks of harm to the child Cafcass/CAFCASS Cymru will carry out safeguarding enquiries. For all child arrangements orders this will include seeking information from local authorities, and carrying out police checks on the parties. For all other applications received from the court on the form C100, Cafcass/CAFCASS Cymru will carry out a screening process and will undertake those checks if in the professional judgment of the Cafcass officer, or the WFPO in Wales, such checks are necessary.

13.4 Cafcass/CAFCASS Cymru will, if possible, undertake telephone risk identification interviews with the parties and if risks of harm are identified, may invite parties to meet separately with the Cafcass Officer, or WFPO in Wales, before the FHDRA to clarify any safety issue.

13.5 Cafcass/CAFCASS Cymru shall record and outline any safety issues for the court, in the form of a Safeguarding letter (in Wales, this is called a 'Safeguarding report').

13.6 The Cafcass officer, or WFPO, will not initiate contact with the child prior to the FHDRA. If contacted by a child, discussions relating to the issues in the case will be postponed to the day of the hearing or after when the Cafcass officer or WFPO will have more knowledge of the issues.

13.7 Within 17 working days of receipt by Cafcass/CAFCASS Cymru of the application, and at least 3 working days before the hearing, the Cafcass Officer or WFPO shall report to the court, in a Safeguarding letter/report, the outcome of the risk identification work which has been undertaken. The letter/report should specify which court forms filed by the parties (C100, C7 and C1A) have been considered.

13.8 Further, Cafcass and CAFCASS Cymru are required, under section 16A Children Act 1989, to undertake (and to provide to the court) risk assessments where an officer of the Service ('Cafcass Officer' or WFPO) suspects that a child is at risk of harm.

[13A Orders under section 91(14) of the Children Act 1989

13A.1 Under section 91(14) of the 1989 Act orders are available to prevent a person from making future applications under that Act without leave of the court. Section 91(14) leaves a discretion to the court to determine the circumstances in which an order should be made. These circumstances may be many and varied. They include circumstances where an application would put the child concerned, or another individual, at risk of harm (as provided in section 91A), such as psychological or emotional harm. The welfare of the child is paramount.

13A.2 These circumstances can also include where one party has made repeated and unreasonable applications; where a period of respite is needed following litigation; where a period of time is needed for certain actions to be taken for the protection of the child or other person; or where a person's conduct overall is such that an order is merited to protect the welfare of the child directly, or indirectly due to damaging effects on a parent carer. Such conduct could include harassment, or other oppressive or distressing behaviour beyond or within the proceedings including via social media and e-mail, and via third parties. Such conduct might also constitute domestic abuse. A future application could also be part of a pattern of coercive or controlling behaviour or other domestic abuse toward the victim, such that a section 91(14) order is also merited due to the risk of harm to the child or other individual.

13A.4 In proceedings in which domestic abuse is alleged or proven, or in which there are allegations or evidence of other harm to a child or other individual, the court should give early and ongoing consideration to whether it would be appropriate to make a section 91(14) order on disposal of the application, even if an application for such an order has not been made (since the court may make an order of its own motion – see section 91A(5)).

13A.5 Section 91(14) orders are a protective filter – not a bar on applications – and there is considerable scope for their use in appropriate cases. The court should refer to Practice Direction 12Q for guidance on section 91(14) applications and orders.][1]

NOTES

Amendments.[1] Paragraphs inserted: FPR Update No 4 of 2022, May 2022.

14 First Hearing Dispute Resolution Appointment (FHDRA)

14.1 The FHDRA may (where time for service on the respondent(s) has been abridged) take place within 4 weeks, but should ordinarily take place in week 5 following the issuing of the application; at the latest it will take place in week 6 following the issuing of the application.

14.2 The respondent(s) shall have at least 14 days' notice of the hearing where practicable, but the court may specify a shorter time.

14.3 …

14.4 Unless the court otherwise directs, any party to proceedings, and any litigation friend of the parties must attend this (and any other) hearing. If a child is a party and represented by a children's guardian, the children's guardian need not attend directions hearings if represented.

14.5 A party may choose to be accompanied at this (or any) hearing by a McKenzie Friend to support them (a McKenzie Friend is someone who can provide moral support at court for the party; take notes; help with case papers; quietly give advice on any aspect of the conduct of the case.) If so, the McKenzie Friend must comply with the relevant Guidance (currently set out in the Practice Guidance: McKenzie Friends (Civil and Family Courts): July 2010: http://www.judiciary.gov.uk/wp-content/uploads/JCO/Documents/Guidance/mckenzie-friends-practice-guidance-july-2010.pdf).

14.6 A Cafcass Officer or WFPO shall attend this hearing. A mediator may attend where available.

14.7 The Cafcass Officer or WFPO shall, where practicable, speak separately to each party at court before the hearing in particular where it has not been possible to conduct a risk identification interview with either party.

14.8 The FHDRA provides an opportunity for the parties to be helped to an understanding of the issues which divide them, and to reach agreement. If agreement is reached:

(1)   The Court will be able to make an order (which in many cases will be a final order) reflecting that agreement;

(2)   The Court will assist the parties (so far as it is able) in putting into effect the agreement/order in a co-operative way.

14.9 The FHDRA is not privileged. That is to say that what is said at the FHDRA may be referred to at later court hearings.

14.10 By the time of the hearing, the Court should have the following documents:

(a)   C100 application, and C1A (if any);
(b)   Notice of Hearing;
(c)   C7 response and C1A (if any);
(d)   Cafcass/CAFCASS Cymru safeguarding letter/report.

14.11 At the FHDRA the judge, working with the Cafcass Officer, or WFPO, will seek to assist the parties in conciliation and in resolution of all or any of the issues between them. Any remaining issues will be identified, the Cafcass Officer or WFPO will advise the court of any recommended means of resolving such issues, and directions will be given for the future resolution of such issues. At all times the decisions of the Court and the work of the Cafcass Officer or WFPO will take account of any risk or safeguarding issues that have been identified.

14.12 The court should have information obtained through safeguarding checks carried out by Cafcass/CAFCASS Cymru and, where applicable, Supplemental Information Forms C1A filed by the parties, to ensure that any agreement between the parties, or any dispute resolution process selected, is in the interests of the child and safe for all concerned.

14.13 The FHDRA will be conducted in the most appropriate way in the interests of the child. In particular the court shall consider the following matters:

•   **Safeguarding**, in this respect:
(a)   The court shall inform the parties of the content of the safeguarding letter/report provided by Cafcass/CAFCASS Cymru, where it has not already been sent by Cafcass/CAFCASS Cymru to the parties, unless it considers that to do so would create a risk of harm to a party or the child. The court may need to consider whether, and if so how, any information contained in the checks should be disclosed to the parties if Cafcass/CAFCASS Cymru have not disclosed the letter/report.
The court will specifically consider, in the light of all the information before the court, including the contents of the safeguarding letter/report provided by Cafcass/CAFCASS Cymru and any Supplemental Information Form(s) C1A filed by the parties.

(b)   The nature and extent of any factual issues and whether a fact-finding hearing is needed to determine allegations which are not accepted, and whose resolution is likely to affect the decision of the court.

(c)   Risk identification followed by active case management including risk assessment, and compliance with the Practice Direction 12J.
        (Specific provisions about directions for a fact-finding hearing are set out in Practice Direction 12J, paragraphs 16 to 20.)

Further:

(d)   If the safeguarding information is (contrary to the arrangements set out in the CAP) not available at the FHDRA, the court should adjourn the application until the safeguarding checks are available. Interim orders (unless to protect the safety of a child) should not be made in the absence of safeguarding checks.

And further:

(e)   Where the court so directs, a safeguarding letter/report ought to be attached to any referral to a supported or supervised child contact centre in the event the court directs supported or supervised contact.

- **MIAM**, specifically:

(a)   Whether, if a MIAM exemption has been claimed, the Applicant has validly claimed the exemption;

(b)   Whether the Respondent has attended a MIAM;

(c)   If the court finds that a MIAM exemption has not been validly claimed the court will direct the applicant or direct the parties to attend a MIAM and if necessary adjourn the proceedings to enable a MIAM to take place, unless the court considers that in all the circumstances of the case, the MIAM requirement should not apply to the application in question; when making the decision the court will have particular regard to the matters contained in rule 3.10(3) FPR.

- **Mediation, At-Court Mediation assessment, and other Dispute Resolution:** allowing the parties the time and opportunity to engage in non-court dispute resolution.

(a)   At the FHDRA, the judge will specifically consider whether, and the extent to which, the parties can safely resolve some or all of the issues with the assistance of the Cafcass Officer, WFPO, or a mediator.

(b)   There will be, at every FHDRA, a period in which the Cafcass Officer, or WFPO, will seek to conciliate and explore with the parties the resolution of all or some of the issues between them if safe to do so. The procedure to be followed in this connection at the hearing will be determined by local arrangements between the Cafcass manager, or equivalent in Wales, and the Designated Family Judge or [a justices' legal adviser][1] where appropriate.

The court will further consider:

(c)   What is the result of any such meeting at Court?

(d)   What other options there are for resolution e.g. may the case be suitable for further intervention by Cafcass/CAFCASS Cymru;

Should a referral for mediation be made? Is collaborative law appropriate? Should the parties be advised to complete a Parenting Plan?

(e)   Would the parties be assisted by attendance at an Activity Separated Parents Information Programme, (or in Wales, Working Together For Children (WT4C)) or other Activity or intervention, whether by formal statutory provision under section 11 Children Act 1989 or otherwise;

(f)   An at-court assessment of the suitability of the parties for mediation.

• **Consent Orders:**

(a)   Where agreement is reached at any hearing or submitted in writing to the court, no order will be made without scrutiny by the court.

(b)   Where safeguarding checks or risk assessment work remain outstanding, the making of a final order may be deferred for such work. In such circumstances the court shall adjourn the case for no longer than 28 days to a fixed date. A written notification of this work is to be provided by Cafcass/CAFCASS Cymru in the form of an updating Safeguarding letter/report, or if deemed relevant by Cafcass/CAFCASS Cymru, a section 16A risk assessment in accordance with the timescale specified by the court. If satisfactory information is then available, the order may be made at the adjourned hearing in the agreed terms without the need for attendance by the parties. If satisfactory information is not available, the order will not be made, and the case will be adjourned for further consideration with an opportunity for the parties to make further representations

• **Reports:**

(a)   Reports may be ordered where there are welfare issues or other specific considerations which should be addressed in a report by Cafcass/CAFCASS Cymru or the Local Authority. Before a report is ordered, the court should consider alternative ways of working with the parties such as are referred to in paragraph 5 ('non-court resolution of disputed arrangements') above.

(b)   If a report is ordered in accordance with section 7 of the Children Act 1989, the Court should direct which specific matters relating to the welfare of the child are to be addressed. Welfare reports will generally only be ordered in cases where there is a dispute as to with whom the child should live, spend time, or otherwise have contact with. A report can also be ordered:

(i)   If there is an issue concerning the child's wishes, and/or

(ii)   If there is an alleged risk to the child, and/or

(iii) Where information and advice is needed which the court considers to be necessary before a decision can be reached in the case.

(c)   General requests for a report on an application should be avoided; the Court should state on the face of the Order the specific factual and/or other issue which is to be addressed in the focused report.

(d) In determining whether a request for a report should be directed to the relevant local authority or to Cafcass/CAFCASS Cymru, the court should consider such information as Cafcass/CAFCASS Cymru has provided about the extent and nature of the local authority's current or recent involvement with the subject of the application and the parties, and any relevant protocol between Cafcass and the Association of Directors of Children's Services.

(e) The court may further consider whether there is a need for an investigation under section 37 Children Act 1989.

(f) A copy of the Order requesting the report and any relevant court documents are to be sent to Cafcass/CAFCASS Cymru or, in the case of the Local Authority to the Legal Adviser to the Director of the Local Authority Children's Services and, where known, to the allocated social worker by the court forthwith.

(g) Is any expert evidence required? If so, section 13 Children and Families Act 2014, and Part 25 of the FPR must be complied with. This is the latest point at which consideration should be given to the instruction of an expert in accordance with Rule 25.6(b) of the FPR; the court will need to consider carefully the future conduct of proceedings where the preparation of an expert report is necessary but where the parties are unrepresented and are unable to fund the preparation of such a report.

- **Wishes and feelings of the child:**
  (a) In line with the Family Justice Young People's Board Charter, children and young people should be at the centre of all proceedings.
  (b) The child or young person should feel that their needs, wishes and feelings have been considered in the court process.
  (c) Each decision should be assessed on its impact on the child.
  (d) The court must consider the wishes and feelings of the child, ascertainable so far as is possible in light of the child's age and understanding and circumstances. Specifically, the Court should ask:
    (i) Is the child aware of the proceedings?
    (ii) Are the wishes and feelings of the child available, and/or to be ascertained (if at all)?
    (iii) How is the child to be involved in the proceedings, and if so, how; for example, should they meet the judge/lay justices? Should they be encouraged to write to the court, or have their views reported by Cafcass/CAFCASS Cymru or by a local authority?
    (iv) Who will inform the child of the outcome of the case, where appropriate?

- **Case Management:**
  (a) What, if any, issues are agreed and what are the key issues to be determined?
  (b) Should the matter be listed for a fact-finding hearing?
  (c) Are there any interim orders which can usefully be made (e.g. indirect, supported or supervised contact) pending Dispute Resolution Appointment or final hearing?

(d) What directions are required to ensure the application is ready for a Dispute Resolution Appointment or final hearing – statements, reports etc?

(e) Should the application be listed for a Dispute Resolution Appointment (it is envisaged that most cases will be so listed)?

(f) Should the application be listed straightaway for a final hearing?

(g) Judicial continuity should be actively considered (especially if there has been or is to be a fact finding hearing or a contested interim hearing).

- **Allocation:**
  (a) The Allocation decision will be considered by the Court;
  (b) If it is necessary to transfer the case to another court within the DFJ area or another area, or re-allocate it, the court shall state the reasons for transfer/re-allocation, and shall specifically make directions for the next hearing in the court.

- **Order (other than a final order):** Where no final agreement is reached, and the court is required to give case management directions, the following shall be included on the order:
  (a) The date, time and venue of the next hearing;
  (b) Whether the author of any section 7 report is required to attend the hearing, in order to give oral evidence. A direction for the Cafcass officer or WFPO to attend court will not be made without first considering the reason why attendance is necessary, and upon what issues the Cafcass officer or WFPO will be providing evidence;
  (c) such other matters as may be included in President's guidance from time to time.

    Where both parties are Litigants in Person, the court may direct HMCTS to produce a Litigant in Person bundle.

    The judge will, as far as possible, provide a copy of the order to both parties before they leave the courtroom, and will, if necessary, go through and explain the contents of the order to ensure they are clearly understood by both parties. The parties should know the date, time and venue of any further hearing before they leave the court.

NOTES

Amendment.[1] Words substituted: Practice Direction, April 2020.

15 Timetable for the child

15.1 Court proceedings should be timetabled so that the dispute can be resolved as soon as safe and possible in the interests of the child.

15.2 The judge shall, at all times during the proceedings, have regard to the impact which the court timetable will have on the welfare and development of the child to whom the application relates. The judge and the parties shall pay particular attention to the child's age, and important landmarks in the immediate life of the child, including:

(a) the child's birthday;
(b) the start of nursery/schooling;

(c)   the start/end of a school term/year;
(d)   any proposed change of school;
and/or
(e)   any significant change in the child's family, or social, circumstances.

15.3 While it is acknowledged that an interim order may be appropriate at an early stage of court proceedings, cases should not be adjourned for a review (or reviews) of contact or other orders/arrangements, &/or for addendum section 7 report, unless such a hearing is necessary and for a clear purpose that is consistent with the timetable for the child and in the child's best interests.

15.4 When preparing a section 7 report, Cafcass/CAFCASS Cymru (or, where appropriate, the local authority) is encouraged to make recommendations for the stepped phasing-in of child arrangements (i.e. recommendations for the medium and longer term future for the child) insofar as they are able to do so safely in the interests of the child concerned;

15.5 Where active involvement or monitoring is needed, the court may consider making:

(1)   An order under section 11H Children Act 1989 (Monitoring);
(2)   A Family Assistance Order under section 16 Children Act 1989) (in accordance with the Practice Direction 12M FPR, and if all the named adults in the order agree to the making of such an order and if the order is directed to a local authority, the child lives (or will live) within that local authority area or the local authority consents to the making of the order.

16 Capacity of Litigants

16.1 In the event that the judge has concerns about the capacity of a litigant before the court, the judge shall consider

(1)   the Guidance issued by the Family Justice Council in relation to assessing the capacity of litigants;
(2)   Practice Direction 15B (Adults Who May Be Protected Parties and Children Who May Become Protected Parties In Family Proceedings).

17 Evidence

17.1 No evidence shall be filed in relation to an application until after the FHDRA unless:

(1)   It has been filed in support of a without notice application;
(2)   It has been directed by the Court by the Directions on Issue;
(3)   It has been directed by the Court for the purposes of determining an interim application.

18 Rule 16.4 children's guardians

18.1 The Court should be vigilant to identify the cases where a rule 16.4 children's guardian should be appointed. This should be considered initially at the FHDRA.

PART II – Statutory instruments

18.2 Where the court is considering the appointment of a children's guardian from Cafcass/CAFCASS Cymru, it should first ensure that enquiries have been made of the appropriate Cafcass/CAFCASS Cymru manager in accordance with paragraph 7.4, Part 4 of the Practice Direction 16A. This should either be in writing before the hearing or by way of case discussion with the relevant Cafcass service manager; for cases in Wales, the 'hotline' protocol agreed with CAFCASS Cymru will ensure that such a discussion can take place. The court should consult with Cafcass/CAFCASS Cymru, so as to consider any advice in connection with the prospective appointment, and the timescale involved.

18.3 When the court decides to appoint a children's guardian, consideration should first be given to appointing an Officer of the Service or WFPO. If Cafcass/CAFCASS Cymru is unable to provide a children's guardian without delay, or if there is some other reason why the appointment of a Cafcass officer is not appropriate, the court should (further to rule 16.24 of the FPR) appoint a person other than the Official Solicitor, unless the Official Solicitor expressly consents.

18.4 In considering whether to make such an appointment the Court shall take account of the demands on the resources of Cafcass/CAFCASS Cymru that such an appointment would make. The court should also make clear on the face of any order the purpose of the appointment and the timetable of any work to be undertaken.

19 Dispute Resolution Appointment (DRA)

19.1 The Court shall list the application for a Dispute Resolution Appointment ('DRA') to follow the preparation of section 7 or other expert report, or Separated Parenting Information Programme (SPIP) (or WT4C in Wales), if this is considered likely to be helpful in the interests of the child.

19.2 The author of the section 7 report will only attend this hearing if directed to do so by the Court.

19.3 At the DRA the Court will:

    (1)   Identify the key issue(s) (if any) to be determined and the extent to which those issues can be resolved or narrowed at the DRA;

    (2)   Consider whether the DRA can be used as a final hearing;

    (3)   Resolve or narrow the issues by hearing evidence;

    (4)   Identify the evidence to be heard on the issues which remain to be resolved at the final hearing;

    (5)   Give final case management directions including:

        (a)   Filing of further evidence;

        (b)   Filing of a statement of facts/issues remaining to be determined;

        (c)   Filing of a witness template and / or skeleton arguments;

        (d)   Ensuring Compliance with Practice Direction 27A (the Bundles Practice Direction);

        (e)   Listing the Final Hearing.

20 Fact-finding hearing

20.1 If the court considers that a fact-finding hearing is necessary it shall conduct that hearing in accordance with revised Practice Direction 12J.

[20.2 Where there is an application for a section 91(14) order, the court should consider whether any particular findings of fact will be needed in order to determine the section 91(14) application.][1]

NOTES

Amendment.[1] Paragraph inserted: FPR Update No 4 of 2022, May 2022.

21 Enforcement of Child Arrangements

21.1 On any application for enforcement of a child arrangements order, the court shall:

- consider whether the facts relevant to the alleged non-compliance are agreed, or whether it is necessary to conduct a hearing to establish the facts;
- consider the reasons for any non-compliance;
- consider how the wishes and feelings of the child are to be ascertained;
- consider whether advice is required from Cafcass/CAFCASS Cymru on the appropriate way forward;
- assess and manage any risks of making further or other child arrangements order;
- consider whether a SPIP or referral for dispute resolution is appropriate;
- consider whether an enforcement order may be appropriate, and
- consider the welfare checklist.

21.2 The Gatekeepers shall list any application for enforcement of a child arrangements order for hearing, before the previously allocated judge if possible, within 20 working days of issue. Enforcement cases should be concluded without delay.

21.3 An application made within existing proceedings in the family court shall be allocated to the level of judge in accordance with rule 17 of the Family Court (Composition and Distribution of Business) Rules 2014.

21.4 The Gatekeepers shall, if considered necessary, direct that further safeguarding checks are required from Cafcass/CAFCASS Cymru. On any application for enforcement issued more than three months after the order which is the subject of the enforcement, safeguarding checks shall be ordered.

21.5 The court has a wide range of powers in the event of a breach of a child arrangements order without reasonable excuse.

21.6 This range of powers includes (but is not limited to):

(a) referral of the parents to a SPIP, or in Wales a WT4C, or mediation;
(b) variation of the child arrangements order (which could include a more defined order and/or reconsidering the contact provision or the living arrangements of the child);
(c) a contact enforcement order or suspended enforcement order under section 11J Children Act 1989 ('Enforcement order' for unpaid work), (see paragraph 21.7 below);
(d) an order for compensation for financial loss (under section 11O Children Act 1989);

(e)   committal to prison; or

(f)   a fine.

21.7 In the event that the court is considering an enforcement order for alleged non-compliance with a court order (under section 11J Children Act 1989) or considering a Compensation order in respect of financial loss (under section 11O Children Act 1989), the court shall (in the absence of agreement between the parties about the relevant facts) determine the facts in order to establish the cause of the alleged failure to comply.

21.8 Section 11L Children Act 1989 provides that if the court finds that a breach has occurred without reasonable excuse it may order the non-compliant party to undertake unpaid work if that is necessary to secure compliance, and if the effect on the non-compliant party is proportionate to the seriousness of the breach. The court must also consider whether unpaid work is available in the locality and the likely effect on the non-compliant party. It is good practice to ask Cafcass/ CAFCASS Cymru to report on the suitability of this order. Section 11L(7) also requires the court to take into account the welfare of the child who is the subject of the order for contact.

22 Court timetable

22.1 Working Day 1: Paperwork received. Court office checks whether the revised form C100 has been completed correctly. The application will not be issued unless the form has been completed correctly.

22.2 Working Day 3: Case considered by Gatekeeping team. Case allocated by Gatekeepers in accordance with the President's Guidance on allocation and the Family Court (Composition and Distribution) Rules 2014. The Gatekeeper(s) undertaking allocation to check whether form C100 has been completed. If there has been no MIAM, and there are reasons to believe that the applicant should have attended a MIAM, the Gatekeeping judge can direct that a MIAM should take place before the FHDRA.

22.2A By Working Day 3 (2 working days after the date of issue): The court shall send to Cafcass/CAFCASS Cymru a copy of the Form C100 (and the Form C1A, if supplied), and the C6 Notice of Hearing. This will be in electronic format where possible.

22.2B On receipt of the Acknowledgement Form C7 and any Form C1A filed by the respondent(s), the court shall send a copy of each form to Cafcass / CAFCASS Cymru, in electronic format where possible, and shall send copies to the applicant.

22.3 17 working days from the date of its receipt of the application Cafcass/ CAFCASS Cymru will provide the safeguarding letter/report to the Court (20 working days in the area of CAFCASS Cymru).

22.4 Week 5 (or latest, week 6): Case listed for FHDRA (before week 5 if requirements of notice have been abridged).

22.5 Thereafter, case may be listed for fact-finding hearing, DRA &/or final hearing.

23 Relevant Family Application (definition)

23.1 A relevant family application for the purposes of the CAP is an application that

(1)   Is made to the court in, or to initiate, family proceedings, and

(2)   Is of a description specified in the Family Procedure Rules.

ANNEX – EXPLANATION OF TERMS

Abuse	Any behaviour which causes harm
Adjourn/ Adjournment	Where the case, or a hearing, is directed to take place or continue at a later time (which might be on the same day or another day)
Allegation	A claim that someone has done something wrong
Applicant	The name given to someone who is asking the court for a court order
Application	How a person asks the court to do something
Cafcass	Cafcass stands for the 'Children and Family Court Advisory and Support Service'. Cafcass is independent of the courts, social services, education and health authorities and all similar agencies. Cafcass workers (sometimes called 'Family Court Advisers' or 'officers') are specialist social workers who help the court by making safeguarding checks, helping parties at the FHDRA to consider solutions, and if necessary writing reports for the court &/or monitoring arrangements after court
CAFCASS Cymru	This is Cafcass in Wales. CAFCASS Cymru is part of the Department of Health and Social Services in the Welsh Government
Child Arrangements Order	This is an order which will set out arrangements relating to (a) with whom a child is to live, spend time or otherwise have contact, and (b) when a child is to live, spend time or otherwise have contact with any other person
Collaborative law	One of the ways of trying to sort out disputes away from court; each party appoints their own lawyer, and you and your lawyers all meet together to work things out face to face
Consent order	When you have reached an agreement with the other parent, which resolves the dispute, the judge may agree to make that agreement into an order called a consent order
Contact centre	A place for a parent to see their child in a neutral and 'safe' environment. 'Supervised' contact centres provide a safe and neutral place for contact. 'Supported' contact centres, which are often run by volunteers, offer a neutral place for contact in cases where no safety concerns exist

Designated Family Judge	This is the judge who has responsibility to provide leadership to the family judiciary within the court centre or group of courts
Dispute Resolution	The method of solving disagreements
Domestic violence	This phrase is used to describe a wide range of behaviours including any incident or pattern of incidents of controlling, coercive or threatening behaviour, violence or abuse between those aged 16 or over who are or have been intimate partners or family members regardless of gender or sexuality.
	This can encompass, but is not limited to, the following types of abuse: psychological, physical, sexual, financial, or emotional
	Controlling behaviour is: a range of acts designed to make a person subordinate and/or dependent by isolating them from sources of support, exploiting their resources and capacities for personal gain, depriving them of the means needed for independence, resistance and escape and regulating their everyday behaviour. Coercive behaviour is: an act or a pattern of acts of assault, threats, humiliation and intimidation or other abuse that is used to harm, punish, or frighten their victim
DRA	Dispute Resolution Appointment. This is a court hearing which takes place towards the end of the court's involvement, and is another opportunity to see if the dispute can be sorted out with the help of a judge
Enforcement	Making sure that an order is complied with
Expert evidence	Evidence and opinions provided by someone with special skills and knowledge (but, for these purposes, does not refer to a social worker employed by, and giving evidence on behalf of, a local authority who is a party to the case)
Fact finding hearing	A court hearing set up for the court to decide on issues of fact or allegations which are in dispute
Family Assistance order	An order of the court which allows Cafcass or local authorities to provide social-work support to help parties to establish contact arrangements which might otherwise fail
FHDRA	First Hearing Dispute Resolution Appointment. This is a court hearing which takes place at the beginning of the court's involvement.
File	This means to send/deliver to the court office
FPR	Family Procedure Rules 2010; the rules of court which govern family cases.
Gatekeeper(s)	The nominated District Judge and/or nominated Legal Adviser responsible for deciding which level of judge in the family court should initially deal with an application

Hearing	The name given to a meeting or court appointment with a judge
Indirect contact	Any contact which is not face-to-face (for example, letters, birthday cards, phone calls)
Interim contact	Contact that takes place between the first court hearing and the final hearing
Investigation under section 37	Where it appears to a judge that a child is or may be at risk of significant harm and it may be appropriate for local authority children's services to apply for a court order giving them responsibilities towards a family, the judge can direct the local authority to investigate the child's circumstances
Judge	Where the term 'Judge' is used, this refers to any judge of the Family Court including lay justices (magistrates) and judges of the High Court
Judgment	The decision of the Judge, and the reasons why the decision has been made
LAA	Legal Aid Agency; this is the body responsible for providing public funding for legal representation
Litigant in Person or LiP	This is the name given to a person in court proceedings who does not have a lawyer
Litigant in Person Bundle	A bundle of court documents, contained in a file, which contains the following: Section A: Applications, Section B: Orders, Section C: Statements, Section D: Cafcass safeguarding letter, analyses and any expert reports, and Section E: Police, medical, other documents
McKenzie Friend	A friend or other person who can help you prepare your case and go to court with you to give you support and take notes
MIAM	Mediation Information and Assessment Meeting. At this meeting, a trained mediator will explain what mediation is and how it works, explain the benefits of mediation and the likely costs, answer questions, assess whether the person is eligible for legal aid for mediation, assess whether mediation is suitable in the case. A MIAM should be held within 15 working days of contacting the mediator
NACCC	National Association of Child Contact Centres: NACCC has in its membership about 350 child contact centres and services throughout England (including the Channel Isles), Wales and Northern Ireland.
	Child contact centres and services are neutral places where children of separated families can enjoy contact with the parent with whom the child does not live and sometimes with other family members, in a comfortable and safe environment

PART II – Statutory instruments

Parental responsibility	All the legal rights and responsibilities normally associated with being a parent
Part-heard	Means a hearing which has started but which has not been finished within the day, and then continues on another day
Party	Someone involved in the court proceedings – either the person who has made the application, or the person(s) against whom the application has been made
Practice Direction	This is a document which sets out good practice in supporting the FPR (Family Procedure Rules) or other Rules (see above) and/or may contain provisions which could otherwise be contained in rules of court and have same effect as rules
Private family law/private law	Family disputes between individuals about arrangements for children
Respondent(s)	This is the name given to the person or people who receive the court application
Review	To look at something again
Rule 16.4 children's guardian	A person (usually a specialist social worker) appointed by the court to look after the interests of a child in the case
Safeguarding	Making sure that people are safe
Section 7 report	A welfare report, prepared under section 7 of the Children Act 1989; the report will be on such matters relating to the welfare of that child as are required to be dealt with in the report; the report may be in writing or oral
Serve	Delivery of court documents
SPIP	Separated Parents Information Programme; this is available across England, and is for both parents and for grandparents
Statement or Witness Statement	A document setting out what you want to say to the Judge about the case. You should sign it and date it. What you say in the statement must be true
Undertaking	A solemn promise to the court to do, or not do, something
WFPO	Welsh Family Proceedings Officer. A Cafcass officer in Wales
WT4C	The Working Together For Children programme which runs in Wales – and is the equivalent of the SPIP (see above)][1]

CHILD ARRANGEMENTS PROGRAMME: FLOWCHART

DISPUTE OVER ARRANGEMENTS FOR CHILDREN

[CAP:X] = reference to relevant paragraph or section in the Child Arrangements Programme

Cases of Exceptional/Extreme Urgency [CAP:12]
where injunction/prohibited steps orders are sought, go straight to issue and consider without notice application
NB: paperwork must be in order

Signposting [CAP:2]
Seek advice from sortingoutseparation.org.uk, a lawyer or a Dispute Resolution Service

Dispute Resolution Services [CAP:5]
Parties attend for Mediation/SPIP or other Dispute Resolution Service. Parties to consider Parenting Plan. Self-referral to Contact Centre if required.

Attendance at MIAM [CAP:5.3]
(Compulsory for Proposed Applicant unless exemption applies. Proposed Respondent notified and encouraged to attend)

Application [CAP:8]
Form C100 and form C1A (if required) to be completed and submitted to the Court, accompanied by any existing Parenting Plan if available (Case will NOT be issued if paperwork not in order)

Allocation/Gatekeeping [CAP:9]
Case allocated within Family Court (in accordance with Guidance and Rules). Papers submitted to CAFCASS (Day 1 after issue)

Safeguarding checks [CAP:13]
Completed by Cafcass (Day 17 after receipt of application)

Directions on Issue (where necessary) [CAP:9.4]
If the Applicant has not attended MIAM and an exemption has not been validly claimed, the Gatekeeping Judge may direct attendance of the parties (or either of them) at MIAM before the FHDRA (below). Other directions may be given.

MIAM [CAP:9.4[1]]
Both or either party may be referred to MIAM (where not complied with requirement to attend)

PART II – Statutory instruments

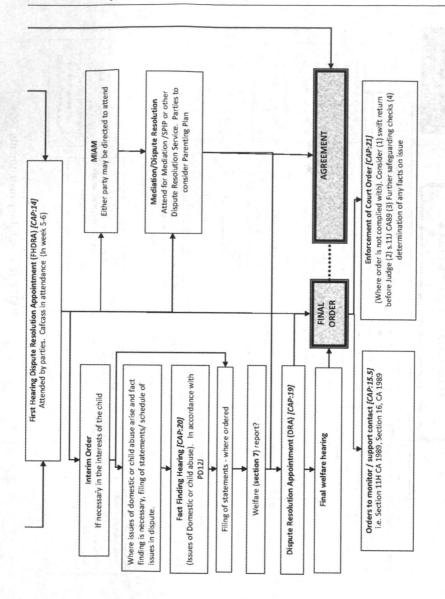

Practice Direction 12C –
Service of Application in Certain Proceedings Relating
to Children

This Practice Direction supplements FPR Part 12 (Procedure Relating to Children except Parental Order Proceedings and Proceedings for Applications in Adoption, Placement and Related Proceedings), rule 12.8 (Service of the application)

Persons who receive copy of application form

1.1 In relation to the proceedings in column 1 of the following table, column 2 sets out the documentation which persons listed in column 3 are to receive –

Proceedings	Documentation	Who receives a copy of the documentation
1 Private law proceedings; public law proceedings; emergency proceedings (except those proceedings referred to in entries 2 and 3 of the Table below); proceedings for a declaration under rule 12.71 as to the existence, or extent, of parental responsibility under Article 16 of the 1996 Hague Convention; an order relating to the exercise of the court's inherent jurisdiction (including wardship proceedings).	Application form (including any supplementary forms); Form C6 (Notice of proceedings); and in private law proceedings, the form of answer.	All the respondents to the application.
2 An enforcement order (section 11J of the 1989 Act); a financial compensation order (section 11O of the 1989 Act).	As above	All the respondents to the application; and where the child was a party to the proceedings in which the [child arrangements order][1] was made – (a) the person who was the children's guardian or litigation friend in those proceedings; or (b) where there was no children's guardian or litigation friend, the person who was the legal representative of the child in those proceedings.
3 A care or a supervision order (section 31 of the 1989 Act) [and other Part 4 proceedings]1.	As above and such of the documents specified in the Annex to [Form C110A][1] as are available.	All the respondents to the application; and Cafcass or CAFCASS Cymru.

Proceedings	Documentation	Who receives a copy of the documentation
4 Proceedings for an order for the return of a child under the 1980 Hague Convention or registration of an order under the European Convention.	As above and the documents referred to in part 2 of the Practice Direction 12F (International Child Abduction).	All the respondents to the application.

(Rule 12.3 sets out who the parties to the proceedings are.)

NOTES

Amendments. Text substituted or inserted: FPR Update, April 2014.

[1.2 When filing the documents referred to in column 2 of the Table in paragraph 1.1, the applicant must also file sufficient copies for one to be served on each respondent and, except for Part 4 proceedings, Cafcass or CAFCASS Cymru. In relation to Part 4 proceedings, the applicant need not file a copy of the documents for Cafcass or CAFCASS Cymru as it is the applicant who sends copies of these documents to Cafcass or CAFCASS Cymru in accordance with Practice Direction 12A.][1]

NOTES

Amendment.[1] Text substituted: FPR Update, April 2014.

1.3 Where the application for an order in proceedings referred to in column 1 of the Table in paragraph 1.1 is made in respect of more than one child all the children must be included in the same application form.

1.4 ...[1] C6A (notice to non parties) [must be served][1] on the persons referred to in the Table in paragraph 3.1 at the same time as serving the documents in column 2 of the Table in paragraph 1.1.

NOTES

Amendments.[1] Text substituted or omitted: FPR Update, April 2014.

Time for serving application

2.1 In relation to the proceedings in column 1 of the following table, column 2 sets out the time period within which the application and accompanying documents must be served on each respondent –

[Proceedings	Minimum number of days prior to hearing or directions appointment for service
1 Private law proceedings; and proceedings for – an order relating to the exercise of the court's inherent jurisdiction (including wardship proceedings);	14 days.

[Proceedings	Minimum number of days prior to hearing or directions appointment for service
a declaration under rule 12.71 as to the existence, or extent, of parental responsibility under Article 16 of the 1996 Hague Convention.	
2 Public law proceedings except proceedings for an interim care order, an interim supervision order or other proceedings referred to in Box 3 below.	7 days.
3 Proceedings for – an interim care order, or the discharge of such an order under section 39(1) of the 1989 Act; an interim supervision order under section 38(1) of the 1989 Act, the discharge or variation of such an order under section 39(2) of the 1989 Act, or the extension or further extension of such an order under paragraph 6(3) of Schedule 3 to that Act; an order varying directions made with an interim care order or interim supervision order under section 38(8)(b) of the 1989 Act; an order under section 39(3) of the 1989 Act varying an interim supervision order in so far as it affects a person with whom the child is living but who is not entitled to apply for the order to be discharged; an order under section 39(3A) of the 1989 Act varying or discharging an interim care order in so far as it imposes an exclusion requirement on a person who is not entitled to apply for the order to be discharged; an order under section 39(3B) of the 1989 Act varying or discharging an interim care order in so far as it confers a power of arrest attached to an exclusion requirement.	3 days.
4 Proceedings for an order for the return of a child under the 1980 Hague Convention or registration of an order under the European Convention.	4 days
5 Emergency proceedings.	1 day][1]

PART II – Statutory instruments

2.2 The court may extend or shorten the time period referred to in column 2 of the table in paragraph 2.1 (see rule 4.1(3)(a)).

2.3 Where the application is to be served on a child, rule 6.33 provides that, in addition to the persons to be served in accordance with rules 6.28 and 6.32, the application must also be served on the persons or bodies listed in rule 6.33(3) unless the court orders otherwise.

NOTES

Amendment.[1] Table substituted: FPR Update, April 2014.

Persons who receive a copy of Form C6A (Notice to Non-Parties)

3.1 [Subject to paragraph 3.2,][2] in relation to each type of proceedings in column 1 of the following table, the persons listed in column 2 are to receive a copy of Form C6A (Notice of Proceedings/Hearing/Directions Appointment to Non-Parties).

[3.2 A person listed in column 2 of the following table shall not receive a copy of Form C6A if the court, on application by any party, directs that such notification is not required.][2]

[Proceedings	Persons to whom notice is to be given
1 All applications.	Subject to separate entries below:
	local authority providing accommodation for the child;
	persons who are caring for the child at the time when the proceedings are commenced; and
	in the case of proceedings brought in respect of a child who is alleged to be staying in a refuge which is certified under section 51(1) or (2) of the 1989 Act, the person who is providing the refuge.
2 An order appointing a guardian (section 5(1) of the 1989 Act).	As for all applications; and
	the father or parent (being a woman who is a parent by virtue of section 43 of the Human Fertilisation and Embryology Act 2008) of the child if that person does not have parental responsibility.
3 A section 8 order (section 8 of the 1989 Act).	As for all applications; and,
	every person whom the applicant believes –
	(i) to be named in a court order with respect to the same child, which has not ceased to have effect;

[Proceedings	Persons to whom notice is to be given
	(ii) to be party to pending proceedings in respect of the same child; or
	(iii) to be a person with whom the child has lived for at least 3 years prior to the application,
	unless, in a case to which (i) or (ii) applies, the applicant believes that the court order or pending proceedings are not relevant to the application.
4 A special guardianship order (section 14A of the 1989 Act);	As for all applications; and every person whom the applicant believes –
variation or discharge of a special guardianship order (section 14D of the 1989 Act).	(i) to be named in a court order with respect to the same child, which has not ceased to have effect;
	(ii) to be party to pending proceedings in respect of the same child; or
	(iii) to be a person with whom the child has lived for at least 3 years prior to the application,
	unless, in a case to which (i) or (ii) applies, the applicant believes that the court order or pending proceedings are not relevant to the application;
	if the child is not being accommodated by the local authority, the local authority in whose area the applicant is ordinarily resident; and
	in the case of an application under section 14D of the 1989 Act, the local authority that prepared the report under section 14A(8) or (9) in the proceedings leading to the order which it is sought to have varied or discharged, if different from any local authority that will otherwise be notified.
5 An order permitting the local authority to arrange for any child in its care to live outside England and Wales (Schedule 2, paragraph 19(1) of the 1989 Act).	As for all applications; and the parties to the proceedings leading to the care order.
6 A care or supervision order (section 31 of the 1989 Act).	As for all applications; and

PART II – Statutory instruments

[Proceedings	Persons to whom notice is to be given
	every person whom the applicant believes to be a party to pending relevant proceedings in respect of the same child; and
	every person whom the applicant believes to be a parent without parental responsibility for the child.
7 A child assessment order (section 43(1) of the 1989 Act).	As for all applications; and
	every person whom the applicant believes to be a parent of the child;
	every person whom the applicant believes to be caring for the child;
	every person in whose favour a [child arrangements order]¹ is in force with respect to the child; and
	every person who is allowed to have contact with the child by virtue of an order under section 34 of the 1989 Act.
8 An order varying or discharging a child assessment order (section 43(12) of the 1989 Act).	The persons referred to in section 43(11)(a) to (e) of the 1989 Act who were not party to the application for the order which it is sought to have varied or discharged.
9 An emergency protection order (section 44(1) of the 1989 Act).	As for all applications above; and every person whom the applicant believes to be a parent of the child.
10 An order varying a direction under section 44(6) in an emergency protection order (section 44(9)(b) of the 1989 Act).	As for all applications; and
	the local authority in whose area the child is living; and
	any person whom the applicant believes to be affected by the direction which it is sought to have varied.
11 A warrant authorising a constable to assist in the exercise of certain powers to search for children and inspect premises (section 102 of the 1989 Act).	The person referred to in section 102(1) of the 1989 Act; and
	any person preventing or likely to prevent such a person from exercising powers under enactments mentioned in subsection (6) of that section.

[Proceedings	Persons to whom notice is to be given
12 An enforcement order (section 11J of the 1989 Act); a financial compensation order (section 11O of the 1989 Act).	Any officer of the Service or Welsh family proceedings officer who is monitoring compliance with a [child arrangements order][1] (in accordance with section 11H(2) of the 1989 Act).
13 An order revoking or amending an enforcement order (Schedule A1, paragraphs 4 to 7 of the 1989 Act) (rule 12.33 makes provision regarding applications under Schedule A1, paragraph 5 of the 1989 Act);	Any officer of the Service or Welsh family proceedings officer who is monitoring compliance with the enforcement order (in accordance with section 11M(1) of the 1989 Act);
an order following a breach of an enforcement order (Schedule A1, paragraph 9 of the 1989 Act).	the responsible officer (as defined in section 197 of the Criminal Justice Act 2003, as modified by Schedule A1 to the 1989 Act).
14 A declaration under rule 12.71 as to the existence, or extent, of parental responsibility under Article 16 of the 1996 Hague Convention.	A person who the applicant believes is a parent of the child.][1]

PART II – Statutory instruments

NOTES

Amendments.[1] Table substituted: FPR Update, April 2014.2 Words and paragraph inserted : Practice Direction, April 2020.

Practice Direction 12D –
Inherent Jurisdiction (including Wardship) Proceedings

This Practice Direction supplements FPR Part 12, Chapter 5

The nature of inherent jurisdiction proceedings

1.1 It is the duty of the court under its inherent jurisdiction to ensure that a child who is the subject of proceedings is protected and properly taken care of. The court may in exercising its inherent jurisdiction make any order or determine any issue in respect of a child unless limited by case law or statute. Such proceedings should not be commenced unless it is clear that the issues concerning the child cannot be resolved under the Children Act 1989.

1.2 The court may under its inherent jurisdiction, in addition to all of the orders which can be made in family proceedings, make a wide range of injunctions for the child's protection of which the following are the most common –

(a)   orders to restrain publicity;
(b)   orders to prevent an undesirable association;
(c)   orders relating to medical treatment;

(d)   orders to protect abducted children, or children where the case has another substantial foreign element; and

(e)   orders for the return of children to and from another state.

1.3 The court's wardship jurisdiction is part of and not separate from the court's inherent jurisdiction. The distinguishing characteristics of wardship are that –

(a)   custody of a child who is a ward is vested in the court; and

(b)   although day to day care and control of the ward is given to an individual or to a local authority, no important step can be taken in the child's life without the court's consent.

Transfer of proceedings to [family][1] court

2.1 Whilst [the family court does][1] not have jurisdiction to deal with applications that a child be made or cease to be a ward of court, consideration should be given to transferring the case in whole or in part to [the family][1] court where a direction has been given confirming the wardship and directing that the child remain a ward of court during his minority or until further order.

2.2 The [family][1] court must transfer the case back to the High Court if a decision is required as to whether the child should remain a ward of court.

2.3 The following proceedings in relation to a ward of court will be dealt with in the High Court unless the nature of the issues of fact or law makes them more suitable for hearing in the [family][1] court –

(a)   those in which an officer of the Cafcass High Court Team or the Official Solicitor is or becomes the litigation friend or children's guardian of the ward or a party to the proceedings;

(b)   those in which a local authority is or becomes a party;

(c)   those in which an application for paternity testing is made;

(d)   those in which there is a dispute about medical treatment;

(e)   those in which an application is opposed on the grounds of lack of jurisdiction;

(f)   those in which there is a substantial foreign element;

(g)   those in which there is an opposed application for leave to take the child permanently out of the jurisdiction or where there is an application for temporary removal of a child from the jurisdiction and it is opposed on the ground that the child may not be duly returned.

NOTES

Amendment.[1] Words substituted: FPR Update, April 2014.

Parties

3.1 Where the child has formed or is seeking to form an association, considered to be undesirable, with another person, that other person should not be made a party to the application. Such a person should be made a respondent only to an application within the proceedings for an injunction or committal. Such a person should not be added to the title of the proceedings nor allowed to see any documents other than those relating directly to the proceedings for the injunction or committal. He or she should be allowed time to obtain representation and any injunction should in the first instance extend over a few days only.

Removal from jurisdiction

4.1 A child who is a ward of court may not be removed from England and Wales without the court's permission. Practice Direction 12F (International Child Abduction) deals in detail with locating and protecting children at risk of unlawful removal.

Criminal Proceedings

[5.1 Case law establishes that:

1. There is no requirement for the police or any other agency carrying out statutory powers of investigation or enforcement to seek the permission of the court to interview a child who is a ward of court. The fact that a child is a ward of court does not affect the powers and duties of the police or other statutory agencies in relation to their investigations. Provided that the relevant statutory requirements are complied with, the police or other agencies are under no duty to take any special steps in carrying out their functions in relation to a child who is a ward of court.

2. Where a child has been interviewed by the police in connection with contemplated criminal proceedings and the child is, or subsequently becomes, a ward of court, the permission of the court is not required for the child to be called as a witness in the criminal proceedings.

For a full review of the relevant case law and principles, see *In the matter of a Ward of Court* [2017] EWHC 1022 (Fam).

5.2 Where the police or other statutory agencies take any action in relation to a child who is a ward of court, the person(s) with day to day care and control of the child, or where applicable the local authority, should bring the relevant information to the attention of the court as soon as practicable. Where wardship proceedings are continuing, any children's guardian appointed for the child must be informed of the situation by the other parties.][1]

NOTES

Amendment.[1] Paragraph substituted: President's Circular, 16 June 2017.

Applications to the Criminal Injuries Compensation Authority

6.1 Where a child who is a ward of court has a right to make a claim for compensation to the Criminal Injuries Compensation Authority ('CICA'), an application must be made by the child's guardian, or, if no guardian has been appointed, the person with care and control of the child, for permission to apply to CICA and disclose such documents on the wardship proceedings file as are considered necessary to establish whether or not the child is eligible for an award plus, as appropriate, the amount of the award.

6.2 Any order giving permission should state that any award made by CICA should normally be paid into court immediately upon receipt and, once that payment has been made, application should made to the court as to its management and administration. If it is proposed to invest the award in any other way, the court's prior approval must be sought.

The role of the tipstaff

7.1 The tipstaff is the enforcement officer for all orders made in the High Court. The tipstaff's jurisdiction extends throughout England and Wales. Every applicable order made in the High Court is addressed to the tipstaff in children and family matters (eg 'The Court hereby directs the Tipstaff of the High Court of Justice, whether acting by himself or his assistants or a police officer as follows…').

7.2 The tipstaff may effect an arrest and then inform the police. Sometimes the local bailiff or police will detain a person in custody until the tipstaff arrives to collect that person or give further directions as to the disposal of the matter. The tipstaff may also make a forced entry although there will generally be a uniformed police officer standing by to make sure there is no breach of the peace.

7.3 There is only one tipstaff (with two assistants) but the tipstaff can also call on any constable or bailiff to assist in carrying out the tipstaff's duties.

7.4 The majority of the tipstaff's work involves locating children and taking them into protective custody, including cases of child abduction abroad.

[Application to set aside an inherent jurisdiction order

8.1 As set out in rule 12.42B, the Part 18 procedure applies to set aside an inherent jurisdiction order. Where such an application was made before rule 12.42B came into force, the Part 18 procedure will still apply subject to any directions that the court might make for the purpose of ensuring that the proceedings are dealt with fairly.

8.2 An application under rule 12.42B should be dealt with by the same level of judge that dealt with the original application. Where reasonably possible, the application should be dealt with by the same judge that dealt with the original application.

8.3 The application should be made promptly upon the party becoming aware of the information or upon the circumstances occurring that give rise to the application.

8.4 An application to set aside an inherent jurisdiction order should only be made where no error of the court is alleged (unless the circumstances set out in rule 18.11 apply). If an error of the court is alleged, an application for permission to appeal under Part 30 should be considered. The grounds on which an inherent jurisdiction order may be set aside are and will remain a matter for decisions by judges. The grounds may include: (i) fraud; (ii) material non-disclosure; (iii) certain limited types of mistake; (iv) a fundamental change in circumstances which undermines the basis on which the order was made; and (v) the welfare of the child requires it.

8.5 The effect of rules 12.42B(1)(a) and (2) is that an application may be made to set aside all or only part of an inherent jurisdiction order, including an inherent jurisdiction order that has been made by consent.

Inherent jurisdiction orders are defined in the rule and include any order, declaration or judgment made under the inherent jurisdiction, including but not limited to orders making a child a ward of court, orders regarding medical treatment of a child and orders for the return or non-return of a child made under the inherent jurisdiction. Inherent jurisdiction orders do not include return orders made under the 1980 Hague Convention (for those orders, see rule 12.42B and paragraphs 4.1A – 4.1B of Practice Direction 12F), but can include orders where the basis to exercise jurisdiction is found in other instruments, such as the 1996 Hague Convention (though the source of power for the return order remains the inherent jurisdiction). Inherent jurisdiction orders do not include orders or judgments made within inherent jurisdiction proceedings for which the power to make such an order or judgment is found in statute (such as the power to make return orders under section 8 of the Children Act 1989) or these Rules (and not the inherent jurisdiction). The power to set aside any such orders would, if it exists, derive either from relevant statutory provisions or form the power to vary or revoke in rule 4.1(6), or from any inherent power of the High Court to set aside its own orders. Rule 12.42B(6) clarifies that any such other power to revoke, discharge or set aside is not ousted by the rule.

8.6 In applications under rule 12.42B, the starting point is that the order which one party is seeking to have set aside was properly made. A mere allegation e.g. that it was obtained by fraud, is not sufficient for the court to set aside the order; evidence must be provided. Only once the ground for setting aside the order has been established (or admitted) can the court set aside the order and rehear the original application. The court has a full range of case management powers and considerable discretion as to how to determine an application to set aside an inherent jurisdiction order, including where appropriate the power to strike out or summarily dispose of an application to set aside. If and when a ground for setting aside has been established, the court may decide to set aside the whole or part of the order there and then, or may delay doing so. Ordinarily, once the court has decided to set aside an inherent jurisdiction order, the court would give directions for a full rehearing to re-determine the original application. However, if the court is satisfied that it has sufficient information to do so, it may proceed to re-determine the original application at the same time as setting aside the inherent jurisdiction order.][1]

NOTES

Amendment.[1] Paragraphs inserted: Practice Direction, April 2020.

PART II – Statutory instruments

Practice Direction 12E –
Urgent Business

This Practice Direction supplements FPR Part 12

Introduction

1.1 This Practice Direction describes the procedure to be followed in respect of urgent and out of hours cases in the Family Division of the High Court. For the avoidance of doubt, it does not relate to cases in respect of adults.

1.2 Urgent or out of hours applications, particularly those which have become urgent because they have not been pursued sufficiently promptly, should be avoided. A judge who has concerns that the urgent or out of hours facilities may have been abused may require a representative of the applicant to attend at a subsequent directions hearing to provide an explanation.

1.3 Urgent applications should whenever possible be made within court hours. The earliest possible liaison is required with the Clerk of the Rules who will attempt to accommodate genuinely urgent applications (at least for initial directions) in the Family Division applications court, from which the matter may be referred to another judge.

1.4 When it is not possible to apply within court hours, contact should be made with the security office at the Royal Courts of Justice (020 7947 6000 or 020 7947 6260) who will refer the matter to the urgent business officer. The urgent business officer can contact the duty judge. The judge may agree to hold a hearing, either convened at court or elsewhere, or by telephone.

1.5 When the hearing is to take place by telephone it should, unless not practicable, be by tape-recorded conference call arranged (and paid for in the first instance) by the applicant's solicitors. Solicitors acting for potential applicants should consider having standing arrangements with their telephone service providers under which such conference calls can be arranged. All parties (especially the judge) should be informed that the call is being recorded by the service provider. The applicant's solicitors should order a transcript of the hearing from the service provider. Otherwise the applicant's legal representative should prepare a note for approval by the judge.

General Issues

2.1 Parents, carers or other necessary respondents should whenever possible be given the opportunity to have independent legal advice or at least to have access to support or counselling.

2.2 In suitable cases, application may be made for directions providing for anonymity of the parties and others involved in the matter in any order or subsequent listing of the case. Exceptionally, a reporting restriction order may be sought.

2.3 Either the Official Solicitor or Cafcass, or CAFCASS Cymru, as the case may be, may be invited by the court to be appointed as advocate to the court.

Medical treatment and press injunction cases

3.1 It may be desirable for a child who is the subject of such proceedings to be made a party and represented through a children's guardian (usually an officer of Cafcass or a Welsh Family Proceedings Officer). Cafcass and CAFCASS Cymru stand ready to arrange for an officer to accept appointment as a children's guardian. They should be contacted at the earliest opportunity where an urgent application is envisaged. For urgent out of hours applications, the urgent business officer will contact a representative of Cafcass. CAFCASS Cymru is not able to deal with cases that arise out of office hours and those cases should be referred to Cafcass who will deal with the matter on behalf of CAFCASS Cymru until the next working day. A child of sufficient understanding to instruct his or her own solicitor should be made a party and given notice of any application.

3.2 Interim declarations/orders under the wardship jurisdiction or Children Act 1989 may be made on application either by an NHS trust, a local authority, an interested adult (where necessary with the leave of the court) or by the child if he or she has sufficient understanding to make the application.

Consultation with Cafcass, CAFCASS Cymru and Official Solicitor

4.1 Cafcass, CAFCASS Cymru and members of the Official Solicitor's legal staff are prepared to discuss cases before proceedings are issued. In all cases in which the urgent and out of hours procedures are to be used it would be helpful if the Official Solicitor, Cafcass or CAFCASS Cymru have had some advance notice of the application and its circumstances.

[4.2 Enquiries about children cases should be directed to the High Court Team Duty Manager at Cafcass National Office, 3rd Floor, 21 Bloomsbury Street, London, WC1B 3HF. DX: Cafcass DX 310101 Bloomsbury 11. Telephone 01753 235273 (Cafcass High Court Team) or 01753 235295 (Cafcass Legal Duty Lawyer). Email HighCourtGM@Cafcass.gsi.gov.uk (office hours only). Enquiries should be marked 'F.A.O. High Court Team' or 'F.A.O. HCT'.][1]]

Enquiries should be marked 'FAO High Court Team or FAO HCT'.

4.3 Enquiries about children cases in Wales should be directed to:

Social Care Team
Legal Services
Welsh Assembly Government
Cathays Park
Cardiff
CF10 3NQ
[Telephone 02920 370888, fax 0872 437 7306.][1]

4.4 Medical and welfare cases relating to an adult lacking capacity in relation to their medical treatment or welfare are brought in the Court of Protection. [Enquiries about adult medical and welfare cases should be addressed to the Court of Protection Healthcare and Welfare Team, Office of the Official Solicitor, Victory House, 30-34 Kingsway, London, WC2B 6EX, telephone 020 3681 2751, fax 020 3681 2762, email enquiries@offsol.gsi.gov.uk.][1]

PART II – Statutory instruments

Reference should also be made to Practice Direction E, accompanying Part 9 of the Court of Protection Rules 2007, and to Practice Direction B accompanying Part 10 of those Rules. Information for parties and practitioners is available on the website of the Ministry of Justice www.justice.gov.uk and general information for members of the public is available on www.direct.gov.uk.

NOTES

Amendment.[1] Text substituted: FPR Update, July 2015.

Practice Direction 12F –
International Child Abduction

This Practice Direction supplements FPR Part 12, Chapters 5 and 6

Part I – Introduction

1.1 This Practice Direction explains what to do if a child has been brought to, or kept in, England and Wales without the permission of anyone who has rights of custody in respect of the child in the country where the child was habitually resident immediately before the removal or retention. It also explains what to do if a child has been taken out of, or kept out of, England and Wales(a) without the permission of a parent or someone who has rights of custody in respect of the child. These cases are called 'international child abduction cases' and are dealt with in the High Court. This Practice Direction also explains what to do if you receive legal papers claiming that you have abducted a child. You can find the legal cases which are mentioned in this Practice Direction, and other legal material, on the website http://www.bailii.org (British and Irish Legal Information Institute).

> (a)   The child must be taken or kept out of the United Kingdom without the permission of a parent or someone who has rights of custody for it to be an international child abduction. This practice direction relates to the law as it applies in England and Wales. If the child has been taken or kept out of the United Kingdom when the child was habitually resident in Scotland, you should contact the Central Authority for Scotland, Scottish Government Justice Directorate, Civil Law Division, St Andrew's House, Regent Road, Edinburgh EH1 3DG Tel: +44 (0) 131 244 4827/4832 Fax: +44 (0)131 244 4848 Website: [http://www.gov.scot/Topics/Justice/law/17867/fm-children-root/18533][1]
>
> If the child has been taken or kept out of the United Kingdom when the child was habitually resident in Northern Ireland, you should contact the Central Authority for Northern Ireland, Northern Ireland Courts and Tribunals Service, Civil Policy and Tribunal Reform Division, 3rd Floor Laganside House, 23-27 Oxford Street, Belfast BT1 3LA [Tel: + 44 (0)28 9072 8808 or + 44 (0) 28 9072 8819; fax +44 (0) 28 9072 8945][1]
>
> Website: http://www.nics.gov.uk or http://www.courtsni.gov.uk/en-GB/Services/ChildAbduction.

1.2 If you have rights of custody in respect of a child and the child has been brought to England or Wales without your permission, or has been brought here with your permission but the person your child is staying with is refusing to return the child, then you can apply to the High Court of Justice, which covers all of England and Wales, for an order for the return of the child.

1.3 How you make an application to the High Court, what evidence you need to provide and what orders you should ask the court to make are all explained in this Practice Direction.

1.4 If your child is under 16 years of age and has been brought to England or Wales from a country which is a party (a 'State party') to the 1980 Hague Convention on the Civil Aspects of International Child Abduction ('the 1980 Hague Convention') then you can make an application to the High Court for an order under that Convention for the return of your child to the State in which he or she was habitually resident immediately before being removed or being kept away. This is explained in Part 2 below.

1.5 If your child is over 16 years of age and under 18, or has been brought to England or Wales from a country which is not a State party to the 1980 Hague Convention, then you can make an application for the return of your child under the inherent jurisdiction of the High Court with respect to children. In exercising this jurisdiction over children, the High Court will make your child's welfare its paramount consideration. How to make an application under the inherent jurisdiction of the High Court with respect to children is explained in Part 3 below.

1.6 It might be necessary for you to make an urgent application to the court if you are not sure where your child is, or you think that there is a risk that the person who is keeping your child away from you might take the child out of the United Kingdom or hide them away. Part 4 below explains how to make an urgent application to the High Court for orders to protect your child until a final decision can be made about returning the child and also how to ask for help from the police and government agencies if you think your child might be taken out of the country.

Rights of Access

1.7 Rights of access to children (also called contact or visitation) may be enforced in England and Wales. [The][2] 1980 Hague Convention expects State parties to comply with orders and agreements concerning access as well as rights of custody. If you have an access order and you want to enforce it in England or Wales, you should read Part 5 below.

NOTES

Amendments.[1] Text substituted: FPR Update, July 2015. [2] Text substituted: FPR Update, March 2019.

Part 2 – Hague Convention Cases

2.1 States which are party to the 1980 Hague Convention have agreed to return children who have been either wrongfully removed from, or wrongfully retained away from, the State where they were habitually resident immediately before the wrongful removal or retention. There are very limited exceptions to this obligation.

2.2 'Wrongfully removed' or 'wrongfully retained' means removed or retained in breach of rights of custody in respect of the child attributed to a person or a body or an institution. 'Rights of custody' are interpreted very widely (see paragraph 2.16 below).

2.3 The text of the 1980 Hague Convention and a list of Contracting States (that is, State parties) can be found on the website of the Hague Conference on Private

PART II – Statutory instruments

International Law at http://www.hcch.net. All Member States of the European Union are State parties to the 1980 Hague Convention, and all but Denmark are bound by an EU Regulation which supplements the operation of the 1980 Hague Convention between the Member States of the EU (Council Regulation (EC) No 2201/2003, see paragraph 2.6).

2.4 In each State party there is a body called the Central Authority whose duty is to help people use the 1980 Hague Convention.

2.5 If you think that your child has been brought to, or kept in, England or Wales, and your State is a State party to the 1980 Hague Convention, then you should get in touch with your own Central Authority who will help you to send an application for the return of your child to the Central Authority for England and Wales. However, you are not obliged to contact your own Central Authority. You may contact the Central Authority for England and Wales directly, or you may simply instruct lawyers in England or Wales to make an application for you. The advantage of making your application through the Central Authority for England and Wales if you are applying from outside the United Kingdom is that you will get public funding ('legal aid') to make your application, regardless of your financial resources.

The Central Authority for England and Wales

2.6 The Child Abduction and Custody Act 1985 brings the 1980 Hague Convention into the law of England and Wales and identifies the Lord Chancellor as the Central Authority. His duties as the Central Authority are carried out by the International Child Abduction and Contact Unit (ICACU). ICACU also carries out the duties of the Central Authority for …[2] the European Convention on Recognition and Enforcement of Decisions concerning Custody of Children signed at Luxembourg on 20 May 1980 (called 'the European Convention' in this Practice Direction but sometimes also referred to as 'the Luxembourg Convention') …[2].

2.7 ICACU is open Mondays to Fridays from 9.00 a.m. to 5.00 p.m. It is located in the Office of the Official Solicitor and Public Trustee and its contact details are as follows:

[International Child Abduction and Contact Unit
Office of the Official Solicitor
Victory House
30–34 Kingsway
London
WC2B 6EX
Email ICACU@offsol.gsi.gov.uk
Tel: + 44 (20) 3681 2608 (10.00am to 4.00pm)
Fax: +44 (20) 3681 2763][1]

In an emergency (including out of normal working hours) contact should be made with the Royal Courts of Justice on one of the following telephone numbers:

+ 44 (0)20 7947 6000, or
+ 44 (0) 20 7947 6260.

In addition, in an emergency or outside normal working hours advice on international child abduction can be sought from reunite International Child Abduction Centre on +44 (0)1162 556 234. Outside office hours you will be directed to the 24 hour emergency service. You can also see information on Reunite's website http://www.reunite.org.

What ICACU Will Do

2.8 When ICACU receives your application for the return of your child, unless you already have a legal representative in England and Wales whom you want to act for you, it will send your application to a solicitor whom it knows to be experienced in international child abduction cases and ask them to take the case for you. You will then be the solicitor's client and the solicitor will make an application for public funding to meet your legal costs. The solicitor will then apply to the High Court for an order for the return of your child.

2.9 You can find out more about ICACU and about the 1980 Hague Convention and the other international instruments mentioned at paragraph 2.6 on two websites: Information for parties and practitioners is available on http://www. justice.gov.uk and general information for members of the public is available on http://[www.gov.uk][1].

Applying to the High Court – the Form and Content of Application

2.10 An application to the High Court for an order under the 1980 Hague Convention must be made in the Principal Registry of the Family Division in Form C67. ...[2]

2.11 The application must include –

(a)   the names and dates of birth of the children;
(b)   the names of the children's parents or guardians;
(c)   the whereabouts or suspected whereabouts of the children;
(d)   the interest of the applicant in the matter (e.g. mother, father, or person with whom the child lives and details of any order placing the child with that person);
(e)   the reasons for the application;
(f)   details of any proceedings (including proceedings not in England or Wales, and including any legal proceedings which have finished) relating to the children;
(g)   where the application is for the return of a child, the identity of the person alleged to have removed or retained the child and, if different, the identity of the person with whom the child is thought to be;
(h)   ...[2]

2.12 The application should be accompanied by all relevant documents including (but not limited to) –

(a)   an authenticated copy of any relevant decision or agreement;
(b)   a certificate or an affidavit from a Central Authority, or other competent authority of the State of the child's habitual residence, or from a qualified person, concerning the relevant law of that State.

2.13 As the applicant you may also file a statement in support of the application, although usually your solicitor will make and file a statement for you on your instructions. The statement must contain and be verified by a statement of truth in the following terms:

'I make this statement knowing that it will be placed before the court, and I confirm that to the best of my knowledge and belief its contents are true.'

(Further provisions about statements of truth are contained in Part 17 of these Rules and in Practice Direction 17A).

The Timetable for the Case

2.14 ...[2] The following procedural steps are intended to ensure that applications under the 1980 Hague Convention ...[2] are handled quickly –

(a) the application must be headed ...[2] 'in the matter of the Child Abduction and Custody Act 1985' ...[2];

(b) the court file will be marked to –
   (i) draw attention to the nature of the application; and
   (ii) state the date on which the 6 week period will expire (the 'hear-by date');

(c) listing priority will, where necessary, be given to such applications;

(d) the trial judge will expedite the transcript of the judgment and its approval and ensure that it is sent to the Central Authority without delay.

...[2]

Applications for Declarations

2.15 If a child has been taken from England and Wales to another State party, the judicial or administrative authorities of that State may ask for a declaration that the removal or retention of the child was wrongful. Or it might be thought that a declaration from the High Court that a child has been wrongfully removed or retained away from the United Kingdom would be helpful in securing his return. The High Court can make such declarations under section 8 of the Child Abduction and Custody Act 1985. An application for a declaration is made in the same way as an application for a return order, the only difference being that the details of relevant legal proceedings in respect of which the declaration is sought (if any), including a copy of any order made relating to the application, should be included in the documentation.

Rights of Custody

2.16 'Rights of custody' includes rights relating to the care of the person of the child and, in particular, the right to determine the child's place of residence. Rights of custody may arise by operation of law (that is, they are conferred on someone automatically by the legal system in which they are living) or by a judicial or administrative decision or as a result of an agreement having legal effect. The rights of a person, an institution or any other body are a matter for the law of the State of the child's habitual residence, but it is for the State which is being asked to return the child to decide: if those rights amount to rights of custody for the purposes of the 1980 Hague Convention; whether at the time of the removal or retention those rights were actually being exercised; and whether there has been a breach of those rights.

2.17 In England and Wales a father who is not married to the mother of their child does not necessarily have 'rights of custody' in respect of the child. An unmarried father in England and Wales who has parental responsibility for a child has rights of custody in respect of that child. In the case of an unmarried father without parental responsibility, the concept of rights of custody may include more than strictly legal rights and where immediately before the removal or retention of the child he was exercising parental functions over a substantial period of time as the only or main carer for the child he may have rights of custody. An unmarried father can ask ICACU or his legal representative for advice on this. It is important to remember that it will be for the State which is being asked to return the child to decide if the father's circumstances meet that State's requirements for the establishment of rights of custody.

2.18 Sometimes, court orders impose restrictions on the removal of children from the country in which they are living. These can be orders under the Children Act 1989 ('section 8' orders) or orders under the inherent jurisdiction of the High Court (sometimes called 'injunctions'). Any removal of a child in breach of an order imposing such a restriction would be wrongful under the 1980 Hague Convention.

2.19 The fact that court proceedings are in progress about a child does not of itself give rise to a prohibition on the removal of the child by a mother with sole parental responsibility from the country in which the proceedings are taking place unless –

(a) the proceedings are Wardship proceedings in England and Wales (in which case removal would breach the rights of custody attributed to the High Court and fathers with no custody rights could rely on that breach); or

(b) the court is actually considering the custody of the child, because then the court itself would have rights of custody.

Particular provisions for European Convention applications

2.20 The European Convention provides for the mutual recognition and enforcement of decisions relating to custody and access, so if a child has been brought here or retained here in breach of a custody order, then that order can be enforced. ...[2] If ...[2] you want to make an application under the European Convention, then you make it in the same way as is described in paragraphs 2.10 and 2.11 above, but in addition you must include a copy of the decision relating to custody (or rights of access – see paragraph 5.1 below) which you are seeking to register or enforce, or about which you are seeking a declaration by the court.

Defending Abduction Proceedings

2.21 If you are served with an application – whether it is under the 1980 Hague or the European Convention or the inherent jurisdiction of the High Court – you

PART II – Statutory instruments

must not delay. You must obey any directions given in any order with which you have been served, and you should seek legal advice at the earliest possible opportunity, although neither you nor the child concerned will automatically be entitled to legal aid.

2.22 It is particularly important that you tell the court where the child is, because the child will not be permitted to live anywhere else without the permission of the court, or to leave England and Wales, until the proceedings are finished.

2.23 It is also particularly important that you present to the court any defence to the application which you or the child might want to make at the earliest possible opportunity, although the orders with which you will have been served are likely to tell you the time by which you will have to do this.

2.24 If the child concerned objects to any order sought in relation to them, and if the child is of an age and understanding at which the court will take account of their views, the court is likely to direct that the child is seen by an officer of the Children and Family Court Advisory and Support Service (Cafcass) or in Wales CAFCASS Cymru. You should cooperate in this process. Children are not usually made parties to abduction cases, but in certain exceptional circumstances the court can make them parties so that they have their own separate legal representation. These are all matters about which you should seek legal advice.

> (Provisions about the power of the court to join parties are contained in rule 12.3 and provisions about the joining and representation of children are contained in Part 16 of these Rules and the Practice Direction 16A (Representation of Children).

NOTES

Amendments.[1] Text substituted: FPR Update, July 2015.2 Words omitted repealed: FPR Update, March 2019.

Part 3 – Non-Convention Cases

3.1 Applications for the return of children wrongfully removed or retained away from States which are not parties to the 1980 Hague Convention or in respect of children to whom that Convention does not apply, can be made to the High Court under its inherent jurisdiction with respect to children. Such proceedings are referred to as 'non-Convention' cases. In proceedings under the inherent jurisdiction of the High Court with respect to children, the child's welfare is the court's paramount consideration. The extent of the court's enquiry into the child's welfare will depend on the circumstances of the case; in some cases the child's welfare will be best served by a summary hearing and, if necessary, a prompt return to the State from which the child has been removed or retained. In other cases a more detailed enquiry may be necessary (see *Re J (Child Returned Abroad: Convention Rights)* [2005] UKHL 40; [2005] 2 FLR 802).

3.2 Every application for the return of a child under the inherent jurisdiction must be made in the Principal Registry of the Family Division and heard in the High Court.

Provision about the inherent jurisdiction is made at Chapter 5 of Part 12 of the Rules and in Practice Direction 12D (Inherent Jurisdiction (including Wardship) Proceedings).

The Form and content of the application

3.3 An application for the return of a child under the inherent jurisdiction must be made in Form C66 and must include the information in paragraph 2.11 above.

3.4 You must file a statement in support of your application, which must exhibit all the relevant documents. The statement must contain and be verified by a statement of truth in the following terms:

'I make this statement knowing that it will be placed before the court, and confirm that to the best of my knowledge and belief its contents are true.'

(Further provisions about statements of truth are contained in Part 17 of these Rules and Practice Direction 17A).

Timetable for Non-Convention Cases

3.5 While the 6 week deadline referred to in paragraph 2.14 is set out in the 1980 Hague Convention …[2], non-Convention child abduction cases must similarly be completed in 6 weeks except where exceptional circumstances make this impossible. Paragraph 2.14 applies to these cases as appropriate for a non-Convention case.

NOTES

Amendment.[1] Words omitted repealed: FPR Update, March 2019.

Part 4 – General Provisions

Urgent applications, or applications out of business hours

4.1 Guidance about urgent and out of hours applications is in Practice Direction 12E (Urgent Business).

[Challenging a return order or non-return order

4.1A If you are a party to a return case and you believe that the court has made an error, it is possible to apply for permission to appeal (see Part 30 of the Rules and Practice Direction 30A).

In rare circumstances, the court might also 'set aside' its own order where it has not made an error but where new information comes to light which fundamentally changes the basis on which the order was made. The threshold for the court to set aside its decision is high, and evidence will be required – not just assertions or allegations.

If the return order or non-return order was made under the 1980 Hague Convention, the court might set aside its decision where there has been fraud, material nondisclosure or mistake (which all essentially mean that there was information that the court needed to know in order to make its decision, but was not told), or where there has been a fundamental change in circumstances which undermines the basis on which the order was made. If you have evidence of such circumstances and wish to apply to the court to set aside its decision, you should use the procedure in Part 18 of the Rules.

If the return order or non-return order was made under the inherent jurisdiction (see Part 3 of this Practice Direction), the court might set aside its decision for similar reasons as with return-non-return orders under the 1980 Hague Convention, but it also might set aside its decision because the welfare of the child or children requires it. If you have evidence of such circumstances and wish to apply to the court to set aside its decision, you should use the procedure in Part 18 of the Rules.

Any such application should be made promptly and the court will also aim to deal with the application as expeditiously as possible.

4.1B If the court has ordered the immediate implementation of the return order and you wish to apply for permission to appeal that return order or for that order to be set aside, you should also consider an application to the court for a "stay" of the return order, or stop it being implemented.][1]

NOTES

Amendment.[1] Paragraphs inserted: Practice Direction, April 2020.

Police assistance to prevent removal from England and Wales

4.2 The Child Abduction Act 1984 sets out the circumstances in which the removal of a child from this jurisdiction is a criminal offence. The police provide the following 24 hour service to prevent the unlawful removal of a child –

(a)   they inform ports directly when there is a real and imminent threat that a child is about to be removed unlawfully from the country; and

(b)   they liaise with Immigration Officers at the ports in an attempt to identify children at risk of removal.

4.3 Where the child is under 16, it is not necessary to obtain a court order before seeking police assistance. The police do not need an order to act to protect the child. If an order has already been obtained it should however be produced to the police. Where the child is between 16 and 18, an order must be obtained restricting or restraining removal before seeking police assistance.

4.4 Where the child is a ward of court (see Practice Direction 12D (Inherent Jurisdiction (including Wardship) Proceedings) the court's permission is needed to remove that child from the jurisdiction. When the court has not given that permission and police assistance is sought to prevent the removal of the ward, the applicant must produce evidence that the child is a ward such as –

(a)   an order confirming wardship;

(b)   an injunction; or

(c)   where the matter is urgent and no order has been made, a certified copy of the wardship application.

4.5 The application for police assistance must be made by the applicant or his legal representative to the applicant's local police station except that applications may be made to any police station –

(a)   in urgent cases;

(b)   where the wardship application has just been issued; or

(c)   where the court has just made the order relied on.

4.6 The police will, if they consider it appropriate, institute the 'port alert' system (otherwise known as 'an all ports warning') to try to prevent removal from the jurisdiction where the danger of removal is –

(a)   real (ie not being sought merely by way of insurance); and

(b)   imminent (ie within 24 to 48 hours).

4.7 The request for police assistance must be accompanied by as much of the following information as possible –

(a)   *the child:* the name, sex, date of birth, physical description, nationality and passport number; if the child has more than one nationality or passport, provide details;

(b)   *the person likely to remove:* the name, age, physical description, nationality, passport number, relationship to the child, and whether the child is likely to assist him or her; if the person has more than one nationality or passport, provide details;

(c)   *person applying for a port alert:* the name, relationship to the child, nationality, telephone number and (if appropriate) solicitor's or other legal representative's name and contact details; if the person has more than one nationality, provide details;

(d)   likely destination;

(e)   likely time of travel and port of embarkation and, if known, details of travel arrangements;

(f)   grounds for port alert (as appropriate) –

   (i)   suspected offence under section 1 or section 2 of the Child Abduction Act 1984;

   (ii) the child is subject to a court order.

(g)   details of person to whom the child should be returned if intercepted.

4.8 If the police decide that the case is one in which the port-alert system should be used, the child's name will remain on the stop list for four weeks. After that time it will be removed automatically unless a further application is made.

[HM Passport Office][1]

4.9 Where the court makes an order prohibiting or otherwise restricting the removal of a child from the United Kingdom, or from any specified part of it, or from a specified dependent territory, the court may make an order under section 37 of the Family Law Act 1986 requiring any person to surrender any UK passport which has been issued to, or contains particulars of, the child.

4.10 [HM Passport Office (HMPO)][1] will take action to prevent a United Kingdom passport or replacement passport being issued only where [HMPO][1] has been served with a court order expressly requiring a United Kingdom passport to be surrendered, or expressly prohibiting the issue of any further United Kingdom passport facilities to the child without the consent of the court, or the holder of such an order. Accordingly, in every case in which such an order has been made,

[HMPO]1 must be served the same day if possible, or at the latest the following day, with a copy of the order. It is the responsibility of the applicant to do this. The specimen form of letter set out below should be used and a copy of the court order must be attached to the letter. Delay in sending the letter to [HMPO]1 must be kept to an absolute minimum.

'[Intelligence Hub
Her Majesty's Passport Office
3 Northgate
96 Milton Street
Glasgow
G4 0BT][1]

Dear Sir/Madam

…………………………..v………………………………..

Case no:……………………………………………….

This is to inform you that the court has today made an order

*prohibiting the issue of a passport/passports to [name(s)] [date of birth (if known)] of [address] without the consent of the holder of the order.

*requiring [name(s)] [date of birth (if known)] of [address] to surrender the passport(s) issued to him/her/them/the following child[ren] / or which contain(s) particulars of the following child[ren]:

Name   Date of Birth

*and has granted an injunction/*made an order restraining the removal of the child[ren] from the jurisdiction.

(*Delete as appropriate)

Please add these names to your records to prevent the issue of further passport facilities for the child[ren]. I enclose a copy of the court order.

Yours faithfully

Applicant's name / Applicant's Solicitor's name'

4.11 Following service on [HMPO][1] of an order either expressly requiring a United Kingdom passport to be surrendered by, or expressly prohibiting the issue of any further United Kingdom passport facilities to the child, [HMPO][1] will maintain a prohibition on issuing a passport, or further passport facilities until the child's 16th birthday. The order should state that a passport must not be granted/applied for without the consent of the court or the holder of the order.

Note: These requests may also be sent to any of the regional Passport Offices.

4.12 Further information on communicating with [HMPO][1] where the court has made a request of, or an order against, [HMPO][1], may be found in [The President's Guidance reissued in October 2014: Communicating with the Home

Office in Family Proceedings. Annex 1 to this Practice Direction contains that Guidance and Annex 2 contains the current version (as at June 2015) of the relevant court form.][1]

4.13 Information about other circumstances, in which [HMPO]1 will agree not to issue a passport to a child if the IPS receives an application, or an order in more general terms than set out at 4.11 above, from a person who claims to have parental responsibility for the child, is available from [HMPO]1 or at [www.gov.uk][1].

The Home Office

4.14 Information about communicating with the Home Office, where a question of the immigration status of a party arises in family proceedings, may be found in the Protocol: Communicating with the Home Office in Family Proceedings (revised and re-issued October 2010).

Press Reporting

4.15 When a child has been abducted and a judge considers that publicity may help in tracing the child, the judge may adjourn the case for a short period to enable representatives of the Press to attend to give the case the widest possible publicity.

4.16. If a Child Rescue Alert has been used concerning a child, within the UK or abroad, it will give rise to media publicity. The court should be informed that this has happened. If there are already court proceedings concerning a child, it is advisable to obtain the agreement of the court before there is publicity to trace a missing child. If the court has not given its permission for a child who is the subject of children proceedings to be identified as the subject of proceedings, to do so would be contempt of court.

Other Assistance

4.17 The Missing Persons Bureau will be participating for the UK in the European Union wide 116 000 hotline for missing children. Parents and children can ring this number for assistance. (It is primarily intended to deal with criminal matters, for example stranger kidnapping.)

4.18 It may also be possible to trace a child by obtaining a court order under the inherent jurisdiction or the wardship jurisdiction of the High Court addressed to certain government departments, as set out in Practice Direction 6C.

NOTES

Amendments.[1] Words substituted: FPR Update, July 2015.

Part 5 – ...[1]

...[1]

NOTES

Amendment.[1] Part repealed: FPR Update, March 2019.

Part 6 – Child abduction cases between the United Kingdom and Pakistan

6.1 A consensus was reached in January 2003 between the President of the Family Division and the Hon. Chief Justice of Pakistan as to the principles to be applied in resolving child abduction cases between the UK and Pakistan.

The Protocol setting out that consensus can be accessed at:

http://www.fco.gov.uk/resources/en/pdf/2855621/3069133

[ANNEX 1

COMMUNICATING WITH UK VISAS AND IMMIGRATION (UKVI) IN FAMILY PROCEEDINGS

Protocol agreed between the President of the Family Division and the Home Office issued on 16 May 2018

1 This Protocol enables the family courts (the Family Division of the High Court of Justice and the Family Court) to communicate with UK VISAS AND IMMIGRATION (UKVI), the relevant division of the Home Office, to obtain immigration and visa information for use in family court proceedings. Although it replaces and supersedes the previous guidance issued in 2002, 2004, 2006, 2010 and 2014, in particular to reflect new UKVI processes and contact details, it does not alter the nature or purpose of the Protocol.

2 There are three parts of the process:

(1) HMCTS form EX660 (rev 04/18), a copy of which is annexed to this Protocol, must be completed by the parties and approved by the judge.

    (a)   The EX660 must be typed, not handwritten.
    (b)   The EX660 must be completed in full, specifying the details of the relevant family members and their relationship to the child(ren). Details of both mother and father/adoptive parents if known should be provided, whether or not they are involved in the proceedings, as this enables UKVI to trace the child(ren)'s records.
    (c)   The EX660 and the order must specify the questions the court wishes to be answered by UKVI.
    (d)   The EX660 must contain the name and contact details of someone who has agreed and is able to provide further information if needed.
    (e)   The EX660 must clearly state the time by which the information is required.

Failure to do this may cause delay in the time it takes UKVI to process the request.

(2) An order in the relevant form, a copy of which is annexed to this Protocol, must be drawn up, approved by the judge and sealed by the court.

    (a)   The order must clearly state the time by which the information is required.
    (b)   The order must specify any additional information or documents, such as a synopsis, which it wishes UKVI to have and set out in the order

that the leave of the court to make disclosure to UKVI has been given. (Note that it may be a contempt of court to disclose this information otherwise.)

(3)   The UKVI SVEC pro-forma must be completed by the court staff utilising the information in the EX660 and the order.

(a)   All relevant fields in the SVEC pro-forma must be completed:
- i.   Section A - All fields to be completed if known
- ii.   Section B - Enquiry Type - Select Standard
- iii.   Section C - Select Subject 1 and complete all fields.
- iv.   Section D - Enter 'Y' in 'Other' field only.
- v.   Section E - Enter 'Please refer to court order and EX660'.
- vi.   For more than one subject, select subject 2 and so on, completing steps C-E for each one.

(b)   In Section B there are two fields, 'Court date' and 'required date', which must be completed. In both fields the date the information is required should be entered, not the court date. These fields generate the target date on UKVI systems and, as the information ordered by the court will be required before the date of the court hearing, this will ensure that the information is provided in time.

3 The EX660 and the order must contain sufficient information to enable UKVI to understand the nature of the case, to identify whether the case involves an adoption, and to identify whether the immigration issues raised relate to an asylum or a non- asylum application.

4 In order to comply with the agreed four (4) week period for UKVI to provide a response to the court, the sealed order should be available to be sent by the court staff to UKVI on the same day that the order is made. Where that is not possible, the court, when stating the required date of receipt by the court of the information requested, must allow any additional time necessary for the preparation, sealing and sending of the order. This is to ensure that UKVI has four (4) weeks to provide a response from the time it receives the order.

5 The sealed order, completed EX660 and SVEC pro-forma should be sent immediately by the court to ICESSVECWorkflow@homeoffice.gsi.gov.uk including EEREQUEST on the subject line of the email. The request for information will be rejected by UKVI if either the sealed order or the SVEC pro-forma is not provided.

6 Where the court wishes to progress a case that may be delayed, it may send an email to SVECManagement@homeoffice.gsi.gov.uk

7 The UKVI official will be personally responsible for either:

(i)   answering the query themselves, by retrieving the file and preparing a statement for the court; or
(ii) forwarding to a caseworker or relevant official with carriage of the particular file.

8 UKVI will ensure that their information is received by the court in time, as instructed by the judge or court making the request.][1]

NOTES

Amendments.[1] Annex inserted: FPR Update, July 2015.

PART II – Statutory instruments

ANNEX 2[1]

Annex 2

Court request for information
to the Home Office

UK Visas & Immigration/HM Passport Office

Name of court	

Please note that all information provided in this form will be forwarded to the Home Office

Case no.	
Serial no.	
Date	

In the matter of the _____ Act

In the matter of | |

To the judge: Each of the following fields must be completed to assist the Home Office find the relevant records. Once completed pass the form to your Court Clerk. The Court Clerk will then produce a separate order directed to the Home Office, using the information provided on this form. The form must be sent **without delay,** together with the court order, to the Home Office Liaison Team.

Name of Judge:

Full name of each party, including relationship to child(ren)	Female/Male (please tick)	Date of birth	Country of origin	Date arrived in UK:	All relevant Home Office reference no's:
	☐ Female ☐ Male				
	☐ Female ☐ Male				
	☐ Female ☐ Male				
	☐ Female ☐ Male				
	☐ Female ☐ Male				
	☐ Female ☐ Male				

continued overleaf

What questions would you like the UKVI/HMPO to answer?	
Please provide a brief summary of case and any other information which will be useful to the UKVI/HMPO in dealing with the request e.g. any details relating to immigration: (Please attach any documents, such as Case Summaries, in respect of which the Court has given leave to disclose to the Home Office).	
Has the court in the order given leave to disclose any supporting documentation to the Home Office?	☐ Yes ☐ No
Contact details of person from whom additional information can be sought:	
By what date is the information required? (Please allow a minimum of 4 weeks from the date of sending to the Home Office Liaison Team)	

To the court clerk
Please send this document, **together with the sealed order** and any attached documents, **without delay** to: Home Office Liaison Team, HM Courts & Tribunal Service, Arnhem House PO Box 6987 Leicester LE1 6ZX. Email: homeofficeliaison@hmcts.gsi.gov.uk Telephone: 0116 249 4177 Fax: 0116 249 4302.

NOTES
Amendments.[1] Annex inserted: FPR Update, July 2015.

[ANNEX 3][1]

NOTES

Amendments.1 Annex renumbered: FPR Update, July 2015.

See paragraph 5.5

Practice Note

5 March 1993

Citations: [1993] 1 FLR 804

Child Abduction Unit: Lord Chancellor's Department

Duties of the Central Authority for England and Wales under Article 21 of the Hague Convention on the Civil Aspects of International Child Abduction

CHILD ABDUCTION AND CUSTODY ACT 1985

In the case of *Re* G (A Minor) (Hague Convention: Access) [1993] 1 FLR 669 the Court of Appeal considered the duties of the Central Authority for England and Wales on receiving an application in respect of rights of access under Art 21 of the Hague Convention.

The Court of Appeal took the view that Art 21 conferred no jurisdiction to determine matters relating to access, or to recognise or enforce foreign access orders. It provides, however, for executive co-operation in the enforcement of such recognition as national law allows.

Accordingly, the duty of the Central Authority is to make appropriate arrangements for the applicant by providing solicitors to act on his behalf in applying for legal aid and instituting proceedings in the High Court under s 8 of the Children Act 1989.

If, during the course of proceedings under Art 21 of the Convention, the applicant decides to seek access instead of the return of the child, but no agreement can be reached and the provisions of the European Convention on the Recognition and Enforcement of Decisions Concerning Custody of Children and on Restoration of Custody of Children are not available, a separate application under s 8 of the Children Act 1989 will have to be made.

Central Authority for England and Wales

NOTES

NB. The Child Abduction Unit is now called ICACU, see paragraph 2.6.

Practice Direction 12G –
Communication of Information

This Practice Direction supplements FPR Part 12, Chapter 7

1.1 Chapter 7 deals with the communication of information (whether or not contained in a document filed with the court) relating to proceedings which relate to children.

1.2 Subject to any direction of the court, information may be communicated for the purposes of the law relating to contempt in accordance with paragraphs 2.1, 3.1 or 4.1.

Communication of information by a party etc. for other purposes

2.1 A person specified in the first column of the following table may communicate to a person listed in the second column such information as is specified in the third column for the purpose or purposes specified in the fourth column –

A party	A lay adviser, a McKenzie Friend, or a person arranging or providing pro bono legal services	Any information relating to the proceedings	To enable the party to obtain advice or assistance in relation to the proceedings
A party	A health care professional or a person or body providing counselling services for children or families		To enable the party or any child of the party to obtain health care or counselling
A party	The Child Maintenance and Enforcement Commission, a McKenzie Friend, a lay adviser or the First-tier Tribunal dealing with an appeal made under section 20 of the Child Support Act 1991		For the purposes of making or responding to an appeal under section 20 of the Child Support Act 1991 or the determination of such an appeal
A party or other person lawfully in receipt of information	The Secretary of State, a McKenzie Friend, a lay adviser or the Upper Tier Tribunal dealing with an appeal under section 24 of the Child Support Act 1991 in respect of a decision of the First-tier Tribunal that was made under section 20 of that Act		For a purpose connected with an appeal under section 24 of the Child Support Act 1991 in respect of a decision of the First-tier Tribunal that was made under section 20 of that Act.
A party	An adoption panel		To enable the adoption panel to discharge its functions as appropriate

PART II – Statutory instruments

A party	A local authority's medical adviser appointed under the Adoption Agencies Regulations 2005 or the Adoption Agencies (Wales) Regulations 2005		To enable the medical adviser to discharge his or her functions as appropriate
A party	The European Court of Human Rights		For the purpose of making an application to the European Court of Human Rights
A party or any person lawfully in receipt of information	The Children's Commissioner or the Children's Commissioner for Wales		To refer an issue affecting the interests of children to the Children's Commissioner or the Children's Commissioner for Wales
[A party or any person lawfully in receipt of information	The Welsh Language Commissioner		To refer an issue so that the Welsh Language Commissioner can consider whether to institute or intervene in legal proceedings or to assist a party or prospective party to legal proceedings.][1]
A party, any person lawfully in receipt of information or a proper officer	A person or body conducting an approved research project		For the purpose of an approved research project
A legal representative or a professional legal adviser	A professional indemnity insurer		To enable the professional indemnity insurer to be notified of a claim or complaint, or potential claim or complaint, in relation to the legal representative or a professional legal adviser, and the legal representative or professional legal adviser to obtain advice in respect of that claim or complaint

A legal representative or a professional legal adviser	A person or body responsible for investigating or determining complaints in relation to legal representatives or professional legal advisers		For the purposes of the investigation or determination of a complaint in relation to a legal representative or a professional legal adviser
A legal representative or a professional legal adviser	A person or body assessing quality assurance systems		To enable the legal representative or professional legal adviser to obtain a quality assurance assessment
A legal representative or a professional legal adviser	An accreditation body	Any information relating to the proceedings providing that it does not, or is not likely to, identify any person involved in the proceedings	To enable the legal representative or professional legal adviser to obtain accreditation
A party	A police officer	The text or summary of the whole or part of a judgment given in the proceedings	For the purpose of a criminal investigation
A party or any person lawfully in receipt of information	A member of the Crown Prosecution Service		To enable the Crown Prosecution Service to discharge its functions under any enactment
A party or an adoption agency	An adoption agency	Any information relating to the proceedings	To enable the sharing of relevant information between adoption agencies for more effective undertaking of their functions

NOTES

Amendment.[1] Entry inserted: FPR Update, April 2020.

Communication for the effective functioning of Cafcass and CAFCASS Cymru

3.1 An officer of the Service or a Welsh family proceedings officer, as appropriate, may communicate to a person listed in the second column such information as is

PART II – Statutory instruments

specified in the third column for the purpose or purposes specified in the fourth column –

A Welsh family proceedings officer	A person or body exercising statutory functions relating to inspection of CAFCASS Cymru	Any information relating to the proceedings which is required by the person or body responsible for the inspection	For the purpose of an inspection of CAFCASS Cymru by a body or person appointed by the Welsh Ministers
An officer of the Service or a Welsh family proceedings officer	The Health and Care Professions Council or the Care Council for Wales	Any information relating to the proceedings providing that it does not, or is not likely to, identify any person involved in the proceedings	For the purpose of initial and continuing accreditation as a social worker of a person providing services to Cafcass or CAFCASS Cymru in accordance with section 13(2) of the Criminal Justice and Courts Services Act 2000 or section 36 of the Children Act 2004 as the case may be
An officer of the Service or a Welsh family proceedings officer	A person or body providing services relating to professional development or training to Cafcass or CAFCASS Cymru	Any information relating to the proceedings providing that it does not, or is not likely to, identify any person involved in the proceedings without that person's consent	To enable the person or body to provide the services, where the services cannot be effectively provided without such disclosure
An officer of the Service or a Welsh family proceedings officer	A person employed by or contracted to Cafcass or CAFCASS Cymru for the purposes of carrying out the functions referred to in column 4 of this row	Any information relating to the proceedings	Engagement in processes internal to Cafcass or CAFCASS Cymru which relate to the maintenance of necessary records concerning the proceedings, or to ensuring that Cafcass or CAFCASS Cymru functions are carried out to a satisfactory standard

Communication to and by Ministers of the Crown and Welsh Ministers

4.1 A person specified in the first column of the following table may communicate to a person listed in the second column such information as is specified in the third column for the purpose or purposes specified in the fourth column –

A party or any person lawfully in receipt of information relating to the proceedings	A Minister of the Crown with responsibility for a government department engaged, or potentially engaged, in an application before the European Court of Human Rights relating to the proceedings	Any information relating to the proceedings of which he or she is in lawful possession	To provide the department with information relevant, or potentially relevant, to the proceedings before the European Court of Human Rights
A Minister of the Crown	The European Court of Human Rights		For the purpose of engagement in an application before the European Court of Human Rights relating to the proceedings
A Minister of the Crown	Lawyers advising or representing the United Kingdom in an application before the European Court of Human Rights relating to the proceedings		For the purpose of receiving advice or for effective representation in relation to the application before the European Court of Human Rights.
A Minister of the crown or a Welsh Minister	Another Minister, or Ministers, of the Crown or a Welsh Minister		For the purpose of notification, discussion and the giving or receiving of advice regarding issues raised by the information in which the relevant departments have, or may have, an interest

5.1 This paragraph applies to communications made in accordance with paragraphs 2.1, 3.1 and 4.1 and the reference in this paragraph to 'the table' means the table in the relevant paragraph.

5.2 A person in the second column of the table may only communicate information relating to the proceedings received from a person in the first column for the purpose or purposes –

(a)　for which he or she received that information; or

(b) of professional development or training, providing that any communication does not, or is not likely to, identify any person involved in the proceedings without that person's consent.

6.1 In this Practice Direction –

'accreditation body' means –
- (a)   The Law Society,
- (b)   Resolution, or
- (c)   the Lord Chancellor in exercise of the Lord Chancellor's functions in relation to legal aid;

'adoption panel' means a panel established in accordance with regulation 3 of the Adoption Agencies Regulations 2005 or regulation 3 of the Adoption Agencies (Wales) Regulations 2005;

'approved research project' means a project of research –
- (a)   approved in writing by a Secretary of State after consultation with the President of the Family Division,
- (b)   approved in writing by the President of the Family Division, or
- (c)   conducted under section 83 of the Act of 1989 or section 13 of the Criminal Justice and Court Services Act 2000;

'body assessing quality assurance systems' includes –
- (a)   The Law Society,
- (b)   the Lord Chancellor in exercise of the Lord Chancellor's functions in relation to legal aid, or
- (c)   The General Council of the Bar;

'body or person responsible for investigating or determining complaints in relation to legal representatives or professional legal advisers' means –
- (a)   The Law Society,
- (b)   The General Council of the Bar,
- (c)   The Institute of Legal Executives,
- (d)   The Legal Services Ombudsman; or
- (e)   The Office of Legal Complaints.

'Cafcass' has the meaning assigned to it by section 11 of the Criminal Justice and Courts Services Act 2000;

'CAFCASS Cymru' means the part of the Welsh Assembly Government exercising the functions of Welsh Ministers under Part 4 of the Children Act 2004;

'criminal investigation' means an investigation conducted by police officers with a view to it being ascertained –
- (a)   whether a person should be charged with an offence, or
- (b)   whether a person charged with an offence is guilty of it;

'health care professional' means –
- (a)   a registered medical practitioner,
- (b)   a registered nurse or midwife,
- (c)   a clinical psychologist, or
- (d)   a child psychotherapist;

'lay adviser' means a non-professional person who gives lay advice on behalf of an organisation in the lay advice sector;

'McKenzie Friend' means any person permitted by the court to sit beside an unrepresented litigant in court to assist that litigant by prompting, taking notes and giving him advice; and 'social worker' has the meaning assigned to it by section 55 of the Care Standards Act 2000.

Practice Direction 12H –
Contribution Orders

This Practice Direction supplements FPR Part 12

1.1 Paragraph 23(6) of Schedule 2 to the 1989 Act provides that where –

(a)   a contribution order is in force;

(b)   the local authority serve another contribution notice; and

(c)   the contributor and the local authority reach an agreement under paragraph 22(7) in respect of that other contribution notice,

the effect of the agreement shall be to discharge the order from the date on which it is agreed that the agreement shall take effect.

1.2 Where a local authority notifies the court of an agreement reached under paragraph 23(6) of Schedule 2 to the 1989 Act, the notification must be sent in writing to the designated officer of the court.

Practice Direction 12I –
Applications for Reporting Restriction Orders

This Practice Direction supplements FPR Part 12

1 This direction applies to any application in the Family Division founded on Convention rights for an order restricting publication of information about children or incapacitated adults.

2 Applications to be heard in the High Court

Orders can only be made in the High Court and are normally dealt with by a Judge of the Family Division. If the need for an order arises in existing proceedings in the [family]1 court, judges should either transfer the application to the High Court or consult their Family Division Liaison Judge. Where the matter is urgent, it can be heard by the Urgent Applications Judge of the Family Division (out of hours contact number 020 7947 6000).

NOTES

Amendment.[1] Text substituted: FPR Update, April 2014.

3 Service of application on the national news media

Section 12(2) of the Human Rights Act 1998 means that an injunction restricting the exercise of the right to freedom of expression must not be granted where the person against whom the application is made is neither present nor represented unless the court is satisfied (a) that the applicant has taken all practicable steps to notify the respondent, or (b) that there are compelling reasons why the respondent should not be notified.

Service of applications for reporting restriction orders on the national media can now be effected via the Press Association's CopyDirect service, to which national newspapers and broadcasters subscribe as a means of receiving notice of such applications.

The court will bear in mind that legal advisers to the media (i) are used to participating in hearings at very short notice where necessary; and (ii) are able to differentiate between information provided for legal purposes and information for editorial use. Service of applications via the CopyDirect service should henceforth be the norm.

The court retains the power to make without notice orders, but such cases will be exceptional, and an order will always give persons affected liberty to apply to vary or discharge it at short notice.

4 Further guidance

The *Practice Note Applications for Reporting Restriction Orders* dated 18 March 2005 and issued jointly by the Official Solicitor and the Deputy Director of Legal Services, provides valuable guidance and should be followed.

5 Issued with the concurrence and approval of the Lord Chancellor.

[Practice Direction 12J – Child Arrangements and Contact Orders: Domestic Abuse and Harm

This Practice Direction supplements FPR Part 12, and incorporates and supersedes the President's Guidance in Relation to Split Hearings (May 2010) as it applies to proceedings for child arrangements orders.

Summary

1 This Practice Direction applies to any family proceedings in the Family Court or the High Court under the relevant parts of the Children Act 1989 or the relevant parts of the Adoption and Children Act 2002 in which an application is made for a child arrangements order, or in which any question arises about where a child should live, or about contact between a child and a parent or other family member, where the court considers that an order should be made.

2 The purpose of this Practice Direction is to set out what the Family Court or the High Court is required to do in any case in which it is alleged or admitted, or there is other reason to believe, that the child or a party has experienced domestic abuse perpetrated by another party or that there is a risk of such abuse.

[Interpretation

2A In this Practice Direction, 'domestic abuse' has the same meaning as in the 2021 Act. Sections 1 and 2 of the 2021 Act provide that:

> '1 Definition of 'domestic abuse'
> (1) This section defines 'domestic abuse' for the purposes of this Act.

(2) Behaviour of a person ('A') towards another person ('B') is 'domestic abuse' if –

    (a)   A and B are each aged 16 or over and are personally connected to each other, and

    (b)   the behaviour is abusive.

(3) Behaviour is 'abusive' if it consists of any of the following –

    (a)   physical or sexual abuse;

    (b)   violent or threatening behaviour;

    (c)   controlling or coercive behaviour;

    (d)   economic abuse (see subsection (4));

    (e)   psychological, emotional or other abuse;

and it does not matter whether the behaviour consists of a single incident or a course of conduct.

(4) 'Economic abuse' means any behaviour that has a substantial adverse effect on B's ability to –

    (a)   acquire, use or maintain money or other property, or

    (b)   obtain goods or services.

(5) For the purposes of this Act A's behaviour may be behaviour 'towards' B despite the fact that it consists of conduct directed at another person (for example, B's child).

(6) References in this Act to being abusive towards another person are to be read in accordance with this section.

(7) For the meaning of 'personally connected', see section 2.

2 Definition of 'personally connected'

(1) For the purposes of this Act, two people are 'personally connected' to each other if any of the following applies –

    (a)   they are, or have been, married to each other;

    (b)   they are, or have been, civil partners of each other;

    (c)   they have agreed to marry one another (whether or not the agreement has been terminated);

    (d)   they have entered into a civil partnership agreement (whether or not the agreement has been terminated);

    (e)   they are, or have been, in an intimate personal relationship with each other;

    (f)   they each have, or there has been a time when they each have had, a parental relationship in relation to the same child (see subsection (2));

    (g)   they are relatives.

(2) For the purposes of subsection (1)(f) a person has a parental relationship in relation to a child if –

    (a)   the person is a parent of the child, or

    (b)   the person has parental responsibility for the child.

(3) In this section –

'child' means a person under the age of 18 years;

'civil partnership agreement' has the meaning given by section 73 of the Civil Partnership Act 2004;

'parental responsibility' has the same meaning as in the Children Act 1989 (see section 3 of that Act);

'relative' has the meaning given by section 63(1) of the Family Law Act 1996.

PART II – Statutory instruments

2B For the avoidance of doubt, it should be noted that 'domestic abuse' includes, but is not limited to, forced marriage, honour-based violence, dowry-related abuse and transnational marriage abandonment.][2]

3 For the purpose of this Practice Direction –

['the 2021 Act' means the Domestic Abuse Act 2021;][2]
…
'abandonment' refers to the practice whereby a husband, in England and Wales, deliberately abandons or 'strands' his foreign national wife abroad, usually without financial resources, in order to prevent her from asserting matrimonial and/or residence rights [and/or rights in relation to childcare][2] in England and Wales. It may involve children who are either abandoned with, or separated from, their mother;

'coercive behaviour' means an act or a pattern of acts of assault, threats, humiliation and intimidation or other abuse that is used to harm, punish, or frighten the victim;

'controlling behaviour' means an act or pattern of acts designed to make a person subordinate and/or dependent by isolating them from sources of support, exploiting their resources and capacities for personal gain, depriving them of the means needed for independence, resistance and escape and regulating their everyday behaviour;

'development' means physical, intellectual, emotional, social or behavioural development;

'harm' means ill-treatment or the impairment of health or development including, for example, impairment suffered from [being a victim of domestic abuse or from][2] seeing or hearing the ill-treatment of another, by domestic abuse or otherwise;

'health' means physical or mental health;

'ill-treatment' includes sexual abuse and forms of ill-treatment which are not physical[;][2]

'judge' includes salaried and fee-paid judges and lay justices sitting in the Family Court and, where the context permits, can include a [justices' legal adviser][1] in the Family Court; and][2]

['victim of domestic abuse' includes, but is not limited to, a child who is a victim of domestic abuse by virtue of section 3 of the 2021 Act, which provides that –

'3 Children as victims of domestic abuse
(1) This section applies where behaviour of a person ('A') towards another person ('B') is domestic abuse.
(2) Any reference in this Act to a victim of domestic abuse includes a reference to a child who –
(a)   sees or hears, or experiences the effects of, the abuse, and
(b)   is related to A or B.
(3) A child is related to a person for the purposes of subsection (2) if –
(a)   the person is a parent of, or has parental responsibility for, the child, or
(b)   the child and the person are relatives.

(4) In this section –

'child' means a person under the age of 18 years;

'parental responsibility' has the same meaning as in the Children Act 1989 (see section 3 of that Act);

'relative' has the meaning given by section 63(1) of the Family Law Act 1996.'

[3A Reference is made at various points in this Practice Direction to making findings of fact in relation to domestic abuse. It should be noted that Part 3A FPR makes provision in relation to victims of domestic abuse in the specific context of participation in proceedings and giving evidence. In that context, it is not necessary for the court to make findings of fact in relation to domestic abuse before assuming that a party or witness is, or is at risk of being, a victim of domestic abuse carried out by a party, relative of another party, or a witness in the proceedings: see rule 3A.2A FPR.][2]

NOTES

Amendment.[1] Words substituted: Practice Direction, April 2020. [2] Heading, paragraphs, definitions and words inserted and definition omitted repealed: FPR Update, 15 July 2021.

General principles

4 Domestic abuse is harmful to children, and/or puts children at risk of harm, [including where they are victims of domestic abuse for example by witnessing]1 one of their parents being violent or abusive to the other parent, or [living in]1 a home in which domestic abuse is perpetrated (even if the child is too young to be conscious of the behaviour). Children may suffer direct physical, psychological and/or emotional harm from living with [and being victims of]1 domestic abuse, and may also suffer harm indirectly where the domestic abuse impairs the parenting capacity of either or both of their parents.

NOTES

Amendment.[1] Words substituted and words inserted: FPR Update, 15 July 2021.

[Orders under section 91(14) of the Children Act 1989

4A.1 Under section 91(14) of the 1989 Act orders are available to prevent a person from making an application under that Act without leave of the court. Section 91(14) leaves a discretion to the court to determine the circumstances in which an order should be made, which may therefore be many and varied. However, section 91A specifies certain circumstances "among others" in which the court may make an order. These circumstances include where an application would put the child concerned, or another individual at risk of harm. This would include, but not be limited to, a risk of harm arising where an application could be used to carry out or continue domestic abuse. A future application could be part of a pattern of coercive or controlling behaviour or other domestic abuse toward the victim, such that a section 91(14) order is merited due to the risk of harm to the child or other individual.

4A.2 Where allegations of domestic abuse are alleged or proven, the court should consider whether a section 91(14) order might be appropriate even if an application for such an order has not been made. (Section 91A(5) of the 1989 Act specifies who can make an application, and provides that the court can make an order of its own motion.)

4A.3 The court should refer to Practice Direction 12Q for guidance on section 91(14) applications and orders.][1]

NOTES

Amendment. [1] Paragraphs inserted: FPR Update No 4 of 2022, May 2022.

5 The court must, at all stages of the proceedings, and specifically at the First Hearing Dispute Resolution Appointment ('FHDRA'), consider whether domestic abuse is raised as an issue, either by the parties or by Cafcass or CAFCASS Cymru or otherwise, and if so must –

- identify at the earliest opportunity (usually at the FHDRA) the factual and welfare issues involved;
- consider the nature of any allegation, admission or evidence of domestic abuse, and the extent to which it would be likely to be relevant in deciding whether to make a child arrangements order and, if so, in what terms;
- give directions to enable contested relevant factual and welfare issues to be tried as soon as possible and fairly;
- ensure that where domestic abuse is admitted or proven, any child arrangements order in place protects the safety and wellbeing of the child and the parent with whom the child is living, and does not expose either of them to the risk of further harm; and
- ensure that any interim child arrangements order (i.e. considered by the court before determination of the facts, and in the absence of admission) is only made having followed the guidance in paragraphs 25–27 below.

In particular, the court must be satisfied that any contact ordered with a parent who has perpetrated domestic abuse does not expose the child and/or other parent to the risk of harm and is in the best interests of the child.

6 In all cases it is for the court to decide whether a child arrangements order accords with Section 1(1) of the Children Act 1989; any proposed child arrangements order, whether to be made by agreement between the parties or otherwise must be carefully scrutinised by the court accordingly. The court must not make a child arrangements order by consent or give permission for an application for a child arrangements order to be withdrawn, unless the parties are present in court, all initial safeguarding checks have been obtained by the court, and an officer of Cafcass or CAFCASS Cymru has spoken to the parties separately, except where it is satisfied that there is no risk of harm to the child and/or the other parent in so doing.

7 In proceedings relating to a child arrangements order, the court presumes that the involvement of a parent in a child's life will further the child's welfare, unless there is evidence to the contrary. The court must in every case consider carefully whether the statutory presumption applies, having particular regard to any allegation or admission of harm by domestic abuse to the child or parent or any evidence indicating such harm or risk of harm.

8 In considering, on an application for a child arrangements order by consent, whether there is any risk of harm to the child, the court must consider all the evidence and information available. The court may direct a report under Section 7 of the Children Act 1989 to be provided either orally or in writing, before it makes its decision; in such a case, the court must ask for information about any advice given by the officer preparing the report to the parties and whether they, or the child, have been referred to any other agency, including local authority children's services. If the report is not in writing, the court must make a note of its substance on the court file and a summary of the same shall be set out in a Schedule to the relevant order.

Before the FHDRA

9 Where any information provided to the court before the FHDRA or other first hearing (whether as a result of initial safeguarding enquiries by Cafcass or CAFCASS Cymru or on form C1A or otherwise) indicates that there are issues of domestic abuse which may be relevant to the court's determination, the court must ensure that the issues are addressed at the hearing, and that the parties are not expected to engage in conciliation or other forms of dispute resolution which are not suitable and/or safe.

10 If at any stage the court is advised by any party (in the application form, or otherwise), by Cafcass or CAFCASS Cymru or otherwise that there is a need for special arrangements to protect the party or child attending any hearing, the court must ensure so far as practicable that appropriate arrangements are made for the hearing (including the waiting arrangements at court prior to the hearing, and arrangements for entering and exiting the court building) and for all subsequent hearings in the case, unless it is advised and considers that these are no longer necessary. [The court should consider Part 3A FPR, in particular the assumption at rule 3A.2A.][1] Where practicable, the court should enquire of the alleged victim of domestic abuse how best she/he wishes to participate.

NOTES

Amendment.[1] Words inserted: FPR Update, 15 July 2021.

First hearing / FHDRA

11 At the FHDRA, if the parties have not been provided with the safeguarding letter/report by Cafcass/CAFCASS Cymru, the court must inform the parties of the content of any safeguarding letter or report or other information which has been provided by Cafcass or CAFCASS Cymru, unless it considers that to do so would create a risk of harm to a party or the child.

12 Where the results of Cafcass or CAFCASS Cymru safeguarding checks are not available at the FHDRA, and no other reliable safeguarding information is available, the court must adjourn the FHDRA until the results of safeguarding checks are available. The court must not generally make an interim child arrangements order, or orders for contact, in the absence of safeguarding information, unless it is to protect the safety of the child, and/or safeguard the child from harm (see further paragraphs 25-27 below).

13 There is a continuing duty on the Cafcass Officer/Welsh FPO which requires them to provide a risk assessment for the court under section 16A Children Act 1989 if they are given cause to suspect that the child concerned is at risk of harm. Specific provision about service of a risk assessment under section 16A of the 1989 Act is made by rule 12.34 of the FPR 2010.

14 The court must ascertain at the earliest opportunity, and record on the face of its order, whether domestic abuse is raised as an issue which is likely to be relevant to any decision of the court relating to the welfare of the child, and specifically whether the child and/or parent would be at risk of harm in the making of any child arrangements order.

Admissions

15 Where at any hearing an admission of domestic abuse toward another person or the child is made by a party, the admission must be recorded in writing by the judge and set out as a Schedule to the relevant order. The court office must arrange for a copy of any order containing a record of admissions to be made available as soon as possible to any Cafcass officer or officer of CAFCASS Cymru or local authority officer preparing a report under section 7 of the Children Act 1989.

Directions for a fact-finding hearing

16 The court should determine as soon as possible whether it is necessary to conduct a fact-finding hearing in relation to any disputed allegation of domestic abuse –

    (a)   in order to provide a factual basis for any welfare report or for assessment of the factors set out in paragraphs 36 and 37 below;

    (b)   in order to provide a basis for an accurate assessment of risk;

    (c)   before it can consider any final welfare-based order(s) in relation to child arrangements; or

    (d)   before it considers the need for a domestic abuse-related Activity (such as a Domestic Violence Perpetrator Programme (DVPP)).

17 In determining whether it is necessary to conduct a fact-finding hearing, the court should consider –

    (a)   the views of the parties and of Cafcass or CAFCASS Cymru;

    (b)   whether there are admissions by a party which provide a sufficient factual basis on which to proceed;

    (c)   if a party is in receipt of legal aid, whether the evidence required to be provided to obtain legal aid provides a sufficient factual basis on which to proceed;

    (d)   whether there is other evidence available to the court that provides a sufficient factual basis on which to proceed;

    (e)   whether the factors set out in paragraphs 36 and 37 below can be determined without a fact-finding hearing;

    (f)   the nature of the evidence required to resolve disputed allegations;

    (g)   whether the nature and extent of the allegations, if proved, would be relevant to the issue before the court; and (h)　whether a separate fact-finding hearing would be necessary and proportionate in all the circumstances of the case.

18 Where the court determines that a finding of fact hearing is not necessary, the order must record the reasons for that decision.

19 Where the court considers that a fact-finding hearing is necessary, it must give directions as to how the proceedings are to be conducted to ensure that the matters in issue are determined as soon as possible, fairly and proportionately, and within the capabilities of the parties. In particular it should consider –

(a)　what are the key facts in dispute;

(b)　whether it is necessary for the fact-finding to take place at a separate (and earlier) hearing than the welfare hearing;

(c)　whether the key facts in dispute can be contained in a schedule or a table (known as a Scott Schedule) which sets out what the applicant complains of or alleges, what the respondent says in relation to each individual allegation or complaint; the allegations in the schedule should be focused on the factual issues to be tried; and if so, whether it is practicable for this schedule to be completed at the first hearing, with the assistance of the judge;

(d)　what evidence is required in order to determine the existence of coercive, controlling or threatening behaviour, or of any other form of domestic abuse;

(e)　directing the parties to file written statements giving details of such behaviour and of any response;

(f)　whether documents are required from third parties such as the police, health services or domestic abuse support services and giving directions for those documents to be obtained;

(g)　whether oral evidence may be required from third parties and if so, giving directions for the filing of written statements from such third parties;

(h)　where (for example in cases of abandonment) third parties from whom documents are to be obtained are abroad, how to obtain those documents in good time for the hearing, and who should be responsible for the costs of obtaining those documents;

(i)　whether any other evidence is required to enable the court to decide the key issues and giving directions for that evidence to be provided;

(j)　what evidence the alleged victim of domestic abuse is able to give and what support the alleged victim may require at the fact-finding hearing in order to give that evidence;

(k)　in cases where the alleged victim of domestic abuse is unable for reasons beyond their control to be present at the hearing (for example, abandonment cases where the abandoned spouse remains abroad), what measures should be taken to ensure that that person's best evidence can be put [before the court;][1] ...[1]

(l)　what support the alleged perpetrator may need in order to have a reasonable opportunity to challenge the evidence; and

(m)　whether a pre-hearing review would be useful prior to the fact-finding hearing to ensure directions have been complied with and all the required evidence is available.

20 Where the court fixes a fact-finding hearing, it must at the same time fix a Dispute Resolution Appointment to follow. Subject to the exception in paragraph 31 below, the hearings should be arranged in such a way that they are conducted by the same judge or, wherever possible, by the same panel of lay justices; where it is not possible to assemble the same panel of justices, the resumed hearing should be listed before at least the same chairperson of the lay justices. Judicial continuity is important.

NOTES

Amendment.[1] Words substituted and words omitted repealed: FPR Update, 15 July 2021.

Reports under Section 7

[21(1) Subject to sub-paragraph (3), sub-paragraph (2) applies in any case where –

(a)   a child being a victim of domestic abuse; or

(b)   a risk of harm to a child resulting from domestic abuse, is raised as an issue.

(2) In such a case, the court should consider directing that a report on the question of contact, or any other matters relating to the welfare of the child [including matters relating to whether a section 91(14) order would be appropriate (see Practice Direction 12Q)][2], be prepared under section 7 of the Children Act 1989 by an Officer of Cafcass or a Welsh family proceedings officer (or local authority officer if appropriate).

(3) Sub-paragraph (2) does not apply where the court is satisfied that it is not necessary to order the preparation of such a report in order to safeguard the child's interests.][1]

22 If the court directs that there shall be a fact-finding hearing on the issue of domestic abuse, the court will not usually request a section 7 report until after that hearing. In that event, the court should direct that any judgment is provided to Cafcass/CAFCASS Cymru; if there is no transcribed judgment, an agreed list of findings should be provided, as set out at paragraph 29.

23 Any request for a section 7 report should set out clearly the matters the court considers need to be addressed.

NOTES

Amendment.[1] Paragraph substituted: FPR Update, 15 July 2021.[2] Words inserted: FPR Update No 4 of 2022, May 2022.

Representation of the child

24 Subject to the seriousness of the allegations made and the difficulty of the case, the court must consider whether it is appropriate for the child who is the subject of the application to be made a party to the proceedings and be separately represented. If the court considers that the child should be so represented, it must review the allocation decision so that it is satisfied that the case proceeds before the correct level of judge in the Family Court or High Court.

Interim orders before determination of relevant facts

25 Where the court gives directions for a fact-finding hearing, or where disputed allegations of domestic abuse are otherwise undetermined, the court should not make an interim child arrangements order unless it is satisfied that it is in the interests of the child to do so and that the order would not expose the child or the other parent to an unmanageable risk of harm (bearing in mind [in particular the definition of 'victim of domestic abuse' and][1] the impact which domestic abuse against a parent can have on the emotional well-being of the child, the safety of the other parent and the need to protect against domestic abuse …[1]).

26 In deciding any interim child arrangements question the court should –

(a) take into account the matters set out in section 1(3) of the Children Act 1989 or section 1(4) of the Adoption and Children Act 2002 ('the welfare check-list'), as appropriate; and

(b) give particular consideration to the likely effect on the child, and on the care given to the child by the parent who has made the allegation of domestic abuse, of any contact and any risk of harm, whether physical, emotional or psychological, which the child and that parent is likely to suffer as a consequence of making or declining to make an order.

27 Where the court is considering whether to make an order for interim contact, it should in addition consider –

(a) the arrangements required to ensure, as far as possible, that any risk of harm to the child and the parent who is at any time caring for the child is minimised and that the safety of the child and the parties is secured; and in particular:

(i) whether the contact should be supervised or supported, and if so, where and by whom; and

(ii) the availability of appropriate facilities for that purpose;

(b) if direct contact is not appropriate, whether it is in the best interests of the child to make an order for indirect contact; and

(c) whether contact will be beneficial for the child.

NOTES

Amendment.[1] Words inserted and words omitted repealed: FPR Update, 15 July 2021.

The fact-finding hearing or other hearing of the facts where domestic abuse is alleged

28 While ensuring that the allegations are properly put and responded to, the fact-finding hearing or other hearing can be an inquisitorial (or investigative) process, which at all times must protect the interests of all involved. At the fact-finding hearing or other hearing –

- each party can be asked to identify what questions they wish to ask of the other party, and to set out or confirm in sworn evidence their version of the disputed key facts; and

PART II – Statutory instruments

- the judge should be prepared where necessary and appropriate to conduct the questioning of the witnesses on behalf of the parties, focusing on the key issues in the case.

29 The court should, wherever practicable, make findings of fact as to the nature and degree of any domestic abuse which is established and its effect on the child, the child's parents and any other relevant person. The court must record its findings in writing in a Schedule to the relevant order, and the court office must serve a copy of this order on the parties. A copy of any record of findings of fact or of admissions must be sent by the court office to any officer preparing a report under Section 7 of the 1989 Act.

30 At the conclusion of any fact-finding hearing, the court must consider, notwithstanding any earlier direction for a section 7 report, whether it is in the best interests of the child for the court to give further directions about the preparation or scope of any report under section 7; where necessary, it may adjourn the proceedings for a brief period to enable the officer to make representations about the preparation or scope of any further enquiries. Any section 7 report should address the factors set out in paragraphs 36 and 37 below, unless the court directs otherwise.

31 Where the court has made findings of fact on disputed allegations, any subsequent hearing in the proceedings should be conducted by the same judge or by at least the same chairperson of the justices. Exceptions may be made only where observing this requirement would result in delay to the planned timetable and the judge or chairperson is satisfied, for reasons which must be recorded in writing, that the detriment to the welfare of the child would outweigh the detriment to the fair trial of the proceedings.

In all cases where domestic abuse has occurred

32 The court should take steps to obtain (or direct the parties or an Officer of Cafcass or a Welsh family proceedings officer to obtain) information about the facilities available locally (to include local domestic abuse support services) to assist any party or the child in cases where domestic abuse has occurred.

33 Following any determination of the nature and extent of domestic abuse, whether or not following a fact-finding hearing, the court must, if considering any form of contact or involvement of the parent in the child's life, consider –

(a)   whether it would be assisted by any social work, psychiatric, psychological or other assessment (including an expert safety and risk assessment) of any party or the child and if so (subject to any necessary consent) make directions for such assessment to be undertaken and for the filing of any consequent report. Any such report should address the factors set out in paragraphs 36 and 37 below, unless the court directs otherwise;

(b)   whether any party should seek advice, treatment or other intervention as a precondition to any child arrangements order being made, and may (with the consent of that party) give directions for such attendance.

34 Further or as an alternative to the advice, treatment or other intervention referred to in paragraph 33(b) above, the court may make an Activity Direction

under section 11A and 11B Children Act 1989. Any intervention directed pursuant to this provision should be one commissioned and approved by Cafcass. It is acknowledged that acceptance on a DVPP is subject to a suitability assessment by the service provider, and that completion of a DVPP will take time in order to achieve the aim of risk-reduction for the long-term benefit of the child and the parent with whom the child is living.

Factors to be taken into account when determining whether to make child arrangements orders in all cases where domestic abuse has occurred

35 When deciding the issue of child arrangements the court should ensure that any order for contact will not expose the child to an unmanageable risk of harm and will be in the best interests of the child.

[36(1) In the light of –

    (a)   any findings of fact,
    (b)   admissions; or
    (c)   domestic abuse having otherwise been established,

the court should apply the individual matters in the welfare checklist with reference to the domestic abuse which has occurred and any expert risk assessment obtained.

(2) In particular, the court should in every case consider any harm –

    (a)   which the child as a victim of domestic abuse, and the parent with whom the child is living, has suffered as a consequence of that domestic abuse; and
    (b)   which the child and the parent with whom the child is living is at risk of suffering, if a child arrangements order is made.

(3) The court should make an order for contact only if it is satisfied –

    (a)   that the physical and emotional safety of the child and the parent with whom the child is living can, as far as possible, be secured before, during and after contact; and
    (b)   that the parent with whom the child is living will not be subjected to further domestic abuse by the other parent.][1]

37 In every case where a finding or admission of domestic abuse is made, or where domestic abuse is otherwise established, the court should consider the conduct of both parents towards each other and towards the child and the impact of the same. In particular, the court should consider –

    (a)   the effect of the domestic abuse on the child and on the arrangements for where the child is living;
    (b)   the effect of the domestic abuse on the child and its effect on the child's relationship with the parents;
    (c)   whether the parent is motivated by a desire to promote the best interests of the child or is using the process to continue a form of domestic abuse against the other parent;

PART II – Statutory instruments

(d)   the likely behaviour during contact of the parent against whom findings are made and its effect on the child; and

(e)   the capacity of the parents to appreciate the effect of past domestic abuse and the potential for future domestic abuse.

NOTES

Amendment.[1] Paragraph substituted: FPR Update, 15 July 2021.

[Orders under section 91(14) of the Children Act 1989

37A.[1] In every case where a finding or admission of domestic abuse is made, or where domestic abuse is otherwise established, the court should consider whether an order under section 91(14) of the Children Act 1989 would be appropriate, even if an application for such an order has not been made. Section 91(14) orders are available to protect a victim of domestic abuse where a further application would constitute or continue domestic abuse. A future application could be part of a pattern of coercive or controlling behaviour or other domestic abuse toward the victim, such that a section 91(14) order is merited due to the risk of harm to the child or other individual. The court should refer to Practice Direction 12Q for direction on section 91(14) applications and orders.]

NOTES

Amendment.[1] Paragraph inserted: FPR Update No 4 of 2022, May 2022.

Directions as to how contact is to proceed

38 Where any domestic abuse has occurred but the court, having considered any expert risk assessment and having applied the welfare checklist, nonetheless considers that direct contact is safe and beneficial for the child, the court should consider what, if any, directions or conditions are required to enable the order to be carried into effect and in particular should consider –

(a)   whether or not contact should be supervised, and if so, where and by whom;

(b)   whether to impose any conditions to be complied with by the party in whose favour the order for contact has been made and if so, the nature of those conditions, for example by way of seeking intervention (subject to any necessary consent);

(c)   whether such contact should be for a specified period or should contain provisions which are to have effect for a specified period; and

(d)   whether it will be necessary, in the child's best interests, to review the operation of the order; if so the court should set a date for the review consistent with the timetable for the child, and must give directions to ensure that at the review the court has full information about the operation of the order.

Where a risk assessment has concluded that a parent poses a risk to a child or to the other parent, contact via a supported contact centre, or contact supported by a parent or relative, is not appropriate.

39 Where the court does not consider direct contact to be appropriate, it must consider whether it is safe and beneficial for the child to make an order for indirect contact.

The reasons of the court

40 In its judgment or reasons the court should always make clear how its findings on the issue of domestic abuse have influenced its decision on the issue of arrangements for the child. In particular, where the court has found domestic abuse proved but nonetheless makes an order which results in the child having future contact with the perpetrator of domestic abuse, the court must always explain, whether by way of reference to the welfare check-list, the factors in paragraphs 36 and 37 or otherwise, why it takes the view that the order which it has made will not expose the child to the risk of harm and is beneficial for the child.][1]

NOTES

Amendment.[1] PD12J substituted: President of Family Division circular, September 2017.

Practice Direction 12K –
Children Act 1989: Exclusion Requirement

This Practice Direction supplements FPR Part 12

Under s 38A(5) and s 44A(5) of the Children Act 1989 the court may attach a power of arrest to an exclusion requirement included in an interim care order or an emergency protection order. In cases where an order is made which includes an exclusion requirement, the following shall apply:

(1) If a power of arrest is attached to the order then unless the person to whom the exclusion requirement refers was given notice of the hearing and attended the hearing, the name of that person and that an order has been made including an exclusion requirement to which a power of arrest has been attached shall be announced in open court at the earliest opportunity. This may be either on the same day when the court proceeds to hear cases in open court or where there is no further business in open court on that day at the next listed sitting of the court.

(2) When a person arrested under a power of arrest cannot conveniently be brought before the relevant judicial authority sitting in a place normally used as a courtroom within 24 hours after the arrest, he may be brought before the relevant judicial authority at any convenient place but, as the liberty of the subject is involved, the press and the public should be permitted to be present, unless security needs make this impracticable.

(3) Any order of committal made otherwise than in public or in a courtroom open to the public, shall be announced in open court at the earliest opportunity. This may be either on the same day when the court proceeds to hear cases in open court or where there is no further business in open court on that day at the next listed sitting of the court. The announcement shall state –
   (a) the name of the person committed,
   (b) in general terms the nature of the contempt of the court in respect of which the order of committal has been made and
   (c) the length of the period of committal.

Practice Direction 12L –
Children Act 1989: Risk Assessments under Section 16A

This Practice Direction supplements FPR Part 12

1 This Practice Direction applies to any family proceedings in the High Court [or the family court][1] in which a risk assessment is made under section 16A of the Children Act 1989 ('the 1989 Act'). It has effect from 1 October 2007.

2 Section 16A(2) of the 1989 Act provides that, if in carrying out any function to which the section applies (as set out in section 16A(1)), an officer of the Service or a Welsh family proceedings officer is given cause to suspect that the child concerned is at risk of harm, the officer must make a risk assessment in relation to the child and provide the risk assessment to the court.

3 The duty to provide the risk assessment to the court arises irrespective of the outcome of the assessment. Where an officer is given cause to suspect that the child concerned is at risk of harm and makes a risk assessment in accordance with section 16A(2), the officer must provide the assessment to the court, even if he or she reaches the conclusion that there is no risk of harm to the child.

4 The fact that a risk assessment has been carried out is a material fact that should be placed before the court, whatever the outcome of the assessment. In reporting the outcome to the court, the officer should make clear the factor or factors that triggered the decision to carry out the assessment.

5 Issued by the President of the Family Division, as the nominee of the Lord Chief Justice, with the agreement of the Lord Chancellor.

NOTES

Amendment.[1] Text substituted: FPR Update, April 2014.

Practice Direction 12M –
Family Assistance Orders: Consultation

This Practice Direction supplements FPR Part 12

1 This Practice Direction applies to any family proceedings in the High Court [or the family court][1] in which the court is considering whether to make a family assistance order under section 16 of the Children Act 1989, as amended ('the 1989 Act'). It has effect from 1 October 2007.

2 Before making a family assistance order the court must have obtained the opinion of the appropriate officer about whether it would be in the best interests of the child in question for a family assistance order to be made and, if so, how the family assistance order could operate and for what period.

3 The appropriate officer will be an officer of the Service, a Welsh family proceedings officer or an officer of a local authority, depending on the category of officer the court proposes to require to be made available under the family assistance order.

4 The opinion of the appropriate officer may be given orally or in writing (for example, it may form part of a report under section 7 of the 1989 Act).

5 Before making a family assistance order the court must give any person whom it proposes be named in the order an opportunity to comment upon any opinion given by the appropriate officer.

6 Issued by the President of the Family Division, as the nominee of the Lord Chief Justice, with the agreement of the Lord Chancellor.

NOTES

Amendment.[1] Text substituted: FPR Update, April 2014.

Practice Direction 12N – Enforcement of Children Act 1989 [Child Arrangements Orders][1]: Disclosure of Information to Officers of the National Probation Service (High Court and County Court)

This Practice Direction supplements FPR Part 12

1 This Practice Direction applies to proceedings in the High Court or [the family][1] court where:

    (a) the court is considering an application for an enforcement order[1] or for an order following an alleged breach of an enforcement order[2] and asks an officer of the Service or a Welsh family proceedings officer to provide information to the court in accordance with section 11L(5) of the Children Act 1989; or

1 Under section 11J of the Children Act 1989.
2 Under paragraph 9 of Schedule A1 to the Children Act 1989.

    (b) the court makes an enforcement order or an order following an alleged breach of an enforcement order and asks an officer of the Service or a Welsh family proceedings officer to monitor compliance with that order and to report to the court in accordance with section 11M of the Children Act 1989.

2 In all cases in which paragraph 1 applies, the officer of the Service or Welsh family proceedings officer will need to discuss aspects of the court case with an officer of the National Probation Service.

3 In order to ensure that the officer of the Service or Welsh family proceedings officer will not potentially be in contempt of court by virtue of such discussions, the court should, when making a request under section 11L(5) or section 11M of the Children Act 1989, give leave to that officer to disclose to the National Probation Service such information (whether or not contained in a document filed with the court) in relation to the proceedings as is necessary.

4 This Practice Direction comes into force on 8 December 2008.

NOTES

Amendments.[1] Text substituted: FPR Update, April 2014.

Practice Direction 12O –
Arrival of Child in England by Air

This Practice Direction supplements FPR Part 12

Where a person seeks an order for the return to him of children about to arrive in England by air and desires to have information to enable him to meet the aeroplane, the judge should be asked to include in his order a direction that the airline operating the flight, and, if he has the information, the immigration officer at the appropriate airport, should supply such information to that person.

To obtain such information in such circumstances in a case where a person already has an order for the return to him of children, that person should apply to a judge ex parte for such a direction.

Practice Direction 12P –
Removal from Jurisdiction: Issue of Passports

This Practice Direction supplements FPR Part 12

1 Removal from jurisdiction

The President has directed that on application for leave to remove from the jurisdiction for holiday periods a ward of court who has been placed by a local authority with foster-parents whose identity the court considers should remain confidential, for example because they are prospective adopters, it is important that such foster-parents should not be identified in the court's order. In such cases the order should be expressed as giving leave to the local authority to arrange for the child to be removed from England and Wales for the purpose of holidays.

It is also considered permissible, where care and control has been given to a local authority, or to an individual, for the court to give general leave to make such arrangements in suitable cases, thereby obviating the need to make application for leave each time it is desired to remove the child from the jurisdiction.

2 Issue of passports

It is the practice of the Passport Department of the Home Office to issue passports for wards in accordance with the court's direction. This frequently results in passports being restricted to the holiday period specified in the order giving leave. It is the President's opinion that it is more convenient for wards' passports to be issued without such restriction.

The Passport Department has agreed to issue passports on this basis unless the court otherwise directs. It will, of course, still be necessary for the leave of the court to be obtained for the child's removal.

****

PART 14 PROCEDURE FOR APPLICATIONS IN ADOPTION, PLACEMENT AND RELATED PROCEEDINGS

14.1 Application of this Part and interpretation

(1) The rules in this Part apply to the following proceedings –

  (a)   adoption proceedings;
  (b)   placement proceedings; and
  (c)   proceedings for –
      (i)   the making of [an]¹ order under section 26 [or an order under section 51A(2)(a)]¹ of the 2002 Act;
      [(iaa) the making of an order under section 51A(2)(b) of the 2002 Act;]¹
      (ii)   the variation or revocation of…¹[–
          (aa) an order under section 27 of the 2002 Act; or
          (bb) an order under section 51A(2) of the 2002 Act in accordance with section 51B(1)(c);]¹
      (iii) an order giving permission to change a child's surname or remove a child from the United Kingdom under section 28(2) and (3) of the 2002 Act;
      (iv)   a section 84 order;
      (v)   a section 88 direction;
      (vi)   a section 89 order; or
      (vii) any other order that may be referred to in a practice direction.

[(1A) This Part is subject to any provision made by or pursuant to Part 41 (proceeding by electronic means).]²

(2) In this Part –

  'Central Authority' means –
      (a)   in relation to England, the Secretary of State; and
      (b)   in relation to Wales, the Welsh Ministers;

  'Convention adoption order' means an adoption order under the 2002 Act which, by virtue of regulations under section 1 of the Adoption (Intercountry Aspects) Act 1999 (regulations giving effect to the Convention on Protection of Children and Co-operation in Respect of Intercountry Adoption, concluded at the Hague on 29th May 1993), is made as a Convention adoption order;
  'guardian' means –
      (a)   a guardian (other than the guardian of the estate of a child) appointed in accordance with section 5 of the 1989 Act; and
      (b)   a special guardian within the meaning of section 14A of the 1989 Act;

  ['provision for contact' has the meaning given to it in rule 13.1(2);]¹
  'section 88 direction' means a direction given by the High Court under section 88 of the 2002 Act that section 67(3) of that Act (status conferred by adoption) does not apply or does not apply to any extent specified in the direction.

PART II – Statutory instruments

NOTES

Amendments.[1] Words substituted, inserted and omitted, sub-paragraphs inserted and definition substituted: SI 2014/843.[2] Paragraph inserted: SI 2020/135.

[14.2 [Assignment of][2] a serial number

(1) This rule applies where –

   (a)   any application in proceedings is made by a person who intends to adopt a child; or

   (b)   an adoption order in respect of the child has been made and an application is made for –

      (i)   a contact order under section 51A(2)(a) of the 2002 Act;

      (ii)   an order prohibiting contact with the child under section 51A(2)(b) of the 2002 Act; or

      (iii)   the variation or revocation of an order under section 51A(2) of the 2002 Act in accordance with section 51B(1)(c).

[(2) In a case under paragraph (1)(a), a serial number must be assigned to identify the person intending to adopt the child in connection with the proceedings in order for the person's identity to be kept confidential in those proceedings.

(3) In a case under paragraph (1)(b), a serial number must be assigned to the person in whose favour the adoption order has been made to keep the identity of the person confidential in proceedings referred to in paragraph (1)(b).][2]

(4) The court may at any time direct that a serial number assigned to a person under paragraph (2) or (3) must be removed.

(5) [When][2] a serial number has been assigned to a person under paragraph (2) or (3) –

   (a)   the court officer will ensure that any notice sent in accordance with these rules does not contain information which discloses, or is likely to disclose, the identity of that person to any other party to that application who is not already aware of that person's identity; and

   (b)   the proceedings on the application will be conducted with a view to securing that the person is not seen by or made known to any party who is not already aware of the person's identity except with the person's consent.][1]

NOTES

Amendment. Rule substituted: SI 2014/843.[2] Words and paragraphs substituted: SI 2016/1013.

14.3 Who the parties are

(1) In relation to the proceedings set out in column 1 of the following table, column 2 sets out who the application may be made by and column 3 sets out who the respondents to those proceedings will be.

Proceedings for	Applicants	Respondents
An adoption order (section 46 of the 2002 Act).	The prospective adopters (sections 50 and 51 of the 2002 Act).	Each parent who has parental responsibility for the child unless that parent has given notice under section 20(4)(a) of the 2002 Act (statement of wish not to be informed of any application for an adoption order) which has effect; any guardian of the child unless that guardian has given notice under section 20(4)(a) of the 2002 Act (statement of wish not to be informed of any application for an adoption order) which has effect; any person in whose favour there is provision for contact; any adoption agency having parental responsibility for the child under section 25 of the 2002 Act; any adoption agency which has taken part at any stage in the arrangements for adoption of the child; any local authority to whom notice under section 44 of the 2002 Act (notice of intention to adopt or apply for a section 84 order) has been given; any local authority or voluntary organisation which has parental responsibility for, is looking after or is caring for, the child; and the child where – – permission has been granted to a parent or guardian to oppose the making of the adoption order (section 47(3) or 47(5) of the 2002 Act); – the child opposes the making of an adoption order; – a children and family reporter recommends that it is in the best interests of the child to be a party to the proceedings and that recommendation is accepted by the court; – the child is already an adopted child;

PART II – Statutory instruments

Proceedings for	Applicants	Respondents
		– any party to the proceedings or the child is opposed to the arrangements for allowing any person contact with the child, or a person not being allowed contact with the child after the making of the adoption order;
		– the application is for a Convention adoption order or a section 84 order;
		– the child has been brought into the United Kingdom in the circumstances where section 83(1) of the 2002 Act applies (restriction on bringing children in);
		– the application is for an adoption order other than a Convention adoption order and the prospective adopters intend the child to live in a country or territory outside the British Islands after the making of the adoption order; or
		– the prospective adopters are relatives of the child.
A section 84 order.	The prospective adopters asking for parental responsibility prior to adoption abroad.	As for an adoption order.
A placement order (section 21 of the 2002 Act).	A local authority (section 22 of the 2002 Act).	Each parent who has parental responsibility for the child: any guardian of the child;
		any person in whose favour an order under the 1989 Act is in force in relation to the child;
		any adoption agency or voluntary organisation which has parental responsibility for, is looking after, or is caring for, the child;
		the child; and
		the parties or any persons who are or have been parties to proceedings for a care order in respect of the child where those proceedings have led to the application for the placement order.

Proceedings for	Applicants	Respondents
An order varying a placement order (section 23 of the 2002 Act).	The joint application of the local authority authorised by the placement order to place the child for adoption and the local authority which is to be substituted for that authority (section 23 of the 2002 Act).	The parties to the proceedings leading to the placement order which it is sought to have varied except the child who was the subject of those proceedings; and any person in whose favour there is provision for contact.
An order revoking a placement order (section 24 of the 2002 Act).	The child; the local authority authorised to place the child for adoption; or where the child is not placed for adoption by the authority, any other person who has the permission of the court to apply (section 24 of the 2002 Act).	The parties to the proceedings leading to the placement order which it is sought to have revoked; and any person in whose favour there is provision for contact.
[An order under section 26 of the 2002 Act.][1]	The child; the adoption agency; any parent, guardian or relative; any person in whose favour there was provision for contact under the 1989 Act which ceased to have effect on an adoption agency being authorised to place a child for adoption, or placing a child for adoption who is less than six weeks old (section 26(1) of the 2002 Act); [if a child arrangements order was in force immediately before the adoption agency was authorised to place the child for adoption or (as the case may be) placed the child for adoption at a time when he or she was less than six weeks old, any person named in the order as a person with whom the child was to live;][1]	The adoption agency authorised to place the child for adoption or which has placed the child for adoption; the person with whom the child lives or is to live; each parent with parental responsibility for the child; any guardian of the child; and the child where – – the adoption agency authorised to place the child for adoption or which has placed the child for adoption or a parent with parental responsibility for the child opposes the making of [the order][1] under section 26 of the 2002 Act; – the child opposes the making of [the order][1] under section 26 of the 2002 Act; – existing provision for contact is to be revoked;

Proceedings for	Applicants	Respondents
	a person who by virtue of an order made in the exercise of the High Court's inherent jurisdiction with respect to children had care of the child immediately before that time; or any person who has the permission of the court to make the application (section 26 of the 2002 Act).	– relatives of the child do not agree to the arrangements for allowing any person contact with the child, or a person not being allowed contact with the child; or – the child is suffering or is at risk of suffering harm within the meaning of the 1989 Act.
An order varying or revoking [an order under section 26 of the 2002 Act][1] (section 27 of the 2002 Act).	The child; the adoption agency; or any person named in [the order][1] (section 27(1) of the 2002 Act).	The parties to the proceedings leading to [the order][1] which it is sought to have varied or revoked; and any person named in [the order][1].
An order permitting the child's name to be changed or the removal of the child from the United Kingdom (section 28(2) and (3) of the 2002 Act).	Any person including the adoption agency or the local authority authorised to place, or which has placed, the child for adoption (section 28(2) of the 2002 Act).	The parties to proceedings leading to any placement order; the adoption agency authorised to place the child for adoption or which has placed the child for adoption; any prospective adopters with whom the child is living; each parent with parental responsibility for the child; and any guardian of the child.
[A contact order under section 51A(2)(a) of the 2002 Act.	The child; or any person who has obtained the court's leave to make the application.	A person who has applied for the adoption order or in whose favour the adoption order is or has been made; and Any adoption agency having parental responsibility for the child under section 25 of the 2002 Act.][1]
[An order prohibiting the person named in the order from having contact with the child (section 51A(2) (b) of the 2002 Act).	A person who has applied for the adoption order or in whose favour the adoption order is or has been made; the child; or any person who has obtained the court's leave to make the application.	A person against whom an application is made who— (but for the child's adoption) would be related to the child by blood (including half-blood), marriage or civil partnership; is a former guardian of the child; is a person who had parental responsibility for the child immediately before the making of the adoption order;

Proceedings for	*Applicants*	*Respondents*
		is a person who was entitled to make an application for an order under section 26 of the 2002 Act in respect of the child (contact with children placed or to be placed for adoption) by virtue of subsection (3)(c), (d) or (e) of that section;
		is a person with whom the child has lived for a period of at least one year; and any adoption agency having parental responsibility for the child under section 25 of the 2002 Act.][1]
[The variation or revocation of a contact order or an order prohibiting contact under section 51A(2) of the 2002 Act (section 51B(1)(c) of that Act).	The child; a person in whose favour the adoption order was made; or a person named in the order.	The parties to the proceedings leading to the contact order or an order prohibiting contact which it is sought to have varied or revoked; and any person named in the contact order or the order prohibiting contact.][1]
A section 88 direction.	The adopted child; the adopters; any parent; or any other person.	The adopters; the parents; the adoption agency; the local authority to whom notice under section 44 of the 2002 Act (notice of intention to apply for a section 84 order) has been given; and the Attorney-General.
A section 89 order.	The adopters; the adopted person; any parent; the relevant Central Authority; the adoption agency;	The adopters; the parents; the adoption agency; and the local authority to whom notice under section 44 of the 2002 Act (notice of intention to adopt or apply for a section 84 order) has been given.

PART II – Statutory instruments

Proceedings for	Applicants	Respondents
	the local authority to whom notice under section 44 of the 2002 Act (notice of intention to adopt or apply for a section 84 order) has been given;	
	the Secretary of State for the Home Department; or any other person.	

(2) The court may at any time direct that a child, who is not already a respondent to proceedings, be made a respondent to proceedings where –

(a)   the child –
   (i)   wishes to make an application; or
   (ii)   has evidence to give to the court or a legal submission to make which has not been given or made by any other party; or
(b)   there are other special circumstances.

(3) The court may at any time direct that –

(a)   any other person or body be made a respondent to proceedings; or
(b)   a party be removed.

(4) If the court makes a direction for the addition or removal of a party, it may give consequential directions about –

(a)   serving a copy of the application form on any new respondent;
(b)   serving relevant documents on the new party; and
(c)   the management of the proceedings.

NOTES

Amendments.[1] Table entries inserted and words substituted: SI 2014/843.

14.4 Notice of proceedings to person with foreign parental responsibility

(1) This rule applies where a child is subject to proceedings to which this Part applies and –

(a)   a parent of the child holds or is believed to hold parental responsibility for the child under the law of another State which subsists in accordance with Article 16 of the 1996 Hague Convention following the child becoming habitually resident in a territorial unit of the United Kingdom; and
(b)   that parent is not otherwise required to be joined as a respondent under rule 14.3.

(2) [Subject to paragraph (2A),][1] the applicant shall give notice of the proceedings to any parent to whom the applicant believes paragraph (1) applies in any case in which a person who was a parent with parental responsibility under the 1989 Act would be a respondent to the proceedings in accordance with rule 14.3.

[(2A) Notice shall not be given to a person to whom the applicant believes paragraph (1) applies if the court directs that such notice is not necessary.][1]

(3) [Unless a direction has been made under paragraph (2A),][1] the applicant and every respondent to the proceedings shall provide such details as they possess as to the identity and whereabouts of any parent they believe to hold parental responsibility for the child in accordance with paragraph (1) to the court officer, upon making, or responding to the application as appropriate.

(4) Where the existence of such a parent only becomes apparent to a party at a later date during the proceedings, that party must notify the court officer of those details at the earliest opportunity.

(5) Where a parent to whom paragraph (1) applies receives notice of proceedings, that parent may apply to the court to be joined as a party using the Part 18 procedure.

NOTES

Amendments.[1] Words and paragraph inserted: SI 2020/135.

14.5 Who is to serve

(1) The general rules about service in Part 6 are subject to this rule.

(2) In proceedings to which this Part applies, a document which has been issued or prepared by a court officer will be served by the court officer except where –

(a) a practice direction provides otherwise; or

(b) the court directs otherwise.

(3) Where a court officer is to serve a document, it is for the court to decide which of the methods of service specified in rule 6.23 is to be used

14.6 What the court or a court officer will do when the application has been issued

(1) As soon as practicable after the application has been issued in proceedings –

(a) the court will –

(i) if section 48(1) of the 2002 Act (restrictions on making adoption orders) applies, consider whether it is proper to hear the application;

(ii) subject to paragraph (4), set a date for the first directions hearing;

(iii) appoint a children's guardian in accordance with rule 16.3(1);

(iv) appoint a reporting officer in accordance with rule 16.30;

(v) consider whether a report relating to the welfare of the child is required, and if so, request such a report in accordance with rule 16.33;

(vi) set a date for the hearing of the application; and

(vii) do anything else that may be set out in a practice direction; and

(b) a court officer will –

(i) subject to receiving confirmation in accordance with paragraph (2) (b)(ii), give notice of any directions hearing set by the court to the

PART II – Statutory instruments

parties and to any children's guardian, reporting officer or children and family reporter;

   (ii)   serve a copy of the application form (but, subject to sub-paragraphs (iii) and (iv), not the documents attached to it) on the persons referred to in Practice Direction 14A;

   (iii) send a copy of the certified copy of the entry in the register of live-births or Adopted Children Register and any health report attached to an application for an adoption order to –

      (aa) any children's guardian, reporting officer or children and family reporter; and

      (bb) the local authority to whom notice under section 44 of the 2002 Act (notice of intention to adopt or apply for a section 84 order) has been given;

   (iv) if notice under rule 14.9(2) has been given (request to dispense with consent of parent or guardian), in accordance with that rule inform the parent or guardian of the request and send a copy of the statement of facts to –

      (aa) the parent or guardian;

      (bb) any children's guardian, reporting officer or children and family reporter;

      (cc) any local authority to whom notice under section 44 of the 2002 Act (notice of intention to adopt or apply for a section 84 order) has been given; and

      (dd) any adoption agency which has placed the child for adoption; and

   (v)   do anything else that may be set out in a practice direction.

(2) In addition to the matters referred to in paragraph (1), as soon as practicable after an application for an adoption order or a section 84 order has been issued the court or the court officer will –

   (a)   where the child is not placed for adoption by an adoption agency –

      (i)   ask either the Service or the Assembly to file any relevant form of consent to an adoption order or a section 84 order; and

      (ii) ask the local authority to prepare a report on the suitability of the prospective adopters if one has not already been prepared; and

   (b)   where the child is placed for adoption by an adoption agency, ask the adoption agency to –

      (i)   file any relevant form of consent to –

         (aa) the child being placed for adoption;

         (bb) an adoption order;

         (cc) a future adoption order under section 20 of the 2002 Act; or

         (dd) a section 84 order;

      (ii) confirm whether a statement has been made under section 20(4)(a) of the 2002 Act (statement of wish not to be informed of any application for an adoption order) and if so, to file that statement;

      (iii) file any statement made under section 20(4)(b) of the 2002 Act (withdrawal of wish not to be informed of any application for an adoption order) as soon as it is received by the adoption agency; and

(iv) prepare a report on the suitability of the prospective adopters if one has not already been prepared.

(3) In addition to the matters referred to in paragraph (1), as soon as practicable after an application for a placement order has been issued –

(a) the court will consider whether a report giving the local authority's reasons for placing the child for adoption is required, and if so, will direct the local authority to prepare such a report; and

(b) the court or the court officer will ask either the Service or the Assembly to file any form of consent to the child being placed for adoption.

(4) Where it considers it appropriate the court may, instead of setting a date for a first directions hearing, give the directions provided for by rule 14.8.

14.7 Date for first directions hearing

Unless the court directs otherwise, the first directions hearing must be within 4 weeks beginning with the date on which the application is issued.

14.8 The first directions hearing

(1) At the first directions hearing in the proceedings the court will –

(a) fix a [timetable for the proceedings including a]² timetable for the filing of –
(i) any report relating to the suitability of the applicants to adopt a child;
(ii) any report from the local authority;
(iii) any report from a children's guardian, reporting officer or children and family reporter;
(iv) if a statement of facts has been filed, any amended statement of facts;
(v) any other evidence, and
(vi) give directions relating to the reports and other evidence;

(b) consider whether the child or any other person should be a party to the proceedings and, if so, give directions in accordance with rule 14.3(2) or (3) joining that child or person as a party;

(c) give directions relating to the appointment of a litigation friend for any protected party or child who is a party to, but not the subject of, proceedings unless a litigation friend has already been appointed;

(d) consider [in accordance with rule 29.17]¹ whether the case needs to be transferred to another court and, if so, give directions to transfer the proceedings to another court …¹;

(e) give directions about –
(i) tracing parents or any other person the court considers to be relevant to the proceedings;
(ii) service of documents;

       (iii) subject to paragraph (2), disclosure as soon as possible of information and evidence to the parties; and

      (iv) the final hearing.

([Under Part 3][2] the court may also direct that the case be adjourned if it considers that [non-court dispute resolution][2] is appropriate.)

(2) Rule 14.13(2) applies to any direction given under paragraph (1)(e)(iii) as it applies to a direction given under rule 14.13(1).

(3) In addition to the matters referred to in paragraph (1), the court will give any of the directions listed in Practice Direction 14B in proceedings for –

    (a)   a Convention adoption order;

    (b)   a section 84 order;

    (c)   a section 88 direction;

    (d)   a section 89 order; or

    (e)   an adoption order where section 83(1) of the 2002 Act applies (restriction on bringing children in).

(4) The parties or their legal representatives must attend the first directions hearing unless the court directs otherwise.

(5) Directions may also be given at any stage in the proceedings –

    (a)   of the court's own initiative; or

    (b)   on the application of a party or any children's guardian or, where the direction concerns a report by a reporting officer or children and family reporter, the reporting officer or children and family reporter.

(6) For the purposes of giving directions or for such purposes as the court directs –

    (a)   the court may set a date for a further directions hearing or other hearing; and

    (b)   the court officer will give notice of any date so fixed to the parties and to any children's guardian, reporting officer or children and family reporter.

(7) After the first directions hearing the court will monitor compliance by the parties with the court's timetable and directions.

NOTES

Amendments.[1] Words inserted and omitted: SI 2013/3204. [2] Words inserted and substituted: SI 2014/843.

14.9 Requesting the court to dispense with the consent of any parent or guardian

(1) This rule applies where the applicant wants to ask the court to dispense with the consent of any parent or guardian of a child to –

    (a)   the child being placed for adoption;

    (b)   the making of an adoption order except a Convention adoption order; or

    (c)   the making of a section 84 order.

(2) The applicant requesting the court to dispense with the consent must –

    (a)   give notice of the request in the application form or at any later stage by filing a written request setting out the reasons for the request; and

    (b)   file a statement of facts setting out a summary of the history of the case and any other facts to satisfy the court that –

        (i)   the parent or guardian cannot be found or is incapable of giving consent; or

        (ii)   the welfare of the child requires the consent to be dispensed with.

(3) If a serial number has been assigned to the applicant under rule 14.2, the statement of facts supplied under paragraph (2)(b) must be framed so that it does not disclose the identity of the applicant.

(4) On receipt of the notice of the request –

    (a)   a court officer will –

        (i)   inform the parent or guardian of the request unless the parent or guardian cannot be found; and

        (ii)   send a copy of the statement of facts filed in accordance with paragraph (2)(b) to –

           (aa)   the parent or guardian unless the parent or guardian cannot be found;

           (bb)   any children's guardian, reporting officer or children and family reporter;

           (cc)   any local authority to whom notice under section 44 of the 2002 Act (notice of intention to adopt or apply for a section 84 order) has been given; and

           (dd)   any adoption agency which has placed the child for adoption; and

    (b)   if the applicant considers that the parent or guardian is incapable of giving consent, the court will consider whether to –

        (i)   appoint a litigation friend for the parent or guardian under rule 15.6(1); or

        (ii)   give directions for an application to be made under rule 15.6(3)

        (iii)   unless a litigation friend is already appointed for that parent or guardian.

14.10 Consent

(1) Consent of any parent or guardian of a child –

    (a)   under section 19 of the 2002 Act, to the child being placed for adoption; and

    (b)   under section 20 of the 2002 Act, to the making of a future adoption order,

must be given in the form referred to in Practice Direction 5A or a form to the like effect.

(2) Subject to paragraph (3), consent –

(a)   to the making of an adoption order; or

(b)   to the making of a section 84 order,

may be given in the form referred to in Practice Direction 5A or a form to the like effect or otherwise as the court directs.

(3) Any consent to a Convention adoption order must be in a form which complies with the internal law relating to adoption of the Convention country of which the child is habitually resident.

(4) Any form of consent executed in Scotland must be witnessed by a Justice of the Peace or a Sheriff.

(5) Any form of consent executed in Northern Ireland must be witnessed by a Justice of the Peace.

(6) Any form of consent executed outside the United Kingdom must be witnessed by –

(a)   any person for the time being authorised by law in the place where the document is executed to administer an oath for any judicial or other legal purpose;

(b)   a British Consular officer;

(c)   a notary public; or

(d)   if the person executing the document is serving in any of the regular armed forces of the Crown, an officer holding a commission in any of those forces.

14.11 Reports by the adoption agency or local authority

(1) The adoption agency or local authority must file the report on the suitability of the applicant to adopt a child within the timetable fixed by the court.

(2) A local authority that is directed to prepare a report on the placement of the child for adoption must file that report within the timetable fixed by the court.

(3) The reports must cover the matters specified in Practice Direction 14C.

(4) The court may at any stage request a further report or ask the adoption agency or local authority to assist the court in any other manner.

(5) A court officer will send a copy of any report referred to in this rule to any children's guardian, reporting officer or children and family reporter.

(6) A report to the court under this rule is confidential.

14.12 Health reports

(1) Reports by a registered medical practitioner ('health reports') made not more than 3 months earlier on the health of the child and of each applicant must be attached to an application for an adoption order or a section 84 order except where –

(a)   the child was placed for adoption with the applicant by an adoption agency;

(b)   the applicant or one of the applicants is a parent of the child; or

(c)   the applicant is the partner of a parent of the child.

(2) Health reports must contain the matters set out in Practice Direction 14D.

(3) A health report is confidential.

14.13 Confidential reports to the court and disclosure to the parties

(1) The court will consider whether to give a direction that a confidential report be disclosed to each party to the proceedings.

(2) Before giving such a direction the court will consider whether any information should be deleted including information which –

(a)   discloses, or is likely to disclose, the identity of a person who has been assigned a serial number under rule 14.2(2) [or (3)][1]; or

(b)   discloses the particulars referred to in rule 29.1(1) where a party has given notice under rule 29.1(2) (disclosure of personal details).

(3) The court may direct that the report will not be disclosed to a party.

NOTES

Amendment.[1] Words inserted: SI 2014/843.

14.14 Communication of information relating to proceedings

For the purposes of the law relating to contempt of court, information (whether or not it is recorded in any form) relating to proceedings held in private may be communicated –

(a)   where the court gives permission;

(b)   unless the court directs otherwise, in accordance with Practice Direction 14E; or

(c)   where the communication is to –

    (i)   a party;

    (ii)   the legal representative of a party;

    (iii)   a professional legal adviser;

    (iv)   an officer of the service or a Welsh family proceedings officer;

    (v)   a welfare officer;

    (vi)   [the Director of Legal Aid Casework (within the meaning of section 4 of the Legal Aid, Sentencing and Punishment of Offenders Act 2012)][1];

    (vii)   an expert whose instruction by a party has been authorised by the court for the purposes of the proceedings; or

    (viii) a professional acting in furtherance of the protection of children.

NOTES

Amendments.[1] Words substituted: SI 2013/534.

14.15 Notice of final hearing

A court officer will give notice to the parties, any children's guardian, reporting officer or children and family reporter and to any other person to whom a practice direction may require such notice to be given –

(a)   of the date and place where the application will be heard; and

(b)   of the fact that, unless the person wishes or the court requires, the person need not attend.

14.16 The final hearing

(1) Any person who has been given notice in accordance with rule 14.15 may attend the final hearing and, subject to paragraph (2), be heard on the question of whether an order should be made.

(2) A person whose application for the permission of the court to oppose the making of an adoption order under section 47(3) or (5) of the 2002 Act has been refused is not entitled to be heard on the question of whether an order should be made.

(3) Any member or employee of a party which is a local authority, adoption agency or other body may address the court at the final hearing if authorised to do so.

(4) The court may direct that any person must attend a final hearing.

(5) Paragraphs (6) and (7) apply to –

(a)   an adoption order;

(b)   a section 84 order; or

(c)   a section 89 order.

(6) Subject to paragraphs (7) and (8), the court cannot make an order unless the applicant and the child personally attend the final hearing.

(7) The court may direct that the applicant or the child need not attend the final hearing.

(8) In a case of adoption by a couple under section 50 of the 2002 Act, the court may make an adoption order after personal attendance of one only of the applicants if there are special circumstances.

(9) The court cannot make a placement order unless a legal representative of the applicant attends the final hearing.

14.17 Proof of identity of the child

(1) Unless the contrary is shown, the child referred to in the application will be deemed to be the child referred to in the form of consent –

(a)   to the child being placed for adoption;

(b)   to the making of an adoption order; or

(c)   to the making of a section 84 order,

where the conditions in paragraph (2) apply.

(2) The conditions are –

(a)   the application identifies the child by reference to a full certified copy of an entry in the registers of live-births;

(b) the form of consent identifies the child by reference to a full certified copy of an entry in the registers of live-births attached to the form; and

(c) the copy of the entry in the registers of live-births referred to in sub-paragraph (a) is the same or relates to the same entry in the registers of live-births as the copy of the entry in the registers of live-births attached to the form of consent.

(3) Where the child is already an adopted child paragraph (2) will have effect as if for the references to the registers of live-births there were substituted references to the Adopted Children Register.

(4) Subject to paragraph (7), where the precise date of the child's birth is not proved to the satisfaction of the court, the court will determine the probable date of birth.

(5) The probable date of the child's birth may be specified in the placement order, adoption order or section 84 order as the date of the child's birth.

(6) Subject to paragraph (7), where the child's place of birth cannot be proved to the satisfaction of the court –

(a) the child may be treated as having been born in [the registration district and sub-district in which the court sits][1] where it is probable that the child may have been born in –
(i) the United Kingdom;
(ii) the Channel Islands; or
(iii) the Isle of Man; or

(b) in any other case, the particulars of the country of birth may be omitted from the placement order, adoption order or section 84 order.

(7) A placement order identifying the probable date and place of birth of the child will be sufficient proof of the date and place of birth of the child in adoption proceedings and proceedings for a section 84 order.

NOTES

Amendments.[1] Words substituted: SI 2013/3204.

14.18 Disclosing information to an adopted adult

(1) The adopted person has the right, on request, to receive from the court which made the adoption order a copy of the following –

(a) the application form for an adoption order (but not the documents attached to that form);

(b) the adoption order and any other orders relating to the adoption proceedings;

(c) orders [containing any provision for contact][1] with the child after the adoption order was made; and

(d) any other document or order referred to in Practice Direction 14F.

PART II – Statutory instruments

(2) The court will remove any protected information from any copy of a document or order referred to in paragraph (1) before the copies are given to the adopted person.

(3) This rule does not apply to an adopted person under the age of 18 years.

(4) In this rule 'protected information' means information which would be protected information under section 57(3) of the 2002 Act if the adoption agency gave the information and not the court.

NOTES

Amendment.[1] Words substituted: SI 2014/843.

14.19 Translation of documents

(1) Where a translation of any document is required for the purposes of proceedings for a Convention adoption order the translation must –

   (a)   unless the court directs otherwise, be provided by the applicant; and
   (b)   be signed by the translator to certify that the translation is accurate.

(2) ...[1]

NOTES

Amendments.[1] Words omitted repealed: SI 2019/517.

14.20 Application for recovery orders

[(1) An application for any of the orders referred to in section 41(2) of the 2002 Act (recovery orders) may be made without notice, in which case the applicant must file the application –

   (a)   where the application is made by telephone, the next business day after the making of the application; or
   (b)   in any other case, at the time when the application is made.][1]

(2) Where the court refuses to make an order on an application without notice it may direct that the application is made on notice in which case the application will proceed in accordance with rules 14.1 to 14.17.

(3) The respondents to an application under this rule are –

   (a)   in a case where –
       (i)   placement proceedings;
       (ii)   adoption proceedings; or
       (iii) proceedings for a section 84 order,
       are pending, all parties to those proceedings;
   (b)   any adoption agency authorised to place the child for adoption or which has placed the child for adoption;
   (c)   any local authority to whom notice under section 44 of the 2002 Act (notice of intention to adopt or apply for a section 84 order) has been given;
   (d)   any person having parental responsibility for the child;

(e)   any person in whose favour there is provision for contact;

(f)   any person who was caring for the child immediately prior to the making of the application; and

(g)   any person whom the applicant alleges to have effected, or to have been or to be responsible for, the taking or keeping of the child.

NOTES

Amendment.[1] Paragraph substituted: SI 2013/3204.

14.21 [Notice to][1] fathers without parental responsibility

Where no proceedings have started an adoption agency or local authority may ask the [court][1] for directions on the need to give a father without parental responsibility notice of the intention to place a child for adoption.

NOTES

Amendments.[1] Words substituted: SI 2020/135.

14.22 Timing of applications for section 89 order

An application for a section 89 order must be made within 2 years beginning with the date on which –

(a)   the Convention adoption or Convention adoption order; or

(b)   the overseas adoption or determination under section 91 of the 2002 Act,

to which it relates was made.

14.23 Custody of documents

All documents relating to proceedings under the 2002 Act must, while they are in the custody of the court, be kept in a place of special security.

14.24 Documents held by the court not to be inspected or copied without the court's permission

Subject to the provisions of these rules, any practice direction or any direction given by the court –

(a)   no document or order held by the court in proceedings under the 2002 Act will be open to inspection by any person; and

(b)   no copy of any such document or order, or of an extract from any such document or order, will be taken by or given to any person.

14.25 Orders

(1) An order takes effect from the date when it is made, or such later date as the court may specify.

(2) In proceedings in Wales a party may request that an order be drawn up in Welsh as well as English.

[(Rule 37.9 makes provision for the court to endorse an order prohibiting contact under section 51A(2)(b) of the 2002 Act with a penal notice on the application of the person entitled to enforce the order.)][1]

NOTES
Amendment.[1] Words inserted: SI 2014/843.

14.26 Copies of orders

(1) Within 7 days beginning with the date on which the final order was made in proceedings, or such shorter time as the court may direct, a court officer will send –

(a)   a copy of the order to the applicant;

(b)   a copy, which is sealed(GL), authenticated with the stamp of the court or certified as a true copy, of –
   (i)   an adoption order;
   (ii)   a section 89 order; or
   (iii) an order quashing or revoking an adoption order or allowing an appeal against an adoption order,
   to the Registrar General;

(c)   a copy of a Convention adoption order to the relevant Central Authority;

(d)   a copy of a section 89 order relating to a Convention adoption order or a Convention adoption to the –
   (i)   relevant Central Authority;
   (ii)   adopters;
   (iii) adoption agency; and
   (iv)   local authority;

(e)   unless the court directs otherwise, [a copy of an order][1] under section 26 of the 2002 Act or a [variation or revocation of such][1] order under section 27 of the 2002 Act to the –
   (i)   person with whom the child is living;
   (ii)   adoption agency; and
   (iii) local authority; ...[1]

[(ee) unless the court directs otherwise, a copy of a contact order under section 51A(2)(a) of the 2002 Act, an order prohibiting contact under section 51A(2)(b) of that Act or a variation or revocation of such orders under section 51B(1)(c) of that Act to the parties to the proceedings; and][1]

(f)   a notice of the making or refusal of –
   (i)   the final order; or
   (ii)   an order quashing or revoking an adoption order or allowing an appeal against an order in proceedings,
   to every respondent and, with the permission of the court, any other person.

(2) The court officer will also send notice of the making of an adoption order or a section 84 order to –

(a)   any court in Great Britain which appears to the court officer to have made any such order as is referred to in section 46(2) of the 2002 Act (order relating to parental responsibility for, and maintenance of, the child); and

---

    (b)   the principal registry, if it appears to the court officer that a parental responsibility agreement has been recorded at the principal registry.

(3) A copy of any final order may be sent to any other person with the permission of the court.

(4) The court officer will send a copy of any order made during the course of the proceedings to the following persons or bodies, unless the court directs otherwise –

    (a)   all the parties to those proceedings;
    (b)   any children and family reporter appointed in those proceedings;
    (c)   any adoption agency or local authority which has prepared a report on the suitability of an applicant to adopt a child;
    (d)   any local authority which has prepared a report on placement for adoption.

(5) If an order has been drawn up in Welsh as well as English in accordance with rule 14.25(2) any reference in this rule to sending an order is to be taken as a reference to sending both the Welsh and English orders.

NOTES

Amendments.[1] Words substituted and omitted and sub-paragraph inserted: SI 2014/843.

14.27 Amendment and revocation of orders

(1) Subject to paragraph (2), an application under –

    (a)   section 55 of the 2002 Act (revocation of adoptions on legitimation); or
    (b)   paragraph 4 of Schedule 1 to the 2002 Act (amendment of adoption order and revocation of direction),

may be made without serving a copy of the application notice.

(2) The court may direct that an application notice be served on such persons as it thinks fit.

(3) Where the court makes an order granting the application, a court officer will send the Registrar General a notice –

    (a)   specifying the amendments; or
    (b)   informing the Registrar General of the revocation,

giving sufficient particulars of the order to enable the Registrar General to identify the case.

14.28

…[1]

NOTES

Amendment.[1] Rule omitted: SI 2013/3204.

Practice Direction 14A –
Who Receives a Copy of the Application Form for Orders in Proceedings

This Practice Direction supplements FPR Part 14, rule 14.6(1)(b)(ii)

Persons who receive copy of application form

1.1 [Subject to paragraph 1.2,][1] in relation to each type of proceedings in column 1 of the following table, column 2 sets out which persons are to receive a copy of the application form.

[1.2 A person listed in column 2 of the following table shall not receive a copy of the application form, if the court, on application by any party, directs that such notification is not required.][1]

NOTES

Amendment.[1] Words and paragraph inserted: Practice Direction, April 2020.

Proceeding for	Who Receives a Copy of the Application Form
An adoption order (section 46 of the Act); or	Any appointed children's guardian, children and family reporter and reporting officer;
a section 84 order	the local authority to whom notice under section 44 (notice of intention to apply to adopt or apply for a section 84 order) has been given;
	the adoption agency which placed the child for adoption with the applicants;
	any other person directed by the court to receive a copy.
A placement order (section 21 of the Act); or	Each parent with parental responsibility for the child or guardian of the child;
an order varying a placement order (section 23 of the Act)	any appointed children's guardian, children and family reporter and reporting officer;
	any other person directed by the court to receive a copy.
An order revoking a placement order (section 24 of the Act)	Each parent with parental responsibility for the child or guardian of the child;
	any appointed children's guardian and children and family reporter;
	the local authority authorised by the placement order to place the child for adoption;
	any other person directed by the court to receive a copy.

Proceeding for	Who Receives a Copy of the Application Form
A contact order (section 26 of the Act); an order varying or revoking a contact order (section 27 of the Act); an order permitting the child's name to be changed or the removal of the child from the United Kingdom (section 28(2) of the Act); a recovery order (section 41(2) of the Act); [a contact order under section 51A(2)(a) of the Act; the making of an order prohibiting contact with the child under section 51A(2)(b) of the Act; the variation or revocation of an order under section 51A(2) of the Act in accordance with section 51B(1)(c) of the Act;][1] a section 89 order; and a section 88 direction	All the parties; any appointed children's guardian and children and family reporter; any other person directed by the court to receive a copy.

NOTES

Amendment.[1] Text inserted: FPR Update, April 2014.

Practice Direction 14B –
The First Directions Hearing – Adoptions with a Foreign Element

This Practice Direction supplements FPR Part 14, rule 14.8(3)

Application

1 This Practice Direction applies to proceedings for:

   (a)   a Convention adoption order;
   (b)   a section 84 order;
   (c)   a section 88 direction;
   (d)   a section 89 order; and
   (e)   an adoption order where the child has been brought into the United Kingdom in the circumstances where section 83(1) of the Act applies.

PART II – Statutory instruments

The first directions hearing

2 At the first directions hearing the court will, in addition to any matters referred to in rule 14.8(1) –

(a) consider whether the requirements of the Act and the Adoptions with a Foreign Element Regulations 2005 (S.I. 2005/392) appear to have been complied with and, if not, consider whether or not [in a case in the family court, it is appropriate that the case should be considered by a puisne judge of the High Court sitting in the family court (who may in turn consider whether or not it is appropriate to transfer the case to the High Court)]²;

(b) consider whether all relevant documents are translated into English and, if not, fix a timetable for translating any outstanding documents;

(c) consider whether the applicant needs to file an affidavit setting out the full details of the circumstances in which the child was brought to the United Kingdom, of the attitude of the parents to the application and confirming compliance with the requirements of The Adoptions with A Foreign Element Regulations 2005;

(d) give directions about –
   (i) the production of the child's passport and visa;
   (ii) the need for [an officer of the Service or a Welsh family proceedings officer]¹ and a representative of the Home Office to attend future hearings; and
   (iii) personal service on the parents (via the Central Authority in the case of an application for a Convention Adoption Order) including information about the role of [the officer of the Service or the Welsh family proceedings officer]¹ and availability of legal aid to be represented within the proceedings; and

(e) consider fixing a further directions appointment no later than 6 weeks after the date of the first directions appointment and timetable a date by which [the officer of the Service or the Welsh family proceedings officer]¹ should file an interim report in advance of that further appointment.

NOTES

Amendments.¹ Words substituted: FPR 2010 2nd Update, 6 April 2012. ² Text substituted: FPR Update, April 2014.

Practice Direction 14C –
Reports by the Adoption Agency or Local Authority

This Practice Direction supplements FPR Part 14, rule 14.11(3)

Matters to be contained in reports

1.1 The matters to be covered in the report on the suitability of the applicant to adopt a child are set out in Annex A to this Practice Direction.

1.2 The matters to be covered in a report on the placement of the child for adoption are set out in Annex B to this Practice Direction.

1.3 Where a matter to be covered in the reports set out in Annex A and Annex B does not apply to the circumstances of a particular case, the reasons for not covering the matter should be given.

ANNEX A – REPORT TO THE COURT WHERE THERE HAS BEEN AN APPLICATION FOR AN ADOPTION ORDER OR AN APPLICATION FOR A SECTION 84 ORDER

Section A: The Report and Matters for the Proceedings

Section B: The Child and the Birth Family

Section C: The Prospective Adopter of the Child

Section D: The Placement

Section E: Recommendations

Section F: Further information for proceedings relating to Convention Adoption Orders, Convention adoptions, section 84 Orders or adoptions where section 83(1) of the 2002 Act applies.

Section A: The Report and Matters for the Proceedings

Part 1 – The report

For each of the principal author/s of the report:

    (i)   name;
    (ii)   role in relation to this case;
    (iii) sections completed in this report;
    (iv) qualifications and experience;
    (v)   name and address of the adoption agency; and
    (vi) adoption agency case reference number.

Part 2 – Matters for the proceedings

    (a)   Whether the adoption agency considers that any other person should be made a respondent or a party to the proceedings, including the child.
    [(a1) Whether the adoption agency or other party considers that any person should not receive notification of the proceedings or should not be made a party. Parties should discuss the matter before proceedings are issued.][1]
    (b)   Whether any of the respondents is under the age of 18.
    (c)   Whether a respondent is a person who, by reason of mental disorder within the meaning of the Mental Health Act 1983, is incapable of managing and administering his or her property and affairs. If so, medical evidence should be provided with particular regard to the effect on that person's ability to make decisions in the proceedings.

NOTES

Amendment.[1] Paragraph inserted: Practice Direction, April 2020.

Section B: The Child and the Birth Family

Part 1

(i) Information about the child

- (a) Name, sex, date and place of birth and address including local authority area.
- (b) Photograph and physical description.
- (c) Nationality.
- (d) Racial origin and cultural and linguistic background.
- (e) Religious persuasion (including details of baptism, confirmation or equivalent ceremonies).
- (f) Details of any siblings, half-siblings and step-siblings, including dates of birth.
- (g) Whether the child is looked after by a local authority.
- (h) Whether the child has been placed for adoption with the prospective adopter by a UK adoption agency.
- (i) Whether the child was being fostered by the prospective adopter.
- (j) Whether the child was brought into the UK for adoption, including date of entry and whether an adoption order was made in the child's country of origin.
- (k) Personality and social development, including emotional and behavioural development and any related needs.
- (l) Details of interests, likes and dislikes.
- (m) A summary, written by the agency's medical adviser, of the child's health history, his current state of health and any need for health care which is anticipated, and date of the most recent medical examination.
- (n) Any known learning difficulties or known general medical or mental health factors which are likely to have, or may have, genetic implications.
- (o) Names, addresses and types of nurseries or schools attended, with dates.
- (p) Educational attainments.
- (q) Any special needs in relation to the child (whether physical, learning, behavioural or any other) and his emotional and behavioural development.
- (r) Whether the child is subject to a statement under the Education Act 1996.
- (s) Previous orders concerning the child –
  - (i) the name of the court;
  - (ii) the order made; and
  - (iii) the date of the order.
- (t) Inheritance rights and any claim to damages under the Fatal Accidents Act 1976 the child stands to retain or lose if adopted.
- (u) Any other relevant information which might assist the court.

(ii) Information about each parent of the child

- (a) Name, date and place of birth and address (date on which last address was confirmed current) including local authority area.
- (b) Photograph, if available, and physical description.
- (c) Nationality.
- (d) Racial origin and cultural and linguistic background.

(e) Whether the mother and father were married to each other at the time of the child's birth or have subsequently married.

(f) Where the parent has been previously married or entered into a civil partnership, dates of those marriages or civil partnerships.

(g) Where the mother and father are not married, whether the father has parental responsibility and, if so, how it was acquired.

(h) If the identity or whereabouts of the father are not known, the information about him that has been ascertained and from whom, and the steps that have been taken to establish paternity.

(i) Past and present relationship with the other parent.

(j) Other information about the parent, where available –

  (i) health, including any known learning difficulties or known general medical or mental health factors which are likely to have, or may have, genetic implications;

  (ii) religious persuasion;

  (iii) educational history;

  (iv) employment history; and

  (v) personality and interests.

(k) Any other relevant information which might assist the court.

Part 2

Relationships, contact arrangements and views.

THE CHILD

(a) If the child is in the care of a local authority or voluntary organisation, or has been, details (including dates) of any placements with foster parents, or other arrangements in respect of the care of the child, including particulars of the persons with whom the child has had his home and observations on the care provided.

(b) The child's wishes and feelings (if appropriate, having regard to the child's age and understanding) about adoption, the application and its consequences, including any wishes in respect of religious and cultural upbringing.

(c) The child's wishes and feelings in relation to contact (if appropriate, having regard to the child's age and understanding).

(d) The child's wishes and feelings recorded in any other proceedings.

(e) Date when the child's views were last ascertained.

THE CHILD'S PARENTS (OR GUARDIAN) AND RELATIVES

(a) The parents' wishes and feelings before the placement, about the placement and about adoption, the application and its consequences, including any wishes in respect of the child's religious and cultural upbringing.

(b) Each parent's (or guardian's) wishes and feelings in relation to contact.

(c) Date/s when the views of each parent or guardian were last ascertained.

(d) Arrangements concerning any siblings, including half-siblings and step-siblings, and whether any are the subject of a parallel application or have been the subject of any orders. If so, for each case give –

    (i)   the name of the court;

    (ii)   the order made, or (if proceedings are pending) the order applied for; and

    (iii) the date of order, or date of next hearing if proceedings are pending.

(e)   Extent of contact with the child's mother and father and, in each case, the nature of the relationship enjoyed.

(f)   The relationship which the child has with relatives, and with any other person considered relevant, including –

    (i)   the likelihood of any such relationship continuing and the value to the child of its doing so; and

    (ii)   the ability and willingness of any of the child's relatives, or of any such person, to provide the child with a secure environment in which the child can develop, and otherwise to meet the child's needs.

(g)   The wishes and feelings of any of the child's relatives, or of any such person, regarding the child.

(h)   Whether the parents (or members of the child's family) have met or are likely to meet the prospective adopter and, if they have met, the effect on all involved of such meeting.

(i)   Dates when the views of members of the child's wider family and any other relevant person were last ascertained.

Part 3

A summary of the actions of the adoption agency

(a)   Brief account of the agency's actions in the case, with particulars and dates of all written information and notices given to the child and his parents and any person with parental responsibility.

(b)   If consent has been given for the child to be placed for adoption, and also consent for the child to be adopted, the names of those who gave consent and the date such consents were given. If such consents were subsequently withdrawn, the dates of these withdrawals.

(c)   If any statement has been made under section 20(4)(a) of the Adoption and Children Act 2002 (the '2002 Act') that a parent or guardian does not wish to be informed of any application for an adoption order, the names of those who have made such statements and the dates the statements were made. If such statements were subsequently withdrawn, the dates of these withdrawals.

(d)   Whether an order has been made under section 21 of the 2002 Act, section 18 of the Adoption (Scotland) Act 1978 or Article 17(1) or 18(1) of the Northern Ireland Order 1987.

(e)   Details of the support and advice given to the parents and any services offered or taken up.

(f)   If the father does not have parental responsibility, details of the steps taken to inform him of the application for an adoption order.

(g)   Brief details and dates of assessments of the child's needs, including expert opinions.

(h)   Reasons for considering that adoption would be in the child's best interests (with date of relevant decision and reasons for any delay in implementing the decision).

Section C: The Prospective Adopter of the Child

Part 1

Information about the prospective adopter, including suitability to adopt

(a) Name, date and place of birth and address (date on which last address was confirmed current) including local authority area.

(b) Photograph and physical description.

(c) Whether the prospective adopter is domiciled or habitually resident in a part of the British Islands and, if habitually resident, for how long they have been habitually resident.

(d) Racial origin and cultural and linguistic background.

(e) Marital status or civil partnership status, date and place of most recent marriage (if any) or civil partnership (if any).

(f) Details of any previous marriage, civil partnership, or relationship where the prospective adopter lived with another person as a partner in an enduring family relationship.

(g) Relationship (if any) to the child.

(h) Where adopters wish to adopt as a couple, the status of the relationship and an assessment of the stability and permanence of their relationship.

(i) If a married person or a civil partner is applying alone, the reasons for this.

(j) Description of how the prospective adopter relates to adults and children.

(k) Previous experience of caring for children (including as a step-parent, foster parent, child-minder or prospective adopter) and assessment of ability in this respect, together where appropriate with assessment of ability in bringing up the prospective adopter's own children.

(l) A summary, written by the agency's medical adviser, of the prospective adopter's health history, current state of health and any need for health care which is anticipated, and date of most recent medical examination.

(m) Assessment of ability and suitability to bring up the child throughout his childhood.

(n) Details of income and comments on the living standards of the household with particulars of the home and living conditions (and particulars of any home where the prospective adopter proposes to live with the child, if different).

(o) Details of other members of the household, including any children of the prospective adopter even if not resident in the household.

(p) Details of the parents and any siblings of the prospective adopter, with their ages or ages at death.

(q) Other information about the prospective adopter –
   (i) religious persuasion;
   (ii) educational history;
   (iii) employment history; and
   (iv) personality and interests.

(r) Confirmation that the applicants have not been convicted of, or cautioned for, a specified offence within the meaning of regulation 23(3) of the Adoption Agencies Regulations 2005 (S.I. 2005/389).

(s) Confirmation that the prospective adopter is still approved.

(t)   Confirmation that any referees have been interviewed, with a report of their views and opinion of the weight to be placed thereon and whether they are still valid.

(u)   Details of any previous family court proceedings in which the prospective adopter has been involved (which have not been referred to elsewhere in this report.)

Part 2

Wishes, views and contact arrangements

Prospective Adopter

(a)   Whether the prospective adopter is willing to follow any wishes of the child or his parents or guardian in respect of the child's religious and cultural upbringing.

(b)   The views of other members of the prospective adopter's household and wider family in relation to the proposed adoption.

(c)   Reasons for the prospective adopter wishing to adopt the child and extent of understanding of the nature and effect of adoption. Whether the prospective adopter has discussed adoption with the child.

(d)   Any hope and expectations the prospective adopter has for the child's future.

(e)   The prospective adopter's wishes and feelings in relation to contact.

Part 3

Actions of the adoption agency

(a)   Brief account of the Agency's actions in the case, with particulars and dates of all written information and notices given to the prospective adopter.

(b)   The Agency's proposals for contact, including options for facilitating or achieving any indirect contact or direct contact.

(c)   The Agency's opinion on the likely effect on the prospective adopter and on the security of the placement of any proposed contact.

(d)   Where the prospective adopter has been approved by an agency as suitable to be an adoptive parent, the agency's reasons for considering that the prospective adopter is suitable to be an adoptive parent for this child (with dates of relevant decisions).

Section D: The Placement

(a)   Where the child was placed for adoption by an adoption agency (section 18 of the 2002 Act), the date and circumstances of the child's placement with prospective adopter.

(b)   Where the child is living with persons who have applied for the adoption order to be made (section 44 of the 2002 Act), the date when notice of intention to adopt was given.

(c)   Where the placement is being provided with adoption support, this should be summarised and should include the plan and timescales for continuing the support beyond the making of the adoption order.

(d) Where the placement is not being provided with adoption support, the reasons why.

(e) A summary of the information obtained from the Agency's visits and reviews of the placement, including whether the child has been seen separately to the prospective adopter and whether there has been sufficient opportunity to see the family group and the child's interaction in the home environment.

(f) An assessment of the child's integration within the family of the prospective adopter and the likelihood of the child's full integration into the family and community.

(g) Any other relevant information that might assist the court.

Section E: Recommendations

(a) The relative merits of adoption and other orders with an assessment of whether the child's long term interests would be best met by an adoption order or by other orders (such as [child arrangements][1] and special guardianship orders).

(b) Recommendations as to whether or not the order sought should be made (and, if not, alternative proposals).

(c) Recommendations as to whether there should be future contact arrangements (or not).

Section F: Further Information for Proceedings Relating to Convention Adoption Orders, Convention Adoptions, Section 84 Orders or an Adoption where Section 83(1) of the 2002 Act applies.

(a) The child's knowledge of their racial and cultural origin.

(b) The likelihood of the child's adaptation to living in the country he/she is to be placed.

(c) Where the UK is the State of origin, reasons for considering that, after possibilities for placement of the child within the UK have been given due consideration, intercountry adoption is in the child's best interests.

(d) Confirmation that the requirements of regulations made under sections 83(4), (5), (6) and (7) and 84(3) and (6) of the 2002 Act have been complied with.

(e) For a Convention adoption or a Convention Adoption Order where the United Kingdom is either the State of origin or the receiving State, confirmation that the Central Authorities of both States have agreed that the adoption may proceed.

(f) Where the State of origin is not the United Kingdom, the documents supplied by the Central Authority of the State of origin should be attached to the report, together with translation if necessary.

(g) Where a Convention adoption order is proposed, details of the arrangements which were made for the transfer of the child to the UK and that they were in accordance with the Adoptions with a Foreign Element Regulations 2005 (S.I. 2005/392).

NOTES

Amendment.[1] Text substituted: FPR Update, April 2014.

ANNEX B – REPORT TO THE COURT WHERE THERE HAS BEEN AN APPLICATION
FOR A PLACEMENT ORDER

Section A: The Report and Matters for the Proceedings

Section B: The Child and the Birth Family

Section C: Recommendations

Section A: The Report and Matters for the Proceedings

Part 1

The report

For each of the principal author/s of the report:

(i)   name;
(ii)   role in relation to this case;
(iii)   section completed in this report;
(iv)   qualifications and experience;
(v)   name and address of the adoption agency; and
(vi)   adoption agency case reference number.

Part 2

Matters for the proceedings

(a)   Whether the adoption agency considers that any other person should be made a respondent or a party to the proceedings.
(b)   Whether any of the respondents is under the age of 18.
(c)   Whether a respondent is a person who, by reason of mental disorder within the meaning of the Mental Health Act 1983, is incapable of managing and administering his or her property and affairs. If so, medical evidence should be provided with particular regard to the effect on that person's ability to make decisions in the proceedings.

Section B: The child and the birth family

Part 1

(i) Information about the child

(a)   Name, sex, date and place of birth and address including local authority area.
(b)   Photograph and physical description.
(c)   Nationality.
(d)   Racial origin and cultural and linguistic background.
(e)   Religious persuasion (including details of baptism, confirmation or equivalent ceremonies).
(f)   Details of any siblings, half-siblings and step-siblings, including dates of birth.
(g)   Whether the child is looked after by a local authority.

(h) Personality and social development, including emotional and behavioural development and any related needs.

(i) Details of interests, likes and dislikes.

(j) A summary, written by the agency's medical adviser, of the child's health history, his current state of health and any need for health care which is anticipated, and date of the most recent medical examination.

(k) Any known learning difficulties or known general medical or mental health factors which are likely to have, or may have, genetic implications.

(l) Names, addresses and types of nurseries or schools attended, with dates.

(m) Educational attainments.

(n) Any special needs in relation to the child (whether physical, learning, behavioural or any other) and his emotional and behavioural development.

(o) Whether the child is subject to a statement under the Education Act 1996.

(p) Previous orders concerning the child:
  (i) the name of the court;
  (ii) the order made; and
  (ii) the date of the order.

(q) Inheritance rights and any claim to damages under the Fatal Accidents Act 1976 the child stands to retain or lose if adopted.

(r) Any other relevant information which might assist the court.

(ii) Information about each parent of the child

(a) Name, date and place of birth and address (date on which last address was confirmed current) including local authority area.

(b) Photograph, if available, and physical description.

(c) Nationality.

(d) Racial origin and cultural and linguistic background.

(e) Whether the mother and father were married to each other at the time of the child's birth, or have subsequently married.

(f) Where the parent has been previously married or entered into a civil partnership, dates of those marriages or civil partnerships.

(g) Where the mother and father are not married, whether the father has parental responsibility and, if so, how it was acquired.

(h) If the identity or whereabouts of the father are not known, the information about him that has been ascertained and from whom, and the steps that have been taken to establish paternity.

(i) Past and present relationship with the other parent.

(j) Other information about the parent, where available –
  (i) health, including any known learning difficulties or known general medical or mental health factors which are likely to have, or may have, genetic implications;
  (ii) religious persuasion;
  (iii) educational history;
  (iv) employment history; and
  (v) personality and interests.

(k) Any other relevant information which might assist the court.

PART II – Statutory instruments

Part 2

Relationships, contact arrangements and views

THE CHILD

- (a)   If the child is in the care of a local authority or voluntary organisation, or has been, details (including dates) of any placements with foster parents, or other arrangements in respect of the care of the child, including particulars of the persons with whom the child has had his home and observations on the care provided.
- (b)   The child's wishes and feelings (if appropriate, having regard to the child's age and understanding) about the application, its consequences, and adoption, including any wishes in respect of religious and cultural upbringing.
- (c)   The child's wishes and feelings in relation to contact (if appropriate, having regard to the child's age and understanding).
- (d)   The child's wishes and feelings recorded in any other proceedings.
- (e)   Date when the child's views were last ascertained.

THE CHILD'S PARENTS (OR GUARDIAN) AND RELATIVES

- (a)   The parents' wishes and feelings about the application, its consequences, and adoption, including any wishes in respect of the child's religious and cultural upbringing.
- (b)   Each parent's (or guardian's) wishes and feelings in relation to contact.
- (c)   Date/s when the views of each parent or guardian were last ascertained.
- (d)   Arrangements concerning any siblings, including half-siblings and step-siblings, and whether any are the subject of a parallel application or have been the subject of any orders. If so, for each case give –
  - (i)   the name of the court;
  - (ii)   the order made, or (if proceedings are pending) the order applied for; and
  - (iii) the date of order, or date of next hearing if proceedings are pending.
- (e)   Extent of contact with the child's mother and father and in each case the nature of the relationship enjoyed.
- (f)   The relationship which the child has with relatives, and with any other person considered relevant, including –
  - (i)   the likelihood of any such relationship continuing and the value to the child of its doing so; and
  - (ii)   the ability and willingness of any of the child's relatives, or of any such person, to provide the child with a secure environment in which the child can develop, and otherwise to meet the child's needs.
- (g)   The wishes and feelings of any of the child's relatives, or of any such person, regarding the child.
- (h)   Dates when the views of members of the child's wider family and any other relevant person were last ascertained.

Part 3

Summary of the actions of the adoption agency

(a) Brief account of the Agency's actions in the case, with particulars and dates of all written information and notices given to the child and his parents and any person with parental responsibility.

(b) If consent has been given for the child to be placed for adoption, and also consent for the child to be adopted, the names of those who gave consent and the date such consents were given. If such consents were subsequently withdrawn, the dates of these withdrawals.

(c) If any statement has been made under section 20(4)(a) of the 2002 Act that a parent or guardian does not wish to be informed of any application for an adoption order, the names of those who have made such statements and the dates the statements were made. If such statements were subsequently withdrawn, the dates of these withdrawals.

(d) Details of the support and advice given to the parents and any services offered or taken up.

(e) If the father does not have parental responsibility, details of the steps taken to inform him of the application for a placement order.

(f) Brief details and dates of assessments of the child's needs, including expert opinions.

(g) Reasons for considering that adoption would be in the child's best interests (with date of relevant decision and reasons for any delay in implementing the decision).

Section C: Recommendations

(a) The relative merits of a placement order and other orders (such as a [child arrangements][1] or special guardianship order) with an assessment of why the child's long term interests are likely to be best met by a placement order rather than by any other order.

(b) Recommendations as to whether there should be future contact arrangements (or not), including whether a contact order under section 26 of the 2002 Act should be made.

NOTES

Amendment.[1] Text substituted: FPR Update, April 2014.

Practice Direction 14D –
Reports by a Registered Medical Practitioner ('Health Reports')

This Practice Direction supplements FPR Part 14, rule 14.12(2)

Matters to be contained in health reports

1.1 Rule 14.12(1) requires that health reports must be attached to an application for an adoption order or a section 84 order except where –

(a) the child was placed for adoption with the applicant by an adoption agency;

(b) the applicant or one of the applicants is a parent of the child; or

(c)   the applicant is the partner of a parent of the child.

1.2 The matters to be contained in the health reports are set out in the Annex to this Practice Direction.

1.3 Where a matter to be contained in the health report does not apply to the circumstances of a particular case, the reasons for not covering the matter should be given.

ANNEX – CONTENTS OF HEALTH REPORTS

This information is required for reports on the health of children and their prospective adopter(s). Its purpose is to build up a full picture of each child's health history and current state of health, including strengths and weaknesses. This will enable local authorities' medical adviser to base their advice to the court on the fullest possible information when commenting on the health implications of the proposed adoption. The reports made by the examining doctor should cover, as far as practicable, the following matters.

1 The child

Name, date of birth, sex, weight and height.

A A health history of each natural parent, so far as is possible, including –

(i)   name, date of birth, sex, weight and height;

(ii)   a family health history, covering the parents, the brothers and sisters and the other children of the natural parent, with details of any serious physical or mental illness and inherited and congenital disease;

(iii) past health history, including details of any serious physical or mental illness, disability, accident, hospital admission or attendance at an out-patient department, and in each case any treatment given;

(iv)   a full obstetric history of the mother, including any problems in the ante-natal, labour and post-natal periods, with the results of any tests carried out during or immediately after pregnancy;

(v)   details of any present illness including treatment and prognosis;

(vi)   any other relevant information which might assist the medical adviser; and

(vii) the name and address of any doctor(s) who might be able to provide further information about any of the above matters.

B A neo-natal report on the child, including –

(i)   details of the birth, and any complications;

(ii)   results of a physical examination and screening tests;

(iii) details of any treatment given;

(iv)   details of any problem in management and feeding;

(v)   any other relevant information which might assist the medical adviser; and

(vi)   the name and address of any doctor(s) who might be able to provide further information about any of the above matters.

C A full health history and examination of the child, including –

(i)   details of any serious illness, disability, accident, hospital admission or attendance at an out-patient department, and in each case any treatment given;

(ii)   details and dates of immunisations;

(iii)   a physical and developmental assessment according to age, including an assessment of vision and hearing and of neurological, speech and language development and any evidence of emotional or conduct disorder;

(iv)   details, if relevant, of the impact of any addiction or substance use on the part of the natural mother before, during or following the pregnancy, and its impact or likely future impact on the child;

(v)   the impact, if any, on the child's development and likely future development of any past exposure to physical, emotional or sexual abuse or neglectful home conditions and/or any non-organic failure to thrive;

(vi)   for a child of school age, the school health history (if available);

(vii)   any other relevant information which might assist the medical adviser; and

(viii)   the name and address of any doctor(s) who might be able to provide further information about any of the above matters.

D The signature, name, address and qualifications of the registered medical practitioner who prepared the report, and the date of the report and of the examinations carried out.

2 The applicant

(If there is more than one applicant, a report on each applicant should be supplied covering all the matters listed below.)

A –

(i)   name, date of birth, sex, weight and height;

(ii)   a family health history, covering the parents, the brothers and sisters and the children of the applicant, with details of any serious physical or mental illness and inherited and congenital disease;

(iii)   marital history, including (if applicable) reasons for inability to have children, and any history of domestic violence;

(iv)   past health history, including details of any serious physical or mental illness, disability, accident, hospital admission or attendance at an out-patient department, and in each case any treatment given;

(v)   obstetric history (if applicable);

(vi)   details of any present illness, including treatment and prognosis;

(vii)   a full medical examination;

(viii)   details of any consumption of alcohol, tobacco and habit-forming drugs;

(ix)   any other relevant information which might assist the medical adviser; and

(x)   the name and address of any doctor(s) who might be able to provide further information about any of the above matters.

PART II – Statutory instruments

B The signature, name, address and qualifications of the registered medical practitioner who prepared the report, and the date of the report and of the examinations carried out.

Practice Direction 14E – Communication of Information Relating to Proceedings

This Practice Direction supplements FPR Part 14, rule 14.14(b)

Communication of information relating to proceedings

1.1 Rule 14.14 deals with the communication of information (whether or not it is recorded in any form) relating to proceedings.

1.2 Subject to any direction of the court, information may be communicated for the purposes of the law relating to contempt in accordance with paragraphs 1.3 or 1.4.

1.3 A person specified in the first column of the following table may communicate to a person listed in the second column such information as is specified in the third column for the purpose or purposes specified in the fourth column.

Communicated by	To	Information	Purpose
A party	A lay adviser or a McKenzie Friend	Any information relating to the proceedings	To enable the party to obtain advice or assistance in relation to the proceedings.
A party	The party's spouse, civil partner, cohabitant or close family member		For the purpose of confidential discussions enabling the party to receive support from his spouse, civil partner, cohabitant or close family member.
A party	A health care professional or a person or body providing counselling services for children or families		To enable the party or any child of the party to obtain health care or counselling.
A party	The Secretary of State, a McKenzie Friend, a lay adviser or an appeal tribunal dealing with an appeal made under section 20 of the Child Support Act 1991¹		For the purposes of making or responding to an appeal under section 20 of the Child Support Act 1991 or the determination of such an appeal.

Communicated by	To	Information	Purpose
[A party or other person lawfully in receipt of information	The Secretary of State, a McKenzie Friend, a lay adviser or the Upper Tier Tribunal dealing with an appeal under section 24 of the Child Support Act 1991 in respect of a decision of the First-tier Tribunal that was made under section 20 of that Act		For a purpose connected with an appeal under section 24 of the Child Support Act 1991 in respect of a decision of the First-tier Tribunal that was made under section 20 of that Act.][3]
A party	An adoption panel		To enable the adoption panel to discharge its functions as appropriate.
[A party	A local authority's medical adviser appointed under the Adoption Agencies Regulations 2005 or the Adoption Agencies (Wales) Regulations 2005		To enable the medical adviser to discharge his or her functions as appropriate.][1]
A party or any person lawfully in receipt of information	The Children's Commissioner or the Children's Commissioner for Wales		To refer an issue affecting the interests of children to the Children's Commissioner or the Children's Commissioner for Wales.
[A party or any person lawfully in receipt of information	The Welsh Language Commissioner		To refer an issue so that the Welsh Language Commissioner can consider whether to institute or intervene in legal proceedings or to assist a party or prospective party to legal proceedings.][5]
A party or a legal representative	A mediator		For the purpose of mediation in relation to the proceedings.
A party, any person lawfully in receipt of information or a proper officer	A person or body conducting an approved research project		For the purpose of an approved research project.

PART II – Statutory instruments

Communicated by	To	Information	Purpose
A party, a legal representative or a professional legal adviser	A person or body responsible for investigating or determining complaints in relation to legal representatives or professional legal advisers		For the purposes of making a complaint or the investigation or determination of a complaint in relation to a legal representative or a professional legal adviser.
[A legal representative or a professional legal adviser	A professional indemnity insurer		To enable the professional indemnity insurer to be notified of a claim or complaint, or potential claim or complaint, in relation to the legal representative or a professional legal adviser, and the legal representative or professional legal adviser to obtain advice in respect of that claim or complaint]4
A legal representative or a professional legal adviser	A person or body assessing quality assurance systems		To enable the legal representative or professional legal adviser to obtain a quality assurance assessment.
A legal representative or a professional legal adviser	An accreditation body	Any information relating to the proceedings providing that it does not, or is not likely to, identify any person involved in the proceedings	To enable the legal representative or professional legal adviser to obtain accreditation.
A party	An elected representative or peer	The text or summary of the whole or part of a judgment given in the proceedings	To enable the elected representative or peer to give advice, investigate any complaint or raise any question of policy or procedure.
A party	The General Medical Council		For the purpose of making a complaint to the General Medical Council.
A party	A police officer		For the purpose of a criminal investigation.
A party or any person lawfully in receipt of information	A member of the Crown Prosecution Service		To enable the Crown Prosecution Service to discharge its functions under any enactment.

Communicated by	To	Information	Purpose
A party or an adoption agency that is not a party	An adoption agency	Any information relating to the proceedings	To enable the sharing of relevant information between adoption agencies for more effective undertaking of their functions

1.4 A person in the second column of the table in paragraph 1.3 may only communicate information relating to the proceedings received from a person in the first column for the purpose or purposes –

(a)   for which he received that information, or

(b)   of professional development or training, providing that any communication does not, or is not likely to, identify any person involved in the proceedings without that person's consent.

1.5 In this Practice Direction

(1)   'accreditation body' means –
    (a)   The Law Society,
    (b)   Resolution, or
    (c)   [the Lord Chancellor in exercise of the Lord Chancellor's functions in relation to legal aid][2];

(1A) 'adoption panel' means a panel established in accordance with regulation 3 of the Adoption Agencies Regulations 2005 or regulation 3 of the Adoption Agencies (Wales) Regulations 2005;

(2)   'approved research project' means a project of research –
    (a)   approved in writing by a Secretary of State after consultation with the President of the Family Division,
    (b)   approved in writing by the President of the Family Division, or
    (c)   conducted under section 83 of the Act of 1989 or section 13 of the Criminal Justice and Court Services Act 2000;

(3)   'body assessing quality assurance systems' includes –
    (a)   The Law Society,
    (b)   [the Lord Chancellor in exercise of the Lord Chancellor's functions in relation to legal aid][2], or
    (c)   The General Council of the Bar;

(4)   'body or person responsible for investigating or determining complaints in relation to legal representatives or professional legal advisers' means –
    (a)   The Law Society,
    (b)   The General Council of the Bar,
    (c)   The Institute of Legal Executives, or
    (d)   The Legal Services Ombudsman;

(5)   'cohabitant' means one of two persons who are neither married to each other nor civil partners of each other but are living together as husband and wife or as if they were civil partners;

(6)   'criminal investigation' means an investigation conducted by police officers with a view to it being ascertained –
    (a)   whether a person should be charged with an offence, or
    (b)   whether a person charged with an offence is guilty of it;

PART II – Statutory instruments

(7)   'elected representative' means –
    (a)   a member of the House of Commons,
    (b)   a member of the National Assembly for Wales, or
    (c)   a member of the European Parliament elected in England and Wales;

(8)   'health care professional' means –
    (a)   a registered medical practitioner,
    (b)   a registered nurse or midwife,
    (c)   a clinical psychologist, or
    (d)   a child psychotherapist;

(9)   'lay adviser' means a non-professional person who gives lay advice on behalf of an organisation in the lay advice sector;

(10)   'McKenzie Friend' means any person permitted by the court to sit beside an unrepresented litigant in court to assist that litigant by prompting, taking notes and giving him advice;

(11)   'mediator' means a family mediator who is –
    (a)   undertaking, or has successfully completed, a family mediation training course approved by the United Kingdom College of Family Mediators, or
    (b)   a member of the Law Society's Family Mediation Panel;

(12)   'peer' means a member of the House of Lords as defined by the House of Lords Act 1999.

NOTES

Amendments.[1] Entry inserted: FPR 2010 5th Update, 20 December 2012. [2] Text substituted: FPR Update, April 2014. [3] Entry inserted: FPR Update, November 2015. [4] Entry inserted: FPR Update, October 2016. [5] Entry inserted: FPR Update, April 2020.

Practice Direction 14F –
Disclosing Information to an Adopted Adult

This Practice Direction supplements FPR Part 14, rule 14.18(1)(d)

How to request for information

1.1 Rule 14.18 states that an adopted person who is over the age of 18 has the right to receive from the court which made the adoption order a copy of –

    (a)   the application form for an adoption order (but not the documents attached to that form);
    (b)   the adoption order and any other orders relating to the adoption proceedings; and
    (c)   orders allowing any person contact with the child after the adoption order was made.

1.2 An application under rule 14.18 must be made in form A64 which is contained in the practice direction supplementing rule 5 and must have attached to it a full certified copy of the entry in the Adopted Children Register relating to the applicant.

1.3 The completed application form must be taken to the court which made the adoption order along with evidence of the applicant's identity showing a photograph and signature, such as a passport or driving licence.

Additional documents that the adopted person is also entitled to receive from the court

2 The adopted adult is also entitled to receive the following documents –

    (a)   any transcript or written reasons of the court's decision; and

    (b)   a report made to the court by –

        (i)   a children's guardian, reporting officer or children and family reporter;

        (ii)   a local authority; or

        (iii)   an adoption agency.

Before the documents are sent to the adopted adult

3 The court will remove protected information from documents before they are sent to the adopted adult.

****

PART 16
REPRESENTATION OF CHILDREN AND REPORTS IN PROCEEDINGS INVOLVING CHILDREN

Chapter 1
Application of this Part

16.1 Application of this Part

This Part –

    (a)   sets out when the court will make a child a party in family proceedings; and

    (b)   contains special provisions which apply in proceedings involving children.

Chapter 2
Child as Party in Family Proceedings

16.2 When the court may make a child a party to proceedings

(1) The court may make a child a party to proceedings if it considers it is in the best interests of the child to do so.

(2) This rule does not apply to a child who is the subject of proceedings –

    (a)   which are specified proceedings; or

    (b)   to which Part 14 applies.

(The Practice Direction 16A sets out the matters which the court will take into consideration before making a child a party under this rule.)

PART II – Statutory instruments

Chapter 3
When a Children's Guardian or Litigation Friend will be Appointed

16.3 Appointment of a children's guardian in specified proceedings or proceedings to which Part 14 applies

(1) Unless it is satisfied that it is not necessary to do so to safeguard the interests of the child, the court must appoint a children's guardian for a child who is –

    (a)   the subject of; and
    (b)   a party to,
        proceedings –
        (i)   which are specified proceedings; or
        (ii)   to which Part 14 applies.

(Rules 12.6 and 14.6 set out the point in the proceedings when the court will appoint a children's guardian in specified proceedings and proceedings to which Part 14 respectively.)

(2) At any stage in the proceedings –

    (a)   a party may apply, without notice to the other parties unless the court directs otherwise, for the appointment of a children's guardian; or
    (b)   the court may of its own initiative appoint a children's guardian.

(3) Where the court refuses an application under paragraph (2)(a) it will give reasons for the refusal and the court or a court officer will –

    (a)   record the refusal and the reasons for it; and
    (b)   as soon as practicable, notify the parties and either the Service or the Assembly of a decision not to appoint a children's guardian.

(4) When appointing a children's guardian the court will consider the appointment of anyone who has previously acted as a children's guardian of the same child.

(5) Where the court appoints a children's guardian in accordance with this rule, the provisions of Chapter 6 of this Part apply.

16.4 Appointment of a children's guardian in proceedings not being specified proceedings or proceedings to which Part 14 applies

(1) [Except in proceedings under section 55A of the 1986 Act and without][1] prejudice to rule 8.42 or 16.6, the court must appoint a children's guardian for a child who is the subject of proceedings, which are not proceedings of a type referred to in rule 16.3(1), if –

    (a)   the child is an applicant in the proceedings;
    (b)   a provision in these rules provides for the child to be a party to the proceedings; or
    (c)   the court has made the child a party in accordance with rule 16.2.

[(1A) Without prejudice to rule 16.6, in proceedings under section 55A of the 1986 Act, the court must appoint a children's guardian for a child where –

(a) the court has made the child a party in accordance with rule 16.2; and

(b) the child is the person whose parentage is in dispute in those proceedings.]¹

(2) The provisions of Chapter 7 of this Part apply where the appointment of a children's guardian is required in accordance with paragraph (1) [or paragraph (1A)]¹.

('children's guardian' is defined in rule 2.3.)

NOTES

Amendments. ¹ Words substituted and inserted, and paragraph inserted: SI 2016/901.

16.5 Requirement for a litigation friend

(1) [Except in proceedings under section 55A of the 1986 Act and without]1 prejudice to rule 16.6, where a child is –

(a) a party to proceedings; but

(b) not the subject of those proceedings,

the child must have a litigation friend to conduct proceedings on the child's behalf.

[(1A) Without prejudice to rule 16.6, where a child is –

(a) a party to proceedings under section 55A of the 1986 Act; but

(b) not the person whose parentage is in dispute in those proceedings,

the child must have a litigation friend to conduct proceedings on the child's behalf.]¹

(2) The provisions of Chapter 5 of this Part apply where a litigation friend is required in accordance with paragraph (1) [or paragraph (1A)]¹.

NOTES

Amendments. ¹ Words substituted and inserted, and paragraph inserted: SI 2016/901.

Chapter 4
Where a Children's Guardian or Litigation Friend is not Required

16.6 Circumstances in which a child does not need a children's guardian or litigation friend

(1) Subject to paragraph (2), a child may conduct proceedings without a children's guardian or litigation friend where the proceedings are proceedings –

(a) under the 1989 Act;

(b) to which Part 11 (applications under Part 4A of the Family Law Act 1996 [or Part 1 of Schedule 2 to the Female Genital Mutilation Act 2003]²) or Part 14 (applications in adoption, placement and related proceedings) of these rules apply; ...¹

(c) relating to the exercise of the court's inherent jurisdiction with respect to children[; or]¹

PART II – Statutory instruments

[(d)   under section 55A of the 1986 Act,]¹

and one of the conditions set out in paragraph (3) is satisfied.

(2) Paragraph (1) does not apply where the child is the subject of and a party to proceedings –

(a)   which are specified proceedings; or
(b)   to which Part 14 applies.

(3) The conditions referred to in paragraph (1) are that either –

(a)   the child has obtained the court's permission; or
(b)   a solicitor –
    (i)   considers that the child is able, having regard to the child's understanding, to give instructions in relation to the proceedings; and
    (ii)   has accepted instructions from that child to act for that child in the proceedings and, if the proceedings have begun, the solicitor is already acting.

(4) An application for permission under paragraph (3)(a) may be made by the child without notice.

(5) Where a child –

(a)   has a litigation friend or children's guardian in proceedings to which this rule applies; and
(b)   wishes to conduct the remaining stages of the proceedings without the litigation friend or children's guardian,

the child may apply to the court, on notice to the litigation friend or children's guardian, for permission for that purpose and for the removal of the litigation friend or children's guardian.

(6) The court will grant an application under paragraph (3)(a) or (5) if it considers that the child has sufficient understanding to conduct the proceedings concerned or proposed without a litigation friend or children's guardian.

(7) In exercising its powers under paragraph (6) the court may require the litigation friend or children's guardian to take such part in the proceedings as the court directs.

(8) The court may revoke any permission granted under paragraph (3)(a) where it considers that the child does not have sufficient understanding to participate as a party in the proceedings concerned without a litigation friend or children's guardian.

(9) Where a solicitor is acting for a child in proceedings without a litigation friend or children's guardian by virtue of paragraph (3)(b) and either of the conditions specified in paragraph (3)(b)(i) or (ii) cease to be fulfilled, the solicitor must inform the court immediately.

(10) Where –

(a) the court revokes any permission under paragraph (8); or

(b) either of the conditions specified in paragraph (3)(b)(i) or (ii) is no longer fulfilled,

the court may, if it considers it necessary in order to protect the interests of the child concerned, appoint a person to be that child's litigation friend or children's guardian.

NOTES

Amendments. [1] Words omitted and inserted, and sub-paragraph inserted: SI 2016/901. [2] Words inserted: SI 2017/413.

Chapter 5
Litigation Friend

16.7 Application of this Chapter

This Chapter applies where a child must have a litigation friend to conduct proceedings on the child's behalf in accordance with rule 16.5.

16.8 Stage of proceedings at which a litigation friend becomes necessary

(1) This rule does not apply in relation to a child who is conducting proceedings without a litigation friend in accordance with rule 16.6.

(2) A person may not without the permission of the court take any step in proceedings except –

(a) filing an application form; or

(b) applying for the appointment of a litigation friend under rule 16.11,

until the child has a litigation friend.

(3) Any step taken before a child has a litigation friend has no effect unless the court orders otherwise.

16.9 Who may be a litigation friend for a child without a court order

(1) This rule does not apply if the court has appointed a person to be a litigation friend.

(2) A person may act as a litigation friend if that person –

(a) can fairly and competently conduct proceedings on behalf of the child;

(b) has no interest adverse to that of the child; and

(c) subject to paragraph (3), undertakes to pay any costs which the child may be ordered to pay in relation to the proceedings, subject to any right that person may have to be repaid from the assets of the child.

(3) Paragraph (2)(c) does not apply to the Official Solicitor, an officer of the Service or a Welsh family proceedings officer.

16.10 How a person becomes a litigation friend without a court order

(1) If the court has not appointed a litigation friend, a person who wishes to act as such must file a certificate of suitability stating that that person satisfies the conditions specified in rule 16.9(2).

(2) The certificate of suitability must be filed at the time when the person who wishes to act as litigation friend first takes a step in the proceedings on behalf of the child.

(3) A court officer will send the certificate of suitability to every person on whom, in accordance with rule 6.28, the application form should be served.

(4) This rule does not apply to the Official Solicitor, an officer of the Service or a Welsh family proceedings officer.

16.11 Appointment of litigation friend by the court

(1) The court may, if the person to be appointed consents, make an order appointing as a litigation friend –

    (a)   the Official Solicitor;
    (b)   an officer of the Service or a Welsh family proceedings officer; or
    (c)   some other person.

(2) An order appointing a litigation friend may be made by the court of its own initiative or on the application of –

    (a)   a person who wishes to be a litigation friend; or
    (b)   a party to the proceedings.

(3) The court may at any time direct that a party make an application for an order under paragraph (2).

(4) An application for an order appointing a litigation friend must be supported by evidence.

(5) Unless the court directs otherwise, a person appointed under this rule to be a litigation friend for a child will be treated as a party for the purpose of any provision in these rules requiring a document to be served on, or sent to, or notice to be given to, a party to the proceedings.

(6) Subject to rule 16.9(3), the court may not appoint a litigation friend under this rule unless it is satisfied that the person to be appointed complies with the conditions specified in rule 16.9(2).

(7) This rule is without prejudice to rule 16.6.

16.12 Court's power to change litigation friend and to prevent person acting as litigation friend

(1) The court may –

    (a)   direct that a person may not act as a litigation friend;

(b)   terminate a litigation friend's appointment; or

(c)   appoint a new litigation friend in substitution for an existing one.

(2) An application for an order or direction under paragraph (1) must be supported by evidence.

(3) Subject to rule 16.9(3), the court may not appoint a litigation friend under this rule unless it is satisfied that the person to be appointed complies with the conditions specified in rule 16.9(2).

16.13   Appointment of litigation friend by court order – supplementary

(1) A copy of the application for an order under rule 16.11 or 16.12 must be sent by a court officer to every person on whom, in accordance with rule 6.28, the application form should be served.

(2) A copy of an application for an order under rule 16.12 must also be sent to –

(a)   the person who is the litigation friend, or who is purporting to act as the litigation friend when the application is made; and

(b)   the person, if not the applicant, who it is proposed should be the litigation friend.

16.14   Powers and duties of litigation friend

(1) The litigation friend –

(a)   has the powers and duties set out in Practice Direction 16A; and

(b)   must exercise those powers and duties in accordance with Practice Direction 16A.

(2) Where the litigation friend is an officer of the Service or a Welsh family proceedings officer, rule 16.20 applies as it applies to a children's guardian appointed in accordance with Chapter 6.

16.15   Procedure where appointment of litigation friend comes to an end

(1) When a child who is not a protected party reaches the age of 18, a litigation friend's appointment comes to an end.

(2) A court officer will send a notice to the other parties stating that the appointment of the child's litigation friend to act has ended.

Chapter 6
Children's Guardian Appointed under Rule 16.3

16.16   Application of this Chapter

This Chapter applies where the court must appoint a children's guardian in accordance with rule 16.3.

16.17   Who may be a children's guardian

Where the court is appointing a children's guardian under rule 16.3 it will appoint an officer of the Service or a Welsh family proceedings officer.

PART II – Statutory instruments

16.18 What the court or a court officer will do once the court has made a decision about appointing a children's guardian

(1) Where the court appoints a children's guardian under rule 16.3 a court officer will record the appointment and, as soon as practicable, will –

    (a)   inform the parties and either the Service or the Assembly; and

    (b)   unless it has already been sent, send the children's guardian a copy of the application and copies of any document filed with the court in the proceedings.

(2) A court officer has a continuing duty to send the children's guardian a copy of any other document filed with the court during the course of the proceedings.

16.19 Termination of the appointment of the children's guardian

(1) The appointment of a children's guardian under rule 16.3 continues for such time as is specified in the appointment or until terminated by the court.

(2) When terminating an appointment in accordance with paragraph (1), the court will give reasons for doing so, a note of which will be taken by the court or a court officer.

16.20 Powers and duties of the children's guardian

(1) The children's guardian is to act on behalf of the child upon the hearing of any application in proceedings to which this Chapter applies with the duty of safeguarding the interests of the child.

(2) The children's guardian must also provide the court with such other assistance as it may require.

(3) The children's guardian, when carrying out duties in relation to specified proceedings, other than placement proceedings, must have regard to the principle set out in section 1(2) and the matters set out in section 1(3)(a) to (f) of the 1989 Act as if for the word 'court' in that section there were substituted the words 'children's guardian'.

(4) The children's guardian, when carrying out duties in relation to proceedings to which Part 14 applies, must have regard to the principle set out in section 1(3) and the matters set out in section 1(4)(a) to (f) of the 2002 Act as if for the word 'court' in that section there were substituted the words 'children's guardian'.

(5) The children's guardian's duties must be exercised in accordance with Practice Direction 16A.

(6) A report to the court by the children's guardian is confidential.

16.21 Where the child instructs a solicitor or conducts proceedings on the child's own behalf

(1) Where it appears to the children's guardian that the child –

    (a)   is instructing a solicitor direct; or

(b)   intends to conduct and is capable of conducting the proceedings on that child's own behalf,

the children's guardian must inform the court of that fact.

(2) Where paragraph (1) applies the children's guardian –

(a)   must perform such additional duties as the court may direct;

(b)   must take such part in the proceedings as the court may direct; and

(c)   may, with the permission of the court, have legal representation in the conduct of those duties.

Chapter 7
Children's Guardian Appointed under Rule 16.4

16.22 Application of this Chapter

This Chapter applies where the court must appoint a children's guardian under rule 16.4.

16.23 Stage of proceedings at which a children's guardian becomes necessary

(1) This rule does not apply in relation to a child who is conducting proceedings without a children's guardian in accordance with rule 16.6.

(2) A person may not without the permission of the court take any step in proceedings except –

(a)   filing an application form; or

(b)   applying for the appointment of a children's guardian under rule 16.24,

until the child has a children's guardian.

(3) Any step taken before a child has a children's guardian has no effect unless the court orders otherwise.

16.24 Appointment of a children's guardian

(1) The court may make an order appointing as a children's guardian, an officer of the Service or a Welsh family proceedings officer or, if the person to be appointed consents –

(a)   a person other than the Official Solicitor; or

(b)   the Official Solicitor.

(2) An order appointing a children's guardian may be made by the court of its own initiative or on the application of –

(a)   a person who wishes to be a children's guardian; or

(b)   a party to the proceedings.

(3) The court may at any time direct that a party make an application for an order under paragraph (2).

PART II – Statutory instruments

(4) An application for an order appointing a children's guardian must be supported by evidence.

(5) The court may not appoint a children's guardian under this rule unless it is satisfied that that person –

> (a)   can fairly and competently conduct proceedings on behalf of the child;
> (b)   has no interest adverse to that of the child; and
> (c)   subject to paragraph (6), undertakes to pay any costs which the child may be ordered to pay in relation to the proceedings, subject to any right that person may have to be repaid from the assets of the child.

(6) Paragraph (5)(c) does not apply to the Official Solicitor, an officer of the Service or a Welsh family proceedings officer.

(7) This rule is without prejudice to rule 16.6 and rule 9.11.

> (Rule 9.11 provides for a child to be separately represented in certain applications for a financial remedy.)

16.25   Court's power to change children's guardian and to prevent person acting as children's guardian

(1) The court may –

> (a)   direct that a person may not act as a children's guardian;
> (b)   terminate the appointment of a children's guardian; or
> (c)   appoint a new children's guardian in substitution for an existing one.

(2) An application for an order or direction under paragraph (1) must be supported by evidence.

(3) Subject to rule 16.24(6), the court may not appoint a children's guardian under this rule unless it is satisfied that the person to be appointed complies with the conditions specified in rule 16.24(5).

16.26   Appointment of children's guardian by court order – supplementary

(1) A copy of the application for an order under rule 16.24 or 16.25 must be sent by a court officer to every person on whom, in accordance with rule 6.28, the application form should be served.

(2) A copy of an application for an order under rule 16.25 must also be sent to –

> (a)   the person who is the children's guardian, or who is purporting to act as the children's guardian when the application is made; and
> (b)   the person, if not the applicant, who it is proposed should be the children's guardian.

16.27   Powers and duties of children's guardian

(1) The children's guardian –

> (a)   has the powers and duties set out in Practice Direction 16A; and

(b)   must exercise those powers and duties in accordance with Practice Direction 16A.

(2) Where the children's guardian is an officer of the Service or a Welsh family proceedings officer, rule 16.20 applies to a children's guardian appointed in accordance with this Chapter as it applies to a children's guardian appointed in accordance with Chapter 6.

16.28 Procedure where appointment of children's guardian comes to an end

(1) When a child reaches the age of 18, the appointment of a children's guardian comes to an end.

(2) A court officer will send a notice to the other parties stating that the appointment of the child's children's guardian to act has ended.

Chapter 8
Duties of Solicitor Acting for the Child

16.29 Solicitor for child

(1) Subject to paragraphs (2) and (4), a solicitor appointed –

(a)   under section 41(3) of the 1989 Act; or
(b)   by the children's guardian in accordance with the Practice Direction 16A,

must represent the child in accordance with instructions received from the children's guardian.

(2) If a solicitor appointed as mentioned in paragraph (1) considers, having taken into account the matters referred to in paragraph (3), that the child –

(a)   wishes to give instructions which conflict with those of the children's guardian; and
(b)   is able, having regard to the child's understanding, to give such instructions on the child's own behalf,

the solicitor must conduct the proceedings in accordance with instructions received from the child.

(3) The matters the solicitor must take into account for the purposes of paragraph (2) are –

(a)   the views of the children's guardian; and
(b)   any direction given by the court to the children's guardian concerning the part to be taken by the children's guardian in the proceedings.

(4) Where –

(a)   no children's guardian has been appointed; and
(b)   the condition in section 41(4)(b) of the 1989 Act is satisfied,

a solicitor appointed under section 41(3) of the 1989 Act must represent the child in accordance with instructions received from the child.

(5) Where a solicitor appointed as mentioned in paragraph (1) receives no instructions under paragraphs (1), (2) or (4), the solicitor must represent the child in furtherance of the best interests of the child.

(6) A solicitor appointed under section 41(3) of the 1989 Act or by the children's guardian in accordance with Practice Direction 16A must serve documents, and accept service of documents, on behalf of the child in accordance with rule 6.31 and, where the child has not been served separately and has sufficient understanding, advise the child of the contents of any document so served.

(7) Where the child wishes an appointment of a solicitor –

   (a)   under section 41(3) of the 1989 Act; or

   (b)   by the children's guardian in accordance with the Practice Direction 16A,

to be terminated –

   (i)   the child may apply to the court for an order terminating the appointment; and

   (ii)   the solicitor and the children's guardian will be given an opportunity to make representations.

(8) Where the children's guardian wishes an appointment of a solicitor under section 41(3) of the 1989 Act to be terminated –

   (a)   the children's guardian may apply to the court for an order terminating the appointment; and

   (b)   the solicitor and, if of sufficient understanding, the child, will be given an opportunity to make representations.

(9) When terminating an appointment in accordance with paragraph (7) or (8), the court will give its reasons for so doing, a note of which will be taken by the court or a court officer.

(10) The court or a court officer will record the appointment under section 41(3) of the 1989 Act or the refusal to make the appointment.

Chapter 9
Reporting Officer

16.30 When the court appoints a reporting officer

In proceedings to which Part 14 applies, the court will appoint a reporting officer where –

   (a)   it appears that a parent or guardian of the child is willing to consent to the placing of the child for adoption, to the making of an adoption order or to a section 84 order; and

   (b)   that parent or guardian is in England or Wales.

16.31 Appointment of the same reporting officer in respect of two or more parents or guardians

The same person may be appointed as the reporting officer for two or more parents or guardians of the child.

16.32 The duties of the reporting officer

(1) The reporting officer must witness the signature by a parent or guardian on the document in which consent is given to –

    (a)   the placing of the child for adoption;

    (b)   the making of an adoption order; or

    (c)   the making of a section 84 order.

(2) The reporting officer must carry out such other duties as are set out in Practice Direction 16A.

(3) A report to the court by the reporting officer is confidential.

(4) The reporting officer's duties must be exercised in accordance with Practice Direction 16A.

Chapter 10
Children and Family Reporter and Welfare Officer

16.33 Request by court for a welfare report in respect of the child

(1) Where the court is considering an application for an order in proceedings, the court may ask –

    (a)   in proceedings to which Parts 12 and 14 apply, a children and family reporter; or

    (b)   in proceedings to which Part 12 applies, a welfare officer,

to prepare a report on matters relating to the welfare of the child, and, in this rule, the person preparing the report is called 'the officer'.

(2) It is the duty of the officer to –

    (a)   comply with any request for a report under this rule; and

    (b)   provide the court with such other assistance as it may require.

(3) A report to the court under this rule is confidential.

(4) The officer, when carrying out duties in relation to proceedings under the 1989 Act, must have regard to the principle set out in section 1(2) and the matters set out in section 1(3)(a) to (f) of that Act as if for the word 'court' in that section there were substituted the words 'children and family reporter' or 'welfare officer' as the case may be.

(5) A party may question the officer about oral or written advice tendered by that officer to the court.

PART II – Statutory instruments

(6) The court officer will notify the officer of a direction given at a hearing at which –

(a)   the officer is not present; and

(b)   the welfare report is considered.

(7) The officer's duties must be exercised in accordance with Practice Direction 16A

('children and family reporter' and 'welfare officer' are defined in rule 2.3)

****

Chapter 12
Supplementary Appointment Provisions

16.36 Persons who may not be appointed as children's guardian, reporting officer or children and family reporter

(1) In [specified proceedings (except where paragraph (2) applies),][1] adoption proceedings or proceedings for a section 84 order or a section 89 order, no person may be appointed as a children's guardian, reporting officer or children and family reporter who –

(a)   is a member, officer or servant of a local authority which is a party to the proceedings;

(b)   is, or has been, a member, officer or servant of a local authority or voluntary organisation who has been directly concerned in that capacity in arrangements relating to the care, accommodation or welfare of the child during the 5 years prior to the start of the proceedings; or

(c)   is a serving probation officer who has, in that capacity, been previously concerned with the child or the child's family.

(2) In placement proceedings, a person described in paragraph (1)(b) or (c) may not be appointed as a children's guardian, reporting officer or children and family reporter.

NOTES

Amendments.[1] Words inserted: SI 2012/679.

16.37 Appointment of the same person as children's guardian, reporting officer and children and family reporter

The same person may be appointed to act as one or more of the following –

(a)   the children's guardian;

(b)   the reporting officer; and

(c)   the children and family reporter.

Chapter 13
Officers of the Service, Welsh Family Proceedings Officers and Local Authority Officers: Further Duties

16.38 Officers of the Service, Welsh family proceedings officers and local authority officers acting under certain duties

(1) This rule applies when –

    (a)   an officer of the Service or a Welsh family proceedings officer is acting under a duty in accordance with –

        (i)   section 11E(7) of the 1989 Act (providing the court with information as to the making of [an][1] activity direction or [an][1] activity condition);

        (ii)   section 11G(2) of the 1989 Act (monitoring compliance with [an][1] activity direction or [an][1] activity condition);

        (iii)   section 11H(2) of the 1989 Act (monitoring compliance with a [child arrangements][1] order);

        (iv)   section 11L(5) of the 1989 Act (providing the court with information as to the making of an enforcement order);

        (v)   section 11M(1) of the 1989 Act (monitoring compliance with an enforcement order);

        (vi)   section 16(6) of the 1989 Act (providing a report to the court in accordance with a direction in a family assistance order); and

        (vii)   section 16A of the 1989 Act (making a risk assessment); and

    (b)   a local authority officer is acting under a duty in accordance with section 16(6) of the 1989 Act (providing a report to the court in accordance with a direction in a family assistance order).

(2) In this rule, –

    (a)   '...[1] activity direction', '...[1] activity condition' and 'enforcement order' have the meanings given in rule 12.2; and

    (b)   references to 'the officer' are to the officer of the Service, Welsh family proceedings officer or local authority officer referred to in paragraph (1).

(3) In exercising the duties referred to in paragraph (1), the officer must have regard to the principle set out in section 1(2) of the 1989 Act and the matters set out in section 1(3)(a) to (f) of the 1989 Act as if for the word 'court' in that section there were substituted the words 'officer of the Service, Welsh family proceedings officer or local authority officer'.

(4) The officer's duties referred to in paragraph (1) must be exercised in accordance with Practice Direction 16A.

NOTES

Amendments.[1] Words substituted and omitted: SI 2014/843.

PART II – Statutory instruments

Chapter 14
Enforcement Orders and Financial Compensation Orders: Persons Notified

16.39 Application for enforcement orders and financial compensation orders: duties of the person notified

(1) This rule applies where a person who was the child's children's guardian, litigation friend or legal representative in the proceedings in which a [child arrangements][1] order was made has been notified of an application for an enforcement order or for a financial compensation order as required by Practice Direction 12C.

(2) The person who has been notified of the application must –

    (a)   consider whether it is in the best interests of the child for the child to be made a party to the proceedings for an enforcement order or a financial compensation order (as applicable); and

    (b)   before the date fixed for the first hearing in the case notify the court, orally or in writing, of the opinion reached on the question, together with the reasons for this opinion.

(3) In this rule, 'enforcement order' and 'financial compensation order' have the meanings given in rule 12.2.

NOTES

Amendment.[1] Words substituted: SI 2014/843.

Practice Direction 16A –
Representation of Children

This Practice Direction supplements FPR Part 16

Part 1
General

Reference in title of proceedings

1.1 Where a litigation friend represents a child in family proceedings in accordance with rule 16.5 and Chapter 5 of Part 16, the child should be referred to in the title of the proceedings as 'A.B. (a child by C.D. his/her litigation friend).

1.2 Where a children's guardian represents a child in family proceedings in accordance with rule 16.4 and Chapter 7 of Part 16, the child should be referred to in the title as 'A.B. (a child by C.D. his/her children's guardian).

1.3 A child who is conducting proceedings on that child's own behalf should be referred to in the title as 'A.B. (a child).'

Part 2
Litigation Friend

Duties of the litigation friend

2.1 It is the duty of a litigation friend fairly and competently to conduct proceedings on behalf of the child. The litigation friend must have no interest in the proceedings adverse to that of the child and all steps and decisions the litigation friend takes in the proceedings must be taken for the benefit of the child.

2.2 ...[1]

NOTES

Amendment.[1] Paragraph omitted: FPR Update, October 2016.

Becoming a litigation friend without a court order

3.1 In order to become a litigation friend without a court order the person who wishes to act as litigation friend must file a certificate of suitability –

  (a) stating that the litigation friend consents to act;
  (b) stating that the litigation friend knows or believes that the [applicant] [respondent] is a child to whom rule 16.5 and Chapter 5 of Part 16 apply;
  (c) stating that the litigation friend can fairly and competently conduct proceedings on behalf of the child and has no interest adverse to that of the child;
  (d) undertaking to pay any costs which the child may be ordered to pay in relation to the proceedings, subject to any right the litigation friend may have to be repaid from the assets of the child; and
  (e) which the litigation friend has verified by a statement of truth.

3.2 Paragraph 3.1 does not apply to the Official Solicitor, an officer of the Service or a Welsh family proceedings officer.

3.3 The court officer will send the certificate of suitability to one of the child's parents or guardians or, if there is no parent or guardian, to the person with whom the child resides or in whose care the child is.

3.4 The litigation friend must file the certificate of suitability at a time when the litigation friend first takes a step in the proceedings on behalf of the child.

Application for a court order appointing a litigation friend

4.1 An application for a court order appointing a litigation friend should be made in accordance with Part 18 and must be supported by evidence.

4.2 The court officer must serve the application notice on the persons referred to in paragraph 3.3.

4.3 The evidence in support must satisfy the court that the proposed litigation friend –

  (a) consents to act;
  (b) can fairly and competently conduct proceedings on behalf of the child;
  (c) has no interest adverse to that of the child; and
  (d) undertakes to pay any costs which the child may be ordered to pay in relation to the proceedings, subject to any right the litigation friend may have to be repaid from the assets of the child.

4.4 Paragraph 4.3(d) does not apply to the Official Solicitor, an officer of the Service of a Welsh family proceedings officer.

PART II – Statutory instruments

4.5 The proposed litigation friend may be one of the persons referred to in paragraph 3.3 where appropriate, or otherwise may be the Official Solicitor, an officer of the Service or a Welsh family proceedings officer. Where it is sought to appoint the Official Solicitor, an officer of the Service or a Welsh family proceedings officer, provision should be made for payment of that person's charges.

Change of litigation friend and prevention of person acting as litigation friend.

5.1 Where an application is made for an order under rule 16.12, the application must set out the reasons for seeking it and the application must be supported by evidence.

5.2 Subject to paragraph 4.4, if the order sought is substitution of a new litigation friend for an existing one, the evidence must satisfy the court of the matters set out in paragraph 4.3.

5.3 The court officer will serve the application notice on –

(a)   the persons referred to in paragraph 3.3; and
(b)   the litigation friend or person purporting to act as litigation friend.

Part 3
Children's Guardian Appointed under Rule 16.3

How the children's guardian exercises duties – investigations and appointment of solicitor

6.1 The children's guardian must make such investigations as are necessary to carry out the children's guardian's duties and must, in particular –

(a)   contact or seek to interview such persons as the children's guardian thinks appropriate or as the court directs; and
(b)   obtain such professional assistance as is available which the children's guardian thinks appropriate or which the court directs be obtained.

6.2 The children's guardian must –

(a)   appoint a solicitor for the child unless a solicitor has already been appointed;
(b)   give such advice to the child as is appropriate having regard to that child's understanding; and
(c)   where appropriate instruct the solicitor representing the child on all matters relevant to the interests of the child arising in the course of proceedings, including possibilities for appeal.

6.3 Where the children's guardian is authorised in the terms mentioned by and in accordance with section 15(1) of the Criminal Justice and Court Services Act 2000 or section 37(1) of the Children Act 2004 (right of officer of the Service or Welsh family proceedings officer to conduct litigation or exercise a right of audience), paragraph 6.2(a) will not apply if the children's guardian intends to have conduct of the proceedings on behalf of the child unless –

(a) the child wishes to instruct a solicitor direct; and

(b) the children's guardian or the court considers that the child is of sufficient understanding to do so.

6.4 Where rule 16.21 (Where the child instructs a solicitor or conducts proceedings on the child's own behalf) applies, the duties set out in paragraph 6.2(a) and (c) do not apply.

How the children's guardian exercises duties – attendance at court, advice to the court and reports

6.5 The children's guardian or the solicitor appointed under section 41(3) of the 1989 Act or in accordance with paragraph 6.2(a) must attend all directions hearings unless the court directs otherwise.

6.6 The children's guardian must advise the court on the following matters –

(a) whether the child is of sufficient understanding for any purpose including the child's refusal to submit to a medical or psychiatric examination or other assessment that the court has the power to require, direct or order;

(b) the wishes of the child in respect of any matter relevant to the proceedings including that child's attendance at court;

(c) the appropriate forum for the proceedings;

(d) the appropriate timing of the proceedings or any part of them;

(e) the options available to it in respect of the child and the suitability of each such option including what order should be made in determining the application; and

(f) any other matter on which the court seeks advice or on which the children's guardian considers that the court should be informed.

6.7 The advice given under paragraph 6.6 may, subject to any direction of the court, be given orally or in writing. If the advice is given orally, a note of it must be taken by the court or the court officer.

6.8 The children's guardian must –

(a) unless the court directs otherwise, file a written report advising on the interests of the child in accordance with the timetable set by the court; and

(b) in proceedings to which Part 14 applies, where practicable, notify any person the joining of whom as a party to those proceedings would be likely, in the opinion of the children's guardian, to safeguard the interests of the child, of the court's power to join that person as a party under rule 14.3 and must inform the court –

(i) of any notification;

(ii) of anyone whom the children's guardian attempted to notify under this paragraph but was unable to contact; and

(iii) of anyone whom the children's guardian believes may wish to be joined to the proceedings.

(Part 18 sets out the procedure for making an application to be joined as a party in proceedings.)

PART II – Statutory instruments

How the children's guardian exercises duties – service of documents and inspection of records

6.9 The children's guardian must serve and accept service of documents on behalf of the child in accordance with rule 6.31 and, where the child has not himself been served and has sufficient understanding, advise the child of the contents of any document so served.

6.10 Where the children's guardian inspects records of the kinds referred to in –

(a)   section 42 of the 1989 Act (right to have access to local authority records); or

(b)   section 103 of the 2002 Act (right to have access to adoption agency records)

the children's guardian must bring all records and documents which may, in the opinion of the children's guardian, assist in the proper determination of the proceedings to the attention of –

(i)   the court; and

(ii)   unless the court directs otherwise, the other parties to the proceedings.

How the children's guardian exercises duties – communication of a court's decision to the child

6.11 The children's guardian must ensure that, in relation to a decision made by the court in the proceedings –

(a)   if the children's guardian considers it appropriate to the age and understanding of the child, the child is notified of that decision; and

(b)   if the child is notified of the decision, it is explained to the child in a manner appropriate to that child's age and understanding.

Part 4
Appointment of Children's Guardian under Rule 16.4

Section 1 – When a child should be made a party to proceedings

7.1 Making the child a party to the proceedings is a step that will be taken only in cases which involve an issue of significant difficulty and consequently will occur in only a minority of cases. Before taking the decision to make the child a party, consideration should be given to whether an alternative route might be preferable, such as asking an officer of the Service or a Welsh family proceedings officer to carry out further work or by making a referral to social services or, possibly, by obtaining expert evidence.

7.2 The decision to make the child a party will always be exclusively that of the court, made in the light of the facts and circumstances of the particular case. The following are offered, solely by way of guidance, as circumstances which may justify the making of such an order –

(a) where an officer of the Service or Welsh family proceedings officer has notified the court that in the opinion of that officer the child should be made a party;

(b) where the child has a standpoint or interest which is inconsistent with or incapable of being represented by any of the adult parties;

(c) where there is an intractable dispute over residence or contact, including where all contact has ceased, or where there is irrational but implacable hostility to contact or where the child may be suffering harm associated with the contact dispute;

(d) where the views and wishes of the child cannot be adequately met by a report to the court;

(e) where an older child is opposing a proposed course of action;

(f) where there are complex medical or mental health issues to be determined or there are other unusually complex issues that necessitate separate representation of the child;

(g) where there are international complications outside child abduction, in particular where it may be necessary for there to be discussions with overseas authorities or a foreign court;

(h) where there are serious allegations of physical, sexual or other abuse in relation to the child or there are allegations of domestic violence not capable of being resolved with the help of an officer of the Service or Welsh family proceedings officer;

(i) where the proceedings concern more than one child and the welfare of the children is in conflict or one child is in a particularly disadvantaged position;

(j) where there is a contested issue about scientific testing.

7.3 It must be recognised that separate representation of the child may result in a delay in the resolution of the proceedings. When deciding whether to direct that a child be made a party, the court will take into account the risk of delay or other facts adverse to the welfare of the child. The court's primary consideration will be the best interests of the child.

7.4 When a child is made a party and a children's guardian is to be appointed –

(a) consideration should first be given to appointing an officer of the Service or Welsh family proceedings officer. Before appointing an officer, the court will cause preliminary enquiries to be made of Cafcass or CAFCASS Cymru. For the relevant procedure, reference should be made to the practice note issued by Cafcass in June 2006 and any modifications of that practice note.

(b) If Cafcass or CAFCASS Cymru is unable to provide a children's guardian without delay, or if for some other reason the appointment of an officer of the Service of Welsh family proceedings officer is not appropriate, rule 16.24 makes further provision for the appointment of a children's guardian.

7.5 ...[1]

NOTES

Amendment.[1] Text omitted: FPR Update, April 2014.

PART II – Statutory instruments

Section 2 – Children's guardian appointed under rule 16.4

DUTIES OF THE CHILDREN'S GUARDIAN

7.6 It is the duty of a children's guardian fairly and competently to conduct proceedings on behalf of the child. The children's guardian must have no interest in the proceedings adverse to that of the child and all steps and decisions the children's guardian takes in the proceedings must be taken for the benefit of the child.

7.7 A children's guardian who is an officer of the Service or a Welsh family proceedings officer has, in addition, the duties set out in Part 3 of this Practice Direction and must exercise those duties as set out in that Part.

BECOMING A CHILDREN'S GUARDIAN WITHOUT A COURT ORDER

7.8 In order to become a children's guardian without a court order the person who wishes to act as children's guardian must file a certificate of suitability –

   (a)   stating that the children's guardian consents to act;
   (b)   stating that the children's guardian knows or believes that the [applicant] [respondent] is a child to whom rule 16.4 and Chapter 7 of Part 16 apply;
   (c)   stating that the children's guardian can fairly and competently conduct proceedings on behalf of the child and has no interest adverse to that of the child;
   (d)   undertaking to pay any costs which the child may be ordered to pay in relation to the proceedings, subject to any right the children's guardian may have to be repaid from the assets of the child; and
   (e)   which the children's guardian has verified by a statement of truth.

7.9 Paragraph 7.8 does not apply to the Official Solicitor, an officer of the Service or a Welsh family proceedings officer.

7.10 The court officer will send the certificate of suitability to one of the child's parents or guardians or, if there is no parent or guardian, to the person with whom the child resides or in whose care the child is.

7.11 The children's guardian must file either the certificate of suitability at a time when the children's guardian first takes a step in the proceedings on behalf of the child.

APPLICATION FOR A COURT ORDER APPOINTING A CHILDREN'S GUARDIAN

7.12 An application for a court order appointing a children's guardian should be made in accordance with Part 18 and must be supported by evidence.

7.13 The court officer must serve the application notice on the persons referred to in paragraph 7.10.

7.14 The evidence in support must satisfy the court that the proposed children's guardian –

   (a)   consents to act;

(b)   can fairly and competently conduct proceedings on behalf of the child;

(c)   has no interest adverse to that of the child; and

(d)   undertakes to pay any costs which the child may be ordered to pay in relation to the proceedings, subject to any right the children's guardian may have to be repaid from the assets of the child.

7.15 Paragraph 7.14 does not apply to the Official Solicitor, an officer of the Service of a Welsh family proceedings officer.

7.16 The proposed children's guardian may be one of the persons referred to in paragraph 7.10 where appropriate, or otherwise may be the Official Solicitor, an officer of the Service or a Welsh family proceedings officer. Where it is sought to appoint the Official Solicitor, an officer of the Service or a Welsh family proceedings officer, provision should be made for payment of that person's charges.

CHANGE OF CHILDREN'S GUARDIAN AND PREVENTION OF PERSON ACTING AS CHILDREN'S GUARDIAN.

7.17 Where an application is made for an order under rule 16.25, the application must set out the reasons for seeking it and must be supported by evidence.

7.18 Subject to paragraph 7.15, if the order sought is substitution of a new children's guardian for an existing one, the evidence must satisfy the court of the matters set out in paragraph 7.14.

7.19 The court officer will serve the application notice on –

(a)   the persons referred to in paragraph 7.10; and

(b)   the children's guardian or person purporting to act as children's guardian.

Part 5
Reporting Officer

How the reporting officer exercises duties

8.1 The reporting officer must –

(a)   ensure so far as reasonably practicable that the parent or guardian is –

   (i)   giving consent unconditionally to the placing of the child for adoption or to the making of an adoption order (as defined in section 46 of the Adoption and Children Act 2002) or a section 84 order; and

   (ii)   with full understanding of what is involved;

(b)   investigate all the circumstances relevant to a parent's or guardian's consent; and

(c)   on completing the investigations the reporting officer must –

   (i)   make a report in writing to the court in accordance with the timetable set by the court, drawing attention to any matters which, in the opinion of the reporting officer, may be of assistance to the court in considering the application; or

(ii)   make an interim report to the court if a parent or guardian of the child is unwilling to consent to the placing of the child for adoption or to the making of an adoption order or section 84 order.

8.2 On receipt of an interim report under paragraph 8.1(1)(c)(ii) a court officer must inform the applicant that a parent or guardian of the child is unwilling to consent to the placing of the child for adoption or to the making of an adoption order or section 84 order.

8.3 The reporting officer may at any time before the final hearing make an interim report to the court if the reporting officer considers it necessary and ask the court for directions.

8.4 The reporting officer must attend hearings as directed by the court.

Part 6
Children and Family Reporter and Welfare Officer

How the children and family reporter or welfare officer exercises powers and duties

9.1 In this Part, the person preparing the welfare report in accordance with rule 16.33 is called 'the officer'.

9.2 The officer must make such investigations as may be necessary to perform the officer's powers and duties and must, in particular –

(a)   contact or seek to interview such persons as appear appropriate or as the court directs; and

(b)   obtain such professional assistance as is available which the children and family reporter thinks appropriate or which the court directs be obtained.

9.3 The officer must –

(a)   notify the child of such contents of the report (if any) as the officer considers appropriate to the age and understanding of the child, including any reference to the child's own views on the application and the recommendation; and

(b)   if the child is notified of any contents of the report, explain them to the child in a manner appropriate to the child's age and understanding.

9.4 The officer must –

(a)   attend hearings as directed by the court;

(b)   advise the court of the child's wishes and feelings;

(c)   advise the court if the officer considers that the joining of a person as a party to the proceedings would be likely to safeguard the interests of the child;

(d)   consider whether it is in the best interests of the child for the child to be made a party to the proceedings, and if so, notify the court of that opinion together with the reasons for that opinion; and

(e)   where the court has directed that a written report be made –

     (i)   file the report; and

     (ii)   serve a copy on the other parties and on any children's guardian,

in accordance with the timetable set by the court.

Part 7
Parental Order Reporter

How the parental order reporter exercises duties – investigations and reports

10.1 The parental order reporter must make such investigations as are necessary to carry out the parental order reporter's duties and must, in particular –

   (a)   contact or seek to interview such persons as the parental order reporter thinks appropriate or as the court directs; and

   (b)   obtain such professional assistance as is available which the parental order reporter thinks appropriate or which the court directs be obtained.

How the parental order reporter exercises duties – attendance at court, advice to the court and reports

10.2 The parental order reporter must attend all directions hearings unless the court directs otherwise.

10.3 The parental order reporter must advise the court on the following matters –

   (a)   the appropriate forum for the proceedings;

   (b)   the appropriate timing of the proceedings or any part of them;

   (c)   the options available to it in respect of the child and the suitability of each such option including what order should be made in determining the application; and

   (d)   any other matter on which the court seeks advice or on which the parental order reporter considers that the court should be informed.

10.4 The advice given under paragraph 10.3 may, subject to any direction of the court, be given orally or in writing. If the advice is given orally, a note of it must be taken by the court or the court officer.

10.5 The parental order reporter must –

   (a)   unless the court directs otherwise, file a written report advising on the interests of the child in accordance with the timetable set by the court; and

   (b)   where practicable, notify any person the joining of whom as a party to those proceedings would be likely, in the opinion of the parental order reporter, to safeguard the interests of the child, of the court's power to join that person as a party under rule 13.3 and must inform the court –

     (i)   of any notification;

     (ii)   of anyone whom the parental order reporter attempted to notify under this paragraph but was unable to contact; and

     (iii) of anyone whom the parental order reporter believes may wish to be joined to the proceedings.

(Part 18 sets out the procedure for making an application to be joined as a party in proceedings.)

Part 8
Officers of the Service, Welsh Family Proceedings Officers and Local Authority Officers: Further Duties

How officers of the Service, Welsh family proceedings officers and local authority officers exercise certain further duties

11.1 This Part applies when an officer of the Service, a Welsh family proceedings officer or a local authority officer is acting under a duty referred to in rule 16.38(1). In this Part, the person acting under a duty referred to in rule 16.38(1) is referred to as 'the officer'.

11.2 The officer must make such investigations as may be necessary to perform the officer's duties and must, in particular –

- (a)   contact or seek to interview such persons as the officer thinks appropriate or as the court directs; and
- (b)   obtain such professional assistance as the officer thinks appropriate or which the court directs.

11.3 The officer must –

- (a)   notify the child of such (if any) of the contents of any report or risk assessment as the officer considers appropriate to the age and understanding of the child;
- (b)   if the child is notified of any contents of a report or risk assessment, explain them to the child in a manner appropriate to the child's age and understanding;
- (c)   consider whether to recommend in any report or risk assessment that the court lists a hearing for the purposes of considering the report or risk assessment;
- (d)   consider whether it is in the best interests of the child for the child to be made a party to the proceedings, and, if so, notify the court of that opinion together with the reasons for that opinion.

11.4 When making a risk assessment, the officer must, if of the opinion that the court should exercise its discretion under rule 12.34(2), state in the risk assessment –

- (a)   the way in which the officer considers the court should exercise its discretion (including the officer's view on the length of any suggested delay in service); and
- (b)   the officer's reasons for that reaching that view.

11.5 The officer must file any report or risk assessment with the court –

- (a)   at or by the time directed by the court;
- (b)   in the absence of any direction, at least 14 days before a relevant hearing; or

(c) where there has been no direction from the court and there is no relevant hearing listed, as soon as possible following the completion of the report or risk assessment.

11.6 In paragraph 11.5, a hearing is relevant if the court officer has given the officer notice that a report prepared by the officer is to be considered at it.

11.7 A copy of any report prepared as a result of acting under a duty referred to in rule 16.38(1)(a)(i) to (vi) or (b) (but not any risk assessment) must, as soon as practicable, be served by the officer on the parties.

(Rule 12.34 makes provision for the service of risk assessments.)

****

PART 18
PROCEDURE FOR OTHER APPLICATIONS IN PROCEEDINGS

18.1 Types of application for which Part 18 procedure may be followed

(1) The Part 18 procedure is the procedure set out in this Part.

(2) An applicant may use the Part 18 procedure if the application is made –

(a) in the course of existing proceedings;
(b) to start proceedings except where some other Part of these rules prescribes the procedure to start proceedings; or
(c) in connection with proceedings which have been concluded.

(3) Paragraph (2) does not apply –

(a) to applications where any other rule in any other Part of these rules sets out the procedure for that type of application;
(b) if a practice direction provides that the Part 18 procedure may not be used in relation to the type of application in question.

[(4) This Part is subject to any provision made by or pursuant to Part 41 (proceeding by electronic means).][1]

NOTES

Amendment.[1] Paragraph inserted: SI 2020/135.

18.2 Applications for permission to start proceedings

An application for permission to start proceedings must be made to the court where the proceedings will be started if permission is granted.

[(Rule 5.4 makes general provision in relation to the court in which proceedings should be started.)][1]

NOTES

Amendment.[1] Words inserted: SI 2013/3204.

18.3 Respondents to applications under this Part

The following persons are to be respondents to an application under this Part –

(a)   where there are existing proceedings or the proceedings have been concluded –
   (i)   the parties to those proceedings; and
   (ii) if the proceedings are proceedings under Part 11, the person who is the subject of those proceedings;

(b)   where there are no existing proceedings –
   (i)   if notice has been given under section 44 of the 2002 Act (notice of intention to adopt or apply for an order under section 84 of that Act), the local authority to whom notice has been given; and
   (ii) if an application is made for permission to apply for an order in proceedings, any person who will be a party to the proceedings brought if permission is granted; and

(c)   any other person as the court may direct.

18.4 Application notice to be filed

(1) Subject to paragraph (2) the applicant must file an application notice.

(2) An applicant may make an application without filing an application notice if –

(a)   this is permitted by a rule or practice direction; or
(b)   the court dispenses with the requirement for an application notice.

18.5 Notice of an application

(1) Subject to paragraph (2), a copy of the application notice must be served on –

(a)   each respondent;
(b)   in relation to proceedings under Part 11, the person who is, or, in the case of an application to start proceedings, it is intended will be, the subject of the proceedings; and
(c)   in relation to proceedings under Parts 12 and 14, the children's guardian (if any).

(2) An application may be made without serving a copy of the application notice if this is permitted by –

(a)   a rule;
(b)   a practice direction; or
(c)   the court.

(Rule 18.8 deals with service of a copy of the application notice.)

18.6 Time when an application is made

When an application must be made within a specified time, it is so made if the court receives the application notice within that time.

18.7 What an application notice must include

(1) An application notice must state –

    (a)   what order the applicant is seeking; and

    (b)   briefly, why the applicant is seeking the order.

(2) A draft of the order sought must be attached to the application notice.

    (Part 17 requires an application notice to be verified by a statement of truth if the applicant wishes to rely on matters set out in his application as evidence.)

18.8 Service of a copy of an application notice

(1) Subject to rule 2.4, a copy of the application notice must be served in accordance with the provisions of Part 6 –

    (a)   as soon as practicable after it is filed; and

    (b)   in any event –

        (i)   where the application is for an …[1] order under rule 9.7 at least 14 days; and

        (ii)   in any other case, at least 7 days;

    before the court is to deal with the application.

(2) The applicant must, when filing the application notice, file a copy of any written evidence in support.

(3) If a copy of an application notice is served by a court officer it must be accompanied by –

    (a)   a notice of the date and place where the application will be heard;

    (b)   a copy of any witness statement in support; and

    (c)   a copy of the draft order which the applicant has attached to the application.

(4) If –

    (a)   an application notice is served; but

    (b)   the period of notice is shorter than the period required by these rules or a practice direction,

the court may direct that, in the circumstances of the case, sufficient notice has been given and hear the application.

(5) This rule does not require written evidence –

    (a)   to be filed if it has already been filed; or

    (b)   to be served on a party on whom it has already been served.

18.9 Applications which may be dealt with without a hearing

(1) The court may deal with an application without a hearing if –

    (a)   the court does not consider that a hearing would be appropriate; or

    (b)   the parties agree as to the terms of the order sought or the parties agree that the court should dispose of the application without a hearing and the court does not consider that a hearing would be appropriate.

(2) Where –

    (a)   an application is made for permission to make an application in proceedings under the 1989 Act; and

    (b)   the court refuses the application without a hearing in accordance with paragraph (1)(a),

the court must, at the request of the applicant, re-list the application and fix a date for a hearing.

(3) …[1]

18.10 Service of application notice following court order where application made without notice

(1) This rule applies where the court has disposed of an application which it permitted to be made without service of a copy of the application notice.

(2) Where the court makes an order, whether granting or dismissing the application, a copy of the application notice and any evidence in support must unless the court orders otherwise, be served with the order on –

    (a)   all the parties in proceedings; and

    (b)   in relation to proceedings under Part 11, the person who is, or, in the case of an application to start proceedings, it is intended will be, the subject of the proceedings.

(3) The order must contain a statement of the right to make an application to set aside[(GL)] or vary the order under rule 18.11.

18.11 Application to set aside or vary order made without notice

(1) A person who was not served with a copy of the application notice before an order was made under rule 18.10 may apply to have the order set aside[(GL)] or varied.

(2) An application under this rule must be made within 7 days beginning with the date on which the order was served on the person making the application.

18.12 Power of the court to proceed in the absence of a party

(1) Where the applicant or any respondent fails to attend the hearing of an application, the court may proceed in the absence of that person.

(2) Where –

(a) the applicant or any respondent fails to attend the hearing of an application; and

(b) the court makes an order at the hearing,

the court may, on application or of its own initiative, re-list the application.

(3) …[1]

NOTES

Amendment.[1] Paragraph omitted: SI 2013/3204.

18.13 Dismissal of totally without merit applications

If the …[1] court dismisses an application (including an application for permission to appeal) and it considers that the application is totally without merit –

(a) the court's order must record that fact; and

(b) the court must at the same time consider whether it is appropriate to make a civil restraint order.

NOTES

Amendment.[1] Words omitted: SI 2013/3204.

Practice Direction 18A –
Other Applications in Proceedings

This Practice Direction supplements FPR Part 18

Application of Part 18

1.1 Part 18 makes general provision for a procedure for making applications. All applications for the court's permission should be made under this Part, with the exception of applications for permission for which specific provision is made in other Parts of the FPR, in which case the application should be made under the specific provision. Examples of where specific provision has been made in another Part of the FPR for applications for permission are rule 11.3 (Permission to apply for a forced marriage protection order) and rule 30.3 (Permission to appeal).

****

Additional requirements in relation to application notices

3.1 In addition to the requirements set out in rule 18.7, the following requirements apply to the applications to which the respective paragraph refers.

3.2 An application notice must be signed and include –

    (a)   the title of the case (if available);

    (b)   the reference number of the case (if available);

    (c)   the full name of the applicant;

    (d)   where the applicant is not already a party, the applicant's address for service, including a postcode. Postcode information may be obtained from www.royalmail.com or the Royal Mail Address Management Guide; and

    (e)   either a request for a hearing or a request that the application be dealt with without a hearing.

3.3 An application notice relating to an application under section 42(6) of the Adoption and Children Act 2002 (permission to apply for an adoption order) must include –

    (a)   the child's name, sex, date of birth and nationality;

    (b)   in relation to each of the child's parents or guardians, their name, address and nationality;

    (c)   the length of time that the child has had his or her home with the applicant;

    (d)   the reason why the child has had his or her home with the applicant;

    (e)   details of any local authority or adoption agency involved in placing the child in the applicant's home; and

    (f)   if there are or have been other court proceedings relating to the child, the nature of those proceedings, the name of the court in which they are being or have been dealt with, the date and type of any order made and, if the proceedings are still ongoing, the date of the next hearing.

3.4 An application notice relating to an application in the High Court by a local authority for permission under section 100(3) of the Children Act 1989 must include a draft of the application form.

3.5 Where permission is required to take any step under the Children Act 1989 (for example an application to be joined as a party to the proceedings) the application notice must include a draft of the application for the making of which permission is sought together with sufficient copies for one to be served on each respondent.

3.6 In an application for permission to bring proceedings under Schedule 1 of the Children Act 1989, the draft application for the making of which permission is sought must be accompanied by a statement setting out the financial details which the person seeking permission believes to be relevant to the request and contain a declaration that it is true to the maker's best knowledge and belief, together with sufficient copies for one to be served on each respondent.

3.7 The provisions in Schedule 1 which require an application for permission to bring proceedings are –

    (a)   paragraph 7(2) – permission is required to make an application for variation of a secured periodical payments order after the death of the parent liable to make the payments if a period of 6 months has passed from the date on which representation in regard to that parent's estate is first taken out; and

(b)   paragraph 11(3) – permission is required to make an application to alter a maintenance agreement following the death of one of the parties if a period of 6 months has passed beginning with the day on which representation in regard to the estate of the deceased is first taken out.

Other provisions in relation to application notices

4.1 On receipt of an application notice containing a request for a hearing, unless the court considers that the application is suitable for consideration without a hearing, the court officer will, if serving a copy of the application notice, notify the applicant of the time and date fixed for the hearing of the application.

4.2 On receipt of an application notice containing a request that the application be dealt with without a hearing, the court will decide whether the application is suitable for consideration without a hearing.

4.3 Where the court –

(a)   considers that the application is suitable for consideration without a hearing; but
(b)   is not satisfied that it has sufficient material to decide the application immediately,

it may give directions for the filing of evidence and will inform the applicant and the respondent(s) of its decision. (Rule 18.11 enables a party to apply for an order made without notice to be set aside or varied.)

4.4 Where the court does not consider that the application is suitable for consideration without a hearing –

(a)   it may give directions as to the filing of evidence; and
(b)   the court officer will notify the applicant and the respondent of the time, date and place for the hearing of the application and any directions given.

4.5 …[1]

4.6 Every application should be made as soon as it becomes apparent that it is necessary or desirable to make it.

4.7 Applications should, wherever possible, be made so that they are considered at any directions hearing or other hearing for which a date has been fixed or for which a date is about to be fixed.

4.8 The parties must anticipate that at any hearing (including any directions hearing) the court may wish to review the conduct of the case as a whole and give any necessary directions. They should be ready to assist the court in doing so and to answer questions the court may ask for this purpose.

4.9 Where a date for a hearing has been fixed, a party who wishes to make an application at that hearing but does not have sufficient time to file an application notice should as soon as possible inform the court (if possible in writing) and, if possible, the other parties of the nature of the application and the reason for it. That party should then make the application orally at the hearing.

NOTES

Amendment.[1] Text omitted: FPR Update, April 2014.

Applications without service of application notice

5.1 An application may be made without service of an application notice only –

    (a)   where there is exceptional urgency;
    (b)   where the overriding objective is best furthered by doing so;
    (c)   by consent of all parties;
    (d)   with the permission of the court;
    (e)   where paragraph 4.9 applies; or
    (f)   where a court order, rule or practice direction permits.

Giving notice of an application

6.1 Unless the court otherwise directs or paragraph 5.1 of this practice direction applies, the application notice must be served as soon as practicable after it has been issued and, if there is to be a hearing, at least 7 days before the hearing date.

6.2 Where an application notice should be served but there is not sufficient time to do so, informal notification of the application should be given unless the circumstances of the application require no notice of the application to be given.

Pre-action applications

7.1 All applications made before proceedings are commenced should be made under this Part.

Telephone hearings

8.1 The court may direct that an application be dealt with by a telephone hearing.

8.2 The applicant should, if seeking a direction under paragraph 8.1, indicate this on the application notice. Where the applicant has not indicated such an intention but nevertheless wishes to seek a direction the request should be made as early as possible.

8.3 A direction under paragraph 8.1 will not normally be made unless every party entitled to be given notice of the application and to be heard at the hearing has consented to the direction.

8.4 No representative of a party to an application being heard by telephone may attend the court in person while the application is being heard unless the other party to the application has agreed that the representative may do so.

8.5 If an application is to be heard by telephone the following directions will apply, subject to any direction to the contrary –

    (a)   the applicant's legal representative is responsible for arranging the telephone conference for precisely the time fixed by the court. The telecommunications provider used must be one of the approved panel of service providers (see HMCS website at www.hmcourts-service.gov. uk);

(b) the applicant's legal representative must tell the operator the telephone numbers of all those participating in the conference call and the sequence in which they are to be called;

(c) it is the responsibility of the applicant's legal representative to ascertain from all the other parties whether they have instructed counsel and, if so the identity of counsel, and whether the legal representative and counsel will be on the same or different telephone numbers;

(d) the sequence in which those involved are to be called will be –

  (i) the applicant's legal representative and (if on a different number) his counsel;

  (ii) the legal representative (and counsel) for all other parties; and

  (iii) the judge or justices, as the case may be;

(e) each speaker is to remain on the line after being called by the operator setting up the conference call. The call may be 2 or 3 minutes before the time fixed for the application;

(f) when the judge has ...[1] been connected the applicant's legal representative (or counsel) will introduce the parties in the usual way;

(g) if the use of a 'speakerphone' by any party causes the court or any other party any difficulty in hearing what is said the judge ...[1] may require that party to use a hand held telephone;

(h) the telephone charges debited to the account of the party initiating the conference call will be treated as part of the costs of the application.

NOTES

Amendments.[1] Text omitted: FPR Update, April 2014.

Video conferencing

9.1 Where the parties to a matter wish to use video conferencing facilities, and those facilities are available in the relevant court, the parties should apply to the court for directions. (Practice Direction 22A provides guidance on the use of video conferencing)

Note of proceedings

10.1 The court or court officer should keep, either by way of a note or a tape recording, brief details of all proceedings before the court, including the dates of the proceedings and a short statement of the decision taken at each hearing.

Evidence

11.1 The requirement for evidence in certain types of applications is set out in some of the rules in the FPR and practice directions. Where there is no specific requirement to provide evidence it should be borne in mind that, as a practical matter, the court will often need to be satisfied by evidence of the facts that are relied on in support of or for opposing the application.

PART II – Statutory instruments

11.2 The court may give directions for the filing of evidence in support of or opposing a particular application. The court may also give directions for the filing of evidence in relation to any hearing that it fixes on its own initiative. The directions may specify the form that evidence is to take and when it is to be served.

11.3 Where it is intended to rely on evidence which is not contained in the application itself, the evidence, if it has not already been served, should be served with the application.

11.4 Where a respondent to an application wishes to rely on evidence, that evidence must be filed in accordance with any directions the court may have given and a court officer will serve the evidence on the other parties, unless the court directs otherwise.

11.5 If it is necessary for the applicant to serve any evidence in reply the court officer will serve it on the other parties unless the court directs otherwise.

11.6 Evidence must be filed with the court as well as served on the parties.

11.7 The contents of an application notice may be used as evidence provided the contents have been verified by a statement of truth.

Consent orders

12.1 The parties to an application for a consent order must ensure that they provide the court with any material it needs to be satisfied that it is appropriate to make the order. Subject to any rule in the FPR or practice direction a letter will generally be acceptable for this purpose.

12.2 Where a judgment or order has been agreed in respect of an application where a hearing date has been fixed, the parties must inform the court immediately.

Other applications considered without a hearing

13.1 Where rule 18.9(1)(b) applies the court will treat the application as if it were proposing to make an order on its own initiative.

13.2 Where the parties agree that the court should dispose of the application without a hearing they should so inform the court in writing and each should confirm that all evidence and other material on which he or she relies has been disclosed to the other parties to the application.

Miscellaneous

14.1 If the case is proceeding in the High Court and the draft order is unusually long or complex it should also be supplied in electronic form on such storage medium as shall be agreed with the judge or court staff, for use by the court office.

14.2 Where rule 18.12 applies the power to re-list the application in rule 18.12(2) is in addition to any other powers of the court with regard to the order (for example to set aside, vary, discharge or suspend the order).

Costs

15.1 Attention is drawn to the CPR costs practice direction and, in particular, to the court's power to make a summary assessment of costs.

15.2 Attention is also drawn to rule 44.13(1) of the CPR which provides that if an order makes no mention of costs, none are payable in respect of the proceedings to which it relates.

PART 19
ALTERNATIVE PROCEDURE FOR APPLICATIONS

19.1 Types of application for which Part 19 procedure may be followed

(1) The Part 19 procedure is the procedure set out in this Part.

(2) An applicant may use the Part 19 procedure where the Part 18 procedure does not apply and –

  (a)   there is no form prescribed by a rule or referred to in Practice Direction 5A in which to make the application;
  (b)   the applicant seeks the court's decision on a question which is unlikely to involve a substantial dispute of fact; or
  (c)   paragraph (5) applies.

[(2A) This Part is subject to any provision made by or pursuant to Part 41 (proceeding by electronic means).][1]

(3) The court may at any stage direct that the application is to continue as if the applicant had not used the Part 19 procedure and, if it does so, the court may give any directions it considers appropriate.

(4) Paragraph (2) does not apply if a practice direction provides that the Part 19 procedure may not be used in relation to the type of application in question.

(5) A rule or practice direction may, in relation to a specified type of proceedings –

  (a)   require or permit the use of the Part 19 procedure; and
  (b)   disapply or modify any of the rules set out in this Part as they apply to those proceedings.

NOTES

Amendments.[1] Paragraph inserted: SI 2020/135.

19.2 Applications for which the Part 19 procedure must be followed

(1) The Part 19 procedure must be used in an application made in accordance with –

  (a)   section 60(3) of the 2002 Act (order to prevent disclosure of information to an adopted person);
  (b)   section 79(4) of the 2002 Act (order for Registrar General to give any information referred to in section 79(3) of the 2002 Act); and

> (c)   rule 14.21 (directions ...[1] regarding fathers without parental responsibility).

(2) The respondent to an application made in accordance with paragraph (1)(b) is the Registrar General.

NOTES

Amendment.[1] Words repealed: SI 2020/135.

19.3 Contents of the application

Where the applicant uses the Part 19 procedure, the application must state –

- (a)   that this Part applies;
- (b)   either –
  - (i)   the question which the applicant wants the court to decide; or
  - (ii)   the order which the applicant is seeking and the legal basis of the application for that order;
- (c)   if the application is being made under an enactment, what that enactment is;
- (d)   if the applicant is applying in a representative capacity, what that capacity is; and
- (e)   if the respondent appears or is to appear in a representative capacity, what that capacity is.

(Part 17 requires a statement of case to be verified by a statement of truth.)

19.4 Issue of application without naming respondents

(1) A practice direction may set out circumstances in which an application may be issued under this Part without naming a respondent.

(2) The practice direction may set out those cases in which an application for permission must be made by application notice before the application is issued.

(3) The application for permission –

- (a)   need not be served on any other person; and
- (b)   must be accompanied by a copy of the application which the applicant proposes to issue.

(4) Where the court gives permission, it will give directions about the future management of the application.

19.5 Acknowledgment of service

(1) Subject to paragraph (2), each respondent must –

- (a)   file an acknowledgment of service within 14 days beginning with the date on which the application is served; and
- (b)   serve the acknowledgment of service on the applicant and any other party.

(2) If the application is to be served out of the jurisdiction, the respondent must file and serve an acknowledgment of service within the period set out in Practice Direction 6B.

(3) The acknowledgment of service must –

(a) state whether the respondent contests the application;

(b) state, if the respondent seeks a different order from that set out in the application, what that order is; and

(c) be signed by the respondent or the respondent's legal representative.

19.6 Consequence of not filing an acknowledgment of service

(1) This rule applies where –

(a) the respondent has failed to file an acknowledgment of service; and

(b) the time period for doing so has expired.

(2) The respondent may attend the hearing of the application but may not take part in the hearing unless the court gives permission.

19.7 Filing and serving written evidence

(1) The applicant must, when filing the application, file the written evidence on which the applicant intends to rely.

(2) The applicant's evidence must be served on the respondent with the application.

(3) A respondent who wishes to rely on written evidence must file it when filing the acknowledgment of service.

(4) A respondent who files written evidence must also, at the same time, serve a copy of that evidence on the other parties.

(5) Within 14 days beginning with the date on which a respondent's evidence was served on the applicant, the applicant may file further written evidence in reply.

(6) An applicant who files further written evidence must also, within the same time limit, serve a copy of that evidence on the other parties.

19.8 Evidence – general

(1) No written evidence may be relied on at the hearing of the application unless –

(a) it has been served in accordance with rule 19.7; or

(b) the court gives permission.

(2) The court may require or permit a party to give oral evidence at the hearing.

(3) The court may give directions requiring the attendance for cross-examination(GL) of a witness who has given written evidence.

(Rule 22.1 contains a general power for the court to control evidence.)

PART II – Statutory instruments

19.9 Procedure where respondent objects to use of the Part 19 procedure

(1) A respondent who contends that the Part 19 procedure should not be used because –

    (a)   there is a substantial dispute of fact; and

    (b)   the use of the Part 19 procedure is not required or permitted by a rule or practice direction,

must state the reasons for that contention when filing the acknowledgment of service.

(2) When the court receives the acknowledgment of service and any written evidence, it will give directions as to the future management of the case.

> (Rule 19.7 requires a respondent who wishes to rely on written evidence to file it when filing the acknowledgment of service.)
> (Rule 19.1(3) allows the court to make an order that the application continue as if the applicant had not used the Part 19 procedure.)

Practice Direction 19A –
Alternative Procedure for Applications

This Practice Direction supplements FPR Part 19

Types of application in which Part 19 procedure must be used

1.1 An applicant must use the Part 19 procedure if the application is for an order under –

    (a)   section 60(3) of the 2002 Act, to prevent disclosure of information to an adopted person;

    (b)   section 79(4) of the 2002 Act, to require the Registrar General to provide information; or

    (c)   rule 14.21 (Inherent jurisdiction and fathers without parental responsibility) in Part 14, to request directions of the High Court regarding fathers without parental responsibility.

Types of application in which Part 19 procedure may be used

1.2 An applicant may use the Part 19 procedure if Part 18 does not apply and if –

    (a)   there is no prescribed form in which to make the application; or

    (b)   the applicant seeks the court's decision on a question which is unlikely to involve a substantial dispute of fact.

1.3 An applicant may also use the Part 19 procedure if a practice direction permits or requires its use for the type of proceedings concerned.

1.4 The practice directions referred to in paragraph 1.3 may in some respects modify or disapply the Part 19 procedure and, where that is so, it is those practice directions, rather than this one, which must be complied with.

1.5 The types of application for which the Part 19 procedure may be used include an application for an order or direction which is unopposed by each respondent before the commencement of the proceedings and the sole purpose of the application is to obtain the approval of the court to the agreement.

1.6 Where it appears to a court officer that an applicant is using the Part 19 procedure inappropriately, the officer may refer the application to the court for consideration of the point.

1.7 The court may at any stage order the application to continue as if the applicant had not used the Part 19 procedure and, if it does so, the court will give such directions as it considers appropriate (see rule 19.1(3)).

The application

2.1 Where an applicant uses the Part 19 procedure, the application form referred to in Practice Direction 5A should be used and must state the matters set out in rule 19.3 and, if paragraphs 1.3 and 1.4 apply, must comply with the requirements of the practice direction in question. In particular, the application form must state that Part 19 applies. A Part 19 application form means an application form which so states.

2.2 An application –

    (a)   in accordance with rule 19.4, to ask the High Court for directions on the need to give a father without parental responsibility notice of the intention to place a child for adoption; or

    (b)   under section 60(3) of the 2002 Act for an order to prevent disclosure of information to an adopted person,

may be issued without naming a respondent.

Responding to the application

3.1 Where a respondent who wishes to respond to a Part 19 application is required to file an acknowledgement of service, that acknowledgement of service should be in form FP5 which is referred to in Practice Direction 5A but can, alternatively be given in an informal document such as a letter.

3.2 Rule 19.5 sets out provisions relating to an acknowledgement of service of a Part 19 application.

3.3 Rule 19.6 sets out the consequence of failing to file an acknowledgement of service.

3.4 A respondent who believes that the Part 19 procedure should not be used because there is a substantial dispute of fact or, as the case may be, because its use is not authorised by any rule in the FPR or any practice direction, must state the reasons for that belief in writing when filing the acknowledgement of service (see rule 19.9). If the statement of reasons includes matters of evidence, it should be verified by a statement of truth.

Managing the application

4.1 The court may give directions immediately a Part 19 application is issued either on the application of a party or of its own initiative. The directions may include fixing a hearing date where –

    (a)   there is no dispute; or

    (b)   where there may be a dispute, but a hearing date could conveniently be given.

4.2 Where the court does not fix a hearing date when the application is issued, it will give directions for the disposal of the application as soon as practicable after the respondent has acknowledged service of the application or, as the case may be, after the period for acknowledging service has expired.

4.3 Certain applications may not require a hearing.

4.4 The court may convene a directions hearing before giving directions.

Evidence

5.1 An applicant wishing to rely on written evidence should file it when the Part 19 application form is issued.

5.2 Evidence will normally be in the form of a witness statement or an affidavit but an applicant may rely on the matters set out in the application form provided it has been verified by a statement of truth.

    (For information about statements of truth see Part 7 and Practice Direction 17A, and about written evidence see Part 22 and Practice Direction 22A.)

5.3 A respondent wishing to rely on written evidence should file it with the acknowledgement of service (see rule 19.7(3)).

5.4 Rule 19.7 sets out the times and provisions for filing and serving written evidence.

5.5 A party may apply to the court for an extension of time to serve and file evidence under rule 19.7 or for permission to serve and file additional evidence under rule 19.8(1).

    (For information about applications see Part 18 and Practice Direction 18A.)

5.6 The parties may, subject to paragraphs 5.7 and 5.8, agree in writing on an extension of time for serving and filing evidence under rule 19.7(3) or rule 19.7(5).

5.7 An agreement extending time for a respondent to file evidence in reply under rule 19.7(3) –

    (a)   must be filed by the respondent at the same time as the acknowledgement of service; and

    (b)   must not extend time by more than 17 days after the respondent files the acknowledgement of service.

5.8 An agreement extending time for an applicant to file evidence in reply under rule 19.7(5) must not extend time to more than 28 days after service of the respondent's evidence on the applicant.

Hearing

6.1 The court may on the hearing date –

(a) proceed to hear the case and dispose of the application;

(b) give case management directions.

****

[PART 25
EXPERTS AND ASSESSORS

25.1

...[1]

NOTES

Amendment.[1] Rule omitted: SI 2014/843.

25.2 Interpretation

(1) In this Part –

...[1]

'children proceedings' means –

(a) proceedings referred to in rules 12.1 and 14.1 and any other proceedings which relate wholly or mainly to the maintenance or upbringing of a minor;

(b) applications for permission to start proceedings mentioned in paragraph (a); and

(c) applications made in the course of proceedings mentioned in paragraph (a);

'expert' means a person who provides expert evidence for use in proceedings;

[(Section 13(8) of the 2014 Act provides for what is not included in reference to providing expert evidence or putting expert evidence before the court in children proceedings)][1]

...[1]

'single joint expert' means a person who provides expert evidence for use in proceedings on behalf of two or more of the parties (including the applicant) to the proceedings.

[(2) The meaning of 'children proceedings' in paragraph (1) is the prescribed meaning for the purposes of section 13(9) of the 2014 Act.][1]

NOTES

Amendments.[1] Definitions omitted, words inserted and paragraph substituted: SI 2014/843.

25.3 Experts – overriding duty to the court

(1) It is the duty of experts to help the court on matters within their expertise.

(2) This duty overrides any obligation to the person from whom experts have received instructions or by whom they are paid.

> (Particular duties of an expert are set out in Practice Direction 25B (The Duties of an Expert, the Expert's Report and Arrangements for an Expert to Attend Court.)

[25.4 Control of expert evidence in proceedings other than children proceedings

(1) This rule applies to proceedings other than children proceedings.

(2) A person may not without the permission of the court put expert evidence (in any form) before the court.

(3) The court may give permission as mentioned in paragraph (2) only if the court is of the opinion that the expert evidence is necessary to assist the court to resolve the proceedings.

> (Provision relating to the control of expert evidence in children proceedings is contained in section 13 of the 2014 Act.)][1]

NOTES

Amendment.[1] Rule substituted: SI 2014/843.

25.5 Further provisions about the court's power to restrict expert evidence

[(1) When deciding whether to give permission as mentioned in section 13(1), (3) or (5) of the 2014 Act or to give a direction under 38(6) of the 1989 Act in children proceedings, the court is to have regard in particular to any failure to comply with rule 25.6 or any direction of the court about expert evidence.][1]

[(1A) The matter referred to in paragraph (1) is a prescribed matter for the purposes of section 13(7)(h) of the 2014 Act and section 38(7B) of the 1989 Act.][1]

(2) When deciding whether to give permission as mentioned in rule 25.4(1) in proceedings other than children proceedings, the court is to have regard in particular to –

    (a)   the issues to which the expert evidence would relate;
    (b)   the questions which the court would require the expert to answer;
    (c)   the impact which giving permission would be likely to have on the timetable, duration and conduct of the proceedings;
    (d)   any failure to comply with rule 25.6 or any direction of the court about expert evidence; and
    (e)   the cost of the expert evidence.

[(3) Provision may be made in a practice direction in relation to permission to put expert evidence in relation to toxicology testing before the court.][2]

25.6 When to apply for the court's permission

[Unless the court directs otherwise, parties must apply for the court's permission as mentioned in section 13(1), (3) or (5) of the 2014 Act or rule 25.4(2) as soon as possible and –

(a) in Part 4 proceedings referred to in rule 12.2 and in so far as practicable other public law proceedings referred to in that rule, no later than a Case Management Hearing;

(b) in private law proceedings referred to in rule 12.2, no later than the First Hearing Dispute Resolution Appointment;

(c) in adoption proceedings and placement proceedings, no later than the first directions hearing;

(d) in proceedings for a financial remedy, no later than the first appointment; and

(e) in a [disputed][2] case referred to in rule 7.1(3), no later than any Case Management Hearing directed by the court under rule [7.14][2].][1]

25.7 What an application notice requesting the court's permission must include

(1) Part 18 applies to an application for the court's permission as mentioned in [section 13(1), (3) or (5) of the 2014 Act or]1 rule 25.4[(2)][1].

(2) In any proceedings –

(a) the application notice requesting the court's permission as mentioned in [section 13(1), (3) or (5) of the 2014 Act or]1 rule 25.4[(2)][1] must state –

    (i) the field in which the expert evidence is required;

    (ii) where practicable, the name of the proposed expert;

    (iii) the issues to which the expert evidence is to relate;

    (iv) whether the expert evidence could be obtained from a single joint expert;

    (v) the other matters set out in Practice Direction 25C or 25D, as the case may be; and

(b) a draft of the order sought is to be attached to the application notice requesting the court's permission and that draft order must set out the matters specified in Practice Direction 25C or 25D, as the case may be.

(3) In children proceedings, an application notice requesting the court's permission as mentioned in [section 13(1), (3) or (5) of the 2014 Act][1] must, in addition to the matters specified in paragraph (2)(a), state the questions which the expert is to be required to answer.

PART II – Statutory instruments

25.8 Where permission is granted

(1) In any proceedings, where the court grants permission as mentioned in [section 13(1), (3) or (5) of the 2014 Act or][1] rule 25.4[(2)][1] –

(a)   it will grant permission only in relation to the expert named or the field identified in the application notice requesting the court's permission; and

(b)   the court will give directions specifying the date by which the expert is to provide a written report.

(2) In children proceedings, in addition to the directions in paragraph (1)(b), the court will give directions –

(a)   approving the questions which the expert is required to answer;

(b)   specifying the date by which the expert is to receive the letter of instruction

NOTES

Amendments.[1] Words inserted: SI 2014/843.

25.9 General requirement for expert evidence to be given in a written report

(1) Expert evidence is to be given in a written report unless the court directs otherwise.

(2) The court will not direct an expert to attend a hearing unless it is necessary to do so in the interests of justice.

25.10 Written questions to experts

(1) A party may put written questions about an expert's report to –

(a)   an expert instructed by another party; or

(b)   a single joint expert appointed under rule 25.11.

(2) Unless the court directs otherwise or a practice direction provides otherwise, written questions under paragraph (1) –

(a)   must be proportionate;

(b)   may be put once only;

(c)   must be put within 10 days beginning with the date on which the expert's report was served;

(d)   must be for the purpose only of clarification of the report; and

(e)   must be copied and sent to the other parties at the same time as they are sent to the expert.

(3) An expert's answers to questions put in accordance with paragraph (1) –

(a)   must be given within the timetable specified by the court; and

(b)   are treated as part of the expert's report.

(4) Where –

(a) a party has put a written question to an expert instructed by another party; and

(b) the expert does not answer that question,

the court may make one or both of the following orders in relation to the party who instructed the expert –

(i) that the party may not rely on the evidence of that expert; or

(ii) that the party may not recover the fees and expenses of that expert from any other party.

25.11 Court's power to direct that evidence is to be given by a single joint expert

(1) Where two or more parties wish to put expert evidence before the court on a particular issue, the court may direct that the evidence on that issue is to be given by a single joint expert.

(2) Where the parties who wish to put expert evidence before the court ('the relevant parties') cannot agree who should be the single joint expert, the court may –

(a) select the expert from a list prepared or identified by the relevant parties; or

(b) direct that the expert be selected in such other manner as the court may direct.

25.12 Instructions to a single joint expert

(1) Where the court gives a direction under rule 25.11(1) for a single joint expert to be used, the instructions are to be contained in a jointly agreed letter unless the court directs otherwise.

(2) Where the instructions are to be contained in a jointly agreed letter, in default of agreement the instructions may be determined by the court on the written request of any relevant party copied to the other relevant parties.

(3) Where the court permits the relevant parties to give separate instructions to a single joint expert, each instructing party must, when giving instructions to the expert, at the same time send a copy of the instructions to the other relevant parties.

(4) The court may give directions about –

(a) the payment of the expert's fees and expenses; and

(b) any inspection, examination or assessments which the expert wishes to carry out.

(5) The court may, before an expert is instructed, limit the amount that can be paid by way of fees and expenses to the expert.

(6) Unless the court directs otherwise, the relevant parties are jointly and severally liable for the payment of the expert's fees and expenses.

25.13 Power of court to direct a party to provide information

(1) Subject to paragraph (2), where a party has access to information which is not reasonably available to another party, the court may direct the party who has access to the information to –

    (a)   prepare and file a document recording the information; and
    (b)   serve a copy of that document on the other party.

(2) In proceedings under Part 14 (procedure for applications in adoption, placement and related proceedings), a court officer will send a copy of the document recording the information to the other party.

25.14 Contents of report

(1) An expert's report must comply with the requirements set out in Practice Direction 25B.

(2) At the end of an expert's report there must be a statement that the expert understands and has complied with the expert's duty to the court.

(3) The instructions to the expert are not privileged against disclosure.

    (Rule 21.1 explains what is meant by disclosure.)

25.15 Use by one party of expert's report disclosed by another

Where a party has disclosed an expert's report, any party may use that expert's report as evidence at any hearing where an issue to which the report relates is being considered.

25.16 Discussions between experts

(1) The court may, at any stage, direct a discussion between experts for the purpose of requiring the experts to –

    (a)   identify and discuss the expert issues in the proceedings; and
    (b)   where possible, reach an agreed opinion on those issues.

(2) The court may specify the issues which the experts must discuss.

(3) The court may direct that following a discussion between the experts they must prepare a statement for the court setting out those issues on which –

    (a)   they agree; and
    (b)   they disagree, with a summary of their reasons for disagreeing.

25.17 Expert's right to ask court for directions

(1) Experts may file written requests for directions for the purpose of assisting them in carrying out their functions.

(2) Experts must, unless the court directs otherwise, provide copies of the proposed requests for directions under paragraph (1) –

    (a)   to the party instructing them, at least 7 days before they file the requests; and

    (b)   to all other parties, at least 4 days before they file them.

(3) The court, when it gives directions, may also direct that a party be served with a copy of the directions.

25.18 Copies of orders and other documents

Unless the court directs otherwise, a copy of any order or other document affecting an expert filed with the court after the expert has been instructed, must be served on the expert by the party who instructed the expert or, in the case of a single joint expert, the party who was responsible for instructing the expert, within 2 days of that party receiving the order or other document.

25.19 Action after final hearing

(1) Within 10 business days after the final hearing, the party who instructed the expert or, in the case of a single joint expert, the party who was responsible for instructing the expert, must inform the expert in writing about the court's determination and the use made by the court of the expert's evidence.

(2) Unless the court directs otherwise, the party who instructed the expert or, in the case of the single joint expert, the party who was responsible for instructing the expert, must send to the expert a copy of the court's final order[, any transcript or written record of the court's decision, and its reasons for reaching its decision, within 10 business days from the date when the party received the order and any such transcript or record.][1] ...[1]

NOTES

Amendments.[1] Words inserted and sub-paragraphs omitted: SI 2014/843.

25.20 Assessors

(1) This rule applies where the court appoints one or more persons under section 70 of the Senior Courts Act 1981 ...[2] as an assessor.

(2) An assessor will assist the court in dealing with a matter in which the assessor has skill and experience.

(3) The assessor will take such part in the proceedings as the court may direct and in particular the court may direct an assessor to –

    (a)   prepare a report for the court on any matter at issue in the proceedings; and

    (b)   attend the whole or any part of the hearing to advise the court on any such matter.

(4) If the assessor prepares a report for the court before the hearing has begun –

    (a)   the court will send a copy to each of the parties; and

    (b)   the parties may use it at the hearing.

(5) Unless the court directs otherwise, an assessor will be paid at the daily rate payable for the time being to a fee-paid deputy district judge of the principal registry and an assessor's fees will form part of the costs of the proceedings.

(6) The court may order any party to deposit in the court office a specified sum in respect of an assessor's fees and, where it does so, the assessor will not be asked to act until the sum has been deposited.

(7) Paragraphs (5) and (6) do not apply where the remuneration of the assessor is to be paid out of money provided by Parliament.][1]

NOTES

Amendments.[1] Part 25 substituted: SI 2012/3061. [2] Words omitted: SI 2014/667.

[Practice Direction 25A – Experts and Assessors in Family Proceedings

This Practice Direction supplements FPR Part 25.

Introduction

1.1 This Practice Direction and Practice Directions 25B to E relate to expert evidence and supplement FPR Part 25. This Practice Direction applies to children proceedings and all other family proceedings.

Emergency and urgent cases

2.1 In emergency or urgent cases – for example, where, before formal issue of proceedings, a without-notice application is made to the court during or out of business hours; or where, after proceedings have been issued, a previously unforeseen need for (further) expert evidence arises at short notice – a party may wish to put expert evidence before the court without having complied with all or any part of Practice Directions 25B to E. In such circumstances, the party wishing to put the expert evidence before the court must apply forthwith to the court – where possible or appropriate, on notice to the other parties – for directions as to the future steps to be taken in respect of the expert evidence in question.

Pre-application instruction of experts

3.1 When experts' reports are commissioned before the commencement of proceedings, it should be made clear to the expert that he or she may in due course be reporting to the court and should therefore consider himself or herself bound by the duties of an expert set out in Practice Direction 25B (The Duties of An Expert, the Expert's Report and Arrangements for An Expert To Attend Court). In so far as possible the enquiries of the expert and subsequent letter of instruction should follow either Practice Direction 25C (Children Proceedings – the Use of Single Joint Experts and the Process Leading to an Expert Being Instructed or Expert Evidence Being Put Before The Court) or 25D (Financial Remedy Proceedings and other Family Proceedings (except Children Proceedings) – the Use of Single Joint Experts and the Process Leading to Expert Evidence Being Put Before The Court).

3.2 In particular, a prospective party to children proceedings (for example, a local authority) should always write a letter of instruction when asking a potential witness for a report or an opinion, whether that request is within proceedings or pre-proceedings (for example, when commissioning specialist assessment materials, reports from a treating expert or other evidential materials); and the letter of instruction should conform to the principles set out in Practice Direction 25C.

3.3 It should be noted that the court's permission is required to put expert evidence (in any form) before the court in all family proceedings [(see section 13(5) of the 2014 Act and FPR 25.4(2))][2]. In children proceedings, the court's permission is also required for an expert to be instructed and for a child to be medically or psychiatrically examined or otherwise assessed for the purposes of the provision of expert evidence in the proceedings ([section 13(1) and (3) of the 2014 Act][2]). Where the court's permission has not been given in accordance with [section 13(1) and (3) of the 2014 Act][2], evidence resulting from such instructions or examination or other assessment is inadmissible unless the court rules otherwise ([section 13(2) and (4) of the 2014 Act][2]). The court's permission will be needed to put any expert evidence before the court which was obtained before proceedings have started.

3.4 Attention is drawn to Practice Direction 15B (Adults Who May Be Protected Parties and Children Who May Become Protected Parties In Family Proceedings) which gives guidance relating to proceedings where an adult party may not have capacity to conduct the litigation or to instruct an expert.][1]

NOTES

Amendment.[1] Practice Direction substituted: FPR 2010 6th Update, 31 January 2013.[2] Text substituted: FPR Update, April 2014.

[Practice Direction 25B –
The Duties of an Expert, The Expert's Report and Arrangements for an Expert to Attend Court

This Practice Direction supplements FPR Part 25.

Scope of this Practice Direction

1.1 This Practice Direction focuses on the duties of an expert including the contents of the expert's report and, where an expert is to attend court, the arrangements for such attendance. Other Practice Directions supporting FPR Part 25 deal with different aspects of experts in family proceedings. The relevant Practice Directions are –

  (a)   Practice Direction 25A (Experts – Emergencies and Pre proceedings Instructions);
  (b)   Practice Direction 25C (Children Proceedings – The Use of Single Joint Experts and the Process Leading to an Expert Being Instructed or Expert Evidence Being Put Before the Court);
  (c)   Practice Direction 25D (Financial Remedy Proceedings and Other Family Proceedings (except Children Proceedings) – The Use of Single

Joint Experts and the Process Leading to Expert Evidence Being Put Before The Court); and

(d)   Practice Direction 25E (Discussions Between Experts in Family Proceedings).

1.2 Practice Direction 15B (Adults Who May Be Protected Parties and Children Who May Become Protected Parties In Family Proceedings) gives guidance relating to proceedings where an adult party may not have capacity to conduct the litigation or to instruct an expert.

[1.3 In accordance with FPR 25.2(1), 'children proceedings' means –

(a)   proceedings referred to in FPR 12.1 and 14.1 and any other proceedings which relate wholly or mainly to the maintenance or upbringing of a minor;

(b)   applications for permission to start proceedings mentioned in paragraph (a);

(c)   applications made in the course of proceedings mentioned in paragraph (a).][3]

The meaning of 'expert'

2.1 In accordance with FPR 25.2(1), 'expert' means a person who provides expert evidence for use in family proceedings. [Section 13(8) of the 2014 Act][2] expressly refers to evidence that is not expert evidence. For example, evidence given by a children's guardian is not expert evidence.

2.2 An expert includes a reference to an expert team which can include ancillary workers in addition to experts. In an expert team, an 'ancillary' worker may be, for example, a play therapist or similar who undertakes work with the child or family for the purpose of the expert assessment. It is perfectly possible that such workers will be experts in their own right and in their own field, but it would be cumbersome to name everyone in that position in an order giving permission for an expert to be instructed, a child to be medically or psychiatrically examined or otherwise assessed or expert evidence to be put before the court or in a letter of instruction to an expert. The purpose of the term 'expert team' is to enable a multi-disciplinary team to undertake the assessment without the order having to name everyone who may be involved. The final expert's report must, however, give information about those persons who have taken part in the assessment and their respective roles and who is responsible for the report.

The expert's overriding duty

3.1 An expert in family proceedings has an overriding duty to the court that takes precedence over any obligation to the person from whom the expert has received instructions or by whom the expert is paid.

Particular duties of the expert

4.1 An expert shall have regard to the following, among other, duties –

(a)   to assist the court in accordance with the overriding duty;

[(aa) in children proceedings, to comply with the Standards for Expert Witnesses in Children Proceedings in the Family Court which are set out in the Annex to this Practice Direction;][3]

(b) to provide advice to the court that conforms to the best practice of the expert's profession;

(c) to answer the questions about which the expert is required to give an opinion (in children proceedings, those questions will be set out in the order of the court giving permission for an expert to be instructed, a child to be examined or otherwise assessed or expert evidence to be put before the court);

(d) to provide an opinion that is independent of the party or parties instructing the expert;

(e) to confine the opinion to matters material to the issues in the case and in relation only to the questions that are within the expert's expertise (skill and experience);

(f) where a question has been put which falls outside the expert's expertise, to state this at the earliest opportunity and to volunteer an opinion as to whether another expert is required to bring expertise not possessed by those already involved or, in the rare case, as to whether a second opinion is required on a key issue and, if possible, what questions should be asked of the second expert;

(g) in expressing an opinion, to take into consideration all of the material facts including any relevant factors arising from ethnic, cultural, religious or linguistic contexts at the time the opinion is expressed;

(h) to inform those instructing the expert without delay of any change in the opinion and of the reason for the change.

The requirement for the court's permission

5.1 The general rule in family proceedings is that the court's permission is required to put expert evidence (in any form) before the court ([see section 13(5) of the 2014 Act for children proceedings and FPR 25.4(2) for other family proceedings][2]). The court is under a duty to restrict expert evidence to that which in the opinion of the court is necessary to assist the court to resolve the proceedings. The overriding objective in FPR 1.1 applies when the court is exercising this duty. In children proceedings, the court's permission is required to instruct an expert and for a child to be medically or psychiatrically examined or otherwise assessed for the purposes of the provision of expert evidence in the proceedings ([section 13(1) and (3) of the 2014 Act][2]).

Preliminary enquiries which the expert should expect to receive

6.1 In good time for the information requested to be available for –

(a) the court hearing when the court will decide whether to give permission for the expert evidence to be put before the court (or also in children proceedings, for the expert to be instructed or the child to be examined or otherwise assessed); or

(b) the advocates' meeting or discussion where one takes place before such a hearing,

PART II – Statutory instruments

the party or parties intending to instruct the expert shall approach the expert with some information about the case.

6.2 The details of the information to be given to the expert are set out in Practice Direction 25C, paragraph 3.2 and Practice Direction 25D paragraph 3.3 and include the nature of the proceedings, the questions for the expert, the time when the expert's report is likely to be required, the timing of any hearing at which the expert may have to give evidence and how the expert's fees will be funded.

6.3 Children proceedings are confidential which means in those proceedings parties raising preliminary enquiries of an expert who has not yet been instructed can only tell the expert information which he or she will need about the case to be able to answer the preliminary questions raised.

Balancing the needs of the court and those of the expert

7.1 It is essential that there should be proper co-ordination between the court and the expert when drawing up the case management timetable: the needs of the court should be balanced with the needs of the expert whose forensic work is undertaken as an adjunct to his or her main professional duties.

The expert's response to preliminary enquiries

8.1 In good time for the court hearing when the court will decide whether or not to give permission for the expert evidence to be put before the court (or also in children proceedings, for the expert to be instructed or the child to be examined or otherwise assessed) or for the advocates' meeting or discussion where one takes place before that hearing, the party or parties intending to instruct the expert will need confirmation from the expert –

(a) that acceptance of the proposed instructions will not involve the expert in any conflict of interest;

(b) that the work required is within the expert's expertise;

(c) that the expert is available to do the relevant work within the suggested time scale;

(d) when the expert is available to give evidence, of the dates and times to avoid and, where a hearing date has not been fixed, of the amount of notice the expert will require to make arrangements to come to court (or to give evidence by telephone conference or video link) without undue disruption to his or her normal professional routines;

(e) of the cost, including hourly or other charging rates, and likely hours to be spent attending experts' meetings, attending court and writing the report (to include any examinations and interviews);

(f) of any representations which the expert wishes to make to the court about being named or otherwise identified in any public judgment given by the court.

Content of the expert's report

9.1 The expert's report shall be addressed to the court and prepared and filed in accordance with the court's timetable and must –

(a)   give details of the expert's qualifications and experience;

(b)   include a statement identifying the document(s) containing the material instructions and the substance of any oral instructions and, as far as necessary to explain any opinions or conclusions expressed in the report, summarising the facts and instructions which are material to the conclusions and opinions expressed;

(c)   state who carried out any test, examination or interview which the expert has used for the report and whether or not the test, examination or interview has been carried out under the expert's supervision;

(d)   give details of the qualifications of any person who carried out the test, examination or interview;

(e)   answer the questions about which the expert is to give an opinion and which relate to the issues in the case;

(f)   in expressing an opinion to the court –

   (i)   take into consideration all of the material facts including any relevant factors arising from ethnic, cultural, religious or linguistic contexts at the time the opinion is expressed, identifying the facts, literature and any other material, including research material, that the expert has relied upon in forming an opinion;

   (ii)   describe the expert's own professional risk assessment process and process of differential diagnosis, highlighting factual assumptions, deductions from the factual assumptions, and any unusual, contradictory or inconsistent features of the case;

   (iii) indicate whether any proposition in the report is an hypothesis (in particular a controversial hypothesis), or an opinion deduced in accordance with peer-reviewed and tested technique, research and experience accepted as a consensus in the scientific community;

   (iv)   indicate whether the opinion is provisional (or qualified, as the case may be), stating the qualification and the reason for it, and identifying what further information is required to give an opinion without qualification;

(g)   where there is a range of opinion on any question to be answered by the expert –

   (i)   summarise the range of opinion;

   (ii)   identify and explain, within the range of opinions, any 'unknown cause', whether arising from the facts of the case (for example, because there is too little information to form a scientific opinion) or from limited experience or lack of research, peer review or support in the relevant field of expertise;

   (iii) give reasons for any opinion expressed: the use of a balance sheet approach to the factors that support or undermine an opinion can be of great assistance to the court;

(h)   contain a summary of the expert's conclusions and opinions;

(i)   contain a statement that the expert –

   (i)   has no conflict of interest of any kind, other than any conflict disclosed in his or her report;

   (ii)   does not consider that any interest disclosed affects his or her suitability as an expert witness on any issue on which he or she has given evidence;

PART II – Statutory instruments

> > (iii)   will advise the instructing party if, between the date of the expert's report and the final hearing, there is any change in circumstances which affects the expert's answers to (i) or (ii) above;
> >
> > (iv)   understands their duty to the court and has complied with that duty; and
> >
> > (v)   is aware of the requirements of FPR Part 25 and this practice direction;
> >
> > [(vi)   in children proceedings, has complied with the Standards for Expert Witnesses in Children Proceedings in the Family Court which are set out in the Annex to this Practice Direction;][3]
>
> (j)   be verified by a statement of truth in the following form –

> 'I confirm that I have made clear which facts and matters referred to in this report are within my own knowledge and which are not. Those that are within my own knowledge I confirm to be true. The opinions I have expressed represent my true and complete professional opinions on the matters to which they refer.'

> [Where the report relates to children proceedings the form of statement of truth must include –

> 'I also confirm that I have complied with the Standards for Expert Witnesses in Children Proceedings in the Family Court which are set out in the Annex to Practice Direction 25B – The Duties of an Expert, the Expert's Report and Arrangements for an Expert to Attend Court'][3]

> (FPR Part 17deals with statements of truth. Rule 17.6 sets out the consequences of verifying a document containing a false statement without an honest belief in its truth.)

Arrangements for experts to give evidence

Preparation

10.1   Where the court has directed the attendance of an expert witness, the party who instructed the expert or party responsible for the instruction of the expert shall, by a date specified by the court prior to the hearing at which the expert is to give oral evidence ('the specified date') or, where in care or supervision proceedings an Issues Resolution Hearing ('the IRH') is to be held, by the IRH, ensure that –

> (a)   a date and time (if possible, convenient to the expert) are fixed for the court to hear the expert's evidence, substantially in advance of the hearing at which the expert is to give oral evidence and no later than a specified date prior to that hearing or, where an IRH is to be held, than the IRH;
>
> (b)   if the expert's oral evidence is not required, the expert is notified as soon as possible;
>
> (c)   the witness template accurately indicates how long the expert is likely to be giving evidence, in order to avoid the inconvenience of the expert being delayed at court;

(d)   consideration is given in each case to whether some or all of the experts participate by telephone conference or video link, or submit their evidence in writing, to ensure that minimum disruption is caused to professional schedules and that costs are minimised.

Experts attending court

10.2 Where expert witnesses are to be called, all parties shall, by the specified date or, where an IRH is to be held, by the IRH, ensure that –

(a)   the parties' advocates have identified (whether at an advocates' meeting or by other means) the issues which the experts are to address;

(b)   wherever possible, a logical sequence to the evidence is arranged, with experts of the same discipline giving evidence on the same day;

(c)   the court is informed of any circumstance where all experts agree but a party nevertheless does not accept the agreed opinion, so that directions can be given for the proper consideration of the experts' evidence and opinion;

(d)   in the exceptional case the court is informed of the need for a witness summons.][1]

[Annex

Standards for Expert Witnesses in Children Proceedings in the Family Court

Subject to any order made by the court, expert witnesses involved in family proceedings (involving children) in England and Wales, whatever their field of practice or country of origin, must comply with the standards (1–11).

1. The expert's area of competence is appropriate to the issue(s) upon which the court has identified that an opinion is required, and relevant experience is evidenced in their CV.

2. The expert has been active in the area of work or practice, (as a practitioner or an academic who is subject to peer appraisal), has sufficient experience of the issues relevant to the instant case, and is familiar with the breadth of current practice or opinion.

3. The expert has working knowledge of the social, developmental, cultural norms and accepted legal principles applicable to the case presented at initial enquiry, and has the cultural competence skills to deal with the circumstances of the case.

4. The expert is up-to-date with Continuing Professional Development appropriate to their discipline and expertise, and is in continued engagement with accepted supervisory mechanisms relevant to their practice.

5. If the expert's current professional practice is regulated by a UK statutory body (See Appendix 1) they are in possession of a current licence to practise or equivalent.

6. If the expert's area of professional practice is not subject to statutory registration (e.g. child psychotherapy, systemic family therapy, mediation, and experts in

PART II – Statutory instruments

exclusively academic appointments) the expert should demonstrate appropriate qualifications and/or registration with a relevant professional body on a case by case basis. Registering bodies usually provide a code of conduct and professional standards and should be accredited by the Professional Standards Authority for Health and Social Care (See Appendix 2). If the expertise is academic in nature (e.g. regarding evidence of cultural influences) then no statutory registration is required (even if this includes direct contact or interviews with individuals) but consideration should be given to appropriate professional accountability.

7. The expert is compliant with any necessary safeguarding requirements, information security expectations, and carries professional indemnity insurance.

8. If the expert's current professional practice is outside the UK they can demonstrate that they are compliant with the FJC 'Guidelines for the instruction of medical experts from overseas in family cases'[1].

1   December 2011. See www.judiciary.gov.uk/about-the-judiciary/advisory-bodies/fjc.

9. The expert has undertaken appropriate training, updating or quality assurance activity – including actively seeking feedback from cases in which they have provided evidence – relevant to the role of expert in the family courts in England and Wales within the last year.

10. The expert has a working knowledge of, and complies with, the requirements of Practice Directions relevant to providing reports for and giving evidence to the family courts in England and Wales. This includes compliance with the requirement to identify where their opinion on the instant case lies in relation to other accepted mainstream views and the overall spectrum of opinion in the UK.

Expectations in relation to experts' fees

11. The expert should state their hourly rate in advance of agreeing to accept instruction, and give an estimate of the number of hours the report is likely to take. This will assist the legal representative to apply expeditiously to the Legal Aid Agency if prior authority is to be sought in a publicly funded case.

Appendix 1 to the standards

UK Health and Social Care Professions and Statutory Regulators with responsibilities within England and Wales

The Professional Standards Authority for Health and Social Care (PSA)[2] (formerly the Council for Healthcare Regulatory Excellence) oversees statutory bodies that regulate health and social care professionals in the UK. It assesses their performance, conducts audits, scrutinises their decisions and reports to Parliament. It also sets standards for organisations holding voluntary registers for health and social care occupations and accredits those that meet them. It shares good practice and knowledge, conducts research and introduces new ideas to the sector including the concept of right-touch regulation. It monitors policy developments in the UK and internationally and provides advice on issues relating to professional standards in health and social care.

2   www.professionalstandards.org.uk

The General Medical Council[3] (GMC) is the independent regulator for doctors in the UK. The GMC's statutory purpose is to protect, promote and maintain the health and safety of the public by ensuring proper standards in the practice of medicine through the Medical Register.

3 www.gmc-uk.org

The General Dental Council[4] regulates dental professionals in the UK. All dentists, dental nurses, dental technicians, clinical dental technicians, dental hygienists, dental therapists and orthodontic therapists must be registered with the GDC to work in the UK.

4 www.gdc-uk.org

The Nursing and Midwifery Council[5] regulates nurses and midwives in the UK, setting standards for work, education and a code of conduct for all registered nurses and midwives.

5 www.nmc-uk.org

Care Council for Wales: The Care Council for Wales is the social care workforce regulator in Wales responsible for promoting and securing high standards across the social services and social care workforce. It regulates social workers in Wales and managers of care services, including residential care homes for children, care homes for adults and domiciliary care for both adults and children. It also regulates social work students and residential child care workers.

The General Optical Council[6] is the regulator for the optical professions in the UK. Its purpose is to protect the public by promoting high standards of education, performance and conduct amongst opticians.

6 www.optical.org

The General Pharmacy Council[7] is the independent regulator for pharmacists, pharmacy technicians and pharmacy premises in Great Britain. Its role is to protect, promote and maintain the health, safety and wellbeing of members of the public by upholding standards and public trust in pharmacy.

7 www.pharmacyregulation.org/about-us

The General Chiropractic Council[8] is a UK-wide statutory body with regulatory powers established by the Chiropractors Act 1994. Its duties are to protect the public by establishing and operating a scheme of statutory regulation for chiropractors, to set the standards of chiropractic education, conduct and practice and to ensure the development of the profession of chiropractic, using a model of continuous improvement in practice.

8 www.gcc-uk.org/page.cfm

The General Osteopathic Council[9] regulates the practice of osteopathy in the United Kingdom. By law osteopaths must be registered with the Council in order to practise in the UK. It works with the public and osteopathic profession to promote patient safety by registering qualified professionals and sets, maintain and develop standards of osteopathic practice and conduct.

9 www.osteopathy.org.uk

PART II – Statutory instruments

The Health and Care Professions Council[10] regulates health and social care professionals with protected titles. Further information is set out in the table below.

10 www.hpc-uk.org/aboutregistration/protectedtitles

Profession	Protected title(s)
Arts therapist An art, music or drama therapist encourages people to express their feelings and emotions through art, such as painting and drawing, music or drama.	• Art psychotherapist • Art therapist • Dramatherapist • Music therapist
Biomedical scientist A biomedical scientist analyses specimens from patients to provide data to help doctors diagnose and treat disease.	• Biomedical scientist
Chiropodist/Podiatrist A chiropodist/podiatrist diagnoses and treats disorders, diseases and deformities of the feet.	• Chiropodist • Podiatrist
Clinical scientist A clinical scientist oversees specialist tests for diagnosing and managing disease. They advise doctors on using tests and interpreting data and they also carry out research to understand diseases.	• Clinical scientist
Dietician A dietician uses the science of nutrition to devise eating plans for patients to treat medical conditions, and to promote good health.	• Dietician
Hearing aid dispenser Hearing aid dispensers assess, fit and provide aftercare for hearing aids.	• Hearing aid dispenser
Occupational therapist An occupational therapist uses specific activities to limit the effects of disability and promote independence in all aspects of daily life.	• Occupational therapist
Operating department practitioner Operating department practitioners participate in the assessment of the patient prior to surgery and provide individualised care.	• Operating department practitioner
Orthoptist Orthoptists specialise in diagnosing and treating visual problems involving eye movement and alignment.	• Orthoptist

Profession	Protected title(s)
Paramedic Paramedics provide specialist care and treatment to patients who are either acutely ill or injured. They can administer a range of drugs and carry out certain surgical techniques.	• Paramedic
Physiotherapist Physiotherapists deal with human function and movement and help people to achieve their full physical potential. They use physical approaches to promote, maintain and restore wellbeing.	• Physiotherapist • Physical therapist
Practitioner psychologist Psychology is the scientific study of people, the mind and behaviour. Psychologists attempt to understand the role of mental functions in individual and social behaviour.	• Practitioner psychologist • Registered psychologist • Clinical psychologist • Counselling psychologist • Educational psychologist • Forensic psychologist • Health psychologist • Occupational psychologist • Sport and exercise psychologist
Prosthetist/Orthotist Prosthetists and orthotists are responsible for all aspects of supplying prostheses and orthoses for patients. A prosthesis is a device that replaces a missing body part. An orthosis is a device fixed to the body.	• Prosthetist • Orthotist
Radiographer Therapeutic radiographers plan and deliver treatment using radiation. Diagnostic radiographers produce and interpret high-quality images of the body to diagnose injuries and diseases.	• Radiographer • Diagnostic radiographer • Therapeutic radiographer
Social workers in England	• Social worker
Speech and language therapist Speech and language therapists assess, treat and help to prevent speech, language and swallowing difficulties.	• Speech and language therapist • Speech therapist

PART II – Statutory instruments

Appendix 2 to the standards

Examples of professional bodies/associations relating to non-statutorily regulated work

Resolution UK

www.resolution.org.uk/

Resolution's members are family lawyers committed to the constructive resolution of family disputes. Members follow a Code of Practice that promotes a non-confrontational approach to family problems, encourage solutions that consider the needs of the whole family and in particular the best interests of children.

Association of Child Psychotherapists (Psychoanalytic)

www.childpsychotherapy.org.uk

The Association of Child Psychotherapists is the professional organisation for Child and Adolescent Psychoanalytic Psychotherapy in the UK. The Association recognises and monitors five training schools in Child and Adolescent Psychotherapy (e.g. the Tavistock and Portman NHS Foundation Trust). Child Psychotherapists who have qualified in one of these trainings (minimum 4 years in-service clinical training, doctoral or doctoral equivalent) are eligible for full membership of the Association and are able to work as autonomous professionals within the NHS or in independent practice. Child Psychotherapists are appointed at similar grades to Clinical Psychologists.

The UK Council for Psychotherapy (UKCP)

www.psychotherapy.org.uk

The UKCP is a membership organisation with over 75 training and listing organisations, and over 7,000 individual practitioners. UKCP holds the national register of psychotherapists and psychotherapeutic counsellors, listing those practitioner members who meet exacting standards and training requirements. Organisational members/associations are grouped together in modality colleges representing all the main traditions in the practice of psychotherapy in the UK including

- Association for Cognitive Analytic Therapy
- Association for Family Therapy and Systemic Practice
- Gestalt Psychotherapy and Training Institute
- Institute of Transactional Analysis
- Institute for Arts in Therapy and Education

The British Association for Counselling & Psychotherapy (BACP)

www.bacp.co.uk

BACP is a membership organisation and a registered charity that sets standards for a wide variety of therapeutic practice and provides information for therapists, clients of therapy, and the general public. It has over 37,000 members and is the largest professional body representing counselling and psychotherapy in the UK. BACP accredits training courses for counsellors and psychotherapists and is dedicated to ensuring its members practice responsibly, ethically and to the highest of standards.

The British Association for Behavioural and Cognitive Psychotherapies (BABCP)

www.babcp.com

The BABCP is the lead organisation for Cognitive Behavioural Therapy in the UK. It is a multi-disciplinary interest group for people involved in the practice and theory of behavioural and cognitive psychotherapy. The BABCP maintain standards for practitioners of Behavioural & Cognitive Psychotherapy by providing the opportunity for members who meet minimum criteria to become accredited.

British Psychoanalytic Council

www.psychoanalytic-council.org

Psychoanalytic or psychodynamic psychotherapy draws on theories and practices of analytical psychology and psychoanalysis. It is a therapeutic process which helps patients understand and resolve their problems by increasing awareness of their inner world and its influence over relationships both past and present. It differs from most other therapies in aiming for deep seated change in personality and emotional development. Psychoanalytic and psychodynamic psychotherapy aim to help people with serious psychological disorders to understand and change complex, deep-seated and often unconsciously based emotional and relationship problems thereby reducing symptoms and alleviating distress.

NAGALRO

www.nagalro.com

Professional association for Family Court Advisers, Children's Guardians and Independent Social Workers.

British Association of Social Workers (BASW);

www.basw.co.uk

UK professional association of social workers.

Confederation of Independent Social Work Agencies UK (CISWA)

www.ciswa-uk.org

CISWA-UK is a not for profit organisation which brings independent social work providers together with the aim of improving the professionalism and expertise of agencies providing services to children and families.][3]

NOTES

Amendment.[1] Practice Direction inserted: FPR 2010 6th Update, 31 January 2013. [2] Text substituted: FPR Update, April 2014. [3] Text inserted: President's Direction, October 2014.

PART II – Statutory instruments

[Practice Direction 25C –
Children Proceedings – The Use of Single Joint Experts and the Process Leading to an Expert Being Instructed or Expert Evidence Being Put Before the Court

This Practice Direction supplements FPR Part 25.

Scope of this Practice Direction

1.1 This Practice Direction applies to children proceedings and contains guidance on –

    (a)   the use of single joint experts;

    (b)   how to prepare for the hearing at which the court will consider whether to give permission for an expert to be instructed, a child to be medically or psychiatrically examined or otherwise assessed for the purposes of provision of expert evidence in the proceedings or for putting expert evidence (in any form) before the court including –

        (i)   preliminary enquiries of experts;

        (ii)   the content of an application for the court's permission in addition to matters mentioned in FPR25.7;

        (iii)   matters to be set out in the draft order to be attached to the application for permission; and

    (c)   the letter of instruction to the expert.

1.2 'Children proceedings' includes proceedings under Schedule 1 to the 1989 Act as those proceedings are proceedings which relate wholly or mainly to the maintenance or upbringing of a minor referred to in FPR25.2(1).

Single joint experts

2.1 [Section 13(1), (3) and (5) of the 2014 Act][2] applies to a single joint expert ('SJE') in addition to an expert instructed by one party. This means that the court's permission is required to put expert evidence from an SJE (in any form) before the court ([section 13(5) of the 2014 Act][2]). The court's permission is also required to instruct an SJE and for a child to be medically or psychiatrically examined or otherwise assessed for the purposes of provision of evidence from an SJE ([section 13(1) and (3) of the 2014 Act][2]). Wherever possible, expert evidence should be obtained from an SJE instructed by both or all the parties. To that end, a party wishing to instruct an expert should as soon as possible after the start of the proceedings first give the other party or parties a list of the names of one or more experts in the relevant speciality whom they consider suitable to be instructed.

2.2 Within 5 business days after receipt of the list of proposed experts, the other party or parties should indicate any objection to one or more of the named experts and, if so, supply the name(s) of one or more experts whom they consider suitable.

2.3 Each party should disclose whether they have already consulted any of the proposed experts about the issue(s) in question.

2.4 Where the parties cannot agree on the identity of the expert, each party should think carefully before seeking the permission of the court to instruct their own expert because of the costs implications. Disagreements about the use and identity of an expert may be better managed by the court in the context of the application for the court's permission to instruct the expert and for directions for the use of an SJE (see paragraph 2.6 below).

Instructing separate experts

2.5 If the parties seek the permission of the court to instruct separate experts –

(a)   they should agree in advance that the reports will be disclosed; and
(b)   the instructions to each expert should comply, so far as appropriate, with paragraphs 4.1 and 6.1 below (Letter of instruction).

Where two or more parties wish to instruct an SJE

2.6 If two or more parties wish to instruct an SJE, before applying to the court for permission and directions for the use of an SJE, the parties should –

(a)   so far as appropriate, comply with the guidance in paragraphs 3.2 (Preliminary enquiries of the expert) and paragraphs 3.10 and 3.11 below;
(b)   receive the expert's confirmation in response to preliminary enquiries referred to in paragraph 8.1 of Practice Direction 25B;
(c)   have agreed in what proportion the SJE's fee is to be shared between them (at least in the first instance) and when it is to be paid; and
(d)   if applicable, have obtained agreement for public funding.

2.7 The instructions to the SJE should comply, so far as appropriate, with paragraphs 4.1 and 6.1 below (Letter of instruction).

Preparation for the permission hearing

3.1 Paragraphs 3.2 to 3.11 give guidance on how to prepare for the hearing at which the court will consider whether to give permission for an expert to be instructed, a child to be examined or otherwise assessed or expert evidence to be put before the court. The purpose of the preparation is to ensure that the court has the information required to enable it to exercise its powers under [section 13(1), (3), (5) and (7) of the 2014 Act and FPR 25.5][2].

Preliminary enquiries of the expert

3.2 In good time for the information requested to be available for the hearing at which the court will consider whether to give permission for an expert to be instructed, a child to be examined or otherwise assessed or expert evidence to be put before the court or for the advocates' meeting or discussion where one takes place before that hearing, the party or parties intending to instruct the expert shall approach the expert with the following information –

(a)   the nature of the proceedings and the issues likely to require determination by the court;

(b)   the issues in the proceedings to which the expert evidence is to relate;

(c)   the questions about which the expert is to be asked to give an opinion (including any ethnic, cultural, religious or linguistic contexts) and which relate to the issues in the case;

(d)   the date when the court is to be asked to give permission for the instruction (or if – unusually – permission has already been given, the date and details of that permission);

(e)   whether permission is to be asked of the court for the instruction of another expert in the same or any related field (that is, to give an opinion on the same or related questions);

(f)   the volume of reading which the expert will need to undertake;

(g)   whether or not permission has been applied for or given for the expert to examine the child;

(h)   whether or not it will be necessary for the expert to conduct interviews – and, if so, with whom;

(i)   the likely timetable of legal and social work steps;

(j)   in care and supervision proceedings, any dates in the Timetable for the Child which would be relevant to the proposed timetable for the assessment;

(k)   when the expert's report is likely to be required;

(l)   whether and, if so, what date has been fixed by the court for any hearing at which the expert may be required to give evidence (in particular the Final Hearing); and whether it may be possible for the expert to give evidence by telephone conference or video link: see paragraphs 10.1 and 10.2 (Arrangements for experts to give evidence) of Practice Direction 25B;

(m)   the possibility of making, through their instructing solicitors, representations to the court about being named or otherwise identified in any public judgment given by the court;

(n)   whether the instructing party has public funding and the legal aid rates of payment which are applicable.

Confidentiality of children proceedings and making preliminary enquiries of an expert

3.3 For the purposes of the law of contempt of court, information relating to children proceedings (whether or not contained in a document filed with the court or recorded in any form) may be communicated only to an expert whose instruction by a party has been permitted by the court (see FPR 12.73(1)(a)(vii) and 14.14(c)(vii)) as children proceedings are confidential.

3.4 Before permission is obtained from the court to instruct an expert in children proceedings, the party seeking permission needs to make the enquiries of the expert referred to above in order to provide the court with information to enable it to decide whether to give permission. In practice, enquiries may need to be made of more than one expert for this purpose. This will in turn require each expert to be given sufficient information about the case to decide whether or not he or she is in a position to accept instructions. Such preliminary enquiries, and the disclosure of information about the case which is a necessary part of such enquiries, will not require the court's permission and will not amount to a contempt of court.

Expert's response to preliminary enquiries

3.5 In good time for the hearing at which the court will consider whether to give permission for an expert to be instructed, a child to be examined or otherwise assessed or expert evidence to be put before the court, the party or parties intending to instruct the expert must obtain the confirmations from the expert referred to in paragraph 8.1 of Practice Direction 25B. These confirmations include that the work is within the expert's expertise, the expert is available to do the work within the relevant timescale and the expert's costs.

3.6 Where the parties cannot agree who should be the single joint expert before the hearing at which the court will consider whether to give permission for an expert to be instructed, a child to be examined or otherwise assessed or expert evidence to be put before the court, they should obtain the above confirmations in respect of all experts whom they intend to put to the court for the purposes of FPR 25.11(2)(a) as candidates for the appointment.

The application for the court's permission mentioned in [section 13(1), (3) and (5) of the 2014 Act][2]

TIMING AND ORAL APPLICATIONS FOR THE COURT'S PERMISSION MENTIONED IN FPR 25.4

3.7 An application for the court's permission for an expert to be instructed, a child to be examined or otherwise assessed or expert evidence to be put before the court should be made as soon as it becomes apparent that it is necessary to make it. FPR 25.6 makes provision about the time by which applications for the court's permission should be made.

3.8 Applications should, wherever possible, be made so that they are considered at any directions hearing or other hearing for which a date has been fixed or for which a date is about to be fixed. It should be noted that one application notice can be used by a party to make more than one application for an order or direction at a hearing held during the course of proceedings. An application for the court's permission for an expert to be instructed, a child to be examined or otherwise assessed or expert evidence to be put before the court may therefore be included in an application notice requesting other orders to be made at such a hearing.

3.9 Where a date for a hearing has been fixed, a party who wishes to make an application at that hearing but does not have sufficient time to file an application notice should as soon as possible inform the court (if possible in writing) and, if possible, the other parties of the nature of the application and the reason for it. The party should provide the court and the other party with as much as possible of the information referred to in FPR 25.7 and paragraph 3.10 below. That party should then make the application orally at the hearing. An oral application of this kind should be the exception and reserved for genuine cases where circumstances are such that it has only become apparent shortly before the hearing that an expert opinion is necessary.

THE APPLICATION

3.10 In addition to the matters specified in FPR 25.7(2)(a) and (3), an application for the court's permission for an expert to be instructed, a child to be examined or otherwise assessed or expert evidence to be put before the court, must state –

(a)   the discipline, qualifications and expertise of the expert (by way of C.V. where possible);

(b)   the expert's availability to undertake the work;

(c)   the timetable for the report;

(d)   the responsibility for instruction;

(e)   whether the expert evidence can properly be obtained by only one party (for example, on behalf of the child);

(f)   why the expert evidence proposed cannot properly be given by an officer of the service, Welsh family proceedings officer or the local authority (social services undertaking a core assessment) in accordance with their respective statutory duties or any other party to the proceedings or an expert already instructed in the proceedings;

(g)   the likely cost of the report on an hourly or other charging basis;

(h)   the proposed apportionment (at least in the first instance) of any jointly instructed expert's fee; when it is to be paid; and, if applicable, whether public funding has been approved.

The terms of the draft order to be attached to the application for the court's permission

3.11 FPR 25.7(2)(b) provides that a draft of the order giving the court's permission as mentioned in [section 13(1), (3) and (5) of the 2014 Act][2] is to be attached to the application for the court's permission. That draft order must set out the following matters –

(a)   the issues in the proceedings to which the expert evidence is to relate and which the court is to identify;

(b)   the questions relating to the issues in the case which the expert is to answer and which the court is to approve ensuring that they –

(i)   are within the ambit of the expert's area of expertise;

(ii)   do not contain unnecessary or irrelevant detail;

(iii)   are kept to a manageable number and are clear, focused and direct;

(c)   the party who is responsible for drafting the letter of instruction and providing the documents to the expert;

(d)   the timetable within which the report is to be prepared, filed and served;

(e)   the disclosure of the report to the parties and to any other expert;

(f)   the organisation of, preparation for and conduct of any experts' discussion (see Practice Direction 25E – Discussions between Experts in Family Proceedings);

(g)   the preparation of a statement of agreement and disagreement by the experts following an experts' discussion;

(h) making available to the court at an early opportunity the expert reports in electronic form;

(i) the attendance of the expert at court to give oral evidence (alternatively, the expert giving his or her evidence in writing or remotely by video link), whether at or for the Final Hearing or another hearing; unless agreement about the opinions given by the expert is reached at or before the Issues Resolution Hearing ('IRH') or, if no IRH is to be held, by a date specified by the court prior to the hearing at which the expert is to give oral evidence.

Letter of instruction

4.1 The party responsible for instructing the expert shall prepare (in agreement with the other parties where appropriate), a letter of instruction to the expert and shall –

(a) set out the context in which the expert's opinion is sought (including any ethnic, cultural, religious or linguistic contexts);

(b) set out the questions approved by the court and which the expert is required to answer and any other linked questions ensuring that they –

    (i) are within the ambit of the expert's area of expertise;

    (ii) do not contain unnecessary or irrelevant detail;

    (iii) are kept to a manageable number and are clear, focused and direct; and

    (iv) reflect what the expert has been requested to do by the court

(Annex A to this Practice Direction sets out suggested questions in letters of instruction to (1) child mental health professionals or paediatricians, and (2) adult psychiatrists and applied psychologists, in Children Act 1989 proceedings);

(c) list the documentation provided, or provide for the expert an indexed and paginated bundle which shall include –

    (i) an agreed list of essential reading; and

    (ii) a copy of this Practice Direction and Practice Directions 25B and E and where appropriate Practice Direction 15B;

(d) identify any materials provided to the expert which have not been produced either as original medical (or other professional) records or in response to an instruction from a party, and state the source of that material (such materials may contain an assumption as to the standard of proof, the admissibility or otherwise of hearsay evidence, and other important procedural and substantive questions relating to the different purposes of other enquiries, for example, criminal or disciplinary proceedings);

(e) identify all requests to third parties for disclosure and their responses in order to avoid partial disclosure, which tends only to prove a case rather than give full and frank information;

(f) identify the relevant people concerned with the proceedings (for example, the treating clinicians) and inform the expert of his or her right to talk to them provided that an accurate record is made of the discussions;

(g) identify any other expert instructed in the proceedings and advise the expert of their right to talk to the other experts provided that an accurate record is made of the discussions;

PART II – Statutory instruments

(h)   subject to any public funding requirement for prior authority, define the contractual basis upon which the expert is retained and in particular the funding mechanism including how much the expert will be paid (an hourly rate and overall estimate should already have been obtained), when the expert will be paid, and what limitation there might be on the amount the expert can charge for the work which they will have to do. In cases where the parties are publicly funded, there may also be a brief explanation of the costs and expenses excluded from public funding by Funding Code criterion 1.3 and the detailed assessment process.

Adult who is a protected party

5.1 Where the adult is a protected party, that party's representative shall be involved in any instruction of an expert, including the instruction of an expert to assess whether the adult, although a protected party, is competent to give evidence (see Practice Direction 15B – Adults Who May Be Protected Parties and Children Who May Become Protected Parties in Family Proceedings).

Asking the court to settle the letter of instruction to a single joint expert

6.1 Where possible, the written request for the court to consider the letter of instruction referred to in rule 25.12(2) should be set out in an e-mail to the court and copied by e-mail to the other instructing parties. The request should be sent to the relevant court or (by prior arrangement only) directly to the judge dealing with the proceedings. [Where a legal adviser has been appointed as the case manager, the request should also be sent to the appointed legal adviser.]2 The court will settle the letter of instruction, usually without a hearing to avoid delay; and will send (where practicable, by e-mail) the settled letter to the lead solicitor for transmission forthwith to the expert, and copy it to the other instructing parties for information.

Annex A

(drafted by the Family Justice Council)

Suggested questions in letters of instruction to child mental health professional or paediatrician in Children Act 1989 proceedings

A. *The Child(ren)*

1. Please describe the child(ren)'s current health, development and functioning (according to your area of expertise), and identify the nature of any significant changes which have occurred

- Behavioural
- Emotional
- Attachment organisation
- Social/peer/sibling relationships
- Cognitive/educational
- Physical
  - Growth, eating, sleep

       – Non-organic physical problems (including wetting and soiling)
       – Injuries
       – Paediatric conditions

2. Please comment on the likely explanation for/aetiology of the child(ren)'s problems/difficulties/injuries

- History/experiences (including intrauterine influences, and abuse and neglect)
- Genetic/innate/developmental difficulties
- Paediatric/psychiatric disorders

3. Please provide a prognosis and risk if difficulties not addressed above.

4. Please describe the child(ren)'s needs in the light of the above

- Nature of care-giving
- Education
- Treatment

in the short and long term (subject, where appropriate, to further assessment later).

B. The parents/primary carers

5. Please describe the factors and mechanisms which would explain the parents' (or primary carers) harmful or neglectful interactions with the child(ren) (if relevant).

6. What interventions have been tried and what has been the result?

7. Please assess the ability of the parents or primary carers to fulfil the child(ren)'s identified needs now.

8. What other assessments of the parents or primary carers are indicated?

- Adult mental health assessment
- Forensic risk assessment
- Physical assessment
- Cognitive assessment

9. What, if anything, is needed to assist the parents or primary carers now, within the child(ren)'s timescales and what is the prognosis for change?

- Parenting work
- Support
- Treatment/therapy

C. Alternatives

10. Please consider the alternative possibilities for the fulfilment of the child(ren)'s needs

- What sort of placement
- Contact arrangements

Please consider the advantages, disadvantages and implications of each for the child(ren).

Suggested questions in letters of instruction to adult psychiatrists and applied psychologists in Children Act 1989 proceedings

1. Does the parent/adult have – whether in his/her history or presentation – a mental illness/disorder (including substance abuse) or other psychological/ emotional difficulty and, if so, what is the diagnosis?

2. How do any/all of the above (and their current treatment if applicable) affect his/her functioning, including interpersonal relationships?

3. If the answer to Q1 is yes, are there any features of either the mental illness or psychological/emotional difficulty or personality disorder which could be associated with risk to others, based on the available evidence base (whether published studies or evidence from clinical experience)?

4. What are the experiences/antecedents/aetiology which would explain his/ her difficulties, if any, (taking into account any available evidence base or other clinical experience)?

5. What treatment is indicated, what is its nature and the likely duration?

6. What is his/her capacity to engage in/partake of the treatment/therapy?

7. Are you able to indicate the prognosis for, time scales for achieving, and likely durability of, change?

8. What other factors might indicate positive change?

(It is assumed that this opinion will be based on collateral information as well as interviewing the adult).][1]

NOTES

Amendment.[1] Practice Direction inserted: FPR 2010 6th Update, 31 January 2013.2 Text substituted: FPR Update, April 2014.

[Practice Direction 25D –
Financial Remedy Proceedings and Other Family Proceedings (Except Children Proceedings) – The Use of Single Joint Experts and the Process Leading to Expert Evidence Being Put Before the Court

This Practice Direction supplements FPR Part 25.

Scope of this Practice Direction

1.1 This Practice Direction applies to financial remedy proceedings and other family proceedings except children proceedings and contains guidance on –

    (a)   the use of single joint experts;

    (b)   how to prepare for the hearing at which the court will consider whether to give permission for putting expert evidence (in any form) before the court including –

      (i)   preliminary enquiries of experts;

      (ii)   information to be given to the court before the hearing;

(c)   the letter of instruction to the expert.

Single joint experts

2.1 FPR 25.4 applies to a single joint expert ('SJE') in addition to an expert instructed by one party. This means that the court's permission is required to put expert evidence from an SJE (in any form) before the court. However, in family proceedings (except children proceedings) there is no requirement for the court's permission to be obtained before instructing an expert. Wherever possible, expert evidence should be obtained from a single joint expert instructed by both or all the parties ('SJE'). To that end, a party wishing to instruct an expert should first give the other party or parties a list of the names of one or more experts in the relevant speciality whom they consider suitable to be instructed.

2.2 Within 10 business days after receipt of the list of proposed experts, the other party or parties should indicate any objection to one or more of the named experts and, if so, supply the name(s) of one or more experts whom they consider suitable.

2.3 Each party should disclose whether they have already consulted any of the proposed experts about the issue(s) in question.

2.4 Where the parties cannot agree on the identity of the expert, each party should think carefully before instructing their own expert and seeking the permission of the court to put that expert evidence before it because of the costs implications. Disagreements about the use and identity of an expert may be better managed by the court in the context of an application for the court's permission to put the expert evidence before the court and for directions for the use of an SJE (see paragraph 2.6 below).

Agreement to instruct separate experts

2.5 If the parties agree to instruct separate experts and to seek the permission of the court to put the separate expert evidence before it –

(a)   they should agree in advance that the reports will be disclosed; and

(b)   the instructions to each expert should comply, so far as appropriate, with paragraphs 4.1 and 6.1 below (Letter of instruction).

Agreement to instruct an SJE

2.6 If there is agreement to instruct an SJE, before applying to the court for permission to put the expert evidence before it and directions for the use of an SJE, the parties should –

(a)   so far as appropriate, comply with the guidance in paragraphs 3.3 (Preliminary enquiries of the expert) and paragraphs 3.11 and 3.12 below;

(b)   receive the expert's confirmation in response to preliminary enquiries referred to in paragraph 8.1 of Practice Direction 25B;

PART II – Statutory instruments

(c)   have agreed in what proportion the SJE's fee is to be shared between them (at least in the first instance) and when it is to be paid; and

(d)   if applicable, have obtained agreement for public funding.

2.7 The instructions to the SJE should comply, so far as appropriate, with paragraphs 4.1 and 6.1 below (Letter of instruction).

The test for permission and preparation for the permission hearing

3.1 The test in [FPR 25.4(3)][2] which the court is to apply to determine whether permission should be given for expert evidence to be put before the court has been altered from one which refers to expert evidence being restricted by the court to that which is reasonably required to resolve the proceedings to one which refers to the expert evidence being in the opinion of the court necessary to assist the court to resolve the proceedings. The overriding objective of the FPR, which is to enable the court to deal with cases justly, having regard to any welfare issues involved, continues to apply when the court is making the decision whether to give permission. In addition, the rules (FPR 25.5(2)) now tell the court what factors it is to have particular regard to when deciding whether to give permission. ...[2]

3.2 Paragraphs 3.3 to 3.12 below give guidance on how to prepare for the hearing at which the court will apply the test in [FPR 25.4(3)][2] and the factors in FPR 25.5(2) and decide whether to give permission for expert evidence to be put before the court. The purpose of the preparation is to ensure that the court has the information required to enable it to exercise its powers under [FPR 25.4(2) and 25.5(2)][2] in line with [FPR 25.4(3)][2].

Preliminary enquiries of the expert

3.3 In good time for the information requested to be available for the hearing at which the court will consider whether to give permission for expert evidence to be put before the court, the party or parties intending to instruct the expert shall approach the expert with the following information –

(a)   the nature of the proceedings and the issues likely to require determination by the court;

(b)   the issues in the proceedings to which the expert evidence is to relate;

(c)   the questions about which the expert is to be asked to give an opinion and which relate to the issues in the case;

(d)   whether permission is to be asked of the court for the use of another expert in the same or any related field (that is, to give an opinion on the same or related questions);

(e)   the volume of reading which the expert will need to undertake;

(f)   whether or not it will be necessary for the expert to conduct interviews and, if so, with whom;

(g)   the likely timetable of legal steps;

(h)   when the expert's report is likely to be required;

(i)   whether and, if so, what date has been fixed by the court for any hearing at which the expert may be required to give evidence (in particular the Final Hearing); and whether it may be possible for the expert to give evidence by telephone conference or video link: see paragraphs 10.1 and 10.2 (Arrangements for experts to give evidence) of Practice Direction 25B;

(j)   the possibility of making, through their instructing solicitors, representations to the court about being named or otherwise identified in any public judgment given by the court;

(k)   whether the instructing party has public funding and the legal aid rates of payment which are applicable.

Expert's response to preliminary enquiries

3.4 In good time for the hearing at which the court will consider whether to give permission for expert evidence to be put before the court, the solicitors or party intending to instruct the expert must obtain the confirmations from the expert referred to in paragraph 8.1 of Practice Direction 25B. These confirmations include that the work is within the expert's expertise, the expert is available to do the work within the relevant timescale and the expert's costs.

3.5 Where parties cannot agree who should be the single joint expert before the hearing at which the court will consider whether to give permission for expert evidence to be put before the court, they should obtain the above confirmations in respect of all experts whom they intend to put to the court for the purposes of rule 25.11(2)(a) as candidates for the appointment.

The application for the court's permission to put expert evidence before the court

TIMING AND ORAL APPLICATIONS FOR THE COURT'S PERMISSION

3.6 An application for the court's permission to put expert evidence before the court should be made as soon as it becomes apparent that it is necessary to make it. FPR 25.6 makes provision about the time by which applications for the court's permission should be made.

3.7 Applications should, wherever possible, be made so that they are considered at any directions hearing or other hearing for which a date has been fixed or for which a date is about to be fixed. It should be noted that one application notice can be used by a party to make more than one application for an order or direction at a hearing held during the course of proceedings. An application for the court's permission to put expert evidence before the court may therefore be included in an application notice requesting other orders to be made at such a hearing.

3.8 Where a date for a hearing has been fixed, a party who wishes to make an application at that hearing but does not have sufficient time to file an application notice should as soon as possible inform the court (if possible in writing) and, if possible, the other parties of the nature of the application and the reason for it. The party should provide the court and the other party with as much as possible of the information referred to in FPR 25.7 and paragraph 3.11 below. That party should then make the application orally at the hearing. An oral application of this kind should be the exception and reserved for genuine cases where circumstances are

PART II – Statutory instruments

such that it has only become apparent shortly before the hearing that an expert opinion is necessary.

3.9 In financial remedy proceedings, unless the court directs otherwise, parties must apply for permission to put expert evidence before the court as soon as possible and no later than the first appointment. The expectation is that the court will give directions extending the time by which permission should be obtained where there is good reason for parties to delay the decision whether to use expert evidence and make an application for the court's permission.

3.10 Examples of situations where the time for requesting permission to put expert evidence before the court is likely to be extended are where –

    (a)   a decision about the need for expert evidence cannot be made until replies to questionnaires in relation to Forms E have been fully considered; or

    (b)   valuations of property are agreed for the purposes of the Financial Dispute Resolution appointment but no agreement is reached to resolve the proceedings at that appointment and the court cannot make a consent order as mentioned in FPR 9.17(8). In these circumstances, it may become clear to a party that he or she will want to use expert valuations of property and an application for the court's permission for such valuation to be put before it may be made orally at the end of the appointment to avoid the need for a separate hearing about this issue. As with other oral applications, the party should provide the court and the other party with as much as possible of the information referred to in FPR 25.7 and paragraph 3.11 below. FPR 9.17(9) requires the court to give directions for the future course of the proceedings where it has not made a consent order including, where appropriate, the filing of evidence.

THE APPLICATION

3.11 In addition to the matters specified in FPR 25.7(2)(a), an application for the court's permission to put expert evidence before the court must state –

    (a)   the discipline, qualifications and expertise of the expert (by way of C.V. where possible);

    (b)   the expert's availability to undertake the work;

    (c)   the timetable for the report;

    (d)   the responsibility for instruction;

    (e)   whether the expert evidence can properly be obtained by only one party;

    (f)   why the expert evidence proposed cannot properly be given by an expert already instructed in the proceedings;

    (g)   the likely cost of the report on an hourly or other charging basis:

    (h)   the proposed apportionment (at least in the first instance) of any jointly instructed expert's fee; when it is to be paid; and, if applicable, whether public funding has been approved.

The draft order to be attached to the application for the court's permission

3.12 FPR 25.7(2)(b) provides that a draft of the order giving the court's permission to put expert evidence before the court is to be attached to the application for the court's permission. That draft order must set out the following matters –

(a) the issues in the proceedings to which the expert evidence is to relate;

(b) the party who is to be responsible for drafting the letter of instruction and providing the documents to the expert;

(c) the timetable within which the report is to be prepared, filed and served;

(d) the disclosure of the report to the parties and to any other expert;

(e) the organisation of, preparation for and conduct of any experts' discussion (see Practice Direction 25E – Discussions between Experts in Family Proceedings);

(f) the preparation of a statement of agreement and disagreement by the experts following an experts' discussion;

(g) making available to the court at an early opportunity the expert reports in electronic form;

(h) the attendance of the expert at court to give oral evidence (alternatively, the expert giving his or her evidence in writing or remotely by video link), whether at or for the Final Hearing or another hearing; unless agreement about the opinions given by the expert is reached by a date specified by the court prior to the hearing at which the expert is to give oral evidence.

Letter of instruction

4.1 The party responsible for instructing the expert shall, within 5 business days after the permission hearing, prepare (in agreement with the other parties where appropriate), file and serve a letter of instruction to the expert which shall –

(a) set out the context in which the expert's opinion is sought (including any ethnic, cultural, religious or linguistic contexts);

(b) set out the questions which the expert is required to answer and ensuring that they –

    (i) are within the ambit of the expert's area of expertise;

    (ii) do not contain unnecessary or irrelevant detail;

    (iii) are kept to a manageable number and are clear, focused and direct; and

    (iv) reflect what the expert has been requested to do by the court;

(c) list the documentation provided, or provide for the expert an indexed and paginated bundle which shall include –

    (i) an agreed list of essential reading; and

    (ii) a copy of this Practice Direction and Practice Directions 25B, 25E and where appropriate Practice Direction 15B;

(d) identify any materials provided to the expert which have not been produced either as original medical (or other professional) records or in response to an instruction from a party, and state the source of that material (such materials may contain an assumption as to the standard of proof, the admissibility or otherwise of hearsay evidence, and other important procedural and substantive questions relating to the different purposes of other enquiries);

(e) identify all requests to third parties for disclosure and their responses in order to avoid partial disclosure, which tends only to prove a case rather than give full and frank information;

(f) identify the relevant people concerned with the proceedings and inform the expert of his or her right to talk to them provided that an accurate record is made of the discussions;

(g) identify any other expert instructed in the proceedings and advise the expert of their right to talk to the other experts provided that an accurate record is made of the discussions;

(h) subject to any public funding requirement for prior authority, define the contractual basis upon which the expert is retained and in particular the funding mechanism including how much the expert will be paid (an hourly rate and overall estimate should already have been obtained), when the expert will be paid, and what limitation there might be on the amount the expert can charge for the work which they will have to do. In cases where the parties are publicly funded, there may also be a brief explanation of the costs and expenses excluded from public funding by Funding Code criterion 1.3 and the detailed assessment process.

Adult who is a protected party

5.1 Where the adult is a protected party, that party's representative shall be involved in any instruction of an expert, including the instruction of an expert to assess whether the adult, although a protected party, is competent to give evidence (see Practice Direction 15B – Adults Who May Be Protected Parties and Children Who May Become Protected Parties in Family Proceedings).

Asking the court to settle the letter of instruction to a single joint expert

6.1 Where possible, the written request for the court to consider the letter of instruction referred to in rule 25.12(2) should be set out in an e-mail to the court and copied by e-mail to the other instructing parties. The request should be sent to the relevant court or (by prior arrangement only) directly to the judge dealing with the proceedings. [Where a legal adviser has been appointed as the case manager, the request should also be sent to the appointed legal adviser.][2] The court will settle the letter of instruction, usually without a hearing to avoid delay; and will send (where practicable, by e-mail) the settled letter to the party responsible for instructing the expert for transmission forthwith to the expert, and copy it to the other instructing parties for information.][1]

NOTES

Amendment.[1] Practice Direction inserted: FPR 2010 6th Update, 31 January 2013. [2] Text substituted: FPR Update, April 2014.

[Practice Direction 25E – Discussions Between Experts in Family Proceedings

This Practice Direction supplements FPR Part 25.

Scope

1.1 This Practice Direction supports FPR 25.16 by providing details about how and when experts discussions are to be arranged, their purpose and content. This Practice Direction applies to children proceedings and all other family proceedings.

Experts' discussion or meeting: purpose

2.1 In accordance with FPR 25.16, the court may, at any stage, direct a discussion between experts for the purpose outlined in paragraph (1) of that rule. FPR 25.16(2) provides that the court may specify the issues which the experts must discuss. The expectation is that those issues will include –

  (a) the reasons for disagreement on any expert question and what, if any, action needs to be taken to resolve any outstanding disagreement or question;

  (b) an explanation of existing evidence or additional evidence in order to assist the court to determine the issues.

One of the aims of specifying the issues for discussion is to limit, wherever possible, the need for the experts to attend court to give oral evidence.

Experts' discussion or meeting: arrangements

3.1 Subject to the directions given by the court under FPR 25.16, the solicitor or other professional who is given the responsibility by the court ('the nominated professional') shall within 15 business days after the experts' reports have been filed and copied to the other parties, make arrangements for the experts to have discussions. Subject to any specification by the court of the issues which experts must discuss under FPR 25.16(2), the following matters should be considered as appropriate –

  (a) where permission has been given for the instruction of experts from different disciplines, a global discussion may be held relating to those questions that concern all or most of them;

  (b) separate discussions may have to be held among experts from the same or related disciplines, but care should be taken to ensure that the discussions complement each other so that related questions are discussed by all relevant experts;

  (c) 5 business days prior to a discussion or meeting, the nominated professional should formulate an agenda including a list of questions for consideration. The agenda should, subject always to the provisions of FPR 25.16(1), focus on those questions which are intended to clarify areas of agreement or disagreement.
  Questions which repeat questions asked in the court order giving permission for an expert to be instructed or expert evidence to be put before the court or the letter of instruction or which seek to rehearse cross-examination in advance of the hearing should be rejected as likely to defeat the purpose of the meeting. The agenda may usefully take the form of a list of questions to be circulated among the other parties in advance and should comprise all questions that each party wishes the experts to consider.
  The agenda and list of questions should be sent to each of the experts not later than 2 business days before the discussion;

  (d) the nominated professional may exercise his or her discretion to accept further questions after the agenda with the list of questions has been circulated to the parties. Only in exceptional circumstances should

PART II – Statutory instruments

questions be added to the agenda within the 2-day period before the meeting. Under no circumstances should any question received on the day of or during the meeting be accepted. This does not preclude questions arising during the meeting for the purposes of clarification. Strictness in this regard is vital, for adequate notice of the questions enables the parties to identify and isolate the expert issues in the case before the meeting so that the experts' discussion at the meeting can concentrate on those issues;

(e)   the discussion should be chaired by the nominated professional. A minute must be taken of the questions answered by the experts. Where the court has given a direction under FPR 25.16(3) and subject to that direction, a Statement of Agreement and Disagreement must be prepared which should be agreed and signed by each of the experts who participated in the discussion. In accordance with FPR25.16(3) the statement must contain a summary of the experts' reasons for disagreeing. The statement should be served and filed not later than 5 business days after the discussion has taken place;

(f)   in each case, whether some or all of the experts participate by telephone conference or video link to ensure that minimum disruption is caused to professional schedules and that costs are minimised.

Meetings or conferences attended by a jointly instructed expert

4.1 Jointly instructed experts should not attend any meeting or conference which is not a joint one, unless all the parties have agreed in writing or the court has directed that such a meeting may be held, and it is agreed or directed who is to pay the expert's fees for the meeting or conference. Any meeting or conference attended by a jointly instructed expert should be proportionate to the case.

(Practice Direction 25C, paragraphs 2.1 to 2.7 deals generally with single joint experts in children proceedings and Practice Direction 25D paragraphs 2.1 to 2.7 deals with single joint experts in relation to other family proceedings).

Court-directed meetings involving experts in public law Children Act cases

5.1 In public law Children Act proceedings, where the court gives a direction that a meeting shall take place between the local authority and any relevant named experts for the purpose of providing assistance to the local authority in the formulation of plans and proposals for the child, the meeting shall be arranged, chaired and minuted in accordance with the directions given by the court.][1]

NOTES

Amendment.[1] Practice Direction inserted: FPR 2010 6th Update, 31 January 2013.

[Practice Direction 25F –
Assessors in Family Proceedings

This Practice Direction supplements FPR Part 25.

Scope of this Practice Direction

1.1 This Practice Direction applies to the appointment of assessors in family proceedings in England and Wales.

Appointment of assessors in family proceedings

2.1 [The power to appoint one or more assessors to assist the court is conferred by section 70(1) of the Senior Courts Act 1981, which applies to the family court via section 31E(1) of the Matrimonial and Family Proceedings Act 1984 (and section 31J(e) of that Act confirms that this is the case).][2] In practice, these powers have been used in appeals from a district judge or costs judge in costs assessment proceedings – although, in principle, the statutory powers permit one or more assessors to be appointed in any family proceedings where the High Court or [the family][2] court sees fit.

2.2 Not less than 21 days before making any such appointment, the court will notify each party in writing of the name of the proposed assessor, of the matter in respect of which the assistance of the assessor will be sought and of the qualifications of the assessor to give that assistance.

2.3 Any party may object to the proposed appointment, either personally or in respect of the proposed assessor's qualifications.

2.4 Any such objection must be made in writing and filed and served within 7 business days of receipt of the notification from the court of the proposed appointment, and will be taken into account by the court in deciding whether or not to make the appointment.][1]

NOTES

Amendment.[1] Practice Direction inserted: FPR 2010 6th Update, 31 January 2013. [2] Text substituted: FPR Update, April 2014.

[Practice Direction 25G – Toxicology Test Evidence

This practice direction supplements Part 25 of the Family Procedure Rules 2010

1 This practice direction applies whenever a person seeks to put before the court, or to instruct a person to provide, expert evidence in the form of or based on toxicology testing carried out on a person with a view to establishing whether such testing provides evidence of the abuse of drugs or alcohol.

2 The court will not give permission to put the evidence before the court, or as the case may be to instruct the person, unless the condition in paragraph 3 or 4 is met.

3 Where the testing has not been carried out and a person is seeking to instruct a person to carry out testing or provide evidence on the basis of such testing, the laboratory which is to carry out the testing must at the time of the application for permission to instruct be accredited to –

(a) International Organisation for Standardisation ISO/IEC 17025: 2017 General Requirements for the competence of testing and calibration laboratories; or

(b) International Organisation for Standardisation ISO 15189: Medical laboratories – Requirements for quality and competence.

PART II – Statutory instruments

4 Where the testing has been carried out and a person is seeking to put the evidence before the court –

(a)   the laboratory which carried out the testing must at the time of the testing have been accredited to –

(i)   International Organisation for Standardisation ISO/IEC 17025: 2017 General Requirements for the competence of testing and calibration laboratories; or

(ii)   International Organisation for Standardisation ISO 15189: Medical laboratories – Requirements for quality and competence; or

(b)   the court must be satisfied that there are exceptional circumstances justifying giving permission to put the evidence before the court.][1]

NOTES

Amendment.[1] Practice Direction inserted: FPR Update, March 2020.

****

PART 27
HEARINGS AND DIRECTIONS APPOINTMENTS

27.1 Application of this Part

This Part is subject to any enactment, any provision in these rules or a practice direction.

(Rule 27.4(7) makes additional provision in relation to requirements to stay proceedings where the respondent does not appear and a relevant European regulation or international convention applies.)

27.2 Reasons for a decision[: proceedings before a lay justice or justices][1]

(1) This rule applies to proceedings [in the family court before a lay justice or justices][1].

(2) After a hearing, the court will make its decision as soon as is practicable.

(3) The court must give written reasons for its decision.

(4) Paragraphs (5) and (6) apply where the functions of the court are being performed by –

(a)   two or three lay justices; or

(b)   by a single lay justice in accordance with these rules and Practice Direction 2A.

(5) The [justices' legal adviser][2] must, before the court makes an order or refuses an application or request, make notes of –

(a)   the names of the [lay][1] justice or justices constituting the court by which the decision is made; and

(b)   in consultation with the [lay][1] justice or justices, the reasons for the court's decision.

(6) The [justices' legal adviser]² must make a written record of the reasons for the court's decision.

(7) When making an order or refusing an application, the court, or one of the [lay]¹ justices constituting the court by which the decision is made, will announce its decision and –

    (a)   the reasons for that decision; or

    (b)   a short explanation of that decision.

(8) Subject to any other rule or practice direction, the court officer will supply a copy of the order and the reasons for the court's decision to the persons referred to in paragraph (9) –

    (a)   by close of business on the day when the court announces its decision; or

    (b)   where that time is not practicable and the proceedings are on notice, no later than 72 hours from the time when the court announced its decision.

(9) The persons referred to in paragraph (8) are –

    (a)   the parties (unless the court directs otherwise);

    (b)   any person who has actual care of a child who is the subject of proceedings, or who had such care immediately prior to the making of the order;

    (c)   in the case of an emergency protection order and a recovery order, the local authority in whose area the child lives or is found;

    (d)   in proceedings to which Part 14 applies –

        (i)   an adoption agency or local authority which has prepared a report on the suitability of the applicant to adopt a child;

        (ii)   a local authority which has prepared a report on the placement of the child for adoption;

    (e)   any other person who has requested a copy if the court is satisfied that it is required in connection with an appeal or possible appeal.

(10) ...¹

(Rule 12.16(5) provides for the applicant to serve a section 8 order and an order in emergency proceedings made without notice within 48 hours after the making of the order. Rule 10.6(1) provides for the applicant to serve the order in proceedings under Part 4 of the 1996 Act. Rule 4.1(3)(a) permits the court to extend or shorten the time limit for compliance with any rule. Rule 6.33 provides for other persons to be supplied with copy documents under paragraph (8).)

NOTES

Amendments.¹ Words substituted and inserted, paragraph omitted: SI 2014/667. ² Words substituted: SI 2020/135.

27.3 Attendance at hearing or directions appointment

Unless the court directs otherwise, a party shall attend a hearing or directions appointment of which that party has been given notice.

PART II – Statutory instruments

27.4 Proceedings in the absence of a party

(1) Proceedings or any part of them shall take place in the absence of any party, including a party who is a child, if –

  (a)   the court considers it in the interests of the party, having regard to the matters to be discussed or the evidence likely to be given; and

  (b)   the party is represented by a children's guardian or solicitor,

and when considering the interests of a child under sub-paragraph (a) the court shall give the children's guardian, the solicitor for the child and, if of sufficient understanding and the court thinks it appropriate, the child, an opportunity to make representations.

(2) Subject to paragraph (3), where at the time and place appointed for a hearing or directions appointment the applicant appears but one or more of the respondents do not, the court may proceed with the hearing or appointment.

(3) The court shall not begin to hear an application in the absence of a respondent unless –

  (a)   it is proved to the satisfaction of the court that the respondent received reasonable notice of the date of the hearing; or

  (b)   the court is satisfied that the circumstances of the case justify proceeding with the hearing.

(4) Where, at the time and place appointed for a hearing or directions appointment, one or more of the respondents appear but the applicant does not, the court may refuse the application or, if sufficient evidence has previously been received, proceed in the absence of the applicant.

(5) Where, at the time and place appointed for a hearing or directions appointment, neither the applicant nor any respondent appears, the court may refuse the application.

(6) Paragraphs (2) to (5) do not apply to a hearing to which paragraphs (5) to (8) of rule 12.14 do not apply by virtue of paragraph (9) of that rule.

(7) Nothing in this rule affects any provision of [an][1] international convention by which the United Kingdom is bound which requires a court to stay proceedings where a respondent in another State has not been adequately served with proceedings in accordance with the requirements of that …[1] convention.

NOTES

Amendments.[1] Words substituted and words omitted repealed: SI 2019/517.

27.5 Application to set aside judgment or order following failure to attend

(1) Where a party does not attend a hearing or directions appointment and the court gives judgment or makes an order against him, the party who failed to attend may apply for the judgment or order to be set aside[(GL)].

(2) An application under paragraph (1) must be supported by evidence.

---

(3) Where an application is made under paragraph (1), the court may grant the application only if the applicant –

- (a) acted promptly on finding out that the court had exercised its power to enter judgment or make an order against the applicant;
- (b) had a good reason for not attending the hearing or directions appointment; and
- (c) has a reasonable prospect of success at the hearing or directions appointment.

(4) …[1]

NOTES

Amendment.[1] Paragraph omitted: SI 2013/3204.

27.6 Court bundles and place of filing of documents and bundles

(1) The provisions of Practice Direction 27A must be followed for the preparation of court bundles and for other related matters in respect of hearings and directions appointments.

(2) …[1]

(3) …[1]

…[1]

NOTES

Amendments.[1] Paragraphs and words omitted: SI 2013/3204.

27.7 Representation of companies or other corporations

A company or other corporation may be represented at a hearing or directions appointment by an employee if –

- (a) the employee has been authorised by the company or corporation to appear at the hearing or directions appointment on its behalf; and
- (b) the court gives permission.

27.8 Impounded documents

(1) Documents impounded by order of the court must not be released from the custody of the court except in compliance with –

- (a) a court order; or
- (b) a written request made by a Law Officer or the Director of Public Prosecutions.

(2) A document released from the custody of the court under paragraph (1)(b) must be released into the custody of the person who requested it.

(3) Documents impounded by order of the court, while in the custody of the court, may not be inspected except by a person authorised to do so by a court order.

27.9 Recording, transcription and informal notes of proceedings

(1) At any hearing, the proceedings will be tape recorded or digitally recorded unless the court directs otherwise.

(2) No party or member of the public may use unofficial recording equipment in any court without the permission of the court. (To do so without permission constitutes a contempt of court under section 9 of the Contempt of Court Act 1981.)

(3) Unless the court directs otherwise, a person to whom paragraph (4) applies may require a transcript of the recording of any hearing in proceedings to be supplied to them, upon payment of the charges authorised by any scheme in force for the making of the recording or the transcript.

(4) This paragraph applies to –

    (a)   a party to the proceedings;
    (b)   the Queen's Proctor; and
    (c)   where a declaration of parentage has been made under section 55A of the 1986 Act, the Registrar General.

(5) A person to whom paragraph (4) does not apply may be provided with a transcript of the recording of any hearing –

    (a)   with the permission of the court; and
    (b)   upon payment of the charges authorised by any scheme in force for the making of the recording or the transcript.

(6) At any hearing, the court may give appropriate directions to assist a party, in particular one who is or has been or may become unrepresented, for the compilation and sharing of a note or other informal record of the proceedings made by another party.][1]

NOTES

Amendment.[1] Rule substituted: SI 2020/135.

27.10 Hearings in private

(1) Proceedings to which these rules apply will be held in private, except –

    (a)   where these rules or any other enactment provide otherwise;
    (b)   subject to any enactment, where the court directs otherwise.

(2) For the purposes of these rules, a reference to proceedings held 'in private' means proceedings at which the general public have no right to be present.

27.11 Attendance at private hearings

(1) This rule applies when proceedings are held in private, except in relation to –

    (a)   hearings conducted for the purpose of judicially assisted conciliation or negotiation;
    (b)   proceedings to which the following provisions apply –

> (i) Part 13 (proceedings under section 54 [or section 54A][1] of the Human Fertilisation and Embryology Act 2008);
> (ii) Part 14 (procedure for applications in adoption, placement and related proceedings); and
> (iii) any proceedings identified in a practice direction as being excepted from this rule.

(2) When this rule applies, no person shall be present during any hearing other than –

> (a) an officer of the court;
> (b) a party to the proceedings;
> (c) a litigation friend for any party, or legal representative instructed to act on that party's behalf;
> (d) an officer of the service or Welsh family proceedings officer;
> (e) a witness;
> (f) duly accredited representatives of news gathering and reporting organisations; ...[2]
> [(ff) a duly authorised lawyer attending for journalistic, research or public legal educational purposes; and][2]
> (g) any other person whom the court permits to be present.

(3) At any stage of the proceedings the court may direct that persons within paragraph (2)(f) [and (ff)][2] shall not attend the proceedings or any part of them, where satisfied that –

> (a) this is necessary –
> > (i) in the interests of any child concerned in, or connected with, the proceedings;
> > (ii) for the safety or protection of a party, a witness in the proceedings, or a person connected with such a party or witness; or
> > (iii) for the orderly conduct of the proceedings; or
> (b) justice will otherwise be impeded or prejudiced.

(4) The court may exercise the power in paragraph (3) of its own initiative or pursuant to representations made by any of the persons listed in paragraph (5), and in either case having given to any person within paragraph (2)(f) [or (ff)][2] who is in attendance an opportunity to make representations.

(5) At any stage of the proceedings, the following persons may make representations to the court regarding restricting the attendance of persons within paragraph (2)(f) [and (ff)][2] in accordance with paragraph (3) –

> (a) a party to the proceedings;
> (b) any witness in the proceedings;
> (c) where appointed, any children's guardian;
> (d) where appointed, an officer of the service or Welsh family proceedings officer, on behalf of the child the subject of the proceedings;
> (e) the child, if of sufficient age and understanding.

(6) This rule does not affect any power of the court to direct that witnesses shall be excluded until they are called for examination.

PART II – Statutory instruments

[(7) In this rule—

'duly accredited' refers to accreditation in accordance with any administrative scheme for the time being approved for the purposes of this rule by the Lord Chancellor; and

'duly authorised lawyer' means a person who meets the criteria specified in Practice Direction 27B.][2]

NOTES

Amendments.[1] Words inserted: SI 2018/1413. [2] Word omitted repealed, words inserted and paragraph substituted: SI 2021/875.

Practice Direction 27A –
Family Proceedings: Court Bundles (Universal Practice to be applied in the High Court and Family Court)

This Practice Direction supplements FPR Part 27.

1.1 The President of the Family Division has issued this practice direction to achieve consistency across the country in the Family Court and the Family Division of the High Court in the preparation of court bundles and in respect of other related matters.

Application of the practice direction

2.1 Except as specified in paragraph 2.4, subject to specific directions given in any particular case and, in relation to electronic bundles, subject to such directions in relation to local arrangements ('the local arrangements') as have been specified by the designated family judge for the relevant area wih the agreement of the President of the Family Division, the following practice applies to:

(a)   all hearings before a judge sitting in the Family Division of the High Court wherever the court may be sitting; and

(b)   all hearings in the Family Court.

2.2 'Hearing' includes all appearances before the court, whether with or without notice to other parties, whether at first instance or (subject to paragraph 5.2A.3) on appeal and whether for directions or for substantive relief.

2.3 This practice direction applies whether a bundle is being lodged for the first time or is being re-lodged for a further hearing (see paragraph 9.2).

2.4 This practice direction does not apply to the hearing of any urgent application if and to the extent that it is impossible to comply with it.

2.5 This practice direction applies whether the bundle is prepared and presented in paper or in electronic format. In relation to a hearing before a High Court Judge an electronic bundle may be used with the permission of the judge and in accordance with directions given by the judge. In relation to all other hearings an electronic bundle may be used only -

(a)   in such cases or classes of case as have been approved by the designated family judge for the relevant area with the agreement of the President of the Family Division; and

(b)   in accordance with the local arrangements.

2.6 In this practice direction, the term "lodged with the Court" and any comparable expression in respect of an electronic bundle means making the electronic bundle available to the Court or Judge (and, where required, to the other parties) in accordance with the local arrangements.

Responsibility for the preparation of the bundle

3.1 A bundle for the use of the court at the hearing shall be provided by the party in the position of applicant at the hearing (or, if there are cross-applications, by the party whose application was first in time) or, if that person is a litigant in person, by the first listed respondent who is not a litigant in person. Where all the parties are litigants in person none of them shall, unless the court otherwise directs, be obliged to provide a bundle, but any bundle which they choose to lodge must be prepared and lodged so as to comply with this practice direction.

3.2 The party preparing the bundle shall paginate it using Arabic numbering throughout. If possible the contents of the bundle shall be agreed by all parties.

Contents of the bundle

4.1 The bundle shall contain copies of only those documents which are relevant to the hearing and which it is necessary for the court to read or which will actually be referred to during the hearing. In particular, copies of the following classes of documents must not be included in the bundle unless specifically directed by the court:

(a)   correspondence (including letters of instruction to experts);

(b)   medical records (including hospital, GP and health visitor records);

(c)   bank and credit card statements and other financial records;

(d)   notes of contact visits;

(e)   foster carer logs;

(f)   social services files (with the exception of any assessment being relied on by any of the parties);

(g)   police disclosure.

This does not prevent the inclusion in the bundle of specific documents which it is necessary for the court to read or which will actually be referred to during the hearing.

4.2 The documents in the bundle shall be arranged in chronological order from the front of the bundle, paginated individually and consecutively (starting with page 1 and using Arabic numbering throughout), indexed and divided into separate sections (each section being separately paginated) as follows:

(a)   preliminary documents (see paragraph 4.3) and any other case management documents required by any other practice direction;

(b)   applications and orders;

PART II – Statutory instruments

(c)   statements and affidavits (which must be dated in the top right corner of the front page) but without exhibiting or duplicating documents referred to in para 4.1;

(d)   care plans (where appropriate);

(e)   experts' reports and other reports (including those of a guardian, children's guardian or litigation friend); and

(f)   other documents, divided into further sections as may be appropriate.

All statements, affidavits, care plans, experts' reports and other reports included in the bundle must be copies of originals which have been signed and dated.

4.3 At the commencement of the bundle there shall be inserted the following documents (the preliminary documents):

(a)   an up to date case summary of the background to the hearing confined to those matters which are relevant to the hearing and the management of the case and limited, if practicable, to four A4 pages;

(b)   a statement of the issue or issues to be determined (1) at that hearing and (2) at the final hearing;

(c)   a position statement by each party including a summary of the order or directions sought by that party (1) at that hearing and (2) at the final hearing;

(d)   an up to date chronology, if it is a final hearing or if the summary under (a) is insufficient, each entry being limited, if practicable, to one sentence and cross-referenced to the relevant page(s) in the bundle;

(e)   skeleton arguments, if appropriate;

(f)   a list of essential reading for that hearing; and

(g)   the time estimate (see paragraph 10.1).

4.3A.1 Copies of all authorities relied on must be contained in a separate composite bundle agreed between the advocates. Unless the court has specifically directed otherwise, being satisfied that such direction is necessary to enable the proceedings to be disposed of justly, the bundle shall not contain more than 10 authorities. Where a case is reported in a law report which contains a headnote, such a report shall be used and transcripts (including transcripts on BAILII) shall not be used. Where the bundle is in electronic format an appropriate hyperlink to each authority should be provided.

4.3A.2 Attention is drawn to paragraph 6 of Practice Direction (Citation of Authorities) [2001] 1 WLR 1001 and to Practice Direction (Citation of Authorities) [2012] 1 WLR 780 (both set out in The Family Court Practice) which must be complied with. The reference to "county court cases" in para 6.1 of the first practice direction should be read as including family court cases decided by a judge other than a judge of High Court judge level. Therefore, a judgment on an application attended by one party only, or on an application for permission to appeal, or that only decides that the application is arguable, or by the county court, or in the family court of a judge other than a judge of High Court judge level, may not be cited or included in the bundle of authorities unless either (i) the judgment clearly indicates that it purports to establish a new principle or to extend the present law or (ii) the court for good reason has specifically directed otherwise.

4.4 Each of the preliminary documents shall be as short and succinct as possible and shall state on the front page immediately below the heading the date when it was prepared and the date of the hearing for which it was prepared. Where proceedings relating to a child are being heard by magistrates the summary of the background shall be prepared in anonymised form, omitting the names and identifying information of every person referred to other than the parties' legal representatives, and stating the number of pages contained in the bundle. Identifying information can be contained in all other preliminary documents.

4.5 The summary of the background, statement of issues, chronology, position statement and any skeleton arguments shall be cross-referenced to the relevant pages of the bundle.

4.6 The summary of the background, statement of issues, chronology and reading list shall in the case of a final hearing, and shall so far as practicable in the case of any other hearing, each consist of a single document in a form agreed by all parties. Where the parties disagree as to the content the fact of their disagreement and their differing contentions shall be set out at the appropriate places in the document.

4.7 Where the nature of the hearing is such that a complete bundle of all documents is unnecessary, the bundle (which need not be repaginated) may comprise only those documents necessary for the hearing, but

   (a)   the summary of the background must commence with a statement that the bundle is limited or incomplete; and

   (b)   the bundle shall if reasonably practicable be in a form agreed by all parties.

4.8 Where the bundle is re-lodged in accordance with paragraph 9.2, before it is re-lodged:

   (a)   the bundle shall be updated as appropriate; and

   (b)   all superseded documents (and in particular all outdated summaries, statements of issues, chronologies, skeleton arguments and similar documents) shall be removed from the bundle.

Format of the bundle

5.1 Unless the court has specifically directed otherwise, being satisfied that such direction is necessary to enable the proceedings to be disposed of justly, the bundle (if a paper bundle) shall be contained in one A4 size ring binder or lever arch file limited to no more than 350 sheets of A4 paper and 350 sides of text and (if an electronic bundle) shall be limited to 350 pages of text.

5.2 All documents in the bundle (including statements, affidavits, care plans and experts' reports and other reports) shall (a) in the case of a paper bundle be copied on one side of paper only, unless the court has specifically directed otherwise, (b) be divided by the author into numbered paragraphs and (c) be typed or printed in a font no smaller than 12 point and with 1½ or double spacing.

5.2A.1 Unless the court has specifically directed otherwise, being satisfied that such direction is necessary to enable the proceedings to be disposed of justly, and subject to paragraph 5.2A.2 below, any of the following documents included in the bundle shall be limited to no more than the number of sheets of A4 paper and sides of text specified below:

Case summary	6
Statement of issues	
Position statement	3
Chronology	10
Skeleton argument	20
List of essential reading	1
Witness statement or affidavit (exclusive of exhibits)	25
Expert's or other report	40
(including executive summary at the beginning of no more than 4 pages)	
Care plan	10

5.2A.2 The length and content of skeleton arguments in financial remedy cases which have been allocated to a High Court Judge shall continue to be governed by paragraph 15 of the Statement on the Efficient Conduct of Financial Remedy Hearings dated 1 February 2016.

5.2A.3 In the case of an appeal the bundle must comply with the relevant paragraphs of PD 30A.

5.3 The ring binder or lever arch file shall have clearly marked on the front and the spine:

(a)   the title and number of the case;
(b)   the place where the case has been listed;
(c)   the hearing date and time;
(d)   if known, the name of the judge hearing the case; and
(e)   where in accordance with a direction of the court there is more than one ring binder or lever arch file, a distinguishing letter (A, B, C etc).

In the case of an electronic bundle the bundle must be clearly identifiable with the title and number of the case and as much of the information set out above as is practical should also be provided in accordance with the local arrangements.

Timetable for preparing and lodging the bundle

6.1 The party preparing the bundle shall, whether or not the bundle has been agreed, provide a paginated index to all other parties not less than 4 working days before the hearing.

6.2 Where counsel is to be instructed at any hearing, a paginated bundle shall (if not already in counsel's possession) be delivered to counsel by the person instructing that counsel not less than 3 working days before the hearing.

6.3 The bundle (with the exception of the preliminary documents if and insofar as they are not then available) shall be lodged with the court not less than 2 working days before the hearing, or at such other time as may be specified by the court.

6.4 The preliminary documents shall be lodged with the court no later than 11 am on the day before the hearing and, where the hearing is before a judge of the High Court and the name of the judge is known, shall (with the exception of the authorities, which are to be lodged in hard copy and not sent by email) at the same time be sent by email to the judge's clerk.

Lodging the bundle

7.1 The bundle shall be lodged at the appropriate office. If the bundle is lodged in the wrong place the court may:

    (a)   treat the bundle as having not been lodged; and

    (b)   take the steps referred to in paragraph 12.

7.2 Unless the court has given some other direction as to where the bundle in any particular case is to be lodged (for example a direction that the bundle is to be lodged with the judge's clerk) the bundle shall be lodged:

    (a)   for hearings at the RCJ, in the office of the Clerk of the Rules, 1st Mezzanine (Rm 1M), Queen's Building, Royal Courts of Justice, Strand, London WC2A 2LL (DX 44450 Strand);

    (b)   for hearings at any other place, at such place as may be designated by the designated family judge responsible for that place and in default of any such designation at the court office for the place where the hearing is to take place.

7.3 Any bundle sent to the court by post, DX or courier shall be clearly addressed to the appropriate office and shall show the date and place of the hearing on the outside of any packaging as well as on the bundle itself.

7.4 Unless the court has given some other direction or paragraph 7.5 applies only one copy of the bundle shall be lodged with the court but the party who is responsible for lodging the bundle shall bring to court at each hearing at which oral evidence may be called a copy of the bundle for use by the witnesses (or in the case of an electronic bundle make appropriate arrangements in accordance with the local arrangements for the use by the witnesses of the electronic bundle).

7.5 In the case of a hearing listed before a bench of magistrates four copies of the bundle shall be lodged with the court.

7.6 In the case of hearings at the RCJ or at any other place where the designated family judge responsible for that place has directed that this paragraph shall apply, parties shall:

    (a)   if the bundle or preliminary documents are delivered personally, ensure that they obtain a receipt from the clerk accepting it or them; and

    (b)   if the bundle or preliminary documents are sent by post or DX, ensure that they obtain proof of posting or despatch.

The receipt (or proof of posting or despatch, as the case may be) shall be brought to court on the day of the hearing and must be produced to the court if requested. If the receipt (or proof of posting or despatch) cannot be produced to the court the

PART II – Statutory instruments

judge may: (a) treat the bundle as having not been lodged; and (b) take the steps referred to in paragraph 12.

Lodging the bundle – additional requirements for Family Division or Family Court cases being heard at the RCJ

8.1 Bundles or preliminary documents delivered after 11 am on the day before the hearing may not be accepted by the Clerk of the Rules and if not shall be delivered:

    (a)   in a case where the hearing is before a judge of the High Court, directly to the clerk of the judge hearing the case;

    (b)   in a case where the hearing is before any other judge, to such place as may be specified by the Clerk of the Rules.

8.2 Upon learning before which judge a hearing is to take place, the clerk to counsel, or other advocate, representing the party in the position of applicant shall no later than 3 pm the day before the hearing:

    (a)   in a case where the hearing is before a judge of the High Court, telephone the clerk of the judge hearing the case;

    (b)   in a case where the hearing is before any other judge email the Clerk of the Rules at RCJ.familyhighcourt@hmcts.gsi.gov.uk;

to ascertain whether the judge has received the bundle (including the preliminary documents) and, if not, shall organise prompt delivery by the applicant's solicitor.

Removing and re-lodging the bundle

9.1 Unless either the court wishes to retain the bundle or specific alternative arrangements have been agreed with the court, the party responsible for the bundle shall, following completion of the hearing, retrieve the bundle from the court immediately or, if that is not practicable, collect it from the court within 5 working days. Bundles which are not collected in due time are liable to be destroyed without further notice. The local arrangements will specify the length of time that an electronic bundle will remain available to the court following a hearing.

9.2 The bundle shall be re-lodged for the next and any further hearings in accordance with the provisions of this practice direction and in a form which complies with para 4.7.

Time estimates

10.1 In every case a time estimate (which shall be inserted at the front of the bundle) shall be prepared which shall so far as practicable be agreed by all parties and shall:

    (a)   specify separately: (i) the time estimated to be required for judicial pre-reading; and (ii) the time required for hearing all evidence and submissions; and (iii) the time estimated to be required for preparing and delivering judgment;

(b) be prepared on the basis that before they give evidence all witnesses will have read all relevant filed statements and reports; and

(c) take appropriate account of any additional time likely to be incurred by the use of interpreters or intermediaries.

10.2 Once a case has been listed, any change in time estimates shall be notified immediately by telephone (and then immediately confirmed in writing):

(a) in the case of hearings in the RCJ, to the Clerk of the Rules; and

(b) in the case of hearings elsewhere, to the relevant listing officer.

Taking cases out of the list

11.1 As soon as it becomes known that a hearing will no longer be effective, whether as a result of the parties reaching agreement or for any other reason, the parties and their representatives shall immediately notify the court by telephone and email which shall be confirmed by letter. The letter, which shall wherever possible be a joint letter sent on behalf of all parties with their signatures applied or appended, shall include:

(a) a short background summary of the case;

(b) the written consent of each party who consents and, where a party does not consent, details of the steps which have been taken to obtain that party's consent and, where known, an explanation of why that consent has not been given;

(c) a draft of the order being sought; and

(d) enough information to enable the court to decide (i) whether to take the case out of the list and (ii) whether to make the proposed order.

Penalties for failure to comply with the practice direction

12.1 Failure to comply with any part of this practice direction may result in the judge removing the case from the list or putting the case further back in the list and may also result in a 'wasted costs' order or some other adverse costs order.

Commencement of the practice direction and application of other practice directions

13.1 This practice direction shall have effect from 23 July 2018.

14.1 This practice direction should where appropriate be read in conjunction with the Public Law Outline 2014 (PD12A) and the Child Arrangements Programme 2014 (PD12B). In particular, nothing in this practice direction is to be read as removing or altering any obligation to comply with the requirements of the Public Law Outline 2014 and the Child Arrangements Programme 2014.

This Practice Direction is issued –

(a) in relation to family proceedings, by the President of the Family Division, as the nominee of the Lord Chief Justice, with the agreement of the Lord Chancellor; and

(b) to the extent that it applies to proceedings to which section 5 of the Civil Procedure Act 1997 applies, by the Master of the Rolls as the nominee of the Lord Chief Justice, with the agreement of the Lord Chancellor

PART II – Statutory instruments

Practice Direction 27B –
Attendance of Media Representatives [or Duly Authorised Lawyers][1] at Hearings in Family Proceedings (High Court and County Courts)

This Practice Direction supplements FPR Part 27

NOTES

Amendment.[1] Words inserted: FPR Update, 15 July 2021.

1 Introduction

1.1 This Practice Direction supplements rule 27.11 of the Family Procedure Rules 2010 ('FPR 2010') and deals with the right of representatives of news gathering and reporting organisations ('media representatives') [and of duly authorised lawyers][1] to attend at hearings of family proceedings which take place in private subject to the discretion of the court to exclude such representatives [or such lawyers][1] from the whole or part of any hearing on specified grounds[1] It takes effect on 27 April 2009.

NOTES

Amendment.[1] Words inserted: FPR Update, 15 July 2021.

2 Matters unchanged by the rule

2.1 Rule 27.11(1) contains an express exception in respect of hearings which are conducted for the purpose of judicially assisted conciliation or negotiation and media representatives [or duly authorised lawyers][2] do not have a right to attend these hearings. Financial Dispute Resolution hearings will come within this exception. First Hearing Dispute Resolution appointments in private law Children Act cases will also come within this exception to the extent that the judge plays an active part in the conciliation process. Where the judge plays no part in the conciliation process or where the conciliation element of a hearing is complete and the judge is adjudicating upon the issues between the parties, media representatives [or duly authorised lawyers][2] should be permitted to attend, subject to the discretion of the court to exclude them on the specified grounds. Conciliation meetings or negotiation conducted between the parties with the assistance of an officer of the service or a Welsh Family Proceedings officer, and without the presence of the judge, are not 'hearings' within the meaning of this rule and media representatives [or duly authorised lawyers][2] have no right to attend such appointments.

The exception in rule 27.11(1) does not operate to exclude media representatives [or duly authorised lawyers][2] from –

- Hearings to consider applications brought under Parts IV and V of the Children Act 1989, including [Case Management Hearings, any Further Case Management Hearings]1 and Issues Resolution Hearings
- Hearings relating to findings of fact
- Interim hearings
- Final hearings.

The rights of media representatives [or duly authorised lawyers]2 to attend such hearings are limited only by the powers of the court to exclude such attendance on the limited grounds and subject to the procedures set out in paragraphs (3)–(5) of rule 27.11.

2.2 During any hearing, courts should consider whether the exception in rule 27.11(1) becomes applicable so that media representatives [or duly authorised lawyers][2] should be directed to withdraw.

2.3 The provisions of the rules permitting the attendance of media representatives [or duly authorised lawyers][2] and the disclosure to third parties of information relating to the proceedings do not entitle a media representative to receive or peruse court documents referred to in the course of evidence, submissions or judgment without the permission of the court or otherwise in accordance with Part 12, Chapter 7 of the Family Procedure Rules 2010 and Practice Direction 12G (rules relating to disclosure to third parties). (This is in contrast to the position in civil proceedings, where the court sits in public and where members of the public are entitled to seek copies of certain documents[1]).

1   See *GIO Services Ltd v Liverpool and London Ltd* [1999] 1 WLR 984.

2.4 The question of attendance of media representatives [or duly authorised lawyers][2] at hearings in family proceedings to which rule 27.11 and this guidance apply must be distinguished from statutory restrictions on publication and disclosure of information relating to proceedings, which continue to apply and are unaffected by the rule and this guidance.

2.5 The prohibition in section 97(2) of the Children Act 1989, on publishing material intended to or likely to identify a child as being involved in proceedings or the address or school of any such child, is limited to the duration of the proceedings[1]. However, the limitations imposed by section 12 of the Administration of Justice Act 1960 on publication of information relating to certain proceedings in private[2] apply during and after the proceedings. In addition, in proceedings to which s 97(2) of the Children Act 1989 applies the court should continue to consider at the conclusion of the proceedings whether there are any outstanding welfare issues which require a continuation of the protection afforded during the course of the proceedings by that provision.

1   See *Clayton v Clayton [2006] EWCA Civ 878*.
2   In particular proceedings which –
   (a) relate to the exercise of the inherent jurisdiction of the High Court with respect to minors;
   (b) are brought under the Children Act 1989; or
   (c) otherwise relate wholly or mainly to the maintenance or upbringing of a minor.

NOTES

Amendment.[1] Text substituted: FPR Update, April 2014. [2] Words inserted: FPR Update, 15 July 2021.

3 Aims of the guidance

3.1 This Practice Direction is intended to provide guidance regarding –

- the handling of applications to exclude media representatives [or duly authorised lawyers][1] from the whole or part of a hearing; and

- the exercise of the court's discretion to exclude media representatives [or duly authorised lawyers][1] whether upon the court's own motion or any such application.

3.2 While the guidance does not aim to cover all possible eventualities, it should be complied with so far as consistent in all the circumstances with the just determination of the proceedings.

NOTES

Amendment.[1] Words inserted: FPR Update, 15 July 2021.

4 Identification of media representatives as 'accredited'

4.1 Media representatives will be expected to carry with them identification sufficient to enable court staff, or if necessary the court itself, to verify that they are 'accredited' representatives of news gathering or reporting organisations within the meaning of the rule.

4.2 By virtue of paragraph (7) of the rule, it is for the Lord Chancellor to approve a scheme which will provide for accreditation. The Lord Chancellor has decided that the scheme operated by the UK Press Card Authority provides sufficient accreditation; a card issued under that scheme will be the expected form of identification, and production of the Card will be both necessary and sufficient to demonstrate accreditation.

4.3 A media representative unable to demonstrate accreditation in accordance with the UK Press Card Authority scheme, so as to be able to attend by virtue of paragraph (2)(f) of the rule, may nevertheless be permitted to attend at the court's discretion under paragraph (2)(g).

[Meaning of 'duly authorised lawyer'

4A.1 In rule 27.11 FPR and in this practice direction–

'duly authorised lawyer' means –
    (a)   a person who is authorised by a practising certificate to conduct litigation or exercise a right of audience in the family court;
    (b)   a lawyer working for the Law School, Faculty or Department of a Higher Education Institution designated as a recognised body pursuant to section 216 of the Education Reform Act 1988; or
    (c)   a lawyer attending on behalf of a registered educational charity the name, objects and registered charity number of which have been provided to the President of the Family Division; and

'lawyer' means a person who –
    (a)   holds a qualifying law degree as defined by the Bar Standards Board or Solicitors Regulation Authority;
    (b)   holds or has completed –
        (i)   the Common Professional Examination (CPE);
        (ii)   an approved Graduate Diploma in Law (GDL) course or the Solicitors Qualifying Examination (SQE);
        (iii)   a postgraduate legal qualification; or

(iv)   the CILEx Level 6 Diploma in Law and Practice or the CILEx Graduate Fast Track Diploma.][1]

NOTES

Amendment.[1] Paragraph inserted: FPR Update, 15 July 2021.

5 Exercise of the discretion to exclude media representatives from all or part of the proceedings

5.1 The rule anticipates and should be applied on the basis that media representatives [or duly authorised lawyers][1] have a right to attend family proceedings throughout save and to the extent that the court exercises its discretion to exclude them from the whole or part of any proceedings on one or more of the grounds set out in paragraph (3) of the rule.

5.2 When considering the question of exclusion on any of the grounds set out in paragraph (3) of the rule the court should –

- specifically identify whether the risk to which such ground is directed arises from the mere fact of media presence [or the attendance of duly authorised lawyers][1] at the particular hearing or hearings the subject of the application or whether the risk identified can be adequately addressed by exclusion of media representatives [or duly authorised lawyers][1] from a part only of such hearing or hearings;
- consider whether the reporting or disclosure restrictions which apply by operation of law, or which the court otherwise has power to order will provide sufficient protection to the party on whose behalf the application is made or any of the persons referred to in paragraph (3)(a) of the rule;
- consider the safety of the parties in cases in which the court considers there are particular physical or health risks against which reporting restrictions may be inadequate to afford protection;
- in the case of any vulnerable adult or child who is unrepresented before the court, consider the extent to which the court should of its own motion take steps to protect the welfare of that adult or child.

5.3 Paragraph (3)(a)(iii) of the rule permits exclusion where necessary 'for the orderly conduct of proceedings'. This enables the court to address practical problems presented by media attendance [or the attendance of duly authorised lawyers][1]. In particular, it may be difficult or even impossible physically to accommodate all (or indeed any) media representatives [or duly authorised lawyers][1] who wish to attend a particular hearing on the grounds of the restricted size or layout of the court room in which it is being heard. Court staff will use their best efforts to identify more suitable accommodation in advance of any hearing which appears likely to attract particular media attention [or the particular attention of duly authorised lawyers][1], and to move hearings to larger court rooms where possible. However, the court should not be required to adjourn a hearing in order for larger accommodation to be sought where this will involve significant disruption or delay in the proceedings.

5.4 Paragraph (3)(b) of the rule permits exclusion where, unless the media [and duly authorised lawyers][1] are excluded, justice will be impeded or prejudiced for some reason other than those set out in sub-paragraph (a). Reasons of administrative inconvenience are not sufficient. Examples of circumstances where the impact on justice of continued attendance might be sufficient to necessitate exclusion may include –

- a hearing relating to the parties' finances where the information being considered includes price sensitive information (such as confidential information which could affect the share price of a publicly quoted company); or
- any hearing at which a witness (other than a party) states for credible reasons that he or she will not give evidence in front of media representatives [or duly authorised lawyers][1], or where there appears to the court to be a significant risk that a witness will not give full or frank evidence in the presence of media representatives [or duly authorised lawyers][1].

5.5 In the event of a decision to exclude media representatives [or duly authorised lawyers][1], the court should state brief reasons for the decision.

NOTES

Amendment.[1] Words inserted: FPR Update, 15 July 2021.

[Identification of lawyers as 'authorised'

5A.1 Lawyers will be expected to carry with them identification sufficient to enable court staff, or if necessary the court itself, to verify that they are 'authorised' lawyers within the meaning of the rule.

5A.2 The following forms of identification provide sufficient information, and production of such identification will be both necessary and sufficient to demonstrate that the lawyer is 'authorised' within the meaning of rule 27.11(7) (b)(i), (ii) and (iii) respectively –

  (a)   a current practising certificate accompanied by picture identification of the lawyer and a signed written statement by the lawyer which complies with paragraph [5A.3][2];
  (b)   confirmation on headed notepaper from the relevant Higher Education Institution (or Law School, Faculty or Department of that Institution) of the lawyer's position and qualification, accompanied by picture identification of the lawyer and a signed written statement by the lawyer which complies with paragraph [5A.3][2];
  (c)   confirmation on headed notepaper from the relevant registered educational charity (specifying the registered charity number) of the lawyer's position and qualification, accompanied by picture identification of the lawyer and a signed written statement by the lawyer which complies with paragraph [5A.3][2].

5A.3 The signed written statement required by paragraph [5A.2][2] must –

  (a)   confirm that the lawyer's attendance is for journalistic, research or public legal educational purposes and that the lawyer has no personal interest in the proceedings and that he or she is not attending in the capacity of agent or instructed lawyer for any client; and

(b)   confirm that the lawyer is aware of and will abide by any restrictions on publication, whether arising by operation of law (for example under section 97 of the Children Act 1989 and section 12 of the Administration of Justice Act 1960) or imposed by order of the court, which follow from the proceedings being in private.

5A.4 The information about a registered educational charity required by rule 27.11(7)(b)(iii) is to be submitted using Form FP300 (Request by educational charity to attend family proceedings for authorisation by the President of the Family Division) by e-mail to pfd.office@judiciary.uk, or by post to: The Office of the President of the Family Division, Royal Courts of Justice, Strand, London WC2A 2LL. It will be entered on a list maintained by that office, and therefore need be submitted only once.][1]

NOTES

Amendment.[1] Paragraph inserted: FPR Update, 15 July 2021. [2] Words substituted: FPR Update, 27 January 2022.

6 Applications to exclude media representatives [or duly authorised lawyers][2] from all or part of proceedings

6.1 The court may exclude media representatives [or duly authorised lawyers][2] on the permitted grounds of its own motion or after hearing representations from the interested persons listed at paragraph (5) of the rule. Where exclusion is proposed, any media representatives [or duly authorised lawyers][2] who are present are entitled to make representations about that proposal. There is, however, no requirement to adjourn proceedings to enable media representatives [or duly authorised lawyers][2] who are not present to attend in order to make such representations, and in such a case the court should not adjourn unless satisfied of the necessity to do so having regard to the additional cost and delay which would thereby be caused.

6.2 Applications to exclude media representatives [or duly authorised lawyers][2] should normally be dealt with as they arise and by way of oral representations, unless the court directs otherwise.

6.3 When media representatives [or duly authorised lawyers][2] are expected to attend a particular hearing (for example, where a party is encouraging media [or duly authorised lawyers][2] interest and attendance) and a party intends to apply to the court for the exclusion of the media [or of duly authorised lawyers][2], that party should, if practicable, give advance notice to the court, to the other parties and (where appointed) any children's guardian, officer of the service or Welsh Family Proceedings officer, NYAS or other representative of the child of any intention to seek the exclusion of media representatives from all or part of the proceedings. Equally, legal representatives and parties should ensure that witnesses are aware of the right of media representatives to attend and should notify the court at an early stage of the intention of any witness to request the exclusion of media representatives

6.4 Prior notification by the court of a pending application for exclusion will not be given to media interests [or to any duly authorised lawyers][2] unless the court so directs. However, where such an application has been made, the applicant must where possible, notify the relevant media organisations [and should do so by means of the Press Association CopyDirect service, following the procedure set out in the Official Solicitor/CAFCASS *Practice Note* dated 18 March 2005][1].

NOTES

Amendments.[1] The additional words were added by the President in *Re Child X* (above), paragraph 87. [2] Words inserted: FPR Update, 15 July 2021.

PART 28
COSTS

28.1 Costs

The court may at any time make such order as to costs as it thinks just.

28.2 Application of other rules

(1) Subject to rule 28.3 ...2, [Parts 44 (except rules 44.2(2) and (3) and 44.10(2) and (3)), 46 and 47 and rule 45.8][1] of the CPR apply to costs in proceedings, with the following modifications –

   [(a)   in the definition of 'authorised court officer' in rule 44.1(1), for the words in sub-paragraph (i) substitute 'the family court';][2]
   (b)   ...[2]
   (c)   in accordance with any provisions in Practice Direction 28A; and
   (d)   any other necessary modifications.

(2) ...[2]

NOTES

Amendments.[1] Words substituted: SI 2013/530. [2] Words substituted, sub-paragraphs substituted and omitted and paragraph (2) omitted: SI 2013/3204.

28.3 Costs in financial remedy proceedings

(1) This rule applies in relation to financial remedy proceedings.

(2) Rule [44.2][1](1), (4) and (5) of the CPR do not apply to financial remedy proceedings.

(3) [Rules 44.2(6) to (8) and 44.12][1] of the CPR apply to an order made under this rule as they apply to an order made under rule 44.3 of the CPR.

(4) In this rule –

   (a)   'costs' has the same meaning as in rule [44.1(1)(c)][1] of the CPR; and
   (b)   'financial remedy proceedings' means proceedings for –
      (i)   a financial order except an order for maintenance pending suit, an order for maintenance pending outcome of proceedings, an interim periodical payments order[, an order for payment in respect of legal services][2] or any other form of interim order for the purposes of rule 9.7(1)(a), (b), (c) and (e);
      (ii)   an order under Part 3 of the 1984 Act;
      (iii) an order under Schedule 7 to the 2004 Act;

      (iv)   an order under section 10(2) of the 1973 Act;

      (v)   an order under section 48(2) of the 2004 Act.

(5) Subject to paragraph (6), the general rule in financial remedy proceedings is that the court will not make an order requiring one party to pay the costs of another party.

(6) The court may make an order requiring one party to pay the costs of another party at any stage of the proceedings where it considers it appropriate to do so because of the conduct of a party in relation to the proceedings (whether before or during them).

(7) In deciding what order (if any) to make under paragraph (6), the court must have regard to –

  (a)   any failure by a party to comply with these rules, any order of the court or any practice direction which the court considers relevant;

  (b)   any open offer to settle made by a party;

  (c)   whether it was reasonable for a party to raise, pursue or contest a particular allegation or issue;

  (d)   the manner in which a party has pursued or responded to the application or a particular allegation or issue;

  (e)   any other aspect of a party's conduct in relation to proceedings which the court considers relevant; and

  (f)   the financial effect on the parties of any costs order.

(8) No offer to settle which is not an open offer to settle is admissible at any stage of the proceedings, except as provided by rule 9.17.

[(9) For the purposes of this rule 'financial remedy proceedings' do not include an application under rule 9.9A.][3]

NOTES

Amendments.[1] Words substituted: SI 2013/530.[2] Words inserted: SI 2013/1472.[3] Paragraph inserted: SI 2016/901.

28.4

...[1]

NOTES

Amendments.[1] Rule omitted: SI 2013/3204.

Practice Direction 28A –
Costs

This Practice Direction supplements FPR Part 28

Application and modification of the CPR

1.1 Rule 28.2 provides that subject to rule 28.3 of the FPR ...[1], Parts 43, 44 (except rules 44.3(2) and (3), 44.9 to 44.12C, 44.13(1A) and (1B) and 44.18 to 20), 47 and 48 and rule 45.6 of the CPR apply to costs in family proceedings with the modifications listed in [rule 28.2(1)(a), (c) and (d)][1]. Rule 28.2(1)(c) refers to modifications in accordance with this Practice Direction.

1.2–1.3 ...[1]

NOTES

Amendments.[1] Text omitted and substituted: FPR Update, April 2014.

Application and modification of the Practice Direction supplementing CPR Parts 43 to 48

2.1 For the purpose of proceedings to which these Rules apply, the Practice Direction about costs which supplements Parts 43 to 48 of the CPR ('the costs practice direction') will apply, but with the exclusions and modifications explained below to reflect the exclusions and modifications to those Parts of the CPR as they are applied by Part 28 of these Rules.

2.2 Rule 28.2(1) applies, with modifications and certain exceptions, Parts 43 to 48 of the CPR to costs in family proceedings. ...[1] Rule 28.3,...[1] by way of exception, ...[1] disapplies CPR rule 44.3(1), (4) and (5) in the case of financial remedy proceedings...[1].

2.3 The costs practice direction does not, therefore, apply in its entirety but with the exclusion of certain sections reflecting the non-application of certain rules of the CPR which those sections supplement.

2.4 The costs practice direction applies as follows –

- to family proceedings generally...[1] with the exception of sections 6, 15, 16 ,17 and 23A;
- ...[1]
- to financial remedy proceedings, other than in magistrates' courts, with the exception of section 6, paragraphs 8.1 to 8.4 of section 8 and sections 15, 16, 17 and 23A;
- to a financial remedy proceedings, in magistrates' courts only, with the exception of section 6, paragraphs 8.1 to 8.4 of section 8, sections 15, 16, 17, 23A and sections 28–49A.

2.5 All subsequent editions of the costs practice direction as and when they are published and come into effect shall in the same way extend to all family proceedings.

2.6 The costs practice direction includes provisions applicable to proceedings following changes in the manner in which legal services are funded pursuant to the Access to Justice Act 1999. It should be noted that although the cost of the premium in respect of legal costs insurance (section 29) or the cost of funding by a prescribed membership organisation (section 30) may be recoverable, family proceedings (within section 58A(2) of the Courts and Legal Services Act 1990) cannot be the subject of an enforceable conditional fee agreement.

2.7 Paragraph 1.4 of section 1 of the costs practice direction shall be modified as follows –

in the definition of 'counsel' for 'High court or in the county courts' substitute 'High Court [or in the Family Court][1].

[2.8 Paragraphs 4.1 and 4.2 of CPR Practice Direction 47 shall be modified as follows:

– for paragraphs 4.1 and 4.2 substitute:

'4.1 For the purposes of rule 47.4(1), 'appropriate office' means the court office of the Designated Family Court for the Designated Family Judge area in which the case was being dealt with when the judgment or order was made, or the event occurred which gave rise to the right to assessment, or to which the case has subsequently been moved.

(Her Majesty's Courts and Tribunals Service will publish information to enable Designated Family Judge areas and Designated Family Courts to be identified).'][1]

NOTES

Amendments.[1] Text omitted, substituted and inserted: FPR Update, April 2014.

General interpretation of references in CPR

3.1 References in the costs practice direction to 'claimant' and 'defendant' are to be read as references to equivalent terms used in proceedings to which these Rules apply and other terms and expressions used in the costs practice direction shall be similarly treated.

3.2 References in CPR Parts 43 to 48 to other rules or Parts of the CPR shall be read, where there is an equivalent rule or Part in these Rules, to that equivalent rule or Part.

Costs in financial remedy proceedings

4.1 Rule 28.3 relates to the court's power to make costs orders in financial remedy proceedings. For the purposes of rule 28.3, 'financial remedy proceedings' are defined in accordance with rule 28.3(4)(b). That definition, which is more limited than the principal definition in rule 2.3(1), includes –

(a) an application for a financial order, except –
  (i) an order for maintenance pending suit or an order for maintenance pending outcome of proceedings;
  (ii) an interim periodical payments order or any other form of interim order for the purposes of rule 9.7(1)(a),(b),(c) and (e);

(b) an application for an order under Part 3 of the Matrimonial and Family Proceedings Act 1984 or Schedule 7 to the Civil Partnership Act 2004; and

(c) an application under section 10(2) of the Matrimonial Causes Act 1973 or section 48(2) of the Civil Partnership Act 2004.

4.2 Accordingly, it should be noted that –

   (a)   while most interim financial applications are excluded from rule 28.3, the rule does apply to an application for an interim variation order within rule 9.7(1)(d),

   (b)   rule 28.3 does not apply to an application for any of the following financial remedies –

       (i)   an order under Schedule 1 to the Children Act 1989;

       (ii)   an order under section 27 of the Matrimonial Causes Act 1973 or Part 9 of Schedule 5 to the Civil Partnership Act 2004;

       (iii) an order under section 35 of the Matrimonial Causes Act 1973 or paragraph 69 of Schedule 5 to the Civil Partnership Act 2004; or

       (iv) an order under Part 1 of the Domestic Proceedings and Magistrates' Courts Act 1978 or Schedule 6 to the Civil Partnership Act 2004.

4.3 Under rule 28.3 the court only has the power to make a costs order in financial remedy proceedings when this is justified by the litigation conduct of one of the parties. When determining whether and how to exercise this power the court will be required to take into account the list of factors set out in that rule. The court will not be able to take into account any offers to settle expressed to be 'without prejudice' or 'without prejudice save as to costs' in deciding what, if any, costs orders to make.

4.4 In considering the conduct of the parties for the purposes of rule 28.3(6) and (7) (including any open offers to settle), the court will have regard to the obligation of the parties to help the court to further the overriding objective (see rules 1.1 and 1.3) and will take into account the nature, importance and complexity of the issues in the case. This may be of particular significance in applications for variation orders and interim variation orders or other cases where there is a risk of the costs becoming disproportionate to the amounts in dispute.

The court will take a broad view of conduct for the purposes of this rule and will generally conclude that to refuse openly to negotiate reasonably and responsibly will amount to conduct in respect of which the court will consider making an order for costs. This includes in a 'needs' case where the applicant litigates unreasonably resulting in the costs incurred by each party becoming disproportionate to the award made by the court. Where an order for costs is made at an interim stage the court will not usually allow any resulting liability to be reckoned as a debt in the computation of the assets.

4.5 Parties who intend to seek a costs order against another party in proceedings to which rule 28.3 applies should ordinarily make this plain in open correspondence or in skeleton arguments before the date of the hearing. In any case where summary assessment of costs awarded under rule 28.3 would be appropriate parties are under an obligation to file a statement of costs in CPR Form N260.

4.6 An interim financial order which includes an element to allow a party to deal with legal fees (see *A v A (maintenance pending suit: provision for legal fees)* [2001] 1 WLR 605; *G v G (maintenance pending suit; costs)* [2002] EWHC 306 (Fam); *McFarlane v McFarlane, Parlour v Parlour* [2004] EWCA Civ 872; *Moses-Taiga v Taiga* [2005] EWCA Civ 1013; C v C (Maintenance Pending Suit: Legal Costs) [2006] Fam Law 739; *Currey v Currey (No 2)* [2006] EWCA Civ 1338) is an order made pursuant to section 22 of the Matrimonial

Causes Act 1973 or an order under paragraph 38 of Schedule 5 of the 2004 Act, and is not a 'costs order' within the meaning of rule 28.3.

4.7 By virtue of rule 28.2(1), where rule 28.3 does not apply, the exercise of the court's discretion as to costs is governed by the relevant provisions of the CPR and in particular rule 44.3 (excluding r 44.3(2) and (3)).

PART 29
MISCELLANEOUS

29.1 Personal details

(1) Unless the court directs otherwise, a party is not required to reveal –

(a) the party's home address or other contact details;
(b) the address or other contact details of any child;
(c) the name of a person with whom the child is living, if that person is not the applicant; or
(d) in relation to an application under section 28(2) of the 2002 Act (application for permission to change the child's surname), the proposed new surname of the child.

(2) Where a party does not wish to reveal any of the particulars in paragraph (1), that party must give notice of those particulars to the court and the particulars will not be revealed to any person unless the court directs otherwise.

(3) Where a party changes home address during the course of proceedings, that party must give notice of the change to the court.

29.2 Disclosure of information under the 1991 Act

Where the [Secretary of State][1] requires a person mentioned in regulation 3(1), 4(2) or 6(2)(a) of the Child Support Information Regulations 2008 to furnish information or evidence for a purpose mentioned in regulation 4(1) of those Regulations, nothing in these rules will –

(a) prevent that person from furnishing the information or evidence sought; or
(b) require that person to seek permission of the court before doing so.

NOTES

Amendments.[1] Words substituted: SI 2012/2007.

29.3 Method of giving notice

(1) Unless directed otherwise, a notice which is required by these rules to be given to a person must be given –

(a) in writing; and
(b) in a manner in which service may be effected in accordance with Part 6.

(2) Rule 6.33 applies to a notice which is required by these rules to be given to a child as it applies to a document which is to be served on a child.

29.4 Withdrawal of applications in proceedings

(1) This rule applies to applications in proceedings –

    (a)   under Part 7;

    (b)   under Parts 10 to 14 or under any other Part where the application relates to the welfare or upbringing of a child or;

    (c)   where either of the parties is a protected party.

(2) Where this rule applies, an application may only be withdrawn with the permission of the court.

(3) Subject to paragraph (4), a person seeking permission to withdraw an application must file a written request for permission setting out the reasons for the request.

(4) The request under paragraph (3) may be made orally to the court if the parties are present.

(5) A court officer will notify the other parties of a written request.

(6) The court may deal with a written request under paragraph (3) without a hearing if the other parties, and any other persons directed by the court, have had an opportunity to make written representations to the court about the request.

29.5 The Human Rights Act 1998

(1) In this rule –

    'the 1998 Act' means the Human Rights Act 1998;
    'Convention right' has the same meaning as in the 1998 Act; and
    'declaration of incompatibility' means a declaration of incompatibility under section 4 of the 1998 Act.

(2) A party who seeks to rely on any provision of or right arising under the 1998 Act or seeks a remedy available under that Act must inform the court in that party's application or otherwise in writing specifying –

    (a)   the Convention right which it is alleged has been infringed and details of the alleged infringement; and

    (b)   the relief sought and whether this includes a declaration of incompatibility.

(3) The High Court may not make a declaration of incompatibility unless 21 days' notice, or such other period of notice as the court directs, has been given to the Crown.

(4) Where notice has been given to the Crown, a Minister, or other person permitted by the 1998 Act, will be joined as a party on giving notice to the court.

(5) Where a claim is made under section 7(1) of the 1998 Act (claim that public authority acted unlawfully) in respect of a judicial act –

    (a)   that claim must be set out in the application form or the appeal notice; and

    (b)   notice must be given to the Crown.

(6) Where paragraph (4) applies and the appropriate person (as defined in section 9(5) of the 1998 Act) has not applied within 21 days, or such other period as the court directs, beginning with the date on which the notice to be joined as a party was served, the court may join the appropriate person as a party.

(7) On any application concerning a committal order, if the court ordering the release of the person concludes that that person's Convention rights have been infringed by the making of the order to which the application or appeal relates, the judgment or order should so state, but if the court does not do so, that failure will not prevent another court from deciding the matter.

(8) Where by reason of a rule, practice direction or court order the Crown is permitted or required –

    (a)   to make a witness statement;

    (b)   to swear an affidavit$^{(GL)}$;

    (c)   to verify a document by a statement of truth; or

    (d)   to discharge any other procedural obligation,

that function will be performed by an appropriate officer acting on behalf of the Crown, and the court may if necessary nominate an appropriate officer.

(Practice Direction 29A (Human Rights – Joining the Crown) makes provision for the notices mentioned in this rule.)

****

29.8 Applications for relief which is precluded by the 1991 Act

(1) This rule applies where an application is made for an order which, in the opinion of the court, it would be prevented from making under section 8 or 9 of the 1991 Act and in this rule, 'the matter' means the question of whether or not the court would be so prevented.

(2) The court will consider the matter without holding a hearing.

(3) Where the court officer receives the opinion of the court, as mentioned in paragraph (1), the court officer must send a notice to the applicant of that opinion.

(4) Paragraphs (5) to (11) apply where the court officer sends a notice under paragraph (3).

(5) Subject to paragraph (6), no requirement of these rules apply except the requirements –

    (a)   of this rule;

    (b)   as to service of the application by the court officer; and

    (c)   as to any procedural step to be taken following the making of an application of the type in question.

(6) The court may direct that the requirements of these rules apply, or apply to such extent or with such modifications as are set out in the direction.

(7) If the applicant informs the court officer, within 14 days of the date of the notice, that the applicant wishes to persist with the application, the court will give appropriate directions for the matter to be heard and determined and may provide for the hearing to be without notice.

(8) Where directions are given in accordance with paragraph (7), the court officer must –

    (a)   inform the applicant of the directions;

    (b)   send a copy of the application to the other parties;

    (c)   if the hearing is to be without notice, inform the other parties briefly –

        (i)   of the nature and effect of the notice given to the applicant under paragraph (3);

        (ii)   that the matter is being resolved without a hearing on notice; and

        (iii) that they will be notified of the result; and

    (d)   if the hearing is to be on notice, inform the other parties of –

        (i)   the circumstances which led to the directions being given; and

        (ii)   the directions.

(9) If the applicant does not inform the court officer as mentioned in paragraph (7), the application shall be treated as having been withdrawn.

(10) Where –

    (a)   the matter is heard in accordance with directions given under paragraph (7); and

    (b)   the court determines that it would be prevented, under section 8 or 9 of the 1991 Act, from making the order sought by the applicant,

the court will dismiss the application.

(11) Where the court dismisses the application –

    (a)   the court must give its reasons in writing; and

    (b)   the court officer must send a copy of the reasons to the parties.

29.9 Modification of rule 29.8 where the application is not freestanding

(1) Where the court officer sends a notice under rule 29.8(3) in relation to an application which is contained in another document ('the document') which contains material extrinsic to the application –

    (a)   subject to paragraph (2), the document will be treated as if it did not contain the application in respect of which the notice was served; and

    (b)   the court officer, when sending copies of the documents to the respondents under any provision of these rules, must attach –

        (i)   a copy of the notice under rule 29.8(3); and

        (ii)   a notice informing the respondents of the effect of paragraph (1)(a).

(2) If the court determines that it is not prevented by section 8 or 9 of the 1991 Act from making the order sought by the application, the court –

(a)   must direct that the document shall be treated as if it contained the application; and

(b)   may give such directions as it considers appropriate for the subsequent conduct of the proceedings.

****

Practice Direction 29A – Human Rights, Joining the Crown

This Practice Direction supplements FPR Part 29, rule 29.5 (The Human Rights Act 1998)

Section 4 of the Human Rights Act 1998

1.1 Where a party has informed the court about –

(a)   a claim for a declaration of incompatibility in accordance with section 4 of the Human Rights Act 1998; or

(b)   an issue for the court to decide which may lead to the court considering making a declaration,

then the court may at any time consider whether notice should be given to the Crown as required by that Act and give directions for the content and service of the notice. The rule allows a period of 21 days before the court will make the declaration but the court may vary this period of time.

1.2 The court will normally consider the issues and give the directions referred to in paragraph 1.1 at a directions hearing.

1.3 The notice must be served on the person named in the list published under section 17 of the Crown Proceedings Act 1947.

1.4 The notice will be in the form directed by the court and will normally include the directions given by the court. The notice will also be served on all the parties.

1.5 The court may require the parties to assist in the preparation of the notice.

1.6 Unless the court orders otherwise, the Minister or other person permitted by the Human Rights Act 1998 to be joined as a party must, if he or she wishes to be joined, give notice of his or her intention to be joined as a party to the court and every other party. Where the Minister has nominated a person to be joined as a party the notice must be accompanied by the written nomination.

(Section 5(2)(a) of the Human Rights Act 1998 permits a person nominated by a Minister of the Crown to be joined as a party. The nomination may be signed on behalf of the Minister.)

Section 9 of the Human Rights Act 1998

2.1 The procedure in paragraphs 1.1 to 1.6 also applies where a claim is made under sections 7(1)(a) and 9(3) of the Human Rights Act 1998 for damages in respect of a judicial act.

2.2 Notice must be given to the Lord Chancellor and should be served on the Treasury Solicitor on his behalf.

2.3 The notice will also give details of the judicial act, which is the subject of the claim for damages, and of the court that made it.

> (Section 9(4) of the Human Rights Act 1998 provides that no award of damages may be made against the Crown as provided for in section 9(3) unless the appropriate person is joined in the proceedings. The appropriate person is the Minister responsible for the court concerned or a person or department nominated by him or her (section 9(5) of the Act).

Practice Direction 29B – Human Rights Act 1998

This Practice Direction supplements FPR Part 29

1 It is directed that the following practice shall apply as from 2 October 2000 in all family proceedings:

Citation of authorities

2 When an authority referred to in s 2 of the Human Rights Act 1998 ('the Act') is to be cited at a hearing –

(a)   the authority to be cited shall be an authoritative and complete report;
(b)   the court must be provided with a list of authorities it is intended to cite and copies of the reports –
    (i)   in cases to which *Practice Direction (Family Proceedings: Court Bundles)* (10 March 2000) [2000] 1 FLR 536 applies, as part of the bundle;
    (ii)   otherwise, not less than 2 clear days before the hearing; and

(c)   copies of the complete original texts issued by the European Court and Commission, either paper based or from the Court's judgment database (HUDOC) which is available on the internet, may be used.

Allocation to judges

3
(1)   The hearing and determination of the following will be confined to a High Court judge [and in the family court to a judge of High Court level]1 –
    (*a*)   a claim for a declaration of incompatibility under s 4 of the Act; or
    (*b*)   an issue which may lead to the court considering making such a declaration.

(2)   The hearing and determination of a claim made under the Act in respect of a judicial act shall be confined in the High Court to a High Court judge …[1].

NOTES

Amendments.[1] Text inserted and omitted: FPR Update, April 2014.

Practice Direction 29C –
Transfer of Proceedings from the Family Court to the High Court

This Practice Direction supplements rule 29.17(3)(b) FPR

1 Rule 29.17(3)(b) FPR provides that a judge other than one to whom rule 29.17(4) applies may make a decision to transfer proceedings from the family court to the High Court where the circumstances specified in this Practice Direction apply.

1.2 The circumstances are that the proceedings are to be transferred solely for the purpose of making an order under the inherent jurisdiction of the High Court to require a Government Department or agency to disclose an address to the court.

NOTES

Amendment.[1] PD29C inserted: FPR Update, April 2014.

[Practice Direction 29D –
Court officers making corrections to orders

This practice direction supplements rule 29.16 FPR 2010

1.1 [Rule 29.16][2] FPR provides that the court may correct an accidental slip or omission in a judgment or order. Corrections under that rule must be approved by a judge, or by a Justices' Legal Adviser where Practice Direction 2C so provides.

1.2 A court officer may make an amendment to an order, without prior reference to a judge or Justices' Legal Adviser (as applicable), in the following circumstances –

(a) where a court officer has wrongly transposed details in the draft order approved by the court;

(b) where the error is obviously typographical such as –

  (i) the spelling of a party's name, a date of birth, a place of birth or marriage, where that can be corrected by reference to the application or supporting evidence on the court file such as a birth or marriage certificate; or

  (ii) a nonsensical word clearly included in error (but see paragraph 1.4);

(c) changes to references in the order to the venue at which a hearing took place, where this can be verified from the court file, court diary or cause list;

(d) the date of the order, where this can be verified from the court file, court diary or cause list;

(e) details of a party's legal representatives at a hearing when this can be verified from the court file or other record of hearing;

(f) the date of a hearing, where the court officer has listed a matter for hearing but transposed the details incorrectly into the order that notifies the parties of the hearing date;

(g) to improve the formatting (but not the numbering) of an order.

1.3 If a court officer concludes that –

(a)   it would be inappropriate to make an amendment to an order even where they consider that a case falls within paragraph 1.2; or

(b)   they are not certain whether or not a case falls within paragraph 1.2 (for example whether an error is obviously typographical),

the court officer must refer the matter to a judge to determine whether to make the amendment.

1.4 Save as specified in paragraph 1.2, a court officer must never make linguistic, grammatical or textual amendments to an order, or alter its numbering, without reference to a judge or, where Practice Direction 2C applies, to a Justices' Legal Adviser.

1.5 A court officer must never make an amendment to a judgment or written ruling without reference to a judge or, where Practice Direction 2C applies, to a Justices' Legal Adviser.][1]

NOTES

Amendments.[1] Practice Direction inserted: FPR Update, 15 July 2021. [2] Numbers substituted: FPR Update, 14 September 2021.

PART 30
APPEALS

30.1 Scope and interpretation

(1) The rules in this Part apply to appeals to –

(a)   the High Court; and

(b)   [the family court][1].

(2) This Part does not apply to an appeal in detailed assessment proceedings against a decision of an authorised court officer.

(Rules [47.21 to 47.24][1] of the CPR deal with appeals against a decision of an authorised court officer in detailed assessment proceedings.)

(3) In this Part –

'appeal court' means the court to which an appeal is made;
'appeal notice' means an appellant's or respondent's notice;
'appellant' means a person who brings or seeks to bring an appeal;
['costs judge' means –

(a)   the Chief Taxing Master;

(b)   a taxing master of the Senior Courts; or

(c)   a person appointed to act as deputy for the person holding office referred to in paragraph (b) or to act as temporary additional officer for any such office;

'district judge' means –

(a)   the Senior District Judge of the Family Division

(b)   a district judge of the Principal Registry of the Family Division;

(c)   a person appointed to act as deputy for the person holding office referred to in paragraph (b) or to act as temporary additional officer for any such office;

(d)   a district judge;

(e)   a deputy district judge appointed under section 102 of the Senior Courts Act 1981 or section 8 of the County Courts Act 1984; or

(f)   a District Judge (Magistrates' Courts);][1]

'lower court' means the court from which, or the person from whom, the appeal lies; and

'respondent' means –

(a)   a person other than the appellant who was a party to the proceedings in the lower court and who is affected by the appeal; and

(b)   a person who is permitted by the appeal court to be a party to the appeal.

(4) This Part is subject to any rule, enactment or practice direction which sets out special provisions with regard to any particular category of appeal.

NOTES

Amendments.[1] Words substituted and definitions inserted: SI 2014/667.

30.2 Parties to comply with the practice direction

All parties to an appeal must comply with Practice Direction 30A.

30.3 Permission

[(1) Paragraphs (1B) and (2) of this rule set out when permission to appeal is, or is not, required under these rules to appeal against a decision or order of the family court.

(1A) This rule does not apply where the route of appeal from a decision or order of the family court is to the Court of Appeal, namely where the appeal is against a decision or order made by a circuit judge or Recorder –

(a)   in proceedings under –

    (i)   Part 4 of the 1989 Act (care and supervision);

    (ii)   Part 5 of the 1989 Act (protection of children);

    (iii)   paragraph 19(1) of Schedule 2 to the 1989 Act (approval by the court of local authority arrangements to assist children to live abroad); or

    (iv)   the 2002 Act (adoption, placement etc.);

(b)   in exercise of the family court's jurisdiction in relation to contempt of court where that decision or order was made in, or in connection with, proceedings referred to in sub-paragraph (a); or

(c)   where that decision or order was itself made on an appeal to the family court.

(Appeals in the cases referred to in this paragraph are outside the scope of these rules. The CPR make provision requiring permission to appeal in those cases.)

(1B) Permission to appeal is required under these rules –

    (a)   unless paragraph (2) applies, where the appeal is against a decision made by a circuit judge, Recorder, district judge or costs judge; or

    (b)   as provided by Practice Direction 30A.][1]

(2) Permission to appeal is not required where the appeal is against –

    (a)   a committal order; ...[3]

    (b)   a secure accommodation order under section 25 of the 1989 Act[; or][3]

    [(c)   a refusal to grant habeas corpus for release in relation to a minor.][3]

(3) An application for permission to appeal may be made –

    (a)   to the lower court at the hearing at which the decision to be appealed was made [or, if the hearing is adjourned to a later date, the hearing on that date][5]; or

    (b)   to the appeal court in an appeal notice.

    (Rule 30.4 sets out the time limits for filing an appellant's notice at the appeal court. Rule 30.5 sets out the time limits for filing a respondent's notice at the appeal court. Any application for permission to appeal to the appeal court must be made in the appeal notice (see rules 30.4(1) and 30.5(3).)

(4) Where the lower court refuses an application for permission to appeal, a further application for permission to appeal may be made to the appeal court.

(5) [Subject to paragraph (5A), where][1] the appeal court, without a hearing, refuses permission to appeal, the person seeking permission may request the decision to be reconsidered at a hearing.

[(5A) Where a judge of the High Court or [in the family court, a judge of the High Court or][2] a Designated Family Judge refuses permission to appeal without a hearing and considers that the application is totally without merit, the judge may make an order that the person seeking permission may not request the decision to be reconsidered at a hearing.

(5B) Rule 4.3(5) will not apply to an order that the person seeking permission may not request the decision to be reconsidered at a hearing made under paragraph (5A).][1]

(6) A request under paragraph (5) must be filed within 7 days beginning with the date on which the notice that permission has been refused was served.

(7) Permission to appeal may be given only where –

    (a)   the court considers that the appeal would have a real prospect of success; or

    (b)   there is some other compelling reason why the appeal should be heard.

(8) An order giving permission may –

    (a)   limit the issues to be heard; and

    (b)   be made subject to conditions.

(9) …²

NOTES

Amendments.¹ Words substituted and paragraphs inserted: SI 2013/530. ² Words inserted and paragraph omitted: SI 2014/667. ³ Word omitted, word and punctuation substituted and sub-paragraph inserted: SI 2014/3296. ⁴ Paragraphs (1), (1A) and (1B) substituted: SI 2016/891. ⁵ Words inserted: SI 2022/44.

30.4 Appellant's notice

(1) Where the appellant seeks permission from the appeal court it must be requested in the appellant's notice.

(2) Subject to paragraph (3), the appellant must file the appellant's notice at the appeal court within –

    (a)   such period as may be directed by the lower court [at the hearing at which the decision to be appealed was made or, if the hearing is adjourned to a later date, the hearing on that date]² (which may be longer or shorter than the period referred to in sub-paragraph (b)); or

    (b)   where the court makes no such direction, 21 days after the date of the decision of the lower court against which the appellant wishes to appeal.

[(3) Where the appeal is against –

    (a)   a case management decision; or

    (b)   an order under section 38(1) of the 1989 Act,

the appellant must file the appellant's notice within 7 days beginning with the date of the decision of the lower court.]¹

(4) Unless the appeal court orders otherwise, an appellant's notice must be served on each respondent and the persons referred to in paragraph (5) –

    (a)   as soon as practicable; and

    (b)   in any event not later than 7 days,

after it is filed.

(5) The persons referred to in paragraph (4) are –

    (a)   any children's guardian, welfare officer, or children and family reporter;

    (b)   a local authority who has prepared a report under section 14A(8) or (9) of the 1989 Act;

    (c)   an adoption agency or local authority which has prepared a report on the suitability of the applicant to adopt a child;

    (d)   a local authority which has prepared a report on the placement of the child for adoption; and

    (e)   …¹

NOTES

Amendments.¹ Paragraph substituted and sub-paragraph omitted: SI 2014/667. ² Words inserted: SI 2022/44.

PART II – Statutory instruments

30.5 Respondent's notice

(1) A respondent may file and serve a respondent's notice.

(2) A respondent who –

(a)   is seeking permission to appeal from the appeal court; or
(b)   wishes to ask the appeal court to uphold the order of the lower court for reasons different from or additional to those given by the lower court,

must file a respondent's notice.

(3) Where the respondent seeks permission from the appeal court it must be requested in the respondent's notice.

(4) [Subject to paragraph (4A), a respondent's notice][1] must be filed within –

(a)   such period as may be directed by the lower court [at the hearing at which the decision to be appealed was made or, if the hearing is adjourned to a later date, the hearing on that date][2]; or
(b)   where the court makes no such direction, 14 days beginning with the date referred to in paragraph (5).

[(4A) Where the appeal is against a case management decision, a respondent's notice must be filed within –

(a)   such period as may be directed by the lower court; or
(b)   where the court makes no such direction, 7 days beginning with the date referred to in paragraph (5).][1]

(5) The date referred to in paragraph (4) is –

(a)   the date on which the respondent is served with the appellant's notice where –
permission to appeal was given by the lower court; or
permission to appeal is not required;

(b)   the date on which the respondent is served with notification that the appeal court has given the appellant permission to appeal; or
(c)   the date on which the respondent is served with notification that the application for permission to appeal and the appeal itself are to be heard together.

(6) Unless the appeal court orders otherwise, a respondent's notice must be served on the appellant, any other respondent and the persons referred to in rule 30.4(5) –

(a)   as soon as practicable; and
(b)   in any event not later than 7 days,

after it is filed.

(7) Where there is an appeal against an order under section 38(1) of the 1989 Act –

(a)   a respondent may not, in that appeal, bring an appeal from the order or ask the appeal court to uphold the order of the lower court for reasons different from or additional to those given by the lower court; and

(b)   paragraphs (2) and (3) do not apply.

NOTES

Amendments.[1] Words substituted and paragraph inserted: SI 2014/667. [2] Words inserted: SI 2022/44.

30.6 Grounds of appeal

The appeal notice must state the grounds of appeal.

30.7 Variation of time

(1) An application to vary the time limit for filing an appeal notice must be made to the appeal court.

(2) The parties may not agree to extend any date or time limit set by –

(a)   these rules;

(b)   Practice Direction 30A; or

(c)   an order of the appeal court or the lower court.

(Rule 4.1(3)(a) provides that the court may extend or shorten the time for compliance with a rule, practice direction or court order (even if an application for extension is made after the time for compliance has expired).)

(Rule 4.1(3)(c) provides that the court may adjourn or bring forward a hearing.)

30.8 Stay

Unless the appeal court or the lower court orders otherwise, an appeal does not operate as a stay[(GL)] of any order or decision of the lower court.

30.9 Amendment of appeal notice

An appeal notice may not be amended without the permission of the appeal court.

30.10 Striking out appeal notices and setting aside or imposing conditions on permission to appeal

(1) The appeal court may –

(a)   strike out[(GL)] the whole or part of an appeal notice;

(b)   set aside[(GL)] permission to appeal in whole or in part;

(c)   impose or vary conditions upon which an appeal may be brought.

(2) The court will only exercise its powers under paragraph (1) where there is a compelling reason for doing so.

(3) Where a party was present at the hearing at which permission was given that party may not subsequently apply for an order that the court exercise its powers under paragraphs (1)(b) or (1)(c).

30.11 Appeal court's powers

(1) In relation to an appeal the appeal court has all the powers of the lower court.

> (Rule 30.1(4) provides that this Part is subject to any enactment that sets out special provisions with regard to any particular category of appeal.)

(2) The appeal court has power to –

    (a)   affirm, set aside(GL) or vary any order or judgment made or given by the lower court;

    (b)   refer any application or issue for determination by the lower court;

    (c)   order a new hearing;

    (d)   make orders for the payment of interest;

    (e)   make a costs order.

(3) The appeal court may exercise its powers in relation to the whole or part of an order of the lower court.

> (Rule 4.1 contains general rules about the court's case management powers.)

(4) If the appeal court –

    (a)   refuses an application for permission to appeal;

    (b)   strikes out an appellant's notice; or

    (c)   dismisses an appeal,

and it considers that the application, the appellant's notice or the appeal is totally without merit, the provisions of paragraph (5) must be complied with.

(5) Where paragraph (4) applies –

    (a)   the court's order must record the fact that it considers the application, the appellant's notice or the appeal to be totally without merit; and

    (b)   the court must at the same time consider whether it is appropriate to make a civil restraint order.

30.12 Hearing of appeals

(1) Every appeal will be limited to a review of the decision of the lower court unless –

    (a)   an enactment or practice direction makes different provision for a particular category of appeal; or

    (b)   the court considers that in the circumstances of an individual appeal it would be in the interests of justice to hold a re-hearing.

(2) Unless it orders otherwise, the appeal court will not receive –

    (a)   oral evidence; or

    (b)   evidence which was not before the lower court.

(3) The appeal court will allow an appeal where the decision of the lower court was –

(a) wrong; or
(b) unjust because of a serious procedural or other irregularity in the proceedings in the lower court.

(4) The appeal court may draw any inference of fact which it considers justified on the evidence.

(5) At the hearing of the appeal a party may not rely on a matter not contained in that party's appeal notice unless the appeal court gives permission.

[30.12A Appeal court's power to order that hearing of appeal be held in public

(1) This rule applies where by virtue of rule 27.10 the hearing of an appeal is to be held in private.

(2) The appeal court may make an order—

(a) for the hearing of the appeal to be in public;
(b) for a part of the hearing of the appeal to be in public; or
(c) excluding any person or class of persons from attending a public hearing of an appeal or any part of it.

(3) Where the appeal court makes an order under paragraph (1), it may in the same order or in a subsequent order—

(a) impose restrictions on the publication of the identity of—
  (i) any party;
  (ii) any child (whether or not a party);
  (iii) any witness; or
  (iv) any other person;
(b) prohibit the publication of any information which may lead to any such person being identified;
(c) prohibit the publication of any information relating to the proceedings from such date as the court may specify; or
(d) impose such other restrictions on the publication of information relating to the proceedings as the court may specify.

(4) A practice direction may provide for—

(a) circumstances (which may be of general application or applicable only to specified appeal courts or proceedings) in which the appeal court will ordinarily make an order under paragraph (1); and
(b) the terms of the order under paragraph (2) which the court will ordinarily make in such circumstances.][1]

NOTES
Amendment.[1] Rule inserted: SI 2018/1172.

30.13 Assignment of appeals to the Court of Appeal

(1) Where the court from or to which an appeal is made or from which permission to appeal is sought ('the relevant court') considers that –

(a)   an appeal which is to be heard by a county court or the High Court would raise an important point of principle or practice; or

(b)   there is some other compelling reason for the Court of Appeal to hear it,

the relevant court may order the appeal to be transferred to the Court of Appeal.

[(2) Paragraph (1) does not allow an application for permission to appeal to be transferred to the Court of Appeal.][1]

NOTES

Amendment.[1] Paragraph substituted: SI 2014/667.

30.14 Reopening of final appeals

(1) The High Court will not reopen a final determination of any appeal unless –

(a)   it is necessary to do so in order to avoid real injustice;

(b)   the circumstances are exceptional and make it appropriate to reopen the appeal; and

(c)   there is no alternative effective remedy.

(2) In paragraphs (1), (3), (4) and (6), 'appeal' includes an application for permission to appeal.

(3) This rule does not apply to appeals to [the family court][1].

(4) Permission is needed to make an application under this rule to reopen a final determination of an appeal.

(5) There is no right to an oral hearing of an application for permission unless, exceptionally, the judge so directs.

(6) The judge will not grant permission without directing the application to be served on the other party to the original appeal and giving that party an opportunity to make representations.

(7) There is no right of appeal or review from the decision of the judge on the application for permission, which is final.

(8) The procedure for making an application for permission is set out in Practice Direction 30A.

NOTES

Amendment.[1] Words substituted: SI 2014/667.

**Practice Direction 30A –
Appeals**

This Practice Direction supplements FPR Part 30

Application and interpretation

1.1 This practice direction applies to all appeals to which Part 30 applies.

1.2 In this Practice Direction in relation to the family court –

'the 1984 Act' means the Matrimonial and Family Proceedings Act 1984;
...²

'authorised' means authorised by the President of the Family Division or nominated by or on behalf of the Lord Chief Justice to conduct particular business in the family court, in accordance with Part 3 of rules relating to the composition of the court and distribution of business made in accordance with section 31D of the 1984 Act;

'costs judge' means –

    (a)   the Chief Taxing Master;

    (b)   a taxing master of the Senior Courts; or

    (c)   a person appointed to act as deputy for the person holding office referred to in paragraph (b) or to act as a temporary additional officer for any such office;

'judge of circuit judge level' means –

    (a)   a circuit judge who, where applicable, is authorised;

    (b)   a Recorder who, where applicable, is authorised;

    (c)   any other judge of the family court authorised to sit as a judge of circuit judge level in the family court;

'judge of district judge level' means –

    (a)   the Senior District Judge of the Family Division;

    (b)   a district judge of the Principal Registry of the Family Division ('PRFD');

    (c)   a person appointed to act as deputy for the person holding office referred to in paragraph (b) or to act as a temporary additional officer for any such office;

    (d)   a district judge who, where applicable, is authorised;

    (e)   a deputy district judge appointed under section 102 of the Senior Courts Act 1981 or section 8 of the County Courts Act 1984 who, where applicable, is authorised;

    (f)   an authorised District Judge (Magistrates' Courts);

    (g)   any other judge of the family court authorised to sit as a judge of district judge level in the family court.

'judge of High Court judge level' means –

    (a)   a deputy judge of the High Court;

    (b)   a puisne judge of the High Court;

    (c)   a person who has been a judge of the Court of Appeal or a puisne judge of the High Court who may act as a judge of the family court by virtue of section 9 of the Senior Courts Act 1981;

    (d)   the Senior President of Tribunals;

    (e)   the Chancellor of the High Court;

    (f)   an ordinary judge of the Court of Appeal (including the vice-president, if any, of either division of that court);

    (g)   the President of the Queen's Bench Division;

    (h)   the President of the Family Division;

    (i)   the Master of the Rolls;

    (j)   the Lord Chief Justice;

PART II – Statutory instruments

['justices' legal adviser' means a person authorised to exercise functions under section 67B of the Courts Act 2003 who has such qualifications as are prescribed by the Authorised Court Staff (Legal Advice Functions) Qualifications Regulations 2020; and][2]
'lay justice' means an authorised justice of the peace who is not a District Judge (Magistrates' Courts).

NOTES

Amendments.[1] Text substituted: FPR Update, April 2014. [2] Definition repealed and definition substituted: Practice Direction, April 2020.

Routes of appeal

[2.1 The following table sets out to which court or judge an appeal is to be made (subject to obtaining any necessary permission) from decisions of the family court][1] –

Decision of judge sitting in the family court	Permission generally required (subject to exception in rules of court, for example, no permission required to appeal against a committal order)	Appeal to
1 A bench of – • two or three lay magistrates; or • a lay justice	No	a judge of circuit judge level sitting in the family court; a judge of High Court judge level sitting in the family court where a Designated Family Judge or a judge of High Court Judge level considers that the appeal would raise an important point of principle or practice. (NB a judge of High Court judge level may hear the appeal in interests of effective and efficient use of local judicial resource and the resource of the High Court bench)
2 A judge of district judge level (except the Senior District Judge of the Family Division ...[4] in proceedings for a financial remedy)	Yes	As above
3 ...[4]	...[4]	...[4]

Decision of judge sitting in the family court	Permission generally required (subject to exception in rules of court, for example, no permission required to appeal against a committal order)	Appeal to
4 Senior District Judge of the Family Division in proceedings for financial remedy	Yes	Judge of High Court judge level sitting in the family court
[4A Circuit judge or Recorder, except where paragraph 5 of this table applies.	Yes	High Court Judge (sitting in the High Court)][2]
[5 Circuit judge or Recorder, where the appeal is from: (a) a decision or order in proceedings under – (i) Part 4 or 5 of, or paragraph 19(1) of Schedule 2 to, the Children Act 1989; or (ii) the Adoption and Children Act 2002; (b) a decision or order in exercise of the court's jurisdiction in relation to contempt of court, where that decision or order was made in, or in connection with, proceedings of a type referred to in sub-paragraph (a); or (c) a decision or order made on appeal to the family court.	Yes	Court of Appeal][2]
6 Costs Judge	Yes	Judge of High Court judge level sitting in the family court
7 Judge of High Court judge level	Yes	Court of Appeal

Decision of judge sitting in the family court	Permission generally required (subject to exception in rules of court, for example, no permission required to appeal against a committal order)	Appeal to
[8 Any other judge of the family court not referred to in paragraphs 1 to 7 of this table.	Yes	Court of Appeal][2]

(Provisions setting out routes of appeal include section 31K(1) of the 1984 Act for appeals against decisions from the family court and section 13(2A) of the Administration of Justice Act 1960 for appeals against decisions or orders from the family court relating to contempt of court.

The Access to Justice Act 1999 (Destination of Appeals) (Family Proceedings) Order 2014 (S.I. 2014/602) routes appeals from certain judges and office holders to the family court instead of to the Court of Appeal and rules relating to the composition of the court and distribution of business made in accordance with section 31 D of the 1984 Act make provision for appeals within the family court.

[Amendments to the 2014 Order (made by the Access to Justice Act 1999 (Destination of Appeals) (Family Proceedings) (Amendment) Order 2016) route certain appeals from Circuit Judges or Recorders to the High Court instead of the Court of Appeal. These appeals are heard by a High Court judge sitting in the High Court (see paragraph 8.4 below).][2]

The leapfrogging provision in section 57 of the Access to Justice Act 1999 applies to appeals where in any proceedings in the family court a person appeals or seeks permission to appeal to a court other than the Court of Appeal or the Supreme Court.)

2.2 The following table sets out to which court or judge an appeal is to be made (subject to obtaining any necessary permission) from decisions of the High Court –

Decision of judge	Permission generally required (subject to exception in rules of court, for example, no permission required to appeal against a committal order)	Appeal to
1 District Judge of the High Court; or	Yes	High Court Judge
• a deputy district judge appointed under section 102 of the Senior Courts Act 1981		

Decision of judge	Permission generally required (subject to exception in rules of court, for example, no permission required to appeal against a committal order)	Appeal to
2 The Senior District Judge of the Family Division; • District Judge of the PRFD; or • a person appointed to act as deputy for a District Judge of the PRFD or to act as a temporary additional officer for such office	Yes	High Court Judge
3 Costs judge; or • a person appointed to act as deputy for a costs judge who is a taxing master of the senior courts or to act as a temporary additional officer for such office	Yes	High Court Judge
4. Judge of the High Court (including a person acting as a judge of the High Court in accordance with section 9(1) or section 9(4) of the Senior Courts Act 1981)	Yes	Court of Appeal

(Provisions setting out routes of appeal include section 16(1) of the Senior Courts Act 1981 (as amended) for appeals against decisions from the High Court and section 13 of the Administration of Justice Act 1960 for appeals against an order or decision of the High Court relating to contempt of court. The Access to Justice Act 1999 (Destination of Appeals) (Family Proceedings) Order 2011 (S.I. 2011/1044) routes appeals against decisions of certain judges to the High Court instead of the Court of Appeal. The leapfrogging provision in section 57 of the Access to Justice Act 1999 referred to above applies.

The general rule is that appeals under section 8(1) of the Gender Recognition Act 2004 must be started in the family court as both the High Court and the family court have jurisdiction to hear the appeal (see section 8 of the 2004 Act and FPR 5.4). The procedure for appeals to the Court of Appeal is governed by the Civil Procedure Rules 1998, in particular CPR Part 52.).

[2.3 Justices' legal advisers are not judges of the family court but they are authorised to exercise functions under section 67B of the Courts Act 2003. Appeals against decisions of a justices' legal adviser are to a judge of circuit judge level sitting in the family court. However, it is expected that such appeals will be rare as a justices' legal adviser may refer a matter to the court as appropriate before making a decision.][3]

2.4 Where the decision to be appealed is a decision in a Part 19 (Alternative Procedure For Applications) application on a point of law in a case which did not involve any substantial dispute of fact, the court to which the appeal lies, where that court is the High Court or the family court and unless the appeal would lie to the Court of Appeal in any event, must consider whether to order the appeal to be transferred to the Court of Appeal under FPR 30.13 (Assignment of Appeals to the Court of Appeal).][1]

NOTES

Amendments.[1] Text substituted: FPR Update, April 2014. [2] Entries inserted and substituted, text inserted: FPR Update, October 2016. [3] Paragraph substituted: Practice Direction, April 2020. [4] Words and entry omitted repealed: FPR Update, April 2021.

Grounds for appeal

3.1 Rule 30.12 (hearing of appeals) sets out the circumstances in which the appeal court will allow an appeal.

3.2 The grounds of appeal should –

(a)   set out clearly the reasons why rule 30.12(3)(a) or (b) is said to apply; and

(b)   specify in respect of each ground, whether the ground raises an appeal on a point of law or is an appeal against a finding of fact.

Permission to appeal

4.1 FPR 30.3 (Permission) sets out the circumstances when permission to appeal is required. At present permission to appeal is required where the decision of the family court appealed against was made by a district judge (including a District Judge (Magistrates' Courts)) or a costs judge. Permission to appeal is required where the decision of the High Court appealed against is a decision of a district judge or a costs judge. However, no permission is required where FPR 30.3(2) (appeals against a committal order or a secure accommodation order under section 25 of the Children Act 1989) applies..

(The requirement of permission to appeal may be imposed by a practice direction – see FPR 30.3(1)(b) (Permission). 'District judge' and 'costs judge' are defined in FPR 30.1(3)).

4.1A FPR Part 30 does not apply to an appeal against the decision or order of a Circuit Judge or Recorder in the family court where the decision or order was made –

(a)   in proceedings under –

(i)   Part 4 or 5 of, or paragraph 19(1) of Schedule 2 to, the Children Act 1989; or

(ii)   the Adoption and Children Act 2002;

(b)   in exercise of the court's jurisdiction in relation to contempt of court, where that decision or order was made in, or in connection with, proceedings of a type referred to in paragraph (a); or

(c)   on appeal to the family court.

(An appeal against a decision by a Circuit Judge or Recorder, where the appeal is from a decision or order referred to in paragraph 4.1A, is to the Court of Appeal and the Civil Procedure Rules 1998 apply.)

[4.1B The court should not ordinarily grant permission to appeal where the matters complained of would be better dealt with on an application to set aside a financial remedy order under rule 9.9A, an inherent jurisdiction order under rule 12.42B or a return order or non-return order under rule 12.52A. Such an application would be appropriate if the proposed appeal does not in fact allege an error of the court on the materials that were before the court at the time the order was made. However, by way of exception, permission to appeal may still be given where (i) a litigant alleges both that the court erred on the materials before it and that a ground for setting aside exists; or (ii) as the case may be, the order which it is sought to set aside includes a pension sharing order or pension compensation sharing order and the court may be asked to consider making orders under s 40A(5) or s 40B(2) of the Matrimonial Causes Act 1973.][1]

NOTES

Amendment.[1] Paragraph substituted: Practice Direction, April 2020.

Court to which permission to appeal application should be made

4.2   An application for permission should be made orally at the hearing at which the decision to be appealed against is made.

4.3   Where –

(a)   no application for permission to appeal is made at the hearing; or

(b)   the lower court refuses permission to appeal,

an application for permission to appeal may be made to the appeal court in accordance with rules 30.3(3) and (4) (Permission).

(Rule 30.1(3) defines 'lower court'.)

4.4   Where no application for permission to appeal has been made in accordance with rule 30.3(3)(a) (Permission) but a party requests further time to make such an application the court may adjourn the hearing to give that party an opportunity to do so.

4.5   There is no appeal from a decision of the appeal court to allow or refuse permission to appeal to that court. However, where the appeal court, without a hearing, refuses permission to appeal, the person seeking permission may request that decision to be reconsidered at a hearing, unless an order has been made under rule 30.3(5A) that the person seeking permission may not do so (where the application for permission is considered to be totally without merit) – see section 54(4) of the Access to Justice Act 1999 and rule 30.3(5), (5A) (Permission).

Permission and case management decisions

4.5A Where the application is for permission to appeal from a case management decision, the factors to which the court is to have particular regard include whether –

(a)   the issue is of sufficient significance to justify an appeal;

(b)   the procedural consequences of an appeal (e.g. the impact upon the timetable) outweigh the significance of the case management decision;

(c)   it would be more convenient to adjourn the determination of the issue.

4.5B Case management decisions include decisions made under FPR 4.1(3) and decisions about disclosure, filing of witness statements or experts' reports, directions about the timetable of the proceedings and adding a party to the proceedings.

Material omission from a judgment of the lower court

4.6 Where a party's advocate considers that there is a material omission from a judgment of the lower court or, where the decision is made by a lay justice or justices, the written reasons for the decision of the lower court (including inadequate reasons for the lower court's decision), the advocate should before the drawing of the order give the lower court which made the decision the opportunity of considering whether there is an omission and should not immediately use the omission as grounds for an application to appeal.

4.7 Paragraph 4.8 below applies where there is an application to the lower court for permission to appeal on the grounds of a material omission from a judgment or written reasons (where a decision is made in the family court by a lay justice or justices) of the lower court. Paragraph 4.9 below applies where there is an application for permission to appeal to the appeal court on the grounds of a material omission from a judgment or written reasons (where a decision is made in the family court by a lay justice or justices)]1 of the lower court.

4.8 Where the application for permission to appeal is made to the lower court, the court which made the decision must –

(a)   consider whether there is a material omission and adjourn for that purpose if necessary; and

(b)   where the conclusion is that there has been such an omission, provide additions to the judgment.

4.9 Where the application for permission to appeal is made to the appeal court, the appeal court –

(a)   must consider whether there is a material omission; and

(b)   where the conclusion is that there has been such an omission, may adjourn the application and remit the case to the lower court with an invitation to provide additions to the judgment.

Consideration of Permission without a hearing

4.10 An application for permission to appeal may be considered by the appeal court without a hearing.

4.11 If permission is granted without a hearing the parties will be notified of that decision and the procedure in paragraphs 6.1 to 6.8 will then apply.

4.12 If permission is refused without a hearing the parties will be notified of that decision with the reasons for it. The decision is subject to the appellant's right to have it reconsidered at an oral hearing. This may be before the same judge. However the appellant has no right to have the application considered at an oral hearing where a High Court Judge or Designated Family Judge refused permission to appeal without a hearing and made an order under rule 30.3(5A) that the appellant may not request the decision to be reconsidered at a hearing because he or she considered the application for permission to be totally without merit.

4.13 A request for the decision to be reconsidered at an oral hearing must be filed at the appeal court within 7 days after service of the notice that permission has been refused. A copy of the request must be served by the appellant on the respondent at the same time. This does not apply where an order has been made under rule 30.3(5A) that the appellant may not request the decision to be reconsidered at a hearing.

Permission hearing

4.14 Where an appellant, who is represented, makes a request for a decision to be reconsidered at an oral hearing, the appellant's advocate must, at least 4 days before the hearing, in a brief written statement –

(a)   inform the court and the respondent of the points which the appellant proposes to raise at the hearing;

(b)   set out the reasons why permission should be granted notwithstanding the reasons given for the refusal of permission; and

(c)   confirm, where applicable, that the requirements of paragraph 4.17 have been complied with (appellant in receipt of legal aid).

4.15 The respondent will be given notice of a permission hearing, but is not required to attend unless requested by the court to do so.

4.16 If the court requests the respondent's attendance at the permission hearing, the appellant must supply the respondent with a copy of the appeal bundle (see paragraph 5.9 or 5.9A as applicable) within 7 days of being notified of the request, or such other period as the court may direct. The costs of providing that bundle shall be borne by the appellant initially, but will form part of the costs of the permission application.

Appellants in receipt of services funded by the legal aid applying for permission to appeal

4.17 Where the appellant is in receipt of legal aid and permission to appeal has been refused by the appeal court without a hearing, the appellant must send a

PART II – Statutory instruments

copy of the reasons the appeal court gave for refusing permission to the Director of legal aid casework as soon as it has been received from the court. The court will require confirmation that this has been done if a hearing is requested to re-consider the question of permission.

Limited permission

4.18 Where a court under rule 30.3 (Permission) gives permission to appeal on some issues only, it will –

    (a)   refuse permission on any remaining issues; or

    (b)   reserve the question of permission to appeal on any remaining issues to the court hearing the appeal.

4.19 If the court reserves the question of permission under paragraph 4.18(b), the appellant must, within 14 days after service of the court's order, inform the appeal court and the respondent in writing whether the appellant intends to pursue the reserved issues. If the appellant does intend to pursue the reserved issues, the parties must include in any time estimate for the appeal hearing, their time estimate for the reserved issues.

4.20 If the appeal court refuses permission to appeal on the remaining issues without a hearing and the applicant wishes to have that decision reconsidered at an oral hearing, the time limit in rule 30.3(6) (Permission) shall apply. Any application for an extension of this time limit should be made promptly. The court hearing the appeal on the issues for which permission has been granted will not normally grant, at the appeal hearing, an application to extend the time limit in rule 30.3(6) for the remaining issues.

4.21 If the appeal court refuses permission to appeal on remaining issues at or after an oral hearing, the application for permission to appeal on those issues cannot be renewed at the appeal hearing (see section 54(4) of the Access to Justice Act 1999).

Respondents' costs of permission applications

4.22 In most cases, applications for permission to appeal will be determined without the court requesting –

    (a)   submissions from; or

    (b)   if there is an oral hearing, attendance by,

the respondent.

4.23 Where the court does not request submissions from or attendance by the respondent, costs will not normally be allowed to a respondent who volunteers submissions or attendance.

4.24 Where the court does request –

    (a)   submissions from; or

    (b)   attendance by the respondent,

the court will normally allow the costs of the respondent if permission is refused.

Allocation – appropriate procedure

4A.1 Where a party is dissatisfied with allocation that party may appeal or request the court to reconsider allocation at a hearing under FPR 29.19.

4A.2 Where allocation was made at a hearing, the party who is dissatisfied may appeal.

4A.3 Where allocation was made without a hearing, the party who is dissatisfied should request the court to reconsider allocation at a hearing.

Appellant's notice

5.1 An appellant's notice must be filed and served in all cases. Where an application for permission to appeal is made to the appeal court it must be applied for in the appellant's notice.

Practice Direction 5A specifies the forms to be used to make an appeal: different forms are to be used, depending on the court to which the appeal lies.

Human Rights

5.2 Where the appellant seeks –

    (a)   to rely on any issue under the Human Rights Act 1998; or
    (b)   a remedy available under that Act,

for the first time in an appeal the appellant must include in the appeal notice the information required by rule 29.5(2).

5.3 Practice Direction 29A (Human Rights, Joining the Crown) will apply as if references to the directions hearing were to the application for permission to appeal.

Extension of time for filing appellant's notice

5.4. If an extension of time is required for filing the appellant's notice the application must be made in that notice. The notice should state the reason for the delay and the steps taken prior to the application being made.

5.5 Where the appellant's notice includes an application for an extension of time and permission to appeal has been given or is not required the respondent has the right to be heard on that application and must be served with a copy of the appeal bundle (see paragraph 5.9). However, a respondent who unreasonably opposes an extension of time runs the risk of being ordered to pay the appellant's costs of that application.

5.6 If an extension of time is given following such an application the procedure at paragraphs 6.1 to 6.8 applies.

Applications

5.7 Notice of an application to be made to the appeal court for a remedy incidental to the appeal (e.g. an interim injunction under rule 20.2 (Orders for

PART II – Statutory instruments

interim remedies)) may be included in the appeal notice or in a Part 18 (Procedure For Other Applications in Proceedings) application notice.

(Paragraph 13 of this practice direction contains other provisions relating to applications.).

Documents: appeals to the family court

5.8 Where the appeal lies to the family court, the appellant must file the following documents together with an appeal bundle (see paragraph 5.9) with his or her appellant's notice –

(a)   Omitted
(b)   one copy of the appellant's notice for each of the respondents;
(c)   one copy of the appellant's skeleton argument for each of the respondents;
(d)   Omitted
(e)   Omitted
(f)   any witness statements or affidavits in support of any application included in the appellant's notice.

5.9 Where the appeal lies to the family court, an appellant must include the following documents in his or her appeal bundle –

(a)   a sealed or stamped copy of the appellant's notice;
(b)   a sealed or stamped copy of the order being appealed, or a copy of the notice of the making of an order;
(c)   a copy of any order giving or refusing permission to appeal, together with a copy of the court's reasons for allowing or refusing permission to appeal;
(d)   any affidavit or witness statement filed in support of any application included in the appellant's notice;
(e)   where the appeal is against a consent order, a statement setting out the change in circumstances since the order was agreed or other circumstances justifying a review or re-hearing;
(f)   a copy of the appellant's skeleton argument;
(g)   a transcript or note of judgment or, in a magistrates' court, written reasons for the court's decision (see paragraph 5.23), and in cases where permission to appeal was given by the lower court or is not required those parts of any transcript of evidence which are directly relevant to any question at issue on the appeal;
(h)   the application form;
(i)   any application notice (or case management documentation) relevant to the subject of the appeal;
(j)   any other documents which the appellant reasonably considers necessary to enable the appeal court to reach its decision on the hearing of the application or appeal; and
(k)   such other documents as the court may direct.

5.10 All documents that are extraneous to the issues to be considered on the application or the appeal must be excluded. The appeal bundle may include affidavits, witness statements, summaries, experts' reports and exhibits but only where these are directly relevant to the subject matter of the appeal.

Documents: appeals to the High Court

5.10A Where an appeal lies to the High Court, the appellant must file the following documents, in the following sequence, as the appeal bundle:

(a)   a sealed or stamped copy of the appellant's notice (including the grounds of appeal);

(b)   a sealed or stamped copy of the order being appealed or a copy of the notice of the making of an order;

(c)   a transcript or note of the judgment (see also paragraphs 5.23 and 5.24);

(d)   copies of any documents specifically referred to in the judgment;

(e)   a copy of the appellant's skeleton argument (see also paragraphs 5.14 and 5.15).

5.10B Subject to paragraphs 5.11 and 6.4(1) and (c), no further documents may be included in the appeal bundle without an order of a High Court Judge sitting in the High Court.

5.10C In addition to the appeal bundle, the appellant must file the following duplicate documents –

(a)   one copy of the appellant's notice for each of the respondents;

(b)   one copy of the appellant's skeleton argument for each of the respondents (see also paragraphs 5.14 and 5.15).

Documents: appeals to the family court or the High Court

5.11 Where the appellant is represented, the appeal bundle must contain a certificate signed by the appellant's solicitor, counsel or other representative to the effect that the appellant has read and understood paragraph 5.10 and that the composition of the appeal bundle complies with it.

5.12 Where it is not possible to file all the above documents, the appellant must indicate which documents have not yet been filed and the reasons why they are not currently available. The appellant must then provide a reasonable estimate of when the missing document or documents can be filed and file them as soon as reasonably practicable.

Skeleton arguments

5.13 As noted in paragraphs 5.9 and 5.10A, the appellant's notice must, subject to paragraphs 5.14 and 5.15, be accompanied by a skeleton argument. Alternatively the skeleton argument may be included in the appellant's notice. Where the skeleton argument is so included it will not form part of the notice for the purposes of rule 30.9 (Amendment of appeal notice).

5.14 Subject to paragraph 5.14A, where it is impracticable for the appellant's skeleton argument to accompany the appellant's notice it must be filed and served on all respondents within 14 days of filing the notice.

PART II – Statutory instruments

5.14A In appeals against case management decisions, where the appellant's skeleton argument cannot accompany the appellant's notice it must be filed as soon as practicable or as directed by the court, but in any event not less than 3 days before the hearing of the appeal.

5.15 An appellant who is not represented need not file a skeleton argument but is encouraged to do so since this will be helpful to the court.

5.16 A skeleton argument must contain a numbered list of the points which the party wishes to make. These should both define and confine the areas of controversy. Each point should be stated as concisely as the nature of the case allows.

5.17 A numbered point must be followed by a reference to any document on which the party wishes to rely.

5.18 A skeleton argument must state, in respect of each authority cited –

    (a)   the proposition of law that the authority demonstrates; and

    (b)   the parts of the authority (identified by page or paragraph references) that support the proposition.

5.19 If more than one authority is cited in support of a given proposition, the skeleton argument must briefly state the reason for taking that course.

5.20 The statement referred to in paragraph 5.19 should not materially add to the length of the skeleton argument but should be sufficient to demonstrate, in the context of the argument –

    (a)   the relevance of the authority or authorities to that argument; and

    (b)   that the citation is necessary for a proper presentation of that argument.

5.21 The cost of preparing a skeleton argument which –

    (a)   does not comply with the requirements set out in this paragraph; or

    (b)   was not filed within the time limits provided by this Practice Direction (or any further time granted by the court),

will not be allowed on assessment except to the extent that the court otherwise directs.

5.22 The appellant should consider what other information the appeal court will need. This may include a list of persons who feature in the case or glossaries of technical terms. A chronology of relevant events will be necessary in most appeals.

Suitable record of the judgment

5.23 Where the judgment to be appealed has been officially recorded by the court, an approved transcript of that record should accompany the appellant's notice. Photocopies will not be accepted for this purpose. However, where there is no officially recorded judgment, the following documents will be acceptable –

Written judgments – Where the judgment was made in writing a copy of that judgment endorsed with the judge's signature.

Written reasons – where a decision is made by a lay justice or justices in the family court, a copy of the written reasons for the court's decision.

Note of judgment – When judgment was not officially recorded or made in writing a note of the judgment (agreed between the appellant's and respondent's advocates) should be submitted for approval to the judge whose decision is being appealed. If the parties cannot agree on a single note of the judgment, both versions should be provided to that judge with an explanatory letter. For the purpose of an application for permission to appeal the note need not be approved by the respondent or the lower court judge.

Advocates' notes of judgments where the appellant is unrepresented – When the appellant was unrepresented in the lower court it is the duty of any advocate for the respondent to make the advocate's note of judgment promptly available, free of charge to the appellant where there is no officially recorded judgment or if the court so directs. Where the appellant was represented in the lower court it is the duty of the appellant's own former advocate to make that advocate's note available in these circumstances. The appellant should submit the note of judgment to the appeal court.

5.24 An appellant may not be able to obtain an official transcript or other suitable record of the lower court's decision within the time within which the appellant's notice must be filed. In such cases the appellant's notice must still be completed to the best of the appellant's ability on the basis of the documentation available. However it may be amended subsequently with the permission of the appeal court in accordance with rule 30.9 (Amendment of appeal notice).

Advocates' notes of judgments

5.25 Advocates' brief (or, where appropriate, refresher) fee includes –

(a) remuneration for taking a note of the judgment of the court;
(b) having the note transcribed accurately;
(c) attempting to agree the note with the other side if represented;
(d) submitting the note to the judge for approval where appropriate;
(e) revising it if so requested by the judge,
(f) providing any copies required for the appeal court, instructing solicitors and lay client; and
(g) providing a copy of the note to an unrepresented appellant.

****

Appeals under section 8(1) of the Gender Recognition Act 2004

5.27 Paragraph 5.28 to 5.30 apply where the appeal is brought under section 8(1) of the Gender Recognition Act 2004 on a point of law against a decision by the Gender Recognition Panel to reject the application under sections 1(1), 5(2), 5A(2) or 6(1) of the 2004 Act. The appeal is to the High Court or to the family court. However, FPR 5.4 provides that where the family court has jurisdiction

PART II – Statutory instruments

to deal with a matter, the proceedings relating to that matter must be started in the family court except where the court otherwise directs, any rule, other enactment or Practice Direction provides otherwise or proceedings relating to the same parties are already being heard by the High Court. Most appeals under section 8(1) of the Gender Recognition Act 2004 are therefore likely to be to the family court and be heard by a judge of High Court Judge level sitting in that court in accordance with the rules relating to the composition of the court and distribution of business made in accordance with section 31D of the 1984 Act.

5.28 Where the appeal is to the High Court, the appeal notice must be –

(a)   filed in the PRFD; and
(b)   served on the Secretary of State and the President of the Gender Recognition Panels.

5.28A Where the appeal is to the family court the appeal notice must be served on the Secretary of State and the President of the Gender Recognition Panels.

5.29 The Secretary of State may appear and be heard in the proceedings on the appeal.

5.30 Where the High Court issues a gender recognition certificate under section 8(3)(a) of the Gender Recognition Act 2004, the court officer must send a copy of that certificate to the Secretary of State.

Transcripts or Notes of Evidence

5.31 When the evidence is relevant to the appeal an official transcript of the relevant evidence must be obtained. Transcripts or notes of evidence are generally not needed for the purpose of determining an application for permission to appeal.

Notes of evidence

5.32 If evidence relevant to the appeal was not officially recorded, a typed version of the judge's or [justices' legal adviser's][1] notes of evidence must be obtained.

NOTES

Amendment.[1] Words substituted: Practice Direction, April 2020.

Transcripts at public expense

5.33 Where the lower court or the appeal court is satisfied that –

(a)   an unrepresented appellant; or
(b)   an appellant whose legal representation is provided free of charge to the appellant and not funded by the Community Legal Service,

is in such poor financial circumstances that the cost of a transcript would be an excessive burden the court may certify that the cost of obtaining one official transcript should be borne at public expense.

5.34 In the case of a request for an official transcript of evidence or proceedings to be paid for at public expense, the court must also be satisfied that there are reasonable grounds for appeal. Whenever possible a request for a transcript at public expense should be made to the lower court when asking for permission to appeal.

Filing and service of appellant's notice

5.35 Rule 30.4 (Appellant's notice) sets out the procedure and time limits for filing and serving an appellant's notice. Subject to paragraph 5.36, the appellant must file the appellant's notice at the appeal court within such period as may be directed by the lower court, which should not normally exceed 14 days or, where the lower court directs no such period within 21 days of the date of the decision that the appellant wishes to appeal.

5.36 Rule 30.4(3) (Appellant's notice) provides that unless the appeal court orders otherwise, where the appeal is against an order under section 38(1) of the 1989 Act or a case management decision in any proceedings, the appellant must file the appellant's notice within 7 days beginning with the date of the decision of the lower court.

5.37 Where the lower court announces its decision and reserves the reasons for its judgment or order until a later date, it should, in the exercise of powers under rule 30.4(2)(a)) (Appellant's notice), fix a period for filing the appellant's notice at the appeal court that takes this into account.

5.38 Except where the appeal court orders otherwise a sealed or stamped copy of the appellant's notice, including any skeleton arguments must be served on all respondents and other persons referred to in rule 30.4(5) (Appellant's notice) in accordance with the timetable prescribed by rule 30.4(4)) (Appellant's notice) except where this requirement is modified by paragraph 5.14 or 5.14A in which case the skeleton argument should be served as soon as it is filed.

5.39 Where the appellant's notice is to be served on a child, then rule 6.33 (supplementary provision relating to service on children) applies and unless the appeal court orders otherwise a sealed or stamped copy of the appellant's notice, including any skeleton arguments must be served on the persons or bodies mentioned in rule 6.33(3). For example, the appeal notice must be served on any children's guardian, welfare officer or children and family reporter who is appointed in the proceedings.

5.40 Unless the court otherwise directs, a respondent need not take any action when served with an appellant's notice until such time as notification is given to the respondent that permission to appeal has been given.

5.41 The court may dispense with the requirement for service of the notice on a respondent.

5.42 Unless the appeal court directs otherwise, the appellant must serve on the respondent the appellant's notice and skeleton argument (but not the appeal bundle), where the appellant is applying for permission to appeal in the appellant's notice.

5.43 Where permission to appeal –

    (a)   has been given by the lower court; or

    (b)   is not required,

PART II – Statutory instruments

the appellant must serve the appeal bundle on the respondent and the persons mentioned in paragraph 5.39 with the appellant's notice.

Amendment of Appeal Notice

5.44 An appeal notice may be amended with permission. Such an application to amend and any application in opposition will normally be dealt with at the hearing unless that course would cause unnecessary expense or delay in which case a request should be made for the application to amend to be heard in advance.

Procedure after permission is obtained

6.1 This paragraph sets out the procedure where –

    (a)   permission to appeal is given by the appeal court; or
    (b)   the appellant's notice is filed in the appeal court and –
        (i)   permission was given by the lower court; or
        (ii)   permission is not required.

6.2 If the appeal court gives permission to appeal, the appeal bundle must be served on each of the respondents within 7 days of receiving the order giving permission to appeal.

6.3 The appeal court will send the parties –

    (a)   notification of the date of the hearing or the period of time (the 'listing window') during which the appeal is likely to be heard;
    (b)   where permission is granted by the appeal court a copy of the order giving permission to appeal; and
    (c)   any other directions given by the court.

6.4 Where the appeal court grants permission to appeal, the appellant must add the following documents to the appeal bundle –

    (a)   the respondent's notice and skeleton argument (if any);
    (b)   those parts of the transcripts of evidence which are directly relevant to any question at issue on the appeal;
    (c)   the order granting permission to appeal and, where permission to appeal was granted at an oral hearing, the transcript (or note) of any judgment which was given; and
    (d)   any document which the appellant and respondent have agreed to add to the appeal bundle in accordance with paragraph 7.16.

6.5 Where permission to appeal has been refused on a particular issue, the appellant must remove from the appeal bundle all documents that are relevant only to that issue.

Time estimates

6.6 If the appellant is legally represented, the appeal court must be notified, in writing, of the advocate's time estimate for the hearing of the appeal.

6.7 The time estimate must be that of the advocate who will argue the appeal. It should exclude the time required by the court to give judgment.

6.8 A court officer will notify the respondent of the appellant's time estimate and if the respondent disagrees with the time estimate the respondent must inform the court within 7 days of the notification. In the absence of such notification the respondent will be deemed to have accepted the estimate proposed on behalf of the appellant.

Respondent

7.1 A respondent who wishes to ask the appeal court to vary the order of the lower court in any way must appeal and permission will be required on the same basis as for an appellant.

(Paragraph 3.2 applies to grounds of appeal by a respondent.).

7.2 A respondent who wishes to appeal or who wishes to ask the appeal court to uphold the order of the lower court for reasons different from or additional to those given by the lower court must file a respondent's notice.

7.3 A respondent who does not file a respondent's notice will not be entitled, except with the permission of the court, to rely on any reason not relied on in the lower court. This paragraph and paragraph 7.2 do not apply where the appeal is against an order under section 38(1) of the 1989 Act (see rule 30.5(7) (Respondent's notice)).

7.4 Paragraphs 5.3 (Human Rights and extension for time for filing appellant's notice) and 5.4 to 5.6 (extension of time for filing appellant's notice) of this practice direction also apply to a respondent and a respondent's notice.

Time limits

7.5 The time limits for filing a respondent's notice are set out in rule 30.5(4) and (5) (Respondent's notice).

7.6 Where an extension of time is required the extension must be requested in the respondent's notice and the reasons why the respondent failed to act within the specified time must be included.

7.7 Except where paragraphs 7.8, 7.9A and 7.10 apply, the respondent must file a skeleton argument for the court in all cases where the respondent proposes to address arguments to the court. The respondent's skeleton argument may be included within a respondent's notice. Where a skeleton argument is included within a respondent's notice it will not form part of the notice for the purposes of rule 30.9 (Amendment of appeal notice).

7.8 Subject to paragraph 7.9A, a respondent who –

    (a)   files a respondent's notice; but

    (b)   does not include a skeleton argument with that notice,

must file the skeleton argument within 14 days of filing the notice.

7.9 Subject to paragraph 7.9A, a respondent who does not file a respondent's notice but who files a skeleton argument must file that skeleton argument at least 7 days before the appeal hearing.

(Rule 30.5(4) (Respondent's notice) sets out the period for filing a respondent's notice.).

7.9A In appeals against case management decisions, where –

(a)   the respondent's skeleton argument cannot accompany the respondent's notice; or

(b)   a respondent does not file a respondent's notice but files a skeleton argument,

the skeleton argument must be filed as soon as practicable or as directed by the court, but in any event not less than 3 days before the hearing of the appeal.

7.10 A respondent who is not represented need not file a skeleton argument but is encouraged to do so in order to assist the court.

7.11 The respondent must serve the skeleton argument on –

(a)   the appellant; and
(b)   any other respondent;

at the same time as the skeleton argument is filed at court. Where a child is an appellant or respondent the skeleton argument must also be served on the persons listed in rule 6.33(3) unless the court directs otherwise.

7.12 A respondent's skeleton argument must conform to the directions at paragraphs 5.16 to 5.22 with any necessary modifications. It should, where appropriate, answer the arguments set out in the appellant's skeleton argument.

Applications within respondent's notices

7.13 A respondent may include an application within a respondent's notice in accordance with paragraph 5.7.

Filing respondent's notices and skeleton arguments

7.14 The respondent must file the following documents with the respondent's notice in every case –

(a)   two additional copies of the respondent's notice for the appeal court; and
(b)   one copy each for the appellant, any other respondents and any persons referred to in paragraph 5.39.

7.15 The respondent may file a skeleton argument with the respondent's notice and –

(a)   where doing so must file two copies; and
(b)   where not doing so must comply with paragraph 7.8.

7.16 If the respondent considers documents in addition to those filed by the appellant to be necessary to enable the appeal court to reach its decision on the appeal and wishes to rely on those documents, any amendments to the appeal bundle should be agreed with the appellant if possible.

7.17 If the representatives for the parties are unable to reach agreement, the respondent may prepare a supplemental bundle.

7.18 The respondent must file any supplemental bundle so prepared, together with the requisite number of copies for the appeal court, at the appeal court –

(a) with the respondent's notice; or
(b) if a respondent's notice is not filed, within 21 days after the respondent is served with the appeal bundle.

7.19 The respondent must serve –

(a) the respondent's notice;
(b) the skeleton argument (if any); and
(c) the supplemental bundle (if any),

on –

(i) the appellant; and
(ii) any other respondent;

at the same time as those documents are filed at the court. Where a child is an appellant or respondent the documents referred to in paragraphs (a) to (c) above must also be served on the persons listed in rule 6.33(2) unless the court directs otherwise.

Appeals to the High Court

Application

8.1 The appellant's notice must be filed at the Family Division of the High Court at the Royal Courts of Justice, Strand, London, WC2A 2LL.

8.2 A respondent's notice must be filed at the court where the appellant's notice was filed.

8.3 In the case of appeals from district judges of the High Court, applications for permission and any other applications in the appeal, appeals may be heard and directions in the appeal may be given by a High Court Judge.

8.4 In cases where paragraph 8.5 applies, appeals, applications for permission to appeal and any other applications in the appeal may be heard, and directions in the appeal or application may be given, by a High Court judge only.

8.5 This paragraph applies in the case of appeals from a Circuit judge or Recorder, except where the appeal is from:

(a) a decision or order in proceedings under –
(i) Part 4 or 5 of, or paragraph 19(1) of Schedule 2 to, the Children Act 1989; or
(ii) the Adoption and Children Act 2002;

PART II – Statutory instruments

(b)   a decision or order in exercise of the court's jurisdiction in relation to contempt of court, where that decision or order was made in, or in connection with, proceedings of a type referred to in sub-paragraph (a); or

(c)   a decision or order made on appeal to the family court.

Appeals to a county court

****

Appeals to the family court from decisions in child support proceedings under section 111A of the Magistrates' Courts Act 1980 ('the 1980 Act')

9.3   Section 111A of the 1980 Act, provides that in proceedings under the Child Support Act 1991 a person may appeal to the family court on the ground that a decision is wrong in law or is in excess of jurisdiction. Section 111A(3)(a) provides that no appeal may be brought under section 111A if there is a right of appeal to the family court against the decision otherwise than under that section. Such an appeal is usually heard by a judge of circuit judge level court in accordance with the rules relating to the composition of the court and distribution of business made in accordance with section 31D of the 1984 Act.

9.4   Subject to section 111A of the 1980 Act and any other enactment, the following rules in Part 30 apply to appeals under section 111A of the 1980 Act –

(a)   30.1 (scope and interpretation);
(b)   30.2 (parties to comply with the practice direction);
(c)   30.4 (appellant's notice);
(d)   30.6 (grounds of appeal);
(e)   30.8 (stay); and
(f)   30.9 (amendment of appeal notice).

9.5   Section 111A(4) of the 1980 Act provides that the notice of appeal must be filed within 21 days after the day on which the decision of the magistrates' court was given. The notice of appeal should also be served within this period of time. The time period for filing the appellant's notice in rule 30.4(2) and (3) does not apply. There can be no extension of this 21 day time limit under rule 4.1(3)(a).

Other statutory rights of appeal from a magistrates' court and the court at which the appellant's notice is to be filed – provisions applying to those appeals and appeals under section 111A of the 1980 Act

9.6, 9.7   Omitted

9.8   Subject to any enactment, a district judge may –

(a)   dismiss an appeal;
  (i)   for want of prosecution; or
  (ii)   with the consent of the parties; or

(b)   give leave for the appeal to be withdrawn,

and may deal with any question of costs arising out of the dismissal or withdrawal.

Unless the court directs otherwise, any interlocutory application in an appeal under section 111A of the 1980 Act may be made to a district judge sitting in the family court in accordance with the rules relating to the composition of the court and distribution of business made in accordance with section 31D of the 1984 Act.

9.9–9.11 Omitted

9.12 This practice direction applies to appeals under section 111A of the 1980 Act with the following modifications and any other necessary modifications –

(a)   after paragraph 5.6 insert –

'5.6A Paragraphs 5.4 to 5.6 do not apply to an appeal to the family court under section 111A of the Magistrates' Courts Act 1980.'

(b)   in paragraph 5.35, insert 'and 5.36A' after ' subject to paragraph 5.36';

(c)   after paragraph 5.36 insert –

'5.36A Where the appeal is to a judge of the family court under section 111A of the Magistrates' Courts Act 1980, the appellant's notice must be filed and served within 21 days after the day on which the decision of the lower court was given.'.

Appeals to the family court from the Secretary of State: Deduction order appeals

9.13 A 'deduction order appeal' is an appeal under regulation 25AB(1)(a) to (d) of the Child Support (Collection and Enforcement) Regulations 1992 (S.I. 1992/1989) ('the Collection and Enforcement Regulations'). A deduction order appeal is an appeal against –

(a)   the making of a regular deduction order under section 32A of the Child Support Act 1991 ('the 1991 Act');

(b)   a decision on an application to review a regular deduction order;

(c)   a decision to withhold consent to the disapplication of sections 32G(1) and 32H(2)(b) of the 1991 Act which has the effect of unfreezing funds in the liable person's account; or

(d)   the making of a final lump sum deduction order under section 32F of the 1991 Act.

A deduction order appeal lies to the family court from the Secretary of State as a result of regulation 25AB(1) of the Collection and Enforcement Regulations.

9.14 The rules in Part 30 apply to deduction order appeals with the amendments set out in paragraphs 9.15 to 9.27 and 9.29 and 9.30 below. The rules in Part 30 also apply to appeals against the decision of a district judge in proceedings relating to a deduction order appeal with the amendments set out in paragraph 9.28 below.

9.15 'The respondent' means –

PART II – Statutory instruments

(a)   the Secretary of State and any person other than the appellant who was served with an order under section 32A(1), 32E(1) or 32F(1) of the 1991 Act; and

(b)   a person who is permitted by the appeal court to be a party to the appeal.

9.16 The appellant will serve the appellant's notice on the Secretary of State and any other respondent.

9.17 The appellant shall file and serve the appellant's notice, within 21 days of –

(a)   where the appellant is a deposit-taker, service of the order;

(b)   where the appellant is a liable person, receipt of the order; or

(c)   where the appellant is either a deposit-taker or a liable person, the date of receipt of notification of the decision.

9.18 For the purposes of paragraph 9.17 –

(a)   references to 'liable person' and 'deposit-taker' are to be interpreted in accordance with section 32E of the 1991 Act and regulation 25A(2) of the Collection and Enforcement Regulations and section 54 of the 1991 Act, respectively; and

(b)   the liable person is to be treated as having received the order or notification of the decision 2 days after it was posted by the Secretary of State.

9.19 Rule 4.1(3)(a) (court's power to extend or shorten the time for compliance with a rule, practice direction or court order) does not apply to an appeal against the making of a lump sum deduction order under section 32F of the 1991 Act in so far as that rule gives the court power to extend the time set out in paragraph 9.17 for filing and serving an appellant's notice after the time for filing and serving the that notice set out in paragraph 9.17 has expired.

9.20 The Secretary of State shall provide to the court and serve on all other parties to the appeal any information and evidence relevant to the making of the decision or order being appealed, within 14 days of receipt of the appellant's notice.

9.21 Subject to paragraph 9.23, a respondent who wishes to ask the appeal court to uphold the order or decision of the Secretary of State for reasons different from or in additional to those given by the Secretary of State must file a respondent's notice.

9.22 A respondent's notice must be filed within 14 days of receipt of the appellant's notice.

9.23 Where the Secretary of State as a respondent, wishes to contend that its order or decision should be –

(a)   varied, either in any event or in the event of the appeal being allowed in whole or in part; or

(b)   affirmed on different grounds from those on which it relied when making the order or decision,

it shall, within 14 days of receipt of the appellant's notice, file and serve on all other parties to the appeal a respondent's notice.

9.24 In so far as rule 30.7 (Variation of time) may permit any application for variation of the time limit for filing an appellant's notice after the time for filing the appellant's notice has expired, that rule shall not apply to an appeal made against an order under section 32F(1) of the Act of 1991.

9.25 Rule 30.8 (stay) shall not apply to an appeal made against an order under section 32F(1) of the Act of 1991.

9.26 Omitted

9.27 Rule 30.11 (appeal court's powers) does not apply to deduction order appeals.

9.28 Rule 30.11(2)(d) (making orders for payment of interest) does not apply in the case of an appeal against a decision of a district judge in proceedings relating to a deduction order appeal.

9.29 In the case of a deduction order appeal –

    (a)   the appeal court has power to –
        (i)   affirm or set aside the order or decision;
        (ii)   remit the matter to the Secretary of State for the order or decision to be reconsidered, with appropriate directions;
        (iii) refer any application or issue for determination by the Secretary of State;
        (iv) make a costs order; and

    (b)   the appeal court may exercise its powers in relation to the whole or part of an order or decision of the Secretary of State.

9.30 In rule 30.12 (Hearing of appeals) –

    (a)   at the beginning of paragraph (1), for 'Every' substitute 'Subject to paragraph (2A), every';
    (b)   at the beginning of paragraph (2), for 'Unless' substitute 'Subject to paragraph (2A), unless';
    (c)   after paragraph (2), insert –

       '(2A) In the case of a deduction order appeal, the appeal will be a re-hearing, unless the appeal court orders otherwise.';

    (d)   in paragraph (3), after 'lower court' insert 'or, in a deduction order appeal, the order or decision of the Secretary of State'; and
    (e)   for sub-paragraph (b) of paragraph (3), substitute –

       '(b) unjust because of a serious procedural or other irregularity in –
          (i)   the proceedings in the lower court; or
          (ii)   the making of an order or decision by the Secretary of State.'

Information about the Secretary of State's decision

9.31 In relation to the deduction order appeals listed in column 1 of the table in Schedule 2 to this Practice Direction –

PART II – Statutory instruments

(a)   the documents to be filed and served by the appellant include the documents set out in Column 3; and

(b)   the relevant information to be provided by the Secretary of State in accordance with paragraph 9.20 above includes the information set out in Column 4.

The court at which the appeal notice is to be filed

9.32 In relation to a deduction order appeal, the appellant's notice and other documents required to be filed with that notice shall be filed in the family court (the Collection and Enforcement Regulations 25AB(1)).

In accordance with the rules relating to the composition of the court and distribution of business made in accordance with section 31D of the 1984 Act, deduction order appeals will be heard at district judge level.

The Secretary of State's address for service

9.33 For the purposes of a deduction order appeal the Commission's address for service is –

Freepost
DWP Child Support Agency 19

All notices or other documents for the Secretary of State relating to a deduction order appeal should be sent to the above address.

9.34 This practice direction applies to deduction order appeals and appeals against the decision of a district judge in proceedings relating to a deduction order appeal with the following modifications and any other necessary modifications –

(a)   in paragraph 5.35, insert 'and 5.36B' after ' subject to paragraph 5.36A';
(b)   after paragraph 5.36A insert –

'5.36A Where the appeal is a deduction order appeal, the appellant's notice must be filed and served within 21 days of –

(a)   where the appellant is a deposit-taker, service of the order;
(b)   where the appellant is a liable person, receipt of the order; or
(c)   where the appellant is either a deposit-taker or a liable person, the date of receipt of notification of the decision the lower court was given.'.

Appeal against the court's decision under rules 31.10, 31.11 or 31.14

10.1 The rules in Part 30 apply to appeals against the court's decision under rules 31.10, 31.11 or 31.14 with the amendments set out in paragraphs 10.2 to 10.5 below. Rules 31.15 and 31.16 apply to these appeals. These modifications do not apply to appeals against the decision made on appeal under rule 31.15.

10.2 Rule 30.3 (permission to appeal) does not apply.

10.3 The time for filing an appellant's notice at the appeal court in rule 30.4(2) does not apply. Rule 31.15 sets out the time within which an appeal against the court's decision under rules 31.10, 31.11 or 31.14 must be made to a judge of the High Court.

10.4 Rule 4.1(3)(a) (court's power to extend or shorten the time for compliance with a rule, practice direction or court order) does not apply to an appeal against the court's decision under rules 31.10, 31.11 or 31.14 in so far as that rule gives the court power to extend the time set out in rule 31.15 for filing an appellant's notice.

10.5 Rules 30.7 (variation), 30.8 (stay of proceedings), 30.10 (striking out appeal notices, setting aside or imposing conditions on permission to appeal) and 30.12 (hearing of appeals) do not apply.

Appeals against pension orders and pension compensation sharing orders

11.1 Paragraph 11.2 below applies to appeals against –

(a) a pension sharing order under section 24B of the Matrimonial Causes Act 1973 or the variation of such an order under section 31 of that Act;

(b) a pension sharing order under Part 4 of Schedule 5 to the Civil Partnership Act 2004 or the variation of such an order under Part 11 of Schedule 5 to that Act;

(c) a pension compensation sharing order under section 24E of the Matrimonial Causes Act 1973 or a variation of such an order under section 31 of that Act; and

(d) a pension compensation sharing order under Part 4 of Schedule 5 to the Civil Partnership Act 2004 or a variation of such an order under Part 11 of Schedule 5 to that Act.

11.2 In appeals to which this paragraph applies, the court may extend the time set out in rule 30.4 for filing and serving an appellant's notice in accordance with rule 4.1(3)(a) (court's power to extend or shorten the time for compliance with a rule, practice direction or court order) or rule 30.7 (Variation of time), even if the pension sharing order or pension compensation sharing order has taken effect. However, where an application is made for variation of the time limit for filing or serving an appellant's notice after the order has taken effect, the court should have particular regard to the matters referred to in sections 40A and 40B of the Matrimonial Causes Act 1973 and paragraphs 79 and 80 of Schedule 5 to the Civil Partnership Act 2004 (which restrict the appeal court's power to set aside or vary an order in certain circumstances where an appeal is begun on or after the day on which the order takes effect but which also allow the appeal court in those circumstances to make such further orders as it thinks fit for putting the parties in the position it considers appropriate).

11.3 Omitted

Appeals to a court under section 20 of the 1991 Act (appeals in respect of parentage determinations)

12.1 The rules in Chapters 1 and 5 of Part 8 will apply as appropriate to an appeal under section 20(1) of the 1991 Act where that appeal must be made to a court in accordance with the Child Support Appeals (Jurisdiction of Courts) Order 2002.

12.2 The respondent to such an appeal will be the Secretary of State.

In accordance with the rules relating to the composition of the court and distribution of business made in accordance with section 31D of the 1984 Act, appeals under section 20 of the 1991 Act will be heard at district judge level.

12.3 Omitted

Applications

13.1 Where a party to an appeal makes an application whether in an appeal notice or by Part 18 (Procedure For Other Applications in Proceedings) application notice, the provisions of Part 18 will apply.

13.2 Omitted

Appeals against consent orders

14.1 The rules in Part 30 and the provisions of this Practice Direction apply to appeals relating to orders made by consent in addition to orders which are not made by consent.

Disposing of applications or appeals by consent

15.1 An appellant who does not wish to pursue an application or an appeal may request the appeal court for an order that the application or appeal be dismissed. Such a request must state whether the appellant is a child, or a protected person.

15.2 The request must be accompanied by a consent signed by the other parties stating whether the respondent is a child, or a protected person and consents to the dismissal of the application or appeal.

Allowing unopposed appeals or applications on paper

16.1 The appeal court will not normally make an order allowing an appeal unless satisfied that the decision of the lower court was wrong, but the appeal court may set aside or vary the order of the lower court with consent and without determining the merits of the appeal, if it is satisfied that there are good and sufficient reasons for doing so. Where the appeal court is requested by all parties to allow an application or an appeal the court may consider the request on the papers. The request should state whether any of the parties is a child, or protected person and set out the relevant history of the proceedings and the matters relied on as justifying the proposed order and be accompanied by a copy of the proposed order.

Summary assessment of costs

17.1 Costs are likely to be assessed by way of summary assessment at the following hearings –

    (a)   contested directions hearings;
    (b)   applications for permission to appeal at which the respondent is present;

(c) appeals from case management decisions or decisions made at directions hearings; and

(d) appeals listed for one day or less.

(Provision for summary assessment of costs is made by section 13 of the Practice Direction supplementing CPR Part 44)

17.2 Parties attending any of the hearings referred to in paragraph 17.1 should be prepared to deal with the summary assessment.

Reopening of final appeals

18.1 This paragraph applies to applications under rule 30.14 (Reopening of final appeals) for permission to reopen a final determination of an appeal.

18.2 In this paragraph, 'appeal' includes an application for permission to appeal.

18.3 Permission must be sought from the court whose decision the applicant wishes to reopen.

18.4 The application for permission must be made by application notice and supported by written evidence, verified by a statement of truth.

18.5 A copy of the application for permission must not be served on any other party to the original appeal unless the court so directs.

18.6 Where the court directs that the application for permission is to be served on another party, that party may within 14 days of the service on him or her of the copy of the application file a written statement either supporting or opposing the application.

18.7 The application for permission, and any written statements supporting or opposing it, will be considered on paper by a single judge, and will be allowed to proceed only if the judge so directs.

****

SCHEDULE 2

Appeal	Relevant legislation	Appellant information	Secretary of State information
Appeal against the making of a regular deduction order (under section 32A of the 1991 Act)	• Section 32C(4)(a) of the 1991 Act The Collection and Enforcement Regulations 25AB(1)(a) (appeals)	• A copy of the order; • A covering letter explaining that the order has been made and the reasons for the order namely that there are arrears of child maintenance and/or no other arrangements have been made for the payment of child maintenance, including arrears	• The amount of the current maintenance calculation, the period of debt and the total amount of arrears (including account breakdown if appropriate) and the reasons for the Secretary of State's decision, details of all previous attempts to negotiate payment i.e. phone calls and letters to the non resident parent, details of any previous enforcement action taken

Right margin: PART II – Statutory instruments

Appeal	Relevant legislation	Appellant information	Secretary of State information
Appeal against a decision on an application for a review of a regular deduction order	• Sections 32C(4)(b) 32C(2)(k) of the 1991 Act • The Collection and Enforcement Regulations 25G (review of a regular deduction order) and 25AB(1)(b) (appeals)	• A decision notification setting out whether or not the review has been agreed by the Secretary of State and the resulting action to be taken if agreed; with an enclosure setting out the specific reasons for the Secretary of State's decision	• The reasons for the Secretary of State's decision in respect of the application for review and any evidence supporting that decision
Appeal against the withholding of consent to the disapplication of sections 32G(1) and 32H(2)(b) of the 1991 Act	• Section 32I(4) of the 1991 Act • The Collection and Enforcement Regulations 25N (disapplication of sections 32G(1) and 32H(2)(b) of the 1991 Act) and 25AB(1)(c) (appeals)	• A decision notification setting out that either: (a) consent has been refused; or (b) consent has been given in relation to part of the application i.e. that only some of the funds which were requested to be released have been agreed to be released (the right of appeal will lie in respect of the part of the application which has been refused). • There will be an enclosure with the notification setting out the reasons for the decision on the application.	• The reasons for the Secretary of State's decision in respect of the application for consent and any evidence supporting that decision
Appeal against the making of a final lump sum deduction order (under section 32F of the 1991 Act)	• Section 32J(5) of the 1991 Act Collection and Enforcement Regulations 25AB(1)(d) (appeals)	• A copy of the order; • A covering letter explaining that the order has been made and the reasons for the order namely that there are arrears of child maintenance and/or no other arrangements have been made for the payment of child maintenance, including arrears	• The amount of the current maintenance calculation (if applicable), the period of debt and the total amount of arrears (including account breakdown if appropriate) and the reasons for the Secretary of State's decision, details of all previous attempts to negotiate payment i.e. phone calls and letters to the non resident parent, details of any previous enforcement action taken.

Practice Direction 30B –
Appeals – Transparency

This practice direction supplements Part 30 of the Family Procedure Rules 2010

NOTE: This Practice Direction refers to orders made under FPR rule 30.12A(2), and terms of orders made under FPR rule 30.12A(3). Those references are correct. Rule 30.12A itself, however, refers in paragraphs (3) and (4)(a) to an order under paragraph (1) of the rule, and in paragraph (4)(b) to the terms of an order under paragraph (2) of the rule. Those references are incorrect and should respectively be to an order under paragraph (2), and the terms of an order under paragraph (3) of the rule. The references in the rule are being corrected, but pending correction, they should be read as referring in paragraphs (3) and (4)(a) to an order under paragraph (2) of the rule, and in paragraph (4)(b) to the terms of an order under paragraph (3) of the rule.

Introduction

1.1 This practice direction is made under rule 30.12A(4). It provides for circumstances in which the appeal court will ordinarily make an order under rule 30.12A(2) and for the terms of the order under 30.12A(3) which the court will ordinarily make in such circumstances

1.2 This practice direction applies to all hearings in appeals within the scope of rule 30.12A(1) from the family court to the High Court.

Standard order

2.1 Subject to paragraph 2.3, the appeal court will ordinarily (and so without any application being made)—

(a)   make an order under rule 30.12A (3)(a) that the hearing of the appeal shall be in public; and
(b)   in the same order, impose restrictions under rule 30.12A(3) in relation to the publication of information about the proceedings.

2.2 An order pursuant to paragraph 2.1 will ordinarily be in the terms of the standard order approved by the President of the Family Division and published on the judicial website at https://www.judiciary.uk/publication-jurisdiction/family-2/, using the variant appropriate to the nature of the proceedings.

2.3 In the case of an appeal against a decision or order made in proceedings for a financial remedy where no minor children are involved, the court will not normally impose restrictions under rule 30.12A(3).

2.4 The court may decide not to make an order pursuant to paragraph 2.1 if it appears to the court that there is good reason for not making the order, but will consider whether it would be appropriate instead to make an order (under rule 30.12A (2)(b) or (c))—

(a)   for a part only of the hearing to be held in public; or
(b)   excluding any persons, or class of persons from the hearing, or from such part of the hearing as is held in public.

PART II – Statutory instruments

2.5 In deciding whether there is good reason not to make an order pursuant to paragraph 2.1 and whether to make an order pursuant to paragraph 2.3 instead, the court will have regard in particular to—

(a) the need to protect any child or another person involved in the proceedings;

(b) the nature of the evidence in the proceedings;

(c) whether earlier hearings in the proceedings have taken place in private;

(d) whether there is any risk of disruption to the hearing if there is general public access to it.

Documents to be provided to court reporters at the hearing of an appeal

3.1 The court will make available to the usher or other court official present in court two copies of the judgment under appeal for provision to accredited law reporters and accredited media reporters in accordance with the provisions of this paragraph.

3.2 Where a party is legally represented at the hearing of an appeal, the legal representative must bring to the hearing two additional copies of the party's skeleton argument (including any supplementary skeleton argument) for provision to accredited law reporters and accredited media reporters in accordance with the provisions of this paragraph.

3.3 The additional copies of skeleton arguments must be supplied before the commencement of the hearing to the usher or other court official present in court.

3.4 The usher or other court official to whom the copies of the judgment and skeleton arguments are supplied under paragraphs 3.1 and 3.3 must provide one copy of each to an accredited law reporter (upon production of their Royal Courts of Justice security pass) and one copy of each to an accredited media reporter (upon production of their press pass), if so requested by them. Those copies are to be provided only for the purpose of reporting the court proceedings and on the basis that the recipients may remove them from the court and make further copies of them for distribution to other accredited reporters in court, again only for the purpose of reporting the court proceedings.

3.5 Any party may apply orally to the court at the commencement of the hearing for a direction lifting or varying the obligations imposed by paragraph 3.4. Where a party intends to make such an application or is notified by another party of the intention to make one, the operation of paragraph 3.4 is suspended pending the ruling of the court.

3.6 In deciding whether to make a direction under paragraph 3.5, the court must take into account all the circumstances of the case and have regard in particular to—

(a) the interests of justice;

(b) the public interest;

(c) the protection of the interests of any child, vulnerable adult or protected party;

(d) the protection of the identity of any person intended to be protected by an order or direction relating to anonymity; and

(e) the nature of any private or confidential information (including information relating to personal financial matters) in the document.

A direction may permit a skeleton argument to be supplied in redacted or anonymised form.

3.7 For the purposes of this paragraph, "the hearing of an appeal" includes a hearing listed as an application for permission to appeal with the appeal to follow immediately if permission is granted.

[3.8 Paragraphs 3.1 to 3.7 apply to duly authorised lawyers who are attending court for journalistic, research or public legal educational purposes, in the same way as those paragraphs apply to accredited law reporters and accredited media reporters.

3.9 For the purposes of paragraph 3.4, a duly authorised lawyer is only to be provided with copies of the documents referred to in that paragraph upon production to the usher or other court official of a form of identification specified in paragraph 5A.2 of Practice Direction 27B.

3.10 In this Practice Direction, 'duly authorised lawyer' has the same meaning as in rule 27.11.][1]

NOTES

Amendments.[1] Paragraphs inserted: FPR Update No 3 of 2022, March 2022.

PART 31
REGISTRATION OF ORDERS UNDER THE COUNCIL REGULATION, THE CIVIL PARTNERSHIP (JURISDICTION AND RECOGNITION OF JUDGMENTS) REGULATIONS 2005[, THE MARRIAGE (SAME SEX COUPLES) (JURISDICTION AND RECOGNITION OF JUDGMENTS) REGULATIONS 2014][1] AND UNDER THE HAGUE CONVENTION 1996

NOTES

Amendments.[1] Words inserted: SI 2014/524.

31.1 Scope

This Part applies to proceedings for the recognition, non-recognition and registration of –

(a) judgments to which the Council Regulation applies;

(b) measures to which the 1996 Hague Convention applies; ...[1]

(c) judgments to which the Jurisdiction and Recognition of Judgments Regulations apply, and which relate to dissolution or annulment of overseas relationships entitled to be treated as a civil partnership, or legal separation of the same[; and][1]

PART II – Statutory instruments

[(d)   judgments to which the 2014 Regulations apply and which relate to divorce, or annulment of a marriage of a same sex couple or the judicial separation of the same.]¹

NOTES

Amendments.¹ Words omitted and inserted and paragraph inserted: SI 2014/524.

31.2 Interpretation

(1) In this Part –

(a)   'judgment' is to be construed –
    (i)   in accordance with the definition in Article 2(4) of the Council Regulation where it applies;
    (ii)   in accordance with regulation 6 of the Jurisdiction and Recognition of Judgments Regulations where those Regulations apply; ...¹
    (iii)   as meaning any measure taken by an authority with jurisdiction under Chapter II of the 1996 Hague Convention where that Convention applies; [or]¹
    [(iv)   in accordance with regulation 4(1)(a) of The Marriage (Same Sex Couples) (Jurisdiction and Recognition of Judgments) Regulations 2014 where those Regulations apply;]¹

(b)   'the Jurisdiction and Recognition of Judgments Regulations' means the Civil Partnership (Jurisdiction and Recognition of Judgments) Regulations 2005;

[(ba)   'the 2014 Regulations' means the Marriage (Same Sex Couples) (Jurisdiction and Recognition of Judgments) Regulations 2014;]¹

(c)   'Member State' means –
    (i)   where registration, recognition or non-recognition is sought of a judgment under the Council Regulation, a Member State of the European Union which is bound by that Regulation or a country which has subsequently adopted it;
    (ii)   where recognition is sought of a judgment to which the Jurisdiction and Recognition of Judgments Regulations apply, a Member State of the European Union to which Part II of those Regulations applies;
    [(iii)   where recognition is sought of a judgment to which the 2014 Regulations apply, a member State of the European Union to which Part II of those Regulations applies;]¹

(d)   'Contracting State' means a State, other than a Member State within the meaning of (c) above, in relation to which the 1996 Hague Convention is in force as between that State and the United Kingdom; and

(e)   'parental responsibility' –
    (i)   where the Council Regulation applies, has the meaning given in Article 2(7) of that Regulation; and
    (ii)   where the 1996 Hague Convention applies, has the meaning given in Article 1(2) of that Convention.

(2) References in this Part to registration are to the registration of a judgment in accordance with the provisions of this Part.

PART II – Statutory instruments

NOTES

Amendments.[1] Words omitted and inserted and sub-paragraphs inserted: SI 2014/524.

31.3 Where to start proceedings

(1) Every application under this Part, except for an application under rule 31.18 for a certified copy of a judgment, or under rule 31.20 for rectification of a certificate issued under Articles 41 or 42, must be made to the principal registry.

(2) Nothing in this rule prevents the determination of an issue of recognition as an incidental question by any court in proceedings, in accordance with Article 21(4) of the Council Regulation.

(3) Notwithstanding paragraph (1), where recognition of a judgment is raised as an incidental question in proceedings under the 1996 Hague Convention[,][1] ...[1] the Jurisdiction and Recognition of Judgments Regulations [or the 2014 Regulations][1] the court hearing those proceedings may determine the question of recognition.

NOTES

Amendments.[1] Punctuation inserted, word omitted and words inserted: SI 2014/524.

31.4 Application for registration, recognition or non-recognition of a judgment

(1) Any interested person may apply to the court for an order that the judgment be registered, recognised or not recognised.

(2) Except for an application under rule 31.7, an application for registration, recognition or non-recognition must be –

    (a)   made to a district judge of the principal registry; and

    (b)   in the form, and supported by the documents and the information required by a practice direction.

31.5 Documents – supplementary

(1) Except as regards a copy of a judgment required by Article 37(1)(a) of the Council Regulation, where the person making an application under this Part does not produce the documents required by rule 31.4(2)(b) the court may –

    (a)   fix a time within which the documents are to be produced;

    (b)   accept equivalent documents; or

    (c)   dispense with production of the documents if the court considers it has sufficient information.

(2) This rule does not apply to applications under rule 31.7.

31.6 Directions

(1) As soon as practicable after an application under this Part has been made, the court may (subject to the requirements of the Council Regulation) give such directions as it considers appropriate, including as regards the following matters –

(a)   whether service of the application may be dispensed with;

(b)   expedition of the proceedings or any part of the proceedings (and any direction for expedition may specify a date by which the court must give its decision);

(c)   the steps to be taken in the proceedings and the time by which each step is to be taken;

(d)   the service of documents; and

(e)   the filing of evidence.

(2) The court or court officer will –

(a)   record the giving, variation or revocation of directions under this rule; and

(b)   as soon as practicable serve a copy of the directions order on every party.

31.7 Recognition and enforcement under the Council Regulation of a judgment given in another Member State relating to rights of access or under Article 11(8) for the return of the child to that State

(1) This rule applies where a judgment has been given in another Member State –

(a)   relating to rights of access: or

(b)   under Article 11(8) of the Council Regulation for the return of a child to that State,

which has been certified, in accordance with Article 41(2) or 42(2) as the case may be, by the judge in the court of origin.

(2) An application for recognition or enforcement of the judgment must be –

(a)   made in writing to a district judge of the principal registry; and

(b)   accompanied by a copy of the certificate issued by the judge in the court of origin.

(3) The application may be made without notice.

(4) Rules 31.5 and 31.8 to 31.17 do not apply to an application made under this rule.

(5) Nothing in this rule shall prevent a holder of parental responsibility from seeking recognition and enforcement of a judgment in accordance with the provisions of rules 31.8 to 31.17.

31.8 Registration for enforcement or order for non-recognition of a judgment

(1) This rule applies where an application is made for an order that a judgment given in another Member State, or a Contracting State, should be registered, or should not be recognised, except where rule 31.7 applies.

(2) Where the application is made for an order that the judgment should be registered –

(a) upon receipt of the application, and subject to any direction given by the court under rule 31.6 the court officer will serve the application on the person against whom registration is sought;

(b) the court will not accept submissions from either the person against whom registration is sought or any child in relation to whom the judgment was given.

(3) Where the application is for an order that the judgment should not be recognised –

(a) upon receipt of the application, and subject to any direction given by the court under rule 31.6, the court officer will serve the application on the person in whose favour judgment was given;

(b) the person in whose favour the judgment was given must file an answer to the application and serve it on the applicant –

(i) within 1 month of service of the application; or

(ii) if the applicant is habitually resident in another Member State, within two months of service of the application.

(4) In cases to which the 1996 Hague Convention applies and the Council Regulation does not apply, the court may extend the time set out in subparagraph (3)(b)(ii) on account of distance.

(5) The person in whose favour the judgment was given may request recognition or registration of the judgment in their answer, and in that event must comply with 31.4(2)(b) to the extent that such documents, information and evidence are not already contained in the application for non-recognition.

(6) If, in a case to which the Council Regulation applies, the person in whose favour the judgment was given fails to file an answer as required by paragraph (3), the court will act in accordance with the provisions of Article 18 of the Council Regulation.

(7) If, in a case to which the 1996 Hague Convention applies and the Service Regulation does not, the person in whose favour the judgment was given fails to file an answer as required by paragraph (3) –

(a) where the Hague Convention of 15th November 1965 on the service abroad of judicial and extrajudicial documents in civil or commercial matters applies, the court shall apply Article 15 of that Convention; and

(b) in all other cases, the court will not consider the application unless –

(i) it is proved to the satisfaction of the court that the person in whose favour judgment was given was served with the application within a reasonable period of time to arrange his or her response; or

(ii) the court is satisfied that the circumstances of the case justify proceeding with consideration of the application.

(8) In a case to which the Jurisdiction and Recognition of Judgments Regulations [or the 2014 Regulations][1] apply, if the person in whose favour judgment was given fails to file an answer as required by paragraph (3), the court will apply the Service Regulation where that regulation applies, and if it does not –

(a) where the Hague Convention of 15th November 1965 on the service abroad of judicial and extrajudicial documents in civil or commercial matters applies, the court shall apply Article 15 of that Convention; and

(b) in all other cases, the court will apply the provisions of paragraph (7)(b).

NOTES

Amendment.[1] Words inserted: SI 2014/524.

31.9 Stay of recognition proceedings by reason of an appeal

Where recognition or non-recognition of a judgment given in another Member State or Contracting State is sought, or is raised as an incidental question in other proceedings, the court may stay the proceedings –

(a) if an ordinary appeal against the judgment has been lodged; or

(b) if the judgment was given in the Republic of Ireland, if enforcement of the judgment is suspended there by reason of an appeal.

31.10 Effect of refusal of application for a decision that a judgment should not be recognised

Where the court refuses an application for a decision that a judgment should not be recognised, the court may –

(a) direct that the decision to refuse the application is to be treated as a decision that the judgment be recognised; or

(b) treat the answer under paragraph (3)(b) of rule 31.8 as an application that the judgment be registered for enforcement if paragraph (5) of that rule is complied with and order that the judgment be registered for enforcement in accordance with rule 31.11.

31.11 Notification of the court's decision on an application for registration or non-recognition

(1) Where the court has –

(a) made an order on an application for an order that a judgment should be registered for enforcement; or

(b) refused an application that a judgment should not be recognised and ordered under rule 31.10 that the judgment be registered for enforcement,

the court officer will as soon as practicable take the appropriate action under paragraph (2) or (3).

(2) If the court refuses the application for the judgment to be registered for enforcement, the court officer will serve the order on the applicant and the person against whom judgment was given in the state of origin.

(3) If the court orders that the judgment should be registered for enforcement, the court officer will –

(a) register the judgment in the central index of judgments kept by the principal registry;

(b) confirm on the order that the judgment has been registered; and

(c) serve on the parties the court's order endorsed with the court officer's confirmation that the judgment has been registered.

(4) A sealed order of the court endorsed in accordance with paragraph (3)(b) will constitute notification that the judgment has been registered under Article 28(2) of the Council Regulation or under Article 26 of the 1996 Hague Convention, as the case may be, and in this Part 'notice of registration' means a sealed order so endorsed.

(5) The notice of registration must state –

(a) full particulars of the judgment registered and the order for registration;

(b) the name of the party making the application and his address for service within the jurisdiction;

(c) the right of the person against whom judgment was given to appeal against the order for registration; and

(d) the period within which an appeal against the order for registration may be made.

31.12 Effect of registration under rule 31.11

Registration of a judgment under rule 31.11 will serve for the purpose of Article 21(3) of the Council Regulation, Article 24 of the 1996 Hague Convention, ...1 regulation 7 of the Jurisdiction and Recognition of Judgments Regulations [or regulation 5 of the 2014 Regulations]¹ (as the case may be) as a decision that the judgment is recognised.

NOTES

Amendments.¹ Word omitted and words inserted: SI 2014/524.

31.13 The central index of judgments registered under rule 31.11

The central index of judgments registered under rule 31.11 will be kept by the principal registry.

31.14 Decision on recognition of a judgment only

(1) Where an application is made seeking recognition of a judgment only, the provisions of rules 31.8 and 31.9 apply to that application as they do to an application for registration for enforcement.

(2) Where the court orders that the judgment should be recognised, the court officer will serve a copy of the order on each party as soon as practicable.

(3) A sealed order of the court will constitute notification that the judgment has been recognised under Article 21(3) of the Council Regulation, Article 24 of the 1996 Hague convention[,]¹ ...¹ regulation 7 of the Jurisdiction and Recognition of Judgments Regulations [or regulation 5 of the 2014 Regulations]¹, as the case may be.

(4) The sealed order shall indicate –

(a)   full particulars of the judgment recognised;

(b)   the name of the party making the application and his address for service within the jurisdiction;

(c)   the right of the person against whom judgment was given to appeal against the order for recognition; and

(d)   the period within which an appeal against the order for recognition may be made.

NOTES

Amendments.[1] Punctuation inserted, word omitted and words inserted: SI 2014/524.

31.15 Appeal against the court's decision under rules 31.10, 31.11 or 31.14

(1) An appeal against the court's decision under rules 31.10, 31.11 or 31.14 must be made to a judge of the High Court –

(a)   within one month of the date of service of the notice of registration; or

(b)   if the party bringing the appeal is habitually resident in another Member State, or a Contracting State, within two months of the date of service.

(2) The court may not extend time for an appeal on account of distance unless the matter is one to which the 1996 Hague Convention applies and the Council Regulation does not apply.

(3) If, in a case to which the 1996 Hague Convention applies and the Service Regulation does not, the appeal is brought by the applicant for a declaration of enforceability or registration and the respondent fails to appear –

(a)   where the Hague Convention of 15th November 1965 on the service abroad of judicial and extrajudicial documents in civil or commercial matters applies, the court shall apply Article 15 of that Convention; and

(b)   in all other cases, the court will not consider the appeal unless –

(i)   it is proved to the satisfaction of the court that the respondent was served with notice of the appeal within a reasonable period of time to arrange his or her response; or

(ii)   the court is satisfied that the circumstances of the case justify proceeding with consideration of the appeal.

(4) This rule is subject to rule 31.16.

(The procedure for applications under rule 31.15 is set out in Practice Direction 30A (Appeals).)

31.16 Stay of enforcement where appeal pending in state of origin

(1) A party against whom enforcement is sought of a judgment which has been registered under rule 31.11 may apply to the court with which an appeal is lodged under rule 31.15 for the proceedings to be stayed where –

(a)   that party has lodged an ordinary appeal in the Member State or Contracting State of origin; or

(b)   the time for such an appeal has not yet expired.

(2) Where an application for a stay is filed in the circumstances described in paragraph (1)(b), the court may specify the time within which an appeal must be lodged.

31.17 Enforcement of judgments registered under rule 31.11

(1) [Subject to paragraph (1A)][1] the court will not enforce a judgment registered under rule 31.11 until after –

- (a) the expiration of any applicable period under rules 31.15 or 31.16; or
- (b) if that period has been extended by the court, the expiration of the period so extended.

[(1A) The court may enforce a judgment registered under rule 31.11 before the expiration of a period referred to in paragraph (1) where urgent enforcement of the judgment is necessary to secure the welfare of the child to whom the judgment relates.][1]

(2) A party applying to the court for the enforcement of a registered judgment must produce to the court a certificate of service of –

- (a) the notice of registration of the judgment; and
- (b) any order made by the court in relation to the judgment.

(Service out of the jurisdiction, including service in accordance with the Service Regulation, is dealt with in chapter 4 of Part 6 and in Practice Direction 6B.)

NOTES

Amendments.[1] Words and paragraph inserted: SI 2012/1462.

31.18 Request for a certificate or a certified copy of a judgment

(1) An application for a certified copy of a judgment, or for a certificate under Articles 39, 41 or 42 of the Council Regulation, must be made to the court which made the order or judgment in respect of which certification is sought and without giving notice to any other party.

(2) The application must be made in the form, and supported by the documents and information required by a practice direction.

(3) The certified copy of the judgment will be an office copy sealed with the seal of the court and signed by [a court officer][1]. It will be issued with a certified copy of any order which has varied any of the terms of the original order.

(4) Where the application is made for the purposes of applying for recognition or recognition and enforcement of the order in another Contracting State, the court must indicate on the certified copy of the judgment the grounds on which it based its jurisdiction to make the order, for the purposes of Article 23(2)(a) of the 1996 Hague Convention.

NOTES

Amendments.[1] Words substituted: SI 2013/3204.

PART II – Statutory instruments

31.19 Certificates issued in England and Wales under Articles 41 and 42 of the Council Regulation

The court officer will serve –

(a)   a certificate issued under Article 41 or 42; or

(b)   a certificate rectified under rule 31.20,

on all parties and will transmit a copy to the Central Authority for England and Wales.

31.20 Rectification of certificate issued under Article 41 or 42 of the Council Regulation

(1) Where there is an error in a certificate issued under Article 41 or 42, an application to rectify that error must be made to the court which issued the certificate.

(2) A rectification under paragraph (1) may be made –

(a)   by the court of its own initiative; or

(b)   on application by –

    (i)   any party to the proceedings; or

    (ii)   the court or Central Authority of another Member State.

(3) An application under paragraph (2)(b) may be made without notice being served on any other party.

31.21 Authentic instruments and agreements under Article 46 of the Council Regulation

This Chapter applies to an authentic instrument and an agreement to which Article 46 of the Council Regulation applies as it applies to a judgment.

31.22 Application for provisional, including protective measures

An application for provisional, including protective, measures under Article 20 of the Council Regulation or Articles 11 or 12 of the 1996 Hague Convention may be made notwithstanding that the time for appealing against an order for registration of a judgment has not expired or that a final determination of any issue relating to enforcement of the judgment is pending.

<h2 style="text-align:center">Practice Direction 31A –
Registration of orders under ...² [...²]¹ ...² the 1996 Hague Convention</h2>

This Practice Direction supplements FPR Part 31.

NOTES

Amendment.¹ Text inserted: FPR Update, April 2014. ² Text omitted repealed: FPR Update, March 2019.

Form of application

1.1 An application under rule 31.4 must be made using the Part 19 procedure, except that the provisions of rules 31.8 to 31.14 and of this Practice Direction shall apply in place of rules 19.4 to 19.9.

1.2 Where the application is for recognition only of an order, it should be made clear that the application does not extend to registration for enforcement.

Evidence in support of all applications for registration, recognition or non-recognition

2.1 ...[2]

2.2 All applications to which rule 31.4(2) applies must be supported by a statement that is sworn to be true or an affidavit, exhibiting the judgment, or a verified, certified or otherwise duly authenticated copy of the judgment. In the case of an application ...[2] [...[2]][1] ...[2] under the 1996 Hague Convention, a translation of the judgment should be supplied.

2.3 Where any other document required by this Practice Direction or by direction of the court under rule 31.5 is not in English, the applicant must supply a translation of that document into English certified by a notary public or a person qualified for the purpose, or accompanied by witness statement or affidavit confirming that the translation is accurate.

NOTES

Amendments.[1] Text inserted: FPR Update, April 2014. [2] Text omitted repealed: FPR Update, March 2019.

...[1]

3.1 ...[1]

3.2 ...[1]

3.3 ...[1]

NOTES

Amendment.[1] Paragraphs omitted repealed: FPR Update, March 2019.

Evidence required in support of an application for registration, recognition or non-recognition of a judgment under the 1996 Hague Convention.

4.1 An application for an order for a judgment to be registered under Article 26 or not recognised under Article 24 of the 1996 Hague Convention must be accompanied by a witness statement or affidavit exhibiting the following documents and giving the information required by 4.2, 4.3 or 4.4 below as appropriate.

4.2 In the case of an application for registration –

(a) those documents necessary to show that the judgment is enforceable according to the law of the Contracting State in which it was given;

(b) a description of the opportunities provided by the authority which gave the judgment in question for the child to be heard, except where that judgment was given in a case of urgency;

(c) where the judgment was given in a case of urgency, a statement as to the circumstances of the urgency that led to the child not having the opportunity to be heard;

(d) details of any measures taken in the non-Contracting State of the habitual residence of the child, if applicable, specifying the nature and effect of the measure, and the date on which it was taken;

(e) in as far as not apparent from the copy of the judgment provided, a statement of the grounds on which the authority which gave the judgment based its jurisdiction, together with any documentary evidence in support of that statement;

(f) where appropriate, a statement regarding whether Article 33 of the 1996 Hague Convention has been complied with, and the identity and address of the authority or authorities from which consent has been obtained, together with evidence of that consent; and

(g) the information referred to at 3.2(c) to (e) above.

4.3 In the case of an application for an order that a judgment should not be recognised –

(a) a statement of the ground or grounds under Article 23 of the 1996 Hague Convention on which it is requested that the judgment be not recognised, the reasons why the applicant asserts that such ground or grounds is or are made out, and any documentary evidence on which the Applicant relies; and

(b) an address within the jurisdiction of the court for service of process on the applicant and stating, in so far as is known to the applicant, the name and usual or last known address or place of business of the person in whose favour judgment was given.

4.4 Where is it sought to apply for recognition only of a judgment under the 1996 Hague Convention, the provisions of paragraph 4.2 apply with the exception that the applicant is not required to produce the document referred to in subparagraph 4.2(a).

...[1]

5.1 ...[1]

5.2 ...[1]

5.3 ...[1]

NOTES

Amendment.[1] Paragraphs omitted repealed: FPR Update, March 2019.

Evidence in support of application ...[1] for a certified copy of a judgment

6.1 ...[1]

6.2 ...[1]

6.3 ...[1]

6.4 ...[1]

6.5 ...[1]

6.6 An application for a certified copy of a judgment for the purposes of recognition and enforcement of the judgment under the 1996 Hague Convention must –

(a) provide a statement of the grounds on which the court based its jurisdiction to make the orders in question;

(b) indicate the age of the child at the time of the judgment and the measures taken, if any, for the child's wishes and feelings to be ascertained; and

(c) indicate which persons were provided with notice of the proceedings and, where such persons were served with the proceedings, attach evidence of such service.

NOTES

Amendment.[1] Text and paragraphs omitted repealed: FPR Update, March 2019.

PART 32
REGISTRATION AND ENFORCEMENT OF ORDERS

****

Chapter 4
Registration and Enforcement of Custody Orders under the 1986 Act

32.23 Interpretation

In this Chapter –

'appropriate court' means, in relation to –

(a) Scotland, the Court of Session;

(b) Northern Ireland, the High Court in Northern Ireland; and

(c) a specified dependent territory, the corresponding court in that territory;

'appropriate officer' means, in relation to –

(a) the Court of Session, the Deputy Principal Clerk of Session;

(b) the High Court in Northern Ireland, the Master (Care and Protection) of that court; and

(c) the appropriate court in a specified dependent territory, the corresponding officer of that court;

'Part 1 order' means an order under Part 1 of the 1986 Act;

'the register' means the register kept for the purposes of Part 1 of the 1986 Act; and

'specified dependent territory' means a dependent territory specified in column 1 of Schedule 1 to the Family Law Act 1986 (Specified Dependent Territories) Order 1991.

32.24 Prescribed officer and functions of the court

(1) The prescribed officer for the purposes of sections 27(4) and 28(1) of the 1986 Act is the family proceedings department manager of the principal registry.

(2) The function of the court under sections 27(3) and 28(1) of the 1986 Act shall be performed by a court officer.

32.25 Application for the registration of an order made by the High Court or [the family court][1]

(1) An application under section 27 of the 1986 Act for the registration of an order made in the High Court or [the family court][1] may be made by sending to a court officer at the court which made the order –

- (a)   a certified copy of the order;
- (b)   a copy of any order which has varied the terms of the original order;
- (c)   a statement which –
    - (i)   contains the name and address of the applicant and the applicant's interest under the order;
    - (ii)   contains –
        - (aa)   the name and date of birth of the child in respect of whom the order was made;
        - (bb)   the whereabouts or suspected whereabouts of the child; and
        - (cc)   the name of any person with whom the child is alleged to be;
    - (iii)   contains the name and address of any other person who has an interest under the order and states whether the order has been served on that person;
    - (iv)   states in which of the jurisdictions of Scotland, Northern Ireland or a specified dependent territory the order is to be registered;
    - (v)   states that to the best of the applicant's information and belief, the order is in force;
    - (vi)   states whether, and if so where, the order is already registered;
    - (vii)   gives details of any order known to the applicant which affects the child and is in force in the jurisdiction in which the order is to be registered;
    - (viii)   annexes any document relevant to the application; and
    - (ix)   is verified by a statement of truth; and
- (d)   a copy of the statement referred to in paragraph (c).

(2) On receipt of the documents referred to in paragraph (1), the court officer will, subject to paragraph (4) –

- (a)   keep the original statement and send the other documents to the appropriate officer;
- (b)   record in the court records the fact that the documents have been sent to the appropriate officer; and
- (c)   file a copy of the documents.

(3) On receipt of a notice that the document has been registered in the appropriate court the court officer will record that fact in the court records.

(4) The court officer will not send the documents to the appropriate officer if it appears to the court officer that –

    (a)   the order is no longer in force; or

    (b)   the child has reached the age of 16.

(5) Where paragraph (4) applies –

    (a)   the court officer must, within 14 days of the decision, notify the applicant of the decision of the court officer in paragraph (4) and the reasons for it; and

    (b)   the applicant may apply to [the court]¹ in private for an order that the documents be sent to the appropriate court.

NOTES

Amendments.¹ Words substituted: SI 2013/3204.

Modification. Rule 32.25 modified in an application under s 27 of the Family Law Act 1986 for the registration and enforcement of a custody order made in a magistrates' court by the Magistrates' Courts (Enforcement or Variation of Orders Made in Family Proceedings and Miscellaneous Provisions) Rules 2011, SI 2011/1329, rr 74, 83.

32.26 Registration of orders made in Scotland, Northern Ireland or a specified dependent territory

(1) This rule applies where the prescribed officer receives, for registration, a certified copy of an order made in Scotland, Northern Ireland or a specified dependent territory.

(2) The prescribed officer will –

    (a)   enter in the register –
        (i)   the name and address of the applicant and the applicant's interest under the order;
        (ii)   the name and date of birth of the child and the date the child will attain the age of 16;
        (iii)   the whereabouts or suspected whereabouts of the child; and
        (iv)   the terms of the order, its date and the court which made it;

    (b)   file the certified copy and accompanying documents; and
    (c)   notify –
        (i)   the court which sent the order; and
        (ii)   the applicant,
        that the order has been registered.

32.27 Revocation and variation of an order made in the High Court or [the family court]¹

(1) Where a Part 1 order, registered in an appropriate court, is varied or revoked, the court officer of the court making the order of variation or revocation will –

    (a)   send a certified copy of the order of variation or revocation to –
        (i)   the appropriate officer; and
        (ii)   if a different court, the court which made the Part 1 order;

PART II – Statutory instruments

(b)   record in the court records the fact that a copy of the order has been sent; and

(c)   file a copy of the order.

(2) On receipt of notice from the appropriate court that its register has been amended, this fact will be recorded by the court officer of –

(a)   the court which made the order of variation or revocation; and

(b)   if different, the court which made the Part 1 order.

NOTES

Amendment.[1] Words substituted: SI 2013/3204.

Modification. Rule 32.27 modified where an order under Part 1 of the Family Law Act 1986 registered in an appropriate court is varied or repealed, by the Magistrates' Courts (Enforcement or Variation of Orders Made in Family Proceedings and Miscellaneous Provisions) Rules 2011, SI 2011/1329, rr 74, 83.

32.28 Registration of varied, revoked or recalled orders made in Scotland, Northern Ireland or a specified dependent territory

(1) This rule applies where the prescribed officer receives a certified copy of an order made in Scotland, Northern Ireland or a specified dependent territory which varies, revokes or recalls a registered Part 1 order.

(2) The prescribed officer shall enter particulars of the variation, revocation or recall in the register and give notice of the entry to –

(a)   the court which sent the certified copy;

(b)   if different, the court which made the Part 1 order;

(c)   the applicant for registration; and

(d)   if different, the applicant for the variation, revocation of recall of the order.

(3) An application under section 28(2) of the 1986 Act must be made in accordance with the Part 19 procedure.

(4) The applicant for the Part 1 order, if not the applicant under section 28(2) of the 1986 Act, must be made a defendant to the application.

(5) Where the court cancels a registration under section 28(2) of the 1986 Act, the court officer will amend the register and give notice of the amendment to the court which made the Part 1 order.

32.29 Interim directions

The following persons will be made parties to an application for interim directions under section 29 of the 1986 Act –

(a)   the parties to the proceedings for enforcement; and

(b)   if not a party to those proceedings, the applicant for the Part 1 order.

32.30 Staying and dismissal of enforcement proceedings

(1) The following persons will be made parties to an application under section 30(1) or 31(1) of the 1986 Act –

(a)   the parties to the proceedings for enforcement which are sought to be stayed$^{(GL)}$; and

(b)   if not a party to those proceedings, the applicant for the Part 1 order.

(2) Where the court makes an order under section 30(2) or (3) or section 31(3) of the 1986 Act, the court officer will amend the register and give notice of the amendment to –

(a)   the court which made the Part 1 order; and

(b)   the applicants for –

(i)   registration;

(ii)   enforcement; and

(iii)   stay$^{(GL)}$ or dismissal of the enforcement proceedings.

32.31 Particulars of other proceedings

A party to proceedings for or relating to a Part 1 order who knows of other proceedings which relate to the child concerned (including proceedings out of the jurisdiction and concluded proceedings) must file a witness statement which –

(a)   states in which jurisdiction and court the other proceedings were begun;

(b)   states the nature and current state of the proceedings and the relief claimed or granted;

(c)   sets out the names of the parties to the proceedings and their relationship to the child;

(d)   if applicable and if known, states the reasons why relief claimed in the proceedings for or relating to the Part 1 order was not claimed in the other proceedings; and

(e)   is verified by a statement of truth.

32.32 Inspection of register

The following persons may inspect any entry in the register relating to a Part 1 order and may request copies of the order any document relating to it –

(a)   the applicant for registration of the Part 1 order;

(b)   a person who, to the satisfaction of a district judge, has an interest under the Part 1 order; and

(c)   a person who obtains the permission of a district judge.

Modification. Rule 32.32 modified in an application under s 27 of the Family Law Act 1986 for the registration and enforcement of a custody order made in a magistrates' court by the Magistrates' Courts (Enforcement or Variation of Orders Made in Family Proceedings and Miscellaneous Provisions) Rules 2011, SI 2011/1329, rr 74, 83.

[Chapter 5
Ability of a court officer to take enforcement proceedings in relation to certain orders for periodical payments

32.33 Court officers and enforcement proceedings

(1) In this rule –

PART II – Statutory instruments

'the 1972 Act' means the Maintenance Orders (Reciprocal Enforcement) Act 1972;

'relevant order' means –

    (a)   any order made by the family court for periodical payments, other than an order made by virtue of Part 2 of the 1972 Act;

    (b)   any order for periodical payments made by the High Court (including an order deemed to be made by the High Court by virtue of section 1(2) of the 1958 Act) and registered under Part 1 of the 1958 Act in the family court; and

    (c)   an order made by a court in Scotland or in Northern Ireland which is registered in the family court under Part 2 of the 1950 Act; and

'the payee' means the person for whose benefit payments under a relevant order are required to be made.

(2) Where –

    (a)   payments under a relevant order are required to be made periodically to the family court; and

    (b)   any sums payable under the order are in arrears,

a court officer will, if the payee so requests in writing, and unless it appears to the court officer that it is unreasonable in the circumstances to do so, proceed in the officer's own name for the recovery of those sums.

(3) Where payments under a relevant order are required to be made periodically to the court, the payee may, at any time during the period in which the payments are required to be so made, give authority in writing to a court officer for the officer to proceed as mentioned in paragraph (4).

(4) Where authority is given under paragraph (3) to a court officer, that officer will, unless it appears unreasonable in the circumstances to do so, proceed in the officer's own name for the recovery of any sums payable to the court under the order in question which, on or after the date of the giving of the authority, fall into arrears.

(5) In any case where –

    (a)   authority under paragraph (3) has been given to a court officer; and

    (b)   the payee gives notice in writing to that court officer cancelling the authority,

the authority will cease to have effect and so the court officer will not continue any proceedings already commenced by virtue of the authority.

(6) The payee shall have the same liability for all of the costs properly incurred in, or in relation to, proceedings taken under paragraph (2) at the payee's request, or under paragraph (3) by virtue of the payee's authority, including any court fees and any costs incurred as a result of any proceedings commenced not being continued, as if the proceedings had been commenced by the payee.

(7) Nothing in paragraph (2) or (4) shall affect any right of a payee to proceed in his or her own name for the recovery of sums payable under an order of any court.][1]

NOTES

Amendment.[1] Chapter inserted: SI 2013/3204.

PART 33
ENFORCEMENT

Chapter 1
General Rules

33.1 Application

(1) The rules in this Part apply to an application made in the High Court and [the family court][1] to enforce an order made in family proceedings.

(2) [Parts 50, 83 and 84][1] of, and Schedules 1 and 2 to, the CPR apply, as far as they are relevant and with necessary modification ...[1], to an application made in the High Court and [the family court][1] to enforce an order made in family proceedings.

NOTES

Amendments.[1] Words substituted and omitted: SI 2014/667.

Section 1
Enforcement of orders for the payment of money

33.2 Application of the Civil Procedure Rules

Part 70 of the CPR applies to proceedings under this Section as if –

  (a) in rule 70.1, in paragraph (2)(d), 'but does not include a judgment or order for the payment of money into court' is omitted; ...[1]

  [(a1) in rule 70.3(1), for 'County Court' there is substituted 'family court'; and][1]

  (b) rule 70.5 is omitted.

NOTES

Amendments.[1] Word omitted and paragraph inserted: SI 2014/667.

33.3 How to apply

(1) Except where a rule or practice direction otherwise requires, an application for an order to enforce an order for the payment of money must be made in a notice of application accompanied by a statement which must –

  (a) state the amount due under the order, showing how that amount is arrived at; and

  (b) be verified by a statement of truth.

(2) The notice of application may either –

(a)   apply for an order specifying the method of enforcement; or

(b)   apply for an order for such method of enforcement as the court may consider appropriate.

(3) If an application is made under paragraph (2)(b), an order to attend court will be issued and rule 71.2 (6) and (7) of the CPR will apply as if the application had been made under that rule.

33.4 Transfer of orders

(1) This rule applies to an application for the transfer –

(a)   to the High Court of an order made in [the family court][1]; and

(b)   to [the family court][1] of an order made in the High Court.

(2) The application must be –

(a)   made without notice; and

(b)   accompanied by a statement which complies with rule 33.3(1).

(3) The transfer will have effect upon the filing of the application.

(4) Where an order is transferred from [the family court][1] to the High Court –

(a)   it will have the same force and effect; and

(b)   the same proceedings may be taken on it,

as if it were an order of the High Court.

(5) This rule does not apply to the transfer of orders for periodical payments or for the recovery of arrears of periodical payments.

NOTES

Amendments.[1] Words substituted: SI 2014/667.

Section 2
Committal and injunction

[33.5 Enforcement of orders by way of committal

Part 37 applies as appropriate for the enforcement by way of committal of an order made in family proceedings.][1]

NOTES

Amendment.[1] Rule 33.5 substituted for Rules 33.5–33.8: SI 2014/667.

****

PRACTICE DIRECTION 33A –
ENFORCEMENT OF UNDERTAKINGS

This Practice Direction supplements FPR Part 33

Enforcement of undertaking to do or abstain from doing any act other than the payment of money

[1 Attention is drawn to the provisions of [Part 37 (in particular rule 37(2)) about contempt applications for the enforcement of undertakings][2.][1]

NOTES

Amendment.[1] Text substituted: FPR Update, April 2014.2 Text substituted: FPR Update, October 2020.

Enforcement of undertaking for the payment of money

2.1 Any undertaking for the payment of money that has effect as if it was an order made under Part 2 of the Matrimonial Causes Act 1973 may be enforced as if it was an order and [Part 33 and Part 37 apply][2] accordingly.

2.2 The form of an undertaking for the payment of money that has effect as if it were an order under Part 2 of the Matrimonial Causes Act 1973 must be endorsed with a notice setting out the consequences of disobedience, as follows –

['If you fail to pay any sum of money which you have promised the court that you will pay, a person entitled to enforce the undertaking may apply to the court for an order. You may be sent to prison if it is proved that you –

(a)   have, or have had since the date of your undertaking, the means to pay the sum; and

(b)   have refused or neglected, or are refusing or neglecting, to pay that sum'][1]

2.3 The person giving the undertaking must make a signed statement to the effect that he or she understands the terms of the undertaking being given and the consequences of failure to comply with it, as follows –

'I understand the undertaking that I have given, and that if I break my promise to the court to pay any sum of money, I may be sent to prison'.

2.4 The statement need not be given before the court in person. It may be endorsed on the court copy of the undertaking or may be filed in a separate document such as a letter.

NOTES

Amendments. [1] Text substituted: FPR 2010 2nd Update, 6 April 2012.2 Text substituted: FPR Update, April 2014.

****

PART II – Statutory instruments

PART 36
TRANSITIONAL ARRANGEMENTS AND PILOT SCHEMES

36.1 Transitional provisions

Practice Direction 36A shall make provision for the extent to which these rules shall apply to proceedings started before the day on which they come into force.

36.2 Pilot schemes

Practice directions may modify or disapply any provision of these rules –

    (a)   for specified periods; and
    (b)   in relation to proceedings in specified courts,

during the operation of pilot schemes for assessing the use of new practices and procedures in connection with proceedings.

[36.3 Temporary modifications for coronavirus or other emergency

Practice Directions may modify or disapply any provision of these rules—

    (a)   for specified periods; and
    (b)   in relation to proceedings in specified courts,

in order to address issues for the work of the courts arising from the coronavirus (SARS-CoV-2) outbreak or any other public emergency.][1]

NOTES

Amendments.[1] Rule inserted: SI 2021/155.

Practice Direction 36A –
Transitional Arrangements

This Practice Direction supplements FPR Part 36

[Chapter 1][2]
Content of this Practice Direction

1.1 This [Chapter][2] deals with the application of the FPR to proceedings started before 6th April 2011 ('existing proceedings').

1.2 In this Practice Direction 'the previous rules' means, as appropriate, the Rules of the Supreme Court 1965 and County Court Rules 1981 as in force immediately before 26 April 1999, and –

    the Maintenance Orders (Facilities for Enforcement) Rules 1922;
    the Magistrates' Courts (Guardianship of Minors) Rules 1974;
    the Magistrates' Courts (Reciprocal Enforcement of Maintenance Orders) Rules 1974;
    the Magistrates' Courts (Reciprocal Enforcement of Maintenance Orders) (Republic of Ireland) Rules 1975;

the Magistrates' Courts (Reciprocal Enforcement of Maintenance Orders) (Hague Convention Countries) Rules 1980;

the Magistrates' Courts (Child Abduction and Custody) Rules 1986;

the Magistrates' Courts (Civil Jurisdiction and Judgments Act 1982) Rules 1986;

the Family Proceedings Rules 1991;

the Family Proceedings Courts (Children Act 1989) Rules 1991;

the Family Proceedings Courts (Matrimonial Proceedings etc.) Rules 1991 (in so far as those rules do not relate to enforcement or variation of orders);

the Magistrates' Courts (Costs Against Legal Representatives in Civil Proceedings) Rules 1991 (in so far as those rules relate to family proceedings);

the Family Proceedings Courts (Child Support Act 1991) Rules 1993;

the Magistrates' Courts (Reciprocal Enforcement of Maintenance Orders) (United States of America) Rules 1995 (subject to the saving in paragraph 3.6 of this Practice Direction);

the Magistrates' Courts (Hearsay Evidence in Civil Proceedings) Rules 1999 (in so far as those rules relate to family proceedings); and

the Family Procedure (Adoption) Rules 2005,

as in force immediately before 6th April 2011.

[1.3 Insofar as they relate to family proceedings, the previous rules are revoked with effect from 6 April 2011 by operation of law and necessary implication. This is the case except where the previous rules continue to apply to existing family proceedings in accordance with this Practice Direction. The revocation of the previous rules arises from –

the repeal of the powers under which the previous rules were made (by section 109(1) and (3) of, and paragraph 245(2) of Schedule 8 and Schedule 10 to, the Courts Act 2003) or in the case of the Family Procedure (Adoption) Rules 2005 by remaking the rules in the FPR, and

the fact that the FPR are stated in terms to be a new procedural code and to apply to family proceedings in the High Court, a county court and a magistrates' court (FPR rules 1.1 and 2.1).][1]

NOTES

Amendments. [1] Paragraph inserted: FPR 2010 2nd Update, 6 April 2012. [2] Text inserted and substituted: FPR Update, April 2014.

General scheme of transitional arrangements

2.1 The general scheme is –

(a) to apply the FPR to existing proceedings so far as is practicable; but

(b) where this is not practicable, to apply the previous rules to such proceedings.

Where the previous rules will normally apply

General principle

3.1 Where an initiating step has been taken in a case before 6th April 2011, in particular a step using forms or other documentation required by the previous rules, the case will proceed in the first instance under the previous rules. Where a party must take a step in response to something done by another party in accordance with the previous rules, that step must also be in accordance with those rules.

Responding to old process

3.2 A party who is served with an old type of originating process (for example, an originating summons) on or after 6th April 2011 must respond in accordance with the previous rules and the instructions on any forms received.

Filing and service of pleadings where old process served

3.3 Where a case has been begun by an old type of originating process (whether served before or after 6th April 2011), filing and service of pleadings will continue according to the previous rules.

Pre-commencement order inconsistent with FPR

3.4 Where a court order has been made before 6th April 2011, that order must still be complied with on or after that date.

Steps taken before commencement

3.5 Where a party has, before 6th April 2011, taken any step in the proceedings in accordance with the previous rules, that step will remain valid on or after that date, and a party will not normally be required to take any action that would amount to taking such a step again under the FPR.

****

Where the FPR will normally apply

General principle

4.1 Where a new step is to be taken in any existing proceedings on or after 6th April 2011, it is to be taken under the FPR.

Part 1 (Overriding objective) to apply

4.2 Part 1 of the FPR (Overriding objective) will apply to all existing proceedings from 6th April 2011 onwards.

Issuing of application forms after the FPR come into force

4.3

    (1) The general rule is that –

        (a) only application forms under the FPR will be issued by the court on or after 6th April 2011; and

(b) if a request to issue an old type of form or originating process (summons, etc.) is received at the court on or after 6th April 2011, it will be returned unissued.

(2) By way of exception to the general rule, the court may in cases of urgency direct that the form or process is to be issued as if the request to issue it had been a request to issue an application form under the FPR and, if it does so, the court may make such supplementary directions as it considers appropriate.

First time before a court on or after 6th April 2011

4.4

(1) When proceedings come before a court (whether at a hearing or on paper) for the first time on or after 6th April 2011, the court may direct how the FPR are to apply to the proceedings and may disapply certain provisions of the FPR. The court may also give case management directions.
(2) The general presumption will be that the FPR will apply to the proceedings from then on unless the court directs or this practice direction provides otherwise.
(3) If an application has been issued before 6th April 2011 and the hearing of the application has been set on or after that date, the general presumption is that the application will be decided having regard to the FPR.
(4) When the first occasion on which existing proceedings are before a court on or after 6th April 2011 is a hearing of a substantive issue, the general presumption is that the hearing will be conducted according to the FPR.

Costs

4.5

(1) Any assessment of costs that takes place on or after 6th April 2011 will be in accordance with FPR Part 28 and the provisions of the Civil Procedure Rules as applied by that Part.
(2) However, the general presumption is that no costs for work undertaken before 6th April 2011 will be disallowed if those costs would have been allowed on detailed assessment before that date.
(3) The decision as to whether to allow costs for work undertaken on or after 6th April 2011 will generally be taken in accordance with FPR Part 28 and the provisions of the Civil Procedure Rules as applied by that Part.

[Chapter 2

4.6

(1) Subject to paragraph (3), the following forms will be returned unissued if received by the court on or after 22 April 2014 –

PART II – Statutory instruments

Number	Name
A (except version 04/14)	Notice of [intention to proceed with] an application for a financial order
A1 (except version 04/14)	Notice of [intention to proceed with] an application for a financial remedy (other than a financial order) in the county or high court
B (except version 04/14)	An application for an order for special protection for respondent in certain separation cases (under section 10(2) of the Matrimonial Causes Act 1973 or under section 48(2) of the Civil Partnership Act 2004
C11	Supplement for an application for an Emergency Protection Order
C110	Application under the Children Act 1989 for a care or supervision order
C110A (except version 04/14)	Application for a Care or Supervision Order and Applications for Other Orders under Part 4 of the Children Act 1989

(2) Subject to paragraph (3), the following forms, if used to request that the proceedings listed in column B are issued, will be returned unissued if received by the court on or after 22 April 2014 –

Number	Proceedings requested to be issued
C1 (Application for an order)	Private law proceedings for: • parental responsibility order (under sections 4(1)(c), 4ZA(1)(c) or 4A(1)(b) of the Children Act 1989) or an order terminating parental responsibility (under sections 4(2A), 4ZA(5) or 4A(3) of that Act); • an order appointing a child's guardian (under section 5(1) of the Children Act 1989) or an order terminating the appointment (under section 6(7) of that Act); • an order giving permission to change a child's surname or remove a child from the United Kingdom (under sections 13(1) or 14C of the Children Act 1989); • a special guardianship order; and • an order varying or discharging such an order (under section 14D of the Children Act 1989), unless a separate Form FM1 of version 04/14 has been filed with the C1 application.

Number	Proceedings requested to be issued
C2 (Application: for permission to start proceedings; for an order or directions in existing proceedings; to be joined as, or cease to be, a party in existing family proceedings under the Children Act 1989)	Private law proceedings for: • a parental responsibility order (under sections 4(1)(c), 4ZA(1)(c) or 4A(1)(b) of the Children Act 1989) or an order terminating parental responsibility (under sections 4(2A), 4ZA(5) or 4A(3) of that Act); • an order appointing a child's guardian (under section 5(1) of the Children Act 1989) or an order terminating the appointment (under section 6(7) of that Act); • an order giving permission to change a child's surname or remove a child from the United Kingdom (under sections 13(1) or 14C of the Children Act 1989); • a special guardianship order; and • an order varying or discharging such an order (under section 14D of the Children Act 1989), unless a separate Form FM1 of version 04/14 has been filed with the C2 application.
C100 (Application under the Children Act 1989 for a residence, contact, prohibited steps, specific issue section 8 order or to vary or discharge a section 8 order	Private law proceedings. Proceedings under section 51A of the Adoption and Children Act 2002.
C100 (Application under the Children Act 1989 for a child arrangements, prohibited steps, specific issue section 8 order or to vary or discharge a section 8 order) (version 04/14)	Proceedings under section 51A of the Adoption and Children Act 2002.

(3) Subject to paragraph (4), the court may in cases of urgency direct that a form specified in paragraph 4.6(1) or 4.6(2) is to be issued as if the request to issue had been made on the form applicable on or after 22 April 2014, and if it does so, may make any supplementary directions as it considers appropriate.

(4) Paragraph (3) does not apply if a form specified in paragraph 4.6(1) or 4.62(3) is issued after a period of six months beginning with the 22 April 2014 has elapsed.]¹

NOTES
Amendments.[1] Text inserted: FPR Update, April 2014.

****

[[PART 37:
APPLICATIONS AND PROCEEDINGS IN RELATION TO CONTEMPT OF COURT

37.1 Scope

(1) This Part sets out the procedure to be followed in proceedings for contempt of court ('contempt proceedings').

(2) This Part does not alter the scope and extent of the jurisdiction of courts determining contempt proceedings, whether inherent, statutory or at common law.

(3) This Part has effect subject to and to the extent that it is consistent with the substantive law of contempt of court.

37.2 Interpretation

In this Part –

'claimant' means a person making a contempt application;

'contempt application' means an application to the court for an order determining contempt proceedings;

'defendant' means the person against whom the application is made;

'order of committal' means the imposition of a sentence of imprisonment (whether immediate or suspended) for contempt of court;

'penal notice' means a prominent notice on the front of an order warning that if the person against whom the order is made (and, in the case of a corporate body, a director or officer of that body) disobeys the court's order, the person (or director or officer) may be held in contempt of court and punished by a fine, imprisonment, confiscation of assets or other punishment under the law.

37.3 How to make a contempt application

(1) A contempt application made in existing High Court or family court proceedings is made by an application under Part 18 in those proceedings, whether or not the application is made against a party to those proceedings.

(2) If the application is made in the High Court, it shall be determined by a High Court judge of the Division in which the case is proceeding. If it is made in the family court, it shall be determined by a judge of the family court.

(The Family Court (Composition and Distribution of Business) Rules 2014(a) make provision for which level of judge may determine a contempt application.)

(3) A contempt application in relation to alleged interference with the due administration of justice, otherwise than in existing High Court or family court proceedings, is made by an application to the High Court under Part 19.

(4) Where an application under Part 19 is made under paragraph (3), the rules in Part 19 apply except as modified by this Part and the defendant is not required to acknowledge service of the application.

(5) Permission to make a contempt application is required where the application is made in relation to –

(a) interference with the due administration of justice, except in relation to existing High Court or family court proceedings;

(b) an allegation of knowingly making a false statement in any affidavit, affirmation or other document verified by a statement of truth or in a disclosure statement.

(6) If permission to make the application is needed, the application for permission shall be included in the contempt application, which will proceed to a full hearing only if permission is granted.

(7) If permission is needed and the application relates to High Court proceedings, the question of permission shall be determined by a single judge of the High Court. If permission is granted the contempt application shall be determined by a single judge or Divisional Court of that Division.

37.4 Requirements of a contempt application

(1) Unless and to the extent that the court directs otherwise, every contempt application must be supported by written evidence given by affidavit or affirmation.

(2) A contempt application must include statements of all the following, unless (in the case of (b) to (g)) wholly inapplicable –

(a) the nature of the alleged contempt (for example, breach of an order or undertaking or contempt in the face of the court);

(b) the date and terms of any order allegedly breached or disobeyed;

(c) confirmation that any such order was personally served, and the date it was served, unless the court or the parties dispensed with personal service;

(d) if the court dispensed with personal service, the terms and date of the court's order dispensing with personal service;

(e) confirmation that any order allegedly breached or disobeyed included a penal notice;

(f) the date and terms of any undertaking allegedly breached;

(g) confirmation of the claimant's belief that the person who gave any undertaking understood its terms and the consequences of failure to comply with it;

(h) a brief summary of the facts alleged to constitute the contempt, set out numerically in chronological order;

(i) that the defendant has the right to be legally represented in the contempt proceedings;

(j) that the defendant is entitled to a reasonable opportunity to obtain legal representation and to apply for legal aid which may be available without any means test;

(k)   that the defendant may be entitled to the services of an interpreter;

(l)   that the defendant is entitled to a reasonable time to prepare for the hearing;

(m)   that the defendant is entitled but not obliged to give written and oral evidence in their defence;

(n)   that the defendant has the right to remain silent and to decline to answer any question the answer to which may incriminate the defendant;

(o)   that the court may proceed in the defendant's absence if they do not attend but (whether or not they attend) will only find the defendant in contempt if satisfied beyond reasonable doubt of the facts constituting contempt and that they do constitute contempt;

(p)   that if the court is satisfied that the defendant has committed a contempt, the court may punish the defendant by a fine, imprisonment, confiscation of assets or other punishment under the law;

(q)   that if the defendant admits the contempt and wishes to apologise to the court, that is likely to reduce the seriousness of any punishment by the court;

(r)   that the court's findings will be provided in writing as soon as practicable after the hearing; and

(s)   that the court will sit in public, unless and to the extent that the court orders otherwise, and that its findings will be made public.

37.5 Service of a contempt application

(1) Unless the court directs otherwise in accordance with Part 6 and except as provided in paragraph (2), a contempt application and evidence in support must be served on the defendant personally.

(2) Where a legal representative for the defendant is on the record in the proceedings in which, or in connection with which, an alleged contempt is committed –

(a)   the contempt application and evidence in support may be served on the representative for the defendant unless the representative objects in writing within seven days of receipt of the application and evidence in support;

(b)   if the representative does not object in writing, they must at once provide to the defendant a copy of the contempt application and the evidence supporting it and take all reasonable steps to ensure the defendant understands them;

(c)   if the representative objects in writing, the issue of service shall be referred to a judge of the court dealing with the contempt application; and the judge shall consider written representations from the parties and determine the issue on the papers, without (unless the judge directs otherwise) an oral hearing.

37.6 Cases where no application is made

(1) If the court considers that a contempt of court (including a contempt in the face of the court) may have been committed, the court of its own initiative shall consider whether to proceed against the defendant in contempt proceedings.

(2) Where the court does so, any other party in the proceedings may be required by the court to give such assistance to the court as is proportionate and reasonable, having regard to the resources available to that party.

(3) If the court proceeds of its own initiative, it shall issue a summons to the defendant which includes the matters set out in rule 37.4(2)(a)-(s) (in so far as applicable) and requires the defendant to attend court for directions to be given.

(4) A summons issued under this rule shall be served on the defendant personally and on any other party, unless the court directs otherwise. If rule 37.5(2) applies, the procedure there set out shall be followed unless the court directs otherwise.

37.7 Directions for hearing of contempt proceedings

(1) The court shall give such directions as it thinks fit for the hearing and determination of contempt proceedings, including directions for the attendance of witnesses and oral evidence, as it considers appropriate.

(2) The court may issue a bench warrant to secure the attendance of the defendant at a directions hearing or at the substantive hearing.

(3) The court may not give any direction compelling the defendant to give evidence either orally or in writing.

37.8 Hearings and judgments in contempt proceedings

(1) All hearings of contempt proceedings shall, irrespective of the parties' consent, be listed and heard in public unless the court otherwise directs, applying the provisions of paragraph (4).

(2) In deciding whether to hold a hearing in private, the court must consider any duty to protect or have regard to a right to freedom of expression which may be affected.

(3) The court shall .take reasonable steps to ensure that all hearings are of an open and public character, save when a hearing is held in private (4) A hearing, or any part of it, must be held in private if, and only to the extent that, the court is satisfied of one or more of the matters set out in sub-paragraphs (a) to (g) and that it is necessary to sit in private to secure the proper administration of justice –

- (a) publicity would defeat the object of the hearing;
- (b) it involves matters relating to national security;
- (c) it involves confidential information (including information relating to personal financial matters) and publicity would damage that confidentiality;
- (d) a private hearing is necessary to protect the interests of any child or protected party;
- (e) it is a hearing of an application made without notice and it would be unjust to any respondent for there to be a public hearing;
- (f) it involves uncontentious matters arising in the administration of trusts or in the administration of a deceased person's estate; or
- (g) the court for any other reason considers this to be necessary to secure the proper administration of justice.

PART II – Statutory instruments

(5) The court must order that the identity of any party or witness shall not be disclosed if, and only if, it considers non-disclosure necessary to secure the proper administration of justice and in order to protect the interests of that party or witness.

(6) Unless and to the extent that the court otherwise directs, where the court acts under paragraph (4) or (5), a copy of the court's order shall be published on the website of the Judiciary of England and Wales (which may be found at www. judiciary.uk). Any person who is not a party to the proceedings may apply to attend the hearing and make submissions, or apply to set aside or vary the order.

(7) Advocates and the judge shall appear robed in all hearings of contempt proceedings, whether or not the court sits in public.

(8) Before deciding to sit in private for all or part of the hearing, the court shall notify the national print and broadcast media, via the Press Association.

(9) The court shall consider any submissions from the parties or media organisations before deciding whether and if so to what extent the hearing should be in private.

(10) If the court decides to sit in private it shall, before doing so, sit in public to give a reasoned public judgment setting out why it is doing so.

(11) At the conclusion of the hearing, whether or not held in private, the court shall sit in public to give a reasoned public judgment stating its findings and any punishment.

(12) The court shall inform the defendant of the right to appeal without permission, the time limit for appealing and the court before which any appeal must be brought.

(13) The court shall be responsible for ensuring that judgments in contempt proceedings are transcribed and published on the website of the judiciary of England and Wales.

37.9 Powers of the court in contempt proceedings

(1) If the court finds the defendant in contempt of court, the court may impose a period of imprisonment (an order of committal), a fine, confiscation of assets or other punishment permitted under the law.

(2) Execution of an order of committal requires issue of a warrant of committal. An order of committal and a warrant of committal have immediate effect unless and to the extent that the court decides to suspend execution of the order or warrant.

(3) An order or warrant of committal must be personally served on the defendant unless the court directs otherwise.

(4) To the extent that the substantive law permits, a court may attach a power of arrest to a committal order.

(5) An order or warrant of committal may not be enforced more than two years after the date it was made unless the court directs otherwise.

37.10 Applications to discharge committal orders

(1) A defendant against whom a committal order has been made may apply to discharge it.

(2) Any such application shall be made by an application notice under Part 18 in the contempt proceedings.

(3) The court hearing such an application shall consider all the circumstances and make such order under the law as it thinks fit.]²]¹

NOTES

Amendments.¹ Part 37 inserted: SI 2014/667.2 Part 37 substituted: SI 2020/758.

[[Practice Direction 37A –
Applications and Proceedings in Relation to Contempt of Court

This Practice Direction supplements FPR Part 37.

Directions for hearings of contempt proceedings

1. Evidence adduced by defendant.

Rule 37.7(3) provides that the court may not give any direction compelling the defendant to give evidence either orally or in writing. The court may, however, direct that, if the defendant wishes to adduce evidence in response to the contempt application, the defendant file and serve witness statements of the witnesses (including himself or herself) on which reliance is intended. Such statements may not be used against the defendant in the contempt application unless and until the defendant deploys them in support of the defendant's case against the contempt application.

2. Striking out and procedural defects.

(1) On application by the defendant or on its own initiative, the court may strike out a contempt application if it appears to the court—

    (a)   that the application and the evidence served in support of it disclose no reasonable ground for alleging that the defendant is guilty of a contempt of court;

    (b)   that the application is an abuse of the court's process or, if made in existing proceedings, is otherwise likely to obstruct the just disposal of those proceedings; or

    (c)   that there has been a failure to comply with a rule, practice direction or court order.

(2) The court may waive any procedural defect in the commencement or conduct of a contempt application if satisfied that no injustice has been caused to the defendant by the defect.

Hearings and judgments in contempt proceedings

3. Informing the defendant of right to appeal, etc.

Paragraph (12) of rule 37.8 does not require the court to inform a defendant who has been acquitted of contempt of the right to appeal and the other matters listed in that paragraph.

4. Responsibility of court for publication of judgments.

While paragraph (13) of rule 37.8 makes the court responsible for the publication of transcripts of judgments in contempt proceedings, it does not require the court to publish a transcript of every judgment, but only in a case where the court makes an order for committal.]²]¹

NOTES

Amendments. ¹ PD37A inserted: FPR Update, April 2014. ² PD37A substituted: FPR Update, October 2020.

Glossary

Scope

This glossary is a guide to the meaning of certain legal expressions as used in these rules, but it does not give the expressions any meaning in the rules which they do not otherwise have in the law.

Expression	Meaning
Affidavit	A written, sworn, statement of evidence.
Cross-examination	Questioning of a witness by a party other than the party who called the witness.
Evidence in chief	The evidence given by a witness for the party who called him.
Injunction	A court order prohibiting a person from doing something or requiring a person to do something.
Official copy	A copy of an official document, supplied and marked as such by the office which issued the original.
Pre-action protocol	Statements of best practice about pre-action conduct which have been approved by the President of the Family Division and which are annexed to a Practice Direction.
Privilege	The right of a party to refuse to disclose a document or produce a document or to refuse to answer questions on the ground of some special interest recognised by law.
Seal	A seal is a mark which the court puts on document to indicate that the document has been issued by the court.
Service	Steps required by rules of court to bring documents used in court proceedings to a person's attention.

Expression	Meaning
Set aside	Cancelling a judgment or order or a step taken by a party in the proceedings.
Stay	A stay imposes a halt on proceedings, apart from the taking of any steps allowed by the rules or the terms of the stay. Proceedings can be continued if a stay is lifted.
Strike out	Striking out means the court ordering written material to be deleted so that it may no longer be relied upon.
Without prejudice	Negotiations with a view to settlement are usually conducted 'without prejudice' which means that the circumstances in which the content of those negotiations may be revealed to the court are very restricted.

[PART 38
RECOGNITION AND ENFORCEMENT OF PROTECTION MEASURES

Chapter 1
Scope and interpretation of this Part

38.1 Scope and interpretation

(1) This Part contains rules about the ...[2] recognition and enforcement of [incoming][2] protection measures ...[2].

(2) In this Part –

...[2]

...[2]

'Article 11 notice' means the notification required by Article 11 of the Protection Measures Regulation;

'Article 14 certificate' means a certificate issued under Article 14 of the Protection Measures Regulation;

...[2]

'person causing the risk' has the meaning given to it in the Protection Measures Regulation; and

'protected person' has the meaning given to it in the Protection Measures Regulation.][1]

NOTES

Amendment.[1] Part 38 inserted: SI 2014/3296. [2] Words omitted repealed and word inserted: SI 2019/517.

[Chapter 2

...[2]

38.2 ...[2]

...[2]][1]

NOTES

Amendment.[1] Part 38 inserted: SI 2014/3296. [2] Chapter 2 repealed: SI 2019/517.

[38.3 ...[2]

...[2]][1]

NOTES

Amendment.[1] Part 38 inserted: SI 2014/3296. [2] Chapter 2 repealed: SI 2019/517.

[38.4 ...[2]

...[2]][1]

NOTES

Amendment.[1] Part 38 inserted: SI 2014/3296. [2] Chapter 2 repealed: SI 2019/517.

[38.5 ...[2]

...[2]][1]

NOTES

Amendment.[1] Part 38 inserted: SI 2014/3296. [2] Chapter 2 repealed: SI 2019/517.

[38.6 ...[2]

...[2]][1]

NOTES

Amendment.[1] Part 38 inserted: SI 2014/3296. [2] Chapter 2 repealed: SI 2019/517.

[38.7 ...[2]

...[2]][1]

NOTES

Amendment.[1] Part 38 inserted: SI 2014/3296. [2] Chapter 2 repealed: SI 2019/517.

[38.8 ...[2]

...[2]][1]

NOTES

Amendment.[1] Part 38 inserted: SI 2014/3296. [2] Chapter 2 repealed: SI 2019/517.

[38.9 ...[2]

...[2]][1]

NOTES

Amendment.[1] Part 38 inserted: SI 2014/3296. [2] Chapter 2 repealed: SI 2019/517.

[38.10 ...[2]

...[2]][1]

NOTES

Amendment.[1] Part 38 inserted: SI 2014/3296. [2] Chapter 2 repealed: SI 2019/517.

[38.11 ...²

...²]¹

NOTES

Amendment.¹ Part 38 inserted: SI 2014/3296. ² Chapter 2 repealed: SI 2019/517.

[Chapter 3
Incoming protection measures

38.12 Application for adjustment under Article 11

A protected person may apply to the court under Article 11 of the Protection Measures Regulation [(as it has effect in the law of England and Wales)]² to adjust the factual elements of an incoming protection measure.]¹

NOTES

Amendment.¹ Part 38 inserted: SI 2014/3296. ² Words inserted: SI 2019/517.

[38.13 Notification of the adjustment under Article 11

(1) Subject to paragraph (2), the court officer must give Article 11 notice to the person causing the risk by serving it in accordance with Chapter 3 of Part 6 and the rules in that Chapter apply to service of the notice as they apply to any other document to be served by a court officer.

(2) If the person causing the risk resides [outside the United Kingdom]², the court officer must give Article 11 notice by sending it by registered letter with acknowledgment of receipt or other confirmation of delivery or equivalent to the last known place of residence of that person.]¹

NOTES

Amendment.¹ Part 38 inserted: SI 2014/3296. ² Words substituted: SI 2019/517.

[38.14 Application for refusal of recognition or enforcement under Article 13

An application by a person causing the risk for refusal of recognition or enforcement under Article 13 of the Protection Measures Regulation [(as it has effect in the law of England and Wales)]² must be made to –

  (a) the family court if –
      (i)   there are proceedings relating to the same protection measure before the family court; or
      (ii) proceedings relating to the same protection measure were dealt with by the family court;

  (b) the High Court if –
      (i)   there are proceedings relating to the same protection measure before the High Court; or
      (ii) proceedings relating to the same protection measure were dealt with by the High Court; or

PART II – Statutory instruments

(c)   the family court, unless, applying rule 5.4, the application should be made to the High Court.][1]

NOTES

Amendment.[1] Part 38 inserted: SI 2014/3296. [2] Words inserted: SI 2019/517.

[38.15 Application under Article 14(2)

(1) This rule applies where an Article 14 certificate has been issued in a Member State of the European Union other than …[2] Denmark.

(2) A protected person or person causing the risk may apply to the court to stay, suspend or withdraw the effects of recognition or, where applicable, the enforcement of the protection measure.

(3) An application under this rule must include a copy of the Article 14 certificate issued in the …[2] Member State.

(4) On an application under this rule, the court must make such orders or give such directions as may be necessary to give effect to the Article 14 certificate.][1]

NOTES

Amendment.[1] Part 38 inserted: SI 2014/3296. [2] Words omitted repealed: SI 2019/517.

[Practice Direction 38A –
Recognition and Enforcement of Protection Measures

This Practice Direction supplements Part 38.

The Protection Measures Regulation

1.1 The Protection Measures Regulation is an EU law which helps a person who has a 'protection measure' obtained in one Member State to have it recognised and enforced in any other EU Member State (except Denmark). The protection can continue in the other Member State for the length of time the 'protection measure' has been ordered, except it cannot continue for longer than twelve months. [The Protection Measures Regulation forms part of retained EU law in the United Kingdom by virtue of the European Union (Withdrawal) Act 2018, and provision is made in the Mutual Recognition of Protection Measures in Civil Matters (Amendment) (EU Exit) Regulations 2019 for its provisions in relation to "incoming" protection measures to continue to have effect so that incoming measures can be enforced in England and Wales.][1]

1.2 The Protection Measures Regulation applies across the United Kingdom. Part 38 and this Practice Direction apply in England and Wales only. If you need information about Scotland you should contact the Scottish Government. If you need information about Northern Ireland you should contact the Northern Ireland Department for Justice.

1.3 A 'protection measure' is a decision that says the 'person causing the risk' must comply with one or more of the three kinds of obligation set out below, to protect another person, the 'protected person', from physical or psychological harm.

The obligations are:

- – a ban or controls on entering the place where the protected person lives or works, or regularly visits or stays;
- – a ban or controls on contact, in any form, with the protected person, including by telephone, post, e-mail, text or social media or any other means;
- – a ban or controls on approaching the protected person closer than a stated distance.

1.4 A 'protected person' is the individual who is protected by the obligation in the protection measure. A 'person causing the risk' is the individual on whom the obligation has been imposed.

1.5 ...[1]

1.6 ...[1]

1.7 ...[1]

NOTES

Amendment.[1] Words inserted and paragraphs omitted repealed: FPR Update, March 2019.

...[1]

2.1 ...[1]

2.2 ...[1]

2.3 ...[1]

2.4 ...[1]

2.5 ...[1]

2.6 ...[1]

2.7 ...[1]

2.8 ...[1]

2.9 ...[1]

2.10 ...[1]

2.11 ...[1]

2.12 ...[1]

2.13 ...[1]

NOTES

Amendment.[1] Paragraphs omitted repealed: FPR Update, March 2019.

PART II – Statutory instruments

Incoming protection measures

3.1 An incoming protection measure for which an Article 5 certificate has been issued in [a][1] Member State, is automatically recognised by the court in England and Wales. This section sets out actions the protected person can take in relation to an incoming protection measure, and the points at which the incoming protection measure and Article 5 certificate must be provided to the court. The applications set out below can be made to the family court, the county court and sometimes to the Family Division of the High Court (see rule 5.4 of the Family Procedure Rules 2010). This practice direction and the Family Procedure Rules apply to the family court and Family Division of the High Court only. Applications to the county court are covered by the Civil Procedure Rules.

3.2 The protected person and the person causing the risk can make applications in relation to incoming protection measures using the procedure in Part 18 (or Part 19 if applicable) of the Family Procedure Rules. There is more information in Practice Directions 18A and 19A. These Practice Directions set out the documents the applicant must provide with the application, in addition to any requirements set out in this Practice Direction. When making an application the protected person or the person causing the risk must also provide a copy of the order containing the incoming protection measure and the Article 5 certificate issued in the Member State of origin. (Explanations of the terms used in the Protection Measures Regulation and the certificates are set out in section 1 above.)

ADJUSTMENT OF 'FACTUAL ELEMENTS' IN THE PROTECTION MEASURE

3.3 The protected person can apply to the court for the adjustment of 'factual elements' in the incoming protection measure to make it effective in England and Wales. 'Factual elements' can, for example, include the address or location the person causing the risk must stay away from, such as the location where the protected person lived or worked in the Member State of origin, or the minimum distance the person causing the risk must keep away from the protected person. To make the protection measure work in England and Wales the protected person can apply for the protection measure to be adjusted to show an address in England or Wales. **ANY ADDRESS OR LOCATION IN THE ADJUSTED PROTECTION MEASURE WILL BE DISCLOSED TO THE PERSON CAUSING THE RISK, BECAUSE THE ADJUSTMENT MUST BE NOTIFIED TO THE PERSON CAUSING THE RISK.**

3.4 The protected person can apply to the court under rule 38.12 using the appropriate form for an adjustment to the factual elements to be made. If you are the protected person, you will need to provide an address for notification. You can decide what address to provide and it does not have to be your own home address. **IF YOU ARE THE PROTECTED PERSON, AND THE ADDRESS YOU PROVIDE IS ALSO IN THE ADJUSTED PROTECTION MEASURE, THAT ADDRESS WILL BE DISCLOSED TO THE PERSON CAUSING THE RISK, BECAUSE THE PERSON CAUSING THE RISK MUST BE NOTIFIED OF THE ADJUSTMENT TO BE ABLE TO COMPLY WITH IT.** When the court adjusts the facts in the protection measure the court officer must notify the person causing the risk of the adjustment in accordance with rule 38.13 (Article 11 notice). A protected person may choose not to apply for an adjustment of a protection measure that contains a specific address or location, and may choose to apply only for adjustments of the factual elements of a protection measure that do not contain such information.

ENFORCEMENT OF THE PROTECTION MEASURE

3.5 If the protected person has an incoming protection measure accompanied by an Article 5 certificate from the Member State of origin and they believe the person causing the risk has disobeyed the protection measure, the protected person can apply to the court under rule 10.11 for the issue of a civil warrant for the arrest of the person causing the risk. **IF YOU ARE THE PROTECTED PERSON AND YOU BELIEVE THE PERSON CAUSING THE RISK HAS COMMITTED A CRIMINAL OFFENCE UNDER THE LAW OF ENGLAND AND WALES YOU SHOULD CONTACT THE POLICE.** If this has happened, the person causing the risk may be subject to criminal punishment under the law of England and Wales.

3.6 Incoming protection measures can be enforced by the family court and the High Court in England and Wales as if they had been ordered by those courts. **IF YOU ARE THE PERSON CAUSING THE RISK AND YOU DISOBEY THE PROTECTION MEASURE, YOU MAY BE HELD TO BE IN CONTEMPT OF COURT IN ENGLAND AND WALES AND YOU MAY BE IMPRISONED OR FINED.** Part 10 and Part 37 of the FPR provide more information.

APPLICATION FOR REFUSAL TO RECOGNISE OR ENFORCE THE PROTECTION MEASURE

3.7 The person causing the risk can apply under rule 38.14 using the appropriate form for the court to refuse to recognise an incoming protection measure or to refuse to enforce it against them. Under the Protection Measures Regulation, the court will only refuse to recognise or enforce the protection measure when to do so would be 'manifestly contrary to public policy' or if recognition of the incoming protection measure is 'irreconcilable' with a judgment that has been given or recognised in the United Kingdom.

SUSPENSION OR WITHDRAWAL OF RECOGNITION OR ENFORCEMENT

3.8 When a protection measure from another Member State has been suspended, limited or withdrawn in the Member State of origin or an Article 5 certificate has been withdrawn there, and an Article 14 certificate has been issued to confirm this, the protected person or the person causing the risk can apply under rule 38.15 using the appropriate form to the court in England and Wales which dealt or is dealing with the incoming protection measure to ask the court to stay, suspend or withdraw the effects of recognition or enforcement. The applicant must provide a copy of the Article 14 certificate. When the court has made orders or given directions to give effect to the Article 14 certificate the court officer will inform the other party.

NOTES

Amendment.[1] Words substituted: FPR Update, March 2019.

PART II – Statutory instruments

APPEALS

4.1 All decisions made by the court in England and Wales under the Protection Measures Regulation are subject to ordinary appeal procedures. In most cases permission to appeal will be required, but there is no need to get permission to appeal a decision made by lay justices. (The issue of an Article 5 certificate is separate and cannot be appealed.) Either the protected person or the person causing the risk can seek permission to appeal using the Part 30 procedure.

NOTES

Amendment.[1] Practice Direction inserted: President's Direction, January 2015.

Part III

PRACTICE GUIDANCE

PRACTICE GUIDANCE
16 JANUARY 2014

PRACTICE GUIDANCE (TRANSPARENCY IN THE FAMILY COURTS: PUBLICATION OF JUDGMENTS) (16 JANUARY 2014)

TRANSPARENCY IN THE FAMILY COURTS: PUBLICATION OF JUDGMENTS

The purpose of this Guidance

1 This Guidance (together with similar Guidance issued at the same time for the Court of Protection) is intended to bring about an immediate and significant change in practice in relation to the publication of judgments in family courts and the Court of Protection.

2 In both courts there is a need for greater transparency in order to improve public understanding of the court process and confidence in the court system. At present too few judgments are made available to the public, which has a legitimate interest in being able to read what is being done by the judges in its name. The Guidance will have the effect of increasing the number of judgments available for publication (even if they will often need to be published in appropriately anonymised form).

3 In July 2011 Sir Nicholas Wall P issued, jointly with Bob Satchwell, Executive Director of the Society of Editors, a paper, *The Family Courts: Media Access & Reporting* (Media Access & Reporting), setting out a statement of the current state of the law. In their preface they recognised that the debate on increased transparency and public confidence in the family courts would move forward and that future consideration of this difficult and sensitive area would need to include the questions of access to and reporting of proceedings by the media, whilst maintaining the privacy of the families involved. The paper is to be found at:

http://www.judiciary.gov.uk/Resources/JCO/Documents/Guidance/family-courts¬media-july2011.pdf

4 In April 2013 I issued a statement, *View from the President's Chambers: the Process of Reform*, [2013] Fam Law 548, in which I identified transparency as one of the three strands in the reforms which the family justice system is currently undergoing. I said:

'I am determined to take steps to improve access to and reporting of family proceedings. I am determined that the new Family Court should not be saddled, as the family courts are at present, with the charge that we are a system of secret and unaccountable justice. Work, commenced by my predecessor, is well underway. I hope to be in a position to make important announcements in the near future.'

5 That applies just as much to the issue of transparency in the Court of Protection.

PART III – Practice guidance

6 Very similar issues arise in both the Family Court (as it will be from April 2014) and the Court of Protection in relation to the need to protect the personal privacy of children and vulnerable adults. The applicable rules differ, however, and this is something that needs attention. My starting point is that so far as possible the same rules and principles should apply in both the family courts (in due course the Family Court) and the Court of Protection.

7 I propose to adopt an incremental approach. Initially I am issuing this Guidance. This will be followed by further Guidance and in due course more formal Practice Directions and changes to the Rules (the Court of Protection Rules 2007 and the Family Procedure Rules 2010). Changes to primary legislation are unlikely in the near future.

8 As provided in paragraph 14 below, this Guidance applies only to judgments delivered by certain judges. In due course, following the introduction of the Family Court, consideration will be given to extending it to judgments delivered by other judges (including lay justices).

The legal framework

9 The effect of section 12 of the Administration of Justice Act 1960 is that it is a contempt of court to publish a judgment in a family court case involving children unless either the judgment has been delivered in public or, where delivered in private, the judge has authorised publication. In the latter case, the judge normally gives permission for the judgment to be published on condition that the published version protects the anonymity of the children and members of their family.

10 In every case the terms on which publication is permitted are a matter for the judge and will be set out by the judge in a rubric at the start of the judgment.

11 The normal terms as described in paragraph 9 may be appropriate in a case where no-one wishes to discuss the proceedings otherwise than anonymously. But they may be inappropriate, for example, where parents who have been exonerated in care proceedings wish to discuss their experiences in public, identifying themselves and making use of the judgment. Equally, they may be inappropriate in cases where findings have been made against a person and someone else contends and/or the judge concludes that it is in the public interest for that person to be identified in any published version of the judgment.

12 If any party wishes to identify himself or herself, or any other party or person, as being a person referred to in any published version of the judgment, their remedy is to seek an order of the court and a suitable modification of the rubric: Media Access & Reporting, para 82; *Re RB (Adult) (No 4)* [2011] EWHC 3017 (Fam), [2012] 1 FLR 466, paras [17], [19].

13 Nothing in this Guidance affects the exercise by the judge in any particular case of whatever powers would otherwise be available to regulate the publication of material relating to the proceedings. For example, where a judgment is likely to be used in a way that would defeat the purpose of any anonymisation, it is open to the judge to refuse to publish the judgment or to make an order restricting its use.

Guidance

14 This Guidance takes effect from 3 February 2014. It applies

(i) in the family courts (and in due course in the Family Court), to judgments delivered by Circuit Judges, High Court Judges and persons sitting as judges of the High Court; and

(ii) to all judgments delivered by High Court Judges (and persons sitting as judges of the High Court) exercising the inherent jurisdiction to make orders in respect of children and incapacitated or vulnerable adults.

15 The following paragraphs of this Guidance distinguish between two classes of judgment:

(i) those that the judge *must* ordinarily allow to be published (paragraphs 16 and 17); and

(ii) those that *may* be published (paragraph 18).

16 Permission to publish a judgment should always be given whenever the judge concludes that publication would be in the public interest and whether or not a request has been made by a party or the media.

17 Where a judgment relates to matters set out in Schedule 1 or 2 below and a written judgment already exists in a publishable form or the judge has already ordered that the judgment be transcribed, the starting point is that permission should be given for the judgment to be published unless there are compelling reasons why the judgment should not be published.

Schedule 1

In the family courts (and in due course in the Family Court), including in proceedings under the inherent jurisdiction of the High Court relating to children, judgments arising from:

(i) a substantial contested fact-finding hearing at which serious allegations, for example allegations of significant physical, emotional or sexual harm, have been determined;

(ii) the making or refusal of a final care order or supervision order under Part 4 of the Children Act 1989, or any order for the discharge of any such order, except where the order is made with the consent of all participating parties;

(iii) the making or refusal of a placement order or adoption order under the Adoption and Children Act 2002, or any order for the discharge of any such order, except where the order is made with the consent of all participating parties;

(iv) the making or refusal of any declaration or order authorising a deprivation of liberty, including an order for a secure accommodation order under section 25 of the Children Act 1989;

(v) any application for an order involving the giving or withholding of serious medical treatment;

(vi) any application for an order involving a restraint on publication of information relating to the proceedings.

PART III – Practice guidance

Schedule 2

In proceedings under the inherent jurisdiction of the High Court relating to incapacitated or vulnerable adults, judgments arising from:

(i)   any application for a declaration or order involving a deprivation or possible deprivation of liberty;

(ii)   any application for an order involving the giving or withholding of serious medical treatment;

(iii)   any application for an order that an incapacitated or vulnerable adult be moved into or out of a residential establishment or other institution;

(iv)   any application for a declaration as to capacity to marry or to consent to sexual relations;

(v)   any application for an order involving a restraint on publication of information relating to the proceedings.

18 In all other cases, the starting point is that permission may be given for the judgment to be published whenever a party or an accredited member of the media applies for an order permitting publication, and the judge concludes that permission for the judgment to be published should be given.

19 In deciding whether and if so when to publish a judgment, the judge shall have regard to all the circumstances, the rights arising under any relevant provision of the European Convention on Human Rights, including Articles 6 (right to a fair hearing), 8 (respect for private and family life) and 10 (freedom of expression), and the effect of publication upon any current or potential criminal proceedings.

20 In all cases where a judge gives permission for a judgment to be published:

(i)   public authorities and expert witnesses should be named in the judgment approved for publication, unless there are compelling reasons why they should not be so named;

(ii)   the children who are the subject of the proceedings in the family courts, and other members of their family, and the person who is the subject of proceedings under the inherent jurisdiction of the High Court relating to incapacitated or vulnerable adults, and other members of their family, should not normally be named in the judgment approved for publication unless the judge otherwise orders;

(iii)   anonymity in the judgment as published should not normally extend beyond protecting the privacy of the children and adults who are the subject of the proceedings and other members of their families, unless there are compelling reasons to do so.

21 Unless the judgment is already in anonymised form or the judge otherwise orders, any necessary anonymisation of the judgment shall be carried out, in the case of judgments being published pursuant to paragraphs 16 and 17 above, by the solicitor for the applicant in the proceedings and, in the case of a judgment being published pursuant to paragraph 18 above, by the solicitor for the party or person applying for publication of the judgment. The anonymised version of the judgment must be submitted to the judge within a period specified by the judge for approval. The version approved for publication will contain such rubric as the judge specifies. Unless the rubric specified by the judge provides expressly to

the contrary every published judgment shall be deemed to contain the following rubric:

'This judgment was delivered in private. The judge has given leave for this version of the judgment to be published on condition that (irrespective of what is contained in the judgment) in any published version of the judgment the anonymity of the children and members of their family must be strictly preserved. All persons, including representatives of the media, must ensure that this condition is strictly complied with. Failure to do so will be a contempt of court.'

22 The judge will need to consider who should be ordered to bear the cost of transcribing the judgment. Unless the judge otherwise orders:

(i)   in cases falling under paragraph 16 the cost of transcribing the judgment is to be at public expense;

(ii)   subject to (i), in cases falling under paragraph 17 the cost of transcribing the judgment shall be borne equally by the parties to the proceedings;

(iii)   in cases falling under paragraph 18, the cost of transcribing the judgment shall be borne by the party or person applying for publication of the judgment.

23 In all cases where permission is given for a judgment to be published, the version of the judgment approved for publication shall be made available, upon payment of any appropriate charge that may be required, to any person who requests a copy. Where a judgment to which paragraph 16 or 17 applies is approved for publication, it shall as soon as reasonably practicable be placed by the court on the BAILII website. Where a judgment to which paragraph 18 applies is approved for publication, the judge shall consider whether it should be placed on the BAILII website and, if so, it shall as soon as reasonably practicable be placed by the court on the BAILII website.

Sir James Munby

President of the Family Division

PART III – Practice guidance

APPOINTING A LITIGATION FRIEND CHECKLIST
4 APRIL 2014

Form for solicitors to complete if a protected party lacks capacity to carry out family proceedings (published 4 April 2014; last updated 21 December 2021)

Checklist for the appointment of a litigation friend (including the Official Solicitor)

This checklist should be completed where there is reason to believe that a party or prospective party to proceedings ('PP') lacks capacity (within the meaning of the Mental Capacity Act 2005) to conduct the proceedings. It should be completed by PP's legal representative or, if none, any person (including a local authority) able to provide the relevant information.

Name of party: ....

Describe briefly the reasons for believing that PP lacks capacity to conduct the proceedings:

....

Evidence and finding as to capacity

Has the court made a finding that PP lacks capacity to conduct the proceedings?

Yes ☐ No ☐

(If so, give the date and attach a copy of the order)

Date ....

Has an assessment of capacity been obtained?

Yes ☐ No ☐

If so, give the date of the assessment, the name and occupation/professional qualification of the author and a concise summary of the conclusion. A copy should be attached if available:

....

Has PP been informed of the assessment?

Yes ☐ No ☐

Does PP accept the assessment?

Yes ☐ No ☐

Has PP been informed of the effect and consequences of the assessment and of being a protected party?

Yes ☐ No ☐

If there is no assessment of capacity, what, if any, evidence was relied on by the court to determine the question of capacity?

....

If an assessment is to be carried out, who is to make the arrangements and when?

....

Litigation friend

Have enquiries been made as to whether any person other than the Official Solicitor is suitable and willing to act as litigation friend?

Yes ☐ No ☐

If so, is there any such person suitable and willing to act?

Yes ☐ No ☐

If yes, state name, address and relationship, if any, to PP:

....

If no enquiries have been made, give reasons and state when and how any enquiries are to be made:

....

Funding

Has a legal aid certificate been granted to PP?

Yes ☐ No ☐

If not, is PP eligible for legal aid?

(a)   without assessment of merit or means

Yes (a) ☐ No ☐

(b)   subject to merit and/or means

Yes (b) ☐ No ☐

If PP is ineligible for legal aid, how is security for costs to be provided to the Official Solicitor or other litigation friend? (eg PP's funds, with Court of Protection authority if required, or undertaking by another party):

....

Information for the Official Solicitor (where invited to consent)

Have the following been provided to the Official Solicitor?

A copy of any court order relating to capacity and/or the appointment of a litigation friend

Yes ☐ No ☐

A copy of any assessment of capacity (including any letter of instruction)

Yes ☐ No ☐

The information set out in this form (to be given in writing and including any relevant attendance note)

Yes ☐ No ☐

The Official Solicitor's referral form (also available on www.gov.uk) explains what information / documents must be sent to the Official Solicitor when making a referral.

If the Official Solicitor consents to act as litigation friend for PP, who is to provide the case papers to the Official Solicitor?

....

This form has been completed by:

Name: ....

Position: ....

Address/Phone/Email: ....

Date: ....

Further information

For further information about the appointment of the Official Solicitor, reference should be made to the Practice Note: The Official Solicitor to the Senior Courts: Appointment in Family Proceedings and Proceedings under the Inherent Jurisdiction in relation to Adults (January 2017).

For the procedure in relation to protected parties, see the Family Procedure Rules 2010, Part 15 and Practice Directions 15A and 15B

Contacting the Official Solicitor

To discuss any question in relation to the appointment of the Official Solicitor in a particular family case, contact may be made by email at osinformation@ospt.gov.uk.

PRESIDENT'S GUIDANCE
22 APRIL 2014

PRESIDENT'S GUIDANCE (ALLOCATION AND GATEKEEPING FOR CARE, SUPERVISION AND OTHER PROCEEDINGS UNDER PART IV OF THE CHILDREN ACT 1989 (PUBLIC LAW)) (22 APRIL 2014)

ALLOCATION AND GATEKEEPING FOR CARE, SUPERVISION AND OTHER PROCEEDINGS UNDER PART IV OF THE CHILDREN ACT 1989 (PUBLIC LAW)

Issued in accordance with rule 21 of the Family Court (Composition and Distribution of Business) Rules 2014

Introduction

1 This Guidance is issued by the President of the Family Division and applies to all care, supervision and other Part IV proceedings commencing on and after 22 April 2014. It is issued following consultation with, and where applicable the agreement of, the Lord Chancellor, in accordance with rule 21 of the Family Court (Composition and Distribution of Business) Rules 2014, and is to be read with those Rules and PD12A (PLO 2014).

2 This Guidance applies to the allocation of all relevant proceedings to judges of the Family Court, including allocation to lay justices working with Justices' Clerks or Assistant Justices' Clerks (referred to in this guidance as 'legal advisers'). The purpose of the Guidance is to ensure that all new care, supervision and other Part IV proceedings are allocated to the appropriate level of judge and, where appropriate, to a named case management judge (or case manager) who shall provide continuity for the proceedings in accordance with the President's Guidance on Judicial Continuity and Deployment (Public Law).

Gatekeeping teams

3 Each Designated Family Judge (DFJ) will lead a gatekeeping team in each Designated Family Centre. A gatekeeping team will consist of the Designated Family Judge, his nominated deputy, the Justices' Clerk (or his nominated legal adviser) and an equal number of District Judges nominated by the Designated Family Judge, and legal advisers who will be identified by the Justices' Clerk in agreement with the Designated Family Judge. The number of legal advisers and District Judges is to be consistent with the needs of the business and the expertise of those who are available. Members of the gatekeeping team are referred to in this guidance as 'gatekeepers'.

4 All applications for care, supervision and other Part IV orders which are received for issue by 4.00 pm will be issued by HMCTS and placed before gatekeepers for their joint consideration on the next working day. Applications that are considered urgent will be allocated to the first available judge of the

PART III – Practice guidance

Family Court (in accordance with rule 16 of the Family Court (Composition and Distribution of Business) Rules 2014).

5 Local Authority applicants are to complete the Allocation Proposal section of the C110A application form when issuing proceedings. The Allocation Proposal section is to be used by the gatekeepers to record their allocation decision.

6 Members of the gatekeeping team are to be available at fixed times on each weekday to allocate jointly all relevant proceedings that have been issued. It is recommended that if they do not sit together at a fixed time in a court list for this purpose, they have a listed time for discussion between each other, for example, an hour at the beginning of the day. The gatekeepers will have access to information about existing allocated case volumes in the family court to help inform allocation decisions, as well as information about when and where Case Management Hearings can be listed. They will consider the file in each new application that has been issued on the preceding day and any outstanding applications and determine, in accordance with the Family Court (Composition and Distribution of Business) Rules 2014 and this guidance, the level of judge, and where possible the identity of the judge to which the proceedings are to be allocated. They will record their allocation decision on the Allocation Proposal section of the C110A application form.

7 When the allocation decision has been made, the case management judge or case manager will issue the Standard Directions on Issue and Allocation (SDO) in accordance with PD12A (PLO 2014) together with any appropriate Notice of Hearing. Court staff will notify by e-mail the relevant local authority of the date, time, location and identity of the allocated case management judge (or case manager) for the case management hearing and will list the case management hearing before an identified case management judge or case manager in accordance with the guidance of the DFJ and the allocation decision that has been made.

8 If the gatekeepers cannot agree on an allocation decision or they require further guidance, they must refer the allocation decision to the Designated Family Judge or his nominated deputy.

9 An allocation decision made by the gatekeepers does not prevent the possibility of a party to the proceedings making a subsequent application for a review of the decision.

10 If a care or supervision application is issued by a local authority as 'urgent' with a request for an early hearing to authorise the removal of a child and permission to abridge time to serve the parties, the application for expedition and any consequential directions will be considered by the gatekeepers. These are exceptional cases which may include newborn babies who are about to be discharged from hospital where the issue of care and supervision order applications is part of planned pre-proceedings involvement with the family. In all other cases where there is an identified real and immediate safety risk to the child, the expectation is that an application will be made for an Emergency Protection Order. This Guidance does not affect the existing procedures for dealing with Emergency Protection Order applications.

11 The Designated Family Judge shall monitor the allocation and gatekeeping process with a consultation group comprising: a Circuit Judge, a District Judge, a District Judge (Magistrates Court), the Justices' Clerk or his nominated deputy, a legal adviser and two members of the administration in the Designated Family Centre. The consultation group will meet at least once a month to identify any allocation questions upon which the advice of the Designated Family Judge or the Family Division Liaison Judge is required to ensure that there is consistency of allocation, effective use of resources and the identification of specific questions, the answers to which will be used as local guidance by the gatekeepers.

Principles

12 Allocation decisions must be made in accordance with the Family Court (Composition and Distribution of Business) Rules 2014.

13 This Guidance is consistent with those Rules, the guidance issued by the President of the Family Division in accordance with PD12A (PLO 2014), and decisions of the superior courts. It is intended to reflect the wide variation in the level of experience and expertise in the Family Court. Cases should be allocated to judges (including lay justices) and case managers with the appropriate level of experience to ensure that judicial resources are used most effectively.

14 In determining allocation, the gatekeepers shall consider each application having regard to the information provided on and with the C110A application form and shall determine the appropriate level of judge of the Family Court, in accordance with the requirements of rule 20 of the Family Court (Composition and Distribution of Business) Rules 2014:

   (a)   the need to make the most effective and efficient use of the local judicial resources that is appropriate, given the nature and type of application;

   (b)   the need to avoid delay;

   (c)   the need for judicial continuity;

   (d)   the location of the parties or of any child relevant to the proceedings; and

   (e)   complexity.

15 In the Family Court, no distinction is to be drawn between proceedings which may be heard by District Judges and District Judges (Magistrates Courts) ('judges of 'district judge level'). There is an expectation that judges of district judge level will Issued 22 April 2014 4 assume personal responsibility for all case management hearings in proceedings allocated to them, in accordance with the President's Guidance on Judicial Continuity and Deployment (Public Law).

Allocation Guidance

16 The factors set out at paragraph (14) above, include at (a) the judicial and HMCTS resources available in each court location, at (b) the needs of the parties to ensure that cases are listed before the appropriate level of judge with the minimum of delay, so that all proceedings are heard within the Timetable for the Child and within a maximum of 26 weeks or any extended Timetable for the Proceedings, as directed by the case management judge, at (c) the President's

PART III – Practice guidance

Guidance on Judicial Continuity and Deployment (Public Law) and at (d) a location that is suitable for the parties, particularly if special requirements or circumstances exist.

17 The schedule to this Guidance sets out matters which are likely to be relevant to the consideration of the 'complexity' factor referred to at paragraph (14)(e) above.

18 Subject to the guidance given below, all care, supervision and other Part IV proceedings may be heard by any judge of the Family Court (including lay justices) who has been authorised or nominated to conduct care and supervision proceedings and may be case managed by any judge or legal adviser who has likewise been authorised or nominated.

19 It is not expected that proceedings described in the schedule to this Guidance will be allocated to lay justices or the legal adviser acting as their case manager unless specifically approved by the Justices' Clerk (or his nominated deputy) in consultation with the Designated Family Judge. There is also an expectation that magistrates will not hear any contested hearing where the ELH is in excess of 3 days without the same having been approved from time to time by the Justices' Clerk (or his nominated deputy) in consultation with the Designated Family Judge.

20 It is expected that proceedings described in column 1 of the schedule to this Guidance will be allocated to a judge of district judge level.

21 It is expected that proceedings described in column 2 of the schedule to this Guidance will be allocated to a judge of circuit judge level or a judge of High Court judge level and will not be allocated to a judge of district judge level unless specifically released by the Designated Family Judge or one of his nominated deputies.

22 Proceedings described in paragraph H of column 2 of the schedule to this Guidance are to be issued in the Family Division of the High Court of Justice.

Schedule to the Allocation and Gatekeeping Guidance

Column 1	Column 2
A) Risk assessment issues	**A) Risk assessment issues**
(1) Allegations or risk of	(1) Allegations of physical or sexual abuse which involve any of the following features:
a) serious physical or sexual abuse causing or likely to cause significant injury to the relevant children, and/or	• Exceptional gravity in relation to the acts alleged or the nature of the harm suffered
b) serious sexual abuse of the relevant children	• Where there is, or is likely to be, conflicting expert opinion from more than two expert witnesses on any key issue

Column 1	Column 2
	• Shaking injuries involving retinal haemorrhage/ brain injury/ fractures • Complex medical questions involving novel issues or the determination of causation
(2) Allegations of serious domestic violence eg. causing significant injury particularly if witnessed by the child	(2) Allegations of extremely serious domestic violence or rape, particularly if witnessed by the child
	(3) Risk of serious physical or emotional harm arising from – • Death of another child in family, a parent or other significant person • A parent or other significant person who may have committed a grave crime e.g. murder, manslaughter or rape
(4) Significant disputed issues relating to psychiatric illness of a parent and/ or a child	
	(5) History of suspicious death of a child in the family
(6) Significant disputed medical issues relating to the relevant child	(6) Complex medical issues, including medical causation issues and medical treatment issues including where any of the parties suffer from psychiatric illness or psychological issues or any significant disability such as profound deafness, blindness or learning disability, or which will require specialist knowledge and services in respect of parenting capacity or the needs of the children
B) Unusual/Complex issues relating to ethnicity or religion	**B) Unusual/Complex issues relating to ethnicity or religion**
None	(7) Significant contested issues in respect of religion, culture or ethnicity or involving medical treatment relating to the same
C) Non-subject child as a party (particularly if under 16)	**C) Non-subject child as a party (particularly if under 16)**
(8) Where a child may be required to give evidence.	(8) Where children (including parents who are under the age of 18) are, or may be, required to give evidence and be joined as a party

PART III – Practice guidance

Column 1	Column 2
D) Capacity issues	**D) Capacity issues**
(9) Where there is a need for the Official Solicitor or another litigation friend to represent the interests of an incapacitated adult	(9) Where there is a need for the Official Solicitor or another litigation friend to represent the interests of more than one incapacitated party
E) Real possibility of conflict of expert evidence or difficulty in resolving conflict in the evidence of witnesses	**E) Real possibility of conflict of expert evidence or difficulty in resolving conflict in the evidence of witnesses**
(10) Where there is an identified need for no more than two expert witnesses to report on the same key issue(s)	(10) Where there is an identified need for more than two expert witnesses to report on the same key issue(s)
F) Novel or difficult point of law	**F) Novel or difficult point of law**
None	(11) Where the case involves a difficult point of law, issues of public policy or unusually complex or sensitive issues
	(12) Allegations of serious abuse where there are, or are likely to be, criminal proceedings and consideration of issues regarding disclosure of information or public interest immunity
	(13) Complex issues as to disclosure – where a party seeks leave to withhold information from another party, or where there is an issue about the release of confidential information involving a difficult point of law, or where disclosure of documentation involves a difficult or sensitive exercise of discretion or public policy issues
	(14) Where there are concurrent criminal proceedings in the Crown Court relevant to the issues between the parties and joint directions hearing(s) may be required.
	(15) Cases not in category H below, but which have significant immigration/status issues.

Column 1	Column 2
G) Existing proceedings relating to the child or a sibling which are proceeding before another court or have been recently completed before another court	**G) Existing proceedings relating to the child or a sibling which are proceeding before another court or have been recently completed before another court**
(16) Consideration must be given to listing the current proceedings before the judge who heard or is hearing the proceedings relating to the child or sibling in order to provide continuity.	(16) Consideration must be given to listing the current proceedings before the judge who heard or is hearing the proceedings relating to the child or sibling in order to provide continuity.
	H) High Court Reserved Jurisdictions
International Proceedings	**International Issues**
	(17) There is an issue concerning placement for adoption of the child outside the jurisdiction
(18) Cases to which Brussels II revised applies	(18) Proceedings with an international element relating to recognition or enforcement of orders, conflict or comity of laws or which have exceptional immigration / asylum status issues
(19) Cases in which placement is limited to temporary removal to a Hague Convention country.	(19) Cases in which an application is made for (a) permanent placement or (b) temporary removal from the jurisdiction to a non-Hague convention country;
	20) Cases in which a child has been brought to this jurisdiction in circumstances which might constitute a wrongful removal or retention either from a EC Member State, a Hague Convention country (a contracting State to the 1980 Hague Child Abduction Convention and/or a contracting State to the 1996 Hague Child Protection Convention) or a non-Convention country;

PART III – Practice guidance

Column 1	Column 2
	(21) Cases in which a child is alleged to have been abducted overseas and applications have been made in this jurisdiction such as for a declaration that the child was habitually resident in this country prior to the abduction or for an order that the child be returned with a request for assistance etc; and
	(22) Cases in which Tipstaff Orders are applied for.
	Inherent Jurisdiction
	(23) Injunctions invoking the inherent jurisdiction of the court
	(24) Interim or substantive relief which requires the inherent jurisdiction of the High Court to be invoked.
	Other
	(25) Applications for Declaratory Relief
	(26) Applications which require the jurisdiction of the Administrative Court to be invoked
	(27) Issues as to publicity (identification of a child or restriction on publication or injunctions seeking to restrict the freedom of the media)
	(28) Applications in medical treatment cases e.g. for novel medical treatment or life saving procedures
I) Other case management issues	**I) Other case management issues**
(29) Where a 'split hearing' or finding of fact hearing is necessary and judicial continuity cannot otherwise be ensured	(29) Where a 'split hearing' or finding of fact hearing is necessary and judicial continuity before a District Judge cannot be ensured
	(30) Where possible local authority failures to progress plans to protect the child(ren) in the case are likely to be addressed critically by the court because it is alleged that there has been systemic failure in the proceedings and other proceedings

PRESIDENT'S GUIDANCE
22 APRIL 2014

PRESIDENT'S GUIDANCE (ALLOCATION AND GATEKEEPING FOR PROCEEDINGS UNDER PART II OF THE CHILDREN ACT 1989 (PRIVATE LAW)) (22 APRIL 2014)

ALLOCATION AND GATEKEEPING FOR PROCEEDINGS UNDER PART II OF THE CHILDREN ACT 1989 (PRIVATE LAW)

Issued in accordance with rule 21 of the Family Court (Composition and Distribution of Business) Rules 2014

Introduction

1 This Guidance is issued by the President of the Family Division and applies to all private law proceedings under Part II of the Children Act 1989 (hereinafter referred to as 'private law proceedings') from 22 April 2014. It is issued following consultation with, and where applicable with the agreement of, the Lord Chancellor, in accordance with rule 21 of the Family Court (Composition and Distribution of Business) Rules 2014, and is to be read with those Rules and PD12B FPR (CAP 2014)).

2 The purpose of the Guidance is to ensure that all new private law proceedings are allocated to the appropriate level of judge and, where appropriate to a named case management judge (or case manager in those cases allocated to lay justices) who shall provide continuity for the proceedings in accordance with the President's Guidance on Judicial Continuity and Deployment (Private Law).

3 This Guidance applies to the allocation of all relevant proceedings to all judges of the Family Court (including lay justices sitting with assistant justices' clerks (referred to in this Guidance as legal advisers). During the implementation and consolidation of arrangements for the Family Court, this includes allocation to legal advisers conducting FHDRAs in court centres where:

(i)   there is agreement between the Designated Family Judge ('DFJ'), HMCTS Head of CFT, the justices' clerk and the relevant Panel Chair(s) that available judicial resources locally require that FHDRAs continue to be listed before the legal advisers; or

(ii)   in areas where the practice does not currently take place, where there is agreement between the DFJ, HMCTS Head of CFT, the justices' clerk and the relevant Panel Chair(s), and specific permission granted from the President of the Family Division and the HMCTS Director for Civil Family and Tribunals, that it be extended to facilitate the appropriate allocation of cases;

And in any event

(iii) provided that such allocation does not restrict the court's ability to make substantive orders on the day of the hearing (i.e. by using parallel or

PART III – Practice guidance

back-to-back lists, so that lay justices or judges are available to consider the case and, where appropriate, make a substantive order).

Allocation and Resources

4 In some DFJ's areas, full implementation of this guidance may result in a significant shift of caseload between levels of the judiciary. Before implementation it will therefore be necessary for the DFJ in consultation with the local judiciary, the justices' clerk, and HMCTS to review the available resources, in terms of courtrooms, court staff and judiciary including lay justices and legal advisers. The extent and timescale of implementation of the guidance should take these factors into account alongside any shift in allocation of public law cases following the implementation of the President's Guidance on Allocation Gatekeeping for Care Supervision and other Proceedings under Part IV of the Children Act 1989 (Public Law). The overarching intention should be to avoid delay in all children's proceedings wherever possible.

Allocation and listing schedules

5 The DFJ in consultation with the judiciary, the justices' clerk and HMCTS should review the family listing schedules in place within the DFJ's area taking into account the plans for the implementation of the Family Court. Where feasible and practical, consideration should be given to arranging listing schedules so that First Hearing Dispute Resolution Appointments (FHDRAs) are taking place in parallel lists (i.e. on the same day and ideally in the same building) before District Judges and lay justices (sitting with a legal adviser), or where appropriate (in accordance with paragraph 3 above) before legal advisers sitting alone. This will allow for re-allocation to be considered up to and including the date of the hearing of the case, so that an alternative judicial level to that selected by the Gatekeeper(s) (see paragraph 6 below) can be arranged if necessary (in particular, should receipt of the Cafcass Safeguarding checks or interview with the parties raise matters of particular significance which justify a revised allocation decision).

Gatekeeping teams

6 Each DFJ will lead a gatekeeping team responsible for private law gatekeeping in each of the Family Hearing Centres that are nominated by the President to be Designated Family Centres. The team will consist of the DFJ and the justices' clerk with as many legal advisers and District Judges as the DFJ considers necessary to carry out the gatekeeping role depending on local demand and conditions. The DFJ in consultation with the District Judges and the justices' clerk will determine whether gatekeeping decisions are to be made by the District Judges or legal advisers acting alone, or together. The District Judge and legal advisers when making gatekeeping and allocation decisions are referred to as 'the Gatekeeper(s)' in this guidance.

7 All applications for private law orders which are received by 4.00 pm will be issued by HMCTS and placed before the Gatekeeper(s) for their consideration on the next working day, except where they are (or have been) dealt with as an urgent application. The Gatekeeper(s) should consider the application on the basis of

the information provided in the application, and shall determine the appropriate level of judiciary in accordance with this guidance, and the requirements of the Family Court (Composition and Distribution of Business) Rules 2014, based on consideration of the relative significance of:

(a) The need to make the most effective and efficient use of the local judicial resources that is appropriate, given the nature and type of application;

(b) The need to avoid delay;

(c) The need for judicial continuity;

(d) The location of the parties or of any child relevant to the proceedings; and

(e) Complexity.

8 The judiciary including lay justices and legal advisers have an ongoing duty to keep allocation decisions under review particularly:

(a) when any response to the application is received;

(b) the safeguarding checks are received; and

(c) at the FHDRA when further information has been ascertained from the parties and Cafcass or CAFCASS Cymru at court.

9 When making an allocation decision the Gatekeepers will enquire into whether a MIAM exemption has been validly claimed, to the extent possible at this stage. If the MIAM exemption has not been validly claimed, the Gatekeepers shall give directions in accordance with rule 3.10(2)/(3) FPR 2010.

10 Prior to making an allocation decision the Gatekeeper(s) shall consider whether to allocate the application to a different location for hearing within the DFJ area, or to transfer the application to another DFJ area, where it appears that the parties, and/or the child(ren) who are the subject of the application, reside(s) in an area other than that covered by the DFJ.

11 Gatekeeper(s) are to be made available for a period of time on each weekday to allocate all private law proceedings which have been issued. Gatekeeper(s) will consider the file in each new application which has been issued on the preceding day and any urgent applications which are outstanding, and determine to which level of judge the proceedings should be allocated, i.e. to lay justices, a judge at District Judge level, a judge at Circuit Judge level or judge at High Court level sitting in the Family Court:

(a) Based on consideration of the relative significance of the matters set out in paragraph 7(a)–(e) (above),

and

(b) When considering complexity, by reference to the schedule to this guidance.

The Gatekeeper(s) will record their allocation decision and reasons on the case papers and make any appropriate arrangements for transfer (between courts) as necessary. In addition, where it appears that a case needs an urgent listing, the Gatekeeper(s) will ensure that the case is listed as a matter of urgency, and will give directions to abridge time for service if necessary.

PART III – Practice guidance

12 The DFJ shall make arrangements to ensure the swift allocation of all cases within the Family Court to a named case manager so that it can be listed (in accordance with this Guidance and the Family Court (Composition and Distribution of Business) Rules 2014) in week 5 or 6 after issue, for an FHDRA, or sooner if an FHDRA is not appropriate.

13 If any Gatekeeper requires further guidance on a particular case, they should refer the allocation decision to the DFJ or his nominated deputy.

14 An allocation decision made by the Gatekeepers does not prevent a party to the proceedings applying for a review of the decision

15 The DFJ shall monitor the allocation and gatekeeping practices in the DFJ area to ensure that there is consistency of allocation, effective use of resources and the capacity to list cases at the earliest opportunity to avoid delay. He/she may issue local guidance to the Gatekeepers from time to time to reflect local circumstances and ensure the best use of resources. The allocation of work between the Circuit Bench, the District Bench, the lay justices and, where appropriate and agreed, the legal advisers may be subject to local directions by the DFJ .

Directions on Issue

16 Gatekeepers shall be able to issue Directions on Issue on Form CAP01 in the following circumstances:

  (a) where the Gatekeeper finds on the basis of the information provided that the exemption from attending a MIAM has not validly been claimed, the Gatekeeper will direct the applicant, or will direct the parties, to attend a MIAM before the FHDRA, unless the Gatekeeper considers that in all the circumstances of the case the MIAM requirement should not apply to the application in question; the Gatekeeper will have regard to the matters set out in rule 3.10(3) FPR when making this decision;

  (b) where it appears that an urgent issue requires determination, the Gatekeeper may give directions for an accelerated hearing;

  (c) exceptionally, where it appears that directions need to be given for the service and filing of evidence, he/she may give directions for the filing of evidence.

Principles of Allocation

17 Allocation decisions must be made in accordance with the Family Court (Composition and Distribution of Business) Rules 2014.

18 This Guidance identifies criteria which are intended to be consistent with the Family Court (Composition and Distribution of Business) Rules 2014, and the decisions of superior courts.

19 In determining allocation, judicial continuity is an important consideration and the President's Guidance on Judicial Continuity and Deployment (Private Law) is to be followed.

20 In determining allocation consideration must be given to the matters set out in paragraph 7(a)–(e) above, in particular the need to avoid delay and provide the earliest possible hearing dates consistent with the welfare of the subject child(ren).

21 No distinction is to be drawn between proceedings which may be heard by District Judges and District Judges (Magistrates' Courts). There is an expectation that District Judges will assume personal responsibility for all case management hearings in proceedings allocated to them in accordance with the President's Guidance on Judicial Continuity and Deployment (Private Law).

Allocation Guidance

22 Subject to the guidance given below, all private law proceedings may be heard by any judge who has been authorised or nominated to conduct such proceedings, and may be case managed by the same judge or legal adviser.

23 When considering specifically the complexity of a case (see paragraph 7(e) above), it is envisaged that all relevant family applications (as defined in CAP paragraph 23) will be heard by lay justices (or at the FHDRA by legal advisers) unless they are of the type set out in the Schedule to this Guidance (see paragraphs 25 and 26 below). Additionally, a relevant family application may:

(a) be allocated to be heard by lay justices where specifically approved by the justices' clerk (or his nominated deputy) in consultation with the DFJ, or

(b) be re-allocated to be heard by lay justices where, at FHDRA or other hearing, it appears to the judge that the case does not fall, or no longer falls, within the Schedule.

24 There is an expectation that lay justices will not hear any contested private law application where the estimated length of the hearing is in excess of 3 days without the same having been approved by the justices' clerk in consultation with the DFJ.

25 When considering specifically the complexity of a case (see paragraph 7(e) above), it is envisaged that:

(c) proceedings described in Part 1 of the schedule to this Guidance will be allocated to a District Judge, or a District Judge (Magistrates' Court). If, on allocation it appears to the District Judge that the particular circumstances of the individual case justify allocation to a Circuit Judge, the District Judge shall so allocate it.

(d) subject to paragraph 27 (below), proceedings described in Part 2 of the schedule to this Guidance will be allocated to either a District Judge, District Judge (Magistrates' Court) or to a Circuit Judge or a High Court Judge.

26 Where the Gatekeeper allocates proceedings described in Part 2 of the schedule to a Circuit Judge or to a High Court Judge sitting in the Family Court, the FHDRA for that case shall be listed before a District Judge or District Judge (Magistrates' Court) unless the Gatekeeper considers (in discussion with the DFJ) that the FHDRA should be conducted by the Circuit Judge or High Court Judge (as appropriate).

27 Proceedings described in Part 3 of the schedule to this Guidance are to be issued in the High Court, not the Family Court. If they are received in the Family

PART III – Practice guidance

Court, then they must be identified and transferred to the Family Division of the High Court.

28 Where it appears to a Court that the issues in a case have developed from the point of initial allocation in such a way as to justify re-allocation, the court shall consider re-allocation in accordance with this Guidance and Schedule, having regard to the matters set out in paragraph 7(a)–(e) above, and taking account to the extent appropriate the principle of judicial continuity, and the need to avoid delay.

Urgent hearings

29 Urgent applications are those in which the applicant for a private law family order invites the court by application C2 either to (a) list the application for a hearing without notice to the respondent, or (b) reduce the normal (14 days) time-limit for service of an application and list a hearing at short notice.

30 If the application is considered by the Gatekeeper(s), they are to have regard generally to the guidance in paragraph 12.1–12.5 of the CAP in relation to the making of without notice orders when considering how to allocate an application that is presented for allocation as 'urgent'.

31 When presented with an application said to be urgent, the Gatekeeper(s) shall upon receipt:

(a)   allocate the application to the appropriate level of judiciary in accordance with rule 16 of the Family Court (Composition and Distribution of Business) Rules 2014, and

(b)   determine whether the application requires

(i)   a hearing on that day, or
(ii)   requires an early hearing in advance of the FHDRA, with a reduced time for service of the application.

If an application for an urgent hearing is refused, reasons shall be given in writing and the application listed for FHDRA; the Gatekeeper may issue further directions in accordance with paragraph 16 above.

Schedule to the Allocation and Gatekeeping Guidance – Private Law

NOTE THAT

When, on allocation, Gatekeepers are considering specifically the issue of complexity, it is envisaged that they will allocate all relevant family applications (as defined in the Child Arrangements Programme paragraph 23) to the lay justices (or at the FHDRA by legal advisers) UNLESS they are of the type set out in this Schedule (below) (See paragraph 23 Guidance on Allocation & Gatekeeping for Proceedings under Part II of the Children Act 1989 (Private Law Proceedings))

Part 1 – District Judge (unless in the opinion of the allocated District Judge, the particular characteristics of the individual case justify transfer to a Circuit Judge)	Part 2 – District Judge but may be by Circuit Judge (or at most serious level by High Court Judge)	Part 3 – High Court and Inherent Jurisdiction
Allegations of significant physical, emotional or sexual abuse, or behaviours which have caused, or are at risk of causing, significant harm to the relevant child.	Cases involving significant factual disputes (including allegations of abuse, violence, alleged or proven criminal activity, gravely inappropriate behaviours, sexual abuse, complex physical and/or mental health issues in relation to relevant adults or children) particularly where a fact finding hearing of 3 days or more is a real possibility and/or where it is likely that more than one expert (not including CAFCASS and/or social worker) will be involved.	Inherent jurisdiction of the court relating to minors

Application to make a child a ward of court, or to bring such an order to an end.

Proceedings under the Child Abduction & Custody Act 1985, and other international abduction cases

Proceedings with an international element relating to or enforcement of Orders, conflict or comity of laws which have exceptional immigration/asylum status issues.

Declarations of incompatibility under the Human Rights Act 1998 |
| Cases where significant factual matters are in issue (including substance misuse, domestic abuse, paternity, physical and/or mental health of relevant adults or children) such that a fact-finding hearing lasting more than one day is likely and the necessity for expert evidence (i.e. beyond the expertise of CAFCASS and/or social worker) is likely to arise. | Cases where there are particularly difficult and unusual immigration or jurisdictional issues.

Cases involving leave to remove (permanently or temporarily) from the jurisdiction to Hague Convention and/or EU countries which are factually or legally complex.

Cases which appear to involve, or have the potential to involve, intractable opposition to contact. | Applications for Declaratory Relief

Registration of foreign judgments under Part 1 of the Foreign Judgments (Reciprocal Enforcement) Act 1920

Registration of judgments given in a different part of the UK under Part 2 of the Civil Jurisdiction and Judgments Act 1982 |
| Cases where the capacity of one of the parents is, or is likely to be, raised as an issue.

Cases where there is a real possibility that the child will have to be joined as a party (see guidelines under rule 16.4 FPR 2010) &/or may be called to give evidence. | Cases seeking enforcement of existing Orders made by a Circuit Judge or Recorder or in cases where a Circuit Judge or Recorder has previously made orders in relation to the same parties. Allocation should be to the same Circuit Judge or Recorder where practicable. | Registration of custody (Part 1) orders made in a court in another part of the UK under the Family Law Act 1986, section 32(1)

Parental Responsibility order prior to adoption abroad (Adoption and Children Act 2002, section 84(1)) |

PART III – Practice guidance

Part 1 – District Judge (unless in the opinion of the allocated District Judge, the particular characteristics of the individual case justify transfer to a Circuit Judge)	Part 2 – District Judge but may be by Circuit Judge (or at most serious level by High Court Judge)	Part 3 – High Court and Inherent Jurisdiction
Cases where there is, or is likely to be, a significant issue in relation to disclosure of documents to or from third parties or outside agencies. Cases where immigration issues are likely to be relevant and significant	Circuit Judge (not District Judge): Cases seeking leave to remove from the jurisdiction [permanently or temporarily] outside of the Hague Convention/ the EU. Where there are particular factual or legal complexities, the cases should ordinarily be allocated to the High Court following consultation with the DFJ.	Application for direction that section 67(3) of the Adoption and Children Act 2002 (status conferred by adoption) does not apply. Application for annulment of overseas or Convention adoption under Adoption and Children Act 2002, section 89
Cases involving leave to remove children (permanently or temporarily) from the jurisdiction to Hague Convention and/or EU countries.		Issuance of letter of request for person to be examined out of the jurisdiction. Applications under Article 15 of the 2201/2003 Council Regulation and Article 9 of the 1996 Hague Convention (request for transfer of jurisdiction).
Cases which involve significant issues to be determined in relation to the disclosure of information to one or other of the parties (e.g. where the Cafcass officer seeks to withhold information contained in a Safeguarding letter).		Applications under Article 16 of the 1996 Hague Convention for a declaration as to the extent or existence of parental responsibility. Applications under Part 31 of the FPR (registration of orders under the 2201/2003 Council Regulation, the 1996 Hague Convention and the Civil Partnership (Jurisdiction and Recognition of Judgments) Regulations 2005).
Cases involving the enforcement of existing orders made by a District Judge or cases where a District Judge has previously made orders in relation to the same parties. Allocation should be to the same District Judge where practicable.		Cases which require the jurisdiction of the Administrative Court to be invoked

Part 1 – District Judge (unless in the opinion of the allocated District Judge, the particular characteristics of the individual case justify transfer to a Circuit Judge)	Part 2 – District Judge but may be by Circuit Judge (or at most serious level by High Court Judge)	Part 3 – High Court and Inherent Jurisdiction
Cases where there is a real possibility that Public Law Orders will be required, where the issues arising are of a type described in Part 1 or Part 2 of the Schedule to the President's Guidance on Allocation and Gatekeeping for Care, Supervision and other Part 4 proceedings.		

PART III – Practice guidance

PRESIDENT'S GUIDANCE
22 APRIL 2014

PRESIDENT'S GUIDANCE (CONTINUITY AND DEPLOYMENT (PRIVATE LAW)) (22 APRIL 2014)

CONTINUITY AND DEPLOYMENT (PRIVATE LAW)

Introduction

1 This Guidance is issued by the President of the Family Division.

2 This Guidance applies to all private law proceedings under Part II of the Children Act 1989 (private children proceedings) heard in the Family Court.

3 Deployment is a judicial function which includes the patterning of judges and lay justices, the management of the workload of the court, allocation and listing.

4 The purpose of this Guidance is to ensure that family proceedings are accorded the appropriate level of priority in their listing and that they are case managed and heard by judges (including lay justices) and legal advisers who provide continuity of the conduct of the proceedings.

Continuity and Docketing

5 In accordance with the Guidance given by HMCTS on the introduction of a system for the docketing of cases (which is annexed to this Guidance) all private children proceedings are to be allocated to a case management judge in the Family Court who will be responsible for any case management hearings in the proceedings.

6 For the lay justices, the case manager is the justices' clerk or assistant justices' clerk (legal adviser) who manages the case. Continuity of the case manager for hearings before lay justices is as essential as continuity of the case management judge for other judges of the Family Court.

7 The name of the case manager(s) or case management judge must be recorded on the outside of the court file by the court staff immediately after the FHDRA or other first hearing.

8 Where possible, the case management judge or the case manager sitting with lay justices is to conduct any contested hearing including the final hearing in all proceedings allocated to them.

9 No hearing at any stage of the proceedings should conclude without a date for the next hearing having been fixed for the earliest possible date, and communicated to the parties at court.

10 It is not good practice for proceedings to have to wait until the case manager or the case management judge is available. Discussions must take place during the FHDRA, DRA or other hearings (and with HMCTS) to ensure that one of

the two case managers or the case management judge is available to hear the proceedings on the date fixed for the next appointment. Legal advisers and judges must fit their availability around the case, not the other way around. Although continuity of representation is important, lawyers will be expected to organise their diaries to ensure that cases are heard without delay.

11 The allocation of private children proceedings is to be undertaken in accordance with the President's Guidance on Allocation and Gatekeeping (Private Law), and the Family Court (Composition and Distribution of Business) Rules 2014.

Deployment

12 Circuit Judges and District Judges hearing private children proceedings should be patterned so as to be able to sit in private children proceedings with a gap of no more than a month so as to provide continuity for their allocated proceedings.

13 District Judges (Magistrates' Court) who sit on private children proceedings are identified by the Chief Magistrate and authorised by the President. The deployment of DJsMC is determined by the Chief Magistrate in consultation with Presiding Judges and the Family Division Liaison Judge (FDLJ) on each Circuit.

14 Legal advisers are generally to be patterned so that they are available to the Family Court for not less than 40% of their time. Those sitting as case managers must sit for 40% or more of their time in public and private law. Each private law application which is allocated to the lay justices must have one and not more than two allocated case managers who are legal advisers.

15 Justices' clerks will be expected to agree the deployment of their lay justices with Designated Family Judges (DFJs) and this should be done in direct meetings between the DFJ and the justices' clerk and his/her tier 4 specialists. Any disagreements are to be referred immediately to the FDLJ and the Regional Delivery Director through his/her Head of Civil, Family and Tribunals

16 The deployment of Circuit Judges and District Judges in the Family Court (i.e. their patterns and itineraries) is decided by the Presiding Judges in consultation with and on the advice of the FDLJ, and the Designated and Resident Judges. DFJs are encouraged to agree a protocol with Resident Judges for the patterning of mixed ticketed judges and their availability to provide judicial continuity.

Continuity by Lay Justices

17 The following arrangements will apply to proceedings heard by lay justices in the Family Court for case management and hearing.

18 Lay justices are patterned to sit by their justices' clerk. Continuity should be provided for in the individual case, where a decision of fact has been made which renders a case theoretically or actually part heard, in accordance with the guidance in *Re B (Children)* [2008] UKHL 35, and rule 8 of the Family Court (Composition and Distribution of Business) Rules 2014. Wherever possible, the

PART III – Practice guidance

court which resumes a hearing shall be composed of the same lay justices as dealt with the previous part of the hearing; alternatively, continuity is to be provided by at least one of the lay justices (preferably the Chairman) as well as the legal adviser who is the case manager for the proceedings.

Appeals

19 Appeals within the Family Court are to be allocated to judges in accordance with the Family Court (Composition and Distribution of Business) Rules 2014. Appeals from Circuit Judges and second appeals will continue to be heard by the Court of Appeal.

PRESIDENT'S GUIDANCE
10 NOVEMBER 2014

THE INTERNATIONAL CHILD ABDUCTION AND
CONTACT UNIT (ICACU)

I am aware that an increasing number of children cases have an international element and that courts often require information from other jurisdictions before being able to proceed. It is not always easy to know how to obtain this information.

While it may not always be possible to obtain the information sufficiently quickly to enable the court to hear these cases within 26 weeks, I am very grateful to the International Child Abduction and Contact Unit (ICACU) for providing the following, which will help practitioners to follow the correct route to obtain information to help the court when necessary. It has been approved by Lady Justice Black and the Senior Master.

Practitioners will also need to be alive to Chapter VI of Part 12 of the Family Procedure Rules 2010 as amended, and to The Parental Responsibility and Measures for the Protection of Children (International Obligations) (England and Wales and Northern Ireland) Regulations 2010.

Sir James Munby
President of the Family Division
10 November 2014

The ICACU

The ICACU is the operational Central Authority for England and Wales for Council Regulation (EC) 2201/2003 ('Brussels IIA' or 'the Revised Brussels II Regulation') and for England only for the 1996 Hague Convention on Jurisdiction, Applicable Law, Recognition, Enforcement and Co-operation in Respect of Parental Responsibility and Measures for the Protection of Children ('the 1996 Hague Convention').[1]

1 The ICACU is also the operational Central Authority for the 1980 Hague Convention on the Civil Aspects of International Child Abduction and the 1980 Hague European Convention on Recognition and Enforcement of Decisions Concerning Custody of Children and Restoration of Custody of Children.

The ICACU provides a standard response/leaflet to enquiries about requests for co-operation from local authorities explaining about other sources of assistance including where to find information and contact details of other bodies which may be able to assist. A copy of that standard response/leaflet is attached as it is a helpful resource.

Can the ICACU help?

The ICACU is a small administrative unit. Its staff are not lawyers or social workers. The ICACU cannot give legal advice.

The ICACU may however be able to help by making a request for co-operation to another country, in particular for the collection and exchange of information if the other country is:

(a)   either a Member State of the European Union (other than Denmark); or

(b)   a State Party to the 1996 Hague Convention;

and

(c)   the request for co-operation is in scope of the Revised Brussels II Regulation or of the 1996 Hague Convention

To decide if the proposed request for co-operation is in scope consider Articles 1, 53–57 of the Revised Brussels II Regulation and Articles 1, 3, 4, 30–37 of the 1996 Hague Convention.

ICACU can have a role in relation to transfers between courts under Article 15 of the Revised Brussels II Regulation or authorities under Articles 8 and 9 the 1996 Hague Convention; this role is not covered by this 'view'.

Requests for co-operation involving the collection and exchange of information under Article 55 of the Revised Brussels II Regulation or under Article 34 of the 1996 Hague Convention must be distinguished from requests for evidence.

If making a request under the 1996 Hague Convention consideration should be given to Article 37 of the 1996 Hague Convention before deciding to contact the ICACU.

If considering placement of a child in another country:

- for an EU Member State you should consider Article 56 of the Revised Brussels II Regulation and the decision of the Court of Justice of the European Union ('CJEU') on the operation of Article 56 in case C-92/12 PPU;

- for a 1996 Hague Convention country you should consider Article 33 of the Convention.

Whether or not placement of a child in another country is considered to be placement in institutional care or with a foster family, is a question for the requested country not for the requesting country. A placement which from a domestic perspective is a private law placement may be regarded as a public law placement by the requested country. A request for co-operation can be made to establish if, in principle, the consent of the other country would be required for placement even if the care plan for the child is not yet fully informed.

The ICACU may have practical knowledge and experience of the processes and procedures in the other country which it can usefully share in response to an enquiry. However before relying on information formerly provided by the ICACU in another case you should bear in mind that the other country's processes and procedures may have changed since you last contacted the ICACU.

If your request is not in scope of the Revised Brussels II Regulation or of the 1996 Hague Convention, it may be in scope of another European Regulation or international Convention and another central authority or body may be able to assist.

For example, in England and Wales:

The **Senior Master** is:

(a) the transmitting agency under Article 2 of Council Regulation (EC) No 1393/2007 of 13 November 2007 on the service in the Member States of judicial and extrajudicial documents in civil or commercial matters, ('the Service Regulation')

(b) the central authority under Article 3 of the 1965 Hague Convention on the Service Abroad of Judicial and Extrajudicial Documents in Civil or Commercial Matters ('the 1965 Hague Convention')

(c) the central body under Article 3 of Council Regulation (EC) No 1206/2001 of 28 May 2001 on cooperation between the courts of the Member States in the taking of evidence in civil or commercial matters ('the Taking of Evidence Regulation')

(d) the central authority under Article 2 of the 1970 Hague Convention on the Taking of Evidence Abroad in Civil or Commercial Matters ('the 1970 Hague Convention').

The administrative unit which supports the Senior Master is the Foreign Process Section based in the Royal Courts of Justice.

Member States have differing views as to what comes within scope of the Revised Brussels II Regulation and what comes within scope of the Taking of Evidence Regulation. If you are in doubt this may be where the ICACU's practical knowledge and experience of the other country's processes and procedures can be of assistance. In such cases you should make an early enquiry to avoid delay at the point the formal request needs to be made.

The **UKCA-ECR** is the central authority for the exchange of criminal records between Member States of the European Union.

What the ICACU does not do

As the ICACU has no role to play in the operation of:

• the Service Regulation, or of
• the 1965 Hague Convention,
• the ICACU will not serve or arrange service of court documents and nor will its counterpart in the other country.

As the mechanism for the taking of evidence abroad is in the Taking of Evidence Regulation or the 1970 Hague Convention, the ICACU will not assist in acquiring evidence.

Please note that the ICACU does not forward requests for co-operation on to other domestic central authorities or bodies when it receives a request which is outside the scope of the Revised Brussels II Regulation or of the 1996 Hague Convention.

The ICACU does not notify consular authorities about proceedings concerning a child of a foreign nationality either pursuant to *Re E (Brussels II Revised: Vienna Convention: Reporting Restrictions)* [2014] EWHC 6 (Fam), [2014] 2 FLR 151

PART III – Practice guidance

or at all as that is not a central authority duty or function. Consular authorities, not the ICACU, should also be contacted about passports and other travel documents such as visas.

A request for an opinion on jurisdiction is not a question for central authorities. The ICACU will not offer an opinion on jurisdiction and nor should a question about jurisdiction form part of a request for the collection and exchange of information.

The ICACU will not transmit a request for formal criminal record checks as that is a request properly directed to the UKCA-ECR.

The ICACU does not become directly involved in the court proceedings. Central authorities are not under any obligation to engage in proceedings and do not require a court order before discharging their duties and responsibilities under the Revised Brussels II Regulation or the 1996 Hague Convention.

Contacting the ICACU

The ICACU's general office telephone number is 0203 681 2608 and can be used by parties seeking "in principle" advice based on the ICACU's experience of the other country. However the ICACU prefers contact to be made by email using the email address: **icacu@offsol.gsi.gov.uk**.

Email contact allows the ICACU to manage their busy workload and to collate information about the types of requests and countries. If an enquiry is made by telephone the ICACU will usually ask that the enquiry also be put in writing but understands that if a matter is urgent a telephone enquiry may first be necessary.

Making a request for co-operation

Requests for co-operation need to be **relevant, focussed, timely and practical**.

You should specify whether the request is being made under the Revised Brussels II Regulation or under the 1996 Hague Convention. You should identify in your request the Article(s) relied on by you for the purpose of making the request. Remember that the request needs to be in scope of the Revised Brussels II Regulation or the 1996 Hague Convention.

Requests for co-operation should be made as early as practicably possible. There is nothing in the Revised Brussels II Regulation or the 1996 Hague Convention which requires a requested State to respond to a request for co-operation within a particular timescale. The ICACU cannot compel the requested central authority or foreign competent authorities to respond within a specific timetable but their counterparts are more likely to be able to offer assistance if the request is focussed and made on a timely basis. The ICACU therefore asks that any request for co-operation is made as early as practicable in the proceedings and that it is informed about the court timetable including the date of any listed hearing.

When fixing the court timetable the timescale for a response from the other jurisdiction needs to be realistic having regard to the number of steps involved in a request for co-operation. In a public law case those steps may involve:

- the decision to make a request for co-operation by the local authority whether following the court's direction or otherwise;
- request received by the ICACU;
- the ICACU requesting any necessary translations;
- the request being transmitted by the ICACU to the requested central authority;
- the requested central authority making any enquiries directly or of its competent authorities to enable it to respond;
- the requested central authority or the ICACU arranging any necessary translations of the response;
- the ICACU transmitting the response to the local authority here;
- the initial response from the requested central authority may include a request for additional information and documents in order to enable a more detailed response to be provided.

A sealed copy of any relevant court order should be provided to the ICACU promptly (to assist in avoiding delay).

In formulating the request for co-operation you should give consideration to what information practically the requested central authority and their competent authorities may require in order to respond to the request. A clear background case summary will assist. You should always provide the full name and date(s) of birth of the child(ren) and of any relevant adult and an explanation of the family relationship(s). If the case involves a more complex family structure (full, half or step siblings, different generations in the same household etc) then a genogram is likely to be of assistance. Additionally:

- for the benefit of the requested central authority you should explain technical language (for example what is meant by section 20 consent) and acronyms;
- for kinship care assessments it may be useful to explain what the local authority or court would find helpful for the assessment to cover but it is unlikely to be appropriate to ask foreign authorities to complete domestic forms;
- for requests to identify potential kinship carers provide as much information as possible to assist the requested State to trace the individuals concerned; if current contact details are not known, then the last known address in the requested country (or as much information as possible as to where the family is from in that country), social security details or passport / foreign identity document details may also assist;
- only the documents relevant to the request should be sent; it is not usually necessary for the whole court bundle to be provided;
- if the court's permission is required to disclose information or documents to the ICACU and to the requested central authority the permission application should be made promptly.

The ICACU has a limited budget for translations. It will arrange translation of the request for co-operation but the parties to the court proceedings will need to agree who is to prepare translations of any supporting documents.

PART III – Practice guidance

If the welfare plan for the child is for placement in the other country you should check if that country's consent to the placement is required under either Article 56 of the Revised Brussels II Regulation or under Article 33 of the 1996 Hague Convention. Whether or not consent is required is a question for the other country. If there is any doubt about whether the consent of the other country will be required a request for co-operation can be made in order to clarify the position.

The ICACU does not require a court order in order to discharge its duties and functions as the operational central authority but it may be helpful if the court directs one party to the proceedings to make the request for co-operation to the ICACU and to do so within a particular time frame. The parties may of course consult with each other as to the content of the request for co-operation.

In public law children cases the ICACU prefers that the local authority (rather than any other party) contact the ICACU about a request for co-operation (or any other request – for example, assistance with an Article 15 transfer request). The ICACU's experience is that a request for co-operation to the other country may be followed by a request from that country about the same child. If the ICACU receives a request from the other country it will transmit it to the local authority and it is administratively more efficient and less likely to give rise to miscommunication if the ICACU is in contact with one party only.

Although the court may request or invite assistance from foreign authorities orders should not be made against foreign authorities including central authorities, consular authorities or other public bodies in another country.

PRESIDENT'S GUIDANCE
26 MARCH 2015

THE ROLE OF THE ATTORNEY GENERAL IN APPOINTING ADVOCATES TO THE COURT OR SPECIAL ADVOCATES IN FAMILY CASES

I have updated guidance first circulated by Mr Justice Holman, when he was Acting President, on 21 November 2012. The roles of Advocate to the Court, and Special Advocate are, of course, quite separate and distinct but each is potentially a burden on the limited public interest funds of the Attorney General.

Advocates to the Court

The Memorandum agreed between Lord Goldsmith and Lord Woolf on 19 December 2001 remains in effect and applies in family as in other cases. It is reproduced in the annual The Family Court Practice. The test or criterion for seeking the assistance of an advocate to the court is at paragraph 3, namely 'when there is a danger of an important and difficult point of law being decided without the court hearing relevant argument'. This requires that the point is both 'important' and 'difficult'. It also requires that there is a danger of the point 'being decided'. This is different and distinct from the point having been decided, but the court being unclear what the decided law is. The Memorandum is very clear, and the Attorney General is clear, that an Advocate to the Court ought not to be requested simply because there are self-represented litigants and the court does not know what the decided law is. We must be very sparing in requests for Advocates to the Court, and ensure that the request does properly fall within the test in the Memorandum.

There may of course be cases (particularly as Litigants in Person are now more common since most private law cases were taken out of scope of Legal Aid in April 2013) in which a judge genuinely perceives that an important and difficult point of law requires to be decided, but he is unaware that the point has already been decided. I have agreed with the Attorney General that in such a case, when responding to the court's request, his office may bring to the court's attention the relevant decided law.

Special Advocates

These are not the subject of the above, or any, Memorandum. Usually a Special Advocate is required because a public body that is party to the litigation, often a local authority or the police, resist disclosure of sensitive documents. The Attorney General has asked that at the point of requesting him to instruct a Special Advocate the court should specifically consider and make provision (after, of course, hearing submissions from the parties) as to which party should pay the costs of the Special Advocate. The essential point is that this is not a service which the Attorney General will normally cover. I can see no reason why he should be expected to do so, and no reason why the court should not

PART III – Practice guidance

fix in advance which party will pay the costs of the Special Advocate. Please, therefore, do this.

It is rare that an Advocate to the Court or Special Advocate is requested by judges below that of the High Court Bench in the Family Court. If these issues arise below the level of the High Court Bench it would be prudent to seek the views of the Family Division Liaison Judge before considering any request.

Sir James Munby
President of the Family Division

PRACTICE DIRECTION
26 MARCH 2015

PRACTICE DIRECTION (COMMITTAL FOR CONTEMPT OF COURT – OPEN COURT) (26 MARCH 2015)

Preamble

1 This Practice Direction applies to all proceedings for committal for contempt of court, including contempt in the face of the court, whether arising under any statutory or inherent jurisdiction and, particularly, supplements the provisions relating to contempt of court in the Civil Procedure Rules 1998, the Family Procedure Rules 2010, the Court of Protection Rules 2007, and the Criminal Procedure Rules 2014 and any related Practice Directions supplementing those various provisions. It applies in all courts in England and Wales, including the Court of Protection, and supersedes the *Practice Guidance: Committal for Contempt* [2013] 1 WLR 1326, dated 3 May 2013; *Practice Guidance (Committal Proceedings: Open Court) (No. 2)* [2013] 1 WLR 1753, dated 4 June 2013; and *President's Circular: Committals* Family Court Practice 2014 at 2976, dated 2 August 2013.

2 Any reference in this Practice Direction to a judgment includes reference to written reasons provided in accordance with rule 27.2 of the Family Procedure Rules 2010.

Open Justice

3 Open justice is a fundamental principle. The general rule is that hearings are carried out in, and judgments and orders are made in, public. This rule applies to all hearings, whether on application or otherwise, for committal for contempt irrespective of the court in which they are heard or of the proceedings in which they arise.

4 Derogations from the general principle can only be justified in exceptional circumstances, when they are strictly necessary as measures to secure the proper administration of justice. Derogations shall, where justified, be no more than strictly necessary to achieve their purpose.

Committal Hearings – in Public

5 (1) All committal hearings, whether on application or otherwise and whether for contempt in the face of the court or any other form of contempt, shall be listed and heard in public.

(2) They shall, except where paragraph 5(3) applies, be listed in the public court list as follows:

> FOR HEARING IN OPEN COURT
> Application by (*full name of applicant*) for
> the Committal to prison of
> (*full name of the person alleged to be in contempt*)

PART III – Practice guidance

(3) In those cases where the person alleged to be in contempt is subject to arrest for an alleged breach of an order, including a location or collection order or an order made under the Family Law Act 1996, the hearing shall be listed in the public court list as follows:

> FOR HEARING IN OPEN COURT [add, where there has been a remand in custody: in accordance with the order of (*name of judge*) dated (*date*)]

> Proceedings for the Committal to prison of
> (*full name of the person alleged to be in contempt*)
> who was arrested on (*date*) in accordance with and for alleged breach
> of a [location/collection/Family Law Act 1996/other] order made by
> (*name of judge*) on (*date*).

6 Where it is not possible to publish the details required by paragraph 5(3) in the public court list in the usual way the day before the hearing i.e., in such circumstances where the alleged contemnor is produced at court by the Tipstaff or a constable on the morning of the hearing, having been arrested over night, the following steps should be taken:

(1) Where, as in the Royal Courts of Justice, the public court list is prepared and accessible in electronic form, it should be updated with the appropriate entry as soon as the court becomes aware that the matter is coming before it;

(2) Notice of the hearing should at the same time be placed outside the door of the court in which the matter is being, or is to be heard, and at whatever central location in the building the various court lists are displayed;

(3) Notice should be given to the national print and broadcast media, via the Press Association's CopyDirect service, of the fact that the hearing is taking or is shortly due to take place.

If an alleged contemnor is produced at court, having been arrested overnight, the person shall immediately be produced before a judge who shall sit in public.

7 Where the committal hearing is brought by way of application notice, the court may authorise any person who is not a party to proceedings to obtain a copy of the application notice, upon request and subject to payment of any appropriate fee. Authorisation shall be granted in all but exceptional circumstances. Where authorisation is refused, the reasons for that refusal shall be set out in writing by the judge and supplied to the person who made the request.

Committal Hearings – in Private

8 Where the court, either on application or otherwise, is considering derogating from the general rule and holding a committal hearing in private, or imposing any other such derogation from the principle of open justice:

(1) it shall in all cases before the hearing takes place, notify the national print and broadcast media, via the Press Association's CopyDirect service, of the fact of the committal hearing (whether it is brought on application or otherwise) when and where it is listed for hearing, and the nature of the proposed derogation; and

(2) at the outset of the committal hearing the court shall hear submissions from the parties and/or the media on the question whether to impose the proposed derogation.

9 In considering the question whether there are exceptional circumstances justifying a derogation from the general rule, and whether that derogation is no more than strictly necessary the fact that the committal hearing is made in the Court of Protection or in any proceedings relating to a child does not of itself justify the matter being heard in private. Moreover the fact that the hearing may involve the disclosure of material which ought not to be published does not of itself justify hearing the application in private if such publication can be restrained by an appropriate order.

10 Where the court decides to exercise its discretion to derogate from the general rule, and particularly where it decides to hold a committal hearing in private, it shall, before it continues to do so, sit in public in order to give a reasoned public judgment setting out why it is doing so.

11 Where, having decided to exercise its discretion to hold a committal hearing in private, the court further decides that the substantive committal application is to be adjourned to a future date, the adjourned hearing shall be listed in the public court list as follows:

FOR HEARING IN PRIVATE
In accordance with the order of (*name of judge*) dated (*date*)
[On the application of (*full name of applicant*)]
Proceedings for the Committal to prison of
(*full name of the person alleged to be in contempt*)

12 Orders directing a committal hearing be heard in private or of other such derogations from the principle of open justice shall not be granted by consent of the parties: see *JIH* v *News Group Newspapers* [2011] EWCA Civ 42, [2011] WLR 1645 at [21].

Judgments

13 (1) In all cases, irrespective of whether the court has conducted the hearing in public or in private, and the court finds that a person has committed a contempt of court, the court shall at the conclusion of that hearing sit in public and state:

(i) the name of that person;

(ii) in general terms the nature of the contempt of court in respect of which the committal order, which for this purpose includes a suspended committal order, is being made;

(iii) the punishment being imposed; and

(iv) provide the details required by (i) to (iii) to the national media, via the CopyDirect service, and to the Judicial Office, at judicialwebupdates@judiciary.gsi.gov.uk, for publication on the website of the Judiciary of England and Wales.

(2) There are no exceptions to these requirements. There are never any circumstances in which any one may be committed to custody or made subject

PART III – Practice guidance

to a suspended committal order without these matters being stated by the court sitting in public.

14 In addition to the requirements at paragraph 13, the court shall, in respect of all committal decisions, also either produce a written judgment setting out its reasons or ensure that any oral judgment is transcribed, such transcription to be ordered the same day as the judgment is given and prepared on an expedited basis. It shall do so irrespective of its practice prior to this Practice Direction coming into force and irrespective of whether or not anyone has requested this.

15 Copies of the written judgment or transcript of judgment shall then be provided to the parties and the national media via the CopyDirect service. Copies shall also be supplied to BAILII and to the Judicial Office at judicialwebupdates@judiciary.gsi.gov.uk for publication on their websites as soon as reasonably practicable.

16 Advocates and the judge (except judges and justices of the peace in the Magistrates' courts) shall be robed for all committal hearings.

This Direction is made by the Lord Chief Justice, following consultation with the Master of the Rolls, President of the Queen's Bench Division, President of the Family Division and of the Court of Protection, and Chancellor of the High Court. It is issued in accordance with the procedure laid down in Part 1 of Schedule 2 to the Constitutional Reform Act 2005.

Lord Thomas LCJ

LITIGATION FRIEND REFERRAL FORM FOR CHILDREN ACT PUBLIC LAW CASES 30 MARCH 2015

Form for solicitors to provide additional information about a protected party, if the Official Solicitor is asked to be a litigation friend (published 30 March 2015; last updated 21 December 2021)

Any referral must be made promptly whenever the Official Solicitor is invited to act as the litigation friend of a protected party (PP) or child. The referral form must be completed by the PP's solicitor or, if none, another legal professional involved in the proceedings (including the local authority).

1. Who are you?

Are you the PP's solicitor?

Yes ☐ No ☐

If you are not the PP's solicitor, who are you and why are you making the referral?

....

2. Court details

Court name, address and email:

....

Case number:

....

Type of proceedings:

....

3. The parties and representatives

Name of PP:	DoB:
PP's solicitor, solicitor's firm, address, telephone number, email and reference:	

You must attach a document with the details of all the parties including their solicitors or give the details below:

Applicant's name:	Name of applicant's solicitor:	Solicitor's firm contact details and reference: ....

PART III – Practice guidance

Respondents' names: .... Name of respondent's solicitor:		Solicitor's firm contact details and reference: ....
Name of child(ren) and DOB:	Name of children's solicitor:	Solicitor's firm contact details and reference: ....
Name of other parties (specify):	Name of other parties' solicitor:	Solicitor's firm contact details and reference: ....

4. The Official Solicitor's criteria for consenting to act as litigation friend:

The acceptance criteria are in the Official Solicitor's 2017 Practice Note: The Official Solicitor to the Senior Courts: Appointment in Family Proceedings and Proceedings under the Inherent Jurisdiction in relation to Adults. The litigation friend checklist must also be completed and sent with the referral. The Practice Note and litigation friend checklist are available on www.gov.uk.

5. Required information and documents

Information and documents required by the Official Solicitor to enable her to discharge her duty as litigation friend:

5(a) Information required:

In all cases you must provide a background summary explaining the local authority's concerns, any precipitating incident(s) which led to the proceedings, what major steps have occurred in the proceedings and what the issues are:

Background summary:

....

5(b) If you represent the PP, you must provide:

- a reading list of what the Official Solicitor's case manager needs to read first by way of introduction to the case and to obtain an overview of the issues from your client's perspective;
- your advice on any assessments already completed - in particular about whether those assessments properly took into account your client's particular's needs;
- your advice about the next steps the Official Solicitor should take as your client's litigation friend, including advice about whether any further assessment or expert opinion should be obtained.

See also 5(c) below.

1. Reading list:

....

2. Your advice (assessments):

....

3. Your advice (next steps):

....

5(c) The client

Please provide a summary of:

Your client's current views and wishes in relation to the proceedings and the matters at issue.

....

The contact your client is having with the child(ren), how that contact is progressing and your client's views in relation to contact. If your client is not having contact, please provide the reasons.

....

Whether any potential alternative carers have been identified for the child(ren) in the event that it is established during the proceedings that the child(ren) cannot be cared for by a parent.

....

5(d) The court timetable

What is the date of the next court hearing? Please also set out the court timetable:

Timetable:

....

Other relevant information (including but not limited to whether one or more of the following is a feature of this case):

- ☐   The client is an intervener not a parent
- ☐   There is a serious medical treatment issue (child or adult)
- ☐   There is a dispute about the child(ren)'s name
- ☐   International element
- ☐   A fact-finding hearing is proposed
- ☐   There is a potential Human Rights Act 1998 claim
- ☐   Concurrent criminal investigation and/or proceedings
- ☐   Non-accidental injury to the child(ren)
- ☐   Court of Protection issues
- ☐   Other

PART III – Practice guidance

Please give details:

Other relevant information:

....

5(e) Required documents:

The referral and litigation friend checklist must be accompanied by each of the following:

Document	Attached
Litigation friend checklist	Yes / No
The order inviting the Official Solicitor to act as litigation friend (a draft approved order if the sealed order is not yet available)	Yes / No
A copy of the letter of instruction to the expert by which an opinion was sought on the PP's capacity to conduct these proceedings	Yes / No
The opinion on PP's capacity to conduct the proceedings (whether a report or the Official Solicitor's capacity certificate)	Yes / No
The attendance note recording your discussion with the client about the capacity evidence (this is to check if the client disputes the opinion as to lack of capacity)	Yes / No
The court bundle (pleadings filed subsequently should be sent to osinformation@ospt.gov.uk until the case is accepted and allocated, following which they are sent to the case manager)	Yes / No
A copy of your client's legal aid certificate (or other document establishing there is security for the costs of legal representation)	Yes / No
A copy of all notes of attendance on your client (personal attendance or telephone): this is to ensure the Official Solicitor is properly informed as to the views and wishes expressed by your client to date.	Yes / No

If any one of the documents listed at (1)–(8) above is not being sent with the referral, please explain why not below:

....

The referral form, litigation friend checklist, bundle and other supporting documents must be emailed to: osinformation@ospt.gov.uk

PRESIDENT'S GUIDANCE
APRIL 2015 (REISSUED 30 JULY 2015)

TAGGING OR ELECTRONIC MONITORING IN FAMILY CASES[1]

Sir James Munby President of the Family Division

1   Annex to *Re X (Children); Re Y (Children)* [2015] EWHC 2265 (Fam).

Occasionally a judge will request a parent or party to the proceedings to be electronically tagged. This is a device that is fitted on the leg and allows the Electronic Monitoring contractor to monitor compliance against a curfew. It is normally referred to as a curfew or tagging order in family proceedings and is only available in High Court matters.

It is usually ordered in children's cases when there is a real risk of one of the parents' abducting the child. These matters clearly need to be dealt with as a PRIORITY and should be processed on day of receipt.

The National Offender Management Service (NOMS) is responsible for the electronic monitoring contract and there is a contract in place with Capita, operating as Electronic Monitoring Services (EMS), who monitors these orders on behalf of agencies. If possible EMS need to be contacted by 15:00hrs to ensure that the tag can be fitted the same day but if they receive the order after this time then they will endeavour to install that same day but they are permitted, under the contract, to install the tag the following day.

This guidance shows you how to deal with such a request once an order has been made.

1. Q: Have family courts the legal power to make such orders?

The judgment of Mrs Justice Parker from March 2009 makes clear that electronic monitoring is available in High Court matters.

2. Q: Is there a specific protocol/contract in place to deal with tagging requests in family proceedings?

Due to the relatively low number of such requests there is not a specific contract in place to provide this service. NOMS have a contract in place with two providers for tagging orders in the criminal courts and we operate within this to get family orders actioned.

3. Q: What are the requirements for the order?

The order or an attachment to the order must contain:

*   Full name of the person to be tagged
*   Date of birth of the person to be tagged.
*   Full address of the place of curfew
*   Date and time which the electronically tagged person agrees to be present at the address to allow the device to be fitted.

PART III – Practice guidance

NOTE: usually the provider will fit the device anytime prior to midnight (22:00 for young people) the day that the curfew is due to start, or the following day.

- A schedule of the times at which the court expects the person to be at home (or any other relevant place), so that the service provider can monitor compliance.
  a)   the start date of the curfew, and if known,
  b)   the end date of the curfew
  c)   the days on which the curfew operates
  d)   the curfew hours each day.

The name and contact details of the relevant officer/ solicitor whom the service provider should report to if there is any breach of the above schedule or if the person appears to have removed, or attempted to remove the tag. NOTE: a named contact must be given – usually the solicitor in the case.

4. Q: Who do I need to contact and by when?

A: Once an order has been made you should contact the service provider directly.

Due the rarity of these orders it is best practice to call the providers initially so they can prepare for the incoming order. EMS can be contacted on 0161 862 1200

Be sure to contact the solicitors in the case, if appropriate, to confirm that the order has been received and has been processed by the provider.

5. Q: What if a tagging order is subsequently extended?

Occasionally, the judge will extend the time of the curfew that is already in place.

REQUIREMENTS:-

- Sealed Order giving further leave to extend the time of the curfew – note any new instructions there may be.
- New schedule, setting out the information as stated above.

Repeat all the actions at point 4.

6. Q: What happens once a curfew has expired?

Unless the provider receives instructions to the contrary once a curfew order has expired the service provider will automatically remove the electronic monitoring device without any further contact from the court.

7. Q: What happens if a curfew is breached?

Depending on the contents of the order the service provider will normally contact the named person on the order to notify them of the breach. This is why it should usually be a solicitor to the case as they will be able to take immediate action. If the named contact is a member of court staff you should notify a member of the judiciary immediately to get further directions.

At annex A there is an example of what a tagging or curfew order may look like

[The annexed form of order is as follows:]

IN THE HIGH COURT OF JUSTICE

FAMILY DIVISION

PRINCIPAL REGISTRY

BEFORE xxxx SITTING IN CHAMBERS AT xxxx ON xxxx.

IN THE MATTER OF xxxx (BORN ON xxxx) (A CHILD)

AND IN THE MATTER OF AN APPLICATION UNDER THE INHERENT JURISDICTION OF THE HIGH COURT

AND IN THE MATTER OF AN APPLICATION UNDER THE SENIOR COURTS ACT 1981

BETWEEN:

xxxx

Applicant

and

xxxx

Respondent

UPON HEARING xxx

BY CONSENT

IT IS ORDERED THAT:

1. EMS is requested to take such steps as are necessary to effect and to continue the electronic tagging of the Respondent xxxx, xxxx (D.O.B. xxxx) in accordance with the schedule of information provided below.

Schedule of information provided for the purposes of effecting and
continuing the electronic tagging of a person

Name and date of birth of person to be electronically tagged	xxxx (D.O.B. xxxx)
Address of the place of curfew	xxxx
Date and time at which the electronically tagged person agrees to be present at the address of the place of curfew for the purposes of the installation of the monitoring device	xxxx
Start date of curfew	xxxx
End date of curfew	xxxx (include time curfew ends)
Days on which curfew is in place	xxxx
Curfew hours	xxxx
Name and contact details of relevant person whom should be contacted if there is a breach of the curfew or if the tag is removed or otherwise interfered with	xxxx

DATED xxxx"

PRACTICE GUIDANCE
24 JUNE 2015

PRACTICE GUIDANCE (COMMITTAL FOR CONTEMPT OF COURT – OPEN COURT) (24 JUNE 2015)

Preamble

1. This Practice Guidance answers various questions which have arisen on the application and interpretation of the Practice Direction: Committal for Contempt-Open Court, dated 26 March 2015 (the Committal PD)

Press Notification – Hearings

2. The Committal PD only requires the press to be notified before a committal hearing in two circumstances:

    (1)   where it is not possible to list the committal hearing in the public court list in the usual way the day before the hearing is to take place, see paragraph 6 of the Committal PD; and

    (2)   where, in advance of a hearing, the court, either on application or of its own initiative, is considering holding the committal hearing in private, see paragraph 8 of the Committal PD.

3. Press notification of a committal hearing is not therefore required in respect of all committal hearings.

Judgments

4. Paragraph 13 of the Committal PD only applies where the court finds that a person has committed a contempt of court and makes either an order for committal or a suspended committal order, see specifically paragraph 13(1)(ii). It does not apply where the court makes any other order having found a person has committed a contempt of court.

5. Where paragraph 13 applies, the following format for providing the required information should be used:

'Pursuant to paragraph 13 of Practice Direction: Committal for Contempt of Court – Open Court

In relation to [*insert case number*] on [*insert date*], at [*insert court*] I, [*insert title and name of judge*] sentence [*insert name of individual subject to the committal or suspended committal order*], to [*an immediate/suspended custodial sentence*] of [*insert term of sentence*] for contempt of court. The basis of that sentence was that [*short, general reasons*].'

6. For the purposes of paragraph 14 of the Committal PD, where it is not the usual practice of a court to give reasoned judgments because, for instance, it is not a court of record, the judgment, should set out the information required by paragraph 13(1)(i) – (iii) of the PD with short, written, reasons why the court

PART III – Practice guidance

arrived at its decision. Annex 1 to this Guidance contains a judgment pro forma for this purpose. This may be of particular assistance in the County Court and Magistrates' courts.

Application to proceedings under CPR r.71 and CCR O.27 and FPR rr.3319, 33.19A and 33.23

7. The Committal PD applies to committal hearings, see paragraph 5(1) of the Committal PD.

8. The Committal PD does not apply to orders made on a written reference to a High Court judge or Circuit judge under the procedure set out in CPR r.71.8(1) and r.71.8(2) and CPR PD71, paragraph 6 and 7. It does not as CPR r.71 provides a process whereby any committal order made on such a written reference must be suspended on terms, amongst other things, that the person subject to the order attend court and is therefore capable of challenge before enforcement: see CPR r. 71.8(3) and r.71.8(4) and *Broomleigh Housing Association Ltd* v *Okonkwo* [2010] EWCA 1113 at [22]. The Committal PD does, as a consequence, apply to any hearing under CPR r.71.8(4)(b)).

9. The Committal PD applies to the attachment of earnings procedure under CCR O.27 r.7 and O.27 r.7A as it does to CPR r.71. It therefore only applies to the adjourned hearing referred to in CCR O.27 r.7B and to any further hearing to deal with a suspended committal order made under that provision.

10. Paragraphs 7–9 apply to FPR rr.33.19, 33.19A and 33.23 in so far as they apply the procedure in CCR O.27 and CPR r.71 to proceedings to which the Family Procedure Rules 2010 apply.

Applications to proceedings under the Policing and Crime Act 2009 and the Anti-Social Behaviour, Crime and Policing Act 2014

11. The Policing and Crime Act 2009 makes provision for civil injunctions to be made in respect of gang-related violence. The Anti-Social Behaviour, Crime and Policing Act 2014 makes provision for civil injunctions to be made in respect of certain types of anti-social behaviour.

12. The Committal PD applies to committal hearings in respect of adults who are alleged to have breached injunctions made under the 2009 Act and the 2014 Act. It does not however apply to hearings arising from alleged breaches of injunctions made under either the 2009 Act or the 2014 Act by individuals under the age of 18 as they are not applications for committal to prison for contempt, but are rather applications for a supervision or detention order under the statutory procedure set out in schedule 5A of the 2009 Act and schedule 2 of the 2014 Act.

13. In certain circumstances section 43 of the 2009 Act and section 9 of 2014 Act may require breach of an injunction to be dealt with by a judge outside the court's normal opening hours, i.e., in the evening, at a weekend or on a bank holiday.

14. Where an 'out of hours' court is open and available, such matters should be listed and heard at that court 'out of hours'. Paragraph 6(3) of the Committal PD applies to such listings.

15. Where no 'out of hours' court is open and available, the judge should consider whether the matter can properly be dealt with, at a location other than an open court, through exercise of the power to remand on bail or in custody, provided under section 43(5) and schedule 5 of the 2009 or section 9(5) and schedule 1 of the 2014 Act. Use of the remand power does not engage the notification requirements of paragraphs 5, 6, 13 or 15 of the Committal PD. Those requirements will be met when the matter comes back before the court as specified below.

16. Where breach of an injunction is dealt with by way of remand on bail, the committal hearing should be listed, in accordance with the provisions of the Committal PD, at the first convenient date when the court is sitting.

17. Where breach of an injunction is dealt with by way of remand in custody, the committal hearing should be listed for hearing, within any applicable statutory time limit and in accordance with the provisions of the Committal PD, in the nearest appropriate court to the place of custody on the first convenient date when the court is sitting.

Review

18. The operation of the Committal PD will be subject to review in October 2015.

Lord Thomas LCJ

Annex 1

IN THE [................] **COURT**   **Case No:**

Sitting at

1. On the ... of ... 201... this court committed the following named person to prison

(2)

2. In relation to an order dated

3. which provided that the Respondent/Defendant should not [set out relevant paras of the order]

i)

ii)

iii)

4. the court found that [following admissions made] (s)he had disobeyed/ breached that order by

i)

ii)

ii)

PART III – Practice guidance

5. and imposed the following sentence(s) for those breach(es)

Breach	Sentence
i)	i)
ii)	ii)
iii)	iii)

6. Accordingly it was ordered that[2]…

> be committed for contempt to Her Majesty's Prison at[3] … for a (total) period of … or until lawfully discharged if sooner, [and that a warrant of arrest and committal be issued forthwith].

OR

> …
> be committed for contempt to prison for a (total) period of …

The order is suspended until …… and will not be put into force if during that time[2] …… complies with the following terms:

i)

ii)

ii)

……

[Insert name and title of judge]

Dated

This form is to be sent to the national media, via the CopyDirect service, and to the Judicial Office, at mailto:judicialwebupdates@judiciary.gsi.gov.uk, for publication on the website of the Judiciary of England and Wales.

PRESIDENT'S GUIDANCE
8 OCTOBER 2015

RADICALISATION CASES IN THE FAMILY COURTS

Guidance issued by Sir James Munby President of the Family Division on 8 October 2015

1 Recent months have seen increasing numbers of children cases coming before the Family Division and the Family Court where there are allegations or suspicions: that children, with their parents or on their own, are planning or attempting or being groomed with a view to travel to parts of Syria controlled by the so-called Islamic State; that children have been or are at risk of being radicalised; or that children have been or at are at risk of being involved in terrorist activities either in this country or abroad.

2 Most of these cases have been brought under the inherent jurisdiction, where the children have been made wards of court. Such cases are necessarily in the High Court. Others have been care cases commenced in the Family Court. Some cases have started out under the inherent jurisdiction but then become care cases.

3 Only a local authority can start care proceedings (see section 31(1) of the Children Act 1989 – the police powers are set out in section 46). However, any person with a proper interest in the welfare of a child can start proceedings under the inherent jurisdiction or apply to make a child a ward of court. Usually, in cases falling within the description in paragraph 1 above, it will be the local authority which starts proceedings under the inherent jurisdiction or applies to make a child a ward of court, and the court would not expect the police (who have other priorities and responsibilities) to do so. There is, however, no reason why in a case where it seems to the police to be necessary to do so, the police should not start such proceedings for the purposes, for example, of making a child a ward of court, obtaining an injunction to prevent the child travelling abroad, obtaining a passport order, or obtaining a Tipstaff location or collection order.

4 Given the complexities of these cases, I have decided that, for the time being at least, all cases falling within the description in paragraph 1 above are to be heard by High Court Judges of the Family Division. For the purpose of this Guidance the expression High Court Judge of the Family Division does not include a judge or other person authorised to sit as a High Court Judge under section 9 of the Senior Courts Act 1981.

5 Where a case falling within the description in paragraph 1 above is issued in the Family Court, or where a case issued in the Family Court becomes a case falling within the description in paragraph 1 above, then:

(a) the Designated Family Judge must be notified immediately;

(b) the Designated Family Judge must immediately notify the Family Division Liaison Judge (who should liaise with the President of the Family Division); and

PART III – Practice guidance

    (c)   urgent steps must be taken, in consultation with the Family Division Liaison Judge, to allocate the case to a High Court Judge of the Family Division.

6 In exceptional circumstances a case falling within the description in paragraph 1 above may be heard by a Designated Family Judge, or a judge authorised to sit as a High Court Judge under section 9 of the Senior Courts Act 1981, but only if this has previously been authorised in relation to that particular case by the President of the Family Division or the Family Division Liaison Judge. Such permission will not normally be given in any case:

    (a)   raising PII issues;

    (b)   requiring a closed hearing or use of a special advocate; or

    (c)   where electronic tagging is proposed.

7 Judges hearing cases falling within the description in paragraph 1 above will wish to be alert to:

    (a)   the need to protect the Article 6 rights of all the parties;

    (b)   the fact that much of the information gathered by the police and other agencies will not be relevant to the issues before the court;

    (c)   the fact that some of the information gathered by the police and other agencies is highly sensitive and such that its disclosure may damage the public interest or even put lives at risk;

    (d)   the need to avoid inappropriately wide or inadequately defined requests for disclosure of information or documents by the police or other agencies;

    (e)   the need to avoid seeking disclosure from the police or other agencies of information or material which may be subject to PII, or the disclosure of which might compromise ongoing investigations, damage the public interest or put lives at risk, unless the judge is satisfied that such disclosure is "necessary to enable the court to resolve the proceedings justly" within the meaning given to those words when used in, for example, sections 32(5) and 38(7A) of the Children Act 1989 and section 13(6) of the Children and Families Act 2014;

    (f)   the need to safeguard the custody of, and in appropriate cases limit access to, any sensitive materials provided to the court by the police or other agencies;

    (g)   the need to consider any PII issues and whether there is a need for a closed hearing or use of a special advocate;

    (h)   the need to safeguard the custody of, and in appropriate cases limit access to, (i) the tape or digital recordings of the proceedings or (ii) any transcripts;

    (i)   the need to ensure that the operational requirements of the police and other agencies are not inadvertently compromised or inhibited either because a child is a ward of court or because of any order made by the court;

    (j)   the assistance that may be gained if the police or other agencies are represented in court, including, in appropriate cases, by suitably expert counsel.

8 Judges hearing cases falling within the description in paragraph 1 above will also wish to consider whether in any particular case there is a need (i) to exclude the media, or (ii) to make a reporting restriction order, or (iii) to make an 'anti-tipping-off' order (for instance when making an order for disclosure against a third party). The media should be excluded only as a last resort and if there is reason to believe that the situation cannot be adequately protected by a reporting restriction order or 'anti-tipping-off' order.

9 Advocates appearing in cases falling within the description in paragraph 1 above need to be alert to and be prepared to argue the issues that may arise, including those referred to in paragraphs 7 and 8 above.

10 I draw attention to what Hayden J has said about "The importance of coordinated strategy, predicated on open and respectful cooperation between all the safeguarding agencies involved" and the need for "open dialogue, appropriate sharing of information, mutual respect for the differing roles involved and inter-agency cooperation" if children in such cases are to be provided with the kind of protection they require.

11 This is a two-way process. The court can expect to continue to receive the assistance it has hitherto been given in these cases by the police and by other agencies. But there must be reciprocity.

12 The police and other agencies recognise the point made by Hayden J that 'n this particular process it is the interest of the individual child that is paramount. This cannot be eclipsed by wider considerations of counter terrorism policy or operations.' The police and other agencies also recognise the point made by Bodey J that 'it is no part of the functions of the Courts to act as investigators, or otherwise, on behalf of prosecuting authorities ... or other public bodies.' But subject to those qualifications, it is important that the family justice system works together in cooperation with the criminal justice system to achieve the proper administration of justice in both jurisdictions, for the interests of the child are not the sole consideration. So the family courts should extend all proper assistance to those involved in the criminal justice system, for example, by disclosing materials from the family court proceedings into the criminal process.

13 In the same way, the police and other agencies will wish to be alert to the need of the court for early access to information, for example, information derived from examination of seized electronic equipment, so far as such information is relevant to the issues in the family proceedings. Accordingly, the court should be careful to identify with as much precision as possible in any order directed to the police or other agencies: the issues which arise in the family proceedings; the types of information it seeks; and the timetable set by the court for the family proceedings.

14 I attach a list in chronological order of relevant judgments which are publicly available on the BAILII website:

Re Y (A Minor: Wardship) [2015] EWHC 2098 (Fam) (17 March 2015 – Hayden J)

Tower Hamlets v M and ors [2015] EWHC 869 (Fam) (27 March 2015 – Hayden J)

Re Y (A Minor: Wardship) [2015] EWHC 2099 (Fam) (23 April 2015 – Hayden J)

Re M (Children) [2015] EWHC 1433 (Fam) (20 May 2015 – Munby P)

Re Z [2015] EWHC 2350 (4 June 2015 – Hayden J)

Re X (Children); Re Y (Children) [2015] EWHC 2265 (Fam) (30 July 2015 – Munby P)

Re X (Children); Re Y (Children) (No 2) [2015] EWHC 2358 (Fam) (04 August 2015 – Munby P)

London Borough of Tower Hamlets v B [2015] EWHC 2491 (21 August 2015 – Hayden J)

15 This Guidance will be reviewed from time to time.

James Munby
President of the Family Division
8 October 2015

PRESIDENT'S GUIDANCE DECEMBER 2016

ALLOCATION OF WORK TO SECTION 9[1] JUDGES

1. Where proceedings are issued in the Family Court but are allocated at the Gatekeeping stage to be heard by a High Court Judge (particularly if they are proceedings described in *Paragraph H of Part 2* of the *Schedule to Public Law Allocation and Gatekeeping Guidance 2013*[2], or *Part 3 of the Schedule to the Allocation and Gatekeeping Guidance – Private Law 2014*[3]), the DFJ must obtain the agreement of the FDLJ (or in a case of urgency from the Urgent Applications Judge of the Family Division, or other Judge of the Family Division) before any hearing in proceedings allocated to High Court level is conducted by a section 9 Judge.

2. Where free-standing proceedings are issued in the Family Division of the High Court on circuit[4], the DFJ must obtain the agreement of the FDLJ (or in a case of urgency from the Urgent Applications Judge of the Family Division, or other Judge of the Family Division) before any hearing in such proceedings is conducted by a section 9 Judge.

3. Where an application is made in the High Court, in the context of and during proceedings which are before the Family Court (e.g. where relief is sought under the inherent jurisdiction ancillary to an application for a public law order before the Family Court), advance authorisation must be sought from the FDLJ (or in a case of urgency from the Urgent Applications Judge of the Family Division, or other Judge of the Family Division) for the High Court application to be heard by the judge (who must be suitably authorised) sitting as a section 9 judge[5].

4. If proceedings are issued in the Family Court but an issue arises as to *transfer* of the proceedings to the High Court, except as provided for in paragraph [5] below, the DFJ shall refer the case to the FDLJ under *rule 29.17(3)/(4) FPR 2010* for decision.

5. A section 9 judge may make a decision to transfer proceedings from the Family Court to the High Court solely for the purpose of making an order under the inherent jurisdiction of the High Court to require a Government Department or agency to disclose an address to the court (*PD29C FPR 2010* at §2).

6. If at any time a judge who is conducting proceedings considers that they should be re-allocated to High Court level for hearing by a High Court Judge or a section 9 judge, the judge shall, before re-allocating the case, discuss the matter with the DFJ, who shall if necessary consult the FDLJ.

7. All orders made by section 9 judges in family proceedings, whether in the Family Court or the High Court, shall specifically state that the order was made by a section 9 judge. The destination for any appeal is affected by the tier of judiciary dealing with the application at first instance.

8. No Tipstaff Orders may be made by a section 9 judge without prior authorisation from the FDLJ (or in a case of urgency from the Urgent Applications Judge of the Family Division, or other Judge of the Family Division).

9. Proceedings under the *Mental Capacity Act 2005* in the Court of Protection shall not be allocated or transferred to a section 9 judge[6] without prior authorisation from the FDLJ (or in a case of urgency from the Urgent Applications Judge of the Family Division, or other Judge of the Family Division).

President of the Family Division

December 2016

NOTES

1 This Guidance refers to 'section 9 Judges' as those appointed under Section 9(1) ('Judge of the High Court') and Section 9(4) ('Deputy Judge of the High Court') of the Senior Courts Act 1981.

2 Public law Guidance: https://www.judiciary.gov.uk/wp-content/uploads/JCO/Documents/family-court-guide/pfd-guidance-on-allocation-and-gatekeeping.pdf, and Public law Schedule, see https://www.judiciary.gov.uk/wp-content/uploads/JCO/Documents/family-court-guide/schedule-to-the-allocation-and-gatekeeping-guidance.pdf

3 Public law Guidance: https://www.judiciary.gov.uk/wp-content/uploads/JCO/Documents/family-court-guide/pfd-guidance-on-allocation-and-gatekeeping.pdf, and Public law Schedule, see https://www.judiciary.gov.uk/wp-content/uploads/JCO/Documents/family-court-guide/schedule-to-the-allocation-and-gatekeeping-guidance.pdf

4 This phrase 'on circuit' means in any court centre in England and Wales other than the Principal Registry of the Family Division, London.

5 This addresses the points considered in RE v North Yorkshire [2015] at §23 and Redcar & Cleveland v B [2013] at §7.

6 Tier 3 Judge: see PD3B CoPR 2007 para.3(viii)

PRACTICE GUIDANCE
18 JANUARY 2017

FAMILY COURT – DURATION OF EX PARTE (WITHOUT NOTICE) ORDERS
18 JANUARY 2017

This Guidance was originally issued on 13 October 2014. This revised Guidance, issued on 18 January 2017, supersedes the previous Guidance.

1 The Magistrates' Association and the National Bench Chairs' Forum have raised with me the question of whether it is proper to grant an ex parte non-molestation injunction for an unlimited period. They suggest that practice varies. They express the view that to grant such an order for an unlimited time is wrong in principle.

2 In expressing that view, the Magistrates' Association and the National Bench Chairs' Forum are entirely correct. To grant an ex parte (without notice) injunction for an unlimited time is wrong in principle. The practice of granting such orders for an unlimited time, if this is still occurring, must stop.

3 Subject only to paragraph 8, the same principles, as set out below, apply to all ex parte (without notice) injunctive orders made by the Family Court or by the Family Division, irrespective of the subject matter of the proceedings or the terms of the order.

4 The law is to be found in *Horgan* v *Horgan* [2002] EWCA Civ 1371, paras 5–6 (Ward LJ), *R (Casey)* v *Restormel Borough Council* [2007] EWHC 2554 (Admin), paras 37–41 (Munby J*), In re C (A Child) (Family Proceedings: Practice)* [2013] EWCA Civ 1412, [2014] 1 WLR 2182, [2014] 1 FLR 1239, para 15 (Ryder LJ) and *Re A (A Child)* [2016] EWCA Civ 572, [2016] 4 WLR 111, paras 49–61, esp paras 59–61 (Munby P).

5 The relevant principles, compliance with which is essential, are as follows:

(i)   An ex parte (without notice) injunctive order must never be made without limit of time. There must be a fixed end date. It is not sufficient merely to specify a return day. The order must specify on its face and in clear terms precisely when it expires (eg, 12 noon on 20 March 2017).

(ii)   The order must also fix a return day. The order must specify the date, time and place of the hearing on the return day. The return day should normally be no more than 14 days after the date when the order was made. How long the hearing on the return day should be listed for must be a matter for the discretion of the judge. However, having regard to paragraph 6, often a very short listing may well be appropriate.

(iii) Careful consideration needs to be given to the duration of any order made ex parte (without notice). Many orders will be of short duration, typically no more than 14 days. But in appropriate cases involving personal protection, such as non-molestation injunctions granted in accordance with Part IV of the Family Law Act 1996, the order itself can be for a longer period, such as 6 or even 12 months, *provided that the order specifies a return day within no more than 14 days*. This must be a matter for the discretion of the judge, but a period longer than 6 months is likely to be appropriate only where the allegation is of long term abuse or where some other good reason is shown. Conversely, a period shorter than 6 months may be appropriate in a case where there appears to be a one-off problem that may subside in weeks rather than months.

(iv)   The order must make it clear that (a) it was made in the absence of the respondent and that the court has considered only the evidence of the applicant and (b) the court has made no finding of fact. Where the evidence is written, it must be identified in the order. Where, exceptionally, the court has received oral or other evidence (eg, a photograph) that evidence should be recorded on the face of the order or reduced to writing and served with the order.

(v)   Where the order has been made in accordance with Part IV of the Family Law Act 1996 it must recite that the court has had regard to sections 45(1) and (2) of the Act.

(vi)   The order (see FPR 18.10(3)) 'must contain a statement of the right to make an application to set aside or vary the order under rule 18.11.' The phrase 'liberty to apply' is not sufficient for this purpose. The order must spell out that the respondent is entitled, without waiting for the return day, to apply to set aside or vary the order.

(vii) If the respondent does apply to set aside or vary the order the court must list the application as a matter of urgency, within a matter of days at most.

6 Experience suggests that in certain types of case, for example, non-molestation or other orders granted in accordance with Part IV of the Family Law Act 1996, the respondent frequently neither applies to set aside or vary the order nor attends the hearing on the return day.

(i)   When, in such cases, there is no attendance by the respondent and the order, having been served, does not require amendment there is no need for re-service. The order made on the return should however record that the respondent, although afforded the opportunity to be heard, has neither attended nor sought to be heard.

(ii)   If, however, variation of the original order is sought by the applicant (eg by extending the ambit or the duration of the order) then:

(a)   Paragraphs 5(i), (iii)-(v) must be complied with in relation to the new order and the new order will need to be served.

(b)   Unless, before the return day, the respondent was given proper notice of the proposed amendments, either in the application or in the initial order, (a) the new order must specify a new return day, and (b) paragraph 5(ii) must be complied with in relation to the new order.

7 I remind all practitioners and judges of the principle, which applies to all ex parte (without notice) injunctive orders made by the Family Court or by the Family Division, irrespective of the subjectmatter of the proceedings or the terms of the order, that a without notice application will normally be appropriate only if:

(a)   there is an emergency or other great urgency, so that it is impossible to give any notice, however short or informal, or

(b)   there is a real risk that, if alerted to what is proposed, if 'tipped off', the respondent will take steps in advance of the hearing to thwart the court's order or otherwise to defeat the ends of justice. In an appropriate case this can justify the grant of a non-molestation injunction without notice, lest the respondent, having been served with an application, further molests his (or her) victim or exerts pressure on her (him) to abandon the proceedings.

8 Nothing in this Guidance derogates from, or otherwise modifies, the principles and safeguards to be observed on an application for an ex parte (without notice) freezing or search order: see *L* v *K* *(Freezing Orders: Principles and Safeguards)* [2013] EWHC 1735 (Fam), [2014] Fam 35.

Sir James Munby
President of the Family Division

PRACTICE NOTE
JANUARY 2017

THE OFFICIAL SOLICITOR TO THE SENIOR COURTS: APPOINTMENT IN FAMILY PROCEEDINGS AND PROCEEDINGS UNDER THE INHERENT JURISDICTION IN RELATION TO ADULTS

Introduction

1. This Practice Note replaces the Practice Note dated March 2013 issued by the Official Solicitor.

2. It concerns:

(a) the appointment of the Official Solicitor as 'litigation friend' of a 'protected party' or child in family proceedings, where the Family Division of the High Court is being invited to exercise its inherent jurisdiction in relation to a vulnerable adult[1] or where proceedings in relation to a child aged 16 or 17 are transferred into the Court of Protection;

(b) requests by the court to the Official Solicitor to conduct *Harbin* v *Masterman*[2] enquiries; and

(c) requests by the court to the Official Solicitor to act as, or appoint counsel to act as, an advocate to the court[3].

The Note is intended to be helpful guidance, but is always subject to legislation including the Rules of Court, to Practice Directions, and to case law.

In this Note 'FPR 2010' means Family Procedure Rules 2010, 'CPR 1998' means Civil Procedure Rules 1998 and 'CoPR 2007' means Court of Protection Rules 2007.

3. For the avoidance of doubt, the Children and Family Court Advisory and Support Service (CAFCASS) has responsibilities in relation to a child in family proceedings in which their welfare is or may be in question (Criminal Justice and Court Services Act 2000, section 12). Since 1 April 2001 the Official Solicitor has not represented a child who is the subject of family proceedings (other than in very exceptional circumstances). In cases of doubt or difficulty, staff of the Official Solicitor's office will liaise with staff of CAFCASS Legal Services to avoid duplication and ensure the most suitable arrangements are made.

Appointment of a litigation friend for a protected party

4. A 'protected party' requires a litigation friend. In family proceedings this requirement appears in Part 15 of the FPR 2010, in proceedings in the Family Division of the High Court of Justice under the court's inherent jurisdiction it appears in Part 21 of the CPR 1998 and in proceedings in the Court of Protection it appears in Part 17 of the CoPR 2007.

5. In family proceedings, a 'protected party' means a party, or an intended party, who lacks capacity (within the meaning of the Mental Capacity Act 2005) to conduct the proceedings: FPR 2010, rule 2.3; and in proceedings under the inherent jurisdiction the expression has the same meaning: CPR 1998, rule 21.2. The following should be noted:

(a)   there must be undisputed evidence the party, or intended party, lacks capacity to conduct the proceedings;

(b)   that evidence, and what flows from the party, or intended party, being a protected party, should have been disclosed to, and carefully explained to, the party or intended party;

(c)   the party, or intended party, is entitled to dispute an opinion that they lack capacity to conduct the proceedings; there may be cases where the party's, or intended party's, capacity to conduct the proceedings is the subject of dispute between competent experts. In either case a formal finding by the court under FPR 2010, rule 2.3, or CPR 1998, rule 21.2 is required.

Vulnerable adult

6. Applications made under the inherent jurisdiction in respect of a 'vulnerable' adult are made to the Family Division of the High Court but are not family proceedings; the CPR 1998 apply to proceedings under the inherent jurisdiction in respect of adults and the application should be made on a Part 8 claim form using the Part 8 alternative procedure.

7. Difficult questions may arise if the 'vulnerable' adult despite having capacity to make the decision or decisions in question nonetheless lacks capacity to conduct the proceedings.

8. A litigation friend is only required if the 'vulnerable' adult does lack capacity to conduct the proceedings and is therefore a protected party as defined in CPR 1998, rule 21.2.

Court of Protection

9. The Court of Protection was established by section 45 Mental Capacity Act 2005. Court of Protection proceedings are not family proceedings. 'P' in Court of Protection proceedings is any person (other than a protected party) who lacks or, so far as consistent with the context, is alleged to lack capacity to make a decision or decisions in relation to any matter that is the subject of an application to the Court of Protection (CoPR 2007, rule 6).

10. A 'protected party' is a party or an intended party (other than P or a child) who lacks capacity to conduct the proceedings (CoPR 2007, rule 6).

Children who require a litigation friend in proceedings

11. Non-subject child: a child who is not the subject of family proceedings may nevertheless be a party and subject to FPR 2010 rule 16.6 (see paragraph 7), requires a litigation friend in family proceedings. The most common examples are:

PART III – Practice guidance

(a)   a child who is also the parent of a child, and who is a respondent to a Children Act 1989 or Adoption and Children Act 2002 application;

(b)   a child who wishes to make an application for a Children Act 1989 order naming another child (typically a child arrangements order for contact with a sibling);

(c)   a child who has been joined as an intervener in a public law children case to respond to allegations;

(d)   a child intervenor in financial remedy proceedings;

(e)   a child party to applications for declarations of status under Part III Family Law Act 1986 other than section 55A applications;

(f)   a child applicant for, or respondent to, an application for an order under Part IV (Family Homes and Domestic Violence) or Part 4A (Forced Marriage) of the Family Law Act 1996;

12. Child parties to applications for declarations of parentage under section 55A Family Law Act 1986: subject to FPR 2010 rule 16.6, in section 55A cases

(a)   any child whose parentage is in dispute and who has been joined as party under FPR 2010 rule 16.2 would have a children's guardian appointed under rule 16.4;

(b)   a child party whose parentage is not in dispute requires a litigation friend.

13. FPR 2010 Part 16 makes provision for the representation of children.

(a)   Rule 16.6 sets out the circumstances in which a child does not need a children's guardian or litigation friend. A child party to proceedings under the Children Act 1989, section 55A Family Law Act 1986, Part 4A Family Law Act 1996, applications in adoption, placement and related proceedings, or proceedings relating to the exercise of the court's inherent jurisdiction with respect to children, may rely on the provisions of rule 16.6.

(b)   However this rule does not apply to those children who are the subject of and party to specified proceedings or proceedings to which Part 14 applies.

14. Children aged 16–17 years: the Mental Capacity Act 2005 (Transfer of Proceedings) Order 2007 (SI 2007/1899) makes provision for the transfer of proceedings from the Court of Protection to a court having jurisdiction under the Children Act 1989. The Order also makes provision for the transfer of the whole or part of the proceedings from a court having jurisdiction under the Children Act 1989 to the Court of Protection where it considers that in all circumstances, it is just and convenient to transfer the proceedings:

(a)   Article 3(3) of the Order lists those factors to which the court must have regard when making a determination about transfer to the Court of Protection either on an application or of its own initiative;

(b)   proceedings transferred under Article 3 are to be treated for all purposes as if they were proceedings under the Mental Capacity Act 2005 which had been started in the Court of Protection;

(c) as Court of Protection proceedings are not family proceedings transfer of proceedings into the Court of Protection means any involvement by CAFCASS in those proceedings will end;

(d) there should be reason to believe that the child lacks capacity (within the meaning of the Mental Capacity Act 2005) in relation to a matter or matters concerning their own welfare and that it is likely that they will still lack capacity to make decisions in respect of that matter when they reach 18.

15. Rules 141(4)–(5) of the CoPR 2007 make provision for a child to be permitted to conduct proceedings in the Court of Protection without a litigation friend. However if the child is 'P' within the meaning of rule 6 of the CoPR 2007 reference should be made to rule 141(1) and rule 147 of those Rules in relation to the appointment of a litigation friend.

The role of a litigation friend

16. The case law and the Rules provide that a litigation friend must fairly and competently conduct the proceedings in the protected party's or child's best interests[4], and must have no interest in the proceedings adverse to that of the protected party or child. The procedure and basis for the appointment of a litigation friend and the duty of a litigation friend are contained in Part 15 (Representation of Protected Parties) FPR 2010 and Part 16 (Representation of Children and Reports in Proceedings Involving Children) FPR 2010 and the associated Practice Directions.

The Official Solicitor's criteria for consenting to act as litigation friend

17. The Official Solicitor is the litigation friend of last resort. No person, including the Official Solicitor, can be appointed to act as litigation friend without their consent. The Official Solicitor will not accept appointment where there is another person who is suitable and willing to act as litigation friend. The Official Solicitor's criteria for consenting to act as litigation friend are:

(a) in the case of an adult that the party or intended party is a protected party[5];

(b) there is security for the costs of legal representation of the protected party which the Official Solicitor considers satisfactory. Sources of security may be:

  (i) the Legal Aid Agency where the protected party or child is eligible for legal aid;

  (ii) the protected party's or child's own funds where they have financial capacity or where they do not where the Court of Protection has given him authority to recover the costs from the adult's or child's funds;

  (iii) an undertaking from another party to pay his costs;

(c) the case is a last resort case.

Invitations to the Official Solicitor: new cases

18. Solicitors who have been consulted by a child or a protected party (or by someone acting on their behalf, or concerned about their interests) should write

to the Official Solicitor setting out the background to the proposed case and explaining the basis on which the Official Solicitor's criteria for acting are met.

Invitations to the Official Solicitor: pending proceedings

19. Where a case is already before the court, an order inviting the Official Solicitor to act should be expressed as being made subject to his consent. The Official Solicitor cannot consent to act unless and until he is satisfied that his criteria are met.

20. If so satisfied, he will allocate public law children cases to a case manager within 2 working days of his criteria being met; all other cases will be allocated within 5 working days. The position in relation to allocation may be subject to change from time to time

Public law children cases

21. Allocation to a case manager does not preclude the need for the case manager to be given sufficient time to become familiar with the facts of, and issues in the case before the Official Solicitor, as litigation friend of the protected party or child, is able to give instructions. The case manager will have existing cases and must make decisions about priorities. Allocation to a case manager in close proximity to a hearing may require that the hearing be re-listed.

22. To enable the Official Solicitor promptly to consider the invitation to him to act, he should be sent as soon as possible the completed referral form for public law children cases (available at www.gov.uk[6]) and the documents that form refers to.

All other cases

23. In all other cases the Official Solicitor should be provided with the following as soon as possible:

   (a)   the sealed court order inviting him to act as litigation friend (with a note of the reasons approved by the Judge if appropriate);
   (b)   (adult party):
         (i)   a copy of the letter of instruction to the expert by which an opinion was sought as to the party's capacity to conduct the proceedings;
         (ii)   the opinion on capacity (the Official Solicitor's pro forma certificate of capacity to conduct proceedings may be requested from his office for the purpose of obtaining an opinion and is available on www.gov.uk[7]);
   (c)   a full explanation as to how the costs of legal representation are to be paid (including any relevant supporting documents) – it is a matter for the Official Solicitor whether the proposed security for costs is satisfactory;
   (d)   confirmation that there is no other person suitable and willing to act as litigation friend (including enquiries made about this);
   (e)   the court file (provision of the court file may not be necessary if the court directs a party to provide a full indexed copy of the bundle to the Official Solicitor on a timely basis).

Litigants in person

24. If one or more of the parties is or are litigants in person, and there is reason to believe that a litigant in person may lack capacity to conduct the proceedings, the court will need to consider, and if necessary give directions as to:

(a) who is to arrange for assessment of their capacity to conduct the proceedings;

(b) how the cost of that assessment is to be funded;

(c) how any invitation to act as litigation friend is to be made either to any suitable and willing person or to the Official Solicitor so as to provide the proposed litigation friend with the documents and relevant information (including information to enable enquiries necessary to establish whether or not funding for legal costs is available);

(d) any resulting timetabling: where the Official Solicitor is being invited to be litigation friend regard should be had to the Official Solicitor's need to investigate whether his acceptance criteria are met including the possibility that an application to the Court of Protection (for authority to pay the costs out of the protected party's or child's funds) may be necessary.

25. The Official Solicitor will notify the court in the event he expects a delay in accepting appointment either because it is not evident that his criteria are met or for any other reason. The court may wish to consider:

(a) making enquiries of the parties as to the steps being taken by them to establish that the Official Solicitor's criteria for acting are met;

(b) whether directions should be made to ensure that the parties progress such enquiries on a timely basis;

(c) fixing a further directions appointment.

26. If, at any time, another litigation friend is appointed before the Official Solicitor is in a position to accept the invitation to him to act, the Official Solicitor should be notified without delay.

Where the Official Solicitor has accepted appointment as litigation friend

27. Once the Official Solicitor is able to accept appointment as litigation friend he will need time to prepare the case on behalf of the protected party or child and may wish to make submissions about any substantive hearing date.

28. In all cases to avoid unnecessary delay in progression of the case, he requires from the solicitors he appoints for the protected party or child:

(a) a reading list identifying the material documents;

(b) identification of the issues including those which require consideration on behalf of the protected party or child;

(c) a summary of the background to, and major steps in the proceedings;

(d) advice as to the steps the Official Solicitor, as litigation friend, should now take in the proceedings on behalf of the protected party or child;

PART III – Practice guidance

(e)   copies of all notes of attendance on the protected party or child (so that the Official Solicitor is properly informed as to the views and wishes expressed by the protected party or child to date);

(f)   confirmation of the protected party's or child's ascertainable present views and wishes in relation to the proceedings.

Advising the court: *Harbin* v *Masterman* enquiries and Advocate to the Court

29. Where the Official Solicitor is invited, with his consent, to conduct enquiries under Harbin v Masterman and it appears to the Official Solicitor that any public body wishes to seek the assistance of the court but is unwilling to carry out the enquiries itself, the Official Solicitor may seek an undertaking from that public body to indemnify him in respect of his costs of carrying out those enquiries.

30. The Official Solicitor may be invited by the court to act or instruct counsel as a friend of the court (advocate to the court) if it appears to the court that such an invitation is more appropriately addressed to him rather than (or in addition to) CAFCASS Legal Services or to the Attorney-General. It is a matter for him whether he accepts that invitation.

Contacting the Official Solicitor

31. It may be helpful to discuss the question of appointment with the Official Solicitor or one of his staff by telephoning 020 3681 2755 (General enquiries: public law family cases) 020 3681 2754 (General enquiries: private law family cases including divorce), or 020 3681 2751 (General enquiries: Court of Protection healthcare & welfare). In particular:

(a)   if in doubt about whether the Official Solicitor's acceptance criteria are met, or

(b)   to request a copy of the Official Solicitor's pro forma certificate of capacity to conduct proceedings and guidance notes[8].

32. Enquiries about the appointment of the Official Solicitor as litigation friend in family proceedings should be addressed:

(a)   (in private law family cases) to the Team Leader, Family Litigation (Private Law);

(b)   (in public law family cases) to the Team Leader, Family Litigation (Public Law).

All other enquiries should be addressed to a family lawyer.

The contact details are:

Office of the Official Solicitor to the Senior Courts
Victory House
30–34 Kingsway
London WC2B 6EX

DX 141423 Bloomsbury 7
Fax: 020 3681 2762
E-mail: enquiries@offsol.gsi.gov.uk

Alastair Pitblado, Official Solicitor
January 2017

https://www.gov.uk/government/organisations/official-solicitor-and-public-trustee

NOTES

1   In this context a 'vulnerable adult' is a person who has mental capacity in respect of the decisions in question but who lacks litigation capacity.
2   [1896] 1 Ch 351.
3   See the Attorney-General's Memorandum of 19 December 2001: 'Requests for the appointment of an advocate to the court'.[2002] Fam Law 229
4   Sir Robert Megarry V-C said in Re E (mental health patient) [1984] 1 All ER 309 at pages 312–3 'The main function of a [litigation] friend appears to be to carry on the litigation on behalf of the plaintiff and in his best interests. For this purpose the [litigation] friend must make all the decisions that the plaintiff would have made, had he been able… the [litigation] friend … is responsible to the court for the propriety and the progress of the proceedings. The [litigation] friend does not, however, become a litigant himself…'
5   The Official Solicitor is able to provide a pro forma certificate of capacity to conduct proceedings and guidance notes. The pro forma is also available on www.gov.uk.
6   https://www.gov.uk/government/publications/official-solicitor-referral-form-for-children-act-public-law-proceedings
7   https://www.gov.uk/government/publications/certificate-as-to-capacity-to-conduct-proceedings
8   Also available online by navigating from: https://www.gov.uk/government/organisations/official-solicitor-and-public-trustee

PRESIDENT'S GUIDANCE
28 FEBRUARY 2018

JURISDICTION OF THE FAMILY COURT: ALLOCATION OF CASES WITHIN THE FAMILY COURT TO HIGH COURT JUDGE LEVEL AND TRANSFER OF CASES FROM THE FAMILY COURT TO THE HIGH COURT

1 There remains considerable confusion concerning the extent and exercise of the power by judges sitting in the family court to transfer a case, or part of a case, to the High Court.

2 A transfer of a case to the High Court to be heard by a judge of that court is not the same thing as an allocation of a case within the family court to a judge of High Court judge level. This is a crucial distinction which still too often appears to be overlooked.

3 This confusion derives in significant part from the complexity of the legislative framework governing the family court. This Guidance seeks to clarify the position. It deals in turn with six topics:

1   The family court and its relationship with the High Court.
2   The jurisdiction of the family court.
3   The allocation of matters as between the family court and the High Court.
4   The allocation of matters within the family court.
5   The transfer of matters from the family court to the High Court.
6   Transfer: general principles.

The family court and its relationship with the High Court

4 The High Court, of which the Family Division is part, is a superior court of record. It has unlimited jurisdiction. The family court, in contrast, is a creature of statute, with its jurisdiction defined by statute. The jurisdiction of the family court, although very extensive, is not unlimited.

5 The family court was created on 22 April 2014 by section 17(3) of the Crime and Courts Act 2013 (the 2013 Act), which, together with Part 1 of Schedule 10, inserted a new Part 4A, sections 31A–31P, in the Matrimonial and Family Proceedings Act 1984 (the 1984 Act).

6 The composition of the family court and those who are entitled to sit as judges of the family court are defined in the Family Court (Composition and Distribution of Business) Rules 2014, SI 2014/840. The puisne judges of the Family Division, the President of the Family Division, and section 9 judges sit in the family court as what are referred to as "judges of High Court level": see rules 2(1) and 3(1)(a)(iii) of the 2014 rules.

7 Because puisne judges of the Family Division, the President of the Family Division, and section 9 judges can, and do, sit both in the Family Division and in the family court, it is important always to be clear as to whether, in a particular

case, they are sitting in the Family Division or in the family court. However, just as a judge can, when appropriate, sit simultaneously in both the Family Division and the Court of Protection, there is nothing to prevent a judge, when appropriate, sitting simultaneously in both the Family Division and the family court.

8 The family court is a single court with power to sit and conduct business at any place in England and Wales: section 31B(1) of the 1984 Act. It is therefore a solecism to refer to "the Barchester Family Court" or to head orders "In the Barchester Family Court." The correct heading is "In the Family Court sitting at Barchester."

9 It is particularly important, when a case is being heard by a judge of High Court level, that the order should accurately record whether the judge is sitting in the High Court or in the family court. If the judge is sitting in the family court, the order must be headed "In the Family Court sitting at ..." and not "In the High Court of Justice Family Division." This is so whether the judge is sitting in the Royal Courts of Justice or anywhere else. Accordingly, when the judge is sitting in the Royal Courts of Justice, but in the family court rather than the High Court, the order must be headed "In the Family Court sitting at the Royal Courts of Justice." In the same way, it is important to ensure that the correct form of neutral citation number is used. When a judge of High Court level is sitting in the Family Division, the correct form of neutral citation number is [2018] EWHC xxx (Fam); when a judge of High Court level is sitting in the family court, the correct form of neutral citation number is [2018] EWFC xx.

The jurisdiction of the family court

10 The jurisdiction of the family court is defined by section 31A(1) of the 1984 Act, which provides that the family court has:

"the jurisdiction and powers conferred on it –

(a) by or under this or any other Act, or

(b) by or under any Act, or Measure, of the National Assembly for Wales."

11 This was implemented by the amendment, in accordance with Part 1 of Schedule 11 of the 2013 Act, headed "Transfer of jurisdiction to family court", of a long list of statutes, starting with the Married Women's Property Act 1882 and ending with the Children and Families (Wales) Measure 2010. These amendments provided, in particular, for the substitution of references to the family court for the previous references to the county court. Thus, for example, the definition in section 52(1) of the Matrimonial Causes Act 1973 of the words "the court" for the purposes of that Act was amended by paragraph 65 of Schedule 11 to read "the High Court or the family court" in place of the previous wording "the High Court or, where a county court has jurisdiction by virtue of the Matrimonial Causes Act 1967, a county court."

12 The Crime and Courts Act 2013 (Family Court: Transitional and Saving Provision) Order 2014, SI 2014/956, provides that:

"2. In this Order –

...

(a)   "original court" means any court exercising transferred jurisdiction before the transfer day;

(b)   "transfer day" means 22nd April 2014;

(c)   "transferred jurisdiction" means any jurisdiction that is transferred to or conferred on the family court by virtue of the 2013 Act; and

(d)   "transferred proceedings" means proceedings which were issued before the transfer day in the original court under transferred jurisdiction.

3(1) On and after the transfer day, transferred proceedings are continued in the family court as if they had been issued in that court."

The effect of this is that all existing proceedings which were now within the jurisdiction of the family court were automatically transferred to the family court on 22 April 2014 and thereafter continued as if they had been issued in the family court. This applied not merely to proceedings commenced before 22 April 2014 in the family proceedings court or the county court but also to proceedings commenced before that date in the High Court: see *Rapisarda v Colladon* [2014] EWFC 1406, [2015] 1 FLR 584, para 2. Thus, for example, a variation application in relation to a periodical payments order made in the High Court before 22 April 2014 must be issued and heard in the family court.

13 Although the list of statutes amended by Schedule 11 is lengthy, it is not all-embracing. There are important statutes which were not amended in this way and where, in consequence, the family court does not have jurisdiction: these include the Inheritance (Provision for Family and Dependants) Act 1975, the Child Abduction and Custody Act 1985 and the Trusts of Land and Appointment of Trustees Act 1996.

14 Part A of the Schedule to this Guidance lists those matters which are not within the jurisdiction of the family court: see paragraph H of column 2 of the schedule to President's Guidance of 22 April 2014, Allocation and Gatekeeping for Care, Supervision and other Proceedings under Part IV of the Children Act 1989 (Public Law) and Part 3 of the schedule to President's Guidance of 22 April 2014, Allocation and Gatekeeping for Proceedings under Part II of the Children Act 1989 (Private Law).

15 Section 31E(1)(a) of the 1984 Act provides that "In any proceedings in the family court, the court may make any order ... which could be made by the High Court if the proceedings were in the High Court." This does not permit the family court to exercise original or substantive jurisdiction in respect of those exceptional matters, including applications under the inherent jurisdiction of the High Court, that must be commenced and heard in the High Court. It does, however, permit the use of the High Court's inherent jurisdiction to make incidental or supplemental orders to give effect to decisions within the jurisdiction of the family court. Thus, for example, the family court can:

(a)   issue a bench warrant to secure the attendance of a judgment creditor at an enforcement hearing: see *Re K (Remo: Power of Magistrates to issue Bench Warrant)* [2017] EWFC 27); and

(b)   require a party to use his or her best endeavours to procure the release of the other party from mortgage covenants: see *CH v WH* [2017] EWHC 2379 (Fam).

The allocation of matters as between the family court and the High Court

16 Rule 5.4 of the Family Procedure Rules 2010 provides as follows:

"(1)   Where both the family court and the High Court have jurisdiction to deal with a matter, the proceedings relating to that matter must be started in the family court.

(2)   Paragraph (1) does not apply where –

(a)   proceedings relating to the same parties are already being heard in the High Court;

(b)   any rule, other enactment or Practice Direction provides otherwise; or

(c)   the court otherwise directs."

Paragraph (1) accordingly does not apply where President's Guidance of 22 April 2014, Allocation and Gatekeeping for Care, Supervision and other Proceedings under Part IV of the Children Act 1989 (Public Law) and President's Guidance of 22 April 2014, Allocation and Gatekeeping for Proceedings under Part II of the Children Act 1989 (Private Law), both of which were issued in accordance with rule 21 of the Family Court (Composition and Distribution of Business) Rules 2014, SI 2014/840, provide otherwise.

17 The following matters **must** be commenced in the Family Division of the High Court rather than in the family court:

(a)   The matters listed in Part A of the Schedule to this Guidance: matters in respect of which the family court does not have jurisdiction and which therefore **must** be commenced in the Family Division.

(b)   The matters listed in Part B of the Schedule to this Guidance **must** be commenced in the Family Division even though the family court has jurisdiction but may at any time be transferred by the High Court to the family court in accordance with section 38 of the 1984 Act.

18 Except as specified in the Schedule to this Guidance every family matter **must** be commenced in the family court and **not** in the High Court. Where a family matter (for example an application under Part III of the 1984 Act) has been commenced in the High Court in circumstances other than those specified in the Schedule to this Guidance, the matter will ordinarily be immediately transferred by the High Court to the family court in accordance with section 38 of the 1984 Act.

19 Where a matter listed in either Part A or Part B of the Schedule to this Guidance has been received in the family court:

(a)   The matter must immediately be transferred by the family court to the Family Division: see paragraph 27 of President's Guidance of 22 April 2014, Allocation and Gatekeeping for Proceedings under Part II of the Children Act 1989 (Private Law).

(b)   Failing such transfer, the matter will be transferred by order of the Family Division in accordance with section 31I of the 1984 Act.

The allocation of matters within the family court

20 The allocation of cases within the family court is regulated by the Family Court (Composition and Distribution of Business) Rules 2014, SI 2014/840, by President's Guidance of 22 April 2014, Allocation and Gatekeeping for Care, Supervision and other Proceedings under Part IV of the Children Act 1989 (Public Law), and by President's Guidance of 22 April 2014, Allocation and Gatekeeping for Proceedings under Part II of the Children Act 1989 (Private Law).

21 These give full power to allocate a case of complexity for hearing in the family court by a "judge of High Court level" or, if appropriate, a judge of the Family Division.

22 In the family court, the following remedies must be heard by a judge of High Court level: an application for a search order; a claim in respect of a judicial act under the Human Rights Act 1998[1]; an action in respect of the interference with the due administration of justice; an application for a warrant of sequestration; and an application under Article 13 of the Protection Measures Regulation in relation to an incoming protection measure: see the Family Court (Composition and Distribution of Business) Rules 2014, Schedule 2, Table 3.

23 In financial remedy cases, the allocation criteria are set out in the Statement dated 1 February 2016 on the Efficient Conduct of Financial Remedy Hearings Allocated to a High Court Judge Whether Sitting at the Royal Courts of Justice or Elsewhere.

24 When a freezing order is sought, the application should always be heard in the family court, normally at District Judge level, but may be allocated to a judge of High Court level by reference to the criteria in the Statement, applied by analogy: see *Tobias v Tobias* [2017] EWFC 46.

25 Although rule 15(1) and Schedule 1 para 4(a) of the Family Court (Composition and Distribution of Business) Rules 2014 state that proceedings under Part III of the 1984 Act, sections 12 and 13 (both permission and substantive applications) should normally be allocated to a judge of High Court level, rule 15(2) provides that this principle is "subject to the need to take into account the need to make the most effective and efficient use of local judicial resource and the resource of the High Court bench that is appropriate given the nature and type of the application." Unless such a case has some special feature, or complexity, or very substantial assets, it should be allocated to a district judge for the permission decision, as well as substantively: see *Barnett v Barnett* [2014] EWHC 2678 (Fam).

The transfer of matters from the family court to the High Court

26 The powers to transfer cases from the family court to the Family Division which are conferred by sections 31I and 38 of the 1984 Act are exercisable only by the Family Division and not by the family court. Section 39 of the 1984 Act confers jurisdiction on the family court to transfer cases to the High Court. The exercise of this power is, however, subject to the stringent limitations imposed by rules 29.17(3) and (4) of the Family Procedure Rules 2010, which provide as follows:

"(3) A case may not be transferred from the family court to the High Court unless –

    (a) the decision to transfer was made by a judge sitting in the family court who is a person to whom paragraph (4) applies; or

    (b) one or more of the circumstances specified in Practice Direction 29C applies.

(4) This paragraph applies to a person who is –

    (a) the President of the Family Division;

    (b) an ordinary judge of the Court of Appeal (including the vice-president, if any, of either division of that court);

    (c) a puisne judge of the High Court."

The expression "a puisne judge of the High Court" does not include a section 9 judge. PD 29C provides as follows:

"1.1 Rule 29.17(3)(b) FPR provides that a judge other than one to whom rule 29.17(4) applies may make a decision to transfer proceedings from the family court to the High Court where the circumstances specified in this Practice Direction apply.

1.2 The circumstances are that the proceedings are to be transferred solely for the purpose of making an order under the inherent jurisdiction of the High Court to require a Government Department or agency to disclose an address to the court."

27 The effect of this is that:

    (a) The only circumstances in which a District judge, a Circuit Judge or a Recorder (even if sitting under section 9) can transfer a case from the family court to the High Court are those specified in paragraph 1.2 of PD 29C (which, in practice, applies only in cases where disclosure is required from HM Revenue and Customs).

    (b) A transfer in accordance with paragraph 1.1 of PD 29C is temporary, being "solely" for the purpose of making the disclosure order. As soon as the order has been made the matter should be re-transferred back to the family court.

28 There are still far too many instances in which, despite the plain and peremptory language of FPR rules 29.17(3) and (4) and of PD 27C, cases are being purportedly transferred from the family court to the High Court by judges other than those authorised to do so under FPR 29.17(4). Such 'transfers' are doubly wrong: (i) the 'transfer' is made without jurisdiction and, in any event (ii) there is almost always no justification for transferring the case to the High Court rather than re-allocating it for hearing in the family court by a "judge of High Court level" or, if appropriate, a judge of the Family Division.

29 In *Re T (A Child)* [2017] EWCA Civ 1889, a section 9 judge had purported to transfer a case to the High Court in order to make, pursuant to the inherent jurisdiction, a geographic exclusion order so as to prevent the natural mother from subverting a care order. That purported transfer was beyond his powers. There was, in any event, no need to transfer the case to the High Court, for it was

within his power, as a judge of the family court, to make that supplemental order pursuant to section 31E of the 1984 Act.

Transfer: general principles

30 It is very important for the family court, which has now been in existence for nearly four years, to gain the respect it deserves as the sole, specialist, court to deal with virtually all family litigation. Except as specified in the Schedule to this Guidance, cases should only need to be heard in the High Court in very limited and exceptional circumstances.

(a) There is no justification for transferring a case from the family court to the High Court merely because it requires to be heard by a judge of the Family Division. The proper course is to re-allocate the case for hearing in the family court by a "judge of High Court level" or, if appropriate, a judge of the Family Division.

(b) There is no justification for transferring a case from the family court to the High Court merely because it is linked with proceedings which are properly in the High Court. The proper course (see paragraph 7 above) is to re-allocate the case for hearing in the family court by a "judge of High Court level" or, if appropriate, a judge of the Family Division, and to ensure that that judge sits simultaneously both in the Family Division and in the family court to hear both sets of proceedings.

(c) There is no justification for transferring a case from the family court to the High Court merely because of some perceived complexity or difficulty. The proper course is to re-allocate the case for hearing in the family court by a "judge of High Court level" or, if appropriate, a judge of the Family Division. It is, for example, virtually impossible to conceive of a divorce or financial remedy case which needs to be transferred from the family court to the High Court.

31 Where a case has been properly commenced in or transferred to the High Court and the substantive decision has been made it is important that any remaining, residual, issues are transferred at the soonest opportunity to the family court, and usually at District or Circuit Judge level, unless there remain exceptional features that justify the case staying in the High Court. Thus, for example, where a case has been commenced in the High Court to obtain a location order, pursuant to the inherent jurisdiction, in respect of a missing child, and where the child has later been found, it will almost certainly not be necessary for the case to remain in the High Court.

The Schedule

Part A : family court does not have jurisdiction; must be commenced in the Family Division	
1	Inherent jurisdiction of the court relating to children (including applications for interim relief and injunctions invoking the inherent jurisdiction of the court and applications to make a child a ward of court or to bring such an order to an end)
2	Cases in which a Tipstaff Order is applied for

3	Applications for Declaratory Relief (other than under Part III of the Family Law Act 1986)	
4	Declarations of incompatibility under the Human Rights Act 1998	
5	Proceedings under the Inheritance (Provision for Family and Dependants) Act 1975	Note
6	Proceedings under the Trusts of Land and Appointment of Trustees Act 1996	Note
7	Proceedings under the Child Abduction and Custody Act 1985 (including under Part II)	
8	Adoptions with a foreign element involving:	
	(a) an issue concerning placement for adoption of the child outside the jurisdiction,	
	(b) application for direction that section 67(3) of the Adoption and Children Act 2002 (status conferred by adoption) does not apply,	
	(c) parental responsibility order prior to adoption abroad (Adoption and Children Act 2002, section 84(1)), or	
	(d) application for annulment of overseas or Convention adoption under Adoption and Children Act 2002, section 89	
9	Registration of:	
	(a) foreign judgments under Part 1 of the Foreign Judgments (Reciprocal Enforcement) Act 1920;	
	(b) judgments given in a different part of the UK under Part 2 of the Civil Jurisdiction and Judgments Act 1982;	
	(c) Part 1 orders made in a court in another part of the UK under the Family Law Act 1986 section 32(1)	
10	Applications under Part 31 of the FPR (registration of orders under the 2201/2003 Council Regulation, the 1996 Hague Convention and the Civil Partnership (Jurisdiction and Recognition of Judgments) Regulations 2005).	
11	Applications under Article 16 of the 1996 Hague Convention for a declaration as to the extent or existence of parental responsibility.	
12	Applications under Article 15 of the 2201/2003 Council Regulation and Articles 8 and 9 of the 1996 Hague Convention (request for transfer of jurisdiction) but only when required by FPR 2010 12.61-12.66 to be made to the High Court	
13	Issuance of letter of request for person to be examined out of the jurisdiction	
Part B : family court has jurisdiction but must be commenced in the Family Division		
14	Cases which require the jurisdiction of the Administrative Court to be invoked	

PART III – Practice guidance

15	Radicalisation cases within the meaning of President's Guidance, Radicalisation cases in the family courts, dated 8 October 2015	
16	Issues as to publicity (identification of a child or restriction on publication or injunctions seeking to restrict the freedom of the media) where this is the principal relief sought	
17	Applications in medical treatment cases e.g. for novel medical treatment or lifesaving procedures	
18	Public law cases in which an application is made for	
	(a) permanent placement or	
	(b) temporary removal from the jurisdiction to a non-Hague convention country	
19	Proceedings with an international element relating to recognition or enforcement of orders, conflict or comity of laws which have exceptional immigration/asylum status issues	
20	Public law cases in which:	
	(a) a child has been brought to this jurisdiction in circumstances which might constitute a wrongful removal or retention either from a EC Member State, a Hague Convention country (a contracting State to the 1980 Hague Child Abduction Convention and/or a contracting State to the 1996 Hague Child Protection Convention) or a non-Convention country, or	
	(b) a child is alleged to have been abducted overseas and applications have been made in this jurisdiction such as for a declaration that the child was habitually resident in this country prior to the abduction or for an order that the child be returned with a request for assistance etc	

Note: These cases can also be commenced in the county court

Sir James Munby,
President of the Family Division
28 February 2018

NOTE

1   A claim in respect of a judicial act by a High Court Judge may only be heard in the Court of Appeal: *Mazhar v The Lord Chancellor* [2017] EWHC 2536 (Fam)

PRACTICE GUIDANCE
13 MARCH 2018

PRACTICE GUIDANCE (CASE MANAGEMENT AND MEDIATION OF INTERNATIONAL CHILD ABDUCTION PROCEEDINGS) (13 MARCH 2018)

1 Introduction

1.1 For the purposes of this Practice Guidance, 'international child abduction proceedings' are proceedings in which the return of a child is sought under any of the following:

(a) The Convention on the Civil Aspects of International Child Abduction of 25 October 1980 ('the 1980 Hague Convention');

(b) The Convention on Jurisdiction, Applicable Law, Recognition, Enforcement and Cooperation in Respect of Parental Responsibility and Measures for the Protection of Children ('the 1996 Hague Convention');

(c) Council Regulation (EC) No 2201/2003 of 27 November 2003 on jurisdiction and the recognition and enforcement of judgments in matrimonial matters and matters of parental responsibility ('the Council Regulation');

(d) The High Court's power to make an order returning the child to another jurisdiction or to make an order for the return of the child to this jurisdiction ('the inherent jurisdiction')

1.2 International child abduction proceedings dealt with under the 1980 Hague Convention must be completed within six weeks of the date of the application. FPR PD12F paragraph 3.5 applies the same time limit to non-Convention cases under the inherent jurisdiction, save where exceptional circumstances make this impossible. This Practice Guidance is issued to ensure all applications are case managed in a manner that facilitates these time limits, both in cases that commence with a without notice application and cases that commence on notice.

1.3 Chapter 6 of Part 12 of the FPR 2010 and PD12F provide the procedural framework for proceedings under the 1980 Hague Convention, the 1996 Hague Convention and the Council Regulation. The rules provide for case management directions in child abduction proceedings to be given 'as soon as practicable' after the application has been made. In particular, the rules provide for:

(a) Directions for the production of the applicant's evidence (r. 12.46)

(b) The giving of case management directions generally (r 12.48) (c) The filing and service of an answer (r 12.49)

(d) The filing and service of written evidence (r 12.50)

2 Case Management – Procedure

(a) Without notice applications

Use of without notice applications

2.1 Commencing proceedings by way of a without notice application pursuant to FPR r 12.47 will be justified only where

(a)   the case is one of exceptional urgency or

(b)   there is a compelling case that the child's welfare will be compromised if the other party is alerted in advance or

(c)   where the whereabouts of the child and the proposed respondent are unknown.

An urgent out of hours without notice application will be justified only where an order is necessary to regulate the position between the moment the order is made and the next available sitting of the court.

Evidence in support of without notice applications

2.2 The evidence in support of a without notice application must be as detailed and precise as possible having regard to the material provided by the applicant and transmitted by the Central Authority of the Requesting State. Unparticularised generalities will not suffice. Sources of hearsay must be identified and expressions of opinion must be supported by evidence and proper reasoning. The evidence should set out the orders sought, together with fully particularised reasons. Specifically, with respect to the narrow circumstances justifying a without notice application set out in para 2.1 above:

(a)   Where the justification for proceeding without notice is said to be exceptional urgency, the evidence in support of the without notice application must identify why the case is exceptionally urgent and why no notice, even short informal notice, can be given to the respondent (with respect to short, informal notice see para 2.8 below).

(b)   Where the justification for proceeding without notice is said to be a compelling case that the child's welfare will be compromised if notice is given, the evidence in support of the without notice application must demonstrate a real risk that if the respondent is alerted in advance the welfare of the child will be compromised, whether by the respondent thwarting the court's order or otherwise. Where the risk is said to be removal of the child from the jurisdiction, the evidence must address (i) the magnitude of the risk that the respondent will be minded to remove, (ii) the magnitude of the risk that, if the respondent is minded to remove, he or she will be able to evade protective measures put in place by the court and (iii) the magnitude of the consequences for the children if the protective measures are evaded.

(c)   Where the justification for proceeding without notice is said to be that the whereabouts of the child and the proposed respondent are unknown, the evidence in support of the without notice application must explain what steps have been taken to locate them, what disclosure orders are required against an identified agency and why there is reason to believe that that agency may be able to provide information which may lead to the location of the child.

Without notice orders

2.3 Before seeking a without notice Tipstaff order the applicant or their legal representative must speak to the Tipstaff. The Tipstaff can be contacted by telephone on 01622 858035.

2.4 Passport orders, location orders and collection orders constitute an interference with the child's and the respondent's fundamental rights. On a without notice application, parties should only seek, and the court can only be expected to grant, such orders as are necessary and proportionate having regard to the risks assessed to exist on the evidence. Where a court makes more than one disclosure order, it may provide for the sequential service of those orders.

Case management directions at without notice hearings

2.5 Where a without notice application is justified and the court grants a Tipstaff or other substantive order, or where a without notice application is justified but the court refuses to grant a Tipstaff or other substantive order on the merits, the court will in each case proceed to give case management directions to progress the matter, which directions may be varied and/or supplemented at the first on notice hearing where appropriate. The directions given will include the following:

(a) A direction that at the first on notice hearing the applicant and the respondent shall each be given the opportunity to speak separately with a mediator, who will be present at the Royal Courts of Justice, to enable the mediator to discuss with the parties the possibility of mediation under the Child Abduction Mediation Scheme and, where appropriate, undertake a screening interview.

(b) A direction pursuant to FPR r 12.46(a) for the filing of any further evidence to be relied on by the applicant in support of the application including, where it is not already contained in the evidence supporting the application, a description of any protective measures (including orders that may be subject to a declaration of enforceability or registration under Art 11 of the 1996 Hague Convention or, where appropriate, undertakings) the applicant is prepared, without prejudice to his or her case, to offer for the purpose of securing the child's return.

(c) A direction pursuant to FPR r 12.50(2)(a) for the filing and serving of the respondent's answer.

(d) A direction pursuant to FPR r 12.50(1) for the filing of the respondent's evidence in support of the answer, to include details of any protective measures the respondent seeks (including, where appropriate, undertakings) in the event that the court orders the child's return.

(e) An order listing the matter for hearing for summary resolution, or in the alternative, further directions, no more than seven days from the date on which the without notice order is made (where a collection order is made the Tipstaff will return the matter to court within 3 days of the order being executed) with a direction that the respondent shall attend this hearing.

(f) A direction for the provision by HMCTS of an interpreter for the hearing where Section 11 of Form C67 indicates that the respondent does not speak English and indicates the language and dialect spoken by the respondent.

(g) Such further or other case management directions that are appropriate in the circumstances of the case. Where it is clear on the face of the application and supporting evidence that it will be appropriate for the child to be heard during the proceedings the court may make directions to ensure the child is given the opportunity to be heard (see paragraph 3.5 below).

(h)   Unless the court directs otherwise, a direction pursuant to FPR r 12.47(3) that the applicant is to effect personal service of the standard directions order together with a record of the without notice hearing (note that where an order provides for service by the Tipstaff it is not sufficient for the order to be served by the applicant).

2.6 It is important that any without notice application is prepared in a manner that maximises the chances of the on notice hearing being effective. To this end, the without notice application and the evidence in support must contain all the information in the possession of the applicant that will or may assist in the prompt execution of any orders made. To further assist in achieving an effective on notice hearing, the directions order resulting from the without notice hearing will be served together with an information sheet, detailing how the respondent can obtain legal advice, public funding from the Legal Aid Agency and, if necessary, pro bono assistance, and a copy of the Child Abduction Mediation Scheme.

2.7 Where the application has been commenced by way of a without notice hearing, at the first effective on notice hearing the court will make further case management directions with input from both parties with a view to addressing each of the matters set out in paragraph 2.11 of this Practice Guidance where those matters have not already been dealt with by way of directions at the without notice hearing.

(b) On notice applications

Notice periods for on notice applications

2.8 FPR r 12.8 and PD12C provide that, in proceedings under the 1980 Hague Convention, service of the application on the respondent must be effected a minimum of 4 days before the first hearing and that, in proceedings under the inherent jurisdiction, service on the respondent must be effected a minimum of 14 days before the first hearing. Pursuant to PD12C para 2.2 the court may extend or shorten these periods for service. Whilst the courts have endorsed the practice of giving short, informal notice of proceedings in preference to proceeding without notice, where short, informal notice is given there must be evidence identifying why it was not possible to serve the application in accordance with the rules or to make an application to abridge time for service.

Standard directions on issue

2.9 Where the application is made on notice (and, accordingly, there is no without notice hearing immediately following the issuing of the application) there is a risk that valuable time will be lost between issue and the first on notice hearing. To minimise this risk, upon the court issuing an on notice application the court will, of its own motion, make standard directions upon issue pursuant to FPR r 12.5(1)(b), to include:

(a)   A direction that at the first on notice hearing the applicant and the respondent shall each be given the opportunity to speak separately with the mediator present at the Royal Courts of Justice to enable the mediator to discuss with the parties the possibility of mediation under the Child Abduction Mediation Scheme and, where appropriate, undertake a screening interview.

(b)   A direction pursuant to FPR r 12.46(a) for the filing of any further evidence to be relied on by the applicant in support of the application including, where it is not already contained in the evidence supporting the application, a description of any protective measures (including orders that may be subject to registration under Art 11 of the 1996 Hague Convention or, where appropriate, undertakings) the applicant is prepared, without prejudice to his or her case, to offer for the purpose of securing the child's return.

(c)   A direction pursuant to FPR r 12.50(2)(a) for the filing and serving of the respondent's answer not less than 2 days prior to the first hearing.

(d)   A direction pursuant to FPR r 12.50(1) for the filing of the respondent's evidence in support of the answer, to include details of any protective measures the respondent seeks (including, where appropriate, undertakings) in the event that the court orders the child's return not less than 2 days prior to the first hearing.

(e)   A direction that upon service of the application the respondent file with the court a notice confirming the respondent's address and the whereabouts of the child (or that they are unaware of the child's whereabouts) and, where the respondent subsequently changes his or her address or becomes aware of any change in the child's whereabouts, a notice of the new address or of the new whereabouts of the child.

(f)   A direction that upon service of the application the respondent serve on the applicant the notice confirming the respondent's address and the whereabouts of the child (or that they are unaware of the child's whereabouts) or file with the court a notice indicating that the respondent objects to serving on the applicant with notice confirming the respondent's address and the whereabouts of the child and the reasons for that objection.

(g)   An order listing the matter for hearing for summary resolution or in the alternative further directions, seven days from the date the application is issued with a direction that the respondent shall attend this hearing.

(h)   A direction for the provision by HMCTS of an interpreter for the hearing where Section 11 of Form C67 indicates that the respondent does not speak English and indicates the language and dialect spoken by the respondent.

(i)   Such further or other case management directions that are appropriate in the circumstances of the case. Where it is clear on the face of the application and supporting evidence that it will be appropriate for the child to be heard during the proceedings the court may make directions to ensure the child is given the opportunity to be heard (see paragraph 3.5 below).

(j)   A direction that the applicant is to effect personal service of the standard directions order.

2.10 The resulting directions order will be served together with an information sheet, detailing how the respondent can obtain legal advice, public funding from

PART III – Practice guidance

the Legal Aid Agency and, if necessary, pro bono assistance, and a copy of the Child Abduction Mediation Scheme.

Directions at first on notice hearing

2.11 At the first hearing, the parties should attend fully prepared to deal with the case management matters that have not been dealt with by way of standard directions upon issue or which have been so dealt with but require variation, together with any additional case management matters that may arise in the circumstances of the case. The court will expect the parties to be able to deal with the following case management issues if applicable:

(a)   Further directions with respect to mediation or other non-court dispute resolution procedure.

(b)   Allocation.

(c)   Any directions required to deal with further disclosure.

(d)   Any further directions with respect to the filing and service of an answer and evidence in support, to include details of any protective measures the respondent seeks (including, where appropriate, undertakings) in the event that the court orders the child's return.

(e)   Any further directions with respect to the filing and service of the applicant's evidence in reply to the answer, including, where it is not already contained in the evidence supporting the application, a description of any protective measures (including orders that may be subject to a declaration of enforceability or registration under Art 11 of the 1996 Hague Convention or, where appropriate, undertakings) the applicant is prepared, without prejudice to his or her case, to offer to secure the child's return. Where the respondent's answer raises a defence under Art 13(b) the applicant should give immediate consideration to, and take steps, in the most expeditious way available, to ensure that information is obtained, whether from the Central Authority of the Requesting State or otherwise, as to the protective measures that are available, or could be put in place to meet the alleged identified risks.

(f)   Directions in respect of expert evidence, if appropriate. Where a party seeks to adduce expert evidence, that party must comply with the requirements of FPR Part 25.

(g)   Directions in respect of oral evidence, if appropriate (in respect of directions for oral evidence see para 3.8 below).

(h)   Directions with respect to ensuring that the child is given the opportunity to be heard during the proceedings, unless this appears inappropriate having regard to his or her age or degree of maturity, including consideration of joinder and separate representation (see paragraph 3.5 below). Any application for joinder and separate representation should be made on notice prior to the first on notice hearing, to be dealt with at that hearing.

(i)   The timetabling of the final hearing prior to the expiry of the six-week deadline, including the appropriate time estimate for the hearing, incorporating time for judicial reading and judgment writing.

(j)   The arrangements for the provision of a court bundle that complies with FPR 2010 PD27A.

(k) The arrangements for the provision, where appropriate, of skeleton arguments and an agreed bundle of authorities in compliance with PD27A.

(l) Ancillary directions making provision where necessary for the attendance of a party not in the jurisdiction, the provision of video-links and the provision for interpreters at the final hearing. Where a video-link it sought, it is the responsibility of the parties to ensure appropriate arrangements are made for the video link and that the connection is made to the court via an ISDN line or, where an ISDN line is not available, that a 'bridging link' is arranged to ensure that a connection with the court can take place.

3 Case Management – Related Matters

(a) Child Abduction Mediation Scheme

3.1 The requirement in FPR r 1.4(2)(f)) that case management includes encouraging the parties to use a non-court dispute resolution procedure if the court considers that appropriate and facilitating the use of such procedure, and the obligation imposed by FPR r 3.3(1) to consider whether non-court dispute resolution is appropriate at every stage of the proceedings, applies to international child abduction proceedings. The Lord Chancellor has set out in regulations provision on the of grant of non-means non-merit tested legal aid for mediation for applicant parents in cases under the 1980 Hague Convention.

3.2 Within this context, the court will, where appropriate, encourage the parties to engage in mediation of their dispute through participation in the Child Abduction Mediation Scheme (see Appendix). In any case where it is alleged or admitted, or there is other reason to believe, that the child or a parent has experienced domestic abuse or that there is a risk of such abuse, the court will have regard to these matters when deciding whether it is appropriate to encourage the parties to mediate. Participation in the Child Abduction Mediation Scheme is voluntary and without prejudice to the parties' right to invite the court to determine the issues between them. An unwillingness to enter into mediation will not have an effect on the outcome of the proceedings. It is important that parties and their representatives note that entering into a process of mediation will not ground a defence of acquiescence (see In Re H (Minors) (Abduction: Acquiescence) [1998] AC 72 at 88-89).

3.3 The Child Abduction Mediation Scheme will operate in parallel with, but independent from, the proceedings. Where parties agree to enter into mediation, the court will give any directions required to facilitate the mediation. The parties or the parties' representatives must be in a position to address the court on the question of mediation at the relevant hearing to enable the court to consider the appropriateness of such directions. The mediation will proceed with the aim of completing that mediation within the applicable timescales. Where the mediation is successful, the resulting Memorandum of Understanding will be drawn up into a consent order for approval by the court. If the mediation is not successful, the court will proceed to determine the application.

PART III – Practice guidance

(b) Issue Identification

3.4 Key to ensuring that the final hearing is dealt with in a manner commensurate with the summary nature of most international child abduction hearings is the identification at the case management stage of what matters are truly in issue between the parties. It is particularly important that the directions hearing(s) preceding the final hearing be used to identify the real issues in the case, so that the judge can give firm and focused case management directions, including as to the form that the hearing will take. Parties can expect the court to be rigorous and robust at the case management stage in requiring parties to consider and identify the issues that the court is required to determine and to make concessions in respect of issues that are capable of agreement.

(b) Participation of the Child

3.5 Art 11(3) of the Council Regulation requires the court to ensure that child is given the opportunity to be heard during the proceedings unless this appears inappropriate having regard to his or her age or degree of maturity. Where it is clear on the face of the application and supporting evidence that it will be appropriate for the child to be heard during the proceedings the court may give directions to facilitate this at a without notice hearing or by way of standard directions on issue. Where directions have not already been given, the question of whether the child is to be given an opportunity to be heard in proceedings having regard to his or her age and degree of maturity, and if so how, must be considered and determined at the first on notice hearing. The methods by which a child may be heard during the proceedings comprise a report from an Officer of the Cafcass High Court Team or party status with legal representation. In most cases where it is appropriate for the child to be given an opportunity to be heard in proceedings an interview of the child by an officer of the Cafcass High Court Team will be sufficient to ensure that the child's wishes and feelings are placed before the court. In only a very few cases will party status be necessary. Where the exception relied on is that of settlement pursuant to Art 12 of the 1980 Hague Convention, the separate point of view of the child will be particularly important. The court should record on the face of any final order the manner in which the child has been heard in the proceedings.

(c) Witness Statements

3.6 Paragraph 2.13 of Practice Direction PD12F recognises that, to avoid delay, the initial statement in support of the application may be in the form of a statement given by the applicant's solicitor based on information transmitted by the Central Authority of the Requesting State. The applicant's initial statement of evidence must however, include the applicant's evidence establishing the necessary requirements for a return, a description of any protective measures (including orders that may be subject to a declaration of enforceability or registration under Art 11 of the 1996 Hague Convention or, where appropriate, undertakings) the applicant is prepared, without prejudice to his or her case, to offer for the purpose of securing the child's return and full details of any proceedings in the Requesting State or in England and Wales of which the applicant is aware.

3.7 Witness statements filed in support of the answer and in reply to the answer should be as economical as possible and should deal only with those factual matters relevant to the issues raised in the answer. The court will rarely be assisted by a detailed account of the history of the parents' relationship. Appropriate translations of exhibits should be provided with the statement. Where the maker of the statement does not speak English, the statement should be prepared and served in the maker's own language and then certified translation into English provided by the party concerned.

(d) Oral Evidence

3.8 The court will rarely make a direction for oral evidence to be given. Any party seeking such direction for oral evidence will need to demonstrate to the satisfaction of the court that oral evidence is necessary to assist the court to resolve the proceedings justly. Any party seeking to rely on oral evidence should raise the issue at the earliest available opportunity and no later than the pre-hearing review.

(e) Bundles

3.9 The court bundle for any hearing must comply with FPR PD 27A. PD27A limits the size of the bundle to a single file containing no more than 350 pages (PD 27A para 5.1). The limit of 350 pages includes the skeleton arguments. Only those documents which are relevant to the hearing and which it is necessary for the court to read, or which will be referred to during the hearing, may be included (PD 27A para 4.1). It will not generally be necessary to include in the bundle the application sent from the home country's Central Authority to ICACU. Where an issue arises as to the inclusion of this document, that issue will be dealt with by direction of the court. Skeleton arguments and other preliminary materials prepared for use in relation to earlier hearings should be excluded. Any separate bundle of all authorities relied on for any hearing must comply with PD 27A para 4.3. Each authority relied on must be provided with the relevant passages highlighted by means of a vertical line in the margin. Skeleton arguments must be filed by no later than 11am on the working day before the hearing (PD 27A para 6.4).

3.10 The time limits set out in FPR PD 27A para 6 for preparing and delivering the bundle and case management documents represent the minimum time limits applicable to this task. Where the hearing is on notice and the respondent is a litigant in person, the applicant should prepare and deliver the bundle pursuant to PD27A para 6 in a timeframe that ensures that the bundle and the case management documents are provided to the litigant in person at least three working days prior to the hearing.

(f) Time estimates

3.11 The time estimate for the final hearing should make reasonable allowance for judicial reading time and judgment writing. In those cases where permission for oral evidence has been given a witness template for the final hearing should also be completed at the time that the direction for oral evidence is made to ensure that the time estimate for the final hearing is accurate.

(g) International Judicial Liaison

3.12 The following matters may appropriately be the subject of direct international judicial liaison:

(a) information concerning the scheduling of the case in the foreign jurisdiction,

(b) seeking to establish whether protective measures are available for the child or other parent in the State to which the child would be returned,

(c) ascertaining whether the foreign court can accept and enforce orders made or undertakings offered by the parties in the initiating jurisdiction,

(d) ascertaining whether the foreign court can make a 'mirror order',

(e) confirming whether orders were made by the foreign court and

(f) verifying whether findings about domestic violence were made by the foreign court.

This is not an exhaustive list. It is important to remember that international judicial liaison is not intended to be a substitute for obtaining legal advice, a means to avoid having to seek expert evidence as to foreign law or procedure, a mechanism for judges to settle welfare disputes or a means of making submissions to a foreign court. All requests for international judicial liaison should be made through the International Family Justice Office (IFJOffice@hmcts.gsi.gov.uk) and should be accompanied by a (preferably agreed) concise case summary and a set of focused questions to be put to the network judge which ask for information of a practical and non-legal nature, phrased in a neutral, non-tactical way.

(h) Final Hearing

3.13 Article 11 of the 1980 Hague Convention requires the judicial or administrative authorities of Contracting States to act expeditiously in proceedings for the return of children. Article 11(3) of the Council Regulation also requires a court to which a return application is made to act expeditiously and stipulates that, unless exceptional circumstances make this impossible, the court must issue its judgment no later than six weeks after the application is lodged. Within this context, whilst the quantity and nature of the evidential material required to reach a proper determination of the application at final hearing will depend on the individual case, as will the format of the final hearing, including the extent to which oral evidence is permitted, the final hearing will be dealt with summarily and in most cases based on the written material then available to the court.

(i) Orders

3.14 The Tipstaff passport, location and collection orders are in a standard format that has been arrived at after careful consultation and revision. It is for the court to draw the relevant Tipstaff order once granted. Legal representatives should not provide a draft of the passport order, location order or collection order sought. Legal representatives should provide drafts of any disclosure orders sought and a separate draft of the case management directions sought alongside the Tipstaff and/or disclosure order(s) applied for. Orders which discharge Tipstaff orders, including orders for the release of passports held by the Tipstaff, will only be accepted by the Tipstaff if they are sealed.

3.15 Where one of the parties is a litigant in person, the advocate for the represented party will need to ensure that any case management and disclosure orders made by court are drafted and submitted for approval by the judge. When the solicitor for the represented party sends a copy of the order to the litigant in person, the solicitor should highlight in writing to the litigant in person any case management steps that the order requires them to take. Counsel instructed on a Direct Access basis cannot conduct litigation on behalf of their client. The obligation on Direct Access counsel ends once the order has been submitted to the court. Case management directions made against the client must accordingly be met by them as a litigant in person.

3.16 Where an order refusing the return of the child (a 'non-return' order) has been made in respect of an applicant from an EU member state on the grounds set out in Art 13 of the 1980 Hague Convention, the procedure set out in Art 11(6) of the Council Regulation, requiring the transmission of certain documents to the court with jurisdiction or Central Authority in the Member State where the child was habitually resident within one month of the date of the nonreturn order, must be complied with.

(j) Appeals and Applications for Stay

3.17 Any application for a stay pending an application for permission to appeal and the application for permission to appeal should be made expeditiously. Any application for permission to appeal and any stay should be made to the judge if possible and, if not possible or if refused, to the Court of Appeal. The filing of the notice of appeal should not be delayed until the appellant has received a copy of the approved transcript of the judgment under appeal.

Sir James Munby
President of the Family Division
13 March 2018

Appendix
Child Abduction Mediation Scheme

Introduction

1 The requirement in FPR r 1.4(2)(f)) that case management includes encouraging the parties to use a non-court dispute resolution procedure if the court considers that appropriate and facilitating the use of such procedure, and the obligation imposed by FPR r 3.3(1) to consider whether non-court dispute resolution is appropriate at every stage of the proceedings, applies to international child abduction proceedings. The 1980 Hague Convention itself, by Arts 7(c) and 10, places weight on the desirability of a negotiated or voluntary return or the amicable resolution of the issues.

2 In 2006, a child abduction Mediation Pilot Scheme run by Reunite, with funding from the Nuffield Foundation, found, in the context of twenty-eight cases which progressed to a concluded mediation, that there is a clear role for mediation in resolving cases of alleged child abduction and that parents were

PART III – Practice guidance

willing to embrace the use of mediation. Seventy-five percent of cases resulted in the parents concerned reaching a Memorandum of Understanding.

3 The Child Abduction Mediation Scheme is a mediation scheme that aims to ensure that parties engaged in child abduction proceedings are able, in an appropriate case, to access a mediation service as an integral part of the court process and in parallel with, but independent from, the proceedings. Whilst mediation will not be appropriate, or suitable, in every case, it is an option that should be explored by the court in all cases of alleged international child abduction.

Child Abduction Mediation Scheme – Key Principles

4 The Child Abduction Mediation Scheme is an independent mediation scheme run with the assistance of Reunite, which organisation provides mediators with specialised knowledge of international child abduction, trained and experienced in mediating cases of this nature. The following key principles apply to the operation of the Child Abduction Mediation Scheme:

(a)   The mediation will run in parallel with, but independent from, the proceedings in court, with the aim of completing the mediation within the timescale applicable to the proceedings.

(b)   Mediation is voluntary and will only be undertaken with the consent of both parents. An unwillingness to enter into mediation will not have an effect on the outcome of the proceedings.

(c)   Mediation will only be undertaken if the mediator considers that it is appropriate and safe to do so, and following an assessment of the parties and their situation during the required screening stage.

(d)   Participation by the parties in mediation is without prejudice to the applicant's right to pursue the return of the child, and without prejudice to the respondent's right to defend the proceedings.

(e)   Participation by the parties in mediation does not prevent the parties from requesting that the court determine the issues between them.

(f)   If the mediation is not successful in resolving the issues then the matter will return to the court arena for determination.

5 The Child Abduction Mediation Scheme complements the proceedings and is only embarked upon once proceedings have been issued (Reunite also runs a mediation scheme that operates independent of court proceedings. Full details of this scheme can be found at http://www.reunite.org/pages/mediation.asp).

6 The operation of the Child Abduction Mediation Scheme will be facilitated by the presence at the Royal Courts of Justice of mediators from Reunite with specialised knowledge of international child abduction who will be available to speak with parties on child abduction matters.

Child Abduction Mediation Scheme – Operation

7 The scheme has three key stages, namely (i) identification, (ii) screening and (iii) mediation. The three key stages operate as follows:

Identification

8 Participation in the Child Abduction Mediation Scheme is voluntary. Mediation will only be undertaken with the consent of both parents and where it can be undertaken safely. However, it is also important that parties to child abduction proceedings are aware of, and have the proper opportunity to indicate their willingness to participate in the Child Abduction Mediation Scheme.

9 Within this context, the following steps will be taken by the court in each case, with a view to identifying those cases in which the parties are willing to consider mediation of their dispute:

(a) At the first without notice hearing, or by way of standard directions following an on notice application, the court will, where appropriate, direct that the applicant and the respondent shall each be given the opportunity at the first on notice hearing to speak with a mediator.

(b) At the first on notice hearing, the court will, where appropriate, encourage the parties to consider the option of mediation and, in an appropriate case, will invite the parties to speak with a mediator.

(c) Where the parties agree to speak with the mediator, the mediator will discuss with the parties the possibility of participating in mediation under the Child Abduction Mediation Scheme and will carry out an initial screening interview (see paragraph 11 below).

(d) Where the parties consent to mediate and the case is suitable for mediation, the court will give any directions necessary to facilitate the mediation and will record on the face of the order the proposed outline timetable for the mediation, in consultation with the parties and the mediator.

10 Where one party is outside the jurisdiction, the steps set out at Paragraph 9 will be accomplished by telephone at the first on notice hearing. Where this is not possible, for example due to a time difference, they will be accomplished on an agreed date shortly after the hearing. If these steps are accomplished on an agreed date shortly after the hearing, the parties will inform the court of the outcome and, where necessary, the court will either approve agreed directions to facilitate any agreement to mediate or list the matter for the purposes of giving any such directions. In any event, the mediator will ensure that the required screening and assessment is carried out prior to the mediation commencing.

11 It is important to note that entering into a process of mediation will not ground a defence of acquiescence (see In Re H (Minors) (Abduction: Acquiescence) [1998] AC 72 at 88-89).

Screening

12 In addition to the parents being willing to mediate, the case must be suitable for mediation. Mediators have a responsibility to ensure that the parents take part in any mediation process willingly, and without fear of violence or harm. The mediator will undertake a screening procedure to confirm that this can be achieved. The mediator will have particular regard to the welfare of the child or children. The mediator will also have particular regard to any allegation or

admission of domestic abuse (as defined in FPR PD12J paragraph 3), or other reason to believe that the child or a parent has experienced domestic abuse or is at risk of such abuse.

13 Within this context, an initial screening interview will be undertaken individually with each of the parents prior to undertaking mediation, in order to ensure that the parent is willing to take part in mediation and to assess whether the case is suitable and safe for mediation. The screening interview will also allow the mediator to confirm to each parent at the conclusion of the interview whether it is appropriate for mediation to be offered and, if so, to ensure that each parent understand the purpose of the mediation and to provide an opportunity for any concerns relevant to mediation to be further discussed.

14 As provided for at paragraphs 8(c) and 10, where possible, the screening interviews will take place at the first on notice hearing when the parents speak with the mediator, either in person or by telephone. However, where the screening interview takes place at a later agreed date, the parties will inform the court of the outcome and, where necessary, the court will either approve agreed directions to facilitate any agreement to mediate or list the matter for the purposes of giving any such directions.

15 Where both parents indicate a willingness to engage in mediation, during the screening interview the mediator will deal with the following matters:

(a)   Whether or not the case is one that is suitable for mediation.

(b)   Whether or not both parents are willing to mediate and to attend mediation with an open mind.

(c)   Whether or not the subject child appears to be of an age and level of maturity at which their voice should be heard.

(d)   Provide information about the mediation and how the mediation process will work in parallel with, but independent from, the proceedings.

(e)   Address any concerns that either parent may have relevant to the conduct of the mediation.

16 Within the context of the matters set out in paragraph 12, the assessment of the suitability of a case for mediation will include an assessment of whether the mediation can be conducted safely. In any case in which the parents are willing to mediate but it is alleged or admitted, or there is other reason to believe, that the child or a parent has experienced domestic abuse (as defined in FPR PD12J paragraph 3) or that there is a risk of such abuse, the mediator will assess, through the screening procedure, whether a mediation can be conducted safely having regard to the matters set out in FPR PD12B paragraphs 5.1 and 5.2 and FPR PD12J. A mediation will take place in such circumstances only after the mediator has undertaken a risk assessment and is satisfied that appropriate measures are in place to protect the safety of those participating in the mediation process.

17 If, during the screening interview, it is identified that the subject child appears to be of an age and level of maturity at which their voice should be heard, the court will direct that the child be interviewed by a member of the Cafcass High Court Team and a report filed with the court and provided to the parents and mediators.

Mediation

18 Where the parties agree to mediate and the case is suitable for mediation, the mediation will be timetabled so as to ensure that the timescales applicable to the proceedings are met.

19 Reunite will contact both parents to arrange appropriate dates for mediation. Where it proves impossible for an applicant to come to this jurisdiction for the purposes of mediation, the mediator will conduct the mediation with the applicant attending by way of a telecommunications application such as Skype.

20 In some circumstances public funding from the Legal Aid Agency may be available to cover the costs of flights and hotel for the applicant parent to come to this jurisdiction for the purposes of mediation, in which case Reunite will co-ordinate travel and accommodation arrangements.

21 Where the parent has requested the services of an interpreter, this will be provided throughout the mediation session(s).

22 Parents are free at any stage during the course of the mediation to consult their respective legal representatives in this jurisdiction or overseas, or any other individual they wish to consult and the mediator may encourage them, as appropriate, to consult.

23 Where a safeguarding issue concerning a child or an adult arises during the course of the mediation, the mediator will, where appropriate, terminate the mediation and will notify the relevant agencies.

24 Where the mediation is successful, the agreement reached between the parents will be set down in the form of a Memorandum of Understanding. Parents will be encouraged to seek advice on the Memorandum of Understanding from their respective legal representatives if they have them. The court will be informed of the outcome of the mediation and the Memorandum of Understanding will be reduced to a consent order which will be placed before the court for approval. Any consent order will explain how the child has been heard in the context of the mediation process.

25 Where the mediation is not successful, the court will proceed to determine the case. Ordinarily, there will be no further reference to the mediation or to anything said during the mediation, save where child protection concerns have been revealed or a report has been prepared by the Cafcass High Court Team pursuant to paragraph 17 above.

PART III – Practice guidance

PRESIDENT'S GUIDANCE
10 APRIL 2018

LISTING FINAL HEARINGS IN ADOPTION CASES

Introduction

1. This Guidance is issued with the purpose of clarifying the legal requirements and practical arrangements for final hearings in adoption applications and adoption visits.

2. In this Guidance:

   (a)   "the 2002 Act" means the Adoption and Children Act 2002;
   (b)   "the 1989 Act" means the Children Act 1989;
   (c)   any reference to a rule by number is a reference to the rule so numbered in the Family Procedure Rules 2010 (FPR 2010);
   (d)   the term 'judge' includes magistrates.

Previous guidance

3. This Guidance replaces the 'President's Guidance: Listing Final Hearings in Adoption cases' of 3 October 2008.

The adoption application

4. An application for an adoption order should, if reasonably practicable, be issued in the Family Court in which any relevant Care Order (Part IV of the 1989 Act) and/or Placement Order (Chapter 3 of the 2002 Act) was made in relation to the child, so as to achieve (where possible) judicial continuity, and easier file management.

First Directions Hearing

5. Once an application for an adoption order is issued, notice will be given to those identified in rule 14.3 (including birth parents with parental responsibility), and rule 14.4 (but note that a parent will not automatically receive a copy of the adoption application form: see para 1 PD14A FPR 2010, though the court may direct this). The court may at any time direct any other person to be a respondent to the proceedings (rule 14.3(3)); this may of course include a birth father without parental responsibility.[1] The obligation is on the court to ensure that each respondent to the application is thereafter given notice of each hearing and that they are kept informed of the progress of the case.[2]

6. Where an adoption application is made in relation to a child who would, by virtue of any order made within the proceedings, acquire British Citizenship, the Court should notify the Home Office of the application and invite the Secretary of State to indicate (within a defined period) whether he/she wishes to intervene.

7. Upon issue of the application, the court will give standard directions (rule 14.6), which may include the listing of the case for a first directions hearing (rule

14.6(1)(a)(ii)); it may also include the listing of a final hearing (rule 14.6(1)(a) (vi)). Where it considers it appropriate to do so, the court may give the directions provided for in rule 14.8 without listing a first directions hearing (rule 14.6(iv)). A first directions hearing should generally be held within 4 weeks beginning with the date on which the application is issued (rule 14.7). If, prior to the first hearing, a parent gives notice of his/her intention to apply for leave to oppose under section 47(3) or section 47(5) of the 2002 Act, the file shall be referred to the allocated judge who shall consider giving directions for the parent to file and serve a short statement setting out their case in relation to change in circumstances.

8. If a first directions hearing is held, the court will give consideration to the matters set out in rule 14.8. If a birth parent with parental responsibility (see section 52(6)) attends that hearing and seeks leave to oppose the adoption under section 47(3) or section 47(5) of the 2002 Act, or otherwise notifies the court (generally in writing, though not necessarily by way of formal application) of a wish to oppose the application, directions will be given for the listing of that application. If it appears that there is no opposition from the birth parent to the adoption, and everything else is in order, the court will list the application for a final hearing.

Notice of final hearing

9. Section 141(3) of the 2002 Act and rule 14.15 place an obligation on the court officer to give to the persons listed in rule 14.3, including birth parent(s) with parental responsibility (unless that parent has given notice under section 20(4)(a) of the 2002 Act), notice of the date and place of the final hearing of an adoption application.

10. The requirement to give notice is mandatory; the general rules about service in Part 6 FPR 2010 apply save as directed by the court or otherwise provided by PD. Notice of the final hearing must be given to any person listed in rule 14.3. If a person to whom service should be effected cannot be found, a formal application should be made for an order that notice of the hearing on that person be dispensed with; this application will be treated as being made under rule 6.36. It is unlikely that service will be dispensed with in relation to a parent with parental responsibility unless there is evidence that significant efforts have been made to trace such a person. The provisions of rule 6.36 (power of court to dispense with service) will be applied exceptionally in relation to notice of the final hearing. By rule 14.16 any person who has been given notice under rule 14.15 has the right to attend the final hearing and, except where rule 14.16(2) applies,[3] to be heard on the question of whether an adoption order should be made.

Application for leave to oppose

11. The court shall never list the parent's application for leave to oppose the adoption application, and the final hearing of the adoption application on the same day.

12. If an application for leave to oppose the adoption is listed and determined, and is unsuccessful, the court may then list the application for final hearing.

13. No fewer than 21 days shall elapse between the refusal of leave and the listing of the final hearing[4] (which is now likely to be the final 'adoption' hearing). It is not appropriate to abbreviate this time-period.

14. While it may be possible for the judge to indicate, when dismissing an application for leave to oppose an adoption application, that an adoption order is likely, on the basis of the current information, to be pronounced at the next hearing,[5] it should not be forgotten that at the listed final hearing it is still open to another party (i.e. one who has not been refused permission to oppose the adoption application) to "attend … and, subject to paragraph (2), be heard on the question of whether an order should be made" (Rule 14.16).

Practical arrangements for the final hearing

15. In some cases, the welfare of the child will require arrangements to be made to ensure that the birth parent(s) and the applicant(s) or the child do not meet at or in the vicinity of the court. This will apply particularly to proceedings in which a serial number has been assigned to the applicant under rule 14.2(2). Rule 14.2(5)(b) provides that, in such a case, the proceedings will be conducted with a view to securing that the applicant is not seen by or made known to any party who is not already aware of his identity except with his consent.

16. Rule 14.16(6) provides that the court cannot make an adoption order unless the applicant and the child personally attend the final hearing. However, rule 14.16(6) is subject to rule 14.16(7), (8), which give the court a discretion to direct that the applicant (or one of them) or the child need not attend the final hearing; this provision permits the court, where appropriate, to direct that the attendance of the applicant or the child or both of them at the final hearing is not required. Special arrangements can of course be made for the attendance of the applicant(s) and/or child (see further para 19 below).

17. When giving directions for the conduct of the final hearing of an adoption application, the court should consider in particular:

(a) whether to give a direction under rule 14.16(7) that the applicant or the child need not attend the hearing;

(b) whether to give a direction under rule 14.16(4) that any person must attend the hearing;

(c) whether arrangements need to be made to ensure that the birth parent(s) and the applicant(s) or the child do not meet at or in the vicinity of the court;

(d) the arrangements for ensuring that the ascertainable wishes and feelings of the child regarding the adoption decision are placed before the court;

(e) the facilities at the place where the final hearing is to take place, including:
   – the availability of suitable accommodation;
   – the use of any electronic information exchange and video or telephone conferencing links

(f) whether any documents filed in any earlier proceedings should be obtained and made available in these proceedings;

(g) whether the social work Annex A report should be disclosed to the parties, and if so in what form..

18. In proceedings in which a serial number has been assigned to the applicant under rule 14.2, it will generally be appropriate to excuse the attendance of the child at the final hearing. It is likely also to be appropriate to excuse the attendance of the applicant, to ensure that confidentiality is preserved. Where in such a case the attendance of the applicant is required, arrangements must be made to ensure that the applicant is not seen by or made known to any party who is not already aware of his identity.

19. In any case in which a direction is given that the applicant or the child need not attend the final hearing, the order and any notice of hearing issued by the court must state clearly that the applicant or the child, as the case may be, should not attend.

20. At a final hearing, if a birth parent with parental responsibility attends and seeks leave to oppose the adoption (and no such application has been made or disposed of during the proceedings), the court will give directions for that application and list it for hearing. If that application is subsequently unsuccessful, the court will then re-list the application for final hearing, giving notice to the birth parent.

21. Each court which hears adoption applications must have arrangements in place to provide information to the relevant parties about any special arrangements made for their attendance at and the conduct of the final hearing.

22. The application for an adoption order should be determined at the hearing of which notice has been given under rule 14.15. If the application is not determined at that hearing, notice of any adjourned final hearing should be given under rule 14.15 and this Guidance shall apply equally to the adjourned hearing.

23. If an adoption order is to be made, it should ordinarily be pronounced at the conclusion of the listed final hearing, but may be deferred for example to enable the applicants to attend in person. The adoption order should be dated and takes effect on the day it is made, unless either the court specifies otherwise (rule 14.25), or grants a stay pending appeal.[6]

24. It is expected that no fewer than 21 days shall elapse after the making of the adoption order before the holding of any adoption visit. However, an adoption visit could exceptionally, in the discretion of the judge, be held within this period; this may be appropriate if, for instance, the birth parent has taken no part in the adoption application proceedings, and some other pressing reason arises for the visit to take place within the 21-day period.

Adoption visit

25. An adoption visit ("adoption visit") which follows the making of an adoption order is an informal celebratory occasion held at the discretion of the judge for the benefit of the adoptive parents and child if they desire it.

26. The adoption visit shall not be held prior to the expiry of the appeal period (generally no fewer than 21 days, or more safely 28 days) following the making of the adoption order. Save for the exceptional circumstances referred to in para 24 above, it is not appropriate to abbreviate this time- period.

PART III – Practice guidance

27. Ideally, the visit should take place at the court where the adoption order was made, and in those circumstances, it should be possible for the visit to be conducted by the judge, or where the order was made by magistrates at least one of the bench, who made the adoption order. It is recognised that for practical reasons, however, the adopters may prefer the adoption visit to take place in the Family Court nearer their home.

28. It is expected that any adoption visit(s) shall take place outside normal court sitting hours. They shall not be listed or referred to in the daily court list.

29. An adoption visit is not a 'court hearing'; it is not specifically provided for in the rules and should not be introduced into, or confused with, the formal steps of the adoption process.

James Munby,
President of the Family Division
10 April 2018

NOTES

1 For example, the father without PR who has nonetheless played a full part in recently concluded placement order proceedings; or the father who has indicated to the Local Authority (while discharging its functions under Regulation 14 of the *Adoption Agencies Regulations 2005*: see specifically regulation 14(3)) a wish to apply for party status; or the parent without PR who properly asserts ECHR rights: see *Keegan v Ireland* (No 16989/90) (1994) 18 EHRR 342, *Re H; Re G (Adoption: Consultation of unmarried fathers)* [2001] 1 FLR 646. See also *Re A and Others (Children) (Adoption)* [2017] EWHC 35 (Fam), [2017] 2 FLR 995, at paras 62-65 generally, and specifically in relation to parents who have a contact order.

2 See *X and Y v A Local Authority (Adoption: Procedure)* [2009] EWHC 47 (Fam), 2 FLR 984.

3 A person whose application for the permission of the court to oppose the making of an adoption order under section 47(3) or (5) of the 2002 Act has been refused is not entitled to be heard on the question of whether an order should be made.

4 McFarlane LJ in *Re B* [2013] EWCA Civ 421.

5 See Sir James Munby P in *Re W (Adoption Order: Leave to Oppose); Re H (Adoption Order: Application for Permission for Leave to Oppose)* [2013] EWCA Civ 1177, [2014] 1 FLR 1266, at para 30; *Re W (Adoption: Procedure: Conditions)* [2015] EWCA Civ 403, [2016] 1 FLR 454.

6 See *Re W (A Child) (No 2)* [2017] EWHC 917 (Fam), *Re W (A Child) (No 3)* [2017] EWHC 1032 (Fam), [2017] 2 FLR 1714 (Sir James Munby P).

PRESIDENT'S GUIDANCE
17 JUNE 2019

FORMS OF ORDERS IN CHILDREN CASES

1. This Guidance is issued by the President of the Family Division.

2. Previous Guidance in relation to Private Law [*President's Guidance – 22 April 2014 – Use of Prescribed Documents (Private Law)*] and Public Law [Family Procedure Rules 2010, PD12A, para 7.1] makes it plain that the President of the Family Division may, from time to time, issue guidance on prescribed templates and orders.

3. The most recent guidance is *Practice Guidance – 6 June 2018 – Standard Children and Other Orders*, which encouraged use of the recently produced templates for orders in all children cases.

4. In addition, the content of orders (other than final orders) made at the FHDRA in Private Law cases relating to children is prescribed by FPR 2010, PD12B, para 14.13.

5. The advent of new ways of working introduced by the Public Law Outline ['PLO'] and the Child Arrangements Programme ['CAP'] embraced the concept of lengthy narrative court orders in children cases. The aim was to encapsulate all of the essential information about a case in the most recent court order so that anyone taking up a case would only need to turn to the latest order to understand the issues, the parties, the state of the proceedings and other key information.

6. The purpose of the 6 June 2018 Practice Guidance and standard orders was to provide a comprehensive menu from which the appropriate orders and directions could be selected and used in shorter form template orders. They were intended to ensure that orders contained the essential information and directions relating to the particular hearing, but without including unnecessary material. Orders 7.3 – 7.7 (Private Law) and Orders 8.3-8.5 (Public Law) are designed to cater for case management orders and final orders in most situations and it is expected that these forms of order will generally be used as the basis for drafting the relevant order, supplemented if necessary from precedents in Orders 7.2 and 8.2.

7. The aim of these requirements is to assist, rather than add to, the burden of those whose task it is in any case to draw up and approve a court order. The laudable intention (with which I agree) was, as the Guidance states, for draft order templates to be available electronically and for these to be used by all at the click of a mouse. For whatever reason, it has become clear to me that many judges and practitioners are not using electronic templates or programs and are, instead, preparing lengthy narrative orders in each case by a more laborious method with the result that the preparation of orders is now taking more time rather than less. In addition, in Private Law cases, there has been a substantial rise in the number of Litigants in Person, with the result that the task of drawing up the court order falls to the Judge or Magistrates Legal Adviser, without assistance from lawyers for the parties, in those cases.

PART III – Practice guidance

8. As is well known, the Family Court is currently experiencing a very high number of children cases. In these circumstances, I have reluctantly come to the view that the detriment, in terms of time taken to prepare lengthy narrative orders after every hearing, outweighs the benefit that such orders bring. In short, in the current climate, the court simply does not have time in every case to meet the need for the preparation of full orders after every hearing. Where, as expected, the standard forms of order are used care should be taken to ensure that only the essential information is included.

9. Despite the pressure on the system, I remain persuaded that the first order made in any child case (public or private law) should comply with the previous Practice Guidance or PD12B, para 14.13, so that the key information in each case is recorded there. For subsequent orders (other than final orders) the court, while following the previous Practice Guidance, should tailor the order to the particular circumstances of the case, without the need to include lengthy narrative material which does not relate to the requirements of the particular order. The minimum required content in an order following a second or subsequent interim hearing will be:

i.   A recital of who attended and their representation;
ii.   A recital of the issues determined at the hearing;
iii.   A record of any agreement or concession made during the hearing;
iv.   A recital of the issues that remain outstanding; and
v.   The text of any orders that were made.

It is expected that this approach will enable the court to limit the content of orders to what is strictly required for effective case management.

10. Following a final hearing, the court order should, as has always been the case, set out in full the orders that the court has made, together with any appropriate recitals.

11. It is my intention that the use of shorter forms of order as explained in this Guidance should be seen as a temporary measure to support the effective preparation of court orders. The ultimate goal remains, as stated in the June 2018 Guidance, for court orders eventually to be drawn with ease from an electronically supported system once such systems are widely available.

Guidance issued by

Sir Andrew McFarlane
President of the Family Division
17 June 2019

PRESIDENT'S GUIDANCE
19 MARCH 2020

COVID 19: NATIONAL GUIDANCE FOR
THE FAMILY COURT

1. This Guidance, which is issued with the approval of the Lord Chief Justice and the Senior Presiding Judge, is intended to be followed with immediate effect by all levels of the Family Court and in the High Court Family Division.

2. The aim of the Guidance is to 'Keep Business Going Safely'. There is a strong public interest in the Family Justice System continuing to function as normally as possible despite the present pandemic. At the same time, in accordance with government guidance, there is a need for all reasonable and sensible precautions to be taken to prevent infection and, in particular, to avoid non-essential personal contact.

3. The government guidance is, however, primarily aimed at the social setting, rather than the business/work environment. Depending on the circumstances there may be the need, and no harm involved, in having a number of people present in court for an oral hearing.

4. Taking these competing factors together, whilst the default position should be that, for the time being, all Family Court hearings should be undertaken remotely either via email, telephone, video or Skype, etc ['remote hearing'], where the requirements of fairness and justice require a court-based hearing, and it is safe to conduct one, then a court-based hearing should take place.

The Rules

5. The Family Procedure Rules 2010 provide for the use of remote hearings in appropriate cases. FPR, r 1.4(e) provides that the court must further the Overriding Objective by making use of technology. FPR r 4.1(3)(e) provides that the court may hold a hearing and receive evidence by telephone or by using any other method of direct oral communication. In public law cases, FPR PD12A para 24 requires that where facilities are available to the court and the parties, the court should consider making full use of technology, including electronic information exchange and video or telephone conferencing. FPR r 22.3 provides that the court may allow a witness to give evidence through a video link or by other means. Annex 3 to FPR PD22A provides detailed guidance as to how video conferencing should be dealt with in court. Lastly, by r 4.3 the court may make orders of its own initiative.

Remote Hearings

6. The facilities to enable remote hearings are discussed in more detail at paragraph 14.

7. In contrast to jury trials in the Crown Court, there is no category of case that may be listed in the Family Court which necessarily requires the physical attendance of key participants in the same courtroom. The determination of

PART III – Practice guidance

whether or not a remote hearing is to take place will not therefore turn on the estimated length of the hearing, but upon other case specific factors.

8. The following categories of hearing are suitable for remote hearing:

a. All directions and case management hearings;
b. Public Law Children:
   i. Emergency Protection Orders
   ii. Interim Care Orders
   iii. Issue Resolution Hearings;
c. Private Law Children:
   i. First Hearing Dispute Resolution Appointments
   ii. Dispute Resolution Appointments
   iii. Other interim hearings
   iv. Simple short contested cases
d. Injunction applications where there is no evidence that is to be heard (or only limited evidence).
e. Financial Cases [see the guidance issued for the Financial Remedies Court by Mostyn J on 17th March at Appendix B below].
f. Appeals.
g. Other hearings as directed by the judge concerned.

9. Where a case in one of the categories listed in paragraph 8 above has already been listed for a hearing at which the parties are due to attend court then, if it is possible to make arrangements for the fixed hearing to be conducted remotely, then the hearing should go ahead remotely without any personal attendance at court. A draft directions order is at Appendix A below.

10. It is possible that other cases may also be suitable to be dealt with remotely. As the current situation is changing so rapidly, and as the circumstances that will impact upon this decision are likely to differ from court to court and from day to day, the question of whether any particular case is heard remotely must be determined on a case-by-case basis.

11. Where a case cannot be listed for a remote hearing as matters stand then any existing listing should be adjourned and the case must be listed promptly for a directions hearing, which should be conducted remotely. The primary aim of the directions hearing should be to identify the optimal method of conducting the court process in order to achieve a fair and just hearing of the issues but, at the same time, minimising as much as possible the degree of inter-personal contact between each participant. In appropriate cases, this may involve the use of a remote hearing where it is possible to conduct the court process in a manner that achieves a fair and just consideration of the issues. Recent experience has demonstrated that it is possible to conduct a complicated extensive multi-party hearing using the Business for Skype system that is available on the judicial laptop. In other cases it may be necessary for the personal attendance at court, for some or all of the hearing, by some or all of the participants.

12. At any directions hearing to discuss the future hearing arrangements, judges and magistrates should also require the parties to focus on the realistic options that are currently available to meet the child's welfare needs during the present straightened circumstances.

Urgent Cases

13. Even where a case is urgent, it should be possible for arrangements to be made for it to be conducted remotely. The default position should be that the hearing is conducted remotely. Where a case is genuinely urgent, and it is not possible to conduct a remote hearing and there is a need for pressing issues to be determined, then the court should endeavour to conduct a face-to-face hearing in circumstances (in terms of the physical arrangement of the court room and in the waiting area) which minimise the opportunity for infection.

Remote Hearings: technical matters

14. Remote hearings may be conducted using the following facilities as appropriate to the individual case:

    a.   By way of an email exchange between the court and the parties;
    b.   By way of telephone using conference calling facilities;
    c.   By way of the court's video-link system, if available;
    d.   The use of the Skype for Business App installed on judicial laptops;
    e.   Any other appropriate means of remote communication, for example BT MeetMe or FaceTime.

The most recent HMCTS update on the use of video and telephone hearings (issued on 18.3.20) during the coronavirus pandemic is at https://www.gov.uk/guidance/hmcts-telephone-and-video-hearings-duringcoronavirus-outbreak

If you are unfamiliar with Skype there is a simple user guide on the Judicial Intranet (under the Practical Matters tab, select Coronavirus (Covid-19) and scroll down) https://www.youtube.com/watch?v=2WUe59-aWI8&feature=youtu.be

https://www.youtube.com/watch?v=9MpqcXAdx0k&feature=youtu.be

https://www.youtube.com/watch?v=qQpQEDYskrc&feature=youtu.be

https://www.youtube.com/watch?v=H8xbgad2q_Q&feature=youtu.be

15. Any arrangement for a remote hearing must make provision for the hearing to be recorded. Where the hearing takes place with the judge/magistrates in a court room, recording will take place in the ordinary manner. If BT Conferencing is used for a telephone hearing then that system will produce a transcript of the hearing. Where Skype for Business is used, there is a facility within the software for the digital record of the hearing to be recorded (this is not the same as a typed transcript but may suffice for most purposes).

16. The responsibility for making technical and other arrangements for a remote hearing and for confirming the details of the arrangements for the hearing to the other parties no later than 24 hours prior to the remote hearing taking place is to be undertaken by the following party liaising with the court:

    a.   The local authority in a public law case;
    b.   The applicant, if legally represented, in a private law case;
    c.   The respondent, if legally represented and where the applicant is not, in a private law case;

> d.   The court where no party is legally represented.

17. When conducting a remote hearing, there is a need for the judge or magistrates to use their best endeavours to ensure that only those who would be allowed into the court room for an oral hearing are privy to the remote hearing and that all parties understand that the system used by the court will record the proceedings and that no other recording is to be made by any of the parties.

18. On the day before a remote hearing the applicant must electronically file a PDF bundle which complies with FPR PD27A, and which in any event must include as a minimum:

> a.   A case summary and chronology;
> b.   The parties' positions statements;
> c.   The previous orders that are relevant to the remote hearing;
> d.   All essential documents that the court requires to determine the issues that fall for determination at the remote hearing;
> e.   A draft order;
> f.   Completed advocates' forms together with the single address that the signed and sealed forms are to be returned to for distribution to the advocates.

Final Observation

19. These are exceptional and unprecedented times. The situation both nationally and in each locality is changing daily, if not hourly. I am well aware of the intensely difficult and highly stressful circumstances that all those working in the Family Justice System are currently experiencing and I am greatly appreciative of their commitment to the continued delivery of justice in circumstances which, only a week or so ago, would have been considered unimaginable. This Guidance is intended to deliver a very significant change of direction in the method of working within the Family Court, whilst at the same time enabling us to continue to operate and to meet the pressing needs of those who turn to the court for protection and justice.

The Rt Hon Sir Andrew McFarlane
President of the Family Division and Head of Family Justice
19th March 2020

Appendix A

In the High Court of Justice No: XXXX Family Division / The Family Court

IN THE MATTER OF XXXX AND IN THE MATTER OF XXXX CHILDREN

BEFORE XXXX SITTING AT XXXX ON XXXX

UPON the Court determining that in the exceptional circumstances of the current national public health emergency this case is suitable for hearing remotely ('remote hearing') by means of [video link]/[Skype]/[telephone]/[other].

BY ITS OWN MOTION / BY CONSENT

IT IS ORDERED THAT:

1. All hearings in this matter shall take place by way of remote hearing pursuant to FPR 2010 r 4.1(e) unless the court directs otherwise.

2. The parties and their representatives shall attend all hearings by way of [video link]/[Skype]/[telephone]/[other].

3. No unauthorised person may be present at this hearing. When asked, each legal representative must be able to confirm that no unauthorised person is in attendance or able to listen to the hearing.

4. This matter shall be listed for a remote hearing on XXXX at XXXX before XXXX sitting at XXXX with a time estimate of XXXX.

5. The parties shall arrange and attend remotely an Advocates Meeting no less than 48 hours before the hearing listed above.

6. The [applicant / respondent] shall be responsible for arranging with the Judge's clerk) the necessary facilities to conduct a remote hearing, allowing sufficient time for any necessary testing to take place. This will include provision to the court of the necessary contact details for the parties and their representatives where these are needed to facilitate the remote hearing.

7. The [applicant / respondent] must confirm the details of the arrangements for the hearing to the other parties by no later than 24 hours prior to the remote hearing taking place.

8. The applicant shall by 1600 hrs on the day before the hearing electronically file a PDF bundle, which must include:

   (a)   A case summary and chronology;
   (b)   The parties positions statements;
   (c)   The previous orders that are relevant to the remote hearing;
   (d)   All essential documents that the court requires to determine the issues that fall for determination at the remote hearing;
   (e)   A draft order;
   (f)   Completed advocates' forms together with the single address that the signed and sealed forms are to be returned to for distribution to the advocates.

9. [Further Directions].../

Dated XXXX

PART III – Practice guidance

Appendix B

Mr Justice Mostyn
National lead judge of the Financial Remedies Courts

In the light of the guidance this morning from the Lord Chief Justice I would like to ask all the zone leaders to propose to FRC judges the following measures.

1.   First appointments should be done wherever possible using the "accelerated" paper-only procedure in the fourth schedule to the FRC protocol (https://www.judiciary.uk/wp-content/uploads/2019/11/FRC-Good-PracticeProtocol-November-2019.pdf). The terms of that schedule do not need to be followed strictly; judicial latitude is encouraged. Judges should accept consent orders dealing with first appointments routinely.

2.   Parties should be encouraged to have their FDRs done privately. Such private FDRs should routinely be done remotely. Most barristers' chambers and solicitors' offices have facilities to enable FDRs to be done remotely.

3.   The default position for other hearings is that they should be done either by Skype (Skype for Business is available on all judicial laptops) or by telephone. The extension of the existing virtual courts project is being actively investigated.

4.   Physical hearing should only take place where this is absolutely unavoidable.

5.   The physical lodging and handling of documents should be avoided. The use of ebundles should be virtually mandatory. See https://www.judiciary.uk/announcements/financial-remedies-courts-ebundles-protocol/

6.   FRC judges should endeavour to do as much work as they possibly can from home.

I would ask that these measures are given wide publicity in your respective FRC zones.

17 March 2020

PRESIDENT'S MEMORANDUM
10 NOVEMBER 2021

PRESIDENT'S MEMORANDUM (DRAFTING ORDERS) (10 NOVEMBER 2021)

1 In my speech to the FLBA on 16 October 2021 I stated:

> 'The task of drafting an order has become a prolonged process. Partly because of remote working, the process of negotiating the order extends for days, with input from instructing solicitors and lay parties. These drafts are embellished to a Byzantine degree.'

I had previously referred to the problems that had arisen in the agreeing and drafting of orders in my Guidance: Forms of Orders in Children Cases (17 June 2019). There I observed that:

> 'Many judges and practitioners are not using electronic templates or programs and are, instead, preparing lengthy narrative orders in each case by a more laborious method with the result that the preparation of orders is now taking more time rather than less.'

2 In that Guidance I proposed that the first order made in any children's case should contain the key information but that subsequent orders should be in short form omitting lengthy narrative material and containing recitals stating only who attended and their representation; the issues determined at the hearing; any agreement or concession made during the hearing; and the issues that remain outstanding. I hoped that this would mitigate the problems.

3 In the field of public law a comparable problem has been addressed by the issue of amended orders 18 April 2021 which should have had the effect of substantially shortening orders made in that sphere with the result that time will have been saved and contention reduced.

4 Yet, it is clear that the problem has persisted in the field of private law, both in relation to litigation about children, and about money, and that the preparation of orders has become a highly adversarial and confrontational process leading to much unnecessary verbiage and great delay in the production of agreed drafts.

5 I have been asked to consider issuing a Practice Direction regulating professional standards in this area.

6 I do not consider that the Family Court needs such a Practice Direction, at least not at the present time. However, the Family Procedure Rule Committee will have to consider introducing such a measure if the principles in this memorandum are not observed and the non-compliance with elementary principles continues.

Standard Orders

7 When drafting orders, whether by consent or following a hearing, the standard order templates should be used, adapted as appropriate to the facts of the case:

PART III – Practice guidance

Practice Guidance: Standard Financial and Enforcement Orders (30 November 2017); Practice Guidance : Standard Children and other Orders (6 June 2018).

8 However, these templates only provide standard clauses for agreements and orders disposing of the case together with rules about formatting. They say nothing about the content of the recitals. This is the area where great controversy seems to arise.

Recitals

9 The first and most basic rule is that where the order follows a hearing its terms (including its recitals) must reflect the result of the hearing, no more, no less.

10 The purpose of a recital is not to summarise what happened at a hearing, but rather to record those essential background matters which are not part of the body of the order.

11 In my Guidance of 17 June 2019 I said that in an ideal world the aim was to encapsulate all of the essential information about a children's case in the most recent court order so that anyone taking up a case would only need to turn to the latest order to understand the issues, the parties, the state of the proceedings and other key information.

12 However, that process has led to delay, expense and confrontation, which has continued notwithstanding the use of short form orders. Therefore, while it remains necessary in children's cases, both domestic and those with an international element, to record the essential background matters, it is essential that this is done as shortly and as neutrally as possible and that the parties should not seek to introduce adversarial and partisan statements in their favour in the recitals to the order. This is the first area of potential conflict.

13 It is not necessary in a financial remedy order to record any background matters, although the court in its discretion may permit the parties to do so. In this event it is, again, essential that this is done as shortly and as neutrally as possible.

14 The second area of potential conflict is the practice of parties seeking to attribute views to the court which did not form part of the court's decision. This is a surprisingly prevalent practice and gives rise to much controversy. It is a practice that must cease.

15 The third area of potential conflict is the practice of a party's representative seeking to record that party's position before, or during, the course of, the hearing. Again, this can give rise to much conflict, but is wholly superfluous. This, too, must cease.

16 More latitude is permissible as regards consent orders but, again, restraint in relation to the content of recitals must be exercised given the cost to the parties and the time of the court that is spent approving them.

When the order must be drafted and lodged

17 Where one or both parties has legal representation at a particular hearing, the order must be agreed, drafted and lodged before the parties leave the court building or, on remote hearings, on the day of the hearing, unless this is wholly impracticable, in which event the order must be agreed, drafted and lodged within two working days of the hearing. The date for the next hearing must be fixed by the parties with the court and stated in the order before the parties leave the court, unless the court otherwise orders.

PRESIDENT'S MEMORANDUM 10 NOVEMBER 2021

PRESIDENT'S MEMORANDUM (WITNESS STATEMENTS) (10 NOVEMBER 2021)

1 Too many witness statements are prepared in breach of proper professional standards.

2 It is clear that this problem is not confined to proceedings in the Family Court. It has become so acute in the Business and Property Courts that it has been necessary to pass a highly prescriptive Practice Direction – CPR PD 57AC – to seek to deal with the problem.

3 I do not consider that the Family Court needs an equivalent Practice Direction, at least not at the present time. However, the Family Procedure Rule Committee will have to consider introducing such a measure if the principles in this memorandum are not observed.

The fundamental requirements

4 Witness statements tell the parties and the court what evidence a party intends to rely on at a final hearing. Their use has the key added benefit of promoting the overriding objective by helping the court to deal with cases justly and proportionately, including by helping to put parties on an equal footing, saving time at the final hearing and promoting settlement in advance of the final hearing.

5 Witness statements must only contain evidence from the maker of the statement.

6 The statement must be expressed in the first person using the witness's own words (PD 22A para 4.1).

7 A witness statement must not:

    a   quote at any length from any document;
    b   seek to argue the case;
    c   take the court through the documents in the case;
    d   set out a narrative derived from the documents;
    e   express the opinions of the witness; or
    f   use rhetoric.

Facts, information and belief

8 A witness statement may only set out matters of fact and matters of information and belief (para 4.3).

9 Matters of fact include past facts (i.e. events which have happened) and future facts (i.e. events which are expected to happen). A statement may state only those matters of fact of which the witness has personal knowledge and which are relevant to the case (para 4.3(a)).

10 The statement must indicate the source of any matters of information and belief (para 4.3(b)). Evidence about proposed child arrangements or, in a financial remedy case, about needs, will be matters of information and belief. Therefore, where such evidence of such information and belief is given, the source or basis for that belief must be stated.

11 Documents

a   The statement must identify in a list appended to it what documents, if any, the witness has referred to, or been referred to, for the purpose of providing the evidence set out in the statement.

b   The statement should identify or describe the documents in such a way that they may be located easily at the final hearing.

c   Documents disclosed in the proceedings should be listed by disclosure reference (e.g. 'reply to questionnaire bundle at page 75'). Such documents must not be annexed to the statement.

d   The requirement to identify documents the witness has referred to, or been referred to, does not affect any privilege that may exist in relation to any of those documents. Privileged documents may be identified by category or general description.

e   Documents in the list which are not privileged and have not been previously disclosed must be disclosed at the same time that the witness statement is filed and served.

Memory

12 A person involved in preparing the statement of a witness must not, subject to the next paragraph, in any way seek to alter or influence the recollection of the witness. This is a rule of fundamental importance, breach of which will be serious professional misconduct.

13 However, the memory of witnesses may be refreshed by showing them a document which they created, or which they saw while the facts stated in the document were still fresh in their mind. Any such document must be listed under para 11.

14 Parties should understand that the court's approach to witness evidence based on human memory will be in accordance with CPR PD 57AC, Appendix para 1.3. This states that human memory:

a   is not a simple mental record of a witnessed event that is fixed at the time of the experience and fades over time, but

b   is a fluid and malleable state of perception concerning an individual's past experiences, and therefore

c   is vulnerable to being altered by a range of influences, such that the individual may or may not be conscious of the alteration.

A person involved in preparing a witness statement should keep this very clearly in mind and, therefore, be wary of categorical statements about past events unless those events are corroborated by contemporaneous documents.

Length of the statement

15 A witness statement must be as concise as possible without omitting anything of significance.

16 As a general standard, a witness statement should not exceed 15 pages in length (excluding exhibits). This page limit is a statement of best practice and does not derogate from the limit of 25 pages in PD 27A para 5.2A.1, which should be regarded as a maximum.

Sanctions

17 The court has a power under FPR 22.1(2) to exclude evidence that would otherwise be admissible. The court will consider excluding under this rule a witness statement which materially fails to comply with the standards in this memorandum. The court also has power under CPR 44.11(1)(b) to disallow the costs incurred in preparation of a non-compliant witness statement.

Template for LIPs in non-complex private law welfare cases

18 A useful template for use by Litigants in Person in non-complex private law welfare cases is attached to this memorandum. Its use in such cases is optional, but is strongly encouraged.

19 It should be noted that a guide for LIPs litigating in the Family Court will be prepared in due course.

10 November 2021

Case No: [Insert]

In the Family Court

Sitting at [place]

Date of next hearing; [complete]

STATEMENT OF THE APPLICANT / RESPONDENT

I (insert name) of (insert address or state 'undisclosed confidential address') make this statement believing the contents to be true to the best of my knowledge and ability and that this statement will stand as my evidence in these court proceedings.

Signed

Date

The children

The children	
1) Please state the full name date of birth and age of each child	1 (name) born on … who is … years old and is my son/daughter (or specify if other relationship)
	2 (repeat these details for each child involved in the case)

2) Please set out where and with whom each child is living	1 (Name or alternatively 'the children') live with (insert the name, relationship to the child and address if different to the address above). 2 (repeat as necessary)
3) Please set out the current arrangements for each child to spend time with the other parent.	
The summary of dispute	
4) Please identify the areas of dispute between you and the other parent.	
5) Please re-read the 'safeguarding Letter' from Cafcass and confirm if the contents of the letter are correct to the best of your knowledge.	YES/NO (delete as appropriate)
6) If your answer to the last question is NO, please set out a summary of what you disagree with or is incorrect.	
7) Has Cafcass or a social worker prepared a further (Section 7) report?	YES/NO (delete as appropriate) Insert the date of the report ….
8) If so, do you accept the recommendations at the end of the report?	YES/NO/PARTLY (delete as appropriate)
9) Are there any relevant facts stated in the report that you disagree with?	YES/NO (delete as appropriate)
10) If so please identify what those facts are	
Courses and mediation	
11 Have you attended the Separated Parents Information Programme (SPIP)?	YES/NO (delete as appropriate)
12) If so, state how this has helped your approach to issues involving the children	
13) Have you attended mediation?	YES/NO (delete as appropriate)
14) If not, would you like to?	YES/NO (delete as appropriate)
Your proposed arrangements	
15) Please set out with whom the children should live	
16) Please set out why your proposed living arrangements will best meet the needs of the child(ren).	

PART III – Practice guidance

17) Please set out your proposed arrangements for the Child(ren) spending contact time with the other parent or relevant adults. You should include proposed arrangements for holidays and special events.	
18) If you are proposing a build up over time in the amount of time that the child(ren) will spend with the parent with whom they are not living please set out you plan and the time periods from which it will increase	
19) Please set out why the above proposed contact arrangements will best meet the needs of the child(ren).	
20) If your proposed arrangements do not include overnight stays, please explain why and how you believe this is in the best interest of the child(ren)	
21) Please set out your proposed arrangements for the collection and the return of the child(ren)	
Further information	
22) The court must make its decision about the child(ren)'s welfare by reference to the welfare checklist under the Children Act (1989). This is set out in the next column. Please provide any additional evidence that you wish to rely on under each heading.	(a) the ascertainable wishes and feelings of the child concerned (considered in the light of his age and understanding); (b) the child's physical, emotional and educational needs; (c) the likely effect on the child of any change in his circumstances; (d) the child's age, sex, background and any characteristics of which the court considers relevant; (e) any harm which the child has suffered or is at risk of suffering; (f) how capable each of the child's parents, and any other person in relation to whom the court considers the question to be relevant, is of meeting the child's needs; (g) the range of powers available to the court under this Act in the proceedings in question.

23) Please list here what documents, if any, you have referred to or been referred to for the purpose of providing the evidence set out in this statement. If the documents have not been previously disclosed you should disclose them when you file and serve this statement	

Note: Please make sure that a copy of this statement is sent to the court and to all parties, and if a report has been prepared, to the Cafcass officer or Social Worker who wrote it. Please make sure that you keep a copy for yourself and bring it to all Court hearings with you

PART III – Practice guidance

PRESIDENT'S GUIDANCE
MARCH 2022

PRESIDENT'S GUIDANCE (LIAISON BETWEEN COURTS IN ENGLAND AND WALES AND BRITISH EMBASSIES AND HIGH COMMISSIONS ABROAD) (MARCH 2022)

(1) This guidance note describes procedures which are to be followed when a court in England and Wales exercising family jurisdiction seeks to invoke consular assistance. The procedures have been agreed between the President of the Family Division and the Foreign, Commonwealth and Development Office (FCDO).

(2) Courts exercising family jurisdiction in England and Wales regularly deal with cases where children have been wrongfully removed to a foreign country or have been retained there wrongfully, most commonly by a parent or relative. Such cases may involve abduction or removal by one or both parents with a view to forced marriage or female genital mutilation, in which case a Forced Marriage Protection Order (FMPO) or Female Genital Mutilation Protection Order (FGMPO) may be appropriate.

(3) When the court is exercising family jurisdiction in such circumstances, consular assistance may be sought, via the FCDO in London, from the relevant British Embassies, High Commissions or Consulates abroad.

(4) Where the country to which the child has been taken is a party to the Convention on the Civil Aspects of International Child Abduction signed at The Hague on 25 October 1980 (1980 Hague Convention), established procedures apply for the making of applications for the return of the child, via the central authority, which for England and Wales is The International Child Abduction and Contact Unit (ICACU), situated in the office of the Official Solicitor and Public Trustee at Post Point 0.53, 102 Petty France, London, SW1H 9AJ, telephone +44 (0)20 3681 2756, email icacu@ospt.gov.uk.

(5) Where the country to which the child has been taken is a party to either of the following Conventions, the court will need to consider the Convention when deciding what steps to take:

- 1980 European Convention on Recognition and Enforcement of Decisions concerning Custody of Children and on the Restoration of Custody of Children (a Convention of the Council of Europe, also known as the 1980 Luxembourg Convention);
- 1996 Hague Convention on jurisdiction, applicable law, recognition, enforcement and cooperation in respect of parental responsibility and measures for the protection of children. Please note that for the 1996 Hague Convention, ICACU is the (operational) central authority for England and the Welsh Government is separately the central authority for Wales (Tel.: +44 (29) 23000 61500) Email: WalesCAHague1996@gov.wales.

(6) ICACU has published explanatory guidance and application forms regarding the assistance which can be provided in respect of the above-named Conventions. The relevant forms for the 1980 and 1996 Hague Conventions can be found at: https://www.gov.uk/government/publications/international-child-abduction-andcontact-unit-application-form https://www.gov.uk/government/publications/international-child-abduction-unitrequest-for-co-operation-form

(7) Where, however, the country concerned is not a party to any of the above Conventions, consideration will need to be given in each case as to what orders if any should be made to seek to secure the return of the child to England and Wales.

(8) It may be possible in appropriate cases for representatives from the relevant British Embassy, High Commission or Consulate to follow-up with the competent safeguarding authority to check the child[ren]'s welfare, engage local police to ascertain what efforts have been made to locate the child[ren], to host consular appointments involving the child[ren], and to advise on travel arrangements for the return of the child[ren] to England and Wales. Such activities will however always be subject to the requirements of the domestic law of the country in question. The Foreign Secretary has discretion in deciding how to conduct international affairs, and the court cannot order the FCDO to exercise consular assistance. There is no general duty for the FCDO to provide consular assistance to British nationals. There may be limits to what the FCDO can do to help when a dual national child is in the country of their other nationality.

(9) Before the court requests assistance from the FCDO, contact should be made with the Child Policy Unit in Consular Directorate (Consular.ChildrensPolicyOfficer@fcdo.gov.uk), or the Forced Marriage Unit (FMU@fcdo.gov.uk) if the case involves forced marriage or female genital mutilation. This is to provide the FCDO with an opportunity to clarify what level of assistance it may be in a position to offer in the country concerned. The FCDO will be able to identify the relevant Embassy, High Commission or Consulate to which any order or request for assistance should be directed, and to forward documents.

(10) The FCDO provides a facilitative role in relation to the return of the child but is not able to care for, take control of, or assist in procuring the return of the child. The naming of specific officials (for example Ambassadors, High Commissioners or other FCDO officials) must be avoided. Instead reference should be made to 'The Consular Directorate of the Foreign, Commonwealth and Development Office'.

(11) Consular staff are not trained to assess the welfare of a child as a professional Social Worker would be. Accordingly, the FCDO cannot conduct welfare visits or safe and well checks. The FCDO can provide information and contact details for the competent safeguarding authority/ies and Non-Governmental Organisations (NGOs) in the relevant country who may be able to undertake welfare checks on the child[ren].

(12) The FCDO will take practical steps to co-operate in any way which is appropriate on UK passport handling. It should be noted that:

PART III – Practice guidance

    (a)   The FCDO is dependent upon the co-operation of the parent or adult to comply with an order. The FCDO is unable to authorise or enforce compliance.

    (b)   The FCDO or UK diplomatic premises should not be used as a depositary for the return of UK passports.

    (c)   The FCDO is not in a position to carry passports across international borders via the diplomatic bag or other means. Arrangements to transport a UK Passport should be made by the passport holder or, if a child passport, those with parental responsibility.

    (d)   On return of the child[rens]'s passport/s no further responsibility lies with the FCDO in relation to the parties' future movements.

(13) The FCDO can provide information and contact details for the competent safeguarding authority and NGOs in the relevant country to assist the court and other parties. Authorities and NGOs in the relevant country may be able to assist in locating the child[ren], and arranging to return the child[ren]. However, Social Services in England and Wales are not authorised to work outside the UK and as such the primary work of returning the child will require the cooperation of in-country authorities.

(14) The FCDO can issue Emergency Travel Documents (ETDs) to British citizens or those with a claim to British nationality providing they meet the eligibility criteria. ETDs do not replace full validity passports, but in issuing them the FCDO is providing consular assistance to a person who urgently needs to travel. ETDs are only issued to those who have not held a British passport before in exceptional circumstances. Ordinarily, first time applicants should apply for a passport to travel. FCDO policy states that ETDs can only be issued to those who are 15 years old and younger when all those with parental responsibility have given consent. This policy is deviated from only in exceptional circumstances. It is helpful to the FCDO if the court can make it clear when an ETD may be issued with the consent of only one person with parental responsibility or, where necessary, without the consent of anyone with parental responsibility. Foreign nationals looking to travel to the UK will need to make the necessary visa arrangements with UK Visas and Immigration (UKVI).

(15) The FCDO can provide advice on the repatriation of a child, including options for financing travel. Financial assistance (such as a loan) can be considered in exceptional circumstances, but will be considered on a case by case basis. The court or those with parental responsibility may contact the FCDO before an order is made to discuss these options.

(16) Whilst the FCDO stands ready to assist the court in any way which is appropriate, the repatriation of foreign nationals from the UK to a third country is outside the scope of consular assistance. Likewise, the submission of visa applications to a third country is the responsibility of the applicant.

(17) In a case where assistance can be given by the FCDO, the order should provide for disclosure of the specific documents required in order for the FCDO to provide the necessary assistance. A copy of all such orders should be sent to the Child Policy Unit, Foreign, Commonwealth and Development Office, King Charles Street, London, SW1A 2AH; Consular.ChildrensPolicyOfficer@fcdo.gov.uk.

(18) If the order relates to the 2003 UK-Pakistan Protocol on Child Contact and Abduction, a copy should in addition be sent by email to the International Family Justice Office IFJOffice@Justice.gov.uk.

(19) The FCDO has published guidance on the assistance which can be provided in respect to international parental child abductions: https://www.gov.uk/government/publications/international-parental-childabduction/international-parental-child-abduction.

(20) Attached is a Schedule of specimen provisions which may be included in orders principally directed to cases where a child has been wrongfully removed to/retained in a foreign country.

The Rt Hon Sir Andrew McFarlane President of the Family Division 14 March 2022

Schedule

Specimen Provisions for Orders

AND WHEREAS [AB] is a Ward of the High Court of England and Wales and is a British citizen; and currently [believed to be] travelling outside England and Wales with a United Kingdom passport

AND WHEREAS in consequence of the fact that this Court has ordered that [AB] remain a Ward of this Court, the High Court of England and Wales, while (until [s]he attains the age of 18 years on [date]) [s]he remains a minor, this Court is empowered and required to exercise its custodial jurisdiction over him/her and to ascertain his/her best interests and to facilitate and protect those best interests

AND WHEREAS it appears from an order made in [details of proceedings] on [date] (of which a copy is attached) that [AB] was habitually resident in England and Wales [on[date]/at the time [s]he was removed from this jurisdiction]

AND WHEREAS the High Court of England and Wales is anxious to protect and secure his/her wellbeing and best interests and to ensure that he/she may freely express his/her wishes concerning his/her country and place of residence

AND WHEREAS the High Court of England and Wales is anxious to ensure that [s]he is not induced or coerced into contracting any marriage or betrothal against his/her will

AND WHEREAS the High Court of England and Wales is satisfied that all interested parties are before the Court including Cafcass (the Children and Family Court Advisory and Support Service) appointed by the Court to represent the Ward

AND WHEREAS the High Court of England and Wales having heard oral evidence from [ ] is of the view that serious grounds exist in the present circumstances to question whether this Court's Ward [AB] is able freely to express his/her views and wishes and in particular with regard to his/her country of residence

AND WHEREAS the High Court of England and Wales has in the interests of [AB] determined that [s]he should so soon as practicable return/be returned to England and Wales

IT IS ORDERED that every person within the jurisdiction of this Court who is in a position to do so shall co-operate in assisting and securing the immediate return to England and Wales of [AB], a Ward of the High Court of England and Wales

AND NOW THEREFORE THIS COURT RESPECTFULLY REQUESTS any person not within the jurisdiction of this Court who is in a position to do so to co-operate in assisting and securing the immediate return to England and Wales of the Ward [AB]

AND THIS COURT RESPECTFULLY REQUESTS all judicial and administrative bodies in the State of [ ] to consider what assistance may be provided pursuant to the exercise of their respective powers, and to provide such assistance that they consider appropriate, with a view to establishing the whereabouts of the Ward of the High Court of England and Wales.

AND NOW THEREFORE THIS COURT RESPECTFULLY REQUESTS all judicial, administrative and law enforcement authorities to consider what assistance may be provided pursuant to the exercise of their respective powers, and to provide such assistance that they consider appropriate, with a view to locating, safeguarding and facilitating the return to England and Wales of the said minor child[ren] pursuant to the laws of England and Wales [and in accordance with the Protocol made on 17 January 2003 in London and signed by the Honourable Chief Justice of the Supreme Court of Pakistan and by the Right Honourable The President of the Family Division of the High Court of Justice of England and Wales].

Other Examples of Helpful Wording

FOR THE AVOIDANCE OF DOUBT the Foreign, Commonwealth and Development Office and/or Her Majesty's Passport Office may grant a passport, travel document or emergency travel document to [names of child/ren] without the consent of [name of parent/mother/father]

PERMISSION IS HEREBY GIVEN to the Foreign, Commonwealth and Development Office of the United Kingdom to share the information disclosed to them in accordance with paragraph [X] above with [named bodies/persons] [and any other relevant agency]

PRESIDENT'S GUIDANCE
5 MAY 2022

PRESIDENT'S GUIDANCE (FACT FINDING HEARINGS AND DOMESTIC ABUSE IN PRIVATE LAW CHILDREN PROCEEDINGS) (5 MAY 2022)

Introduction

In March 2022 I invited Lady Justice Macur to form a small group with the task of producing short, clear and practical guidance for judges and magistrates concerning fact finding hearings and domestic abuse in Private Law children proceedings in the Family Court. I am extremely grateful to Macur LJ and her team who have, in the short time available, conducted a useful survey of salaried and fee-paid judges before producing this guidance, which I now approve and publish.

Sir Andrew McFarlane
President of the Family Division
5th May 2022

General

1 Make every hearing count. Do not sanction short hearings or agree to insufficient preparation time for the first or other case management hearings on the basis that things can be 'sorted out' next time. Seize the opportunity to probe. Remain 'in control' throughout. Strive to achieve judicial continuity and take ownership of the case. Remember delay is inimical to child welfare.

2. As the judge or magistrate, you have the relevant expertise and competence to analyse and determine the necessity for a fact-finding hearing, and if so, the extent of the hearing and the evidence that will be required. The views of the parties, the CAFCASS officer or the advocates may be persuasive, but they are not determinative; interrogate their reasoning.

3 There is a time and a place to determine allegations of domestic abuse, but it may not be in your court. Unless it will be relevant to, and necessary for, your decision regarding the welfare of the child, do not allow the court to be used to litigate such allegations.

At the FHDRA / first directions appointment/ to be considered at gatekeeping

4 Non-court dispute resolution and MIAMs:

 a Has a MIAM taken place? If not, why not? Should it now be required? The court has a duty to consider non-court dispute resolution: FPR r3.3.

 b If a MIAM exemption has been claimed on the ground of domestic abuse, check that evidence exists as specified at FPR PD3A [20]. Is the exemption valid? FPR r.3.10.

PART III – Practice guidance

c   If appropriate, invite an authorised family mediator to advise whether mediation is possible with adaptations such as shuttle diplomacy or protective measures.

5 Identify the real issues in the case. Is one parent denying contact per se or seeking to add conditions for or in relation to contact arrangements? What are the questions pertaining to the child's welfare?

6 What exactly is alleged in terms of domestic abuse and by whom? Consider the definitions at FPR PD 12J [2A] and [3] in addition to PD 12J [14].

7 Has a Form C1A been completed? Is there a response?

a   If so, ensure the forms are considered in their entirety. Are there admissions? Does the form and/or response suggest a possible way forward to the satisfaction of the court that will permit safe continuation of relationships with the child and avoid conflict with other adults?

b   If not, why not? Is it appropriate to obtain a verbal summary of any allegations and/or response during the hearing in order for progress to be made?

8 Collectively, does the information already before the court (for example, the C100, C1A and any safeguarding report) contain sufficient detail to avoid the necessity of directing further evidence/documentation to determine the issue?

9 If further evidence/documentation is required to determine the issue, what is necessary in the fact specific circumstances of the case? The judgment in Re H-N [2021] EWCA Civ 448 (paras 41- 49) cautioned against allowing a Scott Schedule to distort the fact finding process (by becoming the sole focus of a hearing), but the Court of Appeal did not rule out the use of a schedule as a structure to assist in analysing specific allegations.

10 In determining what further evidence/documentation is needed, the nature of the allegations will be important. Allegations that can be clearly defined (such as specific incidents of physical abuse) may be suitable for reduction to a schedule. Other allegations that require the court to take a broad overview and look at patterns of behaviour (such as coercive and controlling behaviour) are likely to require a statement. A hybrid of the two, dividing types of abuse into clusters to provide an overview akin to a threshold document in public law proceedings might be appropriate. However, do not consider only the nature of the allegations, but also practicality and expediency bearing in mind the parties before you. Require a like for like document in response from the alleged perpetrator.

11 Ensure that you obtain the essential information in respect of any allegation at an early stage. What, when, where? What was the effect on the child and the parent? Were there witnesses? What other evidence might be available? Is the behaviour complained of because of the breakdown of the relationship rather than a/the cause of the breakdown?

Is a fact-finding hearing required?

12 When determining whether to order a fact-finding hearing, consider:

a   the nature of the allegations and the extent to which those allegations are likely to be relevant to the making of a child arrangements order;

b   that the purpose of a fact finding is to allow assessment of the future risk to the child and the impact of any abuse on the child;

c   whether fact-finding is necessary or whether other evidence suffices; and,

d   whether fact-finding is proportionate.

13 The fundamentals are relevance, purpose, and proportionality. Consider FPR PD 12J [14] and [17].

14 Allegations that require the assessment of a pattern of behaviour, such as controlling and coercive behaviour, do not justify a different approach. The court only needs to determine allegations of such behaviour to the extent that it is relevant and necessary to determine issues as to a child's future welfare. Even then, the court is only required to assess the overarching issue, rather than every single subsidiary factual allegation that may also be raised.

15 Always consider whether the allegations (at their highest) go to safeguarding in general or to particular circumstances that could be mitigated by supervision of contact or some other measures. If the latter and mitigations are available, why is it said that a fact-finding hearing is required?

16 If your conclusion is that the allegations, if proved and however serious, would not be relevant to the decision, then no fact-finding hearing is required.

17 Record brief reasons for your decision whether or not a fact-finding hearing is necessary on the face of the order.

Case management if a fact-finding hearing is required

18 When determining the specific allegations to be tried, consider relevance, purpose, and proportionality.

19 Robust case management is required from the outset. Remember your case management responsibilities and powers: FPR r1.1, r1.4, r.4.4.

20 It is the court that controls the evidence in the case: FPR r.22.1.

21 Only order third party disclosure where it is necessary and proportionate to do so. Require justification for any requests and refuse fishing exercises. In what respect is it said the proposed evidence supports or undermines an allegation? Ensure that any orders are targeted and precise. For example, is it possible to direct specific disclosure from the police, as opposed to a 'catch all' order? Will a GP summary suffice instead of a party's full GP records?

22 If a party seeks to rely on a witness of fact, only allow evidence that goes to an issue to be determined. Test with the parties and decide what, if any, real value is likely to be brought to your enquiry by the evidence of third parties.

23 No case should be timetabled to a fact-finding hearing without a properly completed witness template. This will assist the parties and manage their expectations.

24 Consider participation directions. Section 63 Domestic Abuse Act 2021 establishes a presumption that where a party or witness is or at risk of being a

PART III – Practice guidance

victim of domestic abuse from a party to the proceedings, the quality of their evidence and / or their participation as a party is likely to be diminished by reason of vulnerability. Consideration of FPR r.3A and PD 3AA are mandatory and the obligation to consider vulnerability is the court's, regardless of whether a party is represented or if participation directions are sought.

25 At the fact-finding hearing itself, control the hearing and keep the parties and advocates on point. Keep in mind the issues / previously identified allegations. Do not permit irrelevant diversions.

26 Always ensure that any summary of findings you have made is fairly and accurately recorded in the order or a document attached to it.

Re-visiting a decision not to have a fact-finding hearing

27 The court must, at all stages in the proceedings, consider whether domestic abuse is raised as an issue: FPR PD 12J [5]. However, guard against attempts to re-argue the question once a decision has been made. What is said to have changed to undermine the original analysis? Proceedings should have judicial continuity, wherever possible, and a consistent approach.

28 If 'new' evidence relating to past events is presented, ask why it was not available or disclosed before. If no good reason is advanced, then you may refuse to admit it. The more significant the evidence is said to be, the more compelling the explanation needs to be for its late receipt.

CALENDARS 2020–2023

2020

JANUARY
M	T	W	T	F	S	S
		1	2	3	4	5
6	7	8	9	10	11	12
13	14	15	16	17	18	19
20	21	22	23	24	25	26
27	28	29	30	31		

FEBRUARY
M	T	W	T	F	S	S
					1	2
3	4	5	6	7	8	9
10	11	12	13	14	15	16
17	18	19	20	21	22	23
24	25	26	27	28	29	

MARCH
M	T	W	T	F	S	S
						1
2	3	4	5	6	7	8
9	10	11	12	13	14	15
16	17	18	19	20	21	22
23	24	25	26	27	28	29
30	31					

APRIL
M	T	W	T	F	S	S
		1	2	3	4	5
6	7	8	9	10	11	12
13	14	15	16	17	18	19
20	21	22	23	24	25	26
27	28	29	30			

MAY
M	T	W	T	F	S	S
				1	2	3
4	5	6	7	8	9	10
11	12	13	14	15	16	17
18	19	20	21	22	23	24
25	26	27	28	29	30	31

JUNE
M	T	W	T	F	S	S
1	2	3	4	5	6	7
8	9	10	11	12	13	14
15	16	17	18	19	20	21
22	23	24	25	26	27	28
29	30					

JULY
M	T	W	T	F	S	S
		1	2	3	4	5
6	7	8	9	10	11	12
13	14	15	16	17	18	19
20	21	22	23	24	25	26
27	28	29	30	31		

AUGUST
M	T	W	T	F	S	S
					1	2
3	4	5	6	7	8	9
10	11	12	13	14	15	16
17	18	19	20	21	22	23
24	25	26	27	28	29	30
31						

SEPTEMBER
M	T	W	T	F	S	S
	1	2	3	4	5	6
7	8	9	10	11	12	13
14	15	16	17	18	19	20
21	22	23	24	25	26	27
28	29	30				

OCTOBER
M	T	W	T	F	S	S
			1	2	3	4
5	6	7	8	9	10	11
12	13	14	15	16	17	18
19	20	21	22	23	24	25
26	27	28	29	30	31	

NOVEMBER
M	T	W	T	F	S	S
						1
2	3	4	5	6	7	8
9	10	11	12	13	14	15
16	17	18	19	20	21	22
23	24	25	26	27	28	29
30						

DECEMBER
M	T	W	T	F	S	S
	1	2	3	4	5	6
7	8	9	10	11	12	13
14	15	16	17	18	19	20
21	22	23	24	25	26	27
28	29	30	31			

2021

JANUARY
M	T	W	T	F	S	S
				1	2	3
4	5	6	7	8	9	10
11	12	13	14	15	16	17
18	19	20	21	22	23	24
25	26	27	28	29	30	31

FEBRUARY
M	T	W	T	F	S	S
1	2	3	4	5	6	7
8	9	10	11	12	13	14
15	16	17	18	19	20	21
22	23	24	25	26	27	28

MARCH
M	T	W	T	F	S	S
1	2	3	4	5	6	7
8	9	10	11	12	13	14
15	16	17	18	19	20	21
22	23	24	25	26	27	28
29	30	31				

APRIL
M	T	W	T	F	S	S
			1	2	3	4
5	6	7	8	9	10	11
12	13	14	15	16	17	18
19	20	21	22	23	24	25
26	27	28	29	30		

MAY
M	T	W	T	F	S	S
					1	2
3	4	5	6	7	8	9
10	11	12	13	14	15	16
17	18	19	20	21	22	23
24	25	26	27	28	29	30
31						

JUNE
M	T	W	T	F	S	S
	1	2	3	4	5	6
7	8	9	10	11	12	13
14	15	16	17	18	19	20
21	22	23	24	25	26	27
28	29	30				

JULY
M	T	W	T	F	S	S
			1	2	3	4
5	6	7	8	9	10	11
12	13	14	15	16	17	18
19	20	21	22	23	24	25
26	27	28	29	30	31	

AUGUST
M	T	W	T	F	S	S
						1
2	3	4	5	6	7	8
9	10	11	12	13	14	15
16	17	18	19	20	21	22
23	24	25	26	27	28	29
30	31					

SEPTEMBER
M	T	W	T	F	S	S
		1	2	3	4	5
6	7	8	9	10	11	12
13	14	15	16	17	18	19
20	21	22	23	24	25	26
27	28	29	30			

OCTOBER
M	T	W	T	F	S	S
				1	2	3
4	5	6	7	8	9	10
11	12	13	14	15	16	17
18	19	20	21	22	23	24
25	26	27	28	29	30	31

NOVEMBER
M	T	W	T	F	S	S
1	2	3	4	5	6	7
8	9	10	11	12	13	14
15	16	17	18	19	20	21
22	23	24	25	26	27	28
29	30					

DECEMBER
M	T	W	T	F	S	S
		1	2	3	4	5
6	7	8	9	10	11	12
13	14	15	16	17	18	19
20	21	22	23	24	25	26
27	28	29	30	31		

2022

JANUARY
M	T	W	T	F	S	S
					1	2
3	4	5	6	7	8	9
10	11	12	13	14	15	16
17	18	19	20	21	22	23
24	25	26	27	28	29	30
31						

FEBRUARY
M	T	W	T	F	S	S
	1	2	3	4	5	6
7	8	9	10	11	12	13
14	15	16	17	18	19	20
21	22	23	24	25	26	27
28						

MARCH
M	T	W	T	F	S	S
	1	2	3	4	5	6
7	8	9	10	11	12	13
14	15	16	17	18	19	20
21	22	23	24	25	26	27
28	29	30	31			

APRIL
M	T	W	T	F	S	S
				1	2	3
4	5	6	7	8	9	10
11	12	13	14	15	16	17
18	19	20	21	22	23	24
25	26	27	28	29	30	

MAY
M	T	W	T	F	S	S
						1
2	3	4	5	6	7	8
9	10	11	12	13	14	15
16	17	18	19	20	21	22
23	24	25	26	27	28	29
30	31					

JUNE
M	T	W	T	F	S	S
		1	2	3	4	5
6	7	8	9	10	11	12
13	14	15	16	17	18	19
20	21	22	23	24	25	26
27	28	29	30			

JULY
M	T	W	T	F	S	S
				1	2	3
4	5	6	7	8	9	10
11	12	13	14	15	16	17
18	19	20	21	22	23	24
25	26	27	28	29	30	31

AUGUST
M	T	W	T	F	S	S
1	2	3	4	5	6	7
8	9	10	11	12	13	14
15	16	17	18	19	20	21
22	23	24	25	26	27	28
29	30	31				

SEPTEMBER
M	T	W	T	F	S	S
			1	2	3	4
5	6	7	8	9	10	11
12	13	14	15	16	17	18
19	20	21	22	23	24	25
26	27	28	29	30		

OCTOBER
M	T	W	T	F	S	S
					1	2
3	4	5	6	7	8	9
10	11	12	13	14	15	16
17	18	19	20	21	22	23
24	25	26	27	28	29	30
31						

NOVEMBER
M	T	W	T	F	S	S
	1	2	3	4	5	6
7	8	9	10	11	12	13
14	15	16	17	18	19	20
21	22	23	24	25	26	27
28	29	30				

DECEMBER
M	T	W	T	F	S	S
			1	2	3	4
5	6	7	8	9	10	11
12	13	14	15	16	17	18
19	20	21	22	23	24	25
26	27	28	29	30	31	

2023

JANUARY
M	T	W	T	F	S	S
						1
2	3	4	5	6	7	8
9	10	11	12	13	14	15
16	17	18	19	20	21	22
23	24	25	26	27	28	29
30	31					

FEBRUARY
M	T	W	T	F	S	S
		1	2	3	4	5
6	7	8	9	10	11	12
13	14	15	16	17	18	19
20	21	22	23	24	25	26
27	28					

MARCH
M	T	W	T	F	S	S
		1	2	3	4	5
6	7	8	9	10	11	12
13	14	15	16	17	18	19
20	21	22	23	24	25	26
27	28	29	30	31		

APRIL
M	T	W	T	F	S	S
					1	2
3	4	5	6	7	8	9
10	11	12	13	14	15	16
17	18	19	20	21	22	23
24	25	26	27	28	29	30

MAY
M	T	W	T	F	S	S
1	2	3	4	5	6	7
8	9	10	11	12	13	14
15	16	17	18	19	20	21
22	23	24	25	26	27	28
29	30	31				

JUNE
M	T	W	T	F	S	S
			1	2	3	4
5	6	7	8	9	10	11
12	13	14	15	16	17	18
19	20	21	22	23	24	25
26	27	28	29	30		

JULY
M	T	W	T	F	S	S
					1	2
3	4	5	6	7	8	9
10	11	12	13	14	15	16
17	18	19	20	21	22	23
24	25	26	27	28	29	30
31						

AUGUST
M	T	W	T	F	S	S
	1	2	3	4	5	6
7	8	9	10	11	12	13
14	15	16	17	18	19	20
21	22	23	24	25	26	27
28	29	30	31			

SEPTEMBER
M	T	W	T	F	S	S
				1	2	3
4	5	6	7	8	9	10
11	12	13	14	15	16	17
18	19	20	21	22	23	24
25	26	27	28	29	30	

OCTOBER
M	T	W	T	F	S	S
						1
2	3	4	5	6	7	8
9	10	11	12	13	14	15
16	17	18	19	20	21	22
23	24	25	26	27	28	29
30	31					

NOVEMBER
M	T	W	T	F	S	S
		1	2	3	4	5
6	7	8	9	10	11	12
13	14	15	16	17	18	19
20	21	22	23	24	25	26
27	28	29	30			

DECEMBER
M	T	W	T	F	S	S
				1	2	3
4	5	6	7	8	9	10
11	12	13	14	15	16	17
18	19	20	21	22	23	24
25	26	27	28	29	30	31

Part IV

MISCELLANEOUS

PART IV – Miscellaneous